Commentary on the Law of the International Criminal Court

Mark Klamberg (editor)

2017
Torkel Opsahl Academic EPublisher
Brussels

EDITOR'S PREFACE

The establishment of international criminal jurisdictions such as the International Criminal Court ('ICC') presents new challenges for legal practitioners as well as scholars in their legal research. High-quality legal commentaries can be of great assistance for both practitioners and scholars.

The Commentary on the Law of the International Criminal Court ('CLICC') has been designed with inspiration from commentaries on domestic law as well as international law. More than forty scholars and experts have contributed to CLICC. Its basic idea is to answer legal questions and issues in an expeditious manner. CLICC does not only address ordinary and recurrent questions of interpretation and application of international criminal law. If the legal issues are more complicated, CLICC informs on relevant preparatory works, case law, expert views and scholarship which may be consulted for further research.

I note with satisfaction that the online version of CLICC has already provided utility to scholars and practitioners in the field. Not all of the original contributors to the online commentary have been available for the completion of this printed version. I would like to express my appreciation for the contributions of Dr. Björn Elberling and Dr. Dominik Zimmerman. Fortunately, we have found well-qualified persons for their replacement. The comments to the articles concerned give due credit to the mentioned persons, where former considerations are used.

The focus has been on case law and contentious issues already resolved or in need of resolution. Provisions that are deemed of greater importance have been covered in more detail.

When you use the printed version of CLICC, it is normally from one of two of the following starting-points. If you know which legal provision is associated with the legal question or issues that you are interested in, go to the Table of Contents and you will find where the relevant provision is commented on. If you are interested in a specific case and to which provisions the case may be relevant, go to the Table of Cases.

If you wish to make reference to the printed version of CLICC, please make the reference to the page and note in this way:

Michael Stile and Carl-Friedrich Stuckenberg, "Article 103: Role of States in Enforcement of Sentences of Imprisonment", in Mark Klamberg (ed.), *Commentary on the Law of the International Criminal Court*, TOAEP, Brussels, 2017, 688–695, p. 691, note 783.

If you wish to make a reference to the online version of CLICC, please do it in this way:

Michael Stile and Carl-Friedrich Stuckenberg, "Article 103: Role of States in Enforcement of Sentences of Imprisonment", in Mark Klamberg (ed.), *Commentary on the Law of the International Criminal Court*, note 783, available at www.cmn-kh.org/clicc, updated 30 April 2017.

CLICC online (www.cmn-kh.org/clicc) is continuously updated and has functionality which allows the user to click on hyperlinks to access case law in full text. CLICC online connects to other services in the CMN Knowledge Hub.

The Faculties of Law at Stockholm University and Uppsala University have provided excellent practical and technical facilities for my work. The publishing of the present commentary has benefited greatly from the competent editing assistance of Josef Svantesson and the funds provided for that purpose by the Foundation SJF (Stiftelsen Juridisk Fakultetslitteratur). I am especially grateful to LIU Sijia who provided editorial assistance to the early work on CLICC. Other members of the editorial team include Camilla Lind and Hanna Szabo. Kiki A. Japutra and MA Xili have contributed to the integration of CLICC in CILRAP's CMN Knowledge Hub. Ralph Hecksteden has provided essential technical assistance with CLICC online. The language of the commentary has benefited greatly from the competent editing of Gareth Richards, TOAEP Senior Editor. I would also like to thank Devasheesh Bais and Nikola Hajdin for their work during the final phase of editing.

Finally, I wish to thank Morten Bergsmo for welcoming CLICC as a part of CILRAP's network and for all his support.

Mark Klamberg

FOREWORD BY JUDGE LENNART ASPEGREN

The Hague is often looked upon as the capital of international law. Aptly enough, it has a statue of the Dutch philosopher Baruch Spinoza, also known as Benedict de Spinoza (1632–1677). The statue can be seen outside his old house in Paviljoensgracht, in the Jewish quarter of the city. It shows him with his head cupped in his right hand and with a gentle look on his face – relaxed and contented. In his own lifetime, Spinoza was a highly controversial figure, assailed not least by people of various religious persuasions and maliciously ridiculed. But in recent centuries he has gained general recognition as a worthy campaigner for rationalism and intellectualism in the spirit of Socrates. The great German philosopher Friedrich Hegel (1770–1831), for example, commends him as a thinker who cast aside "all darkness, all mendacity and falsehood, all brooding and bewildering affectations".

Spinoza's discourse takes human history as its starting point, but with an eye to the future. In the year of his death, we find him writing in *Political Treatise* (1677):

> I sedulously endeavoured neither to deride, nor to pity, nor to loathe human actions, but only to understand them.
>
> Thus I have regarded human passion – such as love, hatred, wrath, envy, glory, mercy and other commotions of human soul – not as vices of human nature, but as qualities that pertain to it, just as warm, cold, tempest, thunder and similar phenomena pertain to weather. Even when they are uncomfortable, they are nevertheless necessary. They are grounded on specific causes.
>
> Through these causes we try to understand their nature. And our mind draws from their true apprehension and understanding as much pleasure as from what is agreeable to our senses.

We think of the twentieth century as the century of democracy's breakthrough and technological progress. But it is to no less a degree an unparalleled age of world wars and bombs – and, moreover, a period when oppression, persecution and terror cost millions of civilian lives. Mass outrages in the form of massacres, rape, torture and other nefarious deeds were perpetrated in many quarters: in the Ottoman Empire, in Nazi

Germany and its vassal states, in the African colonies, in the Soviet Union, in Cambodia, in Yugoslavia, in Rwanda. Many of the international criminals have been brought to justice, but many more certainly remain at large. Sadly, offenders – in the Middle East, in Africa and elsewhere – are still committing new serious violations of human rights and international humanitarian law. In fact, in a wider perspective, the history of international criminal and procedural law is short.

Yet, against this background, an important development took place after the Second World War. Pioneers included the Polish lawyer Raphael Lemkin (1900–1959), who launched the concept of a United Nations ('UN') Convention against what he termed genocide. All over the world, and not least in the past few decades, human rights lawyers have been joining in efforts to keep the apparatus of law in trim, to disseminate knowledge of current law and to move legal development forward, both practically and academically. Many of their contributions have been in a spirit closely akin to the positive intellectual world of Spinoza.

Dr. Mark Klamberg, through his book *Evidence in International Criminal Trials* (Martinus Nijhoff, 2013), has already shed a commendable light on criminal procedure in the weightiest of post-war international fora: the two International Military Tribunals at Nuremberg and Tokyo, the UN *ad hoc* Tribunals for the former Yugoslavia ('ICTY', The Hague) and for Rwanda ('ICTR', Arusha), and the permanent International Criminal Court ('ICC', The Hague). His thesis portrays international judicial procedure as a legal system *sui generis.*

Klamberg is now, in 2017, bringing out a new contribution on a related subject as an editor: a Commentary on the Law of the International Criminal Court ('CLICC'). This is another useful contribution, giving as it does a provision-by-provision analysis of the ICC Statute. Klamberg has for this purpose invited a group of eminent scholars and practitioners to provide comments. They have successfully combined a basically rational and humanist approach with extreme accuracy in every detail, including a huge number of case law references.

Legal commentaries such as CLICC provide for practitioners and scholars an overview of the topic in need of research, help to define the issues and refer to journal articles or primary sources. In addition to setting out general legal principles, CLICC can also provide useful analysis in areas where international criminal law is complex or unclear.

Rabindranath Tagore wrote in 1920: "Knowledge is precious to us, because we shall never have time to complete it". True. But meanwhile we must be grateful for all serviceable contributions. This commentary is unquestionably of such calibre in the field of international criminal justice. Without any doubt it has good prospects of becoming a standard work of reference.

Lennart Aspegren, LL.M., LL.D.h.c.
Former Under-Secretary-General, United Nations
Judge, International Criminal Tribunal for Rwanda

TABLE OF CONTENTS

TABLE OF CASES

Prosecutor v. Francis Kirimi Muthaura, Uhuru Muigai Kenyatta and Mohammed Hussein Ali (Case No. ICC-01/09-02/11)

Situation in Uganda (Case No. ICC-02/04-01/05)

Situation in the Republic of Kenya (Case No. ICC-01/09-19)

ICJ

ICTY

ICTR

PREAMBLE[1]

The States Parties to this Statute,

Conscious that all peoples are united by common bonds, their cultures pieced together in a shared heritage, and concerned that this delicate mosaic may be shattered at any time,[2]

Mindful that during this century millions of children, women and men have been victims of unimaginable atrocities that deeply shock the conscience of humanity,[3]

Recognizing that such grave crimes threaten the peace, security and well-being of the world,[4]

Affirming that the most serious crimes of concern to the international community as a whole must not go unpunished and that their effective prosecution must be ensured by taking measures at the national level and by enhancing international cooperation,[5]

Determined to put an end to impunity for the perpetrators of these crimes and thus to contribute to the prevention of such crimes,[6]

---

[1] The preamble sets the tone of the ICC Statute. Pursuant to Article 31 of the Vienna Convention the preamble is part of the context within the ICC Statute should be interpreted and applied. The Appeals Chamber has stated that when interpreting treaties, including the ICC Statute, the purposes may be gathered from "the wider aims of the law as may be gathered from its preamble and general tenor of the treaty" (*Situation in Democratic Republic of the Congo*, Judgment on the Prosecutor's Application for Extraordinary Review of Pre-Trial Chamber I's 31 March 2006 Decision Denying Leave to Appeal, ICC-01/04-168, 13 July 2006, para. 33). Operative Articles are typically more detailed and thus have higher rank than the preamble. The three first paragraphs of the preamble are more moral and philosophical statements and do not set out prescriptive rules. Similarly, the ninth and eleventh paragraphs do not have real prescriptive significance. The remaining paragraphs have been more prescriptive. To consider the preamble would normally only be necessary in cases of doubt.

[2] The affirmation in this paragraph is a way to highlight the importance of cultures and the need for various peoples of the world to exercise respect and tolerance fore one another. The references to "common bonds" and "shared heritage" recognise that humankind essentially is one despite differences between societies.

[3] The second preambular paragraph which has a reference to the millions of victims of past atrocities is an effort to ensure that the memory of these atrocities remains as a part of the collective human conscience.

[4] The third preambular paragraph uses the term "grave crimes", clarifying that that the "unimaginable atrocities" mentioned in paragraph 2 are not any crimes. Paragraphs 4 and 9 uses the similar term "the most serious crimes of concern", also to be found in Articles 1 and 5(1). The paragraph also mentions the values that the international criminal law seeks to protect: peace, security and well-being of the world. This may be compared with the formula "peace and security" throughout the UN Charter. The addition of "well-being" was done to emphasise more than the narrow concept of security, but also distribution of basic resources.

[5] The fourth preambular paragraph asserts the rule to fight against impunity, an obligation repeated in the fifth and sixth preambular paragraphs. Although this paragraph stresses the need for national measures at the national level and international cooperation, it does not deal with the relationship between the jurisdiction of the ICC and national jurisdictions. This matter is instead dealt with in the tenth preambular paragraph, Articles 1 and 17.

Recalling that it is the duty of every State to exercise its criminal jurisdiction over those responsible for international crimes, [7]

Reaffirming the Purposes and Principles of the Charter of the United Nations, and in particular that all States shall refrain from the threat or use of force against the territorial integrity or political independence of any State, or in any other manner inconsistent with the Purposes of the United Nations, [8]

---

[6] The fifth preambular paragraph is continuation of the previous paragraph, the aim to end impunity. It covers two functions of international criminal law: both the aim of repressing crimes that have been perpetrated and the aim of preventing future crimes from happening.

[7] Preambular paragraph 6 reminds the States of their duty to exercise criminal jurisdiction over those responsible for international crimes. It refers to "international crimes" which may be interpreted as broader concept than the core crimes listed in Article 5. International crimes could also include terrorism, piracy and drug offences. The preamble thus includes a reminder for the states not only to fight core crimes but also other crimes in their mutual interest.

[8] Preambular paragraph 7 reaffirms the States of the purposes and Principles of the Charter of the United Nations, in particular the obligations in Article 2(4) to refrain from the threat or use of force against the territorial integrity or political independence of any State. Article 1 of the UN Charter sets out the purposes of the UN Charter:

The Purposes of the United Nations are:

1. To maintain international peace and security, and to that end: to take effective collective measures for the prevention and removal of threats to the peace, and for the suppression of acts of aggression or other breaches of the peace, and to bring about by peaceful means, and in conformity with the principles of justice and international law, adjustment or settlement of international disputes or situations which might lead to a breach of the peace;
2. To develop friendly relations among nations based on respect for the principle of equal rights and self-determination of peoples, and to take other appropriate measures to strengthen universal peace;
3. To achieve international co-operation in solving international problems of an economic, social, cultural, or humanitarian character, and in promoting and encouraging respect for human rights and for fundamental freedoms for all without distinction as to race, sex, language, or religion; and
4. To be a centre for harmonising the actions of nations in the attainment of these common ends.

Article 2 of the UN Charter sets out the principles of the UN Charter:

The Organisation and its Members, in pursuit of the Purposes stated in Article 1, shall act in accordance with the following Principles.

1. The Organisation is based on the principle of the sovereign equality of all its Members.
2. All Members, in order to ensure to all of them the rights and benefits resulting from membership, shall fulfil in good faith the obligations assumed by them in accordance with the present Charter.
3. All Members shall settle their international disputes by peaceful means in such a manner that international peace and security, and justice, are not endangered.
4. All Members shall refrain in their international relations from the threat or use of force against the territorial integrity or political independence of any state, or in any other manner inconsistent with the Purposes of the United Nations.

Emphasizing in this connection that nothing in this Statute shall be taken as authorizing any State Party to intervene in an armed conflict or in the internal affairs of any State,[9]

Determined to these ends and for the sake of present and future generations, to establish an independent permanent International Criminal Court in relationship with the United Nations system, with jurisdiction over the most serious crimes of concern to the international community as a whole,[10]

Emphasizing that the International Criminal Court established under this Statute shall be complementary to national criminal jurisdictions,[11]

Resolved to guarantee lasting respect for and the enforcement of international justice,[12]

---

5. All Members shall give the United Nations every assistance in any action it takes in accordance with the present Charter, and shall refrain from giving assistance to any state against which the United Nations is taking preventive or enforcement action.

6. The Organisation shall ensure that states which are not Members of the United Nations act in accordance with these Principles so far as may be necessary for the maintenance of international peace and security.

The paragraph appears to be directed to the States, "interests of peace" arguably has less relevance for the Court's activities. Article 16 affords discretion to consider questions of peace, but this is a responsibility of the Security Council, not the Court.

[9] Even though the Court may deal with individual criminal responsibility for acts committed in internal armed conflict, but that does not mean that the Court will intervene in the internal affairs of the state concerned or the armed conflict. Moreover, the ICC Statute does not concern dispute settlement.

[10] The ninth preambular paragraph reaffirms that the ICC is a permanent court as opposed to the temporary character of the military tribunals in Nuremberg, Tokyo and the *ad hoc* tribunals for former Yugoslavia and Rwanda. The ICC is meant to address some of the complaints against its predecessors, namely them being a form of "victor's justice" and alleged use of retroactive legislation. Although there is no specific provision concerning the cessation of the ICC Statute, the parties could consent to terminate the Statute in accordance with the relevant rules of the Vienna Convention on the Law of Treaties.

[11] The tenth preambular paragraph describes one of the main features of the Court, namely that domestic criminal investigations and prosecutions have priority over the ICC provided that such domestic proceedings are genuine. This principle of complementarity may be contrasted with the jurisdictions of the *ad hoc* tribunals who have primacy over national courts. The principle of complementarity is repeated in Article 1 and Article 17 provides a more detailed standard.

[12] The final preambular paragraph uses the broad term "international justice", but from the context it should be understood to mean "international criminal justice". The ICC fills a gap. While the International Court of Justice settle disputes between states the ICC deals with individual criminal responsibility. From this paragraph follows that international criminal justice includes respect as well as enforcement international criminal law at both the domestic and international level.

Doctrine:

1. Tuiloma Neroni Slade and Roger S. Clark, "Preamble and Final Clauses", in Roy S. Lee (ed.), *The International Criminal Court: The Making of the Rome Statute: Issues, Negotiations, Results*, Kluwer Law International, The Hague, 1999, pp. 425–29.

2. Morten Bergsmo and Otto Triffterer, "Preamble", in Otto Triffterer (ed.), *Commentary on the Rome Statute of the International Criminal Court,* 2nd ed., C.H. Beck/Hart/Nomos, Munich/Oxford/Baden-Baden, 2008, pp. 1–47, MN 1–23.

Have agreed as follows:

3. William A. Schabas, *The International Criminal Court: Commentary on the Rome Statute*, Oxford University Press, Oxford, 2010, pp. 29–53.
4. Eric David, "Preamble", in Paul De Hert, Mathias Holvoet, Jean Flamme and Olivia Struyven (eds.), *Code of International Criminal Law and Procedure, Annotated*, Larcier Ghent, Brussels, 2013, pp. 7–10.

Author: Mark Klamberg.

PART 1. ESTABLISHMENT OF THE COURT

Article 1
The Court[13]

An International Criminal Court ("the Court") is hereby established.[14] It shall be a permanent institution[15] and shall have the power to exercise its jurisdiction over persons for the most serious crimes of international concern, [16] as referred to in this Statute, and shall be complementary to national criminal jurisdictions. The jurisdiction and functioning of the Court shall be governed by the provisions of this Statute.[17]

---

[13] *General remarks*:

Article 1 contains the main features of the International Criminal Court, namely it declares that the Court is established, is a permanent institution, that it may exercise jurisdiction for the most serious crimes and is complementary to national jurisdictions. These features are more precisely regulated in other Articles of the ICC Statute as indicated below and Article 1 may thus appear redundant. It also appears superfluous to that state the Court shall be governed by the provisions of this Statute.

[14] This sentence reflects that the Court is established by a treaty in contrast to the *ad hoc* tribunals, since latter are creations of the UN Security Council. The word "hereby" relates to the defined point of time when the Court was established. It follows from Articles 11 and 126 that the Court was established and came in to operation when the treaty entered into force on 1 July 2012. Article 1 uses the term "Court" which is not used consistently through the ICC Statute. In Article 34 the term "Court" refers to the institution as a whole, including the Presidency, the Chambers, the Office of the Prosecutor and the Registry. This also appears to be the understanding in Articles 2 and 16. However, in provisions such as 15(4), 17(1), 19(4) and 19(8) the term "Court" implies the Chambers, or judges.

[15] The ICC is a permanent court as opposed to the temporary character of the military tribunals in Nuremberg, Tokyo and the *ad hoc* tribunals for former Yugoslavia and Rwanda. Although there is no specific provision concerning the cessation of the ICC Statute, the parties could consent to terminate the Statute in accordance with the relevant rules of the Vienna Convention on the Law of Treaties ('VCLT').

[16] The Court's power is limited by the jurisdiction conferred to it. This means that it only has jurisdiction over the crimes listed in Article 5. The wording "persons" implies that the Court only has jurisdiction over natural persons which is supported by Article 25(1).

[17] The Court is complementarity to national criminal jurisdictions. The principle of complementarity is not defined in the present Article but addressed in paragraph 10 of the Preamble and in Articles 12–15 and 17–20.

Cross-references:
Paragraph 10 of the Preamble.

Doctrine:
1. William A. Schabas, *The International Criminal Court: A Commentary on the Rome Statute*, Oxford University Press, Oxford, 2010, pp. 57–62.
2. Otto Triffterer, "Article 1: The Court", in Otto Triffterer (ed.), *Commentary on the Rome Statute of the International Criminal Court: Observers' Notes, Article by Article*, 2nd ed., C.H. Beck/Hart/Nomos, Munich/Oxford/Baden-Baden, 2008, pp. 49–62.

---

3. Micaela Frulli, "Jurisdiction Ratione Personae", in Antonio Cassese, Paola Gaeta and John R.W.D. Jones (eds.), *The Rome Statute of the International Criminal Court: A Commentary*, Oxford University Press, Oxford, 2002, p. 532.
4. Luigi Condorelli and Santiago Villalpando, "Referral and Deferral by the Security Council", in Antonio Cassese, Paola Gaeta and John R.W.D. Jones (eds.), *The Rome Statute of the International Criminal Court: A Commentary*, Oxford University Press, Oxford, 2002, p. 637.
5. John T. Holmes, "Complementarity: National Courts versus the ICC", in Antonio Cassese, Paola Gaeta and John R.W.D. Jones (eds.), *The Rome Statute of the International Criminal Court: A Commentary*, Oxford University Press, Oxford, 2002, pp. 667–668, 671–672.

Author: Mark Klamberg.

Article 2

Relationship of the Court with the United Nations

The Court shall be brought into relationship with the United Nations through an agreement to be approved by the Assembly of States Parties to this Statute and thereafter concluded by the President of the Court on its behalf.[18]

---

[18] *General remarks*:

As the Court is established by way of a multilateral treaty it is an entirely separate institution *vis-à-vis* the United Nations ('UN'). The International Criminal Court derives its power and authority from a treaty and not from the UN. As such the ICC is an independent international organisation. However, the Court is a part of an international system where the United Nations is at the centre. There is a need to coordinate the responsibility of the United Nations to maintain peace and security with the Court's judicial role. This requires a structural link between the two institutions. Article 2 deals with the overall relationship between the Court and the United Nations. More specific matters are dealt with in other provisions. The Security Council can give the Court jurisdiction and trigger proceedings pursuant to Article 13(b). Article 16 provides that the Security Council may suspend or defer proceedings. The International Court of Justice ('ICJ'), the principal judicial organ of the United Nations, may have a role according to Article 119(2) in settling disputes between States Parties. Finally, Article 115(b) provides that the United Nations may provide funds to the Court, subject to the approval of the General Assembly, in particular in relation to the expenses incurred due to Article 13(b) referrals by the Security Council.

Analysis:

On 4 October 2004 the Negotiated Relationship Agreement between the International Criminal Court and the United Nations was adopted and entered into force. The agreement concerns, *inter alia*, reciprocal representation (Article 4), exchange of information (Article 5), reports to the UN (Article 6), proposal from the Court for items for consideration at the United Nations (Article 7), personal arrangements (Article 8), administrative cooperation (Article 9), services and facilities (Article 10), access to the United Nations Headquarters (Article 11), *laissez-passer* (Article 12) and financial matters (Article 13).

Cross-references:

Articles 13(b), 16 and part 12.

Doctrine:

1. Luigi Condorelli and Santiago Villalpando, "Relationship of the Court with the United Nations", in Antonio Cassese, Paola Gaeta and John R.W.D. Jones (eds.), *The Rome Statute of the International Criminal Court: A Commentary*, Oxford University Press, Oxford, 2002, pp. 219–34.
2. William A. Schabas, *The International Criminal Court: A Commentary on the Rome Statute*, Oxford University Press, Oxford, 2010, pp. 57–62.
3. Antonio Marchesi, "Article 2: Relationship of the Court with the United Nations", in Otto Triffterer (ed.), *Commentary on the Rome Statute of the International Criminal Court: Observers' Notes, Article by Article*, 2nd ed., C.H. Beck/Hart/Nomos, Munich, 2008, pp. 49–62.

Author: Mark Klamberg.

Article 3
Seat of the Court

1. The seat of the Court shall be established at The Hague in the Netherlands ("the host State").[19]
2. The Court shall enter into a headquarters agreement with the host State, to be approved by the Assembly of States Parties and thereafter concluded by the President of the Court on its behalf.[20]
3. The Court may sit elsewhere, whenever it considers it desirable, as provided in this Statute.[21]

---

[19] Domestic laws and regulations of the host State do apply within ICC premises unless the parties have contracted otherwise. However, it cannot be enforced by that State without the ICC waiving its relevant immunity in that case.

[20] In contrast to the International Criminal Tribunal for the former Yugoslavia ('ICTY') and the International Criminal Tribunal for Rwanda ('ICTR') the ICC is not an organ of the United Nations. Therefore, the General Convention of Privileges and Immunities of the UN (1945) does not apply and thus a similar general agreement is necessary. Other Articles relevant to the Host State Agreement include Articles 48 and 103. On 19 November 2002 the Registrar of the Court and the Ministry of Foreign Affairs of the Kingdom of the Netherlands exchanged Notes embodying an interim agreement between the ICC and the Kingdom of the Netherlands concerning the headquarters of the Court. The arrangements will continue to apply until the entry into force of the Headquarters Agreement.

Cross-references:
Articles 48 and 103.

[21] It is possible for the Court to sit outside The Hague. According to Article 38(3)(a) it shall be for the Presidency to take decision to arrange for sitting outside the Court.

Cross-references:
Article 38(3)(a).

Doctrine:

1. Adrian Bos, in Antonio Cassese, Paola Gaeta and John R.W.D. Jones (eds.), *The Rome Statute of the International Criminal Court: A Commentary*, Oxford University Press, Oxford, 2002, pp. 199–202.
2. Gerhard A.M. Strijards, in Otto Triffterer (ed.), *Commentary on the Rome Statute of the International Criminal Court*, Nomos Verlagsgesellschaft, Baden-Baden, 1999, pp. 77–88.

Author: Mark Klamberg.

Article 4
Legal status and powers of the Court[22]

---

[22] *General remarks*

International institutional law does not contain a definite set of criteria by which to identify an international organisation. Features that are commonly expected to be present include: the creation through an international agreement or other international instrument, having at least one organ with a will of its own, and being established under international law. Sometimes also the possession of international legal personality is mentioned as separate criteria (Schermers and Blokker, 2003, pp. 21–37, International Law Commission, Draft Articles on Responsibility of States for Internationally Wrongful Acts, in Report of the International Law Commission on the Work of its Fifty-third Session, Supplement No. 10 (A/56/10), Supplement No. 10 (A/56/10), Article 2), as well as the capacity to conclude treaties (Vienna Convention on the Law of Treaties between States and International Organisations or between International Organisations, 21 March 1986, Not yet in force, Article 6).

Article 4 deals with the nature of the ICC as an international actor. It addresses two of the most fundamental (and intertwined) features that assert an institution as an international legal subject and define the extent of the activities of that subject: the possession of legal personality and the exercise of powers.

Ever since the *Reparation for Injuries* case before the International Court of Justice, it has been unquestionable that international organisations can also be international legal subjects (*Reparation for injuries suffered in the service of the United Nations*, Advisory Opinion, 1949 ICJ Reports 174). Express assertion of legal personality is not a prerequisite for the acquisition of legal personality under international law. Nor can a set of prerequisites be identified by which to acquire international legal personality. Instead a more pragmatic approach has been applied. As the ICJ concluded in respect of the United Nations, when an organisation "was intended to exercise and enjoy, and is in fact exercising and enjoying, functions and rights which can only be explained on the basis of the possession of [...] international legal personality", the legal personality of the organisation is confirmed (*Reparation for injuries suffered in the service of the United Nations*, Advisory Opinion, 1949 ICJ Reports 174, p. 179, and Klabbers, 2009, p. 50).

As to the question of legal powers, Article 4 defines both the functional and territorial scope of the powers of the ICC. The totality of the powers of an international organisation is a sum of the explicitly granted powers and those non-express powers that are conferred upon it: "The powers conferred on international organisations are normally the subject of an express statement in their constituent instruments. Nevertheless, the necessities of international life may point to the need for organisations, in order to achieve their objectives, to possess subsidiary powers [...] known as 'implied' powers" (*Legality of the Use by a State of Nuclear Weapons in Armed Conflict*, Advisory Opinion, 8 July 1996, ICJ Reports 1996, para. 25).

In respect of judicial bodies the non-express powers are commonly characterised as inherent powers (or inherent jurisdiction). Whereas implied powers are derived from a perceived necessity for the performance of functions or attainment of objectives, the bulk of inherent powers of institutions are of a customary nature. As soon as an institution comes into existence, the logic is, it will enjoy all of these powers (Seyersted, 2008, p. 35). However, while a distinction between implied and inherent powers can be upheld in principle, a separation of the two categories of non-express powers may be difficult to uphold in practice.

1. The Court shall have international legal personality.[23] It shall also have such legal capacity[24] as may be necessary for the exercise of its functions and the fulfilment of its purposes.[25]

---

[23] The design and functions of the ICC confirm its status as an international legal person and as an international organisation. The ICC is established through an international treaty (Rome Statute of the International Criminal Court, 17 July 1998, 2187 UNTS 90, entered into force July 1, 2002), it has separate organs the will of which is independent from individual state parties (Article 34 ICC and Article 112 ICC), and it has powers to conclude international agreements. The Statute confers upon the Court the powers to conclude an agreement with the UN (Article 2 ICC, Negotiated Relationship Agreement between the International Criminal Court and the United Nations, 20 August 2004, A/58/874), a headquarters agreement (Article 3 ICC, Headquarters Agreement between the International Criminal Court and the Host State, 7 June 2007, entered into force 1 March 2008, ICC-BD/04-01-08), an agreement on privileges and immunities (Article 48 ICC, Agreement on the Privileges and Immunities of the International Criminal Court, 9 September 2002, entered into force 22 July 2004, ICC-ASP/1/3), and *ad hoc* agreements with non-party states (Article 87(5)(a) ICC). The powers of the Court to conclude agreements are not even limited to these instances but extend to the conclusion of a variety of agreements with state parties, non-party states, and international institutions (The ICC has entered into agreements for example with the EU, the Red Cross, and the Organisation internationale de la Francophonie. Agreements on enforcement of sentences have been concluded with several state parties. See the Official Journal of the Court).

The express inclusion in the constituent instrument of a provision granting international legal personality is a rarity among international organisations. It could also be thought of as superfluous given that the performance of functions and exercise of powers confirms the existence of an independent will and a capacity to act at the international level. The express confirmation of the international legal personality of the Court is however an expression of the consensus that was reached during the drafting process on establishing the ICC as an independent international organisation rather than as a UN organ (Schabas, 2010, p. 95). The Agreement on the Privileges and Immunities of the International Criminal Court further confirms both the international and national legal personality of the ICC (Agreement on the Privileges and Immunities of the International Criminal Court, ICC-ASP/1/3, Article 2).

Legal personality indicates a capacity of possessing international rights and duties, but no specific powers (nor the scope of powers) can be derived from the possession of personality as such. This is the essential difference between states and organisations as legal subjects (*Reparation for injuries suffered in the service of the United Nations*, Advisory Opinion, 1949 ICJ Reports 174, p. 179). The difference between states and organisations as legal subjects also affects the scope of their duties. In this respect Trial Chamber II has noted that the ICC is not able to implement the non-refoulement principle – a customary principle binding the Court due to its international legal personality – within its ordinary meaning (*Prosecutor v. Katanga and Ngudjolo*, Decision on an Amicus Curiae application and on the "Requête tendant à obtenir présentations des témoins DRC-D02-P-0350, DRC-D02-P-0236, DRC-D02-P-0228 aux autorités néeriandaises aux fins d'asile" (Articles 68 and 93(7) of the Statute), ICC-01/04-01/07-3003, para. 64).

As no particular legal powers are bestowed upon an organisation merely due to the possession of legal personality, the practical importance of that status rather follows from the obligation that is created for states to recognise the ICC as an autonomous actor. Member states hereby have a duty for example to recognise the binding effect of treaties concluded by the ICC, as well as to grant immunities to the Court (Martines, 2002, p. 208–10).

---

2. The Court may exercise its functions and powers,[26] as provided in this Statute, on the territory of any State Party and, by special agreement, on the territory of any other State.[27]

---

[24] In the absence of personality, the ICC could not make contracts for goods and services, hire employees, or perform its operational activities. While some of these activities require international legal personality, others are performed under domestic law (Gallant, 2003, p. 556). The inclusion of a clause in constituent instruments of organisations that explicitly bestows national legal personality is far more common than the inclusion of such a clause concerning international legal personality. Also preparatory work clearly indicates that the purpose of the passage is to bestow national legal personality (Preparatory Committee Draft Statute, p. 10, Schabas, 2010, p. 96–97) The Headquarters Agreement further specifies the content of the national legal personality by adding that the Court shall: "[…] in particular, have the capacity to contract, to acquire and to dispose of immovable and movable property and to participate in legal proceedings" (Headquarters Agreement between the International Criminal Court and the Host State, ICC-BD/04-01-08, Article 3). Both expressions are standard phrases to be found in constituent instruments and headquarters agreements, confirming the status of an organisation in the domestic legal systems of state parties.

Whereas the Headquarters agreement is key to the proper functioning of the ICC in the host state (the Netherlands), an obligation to recognise acts of the ICC can also arise within the national legal systems of other state parties. The ICC may for example sit elsewhere than in the host state (Article 3(3)), the Court shall enjoy necessary privileges and immunities in the territory of each State Party (Article 48 ICC), the Prosecutor may in some cases act directly within the territory of a state party without having secured cooperation of that party (Articles 54(2) and 57(3) ICC), and the Court may decide on a place of trial other than the seat of the Court (Article 62 ICC). The fact that sentences of imprisonment can be served in a state other than the host state may also imply the national legal personality of the ICC (Article 103(4) ICC, also see commentary by Strijards, 2008, p. 1656). State parties have a duty to cooperate fully with the Court, to ensure that there are certain procedures available under national law, and to comply with requests of various kinds (Part 9, ICC Statute). This cooperation does not however require the exercise of the powers of the ICC on the territory of state parties (Rückert, 2008, p. 125).

[25] The obligation which the Statute lays upon state parties to recognise the Court as a legal person in domestic law, does not define the content of the legal capacity of the Court. In other words, the capacity for performing certain acts on the domestic level does not entail an automatic competence for the ICC to perform that act. The necessity assessment serves first of all to ensure that the ICC will enjoy such capacity that it needs for performing its functions and fulfilling its purposes. This means that although special mention is made in the Headquarters Agreement and the Agreement on Privileges and Immunities of the capacity to contract, to acquire and to dispose of immovable and movable property, and to participate in legal proceedings, the list is not exhaustive. On the other hand, the necessity requirement also restricts the capacity of the ICC by requiring a link to the functions and purposes as defined in the Statute (Schermers and Blokker, 2003, p. 1011, note 111; Rückert, 2008, p. 124). The extent of the capacity of the ICC in domestic legal systems is also limited to the exercise of powers that are "provided in the Statute" (see note 11 on sub-paragraph 2) (Schermers and Blokker, 2003, p. 1016).

[26] The express powers of an organisation are unquestionably "provided in the Statute". However, also the implied powers of an organisation can be characterised as derived from the Statute. Although international case law displays some variation in the semantic construction of implied powers, the link to the statute basically derives from that an implied power can only be exercised when that power can be claimed to be necessary for the attainment of one of the objectives of the organisation. The extent of the implied powers of an organisation can range from powers that are necessary for the exercise of explicit powers (by which to attain the objectives of the or-

ganisation), to completely new powers that supplement the means by which to attain the goals of the organisation. Which implied powers an organisation enjoys, depends on the "needs of the community" (*Reparation for Injuries*, ICJ Reports 1949, p. 178, for a discussion see Engström 2012, Chapter 2).

There are several 'communities' that interpret the ICC Statute. The first community to interpret the extent of ICC powers was the Rome Conference. Authors seem to agree that the reference to "as provided in this Statute" was inserted in order to guard against expansion of the competence of the ICC through the use of implied powers (Rückert, 2008, p. 126; Martines, 2002, p. 215; Schabas, 2010, p. 97). Whether the inclusion of a reference to the Statute can prevent the use of implied powers if agreement on the necessity of such powers is attained is however uncertain. If a claim is made that the reference to the Statute does not exclude the use of more limited implied powers (necessary for the exercise of the expressly provided powers) (Rückert, 2008, p. 126), this inevitably undermines any categorical denial of implied powers. Such a construction of the powers of the ICC turns express powers into purposes, the realisation of which may allow for a range of different implied powers. Further, even if the reference to the statute is read as an express exclusion of any implied powers, that exclusion can lose its limiting effect if agreement on the need for widening the competence of the ICC is later achieved (see White, 2005, pp. 73–74 discussing the OAS Charter. As a matter of treaty law subsequent agreement and practice precedes the merely supplementary role of preparatory work in the interpretation and application of a treaty. Articles 31 and 32, Vienna Convention on the Law of Treaties, 23 May 1969, 1155 UNTS 331, entered into force 27 January 1980).

When dealing with judicial bodies, non-express powers are far more commonly presented as 'inherent' rather than 'implied'. The idea of inherent powers has its origin in common law systems where it has been invoked by courts for a range of different purposes (see Brown, 2005, pp. 205–206). Recourse to inherent powers can also be found in the case law of several international judicial bodies. The ICJ has noted that it: "[...] possesses an inherent jurisdiction enabling it to take such action as may be required, on the one hand to ensure that the exercise of its jurisdiction over the merits [...] shall not be frustrated, and on the other, to provide for the orderly settlement of all matters in dispute, to ensure the observance of the "inherent limitations on the exercise of the judicial function" of the Court, and to "maintain its judicial character". Such inherent jurisdiction, on the basis of which the Court is fully empowered to make whatever findings may be necessary for the purposes just indicated, derives from the mere existence of the Court as a judicial organ established by the consent of states, and is conferred upon it in order that its basic judicial function may be safeguarded" (*Nuclear Tests Case*, ICJ Reports 1974, para. 23). As to the relationship between the implied and inherent powers doctrines, the Appeals Chamber of the ICTY has held that the inherent powers notion would be preferable with respect to those non-express powers which are judicial in nature, whereas the implied powers doctrine seems better suitable for describing the extension of the competence of political organisations (*Prosecutor v. Tihomir Blaškić* (Case No. IT-95-14-AR), ICTY Appeals Chamber, Judgment on the Request of The Republic of Croatia for Review of the Decision of Trial Chamber II of 18 July 1997, 29 October 1997, para. 25, note 27).

A suggestion that Article 4 would exclude the use of implied powers but not reliance on inherent powers raises the question of the nature of and relationship between the implied and inherent powers doctrines. On the face of it, the commonality of some powers of international organisations (to adopt a budget, to conclude treaties, or to bring claims), make them seem inherent in the possession of legal personality (Rama-Montaldo, 1970). As international courts and tribunals display considerably more functional and procedural similarities than international political organisations, it seems only natural that an array of powers can be assumed to follow from their mere existence as such: the power to take interim measures, to request stays of proceedings or to stay its own proceedings, to order discontinuance of a wrongful act or omission, to appraise the credibility of a witness, to pronounce upon instances of contempt of the court, to order compensation, to consider matters or issue orders *proprio motu*, and to rectify material errors in a judgment (For a summary and references, see the Appeals Chamber of the Special Tribunal for Lebanon, El Sayed, (CH/AC/2010/02), Appeals Chamber, Decision on Appeal of Pre-Trial Judge's Order regarding Jurisdiction and Standing, 10 November 2010, para. 46. Also see Brown, 2005).

The Regulations of the Court recognises the existence of inherent powers (Regulations of the Court, ICC-BD/01-01-04, paras. 28(3), and 29(2)). As a point of departure inherent powers can be exercised by all organs of the ICC in carrying out their duties. However, the practice of other tribunals of exercising inherent powers is not automatically indicative of the existence of such inherent powers of the ICC. Somewhat at odds with the idea that inherent powers derive from the mere existence of a judicial body, the exercise and exact scope of any inherent powers must always be determined in relation to the functions of the individual court (Brown, 2005, p. 229; Amerasinghe, 2003, p. 99). This also renders the eventual difference between the implied powers and inherent powers doctrines unclear.

An element that may affect the use of inherent powers in the ICC when compared to the ICTY and ICTR is the more civil law oriented approach to criminal law of the ICC, which brings with it a stricter requirement of codification (Sluiter, 2010, p. 588). Nevertheless, the case law of the Court is rich with examples on the exercise of inherent powers. The ICC Pre-Trial Chamber II has noted that the Chamber has an inherent power to make "necessary alterations to documents issued by the Chamber" (*Prosecutor v. Kony et al.*, Pre-Trial Chamber II, Decision on the Prosecutor's Urgent Application Dated 26 September 2005, ICC-02/04-01/05, 27 September 2005). The Appeals Chamber has indicated that the Chamber may exercise an inherent power to stay proceedings, if (i) the "essential preconditions of a fair trial are missing", and (ii) there is "no sufficient indication that this will be resolved during the trial process" (*Prosecutor v. Lubanga*, Appeals Chamber, Judgment on the appeal of the Prosecutor against the decision of Trial Chamber I entitled "Decision on the consequences of non-disclosure of exculpatory materials covered by Article 54(3)(e) agreements and the application to stay the prosecution of the accused, together with certain other issues raised at the Status Conference on 10 June 2008", ICC-01/04-01/06-1486, 21 October 2008, para. 76, and *Prosecutor v. Kenyatta*, Trial Chamber V, Decision on defence application pursuant to Article 64(4) and related requests, ICC-01/09-02/11-728, 26 April 2013, para. 74). Trial Chamber I has noted, by reference to the practice of the ICTY and ICTR, that a Chamber "can depart from earlier decisions that would usually be binding if they are manifestly unsound and their consequences are manifestly unsatisfactory" (*Prosecutor v. Lubanga*, Decision on the defence request to reconsider the "Order on numbering of evidence" of 12 May 2010, ICC-01/04-01/06, 30 March 2011, para. 18). Pre-Trial Chamber I has held, referring to the practice of the ICTY, that it possesses an inherent power to inform the UN Security Council on lack of cooperation of non-party states (*Prosecutor v. Harun et al.*, Decision informing the United Nations Security Council about the lack of cooperation by the republic of the Sudan, ICC-02/05-01/07, 25 May 2010, p. 6). However, in respect of state parties the ICC has relied on the express mechanism for informing the Security Council provided for by Article 87(7) ICC (*Prosecutor v. Omar Hassan Ahmad Al Bashir*, Decision pursuant to Article 87(7) of the ICC Statute on the refusal of the Republic of Chad to comply with the cooperation requests issued by the Court with respect to the arrest and surrender of Omar Hassan Ahmad Al Bashir, ICC-02/05-01/09, 13 December 2011). As a more general characterisation of the inherent powers of the ICC, Trial Chamber IV has stated that any inherent powers or incidental jurisdiction can only be invoked in a restrictive manner. The reason for this, especially in the case of procedural matters such as stay of proceedings, is that the exercise of non-express powers may contradict the object and purpose of the Court by frustrating the administration of justice (*Prosecutor v. Abdallah Banda Abakaer Nourain and Saleh Mohammed Jerbo*

Jamus, Trial Chamber IV, Decision on the defence request for a temporary stay of proceedings, ICC-02/05-03/09, 26 October 2012, para. 78). This echoes the concern of Judge Blattmann that the exercise of inherent powers imports a discretionary element to the decision-making, potentially undermining procedural certainty (especially if there is an alternative mechanism available in the Statute) (*Prosecutor v. Lubanga*, Separate Opinion of Judge René Blattmann to the Decision on the defence request to reconsider the "Order on numbering of evidence" of 12 May 2010, ICC-01/04-01/06, 30 March 2011, paras. 1 and 7).

27   The ICC can exercise jurisdiction over the crimes listed in Article 5 ICC both in relation to state parties and non-party states (Article 12 ICC). In respect of state parties, the jurisdiction of the ICC is not only exercised *vis-à-vis* the state that has a special link with a crime, but all ICC state parties for example through the summoning of witnesses (Martines, 2002, p. 214). In respect of non-party states, it is a general rule of international law that a treaty cannot create obligations for third states without their consent (Vienna Convention on the Law of Treaties, 23 May 1969, 1155 UNTS 331, entered into force 27 January 1980, Articles 34–36). Therefore, the possibility of extending the legal personality of the ICC also to non-party states is one of the more novel features of the ICC Statute. Non-party states can accept the jurisdiction of the ICC through a declaration (Article 12(3) ICC), the Court can invite non-party states to provide assistance through *ad hoc* arrangements, agreements, or "any other appropriate basis" (Article 87 ICC), and the ICC may come to exercise jurisdiction over non-party states through UN Security Council referral (Article 13(b) ICC). The use of declarations and agreements for extending the jurisdiction of the ICC ensures a consensual basis for the extension. For example, Côte d'Ivoire had, prior to its ratification of the ICC Statute in 2013, accepted the jurisdiction of the Court already in 2005 (ICC, Registrar confirms that the Republic of Côte d'Ivoire has accepted the jurisdiction of the Court, ICC-CPI-20050215-91).

The absence of such expressions of consent does not however necessarily prevent the Prosecutor from acting on a situation. The possibility of extending the jurisdiction of the ICC to non-party states even without their consent through UN Security Council referral is by some authors considered as a true expression of the 'objective' legal personality of the Court (on theories of legal personality, see, for example, Martines, 2002, pp. 206–208 and Klabbers, 2009, pp. 46–51). The UN Security Council has, in referring situations to the ICC, emphasised that States not parties to the ICC Statute have no obligations under the Statute (UN SC Res. 1593 (2005) on the situation in Darfur, 31 March 2005, para. 2, and UN SC Res. 1970 (2011) on the situation in Libya, 17 March 2011, para. 5). The obligation for non-party states to cooperate with the Court rather derives from the UN Charter (Article 25 Charter of the United Nations, 26 June 1945, 1 UNTS XVI, entered into force 24 October 1945, Gallant, 2003, p. 583; Williams and Schabas, 2008, pp. 569–74; and Schabas, 2010, pp. 293–304).

Cross-references:
Articles 2, 3, 5, 12, 13, 34, 48, 54, 57, 62, 87, 89–92, 103 and 112.

Doctrine:

1. Chittharanjan F. Amerasinghe, *Principles of the Institutional Law of International Organizations*, Cambridge University Press, Cambridge, 2005.

2. Chester Brown, "The Inherent Powers of International Courts and Tribunals", in *British Yearbook of International Law*, 2005, vol. 76, pp. 195–244.

3. Viljam Engström, *Constructing the Powers of International Institutions*, Martinus Nijhoff, Leiden, 2012.

4. Kenneth S. Gallant, "The International Criminal Court in the System of States and International Organizations", in *Leiden Journal of International Law*, 2003, vol. 16, pp. 553–591.

5. Jan Klabbers, *An Introduction to International Institutional Law*, Cambridge University Press, Cambridge, 2009.

6. Francesca Martines, "Legal Status and Powers of the Court", in Antonio Cassese, Paola Gaeta and John R.W.D. Jones (eds.), *The Rome Statute of the International Criminal Court: A Commentary*, Oxford University Press, Oxford, 2002, pp. 203–18.

7. Manuel Rama-Montaldo, "International Legal Personality and Implied Powers of International Organizations", in *British Yearbook of International Law*, 1970, vol. 44, pp. 111–55.

8. Wiebke Rückert, "Article 4: Legal Status and Powers of the Court", in Otto Triffterer (ed.), *Commentary on the Rome Statute of the International Criminal Court: Observers' Notes, Article by Article*, 2nd ed., C.H. Beck/Hart/Nomos, Munich/Oxford/Baden-Baden, 2008, pp. 121–27.

9. William A. Schabas, *The International Criminal Court: A Commentary on the Rome Statute*, Oxford University Press, Oxford, 2010.

10. Henry G. Schermers and Niels M. Blokker, *International Institutional Law: Unity within Diversity*, Martinus Nijhoff, Leiden, 2003.

11. Finn Seyersted, *Common Law of International Organizations*, Martinus Nijhoff, Leiden, 2008.

12. Gerard A.M. Strijards, "Article 10: Role of States in Enforcement of Sentences of Imprisonment", in Otto Triffterer (ed.), *Commentary on the Rome Statute of the International Criminal Court: Observers' Notes, Article by Article*, 2nd ed., Beck/Hart/Nomos, Munich/Oxford/Baden-Baden, 2008, pp. 1647–57.

13. Göran Sluiter, "Trends in the Development of a Unified Law of International Criminal Procedure", in Carsten Stahn and Larissa van den Herik (eds.), *Future Perspectives on International Criminal Justice*, TMC Asser Press, The Hague, 2010, pp. 585–99.

14. Nigel D. White, *The Law of International Organisations*, Manchester University Press, Manchester, 2005.

15. Sharon A. Williams and William A. Schabas, "Article 13: Exercise of Jurisdiction", in Otto Triffterer (ed.), *Commentary on the Rome Statute of the International Criminal Court: Observers' Notes, Article by Article*, 2nd ed., Munich/Oxford/Baden-Baden, Beck/Hart/Nomos, 2008, pp. 563–74.

Author: Viljam Engström.

PART 2. JURISDICTION, ADMISSIBILITY AND APPLICABLE LAW

Article 5
Crimes within the jurisdiction of the Court[1]

The jurisdiction of the Court shall be limited to the most serious crimes of concern to the international community as a whole. The Court has jurisdiction in accordance with this Statute with respect to the following crimes:[28]

(a) The crime of genocide;[29]

(b) Crimes against humanity;[30]

(c) War crimes;[31]

(d) The crime of aggression.[32]

---

[1] Paragraph 2 of article 5 ("The Court shall exercise jurisdiction over the crime of aggression once a provision is adopted in accordance with articles 121 and 123 defining the

---

[28] The crimes mentioned in the present provision are considered to be the core crimes of international criminal law.

[29] See comments under Article 6.

[30] See comments under Article 7.

[31] See comments under Article 8.

[32] At the Rome Conference, the informal consultations did not bring the delegations to an agreement on the definition of the crime and under which conditions the Court shall exercise jurisdiction with respect to the crime. Thus, the Court may not exercise jurisdiction with respect to the crime of aggression.

The Court's jurisdiction over the crime was made dependent on the Assembly of State Parties ('ASP') agreeing on a definition in accordance with the now deleted Article 5(2). In 2002 the ASP decided to establish a Special Working Group on the Crime of Aggression (SWGCA), which was to submit proposed provisions to a future Review Conference (Resolution on Continuity of Work in Respect of the Crime of Aggression, 2002). The SWGCA draft amendments were the starting point for the discussions at the Kampala Review Conference in 2010, where Articles 8 *bis*, 15 *bis*, 15 *ter* and 25 (3) *bis* were adopted. It follows from Articles 5 *bis(3)* and 15 *ter(3)* that the Court will have the power by 2017 to exercise jurisdiction over the crime, provided that 30 States Parties have ratified or accepted the amendments.

Doctrine:

1. Gerhard Werle, *Principles of International Criminal Law*, TMC Asser Press, The Hague, 2005, pp. 400–1, MN 1184–85.

2. Herman von Hebel and Darryl Robinson, "Crimes Within the Jurisdiction of the Court", in Roy S. Lee (ed.), *The International Criminal Court: The Making of the Rome Statute: Issues, Negotiations, Results*, Kluwer Law International, The Hague, 1999, pp. 81–85.

3. Andreas Zimmerman, in Otto Triffterer (ed.), *Commentary on the Rome Statute of the International Criminal Court: Observers' Notes, Article by Article*, 2nd ed., C.H. Beck/Hart/Nomos, Munich/Oxford/Baden-Baden, 2008, pp. 129–142, MN 1–41.

Author: Mark Klamberg.

crime and setting out the conditions under which the Court shall exercise jurisdiction with respect to this crime. Such a provision shall be consistent with the relevant provisions of the Charter of the United Nations.") was deleted in accordance with RC/Res.6, annex I, of 11 June.

Article 6
Genocide[33]

---

[33] *General remarks*:

i. The legal and the ordinary concept of genocide

A principal difficulty relating to the interpretation of the concept of genocide arises from the widespread use of the term. The 'ordinary' concept, which exists outside its legal parameters, has been stretched to fit a wide variety of scenarios. The word is commonly employed in particular in reference to campaigns involving the killing of a large number of victims. The legal concept, as it appears in identical phrasing in the texts of Article 6 ICC Statute, Article 4(2) ICTY Statute, Article 2(2) ICTR Statute and Article II of the Genocide Convention, differs from that (see below at C.), but there is evidence that the ordinary concept has influenced the views of tribunals and individual judges. In *Kayishema and Ruzindana* for instance, the ICTR Trial Chamber quoted with approval the opinion that it was "virtually impossible" for genocide to be committed without State involvement, "given the magnitude of this crime" (*Prosecutor v. Clément Kayishema and Obed Ruzindan*a (Case No. ICTR-95-1-T), ICTR T. Ch., Judgment, 21 May 1999, para. 94). For the impact of the ordinary concept of genocide on the ICJ judgment in *Croatia v. Serbia*, see Behrens, 2015). The legal concept, at least pursuant to the literal interpretation of the ICC Statute, requires neither magnitude (on the objective side of the crime) nor State involvement nor even the involvement of more than one perpetrator (But see below at ii. for the contextual element).

ii. Contextual element

An attempt to introduce a contextual element into the legal concept of genocide was made through the Elements of Crime in 2000 (see last element of each of the alternatives of genocide in the Elements of Crime).

A literal reading of the crime as it appears in the ICC Statute does not suggest that organisational structure, pattern, magnitude or other contextual elements have become of the concept of genocide. It is for that reason that the establishment of contextual elements in the Elements of Crime is a problematic feature. Triffterer for one has voiced the view that the requirement of a context is not consistent with the wording of the statute and thus conflicts with Article 9 of the ICC Statute (Triffterer, 2001a, p. 407). In *Al Bashir*, however, the majority of the Pre-Trial Chamber found that the application of the Elements of Crime could only be refused if this would lead to an "irreconcilable contradiction" with the Statute of the court, *Prosecutor v. Omar Al Bashir*, ICC PT. Ch., Decision on the Prosecution's Application for a Warrant of Arrest against Omar Hassan Ahmad Al Bashir, ICC-02/05-01/09-3, 4 March 2009, para. 128), but concluded that, "[i]n the case at hand", such a contradiction did not exist (*ibid.*, para. 132). If a contextual element along these lines were accepted, it would in any event not reflect customary international law that existed before the entry into force of the Elements of Crime (see also *Krstić*, ICTY Appeals Chamber, Judgment, 19 April 2004, para. 224).

On the requirement of a "manifest pattern of similar conduct", the Pre-Trial Chamber noted that the "crime of genocide is only completed when the relevant conduct presents a concrete threat to the existence of the targeted group, or a part thereof" (Pre-Trial Chamber, *Al Bashir*, PT. Ch., 4 March 2009, para. 124). That threat had to be "concrete and real, as opposed to just being latent or hypothetical" (*ibid.*). In her dissenting opinion, Judge Ušacka took exception to the "result-based" reading to which the majority view would lead, and stated that the requirement of a threat "would then duplicate the purpose of the second part" of the contextual element (*Al Bashir*, ICC PT. Ch., Arrest Warrant Decision, ICC-02/05-01/09-3, 4 March 2009, Dissenting Opinion Judge Ušacka, para. 26), that is, "conduct that could itself effect such destruction".

With regard to that element, the majority found that it referred to conduct of "such a nature as to itself effect [...] the total or partial destruction of the targeted group" (*Al Bashir*, Pre-Trial Chamber, Arrest Warrant Decision, ICC-02/05-01/09-3, 4 March 2009, para. 123).

iii. Evidentiary issues

Questions of evidence cause particular problems in relation to the existence of specific genocidal intent (see below, notes 34–38). The ICTR Appeals Chamber has accepted that this element can be proven through circumstantial evidence, but it also emphasised that a finding of intent must still be "the only reasonable inference from the totality of the evidence" (*Prosecutor v. Ferdinand Nahimana, Jean-Bosco Barayagwiza, Hassan Ngeze* (Case No. ICTR-99-52-T), ICTR T. Ch., Judgment, 3 December 2003, para. 524). That requirement allows for a critical approach towards strands of evidence which were accepted by the Trial Chambers as suitable indications for genocidal intent.

With regard to incriminating evidence, the *ad hoc* tribunals have accepted for a long time that genocidal intent can be inferred from the actions of the perpetrator at the time of the commission of the crime (*Prosecutor v. Jean-Paul Akayesu* (Case No. ICTR-96-4-T), ICTR T. Ch., Judgment, 2 September 1998, para. 523).

But even actions of this kind may allow for a range of inferences (Behrens, 2007, 136). The "scale of the atrocities" (see *Prosecutor v. André Ntagerura, Emmanuel Bagambiki, Samuel Imanishimwe* (Case No. ICTR-99-46-T), ICTR T. Ch., Judgment, 25 February 2004, para. 689) and the manner of the killing (see *ibid.*, para. 690) cause particular problems in that regard, as crimes against humanity can be committed in an equally cruel fashion and are, because of their contextual element, likely to result in large-scale atrocities.

The *ad hoc* tribunals have also given weight to statements which the accused had made at the relevant time (*Prosecutor v. Kayishema*, ICTR T. Ch., 21 May 1999, para. 93). In this regard, the fact must be taken into account that a defendant's statements will require interpretation in light of their context (see *ibid.*, para. 539, on the phrases "go to work" or "get down to work").

Preparatory work:

The introduction of the concept of this crime into international law can be traced to the work of the Polish lawyer Raphael Lemkin, who in *Axis Rule in Occupied Europe* (Washington, 1944), used the term 'genocide' to refer to the "destruction of a nation or of an ethnic group" (*ibid.*, chapter 9). Before the International Military Tribunal ('IMT') at Nuremberg, genocide was mentioned in the text of the indictment, but it did not form an independent charge against the defendants – it was rather seen as conduct which fulfilled the parameters of war crimes and crimes against humanity.

In 1946 General Assembly Resolution 96(I) recognised genocide as a "crime under international law" and understood it to mean "the denial of the right of existence of entire human groups" (GA Res 96(I)). In that Resolution, the General Assembly also requested the Economic and Social Council ('ECOSOC') to "undertake the necessary studies, with a view to drawing up a draft convention on the crime of genocide" (*ibid.*).

The UN Secretariat subsequently issued a first draft of a genocide convention, which was then reviewed by an *ad hoc* committee convened by ECOSOC, resulting in a second draft. A third draft was issued by the Sixth Committee of the General Assembly in 1948 and submitted to the General Assembly for adoption. The resulting convention – the Convention on the Prevention and Punishment of the Crime of Genocide – was adopted on 8 December 1948 and entered into force on 12 January 1951. One of the most important changes which materialised during the codification process, was the shifting emphasis of the crime: where the 1946 General Assembly Resolution still put an objective aspect of genocide at the centre of the concept, the crime as enshrined in the Genocide Convention receives its particular characteristic through its

For the purpose of this Statute, "genocide" means any of the following acts committed with intent[34] to destroy,[35] in whole or in part,[36] a national, ethnical, racial or religious group,[37] as such:[38]

---

subjective side ("intent to destroy, in whole or in part, a national, ethnical, racial or religious group, as such").

Further insight into the interpretation of the crime is provided through the International Law Commission ('ILC') commentary on Article 17 of the 1996 Draft Code of Crimes against the Peace and Security of Mankind (YILC. 1996, vol. 2, part 2, p. 44). But the definition of genocide as it appears in Article II of the Genocide Convention has remained textually unchanged in the ICC Statute.

[34] Next to the group element, it is the existence of destructive intent which gives the crime its particular character (cf. *Prosecutor v. Radoslav Brđanin* (Case No. IT-99-36-T), ICTY T. Ch., Judgment, 1 September 2004, para. 699).

The intent element is not merely a counterpart to an already existing factor on the side of the *actus reus*, but has an existence outside and above the latter. The ICTY Trial Chamber in *Prosecutor v. Milomir Stakić* (Case No. IT-97-24-T), ICTY T. Ch., Judgment, 31 July 2003, thus spoke of a crime distinguished "by a 'surplus' of intent" (para. 520).

The precise threshold for genocidal intent has been subject of controversy. A majority of the Chambers of the *ad hoc* tribunals resort to terms which imply a volitional standard: the perpetrator "seeks to achieve" the destruction (for example *Prosecutor v. Goran Jelisić* (Case No. IT-95-10-A), ICTY A. Ch., Judgment, 5 July 2001, paras. 45–46), or he must have had the "goal" of destroying the group (*Prosecutor v. Radislav Krstić* (Case No. IT-98-33-T), ICTY T. Ch., Judgment, 2 August 2001, paras. 571, 572). The ILC expressed a similar view when it found that "a general awareness of the probable consequences" of a genocidal act was not sufficient (YILC, 1996, vol. 2, part 2, 44, Article 17, para. 5).

Supporters of the cognitive opinion focus on the knowledge of the perpetrator: in Jelisić for instance, the Prosecution stated that it was sufficient for the mental element that the perpetrator "knew that his acts were destroying, in whole or in part, the group, as such", and made clear that such knowledge must refer to actual (as opposed to probable) destruction (*Prosecutor v. Jelisić*, ICTY A. Ch., 5 July 2001, para. 42). For further references in the literature, see Behrens, 2012a, pp. 77, 78).

However, the lower cognitive standard has that far not found favour with the international criminal tribunals – with some Trial Chambers stating expressly that knowledge of inevitable or likely destructive consequences was not sufficient for the conviction of the defendant (*Prosecutor v. Vidoje Blagojević and Dragan Jokić* (Case No. IT-02-60-T), ICTY T. Ch., Judgment, 17 January 2005, para. 656).

[35] In the eyes of the ILC, 'destruction' referred only to the "material destruction of a group either by physical or by biological means"; other forms of destruction were expressly dismissed (YILC, 1996, vol. 2, part 2, 46, para. 12). A more inclusive view has been supported by the Constitutional Court of Germany, which in 2000 found that destructive intent extended "beyond physical and biological extermination" (BVerfG, para (III)(4)(a)(aa)). In his partially dissenting opinion in *Krstić*, Judge Shahabuddeen found that the destruction of the group as a 'social unit' was embraced by the intention of the perpetrator (*Prosecutor v. Radislav Krstić* (Case No. IT-98-33-A), ICTY A. Ch., Judgment, 19 April 2004, Partial Dissenting Opinion of Judge Shahabuddeen, para. 51).

In the case law of the *ad hoc* tribunals, there is however a strong tendency to follow the narrower view: in *Prosecutor v. Seromba* (Case No. ICTR-2001-66-I), ICTR T. Ch., Judgment, 13 December 2006, for instance, the Trial Chamber found that the concept of "destruction of the group" (in the context of genocidal intent) referred to the "material destruction of a group either by physical or by biological means [...]" (para. 319. See also Tournaye, 2003, p. 454). It is certainly true that a group can be destroyed in more ways than through the killing of its members or the prevention of births (*Prosecutor v. Blagojević*, ICTY T. Ch., 17 January 2005, para. 666), but the inclusion of all kinds of destruction is also likely to lead to such an extensive understanding of the crime that its threshold disappears. The existence of national groups, for example, could effectively be terminated through mere changes in the legal personality of the State, including its voluntary merger with another State.

Apart from that, the fact cannot be dismissed that the option of including other forms of destruction had existed at drafting stage but was ultimately rejected (see *Prosecutor v. Radislav Krstić* (Case No. IT-98-33-T), ICTY T. Ch., Judgment, 2 August 2001, para. 576, fn. 1284); a comprehensive view of the codification history therefore does not yield a result which supports the wider view.

[36] The phrase "in whole or in part" was introduced at the drafting stage through a suggestion by Norway, which the Sixth Committee accepted (UN GAOR, 3rd session, 6th Committee, 73rd meeting, 92, 97); but its interpretation has ever since been subject of much debate in the literature and the international criminal tribunals.

It does seem well accepted today that the intended destruction must refer at least to a "substantial part" of the relevant group (see for example *Prosecutor v. Radoslav Brđanin* (Case No. IT-99-36-T), ICTY T. Ch., Judgment, 1 September 2004, para. 701; YILC, 1996, vol. 2, part 2, 45, para. 8 and *Prosecutor v. Radislav Krstić* (Case No. IT-98-33-A), ICTY A. Ch., Judgment, 19 April 2004, para. 11). However, the determination of 'substantiality' has caused interpretive problems to the tribunals and commentators. In international case law, three general methods have been established to evaluate substantiality: the numerical, the functional and the geographical approaches.

The Trial Chamber in *Prosecutor v. Kayishema* (Case No. ICTR-95-1-T), ICTR T. Ch., Judgment, 21 May 1999, for instance, promoted the numerical approach, when it found that "in part" required the "intention to destroy a considerable number of individuals who are part of the group" (para. 97; see also Preparatory Committee, Report of the Preparatory Committee on the Establishment of an International Criminal Court, 14 April 1998, A/CONF.183/2/Add.1 – p. 11, Article 5, fn. 1). Later case law was more cautious. The *Krstić* Appeals Chamber for instance, saw it as a "necessary" starting point, but "not in all cases the ending point of the inquiry" (para. 12). In any event, the assessment of the numerical significance of the part is not exhausted by an examination of actual numbers, but also needs to involve an evaluation of the part of the group in relation to the overall group size (*ibid.*).

Under the functional approach, the perpetrator is not necessarily seen as selecting a numerically significant part, but instead a section which has significance for the group because of particular functions associated with it. Whitaker referred in that regard to "a significant section of a group such as its leadership" (Whitaker Report, 1985, para. 29). The precise methods of assessing substantiality under the functional approach vary from situation to situation. In *Brđanin*, reference was made to the "prominence" which the targeted part enjoyed within the group (*Prosecutor v. Radoslav Brđanin* (Case No. IT-99-36-T), ICTY T. Ch., Judgment, 1 September 2004, para. 702); and the Appeals Chamber in *Prosecutor v. Radislav Krstić* (Case No. IT-98-33-A), ICTY A. Ch., Judgment, 19 April 2004, expressed the view that the targeted Bosnian Muslims of Srebrenica were "emblematic of the Bosnian Muslims in general" (para. 37 and see para. 16; see also *Prosecutor v. Zdravko Tolimir* (Case No. IT-05-88/2-A), ICTY A. Ch. Judgment, 8 April 2015, para. 261).

A section which features often in the considerations of the tribunals is the leadership of the group (for example *Brđanin*, ICTY T. Ch., 1 September 2004, para. 703). Other sections which have been mentioned by tribunals and commentators include men of military age – a consideration which played a particular role in *Krstić*, where the killing of the Bosnian Muslim men in Srebrenica was concerned (*Krstić*, ICTY T. Ch., 2 August 2001, para. 579) – and law enforcement or security personnel (Commission of Experts, 1992, para. 94). Like the numerical approach, the assessment of substantiality here also involves an evaluation of the effect that the targeting of this part has on the group as a whole (*Prosecutor v. Goran Jelisić* (Case No. IT-95-10-T), ICTY T. Ch., Judgment, 14 December 1999, para. 82).

A particular concern which attaches to the functional approach is the fact that its application might defeat the very purpose of establishing a threshold through substantiality. The problem gained prominence in the *Krstić* case. According to the Defence, the Trial Chamber had concluded that Krstić had targeted the Bosnian Muslim men of military age of Srebrenica. These formed part of the Bosnian Muslims of Srebrenica, which in turn were part of the actual protected group – the Bosnian Muslims (*Krstić*, ICTY A. Ch., 19 April 2004, para. 18). In the words of the Defence, the Trial Chamber had therefore identified "part of a part" of a group (*Prosecutor v. Radislav Krstić* (Case No. IT-98-33-A), ICTY A. Ch., Judgment, 19 April 2004, Partial Dissenting Opinion of Judge Shahabuddeen, para. 43). If the Bosnian Muslim men of Srebrenica were just seen as part of the protected group as a whole (the Bosnian Muslims), it would not have been acceptable to consider them as fulfilling the substantiality requirement (*Krstić*, ICTY A. Ch., 19 April 2004, para. 18).

The Appeals Chamber did not follow this line of reasoning and concluded that the military-aged men had been considered not as "part of a part" of a group, but that their killing had formed evidence for the fact that the perpetrator had intent to destroy a (substantial) part of the group, that is, the Bosnian Muslims of Srebrenica (*ibid.*). At the same time, the Chamber also clarified that the functional approach was "only one of several" methods to assess the substantiality of the group (*ibid.*, para. 22). In *Tolimir*, the Trial Chamber had referred to the killing of three community leaders as evidence for the existence of genocidal intent (*Prosecutor v. Zdravko Tolimir* (Case No. IT-05-88/2-T), ICTY T. Ch., Judgment, 12 December 2012, paras. 780–82). The Appeals Chamber found that the Trial Chamber had failed to show that the fate of the community leaders had had an impact "on the survival of the group as such" (*Prosecutor v. Zdravko Tolimir* (Case No. IT-05-88/2-A), ICTY A. Ch., Judgment, 8 April 2015, para. 267), but found no legal error in the general derivation of genocidal intent from the targeting of leading figures of a community (*ibid.*, para. 263).

The geographical approach is based on the understanding of genocide as a crime which is by necessity limited by geographical conditions. In 1982, for instance, the General Assembly referred to localised massacres – the killing of Palestinian civilians in the Sabra and Shatila refugee camps – as 'genocide' (UNGA Res 37/123D (1982)) and the ILC pointed out that the intended destruction of a protected group "from every corner of the globe" was not a necessary requirement of the crime (YILC, 1996, vol. 2, part 2, 45, Article 17, para. 8).

The geographical approach has, on the whole, been embraced by the *ad hoc* tribunals (cf. *Prosecutor v. Brđanin*, ICTY T. Ch., 1 September 2004, para. 703). Some Trial Chambers went so far as to find that the 'part' of the group might be limited to a single region or community (*Prosecutor v. Duško Sikirica, Damir Došen, Dragan Kolundžija* (Case No. IT-95-8-T), ICTY T. Ch., Judgment on Defence Motion to Acquit, 3 September 2001, para. 68). In *Prosecutor v. Krstić*, ICTY T. Ch., 19 April 2004, the Trial Chamber outlined the possibility that genocide might be committed even in a municipality, and made express reference to the General Assembly resolution on Sabra and Shatila (para. 589).

Opposition to the geographical method tends not to concern the basic principle that genocidal intent can be limited to a particular area, but rather seeks to introduce certain limitations on the approach. In *Prosecutor v. Brđanin*, ICTY T. Ch., 1 September 2004, the Trial Chamber expressed the view that a limitation of the 'part' of the group to certain municipalities of the Autonomous Region of the Krajina could have a "distorting effect" (para. 966). Similar concerns were voiced by the ICTY Trial Chamber in *Prosecutor v. Milomir Stakić* (Case No. IT-97-24-T), ICTY T. Ch., Judgment, 31 July 2003, which however followed the geographical approach "with some hesitancy" (para. 523).

Additional problems arise from the fact that the perpetrator will in some cases specifically have limited his intent to a particular region and therefore not have targeted the group "as such". Situations of this kind arise when a municipality or other geographic area is selected as the target of a punitive expedition – acts which will usually be covered by crimes against humanity, but might, because of their very limited nature, not fulfil the requirements of genocidal intent.

[37] The Elements of Crime clarify that the 'group element' carries significance both for the objective and the subjective part of the crime. On the objective side, the victim of the perpetrator's conduct must belong to a "particular national, ethnical, racial or religious group" (Elements of Crime, Article 6, element 2 of each alternative); on the subjective side, the perpetrator must have had the intent "to destroy, in whole or in part" a group of this kind (*ibid.*, element 3 of each alternative).

The ICTR Trial Chamber in *Prosecutor v. Akayesu* (Case No. ICTR-96-4-T), Judgment, 2 September 1998, defined a 'national group' as a group whose members are seen as sharing a "legal bond, based on common citizenship, coupled with reciprocity of rights and duties" (para. 512), an ethnic group as a group "whose members share a common language or culture" (para. 513). The characteristics of members of a racial group were seen as their "hereditary physical traits often identified with a geographical region, irrespective of linguistic, cultural, national or religious factors" (*ibid.*, para. 514) and members of a religious group "share the same religion, denomination or mode of worship" (*ibid.*, para. 515).

Apart from the controversial nature inherent in the selection of only certain groups for the protection of international criminal law in this regards (see Behrens, 2012b, pp. 240, 241), the group element has also led to difficulties where its application in practice is concerned.

The attempt to reach a precise distinction between Hutus and Tutsis in Rwanda for instance – groups which shared the same culture and language and which showed a "high rate of mixed marriages" (Cassese, 2003, p. 101) – posed challenges where the parameters of the four enumerated groups were concerned.

But the later case law of the *ad hoc* tribunals has not followed an entirely objective approach. In *Kayishema and Ruzindana*, the ICTR would also have included at least under the category of 'ethnic groups' a group which "distinguishes itself, as such (self identification); or, a group identified as such by others, including perpetrators of the crimes (identification by others)" (*Prosecutor v. Clément Kayishema and Obed Ruzindana* (Case No. ICTR-95-1-T), ICTR T. Ch., Judgment, 21 May 1999, para. 98).

The approach which was eventually adopted by the Trial Chambers is best understood as a contextual approach – referred to in the *Semanza* judgment as a method by which the identification of a group "ought to be assessed on a case-by-case basis by reference to the objective particulars of a given social and historical context, and by the subjective perceptions of the perpetrator" (*Prosecutor v. Laurent Semanza* (Case No. ICTR-97-20-T), ICTR T. Ch., Judgment, 15 May 2003, para. 317). The Chamber found that group identification was to be made "on a case-by-case basis, consulting both objective and subjective criteria" (*ibid.*).

A similar difficulty exists where the identification of members of a group is concerned. In this regard, the existing case law appears to favour a subjective approach: membership of the group was to be considered "from a subjective standpoint, holding that the victim is perceived by the perpetrator of the crime as belonging to the group targeted for destruction" (*Prosecutor v. Seromba*, ICTR T. Ch., 13 December 2006, para. 318).

[38] The inclusion of the words "as such" indicates that the boundaries between genocidal intent and motive, if they do exist, are difficult to identify (see Behrens, 2012c). During the drafting process, the *ad hoc* committee had suggested a list of motives that would form the basis for the genocidal acts. This suggestion triggered considerable debate in the Sixth Committee. In the end, an express reference to motives was not included, but the Committee agreed to a proposal by Venezuela which introduced the words "as such" into the crime. The Venezuelan delegate, speaking to his amendment, stated that he "felt that his amendment should meet the views of those who wished to retain a statement of motives; indeed, the motives were implicitly included in the words 'as such'" (Pérez Perozo (Venezuela), UN doc. A/C.6/SR.76, 124). Subsequently, some Trial Chambers have made use of the language of motives when referring to specific intent: the *Akayesu* Trial Chamber went so far as to refer to an "ulterior motive, which is to destroy, in whole or in part, the group" (*Prosecutor v. Jean-Paul Akayesu* (Case No. ICTR-96-4-T), ICTR T. Ch., Judgment, 2 September 1998, para. 522).

The phrase "as such" also emphasises the fact that the (principal) victim of genocide is the group itself (*Prosecutor v. Radoslav Brđanin* (Case No. IT-99-36-T), ICTY T. Ch., Judgment, 1 September 2004, para. 698) – a notion which is apparent from the codification history of the crime (Ad Hoc Committee on Genocide, Note by the Secretariat, UN doc. E/AC.25/3/Rev.1, 12 April 1948, 6 and YILC, 1996, vol. 2, part 2, 45, Article 17, para. 6). The group must have been targeted as a "separate and distinct entity" (*Prosecutor v. Popović et al.*, ICTY T. Ch., 10 June 2010, paras. 821 and 1177 with further references). The individuals affected by the underlying acts are, by comparison, victims only because of their membership of that particular group (*Prosecutor v. Radislav Krstić* (Case No. IT-98-33-T), ICTY T. Ch., Judgment, 2 August 2001, para. 561).

This prominent role of the group element on the subjective side of the crime raises the question whether genocide is possible if perpetrators attack members of their own group. The issue gained particular prominence in the context of the large-scale crimes which the Khmer Rouge committed on the Khmer people in Cambodia. The UN Commission on Human Rights, reflecting on these events, coined the term 'autogenocide' (Commission on Human Rights, 35th session, Summary Record of the First Part (Public) of the 1510th Meeting, UN doc. E/CN.4/SR.1510 (1979), paras. 22, 24). The term lacks legal currency, but has been at the centre of some debate among commentators of the crime.

In its discussion of genocide, the Group of Experts for Cambodia declined to take a position on the question whether the Khmer Rouge possessed destructive intent with regard to the Khmer people (Report of the Group of Experts for Cambodia established pursuant to General Assembly Resolution 52/135, (1999), Annex, para. 65). Before the Extraordinary Chambers in the Courts of Cambodia ('ECCC'), Ieng Sary and other Khmer Rouge leaders were in 2010 indicted for genocide committed against the Cham and the Vietnamese, but not against the Khmer people (Extraordinary Chambers in the Courts of Cambodia, Office of the Co-Investigating Judges, Closing Order (Case No. 002/19-09-2007-ECCC-OCIJ), 15 December 2010, paras. 1335–49 and 1613).

In the literature, some authors have supported the opinion that autogenocide still qualifies as genocide, as it involves the intended destruction of part of a protected group (Khan and Dixon, 2009, p. 1088, paras. 13–25; Hannum, 1989, pp. 103 ff., 112). The Trial Chambers on the other hand have emphasised that the individual victims must have been targeted "specifically because they belonged" to the protected group (*Prosecutor v. Akayesu*, ICTR T. Ch., 2 September 1998, para. 521). In the Cambodian case, this lends support to the opposing view, since the Khmer victims were selected for political and other reasons, but not on the basis of their membership of a group protected by the Convention (Vest, 1999, p. 356).

(a) Killing members of the group;[39]

(b) Causing serious bodily or mental harm to members of the group;[40]

There is in fact no reason why autogenocide should not be covered by Article 6. But autogenocide, if the concept is to be applied correctly, requires that the perpetrator deliberately made his own group the victim of his actions. There is perhaps a tendency to dismiss too quickly the possibility of self-destructive génocidaires. In the majority of cases, however, the perpetrator will probably have an inflated rather than a dismissive perception of his own people, leaving only a slim realm for the reality of 'genuine' autogenocide.

[39] The Elements of Crime provide that "[t]he term 'killed' is interchangeable with the term 'caused death'" (Article 6(a), note 10). That indicates that the death of the victim is a necessary consequence of the perpetrator's conduct and that a causal link needs to exist between conduct and consequence. To that degree, the elements of 'killing' as one of the alternatives of genocide do not appear to show any significant deviation from the elements identified under 'murder' as a crime against humanity (see *Prosecutor v. Mitar Vasiljević* (Case No. IT-98-32-T), ICTY T. Ch., Judgment, 29 November 2002, para. 205, notes 1 and 2.).

However, the conclusion (suggested by some Trial Chambers) that all elements of that crime against humanity are equivalent to the elements of 'killing' here (see on this *Prosecutor v. Vujadin Popović, Ljubisa Beara, Drago Nikolić, Ljubomir Borovčanin, Radivoje Miletić, Milan Gvero, Vinko Pandurević* (Case No. IT-05-88-T), ICTY T. Ch., Judgment, 10 June 2010, para. 810, referring to paras. 787–89), remains a generalisation. On the side of the *mens rea*, at least, certain differences arise. With regard to murder as a crime against humanity, the intention to cause serious bodily harm which "the accused should reasonably have known might lead to death", has in the past been accepted as a sufficient subjective element (*Popović*, ICTY T. Ch., 10 June 2010, para. 788). If that were the case where genocide is concerned, actual knowledge would no longer be required – even negligence would fulfil the *mens rea* of alternative (a).

Most Trial Chambers however appear to call for intent with regard to the consequence of the killing. In this regard, the findings in *Akayesu* are instructive. When considering both the English and the French version of the Genocide Convention, the Chamber found that the French term ('*meurtre*') was to be preferred to the English term 'killing', as the latter could refer even to unintentional homicides (*Prosecutor v. Jean-Paul Akayesu* (Case No. ICTR-96-4-T), ICTR T. Ch., Judgment, 2 September 1998, para. 500). It consequently interpreted Article 2(2)(a) of the ICTR Statute as meaning homicide "committed with the intent to cause death" (*ibid.*, para. 501). The Chamber had based its opinion on the principle that the interpretation which is more favourable to the accused, had to be preferred (*ibid.*).

[40] The 'harm' to which this alternative of genocide refers, need not be "permanent and irremediable" (*Prosecutor v. Akayesu*, ICTR T. Ch., 2 September 1998, para. 502), but the *Seromba* Appeals Chamber found that it must be so serious as to cause a threat of the "destruction [of a protected group] in whole or in part" (*Prosecutor v. Athanase Seromba* (Case No. ICTR-2001-66-I), ICTR A. Ch., para. 46).

In *Krstić*, the Trial Chamber noted that the relevant harm must go "beyond temporary unhappiness, embarrassment or humiliation" (para. 513; see also *Prosecutor v. Tolimir*, ICTR A. Ch., 8 April 2015, paras. 203, 212) and that it must result "in a grave and long-term disadvantage to a person's ability to lead a normal and constructive life" (*ibid.*). The Elements of Crime and the case law of the tribunals provide examples which qualify in this category, including torture (Elements of Crime, fn. 3 to Article 6(b), 1st element, *Prosecutor v. Radislav Krstić* (Case No. IT-98-33-T), ICTY T. Ch., Judgment, 2 August 2001, para. 513), inhuman and degrading treatment (*ibid.*), rape (*ibid.* and *Prosecutor v. Rutaganda* (Case No ICTR-96-3), ICTR T. Ch., Judgment, 6 December 1999, para. 51) and sexual violence (*ibid.*, and *Prosecutor v. Akayesu* (Case No. ICTR-96-4-T), ICTR T. Ch., Judgment, 2 September 1998, para. 688); but

(c) Deliberately inflicting on the group conditions of life calculated to bring about its physical destruction in whole or in part;[41]

---

persecution (*Akayesu*, ICTR T. Ch., 2 September 1998, para. 504) and deportations (*Krstić*, ICTY T. Ch., 2 August 2001, para. 513) have also been mentioned in this context. Threats of death and "knowledge of impeding death" have been accepted as examples for serious mental harm (*Prosecutor v. Zdravko Tolimir*, Case No. IT-05-88/2-A, ICTY A. Ch., Judgment, 8 April 2015, para. 206). Forcible transfer, too, can cause serious bodily and mental harm (*ibid.*, paras. 208, 209), but a Trial Chamber would also have to find that long-term consequences resulted from such transfer and that there had been a link between the forcible transfer and the physical destruction of the group (*ibid.*, para. 217).

Pursuant to Article 30, intent is required both for conduct and consequence of this alternative of genocide. With regard to the former, this means that the perpetrator must have meant to engage in the relevant act; with regard to the latter – the resulting serious bodily or mental harm – Article 30 provides that the perpetrator must have meant to cause the consequence or must have been "aware that it will occur in the ordinary course of events". The case law of the *ad hoc* tribunals confirms that the harm must have been inflicted intentionally (*Prosecutor v. Popović et al.* (Case No. IT-05-88-T), ICTY T. Ch., Judgment, 10 June 2010, para. 811).

[41] The infliction of conditions of this kind does not need to be an imposition of methods which would immediately lead to the deaths of group members (*Prosecutor v. Kayishema and Ruzindana* (Case No. ICTR-95-1-T), ICTR T. Ch., Judgment, 21 May 1999, para. 116). The *Tolimir* Appeals Chamber went so far as to state that [direct] 'killings' could not be seen as a method of inflicting conditions of life calculated to bring about its destruction under this alternative of the crime (*Prosecutor v. Zdravko Tolimir*, Case No. IT-05-88/2-A, ICTY A. Ch., Judgment, 8 April 2015, para. 228). The *ad hoc* tribunals have accepted that so-called 'slow death' measures would fulfil the required element of this alternative (*Prosecutor v. Kayishema and Ruzindana*, ICTR T. Ch., 21 May 1999, para. 115). Subjecting members of the group to a subsistence diet, the denial of necessary medical services, but also "systematic expulsion from homes" falls in this category (*Prosecutor v. Akayesu* (Case No. ICTR-96-4-T), ICTR T. Ch., Judgment, 2 September 1998, para. 506; *Prosecutor v. Brđanin* (Case No. IT-99-36-T), ICTY T. Ch., Judgment, 1 September 2004, para. 691; *Prosecutor v. Zdravko Tolimir,* Case No. IT-05-88/2-A, ICTY A. Ch., 8 April 2015, para. 226). In *Tolimir*, the Appeals Chamber did, however, clarify that forcible transfer needs to be carried out "with a view to the destruction of the group", as opposed to its geographical removal, if it is to be considered under this alternative of genocide (*Tolimir* (Appeals Chamber), para. 233).

Other examples that have been mentioned include the failure to provide proper housing, clothing or hygiene or imposition of "excessive work or physical exertion" (*Brđanin*, ICTY T. Ch., 1 September 2004, para. 691; *Kayishema*, ICTR T. Ch., 21 May 1999, para. 115). The destruction of religious sites as a method of inflicting such conditions of life has been rejected by the ICTY Appeals Chamber (*Prosecutor v. Zdravko Tolimir*, Case No. IT-05-88/2-A, ICTY A. Ch., 8 April 2015, para. 230).

There is, as the *Brđanin* Trial Chamber confirmed, no need to prove that the group has been physically destroyed in whole or in part (para. 691). On the other hand, it would go too far to conclude from that that 'proof of a result' is not required (but on this, see *Prosecutor v. Stakić* (Case No. IT-97-24-T), ICTY T. Ch., Judgment, 31 July 2003, para. 517). Alternative (c) does envisage a consequence, but the consequence lies not in the destruction of the group, but in the fact that the relevant conditions have come into existence (see on this Article 6 (c) of the Elements of Crime, which in its first paragraph clarifies that the conditions must have been inflicted).

(d) Imposing measures intended to prevent births within the group;[42]

(e) Forcibly transferring children of the group to another group.[43]

As such, this consequence requires a corresponding element on the side of the *mens rea* of the crime. The term 'deliberately' is an express reference to that element (Genocide Application Case, 69, para. 186) which therefore cannot involve a standard lower than intent. However, that does not mean that a requirement of prior planning needs to be read into the adjective (cf. Jessberger, 101).

The term 'calculated', on the other hand, is not a reference to the *mens rea* of the perpetrator – the conditions may well have been calculated by a third party to have this effect (for instance, in cases in which a military commander orders the perpetrator to impose an insufficient diet on inmates of a detention camp). This aspect, relating to the nature of the conditions, is a circumstantial element; the perpetrator must have had knowledge of it as defined in Article 30(3) of the ICC Statute.

Cross-references:

Starvation in Articles 7(1)(b), (j) and (k); 7(2)(b); 8(2)(a)(iii); 8(2)(b)(ii), (v), (xiii) and (xxv).

[42] In the *Akayesu* case, the ICTR Trial Chamber clarified that it is sufficient for this alternative if the relevant measures have mental effects on the victims. It referred in this regard to the example of rape in cases in which "the person raped refuses subsequently to procreate, in the same way that members of a group can be led, through threats or trauma, not to procreate" (*Prosecutor v. Akayesu* (Case No. ICTR-96-4-T), ICTR T. Ch., Judgment, 2 September 1998, para. 508).

In cases of rape, the perpetrator may also achieve the prevention of births in the group through a different chain of causation: in that regard, the ICTR referred to a situation in which female members of a group in a society in which membership of the group was dependent on the identity of the father, were raped by men of another group (*ibid.*, para. 507). In circumstances of this kind, the criminal act might well have been carried out with the intent to impregnate the woman and to "have her give birth to a child who will consequently not belong to its mother's group" (*ibid.*). Other examples include sexual mutilation, sterilisation, sexual segregation, prohibition of marriage and forced birth control (*ibid.*).

The ILC made clear that the term 'imposing' implied an element of coercion: and therefore, this rule could, for instance, not be seen as encompassing "voluntary birth control programmes sponsored by a State as a matter of social policy" (YILC, 1996, vol. 2, part 2, p 46, Article 17, Commentary, para. 16).

Intent is required where the commission of the act (the implementation of the measures) is concerned (*Prosecutor v. Popović* (Case No. IT-05-88-T), ICTY T. Ch., Judgment, 10 June 2010, para. 808), and Article 30(2)(a) appears to call for a strong volitional element in that regard ("means to engage"). The measure itself, on the other hand, is a circumstantial element, and the required mental element which attaches to it, is therefore cognitive in nature: the perpetrator must have known about the nature of the measures (Article 30(3)). A different reading cannot be derived from the word 'intended', which this alternative of genocide employs (but see also *Case Concerning the Application of the Convention on the Prevention and Punishment of the Crime of Genocide (Bosnia and Herzegovina v. Serbia and Montenegro)*, ICJ, Judgment, 26 February 2007, para. 186): the intent to which the wording of Article 6(d) refers may well have been that of a third party. The intent of the perpetrator, on the other hand, is required for the consequence of the act (Article 30(2)(b)), that is, for the fact that such measures have now come into existence in the protected group.

43   The Elements of Crime specify that the act under this alternative consists in the transfer of one or more persons from a protected group to another group, when these persons belonged to the protected group and were below the age of 18 years (Elements of Crime, Article 6, elements 1, 2, 4 and 5.). The potential age range of the victims is therefore more extensive than that envisaged in other international crimes (see, for example, Article 8(2)(b)(xxvi) ICC Statute and Article 8(2)(e)(vii)).

The transfer must have been carried out in a 'forcible' manner. In that regard, however, the *ad hoc* tribunals had already emphasised that it was the aim of the provision not only to protect against "forcible physical transfer", but also against "acts of threats or trauma" which would accomplish the coercive transfer (*Prosecutor v. Jean-Paul Akayesu* (Case No. ICTR-96-4-T), ICTR T. Ch., Judgment, 2 September 1998, para. 509). Today, the Elements of Crime provide that the word 'forcibly' is "not restricted to physical force, but may include threat of force or coercion, such as that caused by fear of violence, duress, detention, psychological oppression or abuse of power, against such person or persons or another person, or by taking advantage of a coercive environment" (Elements of Crime, Article 6, element 1, note 5).

The perpetrator must have had intent with regard to the consequence of the crime, that is, the completed transfer from one group to another group. However, the fact that the victim of the transfer was a child, is a circumstantial element. In this regard, the Elements of Crime make clear that a standard lower than knowledge is sufficient for the subjective element: it is enough that the perpetrator "should have known" that the victim had not yet reached the age of 18 years (Elements of Crime, Article 6(e), 6th element). It is one of the rare cases in which the *mens rea* for one of the underlying acts of genocide deviates from the standard established by Article 30 of the ICC Statute.

Doctrine:

1. Paul Behrens, "A Moment of Kindness? Consistency and Genocidal Intent", in Ralph Henham and Paul Behrens (eds.), *The Criminal Law of Genocide: International, Comparative and Contextual Aspects*, Ashgate, Aldershot, 2007, pp. 125–140.
2. Paul Behrens, "Assessment of International Criminal Evidence: The Case of the Unpredictable Génocidaire", in *Zeitschrift für Ausländisches Öffentliches Recht und Völkerrecht*, 2011, vol. 71, pp. 662–89.
3. Paul Behrens and Ralph Henham (eds.), *Elements of Genocide*, Routledge, New York, 2012.
4. Paul Behrens, "The *Mens Rea* of Genocide", in Paul Behrens and Ralph Henham (eds.), *Elements of Genocide*, Routledge, New York, 2012, pp. 70–96 [Behrens 2012(a)].
5. Paul Behrens, "The Need for a Genocide Law", in Paul Behrens and Ralph Henham (eds.), *Elements of Genocide*, Routledge, New York, 2012, pp. 237–53 [Behrens 2012(b)].
6. Paul Behrens, "Genocide and the Question of Motives", in *Journal of International Criminal Justice*, 2012, vol. 10, pp. 501–23.
7. Paul Behrens, "Between Abstract Event and Individualized Crime: Genocidal Intent in the Case of Croatia", in *Leiden Journal of International Law*, 2015, vol. 28, pp. 923–35.
8. Antonio Cassese, *International Criminal Law,* Oxford University Press, Oxford, 2003.
9. Pieter Drost, *The Crime of State: Penal Protection for Fundamental Freedoms of Persons and Peoples. Book II: Genocide,* A.W. Sythoff, Leiden, 1959, p. 124.
10. Paola Gaeta (ed.), *The UN Genocide Convention: A Commentary*, Oxford University Press, Oxford, 2009.
11. Alexander K.A. Greenawalt, "Rethinking Genocidal Intent: The Case for a Knowledge-Based Interpretation", in *Columbia Law Review*, 1999, vol. 99, p. 2259–94.

12. Hurst Hannum, "International Law and Cambodian Genocide: The Sounds of Silence", in *Human Rights Quarterly*, 1989, vol. 11, no. 1, pp. 82–138.

13. Kevin Jon Heller, "Prosecutor v. Karemera, Ngirumpatse, and Nzirorera, Case No. ICTR-98-44-AR73(C). Decision on Prosecutor's Interlocutory Appeal of Decision on Judicial Notice. International Criminal Tribunal for Rwanda, Appeals Chamber, June 16, 2006", in *American Journal of International Law*, 2007, vol. 101, p. 157–63.

14. Ralph Henham and Paul Behrens (eds.), *The Criminal Law of Genocide: International, Comparative and Contextual Aspects*, Ashgate, Aldershot, 2007.

15. Hans-Heinrich Jescheck, "Die internationale Genocidium-Konvention vom 9. Dezember 1948 und die Lehre vom Völkerstrafrecht", in *Zeitschrift für die gesamte Strafrechtswissenschaft*, 1954, vol. 66, no. 2, p. 193.

16. Florian Jessberger, "The Definition and the Elements of the Crime of Genocide", in Paola Gaeta (ed.), *The UN Genocide Convention: A Commentary*, Oxford University Press, Oxford, 2009, pp. 87–111.

17. Nina H.B. Jørgensen, "The Definition of Genocide: Joining the Dots in the Light of Recent Practice", in *International Criminal Law Review*, 2001, vol. 1, no. 3, pp. 285–313.

18. Karim Khan and Rodney Dixon, *Archbold International Criminal Courts: Practice, Procedure and Evidence*, Sweet and Maxwell, London, 2009.

19. Claus Kreß, "The Darfur Report and Genocidal Intent", in *Journal of International Criminal Justice*, 2005, vol. 3, no. 3, pp. 562–78.

20. Lawrence J. LeBlanc, "The Intent to Destroy Groups in the Genocide Convention: The Proposed U.S. Understanding", in *American Journal of International Law*, 1984, vol. 78, no. 2, pp. 369–85.

21. Raphael Lemkin, *Axis Rule in Occupied Europe*, Carnegie Endowment for International Peace, Washington, DC, 1944.

22. Matthew Lippman, "The Convention on the Prevention and Punishment of Genocide: Fifty Years Later", in *Arizona Journal of International and Comparative Law*, 1998, vol. 15, no. 2, pp. 415–514.

23. David L. Nersessian, "The Razor's Edge: Defining and Protecting Human Groups under the Genocide Convention", in *Cornell International Law Journal*, 2003, vol. 36, no. 2, p. 293–327.

24. John Quigley, *The Genocide Convention: An International Law Analysis*, Ashgate, Aldershot, 2006.

25. Nehemiah Robinson, *The Genocide Convention: A Commentary*, Institute of Jewish Affairs, World Jewish Congress, New York, 1960.

26. William A. Schabas, *Genocide in International Law: The Crime of Crimes*, Cambridge University Press, Cambridge, 2009.

27. Cécile Tournaye, "Genocidal Intent before the ICTY", in *International and Comparative Law Quarterly*, 2003, vol. 52, no. 2, pp. 447–62.

28. Otto Triffterer, "Genocide, Its Particular Intent to Destroy in Whole or in Part the Group as Such", in *Leiden Journal of International Law*, 2001, vol. 14, no. 2, p. 399–408 [Triffterer 2001(a)].

29. Otto Triffterer, "Kriminalpolitische und dogmatische Überlegungen zum Entwurf gleichlautender "Elements of Crimes" für alle Tatbestände des Völkermordes", in Bernd Schünemann (ed.), *Festschrift für Claus Roxin zum 70. Geburtstag am 15. Mai 2001*, Walter de Gruyter, Berlin, 2001, p. 1415 [Triffterer (2001b)].

30. Harmen G. van der Wilt, "Genocide, Complicity in Genocide and International v. Domestic Jurisdiction", in *Journal of International Criminal Justice*, 2006, vol. 4, no. 2, pp. 239–57.

31. Beth Van Schaack, "The Crime of Political Genocide: Repairing the Genocide Convention's Blind Spot", in *Yale Law Journal*, 1997, vol. 106, pp. 2259–91.

32. Hans Vest, "Die bundesrätliche Botschaft zum Beitritt der Schweiz zur Völkermordkonvention – kritische Überlegungen zum Entwurf eines Tatbestandes für den Völkermord", in *Schweizerische Zeitschrift für Strafrecht*, 1999, vol. 117, pp. 351, 356.

33. Hans Vest, *Genozid durch organisatorische Machtapparate*, Nomos, Baden-Baden, 2002.

34. Hans Vest, "A Structure-Based Concept of Genocidal Intent", in *Journal of International Criminal Justice*, 2007, vol. 5, no. 4, p. 781–97.

35. Gerhard Werle, *Principles of International Criminal Law*, Cambridge University Press, Cambridge, 2009.

Other Materials:

1. Draft Code of Crimes Against the Peace and Security of Mankind YILC 1996, vol. 2, part 2, p. 46, Art. 17, Commentary.

2. Report of the Preparatory Committee on the Establishment of an International Criminal Court, 14 April 1998, A/CONF.183/2/Add.1 – p. 11, Art. 5, fn. 1.

3. Report of the Group of Experts for Cambodia established pursuant to General Assembly Resolution 52 / 135, (1999), Annex, para. 63.

4. Report of the International Commission of Inquiry on Darfur to the United Nations Secretary-General pursuant to Security Council resolution 1564 of 18 September 2004, 25 January 2005 ['Darfur Report'].

5. United Nations, Ad Hoc Committee on Genocide, Note by the Secretariat, UN doc. E/AC.25/3/Rev.1, 12 April 1948, p. 6.

6. United Nations, Commission of Experts, Final Report of the Commission of Experts Established Pursuant to Security Council Resolution 780 (1992), UN doc. S/1994/674 ['Commission of Experts'].

7. United Nations, Commission on Human Rights, 35th session, Summary Record of the First Part (Public) of the 1510th Meeting, UN doc. E/CN.4/SR.1510 (1979), paras. 22, 24.

8. United Nations Commission on Human Rights, Sub-Commission on Prevention of Discrimination and Protection of Minorities, 38th session, Item 4 of the provisional agenda, E/CN.4/Sub.2/1985/6. Revised and updated report on the question of the prevention and punishment of the crime of genocide, prepared by Mr B Whitaker (2 July 1985) ['Whitaker Report'], para. 31.

9. United Nations, General Assembly, Resolution 96(I), 11 Dec 1946, UN doc. A/Res/96(I).

10. United Nations, General Assembly, Resolution 37/123D, 16 Dec 1982, UN doc. A/Res/37/123D.

11. United States Congress, Executive Session of the Senate Foreign Relations Committee, Historical Series, vol. 2, US Government Printing Office, 1976, 370.

Author: Paul Behrens.

Article 7
Crimes against humanity

1. For the purpose of this Statute, "crime against humanity" means any of the following acts when committed as part of a widespread or systematic attack directed against any civilian population,[44] with knowledge of the attack:[45]

General remarks:

[44] The general elements in the chapeau of Article 7 elevate an ordinary crime or an inhumane conduct to a crime against humanity. The general elements were extensively dealt with during the drafting of the ICC Statute and are set out in Article 7(1) and (2) of the Statute, as well as in the Elements of Crimes (von Hebel and Robinson, 1999, pp. 91–97; McCormack, 2004, pp. 179–182, 186–189). In the ICC case law, they were analysed by the Pre-Trial Chamber in *Prosecutor v. Bemba* in 2008, and its analysis has been largely followed by other Pre-Trial Chambers and the Trial Chamber in the *Prosecutor v. Katanga*.

Analysis:

i. Definition

Crimes against humanity pursuant to the ICC Statute are any of the enumerated acts in Article 7 "when committed as part of a widespread or systematic attack directed against any civilian population, with knowledge of the attack" (ICC Statute, Article 7(1)). According to Article 7(2)(a), an "attack directed against any civilian population" means "a course of conduct involving the multiple commission of acts referred to in paragraph 1 against any civilian population, pursuant to or in furtherance of a State or organizational policy to commit such attack". These words are repeated in the Elements of Crimes.

For each of the underlying acts, the Elements of Crimes set out that the conduct must have been "committed as part of a widespread or systematic attack directed against a civilian population". Further, they state that the perpetrator must have known "that the conduct was part of or intended the conduct to be part of a widespread or systematic attack against a civilian population".

Based on the above, the Pre-Trial Chambers have identified five general elements: "(i) an attack directed against any civilian population, (ii) a State or organisational policy, (iii) the widespread or systematic nature of the attack, (iv) a nexus between the individual act and the attack, and (v) knowledge of the attack" (*Situation in the Republic of Kenya*, ICC PT. Ch. II, ICC-01/09-19, Decision Pursuant to Article 15 of the Rome Statute on the Authorisation of an Investigation into the Situation in the Republic of Kenya, 31 March 2010, para. 79; *Situation in the Republic of Côte d'Ivoire*, ICC PT. Ch. III, ICC-02/11-14, Decision Pursuant to Article 15 of the Rome Statute on the Authorisation of an Investigation into the Situation in the Republic of Côte d'Ivoire, 3 October 2011, para. 29).

Notably, the general elements do not contain any requirement of a nexus to an armed conflict or any discriminatory element (von Hebel and Robinson, 1999, pp. 92–94; McCormack, 2004, pp. 184–186; Robinson, 1999, pp. 45–47; Schabas, 2010, pp. 144–147, 157).

ii. Requirements

a. Material elements

With regard to the requirement of 'attack', the Elements of Crimes clarify that "[t]he acts need not constitute a military attack". Although the ICC Statute itself defines 'attack' as "course of conduct", the Pre-Trial Chamber in the *Prosecutor v. Bemba* considered that the term referred to "a campaign or operation", although adding that the "appropriate terminology used in [the ICC

Statute] being a 'course of conduct'" (*Prosecutor v. Bemba*, ICC PT. Ch. II, ICC-01/05-01/08-424, Decision Pursuant to Article 61(7)(a) and (b) of the Rome Statute on the Charges of the Prosecutor Against Jean-Pierre Bemba Gombo, 15 June 2009, para. 75). The Pre-Trial Chamber set out that it is the commission of the acts referred to in Article 7(1) that constitute the 'attack' and "beside the commission of the acts, no additional requirement for the existence of an "attack" should be proven" (*ibid.*). This does not necessarily mean that the element of 'attack' is proven as soon as the underlying acts allegedly committed by the perpetrator are proven (see *Prosecutor v. Bemba*, ICC PT. Ch. II, ICC-01/05-01/08-424, Decision Pursuant to Article 61(7)(a) and (b) of the Rome Statute on the Charges of the Prosecutor Against Jean-Pierre Bemba Gombo, 15 June 2009, para. 151). Presumably the Pre-Trial Chamber merely intended to say that an attack must be composed of acts enumerated in Article 7(1) (as opposed to other acts). In this respect, the Pre-Trial Chamber could have found support in the text of Article 7 itself, although it did cite the Akayesu Trial Judgment, which does not support this (see *Akayesu*, ICTR-96-4, ICTR T. Ch., 2 September 1998, para. 581 ("The concept of attack maybe [*sic*] defined as a [*sic*] unlawful act of the kind enumerated in Article 3(a) to (i) of the Statute [...] An attack may also be non violent in nature, like imposing a system of apartheid [...] or exerting pressure on the population to act in a particular manner").

The same Pre-Trial Chamber stated that the requirement of 'directed against' means that "the civilian population must be the primary object of the attack and not just an incidental victim of the attack" (*Prosecutor v. Bemba*, ICC PT. Ch. II, ICC-01/05-01/08-424, Decision Pursuant to Article 61(7)(a) and (b) of the Rome Statute on the Charges of the Prosecutor Against Jean-Pierre Bemba Gombo, 15 June 2009, para. 76, citing ICTY case law, in particular *Prosecutor v. Kunarac et al.*, IT-96-23 and 23/2, ICTY A. Ch., 12 June 2002, paras. 91–92).

With regard to the element of 'population', the Pre-Trial Chamber implied a low threshold by stating that the Prosecutor must demonstrate "that the attack was such that it cannot be characterised as having been directed against only a limited and randomly selected group of individuals". It added that the entire population of the geographical area where the attack is taking place need not have been targeted (*Prosecutor v. Bemba*, ICC PT. Ch. II, ICC-01/05-01/08-424, Decision Pursuant to Article 61(7)(a) and (b) of the Rome Statute on the Charges of the Prosecutor Against Jean-Pierre Bemba Gombo, 15 June 2009, para. 77). In this respect, the Pre-Trial Chamber cited ICTY and ICTR case law, in particular the *Kunarac* Appeal Judgment (*Prosecutor v. Kunarac et al.*, IT-96-23 and 23/2, ICTY A. Ch., 12 June 2002, para. 90).

The Pre-Trial Chamber noted that the term 'civilian' is not defined in the Statute but that according to the well-established principle of international humanitarian law, "[t]he civilian population [...] comprises all persons who are civilians as opposed to members of armed forces and other legitimate combatants" (*Prosecutor v. Bemba*, ICC PT. Ch. II, ICC-01/05-01/08-424, Decision Pursuant to Article 61(7)(a) and (b) of the Rome Statute on the Charges of the Prosecutor Against Jean-Pierre Bemba Gombo, 15 June 2009, para. 78; also cited by *Prosecutor v. Katanga*, ICC T. Ch. II, ICC-01/04-01/07-3436, Jugement rendu en application de l'Article 74 du Statut, 7 March 2014, para. 1102). In this respect, the Pre-Trial Chamber cited the Trial Judgment in the *Kunarac* case (*Prosecutor v. Kunarac et al.*, IT-96-23 and 23/2, ICTY Trial Ch., 22 February 2001, para. 425), although any reference to the ICTY Appeals Chamber's later extensive analysis of this issue is notably absent (see *Prosecutor v. Martić*, IT-95-11, ICTY A. Ch., 8 October 2008, paras. 291–314 and *Prosecutor v. Mrkšić and Šljivančanin*, IT-95-13/1, ICTY A. Ch., 5 May 2009, paras. 23–34).

The requirement of 'widespread or systematic' is disjunctive (see *Situation in the Republic of Kenya*, ICC PT. Ch. II, ICC PT. Ch. II, ICC-01/09-19, Decision Pursuant to Article 15 of the Rome Statute on the Authorisation of an Investigation into the Situation in the Republic of Kenya, 31 March 2010, para. 94). The issue of whether this should be a disjunctive or a conjunctive test was extensively debated by the drafters of the ICC Statute (see, *inter alia*, von Hebel and Robinson, 1999; Robinson, 1999, p. 47).

With regard to 'widespread', the Pre-Trial Chambers in the cases *Prosecutor v. Katanga and Ngudjolo* and *Prosecutor v. Gbagbo* stated that it "connotes the large-scale nature of the attack and the number of targeted persons" (*Prosecutor v. Katanga and Ngudjolo*, ICC PT. Ch. I, ICC-01/04-01/07-717, Decision on the Confirmation of Charges, 30 September 2008, para. 394; *Prosecutor v. Gbagbo*, ICC PT. Ch. I, Decision on the Confirmation of Charges against Laurent Gbagbo, ICC-02/11-01/11-656-Red, 12 June 2014, para. 222). The Pre-Trial Chamber in the *Prosecutor v. Bemba* restricted it further by stating that that it "connotes the large-scale nature of the attack, which should be massive, frequent, carried out collectively with considerable seriousness and directed against a multiplicity of victims" (*Prosecutor v. Bemba*, ICC PT. Ch. II, ICC-01/05-01/08-424, Decision Pursuant to Article 61(7)(a) and (b) of the Rome Statute on the Charges of the Prosecutor Against Jean-Pierre Bemba Gombo, 15 June 2009, para. 83, citing *Prosecutor v. Akayesu*, ICTR-96-4, ICTR T. Ch., 2 September 1998, para. 580).

However, the *Bemba* and *Katanga and Ngudjolo* Pre-Trial Chambers also concluded that a widespread attack entailed "an attack carried out over a large geographical area or an attack in a small geographical area directed against a large number of civilians" (*Prosecutor v. Bemba*, ICC PT. Ch. II, ICC-01/05-01/08-424, Decision Pursuant to Article 61(7)(a) and (b) of the Rome Statute on the Charges of the Prosecutor Against Jean-Pierre Bemba Gombo, 15 June 2009, para. 83; *Prosecutor v. Katanga and Ngudjolo*, ICC PT. Ch. I, ICC-01/04-01/07-717, Decision on the Confirmation of Charges, 30 September 2008, para. 395). Therefore, it appears that the main considerations are the geographical scope of the attack and the number of victims. According to the Katanga Pre-Trial Chamber, even in the context of a systematic attack the requirement of 'multiple acts' would ensure that the attack involves a multiplicity of victims (*Prosecutor v. Katanga and Ngudjolo*, ICC PT. Ch. I, ICC-01/04-01/07-717, Decision on the Confirmation of Charges, 30 September 2008, para. 398).

As for 'systematic', the *Katanga and Ngudjolo* and the *Gbagbo* Pre-Trial Chambers stated that this element refers to "the organised nature of the acts of violence and the improbability of their random occurrence" (*Prosecutor v. Katanga and Ngudjolo*, ICC PT. Ch. I, ICC-01/04-01/07-717, Decision on the Confirmation of Charges , 30 September 2008, para. 394, citing *Kordić and Čerkez*, ICTY A. Ch., 17 December 2004, para. 94, which is citing *Prosecutor v. Kunarac et al.*, IT-96-23 and 23/2, ICTY A. Ch., 12 June 2002, para. 94; *Prosecutor v. Gbagbo*, ICC PT. Ch. I, Decision on the Confirmation of Charges against Laurent Gbagbo, ICC-02/11-01/11-656-Red, 12 June 2014, para. 223).

Regarding the element of 'policy to commit such attack', the Elements of Crimes set out "that the State or organization actively promote or encourage such an attack against a civilian population". In a footnote, the drafters added that "a policy may, in exceptional circumstances, be implemented by a deliberate failure to take action, which is consciously aimed at encouraging such attack" but that "[t]he existence of such a policy cannot be inferred solely from the absence of governmental or organizational action".

The Pre-Trial Chamber in the *Prosecutor v. Katanga and Ngudjolo* correctly linked this element to the elements of widespread or systematic: "in the context of a widespread attack, the requirement of an organizational policy [...] ensures that the attack, [...] must still be thoroughly organised and follow a regular pattern" (Katanga and Ngudjolo, ICC PT. Ch. I, ICC-01/04-01/07-717, Decision on the Confirmation of Charges , 30 September 2008, para. 396).

The Pre-Trial Chamber in the *Prosecutor v. Gbagbo* added: "the concept of 'policy' and that of the 'systematic' nature of the attack [...] both refer to a certain level of planning of the attack. In this sense, evidence of planning, organisation or direction by a State or organisation may be relevant to prove both the policy and the systematic nature of the attack, although the two concepts should not be conflated as they serve different purposes and imply different thresholds under Article 7(1) and (2)(a) of the Statute" (*Gbagbo*, ICC PT. Ch. I, Decision on the Confirmation of Charges against Laurent Gbagbo, ICC-02/11-01/11-656-Red, 12 June 2014, para. 216).

Regardless of this statement by the *Gbagbo* Pre-Trial Chamber, the definition of "attack directed against any civilian population" in Article 7(2) reduces the significance of the disjunctive, as opposed to a conjunctive test, for the characterisation of the attack ('widespread or systematic') (see Schabas, 2010, p. 143).

The Pre-Trial Chamber in the *Prosecutor v. Bemba* discussed the element of policy, stating that it implied that "the attack follows a regular pattern" but that the policy does not have to be formalised (*Prosecutor v. Bemba*, ICC PT. Ch. II, ICC-01/05-01/08-424, Decision Pursuant to Article 61(7)(a) and (b) of the Rome Statute on the Charges of the Prosecutor Against Jean-Pierre Bemba Gombo, 15 June 2009, para. 81; see also *Prosecutor v. Katanga and Ngudjolo*, ICC PT. Ch. I, ICC-01/04-01/07-717, Decision on the Confirmation of Charges , 30 September 2008, para. 396). A number of Pre-Trial Chambers also pointed to two extremes, which does little to clarify the limits of the term 'policy': "an attack which is planned, directed or organized – as opposed to spontaneous or isolated acts of violence – will satisfy this criterion" (*Prosecutor v. Bemba*, ICC PT. Ch. II, ICC-01/05-01/08-424, Decision Pursuant to Article 61(7)(a) and (b) of the Rome Statute on the Charges of the Prosecutor Against Jean-Pierre Bemba Gombo, 15 June 2009, para. 81; *Prosecutor v. Katanga and Ngudjolo*, ICC PT. Ch. I, ICC-01/04-01/07-717, Decision on the Confirmation of Charges, 30 September 2008, para. 396; Gbagbo, ICC PT. Ch. I, Decision on the Confirmation of Charges against Laurent Gbagbo, ICC-02/11-01/11-656-Red, 12 June 2014, para. 215).

Article 7(2)(a) clarifies that it needs to be a State or organisational policy. One Pre-Trial Chamber declared that the term 'State' was self-explanatory but added that the policy did not have to be conceived "at the highest level of the State machinery" (*Situation in the Republic of Kenya*, ICC PT. Ch. II, ICC PT. Ch. II, ICC-01/09-19, Decision Pursuant to Article 15 of the Rome Statute on the Authorisation of an Investigation into the Situation in the Republic of Kenya, 31 March 2010, para. 89, citing *Prosecutor v. Blaškić*, ICTY T. Ch., Judgment, 3 March 2000, para. 205). Therefore, also a policy adopted by regional or local organs of the State could satisfy this requirement (*ibid.*).

With regard to 'organisational', the Pre-Trial Chambers in *Prosecutor v. Bemba* and *Prosecutor v. Katanga and Ngudjolo* stated that the organisation may be "groups of persons who govern a specific territory or [...] any organization with the capability to commit a widespread or systematic attack against a civilian population" (*Prosecutor v. Bemba*, ICC PT. Ch. II, ICC-01/05-01/08-424, Decision Pursuant to Article 61(7)(a) and (b) of the Rome Statute on the Charges of the Prosecutor Against Jean-Pierre Bemba Gombo, 15 June 2009, para. 81; *Prosecutor v. Katanga and Ngudjolo*, ICC PT. Ch. I, ICC-01/04-01/07-717, Decision on the Confirmation of Charges , 30 September 2008, para. 396). It is therefore not limited to State-like organisations (*Situation in the Republic of Kenya*, ICC PT. Ch. II, ICC PT. Ch. II, ICC-01/09-19, Decision Pursuant to Article 15 of the Rome Statute on the Authorisation of an Investigation into the Situation in the Republic of Kenya, 31 March 2010, paras. 90–92; *Prosecutor v. Muthaura et al.*, ICC PT. Ch. II, Decision on the Confirmation of Charges Pursuant to Article 61(7)(a) and (b) of the Rome Statute, 23 January 2012, para. 112; *Ruto et al.*, Decision on the Confirmation of Charges Pursuant to Article 61(7)(a) and (b) of the Rome Statute, 23 January 2012, para. 33. See also Judge Kaul's dissents to these decisions: *Prosecutor v. Ruto et al.*, Dissenting Opinion by Judge Hans-Peter Kaul to Pre-Trial Chamber II's "Decision on the Prosecutor's Application for Summons to Appear for William Samoei Ruto, Henry Kiprono Kosgey and Joshua Arap Sang", 15 March 2011, and *Prosecutor v. Muthaura et al.*, Dissenting Opinion by Judge Hans-Peter Kaul to Pre-Trial Chamber II's "Decision on the Prosecutor's Application for

Summonses to Appear for Francis Kirimi Muthaura, Uhuru Muigai Kenyatta and Mohammed Hussein Ali", 15 March 2011). The Trial Chamber in the *Prosecutor v. Katanga* followed this approach (*Prosecutor v. Katanga*, ICC T. Ch. II, ICC-01/04-01/07-3436, Jugement rendu en application de l'Article 74 du Statut, 7 March 2014, paras. 1117–22).

The *Bemba* Pre-Trial Chamber stated that when determining whether the 'part of' requirement was met it would consider "the characteristics, the aims, the nature or consequences of the act" (*Prosecutor v. Bemba*, ICC PT. Ch. II, ICC-01/05-01/08-424, Decision Pursuant to Article 61(7)(a) and (b) of the Rome Statute on the Charges of the Prosecutor Against Jean-Pierre Bemba Gombo, 15 June 2009, para. 84). It also stated "the underlying offences must [...] not be isolated" (*Prosecutor v. Bemba*, ICC PT. Ch. II, ICC-01/05-01/08-424, Decision Pursuant to Article 61(7)(a) and (b) of the Rome Statute on the Charges of the Prosecutor Against Jean-Pierre Bemba Gombo, 15 June 2009, para. 83), although that ought to follow already from the fact they have to be part of a widespread or systematic attack against a civilian population.

Author: Jonas Nilsson (The views expressed are those of the author alone and do not necessarily reflect the views of the United Nations or the ICTY).

[45] Article 7(1) sets out the mental element as 'knowledge of the attack'. The Elements of Crimes clarify that this requirement "should not be interpreted as requiring proof that the perpetrator had knowledge of all characteristics of the attack or the precise details of the plan or policy of the State or organization".

As stated above, the Elements of Crimes state that the perpetrator must have known "that the conduct was part of or intended the conduct to be part of a widespread or systematic attack against a civilian population". The intent clause is meant to address the situation of "an emerging widespread or systematic attack", that is a situation when the attack has not yet happened and knowledge of it therefore is impossible (Elements of Crimes, p. 5; see also Robinson, 2001, p. 73).

Doctrine:

1. Rodney Dixon and Christopher K. Hall, "Chapeau", in Otto Triffterer (ed.), *Commentary on the Rome Statute of the International Criminal Court: Observers' Notes, Article by Article*, 2nd ed., C.H. Beck/Hart/Nomos, Munich/Oxford/Baden-Baden, 2008, pp. 168–83.

2. Herman von Hebel and Darryl Robinson, "Crimes Within the Jurisdiction of the Court", in Roy S. Lee (ed.), *The International Criminal Court: The Making of the Rome Statute. Issues, Negotiations, Results*, Kluwer Law International, The Hague, 1999, pp. 90–103.

3. Timothy L.H. McCormack, "Crimes Against Humanity", in Dominic McGoldrick, Peter Rowe and Eric Donnelly (eds.), *The Permanent International Criminal Court: Legal and Policy Issues*, Hart Publishing, Oxford, 2004, pp. 179–89.

4. Jonas Nilsson, "Crimes Against Humanity", in Antonio Cassese (ed.), *The Oxford Companion to International Criminal Justice*, Oxford University Press, Oxford, 2009, pp. 284–88.

5. Darryl Robinson, "The Context of Crimes Against Humanity", in Roy S. Lee (ed.), *The International Criminal Court: Elements of Crimes and Rules of Procedure and Evidence*, Transnational Publishers, Ardsley, NY, 2001, pp. 61–80.

6. Darryl Robinson, "Defining 'Crimes Against Humanity' at the Rome Conference", in *American Journal of International Law*, 1999, vol. 93, no. 1, pp. 43–57.

7. William A. Schabas, *The International Criminal Court: A Commentary on the Rome Statute*, Oxford University Press, Oxford, 2010, pp. 139–157.

Author: Jonas Nilsson (The views expressed are those of the author alone and do not necessarily reflect the views of the United Nations or the ICTY.)

(a) Murder;[46]

---

[46] *General remarks*:

Murder has been included as the first crime against humanity in every instrument defining crimes against humanity (Hall, 2008, p. 183). It was included in Article 7 of the ICC Statute without real controversy (von Hebel and Robinson, p. 98; Hall, 2008, p. 184). It was also deemed not to require a clarification of the intended meaning in Article 7(2) (McCormack, 2004, p. 189). Murder as a crime against humanity has been dealt with in one of the judgments before the ICC (*Katanga*, ICC T. Ch. II, ICC-01/04-01/07-3436, Jugement rendu en application de l'Article 74 du Statut, 7 March 2014, paras. 765–782).

Analysis:

i. Definition

Murder as a crime against humanity within the meaning of Article 7(1)(a) is not defined in the Statute. According to the Elements of Crimes, one element of murder is that the perpetrator killed, or caused the death of, one or more persons. Neither Article 7 nor the Elements of Crimes give any clue as to how the *mens rea* should be understood. Therefore Article 30 applies and the material elements must be committed with intent and knowledge (*Prosecutor v. Katanga*, ICC T. Ch. II, ICC-01/04-01/07-3436, Jugement rendu en application de l'Article 74 du Statut, 7 March 2014, para. 780).

ii. Requirements

a. Material elements

According to the Pre-Trial Chamber in the case *Prosecutor v. Bemba* the material elements of murder are that the victim is dead and that the death "result from the act of murder" (*Prosecutor v. Bemba*, ICC PT. Ch. II, Decision Pursuant to Article 61(7)(a) and (b) of the Rome Statute on the Charges of the Prosecutor Against Jean-Pierre Bemba Gombo, 15 June 2009, para. 132). The first element of the crime of murder is thus that the victim is dead. As for the second element, the Pre-Trial Chamber was unhelpful by simply stating that the crime of murder requires "the act of murder". It cited a number of ICTR and ICTY trial judgments (*Prosecutor v. Akayesu*, ICTR T. Ch., 2 September 1998, para. 589; *Prosecutor Rutaganda*, ICTR T. Ch., 6 December 1999, para. 80; *Blaškić*, ICTY T. Ch., 3 March 2000, paras. 216–217; *Prosecutor v. Delalić et al.*, ICTY T. Ch., 16 November 1998, para. 424), which all sets out that the second element is that the death must have been caused by an act of the perpetrator, with the ICTR judgments adding that the death could also be caused by an omission.

The reliance of the Pre-Trial Chamber on ICTY and ICTR trial judgments in this respect is odd considering that the ICTY Appeals Chamber has set out the elements of murder as a crime against humanity. In the case *Prosecutor v. Mirolsav Kvočka et al.*, the Appeals Chamber set out that the first two elements are that the victim is dead and that the death was the result of an act or omission of the perpetrator (*Prosecutor Kvočka et al.*, ICTY A. Ch., 28 February 2005, para. 261).

The *Bemba* Pre-Trial Chamber went on to clarify that the act may be committed by action or omission (*Prosecutor v. Bemba*, ICC PT. Ch. II, Decision Pursuant to Article 61(7)(a) and (b) of the Rome Statute on the Charges of the Prosecutor Against Jean-Pierre Bemba Gombo, 15 June 2009, para. 132). In this respect, the Pre-Trial Chamber did not refer to ICTY or ICTR case law but to a decision by the Pre-Trial Chamber in the case *Prosecutor v. Katanga and Ngudjolo*, discussing the crime of wilful killing as war crime (*Prosecutor v. Bemba*, ICC PT. Ch. II, Decision Pursuant to Article 61(7)(a) and (b) of the Rome Statute on the Charges of the Prosecutor Against Jean-Pierre Bemba Gombo, 15 June 2009, para. 132, citing *Katanga and Ngudjolo*, ICC PT. Ch. I, ICC-01/04-01/07-717, Decision on the Confirmation of Charges , 30 September 2008, para. 287).

(b) Extermination;[47]

b. Mental elements

According to the Pre-Trial Chamber in the case *Prosecutor v. Katanga and Ngudjolo*, the mental element of the crimes against humanity of murder is that the perpetrator intended to kill one or more persons (*Prosecutor v. Katanga and Ngudjolo*, ICC PT. Ch. I, ICC-01/04-01/07-717, Decision on the Confirmation of Charges , 30 September 2008, para. 423). It specified that this encompasses "first and foremost, cases of *dolus directus* of the first and second degree" (*ibid.*). The Pre-Trial Chamber in *Prosecutor v. Bemba*, in its discussion of the mental element, do not use the words "first and foremost" and therefore limits the element to *dolus directus* in the first and second degree (*Prosecutor v. Bemba*, ICC PT. Ch. II, Decision Pursuant to Article 61(7)(a) and (b) of the Rome Statute on the Charges of the Prosecutor Against Jean-Pierre Bemba Gombo, 15 June 2009, para. 135). The Pre-Trial Chamber elaborated further on these concepts. It set out that Article 30(2) and (3) embraces two degrees of *dolus*, namely *dolus directus* in the first degree, or direct intent, and *dolus directus* in the second degree, also known as oblique intention. However, the provision does not cover *dolus eventualis*, also referred to as subjective or advertent recklessness (*ibid.*, paras. 352–369). The author refers to the commentary of Article 30 for further discussion on this.

Cross-references:

Article 8(2)(a)(i) and 8(2)(c)(i).

Doctrine:

1. Christopher K. Hall, "Article 7: Crimes Against Humanity", in Otto Triffterer (ed.), *Commentary on the Rome Statute of the International Criminal Court: Observers' Notes, Article by Article*, 2nd ed., C.H. Beck/Hart/Nomos, Munich/Oxford/Baden-Baden, 2008, pp. 183–90.

2. Timothy L.H. McCormack, "Crimes Against Humanity", in Dominic McGoldrick, Peter Rowe and Eric Donnelly (eds.), *The Permanent International Criminal Court: Legal and Policy Issues*, Hart Publishing, Oxford, 2004, pp. 189–90.

3. Darryl Robinson, "Article 7(a) – Crime Against Humanity of Murder", in Roy S. Lee (ed.), *The International Criminal Court: Elements of Crimes and Rules of Procedure and Evidence*, Transnational Publishers, Ardsley, NY, 2001, pp. 80–81.

4. William A. Schabas, *The International Criminal Court: A Commentary on the Rome Statute*, Oxford University Press, Oxford, 2010, pp. 157–58.

5. Guénaël Mettraux, "Murder", in Antonio Cassese (ed.), *The Oxford Companion to International Criminal Justice*, Oxford University Press, Oxford, 2009, pp. 426–27.

6. Gerhard Werle, *Principles of International Criminal Law*, TMC Asser Press, The Hague, 2005, pp. 232–33, MN 674–77.

Author: Jonas Nilsson (The views expressed are those of the author alone and do not necessarily reflect the views of the United Nations or the ICTY).

[47] *General remarks*:

The crime against humanity of extermination essentially consists of the large-scale killing of members of a civilian population. It has been listed in all instruments concerning crimes against humanity since the Second World War (Hall, 2008, p. 190).

Analysis:

i. Definition

The crime against humanity of extermination is listed in Article 7(1)(b) of the ICC Statute. While Article 7(1)(b) does not elaborate on the definition of extermination, Article 7(2)(b) clarifies that it includes the infliction of conditions of life, *inter alia* the deprivation of access to food and medicine, calculated to bring about the destruction of part of a population. The Elements of Crimes provide further:

1. The perpetrator killed[8] one or more persons, including by inflicting conditions of life calculated to bring about the destruction of part of a population.[9]
2. The conduct constituted, or took place as part of,[10] a mass killing of members of a civilian population.
3. The conduct was committed as part of a widespread or systematic attack directed against a civilian population.
4. The perpetrator knew that the conduct was part of or intended the conduct to be part of a widespread or systematic attack directed against a civilian population.
5. The conduct could be committed by different methods of killing, either directly or indirectly.
6. The infliction of such conditions could include the deprivation of access to food and medicine.
7. The term "as part of" would include the initial conduct in a mass killing.

ii. Distinction between extermination and murder (both as crimes against humanity) and genocide

The only element that distinguishes murder as a crime against humanity from extermination as a crime against humanity is the requirement for extermination that the killings occur on a mass scale (*Prosecutor v. Ntakirutimana and Ntakirutimana*, ICTR A. Ch., 13 December 2004, para. 542). Murder as a crime against humanity does not contain a materially distinct element from extermination as a crime against humanity; each involves killing within the context of a widespread or systematic attack against the civilian population. Consequently, a conviction for murder as a crime against humanity and a conviction for extermination as a crime against humanity, based on the same set of facts, would be impermissibly cumulative (*Prosecutor v. Ntakirutimana and Ntakirutimana*, ICTR A. Ch., 13 December 2004, para. 542; *Prosecutor v. Lukić and Lukić*, ICTY T. Ch. III, 20 June 2009, para. 1045). While extermination differs from murder because extermination concerns a large number of victims, extermination differs from genocide because extermination covers situations in which a group of individuals who do not share any common characteristics are killed (whereas genocide requires a demonstration of the specific intent to destroy a defined group sharing common characteristics) (Hall, 2008, p. 190).

iii. Requirements

In addition to the contextual elements required for all crimes against humanity set out in elements 3 and 4 of the above-listed Elements of Crimes, the following needs to be proven.

a. Material elements

Elements 1 and 2 of the above-listed Elements of Crimes constitute the material elements of extermination.

1. The perpetrator killed one or more persons, including by inflicting conditions of life calculated to bring about the destruction of part of a population.

The Elements of Crimes indicate that the killing may be carried out either directly or indirectly, which would include the infliction of conditions of life calculated to bring about the destruction of part of a population as set out above. The only ICC decision to date to address the crime of extermination in any detail is the first arrest warrant decision in the Al Bashir case (*Prosecutor v. Al Bashir*, ICC PT. Ch. I, Decision on the Prosecution's Application for a Warrant of Arrest against Omar Hassan Ahmad Al Bashir, ICC-02/05-01/09-3, 4 March 2009). Pre-Trial Chamber I found that there were reasonable grounds to believe that the crime of extermination was committed through acts such as the killing of over a thousand civilians in connection with an attack on a town (*Prosecutor v. Al Bashir*, ICC PT. Ch. I, Decision on the Prosecution's Application for a Warrant of Arrest against Omar Hassan Ahmad Al Bashir, ICC-02/05-01/09-3, 4 March

2009, para. 97). The Prosecution also alleged that the systematic destruction of the means of survival of civilian populations in Darfur constituted a form of extermination. However, Pre-Trial Chamber I did not explicitly refer to this means of carrying out extermination when finding reasonable grounds to believe that the crime of extermination was committed (*Prosecutor v. Al Bashir*, ICC PT. Ch. I, Decision on the Prosecution's Application for a Warrant of Arrest against Omar Hassan Ahmad Al Bashir, ICC-02/05-01/09-3, 4 March 2009, paras. 91, 95–97).

In the second arrest warrant decision in the *Al Bashir* case, Pre-Trial Chamber I noted in passing that extermination can be committed through the "infliction of certain conditions of life upon one or more persons" where those conditions are "calculated to bring about the physical destruction of that group, in whole or in part" (*Prosecutor v. Al Bashir*, ICC PT. Ch. I, Second Decision on the Prosecution's Application for a Warrant of Arrest for Omar Hassan Ahmad Al Bashir, ICC-02/05-01/09-94, 12 July 2010, para. 33). Pre-Trial Chamber I concluded (in relation to the genocide charge) that that "one of the reasonable conclusions that can be drawn is that the acts of contamination of water pumps and forcible transfer coupled by resettlement by member of other tribes, were committed in furtherance of the genocidal policy, and that the conditions of life inflicted on the Fur, Masalit and Zaghawa groups were calculated to bring about the physical destruction of a part of those ethnic groups" (*Prosecutor v. Al Bashir*, ICC PT. Ch. I, Second Decision on the Prosecution's Application for a Warrant of Arrest for Omar Hassan Ahmad Al Bashir, ICC-02/05-01/09-94, 12 July 2010, para. 38). It has been recognised at the ICTY and ICTR that the material elements of extermination include "subjecting a widespread number of people or systematically subjecting a number of people to conditions of living that would inevitably lead to death" (*Prosecutor v. Stakić*, ICTY A. Ch., 22 March 2006, para. 259); *Prosecutor v. Ntakirutimana and Ntakirutimana*, ICTR A. Ch., 13 December 2004, para. 522).

2. The conduct constituted, or took place as part of, a mass killing of members of a civilian population.

In the first arrest warrant decision in the *Al Bashir* case, Pre-Trial Chamber I repeated that the killings had to occur as part of a mass killing of a civilian population and noted that this mirrors the jurisprudence of the ICTY and ICTR on extermination (*Prosecutor v. Al Bashir*, ICC PT. Ch. I, Decision on the Prosecution's Application for a Warrant of Arrest against Omar Hassan Ahmad Al Bashir, ICC-02/05-01/09-3, ICC-02/05-01/09-3, 4 March 2009, para. 96). The Elements of Crimes clarify that the term "as part of" would include the initial conduct in a mass killing. Thus already the first killings in a mass killing meet this requirement even though the requirement of a massive killing may not be satisfied until subsequent killings are perpetrated (Schabas, 2010, p. 159).

At the ICTY and ICTR, the jurisprudence concerning the material elements of extermination has focused on the massiveness requirement, which "distinguishes the crime of extermination from the crime of murder" (*Prosecutor v. Lukić and Lukić*, ICTY A. Ch., 4 December 2012, para. 536; *Prosecutor v. Ntakirutimana and Ntakirutimana*, ICTR A. Ch., 13 December 2004, para. 542). It is well established that the massiveness requirement does not suggest a strict numerical approach with a minimum number of victims (*Prosecutor v. Lukić and Lukić*, ICTY A. Ch., 4 December 2012, para. 537). While extermination as a crime against humanity has been found in relation to the killing of thousands of victims, it has also been found in relation to fewer killings, including incidents of around 60 victims and less at the ICTY, ICTR, and SCSL (see *Prosecutor v. Lukić and Lukić*, ICTY A. Ch., 4 December 2012, para. 537). The assessment of the massiveness requirement is made on a case-by-case basis, taking into account the circumstances in which the killings occurred. Relevant factors include, *inter alia*: the time and place of the killings; the selection of the victims and the manner in which they were targeted; and whether the killings were aimed at the collective group rather than victims in their individual capacity (*Prosecutor v. Lukić and Lukić*, ICTY A. Ch., 4 December 2012, para. 538). Where mass kill-

(c) Enslavement;[48]

ings are committed on an extremely large scale, far surpassing the threshold for extermination, this can be taken into account as an aggravating factor in sentencing (*Prosecutor v. Ndinda-bahizi*, ICTR A. Ch., 16 January 2007, para. 135).

It has been recognised that several killing incidents can be accumulated together to constitute extermination (*Prosecutor v. Popović et al.*, ICTY T. Ch. II, 10 June 2010, para. 805, holding that "in light of the temporal and geographical proximity of the killings, the similarities between them and the organized and coordinated manner in which the Bosnian Serb Forces conducted them, [...] they formed part of a single operation"; *Prosecutor v. Tolimir*, ICTY A. Ch., 8 April 2015, para. 147). Killings that are not part of the same attack on a civilian population, and instead are isolated acts, should not be accumulated together (*Prosecutor v. Tolimir*, ICTY A. Ch., 8 April 2015, para. 150).

b. Mental elements

In the absence of a specific provision defining the mental requirements for extermination, Article 30 of the ICC Statute applies. Accordingly, the material elements must be committed with intent and knowledge, as defined in Article 30.

At the ICTY and ICTR it has been held that the mental elements of extermination require the intention to kill on a large scale or to systematically subject a large number of people to conditions of living that would lead to their deaths. The Appeals Chambers of the ICTY and the ICTR have noted that there is no support in customary international law for the requirement of intent to kill a certain threshold number of victims. This is consistent with the fact that there is no numerical threshold established with respect to the material elements of extermination (*Prosecutor v. Stakić*, ICTY A. Ch., 22 March 2006, para. 260; *Prosecutor v. Ntakirutimana and Ntakirutimana*, ICTR A. Ch., 13 December 2004, paras. 516, 522). In the *Al Bashir* case, Pre-Trial Chamber I noted in passing that where extermination is committed through the "infliction of certain conditions of life upon one or more persons", it is necessary to show that those conditions were "calculated to bring about the physical destruction of that group, in whole or in part" (*Prosecutor v. Al Bashir*, ICC PT. Ch. I, Second Decision on the Prosecution's Application for a Warrant of Arrest for Omar Hassan Ahmad Al Bashir, ICC-02/05-01/09-94, 12 July 2010, para. 33).

Cross-references:

Articles 6, 7(1)(a), 7(2), 8(2)(a)(i), 8(2)(b)(xxv), 8(2)(c)(i) and 30.

Doctrine:

1. Christopher K. Hall, "Article 7: Crimes Against Humanity", in Otto Triffterer (ed.), *Commentary on the Rome Statute of the International Criminal Court: Observers' Notes, Article by Article*, 2nd ed., C.H. Beck/Hart/Nomos, Munich/Oxford/Baden-Baden, 2008, pp. 190–91, 237–43.

2. William A. Schabas, *The International Criminal Court: A Commentary on the Rome Statute*, Oxford University Press, Oxford 2010, pp. 158–160.

Author: Matthew Gillett (The views expressed are those of the author alone and do not necessarily reflect the views of the United Nations, the ICTY or the Office of the Prosecutor of the ICTY).

---

[48] *General remarks*:

Enslavement has been included as a crime against humanity in every instrument defining crimes against humanity (Hall, 2008, p. 192). There was a general agreement throughout the drafting process that enslavement should be included in Article 7 of the ICC Statute, although there was discussion about to the exact meaning of the term (Hall, 2008, p. 192). None of the judgments before the ICC have addressed the elements of this crime.

Analysis:

i. Definition

According to one author, the crime of enslavement encompasses three components: slavery, servitude, and forced or compulsory labour (Hall, 2008, p. 193). However, Article 7(2)(b) specifies that 'enslavement' means "the exercise of any or all of the powers attaching to the right of ownership over a person". This reflects the definition of slavery as set out in the Slavery Convention of 1926 (Slavery Convention, Article 1(1)). This would imply that "enslavement" for the purpose of the ICC Statute is limited to slavery in the traditional sense.

That said, the Elements of Crimes provides further specification by the words: "such as by purchasing, selling, lending or bartering [...] a person or persons or by imposing on them a similar deprivation of liberty". It adds that "[i]t is understood that such deprivation of liberty may, in some circumstances, include exacting forced labour or otherwise reducing a person to a servile status as defined in the Supplementary Convention on the Abolition of Slavery, the Slave Trade, and Institutions and Practices Similar to Slavery of 1956". Article 7(2)(b) adds that the definition "includes the exercise of [any or all of the powers attaching to the right of ownership over a person] in the course of trafficking in persons, in particular women and children", which is also repeated in the Elements of Crimes (Elements of Crimes, p. 6, fn. 11). The texts in Article 7(2)(b) and the Elements of Crimes appear to broaden the definition of "enslavement" beyond the traditional notion of slavery.

Neither Article 7 nor the Elements of Crimes give any guidance as to how the *mens rea* should be understood. Therefore Article 30 applies and the material elements must be committed with intent and knowledge.

ii. Requirements

a. Material elements

As explained above, the main area of contention is whether "enslavement" includes something additional to the concept of slavery in the traditional sense. One author comments on the relevant provisions in the ICC Statute and the Elements of Crimes: "The enslavement provision is somewhat convoluted and inelegant, involving a broad general test, a restrictive-sounding list, and an expansive footnote. This reflects the contradictory pressures of the intense negotiations on these issues" (Robinson, 2001, p. 86). As of now, there is no ICC case law addressing this matter.

In the case *Prosecutor v. Dragoljub Kunarac et al.*, the Trial Chamber defined enslavement as "the exercise of any or all of the powers attaching to the right of ownership over a person" and that the *actus reus* of the crime therefore was "the exercise of any or all of the powers attaching to the right of ownership over a person" (*Prosecutor v. Kunarac et al.*, ICTY T. Ch., 22 February 2001, paras. 539–40). Having reviewed international instruments and case law, the Trial Chamber added that the definition "may be broader that the traditional and sometimes apparently distinct definitions of either slavery, the slave trade and servitude or forced or compulsory labour found in the areas of international law" (*ibid.*, paras. 518–38, 541). The Appeals Chamber accepted the Trial Chamber's "chief thesis [...] that the traditional concept of slavery, as defined in the 1926 Slavery Convention and often referred to as 'chattel slavery' (fn. omitted), has evolved to encompass various contemporary forms of slavery which are also based on the exercise of any or all of the powers attaching to the right of ownership" (*Prosecutor v. Kunarac et al.*, ICTY A. Ch., 12 June 2002, para. 117). It added that "[i]n the case of these various contemporary forms of slavery, the victim is not subject to the exercise of the more extreme rights of ownership associated with 'chattel slavery', but in all cases, as a result of the exercise of any or all of the powers attaching to the right of ownership, there is some destruction of the juridical personality; (fn. omitted) the destruction is greater in the case of 'chattel slavery' but the difference is one of degree" (*ibid.*). Thus, the ICTY Appeals Chamber found that not only enslave-

(d) Deportation or forcible transfer of population;[49]

ment but also slavery, as defined in the Slavery Convention of 1926, had a broader meaning than the traditional notion of slavery.

The Pre-Trial Chamber in the case *Prosecutor v. Katanga and Ngudjolo* hinted at a similar broad understanding of enslavement. When discussing 'sexual slavery' (Article 7(1)(g)), it concluded that this crime may be regarded as a particular form of enslavement and therefore what is encompassed with 'sexual slavery' must also be encompassed with 'enslavement' (*Katanga and Ngudjolo*, ICC PT. Ch. I, ICC-01/04-01/07-717, Decision on the Confirmation of Charges , 30 September 2008, para. 430). The Pre-Trial Chamber then lists a number of institutions and practices referred to the 1956 Supplementary Convention: "debt bondage, serfdom, forced marriage practices and forms of child labour" (*ibid.*). It adds that, in its view, sexual slavery (and therefore, presumably enslavement) also encompasses "situations where women and girls are forced into 'marriage', domestic servitude or other forced labour involving sexual activity, including rape, by their captors" (fn. omitted). Forms of sexual slavery can, for example, be "practices such as the detention of women in 'rape camps' or 'comfort stations', forced temporary 'marriages' to soldiers and other practices involving the treatment of women as chattel" (fn. omitted) (*Katanga and Ngudjolo*, ICC PT. Ch. I, ICC-01/04-01/07-717, Decision on the Confirmation of Charges , 30 September 2008, para. 431).

b. Mental elements

See the commentary of Article 30 for discussion on the *mens rea* for enslavement as a crime against humanity.

Cross-references:

Articles 8(2)(b)(xxi) and 8(2)(c)(ii).

Doctrine:

1. M. Cherif Bassiouni, *Crimes Against Humanity: Historical Evolution and Contemporary Application*, Cambridge University Press, Cambridge, 2011, pp. 374–81.
2. Christopher K. Hall, "Article 7: Crimes Against Humanity", in Otto Triffterer (ed.), *Commentary on the Rome Statute of the International Criminal Court: Observers' Notes, Article by Article*, 2nd ed., C.H. Beck/Hart/Nomos, Munich/Oxford/Baden-Baden, 2008, pp. 191–94, 244–47.
3. Timothy L.H. McCormack, "Crimes Against Humanity", in Dominic McGoldrick, Peter Rowe and Eric Donnelly (eds.), *The Permanent International Criminal Court: Legal and Policy Issues*, Hart Publishing, Oxford, 2004, p. 191.
4. Darryl Robinson, "Article 7(a) – Crime Against Humanity of Murder", in Roy S. Lee (ed.), *The International Criminal Court: Elements of Crimes and Rules of Procedure and Evidence*, Transnational Publishers, Ardsley, NY, 2001, pp. 84–86.
5. William A. Schabas, *The International Criminal Court: A Commentary on the Rome Statute*, Oxford University Press, Oxford, 2010, pp. 160–163.
6. Gerhard Werle, *Principles of International Criminal Law*, TMC Asser Press, The Hague, 2005, pp. 236–38, MN 683–89.
7. Alexander Zahar, "Slavery", in Antonio Cassese (ed.), *The Oxford Companion to International Criminal Justice*, Oxford University Press, Oxford, 2009, pp. 514–15.

Author: Jonas Nilsson (The views expressed are those of the author alone and do not necessarily reflect the views of the United Nations or the ICTY).

49 *General remarks*:

Article 7(1)(d) concerns forced displacement of persons from where they are lawfully present, without grounds permitted under international law.

Deportation, which is commonly understood as forced displacement from one country to another, was already recognised as a crime against humanity in the Nuremberg Charter (Hall, 2008, pp. 194–95). In addition to deportation, forcible transfer of population was included in the ICC Statute to make clear that transfers within a State's borders can also constitute a crime against humanity (Robinson, 2001, p. 86). In contrast, the statutes of the ICTY and the ICTR only explicitly list deportation as a crime against humanity. However, the jurisprudence has recognised that forcible transfer can constitute the crime against humanity of "other inhumane acts" or an underlying act of persecution (*Prosecutor v. Stakić* (Case No. IT-97-24-A), ICTY A. Ch., Judgment, 22 March 2006, para. 317; *Prosecutor v. Krnojelac* (Case No. IT-97-25-A), ICTY A. Ch., Judgment, 17 September 2003, para. 218; *Prosecutor v. Naletilić and Martinović* (Case No. IT-98-34-A), ICTY A. Ch., Judgment, 3 May 2006, paras. 153–54). The protected interests underlying the prohibition of deportation and forcible transfer include the rights to stay in one's home and community and not to be deprived of one's property by forcible displacement to another location (*Prosecutor v. Stakić*, ICTY A. Ch., 22 March 2006, para. 277; Hall, 2008, p. 195; see also *Prosecutor v. Krnojelac*, ICTY A. Ch., 17 September 2003, para. 218; Schabas, 2010, p. 163).

Analysis:

i. Definition

According to Article 7(2)(d), "'[d]eportation or forcible transfer of population' means forced displacement of the persons concerned by expulsion or other coercive acts from the area in which they are lawfully present, without grounds permitted under international law". The Elements of Crimes provide further:

1. The perpetrator deported or forcibly[12] transferred,[13] without grounds permitted under international law, one or more persons to another State or location, by expulsion or other coercive acts.
2. Such person or persons were lawfully present in the area from which they were so deported or transferred.
3. The perpetrator was aware of the factual circumstances that established the lawfulness of such presence.
4. The conduct was committed as part of a widespread or systematic attack directed against a civilian population.
5. The perpetrator knew that the conduct was part of or intended the conduct to be part of a widespread or systematic attack directed against a civilian population.

[12] The term "forcibly" is not restricted to physical force, but may include threat of force or coercion, such as that caused by fear of violence, duress, detention, psychological oppression or abuse of power against such person or persons or another person, or by taking advantage of a coercive environment.

[13] "Deported or forcibly transferred" is interchangeable with "forcibly displaced".

ii. Distinction between deportation and forcible transfer

Article 7(2)(d) provides a single definition for "[d]eportation or forcible transfer of population". This raises the question whether there is a need to distinguish between the two alternatives (see Acquaviva, 2011, p. 18). ICC case law supports the need for such a distinction (see also Werle and Jessberger, 2014, p. 359 and Hall, 2008, p. 247 who refer to distinct crimes). In *Ruto et al.* and *Muthaura et al.* the Prosecution charged and Pre-Trial Chamber II confirmed charges for "deportation or forcible transfer of population" (*Prosecutor v. Ruto et al.*, ICC PT. Ch. II, Decision on the Confirmation of Charges Pursuant to Article 61(7)(a) and (b) of the Rome Statute, ICC-01/09-01/11-373, 23 January 2012, paras. 22, 268, 299, 349, 350, 367; *Prosecutor v. Muthaura et al.*, ICC PT. Ch. II, Decision on the Confirmation of Charges Pursuant to Article 61(7)(a) and (b) of the Rome Statute, ICC-01/09-02/11-382-Red, 23 January 2012, paras. 21,

241, 298, 428). The Defence in *Ruto et al.* challenged this alternative formulation of the charges. Pre-Trial Chamber II saw "no apparent prejudice caused by this formulation at this particular stage of the proceedings and in relation to this unique crime". The Pre-Trial Chamber pointed out, however, that the Trial Chamber will ultimately have to draw a distinction between deportation and forcible transfer (*Prosecutor v. Ruto et al.*, ICC PT. Ch. II, ICC-01/09-01/11-373, 23 January 2012, para. 268). In other cases, the legal characterisation was already limited to forcible transfer at the pre-trial stage. In *Al Bashir, Harun and Kushayb*, and *Hussein*, Pre-Trial Chamber I issued warrants of arrest for alleged responsibility for forcible transfer as a crime against humanity (*Prosecutor v. Al Bashir*, ICC PT. Ch. I, Decision on the Prosecution's Application for a Warrant of Arrest against Omar Hassan Ahmad Al Bashir, ICC-02/05-01/09-3, 4 March 2009, p. 92; *Prosecutor v. Al Bashir*, ICC PT. Ch. I, Warrant of Arrest for Omar Hassan Ahmad Al Bashir, ICC-02/05-01/09-1, 4 March 2009, pp. 7–8; *Prosecutor v. Harun and Kushayb*, ICC PT. Ch. I, Decision on the Prosecution Application under Article 58(7) of the Statute, ICC-02/05-01/07-1-Corr, 27 April 2007, pp. 45, 48, 56; *Prosecutor v. Harun and Kushayb*, ICC PT. Ch. I, Warrant of Arrest for Ahmad Harun, ICC-02/05-01/07-2, 27 April 2007, pp. 7, 10, 15–16; *Prosecutor v. Harun and Kushayb*, ICC PT. Ch. I, Warrant of Arrest for Ali Kushayb, ICC-02/05-01/07-3-Corr, 27 April 2007, pp. 8, 10, 16–17; *Prosecutor v. Hussein*, ICC PT. Ch. I, Public redacted version of "Decision on the Prosecutor's application under article 58 relating to Abdel Raheem Muhammad Hussein", ICC-02/05-01/12-1-Red, 1 March 2012, pp. 29–30; *Prosecutor v. Hussein*, ICC PT. Ch. I, Warrant of Arrest for Abdel Raheem Muhammad Hussein, ICC-02/05-01/12-2, 1 March 2012, pp. 8, 11; see also *Prosecutor v. Al Bashir*, ICC PT. Ch. I, Second Warrant of Arrest for Omar Hassan Ahmad Al Bashir, ICC-02/05-01/09-95, 12 July 2010, p. 6). Similarly, Pre-Trial Chamber II in *Ntaganda* confirmed charges for forcible transfer of population as a crime against humanity (*Prosecutor v. Ntaganda*, ICC PT. Ch. II, Decision Pursuant to Article 61(7)(a) and (b) of the Rome Statute on the Charges of the Prosecutor Against Bosco Ntaganda, ICC-01/04-02/06-309, 9 June 2014, paras. 36, 64–68, p. 63).

The next question is then how to distinguish between deportation and forcible transfer. The distinction between deportation and forcible transfer is commonly seen in whether the victims are forced across a State border, which is considered as deportation, whereas forcible transfer typically refers to displacements within a State (see Hall, 2008, p. 194). As noted above, the definition contained in Article 7(2)(d) does not explicitly make this distinction. While element 1 of the Elements of Crimes provides that the victims must be displaced "to another State or location", it does not explicitly limit deportation to displacement to another State, nor does it limit forcible transfer to displacement within a State (see Hall, 2008, fn. 178). Nevertheless, Pre-Trial Chamber II in *Ruto et al.* distinguished between forcible transfer and deportation based on "where [the victims] have finally relocated as a result of these acts (that is, within the State or outside the State)" (*Prosecutor v. Ruto et al.*, ICC PT. Ch. II, ICC-01/09-01/11-373, 23 January 2012, para. 268. For this distinction also Werle and Jessberger, 2014, pp. 358–59; Hall, 2008, pp. 198–99 with reference to the drafting history; Schabas, 2010, pp. 163–64). The distinction made by Pre-Trial Chamber II in *Ruto et al.* might suggest that it viewed deportation and forcible transfer as mutually exclusive. At the ICTY, the Appeals Chamber confirmed in *Đorđević* that for forcible transfer "the displacement *may* take place within national boundaries but is not so restricted" (*Prosecutor v. Đorđević* (Case No. IT-05-87/1-A), ICTY A. Ch., Judgment, 27 January 2014, fn. 2159, emphasis in original, referring to *Prosecutor v. Stakić*, ICTY A. Ch., 22 March 2006, para. 317). According to this definition, the ultimate location does not form part of the elements of forcible transfer; deportation thus has an additional element: the transfer across a border (see (Case No. IT-05-88-T), ICTY T. Ch. II, Judgment, 10 June 2010, paras. 892, 904). Deportation at the ICTY does not require displacement across a *de jure* State border. Rather, under certain circumstances, displacement across a *de facto* border suffices. This is to be examined on a case-by-case basis in light of customary international law, which, for example, recognises displacement from occupied territory as deportation (see for the ICC Article 8(2)(b)(viii)), while displacement across constantly changing frontlines is not sufficient (*Prosecutor v. Stakić*, ICTY A. Ch., 22 March 2006, paras. 278, 300–3).

iii. Requirements

In addition to the contextual elements required for all crimes against humanity set out in elements 4 and 5 of the above-listed Elements of Crimes, the following needs to be proven:
a. Material elements

Elements 1 and 2 of the above-listed Elements of Crimes constitute the material elements of deportation and forcible transfer.

1. The perpetrator deported or forcibly transferred, without grounds permitted under international law, one or more persons to another State or location, by expulsion or other coercive acts.

According to the Elements of Crimes, the term 'forcibly' is to be interpreted broadly and is "not restricted to physical force, but may include threat of force or coercion, such as that caused by fear of violence, duress, detention, psychological oppression or abuse of power against such person or persons or another person, or by taking advantage of a coercive environment" (Elements of Crimes, fn. 12). Similarly, at the ICTY forced displacement "is not 'limited to physical force but includes the threat of force or coercion, such as that caused by fear of violence, duress, detention, psychological oppression or abuse of power against such person or persons or another person, or by taking advantage of a coercive environment'" (*Prosecutor v. Đorđević*, ICTY A. Ch., 27 January 2014, para. 727 quoting *Prosecutor v. Stakić*, ICTY A. Ch., 22 March 2006, para. 281). The question is whether the victims had no genuine choice (*Prosecutor v. Đorđević*, ICTY A. Ch., 27 January 2014, para. 727; *Prosecutor v. Stakić*, ICTY A. Ch., 22 March 2006, para. 279). According to Pre-Trial Chamber II in *Ruto et al.*, various conduct can amount to "expulsion or other coercive acts", forcing the victim to leave (*Prosecutor v. Ruto et al.*, ICC PT. Ch. II, ICC-01/09-01/11-373, 23 January 2012, para. 244). The Pre-Trial Chamber considered killing, looting, burning and destruction of property as the coercive acts through which the displacement occurred (*Prosecutor v. Ruto et al.*, ICC PT. Ch. II, ICC-01/09-01/11-373, 23 January 2012, paras. 251, 255, 260–261, 265–266, 277). In *Muthaura et al.* Pre-Trial Chamber II held that the destruction of homes, killings, injuries, rapes and public announcements that people of a certain ethnicity must leave amounted to coercion causing the residents to leave their homes (*Prosecutor v. Muthaura et al.*, ICC PT. Ch. II, ICC-01/09-02/11-382-Red, 23 January 2012, paras. 244, 279).

Pre-Trial Chamber II in *Ruto et al.* emphasised that to prove deportation or forcible transfer a link needs to be established between the perpetrator's conduct and the resulting effect of forcing the victim to leave the area to another State or location (*Prosecutor v. Ruto et al.*, ICC PT. Ch. II, ICC-01/09-01/11-373, 23 January 2012, para. 245; see also *Prosecutor v. Popović et al.*, ICTY T. Ch. II, 10 June 2010, para. 893).

Although Article 7(1)(d) refers to deportation or forcible transfer of *population*, the Elements of Crimes clarify that the transfer of one person can suffice (Werle and Jessberger, 2014, p. 358).

The displacement has to occur without grounds permitted under international law. The ICTY Appeals Chamber in *Đorđević* pointed out that – as with all other elements of the crime – this is for the Prosecution to prove (see *Prosecutor v. Đorđević*, ICTY A. Ch., 27 January 2014, para. 705). International humanitarian law, for example, permits displacement for certain reasons, such as for the security of the population/civilians involved or in case of imperative military reasons, and under certain conditions (for example Article 49 Geneva Convention IV, Article 17 Additional Protocol II). Pre-Trial Chamber II in *Ntaganda* considered that the acts of displacement "were not justified by the security of the civilians involved or by military necessity, as there [was] no indication of any precautionary measures having been taken before these acts of displacement were carried out or any reasons linked to the conduct of military operations" (*Prosecutor v. Ntaganda*, ICC PT. Ch. II, ICC-01/04-02/06-309, 9 June 2014, para. 68). Although displacement for humanitarian reasons is allowed in certain situations, the ICTY Appeals Chamber has held that this does not apply "where the humanitarian crisis that caused the displacement is itself the result of the accused's own unlawful activity" (*Prosecutor v. Stakić*, ICTY A. Ch., 22 March 2006, para. 287). Human rights instruments provide for other grounds permitting displacement in certain circumstances (see, for example, Article 12(3) ICCPR; Hall, 2008, p. 251; Werle and Jessberger, 2014, p. 359).

2. Such person or persons were lawfully present in the area from which they were so deported or transferred.

The question of whether the lawfulness of the victims' presence is to be determined under national or international law was debated during the negotiations of the ICC Statute, but was ultimately left for the Court to decide (Robinson, 2001, p. 87 setting out the different positions during the negotiations; for a determination under international law, Werle and Jessberger, 2014 p. 360; considering lawful presence under national or international law sufficient, Hall, 2008, p. 248; see also Cryer *et al.*, 2014, fn. 147). For the purpose of confirming charges against Bosco Ntaganda, Pre-Trial Chamber II considered that "absent any indication to the contrary in the evidence", the civilians displaced were lawfully present in the relevant locations (*Prosecutor v. Ntaganda*, ICC PT. Ch. II, ICC-01/04-02/06-309, 9 June 2014, para. 68; see also *Prosecutor v. Ruto et al.*, ICC PT. Ch. II, ICC-01/09-01/11-373, 23 January 2012, paras. 251, 255, 261). ICTY Trial Chamber II in *Popović et al.* opined that "lawfully present" should not be equated to the legal concept of lawful residence, but understood in its common meaning (*Prosecutor v. Popović et al.*, ICTY T. Ch. II, 10 June 2010, para. 900).

b. Mental elements

With respect to the first material element, Article 30 applies (Robinson, 2001, p. 88). At the ICTY, the intent to displace the victim permanently is not required for deportation or forcible transfer (*Prosecutor v. Stakić*, ICTY A. Ch., 22 March 2006, paras. 278, 307, 317; see, however, Werle and Jessberger, 2014, p. 361).

With respect to the second material element, element 3 of the Elements of Crimes clarifies that awareness of the factual circumstances establishing the lawfulness of the victims' presence suffices. It is not required that the perpetrator make any legal evaluation of the lawfulness of the victims' presence (Robinson, 2001, p. 88).

Cross-references:

Articles 7(2)(d), 8(2)(a)(vii), 8(2)(b)(viii), 8(2)(e)(viii) and 30.

Doctrine:

1. Guido Acquaviva, "Forced Displacement and International Crimes", UNHCR Legal and Protection Policy Research Series, Division of International Protection, June 2011.

2. Robert Cryer, Håkan Friman, Daryll Robinson and Elizabeth Wilmshurst, *An Introduction to International Criminal Law and Procedure*, 3rd ed., Cambridge University Press, Cambridge, 2014, pp. 247–48.

3. Christopher K. Hall, "Article 7: Crimes Against Humanity", B.I.2 (d) "Deportation or forcible transfer of population", and B.II.(d) "Prohibited movements of population", in Otto Triffterer (ed.), *Commentary on the Rome Statute of the International Criminal Court: Observers' Notes, Article by Article,* 2nd ed., C.H. Beck/Hart/Nomos, Munich/Oxford/Baden-Baden, 2008, pp. 194–200, 247–51.

4. Darryl Robinson, "Article 7(1)(d) – Crime Against Humanity of Deportation or Forcible Transfer of Population", in Roy S. Lee (ed.), *The International Criminal Court: Elements of*

(e) Imprisonment or other severe deprivation of physical liberty in violation of fundamental rules of international law;[50]

Crimes and Rules of Procedure and Evidence, Transnational Publishers, Ardsley, NY, 2001, pp. 86–88.

5. William A. Schabas, *The International Criminal Court: A Commentary on the Rome Statute*, Oxford University Press, Oxford, 2010, pp. 163–65.

6. Gerhard Werle and Florian Jessberger, *Principles of International Criminal Law*, 3rd ed., Oxford University Press, Oxford, 2014, pp. 357–61.

Author: Barbara Goy (The views expressed are those of the author alone and do not necessarily reflect the views of the Mechanism for International Criminal Tribunals ('MICT'), the ICTY or the United Nations in general.)

[50] *General remarks*:

Although imprisonment was not included in the Nuremberg and Tokyo Charters, it has been included as a crime against humanity in subsequent instruments, including the ICTY and ICTR statutes (Hall, 2008, p. 200). None of the judgments before the ICC has addressed the elements of this crime.

Analysis:

i. Definition

The full text of Article 7(1)(e) reads "Imprisonment or other severe deprivation of physical liberty in violation of fundamental rules of international law". There is no provision in Article 7(2) further addressing this crime.

ii. Requirements

a. Material elements

The two alternatives of 'imprisonment' and 'sever deprivation of physical liberty' seem to suggest that the term 'imprisonment' should be understood in a narrow sense, as imprisonment after conviction by a court (Hall, 2008, p. 201). However, according to the definition, this imprisonment has to be in violation of fundamental rules of international law. Together the two concepts cover a broad range of arbitrary deprivations of liberty (Hall, 2008, p. 202).

The Statute does not contain any clear guidance as to what constitute a 'severe' deprivation of liberty. The use of the word 'other' indicates that 'imprisonment' already meets the threshold for 'severe' and this might be of some assistance in interpreting the term. Furthermore, according to the Elements of Crimes, one of the elements are that "[t]he gravity of the conduct was such that it was in violation of fundamental rules of international law". Presumably the drafters did not intend to introduce a new gravity-element that was not foreseen in the Statute (see Hall, 2008, p. 204). Therefore, this element must be a reference to 'severe' in the Statute. The meaning of the term 'severe' is then merely that the severe deprivation of liberty (including imprisonment) must be in violation of fundamental rules of international law.

Neither the Statute nor the Elements of Crimes specify which the fundamental rules of international law are.

b. Mental elements

Article 7 does not give any guidance as to how the *mens rea* should be understood. In this respect, Article 30 applies and the material elements must be committed with intent and knowledge. The author refers to the commentary of Article 30 for discussion on the *mens rea* for imprisonment as a crime against humanity.

In addition, the Elements of Crimes specifies that the perpetrator must have been "aware of the factual circumstances that established the gravity of the conduct". In this respect, one author commented that there was general agreement among the drafters "that the prosecutor need not

(f) Torture;[51]

---

prove that the perpetrator made any legal evaluation that the imprisonment was in violation of fundamental rules of international law" (Robinson, 2001, p. 89).

Cross-references:
Article 8(2)(a)(vii).

Doctrine:

1. M. Cherif M. Bassiouni, *Crimes Against Humanity: Historical Evolution and Contemporary Application*, Cambridge University Press, Cambridge, 2011, pp. 443–45.

2. Christopher K. Hall, "Article 7: Crimes against humanity, (e) 'Imprisonment or other severe deprivation of physical liberty'", in Otto Triffterer (ed.), *Commentary on the Rome Statute of the International Criminal Court: Observers' Notes, Article by Article*, 2nd ed., C.H. Beck/Hart/Nomos, Munich/Oxford/Baden-Baden, 2008, pp. 200–5.

3. Timothy L.H. McCormack, "Crimes Against Humanity", in Dominic McGoldrick, Peter Rowe and Eric Donnelly (eds.), *The Permanent International Criminal Court: Legal and Policy Issues*, Hart Publishing, Oxford, 2004, p. 193.

4. Darryl Robinson, "Article 7(1)(e) – Crime Against Humanity of Imprisonment or Other Severe Deprivation of Physical Liberty", in Roy S. Lee (ed.), *The International Criminal Court: Elements of Crimes and Rules of Procedure and Evidence*, Transnational Publishers, Ardsley, NY, 2001, pp. 88–89.

5. William A. Schabas, *The International Criminal Court: A Commentary on the Rome Statute*, Oxford University Press, Oxford, 2010, pp. 165–66.

Author: Jonas Nilsson (The views expressed are those of the author alone and do not necessarily reflect the views of the United Nations or the ICTY.)

[51] *General remarks:*

According to one author, there was a general support throughout the drafting process for the inclusion of torture as a crime against humanity (Hall, 2008, p. 205). There was, however, a considerable debate about the definition of this crime (Hall, 2008, p. 205).

Analysis:

i. Definition

According to Article 7(2)(e) and Elements of Crimes, torture means "the intentional infliction of severe pain or suffering, whether physical or mental, upon a person in the custody or under the control of the accused; except that torture shall not include pain or suffering arising only from, inherent in or incidental to, lawful sanctions". Notably, the definition in the Statute does not include a requirement that the infliction of pain or suffering was done for a specific purpose (Elements of Crimes, fn. 14). Such a requirement is included in the torture definition in the Torture Convention, as well as in the definition of torture as a war crime in the Statute. Further, the definition does not include a requirement of a connection to a public official (see von Hebel and Robinson, 1999, p. 99).

ii. Requirements

a. Material elements

The two material elements are: 1) the infliction of severe physical or mental pain or suffering, and 2) that this infliction is on a person in custody or under the control of the perpetrator. With regard to the severity requirement, the Pre-Trial Chamber in the case *Prosecutor v. Bemba* considered that "it is constantly accepted in applicable treaties and jurisprudence that an important degree of pain and suffering has to be reached" (*Prosecutor v. Bemba*, ICC PT. Ch. II, Decision Pursuant to Article 61(7)(a) and (b) of the Rome Statute on the Charges of the Prosecutor

---

(g) Rape,[52] sexual slavery,[53] enforced prostitution,[54] forced pregnancy,[55] enforced steriliza-tion,[56] or any other form of sexual violence of comparable gravity;[57]

Against Jean-Pierre Bemba Gombo, ICC-01/05-01/08-424, 15 June 2009, para. 193). Arguably, this adds very little or nothing to the understanding of the word 'severe' in the definition.

Torture in the sense of the Statute does not include infliction of pain or suffering that arises only from, are inherent in or incidental to, lawful sanctions. According to one author, 'lawful' refers to international law or national law, which is consistent with international law and stand-ards (Hall, 2008, p. 253). However, the Statute itself, as well as the Elements of Crimes, are si-lent on this issue.

b. Mental elements

Article 7(2)(e) includes the word 'intentional', which means that Article 30, stating "[u]nless otherwise provided", is not applicable with regard to the crime of torture. The Pre-Trial Cham-ber in the case *Prosecutor v. Bemba* concluded that the use of the term 'intentional' excluded the separate requirement of knowledge set out in Article 30(2) of the Statute and that it was therefore not necessary to demonstrate that the perpetrator knew that the harm inflicted was se-vere (*Prosecutor v. Bemba*, ICC PT. Ch. II, Decision Pursuant to Article 61(7)(a) and (b) of the Rome Statute on the Charges of the Prosecutor Against Jean-Pierre Bemba Gombo, ICC-01/05-01/08-424, 15 June 2009, para. 194).

Cross-references:

Articles 8(2)(a)(ii) and 8(2)(c)(i).

Doctrine:

1. M. Cherif Bassiouni, *Crimes Against Humanity: Historical Evolution and Contemporary Application*, Cambridge University Press, Cambridge, 2011, pp. 411–19.
2. Christopher K. Hall, "Article 7 Crimes Against Humanity, (f) 'Torture' and (e) 'Torture'", in Otto Triffterer (ed.), *Commentary on the Rome Statute of the International Criminal Court: Observers' Notes, Article by Article*, 2nd ed., C.H. Beck/Hart/Nomos, Mu-nich/Oxford/Baden-Baden, 2008, pp. 205–6, 251–55.
3. Timothy L.H. McCormack, "Crimes Against Humanity", in Dominic McGoldrick, Peter Rowe and Eric Donnelly (eds.), *The Permanent International Criminal Court: Legal and Policy Issues*, Hart Publishing, Oxford, 2004, pp. 194–95.
4. Darryl Robinson, "Article 7(1)(f) – Crime Against Humanity of Torture", in Roy S. Lee (ed.), *The International Criminal Court: Elements of Crimes and Rules of Procedure and Evidence,* Transnational Publishers, Ardsley, NY, 2001, pp. 90–92.
5. William A. Schabas, *The International Criminal Court: A Commentary on the Rome Statute*, Oxford University Press, Oxford, 2010, pp. 166–69.
6. Alexander Zahar, "Torture", in Antonio Cassese (ed.), *The Oxford Companion to Interna-tional Criminal Justice,* Oxford University Press, Oxford, 2009, pp. 537–38.

Author: Jonas Nilsson (The views expressed are those of the author alone and do not necessarily reflect the views of the United Nations or the ICTY.)

[52] Rape is considered the most severe form of sexual violence. Sexual violence is a broad term that covers all forms of acts of a sexual nature under coercive circumstances, including rape. The key element that separates rape from other acts is penetration. The Elements of Crime provide a more specific definition of the criminal conduct. Rape falls under the chapeaus of genocide, crimes against humanity or war crimes under specific circumstances, confirmed both through the ICC Statute and through the case law of the ICTR and the ICTY. In order for rape to rise to the level of a crime against humanity, it must be perpetrated within the context of a widespread or systematic attack aimed at a civilian population. Combatants cannot thus be victims of rape

as a crime against humanity. The attack must also aim at a significant number of victims. This does not preclude a single rape from constituting a crime against humanity, if perpetrated within the context of a widespread or systematic attack. The underlying act, such as rape, does not have to be the same as the other acts committed during the attack.

For the mental element of rape Article 30 applies. The perpetrator has to have knowledge of the act being part of a systematic attack or the factual circumstances of a widespread attack. It is sufficient if he or she intended to further such an attack. He or she must also have intended to penetrate the victim's body and be aware that the penetration was by force or threat of force.

The definition of rape is the same regarding rape as genocide, crimes against humanity and war crimes, albeit the contextual elements of the chapeaus differ. The *actus reus* of the violation is found in the Elements of Crimes. The definition focuses on penetration with 1) a sexual organ of any body part, or 2) with the use of an object or any other part of the body of the anal or genital opening of the victim, committed by force or threat or force or coercion. "Any part of the body" under point 1 refers to vaginal, anal and oral penetration with the penis and may also be interpreted as ears, nose and eyes of the victim. Point 2 refers to objects or the use of fingers, hands or tongue of the perpetrator. Coercion may arise through fear of violence, duress, detention, psychological oppression or abuse of power. These situations are provided as examples, apparent through the use of the term 'such as'. Consent is automatically vitiated in such situations. The definition is intentionally gender-neutral, indicating that both men and women can be perpetrators or victims. The definition of rape found in the Elements of Crimes is heavily influenced by the legal reasoning in cases regarding rape of the ICTY and the ICTR. Such cases can thus further elucidate the interpretation of the elements of the crime, meanwhile also highlighting different approaches to the main elements of rape, including 'force' and 'non-consent'. See, for example, *Furundzija*, in which the Trial Chamber of the ICTY held that force or threat of force constitutes the main element of rape (*Prosecutor v. Furundzija* (Case No. IT-95-17/1-T), ICTY T. Ch., 10 December 1998). To the contrary, the latter case of *Kunarac* emphasised the element of non-consent as the most essential in establishing rape, in that it corresponds to the protection of sexual autonomy (*Prosecutor v. Kunarac, Kovac and Vukovic* (Case No. IT-96-23 and 23/1) ICTY T. J, 22 February 2001). As to the term 'coercion' the ICTR Trial Chamber in *Akayesu* held that a coercive environment does not require physical force. It also adopted a broad approach to the *actus reus*, including also the use of objects, an approach that has been embraced also by the ICTY and the ICC (*Prosecutor v. Jean-Paul Akayesu* (Case No. ICTR-96-4-T), ICTR T. Ch., 2 September 1998, para. 598).

Rule 63 is of importance which holds that the Court's Chambers cannot require corroboration to prove any crime within its jurisdiction, particularly crimes of sexual violence. Rule 70 further delineates the possibility of introducing evidence of consent as a defence. This is highly limited, emphasising that consent cannot be inferred in coercive circumstances. Rule 71 forbids evidence of prior sexual conduct.

Several cases at the ICC include charges of rape as a crime against humanity. This includes Pre-Trial Chamber III in *Bemba*, for crimes committed in the Central African Republic, 2002–2003. Bemba is charged with rape as a crime against humanity and war crime. In the 2009 confirmation of charges decision in the Bemba case, Pre-Trial Chamber II dismissed charges of rape as torture and outrages upon personal dignity, solely confirming charges of rape. The Chamber held that including the distinctive charges would constitute cumulative charging and be "detrimental to the rights of the Defence" (*Prosecutor v. Bemba*, PT Ch. I, Decision Pursuant to Article 61(7)(a) and (b) of the Rome Statute, ICC-01/05-01/08-424, 15 June 2009, para. 202).

In *Prosecutor v. Katanga*, the Chamber referred to the *Akayesu* judgment on the interpretation of a coercive environment. It held that "threats, intimidation, extortion and other forms of duress which prey on fear or desperation may constitute coercion, and coercion may be inherent in certain circumstances, such as armed conflict or military presence" (*Prosecutor v. Katanga*, ICC PT. Ch. I. Decision on the Confirmation of Charges, ICC-01/04-01/07-717, 30 September 2008, para. 440. See also *Prosecutor v. Akayesu* (Case No IT-96-4-T), ICTR T. Ch. I, Trial Judgment, 2 September 1998, para. 688). The Chamber found sufficient evidence to confirm charges that members of the FNI and FRPI by force or threat invaded the body of women and girls abducted in the village of Bogoro (see para. 442).

In *Prosecutor v. Kenyatta*, the Chamber confirmed that there were substantial grounds to believe widespread rapes had been perpetrated sufficient to rise to the level of crimes against humanity (*Prosecutor v. Kenyatta*, ICC PT. Ch. I. Decision on the Confirmation of Charges Pursuant to Article 61 (7)(a) and (b) of the Rome Statute Against Kenyatta, ICC-01/09-02/11, 23 January 2012, para. 257).

Several arrest warrants confirm reasonable grounds to believe that rape as crimes against humanity have been committed. See, for example, *Prosecutor v. Gbagbo*, Warrant of Arrest ICC-02/11, 23 November 2011, para. 8; *Prosecutor v. Ntaganda*, ICC PT. Ch. II., Decision on ther Prosecutor's Application under Article 58, ICC-01/04-02/06, 13 July 2012, para. 38: "reasonable grounds to believe, that crimes of rape and sexual slavery were committed as part of the attacks in different locations in Ituri"; *Prosecutor v. Ahmad Harun and Ali Kushayb*, ICC PT. Ch. I., Warrant of Arrest, ICC-02/05-01/07, 27 April 2007 found reasonable grounds to believe that Harun and Kushayb, through the direction of the Sudanese Armed Forces and the Janjaweed committed rapes of women and girls of certain ethnic groups. In *Prosecutor v. Al Bashir*, ICC PT Ch. I., Second Warrant of Arrest, ICC-02/05-01/09, 12 July 2010, the Pre-Trial Chamber found reasonable grounds to establish rape as a crime against humanity. In *Prosecutor v. Kony*, ICC PT. Ch. II, Warrant of Arrest, ICC-02/04-01/05, 27 September 2005, the chamber also found reasonable grounds to establish rape and sexual slavery as crimes against humanity.

Cross-references:

Articles 8(2)(b)(xxii) and 8(2)(e)(vi).

Doctrine:

1. Antonio Cassese, in Antonio Cassese, Paola Gaeta and John R.W.D. Jones (eds.), *The Rome Statute of the International Criminal Court: A Commentary*, Oxford University Press, Oxford, 2002, pp. 374–75.

2. Gerhard Werle, *Principles of International Criminal Law*, TMC Asser Press, The Hague, 2005, pp. 248–50, MN 723–27.

3. Machteld Boot, in Otto Triffterer (ed.), *Commentary on the Rome Statute of the International Criminal Court: Observers' Notes, Article by Article*, 2nd ed., C.H. Beck/Hart/Nomos, Munich/Oxford/Baden-Baden, 2008, pp. 209–11.

4. Anne-Marie L.M. de Brouwer, *Supranational Criminal Prosecution of Sexual Violence: The ICC and the Practice of the ICTY and the ICTR*, Antwerp, Intersentia, 2005, pp. 103–35.

5. M. Cherif Bassiouni, *Crimes Against Humanity, Historical Evolution and Contemporary Application*, Cambridge University Press, Cambridge, 2011, pp. 440–42.

Author: Maria Sjöholm.

[53] Sexual slavery is a particular form of enslavement which includes limitations on one's autonomy, freedom of movement and power to decide matters relating to one's sexual activity. Although it is listed as a separate offence in the ICC Statute, it is regarded as a particular form of enslavement. However, whereas enslavement is solely considered a crime against humanity, sexual slavery may constitute either a war crime or a crime against humanity. It is partly based on the definition of enslavement identified as customary international law by the ICTY in the Kunarac case (*Prosecutor v. Kunarac, Kovac and Vukovic* (Case No. IT-96-23), ICTY T. Ch., 22 February 2001, para. 543). Sexual slavery is thus considered a form of enslavement with a

sexual component. Its definition is found in the Elements of Crimes and includes the exercise of any or all of the powers attached to the right of ownership over one or more persons, "such as by purchasing, selling, lending or bartering such a person or persons, or by imposing on them a similar deprivation of liberty". The person should have been made to engage in acts of a sexual nature. The crime also includes forced marriages, domestic servitude or other forced labour that ultimately involves forced sexual activity. In contrast to the crime of rape, which is a completed offence, sexual slavery constitutes a continuing offence.

In *Prosecutor v. Katanga and Ngudjolo*, The Pre-Trial chamber held that "sexual slavery also encompasses situations where women and girls are forced into 'marriage', domestic servitude or other forced labour involving compulsory sexual activity, including rape, by their captors (*Prosecutor v. Katanga and Ngudjolo*, ICC PT. Ch. I, Decision on the Confirmation of Charges, ICC-01/04-01/07-717, 30 September 2008, para. 431). Forms of sexual slavery can, for example, be practices such as the detention of women in 'rape camps' or 'comfort stations', forced temporary 'marriages' to soldiers and other practices involving the treatment of women as chattel, and as such, violations of the peremptory norm prohibiting slavery". The Chamber found sufficient evidence to affirm charges of sexual slavery as crimes against humanity in the form of women being abducted for the purpose of using them as wives, being forced or threatened to engage in sexual intercourse with combatants, to serve as sexual slaves and to work in military camps servicing soldiers (see para. 434).

The SCSL Appeals Chamber in the *Brima* case has found the abduction and confinement of women to constitute forced marriage and consequently a crime against humanity. The Chamber concluded that forced marriage was distinct from sexual slavery. Accordingly, "While forced marriage shares certain elements with sexual slavery such as non-consensual sex and deprivation of liberty, there are also distinguishing factors. First, forced marriage involves a perpetrator compelling a person by force or threat of force, through the words or conduct of the perpetrator or those associated with him, into a forced conjugal association with another person resulting in great suffering, or serious physical or mental injury on the part of the victim. Second, unlike sexual slavery, forced marriage implies a relationship of exclusivity between the 'husband' and 'wife', which could lead to disciplinary consequences for breach of this exclusive arrangement" (see *Prosecutor v. Brima* (Case No. SCSL-2004-16-A), SCSL A. Ch., Appeals Judgment, 22 February 2008, para. 195). In 2012 the Court in a decision on the *Charles Taylor* case declared its preference for the term "forced conjugal slavery". The Trial Chamber did not find the term 'marriage' to be helpful in describing the events that had occurred, in that it did not constitute marriage in the universally understood sense (*Prosecutor v. Taylor* (Case No. SCSL-03-01-T), SCSL T. Ch., Judgment, 18 May 2012, para. 427).

Several arrest warrants at the ICC confirm reasonable grounds to believe that sexual slavery has been committed as part of attacks on civilian population and thus constituting crimes against humanity (see *Prosecutor v. Bosco Ntaganda*, ICC PT. Ch. II, Decision on Prosecutor's Application under Article 58, ICC-01/04-02/06-36-Red, 13 July 2012; *Warrant of Arrest for Joseph Kony*, ICC PT. Ch. II, ICC-02/04-01/05, 27 September 2005, para. 38; and *Warrant of Arrest against Vincent Otti*, ICC PT. Ch. II, ICC-02/04, 8 July 2005, para. 17).

Cross-references:

Articles 8(2)(b)(xxii) and 8(2)(e)(vi).

Doctrine:

1. Machteld Boot, revised by Christopher K. Hall, in Otto Triffterer (ed.), *Commentary on the Rome Statute of the International Criminal Court: Observers' Notes, Article by Article*, 2nd ed., C.H. Beck/Hart/Nomos, Munich/Oxford/Baden-Baden, 2008, pp. 211–12.

2. Gerhard Werle, *Principles of International Criminal Law*, TMC Asser Press, The Hague, 2005, pp. 250–51, MN 728.

3. Robert Cryer, Håkan Friman, Daryll Robinson and Elizabeth Wilmshurst, *An Introduction to International Criminal Law and Procedure*, 3rd ed., Cambridge University Press, Cambridge, 2014, p. 256.

4. Anne-Marie L.M. de Brouwer, *Supranational Criminal Prosecution of Sexual Violence: The ICC and the Practice of the ICTY and the ICTR*, Intersentia, Antwerp/Oxford, 2005, pp. 137–41.

Author: Maria Sjöholm.

[54] The Elements of Crimes requires the 1) causing or a person to engage in acts of a sexual nature, 2) by force or threat of force or under coercive circumstances, and 3) the perpetrator or another person obtained or expected to obtain pecuniary or other advantage in exchange for or in connection with the acts. Primarily, the latter point distinguishes it from sexual slavery. It can also be distinguished in that sexual slavery requires the exercise or any or all of the powers attaching to the rights of ownership. Enforced prostitution could, however, rise to the level of sexual slavery, should the elements of both crimes exist. In comparison with rape and sexual slavery, enforced prostitution can either be a continuing offence or constitute a separate act. Enforced prostitution is prohibited in the Geneva Convention IV 1949 as an example of an attack on a woman's honour and in Additional Protocol I as an outrage upon personal dignity.

Cross-references:

Articles 8(2)(b)(xxii) and 8(2)(e)(vi).

Doctrine:

1. Machteld Boot revised by Christopher K. Hall, in Otto Triffterer (ed.), *Commentary on the Rome Statute of the International Criminal Court: Observers' Notes, Article by Article*, 2nd ed., C.H. Beck/Hart/Nomos, Munich/Oxford/Baden-Baden, 2008, pp. 212–13.

2. Gerhard Werle, *Principles of International Criminal Law*, TMC Asser Press, The Hague, 2005, p. 251, MN 729–30.

3. Robert Cryer, Håkan Friman, Daryll Robinson and Elizabeth Wilmshurst, *An Introduction to International Criminal Law and Procedure*, 3rd ed., Cambridge University Press, Cambridge, 2014, pp. 256–57.

4. Anne-Marie L.M. de Brouwer, *Supranational Criminal Prosecution of Sexual Violence: The ICC and the Practice of the ICTY and the ICTR*, Antwerp, Intersentia, 2005, pp. 141–42.

Author: Maria Sjöholm.

[55] According to Article 7(2)(f) forced pregnancy means the unlawful confinement of a woman forcibly made pregnant. Unlawful confinement should be interpreted as any form of deprivation of physical liberty contrary to international law. The deprivation of liberty does not have to be severe and no specific time frame is required. The use of force is not required, but some form of coercion. To complete the crime, it is sufficient if the perpetrator holds a woman imprisoned who has been impregnated by someone else. The forcible impregnation may involve rape or other forms of sexual violence of comparable gravity. In addition to the mental requirements in Article 30, the perpetrator must act with the purpose of affecting the ethnic composition of any population or carrying out other grave violations of international law. National laws prohibiting abortion do not amount to forced pregnancy.

Cross-references:

Articles 8(2)(b)(xxii) and 8(2)(e)(vi).

Doctrine:

1. Machteld Boot, revised by Christopher K. Hall, in Otto Triffterer (ed.), *Commentary on the Rome Statute of the International Criminal Court: Observers' Notes, Article by Article*, 2nd ed., C.H. Beck/Hart/Nomos, Munich/Oxford/Baden-Baden, 2008, pp. 213 and 255–56.

2. Gerhard Werle, *Principles of International Criminal Law*, TMC Asser Press, The Hague, 2005, pp. 251–52, MN 731–32.

3. Robert Cryer, Håkan Friman, Daryll Robinson and Elizabeth Wilmshurst, *An Introduction to International Criminal Law and Procedure*, 3rd ed., Cambridge University Press, Cambridge, 2014, p. 257.

4. Anne-Marie L.M. de Brouwer, *Supranational Criminal Prosecution of Sexual Violence: The ICC and the Practice of the ICTY and the ICTR*, Antwerp, Intersentia, 2005, pp. 143–46.

Author: Maria Sjöholm.

[56] Enforced sterilisation is a form of "[i]mposing measures intended to prevent births within the group" within the meaning of Article 6(e). It is carried out without the consent of a person. Genuine consent is not given when the victim has been deceived. Enforced sterilisation includes depriving a person of their biological reproductive capacity, which is not justified by the medical treatment of the person. It does not include non-permanent birth-control methods. It is not restricted to medical operations but can also include the intentional use of chemicals for this effect. It arguably includes vicious rapes where the reproductive system has been destroyed. The Elements of Crime provide a more specific definition of the criminal conduct. For the mental element Article 30 applies. Enforced sterilisation may also fall under the chapeau of genocide if such intent is present.

Cross-references:

Articles 8(2)(b)(xxii) and 8(2)(e)(vi).

Doctrine:

1. Machteld Boot, revised by Christopher K. Hall, in Otto Triffterer (ed.), *Commentary on the Rome Statute of the International Criminal Court: Observers' Notes, Article by Article*, 2nd ed., C.H. Beck/Hart/Nomos, Munich/Oxford/Baden-Baden, 2008, pp. 213–14.

2. Gerhard Werle, *Principles of International Criminal Law*, TMC Asser Press, The Hague, 2005, p. 252, MN 733.

3. Robert Cryer, Håkan Friman, Daryll Robinson and Elizabeth Wilmshurst, *An Introduction to International Criminal Law and Procedure*, 3rd ed., Cambridge University Press, Cambridge, 2014, pp. 257–58.

4. Anne-Marie L.M. de Brouwer, *Supranational Criminal Prosecution of Sexual Violence: The ICC and the Practice of the ICTY and the ICTR*, Antwerp, Intersentia, 2005, p. 146.

Author: Maria Sjöholm.

[57] The provision has a catch-all character and requires that the conduct is comparable in gravity to the other acts listed in Article 7(1)(g). It concerns acts of a sexual nature against a person through the use of force or threat of force or coercion. The importance of distinguishing the different forms of sexual violence primarily lies in the level of harm to which the victim is subjected and the degree of severity, and therefore becomes a matter of sentencing.

It is generally held to include forced nudity, forced masturbation or forced touching of the body. The ICTR in *Akayesu* held that "sexual violence is not limited to physical invasion of the human body and may include acts which do not involve penetration or even physical contact" (see *Prosecutor v. Akayesu* (Case No. ICTR-96-4-T) ICTR T. Ch., 2 September 1998, para. 688). The Trial Chamber in the case confirmed that forced public nudity was an example of sexual violence within its jurisdiction (para. 10A). Similarly, the Trial Chamber of the ICTY in its *Kvocka* decision declared: "sexual violence is broader than rape and includes such crimes as sexual slavery or molestation, and also covers sexual acts that do not involve physical contact, such as forced public nudity (*Prosecutor v. Kvocka* (Case No. IT-98-30/1-T) ICTY T. Ch., 2 November 2001, para. 180). To the contrary, in the decision on the Prosecutor's application for

(h) Persecution against any identifiable group or collectivity on political, racial, national, ethnic, cultural, religious, gender as defined in paragraph 3, or other grounds that are universally recognized as impermissible under international law, in connection with any act referred to in this paragraph or any crime within the jurisdiction of the Court;[58]

---

a warrant of arrest in the *Bemba* case, the Pre-Trial Chamber of the ICC did not include a charge of sexual violence as a crime against humanity in the arrest warrant, which had been based on allegations that the troops in question had forced women to undress in public in order to humiliate them, stating that "the facts submitted by the Prosecutor do not constitute other forms of sexual violence of comparable gravity to the other forms of sexual violence set forth in Article 7(1)(g)" (*Prosecutor v. Bemba*, ICC PT. Ch. I, Decision on the Prosecutor's Application for a Warrant of Arrest against Jean-Pierre Bemba Gombo, ICC-01/05-01/08, 10 June 2008, para. 40).

In the *Lubanga* case of the ICC, evidence of sexual violence was presented during the trial, including various forms of sexual abuse of girl soldiers who were forcefully conscripted. However, no charges of sexual violence were brought. The Prosecution rather encouraged the Trial Chamber to consider evidence of sexual violence as an integral element of the recruitment and use of child soldiers (*Prosecutor v. Lubanga*, ICC T. Ch. I, Prosecution's Closing Brief, ICC-01/04-01/06-2748-Red, 1 June 2011, paras. 139, 142 and 205). In the confirmation of charges in the *Muthaura and Kenyatta* case, Pre-Trial Chamber II chose not to charge forced male circumcision and penile amputation as sexual violence, but rather as inhumane acts. The Chamber held that "the evidence placed before it does not establish the sexual nature of the acts of forcible circumcision and penile amputation. Instead, it appears from the evidence that the acts were motivated by ethnic prejudice" (*Prosecutor v. Muthaura and Kenyatta*, ICC PT. Ch. I, Decision on the Confirmation of Charges Pursuant to Article 61(7)(a) and (b) of the Rome Statute, ICC-01/09-02/11-382-Red, 23 January 2012, para. 266). It argued that "not every act of violence which targets parts of the body commonly associated with sexuality should be considered an act of sexual violence" (see para. 265).

Cross-references:

Articles 8(2)(b)(xxii) and 8(2)(e)(vi).

Doctrine:

1. Machteld Boot, revised by Christopher K. Hall, in Otto Triffterer (ed.), *Commentary on the Rome Statute of the International Criminal Court: Observers' Notes, Article by Article*, 2nd ed., C.H. Beck/Hart/Nomos, Munich/Oxford/Baden-Baden, 2008, pp. 214–15.

2. Gerhard Werle, *Principles of International Criminal Law*, TMC Asser Press, The Hague, 2005, pp. 252–53, MN 734.

3. Robert Cryer, Håkan Friman, Daryll Robinson and Elizabeth Wilmshurst, *An Introduction to International Criminal Law and Procedure*, 3rd ed., Cambridge University Press, Cambridge, 2014, pp. 258–59.

4. Anne-Marie L.M. de Brouwer, *Supranational Criminal Prosecution of Sexual Violence: The ICC and the Practice of the ICTY and the ICTR*, Antwerp, Intersentia, 2005, pp. 147–52.

Author: Maria Sjöholm.

[58] *General remarks*

Persecution has been included in every instrument defining crimes against humanity. Arguably, it is central to the concept of crimes against humanity, as being an act not criminalised also as a war crime or as an ordinary crime. It seeks to criminalise massive violations of human rights, committed on discriminatory grounds. There was controversy among the drafters with regard to including persecution as a crime against humanity in the ICC Statute, as well as to the crime's exact definition (von Hebel and Robinson, 1999, p. 101). The crime of persecution has been extensively dealt with in the case law of the ICTY (see Nilsson, 2011). None of the judgments before the ICC have addressed the elements of this crime.

Analysis:

i. Definition

The full text of the definition of persecution in Article 7(1)(h) reads: "Persecution against any identifiable group or collectivity on political, racial, national, ethnic, cultural, religious, gender as defined in paragraph 3, or other grounds that are universally recognized as impermissible under international law, in connection with any act referred to in this paragraph or any crime within the jurisdiction of the Court". Article 7(2)(g) sets out that persecution means "the intentional and severe deprivation of fundamental rights contrary to international law by reason of the identity of the group or collectivity".

In this respect, the ICC Statute differs significantly from other legal instruments, which include a considerably more succinct provision. For example, the equivalent provision in the Nuremberg Charter (reproduced in the ICTY and ICTR Statutes), reads: "persecution on political, racial or religious grounds". The reason for the more elaborate definition was a concern among many delegations at the Rome Conference that persecution might be interpreted to include any kind of discriminatory practices (Witschel and Rückert, 2001, pp. 94–95).

The Elements of Crimes clarifies that the perpetrator must have targeted "one or more persons" (Elements of Crimes, Article 7(1)(h), nos. 1–2). Besides that, the Elements of Crimes do not add anything to the text in the Statute itself.

ii. Requirements

a. Material elements

The material elements of persecution are: 1) severe deprivation of fundamental rights contrary to international law; 2) on political, racial, national, ethnic, cultural, religious, gender as defined in paragraph 3, or other grounds that are universally recognised as impermissible under international law; and 3) in connection with any act referred to in Article 7(1) or any crime within the jurisdiction of the Court. According to one commentator, the requirement of connection with other crimes means in practice war crimes, as "[p]rosecuting persecution in the presence of genocide would also be totally redundant" (Schabas, 2010, p. 177). Another commentator argues that "[i]n practical terms, the requirement should not prove unduly restrictive, as a quick review of historical acts of persecution shows that persecution is inevitably accompanied by such inhumane acts" (Robinson, 1999, p. 55).

With regard to the element of "severe deprivation of fundamental rights", the charges confirmed before the ICC until now have been limited to such crimes which have also been charged separately as other crimes against humanity (*Prosecutor v. Gbagbo*, ICC PT. Ch. I, Decision on the Confirmation of Charges against Laurent Gbagbo, ICC-02/11-01/11-656-Red, 12 June 2014, para. 204, compared with paras. 193–199; *Prosecutor v. Muthaura et al.*, ICC PT. Ch. II, ICC-01/09-02/11-382-Red, Decision on the Confirmation of Charges Pursuant to Article 61(7)(a) and (b) of the Rome Statute, 23 January 2012, para. 283, compared with paras. 233, 243, 257, 270–271, 275–277; *Prosecutor v. Ruto et al.*, ICC PT. Ch. II, ICC-01/09-01/11-373, Decision on the Confirmation of Charges Pursuant to Article 61(7)(a) and (b) of the Rome Statute, 23 January 2012, paras. 271–272, compared with paras. 225–226, 228–239, 241–242, 248–251, 253–266).

b. Mental elements

The definition in Article 7 sets out that the severe deprivation of fundamental rights must be committed intentionally. In addition, it expresses that the deprivation must be committed on discriminatory grounds. Finally, with regard to the third material element mentioned above ("in connection with any act referred to in Article 7(1) or any crime within the jurisdiction of the

(i) Enforced disappearance of persons;[59]

Court"), the Elements of Crimes clarifies that no additional mental element is necessary (Elements of Crimes, p. 10, fn. 22).

Doctrine:

1. Dermot Groome, "Persecution", in Antonio Cassese (ed.), *The Oxford Companion to International Criminal Justice*, Oxford University Press, Oxford, 2009, pp. 453–54.

2. Christopher K. Hall, "Article 7 Crimes against Humanity, (h) 'Persecution'", in Otto Triffterer (ed.), *Commentary on the Rome Statute of the International Criminal Court: Observers' Notes, Article by Article,* 2nd ed., C.H. Beck/Hart/Nomos, Munich/Oxford/Baden-Baden, 2008, pp. 216–21.

3. Herman von Hebel and Darryl Robinson, in Roy S. Lee (ed.), *The International Criminal Court: The Making of the Rome Statute. Issues, Negotiations, Results,* Kluwer Law International, Leiden, 1999, pp. 90–103.

4. Timothy L.H. McCormack, "Crimes Against Humanity", in Dominic McGoldrick, Peter Rowe and Eric Donnelly (eds.), *The Permanent International Criminal Court: Legal and Policy Issues*, Hart Publishing, Oxford, 2004, pp. 196–97.

5. Jonas Nilsson, "The Crime of Persecution in the ICTY Case law", in Bert Swart, Alexander Zahar and Göran Sluiter (eds.), *The Legacy of the International Criminal Tribunal for the Former Yugoslavia*, Oxford University Press, Oxford, 2011, pp. 219–46.

6. William A. Schabas, *The International Criminal Court: A Commentary on the Rome Statute*, Oxford University Press, Oxford, 2010, pp. 175–80.

7. Georg Witschel and Wiebke Rückert, "Article 7(1)(h) – Crime Against Humanity of Persecution", in Roy S. Lee (ed.), *The International Criminal Court: Elements of Crimes and Rules of Procedure and Evidence*, Transnational Publishers, Ardsley, NY, 2001, pp. 94–97.

Author: Jonas Nilsson (The views expressed are those of the author alone and do not necessarily reflect the views of the United Nations or the ICTY.)

[59] *General remarks*:

The 'systematic practice' of enforced disappearance was considered "the nature of crimes against humanity" by the UN General Assembly through a resolution in 1992 (UN GA res. 47/133, 18 December 1992, preamble). Similarly, the International Convention for the Protection of All Persons from Enforced Disappearance states that enforced disappearance "in certain circumstances defined in international law" constitutes a crime against humanity. None of the judgments before the ICC have addressed the elements of this crime.

The complex nature of the crime is acknowledged in the Elements of Crimes: "it is recognized that its commission will normally involve more than one perpetrator as a part of a common criminal purpose" (Elements of Crimes, fn. 23).

Analysis:

i. Definition

According to Article 7(2)(i), enforced disappearance of persons means "the arrest, detention or abduction of persons by, or with the authorization, support or acquiescence of, a State or political organization, followed by a refusal to acknowledge that deprivation of freedom or to give information on the fate or whereabouts of those persons, with the intention of removing them from the protection of the law for a prolonged period of time". The Elements of Crimes clarifies that both the deprivation of liberty and the refusal to acknowledge this deprivation or to give information on the fate or whereabouts of such person or persons must have been carried out by, or with the authorisation, support or acquiescence of, a State or political organisation.

ii. Requirements

(j) The crime of apartheid;[60]

---

a. Material elements

The two central material elements are 1) an arrest, detention or abduction of a person or persons, and 2) a refusal to acknowledge that deprivation of freedom or to give information on the fate or whereabouts of those persons. According to the Elements of Crimes, there must be an objective nexus between these material elements (Elements of Crimes, Article 7(1)(i), item 2).

Furthermore, the deprivation of liberty needs to have been carried out by, or with the authorisation, support or acquiescence of, a State or political organisation. In this respect, there is an overlap with one of the general elements of crimes against humanity: "part of a widespread or systematic attack directed against any civilian population", with 'attack' being defined as "a course of conduct [...] pursuant to or in furtherance of a State or organizational policy to commit such attack" (Article 7(1), and (2)(a)).

b. Mental elements

According to the Elements of Crimes, the perpetrator must be aware that the deprivation of liberty "would be followed in the ordinary course of events by a refusal to acknowledge that deprivation of freedom or to give information on the fate or whereabouts of such person or persons" or that "[s]uch refusal was preceded or accompanied by that deprivation of freedom".

In addition, the definition adds a specific intent for this crime: "the intention of removing [the person or persons deprived of their liberty] from the protection of the law for a prolonged period of time".

Doctrine:

1. M. Cherif Bassiouni, *Crimes Against Humanity: Historical Evolution and Contemporary Application*, Cambridge University Press, Cambridge, 2011, pp. 448–52.
2. Christopher K., Hall, "Article 7 Crimes Against Humanity, (i) 'Enforced Disappearance of Persons'", in Otto Triffterer (ed.), *Commentary on the Rome Statute of the International Criminal Court: Observers' Notes, Article by Article*, 2nd ed., C.H. Beck/Hart/Nomos, Munich/Oxford/Baden-Baden, 2008, pp. 221–26, 266–73.
3. Timothy L.H. McCormack, "Crimes Against Humanity", in Dominic McGoldrick, Peter Rowe and Eric Donnelly (eds.), *The Permanent International Criminal Court: Legal and Policy Issues*, Hart Publishing, Oxford, 2004, pp. 197–98.
4. William A. Schabas, *The International Criminal Court: A Commentary on the Rome Statute*, Oxford University Press, Oxford, 2010, pp. 180–82.
5. Marieke Wierda and Thomas Unger, "Enforced Disappearances", in Antonio Cassese (ed.), *The Oxford Companion to International Criminal Justice*, Oxford University Press, Oxford, 2009, pp. 309–10.
6. Georg Witschel and Wiebke Rückert, "Article 7(1)(i) – Crime Against Humanity of Enforced Disappearance of Persons", in Roy S. Lee (ed.), *The International Criminal Court: Elements of Crimes and Rules of Procedure and Evidence*, Transnational Publishers, Ardsley, NY, 2001, pp. 98–103.

Author: Jonas Nilsson (The views expressed are those of the author alone and do not necessarily reflect the views of the United Nations or the ICTY.)

[60] *General remarks*:

The crime of apartheid was condemned as a crime against humanity by the UN General Assembly through a resolution in 1966 (UN GA res. 2202 (XXI), 16 December 1966, para. 1) and in the International Convention on the Suppression and Punishment of the Crime of Apartheid. None of the judgments before the ICC have addressed the elements of this crime.

A number of authors have criticised the inclusion of "the crime of apartheid" in the list of crimes against humanity in the ICC Statute as legally unsound (Zahar, 2009, pp. 245–46 and McCormack, 2004, pp. 198–200). Essentially, the critique is that the crime is fully covered by the crime of persecution as a crime against humanity and that there is therefore no need for it.

Analysis:

i. Definition

According to Article 7(2)(h), the crime of apartheid encompasses "inhumane acts of a character similar to those referred to in paragraph 1 (of Article 7), committed in the context of an institutionalized regime of systematic oppression and domination by one racial group over any other racial group or groups and committed with the intention of maintaining that regime". The Elements of Crimes clarifies that the crime may be committed by an act against one or more persons, that 'character' refers to the nature and gravity of the act, and that the perpetrator need to be aware of the factual circumstances that established the character of the act.

ii. Requirements

a. Material elements

The material elements of the crime of apartheid bear similarities with the crimes of persecution and other inhumane acts, in that it overlaps substantially with other crimes against humanity. With regard to which acts it encompasses, the definition itself points to the other crimes against humanity. The act or acts of the crime of apartheid must be of "a character similar to those referred to in paragraph 1 [of Article 7]", meaning of the same nature and gravity as those acts. Therefore, the acts of the crime of apartheid could also be one of those listed acts, for example murder and torture.

According to the definition the act or acts must be "committed in the context of an institutionalized regime of systematic oppression and domination by one racial group over any other racial group or groups". With regard to this element there is a clear overlap with one of the general elements of crimes against humanity: "part of a widespread or systematic attack directed against any civilian population", with 'attack' being defined as "a course of conduct [...] pursuant to or in furtherance of a State or organizational policy to commit such attack" (Article 7(1) and (2)(a)). It is difficult to imagine any scenario in which the general elements have been proven (which they have to for the act to qualify as a crime against humanity), but the specific element of the crime of apartheid has not. Therefore, at least in practice, this element of the crime of apartheid does not amount to a distinct element of the crime.

b. Mental elements

Besides the mental elements of the crime, as set out in Article 30 of the ICC Statute, the definition adds a specific intent for this crime: "the intention of maintaining [the institutionalized regime of systematic oppression and domination by one racial group over any other racial group or groups]".

Doctrine:

1. M. Cherif Bassiouni, *Crimes Against Humanity: Historical Evolution and Contemporary Application*, Cambridge University Press, Cambridge, 2011, pp. 448–52.
2. Christopher K. Hall, "Article 7: Crimes Against Humanity, (j) 'The Crime of Apartheid'", in Otto Triffterer (ed.), *Commentary on the Rome Statute of the International Criminal Court: Observers' Notes, Article by Article*, 2nd ed., C.H. Beck/Hart/Nomos, Munich/Oxford/Baden-Baden, 2008, pp. 227–29, 263–66.
3. Timothy L.H. McCormack, "Crimes Against Humanity", in Dominic McGoldrick, Peter Rowe and Eric Donnelly (eds.), *The Permanent International Criminal Court: Legal and Policy Issues*, Hart Publishing, Oxford, 2004, pp. 198–200.

(k) Other inhumane acts of a similar character intentionally causing great suffering, or serious injury to body or to mental or physical health.[61]

---

4. William A. Schabas, *The International Criminal Court: A Commentary on the Rome Statute*, Oxford University Press, Oxford, 2010, pp. 182–83.
5. Gerhard Werle, *Principles of International Criminal Law*, TMC Asser Press, The Hague, 2005, pp. 262–64, MN 758–65.
6. Georg Witschel and Wiebke Rückert, "Article 7(1)(j) – Crime Against Humanity of Apartheid", in Roy S. Lee (ed.), *The International Criminal Court: Elements of Crimes and Rules of Procedure and Evidence*, Transnational Publishers, Ardsley, NY, 2001, pp. 103–6.
7. Alexander Zahar, "Apartheid as an International Crime" in Antonio Cassese (ed.), *The Oxford Companion to International Criminal Justice*, Oxford University Press, Oxford, 2009, pp. 245–46.

Author: Jonas Nilsson (The views expressed are those of the author alone and do not necessarily reflect the views of the United Nations or the ICTY.)

[61] *General remarks*:

The definitions of crimes against humanity in the Nuremberg Charter, Control Council Law No. 10, and the ICTY and ICTR Statutes, have all included a residual provision of this kind, indicating that the list of expressly named acts is not exhaustive. It reflects the sentiment that it is not possible to create such an exhaustive list. According to one Author: "The capacity of human beings to concoct novel forms of atrocity is a constant source of discomfort and shame and it is critical that provisions exist to facilitate prosecution of such actions not currently known or experienced" (McCormack, 2004, p. 201).

The risk of creating an open-ended definition was countered in the drafting of the ICC Statute by clarifying the terms with the ejusdem generis rule (von Hebel and Robinson, 1999, p. 102). By linking it with the other crimes against humanity, the drafters sought to achieve a more precise definition and thus consistency with the principle of nullum crimen sine lege (Witschel and Rückert, 2001, p. 107).

Analysis:

i. Definition

The definition in Article 7(1)(k) reads: "[o]ther inhumane acts of a similar character intentionally causing great suffering, or serious injury to body or to mental or physical health". Article 7(2) does not contain any further clarification of the provision. The Elements of Crimes clarifies that 'character' refers to the nature and gravity of the act (Elements of Crimes, fn. 30). Further, the perpetrator must be aware of the factual circumstances that established the character of the act (Elements of the Crimes, p. 12).

ii. Requirements

a. Material elements

There are two material elements for this crime: 1) an act causing great suffering, or serious injury to body or to mental or physical health; and 2) an act of similar character (nature and gravity) to any other act in Article 7(1).

The Pre-Trial Chamber in *Prosecutor v. Katanga and Ngudjolo* contrasted the provision in the ICC Statute with the equivalent provision in the Nuremberg Charter and the ICTY and ICTR Statutes: the [ICC] Statute has given to "other inhumane acts" a different scope than its antecedents like the Nuremberg Charter and the ICTR and ICTY Statutes. The latter conceived "other inhumane acts" as a "catch-all provision", leaving a broad margin for the jurisprudence to determine its limits. In contrast, the ICC Statute contains certain limitations, as regards to the action constituting an inhumane act and the consequences required as a result of that action (*Ka-*

tanga and Ngudjolo, ICC PT. Ch. I, Decision on the Confirmation of Charges, ICC PT. Ch. I, ICC-01/04-01/07-717, 30 September 2008, para. 450).

In this respect, it first clarified that none of the acts constituting crimes against humanity according to Article 7(1)(a) to (j) could simultaneously be considered as an other inhumane act (*ibid.*, para. 452). Referring to the principle of *nullum crimen sine lege*, it added that inhumane acts are to be considered "as serious violations of international customary law and the basic rights pertaining to human beings, drawn from the norms of international human rights law" (*ibid.*, para. 448). Whether a particular act meets these requirements has to be determined with considerations given to all the factual circumstances (*ibid.*, para. 449). In this respect, the Pre-Trial Chamber referred primarily to ICTY case law ((Case No. IT-95-16), ICTY T. Ch., Judgment, 14 January 2000, para. 566; *Prosecutor v. Stakić* (Case No. IT-97-24), ICTY T. Ch., Judgment, 31 July 2003, para. 721; *Prosecutor v. Vasiljević* (Case No. IT-98-32), ICTY A. Ch., 25 February 2004, para. 165), which might appear odd considering that the Pre-Trial Chamber expressly attempted to distinguish the ICTY provision from that in the ICC Statute. With regard to consequences, the Pre-Trial Chamber merely reiterated the words from the Statute: "great suffering, or serious injury to body or to mental or physical health" (*ibid.*, para. 453).

The Pre-Trial Chamber in *Prosecutor v. Muthaura et al.* did not contrast the provision on "other inhumane acts" with the equivalent provisions in other legal instruments. It did, however, consider that the provision "must be interpreted conservatively and must not be used to expand uncritically the scope of crimes against humanity" (*Prosecutor v. Mathaura et al.*, ICC PT. Ch. II, Decision on the Confirmation of Charges Pursuant to Article 61(7)(a) and (b) of the Rome Statute, ICC-01/09-02/11-382-Red, 23 January 2012, para. 269). It also considered that if a conduct could be charged as another crime against humanity, its charging as other inhumane acts would be impermissible (*ibid.*). The Pre-Trial Chamber confirmed charges of acts causing physical injury (including forcible circumcision, penile amputation, and mutilations) and acts causing mental suffering on the part of victims whose family members were killed in front of their eyes (*ibid.*, paras. 267–68, 270–77). However, with regard to the destruction or vandalising of property and businesses the Pre-Trial Chamber did not consider that this conduct caused "serious injury to mental health" within the definition of other inhumane acts.

b. Mental elements

The definition in the Statute and the Elements of Crimes sets out that the perpetrator must have inflicted great suffering, or serious injury to body or to mental or physical health intentionally. Further, the perpetrator must have been aware of the factual circumstances that established the character similar to any other act referred to in Article 7(1) of the Statute.

The Pre-Trial Chamber in the case *Prosecutor v. Katanga and Ngudjolo* declined to confirm charges of attempted murder under the provision of other inhumane acts, for reasons of lack of *mens rea*: "the clear intent to kill persons cannot be transformed into intent to severely injure persons by means of inhumane acts solely on the basis that the result of the conduct was different from that which was intended and pursued by the perpetrators" (*Katanga and Ngudjolo*, ICC PT. Ch. I, Decision on the Confirmation of Charges, ICC-01/04-01/07-717, 30 September 2008, para. 463).

Cross-references:

Starvation in Articles 6(c), 7(1)(b)and (j), 7(2)(b), 8(2)(a)(iii), 8(2)(b)(ii), (v), (xiii) and (xxv), and 8(2)(c)(i).

Doctrine:

1. Christopher K. Hall, "Article 7: Crimes Against Humanity, (k) 'Other Inhumane Acts'", in Otto Trifterer (ed.), *Commentary on the Rome Statute of the International Criminal Court: Observers' Notes, Article by Article*, 2nd ed., C.H. Beck/Hart/Nomos, Munich/Oxford/Baden-Baden, 2008, pp. 230–34.

2. For the purpose of paragraph 1:

(a) "Attack directed against any civilian population" means a course of conduct involving the multiple commission of acts referred to in paragraph 1 against any civilian population, pursuant to or in furtherance of a State or organizational policy to commit such attack;[62]

---

2. Herman von Hebel and Darryl Robinson, in Roy S. Lee (ed.), *The International Criminal Court: The Making of the Rome Statute. Issues, Negotiations, Results*, Kluwer Law International, Alphen aan Den Rijn, 1999, pp. 90–103.

3. Timothy L.H. McCormack, "Crimes Against Humanity", in Dominic McGoldrick, Peter Rowe and Eric Donnelly (eds.), *The Permanent International Criminal Court: Legal and Policy Issues*, Hart Publishing, Oxford, 2004, pp. 200–1.

4. William A. Schabas, *The International Criminal Court: A Commentary on the Rome Statute*, Oxford University Press, Oxford, 2010, pp. 183–86.

5. Georg Witschel and Wiebke Rückert, "Article 7(1)(k) – Crime Against Humanity of Other Inhumane Acts", in Roy S. Lee (ed.), *The International Criminal Court: Elements of Crimes and Rules of Procedure and Evidence*, Transnational Publishers, Ardsley, NY, 2001, pp. 106–8.

6. Alexander Zahar, "Other Inhumane Acts", in Antonio Cassese (ed.), *The Oxford Companion to International Criminal Justice*, Oxford University Press, Oxford, 2009, p. 448.

[62] Article 7(2)(a) clarifies that it needs to be a State or organisational policy. One Pre-Trial Chamber declared that the term 'State' was self-explanatory but added that the policy did not have to be conceived "at the highest level of the State machinery" (*Situation in the Republic of Kenya*, ICC PT. Ch. II, Decision Pursuant to Article 15 of the Rome Statute on the Authorisation of an Investigation into the Situation in the Republic of Kenya, ICC-01-09, 31 March 2010, para. 89, citing *Prosecutor v. Blaškić*, ICTY T. Ch., Judgment, 3 March 2000, para. 205). Therefore, also a policy adopted by regional or local organs of the State could satisfy this requirement (*ibid.*).

With regard to 'organisational', the Pre-Trial Chambers in *Prosecutor v. Bemba* and *Prosecutor v. Katanga and Ngudjolo* stated that it may be "groups of persons who govern a specific territory or […] any organization with the capability to commit a widespread or systematic attack against a civilian population" (*Prosecutor v. Bemba*, ICC PT. Ch. II, Decision Pursuant to Article 61(7)(a) and (b) of the Rome Statute on the Charges of the Prosecutor Against Jean-Pierre Bemba Gombo, 15 June 2009, para. 81; Katanga and Ngudjolo, ICC PT. Ch. I, Decision on the Confirmation of Charges, ICC-01/04-01/07-717, 30 September 2008, para. 396). It is therefore not limited to State-like organisations (*Situation in the Republic of Kenya*, ICC PT. Ch. II, Decision Pursuant to Article 15 of the Rome Statute on the Authorisation of an Investigation into the Situation in the Republic of Kenya, 31 March 2010, paras. 90–92; *Prosecutor v. Muthaura et al.*, ICC PT. Ch. II, Decision on the Confirmation of Charges Pursuant to Article 61(7)(a) and (b) of the Rome Statute, 23 January 2012, para. 112; *Prosecutor v. Ruto et al.*, Decision on the Confirmation of Charges Pursuant to Article 61(7)(a) and (b) of the Rome Statute, 23 January 2012, para. 33 (See also Judge Kaul's dissents to these decisions: *Prosecutor v. Ruto et al.* Dissenting Opinion by Judge Hans-Peter Kaul to Pre-Trial Chamber II's "Decision on the Prosecutor's Application for Summons to Appear for William Samoei Ruto, Henry Kiprono Kosgey and Joshua Arap Sang", 15 March 2011, and *Prosecutor v. Muthaura et al.*, Dissenting Opinion by Judge Hans-Peter Kaul to Pre-Trial Chamber II's "Decision on the Prosecutor's Application for Summonses to Appear for Francis Kirimi Muthaura, Uhuru Muigai Kenyatta and Mohammed Hussein Ali", 15 March 2011). The Trial Chamber in the *Prosecutor v. Katanga* followed this approach (*Prosecutor v. Katanga*, ICC T. Ch. II, ICC-01/04-01/07-3436, Jugement rendu en application de l'Article 74 du Statut, 7 March 2014, paras. 1117–1122).

(b) "Extermination" includes the intentional infliction of conditions of life, *inter alia* the deprivation of access to food and medicine, calculated to bring about the destruction of part of a population;

(c) "Enslavement" means the exercise of any or all of the powers attaching to the right of ownership over a person and includes the exercise of such power in the course of trafficking in persons, in particular women and children;

(d) "Deportation or forcible transfer of population" means forced displacement of the persons concerned by expulsion or other coercive acts from the area in which they are lawfully present, without grounds permitted under international law;

(e) "Torture" means the intentional infliction of severe pain or suffering, whether physical or mental, upon a person in the custody or under the control of the accused; except that torture shall not include pain or suffering arising only from, inherent in or incidental to, lawful sanctions;

(f) "Forced pregnancy" means the unlawful confinement of a woman forcibly made pregnant, with the intent of affecting the ethnic composition of any population or carrying out other grave violations of international law. This definition shall not in any way be interpreted as affecting national laws relating to pregnancy;

(g) "Persecution" means the intentional and severe deprivation of fundamental rights contrary to international law by reason of the identity of the group or collectivity;

(h) "The crime of apartheid" means inhumane acts of a character similar to those referred to in paragraph 1, committed in the context of an institutionalized regime of systematic oppression and domination by one racial group over any other racial group or groups and committed with the intention of maintaining that regime;

(i) "Enforced disappearance of persons" means the arrest, detention or abduction of persons by, or with the authorization, support or acquiescence of, a State or a political organization, followed by a refusal to acknowledge that deprivation of freedom or to give information on the fate or whereabouts of those persons, with the intention of removing them from the protection of the law for a prolonged period of time.

3. For the purpose of this Statute, it is understood that the term "gender" refers to the two sexes, male and female, within the context of society. The term "gender" does not indicate any meaning different from the above.[63]

The *Bemba* Pre-Trial Chamber stated that when determining whether the 'part of' requirement was met it would consider "the characteristics, the aims, the nature or consequences of the act" (*Prosecutor v. Bemba*, ICC PT. Ch. II, Decision Pursuant to Article 61(7)(a) and (b) of the Rome Statute on the Charges of the Prosecutor Against Jean-Pierre Bemba Gombo, 15 June 2009, para. 84). It also stated "the underlying offences must [...] not be isolated" (*Prosecutor v. Bemba*, ICC PT. Ch. II, Decision Pursuant to Article 61(7)(a) and (b) of the Rome Statute on the Charges of the Prosecutor Against Jean-Pierre Bemba Gombo, 15 June 2009, para. 83), although that ought to follow already from the fact they have to be part of a widespread or systematic attack against a civilian population.

Author: Jonas Nilsson (The views expressed are those of the author alone and do not necessarily reflect the views of the United Nations or the ICTY.)

[63] The term "gender" refers to socially constructed roles played by women and men.

Doctrine:
1. Machteld Boot, in Otto Triffterer (ed.), *Commentary on the Rome Statute of the International Criminal Court: Observers' Notes, Article by Article*, 2nd ed., C.H. Beck/Hart/Nomos, Munich/Oxford/Baden-Baden, 2008, p. 273.

Author: Mark Klamberg.

Article 8
War crimes[2]

1. The Court shall have jurisdiction in respect of war crimes in particular when committed as part of a plan or policy or as part of a large-scale commission of such crimes.[64]

2. For the purpose of this Statute, "war crimes" means:

    (a) Grave breaches of the Geneva Conventions of 12 August 1949, namely, any of the following acts against persons or property protected under the provisions of the relevant Geneva Convention:[65]

---

[64] In contrast to crimes against humanity, plan, policy and scale are not elements of war crimes. One single act may constitute a war crime. However, it is unlikely that a single act would meet the gravity threshold in Article 17(1)(d).

Doctrine:

1. Michael, Bothe, in Antonio Cassese, Paola Gaeta and John R.W.D. Jones (eds.), *The Rome Statute of the International Criminal Court: A Commentary*, Oxford University Press, Oxford, 2002, pp. 380–381.

2. Michael Cottier, "Article 8, War Crimes", in Otto Triffterer (ed.), *Commentary on the Rome Statute of the International Criminal Court: Observers' Notes, Article by Article*, 2nd ed., C.H. Beck/Hart/Nomos, Munich/Oxford/Baden-Baden, 2008, pp. 299–300.

3. Gerhard Werle, *Principles of International Criminal Law,* TMC Asser Press, The Hague, 2005, p. 269, MN 773.

Author: Mark Klamberg.

[65] *General remarks:*

War crimes are crimes committed in time of armed conflict. As there is no general definition of an armed conflict in the ICC Statute or the Elements of Crimes the Court has relied on ICTY jurisprudence to define "armed conflict": "an armed conflict exists whenever there is a resort to armed force between States or protracted violence between governmental authorities and organized armed groups or between such groups within a State" (*Prosecutor v. Lubanga*, ICC T. Ch. I, Judgment, ICC-01/04-01/06, 14 March 2012, para. 533).

The crimes listed in Article 8(2) can be perpetrated in both international and non-international armed conflicts (*Prosecutor v. Bemba*, ICC PT. Ch. II, Decision Pursuant to Article 61(7)(a) and (b) of the Rome Statute on the Charges of the Prosecutor Against Jean-Pierre Bemba Gombo, ICC-01/05-01/08-424, ICC-01/05-01/08-424, 15 June 2009, para. 216). While Articles 8(2)(a) and (b) cover acts committed in an international armed conflict, Articles 8(2)(c) and (e) refer to acts committed in a non-international armed conflict.

Following the *Tadić* jurisprudence of the ICTY that refers to mixed conflicts, that is, conflicts that are both international and non-international (*Prosecutor v. Tadić* (Case No. IT-94-1-I), ICTY A. Ch., Decision on the Defence Motion for Interlocutory Appeal on Jurisdiction, 2 October 1995, para. 77), the ICC has stated that(1) the nature of a conflict can change over time (*Prosecutor v. Katanga*, ICC T. Ch. II, Jugement, ICC-01/04-01/07-3436, 7 March 2014, para. 1181), and (2) conflicts of different nature can take place on the same territory (*Lubanga*, ICC T. Ch. I, Judgment, ICC-01/04-01/06, 14 March 2012, para. 540; *Katanga*, ICC T. Ch. II, Jugement, ICC-01/04-01/07-3436, 7 March 2014, paras. 1174 and 1182; *Prosecutor v. Ntaganda*, ICC PT. Ch. II, Decision on the Confirmation of Charges, ICC-01/04-02/06-309, 9 June 2014, para. 33). As a result, any determination of the qualification of an armed conflict must be based on an evaluation of the facts at the relevant time.

Analysis:

Article 8(2)(a) states that "For the purpose of this Statute, 'war crimes' means: (a) Grave breaches of the Geneva Conventions of 12 August 1949, namely, any of the following acts against persons or property protected under the provisions of the relevant Geneva Convention [...]".

i) Scope of Application

The four Geneva Conventions of 1949 apply in international armed conflict. Neither the Statute nor the Elements of Crimes define the concepts of "armed conflict" and "international armed conflict" and thus recourse must be had to the principles and rules of international law, and more specifically, Common Article 2 of the Geneva Conventions which state that international armed conflicts involve two or more State parties to the conventions and do not necessitate a threshold of violence to apply (*Lubanga*, ICC T. Ch. I, Judgment, ICC-01/04-01/06, 14 March 2012, para. 541; *Katanga*, ICC T. Ch. II, Judgment, ICC-01/04-01/07-3436, 7 March 2014, para. 1177).

The concept of an international armed conflict also includes military occupation (fn. 34 of the Elements of Crimes; *Katanga*, ICC T. Ch. II, Jugement, ICC-01/04-01/07-3436, 7 March 2014, para. 1179): a "territory is considered to be occupied when it is actually placed under the authority of the hostile army, and the occupation extends only to the territory where such authority has been established and can be exercised" (*Prosecutor v. Lubanga*, ICC PT. Ch. I, Decision on the Confirmation of Charges, ICC-01/04-01/06-803, 29 January 2007, para. 212; *Lubanga*, ICC T. Ch. I, Judgment, ICC-01/04-01/06, 14 March 2012, para. 542; *Katanga*, ICC T. Ch. II, Jugement, ICC-01/04-01/07-3436, 7 March 2014, para. 1179). In *Katanga* the ICC developed a list of elements to be taken into consideration when applying this definition (*Katanga*, ICC T. Ch. II, Jugement, ICC-01/04-01/07-3436, 7 March 2014, para. 1180).

Following the *Tadić* jurisprudence of the ICTY (*Prosecutor v. Tadić* (Case No. IT-94-1-A), ICTY A. Ch., Judgment, 15 July 1999, para. 84) the ICC has interpreted the definition of an international armed conflict to include conflicts opposing a State against an armed opposition group when "(i) another State intervenes in that conflict through its troops (direct intervention), or (ii) some of the participants in the internal armed conflict on behalf of that other State (indirect intervention)" (*Lubanga*, ICC T. Ch. I, Judgment, ICC-01/04-01/06, 14 March 2012, para. 541; *Bemba*, ICC PT. Ch. II, Decision Pursuant to Article 61(7)(a) and (b) of the Rome Statute on the Charges of the Prosecutor Against Jean-Pierre Bemba Gombo, ICC-01/05-01/08-424, 15 June 2009, para. 220; *Katanga*, ICC T. Ch. II, Jugement, ICC-01/04-01/07-3436, 7 March 2014, para. 1177); in this instance the conflict is internationalised. However, assistance provided by foreign States to the State fighting an armed opposition group does not lead to the internationalisation of the conflict (*Bemba*, ICC PT. Ch. II, ICC-01/05-01/08-424, 15 June 2009, para. 246; *Prosecutor v. Mbarushimana*, ICC PT. Ch. I, Decision on the Confirmation of Charges, ICC-01/04-01/10-465-Red, 16 December 2011, para. 101). To determine whether a situation falls within situation (ii) the ICC follows the 'overall control' test that was devised by the ICTY in *Tadić* (*Tadić*, ICTY A. Ch., Judgment, 15 July 1999, para. 137) (*Lubanga*, ICC PT. Ch. I, Decision on the Confirmation of Charges, 29 January 2007, para. 211; *Prosecutor v. Lubanga*, ICC T. Ch. I, Judgment, ICC-01/04-01/06, 14 March 2012, para. 541). It specifies that when a State plays a role "in organising, coordinating or planning the military actions of the military group, in addition to financing, training and equipping or providing operational support to that group" then the conflict becomes international (*Lubanga*, ICC PT. Ch. I, Decision on the Confirmation of Charges, ICC-01/04-01/06-803, 29 January 2007, para. 211; *Lubanga*, ICC T. Ch. I, Judgment, ICC-01/04-01/06, 14 March 2012, para. 541; *Katanga*, ICC T. Ch. II, Jugement, ICC-01/04-01/07-3436, 7 March 2014, para. 1178).

To sum up "an international armed conflict exists in case of armed hostilities between States through their respective armed forces or other actors acting on behalf of the State" (*Bemba*, ICC PT. Ch. II, ICC-01/05-01/08-424, 15 June 2009, para. 223; *Katanga*, ICC T. Ch. II, Jugement, ICC-01/04-01/07-3436, 7 March 2014, para. 1177).

ii) Concept of Grave Breaches

Each Geneva Convention has its own list of grave breaches (Article 50 GC I, Article 51 GC II, Article 130 GC III and Article 147 GC IV). The ICC Statute is an accurate reflection of the grave breaches provisions of the four Geneva Conventions.

iii) Acts against Persons or Property Protected under Geneva Conventions

For the grave breaches regime under the Geneva Conventions to apply the acts must have been committed against protected persons (for example, wounded, injured, sick and/or shipwrecked combatants, prisoners of war and civilians in occupied territory) and property (for example, movable and non-movable property in occupied territory (see, for example, *Prosecutor v. Blaškić* (Case No. IT-95-14), ICTY T. Ch., Judgment, 3 March 2000, para. 157)). This is repeated in fn. 35 of the Elements of Crimes: "all victims must be 'protected persons' under one or more of the Geneva Conventions of 1949".

While the Geneva Conventions I, II and III do not refer to the nationality of the member of the armed forces, Article 4 GC IV explicitly considers protected persons as those who "find themselves, in case of a conflict or occupation, in the hands of a Party to the conflict of Occupying Power of which they are not nationals". Footnote 33 of the Elements of Crimes explains that "[w]ith respect to nationality, it is understood that the perpetrator needs only to know that the victim belonged to an adverse party to the conflict" thereby seemingly adopting the broad definitional approach of the ICTY whereby allegiance, rather than nationality, is key to determining whether the individual is to be granted protection under the Geneva Convention IV (*Tadić*, ICTY A. Ch., Decision on the Defence Motion for Interlocutory Appeal on Jurisdiction, 2 October 1995, para. 76; *Tadić*, ICTY A. Ch., Judgment, 15 July 1999, paras. 164–66). In *Katanga and Chui*, the ICC endorsed this approach, specifying that "individual civilians […] automatically become protected persons within the meaning of Article 4 GC IV, provided they do not claim allegiance to the party in question" (*Prosecutor v. Katanga and Chui*, ICC PT. Ch. I, Decision on the Confirmation of Charges, ICC-01/04-01/07-717, 30 September 2008, para. 293).

So far no such cases have been decided by the ICC. Generally, it is rather rare for international criminal tribunals to deal with violations of the first three Geneva Conventions.

iv) Awareness

Unlike for crimes prosecuted before the ICTY which requires that the perpetrator was aware that that his or her acts were linked to a conflict of an international nature (*Prosecutor v. Naletilić and Martinović* (Case No. IT-98-34-A), ICTY A. Ch., Judgment, 3 May 2006, paras. 110–20) the ICC Statute only requires the "awareness of the factual circumstances that established the existence of an armed conflict that is implicit in the terms 'took place in the context of and was associated with'" (Elements of Crimes, Article 8, Introduction). There must however be a nexus between the act and the conflict.

However, both courts require that the individual was aware that the individuals/property were protected under one or more of the Geneva Conventions (Elements of Crimes, Article 8(2)(a)(i), fn. 32). It is sufficient to show that the perpetrator was aware of the "factual circumstances that established [the] status [of the individuals]".

Doctrine:

(i) Wilful killing;[66]

(ii) Torture[67] or inhuman treatment,[68] including biological experiments;[69]

1. Dapo Akande, "Classification of Armed Conflicts: Relevant Legal Concepts", in Elizabeth Wilmhurst (ed.), *International Law and the Classification of Conflicts*, Oxford University Press, Oxford, 2012, pp. 32–79.

2. Michael Bothe, "War Crimes", in Antonio Cassese, Paola Gaeta and John R.W.D. Jones (eds.), *The Rome Statute of the International Criminal Court: A Commentary*, Oxford University Press, Oxford, 2002, pp. 379–426.

3. Knut Dörmann, "Article 8, War Crimes", in Otto Triffterer (ed.), *Commentary on the Rome Statute of the International Criminal Court: Observers' Notes, Article by Article*, 2nd ed., C.H. Beck/Hart/Nomos, Munich/Oxford/Baden-Baden, 2008, pp. 300–5.

4. Antonio Cassese, Paola Gaeta and John R.W.D. Jones (eds.), *International Criminal Law*, Oxford University Press, Oxford, 2013, pp. 63–83.

5. Robert Cryer, Håkan Friman, Daryll Robinson and Elizabeth Wilmshurst, *An Introduction to International Criminal Law and Procedure*, 3rd ed., Cambridge University Press, Cambridge, 2014, pp. 264–284.

6. Anthony Cullen, "War Crimes", in William and Nadia Bernaz (eds.), *Routledge Handbook of International Criminal Law*, Routledge, London, 2011, pp. 139–54.

7. Knut Dörmann, *Elements of War Crimes under the Rome Statute of the International Criminal Court*, Cambridge University Press, Cambridge, 2002, pp. 17–37.

8. William A. Schabas, *An Introduction to the International Criminal Court*, Cambridge University Press, Cambridge, 2011, pp. 131–33.

9. William A. Schabas, *The International Criminal Court: A Commentary on the Rome Statute*, Oxford University Press, Oxford, 2010, pp. 188–257.

Author: Noëlle Quénivet.

[66] The term 'killing' is interchangeable with the term 'causing death'. Killing in actual fighting between combatants (which is not a prisoner of war, wounded or sick) is not covered by the provision. The present provision is more clear than Article 7(1)(a) regarding the mental element by the use of the notion 'wilful'. Thus, the perpetrator must either act intentionally or recklessly.

In *Prosecutor v. Katanga and Ngudjolo*, ICC PT. Ch. I, Decision on the Confirmation of Charges, ICC-01/04-01/07-717, 30 September 2008, para. 294, PTC I stated that "Article 8(2)(a)(i) of the Statute also applies to the wilful killing of the protected persons by an attacking force, when such killings occur after the overall attack has ended, and defeat or full control of the targeted village has been secured".

Cross-references:
Article 7(1)(a) and 8(2)(c)(i).

Doctrine:

1. Michael Bothe, "War Crimes", in Antonio Cassese, Paola Gaeta and John R.W.D. Jones (eds.), *The Rome Statute of the International Criminal Court: A Commentary*, Oxford University Press, Oxford, 2002, p. 392.

2. William J. Fenrick, "Article 8, War Crimes", in Otto Triffterer (ed.), *Commentary on the Rome Statute of the International Criminal Court: Observers' Notes, Article by Article*, 2nd ed., C.H. Beck/Hart/Nomos, Munich/Oxford/Baden-Baden, 2008, pp. 305–6.

3. Gerhard Werle, *Principles of International Criminal Law*, TMC Asser Press, The Hague, 2005, pp. 302–3, MN 875–78.

Author: Mark Klamberg.

[67] Torture is the infliction of severe physical or mental pain or suffering upon one or more persons. The standard for torture is set in the Torture Convention. In contrast to the aforementioned convention, it is not necessary that perpetrator acted in an official capacity. The Elements of Crimes provides a non-exclusive listing of which purposes the torture serve, which distinguishes it from torture as a crime against humanity which does not require a purpose.

Cross-references:

Articles 7(1)(f) and 8(2)(c)(i).

Doctrine:

1. Michael Bothe, "War Crimes", in Antonio Cassese, Paola Gaeta and John R.W.D. Jones (eds.), *The Rome Statute of the International Criminal Court: A Commentary*, Oxford University Press, Oxford, 2002, pp. 392–93.
2. Knut Dörmann, "Article 8, War Crimes", in Triffterer (ed.), *Commentary on the Rome Statute of the International Criminal Court: Observers' Notes, Article by Article*, 2nd ed., C.H. Beck/Hart/Nomos, Munich/Oxford/Baden-Baden, 2008, pp. 306–8.
3. Gerhard Werle, *Principles of International Criminal Law*, TMC Asser Press, The Hague, 2005, pp. 305–6, MN 887–90.

Author: Mark Klamberg.

[68] Inhuman treatment means the infliction of severe physical or mental pain or suffering upon one or more persons. The protected interest is the human dignity. For the mental element Article 30 applies.

In *Prosecutor v. Katanga and Chui*, ICC-01/04-01/07-717, Decision on the Confirmation of Charges, 30 September 2008, para. 364, PTC I was of the "that there is sufficient evidence to establish substantial grounds to believe that the war crime of inhuman treatment, as defined in Article 8(2)(a)(ii) of the Statute".

Cross-references:

Article 8(2)(c)(i).

Doctrine:

1. Michael Bothe, "War Crimes", in Antonio Cassese, Paola Gaeta and John R.W.D. Jones (eds.), *The Rome Statute of the International Criminal Court: A Commentary*, Oxford University Press, Oxford, 2002, pp. 392–93.
2. Knut Dörmann, "Article 8, War Crimes", in Otto Triffterer (ed.), *Commentary on the Rome Statute of the International Criminal Court: Observers' Notes, Article by Article*, 2nd ed., C.H. Beck/Hart/Nomos, Munich/Oxford/Baden-Baden, 2008, pp. 308–9.
3. Gerhard Werle, *Principles of International Criminal Law*, TMC Asser Press, The Hague, 2005, pp. 310–11, MN 903–9.

Author: Mark Klamberg.

[69] The prohibition of biological experiments covers the use of therapeutic methods which are not justified on medical grounds and not carried out in the interest of the affected person. The consent of the victim is not relevant.

Cross-references:

Article 8(2)(b)(x) and 8(2)(e)(xi).

Doctrine:

1. Michael Bothe, "War Crimes", in Antonio Cassese, Paola Gaeta and John R.W.D. Jones (eds.), *The Rome Statute of the International Criminal Court: A Commentary*, Oxford University Press, Oxford, 2002, p. 393.

(iii) Wilfully causing great suffering, or serious injury to body or health;[70]

(iv) Extensive destruction and appropriation of property, not justified by military necessity and carried out unlawfully and wantonly;[71]

(v) Compelling a prisoner of war or other protected person to serve in the forces of a hostile Power;[72]

---

2. Knut Dörmann, "Article 8, War Crimes", in Otto Triffterer (ed.), *Commentary on the Rome Statute of the International Criminal Court: Observers' Notes, Article by Article*, 2nd ed., C.H. Beck/Hart/Nomos, Munich/Oxford/Baden-Baden, 2008, pp. 309–10.

3. Gerhard Werle, *Principles of International Criminal Law*, TMC Asser Press, The Hague, 2005, pp. 308–9, MN 898–901.

Author: Mark Klamberg.

[70] This provision covers acts such as rape, mutilation of the wounded or their exposure to useless and unnecessary suffering. It differs from the war crime of torture mainly in that the act does not need to serve a specific purpose. The mental element requires at least recklessness.

Cross-references:

Article 8(2)(c)(i).

Starvation in Articles 6(c), 7(1)(b), (j) and (k), 7(2)(b); 8(2)(b)(ii), (v), (xiii) and (xxv), and 8(2)(c)(i).

Doctrine:

1. Michael Bothe, "War Crimes", in Antonio Cassese, Paola Gaeta and John R.W.D. Jones (eds.), *The Rome Statute of the International Criminal Court: A Commentary*, Oxford University Press, Oxford, 2002, p. 393.

2. Knut Dörmann, "Article 8, War Crimes", in Otto Triffterer (ed.), *Commentary on the Rome Statute of the International Criminal Court: Observers' Notes, Article by Article*, 2nd ed., C.H. Beck/Hart/Nomos, Munich/Oxford/Baden-Baden, 2008, pp. 310–11.

3. Gerhard Werle, *Principles of International Criminal Law*, TMC Asser Press, The Hague, 2005, pp. 306–7, MN 891–94.

Author: Mark Klamberg.

[71] The destruction of property is also criminalised through offences that cover methods of warfare. The term appropriation is interchangeable with confiscation. The seizure of property in armed conflict is not prohibited under all circumstances. Nevertheless, pillaging is expressly forbidden and cannot be justified on the basis of military necessity, see Articles 8(2)(b)(xvi) and 8(2)(e)(v). The mental element requires at least recklessness.

Cross-references:

Articles 8(2)(b)(xiii), 8(2)(b)(xvi), 8(2)(e)(v) and 8(2)(e)(xii).

Doctrine:

1. Michael Bothe, "War Crimes", in Antonio Cassese, Paola Gaeta and John R.W.D. Jones (eds.), *The Rome Statute of the International Criminal Court: A Commentary*, Oxford University Press, Oxford, 2002, p. 394.

2. Knut Dörmann, "Article 8, War Crimes", in Otto Triffterer (ed.), *Commentary on the Rome Statute of the International Criminal Court: Observers' Notes, Article by Article*, 2nd ed., C.H. Beck/Hart/Nomos, Munich/Oxford/Baden-Baden, 2008, pp. 311–13.

3. Gerhard Werle, *Principles of International Criminal Law*, TMC Asser Press, The Hague, 2005, pp. 334–40, MN 987–1004.

Author: Mark Klamberg.

(vi) Wilfully depriving a prisoner of war or other protected person of the rights of fair and regular trial;[73]

---

[72] The expression "forces" should be given a broad interpretation.

Cross-references:

Article 8(2)(b)(xv).

Doctrine:

1. Michael Bothe, "War Crimes", in Antonio Cassese, Paola Gaeta and John R.W.D. Jones (eds.), *The Rome Statute of the International Criminal Court: A Commentary*, Oxford University Press, Oxford, 2002, p. 394.
2. Knut Dörmann, "Article 8, War Crimes", in Otto Triffterer (ed.), *Commentary on the Rome Statute of the International Criminal Court: Observers' Notes, Article by Article*, 2nd ed., C.H. Beck/Hart/Nomos, Munich/Oxford/Baden-Baden, 2008, pp. 313–14.
3. Gerhard Werle, *Principles of International Criminal Law*, TMC Asser Press, The Hague, 2005 pp. 316–17, MN 924–28.

Author: Mark Klamberg.

[73] The Elements of Crime refers to the guarantees laid down in Geneva Conventions III (GC III) and IV (GC IV), stating that the right to fair trial include: the right to an independent and impartial court (Article 84(2) of GC III), the right to timely notification by the detaining power about any planned trial of a prisoner of war (Article 104 of GC III), the right to immediate information on the charges (Article 104 of GC III and Article 71(2) of GC IV), the prohibition of collective punishment (Article 87(3) of GC III and Article 33 of GC IV), the principle of legality (Article 99(1) of GC III and Article 67 of GC IV), the ne bis in idem principle (Article 86 of GC III and Article 117(3) of GC IV), the right to appeal or petition and information on the possibility thereof (Article 106 of GC III and Article 73 of GC IV), the possibility of presenting a defence and having assistance of qualified counsel (Article 99(3) of GC III), the right to receive the charges and other trial documents in good time an din understandable language (Article 105(4) of GC III), the right of an accused prisoner of war to assistance by one of his prisoner comrades (Article 105(1) of GC III), the defendant's right to representation by an advocate of his own choice (Article 105(1) of GC III and Article 72(1) of GC IV), the right of the defendant to present necessary evidence and especially to call and question witnesses (Article 105(1) of GC III and Article 72(1) of GC IV), and the right to the services of an interpreter (Article 105(1) of GC III and Article 72(3) of GC IV). The death penalty may only be imposed under specific circumstances (Article 100 of GC III and Article 68 of GC IV), and prisoners of war must be tried in the same courts and according to the same procedure as members of the armed forces of the detaining power (Article 102 of GC III). These rules should be supplemented by the rules on a fair trial contained in Article 75(3) and (4) of Additional Protocol I. The mental element requires at least recklessness.

Cross-references:

Articles 8(2)(b)(xiv) and 8(2)(c)(iv).

Doctrine:

1. Michael Bothe, "War Crimes", in Antonio Cassese, Paola Gaeta and John R.W.D. Jones (eds.), *The Rome Statute of the International Criminal Court: A Commentary*, Oxford University Press, Oxford, 2002, pp. 394–95.
2. Knut Dörmann, "Article 8, War Crimes", in Otto Triffterer (ed.), *Commentary on the Rome Statute of the International Criminal Court: Observers' Notes, Article by Article*, 2nd ed., C.H. Beck/Hart/Nomos, Munich/Oxford/Baden-Baden, 2008, pp. 314–16.

(vii) Unlawful deportation or transfer[74] or unlawful confinement;[75]

(viii) Taking of hostages.[76]

---

3. Gerhard Werle, *Principles of International Criminal Law*, TMC Asser Press, The Hague, 2005 pp. 320–22, MN 938–43.

Author: Mark Klamberg.

[74] The material element requires the transfer of persons from one territory to another. The difference between deportation and forcible transfer lies only in whether a border is crossed. Deportation requires that a border is crossed, while as forcible transfer means the transfer of one or more persons within the same state's territory. For the mental element Article 30 applies.

Cross-references:
Articles 7(1)(d), 8(2)(b)(viii) and 8(2)(e)(viii).

Doctrine:

1. Michael Bothe, "War Crimes", in Antonio Cassese, Paola Gaeta and John R.W.D. Jones (eds.), *The Rome Statute of the International Criminal Court: A Commentary*, Oxford University Press, Oxford, 2002, p. 395.

2. Knut Dörmann, "Article 8, War Crimes", in Otto Triffterer (ed.), *Commentary on the Rome Statute of the International Criminal Court: Observers' Notes, Article by Article*, 2nd ed., C.H. Beck/Hart/Nomos, Munich/Oxford/Baden-Baden, 2008, pp. 316–18.

3. Gerhard Werle, *Principles of International Criminal Law*, TMC Asser Press, The Hague, 2005 pp. 327–28, MN 963–67.

Author: Mark Klamberg.

[75] In certain circumstances confinement of protected persons may be legitimate, for example, if a civilian threatens one of the parties in a conflict.

Cross-references:
Article 7(1)(e).

Doctrine:

1. Michael Bothe, "War Crimes", in Antonio Cassese, Paola Gaeta and John R.W.D. Jones (eds.), *The Rome Statute of the International Criminal Court: A Commentary*, Oxford University Press, Oxford, 2002, p. 395.

2. Knut Dörmann, "Article 8, War Crimes", in Otto Triffterer (ed.), *Commentary on the Rome Statute of the International Criminal Court: Observers' Notes, Article by Article*, 2nd ed., C.H. Beck/Hart/Nomos, Munich/Oxford/Baden-Baden, 2008, pp. 318–21.

3. Gerhard Werle, *Principles of International Criminal Law*, TMC Asser Press, The Hague, 2005, pp. 323–25, MN 950–54.

Author: Mark Klamberg.

[76] Hostage taking involves the seizure and detainment of one or more protected persons and a threat to kill, injure or continue to detain such person or persons. In addition to the general mental requirement in Article 30 the purpose of the hostage taking is to compel a State, an international organisation, a natural or legal person or a group of persons to act or refrain from acting as an explicit or implicit condition for the safety or the release of such person or persons.

Cross-references:
Article 8(2)(c)(iii).

Doctrine:

1. Michael Bothe, "War Crimes", in Antonio Cassese, Paola Gaeta and John R.W.D. Jones (eds.), *The Rome Statute of the International Criminal Court: A Commentary*, Oxford University Press, Oxford, 2002, p. 395.

(b) Other serious violations of the laws and customs applicable in international armed conflict, within the established framework of international law, namely, any of the following acts:[77]

---

2. Knut Dörmann, "Article 8, War Crimes", in Otto Triffterer (ed.), *Commentary on the Rome Statute of the International Criminal Court: Observers' Notes, Article by Article*, 2nd ed., C.H. Beck/Hart/Nomos, Munich/Oxford/Baden-Baden, 2008, pp. 321–22.

3. Gerhard Werle, *Principles of International Criminal Law*, TMC Asser Press, The Hague, 2005, pp. 325–27, MN 958–62.

Author: Mark Klamberg.

[77] *General remarks*:

Along with Article 8(2)(a), Article 8(2)(b) lists war crimes that take place in the context of an international armed conflict.

Analysis:

Article 8(2)(b) reads: "Other serious violations of the laws and customs applicable in international armed conflict, within the established framework of international law, namely, any of the following acts".

i) Scope of Application

The scope of sub-paragraph (b) is the same as sub-paragraph (a): it is applicable in times of an international armed conflict. This is supported by the Elements of Crimes that repeat that "[t]he conduct took place in the context of and was associated with an international armed conflict" (Article 8(2)(b)) and by the case law (*Prosecutor v. Katanga and Chui*, ICC PT. Ch. I, Decision on the Confirmation of Charges, ICC-01/04-01/07-717, 30 September 2008, para. 244). In fact, in *Katanga and Chui* the ICC, after stating that the conflict was international, proceeds to examine offences charged under Article 8(2)(a) and (b) (*Katanga and Chui*, ICC PT. Ch. I, Decision on the Confirmation of Charges, ICC-01/04-01/07-717, 30 September 2008, para. 243).

ii) Acts Prohibited

The use of the word 'other' indicates that this list of prohibited acts is additional to the grave breaches (which are also "serious violations of the laws and customs applicable in international armed conflict") list included in sub-paragraph (a). Yet, while some of the grave breaches of the Protocol Additional to the Geneva Conventions of 12 August 1949, and relating to the Protection of Victims of International Armed Conflicts (AP I) are referred to in Article 8(2)(b) (for example, Article 85(3)(b) AP I "launching an indiscriminate attack affecting the civilian population or civilian objects in the knowledge that such attack will cause excessive loss of life, injury to civilians, or damage to civilian objects, as defined in Article 57 paragraph 2(a)(iii)" is reflected in Article 8(2)(b)(iv)) others are not (for example, Article 85(4)(b) AP I "unjustifiable delay in the repatriation of prisoners of war or civilians"). This lack of full incorporation in the ICC Statute of the grave breaches mentioned in AP I may be due to the fact that AP I enjoys far less unanimity with States than the Geneva Conventions do.

In fact, the acts enumerated under Article 8(2) (b) are a patchwork of 26 serious violations of international law. Such acts are prohibited by either or both treaty and customary international law. For example, some sub-provisions expressly mention the Geneva Conventions (for example, Articles (2)(b)(xxii) and (xxv)); others are drawn from AP I. For example, Article 8(2)(b)(xxvi) that refers to the crime of recruiting and using children under the age of 15 years is based on Article 77(2) AP I (*Prosecutor v. Lubanga*, ICC T. Ch. I, Judgment, ICC-01/04-01/06, 14 March 2012, para. 542). Most of the sub-provisions relate to means and methods of warfare and are drawn from the Convention Relating to the Laws and Customs of War on Land (Hague IV). Yet there are also a number of new crimes under Article 8(2)(b) such as the prohibition of

(i) Intentionally directing attacks against the civilian population as such or against individual civilians not taking direct part in hostilities;[78]

---

attacks against humanitarian or peacekeeping missions (Article 8(2)(b)(iii)) and against the environment (Article 8(2)(b)(iv)).

Unlike for Article 8(2)(a) there is no requirement for the victims or objects to have protected status.

iii) Awareness

Similar to Article 8(2)(a) the Elements of Crime only require the perpetrator to have been "aware of factual circumstances that established the existence of an armed conflict". The ICC specifically explains that this element of the crime is "common to all war crimes provided for in Article 8(2)(a) and (b) of the Elements of Crimes" (*Katanga and Chui*, ICC PT. Ch. I, Decision on the Confirmation of Charges, ICC-01/04-01/07-717, 30 September 2008, para. 244).

Doctrine:

1. Dapo Akande, "Classification of Armed Conflicts: Relevant Legal Concepts", in Elizabeth Wilmhurst (ed.), *International Law and the Classification of Conflicts,* Oxford University Press, Oxford, 2012, pp. 32–79.

2. Michael Bothe, "War Crimes", in Antonio Cassese, Paola Gaeta and John R.W.D. Jones (eds.), *The Rome Statute of the International Criminal Court: A Commentary*, Oxford University Press, Oxford, 2002, pp. 395–97.

3. Antonio Cassese, Paola Gaeta and John R.W.D. Jones (eds.), *International Criminal Law*, Oxford University Press, Oxford, 2013, pp. 62–83.

4. Robert Cryer, Håkan Friman, Daryll Robinson and Elizabeth Wilmshurst, *An Introduction to International Criminal Law and Procedure*, 3rd ed., Cambridge University Press, Cambridge, 2014, pp. 264–84.

5. Anthony Cullen, "War Crimes", in William A. Schabas and Nadia Bernaz (eds.), *Routledge Handbook of International Criminal Law*, Routledge, London, 2011, pp. 139–54,

6. Knut Dörmann, *Elements of War Crimes under the Rome Statute of the International Criminal Court*, Cambridge University Press, Cambridge, 2002, pp. 17–37.

7. Knut Dörmann, "Article 8, War Crimes", in Otto Triffterer (ed.), *Commentary on the Rome Statute of the International Criminal Court: Observers' Notes, Article by Article*, 2nd ed., C.H. Beck/Hart/Nomos, Munich/Oxford/Baden-Baden, 2008, p. 323.

8. Leena Grover, *Interpreting Crimes in the Rome Statute of the International Criminal Court*, Cambridge University Press, Cambridge, 2014, pp. 279–85.

9. William A. Schabas, *An Introduction to the International Criminal Court*, Cambridge University Press, Cambridge, 2011, pp. 133–42.

10. William A. Schabas, *The International Criminal Court: A Commentary on the Rome Statute*, Oxford University Press, Oxford, 2010, pp. 188–257.

Author: Noëlle Quénivet.

[78] *General remarks*:

The war crime of attacking the civilian population and civilians not taking direct part in hostilities "is the first in the series of war crimes for which one essential element is that the crime must be committed during the conduct of hostilities (commonly known as 'conduct of hostilities crimes')" (*Prosecutor v. Katanga and Chui*, ICC PT. Ch. I, Decision on the Confirmation of Charges, ICC-01/04-01/07-717, 30 September 2008, para. 267). Under international humanitarian law the act of "making the civilian population or individual civilians the object of attack" "when committed wilfully [...] and causing death or serious injury to body or health" is a grave

---

breach (Article 85(3)(a) of Protocol Additional to the Geneva Conventions of 12 August 1949, and relating to the Protection of Victims of International Armed Conflicts (AP I)).

Article 8(2)(b)(i) is a reflection of the principle of distinction in attack in an international armed conflict. While the principle is enshrined in Articles 48 and 51 AP I it is also of customary nature (Rule 1 of the ICRC Study on Customary International Humanitarian Law; *Prosecutor v. Galić* (Case No. IT-98-29-A), ICTY A. Ch., Judgment, 30 November 2006, para. 87). The International Court of Justice has stressed that deliberate attacks on civilians are absolutely prohibited by international humanitarian law (*Legality of the Threat or Use of Nuclear Weapons*, ICJ Advisory Opinion, 8 July 1996, (1996) ICJ Rep. 226, at 257 (para. 78)). Further, as the ICTY highlighted "the principles underlying the prohibition of attacks on civilians, namely the principles of distinction and protection ... incontrovertibly form the basic foundation of international humanitarian law and constitute 'intransgressible principles of international customary'" (*Galić*, ICTY A. Ch., Judgment, 30 November 2006, para. 87).

Analysis:

Article 8(2)(b)(i) states that the ICC has jurisdiction overs acts of "[i]ntentionally directing attacks against the civilian population as such or against individual civilians not taking direct part in hostilities".

i) Material Elements

a. Definition of an Attack

The first element of the Elements of Crimes requires that "the perpetrator directed an attack" (Elements of Crimes, p. 18). Yet, neither the Statute nor the Elements of Crimes define the term "attack". The Court has used Article 49(1) AP I to define an attack as "acts of violence against the adversary, whether in offence or in defence" (*Katanga and Chui*, ICC PT. Ch. I, Decision on the Confirmation of Charges, ICC-01/04-01/07-717, 30 September 2008, para. 266).

As the ICC Statute does not provide for a specific offence of acts whose primary purpose is to spread terror among the civilian population, it is likely that such acts fall within the broad scope of Article 8(2)(b)(i). As Article 8(2)(b)(i) is a reflection of the principle of distinction enshrined in Articles 48 and 51 AP I and Article 8(2)(b) must be read "within the established framework of international law" it is likely that it will also cover the second sentence of the Article 51(2) AP I: "Acts or threats of violence the primary purpose of which is to spread terror among the civilian population are prohibited". This approach was espoused by the ICTY inasmuch as it explained that the prohibition of terror amounts to "a specific prohibition within the general (customary) prohibition of attack on civilians" (*Prosecutor v. Galić* (Case No. IT-98-29-T), ICTY T. Ch. I, Judgment and Opinion, 5 December 2003, para. 98, upheld in *Galić*, ICTY A. Ch., Judgment, 30 November 2006, para. 87).

To establish the link between the attack and the conduct of the hostilities, the Court has stipulated that these civilians must be those "who [have] not fallen yet into the hands of the adverse or hostile party to the conflict to which the perpetrator belongs" (*Katanga and Chui*, ICC PT. Ch. I, Decision on the Confirmation of Charges, ICC-01/04-01/07-717, 30 September 2008, para. 267). Following the ICTY case law, the Court has stated that the litmus test is whether the individual is under the control of the members of the hostile party to the conflict (*Katanga and Chui*, ICC PT. Ch. I, Decision on the Confirmation of Charges, ICC-01/04-01/07-717, 30 September 2008, para. 268). Acts committed against civilians who have fallen into the hands of the enemy cannot be classified as attacks as they are not methods of warfare. They can however be prosecuted under other appropriate legal provisions (*Katanga and Chui*, ICC PT. Ch. I, Decision on the Confirmation of Charges, ICC-01/04-01/07-717, 30 September 2008, para. 269).

There must be a causal link between the perpetrator's conduct and the consequence of the attack (by analogy in relation to Article 8(2)(e)(i), *Prosecutor v. Abu Garda*, ICC PT. Ch. I, Public Redacted Version, Decision on the Confirmation of Charges, ICC-02/05-02/09-243-Red,

8 February 2010, para. 66). That being said, the attack does not need to lead to civilian casualties; it is sufficient to prove that the author launched the attack towards the civilian population or individual civilians. As the Court explained "it does not require any material result or a 'harmful' impact on the civilian population or on the individual civilians targeted by the attack [...]"' (*Katanga and Chui*, ICC PT. Ch. I, Decision on the Confirmation of Charges, ICC-01/04-01/07-717, 30 September 2008, para. 270). It is the intention that counts as the third element of the Elements of Crimes requires that "the perpetrator intended the civilian population as such or individual civilians not taking direct part in hostilities to be the object of the attack". As noted by the Court in *Katanga and Chui* (*Katanga and Chui*, ICC PT. Ch. I, Decision on the Confirmation of Charges, ICC-01/04-01/07-717, 30 September 2008, para. 270) this stands in contrast to Article 85(3) AP I that requires "death or serious injury to body or health" and the jurisprudence of the ICTY (for example, *Prosecutor v. Kordić and Čerkez* (Case IT-95-14/2-T), ICTY T. Ch., Judgment, 26 February 2001, para. 328 as reiterated in *Prosecutor v. Kordić and Čerkez* (Case IT-95-14/2-A), ICTY A. Ch., Judgment, 17 December 2004, para. 40).

b. Object of the Attack is a Civilian Population and Civilians Not Taking Direct Part in the Hostilities

The second element of the Elements of Crimes specifies that "the object of the attack was a civilian population as such or individual civilians not taking direct part in hostilities" (Elements of Crimes, p. 18). This is an absolute prohibition that cannot be counterbalanced by military necessity (*Prosecutor v. Katanga*, ICC Tr. Ch. II, Judgment pursuant to Article 74 of the Statute, ICC-01/04-01/07-3436-T, 7 March 2014, para. 800). This position is reinforced by the fact that in the context of a non-international armed conflict (and thus likely to apply in an international armed conflict too) the ICC has indicated that reprisals are prohibited in all circumstances (*Prosecutor v. Mbarushimana*, ICC PT. Ch. I, Decision on the Confirmation of Charges, ICC-01/04-01/10-465-Red, 16 December 2011, para. 143).

Civilians are defined by reference to Article 50(1) AP I and the civilian population by reference to Articles 50(2) and (3) AP I (*Katanga and Chui*, Decision on the Confirmation of Charges, ICC PT. Ch. I, ICC-01/04-01/07-717, 30 September 2008, fn. 366 and 368 respectively; *Mbarushimana*, ICC PT. Ch. I, Decision on the Confirmation of Charges, ICC-01/04-01/10-465-Red, 16 December 2011, para. 148 in relation to the civilian population). In case of doubt an individual must be considered a civilian (*Katanga and Chui*, ICC PT. Ch. I, Decision on the Confirmation of Charges, ICC-01/04-01/07-717, 30 September 2008, fn. 366 and 375; *Mbarushimana*, ICC PT. Ch. I, ICC-01/04-01/10-465-Red, 16 December 2011, para. 148). The presence among the civilian population of individuals who do not fit within the definition of a civilian, however, does not deprive the entire population of its civilian character (*Katanga and Chui*, ICC PT. Ch. I, Decision on the Confirmation of Charges, ICC-01/04-01/07-717, 30 September 2008, fn. 375; *Mbarushimana*, ICC PT. Ch. I, Decision on the Confirmation of Charges, ICC-01/04-01/10-465-Red, 16 December 2011, para. 148).

Article 8(2)(b)(i) refers to "individual civilians not taking direct part in direct hostilities", thereby introducing the concept of direct participation in hostilities in the context of an international armed conflict. Although the adjective "active", rather than "direct", appears in international humanitarian law in relation to participation in hostilities the Court treats them as synonyms (*Katanga and Chui*, ICC PT. Ch. I, Decision on the Confirmation of Charges, ICC-01/04-01/07-717, 30 September 2008, fn. 367). The Court explains that such participation leads to a temporary loss of protection of civilian status "for such time [such individuals] take direct part in the hostilities" (*Katanga and Chui*, ICC PT. Ch. I, Decision on the Confirmation of Charges, ICC-01/04-01/07-717, 30 September 2008, fn. 375; *Mbarushimana*, ICC PT. Ch. I, Decision on the Confirmation of Charges, ICC-01/04-01/10-465-Red, 16 December 2011, para. 148). Examples of such acts are when a "civilian uses weapons or other means to commit violence against human or material enemy forces" but not when the civilians are supplying food and shelter or sympathising with a belligerent party (*Mbarushimana*, ICC PT. Ch. I, Decision on the Confirmation of Charges, ICC-01/04-01/10-465-Red, 16 December 2011, para. 148). Moreover, the status is not lost when a civilian is defending him/herself.

The ICC has explained that in cases where the attack is directed towards a legitimate military objective within the meaning of Articles 51-52 AP I and simultaneously the civilian population or civilians not taking direct part in the hostilities, the perpetrator can still be prosecuted under Article 8(2)(b)(i) (*Katanga and Chui*, Decision on the Confirmation of Charges, ICC PT. Ch. I, ICC-01/04-01/07-717, 30 September 2008, para. 273). This situation must nonetheless be distinguished from attacks against military objectives with the awareness that they will or may result in the incidental loss of life or injury to civilians (*Katanga and Chui*, ICC PT. Ch. I, Decision on the Confirmation of Charges, ICC-01/04-01/07-717, 30 September 2008, para. 274). The Court has thus distinguished between a violation of the principle of discrimination and a violation of the principle of proportionality, the latter being prosecuted under Article 8(2)(b)(iv) of the Statute.

ii) Subjective Elements

a. "[I]ntentionally" Directing an Attack

The crime must be committed with intention and knowledge, as indicated in Article 30 ICC Statute. Additionally, the third element of the Elements of Crimes (Elements of Crimes, p. 18) requires the perpetrator to have "intended" the attack. The Court has specified that this intention to attack the civilian population is in addition to the standard *mens rea* requirement provided in Article 30 ICC Statute, that is, there must be a *dolus directus* of first degree, that is, a concrete intent (*Abu Garda*, ICC PT. Ch. I, Redacted Version, Decision on the Confirmation of Charges, ICC-02/05-02/09-243-Red, 8 February 2010, para. 93; *Katanga and Chui*, ICC PT. Ch. I, Decision on the Confirmation of Charges, ICC-01/04-01/07-717, 30 September 2008, para. 271). In more recent case law, albeit relating to non-international armed conflict, the Court has argued that the third element in the Elements of Crimes (Elements of Crimes, p. 34) does not constitute a specific *dolus* (*Katanga*, ICC Tr. Ch. II, Judgment pursuant to Article 74 of the Statute, ICC-01/04-01/07-3436-T, 7 March 2014, para. 806; see Commentary to Article 8(2)(e)(i)). According to the Elements of Crimes and the case law so far recklessness does not appear to suffice to fulfil the test. That being said, the Office of the Prosecutor has indicated that "[a]n argument could be made that a pattern of indifference and recklessness with respect to civilian life and property should eventually satisfy the intent requirements of Articles 30 and 8(2)(b)(i) and (ii)" (Office of the Prosecutor, *Situation in the Republic of Korea*. Article 5 Report, June 2014, para. 65).

The Court nonetheless distinguishes two situations. The first is when the civilian population is the sole target of the attack. In this case the moment the attack is launched the crime is committed (*Katanga and Chui*, Decision on the Confirmation of Charges, ICC PT. Ch. I, ICC-01/04-01/07-717, 30 September 2008, para. 272); the second is when the attack is launched simultaneously against two distinct aims: a military objective (according to Articles 51-52 AP I) and a civilian population. In this case a number of requirements must be fulfilled for the crime to be committed. First, the village must have a significant military value; and second, it must contain two distinct targets: the defending forces of the adverse or hostile party in control of the village and the civilian population of the village which shows allegiance to the adverse or hostile party (*Katanga and Chui*, ICC PT. Ch. I, Decision on the Confirmation of Charges, ICC-01/04-01/07-717, 30 September 2008, para. 273).

b. Intention that the Object of the Attack Is the Civilian Population or Civilians

This requirement, which is the second element in the Elements of Crimes (Elements of Crimes, p. 18), must be analysed as a behaviour (*Prosecutor v. Chui*, ICC PT. Ch. I, Sous scellés Décision concernant les éléments de preuve et les renseignements fournis par l'Accusation aux fins de délivrance d'un mandat d'arrêt à l'encontre de Germain Katanga, ICC-01/04-01/07-4-tFRA, 6 July 2007, para. 41). "[T]he crime described in Article 8(2)(c)(i) of the Statute [...] is a crime of mere action" (*Katanga and Chui*, ICC PT. Ch. I, Decision on the Confirmation of Charges, ICC-01/04-01/07-717, 30 September 2008, fn. 374).

Elements assisting in ascertaining the intention of attacking the civilian population or civilians are the means and methods used during the attack (for example, blocking roads to and from the village and order to kill civilians attempting to flee (*Katanga and Chui*, ICC PT. Ch. I, Decision on the Confirmation of Charges, ICC-01/04-01/07-717, 30 September 2008, para. 281)), the number and status of victims (killing of women and children (*Katanga and Chui*, ICC PT. Ch. I, Decision on the Confirmation of Charges, ICC-01/04-01/07-717, 30 September 2008, para. 282)), the discriminatory character of the attack (for example, chanting songs with lyrics indicating that specific groups should be killed while others shown mercy (*Katanga and Chui*, ICC PT. Ch. I, Decision on the Confirmation of Charges, ICC-01/04-01/07-717, 30 September 2008, para. 280) and the nature of the act (for example, killing civilians and destroying their property (*Katanga and Chui*, ICC PT. Ch. I, Decision on the Confirmation of Charges, ICC-01/04-01/07-717, 30 September 2008, paras. 277 and 282).

c. Awareness of the Civilian Status of the Population or Individuals

By analogy with the requirements for the crime of attacking the civilian population or individual civilians not taking direct part in the hostilities in a non-international armed conflict under Article 8(2)(e)(i) it can be argued that the Court further requires that the perpetrator must be aware of the civilian status of the victims (*Mbarushimana*, ICC PT. Ch. I, Decision on the Confirmation of Charges, ICC-01/04-01/10-465-Red, 16 December 2011, paras. 151 and 219; *Katanga*, ICC Tr. Ch. II, Judgment pursuant to Article 74 of the Statute, ICC-01/04-01/07-3436-tENG, 7 March 2014, para. 808). In the report of the Office of the Prosecutor (OTP) on the *Situation in the Republic of Korea*, the OTP noted that the ICTY had explained that "[The] attack must have been conducted intentionally in the knowledge, or when it was impossible not to know, that civilians or civilian property were being targeted not through military necessity" (Office of the Prosecutor, *Situation in the Republic of Korea*, Article 5 Report, June 2014, para. 62).

d. Awareness of the Circumstances that Established the Existence of the Armed Conflict

According to element 5 of the Elements of Crimes for the war crime of attacking civilians, the perpetrator must be aware of factual circumstances that established the existence of an armed conflict (Elements of Crimes, p. 18). This has been reiterated by the Court (*Katanga and Chui*, ICC PT. Ch. I, Decision on the Confirmation of Charges, ICC-01/04-01/07-717, 30 September 2008, para. 265).

Cross-references:

Article 8(2)(b)(ii), 8(2)(b)(ix) and 8(2)(e)(i).

Doctrine:

1. Michael Bothe, "War Crimes", in Antonio Cassese, Paola Gaeta and John R.W.D. Jones (eds.), *The Rome Statute of the International Criminal Court: A Commentary*, Oxford University Press, Oxford, 2002, p. 397.

2. Knut Dörmann, "Article 8, War Crimes", in Otto Triffterer (ed.), *Commentary on the Rome Statute of the International Criminal Court: Observers' Notes, Article by Article*, 2nd ed., C.H. Beck/Hart/Nomos, Munich/Oxford/Baden-Baden, 2008, pp. 323–327.

3. Gerhard Werle and Florian Jessberger, *Principles of International Criminal Law*, Oxford University Press, Oxford, 2014, pp. 475–85 MN 1278–1304.

4. William A. Schabas, *The International Criminal Court: A Commentary on the Rome Statute*, Oxford University Press, Oxford, 2010, pp. 188–257.

(ii)   Intentionally directing attacks against civilian objects, that is, objects which are not military objectives;[79]

---

5.   Daniel Frank, "The Elements of War Crimes – Article 8(2)(b)(i)", in Roy S. Lee (ed.), *The International Criminal Court, Elements of Crimes and Rules of Procedure and Evidence*, Transnational Publishers, Ardsley, NY, 2001, p. 140.

Author: Noëlle Quénivet.

[79]   *General remarks:*

The war crime of attacking civilian objects is a crime committed during the conduct of hostilities. Unlike attacks on the civilian population and individual civilians taking a direct part in the hostilities (see Article 8(2)(b)(i)) the crime of attacking civilian objects is not a grave breach of the Protocol Additional to the Geneva Conventions of 12 August 1949, and relating to the Protection of Victims of International Armed Conflicts (AP I). Further there is no equivalent provision in the Statute that deals with non-international armed conflict (*Prosecutor v. Abu Garda*, ICC PT. Ch. I, Public Redacted Version, Decision on the Confirmation of Charges, ICC-02/05-02/09-243-red, 8 February 2010, para. 85).

Article 8(2)(b)(ii) is a reflection of the principle of distinction in attack in an international armed conflict. While the principle is enshrined in Articles 48 and 52 AP I it is also of customary nature (Rule 7 of the ICRC Study on Customary International Humanitarian Law). The International Court of Justice has stressed that deliberate attacks on civilian objects are absolutely prohibited by international humanitarian law (*Legality of the Threat or Use of Nuclear Weapons* ICJ Advisory Opinion, 8 July 1996, (1996) ICJ Rep. 226, p. 257, para. 78.

Analysis:

Article 8(2)(b)(ii) states that the ICC has jurisdiction overs acts of "[i]ntentionally directing attacks against civilian objects, that is, objects which are not military objectives".

i) Material Elements

a. Definition of an Attack

The first element of the Elements of Crimes requires that "the perpetrator directed an attack" (Elements of Crimes, p. 18). Yet, neither the Statute nor the Elements of Crimes define the term "attack". Although the Court has not defined the concept of "attack" in the context of Article 8(2)(b)(ii) it is likely that, alike for Article 8(2)(b)(i), it will refer to Article 49(1) AP I which asserts that an attack are "acts of violence against the adversary, whether in offence or in defence" (*Prosecutor v. Katanga and Chui*, ICC PT. Ch. I, Decision on the Confirmation of Charges, ICC-01/04-01/07-717, 30 September 2008, para. 266). In its report on the *Situation on Registered Vessels of Comoros, Greece and Cambodia*, the Office of the Prosecutor found that "an attack includes all acts of violence against an adversary" (Office of the Prosecutor, *Situation on Registered Vessels of Comoros, Greece and Cambodia*. Article 53(1) Report, 6 November 2014, para. 93).

There must be a causal link between the perpetrator's conduct and the consequence of the attack. As in the case with the war crime of attacking the civilian population and civilians taking a direct part in hostilities (see Commentary to Article 8(2)(b)(i)) there does not seem to be a requirement that the attack results in some damage or destruction (see discussion in *Prosecutor v. Kordić and Čerkez* (Case IT-95-14/2-A), ICTY A. Ch., Judgment, 17 December 2004, paras. 59–62). It is the intention that counts as the third element of the Elements of Crimes requires that "the perpetrator intended such civilian objects to be the object of the attack" (Elements of Crimes, p. 18). In contrast Article 8(2)(b)(xiii) which covers both military and civilian objects require the destruction, by action or omission, of the property (*Katanga and Chui*, ICC PT. Ch. I, Decision on the Confirmation of Charges, ICC-01/04-01/07-717, 30 September 2008, para. 310).

b. Object of the Attack is Civilian Objects

The second element of the Elements of Crimes specifies that "the object of the attack was civilian objects, that is, objects which are not military objectives" (Elements of Crimes, p. 18). In *Gotovina* the ICTY had explained that the targeting of civilian objects may never be justified by military necessity (*Prosecutor v. Gotovina, Čermak and Markač* (Case No. IT-06-90-T), ICTY T. Ch., Judgment, 15 April 2011, para. 1766). Given that the ICC has also dismissed the justification of military necessity, though in the context of attacks on civilians, it is likely that it will espouse the same approach with regard to objects and follow the *Gotovina* jurisprudence.

Civilian objects are defined in Article 8(2)(b)(ii) in the negative, as "objects which are not military objectives", thereby espousing the international humanitarian law approach (see Article 52(1) AP I and Rule 8 of the ICRC Study on Customary International Humanitarian Law). Military objectives are thus "limited to those objects which by their nature, location, purpose or use make an effective contribution to military action and whose total or partial destruction, capture or neutralization, in the circumstances ruling at the time, offers a definite military advantage" (Article 52(2) AP I). It must be noted that the Court has found that this definition also applies in the context of a non-international armed conflict in relation to attacks on "installations, material, units or vehicles involved in a peacekeeping mission" (*Abu Garda*, ICC PT. Ch. I, Decision on the Confirmation of Charges, ICC-02/05-02/09-243-red, 8 February 2010, para. 89).

There are three elements in assessing whether an object is a military objective:

- The object's nature, location, purpose or use makes a contribution to military action. Usually weapons, military equipment, military transport, military communication centres and army headquarters fulfil his requirements. Other objects that are often called "dual-use objects" (for example, bridges, airports, power plants, manufacturing plants, and integrated power grids) must be examined on a case-by-case basis. As for objects that normally serve civilian purposes such as schools and hospitals they must also be assessed on a case-by-case basis. That being said, referring to *Galić* (*Prosecutor v. Galić* (Case No. IT-98-29-T), ICTY T. Ch. I, Judgment and Opinion, 5 December 2003, para. 51) the Court has explained that in case of doubt an object that is "normally dedicated to civilian purposes" must be considered civilian (*Abu Garda*, ICC PT. Ch. I, Public Redacted Version, Decision on the Confirmation of Charges, ICC-02/05-02/09-243-red, 8 February 2010, fn. 131). This again reflects the approach taken by international humanitarian law in Article 52(3) AP I.

- The object must make an effective contribution to military action. This means that there must be a proximate nexus between the object and the military action.

- The attack on the military objective must offer a definite military advantage in the sense that it is not potential or indeterminate. It is however unclear whether the definition of military advantage relates to one specific military operation or can be viewed in light of a wider operation or military action more generally. Military advantage usually includes gaining ground or weakening the military forces of the adversary.

Examples of civilian objects falling within the purview of Article 8(2)(b)(ii) are houses and parts thereof, personal items and furniture (see *Situation in the Democratic Republic of Congo*, ICC PT. Ch. I, Public Document, Decision on the Applications for Participation Filed in Connection with the Investigation in the Democratic Republic of Congo by Applicants a/0047/06 to a/0052/06, a/0163/06 to a/0187/06, a/0221/06, a/0225/06, a/0226/06, a/0231/06 to a/0233/06, a/0237/06 to a/0239/06, and a/0241/06 to a/0250/06, ICC-01/04-504, 3 July 2008).

Article 8(2)(b)(ii) must be distinguished from attacks against military objectives with the awareness that they will or may result in the incidental destruction of civilian property as this is covered by Article 8(2)(b)(iv) which reflects the principle of proportionality.

ii) Subjective Elements

a. "[I]ntentionally" Directing an Attack

The crime must be committed with intention and knowledge, as indicated in Article 30 ICC Statute. Additionally, the third element of the Elements of Crimes (Elements of Crimes, p. 18) requires the perpetrator to have "intended" the attack. In relation to Article 8(2)(b)(i) (see Commentary on Article 8(2)(b)(i)) the Court has specified that this intention is in addition to the standard *mens rea* requirement provided in Article 30 ICC Statute, that is, there must be a *dolus directus* of first degree, that is, a concrete intent (*Abu Garda*, ICC PT. Ch. I, Decision on the Confirmation of Charges, ICC-02/05-02/09-243-red, 8 February 2010, para. 93; *Katanga and Chui*, ICC PT. Ch. I, Decision on the Confirmation of Charges, ICC-01/04-01/07-717, 30 September 2008, para. 271). As the same terminology is used and Article 8(2)(b)(ii) also deals with civilian status (of objects rather than persons) it is likely that the Court will adopt the same approach. However, in more recent case law, albeit relating to attack on civilians in the context of a non-international armed conflict, the Court has argued that the third element in the Elements of Crimes (Elements of Crimes, p. 34) does not constitute a specific *dolus* (*Prosecutor v. Katanga*, ICC Tr. Ch. II, Jugment, ICC-01/04-01/07-3436, 7 March 2014, para. 806; see Commentary to Article 8(2)(e)(i)).

According to the Elements of Crimes and the case law so far recklessness does not appear to suffice to fulfil the test. That being said, the Office of the Prosecutor has indicated that "[a]n argument could be made that a pattern of indifference and recklessness with respect to civilian life and property should eventually satisfy the intent requirements of Articles 30 and 8(2)(b)(i) and (ii)" (Office of the Prosecutor, *Situation in the Republic of Korea*, Article 5 Report, June 2014, para. 65).

b. Intention that the Object of the Attack Is Civilian Objects

The second element in the Elements of Crimes (Elements of Crimes, p. 18), that is that the object of the attack was civilian objects, must be analysed as a behaviour (*Prosecutor v. Chui*, ICC PT. Ch. I, Sous scellés Décision concernant les éléments de preuve et les renseignements fournis par l'Accusation aux fins de délivrance d'un mandat d'arrêt à l'encontre de Germain Katanga, ICC-01/04-01/07-4-tFRA, 6 July 2007, para. 41).

c. Awareness of the Civilian Status of the Object

In the report of the Office of the Prosecutor (OTP) on the *Situation in the Republic of Korea*, the OTP noted that the ICTY had explained that "[the] attack must have been conducted intentionally in the knowledge, or when it was impossible not to know, that civilians or civilian property were being targeted not through military necessity" (Office of the Prosecutor, *Situation in the Republic of Korea*, Article 5 Report, June 2014, para. 62).

d. Awareness of the Circumstances that Established the Existence of the Armed Conflict

According to element 5 of the Elements of Crimes for the war crime of attacking civilians, the perpetrator must be aware of factual circumstances that established the existence of an armed conflict (Elements of Crimes, p. 18).

Cross-references:

Article 8(2)(b)(i), 8(2)(b)(ix) and 8(2)(e)(i).

Starvation in Articles 6(c), 7(1)(b), (j) and (k), 7(2)(b), 8(2)(a)(iii), 8(2)(b)(v), (xiii) and (xxv).

Doctrine:

1. Michael Bothe, "War Crimes", in Antonio Cassese, Paola Gaeta and John R.W.D. Jones (eds.), *The Rome Statute of the International Criminal Court: A Commentary*, Oxford University Press, Oxford, 2002, pp. 397–98.

2. Knut Dörmann, "Article 8, War Crimes", in Otto Triffterer (ed.), *Commentary on the Rome Statute of the International Criminal Court: Observers' Notes, Article by Article*, 2nd ed., C.H. Beck/Hart/Nomos, Munich/Oxford/Baden-Baden, 2008, pp. 328–30.

(iii)   Intentionally directing attacks against personnel, installations, material, units or vehicles involved in a humanitarian assistance or peacekeeping mission in accordance with the Charter of the United Nations, as long as they are entitled to the protection given to civilians or civilian objects under the international law of armed conflict;[80]

---

3.   Gerhard Werle/Florian Jessberger, *Principles of International Criminal Law*, Oxford University Press, Oxford, 2014, pp. 486–88, MN 1305–12.

4.   William Schabas, *The International Criminal Court: A Commentary on the Rome Statute*, Oxford University Press, Oxford, 2010, pp. 188–257.

5.   Daniel Frank, "The Elements of War Crimes – Article 8(2)(b)(ii)", in Roy S. Lee (ed.), *The International Criminal Court, Elements of Crimes and Rules of Procedure and Evidence*, Transnational Publishers, Ardsley, NY, 2001, pp. 143–44.

Author: Noëlle Quénivet.

[80]   *General remarks*:

Attacking personnel or objects involved in humanitarian assistance or peacekeeping missions, entitled to the protection of civilians or civilian objects, is not a new crime under international humanitarian law. It is rather evidence of the need to specify a group of civilians that because of its missions deserves a specific protection (Report of the Secretary-General on the establishment of a Special Court for Sierra Leone, UN doc., S/2000/915, 4 October 2000, para. 16). During the negotiations of the ICC Statute, the Convention of the Safety on United Nations and Associated Personnel was included in the Draft Statute as one out of three treaty crimes. When decided that no treaty crime would be included in the Statute the delegations began to concentrate on treating and including attacks against UN personnel as a war crime. The crime of attacking peacekeepers was the only one of the three treaty crimes that "survived" this change, which is evidence of its strong symbolic character. A crime with the same definition as in the ICC Statute was included in the Statute of the Special Court for Sierra Leone ('SCSL').

Analysis:

a) Objective Elements

i. The perpetrator directed an attack

The Elements of Crimes do not include a definition of the term 'attack'. The ICC Pre-Trial Chamber has, by reference *inter alia* to the "applicable treaties and the principles and rules of international law, including the established principles of the international law of armed conflict" in Article 21(1)(b) of the Statute found guidance in Article 49 of AP I, applicable in international armed conflicts (IACs) where the term "attack" is defined as "acts of violence against the adversary, whether in offence or in defence". The term has been given the same definition in Article 13(2) of AP II applicable in non-international armed conflicts ('NIACs'). There is no requirement of any harmful impact on the personnel or material. There is a need to establish a causal link between the conduct of the perpetrator and the consequence "so that the concrete consequence, the attack in this case, can be seen as having been caused by the perpetrator" (*Prosecutor v. Abu Garda*, PT. Ch., Decision on the Confirmation of Charges, Public Redacted Version, doc., ICC-02/05-02/09, 8 February 2010, paras. 64–66).

ii. The object of the attack was personnel, installations, material, units or vehicles involved in a humanitarian assistance or peacekeeping mission in accordance with the Charter of the United Nations

There is no generally accepted definition on the notion 'humanitarian assistance', but it includes measures taken with the purpose of preventing or alleviating human suffering of victims of an armed conflict. In practice the object of attacks has so far been personnel and objects involved in a peacekeeping mission. The term 'peacekeeping' is not mentioned in the UN Charter but has

---

developed in practice. The reference to "in accordance with the Charter of the United Nations" does not mean that the mission needs to be established by the UN but includes also missions established by regional organisations (*Abu Garda*, para. 124). While the term lack a simple definition three basic principles are accepted as constituting a peacekeeping mission; consent of the parties; impartiality; and use of force only in self-defence, (*Abu Garda*, para. 71) although there is now a change in UN doctrine regarding definition of such missions (*Prosecutor v. Sesay, Kallon and Gbao (RUF)*, Case No. SCSL-04-15-T, Judgment, 2 March 2009 (*RUF*, paras. 224–225). Consent of the host state is a legal requirement but in practice the consent of the main parties to the conflict is also sought to ensure the effectiveness of the operation. Regarding impartiality, the Report of the Panel of the United Nations Peace Operations (UN doc., A/55/305-S/2000/809 (Brahimi Report)) states, *inter alia*, that "impartiality for such operations must therefore mean adherence to the principles of the Charter and to the objectives of a mandate that is rooted in those Charter principles. Such impartiality is not the same as neutrality or equal treatment of all parties in all cases for all time, which can amount to a policy of appeasement" (Brahimi Report, para. 50 and *Abu Garda*, para. 73 not 106). The majority in the ICC Pre-Trial Chamber noted that peacekeeping missions were only entitled to use force in self-defence compared to peace enforcement missions decided under Chapter VII of the UN Charter which may use force beyond the concept of self-defence in order to achieve their mandates (*Abu Garda*, para. 74). In UN doctrine the right of self-defence includes a "right to resist attempts by forceful means to prevent the peacekeeping operation from discharging its duties under the mandate of the Security Council" although it is doubtful if it has developed to become settled law (international or national) (*RUF*, para. 228).

The development in practice where operations are often authorised by the Security Council under Chapter VII to use all necessary measures for certain purposes is reflected in the UN doctrine by references to robust peacekeeping. Recent UN doctrine considers that the tendency to refer to peacekeeping operations as Chapter VI operations and peace enforcement operations as Chapter VII operations is somewhat misleading. It is now the usual practice, both in peacekeeping and in peace enforcement, "for a Chapter VII mandate to be given" and a distinction is instead made between "operations in which the robust use of force is integral to the mission from the outset [...] and operations in which there is a reasonable expectation that force may not be needed at all" (A More Secure World: Our Shared Responsibility, UN doc., A/59/565 (2004) para. 211). The Capstone Doctrine, as it is known, draws a distinction between peace enforcement and robust peacekeeping. Peacekeeping operations with a robust mandate have been authorised to "use all necessary means to deter forceful attempts to disrupt the political process, and/or assist the national authorities in maintaining law and order. The concept of robust peacekeeping is defined as involving "the use of force at the tactical level with the authorization of the Security Council and consent of the host nation and/or the main parties to the conflict". A peace enforcement operation on the other hand "does not require the consent of the main parties and may involve the use of military force at the strategic level, which is generally prohibited for Member States under Article 2(4) of the Charter, unless authorized by the Security Council" (United Nations Peacekeeping Operations: Principles and Guidelines (2008) p. 34).

The difference between these types of operation is thus not whether they have been established under Chapter VII of the UN Charter, but whether they are dependent on the existence of consent and the use of force at a strategic level. The concept of robust peacekeeping therefore challenges the traditional borders between the concepts of peacekeeping and peace enforcement (traditionally regarded as Chapter VI operations and Chapter VII operations). This may ultimately have an effect on the interpretation of the term peacekeeping mission in the ICC statute. It is telling that the Trial Chamber in the *RUF* case found that the mandate of the UNAMSIL even after it has been expanded through the Resolution 1279 which clearly was decided under Chapter VII and included the expression "use of all necessary measures" was regarded a peacekeeping mission for the purpose of the crime of attacking personnel in such missions (*RUF*, para. 1888).

iii. Such personnel, installations, material, units or vehicles were entitled to the protection given to civilians or civilian objects under the international law of armed conflict

Personnel in humanitarian assistance and peacekeeping missions are presumed to be entitled to the protection of civilians. This is particularly so regarding humanitarian assistance personnel. The authority to use force by peacekeepers, in self-defence or based on a resolution adopted under Chapter VII of the UN Charter (depending on the definition of a peacekeeping mission) naturally raise questions if the use of force by peacekeepers could affect their protection as civilians under international humanitarian law. Personnel in humanitarian assistance and peacekeeping missions are entitled to the protection of civilians as long as they are not taking a direct part in hostilities. Their protection would not be affected by exercising their individual right of self-defence – nor the use of force "in self-defence in the discharge of their mandate, provided that it is limited to such use" (*RUF*, para. 233) It should in this respect be noted that the use of force in defence of the mandate is inherently difficult to define. Determining whether peacekeeping personnel or objects of such a mission were entitled to the protection of civilians or civilian objects, the Trial Chamber in the *RUF* case found that it needed to consider the totality of circumstances existing at the time of the alleged offence including "inter alia, the relevant Security Council resolutions for the operation, the specific operational mandates, the role and practices actually adopted by the peacekeeping mission during the particular conflict, their rules of engagement and operational orders, the nature of the arms and equipment used by the peacekeeping force, the interaction between the peacekeeping force and the parties involved in the conflict, any use of force between the peacekeeping force and the parties in the conflict, the nature and frequency of such force and the conduct of the alleged victim(s) and their fellow personnel" (*RUF*, para. 234) It can be questioned if indeed all these aspects are valid for the determination whether personnel or objects are entitled to the protection of civilians since this a question decided under international humanitarian law.

The Majority in the ICC Pre-Trial exemplified "direct participation in hostilities" to include "bearing, using or taking up arms, taking part in military or hostile acts, activities, conduct or operations, armed fighting or combat, participating in attacks against enemy personnel, property or equipment, transmitting military information for immediate use of a belligerent, and transporting weapons in proximity to combat operations" (*Abu Garda*, para. 81). The determination of whether a person is directly participating in hostilities requires a case-by-case analysis (*Abu Garda*, para. 83).

Based on the definition of civilian objects in Article 52(2) of AP I and the ICRC customary law study, the Majority in the ICC Pre-Trial Chamber found that "installations, material, units or vehicles involved in a peacekeeping mission the context of an armed conflict not of an international character shall not be considered military objectives, and thus shall be entitled to the protection given to civilian objects, unless and for such time as their nature, location, purpose or use make an effective contribution to the military action of a party to a conflict and insofar as their total or partial destruction, capture or neutralization, in the circumstances ruling at the time, offers a definite military advantage" (*Abu Garda*, para. 89).

Given the military structure and organisation of peacekeeping missions it may in fact be questioned if such personnel should be regarded as civilians taking direct part in hostilities if they become involved in armed conflict. Military personnel organised and commanded by a state or an intergovernmental organisation within a traditional military structure may rather be regarded as members of a military force under command of party to an armed conflict than civilians directly participating in an armed conflict. The former has also the legal effect of a

(iv)   Intentionally launching an attack in the knowledge that such attack will cause incidental loss of life or injury to civilians or damage to civilian objects or widespread, long-term and severe damage to the natural environment which

---

change in status of the personnel in a more permanent manner than the latter where civilians directly participating in hostilities only temporarily.

b) Subjective elements

i. The perpetrator intended such personnel, installations, material, units or vehicles so involved to be the object of the attack

The Majority in the ICC Pre-Trial Chamber found that this subjective element was of similar character to that of the Elements of the Crimes for Articles 8(2)(b)(i) and 8(2)(e)(i) dealing with attacks on civilians in both international and non-international armed conflicts. The offence first and foremost encompasses dolus directus of the first degree. The finding of the Majority was also applicable in NIACs (*Abu Garda*, para. 93).

ii. The perpetrator was aware of the factual circumstances that established the protection

The necessary knowledge required by the perpetrator pertains to the facts establishing that the installations, materials, units or vehicles and personnel were involved in a peacekeeping mission but there is no need of legal knowledge regarding their protection.

iii. The perpetrator was aware of factual circumstances that established the existence of an armed conflict

There is no requirement on behalf of the perpetrator to conclude "on the basis of a legal assessment of the said circumstances, that there was an armed conflict" (*Abu Garda,* para. 96) (*RUF,* para. 235).

Cross-references:

Article 8(2)(e)(iii).

Doctrine:

1. Michael Bothe, "War Crimes", in Antonio Cassese, Paola Gaeta and John R.W.D. Jones (eds.), *The Rome Statute of the International Criminal Court: A Commentary*, Oxford University Press, Oxford, 2002, p. 412.
2. Michael Cottier, "Attacks on Humanitarian Assistance or Peacekeeping Missions", in Otto Triffterer (ed.), *Commentary on the Rome Statute of the International Criminal Court: Observers' Notes, Article by Article*, 2nd ed., C.H. Beck/Hart/Nomos, Munich/Oxford/Baden-Baden, 2008, pp. 330–38.
3. Knut Dörmann, *Elements of War Crimes under the Rome Statute of the International Criminal Court: Sources and Commentary*, Cambridge University Press, Cambridge, 2003, pp. 453–56.
4. Ola Engdahl, "Prosecution of Attacks against Peacekeepers in International Courts and Tribunals", in *Military Law and Law of War Review*, 2012, vol. 249, p. 51.
5. Daniel Frank, "Article 8(2)(b)(iii) – Attacking Personnel or Objects Involved in a Humanitarian Assistance or Peacekeeping Mission", in Roy S. Lee (ed.), *The International Criminal Court: Elements of Crimes and Rules of Procedure and Evidence*, Transnational Publishers, Ardsley, NY, 2001, pp. 146.
6. Herman von Hebel and Darryl Robinson, "Crimes within the Jurisdiction of the Court", in Roy S. Lee (ed.), *The International Criminal Court: The Making of the Rome Statute*, Kluwer Law International, The Hague, 1999, pp. 110.

Author: Ola Engdahl.

would be clearly excessive in relation to the concrete and direct overall military advantage anticipated;[81]

(v) Attacking or bombarding, by whatever means, towns, villages, dwellings or buildings which are undefended and which are not military objectives;[82]

(vi) Killing or wounding a combatant who, having laid down his arms or having no longer means of defence, has surrendered at discretion;[83]

---

[81] The provision reflects the principle of proportionality (Articles 51(5)(b) and 85(3)(b) of Additional Protocol I) and brings environment into the equation (Articles 35(3) and 55 of Additional Protocol I).

Doctrine:

1. Michael Bothe, "War Crimes", in Antonio Cassese, Paola Gaeta and John R.W.D. Jones (eds.), *The Rome Statute of the International Criminal Court: A Commentary*, Oxford University Press, Oxford, 2002, pp. 398–401.

2. Roberta Arnold, "Article 8, War Crimes", in Otto Triffterer (ed.), *Commentary on the Rome Statute of the International Criminal Court: Observers' Notes, Article by Article*, 2nd ed., C.H. Beck/Hart/Nomos, Munich/Oxford/Baden-Baden, 2008, pp. 338–41.

3. Gerhard Werle, "Principles of International Criminal Law", TMC Asser Press, The Hague, 2005, pp. 349–52, MN 1040–47.

Author: Mark Klamberg.

[82] A place is considered undefended when it is inhabited, located in a war zone or nearby, and open to occupation by an adverse party. Thus, the provision does not cover objects behind enemy lines, even if there are no combatants or weapons located in or nearby the objects.

Cross-references:

Starvation in Articles 6(c); 7(1)(b), (j)and (k), 7(2)(b), 8(2)(a)(iii), 8(2)(b)(ii), (xiii) and (xxv).

Doctrine:

1. Michael Bothe, "War Crimes", in Antonio Cassese, Paola Gaeta and John R.W.D. Jones (eds.), *The Rome Statute of the International Criminal Court: A Commentary*, Oxford University Press, Oxford, 2002, pp. 401–2.

2. Roberta Arnold, "Article 8, War Crimes", in Otto Triffterer (ed.), *Commentary on the Rome Statute of the International Criminal Court: Observers' Notes, Article by Article*, 2nd ed., C.H. Beck/Hart/Nomos, Munich/Oxford/Baden-Baden, 2008, pp. 341–44.

3. Gerhard Werle, *Principles of International Criminal Law*, TMC Asser Press, The Hague, 2005, pp. 352–354, MN 1049–52.

Author: Mark Klamberg.

[83] The scope of the provision protecting combatants not involved in combat, hors de combat, covers to a large extent the war crime of declaring that no quarter will be given, Article 8(2)(b)(xii). The mental element requires at least recklessness.

Cross-references:

Article 8(2)(b)(xii).

Doctrine:

1. Michael Bothe, "War Crimes", in Antonio Cassese, Paola Gaeta and John R.W.D. Jones (eds.), *The Rome Statute of the International Criminal Court: A Commentary*, Oxford University Press, Oxford, 2002, pp. 405–6.

2. Michael Cottier, in Otto Triffterer (ed.), *Commentary on the Rome Statute of the International Criminal Court: Observers' Notes, Article by Article*, 2nd ed., C.H. Beck/Hart/Nomos, Munich/Oxford/Baden-Baden, 2008, pp. 344–50.

(vii)   Making improper use of a flag of truce,[84] of the flag or of the military insignia and uniform of the enemy[85] or of the United Nations,[86] as well as of the dis-

---

3. Gerhard Werle, *Principles of International Criminal Law*, TMC Asser Press, The Hague, 2005, pp. 304–305, MN 879–84.

Author: Mark Klamberg.

[84] Envoys, identifying themselves by a white flag, authorised to negotiate with the enemy are protected.

Cross-references:

Articles 8(2)(b)(xi) and 8(2)(e)(ix).

Doctrine:

1. Michael Bothe, "War Crimes", in Antonio Cassese, Paola Gaeta and John R.W.D. Jones (eds.), *The Rome Statute of the International Criminal Court: A Commentary*, Oxford University Press, Oxford, 2002, pp. 403–5.
2. Michael Cottier, in Otto Triffterer (ed.), *Commentary on the Rome Statute of the International Criminal Court: Observers' Notes, Article by Article*, 2nd ed., C.H. Beck/Hart/Nomos, Munich/Oxford/Baden-Baden, 2008, pp. 350–57.
3. Gerhard Werle, *Principles of International Criminal Law*, TMC Asser Press, The Hague, 2005, p. 358, MN 1064–65.

Author: Mark Klamberg

[85] According to the Elements of Crime the use of enemy flags, military insignias, and uniforms is prohibited while engaged in an attack, which makes the prohibition less strict in comparison with the use of protective emblems.

Cross-references:

Articles 8(2)(b)(xi) and 8(2)(e)(ix).

Doctrine:

1. Michael Bothe, "War Crimes", in Antonio Cassese, Paola Gaeta and John R.W.D. Jones (eds.), *The Rome Statute of the International Criminal Court: A Commentary*, Oxford University Press, Oxford, 2002, pp. 403–5.
2. Michael Cottier, in Otto Triffterer (ed.), *Commentary on the Rome Statute of the International Criminal Court: Observers' Notes, Article by Article*, 2nd ed., C.H. Beck/Hart/Nomos, Munich/Oxford/Baden-Baden, 2008, pp. 357–59.
3. Gerhard Werle, *Principles of International Criminal Law*, TMC Asser Press, The Hague, 2005, p. 358, MN 1066–67.

Author: Mark Klamberg.

[86] According to the wording only UN military insignia is included, which appears to be an editorial error. It is submitted that the provision also includes non-military UN personnel.

Cross-references:

Articles 8(2)(b)(xi) and 8(2)(e)(ix).

Doctrine:

1. Michael Bothe, "War Crimes", in Antonio Cassese, Paola Gaeta and John R.W.D. Jones (eds.), *The Rome Statute of the International Criminal Court: A Commentary*, Oxford University Press, Oxford, 2002, pp. 403–5.
2. Michael Cottier, in Otto Triffterer (ed.), *Commentary on the Rome Statute of the International Criminal Court: Observers' Notes, Article by Article*, 2nd ed., C.H. Beck/Hart/Nomos, Munich/Oxford/Baden-Baden, 2008, pp. 359–60.

tinctive emblems of the Geneva Conventions,[87] resulting in death or serious personal injury;[88]

(viii) The transfer, directly or indirectly, by the Occupying Power of parts of its own civilian population into the territory it occupies, or the deportation or transfer of all or parts of the population of the occupied territory within or outside this territory;[89]

---

3. Gerhard Werle, *Principles of International Criminal Law*, TMC Asser Press, The Hague, 2005, p. 359, MN 1070.

Author: Mark Klamberg.

[87] The distinctive emblems of the Geneva Conventions are the red cross, the red crescent, the red lion and sun, and the red crystal. The latter emblem was added by the adoption of a third additional Protocol to the Geneva Conventions, 8 December 2005. The Protocol was partly adopted in response to the Israeli argument that it should be able to use the red shield of David in national operations. The third additional Protocol enables the Israeli Society to continue to use its red shield of David as its sole emblem inside Israel. When working outside Israel the Society would need to work according to the requirements of the host country. Normally this would mean that it could display the red shield of David incorporated within the red crystal, or use the red crystal alone (Article 3 of the third additional Protocol). The emblems mark medical and spiritual personnel, medical units and transports, equipment or supplies. The emblems may in principle only be used by persons who do not themselves participate in hostilities.

Cross-references:
Articles 8(2)(b)(xi) and 8(2)(e)(ix).

Doctrine:
1. Michael Bothe, "War Crimes", in Antonio Cassese, Paola Gaeta and John R.W.D. Jones (eds.), *The Rome Statute of the International Criminal Court: A Commentary*, Oxford University Press, Oxford, 2002, pp. 403–5.
2. Michael Cottier, in Otto Triffterer (ed.), *Commentary on the Rome Statute of the International Criminal Court: Observers' Notes, Article by Article*, 2nd ed., C.H. Beck/Hart/Nomos, München/Oxford/Baden-Baden, 2008, pp. 360–62.
3. Gerhard Werle, *Principles of International Criminal Law*, TMC Asser Press, The Hague, 2005, p. 359, MN 1068–69.

Author: Mark Klamberg.

[88] The conduct is only criminal under Article 8(2)(b)(vii) when it led to a person's death or injury.

Doctrine:
1. Michael Bothe, "War Crimes", in Antonio Cassese, Paola Gaeta and John R.W.D. Jones (eds.), *The Rome Statute of the International Criminal Court: A Commentary*, Oxford University Press, Oxford, 2002, pp. 403–5.
2. Michael Cottier, in Otto Triffterer (ed.), *Commentary on the Rome Statute of the International Criminal Court: Observers' Notes, Article by Article*, 2nd ed., C.H. Beck/Hart/Nomos, Munich/Oxford/Baden-Baden, 2008, pp. 353 and 355.
3. Gerhard Werle, *Principles of International Criminal Law*, TMC Asser Press, The Hague, 2005, p. 360, MN 1072.

Author: Mark Klamberg.

[89] The transfer by the Occupying Power of parts of its own civilian population into the territory it occupies violates the principle of international law that an Occupying Power is only permitted to a position of trust as an interim military administrator. The material element requires the trans-

---

(ix)   Intentionally directing attacks against buildings dedicated to religion, education, art, science or charitable purposes, historic monuments, hospitals and
places where the sick and wounded are collected, provided they are not military objectives;[90]

---

fer of persons from one territory to another. Article 49(2) of the Fourth Geneva Convention allows the Occupying Power to undertake total or partial evacuation of a given area if the security
of the population or imperative military reasons so demand. Such evacuations may not involve
the displacement of protected persons outside the bounds of the occupied territory except when
for material reasons it is impossible to avoid such displacement. Persons thus evacuated shall be
transferred back to their homes as soon as hostilities in the area in question have ceased.

Cross-references:
Articles 7(1)(d), 8(2)(a)(vii) and 8(2)(e)(viii).

Doctrine:

1.   Michael Bothe, "War Crimes", in Antonio Cassese, Paola Gaeta and John R.W.D. Jones
(eds.), *The Rome Statute of the International Criminal Court: A Commentary*, Oxford University Press, Oxford, 2002, pp. 395–97.

2.   Michael Cottier, in Otto Triffterer (ed.), *Commentary on the Rome Statute of the International Criminal Court: Observers' Notes, Article by Article*, 2nd ed., C.H.
Beck/Hart/Nomos, München/Oxford/Baden-Baden, 2008, pp. 362–75.

3.   Gerhard Werle, *Principles of International Criminal Law*, TMC Asser Press, The Hague,
2005, pp. 327–28 and 329–31, MN 964–66 and 971–76.

Author: Mark Klamberg.

[90]   *General remarks*:

With this Article the drafters of the ICC Statute included a provision criminalising violations of
the rules protecting cultural property, which have been established by international humanitarian
law as well as several UNESCO treaties over the years. The purpose of this provision is to specifically criminalise the destruction of cultural property as opposed to civilian property and
therefore, it constitutes a *lex specialis* to Articles 8(2)(a)(iv), 8(2)(b)(ii) and 8(2)(b)(xiii).

Analysis:

i. Definition

Pursuant to the ICC Elements of Crime, the following criteria need to be met in order to fulfil
the Article at hand: 1) The perpetrator directed an attack. 2) The object of the attack was one or
more buildings dedicated to religion, education, art, science or charitable purposes, historic
monuments, hospitals or places where the sick and wounded are collected, which were not military objectives. 3) The perpetrator intended such building or buildings dedicated to religion, education, art, science or charitable purposes, historic monuments, hospitals or places where the
sick and wounded are collected, which were not military objectives, to be the object of the attack. 4) The conduct took place in the context of and was associated with an international armed
conflict. 5) The perpetrator was aware of factual circumstances that established the existence of
an armed conflict.

ii. Requirements

a. Material elements

The object of the offence has to be specially protected. The institutions enlisted in the ICC Statute can be classified into four main categories: cultural objects, places for the collection of those
in need (for example, hospitals), institutions dedicated to religion and others dedicated to education. The ICTY defined 'cultural objects' by referring the definition of cultural property in treaty law (for example, the 1954 Hague Convention for the Protection of Cultural Property in the

Event of Armed Conflict) (*Prosecutor v. Strugar* (Case No. IT-01-42), ICTY T. Ch. Judgment of 31 January 2005, para. 230). According to the case law of the ICTY, religious and educational institutions are protected as long as they meet the special requirement of "cultural heritage of people", meaning "objects whose value transcends geographical boundaries, and which are unique in character and are intimately associated with the history and culture of a people" (*Prosecutor v. Martić* (Case No. IT-95-11), ICTY T. Ch. Judgment of 12 June 2007, para. 97). Additionally, these institutions must "clearly be identified as dedicated to religion or education" (*Prosecutor v. Blaškić* (Case No. IT-95-14), ICTY T. Ch. Judgment of 3 March 2000, para. 185).

Furthermore, the object of the offence cannot be a military objective. Military objectives are defined by Article 52(3) Additional Protocol I as objects "which by their nature, location, purpose or use make an effective contribution to military action and whose total or partial destruction, capture or neutralization, in the circumstances ruling at the time, offers a definite military advantage".

Concerning the nature of the offence the ICC Statute penalises the directing of attacks against such institutions. The term 'attack' is defined in Article 49(1) Additional Protocol I and means "acts of violence against the adversary, whether in offence or in defence". Hence, the scope of the Article is extremely broad and almost all acts of hostility fall under this provision. Furthermore, no actual damage to the protected institutions is required. In order for the Article at hand to be fulfilled it is sufficient that the attack was directed against the respective protected institution.

b. Mental elements

Additionally, to the mental elements concerning the general requirements of war crimes, the perpetrator has to fulfil the mental elements of the underlying offence at hand. Namely, the attack against the protected institutions has to be committed "intentionally". A controversial issue while drafting the ICC Statute was whether the term "intentionally" was related solely to the directing of an attack or also to the object of the attack. The *travaux préparatoires* adopted the latter approach. Therefore, the ICC Elements of the Crime require that the perpetrator must have known about the protected status of the institution. Additionally, the perpetrator must have knowledge of the institution's failure to qualify as a military objective, and nevertheless carry out the attack. However, he does not have to make a legal assessment of the protected status of the institutions. He merely needs to know the factual circumstances, which give the object a special status (see *Prosecutor v. Blaškić* (Case No. IT-95-14), ICTY T. Ch. Judgment of 3 March 2000, para. 185).

Cross-references:

Article 8(2)(b)(i), 8(2)(b)(ii), 8(2)(e)(i) and 8(2)(e)(iv).

Doctrine:

1. Roberta Arnold, "Article 8, Paragraph 2 (b)(ix)", in Otto Triffterer (ed.), *Commentary on the Rome Statute of the International Criminal Court: Observers' Notes, Article by Article*, 2nd ed., C.H. Beck/Hart/Nomos, Munich/Oxford/Baden-Baden, 2008, pp. 375–80.

2. Gideon Boas, James L. Biscoff and Nathalie L. Reid, *International Criminal Law Practitioner Library*. Vol. II: *Elements of Crime under International Criminal Law*, Cambridge University Press, Cambridge, 2008.

3. Caroline Ehlert, *Prosecuting the Destruction of Cultural Property in International Criminal Law* Martinus Nijhoff, Leiden, 2014, pp. 121–40.

4. Micaela Frulli, "The Criminalization of Offences against Cultural Heritage in Times of Armed Conflict: The Quest of Consistency", in *European Journal of International Law*, 2011, vol. 22, pp. 203–17.

(x)   Subjecting persons who are in the power of an adverse party to physical mutilation[91] or to medical or scientific experiments[92] of any kind which are neither justified by the medical, dental or hospital treatment of the person concerned

---

5. Mireille Hector, "Enhancing Individual Criminal Responsibility for Offences Involving Cultural Property – The Road to the Rome Statute and the 1999 Second Protocol", in Nout Van Woudenberg and Liesbeth Lijnzaad (eds.), *Protecting Cultural Armed Conflict: An Insight into the 1999 Second Protocol to the Hague Convention of 1954 for the Protection of Cultural Property in the Event of Armed Conflict*, Brill, Leiden, 2010, pp. 375–80.

6. Theodor Meron, "The Protection of Cultural Property in the Event of Armed Conflict within the Case law of the International Criminal Tribunal for the Former Yugoslavia", in *Museum International*, 2005, vol. 57, pp. 41–59.

7. Roger O'Keefe, "Protection of Cultural Property under International Criminal Law", in *Melbourne Journal of International Law*, 2010, vol. 11, pp. 1–54.

8. Rüdiger Wolfrum, "Protection of Cultural Property in Armed Conflict", in Rüdiger Wolfrum (ed.), *The Max Planck Encyclopedia of Public International Law*, Oxford University Press, Oxford, 2008.

Author: Caroline Ehlert.

[91] The term 'physical mutilation' cover acts such as amputations, injury to limbs, removal of organs, and forms of sexual mutilations. The victim's consent is not an excusable defence.

Cross-references:

Articles 8(2)(c)(i) and 8(2)(e)(xi).

Doctrine:

1. Michael Bothe, "War Crimes", in Antonio Cassese, Paola Gaeta and John R.W.D. Jones (eds.), *The Rome Statute of the International Criminal Court: A Commentary*, Oxford University Press, Oxford, 2002, pp. 395–97.

2. Andreas Zimmerman, in Otto Triffterer (ed.), *Commentary on the Rome Statute of the International Criminal Court: Observers' Notes, Article by Article*, 2nd ed., C.H. Beck/Hart/Nomos, Munich/Oxford/Baden-Baden, 2008, pp. 380–83.

3. Gerhard Werle, *Principles of International Criminal Law*, TMC Asser Press, The Hague, 2005, pp. 307–8, MN 895–97.

Author: Mark Klamberg.

[92] The prohibition of medical or scientific experiments cover the use of therapeutic methods which are not justified on medical grounds and not carried out in the interest of the affected person. The consent of the victim is not relevant.

Cross-references:

Article 8(2)(a)(ii) and 8(2)(e)(xi).

Doctrine:

1. Michael Bothe, "War Crimes", in Antonio Cassese, Paola Gaeta and John R.W.D. Jones (eds.), *The Rome Statute of the International Criminal Court: A Commentary*, Oxford University Press, Oxford, 2002, p. 395–97.

2. Andreas Zimmerman, in Otto Triffterer (ed.), *Commentary on the Rome Statute of the International Criminal Court: Observers' Notes, Article by Article*, 2nd ed., C.H. Beck/Hart/Nomos, Munich/Oxford/Baden-Baden, 2008, p. 382.

3. Gerhard Werle, *Principles of International Criminal Law*, TMC Asser Press, The Hague, 2005, pp. 308–10, MN 898–902.

Author: Mark Klamberg.

---

nor carried out in his or her interest, and which cause death to or seriously endanger the health of such person or persons;[93]

(xi) Killing or wounding treacherously individuals belonging to the hostile nation or army;[94]

---

[93] The acts in Article 8(2)(b)(x) can only be justified if undertaken in the interest of the person concerned, for example, amputations may be lawful if performed to save the live or overall health of the patient.

Cross-references:
Article 8(2)(e)(xi).

Doctrine:

1. Michael Bothe, "War Crimes", in Antonio Cassese, Paola Gaeta and John R.W.D. Jones (eds.), *The Rome Statute of the International Criminal Court: A Commentary*, Oxford University Press, Oxford, 2002, p. 395–97.

2. Andreas Zimmerman, in Otto Triffterer (ed.), *Commentary on the Rome Statute of the International Criminal Court: Observers' Notes, Article by Article*, 2nd ed., C.H. Beck/Hart/Nomos, Munich/Oxford/Baden-Baden, 2008, pp. 382–83.

3. Gerhard Werle, *Principles of International Criminal Law*, TMC Asser Press, The Hague, 2005, pp. 308–10, MN 898–902.

Author: Mark Klamberg.

[94] Treachery, also synonymous with perfidy, involves a breach of good faith of the combatants. In practice, it is typically cases in which the accused in deception claims a right to protection for him or herself, and uses this for his or her advantage in the combat. It includes:

- pretending to be a civilian;
- fake use of a flag of truce, the flag or of the military insignia and uniform of the enemy or of the United Nations, as well as of the distinctive emblems of the Geneva Conventions;
- fake use of the protective emblem of cultural property;
- fake use of other internationally recognised protective emblems, signs or signals;
- pretending to surrender;
- pretending to be incapacitated by wounds or sickness;
- pretending to belong to a neutral state or other State not party to the conflict by the use of their signs;
- pretending to belong to the enemy by the use of their signs;

The wording of the provision indicates that the prohibition of treachery protect enemy combatants, as well as civilians. Perfidious acts are only punishable if the perpetrator intentionally killed or wounded an adversary.

Cross-references:
Articles 8(2)(b)(vii) and 8(2)(e)(ix).

Doctrine:

1. Michael Bothe, "War Crimes", in Antonio Cassese, Paola Gaeta and John R.W.D. Jones (eds.), *The Rome Statute of the International Criminal Court: A Commentary*, Oxford University Press, Oxford, 2002, p. 405.

2. Michael Cottier, in Otto Triffterer (ed.), *Commentary on the Rome Statute of the International Criminal Court: Observers' Notes, Article by Article*, 2nd ed., C.H. Beck/Hart/Nomos, Munich/Oxford/Baden-Baden, 2008, pp. 383–90.

(xii)   Declaring that no quarter will be given;[95]

(xiii) Destroying or seizing the enemy's property unless such destruction or seizure be imperatively demanded by the necessities of war;[96]

---

3. Gerhard Werle, *Principles of International Criminal Law*, TMC Asser Press, The Hague, 2005, p. 354–56, MN 1054–58.

Author: Mark Klamberg.

[95] The offence covers 'take no prisoners' warfare. The material element will typically be fulfilled by a declaration that any surrender by the enemy shall be refused even if it is reasonable to accept. In addition to declarations, the provision should be including order and threats that no quarter shall be refused. Combatants are not required to provide the enemy with the opportunity to surrender.

Cross-references:

Article 8(2)(b)(vi) and 8(2)(e)(x).

Doctrine:

1. Michael Cottier, in Otto Triffterer (ed.), *Commentary on the Rome Statute of the International Criminal Court: Observers' Notes, Article by Article*, 2nd ed., C.H. Beck/Hart/Nomos, Munich/Oxford/Baden-Baden, 2008, pp. 391–95.

2. Gerhard Werle, *Principles of International Criminal Law*, TMC Asser Press, The Hague, 2005, pp. 360–62, MN 1074–79.

Author: Mark Klamberg.

[96] The individual elements of the prohibition should be interpreted in light of the relevant rules of customary international law, such as those embodied *inter alia* in Articles 46, 52, 53, 54, 55 and 56 of the 1907 Hague Convention Respecting the Laws and Customs of War on Land. Acts otherwise prohibited may me justified if "imperatively demanded by the necessities of war". The exception should be interpreted restrictively, not every situation of military necessity is covered.

In *Prosecutor v. Katanga and Chui*, ICC PT. Ch. I, ICC-01/04-01/07-717, Decision on the Confirmation of Charges, 30 September 2008, paras. 310–311, the Pre-Trial Chamber held "that the property in question – whether moveable or immoveable, private or public – must belong to individuals or entities aligned with or with allegiance to a party to the conflict adverse or hostile to the perpetrator. Article 8(2)(b)(xiii) of the Statute applies not only when the attack is specifically directed at a military objective but also when it targets and destroys civilian property". PTC I also stated that "in the view of the Chamber, the provision does not apply to incidental destruction of civilian property during an attack specifically directed at a military objective, as long as the destruction does not violate the proportionality rule provided for in Article 51 AP I and in Article 8(2)(b)(iv) of the Statute (para. 313)".

Cross-references:

Articles 8(2)(a)(iv), 8(2)(b)(xvi), 8(2)(e)(v) and 8(2)(e)(xii).

Starvation in Articles 6(c); 7(1)(b), (j)and (k); 7(2)(b); 8(2)(a)(iii); 8(2)(b)(ii), (v)and (xxv).

Doctrine:

1. Michael Bothe, "War Crimes", in Antonio Cassese, Paola Gaeta and John R.W.D. Jones (eds.), *The Rome Statute of the International Criminal Court: A Commentary*, Oxford University Press, Oxford, 2002, p. 403.

2. Andreas Zimmerman, in Otto Triffterer (ed.), *Commentary on the Rome Statute of the International Criminal Court: Observers' Notes, Article by Article*, 2nd ed., C.H. Beck/Hart/Nomos, Munich/Oxford/Baden-Baden, 2008, pp. 395–400.

(xiv)   Declaring abolished, suspended or inadmissible in a court of law the rights and actions of the nationals of the hostile party;[97]

(xv)   Compelling the nationals of the hostile party to take part in the operations of war directed against their own country, even if they were in the belligerent's service before the commencement of the war;[98]

(xvi)   Pillaging a town or place, even when taken by assault;[99]

---

3.   Gerhard Werle, *Principles of International Criminal Law*, TMC Asser Press, The Hague, 2005, pp. 338–40, MN 1000–4.

Author: Mark Klamberg.

[97]   The term 'actions' refers to the right of access to courts of law. This provision is similar Article 8(a)(vi). The difference between the provisions would appear that the present provision covers civil claims as opposed to criminal cases.

Cross-references:
Articles 8(a)(vi) and 8(2)(c)(iv).

Doctrine:

1.   Michael Bothe, "War Crimes", in Antonio Cassese, Paola Gaeta and John R.W.D. Jones (eds.), *The Rome Statute of the International Criminal Court: A Commentary*, Oxford University Press, Oxford, 2002, p. 396.

2.   Michael Cottier, in Otto Triffterer (ed.), *Commentary on the Rome Statute of the International Criminal Court: Observers' Notes, Article by Article*, 2nd ed., C.H. Beck/Hart/Nomos, Munich/Oxford/Baden-Baden, 2008, pp. 400–5.

3.   Gerhard Werle, *Principles of International Criminal Law*, TMC Asser Press, The Hague, 2005, pp. 340–41, MN 1005–7.

Author: Mark Klamberg.

[98]   This offence can also be charged under Article 8(a)(v). There is disagreement whether the prohibition covers more than compelling nationals to serve in the armed forces of the adversary, for example, war-related work.

Cross-references:
Article 8(a)(v).

Doctrine:

1.   Michael Bothe, "War Crimes", in Antonio Cassese, Paola Gaeta and John R.W.D. Jones (eds.), *The Rome Statute of the International Criminal Court: A Commentary*, Oxford University Press, Oxford, 2002, p. 394.

2.   Michael Cottier, in Otto Triffterer (ed.), *Commentary on the Rome Statute of the International Criminal Court: Observers' Notes, Article by Article*, 2nd ed., C.H. Beck/Hart/Nomos, Munich/Oxford/Baden-Baden, 2008, pp. 405–8.

3.   Gerhard Werle, *Principles of International Criminal Law*, TMC Asser Press, The Hague, 2005, pp. 316–18, MN 924–31.

Author: Mark Klamberg.

[99]   The term 'pillage' means appropriation of property for private, personal use and embraces acts of plundering, looting and sacking. There is no substantive difference between appropriation and confiscation. Article 8(2)(e)(v) is an identical provision to the present provision, but applies in non-international armed conflicts. In comparison with Articles 8(2)(a)(iv), 8(2)(b)(xiii) and 8(2)(e)(xii), pillage differs from appropriation and confiscation in regard to the perpetrator's intent to obtain the property for private or personal use.

(xvii) Employing poison or poisoned weapons;[100]

(xviii) Employing asphyxiating, poisonous or other gases, and all analogous liquids, materials or devices;[101]

In *Prosecutor v. Katanga and Chui*, ICC PT. Ch. I, ICC-01/04-01/07-717, Decision on the Confirmation of Charges, 30 September 2008, para. 329, the Pre-Trial Chamber stated that the "war crime of pillaging under Article 8(2)(b)(xvi) of the Statute requires that the property subject to the offence belongs to an 'enemy' or 'hostile' party to the conflict".

Cross-references:

Articles 8(2)(a)(iv), 8(2)(b)(xiii), 8(2)(e)(v) and 8(2)(e)(xii).

Doctrine:

1. Michael Bothe, "War Crimes", in Antonio Cassese, Paola Gaeta and John R.W.D. Jones (eds.), *The Rome Statute of the International Criminal Court: A Commentary*, Oxford University Press, Oxford, 2002, p. 413.

2. Andreas Zimmerman, in Otto Triffterer (ed.), *Commentary on the Rome Statute of the International Criminal Court: Observers' Notes, Article by Article*, 2nd ed., C.H. Beck/Hart/Nomos, Munich/Oxford/Baden-Baden, 2008, pp. 408–10.

3. Gerhard Werle, *Principles of International Criminal Law*, TMC Asser Press, The Hague, 2005, pp. 334–38, MN 986–99.

Author: Mark Klamberg.

[100] This offence could, for example, include the poisoning of water supplies. The production and storage of poison is not prohibited. There is no agreement whether the prohibition on the use of poison covers poison gas. The provision does not prohibit chemical and biological weapons of mass destruction. Instead this is covered by Article 8(2)(b)(xx), but which is not yet in force. This may be explained the lack of agreement on the prohibition on of nuclear weapons and a following compromise during the Rome conference, with the result that weapons of mass destruction are not subject to an explicit and binding provision in the ICC Statute.

Cross-references:

Article 8(2)(b)(xviii) and 8(2)(b)(xx)/

Doctrine:

1. Michael Bothe, "War Crimes", in Antonio Cassese, Paola Gaeta and John R.W.D. Jones (eds.), *The Rome Statute of the International Criminal Court: A Commentary*, Oxford University Press, Oxford, 2002, p. 406.

2. Michael Cottier, in Otto Triffterer (ed.), *Commentary on the Rome Statute of the International Criminal Court: Observers' Notes, Article by Article*, 2nd ed., C.H. Beck/Hart/Nomos, Munich/Oxford/Baden-Baden, 2008, pp. 410–14.

3. Gerhard Werle, *Principles of International Criminal Law*, TMC Asser Press, The Hague, 2005, pp. 369–72, MN 1100–6.

Author: Mark Klamberg.

[101] The wording of the present provision is basically identical the Geneva Protocol of 17 June 1925 for the prohibition of the use in war of asphyxiating, poisonous or other gases, and of bacteriological methods of warfare. It is generally understood that the wording "asphyxiating, poisonous or other gases, and all analogous liquids, materials or devices" in the 1925 Geneva Protocol includes chemical weapons which nullifies the compromise mentioned in the previous commentary (Article 8(2)(b)(xvii)). Even though biological weapons are covered by the Geneva Protocol of 17 June 1925, it is doubtful that the present provision covers these weapons. This is supported by the fact that the relevant passage on biological weapons in the Geneva Protocol of 17 June 1925 was not included in Article 8(2)(b)(xvii).

(xix)   Employing bullets which expand or flatten easily in the human body, such as bullets with a hard envelope which does not entirely cover the core or is pierced with incisions;[102]

(xx)   Employing weapons, projectiles and material and methods of warfare which are of a nature to cause superfluous injury or unnecessary suffering or which are inherently indiscriminate in violation of the international law of armed conflict, provided that such weapons, projectiles and material and methods of warfare are the subject of a comprehensive prohibition and are included in an annex to this Statute, by an amendment in accordance with the relevant provisions set forth in articles 121 and 123;[103]

Cross-references:
Article 8(2)(b)(xvii).

Doctrine:

1. Michael Cottier, in Otto Triffterer (ed.), *Commentary on the Rome Statute of the International Criminal Court: Observers' Notes, Article by Article*, 2nd ed., C.H. Beck/Hart/Nomos, Munich/Oxford/Baden-Baden, 2008, pp. 414–20.

2. Gerhard Werle, *Principles of International Criminal Law*, TMC Asser Press, The Hague, 2005, pp. 372–73, MN 1107–10.

Author: Mark Klamberg.

[102] The 'dum-dum' bullet is a type of bullet covered by the present provision, as well as customary law. The prohibition equally applies to standard bullets converted on the battlefield by piercing them with incisions, as well as to other types of bullets which expand or flatten easily in the human body.

Doctrine:

1. Michael Bothe, "War Crimes", in Antonio Cassese, Paola Gaeta and John R.W.D. Jones (eds.), *The Rome Statute of the International Criminal Court: A Commentary*, Oxford University Press, Oxford, 2002, p. 408.

2. Michael Cottier, in Otto Triffterer (ed.), *Commentary on the Rome Statute of the International Criminal Court: Observers' Notes, Article by Article*, 2nd ed., C.H. Beck/Hart/Nomos, Munich/Oxford/Baden-Baden, 2008, pp. 420–23.

3. Gerhard Werle, *Principles of International Criminal Law*, TMC Asser Press, The Hague, 2005, pp. 373–74, MN 1111–13.

Author: Mark Klamberg.

[103] This is a catch-all prohibition which requires an amendment in the form of annex in order to be binding. Thus, the provision is at the present time not applicable. The present provision was part of the compromise mentioned in the commentary to Article 8(2)(b)(xvii). A great number of delegations at the Rome Conference wanted to include additional weapons such as biological weapons, chemical weapons, land mines and laser-blinding weapons. The provision may be amended in a future review conference.

Cross-references:
Article 8(2)(b)(xvii).

Doctrine:

1. Michael Bothe, "War Crimes", in Antonio Cassese, Paola Gaeta and John R.W.D. Jones (eds.), *The Rome Statute of the International Criminal Court: A Commentary*, Oxford University Press, Oxford, 2002, pp. 408–9.

(xxi)   Committing outrages upon personal dignity, in particular humiliating and de-grading treatment;[104]

(xxii) Committing rape,[105] sexual slavery,[106] enforced prostitution,[107] forced preg-nancy, as defined in article 7, paragraph 2 (f),[108] enforced sterilization,[109] or

---

2. Michael Cottier, in Otto Triffterer (ed.), *Commentary on the Rome Statute of the Interna-tional Criminal Court: Observers' Notes, Article by Article*, 2nd ed., C.H. Beck/Hart/Nomos, Munich/Oxford/Baden-Baden, 2008, pp. 410–413 and 423–425, MN 179–181 and 185–88.

3. Gerhard Werle, *Principles of International Criminal Law*, TMC Asser Press, The Hague, 2005, p. 374, MN 1114–15.

Author: Mark Klamberg.

[104]   Humiliating and degrading treatment is prohibited even if the victim overcomes the conse-quences relatively quickly. In *Prosecutor v. Katanga and Chui*, ICC PT. Ch. I, ICC-01/04-01/07-717, Decision on the Confirmation of Charges, 30 September 2008, para. 369, the Pre-Trial Chamber quoted ICTY jurisprudence when it stated that "there is no requirement that such suffering be lasting". There is no special intent requirement in addition to the general require-ment of Article 30.

Cross-references:
Articles 7(1)(c) and 8(2)(c)(ii).

Doctrine:

1. Michael Bothe, "War Crimes", in Antonio Cassese, Paola Gaeta and John R.W.D. Jones (eds.), *The Rome Statute of the International Criminal Court: A Commentary*, Oxford Uni-versity Press, Oxford, 2002, pp. 414–15.

2. Patricia Viseur Sellers and Elizabeth Bennion, in Otto Triffterer (ed.), *Commentary on the Rome Statute of the International Criminal Court: Observers' Notes, Article by Article*, 2nd ed., C.H. Beck/Hart/Nomos, Munich/Oxford/Baden-Baden, 2008, pp. 425–31.

3. Gerhard Werle, *Principles of International Criminal Law*, TMC Asser Press, The Hague, 2005, p. 314–16, MN 917–23.

Author: Mark Klamberg.

[105]   Rape is considered the most severe form of sexual violence. Sexual violence is a broad term that covers all forms of acts of a sexual nature under coercive circumstances, including rape. The key element that separates rape from other acts is penetration. The Elements of Crime provide a more specific definition of the criminal conduct. Rape falls under the chapeaus of genocide, crimes against humanity or war crimes under specific circumstances, confirmed both through the ICC Statute and through the case law of the ICTR and the ICTY. Rape as a war crime differs from the definition of rape as a crime against humanity only in terms of the context in which the crime is committed. The rape must have been perpetrated in the context of and in association with an international armed conflict.

For the mental element of rape Article 30 applies. The perpetrator has to be aware of the factual circumstances that established the existence of an armed conflict. He or she must also have intended to penetrate the victim's body and be aware that the penetration was by force or threat of force.

The definition of rape is the same regarding rape as genocide, crimes against humanity and war crimes, albeit the contextual elements of the chapeaus differ. The *actus reus* of the violation is found in the Elements of Crimes. The definition focuses on penetration with 1) a sexual organ of any body part, or 2) with the use of an object or any other part of the body of the anal or geni-tal opening of the victim, committed by force or threat or force or coercion. "Any part of the body" under point 1 refers to vaginal, anal and oral penetration with the penis and may also be interpreted as ears, nose and eyes of the victim. Point 2 refers to objects or the use of fingers, hands or tongue of the perpetrator. Coercion may arise through fear of violence, duress, detention, psychological oppression or abuse of power. These situations are provided as examples, apparent through the use of the term "such as". Consent is automatically vitiated in such situations. The definition is intentionally gender neutral, indicating that both men and women can be perpetrators or victims. The definition of rape found in the Elements of Crimes is heavily influenced by the legal reasoning in cases regarding rape of the ICTY and the ICTR. Such cases can thus further elucidate the interpretation of the elements of the crime, meanwhile also highlighting different approaches to the main elements of rape, including 'force' and 'non-consent'. See, for example, *Furundžija*, in which the Trial Chamber of the ICTY held that force or threat of force constitutes the main element of rape (*Prosecutor v. Furundžija* (Case No. IT-95-17/1-T), ICTY T. Ch. I, Judgment,10 December 1998). To the contrary, the latter case of *Kunarac* emphasised the element of non-consent as the most essential in establishing rape, in that it corresponds to the protection of sexual autonomy (*Prosecutor v. Kunarac, Kovac and Vukovic* (Case No. IT-96-23 and 23/122), ICTY T. Ch. I, Judgment, 22 February 2001). As to the term 'coercion' the ICTR Trial Chamber in *Prosecutor v. Akayesu* held that a coercive environment does not require physical force. It also adopted a broad approach to the *actus reus*, including also the use of objects, an approach that has been embraced also by the ICTY and the ICC (*Prosecutor v. Jean-Paul Akayesu* (Case No. ICTR-96-4-T), ICTR T. Ch. I, Judgment, 2 September 1998, para. 598).

Rule 63 is of importance which holds that the Court's Chambers cannot require corroboration to prove any crime within its jurisdiction, particularly crimes of sexual violence. Rule 70 further delineates the possibility of introducing evidence of consent as a defence. This is highly limited, emphasising that consent cannot be inferred in coercive circumstances. Rule 71 forbids evidence of prior sexual conduct.

In *Prosecutor v. Katanga and Chui*, ICC PT. Ch, Decision on the Confirmation of Charges, ICC-01/04-01/07-717, 30 September 2008, para. 347, the Pre-Trial Chamber found sufficient evidence to affirm charges of rape as a war crime. This included the invasion of the body of civilian women by the penetration of the perpetrator's sexual organ or other body parts, through force, threat or fear of violence or death (see paras. 351–52).

Cross-references:

Articles 7(1)(g) and 8(2)(e)(vi).

Doctrine:

1. Antonio Cassese, in Antonio Cassese, Paola Gaeta and John R.W.D. Jones (eds.), *The Rome Statute of the International Criminal Court: A Commentary*, Oxford University Press, Oxford, 2002, pp. 374–375.

2. Michael Bothe, in Antonio Cassese, Paola Gaeta and John R.W.D. Jones (eds.), *The Rome Statute of the International Criminal Court: A Commentary*, Oxford University Press, Oxford, 2002, pp. 415–16.

3. Machteld Boot revised by Christopher K. Hall, in Otto Triffterer (ed.), *Commentary on the Rome Statute of the International Criminal Court: Observers' Notes, Article by Article*, 2nd ed., C.H. Beck/Hart/Nomos, Munich/Oxford/Baden-Baden, 2008, pp. 206–11.

4. Michael Cottier, in Otto Triffterer (ed.), *Commentary on the Rome Statute of the International Criminal Court: Observers' Notes, Article by Article*, 2nd ed., C.H. Beck/Hart/Nomos, Munich/Oxford/Baden-Baden, 2008, pp. 431–41.

5. Gerhard Werle, *Principles of International Criminal Law*, TMC Asser Press, The Hague, 2005, pp. 248–50; 313, MN 723–27, 912–13.

6. Robert Cryer, Håkan Friman, Daryll Robinson and Elizabeth Wilmshurst, *An Introduction to International Criminal Law and Procedure*, 3rd ed., Cambridge University Press, Cambridge, 2014, p. 292.

7. Anne-Marie L.M. de Brouwer, *Supranational Criminal Prosecution of Sexual Violence: The ICC and the Practice of the ICTY and the ICTR*, Antwerp, Intersentia, 2005, pp. 199–201.

Author: Maria Sjöholm.

[106] Sexual slavery is a particular form of enslavement which includes limitations on one's autonomy, freedom of movement and power to decide matters relating to one's sexual activity. Although it is listed as a separate offence in the ICC Statute, it is regarded as a particular form of enslavement. However, whereas enslavement is solely considered a crime against humanity, sexual slavery may constitute either a war crime or a crime against humanity. It is partly based on the definition of enslavement identified as customary international law by the ICTY in the *Kunarac* case (*Prosecutor v. Kunarac, Kovac and Vukovic* (Case No. IT-96-23 and 23/1), ICTY T. Ch. I, Judgment, 22 February 2001, para. 543). Sexual slavery is thus considered a form of enslavement with a sexual component. Its definition is found in the Elements of Crimes and includes the exercise of any or all of the powers attached to the right of ownership over one or more persons, "such as by purchasing, selling, lending or bartering such a person or persons, or by imposing on them a similar deprivation of liberty". The person should have been made to engage in acts of a sexual nature. The crime also includes forced marriages, domestic servitude or other forced labour that ultimately involves forced sexual activity. In contrast to the crime of rape, which is a completed offence, sexual slavery constitutes a continuing offence. Sexual slavery as a war crime differs from the definition of sexual slavery as a crime against humanity only in terms of the context in which the crime is committed.

In *Prosecutor v. Katanga and Chui*, ICC PT. Ch. I, ICC-01/04-01/07-717, Decision on the Confirmation of Charges, 30 September 2008, para. 431. The Pre-Trial Chamber held that "sexual slavery also encompasses situations where women and girls are forced into 'marriage', domestic servitude or other forced labour involving compulsory sexual activity, including rape, by their captors. Forms of sexual slavery can, for example, be practices such as the detention of women in 'rape camps' or 'comfort stations', forced temporary 'marriages' to soldiers and other practices involving the treatment of women as chattel, and as such, violations of the peremptory norm prohibiting slavery". The Chamber found sufficient evidence to affirm charges of sexual slavery as a war crime in the form of women being abducted for the purpose of using them as wives, being forced or threatened to engage in sexual intercourse with combatants, to serve as sexual slaves and to work in military camps servicing soldiers (see para. 347).

The SCSL Appeals Chamber in the *Brima* case has found the abduction and confinement of women to constitute forced marriage and consequently a crime against humanity. The Chamber concluded that forced marriage was distinct from sexual slavery. Accordingly, "While forced marriage shares certain elements with sexual slavery such as non-consensual sex and deprivation of liberty, there are also distinguishing factors. First, forced marriage involves a perpetrator compelling a person by force or threat of force, through the words or conduct of the perpetrator or those associated with him, into a forced conjugal association with another person resulting in great suffering, or serious physical or mental injury on the part of the victim. Second, unlike sexual slavery, forced marriage implies a relationship of exclusivity between the 'husband' and 'wife', which could lead to disciplinary consequences for breach of this exclusive arrangement" (*Prosecutor v. Brima*, SCSL A. Ch., Judgment, 22 February 2008, para. 195). In 2012 the Court in a decision on the Charles Taylor case declared its preference for the term 'forced conjugal slavery'. The Trial Chamber did not find the term 'marriage' to be helpful in describing the events that had occurred, in that it did not constitute marriage in the universally understood sense (*Prosecutor v. Charles Taylor* (Case No. SCSL-03-01-T), SCSL T. Ch. II, Judgment, 18 May 2012, para. 427).

Cross-references:
Articles 7(1)(g) and 8(2)(e)(vi).

Doctrine:

1. Michael Bothe, "War Crimes", in Antonio Cassese, Paola Gaeta and John R.W.D. Jones (eds.), *The Rome Statute of the International Criminal Court: A Commentary*, Oxford University Press, Oxford, 2002, p. 415.

2. Machteld Boot, revised by Christopher K. Hall, in Otto Triffterer (ed.), *Commentary on the Rome Statute of the International Criminal Court: Observers' Notes, Article by Article*, 2nd ed., C.H. Beck/Hart/Nomos, Munich/Oxford/Baden-Baden, 2008, pp. 211–12.

3. Michael Cottier, in Otto Triffterer (ed.), *Commentary on the Rome Statute of the International Criminal Court: Observers' Notes, Article by Article*, 2nd ed., C.H. Beck/Hart/Nomos, Munich/Oxford/Baden-Baden, 2008, pp. 441–47.

4. Gerhard Werle, *Principles of International Criminal Law*, TMC Asser Press, The Hague, 2005, pp. 250–51 and 313, MN 728 and 914–16.

5. Anne-Marie L.M. de Brouwer, *Supranational Criminal Prosecution of Sexual Violence: The ICC and the Practice of the ICTY and the ICTR*, Antwerp, Intersentia, 2005, pp. 199–201.

Author: Maria Sjöholm.

[107] The Elements of Crimes requires the 1) causing or a person to engage in acts of a sexual nature 2) by force or threat of force or under coercive circumstances and 3) the perpetrator or another person obtained or expected to obtain pecuniary or other advantage in exchange for or in connection with the acts. Primarily the latter point distinguishes it from sexual slavery. It can also be distinguished in that sexual slavery requires the exercise or any or all of the powers attaching to the rights of ownership. Enforced prostitution could, however, rise to the level of sexual slavery, should the elements of both crimes exist. In comparison with rape and sexual slavery, enforced prostitution can either be a continuing offence or constitute a separate act. Enforced prostitution is prohibited in the Geneva Convention IV 1949 as an example of an attack on a woman's honour and in Additional Protocol I as an outrage upon personal dignity. Forced prostitution as a war crime differs from the definition of forced prostitution as a crime against humanity only in terms of the context in which the crime is committed.

Cross-references:
Articles 7(1)(g) and 8(2)(e)(vi).

Doctrine:

1. Michael Bothe, "War Crimes", in Antonio Cassese, Paola Gaeta and John R.W.D. Jones (eds.), *The Rome Statute of the International Criminal Court: A Commentary*, Oxford University Press, Oxford, 2002, p. 415.

2. Machteld Boot, revised by Christopher K. Hall, in Otto Triffterer (ed.), *Commentary on the Rome Statute of the International Criminal Court: Observers' Notes, Article by Article*, 2nd ed., C.H. Beck/Hart/Nomos, Munich/Oxford/Baden-Baden, 2008, pp. 212–13, MN 48–50.

3. Michael Cottier, in Otto Triffterer (ed.), *Commentary on the Rome Statute of the International Criminal Court: Observers' Notes, Article by Article*, 2nd ed., C.H. Beck/Hart/Nomos, Munich/Oxford/Baden-Baden, 2008, pp. 447–48.

4. Gerhard Werle, *Principles of International Criminal Law*, TMC Asser Press, The Hague, 2005, pp. 251, 313, MN 729–30 and 914–16.

5. Anne-Marie L.M. de Brouwer, *Supranational Criminal Prosecution of Sexual Violence: The ICC and the Practice of the ICTY and the ICTR*, Antwerp, Intersentia, 2005, pp. 199–201.

Author: Maria Sjöholm.

[108] Forced pregnancy means the unlawful confinement of a woman forcibly made pregnant. Unlawful confinement should be interpreted as any form of deprivation of physical liberty contrary to international law. The deprivation of liberty does not have to be severe and no specific time frame is required. The use of force is not required, but some form of coercion. To complete the crime, it is sufficient if the perpetrator holds a woman imprisoned who has been impregnated by someone else. The forcible impregnation may involve rape or other forms of sexual violence of comparable gravity. In addition to the mental requirements in Article 30, the perpetrator must act with the purpose of affecting the ethnic composition of any population or carrying out other grave violations of international law. National laws prohibiting abortion do not amount to forced pregnancy. Forced pregnancy as a war crime differs from the definition of forced pregnancy as a crime against humanity only in terms of the context in which the crime is committed.

Cross-references:
Articles 7(1)(g) and 8(2)(e)(vi).

Doctrine:

1. Michael Bothe, "War Crimes", in Antonio Cassese, Paola Gaeta and John R.W.D. Jones (eds.), *The Rome Statute of the International Criminal Court: A Commentary*, Oxford University Press, Oxford, 2002, p. 415.

2. Machteld Boot, revised by Christopher K. Hall, in Otto Triffterer (ed.), *Commentary on the Rome Statute of the International Criminal Court: Observers' Notes, Article by Article*, 2nd ed., C.H. Beck/Hart/Nomos, Munich/Oxford/Baden-Baden, 2008, pp. 213 and 255–56.

3. Michael Cottier, in Otto Triffterer (ed.), *Commentary on the Rome Statute of the International Criminal Court: Observers' Notes, Article by Article*, 2nd ed., C.H. Beck/Hart/Nomos, Munich/Oxford/Baden-Baden, 2008, pp. 448–51.

4. Gerhard Werle, *Principles of International Criminal Law*, TMC Asser Press, The Hague, 2005, pp. 251–52 and 313, MN 731–32 and 914–16.

5. Anne-Marie L.M. de Brouwer, *Supranational Criminal Prosecution of Sexual Violence: The ICC and the Practice of the ICTY and the ICTR*, Antwerp, Intersentia, 2005, pp. 199–201.

Author: Maria Sjöholm.

[109] Enforced sterilisation is a form of "[i]mposing measures intended to prevent births within the group" within the meaning of Article 6(e). It is carried out without the consent of a person. Genuine consent is not given when the victim has been deceived. Enforced sterilisation includes depriving a person of their biological reproductive capacity, which is not justified by the medical treatment of the person. It does not include non-permanent birth-control methods. It is not restricted to medical operations but can also include the intentional use of chemicals for this effect. It arguably includes vicious rapes where the reproductive system has been destroyed. The Elements of Crime provide a more specific definition of the criminal conduct. For the mental element Article 30 applies. Enforced sterilisation may also fall under the chapeau of genocide if such intent is present. Enforced sterilisation as a war crime differs from the definition of enforced sterilisation as a crime against humanity only in terms of the context in which the crime is committed.

Cross-references:
Articles 7(1)(g) and 8(2)(e)(vi).

Doctrine:

any other form of sexual violence[110] also constituting a grave breach of the Geneva Conventions;

---

1. Michael Bothe, "War Crimes", in Antonio Cassese, Paola Gaeta and John R.W.D. Jones (eds.), *The Rome Statute of the International Criminal Court: A Commentary*, Oxford University Press, Oxford, 2002, p. 415.

2. Machteld Boot, revised by Christopher K. Hall, in Otto Triffterer (ed.), *Commentary on the Rome Statute of the International Criminal Court: Observers' Notes, Article by Article*, 2nd ed., C.H. Beck/Hart/Nomos, Munich/Oxford/Baden-Baden, 2008, p. 213–14.

3. Michael Cottier, in Otto Triffterer (ed.), *Commentary on the Rome Statute of the International Criminal Court: Observers' Notes, Article by Article*, 2nd ed., C.H. Beck/Hart/Nomos, Munich/Oxford/Baden-Baden, 2008, p. 451.

4. Gerhard Werle, *Principles of International Criminal Law*, TMC Asser Press, The Hague, 2005, pp. 252 and 313, MN 733 and 914–16.

5. Anne-Marie L.M. de Brouwer, *Supranational Criminal Prosecution of Sexual Violence: The ICC and the Practice of the ICTY and the ICTR*, Antwerp, Intersentia, 2005, pp. 199–201.

Author: Maria Sjöholm.

[110] The provision has a catch-all character and requires that the conduct is comparable in gravity to the other acts listed in Article 8(2)(b)(xxii). It concerns acts of a sexual nature against a person through the use of force or threat of force or coercion. The importance of distinguishing the different forms of sexual violence primarily lies in the level of harm to which the victim is subjected and the degree of severity, and therefore becomes a matter of sentencing. Sexual violence as a war crime differs from crimes against humanity in terms of the context in which the crime is committed, in this case in the context of an international armed conflict.

It is generally held to include forced nudity, forced masturbation or forced touching of the body. The ICTR in *Akayesu* held that "sexual violence is not limited to physical invasion of the human body and may include acts which do not involve penetration or even physical contact" (see *Prosecutor v. Jean-Paul Akayesu* (ICTR-96-4-T), ICTR T. Ch. I, Judgment, 2 September 1998, para. 688). The Trial Chamber in the case confirmed that forced public nudity was an example of sexual violence within its jurisdiction (see para. 10 A). Similarly, the Trial Chamber of the ICTY in its *Kvocka* decision declared: "sexual violence is broader than rape and includes such crimes as sexual slavery or molestation, and also covers sexual acts that do not involve physical contact, such as forced public nudity (see *Prosecutor v. Miroslav Kvocka* (Case No. IT-98-30/1-T), ICTY T. Ch, Judgment, 2 November 2001, para. 180). To the contrary, in the decision on the Prosecutor's application for a warrant of arrest in the *Bemba* case, the Pre-Trial Chamber of the ICC did not include a charge of sexual violence as a crime against humanity in the arrest warrant, which had been based on allegations that the troops in question had forced women to undress in public in order to humiliate them, stating that "the facts submitted by the Prosecutor do not constitute other forms of sexual violence of comparable gravity to the other forms of sexual violence set forth in Article 7(1)(g)" (*Prosecutor v. Jean-Pierre Bemba Gombo*, ICC PT. Ch. III, Decision on the Prosecutor's Application for a Warrant of Arrest against Jean-Pierre Bemba Gombo, ICC-01/05-01/08), 10 June 2008, para. 40).

In the *Lubanga* case of the ICC, evidence of sexual violence was presented during the trial, including various forms of sexual abuse of girl soldiers who were forcefully conscripted. However, no charges of sexual violence were brought. The Prosecution rather encouraged the Trial Chamber to consider evidence of sexual violence as an integral element of the recruitment and use of child soldiers. In the confirmation of charges in the *Muthaura and Kenyatta* case, Pre-Trial Chamber II chose not to charge forced male circumcision and penile amputation as sexual

(xxiii) Utilizing the presence of a civilian or other protected person to render certain points, areas or military forces immune from military operations;[111]

(xxiv) Intentionally directing attacks against buildings, material, medical units and transport, and personnel using the distinctive emblems of the Geneva Conventions in conformity with international law;[112]

violence, but rather as inhumane acts. The Pre-Trial Chamber held that "the evidence placed before it does not establish the sexual nature of the acts of forcible circumcision and penile amputation. Instead, it appears from the evidence that the acts were motivated by ethnic prejudice" (*Prosecutor v. Uhuru Muigai Kenyatta and Mohammed Hussein Ali*, ICC PT. Ch, Decision on the Confirmation of Charges Pursuant to Article 61(7)(a) and (b) of the Rome Statute, ICC-01/09-02/11-382-Red, 23 January 2012, para. 266). It argued that "not every act of violence which targets parts of the body commonly associated with sexuality should be considered an act of sexual violence" (para. 265).

In *Prosecutor v. Katanga and Chui*, ICC-01/04-01/07-717, Decision on the Confirmation of Charges, 30 September 2008, para. 375 PTC I, the defendants were charged with outrages upon personal dignity, as defined in Article 8(2)(b)(xxi), rather than sexual violence for making a woman walk through town, dressed solely in a blouse, without underwear.

Cross-references:
Articles 7(1)(g) and 8(2)(e)(vi).

Doctrine:

1. Michael Bothe, "War Crimes", in Antonio Cassese, Paola Gaeta and John R.W.D. Jones (eds.), *The Rome Statute of the International Criminal Court: A Commentary*, Oxford University Press, Oxford, 2002, pp. 415–16.

2. Machteld Boot, revised by Christopher K. Hall, in Otto Triffterer (ed.), *Commentary on the Rome Statute of the International Criminal Court: Observers' Notes, Article by Article*, 2nd ed., C.H. Beck/Hart/Nomos, Munich/Oxford/Baden-Baden, 2008, pp. 214–15.

3. Michael Cottier, in Otto Triffterer (ed.), *Commentary on the Rome Statute of the International Criminal Court: Observers' Notes, Article by Article*, 2nd ed., C.H. Beck/Hart/Nomos, Munich/Oxford/Baden-Baden, 2008, pp. 451–54

4. Gerhard Werle, *Principles of International Criminal Law*, TMC Asser Press, The Hague, 2005, pp. 252–53 and 313, MN 734 and 914–16.

5. Anne-Marie L.M. de Brouwer, *Supranational Criminal Prosecution of Sexual Violence: The ICC and the Practice of the ICTY and the ICTR*, Antwerp, Intersentia, 2005, pp. 199–201.

Author: Maria Sjöholm.

[111] In addition to civilians, it is prohibited to use the presence of prisoners of war and military medical personnel as a shield. If a party violates this provision, the attacking party must still uphold the rules of humanitarian law, including the rule of proportionality and consider additional incidental casualties which may arise due to an attack. In addition to mental requirement of Article 30 the perpetrator must act to protect, aid or prevent a military objective or operation.

Doctrine:

1. Roberta Arnold, "Article 8, War Crimes", in Otto Triffterer (ed.), *Commentary on the Rome Statute of the International Criminal Court: Observers' Notes, Article by Article*, 2nd ed., C.H. Beck/Hart/Nomos, Munich/Oxford/Baden-Baden, 2008, pp. 454–56.

2. Gerhard Werle, *Principles of International Criminal Law*, TMC Asser Press, The Hague, 2005, pp. 365–67, MN 1090–94.

Author: Mark Klamberg.

(xxv) Intentionally using starvation of civilians as a method of warfare by depriving them of objects indispensable to their survival, including wilfully impeding relief supplies as provided for under the Geneva Conventions;[113]

(xxvi) Conscripting or enlisting children under the age of fifteen years into the national armed forces or using them to participate actively in hostilities.[114]

---

[112] The term 'attack' corresponds to the offence of attacks on a civilian population (Article 8(2)(b)(i)). The recognised emblems are the emblem of the Red Cross, the red crescent, the red lion and the sun and the red crystal (the third additional Protocol).

Cross-references:
Articles 8(2)(b)(i) and 8(2)(e)(ii).

Doctrine:

1. Roberta Arnold, "Article 8, War Crimes", in Otto Triffterer (ed.), *Commentary on the Rome Statute of the International Criminal Court: Observers' Notes, Article by Article*, 2nd ed., C.H. Beck/Hart/Nomos, Munich/Oxford/Baden-Baden, 2008, pp. 456–58.

2. Gerhard Werle, *Principles of International Criminal Law*, TMC Asser Press, The Hague, 2005, pp. 348–49, MN 1035–38.

Author: Mark Klamberg.

[113] In addition to deprivation of food, the term 'starvation' may include non-food objects indispensible to the survival of civilians, for example, medicines, blankets or clothing. Acts prohibited under this provision may also be covered by Articles 6(c); 7(1)(b), (j)and (k); 7(2)(b); 8(2)(a)(iii); 8(2)(b)(ii), (v) and (xiii). Starvation can take many forms, including removal or destruction of essential supplies, the prevention of the production of food, impeding relief supplies, and not fulfilling a duty under international law to provide supplies. In addition to mental requirement of Article 30 the perpetrator must intend to starve civilians as a method of warfare.

Cross-references:
Articles 6(c); 7(1)(b), (j)and (k); 7(2)(b); 8(2)(a)(iii); 8(2)(b)(ii), (v) and (xiii).

Doctrine:

1. Michael Cottier, in Otto Triffterer (ed.), *Commentary on the Rome Statute of the International Criminal Court: Observers' Notes, Article by Article*, 2nd ed., C.H. Beck/Hart/Nomos, Munich/Oxford/Baden-Baden, 2008, pp. 458–66.

2. Gerhard Werle, *Principles of International Criminal Law*, TMC Asser Press, The Hague, 2005, pp. 362–65, MN 1081–87.

Author: Mark Klamberg.

[114] *General remarks*:

Article 8(2)(b)(xxvi) concerns the conscription, recruitment or use of children younger than 15 years of age, in the context of an international conflict. The crime also appears in Article 8(2)(b)(vii) to cover the same crime in the context of an internal conflict. The act of conscripting or enlisting a child under the age of 15 years into a national or non-governmental force is therefore a crime, regardless of whether it is committed in the context of an international or internal armed conflict.

Preparatory works:

As the practice of child soldier recruitment/conscription/use had not been previously expressly recognised as criminalised, its inclusion was naturally a controversial point of debate during Statute negotiations. The United States in particular was against the inclusion of the crime, arguing that it was not a crime under customary international law and represented an area of legislative action "outside the purview of the Conference" (Committee of the Whole Meeting Records,

---

4th meeting (Wednesday, 17 June 1998), 54). However, agreement on inclusion was eventually reached due to its position as a well-established treaty law provision (Additional Protocol I, Article 77(2); Additional Protocol II, Article 4(3)(c) and Convention on the Rights of the Child, Article 38(3)). In 2002 the crime was included as a serious violation of international humanitarian law in Article 4(c) of the Statute of the Special Court for Sierra Leone (Statute of the Special Court for Sierra Leone, UN doc. S/2002/246). In a split decision in May 2004, the Special Court held that the provision was already customary international law prior to the adoption of the ICC Statute in 1998; that is to say that the Statute codified an existing customary norm rather than forming a new one (*Prosecutor v. Sam Hinga Norman* (SCSL-04-14-AR72) SCSL App. Ch, Fourth Defence Preliminary Motion Based on Lack of Jurisdiction (Child Recruitment), 31 May 2004).

Analysis:

i. Definition

According to Article 8(2)(b)(xxvi) the crime has three components: recruitment, conscription or use. This is in contrast to both Additional Protocol I and Article 38 of the Convention on the Rights of the Child, which make reference to the singular act of 'recruiting'. The Elements of Crime provide further:

1. The perpetrator conscripted or enlisted one or more persons into the national armed forces or used one or more persons to participate actively in hostilities.
2. Such person or persons were under the age of 15 years.
3. The perpetrator knew or should have known that such person or persons were under the age of 15 years.
4. The conduct took place in the context of and was associated with an international armed conflict.
5. The perpetrator was aware of factual circumstances that established the existence of an armed conflict.

The Pre-Trial Chamber in *Prosecutor v. Thomas Lubanga* determined that the term 'conscripting' refers to a forcible act, 'enlisting' encompasses a 'voluntary' decision to join a military force, and the act of 'enlisting' includes "any conduct accepting the child as part of the militia" (*Prosecutor v. Thomas Dyilo Lubanga*, ICC T. Ch. I, ICC-01/04-01/06, Decision on the Confirmation of Charges, 29 January 2007).

ii. Consent of the child as a mitigating factor

While alleged voluntariness may be negated by force or intimidation, the consent of the child creates the legal characterisation of the conduct as enlistment rather than conscription. Consent is therefore not irrelevant, but nonetheless places the admission of a child to the armed forces firmly within the realm of Article 8 regardless of the means of admission. The specific mode of admission, whether "the result of governmental policy, individual initiative or acquiescence in demands to enlist" (Happold, 2006, p. 8) is, for the most part irrelevant. Happold suggests that this distinction between the means of committing the material element of this crime may become pertinent during sentencing (*ibid.*, p. 12). In its judgment in *Prosecutor v. Thomas Lubanga Dyilo* the ICC Trial Chamber intimated that it would follow this path when determining the sentence, but found no aggravating factors when delivering the sentencing order on 10 July 2012, instead finding that the factors that are relevant for determining the gravity of the crime cannot additionally be taken into account as aggravating circumstances (*Prosecutor v. Thomas Lubanga*, ICC T. Ch. I, Judgment pursuant to Article 74 of the Statute, ICC-01/04-01/06-2842, 14 March 2012, para. 617; *Prosecutor v. Thomas Lubanga*, ICC T. Ch, Sentencing Order, ICC-01/04-01/06-2901, 10 July 2012, paras. 78 and 96).

iii. Continuing crime

There are a number of different ways in which these two concepts are interrelated or occur concurrently in the context of the crime. Conscription and enlistment can be viewed as continuing crimes that begin from the moment a child joins an armed group and end upon demobilisation or attainment of 15 years of age, with all intermittent time additionally constituting 'use'. This is therefore a continuing crime: a state of affairs where a crime has been committed and then maintained. The crime is committed from the moment that a child is entered into an armed force or group, through enlistment or conscription, and continues for as long as that child remains a 'child soldier', ending either through demobilisation or the attainment of 15 years of age. This places liability on the person who recruited the child, whether by enlisting or conscripting, regardless of whether they were involved in the 'use' of the child in an armed conflict. The act of recruitment triggers responsibility for all subsequent use, even if by other commanders. An alternative interpretation is that the crime is not a composite one, as it is capable of being committed by either the initial conscription or enlistment step, or through the subsequent 'use' of the given child, and not necessarily through demonstrating a combination of the two. This expands the liability for the crime to incorporate not just the person who actually undertakes the recruitment process of a given child, but also includes others who later use the child for military purposes.

iii. Requirements

In addition to the contextual elements required for all war crimes of an international nature set out in elements 4 and 5 of the above-listed Elements of Crimes, the following needs to be proven.

a. Material elements

The first two elements listed above set out the material elements of child soldier conscription/enlistment/use:

1. The perpetrator conscripted or enlisted one or more persons into the national armed forces or used one or more persons to participate actively in hostilities.
2. Such person or persons were under the age of 15 years.
3. The perpetrator knew or should have known that such person or persons were under the age of 15 years.

The war crimes established by the ICC Statute are limited to the conscription or enlistment and use of children under the age of fifteen years. However, the acts of 'conscription' and 'enlistment' are not defined in the Statute, nor in the Elements of Crimes, leaving elaboration to judicial interpretation. The Pre-Trial Chamber (*Prosecutor v. Lubanga*, ICC PT. Ch, Decision on the Confirmation of Charges, ICC-01/04-01/06, 29 January 2007, paras. 246–247) determined that the term 'conscripting' refers to a forcible act, whereas 'enlisting' encompasses a 'voluntary' decision to join a military force. The act of 'enlisting' includes "any conduct accepting the child as part of the militia" (*Prosecutor v. Lubanga*, Decision on the Confirmation of Charges, para. 114). While alleged voluntariness may be negated by force or intimidation, the consent of the child creates the legal characterisation of the conduct as enlistment rather than conscription. Consent is therefore not irrelevant, but nonetheless places the admission of a child to the armed forces firmly within the realm of Article 8 regardless of the means of admission.

Finally, Participation by combatant and non-combatant children are covered equally by the ICC Statute due to its use of the term 'participate actively'. However, their participation must be within the context of an armed conflict. The Elements of Crime require that the participation be conduct "associated with an armed conflict", while the *travaux préparatoires* noted above specifies that participation in the armed confrontations is not necessary, but a link to combat is required (UN doc. A/CONF.183/2/Add.1, 14 April 1998).

(c) In the case of an armed conflict not of an international character, serious violations of article 3 common to the four Geneva Conventions of 12 August 1949, namely, any of the following acts committed against persons taking no active part in the hostilities, including members of armed forces who have laid down their arms and those placed hors de combat by sickness, wounds, detention or any other cause:[115]

---

b. Mental elements

While Article 30(3) provides that a perpetrator must have had positive knowledge of the child's age, the Elements of Crimes merely require that he "knew or should have known" that the child was under 15. In *Prosecutor v. Lubanga* it was determined that the Elements of Crimes provides for situations where the perpetrator fails to possess knowledge of the given child's age due to a failure to exercise due diligence in the circumstances (*Prosecutor v. Lubanga*, Decision on the Confirmation of Charges, para. 348). Therefore, the Pre-Trial Chamber considered this element of negligence to be an exception to the "intent and knowledge" standard provided in Article 30(1).

Cross-references:
Article 8(2)(e)(vii).

Doctrine:

1. Julie McBride, *The War Crime of Child Soldier Recruitment*, Springer, New York, 2013.

2. Matthew Happold, "Child Recruitment as a Crime under the Rome Statute of the International Criminal Court", in José Doria, Hans-Peter Gasser and M. Cherif Bassiouni (eds.), *The Legal Regime of the International Criminal Court: Essays in Memory of Igor Blischenko*, Brill, Leiden, 2009.

3. Gerhard Werle, *Principles of International Criminal Law*, TMC Asser Press, The Hague, 2009.

Author: Julie McBride.

[115] *General remarks*:

Two provisions in the ICC Statute relate to war crimes committed in non-international armed conflict, sub-paragraphs (c) and (e). A literal interpretation of these sub-paragraphs shows that there are two thresholds of applicability, that is, two types of non-international armed conflicts. However, it seems that the Court does not distinguish between the two types of non-international armed conflicts (*Prosecutor v. Bemba*, ICC PT. Ch. II, Decision Pursuant to Article 61(7)(a) and (b) of the Rome Statute on the Charges of the Prosecutor Against Jean-Pierre Bemba Gombo, ICC-01/05-01/08-424, 15 June 2009, paras. 216 and 224; *Prosecutor v. Mbarushimana*, ICC PT. Ch. I, Decision on the Confirmation of Charges, ICC-01/04-01/10-465-Red, 16 December 2011, para. 103). This may be so because the sub-paragraph (d) (which explains sub-paragraph (c)) threshold appears lower, not requiring the conflict to be protracted. For example in *Katanga* the ICC only refers to Article 8(2)(f) to characterise the nature of the conflict (*Prosecutor v. Katanga*, ICC T. Ch. II, Jugement, ICC-01/04-01/07-3436, 7 March 2014, paras. 1183-1187) and yet probes offences under Article 8(2)(c) (*Katanga*, ICC T. Ch. II, Jugement, ICC-01/04-01/07-3436, 7 March 2014, para. 1231).

Sub-paragraph (c) must be read in conjunction with Article 8(2)(d) as the latter removes specific situations from its scope of application. As a result, the following situations are not covered by sub-paragraph (c):

• International armed conflicts. This explains why the assessment of the characterisation of the conflict under Article 8(2)(c) takes place in a wider discussion, notably in contradistinction to international armed conflicts (see Article 8(2)(a) ICC Statute). The problem may arise in particular in armed conflicts where there is fighting between governmental forces on one side and organised armed groups on the other where at the same time a third State is involved in the conflict intervening in support of the organised armed groups. The way the Court distinguishes between a non-international and an international armed conflict is by using the "overall control" test as opposed to the "effective control" test that was established by the International Court of Justice in the *Nicaragua Case* (*Case Concerning the Military and Paramilitary Activities in and Against Nicaragua* (*Nicaragua v. United States*), ICJ Merits, Judgment, 27 June 1986, para. 115). The 'overall control' test was devised and developed by the ICTY (*Prosecutor v. Tadić* (Case No. IT-94-1-I), ICTY A. Ch., Decision on the Defence Motion for Interlocutory Appeal on Jurisdiction, 2 October 1995, para. 137) and readily adopted by the ICC (*Prosecutor v. Lubanga*, ICC PT. Ch. I, Decision on the Confirmation of Charges, ICC-01/04-01/06-803, 29 January 2007, para. 211; *Prosecutor v. Lubanga*, ICC T. Ch. I, Judgment, ICC-01/04-01/06, 14 March 2012, para. 541; *Katanga*, ICC T. Ch. II, Jugement, ICC-01/04-01/07-3436, 7 March 2014, para. 1178).

- Internal disturbances and tensions. This is confirmed by Article 8(3) which clearly states to "Nothing in paragraph 2 (c) and (e) shall affect the responsibility of a Government to maintain or re-establish law and order in the State or to defend the unity and territorial integrity of the State, by all legitimate means". The aim of this Article is to ensure that acts committed in times of internal disturbances and tensions are not to be prosecuted as war crimes.

Analysis:

Article 8(2)(c) reads: "In the case of an armed conflict not of an international character, serious violations of Article 3 common to the four Geneva Conventions of 12 August 1949, namely, any of the following acts committed against persons taking no active part in the hostilities, including members of armed forces who have laid down their arms and those placed hors de combat by sickness, wounds, detention or any other cause".

i) Scope of Application: Existence of an Armed Conflict not of an International Character

For this sub-provision to apply the ICC must determine that the acts were committed in the context of an armed conflict not of an international character, which means that the Court will examine 1) whether the conflict is international or has been internationalised, and then 2) whether a number of criteria to consider the events as a non-international armed conflict are fulfilled (see *Bemba*, ICC PT. Ch. II, Decision Pursuant to Article 61(7)(a) and (b) of the Rome Statute on the Charges of the Prosecutor Against Jean-Pierre Bemba Gombo, ICC-01/05-01/08-424, 15 June 2009, paras. 220–37).

In *Bemba*, the Court after reviewing the limits set by the ICC Statute to Article 8(2)(c) and (e) by Article 8(2)(d) and (f) respectively (*Bemba*, ICC PT. Ch. II, Decision Pursuant to Article 61(7)(a) and (b) of the Rome Statute on the Charges of the Prosecutor Against Jean-Pierre Bemba Gombo, ICC-01/05-01/08-424, 15 June 2009, paras. 224–226), Common Article 3 (*Bemba*, ICC PT. Ch. II, ICC-01/05-01/08-424, 15 June 2009, para. 227), AP II (*Bemba*, ICC PT. Ch. II, ICC-01/05-01/08-424, 15 June 2009, para. 228), the ICTY case law (*Bemba*, ICC PT. Ch. II, ICC-01/05-01/08-424, 15 June 2009, para. 229 referring to *Tadić*, ICTY A. Ch., Decision on the Defence Motion for Interlocutory Appeal on Jurisdiction, 2 October 1995, para. 70) and ICTR case law (*Bemba*, ICC PT. Ch. II, ICC-01/05-01/08-424, 15 June 2009, para. 230 referring to *Prosecutor v. Akayesu* (Case No. ICTR-96-4-T), ICTR Ch. I, Judgment, 2 September 1998, para. 620) states that a non-international armed conflict is characterised by the following elements (*Bemba*, ICC PT. Ch. II, ICC-01/05-01/08-424, 15 June 2009, para. 231):

1) The armed hostilities reach "a certain level of intensity, exceeding that of internal disturbances and tensions, such as riots, isolated acts of violence or other acts of a similar nature" (see also *Mbarushimana*, ICC PT. Ch. I, Decision on the Confirmation of Charges, ICC-01/04-01/10-465-Red, 16 December 2011, para. 103);

2) The armed hostilities take "place within the confines of a State territory" (see also *Mbarushimana*, ICC PT. Ch. I, ICC-01/04-01/10-465-Red, 16 December 2011, para. 103);

3) The armed hostilities break out either "between government authorities and organised dissident armed groups" or "between such groups" (see also *Mbarushimana*, ICC PT. Ch. I, ICC-01/04-01/10-465-Red, 16 December 2011, para. 103). While sub-paragraph (d) does not refer to two opposing sides to the conflict the ICC in *Bemba* explained that this element also applies as a matter of customary law (*Bemba*, ICC PT. Ch. II, Decision Pursuant to Article 61(7)(a) and (b) of the Rome Statute on the Charges of the Prosecutor Against Jean-Pierre Bemba Gombo, ICC-01/05-01/08-424, 15 June 2009, para. 232). The notion of "organised armed group" is understood as covering armed groups that

   a) have the ability to plan and carry out military operations for a prolonged period of time (*Prosecutor v. Lubanga*, ICC PT. Ch. I, Decision on the Confirmation of Charges, ICC-01/04-01/06-803, 29 January 2007, para. 234; *Bemba*, ICC PT. Ch. II, ICC-01/05-01/08-424, 15 June 2009, para. 233). The existence of a centre that coordinates the operations of the different actors attests to the group's ability to plan and carry out military operations (*Bemba*, ICC PT. Ch. II, ICC-01/05-01/08-424, 15 June 2009, para. 259); and

   b) must be under responsible command. This notably entails the capacity to impose discipline and the ability to plan and carry out military operations (*Lubanga*, ICC PT. Ch. I, Decision on the Confirmation of Charges, ICC-01/04-01/06-803, 29 January 2007, para. 232; *Bemba*, ICC PT. Ch. II, ICC-01/05-01/08-424, 15 June 2009, para. 234). The group must have a hierarchical structure and a high level of internal organisation (*Mbarushimana*, ICC PT. Ch. I, Decision on the Confirmation of Charges, ICC-01/04-01/10-465-Red, 16 December 2011, para. 104) which means that a group that is structured like a conventional army easily fulfils this requirement (*Bemba*, ICC PT. Ch. II, ICC-01/05-01/08-424, 15 June 2009, paras. 258 and 261). Constitutive instruments as well as the existence and knowledge by the members of the group of disciplinary and military codes demonstrate that the group has an internal disciplinary system (*Mbarushimana*, ICC PT. Ch. I, ICC-01/04-01/10-465-Red, 16 December 2011, para. 104; *Bemba*, ICC PT. Ch. II, ICC-01/05-01/08-424, 15 June 2009, para. 261).

It is unclear whether the requirement of "protracted armed conflict" that is expressly mentioned in sub-paragraph (f) as a limitation to sub-paragraph (e) also applies as a limitation to sub-paragraph (c). A literal approach of the ICC Statute would conclude that there is no need for an Article 8(2)(c) conflict to be protracted. However the ICC in *Bemba* raised the issue, without answering it properly; it circumvented the issue by stating that the conflict it was examining appeared to fulfil the "higher or additional threshold" of being protracted under Article 8(2)(e) combined with Article 8(2)(f) and thus there was no need to discuss the applicability of this threshold to Article 8(2)(c) (*Bemba*, ICC PT. Ch. II, Decision Pursuant to Article 61(7)(a) and (b) of the Rome Statute on the Charges of the Prosecutor Against Jean-Pierre Bemba Gombo, ICC-01/05-01/08-424, 15 June 2009, para. 235). In *Mbarushimana* the ICC simply mentioned the requirement of 'protracted' without giving any justification for its application (*Mbarushimana*, ICC PT. Ch. I, Decision on the Confirmation of Charges, ICC-01/04-01/10-465-Red, 16 December 2011, para. 103). That being said there is no requirement under the ICC Statute for the armed group "to exert control over a part of the territory" (*Bemba*, ICC PT. Ch. II, ICC-01/05-01/08-424, 15 June 2009, para. 236).

Since 2012 the Court has consistently defined a non-international armed conflict by reference to Article 8(2)(e) and (f) and it is unclear what has happened to the *Bemba* and *Mbarushimana* jurisprudence. The commentaries of sub-paragraphs (e) and (f) examine in detail the current state of the law regarding the definition of a non-international armed conflict.

ii) Serious Violations of Article 3 Common to the four Geneva Conventions of 12 August 1949
As specified in Article 8(2)(c) and acknowledged by the case law (*Katanga*, ICC T. Ch. II, Jugement, ICC-01/04-01/07-3436, 7 March 2014, para. 785) the crimes listed thereunder are the acts specified under (a), (b), (c) and (d) of Common Article 3(1) of the Geneva Conventions, though not in the same order. Such crimes are also prohibited under customary international law all the more as Common Article 3 is viewed as a "mandatory minimum code applicable to internal conflict" (*Prosecutor v. Delalic* (Case No. IT-96-21-A), ICTY A. Ch., Judgment, 20 February 2001, para. 140).

iii) Acts Committed against Persons Taking No Active Part in the Hostilities
The offences listed in Article 8(2)(c) must be committed against persons taking no active part in the hostilities and these include "members of armed forces who have laid down their arms and those placed hors de combat by sickness, wounds, detention or any other cause". As the word 'including' is used it means that this list is only illustrative. Indeed, the Elements of Crime refers to "persons [who are] either hors de combat, or [...] civilians, medical personnel, or religious personnel taking no active part in the hostilities" (Elements of Crimes, Article 8, p. 33; see also *Katanga*, ICC T. Ch. II, Jugement, ICC-01/04-01/07-3436, 7 March 2014, para. 786)

The ICC examines the status of individuals on a case-by-case basis, as a constituent element of the offences (*Bemba*, ICC PT. Ch. II, Decision Pursuant to Article 61(7)(a) and (b) of the Rome Statute on the Charges of the Prosecutor Against Jean-Pierre Bemba Gombo, ICC-01/05-01/08-424, 15 June 2009, para. 237). Some general comments can however be made.

In *Katanga*, the ICC, after noting that while Article 8(2)(c) refers to 'direct participation' the Elements of Crimes use the terminology of 'active participation', explains that as Article 8(2)(c) reflects offences under Common Article 3 the concept that applies under Article 8(2)(c) is that of 'direct participation', an interpretation further supported by the case law of the ICTY and ICTR that does not distinguish between 'direct' and 'active' participation (*Katanga*, ICC T. Ch. II, Jugement, ICC-01/04-01/07-3436, 7 March 2014, para. 789). In other words persons protected under Article 8(2)(c) only lose their protection if they take a direct, rather, than an active part in the hostilities and for the duration of their participation (*Katanga*, ICC T. Ch. II, Jugement, ICC-01/04-01/07-3436, 7 March 2014, para. 790). In the absence of a treaty or customary definition of direct participation in hostilities, the ICC uses the Commentary to Article 13(3) AP II that states that these are "acts of war that by their nature or purpose struck at the personnel and 'matériel' of enemy armed forces" (*Katanga*, ICC T. Ch. II, Jugement, ICC-01/04-01/07-3436, 7 March 2014, para. 790).

The persons specifically included in the list in Article 8(2)(c) are known as persons hors de combat, that is, members of the armed forces who have surrendered and/or are sick, wounded or detained. While it is clear that those who have surrendered or are detained are no threat to the opposing party anymore and thus hors de combat it must be noted that under international humanitarian law combatants who are sick or wounded are only considered hors de combat if they refrain from hostile conduct (Yves Sandoz *et al* (eds.), *Commentary on the Additional Protocols to the Geneva Conventions*, Martinus Nijhoff, Geneva, 1987, para. 1409). So far the ICC has not had the opportunity to examine any such cases.

The Elements of Crime further refer to:

- civilians who have been defined in *Katanga* as persons who are not members of State and non-State armed forces (*Katanga*, ICC T. Ch. II, Jugement, ICC-01/04-01/07-3436, 7 March 2014, paras. 788 and 801). The cases presented to the ICC were rather straight forward in the sense that there was no doubt that the civilians were not taking part in the hostilities and therefore the Court did not have to apply the aforementioned test of 'direct' participation. It should be noted that under Common Article 3 and customary law the adjectives 'wounded' and 'sick' also apply to civilians.

- medical and religious personnel, the latter being defined as "non-confessional non-combatant military personnel carrying out a similar function" (Elements of Crimes, Article 8, fn. 56)

iv) Awareness

The ICC Statute requires the "awareness of the factual circumstances that established the existence of an armed conflict that is implicit in the terms 'took place in the context of and was associated with'", that is, there must be a nexus between the act and the conflict (Elements of Crimes, Article 8, p. 34; *Bemba*, ICC PT. Ch. II, Decision Pursuant to Article 61(7)(a) and (b) of the Rome Statute on the Charges of the Prosecutor Against Jean-Pierre Bemba Gombo, ICC-01/05-01/08-424, 15 June 2009, para. 263; *Katanga*, ICC T. Ch. II, Jugement, ICC-01/04-01/07-3436, 7 March 2014, paras. 791, 794, 1176 and 1231). Further the perpetrator must be aware that the acts were perpetrated in the context of a non-international armed conflict (Elements of Crimes, Article 8, p. 34).

What is more the perpetrator must be aware of "the factual circumstances that established the [status of the persons against whom the acts were committed]" (Elements of Crime, Article 8, p. 34). In other words, the perpetrator could easily draw from the circumstances that the individuals had, for example, civilian status (see, for example, *Mbarushimana*, ICC PT. Ch. I, Decision on the Confirmation of Charges, ICC-01/04-01/10-465-Red, 16 December 2011, paras. 191 and 219).

Cross-references:

Article 8(2)(e).

Doctrine:

1. Dapo Akande, "Classification of Armed Conflicts: Relevant Legal Concepts", in Elizabeth Wilmhurst (ed.), *International Law and the Classification of Conflicts,* Oxford University Press, Oxford, 2012, pp. 32–79.

2. Michael Bothe, "War Crimes", in Antonio Cassese, Paola Gaeta and John R.W.D. Jones (eds.), *The Rome Statute of the International Criminal Court: A Commentary,* Oxford University Press, Oxford, 2002, pp. 417–18.

3. Antonio Cassese, Paola Gaeta and John R.W.D. Jones (eds.), *International Criminal Law,* Oxford University Press, Oxford, 2013, pp. 62–83.

4. Robert Cryer, Håkan Friman, Daryll Robinson and Elizabeth Wilmshurst, *An Introduction to International Criminal Law and Procedure*, 3rd ed., Cambridge University Press, Cambridge, 2014, pp. 264–84.

5. Anthony Cullen, "War Crimes", in William A. Schabas and Nadia Bernaz (eds.), *Routledge Handbook of International Criminal Law*, Routledge, London, 2011, pp. 139–54.

6. Knut Dörmann, *Elements of War Crimes under the Rome Statute of the International Criminal Court*, Cambridge University Press, Cambridge, 2002, pp. 382–93.

7. Leena Grover, *Interpreting Crimes in the Rome Statute of the International Criminal Court*, Cambridge University Press, Cambridge, 2014, pp. 279–85.

8. William A. Schabas, *An Introduction to the International Criminal Court*, Cambridge University Press, Cambridge, 2011, pp. 142–44.

9. William A. Schabas, *The International Criminal Court: A Commentary on the Rome Statute*, Oxford University Press, Oxford, 2010, pp. 188–257.

10. Sandesh Sivakumaran, *The Law of Non-International Armed Conflict*, Oxford University Press, Oxford, 2014, pp. 192–95, 273–80.

(i) Violence to life and person, in particular murder of all kinds,[116] mutilation,[117] cruel treatment[118] and torture;[119]

---

11. Andreas Zimmermann, "Article 8, War Crimes", in Otto Triffterer (ed.), *Commentary on the Rome Statute of the International Criminal Court: Observers' Notes, Article by Article*, 2nd ed., C.H. Beck/Hart/Nomos, Munich/Oxford/Baden-Baden, 2008, pp. 476–88.

Author: Noëlle Quénivet.

[116] The term 'killed' in the Elements of Crime is interchangeable with the term 'caused death'. The *mens rea* for murder is neither fully clarified in the present provision nor in the Elements of Crime. The standard of Article 30 applies to mental element. The main question is whether to apply the common law concept of 'wilful blindness' and 'recklessness' or civil law concepts such as *dolus eventualis*. During the negotiations of the Statute and the Elements of Crime it was decided to leave such details for the Court to interpret Article 30. Murder as a war crime differs from the definition of murder as a crime against humanity only in terms of the context in which the crime is committed.

Cross-references:
Article 7(1)(a) and 8(2)(a)(i).

Doctrine:
1. Michael Bothe, "War Crimes", in Antonio Cassese, Paola Gaeta and John R.W.D. Jones (eds.), *The Rome Statute of the International Criminal Court: A Commentary*, Oxford University Press, Oxford, 2002, p. 419.
2. Christopher K. Hall, Andreas Zimmerman, in Otto Triffterer (ed.), *Commentary on the Rome Statute of the International Criminal Court: Observers' Notes, Article by Article*, 2nd ed., C.H. Beck/Hart/Nomos, Munich/Oxford/Baden-Baden, 2008, pp. 183–90, 489.
3. Gerhard Werle, *Principles of International Criminal Law*, TMC Asser Press, The Hague, 2009, pp. 232–33 MN 674–77, pp. 302–3 MN 875–78.

Author: Mark Klamberg.

[117] The term 'mutilation' should be understood to have synonymous meaning as 'physical mutilation' in Article 8(2)(b)(x), covering acts such as amputations, injury to limbs, removal of organs, and forms of sexual mutilations. The victim's consent is not an excusable defence.

Cross-references: :
Article 8(2)(b)(x) and 8(2)(e)(xi).

Doctrine:
1. Michael Bothe, "War Crimes", in Antonio Cassese, Paola Gaeta and John R.W.D. Jones (eds.), *The Rome Statute of the International Criminal Court: A Commentary*, Oxford University Press, Oxford, 2002, pp. 395–97; 419.
2. Andreas Zimmerman, in Otto Triffterer (ed.), *Commentary on the Rome Statute of the International Criminal Court: Observers' Notes, Article by Article*, 2nd ed., C.H. Beck/Hart/Nomos, Munich/Oxford/Baden-Baden, 2008, pp. 489–90.
3. Gerhard Werle, *Principles of International Criminal Law*, TMC Asser Press, The Hague, 2009, pp. 307–8, MN 895–97.

Author: Mark Klamberg.

[118] The offence of cruel treatment carries the same meaning as inhuman treatment (Article 8(2)(a)(ii), namely the infliction of severe physical or mental pain or suffering upon one or more persons. The protected interest is the human dignity. For the mental element Article 30 applies.

In *Prosecutor v. Katanga and Chui*, ICC-01/04-01/07-717, Decision on the Confirmation of Charges, 30 September 2008, para. 364, PTC I was of the "that there is sufficient evidence to

---

(ii) Committing outrages upon personal dignity, in particular humiliating and degrading treatment;[120]

---

establish substantial grounds to believe that the war crime of inhuman treatment, as defined in Article 8(2)(a)(ii) of the Statute".

Cross-references:
Articles 7(1)(k) and Article 8(2)(a)(ii).

Doctrine:

1. Michael Bothe, "War Crimes", in Antonio Cassese, Paola Gaeta and John R.W.D. Jones (eds.), *The Rome Statute of the International Criminal Court: A Commentary*, Oxford University Press, Oxford, 2002, pp. 392–93, 419.

2. Andreas Zimmerman, in Otto Triffterer (ed.), *Commentary on the Rome Statute of the International Criminal Court: Observers' Notes, Article by Article*, 2nd ed., C.H. Beck/Hart/Nomos, Munich/Oxford/Baden-Baden, 2008, p. 205–6, 490.

3. Gerhard Werle, *Principles of International Criminal Law*, TMC Asser Press, The Hague, 2009, pp. 310–11, MN 903–6.

Author: Mark Klamberg.

[119] Torture is the infliction of severe physical or mental pain or suffering upon one or more persons. The standard for torture is set in the Torture Convention. In contrast to the aforementioned convention, it is not necessary that perpetrator acted in an official capacity. The Elements of Crime provide a non-exclusive listing of which purposes the torture serve, which distinguishes it from torture as a crime against humanity which does not require a purpose.

Cross-references:
Articles 7(1)(f) and 8(2)(a)(ii).

Doctrine:

1. Michael Bothe, in Antonio Cassese, Paola Gaeta and John R.W.D. Jones (eds.), *The Rome Statute of the International Criminal Court: A Commentary*, Oxford University Press, Oxford, 2002, pp. 392–93, 419.

2. William J. Fenrick and Andreas Zimmerman, in Otto Triffterer (ed.), *Commentary on the Rome Statute of the International Criminal Court: Observers' Notes, Article by Article*, 2nd ed., C.H. Beck/Hart/Nomos, Munich/Oxford/Baden-Baden, 2008, pp. 205–6, 490.

3. Gerhard Werle, *Principles of International Criminal Law*, TMC Asser Press, The Hague, 2009, pp. 305–6, MN 887–90.

Author: Mark Klamberg.

[120] The humiliating and degrading treatment is prohibited even if the victim overcomes the consequences relatively quickly. In *Prosecutor v. Katanga and Chui*, ICC-01/04-01/07-717, Decision on the Confirmation of Charges, 30 September 2008, para. 369, PTC I quoted ICTY jurisprudence when it stated that "there is no requirement that such suffering be lasting". There is no special intent requirement in addition to the general requirement of Article 30. The wording of the provision is identical to Article 8(2)(b)(xxi).

Cross-references:
Articles 7(1)(c) and 8(2)(b)(xxi).

Doctrine:

1. Michael Bothe, in Antonio Cassese, Paola Gaeta and John R.W.D. Jones (eds.), *The Rome Statute of the International Criminal Court: A Commentary*, Oxford University Press, Oxford, 2002, pp. 414–15, 419.

(iii)   Taking of hostages;[121]

(iv)   The passing of sentences and the carrying out of executions without previous judgement pronounced by a regularly constituted court, affording all judicial guarantees which are generally recognized as indispensable.[122]

---

2.   Patricia Viseur Sellers, in Otto Triffterer (ed.), *Commentary on the Rome Statute of the International Criminal Court: Observers' Notes, Article by Article*, 2nd ed., C.H. Beck/Hart/Nomos, Munich/Oxford/Baden-Baden, 2008, pp. 425–31.

3.   Gerhard Werle, *Principles of International Criminal Law*, TMC Asser Press, The Hague, 2009, pp. 314–16, MN 917–23.

4.   Andreas Zimmerman, in Otto Triffterer (ed.), *Commentary on the Rome Statute of the International Criminal Court: Observers' Notes, Article by Article*, 2nd ed., C.H. Beck/Hart/Nomos, Munich/Oxford/Baden-Baden, 2008, p. 491.

Author: Mark Klamberg.

[121]   Hostage taking involves the seizure and detainment of one or more protected persons and a threat to kill, injure or continue to detain such person or persons. In addition to the general mental requirement in Article 30 the purpose of the hostage taking is to compel a State, an international organisation, a natural or legal person or a group of persons to act or refrain from acting as an explicit or implicit condition for the safety or the release of such person or persons. The wording of the provision is identical to Article 8(2)(a)(viii).

Cross-references:
Article 8(2)(a)(viii).

Doctrine:

1.   Michael Bothe, in Antonio Cassese, Paola Gaeta and John R.W.D. Jones (eds.), *The Rome Statute of the International Criminal Court: A Commentary*, Oxford University Press, Oxford, 2002, pp. 395, 419.

2.   Andreas Zimmerman, in Otto Triffterer (ed.), *Commentary on the Rome Statute of the International Criminal Court: Observers' Notes, Article by Article*, 2nd ed., C.H. Beck/Hart/Nomos, Munich/Oxford/Baden-Baden, 2008, p. 491.

3.   Gerhard Werle, *Principles of International Criminal Law*, TMC Asser Press, The Hague, 2009, pp. 325–27, MN 958–62.

Author: Mark Klamberg.

[122]   The provision guarantees certain minimum due process rights before a sentence is passed or an execution against a protected person takes place. The Elements of Crime distinguishes three separate criminal acts, namely 1) there was no previous judgment pronounced by a court, 2) the court was not regularly constituted, and 3) the court that rendered judgment did not afford other generally recognised judicial guarantees. The provision offers similar, but not identical protection as Article 8(2)(a)(vi). State authorities retains the right to criminally prosecute fighters or civilians for crimes committed in connection with internal armed conflicts.

Cross-references:
Articles 8(2)(a)(vi) and 8(2)(b)(xiv).

Doctrine:

1.   Michael Bothe, in Antonio Cassese, Paola Gaeta and John R.W.D. Jones (eds.), *The Rome Statute of the International Criminal Court: A Commentary*, Oxford University Press, Oxford, 2002, pp. 395, 419.

(d) Paragraph 2 (c) applies to armed conflicts not of an international character and thus does not apply to situations of internal disturbances and tensions, such as riots, isolated and sporadic acts of violence or other acts of a similar nature.[123]

---

2. Andreas Zimmerman, in Otto Triffterer (ed.), *Commentary on the Rome Statute of the International Criminal Court: Observers' Notes, Article by Article*, 2nd ed., C.H. Beck/Hart/Nomos, Munich/Oxford/Baden-Baden, 2008, pp. 491–92.

3. Gerhard Werle, *Principles of International Criminal Law*, TMC Asser Press, The Hague, 2009, pp. 322–23, MN 944–49.

Author: Mark Klamberg.

[123] *General remarks*:

Article 8(2)(d) limits the application of sub-paragraph (c) to certain situations (*Prosecutor v. Bemba*, ICC PT. Ch. II, Decision Pursuant to Article 61(7)(a) and (b) of the Rome Statute on the Charges of the Prosecutor Against Jean-Pierre Bemba Gombo, ICC-01/05-01/08-424, 15 June 2009, para. 225). As sub-paragraph (c) which relates to crimes committed in situations of a non-international armed conflict lacks any definition sub-paragraph (d) appears welcome. Further it must be noted that sub-paragraph (d) is repeated verbatim as the first sentence of sub-paragraph (f).

Analysis:

Article 8(2)(d) states that "Paragraph 2 (c) applies to armed conflicts not of an international character and thus does not apply to situations of internal disturbances and tensions, such as riots, isolated and sporadic acts of violence or other acts of a similar nature".

Scope of Application:

For a situation to fall within the purview of sub-paragraph (c) it must be above the lower threshold specified in sub-paragraph (d). The lower threshold differentiates a non-international armed conflict from "situations of internal disturbances and tensions". In other words, it excludes specific situations from the realm of application of sub-paragraph (c). The provision provides some examples: riots, isolated and sporadic acts of violence or other acts of a similar nature.

Case law in relation to sub-paragraph (d) exclusively is rather sparse. In *Bemba* while the Court explains that a certain level of intensity must be reached for sub-paragraph (c) to apply (*Bemba*, ICC PT. Ch. II, Decision Pursuant to Article 61(7)(a) and (b) of the Rome Statute on the Charges of the Prosecutor Against Jean-Pierre Bemba Gombo, ICC-01/05-01/08-424, 15 June 2009, para. 225) it considers this a limitation on its jurisdiction (para. 225) rather than a description of an armed conflict of a non-international character. In contrast, in *Mbarushimana* the Court, while also considering that sub-paragraph (d) requires the conflict to be of a certain level of intensity, examines the sub-paragraph in a broader discussion on the nature of the armed conflict (*Prosecutor v. Mbarushimana*, ICC PT. Ch. I, Decision on the Confirmation of Charges, ICC-01/04-01/10-465-Red, 16 December 2011, para. 103). In fact, it seems that the criterion of intensity is an element in the determination of a conflict of non-international armed conflict as well as a jurisdictional requirement.

Further although sub-paragraph (c) covers acts listed in Common Article 3 to the Geneva Conventions, sub-paragraph (d) directly stems from Article 1(2) AP II which is deemed to have a higher threshold of applicability than Common Article 3. In other words, there does not seem to be a distinction between non-international armed conflicts falling under the purview of sub-paragraph (c) limited by sub-paragraph (d) on the one hand and of sub-paragraph (e) limited by sub-paragraph (f) on the other. As a result, bearing in mind that the first sentences of sub-paragraphs (d) and (f) are identical ICC case law relating to sub-paragraph (f) can be used. In *Lubanga* (*Prosecutor v. Lubanga*, ICC T. Ch. I, Judgment, ICC-01/04-01/06, 14 March 2012, para. 538) the Court refers to the ICTY jurisprudence, holding that the intensity of the conflict is used to distinguish an armed conflict from situations that are not subject to international humanitarian law (*Prosecutor v. Đorđević* (Case No. IT-05-87/1-T), ICTY T. Ch., Public Judgment with Confidential Annex – Volume I of II, 23 February 2011, para. 1522). In the same paragraph of the judgment (which refers to *Prosecutor v. Mrkšić et al.* (Case No. IT-95-13/1-T), ICTY T. Ch., Judgment, 27 September 2007, para. 407) the Court also accepts that indicators of intensity are "the seriousness of attacks and potential increase in armed clashes, their spread over territory and over a period of time, the increase in the number of government forces, the mobilisation and the distribution of weapons among both parties to the conflict, as well as whether the conflict has attracted the attention of the United Nations Security Council, and, if so, whether any resolutions on the matter have been passed". These indicators are spelled out (para. 1187) and applied (paras. 1216–18) in *Katanga* too (*Prosecutor v. Katanga*, ICC T. Ch. II, Jugement, ICC-01/04-01/07-3436, 7 March 2014).

In addition, the Court has read into Article 8(2)(d) the requirement that for a non-international armed conflict to be established there must be two opposing sides to the conflict (*Bemba*, ICC PT. Ch. II, Decision Pursuant to Article 61(7)(a) and (b) of the Rome Statute on the Charges of the Prosecutor Against Jean-Pierre Bemba Gombo, ICC-01/05-01/08-424, 15 June 2009, para. 232). In *Bemba* it has however avoided examining whether the stricter requirement of the conflict being 'protracted' (that applies in the context of sub-paragraph (e) limited by sub-paragraph (f)) applies to sub-paragraph (c) limited by sub-paragraph (d) (*Bemba*, ICC PT. Ch. II, ICC-01/05-01/08-424, 15 June 2009, para. 235) though it has applied it in other cases (*Mbarushimana*, ICC PT. Ch. I, Decision on the Confirmation of Charges, ICC-01/04-01/10-465-Red, 16 December 2011, para. 103 and *Katanga*, ICC T. Ch. II, Jugement, ICC-01/04-01/07-3436, 7 March 2014, para. 1217).

Cross-references:
Article 8(2)(f).

Doctrine:
1. Dapo Akande, "Classification of Armed Conflicts: Relevant Legal Concepts", in Elizabeth Wilmhurst (ed.), *International Law and the Classification of Conflicts*, Oxford University Press, Oxford, 2012, pp. 32–79.

2. Michael Bothe, "War Crimes", in Antonio Cassese, Paola Gaeta and John R.W.D. Jones (eds.), *The Rome Statute of the International Criminal Court: A Commentary*, Oxford University Press, Oxford, 2002, pp. 417–18.

3. Antonio Cassese, Paola Gaeta and John R.W.D. Jones (eds.), *International Criminal Law*, Oxford University Press, Oxford, 2013, pp. 62–83.

4. Robert Cryer, Håkan Friman, Daryll Robinson and Elizabeth Wilmshurst, *An Introduction to International Criminal Law and Procedure*, 3rd ed., Cambridge University Press, Cambridge, 2014, pp. 264–84.

5. Anthony Cullen, "War Crimes", in William A. Schabas and Nadia Bernaz (eds.), *Routledge Handbook of International Criminal Law*, Routledge, London, 2011, pp. 139–54, 264–84.

6. Knut Dörmann, *Elements of War Crimes under the Rome Statute of the International Criminal Court*, Cambridge University Press, Cambridge, 2002, pp. 382–93.

7. Leena Grover, *Interpreting Crimes in the Rome Statute of the International Criminal Court*, Cambridge University Press, Cambridge, 2014, pp. 279–85.

8. William A. Schabas, *An Introduction to the International Criminal Court*, Cambridge University Press, Cambridge, 2011, pp. 142–44.

9. William A. Schabas, *The International Criminal Court: A Commentary on the Rome Statute*, Oxford University Press, Oxford, 2010, pp. 188–257.

(e) Other serious violations of the laws and customs applicable in armed conflicts not of an international character, within the established framework of international law, namely, any of the following acts:[124]

---

10. Sandesh Sivakumaran, *The Law of Non-International Armed Conflict*, Oxford University Press, Oxford, 2014, pp. 192–95, 273–80.
11. Andreas Zimmermann, "Article 8, War Crimes", in Otto Triffterer (ed.), *Commentary on the Rome Statute of the International Criminal Court: Observers' Notes, Article by Article*, 2nd ed., C.H. Beck/Hart/Nomos, Munich/Oxford/Baden-Baden, 2008, pp. 476–88.

Author: Noëlle Quénivet.

[124] *General remarks*:

Two provisions in the ICC Statute relate to war crimes committed in non-international armed conflict, sub-paragraphs (c) and (e). A literal interpretation of these sub-paragraphs shows that there are two thresholds of applicability, that is, two types of non-international armed conflicts. However it seems that the Court does not distinguish between the two types of non-international armed conflicts (*Prosecutor v. Bemba*, ICC PT. Ch. II, Decision Pursuant to Article 61(7)(a) and (b) of the Rome Statute on the Charges of the Prosecutor Against Jean-Pierre Bemba Gombo, ICC-01/05-01/08-424, 15 June 2009, paras. 216 and 224; *Prosecutor v. Mbarushimana*, ICC PT. Ch. I, Decision on the Confirmation of Charges, ICC-01/04-01/10-465-Red, 6 December 2011, para. 103) specified in sub-paragraphs (c) and (e).

Sub-paragraph (e) must be read in conjunction with sub-paragraphs (f) and Article 8(3). As a result, the following situations are not covered by sub-paragraph (e):

- International armed conflicts. This explains why the assessment of the characterisation of the conflict under Article 8(2)(e) takes place in a wider discussion, notably in contradistinction to international armed conflicts (see Article 8(2)(a) ICC Statute). The problem may arise in particular in armed conflicts where there is fighting between governmental forces on one side and organised armed groups on the other where at the same time a third State is involved in the conflict intervening in support of the organised armed groups. The way the Court distinguishes between a non-international and an international armed conflict is by using the "overall control" test as opposed to the "effective control" test that was established by the International Court of Justice in the *Nicaragua Case* (*Case Concerning the Military and Paramilitary Activities in and Against Nicaragua* (*Nicaragua v. United States*), ICJ Merits, Judgment, 27 June 1986, para. 115). The 'overall control' test was devised and developed by the ICTY (*Prosecutor v. Tadić* (Case No. IT-94-1-I), ICTY A. Ch., Decision on the Defence Motion for Interlocutory Appeal on Jurisdiction, 2 October 1995, para. 137) and readily adopted by the ICC (*Prosecutor v. Lubanga*, ICC PT. Ch. I, Decision on the Confirmation of Charges, ICC-01/04-01/06-803, 29 January 2007, para. 211; *Prosecutor v. Lubanga*, ICC T. Ch. I, Judgment, ICC-01/04-01/06, 14 March 2012, para. 541; *Prosecutor v. Katanga*, ICC Tr. Ch. II, Jugement, ICC-01/04-01/07-3436, 7 March 2014, para. 1178).

- Internal disturbances and tensions. This is confirmed by Article 8(3) which clearly states to "Nothing in paragraph 2 (c) and (e) shall affect the responsibility of a Government to maintain or re-establish law and order in the State or to defend the unity and territorial integrity of the State, by all legitimate means". The aim of this Article is to ensure that acts committed in times of internal disturbances and tensions are not to be prosecuted as war crimes.

Analysis:

Article 8(2)(e) states that "Other serious violations of the laws and customs applicable in armed conflicts not of an international character, within the established framework of international law, namely, any of the following acts".

i) Scope of Application: Existence of an Armed Conflict not of an International Character
For this sub-provision to apply the ICC must determine that the acts were committed in the context of an armed conflict not of an international character.

At first sight, the Court seems to have produced two sets of case law in relation to non-international armed conflicts, one for sub-paragraph (c) and one for sub-paragraph (e). Indeed in some instances the Court's approach to sub-paragraph (e) is that explained in the Commentary to Article 8(2)(c). Two differences are however worth being mentioned. First, the Court explained that for sub-paragraph (e) to apply the conflict must be protracted (*Bemba*, ICC PT. Ch. II, Decision Pursuant to Article 61(7)(a) and (b) of the Rome Statute on the Charges of the Prosecutor Against Jean-Pierre Bemba Gombo, ICC-01/05-01/08-424, 15 June 2009, para. 235; *Mbarushimana*, ICC PT. Ch. I, Decision on the Confirmation of Charges, ICC-01/04-01/10-465-Red, 16 December 2011, para. 103). In the instant case the Court found that five months was to be regarded as 'protracted' (*Bemba*, ICC PT. Ch. II, ICC-01/05-01/08-424, 15 June 2009, para. 255). Second, the Court specified that the organised armed group must be under responsible command (*Bemba*, ICC PT. Ch. II, ICC-01/05-01/08-424, 15 June 2009, para. 234), a requirement later dismissed by the Court in *Lubanga* (*Lubanga*, ICC T. Ch. I, Judgment, ICC-01/04-01/06, 14 March 2012, para. 536).

In other instances, in fact in all cases from *Lubanga* (*Lubanga*, ICC T. Ch. I, Judgment, ICC-01/04-01/06, 14 March 2012; *Katanga*, ICC Tr. Ch. II, Jugement, ICC-01/04-01/07-3436, 7 March 2014; *Prosecutor v. Ntaganda*, ICC PT. Ch. II, Decision on the Confirmation of Charges, ICC-01/04-02/06-309, 9 June 2014) onwards, the Court extensively refers to the ICTY case law (thereby using an interpretation "within the established framework of international law" specified in sub-paragraph (e)) and follows Article 8(2)(f) as explained in the Commentary to sub-paragraph (f). It is believed that this is the leading approach to defining a conflict (paras. 533–38).

The relevant criteria are:

1. The hostilities must be between governmental authorities and organised armed groups or between such groups within a State (*Lubanga*, ICC T. Ch. I, Judgment, ICC-01/04-01/06, 14 March 2012, para. 533). In *Katanga* the Court specifies that this provides for two types of non-international armed conflicts: those opposing the authorities of the government of the State where the hostilities occur against organised armed groups and those opposing organised armed groups, the former also encompassing situations where a State intervenes on a foreign territory in a conflict opposing the governmental authorities to armed opposition group(s), yet with the consent of the governmental authorities (*Katanga*, ICC Tr. Ch. II, Jugement, ICC-01/04-01/07-3436, 7 March 2014, paras. 1184 and 1228).

2. The conflict must be protracted (*Lubanga*, ICC T. Ch. I, Judgment, ICC-01/04-01/06, 14 March 2012, para. 536; *Katanga*, ICC Tr. Ch. II, Jugement, ICC-01/04-01/07-3436, 7 March 2014, para. 1185). The Court has however never explained well what is meant by 'protracted' in this context and seems to be subsumed in the definition of an organised armed group (*Katanga*, ICC Tr. Ch. II, Jugement, ICC-01/04-01/07-3436, 7 March 2014, para. 1185) and the intensity of the conflict (*Katanga*, ICC Tr. Ch. II, Jugement, ICC-01/04-01/07-3436, 7 March 2014, para. 1217) (see Commentary on sub-paragraph (f));

3. The 'organised armed groups' must have a sufficient degree of organisation, in order to enable them to carry out "protracted armed violence" (*Lubanga*, ICC T. Ch. I, Judgment, ICC-01/04-01/06, 14 March 2012, para. 536; *Katanga*, ICC Tr. Ch. II, Jugement, ICC-01/04-01/07-3436, 7 March 2014, para. 1185). There is however no requirement for the group to be "under a responsible command" as expounded in *Bemba* (*Bemba*, ICC PT. Ch. II, ICC-01/05-01/08-424, 15 June 2009, para. 234) and in Article 1(1) of Protocol Additional to the Geneva Conventions of 12 August 1949, and relating to the Protection of Victims of Non-

International Armed Conflicts (AP II) (*Lubanga*, ICC T. Ch. I, Judgment, ICC-01/04-01/06, 14 March 2012, para. 536; *Katanga*, ICC Tr. Ch. II, Jugement, ICC-01/04-01/07-3436, 7 March 2014, para. 1186) though in *Katanga* the Court mentions that the group must present a certain level or organisation such that it is able to implement humanitarian law relating to non-international armed conflicts (*Katanga*, ICC Tr. Ch. II, Jugement, ICC-01/04-01/07-3436, 7 March 2014, para. 1185). There is no requirement under the ICC Statute for the armed group "to exert control over a part of the territory" (*Bemba*, ICC PT. Ch. II, ICC-01/05-01/08-424, 15 June 2009, para. 236; *Lubanga*, ICC T. Ch. I, Judgment, ICC-01/04-01/06, 14 March 2012, para. 536; *Katanga*, ICC Tr. Ch. II, Jugement, ICC-01/04-01/07-3436, 7 March 2014, para. 1186). As noted by the Court itself (*Bemba*, ICC PT. Ch. II, ICC-01/05-01/08-424, 15 June 2009, para. 236; *Lubanga*, ICC T. Ch. I, Judgment, ICC-01/04-01/06, 14 March 2012, para. 536) this clearly departs from Article 1(1) AP II. The ICC has drawn a non-exhaustive list of factors that assist in determining whether the group was organised. The list includes: "the force or group's internal hierarchy; the command structure and rules; the extent to which military equipment, including firearms, are available; the force or group's ability to plan military operations and put them into effect; and the extent, seriousness, and intensity of any military involvement" and each criterion is to be applied with some flexibility and each situation must be assessed on a case-by-case basis (*Lubanga*, ICC T. Ch. I, Judgment, ICC-01/04-01/06, 14 March 2012, para. 537; *Katanga*, ICC Tr. Ch. II, Jugement, ICC-01/04-01/07-3436, 7 March 2014, para. 1186).

4. The conflict must reach a certain level of intensity (*Lubanga*, ICC T. Ch. I, Judgment, ICC-01/04-01/06, 14 March 2012, para. 538; *Katanga*, ICC Tr. Ch. II, Jugement, ICC-01/04-01/07-3436, 7 March 2014, para. 1187). Again, referring back to the ICTY jurisprudence in line with the "within the established framework of international law" requirement set out in sub-paragraph (e) the Court explains that this minimum threshold spelled out in sub-paragraph (f) removes sporadic and isolated situations which are not subject to international humanitarian law (*Prosecutor v. Ðorđević* (Case No. IT-05-87/1-T), ICTY T. Ch., Public Judgment with Confidential Annex – Volume I of II, 23 February 2011, para. 1522) from the jurisdiction of the ICC and that a number of factors must be taken into account (*Prosecutor v. Mrkšić et al.* (Case No. IT-95-13/1-T), ICTY T. Ch., Judgment, 27 September 2007, para. 407) when assessing the intensity of the conflict. These are "the seriousness of attacks and potential increase in armed clashes, their spread over territory and over a period of time, the increase in the number of government forces, the mobilisation and the distribution of weapons among both parties to the conflict, as well as whether the conflict has attracted the attention of the United Nations Security Council, and, if so, whether any resolutions on the matter have been passed" (*Lubanga*, ICC T. Ch. I, Judgment, ICC-01/04-01/06, 14 March 2012, para. 538; *Katanga*, ICC Tr. Ch. II, Jugement, ICC-01/04-01/07-3436, 7 March 2014, para. 1187)

ii) Crimes

The crimes that are mentioned in Article 8(2)(e) are serious violations prohibited by either or both customary and treaty law. The word "other" relates to serious violations of Common Article 3, thereby indicating that the roots of the provision stem from other sources (see also *Bemba*, ICC PT. Ch. II, Decision Pursuant to Article 61(7)(a) and (b) of the Rome Statute on the Charges of the Prosecutor Against Jean-Pierre Bemba Gombo, ICC-01/05-01/08-424, 15 June 2009, para. 224), including Additional Protocol II. However, while the list is mainly drawn from AP II not all violations contained in the treaty have been included in sub-paragraph (e) and while the list is exhaustive for ICC jurisdiction purposes it does not provide an exhaustive list of war crimes in non-international armed conflict. This is recognised by Article 10 ICC Statute that explains that "[n]othing in this Part shall be interpreted as limiting or prejudicing in any way existing or developing rules of international law for purposes other than this Statute". In fact, Resolution RC/Res. 5 has expanded the list to includes Articles 8(2)(e) (xiii), (xiv) and (xv), thereby proving that the list is exhaustive for ICC jurisdiction purposes only and that further crimes can and could be added onto the list.

iii) Awareness

The ICC Statute requires the "awareness of the factual circumstances that established the existence of an armed conflict that is implicit in the terms 'took place in the context of and was associated with'", that is, there must be a nexus between the act and the conflict (see, for example, Elements of Crime in relation to Article 8(2)(e)(i); *Bemba*, ICC PT. Ch. II, Decision Pursuant to Article 61(7)(a) and (b) of the Rome Statute on the Charges of the Prosecutor Against Jean-Pierre Bemba Gombo, ICC-01/05-01/08-424, 15 June 2009, para. 263; *Katanga*, ICC Tr. Ch. II, Jugement, ICC-01/04-01/07-3436, 7 March 2014, paras. 1176 and 1231). Further the perpetrator must be aware that the acts were perpetrated in the context of a non-international armed conflict (see, for example, Elements of Crime in relation to Article 8(2)(e)(i)).

Cross-references:

Article 8(2)(c).

Doctrine:

1. Dapo Akande, "Classification of Armed Conflicts: Relevant Legal Concepts", in Elizabeth Wilmhurst (ed.), *International Law and the Classification of Conflicts*, Oxford University Press, Oxford, 2012, pp. 32–79.

2. Michael Bothe, "War Crimes", in Antonio Cassese, Paola Gaeta and John R.W.D. Jones (eds.), *The Rome Statute of the International Criminal Court: A Commentary*, Oxford University Press, Oxford, 2002, pp. 417–18.

3. Antonio Cassese, Paola Gaeta and John R.W.D. Jones (eds.), *International Criminal Law*, 3rd ed., Oxford University Press, Oxford, 2013, pp. 62–83.

4. Robert Cryer, Håkan Friman, Daryll Robinson and Elizabeth Wilmshurst, *An Introduction to International Criminal Law and Procedure*, 3rd ed., Cambridge University Press, Cambridge, 2014, pp. 264–84.

5. Anthony Cullen, "War Crimes", in William A. Schabas and Nadia Bernaz (eds.), *Routledge Handbook of International Criminal Law*, Routledge, London, 2011, pp. 139–54.

6. Knut Dörmann, *Elements of War Crimes under the Rome Statute of the International Criminal Court*, Cambridge University Press, Cambridge, 2002, pp. 382–93.

7. Leena Grover, *Interpreting Crimes in the Rome Statute of the International Criminal Court*, Cambridge University Press, Cambridge, 2014, pp. 279–85.

8. William A. Schabas, *An Introduction to the International Criminal Court*, Cambridge University Press, Cambridge, 2011, pp. 142–45.

9. William A. Schabas, *The International Criminal Court: A Commentary on the Rome Statute*, Oxford University Press, Oxford, 2010, pp. 188–257.

10. Sandesh Sivakumaran, *The Law of Non-International Armed Conflict*, Oxford University Press, Oxford, 2014, pp. 192–95; 481–83.

11. Sylvain Vité, "Typology of Armed Conflicts in International Humanitarian Law: Legal Concepts and Actual Situations", in *International Review of the Red Cross*, 2009, vol. 91, pp. 69–94.

12. Andreas Zimmermann, Preliminary Remarks on para. 2(c)–(f) and para. 3: "War Crimes Committed in an Armed Conflict not of an International Character", in Otto Triffterer (ed.), *Commentary on the Rome Statute of the International Criminal Court: Observers' Notes, Article by Article*, 2nd ed., C.H. Beck/Hart/Nomos, Munich/Oxford/Baden-Baden, 2008, pp. 475–78.

(i) Intentionally directing attacks against the civilian population as such or against individual civilians not taking direct part in hostilities;[125]

Author: Noëlle Quénivet.

[125] *General remarks:*

The war crime of attacking the civilian population and civilians not taking direct part in hostilities "belongs to the category of offences committed during the actual conduct of hostilities by resorting to prohibited methods of warfare" (*Prosecutor v. Ntaganda*, ICC PT. Ch. II, Decision on the Confirmation of Charges, ICC-01/04-02/06-309, 9 June 2014, para. 45).

Article 8(2)(e)(i) is a reflection of the principle of distinction in attack in a non-international armed conflict. While the principle is enshrined in Article 13(2) of Protocol Additional to the Geneva Conventions of 12 August 1949, and relating to the Protection of Victims of Non-International Armed Conflicts (AP II) it is also of customary nature (Rule 1 of the ICRC Study on Customary International Humanitarian Law; *Prosecutor v. Galić* (Case No. IT-98-29-A), ICTY A. Ch., Judgment, 30 November 2006, para. 87). The International Court of Justice has stressed that deliberate attacks on civilians are absolutely prohibited by international humanitarian law (*Legality of the Threat or Use of Nuclear Weapons*, ICJ Advisory Opinion, 8 July 1996, (1996) ICJ Rep. 226, at 257 (para. 78)). Further, as the ICTY highlighted "the principles underlying the prohibition of attacks on civilians, namely the principles of distinction and protection [...] incontrovertibly form the basic foundation of international humanitarian law and constitute 'intransgressible principles of international customary'" (*Galić*, ICTY A. Ch., 30 November 2006, para. 87).

Article 8(2)(e)(i) mirrors Article 8(2)(b)(i) that applies in an international armed conflict. Both Articles give the Court jurisdiction over attacks against civilians and the civilian population. That being said there is no equivalent in Article 8(2)(e) to Article 8(2)(b)(ii) that prohibits attacks against civilian objects. Given that Article 8(2)(e)(i) specifically refers to the "civilian population" and "individual civilians", that is individuals, it cannot be interpreted so as to cover also civilian objects.

Analysis:

Article 8(2)(e)(i) states that the ICC has jurisdiction overs acts of "[i]ntentionally directing attacks against the civilian population as such or against individual civilians not taking direct part in hostilities".

i) Material Elements

In *Katanga* (*Prosecutor v. Katanga*, ICC Tr. Ch. II, Jugement, ICC-01/04-01/07-3436, 7 March 2014, para. 796) the Court has expounded that the material elements of the crime are:

- The perpetrator has launched an attack;

- The aim of the attack was the civilian population or civilians not taking direct part in hostilities.

a. Definition of an Attack

The first element of the Elements of Crimes requires that "the perpetrator directed an attack" (Elements of Crimes, p. 34). Yet, neither the Statute nor the Elements of Crimes define the term "attack". Referring to the "established framework of international law" mentioned in the chapeau of Article 8(2)(e) the Court has used Article 49 of the Protocol Additional to the Geneva Conventions of 12 August 1949, and relating to the Protection of Victims of Non-International Armed Conflicts and applied it by analogy to Article 13(2) AP II to define an attack as "acts of violence against the adversary, whether in offence or in defence" (*Prosecutor v. Abu Garda*, ICC PT. Ch. I, Public Redacted Version, Decision on the Confirmation of Charges, ICC-02/05-02/09-243-red, 8 February 2010, para. 65; *Katanga*, ICC Tr. Ch. II, ICC-01/04-01/07-3436, 7 March 2014, para. 798; *Ntaganda*, ICC PT. Ch. II, ICC-01/04-02/06-309, 9 June 2014, para. 45).

To establish the link between the attack and the conduct of the hostilities, the Court has stipulated that these civilians must be those "who have not fallen yet into the hands of the attacking party" (*Prosecutor v. Katanga* (Case No. ICC-01/04-01/07), ICC PT. Ch. I, Decision on the Evidence and Information Provided by the Prosecution for the Issuance of a Warrant of Arrest for Germain Katanga, ICC-01/04-01/07-55, 7 July 2007, para. 37; *Ntaganda*, ICC PT. Ch. II, ICC-01/04-02/06-309, 9 June 2014, paras. 45 and 47). Acts committed against civilians who have fallen into the hands of the enemy or are committed far from the combat area cannot be classified as attacks as they are not methods of warfare. They can, however, be prosecuted under other appropriate legal provisions (*Ntaganda*, ICC PT. Ch. II, ICC-01/04-02/06-309, 9 June 2014, para. 47).

The Court has spelled out that in order to characterise a certain conduct as an attack it is important to look at the intended and foreseeable consequences (*Ntaganda*, ICC PT. Ch. II, ICC-01/04-02/06-309, 9 June 2014, para. 46). In other words, there must be a causal link between the perpetrator's conduct and the consequence of the attack (*Abu Garda*, Decision on the Confirmation of Charges, ICC PT. Ch. I, ICC-02/05-02/09-243-red, 8 February 2010, para. 66). Examples of acts falling within the purview of an attack under Article 8(2)(e)(i) are "shelling, sniping, murder, rape, pillage, attacks on protected objects and destruction of property" provided they are linked to the conduct of hostilities (*Ntaganda*, ICC PT. Ch. II, ICC-01/04-02/06-309, 9 June 2014, para. 46).

As the ICC Statute does not provide for a specific offence of acts whose primary purpose is to spread terror among the civilian population, it is likely that such acts fall within the broad scope of Article 8(2)(e)(i). As Article 8(2)(e)(i) is a reflection of the principle of distinction enshrined in Article 13(2) AP II and Article 8(2)(e) must be read "within the established framework of international law" it is likely that it will also cover the second sentence of the Article 13(2) AP II: "Acts or threats of violence the primary purpose of which is to spread terror among the civilian population are prohibited". This approach was espoused by the ICTY inasmuch as it explained that the prohibition of terror amounts to "a specific prohibition within the general (customary) prohibition of attack on civilians" (*Prosecutor v. Galić* (Case No. IT-98-29-T), ICTY T. Ch. I, Judgment and Opinion, 5 December 2003, para. 98, upheld in *Prosecutor v. Galić*, ICTY A. Ch., 30 November 2006, para. 87).

The attack does not need to lead to civilian casualties; it is sufficient to prove that the author directed the attack towards the civilian population or individual civilians. This is in line with Article 13(2) AP II which specifies that "the civilian population as such, as well as individual civilians, shall not be the object of attack", thereby not requiring for harm to occur. As the Court explained "the crime provided for under Article [...] 8(2)(e)(i) of the Statute does not require any harmful impact on the civilian population or on the individual civilians targeted by the attack, and is committed by the mere launching of the attack [...]" (*Katanga*, ICC PT. Ch. I, ICC-01/04-01/07-55, 6 July 2007, para. 37; see also *Katanga*, ICC Tr. Ch. II, ICC-01/04-01/07-3436, 7 March 2014, para. 799). It is the intention that counts as the Elements of Crimes require that "the perpetrator intended the civilian population as such or individual civilians not taking direct part in hostilities to be the object of the attack". This stands in contrast to the ICTY jurisprudence that required the attack to result in death, serious bodily injury or equivalent harm (*Prosecutor v. Kordić and Čerkez* (Case No. IT-95-14/2-A), ICTY A. Ch., Judgment, 17 December 2004, paras. 55–68).

b. Object of the Attack is a Civilian Population and Civilians Not Taking Direct Part in the Hostilities

The second element of the Elements of Crimes specifies that "the object of the attack was a civilian population as such or individual civilians not taking direct part in hostilities" (Elements of Crimes, p. 34). This is an absolute prohibition that cannot be counterbalanced by military necessity (*Katanga*, ICC Tr. Ch. II, ICC-01/04-01/07-3436, 7 March 2014, para. 800). This position is reinforced by the fact that the ICC has, in contrast to the ICTY *Kupreskic* case (*Prosecutor v. Kupreškić et al.* (Case No. IT-95-16-R), ICTY T. Ch., Judgment, 14 January 2000, paras. 527-535), indicated in clear terms that reprisals are prohibited in all circumstances (*Prosecutor v. Mbarushimana*, ICC PT. Ch. I, Decision on the Confirmation of Charges, ICC-01/04-01/10-465-Red, 16 December 2011, para. 143), relying notably on the ICTY Martic decision (*Prosecutor v. Martic* (Case No. IT-95-11-R61), ICTY T. Ch., Decision, 8 March 1996, paras. 15–17).

As there is no definition of a combatant in a non-international armed conflict there is no definition of a civilian under the treaties. While the ICTY defined a civilian as "anyone who is not a member of the armed forces or of an organized military group belonging to a party to the conflict" (*Galić*, ICTY T. Ch. I, 5 December 2003, para. 47) the ICC considers as a civilian anyone who is not a member of the State or non-State armed forces (*Katanga*, ICC Tr. Ch. II, ICC-01/04-01/07-3436, 7 March 2014, para. 788) and a civilian population as "all civilians as opposed to members of armed forces and any other legitimate combatants" (*Mbarushimana*, ICC PT. Ch. I, ICC-01/04-01/10-465-Red, 16 December 2011, para. 148; *Prosecutor v. Bemba*, ICC PT. Ch. II, Decision Pursuant to Article 61(7)(a) and (b) of the Rome Statute on the Charges of the Prosecutor Against Jean-Pierre Bemba Gombo, ICC-01/05-01/08-424, 15 June 2009, para. 78). In case of doubt an individual must be considered a civilian (*Mbarushimana*, ICC PT. Ch. I, ICC-01/04-01/10-465-Red, 16 December 2011, para. 148). The presence among the civilian population of individuals who do not fit within the definition of a civilian, however, does not deprive the entire population of its civilian character (*Mbarushimana*, ICC PT. Ch. I, ICC-01/04-01/10-465-Red, ICC-01/04-01/10-465-Red, 16 December 2011, para. 148) though the Court will take into account factors such as the number and the behaviour of the fighters present among the population (*Katanga*, ICC Tr. Ch. II, ICC-01/04-01/07-3436, 7 March 2014, para. 801).

Article 8(2)(e)(i) refers to "individual civilians not taking direct part in direct hostilities", thereby introducing the concept of direct participation in hostilities in a non-international armed conflict (which also appears in the chapeau of Article 8(2)(c)). There is no customary or treaty law definition of the concept (*Abu Garda*, Decision on the Confirmation of Charges, ICC PT. Ch. I, ICC-02/05-02/09-243-red, 8 February 2010, para. 80; *Katanga*, ICC Tr. Ch. II, ICC-01/04-01/07-3436, 7 March 2014, para. 789 (though in the context of Article 8(2)(c))). Such participation leads to a temporary loss of protection of civilian status, unless the act is in self-defence (*Mbarushimana*, ICC PT. Ch. I, ICC-01/04-01/10-465-Red, 16 December 2011, para. 148). It is indeed recognised that a civilian is allowed to defend him/herself (*Prosecutor v. Bagosora et al.* (Case No. ICTR-98-41-T), ICTR T. Ch. I, Judgment and Sentence, 18 December 2008, paras. 2238-2239).

The Court has stressed that in line with the Commentary of Article 13(3) AP II which explains that "[h]ostilities have been defined as 'acts of war' that by their nature or purpose struck at the personnel and 'matériel' of enemy armed forces" there must be a sufficient causal relationship between the act and its immediate consequences (*Abu Garda*, Decision on the Confirmation of Charges, ICC PT. Ch. I, ICC-02/05-02/09-243-red, 8 February 2010, para. 80; *Katanga*, ICC Tr. Ch. II, ICC-01/04-01/07-3436, 7 March 2014, para. 790). The assessment of whether an individual takes a direct part in hostilities must be carried out on a case-by-case basis (*Abu Garda*, ICC PT. Ch. I, ICC-02/05-02/09-243-red, 8 February 2010, para. 83). For example, the Court has spelled out that "using weapons or other means to commit violence against human or material enemy forces" will qualify as direct participation in hostilities while supplying food and shelter, sympathising with one belligerent party will not (*Mbarushimana*, ICC PT. Ch. I, ICC-01/04-01/10-465-Red, 16 December 2011, para. 148).

The ICC has explained that in cases where the attack is directed towards a legitimate military objective and simultaneously the civilian population or civilians not taking direct part in the hostilities, the author can still be prosecuted under Article 8(2)(e)(i) (*Katanga*, ICC Tr. Ch. II, ICC-01/04-01/07-3436, 7 March 2014, para. 802; *Mbarushimana*, ICC PT. Ch. I, ICC-01/04-01/10-465-Red, 16 December 2011, para. 142). It must however be proven that the principal target of the attack was the civilian population (*Katanga*, ICC Tr. Ch. II, ICC-01/04-01/07-3436, 7 March 2014, para. 802). This situation must nonetheless be distinguished from attacks against military objectives with the awareness that they will or may result in the incidental loss of life or injury to civilians (*Mbarushimana*, ICC PT. Ch. I, ICC-01/04-01/10-465-Red, 16 December 2011, paras. 142 and 218). The Court has thus distinguished between a violation of the principle of discrimination and a violation of the principle of proportionality. While in an international armed conflict the violation of the principle of proportionality can be prosecuted under Article 8(2)(b)(vi) this is not the case in a non-international armed conflict, despite the fact that the principle is recognised to be of customary nature in both international and non-international armed conflicts (see discussion in *Mbarushimana*, ICC PT. Ch. I, ICC-01/04-01/10-465-Red, 16 December 2011, fn. 290). That being said the Court has also argued that in some instances the incidental effect on the civilian population or civilians not taking direct part in hostilities might be so disproportionate that it amounts to a direct attack against such a population or individuals, thereby revealing the author's intention to make the civilian population the object of his or her attack (*Katanga*, ICC Tr. Ch. II, ICC-01/04-01/07-3436, 7 March 2014, para. 802).

ii) Subjective Elements

In *Katanga* (*Prosecutor v. Katanga*, ICC Tr. Ch. II, ICC-01/04-01/07-3436, 7 March 2014, para. 808) the Court explained that for the subjective element to be fulfilled four requirements must be present.

a. "[I]ntentionally" Directing an Attack

The crime must be committed with intention and knowledge, as indicated in Article 30 ICC Statute. The Court has however noted that Article 8(2)(e)(i) specifies that the crime has to be committed 'intentionally'. While in some cases (those relating to Article 8(2)(b)(i)) the Court has explained that this intention to attack the civilian population is in addition to the standard *mens rea* requirement provided in Article 30 ICC Statute, that is, there must be a *dolus directus* of first degree, that is, a concrete intent (*Abu Garda*, Decision on the Confirmation of Charges, ICC PT. Ch. I, ICC-02/05-02/09-243-red, 8 February 2010, para. 93; *Prosecutor v. Katanga and Chui*, ICC PT. Ch. I, Decision on the Confirmation of Charges, ICC-01/04-01/07-717, 30 September 2008, para. 271), in other cases it has argued that the word 'intentionally' is nothing but a repetition of Article 30(2)(a) (*Katanga*, ICC Tr. Ch. II, ICC-01/04-01/07-3436, 7 March 2014, para. 806). The Court has argued that the third element in the Elements of Crimes (Elements of Crimes, p. 34) does not constitute a specific *dolus* but is justified by the use of the word 'intentionally' at the beginning of the sentence and by the need to distinguish this crime from other acts violating the principles of proportionality and/or precautions (*Katanga*, ICC Tr. Ch. II, ICC-01/04-01/07-3436, 7 March 2014, fn. 1851).

b. Intention that the Object of the Attack Is the Civilian Population or Civilians

The Court has stated that this requirement, which is the second element in the Elements of Crimes (Elements of Crimes, p. 34), must be analysed as a behaviour (*Prosecutor v. Chui* (Case No. ICC-01/04-01/07), ICC PT. Ch. I, Sous scellés Décision concernant les éléments de preuve et les renseignements fournis par l'Accusation aux fins de délivrance d'un mandat d'arrêt à l'encontre de Germain Katanga, ICC-01/04-01/07-4-tFRA, 6 July 2007, para. 41). Elements assisting in ascertaining the intention are the means and methods used during the attack, the number and status of victims, the discriminatory character of the attack and the nature of the act (*Katanga*, ICC Tr. Ch. II, ICC-01/04-01/07-3436, 7 March 2014, para. 807). For example, in *Mbarushimana* (*Mbarushimana*, ICC PT. Ch. I, ICC-01/04-01/10-465-Red, 16 December 2011) intention could be inferred from the fact that the armed group wanted to exact revenge on both ci-

(ii) Intentionally directing attacks against buildings, material, medical units and transport, and personnel using the distinctive emblems of the Geneva Conventions in conformity with international law;[126]

---

vilians and soldiers (dubbed operation "eye for eye", para. 144), the orders were to kill all individuals (for example, "everything that moves should be killed", "everything which has breath shouldn't be there at all") (para. 144) and the troops were congratulated for achieving the objective, that is, killing civilians (para. 150).

c. Awareness of the Civilian Status of the Population or Individuals
The Court further requires that the perpetrator attacking the civilian population or individual civilians not taking direct part in the hostilities must be aware of the civilian status of the victims (*Mbarushimana*, ICC PT. Ch. I, ICC-01/04-01/10-465-Red, 16 December 2011, paras. 151 and 219; *Katanga*, ICC Tr. Ch. II, ICC-01/04-01/07-3436, 7 March 2014, para. 808).

d. Awareness of the Circumstances that Established the Existence of the Armed Conflict
According to element 5 of the Elements of Crimes for the war crime of attacking civilians, the perpetrator must be aware of factual circumstances that established the existence of an armed conflict (Elements of Crimes, p. 34).

Cross-references:
Article 8(2)(b)(ii), 8(2)(b)(ix), 8(2)(b)(i) and 8(2)(c).

Doctrine:
1. Michael Bothe, "War Crimes", in Antonio Cassese, Paola Gaeta and John R.W.D. Jones (eds.), *The Rome Statute of the International Criminal Court: A Commentary*, Oxford University Press, Oxford, 2002, p. 397
2. Knut Dörmann, in Otto Triffterer (ed.), *Commentary on the Rome Statute of the International Criminal Court: Observers' Notes, Article by Article*, 2nd ed., C.H. Beck/Hart/Nomos, Munich/Oxford/Baden-Baden, 2008, pp. 323–27.
3. Andreas Zimmerman, in Otto Triffterer (ed.), *Commentary on the Rome Statute of the International Criminal Court: Observers' Notes, Article by Article*, 2nd ed., C.H. Beck/Hart/Nomos, Munich/Oxford/Baden-Baden, 2008, p. 494.
4. Gerhard Werle and Florian Jessberger, *Principles of International Criminal Law*, Oxford University Press, Oxford, 2014, pp. 475–87, MN 1278–1304.
5. William A. Schabas, *The International Criminal Court: A Commentary on the Rome Statute*, Oxford University Press, Oxford, 2010, pp. 188–257.
6. Sandesh Sivakumaran, *The Law of Non-International Armed Conflict*, Oxford University Press, Oxford, 2014, pp. 338–41.

Author: Noëlle Quénivet.

[126] The term 'attack' corresponds to the offence of attacks on a civilian population (Article 8(2)(e)(i)). The recognised emblems are the emblem of the Red Cross, the red crescent, the red lion and the sun and the red crystal (the third additional Protocol). The provision is identical to Article 8(2)(b)(xxiv) and differs only in terms of the context in which the crime is committed.

Cross-references:
Articles 8(2)(e)(i) and 8(2)(b)(xxiv).

Doctrine:
1. Roberta Arnold, in Otto Triffterer (ed.), *Commentary on the Rome Statute of the International Criminal Court: Observers' Notes, Article by Article*, 2nd ed., C.H. Beck/Hart/Nomos, Munich/Oxford/Baden-Baden, 2008, pp. 456–58.

(iii) Intentionally directing attacks against personnel, installations, material, units or vehicles involved in a humanitarian assistance or peacekeeping mission in accordance with the Charter of the United Nations, as long as they are entitled to the protection given to civilians or civilian objects under the international law of armed conflict;[127]

---

2. Andreas Zimmerman, in Otto Triffterer (ed.), *Commentary on the Rome Statute of the International Criminal Court: Observers' Notes, Article by Article*, 2nd ed., C.H. Beck/Hart/Nomos, Munich/Oxford/Baden-Baden, 2008, p. 494,

3. Gerhard Werle, *Principles of International Criminal Law*, TMC Asser Press, The Hague, 2009, pp. 348–49, MN 1035–38.

Author: Mark Klamberg.

[127] *General remarks*:

Attacking personnel or objects involved in humanitarian assistance or peacekeeping missions, entitled to the protection of civilians or civilian objects, is not a new crime under international humanitarian law. It is rather evidence of the need to specify a group of civilians that because of its missions deserves a specific protection (Report of the Secretary-General on the establishment of a Special Court for Sierra Leone, UN doc., S/2000/915 4 October 2000, para. 16). During the negotiations of the ICC Statute, the Convention of the Safety on United Nations and Associated Personnel was included in the Draft Statute as one out of three treaty crimes. When decided that no treaty crime would be included in the Statute the delegations began to concentrate on treating and including attacks against UN personnel as a war crime. The crime of attacking peacekeepers was the only one of the three treaty crimes that 'survived' this change, which is evidence of its strong symbolic character. A crime with the same definition as in the ICC Statute was in included in the Statute of the Special Court for Sierra Leone.

Analysis:

a) Objective Elements

i. The perpetrator directed an attack

The Elements of Crimes do not include a definition of the term "attack". The ICC Pre-Trial Chamber has, by reference *inter alia* to the "applicable treaties and the principles and rules of international law, including the established principles of the international law of armed conflict" in Article 21(1)(b) of the Statute found guidance in Article 49 of AP I, applicable in international armed conflicts (IACs) where the term "attack" is defined as "acts of violence against the adversary, whether in offence or in defence". The term has been given the same definition in Article 13(2) of AP II applicable in non-international armed conflicts ('NIACs'). There is no requirement of any harmful impact on the personnel or material. There is a need to establish a causal link between the conduct of the perpetrator and the consequence "so that the concrete consequence, the attack in this case, can be seen as having been caused by the perpetrator" (*Prosecutor v. Abu Garda*, Decision on the Confirmation of Charges, ICC-02/05- 02/09, PT. Ch., 8 February 2010, paras. 64–66).

ii. The object of the attack was personnel, installations, material, units or vehicles involved in a humanitarian assistance or peacekeeping mission in accordance with the Charter of the United Nations

There is no generally accepted definition on the notion "humanitarian assistance", but it includes measures taken with the purpose of preventing or alleviating human suffering of victims of an armed conflict. In practice the object of attacks has so far been personnel and objects involved in a peacekeeping mission. The term "peacekeeping" is not mentioned in the UN Charter but has developed in practice. The reference to "in accordance with the Charter of the United Nations" does not mean that the mission needs to be established by the UN but includes also missions established by regional organisations (*Abu Garda*, para. 124). While the term lack a simple definition three basic principles are accepted as constituting a peacekeeping mission; consent of the parties; impartiality; and use of force only in self-defence (*Prosecutor v. Abu Garda*, para. 71) although there is now a change in UN doctrine regarding definition of such missions (*Sesay, Kallon and Gbao (RUF)*, Case No. SCSL-04-15-T, Judgment, 2 March 2009 (*RUF*, paras. 224–25). Consent of the host state is a legal requirement but in practice the consent of the main parties to the conflict is also sought to ensure the effectiveness of the operation. Regarding impartiality, the Report of the Panel of the United Nations Peace Operations (UN doc., A/55/305-S/2000/809 (Brahimi Report)) states *inter alia* that "impartiality for such operations must therefore mean adherence to the principles of the Charter and to the objectives of a mandate that is rooted in those Charter principles. Such impartiality is not the same as neutrality or equal treatment of all parties in all cases for all time, which can amount to a policy of appeasement" (Brahimi Report, para. 50 and *Prosecutor v. Abu Garda*, para. 73 not 106). The Majority in the ICC Pre-Trial Chamber noted that peacekeeping missions were only entitled to use force in self-defence compared to peace enforcement missions decided under Chapter VII of the UN Charter which may use force beyond the concept of self-defence in order to achieve their mandates (*Prosecutor v. Abu Garda*, para. 74). In UN doctrine the right of self-defence includes a "right to resist attempts by forceful means to prevent the peacekeeping operation from discharging its duties under the mandate of the Security Council" although it is doubtful if it has developed to become settled law (international or national) (*RUF*, para. 228).

The development in practice where operations are often authorised by the Security Council under Chapter VII to use all necessary measures for certain purposes is reflected in the UN doctrine by references to robust peacekeeping. Recent UN doctrine considers that the tendency to refer to peacekeeping operations as Chapter VI operations and peace enforcement operations as Chapter VII operations is somewhat misleading. It is now the usual practice, both in peacekeeping and in peace enforcement, "for a Chapter VII mandate to be given" and a distinction is instead made between "operations in which the robust use of force is integral to the mission from the outset [...] and operations in which there is a reasonable expectation that force may not be needed at all" (A More Secure World: Our Shared Responsibility, UN doc., A/59/565 (2004) para. 211). The Capstone Doctrine, as it is known, draws a distinction between peace enforcement and robust peacekeeping. Peacekeeping operations with a robust mandate have been authorised to "use all necessary means to deter forceful attempts to disrupt the political process, and/or assist the national authorities in maintaining law and order. The concept of robust peacekeeping is defined as involving "the use of force at the tactical level with the authorization of the Security Council and consent of the host nation and/or the main parties to the conflict". A peace enforcement operation on the other hand "does not require the consent of the main parties and may involve the use of military force at the strategic level, which is generally prohibited for Member States under Article 2(4) of the Charter, unless authorized by the Security Council" (United Nations Peacekeeping Operations: Principles and Guidelines, 2008, p. 34).

The difference between these types of operation is thus not whether they have been established under Chapter VII of the UN Charter, but whether they are dependent on the existence of consent and the use of force at a strategic level. The concept of robust peacekeeping therefore challenges the traditional borders between the concepts of peacekeeping and peace enforcement (traditionally regarded as Chapter VI operations and Chapter VII operations). This may ultimately have an effect on the interpretation of the term peacekeeping mission in the ICC statute. It is telling that the Trial Chamber in the *RUF* case found that the mandate of the UNAMSIL even after it has been expanded through the Resolution 1279 which clearly was decided under Chapter VII and included the expression "use of all necessary measures" was regarded a peacekeeping mission for the purpose of the crime of attacking personnel in such missions (*RUF*, para. 1888).

iii. Such personnel, installations, material, units or vehicles were entitled to the protection given to civilians or civilian objects under the international law of armed conflict

Personnel in humanitarian assistance and peacekeeping missions are presumed to be entitled to the protection of civilians. This is particularly so regarding humanitarian assistance personnel. The authority to use force by peacekeepers, in self-defence or based on a resolution adopted under Chapter VII of the UN Charter (depending on the definition of a peacekeeping mission) naturally raise questions if the use of force by peacekeepers could affect their protection as civilians under international humanitarian law. Personnel in humanitarian assistance and peacekeeping missions are entitled to the protection of civilians as long as they are not taking a direct part in hostilities. Their protection would not be affected by exercising their individual right of self-defence – nor the use of force "in self-defence in the discharge of their mandate, provided that it is limited to such use" (*RUF*, para. 233) It should in this respect be noted that the use of force in defence of the mandate is inherently difficult to define. Determining whether peacekeeping personnel or objects of such a mission were entitled to the protection of civilians or civilian objects, the Trial Chamber in the *RUF* case found that it needed to consider the totality of circumstances existing at the time of the alleged offence including "inter alia, the relevant Security Council resolutions for the operation, the specific operational mandates, the role and practices actually adopted by the peacekeeping mission during the particular conflict, their rules of engagement and operational orders, the nature of the arms and equipment used by the peacekeeping force, the interaction between the peacekeeping force and the parties involved in the conflict, any use of force between the peacekeeping force and the parties in the conflict, the nature and frequency of such force and the conduct of the alleged victim(s) and their fellow personnel" (*RUF*, para. 234) It can be questioned if indeed all these aspects are valid for the determination whether personnel or objects are entitled to the protection of civilians since this a question decided under international humanitarian law.

The Majority in the ICC Pre-Trial exemplified "direct participation in hostilities" to include "bearing, using or taking up arms, taking part in military or hostile acts, activities, conduct or operations, armed fighting or combat, participating in attacks against enemy personnel, property or equipment, transmitting military information for immediate use of a belligerent, and transporting weapons in proximity to combat operations" (*Abu Garda*, para. 81). The determination of whether a person is directly participating in hostilities requires a case-by-case analysis (*Prosecutor v. Abu Garda*, para. 83).

Based on the definition of civilian objects in Article 52(2) of AP I and the ICRC customary law study, the Majority in the ICC Pre-Trial Chamber found that "installations, material, units or vehicles involved in a peacekeeping mission the context of an armed conflict not of an international character shall not be considered military objectives, and thus shall be entitled to the protection given to civilian objects, unless and for such time as their nature, location, purpose or use make an effective contribution to the military action of a party to a conflict and insofar as their total or partial destruction, capture or neutralization, in the circumstances ruling at the time, offers a definite military advantage" (*Abu Garda*, para. 89).

Given the military structure and organisation of peacekeeping missions it may in fact be questioned if such personnel should be regarded as civilians taking direct part in hostilities if they become involved in armed conflict. Military personnel organised and commanded by a state or an intergovernmental organisation within a traditional military structure may rather be regarded as members of a military force under command of party to an armed conflict than civilians directly participating in an armed conflict. The former has also the legal effect of a change in status of the personnel in a more permanent manner than the latter where civilians directly participating in hostilities only temporarily.

b) Subjective elements

(iv) Intentionally directing attacks against buildings dedicated to religion, education, art, science or charitable purposes, historic monuments, hospitals and places where the sick and wounded are collected, provided they are not military objectives;[128]

---

i. The perpetrator intended such personnel, installations, material, units or vehicles so involved to be the object of the attack

The Majority in the ICC Pre-Trial Chamber found that this subjective element was of similar character to that of the Elements of the Crimes for Articles 8(2)(b)(i) and 8(2)(e)(i) dealing with attacks on civilians in both international and non-international armed conflicts. The offence first and foremost encompasses dolus directus of the first degree. The finding of the Majority was also applicable in NIACs (*Abu Garda*, para. 93)

ii. The perpetrator was aware of the factual circumstances that established the protection

The necessary knowledge required by the perpetrator pertains to the facts establishing that the installations, materials, units or vehicles and personnel were involved in a peacekeeping mission but there is no need of legal knowledge regarding their protection.

iii. The perpetrator was aware of factual circumstances that established the existence of an armed conflict

There is no requirement on behalf of the perpetrator to conclude "on the basis of a legal assessment of the said circumstances, that there was an armed conflict" (*Prosecutor v. Abu Garda,* para. 96) (*RUF*, para. 235)

Cross-references:
Article 8(2)(b)(iii).

Doctrine:

1. Michael Bothe, "War Crimes", in Antonio Cassese, Paola Gaeta and John R.W.D. Jones (eds.), *The Rome Statute of the International Criminal Court: A Commentary*, Oxford University Press, Oxford, 2002, p. 412.

2. Michael Cottier, "Attacks on Humanitarian Assistance or Peacekeeping Missions", in Otto Triffterer (ed.), *Commentary on the Rome Statute of the International Criminal Court: Observers' Notes, Article by Article*, 2nd ed., C.H. Beck/Hart/Nomos, Munich/Oxford/Baden-Baden, 2008, pp. 330–38.

3. Knut Dörmann, *Elements of War Crimes under the Rome Statute of the International Criminal Court,* Cambridge University Press, Cambridge, 2003, pp. 453–56.

4. Ola Engdahl, "Prosecution of Attacks against Peacekeepers in International Courts and Tribunals", in *Military Law and Law of War Review*, 2012, vol. 51, p. 249.

5. Daniel Frank, "Article 8(2)(b)(iii) – Attacking Personnel or Objects Involved in a Humanitarian Assistance or Peacekeeping Mission", in Roy S. Lee (ed.), *The International Criminal Court: Elements of Crimes and Rules of Procedure and Evidence*, Transnational Publishers, Ardsley, NY, 2001, p. 146.

6. Herman von Hebel and Darryl Robinson, "Crimes Within the Jurisdiction of the Court", in Roy S. Lee (ed.), *The International Criminal Court: The Making of the Rome Statute*, Kluwer Law International, The Hague, 1999, p. 110.

Author: Ola Engdahl.

[128] *General remarks*:

With this Article the drafters of the ICC Statute included a provision criminalising violations of the rules protecting cultural property, which have been established by international humanitarian law as well as several UNESCO treaties over the years. The purpose of this provision is to specifically criminalise the destruction of cultural property as opposed to civilian property and therefore, it constitutes a *lex specialis* to Article 8(2)(e)(xii).

Analysis:

i. Definition

Pursuant to the ICC Elements of Crime, the following criteria need to be met in order to fulfil the Article at hand: 1) The perpetrator directed an attack. 2) The object of the attack was one or more buildings dedicated to religion, education, art, science or charitable purposes, historic monuments, hospitals or places where the sick and wounded are collected, which were not military objectives. 3) The perpetrator intended such building or buildings dedicated to religion, education, art, science or charitable purposes, historic monuments, hospitals or places where the sick and wounded are collected, which were not military objectives, to be the object of the attack. 4) The conduct took place in the context of and was associated with an armed conflict not of an international character. 5) The perpetrator was aware of factual circumstances that established the existence of an armed conflict.

ii. Requirements

a. Material elements

The object of the offence has to be specially protected. The institutions enlisted in the ICC Statute can be classified into four main categories: cultural objects, places for the collection of those in need (for example, hospitals), institutions dedicated to religion and others dedicated to education. The ICTY defined 'cultural objects' by referring the definition of cultural property in treaty law (for example, the 1954 Hague Convention for the Protection of Cultural Property in the Event of Armed Conflict) (*Prosecutor v. Strugar* (Case No. IT-01-42), ICTY T. Ch. Judgment of 31 January 2005, para. 230). According to the case law of the ICTY, religious and educational institutions are protected as long as they meet the special requirement of "cultural heritage of people", meaning "objects whose value transcends geographical boundaries, and which are unique in character and are intimately associated with the history and culture of a people" (*Prosecutor v. Martić* (Case No. IT-95-11), ICTY T. Ch. Judgment of 12 June 2007, para. 97). Additionally, these institutions must "clearly be identified as dedicated to religion or education" (*Prosecutor v. Blaškić* (Case No. IT-95-14), ICTY T. Ch. Judgment, 3 March 2000, para. 185).

Furthermore, the object of the offence cannot be a military objective. Military objectives are defined by Article 52(3) Additional Protocol I as objects "which by their nature, location, purpose or use make an effective contribution to military action and whose total or partial destruction, capture or neutralization, in the circumstances ruling at the time, offers a definite military advantage".

Concerning the nature of the offence the ICC Statute penalises the directing of attacks against such institutions. The term "attack" is defined in Article 49(1) Additional Protocol I and means "acts of violence against the adversary, whether in offence or in defence". Hence, the scope of the Article is extremely broad and almost all acts of hostility fall under this provision. Furthermore, no actual damage to the protected institutions is required. In order for the Article at hand to be fulfilled it is sufficient that the attack was directed against the respective protected institution.

b. Mental elements

Additionally, to the mental elements concerning the general requirements of war crimes, the perpetrator has to fulfil the mental elements of the underlying offence at hand. Namely, the attack against the protected institutions has to be committed "intentionally". A controversial issue while drafting the ICC Statute was whether the term "intentionally" was related solely to the directing of an attack or also to the object of the attack. The *travaux préparatoires* adopted the latter approach. Therefore, the ICC Elements of the Crime require that the perpetrator must have

(v)   Pillaging a town or place, even when taken by assault;[129]

---

known about the protected status of the institution. Additionally, the perpetrator must have knowledge of the institution's failure to qualify as a military objective, and nevertheless carry out the attack. However, he does not have to make a legal assessment of the protected status of the institutions. He merely needs to know the factual circumstances, which give the object a special status (see *Prosecutor v. Blaškić* (Case No. IT-95-14), ICTY T. Ch. Judgment, 3 March 2000, para. 185).

Cross-references:

Article 8(2)(b)(ix).

Doctrine:

1.   Roberta Arnold, "Article 8, Paragraph 2 (b)(ix)", in Otto Triffterer (ed.), *Commentary on the Rome Statute of the International Criminal Court: Observers' Notes, Article by Article*, 2nd ed., C.H. Beck/Hart/Nomos, Munich/Oxford/Baden-Baden, 2008, pp. 375–80.

2.   Gideon Boas, James L. Biscoff and Nathalie L. Reid, *International Criminal Law Practitioner Library*. Vol. II: *Elements of Crime under International Criminal Law*, Cambridge University Press, Cambridge, 2008.

3.   Caroline Ehlert, *Prosecuting the Destruction of Cultural Property in International Criminal Law*, Martinus Nijhoff Publishers, Leiden, 2014.

4.   Micaela Frulli, "The Criminalization of Offences against Cultural Heritage in Times of Armed Conflict: The Quest of Consistency", in *European Journal of International Law*, 2011, vol. 22, pp. 203–17.

5.   Mireille Hector, "Enhancing Individual Criminal Responsibility for Offences Involving Cultural Property – the Road to the Rome Statute and the 1999 Second Protocol", in Nout Van Woudenberg and Liesbeth Lijnzaad (eds.), *Protecting Cultural Armed Conflict: An Insight into the 1999 Second Protocol to the Hague Convention of 1954 for the Protection of Cultural Property in the Event of Armed Conflict*, Koninklijke Brill, Leiden, 2010, pp. 21–42.

6.   Theodor Meron, "The Protection of Cultural Property in the Event of Armed Conflict within the Case law of the International Criminal Tribunal for the Former Yugoslavia", in *Museum International*, 2005, vol. 57, pp. 41–59.

7.   Roger O'Keefe, "Protection of Cultural Property under International Criminal Law", in *Melbourne Journal of International Law*, 2010, vol. 11, pp. 1–54.

8.   Rüdiger Wolfrum, "Protection of Cultural Property in Armed Conflict", in Rüdiger Wolfrum (ed.), *The Max Planck Encyclopedia of Public International Law*, Oxford University Press, Oxford, 2008.

Author: Caroline Ehlert.

[129]   The term "pillage" means appropriation of property for private, personal use and embraces acts of plundering, looting and sacking. There is no substantive difference between appropriation and confiscation. Article 8(2)(b)(xvi) is an identical provision to the present provision, but applies in international armed conflicts. In comparison with Articles 8(2)(a)(iv), 8(2)(b)(xiii) and 8(2)(e)(xii), pillage differs from appropriation and confiscation in regard to the perpetrator's intent to obtain the property for private or personal use.

In *Prosecutor v. Katanga and Chui*, the Pre-Trial chamber stated that the "war crime of pillaging under Article 8(2)(b)(xvi) of the Statute requires that the property subject to the offence belongs to an 'enemy' or 'hostile' party to the conflict" (ICC PT. Ch. I, Decision on the Confirmation of Charges, ICC-01/04-01/07, 30 September 2008, para. 329).

(vi) Committing rape,[130] sexual slavery,[131] enforced prostitution,[132] forced pregnancy, as defined in article 7, paragraph 2 (f),[133] enforced sterilization,[134] and any other

---

Cross-references:

Articles 8(2)(a)(iv), (8)(2)(b)(xiii), 8(2)(b)(xvi) and 8(2)(e)(xii).

Doctrine:

1. Michael Bothe, "War Crimes", in Antonio Cassese, Paola Gaeta and John R.W.D. Jones (eds.), *The Rome Statute of the International Criminal Court: A Commentary*, Oxford University Press, Oxford, 2002, pp. 413, 422.

2. Andreas Zimmerman, in Otto Triffterer (ed.), *Commentary on the Rome Statute of the International Criminal Court: Observers' Notes, Article by Article*, 2nd ed., C.H. Beck/Hart/Nomos, Munich/Oxford/Baden-Baden, 2008, pp. 408–10, 495.

3. Gerhard Werle, *Principles of International Criminal Law*, TMC Asser Press, The Hague, 2009, pp. 334–38, MN 986–99.

Author: Mark Klamberg.

[130] Rape is considered the most severe form of sexual violence. Sexual violence is a broad term that covers all forms of acts of a sexual nature under coercive circumstances, including rape. The key element that separates rape from other acts is penetration. The Elements of Crime provide a more specific definition of the criminal conduct. Rape falls under the chapeaus of genocide, crimes against humanity or war crimes under specific circumstances, confirmed both through the ICC Statute and through the case law of the ICTR and the ICTY. Rape as a war crime differs from the definition of rape as a crime against humanity only in terms of the context in which the crime is committed. The rape must have been perpetrated in the context of and in association with a non-international armed conflict. In Kunarac, a sufficient nexus to the armed conflict was considered to exist in a situation where combatants took advantage of their positions of military authority to rape individuals, whose displacement was an express goal of the military campaign of which they were part (see *Prosecutor v. Dragoljub Kunarac, Radomir Kovac and Zoran Vukovic* (Case No. IT-96-23 and IT-96-23/1-A), Appeal Judgment, 12 June 2002, paras. 58–59).

For the mental element of rape Article 30 applies. The perpetrator has to be aware of the factual circumstances that established the existence of an armed conflict. He or she must also have intended to penetrate the victim's body and be aware that the penetration was by force or threat of force. The definition of rape is the same regarding rape as genocide, crimes against humanity and war crimes, albeit the contextual elements of the chapeaus differ. The *actus reus* of the violation is found in the Elements of Crimes. The definition focuses on penetration with 1) a sexual organ of any body part, or 2) with the use of an object or any other part of the body of the anal or genital opening of the victim, committed by force or threat or force or coercion. "Any part of the body" under point 1 refers to vaginal, anal and oral penetration with the penis and may also be interpreted as ears, nose and eyes of the victim. Point 2 refers to objects or the use of fingers, hands or tongue of the perpetrator. Coercion may arise through fear of violence, duress, detention, psychological oppression or abuse of power. These situations are provided as examples, apparent through the use of the term "such as". Consent is automatically vitiated in such situations. The definition is intentionally gender-neutral, indicating that both men and women can be perpetrators or victims. The definition of rape found in the Elements of Crimes is heavily influenced by the legal reasoning in cases regarding rape of the ICTY and the ICTR. Such cases can thus further elucidate the interpretation of the elements of the crime, meanwhile also highlighting different approaches to the main elements of rape, including "force" and "non-consent". See, for example, *Furundzija*, in which the Trial Chamber of the ICTY held that force or threat of force constitutes the main element of rape (*Prosecutor v. Furundzija* (Case No. IT-95-17/1-T. 10), ICTY T. Ch, Judgment, 10 December 1998). To the contrary, the latter case of *Kunarac* emphasised the element of non-consent as the most essential in establishing rape, in

---

that it corresponds to the protection of sexual autonomy (*Prosecutor v. Kunarac, Kovac and Vukovic* (Case No. IT-96-23 and 23/122) ICTY T. Ch, Judgment, 22 February 2001). As to the term "coercion" the ICTR Trial Chamber in *Akayesu* held that a coercive environment does not require physical force. It also adopted a broad approach to the *actus reus*, including also the use of objects, an approach that has been embraced also by the ICTY and the ICC (*Prosecutor v. Jean-Paul Akayesu* (Case No. ICTR-96-4-T), ICTR T. Ch, Judgment, 2 September 1998, para. 598).

Rule 63 is of importance which holds that the Court's Chambers cannot require corroboration to prove any crime within its jurisdiction, particularly crimes of sexual violence. Rule 70 further delineates the possibility of introducing evidence of consent as a defence. This is highly limited, emphasising that consent cannot be inferred in coercive circumstances. Rule 71 forbids evidence of prior sexual conduct.

The ICC has in several arrest warrants found reasonable grounds to believe that rape as a war crime within the meaning of Article 8(2)(e)(vi) has been committed. See Second Arrest Warrant against Ntaganda, where the Chamber found reasonable grounds to believe that rape and sexual slavery were committed in different locations in Ituri, *Prosecutor v. Ahmad Harun and Ali Kushayb* (Case No. ICC-02/05-01/07), ICC PT. Ch. I, Warrant of Arrest against Ahmad Harun and Ali Kushayb, 27 April 2007; reasonable grounds to believe that Harun, through the direction of the Sudanese Armed Forces and the Janjaweed committed rapes of women and girls. See also Warrant of Arrest against Joseph Kony (Case No. ICC-02/04-01/05), PT. Ch. II, 27 September 2005; Warrant of Arrest against Vincent Otti (Case No. ICC-02/04), PT. Ch. II, 8 July 2005, para. 17; *Prosecutor v. Sylvestre Mudacumura*, Decision on the Prosecutor's Application under Article 58, ICC-01/04-01/12, 13 July 2012, para. 47.

Cross-references:

Articles 7(1)(g) and 8(2)(b)(xxii).

Doctrine:

1. Antonio Cassese, in Antonio Cassese, Paola Gaeta and John R.W.D. Jones (eds.), *The Rome Statute of the International Criminal Court: A Commentary*, Oxford University Press, Oxford, 2002, pp. 374–75.

2. Michael Bothe, in Antonio Cassese, Paola Gaeta and John R.W.D. Jones (eds.), *The Rome Statute of the International Criminal Court: A Commentary*, Oxford University Press, Oxford, 2002, pp. 415–16, 422.

3. Machteld Boot, revised by Christopher K. Hall, in Otto Triffterer (ed.), *Commentary on the Rome Statute of the International Criminal Court: Observers' Notes, Article by Article*, 2nd ed., C.H. Beck/Hart/Nomos, Munich/Oxford/Baden-Baden, 2008, pp. 206–11.

4. Michael Cottier, in Otto Triffterer (ed.), *Commentary on the Rome Statute of the International Criminal Court: Observers' Notes, Article by Article*, 2nd ed., C.H. Beck/Hart/Nomos, Munich/Oxford/Baden-Baden, 2008, pp. 431–47.

5. Andreas Zimmerman, in Otto Triffterer (ed.), *Commentary on the Rome Statute of the International Criminal Court: Observers' Notes, Article by Article*, 2nd ed., C.H. Beck/Hart/Nomos, Munich/Oxford/Baden-Baden, 2008, pp. 495–96.

6. Gerhard Werle, *Principles of International Criminal Law*, TMC Asser Press, The Hague, 2009, pp. 248–50, 313, MN 723–27; 912–13.

7. Anne-Marie L.M. de Brouwer, *Supranational Criminal Prosecution of Sexual Violence: The ICC and the Practice of the ICTY and the ICTR*, Antwerp, Intersentia, 2005, pp. 202–20.

Author: Maria Sjöholm.

[131] Sexual slavery is a particular form of enslavement which includes limitations on one's autonomy, freedom of movement and power to decide matters relating to one's sexual activity. Although it is listed as a separate offence in the ICC Statute, it is regarded as a particular form of enslavement. However, whereas enslavement is solely considered a crime against humanity, sexual slavery may constitute either a war crime or a crime against humanity. It is partly based on the definition of enslavement identified as customary international law by the ICTY in the *Kunarac* case (*Prosecutor v. Kunarac, Kovac and Vukovic* (Case No. IT-96-23 and 23/1), ICTY T. Ch, Judgment, 22 February 2001, para. 543). Sexual slavery is thus considered a form of enslavement with a sexual component. Its definition is found in the Elements of Crimes and includes the exercise of any or all of the powers attached to the right of ownership over one or more persons, "such as by purchasing, selling, lending or bartering such a person or persons, or by imposing on them a similar deprivation of liberty". The person should have been made to engage in acts of a sexual nature. The crime also includes forced marriages, domestic servitude or other forced labour that ultimately involves forced sexual activity. In contrast to the crime of rape, which is a completed offence, sexual slavery constitutes a continuing offence. The provision is identical to Article 8(2)(b)(xxii) and differs only in terms of the context in which the crime is committed.

In *Prosecutor v. Katanga and Chui*, the Pre-Trial chamber held that "sexual slavery also encompasses situations where women and girls are forced into 'marriage', domestic servitude or other forced labour involving compulsory sexual activity, including rape, by their captors. Forms of sexual slavery can, for example, be practices such as the detention of women in 'rape camps' or 'comfort stations', forced temporary 'marriages' to soldiers and other practices involving the treatment of women as chattel, and as such, violations of the peremptory norm prohibiting slavery" (*Prosecutor v. Katanga and Chui*, ICC PT. Ch, Decision on the Confirmation of Charges, ICC-01/04-01/07-717, 30 September 2008, para. 431).

The SCSL Appeals Chamber in the *Brima* case has found the abduction and confinement of women to constitute forced marriage. The Chamber concluded that forced marriage was distinct from sexual slavery. Accordingly, "While forced marriage shares certain elements with sexual slavery such as non-consensual sex and deprivation of liberty, there are also distinguishing factors. First, forced marriage involves a perpetrator compelling a person by force or threat of force, through the words or conduct of the perpetrator or those associated with him, into a forced conjugal association with another person resulting in great suffering, or serious physical or mental injury on the part of the victim. Second, unlike sexual slavery, forced marriage implies a relationship of exclusivity between the "husband" and "wife", which could lead to disciplinary consequences for breach of this exclusive arrangement" (*Prosecutor v. Brima* (Case No. SCSL-2004-16-A), SCSL A. Ch, Judgment, 22 February 2008, para. 195). In 2012 the Court in a decision on the Charles Taylor case declared its preference for the term "forced conjugal slavery". The Trial Chamber did not find the term "marriage" to be helpful in describing the events that had occurred, in that it did not constitute marriage in the universally understood sense (*Prosecutor v. Charles Taylor* (Case No. SCSL-03-01-T), SCSL T. Ch, Judgment, 18 May 2012, para. 427).

Cross-references:

Articles 7(1)(g) and 8(2)(b)(xxii).

Doctrine:

1. Michael Bothe, in Antonio Cassese, Paola Gaeta and John R.W.D. Jones (eds.), *The Rome Statute of the International Criminal Court: A Commentary*, Oxford University Press, Oxford, 2002, pp. 415, 422.

2. Machteld Boot, revised by Christopher K. Hall, in Otto Triffterer (ed.), *Commentary on the Rome Statute of the International Criminal Court: Observers' Notes, Article by Article*, 2nd ed., C.H. Beck/Hart/Nomos, Munich/Oxford/Baden-Baden, 2008, pp. 211–12.

3. Michael Cottier, in Otto Trifftterer (ed.), *Commentary on the Rome Statute of the International Criminal Court: Observers' Notes, Article by Article*, 2nd ed., C.H. Beck/Hart/Nomos, Munich/Oxford/Baden-Baden, 2008, pp. 441–47.

4. Andreas Zimmerman, in Otto Triffterer (ed.), *Commentary on the Rome Statute of the International Criminal Court: Observers' Notes, Article by Article*, 2nd ed., C.H. Beck/Hart/Nomos, Munich/Oxford/Baden-Baden, 2008, pp. 495–96.

5. Gerhard Werle, *Principles of International Criminal Law*, TMC Asser Press, The Hague, 2009, pp. 250–51, 313, MN 728; 914–16.

6. Anne-Marie L.M. de Brouwer, *Supranational Criminal Prosecution of Sexual Violence: The ICC and the Practice of the ICTY and the ICTR*, Antwerp, Intersentia, 2005, pp. 202–20.

Author: Maria Sjöholm.

[132] The Elements of Crimes requires the 1) causing or a person to engage in acts of a sexual nature 2) by force or threat of force or under coercive circumstances and 3) the perpetrator or another person obtained or expected to obtain pecuniary or other advantage in exchange for or in connection with the acts. Primarily the latter point distinguishes it from sexual slavery. It can also be distinguished in that sexual slavery requires the exercise or any or all of the powers attaching to the rights of ownership. Enforced prostitution could, however, rise to the level of sexual slavery, should the elements of both crimes exist. In comparison with rape and sexual slavery, enforced prostitution can either be a continuing offence or constitute a separate act. Enforced prostitution is prohibited in the Geneva Convention IV 1949 as an example of an attack on a woman's honour and in Additional Protocol I as an outrage upon personal dignity. The provision is identical to Article 8(2)(b)(xxii) and differs only in terms of the context in which the crime is committed.

Cross-references:
Articles 7(1)(g) and 8(2)(b)(xxii).

Doctrine:

1. Michael Bothe, in Antonio Cassese, Paola Gaeta and John R.W.D. Jones (eds.), *The Rome Statute of the International Criminal Court: A Commentary*, Oxford University Press, Oxford, 2002, pp. 415, 422.

2. Machteld Boot, revised by Christopher K. Hall, in Otto Triffterer (ed.), *Commentary on the Rome Statute of the International Criminal Court: Observers' Notes, Article by Article*, 2nd ed., C.H. Beck/Hart/Nomos, Munich/Oxford/Baden-Baden, 2008, pp. 212–13

3. Michael Cottier, in Otto Triffterer (ed.), *Commentary on the Rome Statute of the International Criminal Court: Observers' Notes, Article by Article*, 2nd ed., C.H. Beck/Hart/Nomos, Munich/Oxford/Baden-Baden, 2008, pp. 447–48.

4. Andreas Zimmerman, in Otto Triffterer (ed.), *Commentary on the Rome Statute of the International Criminal Court: Observers' Notes, Article by Article*, 2nd ed., C.H. Beck/Hart/Nomos, Munich/Oxford/Baden-Baden, 2008, pp. 495–96.

5. Gerhard Werle, *Principles of International Criminal Law*, TMC Asser Press, The Hague, 2009, pp. 251, 313, MN 729–30; 914–16.

6. Anne-Marie L.M. de Brouwer, *Supranational Criminal Prosecution of Sexual Violence: The ICC and the Practice of the ICTY and the ICTR*, Antwerp, Intersentia, 2005, pp. 202–20.

Author: Maria Sjöholm.

[133] Forced pregnancy means the unlawful confinement of a woman forcibly made pregnant. Unlawful confinement should be interpreted as any form of deprivation of physical liberty contrary to international law. The deprivation of liberty does not have to be severe and no specific time frame is required. The use of force is not required, but some form of coercion. To complete the crime, it is sufficient if the perpetrator holds a woman imprisoned who has been impregnated by someone else. The forcible impregnation may involve rape or other forms of sexual violence of comparable gravity. In addition to the mental requirements in Article 30, the perpetrator must act with the purpose of affecting the ethnic composition of any population or carrying out other grave violations of international law. National laws prohibiting abortion do not amount to forced pregnancy. The provision is identical to Article 8(2)(b)(xxii)and differs only in terms of the context in which the crime is committed.

Cross-references:
Articles 7(1)(g) and 8(2)(b)(xxii).

Doctrine:

1. Michael Bothe, in Antonio Cassese, Paola Gaeta and John R.W.D. Jones (eds.), *The Rome Statute of the International Criminal Court: A Commentary*, Oxford University Press, Oxford, 2002, pp. 415, 422.

2. Machteld Boot, revised by Christopher K. Hall, in Otto Triffterer (ed.), *Commentary on the Rome Statute of the International Criminal Court: Observers' Notes, Article by Article*, 2nd ed., C.H. Beck/Hart/Nomos, Munich/Oxford/Baden-Baden, 2008, pp. 213 and 255–56.

3. Michael Cottier, in Otto Triffterer (ed.), *Commentary on the Rome Statute of the International Criminal Court: Observers' Notes, Article by Article*, 2nd ed., C.H. Beck/Hart/Nomos, Munich/Oxford/Baden-Baden, 2008, pp. 448–50.

4. Andreas Zimmerman, in Otto Triffterer (ed.), *Commentary on the Rome Statute of the International Criminal Court: Observers' Notes, Article by Article*, 2nd ed., C.H. Beck/Hart/Nomos, Munich/Oxford/Baden-Baden, 2008, pp. 495–96.

5. Gerhard Werle, *Principles of International Criminal Law*, TMC Asser Press, The Hague, 2009, pp. 251–52, 313, MN 731–732; 914–16.

6. Anne-Marie L.M. de Brouwer, *Supranational Criminal Prosecution of Sexual Violence: The ICC and the Practice of the ICTY and the ICTR*, Antwerp, Intersentia, 2005, pp. 202–20.

Author: Maria Sjöholm

[134] Enforced sterilisation is a form of "[i]mposing measures intended to prevent births within the group" within the meaning of Article 6(e). It is carried out without the consent of a person. Genuine consent is not given when the victim has been deceived. Enforced sterilisation includes depriving a person of their biological reproductive capacity, which is not justified by the medical treatment of the person. It does not include non-permanent birth-control methods. It is not restricted to medical operations but can also include the intentional use of chemicals for this effect. It arguably includes vicious rapes where the reproductive system has been destroyed. The Elements of Crime provide a more specific definition of the criminal conduct. For the mental element Article 30 applies. Enforced sterilisation may also fall under the chapeau of genocide if such intent is present. The provision is identical to Article 8(2)(b)(xxii) and differs only in terms of the context in which the crime is committed.

Cross-references:
Articles 7(1)(g) and 8(2)(b)(xxii).

Doctrine:

1. Michael Bothe, in Antonio Cassese, Paola Gaeta and John R.W.D. Jones (eds.), *The Rome Statute of the International Criminal Court: A Commentary*, Oxford University Press, Oxford, 2002, pp. 415, 422.

form of sexual violence also constituting a serious violation of article 3 common to the four Geneva Conventions;[135]

---

2. Machteld Boot, revised by Christopher K. Hall, in Otto Triffterer (ed.), *Commentary on the Rome Statute of the International Criminal Court: Observers' Notes, Article by Article*, 2nd ed., C.H. Beck/Hart/Nomos, Munich/Oxford/Baden-Baden, 2008, pp. 213–14.

3. Michael Cottier, in Otto Triffterer (ed.), *Commentary on the Rome Statute of the International Criminal Court: Observers' Notes, Article by Article*, 2nd ed., C.H. Beck/Hart/Nomos, Munich/Oxford/Baden-Baden, 2008, 2008, p. 451.

4. Andreas Zimmerman, in Otto Triffterer (ed.), *Commentary on the Rome Statute of the International Criminal Court: Observers' Notes, Article by Article*, 2nd ed., C.H. Beck/Hart/Nomos, Munich/Oxford/Baden-Baden, 2008, pp. 495–96.

5. Gerhard Werle, *Principles of International Criminal Law*, TMC Asser Press, The Hague, 2009, pp. 252, 313, MN 733; 914–16.

6. Anne-Marie L.M. de Brouwer, *Supranational Criminal Prosecution of Sexual Violence: The ICC and the Practice of the ICTY and the ICTR*, Antwerp, Intersentia, 2005, pp. 202–20.

Author: Maria Sjöholm.

[135] The provision has a catch-all character and requires that the conduct is comparable in gravity to the other acts listed in Article 8(2)(e)(vi). It concerns acts of a sexual nature against a person through the use of force or threat of force or coercion. The importance of distinguishing the different forms of sexual violence primarily lies in the level of harm to which the victim is subjected and the degree of severity, and therefore becomes a matter of sentencing. Common Article 3 is considered part of customary international law.

It is generally held to include forced nudity, forced masturbation or forced touching of the body. The ICTR in *Akayesu* held that "sexual violence is not limited to physical invasion of the human body and may include acts which do not involve penetration or even physical contact" (*Prosecutor v. Jean-Paul Akayesu* (Case No. ICTR-96-4-T), ICTR T. Ch, Judgment, 2 September 1998, para. 688). The Trial Chamber in the case confirmed that forced public nudity was an example of sexual violence within its jurisdiction (para. 10 A). Similarly, the Trial Chamber of the ICTY in its *Kvocka* decision declared: "sexual violence is broader than rape and includes such crimes as sexual slavery or molestation, and also covers sexual acts that do not involve physical contact, such as forced public nudity (*Prosecutor v. Miroslav Kvocka* (Case No. IT-98-30/1-T) ICTY T. Ch, Judgment, 2 November 2001, para. 180). To the contrary, in the decision on the Prosecutor's application for a warrant of arrest in the *Bemba* case, the Pre-Trial Chamber of the ICC did not include a charge of sexual violence as a crime against humanity in the arrest warrant, which had been based on allegations that the troops in question had forced women to undress in public in order to humiliate them, stating that "the facts submitted by the Prosecutor do not constitute other forms of sexual violence of comparable gravity to the other forms of sexual violence set forth in Article 7(1)(g)" (*Prosecutor v. Jean-Pierre Bemba Gombo*, ICC PT. Ch. I, Decision on the Prosecutor's Application for a Warrant of Arrest against Jean-Pierre Bemba Gombo, ICC-01/05-01/08, 10 June 2008, para. 40). In the *Lubanga* case of the ICC, evidence of sexual violence was presented during the trial, including various forms of sexual abuse of girl soldiers who were forcefully conscripted. However, no charges of sexual violence were brought. The Prosecution rather encouraged the Trial Chamber to consider evidence of sexual violence as an integral element of the recruitment and use of child soldiers. In the confirmation of charges in the *Muthaura and Kenyatta* case, Pre-Trial Chamber II chose not to charge forced male circumcision and penile amputation as sexual violence, but rather as inhumane acts. The Chamber held that "the evidence placed before it does not establish the sexual nature of the acts of forcible circumcision and penile amputation. Instead, it appears from the evidence that the

(vii) Conscripting or enlisting children under the age of fifteen years into armed forces or groups or using them to participate actively in hostilities;[136]

---

acts were motivated by ethnic prejudice" It argued that "not every act of violence which targets parts of the body commonly associated with sexuality should be considered an act of sexual violence" (para. 265).

Cross-references:

Articles 7(1)(g) and 8(2)(b)(xxii).

Doctrine:

1. Michael Bothe, in Antonio Cassese, Paola Gaeta and John R.W.D. Jones (eds.), *The Rome Statute of the International Criminal Court: A Commentary*, Oxford University Press, Oxford, 2002, pp. 415–16, 422.

2. Machteld Boot, revised by Christopher K. Hall, in Otto Triffterer (ed.), *Commentary on the Rome Statute of the International Criminal Court: Observers' Notes, Article by Article*, 2nd ed., C.H. Beck/Hart/Nomos, Munich/Oxford/Baden-Baden, 2008, pp. 214–15.

3. Michael Cottier, in Otto Triffterer (ed.), *Commentary on the Rome Statute of the International Criminal Court: Observers' Notes, Article by Article*, 2nd ed., C.H. Beck/Hart/Nomos, Munich/Oxford/Baden-Baden, 2008, pp. 451–54.

4. Andreas Zimmerman, in Otto Triffterer (ed.), *Commentary on the Rome Statute of the International Criminal Court: Observers' Notes, Article by Article*, 2nd ed., C.H. Beck/Hart/Nomos, Munich/Oxford/Baden-Baden, 2008, pp. 495–96.

5. Gerhard Werle, *Principles of International Criminal Law*, TMC Asser Press, The Hague, 2009, pp. 252–53, 313, MN 734; 914–16.

6. Anne-Marie L.M. de Brouwer, *Supranational Criminal Prosecution of Sexual Violence: The ICC and the Practice of the ICTY and the ICTR*, Antwerp, Intersentia, 2005, pp. 202–20.

Author: Maria Sjöholm

[136] *General remarks*:

Article 8(2)(e)(vii) concerns the conscription, recruitment or use of children younger than fifteen years of age, in the context of an internal conflict. The crime also appears in Article 8(2)(b)(xxvi) to cover the same crime in the context of an international conflict.

Preparatory works:

As the practice of child soldier recruitment/conscription/use had not been previously expressly recognised as criminalised, its inclusion was naturally a controversial point of debate during Statute negotiations. The United States in particular was against the inclusion of the crime, arguing that it was not a crime under customary international law and represented an area of legislative action "outside the purview of the Conference" (Committee of the Whole Meeting Records, 4th meeting Wednesday 17 June 1998, 54). However, agreement on inclusion was eventually reached due to its position as a well-established treaty law provision (Additional Protocol I, Article 77(2); Additional Protocol II, Article 4(3)(c) and Convention on the Rights of the Child, Article 38(3)). In 2002 the crime was included as a serious violation of international humanitarian law in Article 4(c) of the Statute of the Special Court for Sierra Leone (Statute of the Special Court for Sierra Leone, UN doc. S/2002/246). In a split decision in May 2004, the Special Court held that the provision was already customary international law prior to the adoption of the ICC Statute in 1998; that is to say that the Statute codified an existing customary norm rather than forming a new one (*Prosecutor v. Sam Hinga Norman,* Fourth Defence Preliminary Motion Based on Lack of Jurisdiction (Child Recruitment), SCSL-04-14-AR72, 31 May 2004).

Analysis:

i. Definition

According to Article 8(2)(b)(xxvi) the crime has three components: recruitment, conscription or use. This is in contrast to both Additional Protocol I and Article 38 of the Convention on the Rights of the Child, which make reference to the singular act of 'recruiting'. The Elements of Crime provide further:

1. The perpetrator conscripted or enlisted one or more persons into the national armed forces or used one or more persons to participate actively in hostilities.
2. Such person or persons were under the age of 15 years.
3. The perpetrator knew or should have known that such person or persons were under the age of 15 years.
4. The conduct took place in the context of and was associated with an international armed conflict.

The perpetrator was aware of factual circumstances that established the existence of an armed conflict. The Pre-Trial Chamber in *Prosecutor v. Thomas Lubanga* determined that the term 'conscripting' refers to a forcible act, 'enlisting' encompasses a 'voluntary' decision to join a military force, and the act of 'enlisting' includes "any conduct accepting the child as part of the militia" (*Prosecutor v. Thomas Dyilo Lubanga*, ICC PT. Ch, Decision on the Confirmation of Charges, ICC-01/04-01/06, 29 January 2007).

ii. Consent of the child as a mitigating factor

While alleged voluntariness may be negated by force or intimidation, the consent of the child creates the legal characterisation of the conduct as enlistment rather than conscription. Consent is therefore not irrelevant, but nonetheless places the admission of a child to the armed forces firmly within the realm of Article 8 regardless of the means of admission. The specific mode of admission, whether "the result of governmental policy, individual initiative or acquiescence in demands to enlist" (Happold, 2009, p. 8) is, for the most part irrelevant. Happold suggests that this distinction between the means of committing the material element of this crime may become pertinent during sentencing (*ibid.*, p. 12). In its judgment in *Prosecutor v. Thomas Lubanga Dyilo* the ICC Trial Chamber intimated that it would follow this path when determining the sentence, but found no aggravating factors when delivering the sentencing order on 10 July 2012, instead finding that the factors that are relevant for determining the gravity of the crime cannot additionally be taken into account as aggravating circumstances (*Prosecutor v. Thomas Lubanga*, ICC T. Ch. I, Judgment pursuant to Article 74 of the Statute, ICC-01/04-01/06-2842, 14 March 2012, para. 617; *Prosecutor v. Thomas Lubanga,* Sentencing Order, Decision on Sentence Pursuant to Article 76 of the Statute, ICC-01/04-01/06-2901, 10 July 2012, paras. 78 and 96).

iii. Continuing crime

There are a number of different ways in which these two concepts are interrelated or occur concurrently in the context of the crime. Conscription and enlistment can be viewed as continuing crimes that begin from the moment a child joins an armed group and end upon demobilisation or attainment of 15 years of age, with all intermittent time additionally constituting 'use'. This is therefore a continuing crime: a state of affairs where a crime has been committed and then maintained. The crime is committed from the moment that a child is entered into the armed forces, through enlistment or conscription, and continues for as long as that child remains a 'child soldier', ending either through demobilisation or the attainment of 15 years of age. This places liability on the person who recruited the child, whether by enlisting or conscripting, regardless of whether they were involved in the use of the child in an armed conflict. The act of recruitment triggers responsibility for all subsequent use, even if by other commanders. An alternative interpretation is that the crime is not a composite one, as it is capable of being committed by either the initial conscription or enlistment step, or through the subsequent 'use' of the given child, and not necessarily through demonstrating a combination of the two. This expands the liability for the crime to incorporate not just the person who actually undertakes the recruitment process of a given child, but also includes others who later use the child for military purposes.

iii. Requirements

In addition to the contextual elements required for all war crimes of an international nature set out in elements 4 and 5 of the above-listed Elements of Crimes, the following needs to be proven:

a. Material elements

The first two elements listed above set out the material elements of child soldier conscription/enlistment/use.

1. The perpetrator conscripted or enlisted one or more persons into the national armed forces or used one or more persons to participate actively in hostilities.
2. Such person or persons were under the age of 15 years.

The war crimes established by the ICC Statute are limited to the conscription or enlistment and use of children under the age of fifteen years. However, the acts of 'conscription' and 'enlistment' are not defined in the Statute, nor in the Elements of Crimes, leaving elaboration to judicial interpretation. The Pre-Trial Chamber, (*Prosecutor v. Lubanga*, ICC PT. Ch, Decision on the Confirmation of Charges, ICC-01/04-01/06, 29 January 2007) determined that the term 'conscripting' refers to a forcible act, whereas 'enlisting' encompasses a 'voluntary' decision to join a military force (*Lubanga*, Decision on the Confirmation of Charges, paras. 246–47). The act of 'enlisting' includes "any conduct accepting the child as part of the militia" (*Lubanga*, Decision on the Confirmation of Charges, para. 114). While alleged voluntariness may be negated by force or intimidation, the consent of the child creates the legal characterisation of the conduct as enlistment rather than conscription. Consent is therefore not irrelevant, but nonetheless places the admission of a child to the armed forces firmly within the realm of Article 8 regardless of the means of admission.

Finally, Participation by combatant and non-combatant children are covered equally by the ICC Statute due to its use of the term 'participate actively'. However, their participation must be within the context of an armed conflict. The Elements of Crime require that the participation be conduct "associated with an armed conflict", while the *travaux préparatoires* noted above specifies that participation in the armed confrontations is not necessary, but a link to combat is required (UN doc. A/CONF.183/2/Add.1, 14 April 1998).

b. Mental elements

The perpetrator knew or should have known that such person or persons were under the age of 15 years.

While Article 30(3) provides that a perpetrator must have had positive knowledge of the child's age, the Elements of Crimes merely require that he 'knew or should have known' that the child was under fifteen. In *Lubanga* it was determined that the Elements of Crimes provides for situations where the perpetrator fails to possess knowledge of the given child's age due to a failure to exercise due diligence in the circumstances (*Prosecutor v. Lubanga*, Decision on the Confirmation of Charges, para. 348). Therefore, the Pre-Trial Chamber considered this element of negligence to be an exception to the 'intent and knowledge' standard provided in Article 30(1).

Cross-references:
Article 8(2)(b)(xxvi).

Doctrine:
1. Julie McBride, *The War Crime of Child Soldier Recruitment*, Springer, New York, 2013.

(viii) Ordering the displacement of the civilian population for reasons related to the conflict, unless the security of the civilians involved or imperative military reasons so demand;[137]

---

2. Matthew Happold, "Child Recruitment as a Crime under the Rome Statute of the International Criminal Court", in José Doria, Hans-Peter Gasser and M. Cherif Bassiouni (eds.), *The Legal Regime of the International Criminal Court: Essays in Memory of Igor Blischenko*, Brill, Leiden, 2009.

3. Gerhard Werle, *Principles of International Criminal Law*, TMC Asser Press, The Hague, 2009.

Author: Julie McBride.

[137] Article 8(2)(e)(viii), parallel to Article 8(2)(b)(viii), prohibits the displacement of the civilian population in the context of a non-international armed conflict, unless the security of the civilians involved or imperative military reasons so demand. This conduct is prohibited under the same terms in Article 17 Additional Protocol II and reflects customary international humanitarian law (Rule 129 of the ICRC Study, see also Henckaerts and Doswald-Beck, 2005).

The ICC Elements of Crimes clarify that to prove the war crime of displacing a civilian population it is necessary that 1) the perpetrator ordered a displacement of a civilian population; 2) such an order was not justified by the security of the civilians involved or by military necessity; 3) the perpetrator was in a position to effect such displacement by giving such order; 4) the conduct took place in the context and was associated with a non-international armed conflict; and 5) the perpetrator was aware of factual circumstances that established the existence of an armed conflict.

The term "displacement" shall be interpreted in light of international humanitarian law as to include the evacuation of the civilian population both within and outside the national territory. Article 17(2) AP II proscribes the displacement of civilians outside their national territory.

Differently from the wording used in the ICC Statute, the Elements of Crimes refer to the displacement of "a civilian population" as opposed to "the civilian population". This discrepancy shall be construed as to criminalise conducts of displacement of civilians not necessarily involving the whole civilian population (on the point, cf. Dörmann, 2003, p. 473).

However, the number of civilians involved in the displacement shall exceed individual occurrences. This results from the systemic reading of the Elements of Crimes where, for example, Article 8(2)(a)(vii) refers to "one or more persons" as opposed to "a civilian population" (cf. Dörmann, 2003, p. 472). Arguably, since the letter of Article 8(2)(e)(vii) does not resort to the same expression, only the civilian population and not individual civilians shall be affected by the displacement in order for the conduct to fall under the scope of the provision. This proposition finds support in the *travaux préparatoires* to the ICC Statute where the expression "civilian population" was deliberately chosen against the "one or more civilians" as the drafters considered the displacement of one civilian to be insufficient to constitute the war crime of displacement of civilians (Dörmann, 2003, p. 472).

A salient issue which has been recently elucidated by the ICC case law relates to the existence of an actual order to displace a civilian population as a constitutive element of the war crime under Article 8(2)(e)(viii). In the case *Prosecutor v. Bosco Ntaganda*, the Pre-Trial Chamber has clarified what follows:

the conduct by which the perpetrator(s) force(s) civilians to leave a certain area is not limited to an order, as referred to in element 1 of the relevant Elements of Crimes. The Chamber considers that, should this not be the case, the actual circumstances of civilian displacement in the course of an armed conflict would be unduly restricted. This is specifically reflected in the general introduction to the Elements of Crimes, which states

(ix)   Killing or wounding treacherously a combatant adversary;[138]

---

that "[t]he elements [...] apply '*mutatis mutandis*' to all those whose criminal responsi-bility may fall under Articles 25 and 28 of the Statute" (*Prosecutor v. Ntaganda*, ICC PT. Ch. II, Decision Pursuant to Article 61(7)(a) and (b) of the Rome Statute on the Charges of the Prosecutor Against Bosco Ntaganda, ICC-01/04-02/06-309, 9 June 2014, para. 64).

Nothing in the Elements of Crimes indicates the nature of the position which the alleged perpe-trator has to cover in order to effect the displacement of civilians under Article 8(2)(e)(viii). Yet, the wording "to effect the displacement" seems to privilege a de facto appraisal of such a posi-tion. Therefore, both de jure and de facto positions can be reasonably contemplated under the terms of the provision. This finds support in the pronouncement of the Pre-Trial Chamber in the case *Prosecutor v. Bosco Ntaganda* (*Ntaganda*, ICC PT. Ch. II, Decision Pursuant to Article 61(7)(a) and (b) of the Rome Statute on the Charges of the Prosecutor Against Bosco Ntagan-da, ICC-01/04-02/06-309, 9 June 2014, para. 68) stating "the means used [...] and the modus operandi show that the UPC/FPLC soldiers were in a position to displace civilians, as further demonstrated by the large number of civilians who were in fact displaced".

Article 8(2)(e)(viii) admits the displacement of a civilian population for reasons connected to the conflict only in two exceptional circumstances: 1. When the security of the civilians in-volved so demands, (for example, when the civilians are located in areas likely to be subjected to bombings; 2. When imperative military reasons so demand, where the term "imperative" im-poses a restrictive interpretation of this exception (Dörmann, 2003, pp. 474–75).

Cross-references:
Articles 7(1)(d), 8(2)(a)(vii) and 8(2)(b)(viii).

Doctrine:
1.   Knut Dörmann, *Elements of War Crimes under the Rome Statute of the International Crim-inal Court: Sources and Commentary*, Cambridge University Press, Cambridge, 2003.
2.   Jean-Marie Henckaerts and Louise Doswald-Beck, *Customary International Humanitarian Law*, ICRC, Cambridge University Press, Cambridge, 2005, repr. 2009.

Author: Letizia Lo Giacco.

[138]   Treachery, also synonymous with perfidy, involves a breach of good faith of the combatant adversaries. In practice, it is typically cases in which the accused in deception claims a right to protection for him or herself, and uses this for his or her advantage in the combat. It includes:

*   pretending to be a civilian;
*   fake use of a flag of truce, the flag or of the military insignia and uniform of the enemy or of the United
*   Nations, as well as of the distinctive emblems of the Geneva Conventions;
*   fake use of the protective emblem of cultural property;
*   fake use of other internationally recognised protective emblems, signs or signals;
*   pretending to surrender;
*   pretending to be incapacitated by wounds or sickness;
*   pretending to belong to the enemy by the use of their signs.

The provision is similar, but not identical to Article 8(2)(b)(xi). The prohibition on perfidy in the present only extends to "combatant adversaries", while Article 8(2)(b)(xi) also prohibits the killing and wounding of civilians. The use of the notion "combatant adversary" should be distinguished from "enemy combatants", indicating that there is notion "combatant" is not ap-

---

(x)   Declaring that no quarter will be given;[139]

(xi) Subjecting persons who are in the power of another party to the conflict to physical mutilation[140] or to medical or scientific experiments[141] of any kind which are

---

plicable in internal armed conflicts. Perfidious acts are only punishable if the perpetrator intentionally killed or wounded an adversary.

Cross-references:
Article 8(2)(b)(vii) and 8(2)(b)(xi).

Doctrine:
1. Michael Bothe, in Antonio Cassese, Paola Gaeta and John R.W.D. Jones (eds.), *The Rome Statute of the International Criminal Court: A Commentary*, Oxford University Press, Oxford, 2002, pp. 405, 421.
2. Michael Cottier, in Otto Triffterer (ed.), *Commentary on the Rome Statute of the International Criminal Court: Observers' Notes, Article by Article*, 2nd ed., C.H. Beck/Hart/Nomos, Munich/Oxford/Baden-Baden, 2008, pp. 383–90.
3. Andreas Zimmerman, in Otto Triffterer (ed.), *Commentary on the Rome Statute of the International Criminal Court: Observers' Notes, Article by Article*, 2nd ed., C.H. Beck/Hart/Nomos, Munich/Oxford/Baden-Baden, 2008, pp. 498–99.
4. Gerhard Werle, *Principles of International Criminal Law*, TMC Asser Press, The Hague, 2009, p. 354–57, MN 1054–60.

Author: Mark Klamberg.

[139] The offence covers 'take no prisoners' warfare. The material element will typically be fulfilled by a declaration that any surrender by the enemy shall be refused even if it is reasonable to accept. In addition to declarations, the provision should be including order and threats that no quarter shall be refused. Combatant adversaries are not required to provide the enemy with the opportunity to surrender.

Cross-references:
Article 8(2)(b)(vi) and 8(2)(b)(xii).

Doctrine:
1. Michael Bothe, in Antonio Cassese, Paola Gaeta and John R.W.D. Jones (eds.), *The Rome Statute of the International Criminal Court: A Commentary*, Oxford University Press, Oxford, 2002, p. 421.
2. Michael Cottier, in Otto Triffterer (ed.), *Commentary on the Rome Statute of the International Criminal Court: Observers' Notes, Article by Article*, 2nd ed., C.H. Beck/Hart/Nomos, Munich/Oxford/Baden-Baden, 2008, pp. 391–95.
3. Andreas Zimmerman, in Otto Triffterer (ed.), *Commentary on the Rome Statute of the International Criminal Court: Observers' Notes, Article by Article*, 2nd ed., C.H. Beck/Hart/Nomos, Munich/Oxford/Baden-Baden, 2008, p. 499.
4. Gerhard Werle, *Principles of International Criminal Law*, TMC Asser Press, The Hague, 2009, pp. 360–62, MN 1074–79.

Author: Mark Klamberg.

[140] The term "physical mutilation" cover acts such as amputations, injury to limbs, removal of organs, and forms of sexual mutilations. The victim's consent is not an excusable defence.

Cross-references:
Articles 8(2)(b)(x) and 8(2)(e)(xi).

Doctrine:

neither justified by the medical, dental or hospital treatment of the person concerned nor carried out in his or her interest, and which cause death to or seriously endanger the health of such person or persons;[142]

(xii) Destroying or seizing the property of an adversary unless such destruction or seizure be imperatively demanded by the necessities of the conflict;[143]

---

1. Michael Bothe, in Antonio Cassese, Paola Gaeta and John R.W.D. Jones (eds.), *The Rome Statute of the International Criminal Court: A Commentary*, Oxford University Press, Oxford, 2002, p. 422.

2. Andreas Zimmerman, in Otto Triffterer (ed.), *Commentary on the Rome Statute of the International Criminal Court: Observers' Notes, Article by Article*, 2nd ed., C.H. Beck/Hart/Nomos, Munich/Oxford/Baden-Baden, 2008, p. 499.

3. Gerhard Werle, *Principles of International Criminal Law*, TMC Asser Press, The Hague, 2009, pp. 307–8, MN 895–97.

Author: Mark Klamberg.

[141] The prohibition of medical or scientific experiments cover the use of therapeutic methods which are not justified on medical grounds and not carried out in the interest of the affected person. The consent of the victim is not relevant.

Cross-references:
Article 8(2)(a)(ii) and 8(2)(e)(xi).

Doctrine:

1. Michael Bothe, in Antonio Cassese, Paola Gaeta and John R.W.D. Jones (eds.), *The Rome Statute of the International Criminal Court: A Commentary*, Oxford University Press, Oxford, 2002, pp. 422.

2. Andreas Zimmerman, in Otto Triffterer (ed.), *Commentary on the Rome Statute of the International Criminal Court: Observers' Notes, Article by Article*, 2nd ed., C.H. Beck/Hart/Nomos, Munich/Oxford/Baden-Baden, 2008, pp. 382, 499.

3. Gerhard Werle, *Principles of International Criminal Law*, TMC Asser Press, The Hague, 2009, pp. 308–10, MN 898–902.

Author: Mark Klamberg.

[142] The acts in Article 8(2)(e)(xi) can only be justified if undertaken in the interest of the person concerned, for example, amputations may be lawful if performed to save the live or overall health of the patient. Any physical mutilation or unwarranted medical or scientific experiments undertaken of either governmental authorities or on non-state groups are covered by Article 8(2)(e)(xi).

Cross-references:
Articles 8(2)(b)(x).

Doctrine:

1. Michael Bothe, in Antonio Cassese, Paola Gaeta and John R.W.D. Jones (eds.), *The Rome Statute of the International Criminal Court: A Commentary*, Oxford University Press, Oxford, 2002, pp. 422.

2. Andreas Zimmerman, in Otto Triffterer (ed.), *Commentary on the Rome Statute of the International Criminal Court: Observers' Notes, Article by Article*, 2nd ed., C.H. Beck/Hart/Nomos, Munich/Oxford/Baden-Baden, 2008, pp. 382–83, 499.

3. Gerhard Werle, *Principles of International Criminal Law*, TMC Asser Press, The Hague, 2009, pp. 308–10, MN 898–902.

Author: Mark Klamberg.

---

143 This provision is parallel, *mutatis mutandis*, to Article 8(2)(b)(xiii) ICC Statute and reflects customary international humanitarian law (Rule 50 ICRC Study, see also Henckaerts and Doswald-Beck, 2005).

The ICC Elements of Crimes set out the constitutive elements of the war crime of destroying or seizing the enemy's property: 1) The perpetrator destroyed or seized certain property; 2) such a property was of an adversary; 3) such property was protected from the destruction or seizure under the international law of armed conflict; 4) the perpetrator was aware of the factual circumstances that established the status of the property; the destruction of the property was not required by military necessity; 5) the conduct took place in the context and was associated with an armed conflict not of an international character; 6) the perpetrator was aware of factual circumstances that established the existence of an armed conflict.

Article 8(2)(e)(xii) has been invoked as ground of charges against, *inter alia*, Callixte Mbarushimana (*Prosecutor v. Mbarushimana*, ICC PT. Ch. I, Decision on the Confirmation of Charges, ICC-01/04-01/10-465-Red, 16 December 2011) and Bosco Ntaganda (*Prosecutor v. Ntaganda*, ICC PT. Ch. II, Decision Pursuant to Article 61(7)(a) and (b) of the Rome Statute on the Charges of the Prosecutor Against Bosco Ntaganda, ICC-01/04-02/06-309, 9 June 2014, para. 72 ff.). Likewise, the crime of destruction of enemy's property has been imputed to German Katanga and Mathieu Ngudjolo Chui under Article 8(2)(b)(xiii). Such a legal basis was subsequently modified into Article 8(2)(e)(xii) after the requalification of the conflict from international to non-international.

In the judgment in the case *Prosecutor v. Katanga* (*Prosecutor v. Germain Katanga*, ICC T. Ch. II, Jugement rendu en application de l'Article 74 du Statut, ICC-01/04-01/07-3436, 7 March 2014, para. 889 ff.), the Trial Chamber clarified the scope of Article 8(2)(e)(xii) stating that "*rien n'indique que les éléments constitutifs du crime visé à l'Article 8-2-e-xii sont différents de ceux du crime de destruction des biens de l'ennemi commis dans le cadre d'un conflit armé international et visé à l'Article 8-2-b-xiii*" (para. 889). Such a statement is supported by authoritative doctrine (see Dörmann, pp. 485–86). Based on this, the analysis of Article 8(2)(e)(xii) may occur by analogy with Article 8(2)(b)(xiii) ICC Statute.

The provision criminalises the destruction or seizure of enemy's property protected by the law of armed conflicts. There exists a plurality of ways in which the destruction of property may be carried out. The Trial Chamber has exemplified some of them, namely, "*par des acts tels que l'incendie, le démantèlement ou toute autre forme de dégradation de biens*" (*Prosecutor v. Katanga*, T. Ch. II, Jugement rendu en application de l'Article 74 du Statut, ICC-01/04-01/07-3436, 7 March 2014, para. 891), concluding that property heavily damaged can be assimilated to partly destroyed property and can thus fall under the terms of Article 8(2)(e)(xii) (*Prosecutor v. Katanga*, T. Ch. II, Jugement rendu en application de l'Article 74 du Statut, ICC-01/04-01/07-3436, March 2014, para. 891). In the case *Prosecutor v. Bosco Ntaganda*, the Pre-Trial Chamber confirmed the charge of destruction of property against the defendant for having destroyed houses, buildings and other permanent structures, set on fire houses or removed their metal roofs, destroyed fields, destroyed and burned villages (*Prosecutor v. Ntaganda*, ICC PT. Ch. II, Decision Pursuant to Article 61(7)(a) and (b) of the Rome Statute on the Charges of the Prosecutor Against Bosco Ntaganda, ICC-01/04-02/06-309, 9 June 2014, paras. 72–73). Similarly, destruction of property may occur by "setting fire to, pulling down, or otherwise damaging the adversaries' property" (*Prosecutor v. Mbarushimana*, ICC PT. Ch. I, Decision on the Confirmation of Charges, ICC-01/04-01/10-465-Red, 16 December 2011, para. 171).

As to the "seizure" of property, neither the ICC Statute nor the Elements of Crimes help clarify the meaning of the term. According to the ICRC Commentary, seizure is to be distinguished from requisition because the former relates to public property and is a temporary sequestration followed by restitution and indemnity; the latter affects private property and consists

(xiii) Employing poison or poisoned weapons;[144]

---

in a passage of ownership (Pictet, 1958, p. 296). However, this point remains debated in the literature and unclarified by the ICC case law (for a recollection of relevant positions, cf. Dörmann, 2003, pp. 256–57).

The notion of property is quiet broad. It includes property of natural and legal persons, moveable and immoveable, public and private, provided that they are of the adverse party (*Prosecutor v. Katanga*, Jugement, para. 892). The Trial Chamber has shed light of the meaning of adverse, notably, "*alliées ou faisant allégeance à une partie au conflit opposée ou hostile à l'auteur du crime*" (in *Katanga* Judgment, para. 892). Such an adverse character can be established by virtue of the ethnic origin of the persons whose property has been destroyed (or partly destroyed) or seized or based on their place of residence (*Prosecutor v. Katanga*, Jugement, para. 892).

Article 8(2)(e)(xii) applies to individual acts of destruction or seizure of enemy's property which are protected by the law of armed conflict and does not require any element of extensiveness as opposed to Article 8(2)(a)(iv)) ("Extensive destruction and appropriation of property [...] carried out unlawfully and wantonly").

The destruction of enemy property does not constitute a crime under the terms of the Statute if such a destruction was "imperatively demanded by the necessities of the conflict". Such an expression has been regarded as substantively equivalent to "military necessity" and interpreted in line with the ICTY case law (*Prosecutor v. Katanga*, T. Ch. II, Jugement rendu en application de l'Article 74 du Statut, ICC-01/04-01/07-3436, March 2014, para. 894). Military necessity is therefore meant as "*nécessité de measures indispensables pour attaindre les buts de guerre, et légales selon les lois et coutumes de la guerre*" (Lieber Code, Article 14, cited in *Prosecutor v. Katanga*, T. Ch. II, Jugement rendu en application de l'Article 74 du Statut, ICC-01/04-01/07-3436, 7 March 2014, para. 894).

Cross-references:

Articles 8(2)(a)(iv), (8)(2)(b)(xiii), 8(2)(b)(xvi) and 8(2)(e)(v).

Doctrine:

1. Knut Dörmann, *Elements of War Crimes under the Rome Statute of the International Criminal Court: Sources and Commentary*, Cambridge University Press, Cambridge, 2003.

2. Jean-Marie Henckaerts and Louise Doswald-Beck, *Customary International Humanitarian Law*, Cambridge University Press, Cambridge, 2005, repr. 2009.

3. Jean Pictet, *Commentary to I Geneva Convention for the Amelioration of the Condition of the Wounded and Sick in Armed Forces in the Field*, ICRC, Geneva, 1958.

Author: Letizia Lo Giacco.

[144] This offence could, for example, include the poisoning of water supplies. The production and storage of poison is not prohibited. There is no agreement whether the prohibition on the use of poison covers poison gas. Article 8(2)(b)(xvii) is an identical provision to the present provision, but applies in international armed conflicts.

The provision does not prohibit chemical and biological weapons of mass destruction. This may be explained the lack of agreement on the prohibition on of nuclear weapons and a following compromise during the Rome conference, with the result that weapons of mass destruction are not subject to an explicit and binding provision in the ICC Statute.

Cross-references:

Article 8(2)(b)(xvii), 8(2)(b)(xviii) and 8(2)(b)(xx).

Doctrine:

(xiv) Employing asphyxiating, poisonous or other gases, and all analogous liquids, materials or devices;[145]

(xv) Employing bullets which expand or flatten easily in the human body, such as bullets with a hard envelope which does not entirely cover the core or is pierced with incisions.[146]

1. Michael Bothe, in Antonio Cassese, Paola Gaeta and John R.W.D. Jones (eds.), *The Rome Statute of the International Criminal Court: A Commentary*, Oxford University Press, Oxford, 2002, pp. 406.

2. Michael Cottier, in Otto Triffterer (ed.), *Commentary on the Rome Statute of the International Criminal Court: Observers' Notes, Article by Article*, 2nd ed., C.H. Beck/Hart/Nomos, Munich/Oxford/Baden-Baden, 2008, pp. 413–14.

3. Gerhard Werle, *Principles of International Criminal Law*, TMC Asser Press, The Hague, 2009, at pp. 369–72, MN 1100–6.

Author: Mark Klamberg.

[145] The wording of the present provision is basically identical the Geneva Protocol of 17 June 1925 for the prohibition of the use in war of asphyxiating, poisonous or other gases, and of bacteriological methods of warfare. Article 8(2)(b)(xviii) is also an identical provision to the present provision, but applies in international armed conflicts.

It is generally understood that the wording "asphyxiating, poisonous or other gases, and all analogous liquids, materials or devices" in the 1925 Geneva Protocol includes chemical weapons which nullifies the compromise mentioned in the previous commentary (Article 8(2)(e)(xiv)). Even though biological weapons are covered by the Geneva Protocol of 17 June 1925, it is doubtful that the present provision covers these weapons. This is supported by the fact that the relevant passage on biological weapons in the Geneva Protocol of 17 June 1925 was not included in Article 8(2)(b)(xvii).

Cross-references:
Article 8(2)(b)(xvii) and 8(2)(b)(xviii).

Doctrine:

1. Michael Cottier, in Otto Triffterer (ed.), *Commentary on the Rome Statute of the International Criminal Court: Observers' Notes, Article by Article*, 2nd ed., C.H. Beck/Hart/Nomos, Munich/Oxford/Baden-Baden, 2008, pp. 414–20.

2. Gerhard Werle, *Principles of International Criminal Law*, TMC Asser Press, The Hague, 2009, pp. 372–73, MN 1107–10.

Author: Mark Klamberg.

[146] The 'dum-dum' bullet is type of bullet covered by the present provision, as well as customary law. The prohibition equally applies to standard bullets converted on the battlefield by piercing them with incisions, as well as to other types of bullets which expand or flatten easily in the human body. Article 8(2)(b)(xix) is an identical provision to the present provision, but applies in international armed conflicts.

Cross-references:
Article 8(2)(b)(xix).

Doctrine:

1. Michael Bothe, in Antonio Cassese, Paola Gaeta and John R.W.D. Jones (eds.), *The Rome Statute of the International Criminal Court: A Commentary*, Oxford University Press, Oxford, 2002, p. 408.

(f) Paragraph 2 (e) applies to armed conflicts not of an international character and thus does not apply to situations of internal disturbances and tensions, such as riots, isolated and sporadic acts of violence or other acts of a similar nature. It applies to armed conflicts that take place in the territory of a State when there is protracted armed conflict between governmental authorities and organized armed groups or between such groups.[147]

---

2. Michael Cottier, in Otto Triffterer (ed.), *Commentary on the Rome Statute of the International Criminal Court: Observers' Notes, Article by Article*, 2nd ed., C.H. Beck/Hart/Nomos, Munich/Oxford/Baden-Baden, 2008, pp. 420–23.

3. Gerhard Werle, *Principles of International Criminal Law*, TMC Asser Press, The Hague, 2009, pp. 373–374, MN 1111–13.

Author: Mark Klamberg.

[147] *General remarks:*

Sub-paragraph (f) is an express limitation to the scope of application of sub-paragraph (e) that enumerates crimes committed in a non-international armed conflict (*Prosecutor v. Bemba*, ICC PT. Ch. II, Decision Pursuant to Article 61(7)(a) and (b) of the Rome Statute on the Charges of the Prosecutor against Jean-Pierre Bemba Gombo, ICC-01/05-01/08-424, 15 June 2009, para. 225). It is undoubtedly the most discussed Article in academic literature as:

1. It conveys the impression that there are two types of non-international armed conflicts under the ICC Statute, Article 8(2)(c) conflicts as limited by sub-paragraph (d) and Article 8(2)(e) conflicts as limited by sub-paragraph (f).

2. It appears to adopt the *Tadić* jurisprudence (*Prosecutor v. Tadić* (Case No. IT-94-1-AR72), ICTY A. Ch., Decision on the Defence Motion for Interlocutory Appeal on Jurisdiction, 2 October 1995, para. 70) though with a difference in the wording.

Analysis:

Article 8(2)(f) states that "Paragraph 2 (e) applies to armed conflicts not of an international character and thus does not apply to situations of internal disturbances and tensions, such as riots, isolated and sporadic acts of violence or other acts of a similar nature. It applies to armed conflicts that take place in the territory of a State when there is protracted armed conflict between governmental authorities and organized armed groups or between such groups".

i) Scope of Application

Article 8(2)(f) limits the application of sub-paragraph (e) by first providing a minimum threshold of applicability and secondly spelling out the requirements for a conflict to be characterised as an armed conflict of a non-international nature. The first sentence is identical to that expressed in sub-paragraph (d) and has been interpreted in the same way (*Prosecutor v. Katanga*, ICC Tr. Ch. II, Jugement rendu en application de l'Article 74 du Statut, ICC-01/04-01/07-3436, 7 March 2014, paras. 1187 and 1216; *Prosecutor v. Lubanga*, ICC T. Ch. I, Judgment, ICC-01/04-01/06, 14 March 2012, para. 538).

The second sentence was initially considered by the Court as adducing an additional requirement (*Bemba*, ICC PT. Ch. II, Decision Pursuant to Article 61(7)(a) and (b) of the Rome Statute on the Charges of the Prosecutor against Jean-Pierre Bemba Gombo, ICC-01/05-01/08-424, 15 June 2009, para. 235), raising the threshold of a non-international armed conflict. Yet, later case law suggests that this is not the case and there is only one type of non-international armed conflict (see Commentaries on sub-paragraph (c) and (e)) and that its definition is to be found in sub-paragraph (f).

Sub-paragraph (f) second sentence requires:

- the armed conflict to take place between governmental authorities and organised armed groups or between such groups (see Commentary on sub-paragraph (e)); and
- the armed conflict to be protracted (see also *Lubanga*, ICC T. Ch. I, Judgment, ICC-0/04-01/06, 14 March 2012, para. 536). While in sub-paragraph (f) it is the armed conflict that needs to be protracted, in the ICTY case law it is the violence that must be protracted (*Tadić*, ICTY A. Ch., Decision on the Defence Motion for Interlocutory Appeal on Jurisdiction, 2 October 1995, para. 70). It is unclear whether the ICC has paid much attention to this difference in terminology. Indeed, the only time the ICC makes a reference to "armed violence" in relation to sub-paragraph (f) is when it explains the requirement of an organised armed group to be organised enough "in order to enable [it] to carry out protracted armed violence" (*Lubanga*, ICC T. Ch. I, Judgment, ICC-0/04-01/06, 14 March 2012, para. 536). Moreover, the ICTY has used the notion of "protracted" as an intensity element, having overlooked its temporal connotation (as acknowledged by the ICTY in *Prosecutor v. Boškoski and Tarčulovski* (Case No IT-04-82-T), T. Ch. Judgment, 10 July 2008, para. 186).

That being said, the temporal connotation is implied in two separate, though related contexts:

1. Linked to the requirement that the conflict be of a certain intensity. It is indeed unclear whether the intensity requirement is embedded in the first or second sentence of sub-paragraph (f). Given that the majority of the cases (barring the example of *Bemba* (ICC PT. Ch. II, Decision Pursuant to Article 61(7)(a) and (b) of the Rome Statute on the Charges of the Prosecutor against Jean-Pierre Bemba Gombo, ICC-01/05-01/08-424, 15 June 2009) which links intensity to the first sentence (para. 225)) do not distinguish between conflicts under sub-paragraph (c) and (e) the answer to this question does not seem to have any practical implications. In practice the ICC, when discussing the intensity requirement, examines the length of the conflict as one (that is, "the spread [of attacks] [...] over a period of time" (*Lubanga*, ICC T. Ch. I, Judgment, ICC-0/04-01/06, 14 March 2012, para. 538) of many other elements. It has found that hostilities covering a period of five months (*Bemba*, ICC PT. Ch. II, 15 June 2009, paras. 235 and 255), seven months (*Prosecutor v. Lubanga*, ICC PT. Ch. I, Decision on the Confirmation of Charges, ICC-01/04-01/06-803, 29 January 2007, paras. 236–327), 12 months (*Prosecutor v. Mbarushimana*, ICC PT. Ch. I, Decision on the Confirmation of Charges , ICC-01/04-01/10-465-Red, 16 December 2011, para. 107), 16 months (*Prosecutor v. Ntaganda*, ICC PT. Ch. II, Decision Pursuant to Article 61(7)(a) and (b) of the Rome Statute on the Charges of the Prosecutor Against Bosco Ntaganda, ICC-01/04-02/06-309, 9 June 2014, para. 33) and 17 months (*Katanga*, ICC Tr. Ch. II, Jugement rendu en application de l'Article 74 du Statut, ICC-01/04-01/07-3436, 7 March 2014, para. 1217) are protracted but this may not solely be due to the length of the conflict. Other factors play a role in deciding whether the conflict has reached the required intensity (see Commentary on sub-paragraph (e)).

2. Linked to the requirement that the armed group be organised: Directly referring to the adjective "protracted" in sub-paragraph (f) the ICC explains that the organised armed group must "have the ability to plan and carry out military operations for a prolonged period of time" (*Lubanga*, ICC PT. Ch. I, Decision on the Confirmation of Charges, ICC-01/04-0106-803, 29 January 2007, para. 234 (emphasis added); *Mbarushimana*, ICC PT. Ch. I, Decision on the Confirmation of Charges, ICC-01/04-01/10-465-Red, 16 December 2011, para. 103; see also *Katanga*, ICC Tr. Ch. II, Jugement rendu en application de l'Article 74 du Statut, ICC-01/04-01/07-3436, 7 March 2014, para. 1185; *Lubanga*, ICC T. Ch. I, Judgment, ICC-0/04-01/06, 14 March 2012, para. 536). This interpretation is based on Article 1(1) of Protocol Additional to the Geneva Conventions of 12 August 1949, and relating to the Protection of Victims of Non-International Armed Conflicts that requires the dissident armed forces to be able "to carry out sustained and concerted military operations", (albeit decou-

pled from the requirement of territorial control) which is at odds with the *Tadić* definition (*Tadić*, ICTY A. Ch., Decision on the Defence Motion for Interlocutory Appeal on Jurisdiction, 2 October 1995, para. 70). It must be added that the words 'prolonged' and 'protracted' have both been translated into French as '*prolongé*' but do not seem to have been given a specific temporal connotation.

The Court has specifically mentioned that there is no requirement under the ICC Statute for the armed group "to exert control over a part of the territory" (*Bemba*, ICC PT. Ch. II, Decision Pursuant to Article 61(7)(a) and (b) of the Rome Statute on the Charges of the Prosecutor against Jean-Pierre Bemba Gombo, ICC-01/05-01/08-424, 15 June 2009, para. 236; *Lubanga*, ICC T. Ch. I, Judgment, ICC-0/04-01/06, 14 March 2012, para. 536; *Katanga*, ICC Tr. Ch. II, Jugement rendu en application de l'Article 74 du Statut, ICC-01/04-01/07-3436, 7 March 2014, para. 1186). As noted by the Court itself (*Bemba*, ICC PT. Ch. II, ICC-01/05-01/08-44, 15 June 2009, para. 236; *Lubanga*, ICC T. Ch. I, Judgment, ICC-0/04-01/06, 14 March 2012, para. 536) this clearly departs from Article 1(1) AP II. That being said, territorial control is sometimes mentioned (for example, *Ntaganda*, ICC PT. Ch. II, Decision Pursuant to Article 61(7)(a) and (b) of the Rome Statute on the Charges of the Prosecutor Against Bosco Ntaganda, ICC-01/04-02/06-309, 9 June 2014, para. 34). Likewise, the Court has specified that there is no need for the organised armed group to be under responsible command (*Lubanga*, ICC T. Ch. I, Judgment, ICC-0/04-01/06, 14 March 2012, para. 536) despite referring to that requirement in the earlier case of *Bemba* (*Bemba*, ICC PT. Ch. II, Decision Pursuant to Article 61(7)(a) and (b) of the Rome Statute on the Charges of the Prosecutor against Jean-Pierre Bemba Gombo, ICC-01/05-01/08-424, 15 June 2009, para. 234).

Cross-references:
Article 8(2)(d).

Doctrine:

1. Dapo Akande, "Classification of Armed Conflicts: Relevant Legal Concepts", in Elizabeth Wilmhurst (ed.), *International Law and the Classification of Conflicts,* Oxford University Press, Oxford, 2012, pp. 32–79.
2. Michael Bothe, in Antonio Cassese, Paola Gaeta and John R.W.D. Jones (eds.), *The Rome Statute of the International Criminal Court: A Commentary*, Oxford University Press, Oxford, 2002, pp. 417–18.
3. Antonio Cassese, Paola Gaeta and John R.W.D. Jones (eds.), *International Criminal Law*, 3rd ed., Oxford University Press, Oxford, 2013, pp. 62–83.
4. Robert Cryer, Håkan Friman, Daryll Robinson and Elizabeth Wilmshurst, *An Introduction to International Criminal Law and Procedure*, 3rd ed., Cambridge University Press, Cambridge, 2014, pp. 264–84.
5. Anthony Cullen, "War Crimes", in William A. Schabas and Nadia Bernaz (eds.), *Routledge Handbook of International Criminal Law*, Routledge, London, 2011, pp. 139–54.
6. Knut Dörmann, *Elements of War Crimes under the Rome Statute of the International Criminal Court*, Cambridge University Press, Cambridge, 2002, pp. 82–393.
7. Leena Grover, *Interpreting Crimes in the Rome Statute of the International Criminal Court*, Cambridge University Press, Cambridge, 2014, pp. 279–85.
8. William A. Schabas, *An Introduction to the International Criminal Court*, 4th edition, Cambridge University Press, Cambridge, 2011, pp. 142–44.
9. William A. Schabas, *The International Criminal Court: A Commentary on the Rome Statute*, Oxford University Press, Oxford, 2010, pp. 188–257.
10. Sandesh Sivakumaran, *The Law of Non-International Armed Conflict*, Oxford University Press, Oxford, 2014, pp. 192–95.

3. Nothing in paragraph 2 (c) and (e) shall affect the responsibility of a Government to maintain or re-establish law and order in the State or to defend the unity and territorial integrity of the State, by all legitimate means.[148]

* Paragraphs 2 (e) (xiii) to 2 (e) (xv) were amended by resolution RC/Res.5 of 11 June 2010 (adding paragraphs 2 (e) (xiii) to 2 (e) (xv)).

---

11. Sylvain Vité, "Typology of Armed Conflicts in International Humanitarian Law: Legal Concepts and Actual Situations", in *International Review of the Red Cross*, 2009, vol. 91, pp. 69–94.

12. Andreas Zimmermann, in Otto Triffterer (ed.), *Commentary on the Rome Statute of the International Criminal Court: Observers' Notes, Article by Article*, 2nd ed., C.H. Beck/Hart/Nomos, Munich/Oxford/Baden-Baden, 2008, pp. 475–78.

Author: Noëlle Quénivet.

[148] Paragraph 3 is a saving clause taken from Article 3(1) of the second additional protocol. The provision may justify legitimate actions taken on behalf of the Government of a State in which an internal armed conflict is taking place and its armed forces, but not actions taken by non-state groups. The reference to "legitimate means" should be interpreted in a way that the saving clause does not destroy the object and purpose of sub-paragraphs 2(c) and (e).

Doctrine:

1. Michael Bothe, in Antonio Cassese, Paola Gaeta and John R.W.D. Jones (eds.), *The Rome Statute of the International Criminal Court: A Commentary*, Oxford University Press, Oxford, 2002, pp. 423–24.

2. Andreas Zimmerman in Otto Triffterer (ed.), *Commentary on the Rome Statute of the International Criminal Court: Observers' Notes, Article by Article*, 2nd ed., C.H. Beck/Hart/Nomos, Munich/Oxford/Baden-Baden, 2008, pp. 502–3.

Author: Mark Klamberg.

Article 8 *bis*[3]
Crime of aggression[149]

---

[149] *General remarks*:

The crime of aggression criminalises the planning, preparation, initiation and execution of aggressive use of force from one State against another. The crime of aggression is a leadership crime, requiring the perpetrator to have been in a powerful position in the State that committed the act of aggression. Unlike other crimes in the ICC Statute, it is without application to leaders of non-State groups. The Court will exercise jurisdiction of the crime of aggression in accordance with Articles 15 *bis* and 15 *ter*. The definition of aggression in this Article is based largely on the Definition of Aggression annexed to United Nations General Assembly resolution 3314 (XXIX) of 14 December 1974.

Preparatory works:

The crime of aggression has been listed as a crime under Article 5 of the ICC Statute since 1998, however the Court's jurisdiction over the crime was made dependent on the Assembly of States Parties ('ASP') agreeing on a definition in accordance with the now deleted Article 5(2). In 2002 the ASP decided to establish a Special Working Group on the Crime of Aggression ('SWGCA'), which was to submit proposed provisions to a future Review Conference (Resolution on Continuity of Work in Respect of the Crime of Aggression, 2002). The SWGCA draft amendments were the starting point for the discussions at the Kampala Review Conference in 2010, where Articles 8 *bis*, 15 *bis*, 15 *ter* and 25 (3) *bis* were adopted.

The main areas of controversy for the SWGCA, and later for the Review Conference, were the definition of "an act of aggression"; the individual conduct within the act; and the exercise of jurisdiction. The first two sets of issues are covered by this Article, whereas the question of jurisdiction is dealt with under Articles 15 *bis* and 15 *ter*.

The challenge for the SWGCA when defining "act of aggression" for the purpose of the ICC Statute was to find a definition inclusive enough to be effective, but narrow enough to exclude potentially justifiable uses of force. It was also considered as important that it should remain close to the definition under customary international law.

Acts of aggression have long been held to be grave violations of the prohibition of the use of force as regulated in Article 2(4) of the UN Charter. While it has been agreed that not all acts prohibited by Article 2(4) constitute aggression, it has proven difficult to draw the line between aggression and "mere uses of force". This has not been made easier by the uncertainty surrounding the scope and definition of prohibition of the use of force and its exceptions. However, despite significant disagreements, there are some uses of force that lie outside of this sphere of uncertainty and it has been possible to reach at least some agreement on how to define "act of aggression".

In 1974 the General Assembly unanimously agreed on the definition of aggression annexed to Resolution 3314 (XXIX) of 14 December 1974 ('3314 Definition'), which sought to define aggression for the purposes of determinations by the Security Council under Chapter VII of the UN Charter. While most agreed that the 3314 Definition was the most effective starting point for finding a definition of aggression for the purpose of this Statute, it was held to be problematic since it was written for the determination of State acts rather than for individual criminal responsibility. It was further questioned due to its ambiguity and questionable status as customary international law. Despite suggestions to find a generic definition in customary international law on the crime of aggression, or to leave for the Security Council to determine whether an act of aggression had been committed, the solution was to keep the core Articles of the 3314 Definition in Article 8 *bis*(2) and to contextualise the definition for the purpose of the ICC Statute (Barriga, 2012, pp. 18–20).

---

³ Inserted by resolution RC/Res.6 of 11 June 2010.

1. For the purpose of this Statute, "crime of aggression"[150] means the planning,[151] preparation,[152] initiation[153] or execution,[154] by a person in a position effectively to exercise control

---

The second set of issues for the SWGCA to consider was the individual elements of the crime. As an act of aggression generally is committed by a collective, it is essential to have tools to ascertain that every person is treated fairly in relation to his or her individual conduct. To agree on the individual elements proved to be less difficult than agreeing on a definition of "act of aggression", partly because the customary crime of aggression here could provide more guidance. The requirements for a perpetrator to have been involved in "the planning, preparation, initiation or execution" of the act was based on Article 6a of the Charter of the International Military Tribunal in Nuremberg with "execution" being held to be a modern synonym of "waging". Still, there was some discussion on the level of influence that the leader needed to have over the acts of the State to be in a position to commit a crime of aggression. The crime of aggression has historically been a leadership crime, and with few exceptions it was also widely held in the negotiations that its application should be limited to leaders of States, rather than of non-State entities such as armed rebel groups (Kress and Holtzendorff, 2010, p. 1090). While the majority promoted the now adopted "control or direct" test, some favoured the broader "power to shape or influence" test which was held to be more consistent with the customary definition of the crime of aggression (Heller, 2007, p. 479).

Author: Marie Aronsson-Storrier.

[150] Article 8 *bis*(1) is to be read together with Article 8 *bis*(2), which defines "act of aggression" for the purpose of this Statute.

The first paragraph aims to define the role that a person played in the act of aggression and the level of power he or she had within the State. The wording in Article 8 *bis(1)* reflects that a perpetrator does not have to take part of the whole process from beginning to end, but rather he or she needs to have planned, prepared, initiated or executed the act. The conduct verbs are taken directly from the London Charter's Article 6(a), as well as from the ICL Draft Code on Crimes against the Peace and Security of Mankind, with the exemption of "execution", which has replaced "waging" in order to take into account the modernisation of the language. In assessing the individual conduct, Article 8 *bis*(1) should be read together with Article 25(3), 25(3) *bis* and Article 28, although the latter has been held to be very unlikely to apply in practice (McDougall, 2013, p. 184).

There is some uncertainty regarding the scope of the different modes of participation, and it has been considered difficult to receive much guidance from the Post-Second World War Tribunals in Nuremberg and Tokyo, which took a very broad approach to the interpretation of these verbs. It will be for the Court to make a more detailed determination of the nature and scope of the conduct verbs, while taking into account Article 22(2) in cases of ambiguity.

Author: Marie Aronsson-Storrier.

[151] The *planning* of an act of aggression can, for example, consist of participation in meetings where plans to attack another State are formulated. While it does not require the person to be alone in planning the act, it seems not to be sufficient that a person in a powerful position has verbally supported a plan that was already under way, unless in a way their conduct would be caught by Article 25(3) (McDougall, 2013, p. 187).

Author: Marie Aronsson-Storrier.

[152] The *preparation* of an act of aggression includes a wide range of activities leading to a State having the capacity and possibility to commit the act. This includes military, economic, and diplomatic conduct and can, for example, consist of traditional assembling of troops on a border to

over or to direct the political or military action of a State,[155] of an act of aggression which, by its character, gravity and scale,[156] constitutes a manifest violation of the Charter of the United Nations.[157]

---

the State to be attacked, as well as acts such as acquisition of weapons and the liquidation of State assets in order to fund such purchases when this is done for the purpose of committing the act of aggression. It further includes diplomatic attempts to conceal the State's intentions to gain military advantage before an attack (Shukri, 2010, p. 528; *United States et al v. Göring et al*, IMT, 1 October 1946, pp. 108–9).

Author: Marie Aronsson-Storrier.

[153] The *initiation* of an act of aggression refers to the decision taken immediately before the act to actually move ahead and commit it. This covers decisions on a strategic level, but not necessarily on an operational or tactical level. It may, for example, criminalise the conduct of a defence minister, military leader, or a president giving final orders to commit the act (Shukri, 2010, p. 528; McDougall, 2013, p. 188).

Author: Marie Aronsson-Storrier.

[154] The *execution* of an act of aggression includes decisions taken after commencement of the act, such as annexing occupied territory or to occupy territory after an initial aggressive act. This can notably include conduct by persons who were not at all involved in the initial stages of the act (McDougall, 2013, p. 188).

Author: Marie Aronsson-Storrier.

[155] The leadership requirement in Article 8 *bis*(1) states that a "perpetrator was a person in a position effectively to exercise control over or to direct the political or military action of the State which committed the act of aggression". That leaders can be convicted under the ICC Statute is not exclusive for the crime of aggression, but it is the only crime where the perpetrator has to be in a leadership position.

"In a position to effectively exercise" requires the perpetrator to be in a *de facto* position, and includes not only people in formal positions, but rather anyone with a certain level of influence over the act of the State. It also excludes formal holders of office who are lacking real power. Suggested examples of non-governmental figures with de facto influence are prominent figures in business and religion. It should be noted, however, that the requirement that they should be in a position to "exercise control over or to direct the political and military action of the State" has been held to be a very high threshold for non-formal office holders, making it unlikely that Article 8 *bis* will apply to such actors (McDougall, 2013, p. 181; Heller, 2007 p. 490; Politi, 2012 p. 285).

There are some uncertainties as to the application of the "control or direct" test. Whereas, the ICJ, with regard to a state's level of control over an armed group, has applied an "effective control" test in *Nicaragua* (*Case Concerning Military and Paramilitary Activities in and Against Nicaragua*, (*Nicaragua v. United States of America*), ICJ, Judgment, 27 June 1986) with regard to a State's level of control over an armed group, and used it again in the *Genocide Case* (*Application of the Convention on the Prevention and Punishment of the Crime of Genocide*, (*Bosnia and Herzegovina v. Serbia and Montenegro*), ICJ, Judgment, 26 February 2007), the ICTY instead preferred an "overall control" test in *Tadić* (*Prosecutor v. Tadić* (Case No IT-94-1-A), ICTY, Judgment, 15 July 1999). It remains to be seen to what extent the ICC will take guidance from these judgments when applying the "control or to direct" test in Article 8 *bis*(1).

A further requirement under this paragraph is that a perpetrator needs to have had the certain position in the State which committed the act of aggression, and in cases where an entities status as a State will need to be decided upon, it will be for the Court to do so. The exclusion of non-State actors from the crime of aggression is an important difference from the other crimes in the Statute and, despite being a largely undisputed solution, it has been criticised for not accounting for the reality of contemporary uses of force (Weisbord, 2009, p. 7).

Author: Marie Aronsson-Storrier.

[156] According to Understanding 7, the three components of character, gravity and scale "must be sufficient to justify a "manifest" determination", and the presence of one component will not suffice on its own (Resolutions RC/Res.6, Annex III, Understanding 7). While some argue that the "and" in "character, gravity and scale" should be read as though they all must reach the "manifest violation" threshold, the majority of scholars hold as sufficient that two of the three components are present, as long as they together are strong enough to satisfy the standard (McDougall, 2013, pp. 128–130; Kress and von Holtzendorff, 2010, p. 1207).

Author: Marie Aronsson-Storrier.

[157] In order for a crime of aggression to have been committed, an act of aggression as defined in paragraph 2 must have constituted a "manifest violation" of the UN Charter by its character, gravity and scale. According to the drafted elements, this is an objective qualification, and the subjective experience of the victim State as a manifest violation is not sufficient. As the elements also state that "any of the acts referred to in Article 8 *bis*(2), qualify as an act of aggression", there has been some debate as to whether or not the "manifest violation" requirement changes the threshold compared to the 3314 Definition of Aggression, and compared to customary international law. Some argue that since the 3314 Definition already has a high threshold, and as only grave violations of the prohibition of the use of force constitutes aggression under *jus ad bellum*, it is not inconsistent with the law applicable on State conduct to require a violation to be "manifest". Others similarly suggest that the "manifest violation" requirement is a safeguard to make sure to exclude 'grey areas' of the law on the use of force, especially with regards to Humanitarian Intervention (O'Connell and Niyazmatov, 2012, pp. 203–4; Cryer *et al.*, 2014, p. 321). The influence of discussions on humanitarian intervention can also be seen in Understanding 6, which states that a determination of an act of aggression shall take into consideration the "circumstances of each particular case, including the gravity of the acts concerned and their consequences, in accordance with the Charter of the United Nations" (Resolutions RC/Res.6, Annex III, Understanding 6). While a suggestion to have an explicit exclusion for Humanitarian Interventions failed to gain support of the majority, this understanding aims to exclude acts with positive humanitarian consequences. It should be noted that the legal value of the understandings in Annex III is contested, and although it seems to be clear that they are not considered to be part of the text of the ICC Statute itself, there is disagreement on to what extent they bind the Court (Heinsch, 2010, p. 729–30; Heller, 2012, pp. 230–31; McDougall, 2013, pp. 113–19; Van Schaack, 2011, p. 487). According to some scholars, the understandings are purely suggestions for interpretation, whereas others hold them as part of the context in which the crime of aggression is to be interpreted. It remains to be seen how they will be treated by the Court.

Another 'grey area' of *jus ad bellum* is the right to anticipatory self-defence. Despite some still arguing Article 51 of the UN Charter requires the actual occurrence of an armed attack, and that the adoption of the Article overrode the previous customary right to anticipatory self-defence, there is growing acceptance of the right to use force in anticipatory self-defence as long as it is conducted as a last resort where no peaceful means are available (Wilmshurst, 2005, pp. 4–5). Thus, it is possible that anticipatory self-defence adhering to the principle of necessity and conducted in a proportionate manner will not be considered a "manifest violation" of the Charter rules.

Mens rea

The *mens rea* requirement is found in Article 30 with some clarifying notes on the interpretation with regard to the Crime of Aggression in Annex II. There is no requirement to prove that the

2. For the purpose of paragraph 1, "act of aggression" means the use of armed force by a State against the sovereignty, territorial integrity or political independence of another State, or in any other manner inconsistent with the Charter of the United Nations. Any of the following acts, regardless of a declaration of war, shall, in accordance with United Nations General Assembly resolution 3314 (XXIX) of 14 December 1974, qualify as an act of aggression:[158]

---

perpetrator has made a legal evaluation as to whether or not the use of armed force was inconsistent with (Resolution RC/Res.6, 2010, Annex II, para. 2). There is also no need to prove that the perpetrator has made a legal evaluation as to the "manifest" nature of the violation of the UN Charter (Resolution RC/Res.6, 2010, Annex II, para. 4). What is required is that the perpetrator was aware of the factual circumstances that established that the use of armed force was not only inconsistent with, but also a manifest violation of, the UN Charter (Resolution RC/Res.6, 2010, Annex II, Elements 5 and 6). A mistake of fact leading to a lack of *mens rea* is ground for excluding criminal responsibility in accordance with Article 32.

Author: Marie Aronsson-Storrier.

[158] Article 8 *bis*(2) defines "act of aggression" for the purpose of the ICC Statute. In deciding what constitutes an act of aggression, the paragraph relies heavily on Article 1 and 3 of the 3314 Definition and should be read together with Article 8 *bis*(1), which requires the act to be a "manifest violation" of the rules of the UN Charter. Although there has been some discussion on how to interpret the insertion of "in accordance with Resolution 3314", this is not held to mean that the parts of the 3314 Definition that are not repeated in Article 8 *bis*(2) are directly applicable to the Court (Kress and Holtzendorff, 2010, p. 1191).

The examples of acts of aggression listed in Article 3 of the 3314 Definition and in the present paragraph, have previously been criticised for not being consistent with the definition of aggression under customary international law. While there seem to be little debate on whether occupation following a military intervention, bombardment of another State's territory, and the sending of armed groups to use substantial force on another State's territory, all constitute aggression under customary international law, other acts such as the allowance of territory to be used for act of aggression against third state are held to be more uncertain (*Armed Activities on the territory of Congo* (*Democratic Republic of the Congo v. Uganda*), ICJ, Judgment, 19 December 2005, Judge Kooijimans and Judge Elaraby, Separate opinions). This is not problematic with regard to States Parties, though it can create a potential defence for individuals from non-States Parties, where a situation has been referred to the Court by the Security Council in accordance with Article 15 *ter* (Milanović, 2012, pp. 174–75). While the adoption of Article 8 *bis* strengthens the status of the listed examples as acts of aggression under customary international law, especially if it is ratified by a high number of States, this is not necessarily sufficient to change the customary definition.

Even though determinations of an act of aggression are not binding upon the Court, in accordance with Article 15 *bis*(9) and Article 15 *ter* (4), determinations by the Security Council and the International Court of Justice ('ICJ') can still serve as significant guidance for the ICC when assessing whether an act of aggression has been committed. Yet, it is important to remain careful when interpreting judgments and decisions of acts of aggression by the Security Council and the ICJ, as they are made in the context of *jus ad bellum*, rather than under international criminal law. It is often not necessary for the Security Council to determine whether there has been an act of aggression, as it is sufficient that it has been a "threat or breach to the peace" in accordance with Article 39 of the UN Charter for the full spectrum of Chapter VII measures to be available to the Council. That the Security Council or the ICJ has labelled an act as unlawful "use of force" or "threat or breach of the peace" rather than "act of aggression" should therefore not be taken as a negative determination of whether an act of aggression has been committed.

(a) The invasion or attack by the armed forces of a State of the territory of another State, or any military occupation, however temporary, resulting from such invasion or attack, or any annexation by the use of force of the territory of another State or part thereof;[159]

The definition of acts as "armed attacks" for the purpose of Article 51 of the UN Charter might provide some guidance. The ICJ has referred to the 3314 Definition in determining whether there has been an armed attack giving right to self-defence both in *Nicaragua* and in *Armed Activities* (*Case Concerning Military and Paramilitary Activities in and Against Nicaragua* (*Nicaragua v. United States of America*), ICJ, Judgment, 27 June 1986; *Armed Activities on the Territory of Congo* (*Democratic Republic of the Congo v. Uganda*) ICJ, Judgment, 19 December 2005). It should be noted, however, that while the ICJ has used the 3314 Definition when assessing the existence of an armed attack, the relationship between "act of aggression" and "armed attack" is contested. Some consider the difference between "act of aggression" and "armed attack" to be purely contextual (O'Connell and Niyazmatove, 2012, p. 198), whereas others hold that an "armed attack" triggering a right to self-defence not necessarily would constitute an "act of aggression" (Ruys, 2010, p. 139).

Though there was initially some discussion of whether or not the list in Article 8 *bis(2)* should be considered exhaustive, the list is by most read as open ended, a view supported by the wording of the Article. However, as regard all crimes, care shall still be taken in accordance with the principle of *nullum crime sine lege*, found in Article 22 of the Statute (McDougall, 2013, p. 103; Kress and Holzendorff, 2010, p. 1191).

One area of particular interest with regard to the reading of the list in this paragraph is that of cyber-attacks. Since such attacks do not fit directly with any of the examples given in the list below, it has been suggested that they might be covered under Article 8 *bis* with the use of analogy, or alternatively through the application of a broad interpretation of "armed attack" to include cases where a cyber-attack is a manifest violation of the rules of the UN Charter (Weisbord, 2009, pp. 19–20). It is to be seen which approach the Court will take to cyber-attacks in the future.

Author: Marie Aronsson-Storrier.

[159] Invasion by armed forces, military occupation, or annexation of territory through the use of force are uncontroversial types of aggression. It has, however, been suggested that the requirement for an occupation to follow from an "armed attack" is limiting and would exclude occupation following from threats and other coercive means (McDougall, 2013, p. 76).

The General Assembly explicitly referred to Article 3(a) of the 3314 Definition in a series of Resolutions from 1981 to 1992, when holding that Israel's occupation of the Syrian Golan Heights constituted an act of aggression. It also referred to the 3314 Definition of Aggression regarding South Africa's occupation of Namibia in 1982 (General Assembly Resolution 37/43, 3 December 1982).

The Security Council, which often avoids the term "aggression", has used it on a number of occasions such as Resolution 546 (Security Council Resolution 546, 6 January 1984) regarding the military occupation and bombings by South Africa in Angola and Resolution 424 on Southern Rhodesia's invasion of Zambia (Security Council Resolution 424, 17 March 1978).

Even though the Security Council did not describe Iraq's invasion of Kuwait in 1990, as aggression, but merely as an illegal use of force triggering the need for collective action, (Security Council Resolution 660 2 August 1990), the invasion is still widely held as an act of aggression (Cassese, 2007, p. 845). The same is true for the invasion of Falkland Islands by Argentina in 1982, which was deemed a "breach of peace" by the Security Council (Security Council Resolution 502, 3 April 1982).

Author: Marie Aronsson-Storrier.

(b) Bombardment by the armed forces of a State against the territory of another State or the use of any weapons by a State against the territory of another State;[160]

(c) The blockade of the ports or coasts of a State by the armed forces of another State;[161]

(d) An attack by the armed forces of a State on the land, sea or air forces, or marine and air fleets of another State;[162]

(e) The use of armed forces of one State which are within the territory of another State with the agreement of the receiving State, in contravention of the conditions provided for in the agreement or any extension of their presence in such territory beyond the termination of the agreement;[163]

(f) The action of a State in allowing its territory, which it has placed at the disposal of another State, to be used by that other State for perpetrating an act of aggression against a third State;[164]

---

[160] The use of any weapons against the territory of another State which meets the criteria of manifest violation in Article 8 *bis*(1) constitutes an act of aggression. There are numerous examples of acts deemed as aggression that would fall under this section should the Court hold them to be sufficiently severe. Some examples are the Israeli bombing of the Osirak nuclear reactor in Iraq 1981 (General Assembly Resolution 36/27, 13 November 1981), the attacks by Southern Rhodesia into Zambia (Security Council Resolution 424, 17 March 1978), and the air raid by Israel over Tunisia (Security Council Resolution 573, 4 October 1985).
Author: Marie Aronsson-Storrier.

[161] A blockade of ports and coasts are activities that halt the maritime transport to and from another State. A common example of this is the presence of warships controlling traffic in and out of a harbour or of coastal, territorial waters, as well as the mining of a harbour stopping boats and ships from entering or leaving. Two examples of blockade are those by the US of Cuba during the Missile Crisis 1962 and again of the Dominican Republic in 1965 (Glennon, 2010, p. 93).
Author: Marie Aronsson-Storrier.

[162] This sub-paragraph concerns the attack of the forces or fleets of a State, even where they are stationed in, or in transit through, a third State. There is no set requirement for the level of damage, or for the size of the force or fleet that is subject for attack, in order for this provision to apply. The ICJ has not ruled out the possibility for the destruction of a "single military vessel" to constitute an "armed attack" for the purpose of Article 51 of the UN Charter (*Oil Platforms (Islamic Republic of Iran v. United States of America*) ICJ, Judgment, 6 November 2003, para. 72). It has, however, been suggested that the use of the term "fleets" in this provision aims to exclude attacks on a single, or a small group of, commercial vessels (Dinstein, 2011, p. 217).
Author: Marie Aronsson-Storrier.

[163] Article 8 *bis(2)*(e) is applicable in situations where a State initially has consented to the presence of the armed forces of another State, but where the second State either overstays its welcome, or in other ways uses its armed forces in breach of this agreement. A contravention of conditions can include both geographical scope and activities (*Armed Activities on the Territory of Congo (Democratic Republic of the Congo v. Uganda*) ICJ, Judgment, 19 December 2005).
Author: Marie Aronsson-Storrier.

[164] This provision establishes responsibility where a State has approved the use of its territory by another State for the purpose of attacking a third State. The provision has been criticised for confusing the use of force with assistance of the use of force by the means of State action (McDougall, 2013, p. 76). It should be noted that acts under this provision also include cases

(g) The sending by or on behalf of a State of armed bands, groups, irregulars or mercenaries, which carry out acts of armed force against another State of such gravity as to amount to the acts listed above, or its substantial involvement therein.[165]

---

where a State allows another State to attack a third State's forces or fleets as regulated under Article 8 *bis*(2)(d).

Author: Marie Aronsson-Storrier.

[165] Article 8 *bis(2)*(g) regulates "indirect aggression", where a state instead of using its armed troops uses armed bands, groups, irregulars or mercenaries to conduct the act of aggression. Similar provisions can be found in the Friendly Relations Declaration of 1970, as well as in the ILC Draft Code on Offences against the Peace and Security of Mankind of 1954. The inclusion of both groups and mercenaries shows that the aims of the group, whether political, ideological or economical, are unimportant for the application of this Statute; what matter is the extent to which the State in question has control over their actions.

While many violent activities by non-State actors do not meet the requirement of gravity and scale, this section asserts that when they do, a State controlling the non-State actor should not avoid responsibility because its own troops did not conduct the violent act (Weisbord, 2009, p. 13). Further, while it is uncommon for non-State actors to commit acts that in themselves meet the threshold for an act of aggression, the ICJ has held that a series of incidents breaching the prohibition of the use of force can collectively amount to an armed attack. This might provide some guidance for the interpretation of this sub-paragraph (Dinstein. 2005, p. 202; *Armed Activities Armed Activities on the Territory of Congo (Democratic Republic of the Congo v. Uganda)*, ICJ, Judgment, 19 December 2005, para. 146).

With regard to attribution, the ICJ, in *Nicaragua*, invented and applied the "effective control" test in examining the required level of control for actions being attributable for the State (*Nicaragua*, ICJ, 27 June 1986). The test was later rejected by the ICTY in *Tadić* which favoured a test of "overall control" since it held the "effective control" test to lack flexibility, but was reinforced by the ICJ in the *Genocide Case* in 2007, then acknowledging the importance of flexibility as to the circumstances of each case (*Prosecutor v. Tadić* (Case No IT-94-1-A) ICTY, Judgment, 15 July 1999); (*Application of the Convention on the Prevention and Punishment of the Crime of Genocide (Bosnia and Herzegovina v. Serbia and Montenegro)*, ICJ, Judgment, 26 February 2007). The alternative basis "or substantial involvement therein" seems to open up for less direct involvement in the activities of an armed group, and include activities such as financing, providing of arms or other means, and training. Such activities failed to meet the threshold for an "armed attack" in Nicaragua, which was criticised in the dissenting opinion of Judge Schwebel for failing to account for "the realities of the use of force in international relations" (*Case Concerning Military and Paramilitary Activities in and Against Nicaragua (Nicaragua v. United States of America)*, ICJ, Judgment, 27 June 1986, Dissenting Opinion of Judge Schwebel, para. 155). It remains to be seen how the ICC will interpret "substantial involvement" in relation to the requirements in Article 8 *bis*(1).

Cross-references:

Article 5(1)(d), 15 *bis*, 15 *ter* and 25(3) *bis*.

Doctrine:

1. Stefan Barriga, "Negotiating the Amendments on the Crime of Aggression", in Stefan Barriga and Claus Kreß (eds.), *The Travaux Preparatoires of the Crime of Aggression*, Cambridge University Press, Cambridge, 2012, pp. 3–57.

2. Robert Cryer, Håkan Friman, Daryll Robinson and Elizabeth Wilmshurst, *An Introduction to International Criminal Law and Procedure*, 3rd ed., Cambridge University Press, Cambridge, 2014, p. 321.

3. Yorah Dinstein, *War, Aggression and Self-Defence,* 5th ed., Cambridge University Press, Cambridge, 2011, p. 217.

4. Michael Glennon, "The Blank-Prose Crime of Aggression", in *Yale Journal of International Law*, 2010, vol. 35, pp. 71–114.

5. Robert Heinsch, "The Crime of Aggression After Kampala: Success or Burden for the Future?", in *Goettingen Journal of International Law*, 2010, vol. 2, no. 2, pp. 713–43.

6. Kevin Jon Heller, "The Uncertain Legal Status of the Aggression Understandings", in *Journal of International Criminal Justice*, 2012, vol. 10, pp. 229–48.

7. Kevin Jon Heller, "Retreat from Nuremberg: The Leadership Requirement in the Crime of Aggression", *European Journal of International Law*, 2007, vol. 18, pp. 477–97.

8. Claus Kreß and Leonie von Holtzendorff, "The Kampala Compromise on the Crime of Aggression", *Journal of International Criminal Justice*, 2010, vol. 8, no. 5, pp. 1179–1217.

9. Carrie McDougall, *The Crime of Aggression under the Rome Statute of the International Criminal Court*, Cambridge University Press, Cambridge, 2013, pp. 76, 103, 113–19, 128–30, 181, 184, 187–88.

10. Marko Milanović, "Aggression and Legality Custom in Kampala", in *Journal of International Criminal Justice*, 2012, vol. 10, pp. 165–87.

11. Mary Ellen O'Connell and Mirakmal Niyazmatov, "What is Aggression? Comparing the Jus ad Bellum and the ICC Statute", in *Journal of International Criminal Justice*, 2012, vol. 10, pp. 189–207.

12. Mauro Politi, "The ICC and the Crime of Aggression: A Dream that Came Through and the Reality Ahead", in *Journal of International Criminal Justice*, 2012, vol. 10, pp. 267–88.

13. Tom Ruys, *'Armed Attack' and Article 51 of the UN Charter, Evolutions in Customary Law and Practice*, Cambridge University Press, Cambridge, 2010, p. 139.

14. Muhammad Aziz Shukri, "Individual Criminal Responsibility for the Crime of Aggression", in Roberto Bellelli (ed.), *International Criminal Justice: Law and Practice from the Rome Statute to Its Review*, Ashgate, Farnham, 2010, pp. 519–45.

15. Beth Van Schaack, "Crime of Aggression and Humanitarian Intervention on Behalf of Women", in *International Criminal Law Review*, 2011, vol. 11, pp. 477–94.

16. Noah Weisbord, "Conceptualizing Aggression", in *Duke Journal of Comparative and International Law*, 2009, vol. 20, pp. 1–48.

17. Elisabeth Wilmshurst, *Principles of International Law on the Use of Force by States in Self-Defence*, Chatham House, ILP Working Paper 05/01, 2005, pp. 4–5.

Author: Marie Aronsson-Storrier.

Article 9
Elements of Crimes[4]

1. Elements of Crimes shall assist the Court in the interpretation and application of articles 6, 7, 8 and 8 *bis*. They shall be adopted by a two-thirds majority of the members of the Assembly of States Parties.[166]

2. Amendments to the Elements of Crimes may be proposed by:

   (a) Any State Party;[167]

   (b) The judges acting by an absolute majority;[168]

---

[166] The main purpose of the Elements of Crime is to define the crimes with clarity, precision and specificity in order to meet the principle of legality, required for by criminal law. In both civil and common law systems a crime consists of material elements (the objective requirements, the *actus reus*) and mental elements (the subjective requirements: intent and/or knowledge, or *mens rea*).

The Elements of Crime include material elements of three different types, which relate to conduct, consequence and circumstance (see reference in Article 30).

Unless otherwise provided, Article 30 provides the mental requirement. Thus, the principal mental elements in the Elements of Crime stem from Article 30.

The wording "shall assist the Court" makes clear the non-binding nature of the Elements of Crime. The provision appears to contradict Article 21(1)(a) which states that: "The Court shall apply: In the first place, this Statute, Elements of Crime and its Rules of Procedure and Evidence". However, in light of the negotiating history, the Elements of Crime should be understood to have only persuasive value rather than binding force.

The present provision should be contrasted to Article 112(7)(a) which states: "Decisions on matters of substance must be approved by a two-thirds majority of those present and voting provided that an absolute majority of States Parties constitutes the quorum for voting". The wording of Article 9(1) makes it clear that a two-thirds majority of the total members of the Assembly of States Parties, not just the States present and voting, is required for the adoption of the Elements of Crime.

Author: Mark Klamberg.

[167] The right for any State Party to propose an amendment to a treaty stems from the sovereign equality of States. It should be noted that the Elements of Crime are subject to a different procedure than the one designed for amendments of the ICC Statute.

It is not specified in regulation 5(1) whether proposals from State Parties should be submitted to the Advisory Committee on Legal Texts. It appears likely that a State Party would submit a proposal for an amendment to an organ of the Assembly of States Parties. One alternative would be to adopt the same procedure as used for amendments of the Rules of Procedure and Evidence (Rule 3), whereby State Parties submit their proposals to the President of the Bureau of the Assembly of States Parties.

Cross-references:
Regulation 5(1) Amendments to the Rules.

Author: Mark Klamberg.

[168] Provided that there are 18 judges, an absolute majority requires the support of 10 judges. According to regulation 5(1) any proposal for amendments to the Elements of Crime pursuant to Article 9 shall be submitted by a judge to the Advisory Committee on Legal Texts.

(c) The Prosecutor.[169]

Such amendments shall be adopted by a two-thirds majority of the members of the Assembly of States Parties.[170]

3. The Elements of Crimes and amendments thereto shall be consistent with this Statute.[171]

[4] As amended by resolution RC/Res.6 of 11 June 2010 (inserting the reference to article 8 *bis*).

Cross-references:
Regulation 5(1) Amendments to the Rules.

Author: Mark Klamberg.

[169] In contrast to proposals from the Judges, the use of the word "may" instead of "shall" in regulation 5(1) appear to indicate that proposals for amendments to the Elements of Crime can be submitted by the Prosecutor both to the Advisory Committee on Legal Texts and the appropriate organ of the Assembly of States Parties.

Cross-references:
Regulation 5(1) Amendments to the Rules.

Author: Mark Klamberg.

[170] The procedure for amending the Elements of Crime is identical for the procedure of the adoption of the Elements of Crime stated in paragraph 1. Thus, it is clear that a two-thirds majority of the total members of the Assembly of States Parties, not just the States present and voting, is required for the amendment of the Elements of Crime.

Author: Mark Klamberg.

[171] The present provision indicates the relation between the ICC Statute and the Elements of Crime is *lex superior derogat legi inferiori*, rather than *lex posterior derogat legi priori*. In other words, in the event of an conflict between the ICC Statute and the Elements of Crime, the ICC Statute shall prevail. Thus, the non-binding nature of the Elements of Crime is affirmed.

Doctrine:

1. Erkin Gadirov, in Otto Triffterer (ed.), *Commentary on the Rome Statute of the International Criminal Court: Observers' Notes, Article by Article*, 2nd ed., C.H. Beck/Hart/Nomos, Munich/Oxford/Baden-Baden, 2008, pp. 505–29.

2. Herman von Hebel and Maria Kelt, in Roy S. Lee (ed.), *The International Criminal Court: Elements of Crimes and Rules of Procedure and Evidence*, Transnational Publishers, Ardsley, New York, 2001, pp. 7–14.

3. Alain Pellet, in Antonio Cassese, Paola Gaeta and John R.W.D. Jones (eds.), *The Rome Statute of the International Criminal Court: A Commentary*, Oxford University Press, Oxford, 2002, pp. 1059–62; 1077–78.

Author: Mark Klamberg.

Article 10

Nothing in this Part shall be interpreted as limiting or prejudicing in any way existing or developing rules of international law for purposes other than this Statute.[172]

---

[172] *General remarks*

Article 10 has no heading that would enlighten the purpose of the provision or clarify its content. When draft Article Y – eventually adopted as Article 10 – was suggested, it was namely envisaged that the provision could be a sub-paragraph to Article 5 (enumerating the crimes within the jurisdiction of the Court) and as such it would not have needed a heading (UN doc. A/CONF.183/2, p. 20. See further Triffterer, 2008, p. 532). The formulation "for purposes other than this Statute", however, gives forth that the provision was adopted to affect the status given to Part 2 of the ICC Statute outside the ICC context. According to Sadat, the desire was to ensure that "the codification of [...] international criminal law in the ICC Statute would not negatively impact either the existing customary international framework or the development of new customary law" (Sadat, 2000, pp. 910-911). Draft Article Y hence made the ICC negotiations easier by emphasising that the goal of the negotiations was to adopt crime definitions for the purpose of ICC proceedings only and not to influence international law more generally. Article 10 is thus an Article that postulates the "existence of two [...] regimes or corpora of international criminal law" (Cassese, 1999, p. 157), that is, an ICC regime and a customary international law regime.

While there is general agreement that the pivotal function of draft Article Y was to preserve existing international law in situations where the ICC Statute fell short of it (most notably in relation to war crimes), there are different opinions about the extent to which the goal also was to prevent other types of legal changes. In this regard, Sadat has held that "the framers apparently intended that only the restrictive portions of the definitions of the crimes would remain locked within the ICC structure, not more progressive elements" (Sadat, 2000, p. 918). Bennouna, on his part, has argued that the aim of Article 10 was not only to "protect the position of the countries favouring a broader definition of war crimes", but also to hinder "unease among those adhering to a more restrictive definition of crimes against humanity" (Bennouna, 2002, p. 1102). Bennouna's interpretation finds support in the fact that the provision does not only address existing rules of international law, but also applies to developing rules. Sadat's, on the other hand, in that the Article only refers to limiting or prejudicing interpretation (Sadat, 2002, p. 269). While the drafters' intention with the provision is open to debate, the present author finds Sadat's interpretation to be more functional in that it entails that international criminal law is not unnecessarily fragmented. To preserve the unity of international criminal law is important in that the ICC may have jurisdiction over individuals based on Security Council referrals of situations (Article 13) in which cases it is problematic if the ICC law departs from customary international law (see further Milanović, 2011, p. 25 ff., and Sadat, 2002, pp. 262 and 269-71). It should also be noted that when amendments to the ICC Statute were adopted in 2010, including a definition of the crime of aggression, an understanding was attached to the amendment in which it was reaffirmed that the crime of aggression also can be prosecuted in relation to situations referred by the Security Council. At the same time, however, Article 10 is mentioned in relation to domestic jurisdiction over the crime of aggression, and it is emphasised that the ICC definition of the crime has been accepted "for the purpose of [..., the] Statute only" (Resolution RC/Res. 6, Annex III). As such, the understanding sends a conflicting message about the customary law relevance of ICC law and does not really answer how Article 10 should be interpreted.

The fact that the Article's primary addressees are actors outside the Court makes it necessary to ask to what extent such actors are bound to follow provisions in the ICC Statute. It is, for sure, possible to have treaty provisions explaining the drafters' intentions and to try to influence interpretations (see also Articles 22(3), 25(4) and 80). This being said, the behaviour of States in connection to the negotiation and ratification of international treaties plays a central role when State practice and opinio juris are assessed in connection to customary international law. As such, the participation of numerous States in the ICC negotiations and their subsequent ratification of the ICC Statute is something that cannot be completely ignored when the content of customary international law is considered (see for example, Bennouna, 2002, p. 1106). The same also applies to State behaviour in treaty amendment procedures. From this perspective, it is not surprising that the case law of many international and regional courts contain references to Part 2 of the ICC Statute (for such references, see Schabas, 2010, p. 271). In the *Furundžija* case, a Trial Chamber of the ICTY explicitly commented upon the legal relevance of Article 10 and found that:

> [The ICC Statute] was adopted by an overwhelming majority of the States attending the Rome Diplomatic Conference and was substantially endorsed by the General Assembly's Sixth Committee on 26 November 1998. In many areas the Statute may be regarded as indicative of the legal views, that is, opinio juris of a great number of States. Notwithstanding Article 10 of the Statute, the purpose of which is to ensure that existing or developing law is not "limited" or "prejudiced" by the Statute's provisions, resort may be had cum grano salis to these provisions to help elucidate customary international law. Depending on the matter at issue, the Rome Statute may be taken to restate, reflect or clarify customary rules or crystallise them, whereas in some areas it creates new law or modifies existing law. At any event, the Rome Statute by and large may be taken as constituting an authoritative expression of the legal views of a great number of States (*Prosecutor v. Furundžija*, ICTY T. Ch., 10 December 1998, para. 227. See also Cryer, 2006, p. 251).

The case law of the various international and regional courts has made Schabas submit that "Article 10 appears to be largely ignored by the very bodies to whom it is directed, namely specialized tribunals engaged in the interpretation of international law" (Schabas, 2010, p. 271).

As Article 10 of the ICC Statute primarily is directed to actors outside the Court, it is rarely mentioned in the case law of the ICC. In the *Al Bashir* case, the majority of the Pre-Trial Chamber, however, found that the Article "becomes meaningful insofar as it provides that the definition of the crimes in the Statute and the Elements of Crimes shall not be interpreted "as limiting or prejudicing in any way existing or developing rules of international law for purposes other than this Statute" (*Prosecutor v. Al Bashir*, ICC PT. Ch., 4 March 2009, para. 127). What the judges exactly meant by this reference to Article 10 is not evident to the present commentator. Schabas, however, interprets the pronouncement to mean that the judges held that Article 10 supported their claim that it was not necessary to take into consideration customary international law when interpreting the ICC provision on genocide (Schabas, 2011, p. 93). Furthermore, Article 10 has been mentioned in a dissenting opinion by Judge Kaul, where he found that Article 10 "reinforces the assumption that the drafters of the Statute may have deliberately deviated from customary rules" (*Situation in the Republic of Kenya*, ICC PT. Ch (Diss. Op. Kaul), ICC-01/09-19, 31 March 2010, para. 32). As noted above, Article 10 indeed envisages a fragmented international criminal law.

Finally, it should be noted that Article 10 limits its applicability to "this Part" referring to Part 2 of the ICC Statute containing provisions on jurisdiction, admissibility and applicable law. The international crimes definitions are placed in Part 2, but, for example, the provisions on individual criminal responsibility and grounds for excluding criminal responsibility are situated elsewhere (in Part 3). This gives rise to the question of to what extent the implications of the ICC Statute on the existing or developing rules of international law are different in other parts of the Statute. In this regard, Triffterer has argued that the legal principle enshrined in Article 10 is applicable to the whole Statute. He bases his argument of the drafting process of the provision:

> by its drafting process it may be assumed that a limiting or prejudicing interpretation of all Articles outside Part 2, adopted as a compromise or those describing a status quo, should equally not bar the interpretation of "existing or developing rules of international law for purposes other than this Statute". This goes without saying, for instance, with regard to Article 25 [on individual criminal responsibility.] (Triffterer, 2008, p. 535, see also p. 537)

While a detailed analysis of the relationship between customary international law and the ICC Statute lies beyond the scope of this commentary, the following should be noted. First, Part 3 of the ICC Statute contains a provision similar to Article 10, namely Article 22(3), which stipulates that the nullum crimen sine lege provision shall not affect the characterisation of any conduct as criminal under international law independently of the Statute (on the relationship between Article 10 and 22(3), see Broomhall, 2008, p. 726, and Lamb, 2002, p. 754). Second, when it comes to the modes of responsibility and grounds for excluding criminal responsibility, it is generally accepted that customary international law and ICC law do not always concur. For example, in connection to commission responsibility, the ICC has not adopted the joint criminal enterprise doctrine of the *ad hoc* tribunals (*Prosecutor v. Lubanga*, ICC PT. Ch., 29 January 2007, paras. 329, 335 and 338) and the ICTY, on its part, has found that co-perpetratorship responsibility à la ICC Article 25(3)(a) "does not have support in customary international law" (*Prosecutor v. Stakić*, ICTY A. Ch., 22 March 2006, paras. 59 and 62). As, however, the today functioning *ad hoc* international criminal tribunals primarily have addressed atrocities that have occurred before the adoption of the ICC Statute, these tribunals have not had any reason to in detail consider to what extent, if any, the State Practice in connection to the adoption and ratification of the ICC Statute, or its amendment procedures, have changed customary international law.

Cross-references:
Articles 21(3) and 22(3).

Doctrine:

1. Mohamed Bennouna, "The Statute's Rules on Crimes and Existing or Developing International Law", in Antonio Cassese, Paola Gaeta and John R.W.D. Jones (eds.), *The Rome Statute of the International Criminal Court: A Commentary*, 2nd ed., Oxford University Press, Oxford, 2002, pp. 1101–7.

2. Bruce Broomhall, "Article 22, *Nullum Crimen Sine Lege*", in Otto Triffterer (ed.), *Commentary on the Rome Statute of the International Criminal Court: Observers' Notes, Article by Article*, 2nd ed., C.H. Beck/Hart/Nomos, Munich/Oxford/Baden-Baden, 2008, pp. 713–29.

3. Antonio Cassese, "The Statute of the International Criminal Court: Some Preliminary Reflections", in *European Journal of International Law*, 1999, vol. 10, no. 1, pp. 144–71.

4. Robert Cryer, "Of Custom, Treaties, Scholars and the Gavel: The Influence of the International Criminal Tribunals on the ICRC Customary Law Study", in *Journal of Conflict and Security Law*, 2006, vol. 11, no. 2, pp. 239–63.

5. Susan Lamb, "*Nullum Crimen, Nulla Poena Sine Lege* in International Criminal Law", in Antonio Cassese, Paola Gaeta and John R.W.D. Jones (eds.), *The Rome Statute of the International Criminal Court: A Commentary*, Oxford University Press, Oxford, 2002, pp. 733–66.

6. Marko Milanović, "Is the Rome Statute Binding on Individuals? (And Why We Should Care)", in *Journal of International Criminal Justice*, 2011, vol. 9, no. 1, pp. 25–52.

7. Leyia Nadya Sadat, "Custom, Codification and Some Thoughts about the Relationship between the Two: Article 10 of the ICC Statute", in *DePaul Law Review*, 2000, vol. 49, pp. 909–23.

8. Leila Nadya Sadat, *The International Criminal Court and the Transformation of International Law: Justice for the New Millennium*, Transnational Publishers, Ardsley, NY, 2002.

9. William A. Schabas, *The International Criminal Court: A Commentary on the Rome Statute*, Oxford University Press, Oxford, 2010.

10. William A. Schabas, *An Introduction to the International Criminal Court*, 4th ed., Cambridge University Press, Cambridge, 2011.

11. Otto Triffterer, "Article 10", in Otto Triffterer (ed.), *Commentary on the Rome Statute of the International Criminal Court: Observers' Notes, Article by Article*, 2nd ed., C.H. Beck/Hart/Nomos, Munich/Oxford/Baden-Baden, 2008, pp. 531–37.

Author: Mikaela Heikkilä.

Article 11

Jurisdiction *ratione temporis*

1. The Court has jurisdiction only with respect to crimes committed after the entry into force of this Statute.[173]
2. If a State becomes a Party to this Statute after its entry into force, the Court may exercise its jurisdiction only with respect to crimes committed after the entry into force of this Statute for that State, unless that State has made a declaration under article 12, paragraph 3.[174]

---

[173] The Court has the power to exercise jurisdiction following the 1 July 2002, when the ICC Statute was ratified by 60 States and thus entered into force (Article 126). Thus, the ICC Statute is based on the non-retroactivity principle and the temporal jurisdiction of the Court is prospective (Article 24(1)).

The ICC Statute is silent in regard to violations which are committed prior to the entry into force of the Statute and continued afterwards. It is submitted that references in future cases to acts pre-dating the entry into force of the Statute may be useful in establishing the historical context but they may not be form the basis of a charge.

The jurisdiction *ratione temporis* may be limited in two ways. The Security Council may according to Article 16 prevent the Court from exercising jurisdiction for a fixed period of time. A State may also upon ratification of the ICC Statute make a declaration in accordance with Article 124 and opt out for a period of seven years from the jurisdiction of the Court in relation to war crimes.

Cross-references:
Articles 16, 24(1), 124 and 126.

Author: Mark Klamberg.

[174] A precondition to the Court's exercise of jurisdiction is that the State has accepted the jurisdiction of the Court (Article 12). In addition, the Security Council may refer a situation to the Court (Article 13). The requirement on consent on behalf of the State has implications for the temporal jurisdiction of the Court. In regard to States that accepts the jurisdiction of the Court two exceptions may be noted in relation to the jurisdiction *ratione temporis* set by the entry into force of the ICC Statute.

The first exception concerns States Parties. When a State becomes a party, the Court's temporal jurisdiction is limited to the crimes committed after the entry into force of the ICC Statute for that State, unless that State in accordance with Article 12(3) accepts jurisdiction for acts committed prior to ratification but after the entry into force of the Statute. It is submitted that the declaration must be explicit, which was the case in the situation in Uganda and the situation in the Democratic Republic of Congo, see letter of the Prosecutor of 17 June 2004 attached to the Decision Assigning the Situation in Uganda to Pre-Trial Chamber II, 5 July 2004 (p. 4) and Decision Assigning the Situation in the Democratic Republic of Congo to Pre-Trial Chamber I, 5 July 2004 (p. 4).

The second exception, concerning States Not Parties to the ICC Statute, is examined in the comment to Article 12.

Cross-references:
Articles 12 and 13.

Doctrine:

1. Sharon A. Williams, in Otto Triffterer (ed.), *Commentary on the Rome Statute of the International Criminal Court: Observers' Notes, Article by Article*, 2nd ed., C.H. Beck/Hart/Nomos, Munich/Oxford/Baden-Baden, 2008, pp. 539–45.

2. Stéphane Bourgon, in Antonio Cassese, Paola Gaeta and John R.W.D. Jones (eds.), *The Rome Statute of the International Criminal Court: A Commentary*, Oxford University Press, Oxford, 2002, pp. 543–52.

Author: Mark Klamberg.

Article 12
Preconditions to the exercise of jurisdiction[175]

---

[175] *General remarks*:

Article 12 sets the preconditions for the exercise of jurisdiction of the Court. As such, the provision has been called "one of the cornerstone provisions of the Statute" (Bergsmo, 1998, p. 30). In addition to specifying the general preconditions for the exercise of jurisdiction, Article 12 must furthermore be seen as the main provision governing the territorial jurisdiction (*ratione loci* jurisdiction) of the ICC. Given that the ICC Statute does not provide for a separate and exclusive provision dealing in toto with the *ratione loci* jurisdiction of the Court (Bourgon, 2002, p. 560) – such as Article 11 on the temporal jurisdiction (*ratione temporis* jurisdiction) – Article 12 is the central legal source when it comes to determining the territorial jurisdiction of the ICC.

On the basis of this dogmatic structure Article 12 may be divided into two separate yet intertwined stipulations. First, Article 12(1) determines how a State may accept the jurisdiction of the ICC concerning the core crimes, namely by becoming a party to the ICC Statute. Second, in order for the ICC to be able to exercise this jurisdiction, Article 12(2) requires either the territorial State or the nationality State to be among the State Parties. To further extend the possibility of the ICC to exercise jurisdiction Article 12(3) ICC Statute provides for territorial and nationality non-State Parties to *ad hoc* accept the exercise of jurisdiction by the ICC.

With this understanding, Article 12 demonstrates an apparent respect for the sovereignty of States (Malanczuk, 1997, p. 17) and confirms the role of the principle of State sovereignty as a limiting factor for the jurisdiction of the ICC. Thus, Article 12 is the result of a "compromise between State sovereignty and the needs of international justice" (Bourgon, 2002, p. 560). In the ICC Statute's current structure State sovereignty, as underlined in particular in Article 12(2)–(3), may be pierced only by the referral of a situation to the prosecutor by the United Nations Security Council ('UNSC'), pursuant to Article 13(b).

A temporary opt-out from the automatic jurisdiction under Article 12(1) is possible for war crimes pursuant to Article 124 if a declaration to this effect is made by a State upon becoming a Party to the ICC Statute. Such an opt out can be made for a maximum seven years and may be withdrawn at any time. For example, France has declared that "[p]ursuant to Article 124 of the Statute of the International Criminal Court, the French Republic declares that it does not accept the jurisdiction of the Court with respect to the category of crimes referred to in Article 8 when a crime is alleged to have been committed by its nationals or on its territory" (Reservation of 9 June 2000).

Preparatory works:

The drafting history of Article 12 was not straightforward. There were several alternatives.

Germany represented one extreme in the alternative that may be described as "universal jurisdiction". Germany held the view that States could delegate their jurisdiction they are entitled under customary international law to the Court. Since several States exercise universal jurisdiction over genocide, crimes against humanity and war crimes this jurisdiction could be delegated to the Court. They were supported by States such as Sweden, Czech Republic, Latvia, Costa Rica, Albania, Ghana, Namibia, Italy, Hungary, Azerbaijan, Belgium, Ireland, Netherlands, Luxembourg, Bosnia and Herzegovina and Ecuador.

At the other extreme was the United States that held that the State of nationality had to give its consent in all cases, except for Security Council referrals. India, Indonesia, Gabon, Russia, Jamaica, Nigeria, Vietnam, Algeria, Egypt, Israel, Sri Lanka, Pakistan, Afghanistan, Iran and China advanced similar positions in preference of a narrower jurisdiction. Other States, such as the United Kingdom and Korea, tried to find a compromise. As indicated above, the result as

1. A State which becomes a Party to this Statute thereby accepts the jurisdiction of the Court with respect to the crimes referred to in article 5.[176]

2. In the case of article 13, paragraph (a) or (c), the Court may exercise its jurisdiction if one or more of the following States are Parties to this Statute or have accepted the jurisdiction of the Court in accordance with paragraph 3:[177]

---

manifested in Article 12 demonstrates respect for the sovereignty of States, a narrower jurisdiction for the Court.

Author: Dominik Zimmerman, revised by Mark Klamberg.

[176] The main content of Article 12 is the codification of the principle of automatic jurisdiction of the ICC *vis-à-vis* State Parties with respect to the most serious crimes of concern to the international community (the jurisdictional mechanism of "automatic jurisdiction" is sometimes referred to as "inherent" jurisdiction, see, for example, Wagner, 2003, p. 477). As such Article 12(1) merely refers to Article 5 which in turn contains the offences triggering the *ratione materiae* jurisdiction of the ICC. Article 12(1) thus does not itself codify the *ratione materiae* jurisdiction of the Court but instead expresses the central implication for States of becoming a Party to the ICC Statute, namely the fulfillment of the preconditions for the exercise of jurisdiction of the ICC in relation to every new State party. Through the codification of automatic jurisdiction, Article 12(1) furthermore puts emphasis on the understanding of the ICC as being "an independent permanent International Criminal Court" (see Preamble of the ICC Statute). Pursuant to Article 120 no reservation is permitted with the exception of the "opt-out" possibility for war crimes provided for in Article 124.

Due to the reference of Article 12(1) to Article 5, the exercise of jurisdiction of the Court may be limited as far as the crime of aggression is concerned if and when, pursuant to Article 121(5), the ICC Statute has been amended by a definition of this crime (cf. Articles 5(2), 121(5) and 123).

Author: Dominik Zimmerman, revised by Mark Klamberg.

[177] Article 12(2) applies to the circumstances in Article 13(a) or (c) but not to Article 13(b). By omitting Article 13(b) the Court can, when authorised by the Security Council, exercise jurisdiction over crimes committed on the territory of non-Party States.

The second subsection of Article 12 provides guidance as to which State(s) has (have) to accept the ICC's jurisdiction in order for the Court to be able to exercise it in a particular situation. Article 12(2) contains two separate, but alternative, categories of State parties related to a conduct possibly constituting a crime under Article 5, that may constitute the necessary precondition for the ICC's jurisdiction: (a) the State on whose territory the relevant conduct has occurred (so-called territorial State); and (b) the State of which the accused person(s) is (are) national(s) (so-called nationality State). By adhering to these categories, the Statute does not provide for the exercise of jurisdiction if only the State in whose custody a suspect is being held (so-called custodial State), or the State whose national was a victim of the relevant conduct (so-called victim's State) is a State Party. In these cases, however, a referral of the relevant situation to the Prosecutor by the UNSC according to Article 13(b) may still trigger the exercise of jurisdiction. Although such situations are likely to be relatively rare, due also to the difficulty of finding political consensus within the UNSC, this possibility might prove to be valuable in the future in order to reach the ambitious goal of ending impunity for the perpetrators of the most serious crimes of concern to the international community. Similarly, an *ad hoc* acceptance of an affected territorial or nationality non-State Party to the ICC Statute pursuant to Article 12(3) does have this same effect, that is, enabling the ICC to exercise its jurisdiction.

Following from the alternative wording "one or more" contained in Article 12(2) the Court may come to exercise its jurisdiction in cases where States not being Parties to the Statute are

---

(a) The State on the territory of which the conduct in question occurred or, if the crime was committed on board a vessel or aircraft, the State of registration of that vessel or aircraft;[178]

---

involved and which do not, pursuant to Article 12(3), *ad hoc* accept the exercise of jurisdiction. This may, for example, be the case where a crime is committed in the territory of a State party by a national of a non-State Party, or where a national of a State Party commits a serious crime in the territory of a non-State Party. Notwithstanding the influence this might imply on a State not being a party to the ICC Statute, due to the anchorage of both the principle of territoriality and nationality in general international law, such exercise of jurisdiction cannot, however, be in violation of Article 34 Vienna Convention on the Law of Treaties (concluded 23 May 1969, entered into force 27 January 1980, 1155 UNTS 331).

Author: Dominik Zimmerman, revised by Mark Klamberg.

[178] The first basis for the exercise of jurisdiction is the membership of the territorial State to the ICC Statute. This provision is mainly based on the assertion of territorial jurisdiction as one of the main implications of the principle of State sovereignty (Shaw, 2003, p. 579; Lowe, 2006, p. 342–45). The consideration that "all individuals staying on the territory of a state are subjected to the law of that State" (Kelsen, 1952, p. 309) forms a necessary precondition in this regard. Under international law States may exercise this jurisdiction within their own municipal organisational structure or delegate this right in international agreements. Closely connected to the delegation of the sovereign ability to prosecute crimes committed on a State's territory is the granting of full exercise of the ICC's function and powers on the territory of the State Party pursuant to Article 4(2). According to the principle of territorial jurisdiction the territorial State may exercise jurisdiction regardless of the nationality of the person accused of the crime (there is no difference between citizens and aliens with respect to the exercise of the criminal jurisdiction of a State; see Kelsen, 1952, p. 310). With regard to the ICC this means that the Court may take jurisdiction over a conduct which occurred in the territory of a State Party, regardless of whether the person accused of the crime is a citizen of that same State or of a non-State Party. Furthermore, the exercise of jurisdiction is independent of the victim's nationality and whether the alleged criminal remains in a custodial State which is a State party or non-State Party.

Whether or not the nationality State or custodial State is a State Party to the ICC Statute is thus not of any relevance to the possibility of the ICC to exercise jurisdiction but instead has an influence on the obligation to co-operate with the ICC. Whereas State Parties, pursuant to Part 9 are obliged to fully co-operate with the Court in its investigation and prosecution of crimes, the same rules also apply to non-State Parties if they lodge an *ad hoc* declaration under Article 12(3), according to which the exercise of jurisdiction of the ICC is accepted in a particular case (see below).

However, the United Nations Security Council may under the powers in Article 25 and Chapter VII of the UN Charter decide that all States, including non-State parties, shall co-operate fully with and provide any necessary assistance to the Court and the Prosecutor. The Security Council used this power when it referred the situation of Darfur to the Court in Resolution 1593 (2005).

As far as crimes that have been committed on board a vessel or aircraft are concerned the State of registration of the vessel or aircraft is equated with the territorial State. This is in line with Article 91(1) United Nations Convention on the Law of the Sea (concluded 10 December 1982, entered into force 16 November 1994, 1833 UNTS 3) and Article 17 Convention on International Civil Aviation (signed 7 December 1944, entered into force 4 April 1947, 15 UNTS 295) according to which ships have the nationality of the State whose flag they are entitled to fly and an aircraft has the nationality of the State in which it is registered. There is no require-

(b) The State of which the person accused of the crime is a national.[179]

3.   If the acceptance of a State which is not a Party to this Statute is required under paragraph 2, that State may, by declaration lodged with the Registrar, accept the exercise of jurisdiction by the Court with respect to the crime in question. The accepting State shall cooperate with the Court without any delay or exception in accordance with Part 9.[180]

---

ment that the territorial jurisdiction delegated to the Court is under the effective control of the State. Northern Cyprus is an example where this issue might arise (Schabas, 2010, p. 285).

Author: Dominik Zimmerman, revised by Mark Klamberg.

[179] The concept of nationality underlying Article 12(2)(b) is a confirmation of the legal link between a sovereign State and the individuals remaining on its territory (Shaw, 2003, p. 584; Lowe, 2006, pp. 345–47). This linkage does not only entitle a person to a series of rights, but moreover forms the basis for prosecution for crimes committed outside the territory of the State.

The nationality principle is widely used by civil law States as a model to claim jurisdiction over crimes committed by their nationals abroad. As far as serious crimes are concerned also the common law countries adhere to the nationality principle and have furthermore not protested against the use of this principle in criminal matters by other States (Shaw, 2003, p. 589).

The possibility to exercise extraterritorial jurisdiction pursuant to Article 12(2)(b) does not extend to the case where only the State of which the victim is a national is a State party (so-called passive personality principle). Instead the provision is reduced to the active personality principle.

The issue of a possible obligation to co-operate with the ICC is handled in the same way as in the case of territorial jurisdiction, that is, only the State parties to the ICC Statute are obliged to co-operate.

The Prosecutor has considered the possibility to prosecute in relation to alleged acts in Iraq (a non-party State) by nationals of the United Kingdom, a State Party. On the basis of the admissibility assessment pertaining to gravity, the Prosecutor decided not to proceed with an investigation into the situation in Iraq, (Annex to Update on Communications Received by the Office of the Prosecutor: Iraq Response, 9 February 2006). The preliminary examination was reopened in 2014 (OTP Press Release: Prosecutor of the International Criminal Court, Fatou Bensouda, Re-opens the preliminary examination of the situation in Iraq, 13 May 2014).

Author: Dominik Zimmerman, revised by Mark Klamberg.

[180] Article 12(3) concerns non-Party States. It is a residue of the 1994 draft statute of the International Law Commission where consent was required by States on a case-by-case basis.

In situations where neither the relevant territorial State nor the relevant nationality State is a party to the Statute, and where the UNSC does not refer the situation to the Prosecutor the ICC may still exercise jurisdiction provided the territorial State and/or the nationality State (being a non-State Party) on an *ad hoc* basis accepts the exercise of jurisdiction of the ICC. The declaration by which the approval of jurisdiction of the Court is being affirmed "must be express, unequivocal, and precise as to the crime(s) or situation it applies to" (Bourgon, 2002, p. 563).

Provided a declaration has been lodged with the Registrar of the ICC pursuant to Article 12(3), the accepting State thereby commits itself to co-operate with the ICC as if it were a State Party. This commitment is limited, however, to the crime(s) in question and does thus not embrace any investigation and/or prosecution of crimes other than those covered by the declaration. This facultative obligation to co-operate is in line with Article 34 Vienna Convention on the Law of Treaties according to which "[a] treaty does not create either obligations or rights for a third State without its consent".

The wording "the crime in question" contained in Article 12(3) must furthermore be interpreted in accordance with Rule 44. Accordingly, the Article 12(3)-declaration made by a non-State Party implies the "acceptance of jurisdiction with respect to the crimes referred to in Article 5 of relevance to the situation", rather than individual crimes or specific incidents (Stahn *et al.*, 2005, pp. 427–28; Kaul, 2002, p. 611). As an example, Côte d'Ivoire, while not being a party to the ICC Statute, accepted the exercise of jurisdiction by the Court regarding crimes committed on its territory since the events of 19 September 2002 (see Press Release of 15 February 2005, Declaration under Article 12(3) of the Rome Statute, 18 April 2003 and *Situation in the Republic of Côte d'Ivoire*, ICC PT. Ch. III, Decision Pursuant to Article 15 of the Rome Statute on the Authorisation of an Investigation into the Situation in the Republic of Côte d'Ivoire, ICC-02/11-14, 3 October 2011, para. 10). A similar declaration, extending the temporal jurisdiction back to the time of the entry into force of the Statute, was made by the Ugandan government in December 2003 (see letter of the Prosecutor of 17 June 2004 attached to the Decision Assigning the Situation in Uganda to Pre-Trial Chamber II, ICC-02/04-1, 5 July 2004) as well as by the government of the Democratic Republic of the Congo (see letter of the Prosecutor of 17 June 2004 attached to the Decision Assigning the Situation in the Democratic Republic of Congo to Pre-Trial Chamber I, ICC-01/04-1, 5 July 2004). Due to its facultative character, Article 12(3) is in line with the overall State sovereignty-friendliness of Article 12.

Article 12(3) moreover provides the possibility for States to extend the *ratione temporis* jurisdiction of the Court. Pursuant to Article 11(1) the Court has jurisdiction only over crimes committed after the entry into force of the Statute. With regard to States that have become parties to the ICC Statute after its entry into force the jurisdiction only extends to crimes committed after the entry into force of the ICC Statute for that State, unless that State in accordance with Article 12(3) accepts jurisdiction for acts committed prior to ratification but after the entry into force of the Statute. However, it is likely that the Court may also consider facts that occurred prior to the time specified in an Article 12(3)-declaration—for the purpose of securing evidence or uncovering acts of a continuing nature—provided that these facts are linked to events that occurred after that time (Stahn *et al.*, 2005, p. 429–31).

Cross-references:
Rule 44.

Doctrine:

1. Sharon A. Williams, in Otto Triffterer (ed.), *Commentary on the Rome Statute of the International Criminal Court: Observers' Notes, Article by Article*, 2nd ed., C.H. Beck/Hart/Nomos, Munich/Oxford/Baden-Baden, 2008, pp. 547–61.

2. Stéphane Bourgon, in Antonio Cassese, Paola Gaeta and John R.W.D. Jones (eds.), *The Rome Statute of the International Criminal Court. A Commentary*, Oxford University Press, Oxford, 2002, pp. 559–60, 562–65.

3. Hans-Peter Kaul, in Antonio Cassese, Paola Gaeta and John R.W.D. Jones (eds.), *The Rome Statute of the International Criminal Court. A Commentary*, Oxford University Press, Oxford, 2002, pp. 595–96, 607–11.

4. Peter Malanczuk, *Akehurst's Modern Introduction to International Law*, Routledge, New York, 1997, p. 17.

5. Morten Bergsmo, "The Jurisdictional Régime of the International Criminal Court" (Part II, Articles 11–19), in *European Journal of Crime, Criminal Law and Criminal Justice*, 1998, vol. 6, pp. 29–47.

6. Carsten Stahn, Mohamed M. El Zeidy and Héctor Olásolo, "The International Criminal Court's Ad Hoc Jurisdiction Revisited", in *American Journal of International Law*, 2005, vol. 99, no. 2, pp. 421–31.

7. William A. Schabas, *The International Criminal Court: A Commentary on the Rome Statute*, Oxford University Press, Oxford, 2010, pp. 277–292.

8. Markus Wagner, "The ICC and its Jurisdiction – Myths, Misperceptions and Realities", in Armin von Bogdandy and Rüdiger Wolfrum (eds.), *Max Planck Yearbook of United Nations Law*, 2003, vol. 7, pp. 409–512.

9. Malcolm Shaw, *International Law*, 5th ed., Cambridge University Press, Cambridge, 2003, pp. 579, 589.

10. Vaughan Lowe, in Malcolm D. Evans, *International Law*, 2nd ed., Oxford University Press, Oxford, 2006, pp. 342–45.

11. Hans Kelsen, *Principles of International Law*, Rinehart, New York, 1952.

Author: Dominik Zimmerman, revised by Mark Klamberg.

Article 13

Exercise of jurisdiction

The Court may exercise its jurisdiction with respect to a crime referred to in article 5 in accordance with the provisions of this Statute if:

(a) A situation in which one or more of such crimes appears to have been committed is referred to the Prosecutor by a State Party in accordance with article 14;[181]

(b) A situation in which one or more of such crimes appears to have been committed is referred to the Prosecutor by the Security Council acting under Chapter VII of the Charter of the United Nations; or[182]

---

[181] States Parties can trigger the Court's jurisdiction over a particular situation. This entails an ability to direct the Court's attention to events in a particular time and place, possibly involving criminal acts, with a view to initiate an exercise of jurisdiction over those acts.

In *Prosecutor v. Lubanga*, Decision Concerning Pre-Trial Chamber I's Decision of 10 February 2006 and the Incorporation of Documents into the Record of the Case against Mr. Thomas Lubanga Dyilo, 24 February 2006, para. 21, PTC I stated that a situation is defined by "territorial, temporal and possibly personal parameters". This was repeated in *Prosecutor v. Katanga*, Decision on the evidence and information provided by the Prosecution for the issuance of a warrant of arrest for Germain Katanga, 5 November 2007, para. 9. See also *Prosecutor v. Bemba*, Decision on the Prosecutor's Application for a Warrant of Arrest against Jean-Pierre Bemba Gombo, 10 June 2008, para. 16.

This power is restricted to States Parties and there can be no *ad hoc* referrals by non-States Parties, even those that have made declarations pursuant to Article 12(3). This power is not restricted to States with a direct interest or involvement in the situation. State Party referrals must be done in accordance with Article 14.

Author: Mark Klamberg.

[182] The Security Council may trigger the Court's jurisdiction under Article 13(b), but also create jurisdiction, in the case of crimes committed on the territory of non-States Parties. This is an acknowledgement of the fundamental role of the Security Council to confront situations of threats to the peace, breaches of the peace and acts of aggression. The requirement in Article 12(2) on acceptance by States Parties only applies to cases when a situation is referred to the Prosecutor by a State Party or where the Prosecutor has initiated an investigation *proprio motu*. It does not apply to Security Council referrals. Article 13(b) requires that the Security Council act under Chapter VII of UN Charter.

The Security Council made use of Article 13(b) when it acted under chapter VII of the UN charter and referred to the Prosecutor the situation in Darfur, Sudan (resolution 1593(2005)).

In *Prosecutor v. Lubanga*, Decision Concerning Pre-Trial Chamber I's Decision of 10 February 2006 and the Incorporation of Documents into the Record of the Case against Mr. Thomas Lubanga Dyilo, 24 February 2006, para. 21, PTC I stated that a situation is defined by "territorial, temporal and possibly personal parameters". This was repeated in *Prosecutor v. Katanga*, Decision on the evidence and information provided by the Prosecution for the issuance of a warrant of arrest for Germain Katanga, 5 November 2007, para. 9. See also Bemba, Decision on the Prosecutor's Application for a Warrant of Arrest against Jean-Pierre Bemba Gombo, 10 June 2008, para. 16.

(c) The Prosecutor has initiated an investigation in respect of such a crime in accordance with article 15.[183]

Cross-references:
Rule 162.

Author: Mark Klamberg.

[183] The Prosecutor may initiate proceedings *ex officio* (by virtue of his or her office). The Prosectuor's exercise of this power must be done in accordance with Article 15, which is a safeguard against abuse of this function.

In *Prosecutor v. Lubanga*, Decision Concerning Pre-Trial Chamber I's Decision of 10 February 2006 and the Incorporation of Documents into the Record of the Case against Mr. Thomas Lubanga Dyilo, 24 February 2006, para. 21, PTC I stated that a situation is defined by "territorial, temporal and possibly personal parameters". This was repeated in *Prosecutor v. Katanga*, Decision on the evidence and information provided by the Prosecution for the issuance of a warrant of arrest for Germain Katanga, 5 November 2007, para. 9. See also Bemba, Decision on the Prosecutor's Application for a Warrant of Arrest against Jean-Pierre Bemba Gombo, 10 June 2008, para. 16.

Doctrine:

1. Sharon A. Williams and William A. Schabas, in Otto Triffterer (ed.), *Commentary on the Rome Statute of the International Criminal Court: Observers' Notes, Article by Article*, 2nd ed., C.H. Beck/Hart/Nomos, Munich/Oxford/Baden-Baden, 2008, pp. 563–74.

2. Philippe Kirsch and Darryl Robinson, in Antonio Cassese, Paola Gaeta and John R.W.D. Jones (eds.), *The Rome Statute of the International Criminal Court: A Commentary,* Oxford University Press, Oxford, 2002, pp. 619, 657.

3. Luigi Condorelli and Santiago Villalpando, in Antonio Cassese, Paola Gaeta and John R.W.D. Jones (eds.), *The Rome Statute of the International Criminal Court: A Commentary,*, Oxford University Press, Oxford, 2002, pp. 627–44.

Author: Mark Klamberg.

Article 14
Referral of a situation by a State Party[184]

1. A State Party may refer to the Prosecutor a situation in which one or more crimes within the jurisdiction of the Court appear to have been committed requesting the Prosecutor to investigate the situation for the purpose of determining whether one or more specific persons should be charged with the commission of such crimes.[185]

---

[184] *General remarks*:

State referrals are mentioned as one of the three trigger mechanisms under Article 13(a) and 14 of the ICC Statute. Article 14 complements Article 13(a).

State referrals were thought to have little potential for use, but the law-in-action has proven such expectations wrong. As a matter of fact, five out of nine situations before the ICC are based upon State referrals (Uganda, Democratic Republic of Congo, Central African Republic I and II and Mali).

Preparatory works:

A mechanism for States to trigger the ICC's jurisdiction was uncontroversial, but the original idea focused primarily on "complaints" by injured States against other States [Article 25 of the ILC Draft Statute 1994]. During *ad hoc* committee meetings in 1995, possibilities for trigger mechanisms were further discussed. Some delegations favoured a broad referral tool, while others wanted to restrict the referral to "interested States". Numerous options were included in brackets in Article 45 (25) of the Zutphen Draft 1998, which found its way into Article 11 of the Preparatory Committee's Draft Statute 1998.

An alternative draft by the United Kingdom, entitled "Referral of a situation by a State", was included into the Draft Statute 1998. This proposal suggested that "situations" rather than single cases should be referred, a phrasing that found its way into the final version of the ICC Statute. The UK's proposal, intentionally or not, also altered the language moving away from the term "complaint". It was changed to "State referring a situation". No reference to self-referrals or the like can be found in the discussions.

Analysis of provisions and sub-provisions:

Article 14 partly repeats Article 13(a). The object of the referral is a "situation". The neutral wording "situation" was introduced to avoid complaint against specific individuals and as such reduces the prospect of States Parties referring individualised complaints rather than a conflict situation as a whole. Any State Party may refer such a conflict situation to the ICC under mentioned Articles. In accordance with paragraph 2 of Article 14, the relevant circumstances shall be specified and the referral shall be accompanied by supporting documentation.

Author: Ignaz Stegmiller.

[185] "A State Party" refers to any State that has ratified the ICC Statute. A limitation to a certain State, that is, the territorial or national State, was not included.

In the context of Article 12(3) of the ICC Statute the OTP initially denied an investigation with regard to Palestine due to its unclear status under international law (Decision by the Prosecutor, Situation in Palestine, 3 April 2012). In the context of Article 14, this question would have to be solved already beforehand when a State seeks to become a member of the ICC Statute in accordance with Article 125(3) ICC Statute. It is clear that only State Parties may use the trigger mechanism under Article 14. Non-State Parties are limited to a declaration under Article 12(3) and the appropriate trigger mechanism falls under Article 13(c), 15 of the ICC Statute.

In accordance with Article 125 (3) ICC Statute, Palestine then acceded to the ICC Statute (The State of Palestine accedes the Rome Statute, 7 January 2015). It is worthy to note that, despite its unclear status under international law, the accession was accepted and not only discussed during the Assembly of State Parties. Be that as it may, the OTP opened a new preliminary examination, this time on the basis of Article 14 ICC Statute (The Prosecutor of the International Criminal Court, Fatou Bensouda, opens a preliminary examination of the situation in Palestine, 16 January 2015).

Referrals of State Parties can be divided into two categories: third party referrals and self-referrals. Earlier drafting history focused on third party referrals, but practice shows an increasing tendency towards self-referrals by States. According to the prevailing interpretations of Articles 13(a) and 14, self-referrals are referrals by a State Party of a situation in which crimes falling within the jurisdiction of the Court appear to have been committed on that State Party's territory (Müller/Stegmiller, 2010, p. 1272). The Office of the Prosecutor adopted a policy of inviting and encouraging such voluntary self-referrals (Paper on Some Policy Issue before the Office of the Prosecutor, September 2003).

To date, all referrals under Article 14 are such self-referrals, except Palestine. In Palestine, crimes were allegedly committed by Israel, and if this referral leads to full investigations, it would constitute the first referral in the sense of a "complaint" against a third state. In five situations referred to it under Article 14 the Office of the Prosecutor initiated (full) investigations pursuant to Article 53(1) ICC Statute.

In the *Situation of Uganda*, the President of Uganda referred "the situation concerning the LRA" to the ICC in 2004 (ICC – President of Uganda refers situation concerning the Lord's Resistance Army (LRA) to the ICC, 29 January 2004 (ICC-20040129-44)). Despite the wording of the referral ("concerning the LRA"), the Prosecutor is conducting investigations against all involved parties (Statement by Luis Moreno Ocampo, Prosecutor of the ICC – Informal meeting of Legal Advisors of Ministries of Foreign Affairs, 24 October 2005, p. 7). The Prosecutor thus redefines the situation referred to him as encompassing "all crimes committed in Northern Uganda in the context of the ongoing conflict involving the LRA" (*Prosecutor v. Kony et al.*, ICC PT. Ch. II, Decision to Convene a Status Conference on the Investigation in the Situation in Uganda in Relation to the Application of Article 53, ICC-02/04-01/05-68, 02.12.2005, para. 5).

The second referral concerned the *Situation in the Democratic Republic of Congo* where the Chief Prosecutor received a letter signed by the President in 2004 (Prosecutor receives referral of the situation in the Democratic Republic of Congo, 19 April 2004 (ICC-OTP-20040419-50)).

A third self-referral was received by the Chief Prosecutor on behalf of the government of the Central African Republic in 2005 (ICC – Prosecutor receives referral concerning Central African Republic, 07 January 2005 (ICC-OTP-20050107-86)), and a fourth referral regarding the Central African Republic ("Situation in the CAR II") was received in May 2014 (Referral under Articles 13 (a) and 14, 30 May 2014).

A fifth referral by Mali was received in 2012 (Referral letter by the Government of Mali, 13 July 2012).

Another self-referral by the Comoros "with respect to the 31 May 2010 Israeli raid on the Humanitarian Aid Flotilla bound for Gaza Strip, requesting the Prosecutor of the International Criminal Court pursuant to Articles 12, 13 and 14 of the ICC Statute to initiate an investigation into the crimes committed within the Court's jurisdiction, arising from this raid" was also under scrutiny by the Office of the Prosecutor (Referral under Articles 14 and 12(2)(a) of the Rome Statute arising from the 31 May 2010, Gaza Freedom Flotilla situation, 14 May 2013). The referral by the Comoros was rejected on the basis of Article 53(1) ICC Statute (Statement of the Prosecutor of the International Criminal Court, Fatou Bensouda, on concluding the preliminary examination of the situation referred by the Union of Comoros: "Rome Statute legal requirements have not been met", 6 November 2014). However, as noted above, the situation of Palestine as a whole has now been referred (again) by Palestine itself and is pending before the ICC-OTP.

It may be noted that in the *Situation of Kenya*, the Office of the Prosecutor initially also favoured a self-referral (Agreed Minutes of the Meeting between Prosecutor Moreno Ocampo and the delegation of the Kenyan government, 3 July 2009).

The practice of self-referrals was highly disputed among scholars and practitioners (see, for example, Schabas. 2010, Article 14, 306 ff.), but according to the Chambers in *Lubanga* and *Katanga* does not face legality concerns (*Prosecutor v. Lubanga*, ICC PT. Ch. I, Decision concerning Pre-Trial Chamber I's Decision of 10 February 2006 and the Incorporation of Documents into the Record of the Case against Mr Thomas Lubanga Dyilo, ICC-01/04-01/06-8-US-Corr, 24 February 2006, para. 35; *Prosecutor v. Katanga and Chui*, ICC T. Ch. II, Reasons for the Oral Decision on the Motion Challenging the Admissibility of the Case (Article 19 of the Statute), ICC-01/04-01/07-1213, 16 June 2009, paras. 79–80).

Despite the unclear drafting history, that is only supplementary in nature, the terminology "referral" and "refer" rather than "complaint" is neutral and allows for action by any State Party, be it the State Party on which territory the conflict took place. In *Lubanga*, PT. Ch. I mentioned that "the self-referral of the DRC appears consistent with the ultimate purpose of the complementarity regime" (*Prosecutor v. Lubanga*, ICC PT. Ch. I, Decision concerning Pre-Trial Chamber I's Decision of 10 February 2006 and the Incorporation of Documents into the Record of the Case against Mr Thomas Lubanga Dyilo, ICC-01/04-01/06-8-US-Corr, 24 February 2006, para. 35). In *Katanga*, T. Ch. II further clarified, in the context of an admissibility challenge by the Defence:

> However, if a State considers that it is more opportune for the Court to carry out an investigation or prosecution, that State will still be complying with its duties under the complementarity regime, if it surrenders the suspect to the Court in good time and cooperates fully with the Court in accordance with Part IX of the Statute. [...] The Chamber is not in a position to ascertain the real motives of a State which expresses its unwillingness to prosecute a particular case. A State may, without breaching the complementarity principle, refer a situation concerning its territory to the Court if it considers it opportune to do so, just as it may decide to carry out an investigation or prosecution of a particular case (*Prosecutor v. Katanga and Chui*, ICC T. Ch. II, Reasons for the Oral Decision on the Motion Challenging the Admissibility of the Case (Article 19 of the Statute), ICC-01/04-01/07-1213, 16 June 2009, paras. 79–80).

The possibility of self-referrals was upheld by the Appeals Chamber in *Katanga and Chui* stating that "the Statute does not prevent a State from relinquishing its jurisdiction in favour of the Court" (*Prosecutor v. Katanga and Chui*, ICC A. Ch., Judgment on the Appeal of Mr. Germain Katanga against the Oral Decision of Trial Chamber II of 12 June 2009 on the Admissibility of the Case, ICC-01/04-01/07-1497, 25 September 2009, para. 85; in the situation in Central African Republic, *Prosecutor v. Bemba*, ICC A. Ch., Decision on the Admissibility and Abuse of Process Challenges, ICC-01/05-01/08-802, 24 June 2010, paras. 259–60).

Policy concerns of the practice of self-referral are further discussed in doctrine and evaluated more critically (Schabas, 2010, pp. 309–12; Stegmiller, 2011, pp. 131–34; Arsanjani and Reismann, 2005, p. 394; Apuuli, 2006, p. 185; Akhavan, 2005, p. 411). Similarly, withdrawals of self-referrals, meaning that the State attempts to regain its ius puniendi by taking its former referral back, have gained academic interest (Maged, 2006, pp. 419–22; El Zeidy, 2009, pp. 55–56). The issue could have arisen in the Ugandan situation, where Museveni threatened to withdraw the case and solve the Kony problem by himself, but was never taken to the level of challenging the ICC's jurisdiction or admissibility. Article 127(1) of the ICC Statute states that a State that withdraws from the Statute shall not be discharged from the obligations arising from

2. As far as possible, a referral shall specify the relevant circumstances and be accompanied by such supporting documentation as is available to the State referring the situation.[186]

---

the Statute while it was a party. From a contextual point of view, withdrawals of referrals are not consistent with the procedural system of the ICC, which provides for challenges under Articles 18 and 19 of the ICC Statute. Furthermore, Article 16 ICC Statute regulates a deferral mechanism for the Security Council. Any other withdrawal or deferral possibility cannot be found in the ICC's procedural system.

Author: Ignaz Stegmiller.

[186] The formalities regulated in paragraph 2 are not further specified in the Rules of Procedure and Evidence. Rule 45 foresees a submission in writing. There is little practical relevance of this provision so far. It regulates the accompanying information that a State has to provide to the Office of the Prosecutor. The wording ("shall") implies a duty to provide information, however the extent remains unclear and should have been further specified by the Rules of Procedure and Evidence. "As far as possible" and "as is available" allow for a variation of a strict duty. "Supporting" and "relevant" are also open to interpretation.

The Presidency needs to be informed by the Prosecutor pursuant to Regulation 45. Furthermore, OTP Regulation 30 foresees a notification of UN Security Council if a State referral reaches the level of a "reasonable basis" to initiate an investigation under Article 53(1) ICC Statute.

Cross-references:

Article 13(a).

Rule 45.

Regulation 45.

OTP Regulations 25, 30.

Doctrine:

1. Jann Kleffner, *Complementarity in the Rome Statute and National Criminal Jurisdictions*, Oxford University Press, Oxford, 2008.

2. Héctor Olásolo, *The Triggering Procedure of the International Criminal Court*, Martinus Nijhoff Publishers, Leiden, 2005.

3. Ignaz Stegmiller, *The Pre-Investigation Stage of the ICC, Criteria for Situation Selection*, Duncker and Humblot, Berlin, 2011.

4. Payam Akhavan, "Self-referrals before the International Criminal Court: Are States Villains or the Victims of Atrocities", in *Criminal Law Forum*, 2010, vol. 21, no. 1, pp. 103–20.

5. Payam Akhavan, "Developments at the ICC: The Lord's Resistance Army Case: Uganda's Submission of the First State Referral to the ICC", in *American Journal of International Law*, 2005, vol. 99, no. 2, pp. 403–21.

6. Kasaija Phillip Apuuli, "The ICC Arrest Warrants for the Lord's Resistance Army Leaders and Peace Prospects in Northern Uganda", in *Journal of International Criminal Justice*, 2006, vol. 4, no 1, pp. 179–87.

7. Mahnoush Arsanjani and Michael Reismann, "Developments at the International Criminal Court: The law-in-action of the ICC", in *American Journal of International Law*, 2005, vol. 99, no. 2, pp. 385–403.

8. Mohamed El Zeidy, "The Ugandan Government Triggers the First Test of the Complementarity Principle: An Assessment of the First State Party's Referral to the ICC", in *International Criminal Law Review*, 2005, vol. 5, no. 1, pp. 83–119.

---

9. Paola Aeta, "Is the Practice of Self-Referrals a Sound Start for the ICC?", in *Journal of International Criminal Justice*, 2006, vol. 4, no. 4, pp. 949–52.

10. Claus Kreß, ""Self-Referrals' and 'Waivers of Complementarity': Some Considerations in Law and Policy", in *Journal of International Criminal Justice*, 2006, vol. 4, no. 4, pp. 944–48.

11. Adel Maged, "Withdrawals of Referrals: A Serious Challenge to the Function of the ICC", in *International Criminal Law Review*, 2006, vol. 6, no. 3, pp. 419–46.

12. Andreas Th. Müller and Ignaz Stegmiller, "Self-referrals on Trial, From Panacea to Patient", in *Journal of International Criminal Justice*, 2010,vol. 8, no. 5, pp. 1267–94.

13. Darryl Robinson, "Editor's Choice: The Controversy over Territorial State Referrals and Reflections on ICL Discourse", in *Journal of International Criminal Justice*, 2011, vol. 9, no. 2, pp. 355–84.

14. William A. Schabas, "Complementarity in Practice: Some Uncomplimentary Thoughts", in *Criminal Law Forum*, 2008, vol. 19, no. 1, pp. 5–33.

15. Ignaz Stegmiller, "The International Criminal Court and Mali: Towards More Transparency in International Criminal Law Investigations?", in *Criminal Law Forum*, 2013, vol. 24, no. 4, pp. 475–99.

16. Phil Clark, "Chasing Cases, The ICC and the Politics of State Referral in the Democratic Republic of the Congo and Uganda", in Carsten Stahn and Mohamed El Zeidy (eds.), *The International Criminal Court and Complementarity*, 2nd ed., Cambridge University Press, Cambridge, 2011, pp. 1180–203.

17. Mohamed El Zeidy, "The Legitimacy of Withdrawing State Party Referrals and Ad Hoc Declarations under the Statute of the International Criminal Court", in Carsten Stahn and Göran Sluiter (eds.), *The Emerging Practice of the International Criminal Court*, Brill, Leiden, 2009, pp. 55–78.

18. Philippe Kirsch and Darryl Robinson, "Referral by State Parties", in Antonio Cassese, Paola Gaeta and John R.W.D. Jones (eds.), *The Rome Statute of the International Criminal Court*, Oxford University Press, Oxford, 2002, pp. 619–25.

19. Jann Kleffner, "Auto-Referrals and the Complementary Nature of the ICC", in Carsten Stahn and Göran Sluiter (eds.), *The Emerging Practice of the International Criminal Court,* Brill, Leiden, 2009, pp. 41–53.

20. Antonio Marchesi, "Article 14", in Otto Triffterer (ed.), *Commentary on the Rome Statute of the International Criminal Court: Observers' Notes, Article by Article*, 2nd ed., C.H. Beck/Hart/Nomos, Munich/Oxford/Baden-Baden, 2008, pp. 575–79.

21. William A. Schabas, *The International Criminal Court, A Commentary on the Rome Statute*, Oxford University Press, Oxford, 2010, pp. 305–13.

Author: Ignaz Stegmiller.

Article 15
Prosecutor[187]

---

[187] *General remarks*:

Article 15 of the ICC Statute deals with one of the three ways of initiating an investigation. In combination with Article 13(c) ICC Statute it outlines the proprio motu power of the Prosecutor. The expression *proprio motu* means "on his own motion".

The provision regulates a complex preliminary examination procedure. In contrast to the trigger mechanisms of a State or Security Council referral, the Pre-Trial Chamber must authorise an investigation (Article 15(3), (4) ICC Statute). To-date, such decisions were rendered in the situations of Kenya and Côte d'Ivoire. In the Kenya situation, PTC II highlighted that Article 15 of the ICC Statute is "one of the most delicate provisions of this Statute" (*Situation in the Republic of Kenya*, ICC PT. Ch. II, Decision Pursuant to Article 15 of the Rome Statute on the Authorisation of an Investigation into the Situation in the Republic of Kenya, ICC-01/09-19, 31 March 2010, para. 17). The (former) Chief Prosecutor was very reluctant to make practical use of the *proprio motu* power during the first eight years of the ICC's activities.

Preparatory works:

The *proprio motu* power was one of the most controversial aspects during the Rome Conference and political issues had to be resolved before the adoption of the ICC Statute. Opponents and proponents of the mechanism did agree that the inclusion or absence of the mechanism would fundamentally affect the ICC system (Bergsmo and Pejić, 2008, p. 582).

The International Law Commission discussions in 1994 did not even foresee a prosecutorial proprio motu power and provided only for State Party and Security Council referrals. This changed during the Ad Hoc Committee debates in 1995 and the autonomous power of initiating investigations by the Prosecutor was brought to the negotiation table for the first time. A draft proposal was then adopted at the Preparatory Committee's 1996 session, followed by Article 25 *bis* of the Preparatory Committee's session in 1997, which was subsequently reproduced without change in Article 46 Zutphen Draft Statute:

Article 25 bis:

The Prosecutor [may] [shall] initiate investigations [*ex officio*] [*proprio motu*] [or] on the basis of information [obtained] [he may seek] from any source, in particular from Governments, United Nations organs [and intergovernmental and non-governmental organizations]. The Prosecutor shall assess the information received or obtained and decide whether there is sufficient basis to proceed. [The Prosecutor may, for the purpose of initiating an investigation, receive information on alleged crimes under Article 20(a) to (d) from Governments, intergovernmental and non-governmental organizations, victims and associations representing them, or other reliable sources.

The Preparatory Committee's meetings from 1996 to 1998 were characterised by opposing debates. Two groups crystallised, the so-called "like-minded" States in favour of a proprio motu power and a strong Prosecutor, and an opposing group that feared politically motivated or frivolous proceedings by the Chief Prosecutor (*Situation in the Republic of Kenya*, ICC PT. Ch. II, Decision Pursuant to Article 15 of the Rome Statute on the Authorisation of an Investigation into the Situation in the Republic of Kenya, ICC-01/09-19, 31 March 2010, para. 18 with fn. 23). A joint Argentine-German proposal of 25 March 1998 led to broader acceptance of a prosecutorial proprio motu power. The proposal limited the Prosecutor's preliminary examinations to "information received from other parties" and introduced the approval by the Pre-Trial Chamber. The current version of Article 15 is largely identical to the Argentine-German proposal.

During the Rome Conference, 76 per cent of the participating countries – in total numbers 61 States – supported a *proprio motu* power. It was yet unclear until the end of the negotiations whether the mechanism would find its way into the ICC Statute. Despite opposition by States, such as the United States, China, India and Japan, Article 15 was finally adopted.

Analysis of provisions and sub-provisions:

Preliminary examinations are ongoing in Afghanistan, Honduras, Iraq, Ukraine, Palestine, Colombia, Georgia, Guinea, and Nigeria (Report on Preliminary Examination Activities 2013, Office of the Prosecutor, November 2013; see also the ICC-OTP website on Preliminary Examinations). Examinations with regard to the Comoros, Korea and Venezuela were closed.

It is worth noting that preliminary examinations (pre-investigations) are conducted with regard to all three trigger mechanisms. Rules 48 and 104 of the Rules of Procedure and Evidence lead to a partial overlap between Article 15 and 53 ICC Statute and the same factors need to be assessed (*Situation in the Republic of Kenya*, ICC PT. Ch. II, Decision Pursuant to Article 15 of the ICC Statute on the Authorisation of an Investigation into the Situation in the Republic of Kenya, ICC-01/09-19, 31 March 2010, para. 23; *Situation in the Republic of Côte d'Ivoire*, ICC PT. Ch. III, Decision Pursuant to Article 15 of the Rome Statute on the Authorisation of an Investigation into the Situation in the Republic of Côte d'Ivoire, ICC-02/11-14, 3 October 2011, para. 17; *Situation in the Republic of Côte d'Ivoire*, ICC PT. Ch. III, Judge Fernàndez de Gurmendi's separate and partially dissenting opinion to the Decision Pursuant to Article 15 of the Rome Statute on the Authorisation of an Investigation into the Situation in the Republic of Côte d'Ivoire, ICC-02/11-15, 3 October 2011, para. 24; Stegmiller, 2011, pp. 209 ff.).

Regulation 25 of the OTP Regulations states:

The preliminary examination and evaluation of a situation by the Office may be initiated on the basis of:

(a) any information on crimes, including information sent by individuals or groups, States, intergovernmental or non- governmental organisations;

(b) a referral from a State Party or the Security Council; or

(c) a declaration pursuant to Article 12, paragraph 3 by a State which is not a Party to the Statute.

Moreover, Regulation 29(1) OTP Regulations spells out:

In acting under Article 15, paragraph 3, or Article 53, paragraph 1, the Office shall produce an internal report analysing the seriousness of the information and considering the factors set out in Article 53, paragraph 1(a) to (c), namely issues of jurisdiction, admissibility (including gravity), as well as the interests of justice, pursuant to rules 48 and 104. The report shall be accompanied by a recommendation on whether there is a reasonable basis to initiate an investigation.

A first report under regulation 29(1) OTP Regulations was published in the Mali Situation (*Situation in Mali*, Article 53(1) Report, 16 January 2013). The process and criteria are thus similar with regard to all trigger mechanisms. However, the process under Article 15 with regard to *proprio motu* information takes significantly longer in practice.

In fact, no provision in the ICC Statute or the Rules of Procedure and Evidence regulates a specific time period for the completion of a preliminary examination. Regulation 19(4) OTP Regulations states, rather generally, that the evaluation shall continue as long as the situation is investigated. The decision whether or not a "reasonable basis" is reached marks the line between preliminary examinations and investigations, but the question remains what happens if the Prosecutor does not officially announce such a decision. The matter led to a controversy in the situation in the Central African Republic when the Prosecutor gave no information on the situation under scrutiny for over two years. The Pre-Trial Chamber emphasised that a preliminary examination must be completed within "reasonable time", regardless of its complexity (*Situation in the Central African Republic*, ICC PT. Ch. III, Decision Requesting Information on the Status of

1. The Prosecutor may initiate investigations proprio motu on the basis of information on crimes within the jurisdiction of the Court.[188]

2. The Prosecutor shall analyse the seriousness of the information received.[189] For this purpose, he or she may seek additional information from States, organs of the United Nations,

---

the Preliminary Examination of the Situation in the Central African Republic, ICC-01/05-6, 30 November 2006, p. 4). The Prosecutor provided information on the status of the preliminary examination, but pointed out that this information was given on a voluntary basis as the Pre-Trial Chamber has no supervisory function with regard to this early stage and that the decision to seek the opening of investigations lies within the discretion of the Prosecution alone (*Situation in the Central African Republic*, ICC PT. Ch. III, Decision Requesting Information on the Status of the Preliminary Examination of the Situation in the Central African Republic, ICC-01/05-6, 30 November 2006). The disagreement was neither explicitly settled by jurisprudence nor by an amendment of the Rules of Procedure and Evidence. The status and length of preliminary examinations could be (partly) resolved by a new rule or regulation (Stegmiller, 2011, p. 235).

Author: Ignaz Stegmiller.

[188] "May initiate" suggests discretion of the Prosecutor. Commentators have stated that the Prosecutor's initiation right is "unconditional and discretionary, but carefully balanced by the need for authorization by a Pre-Trial Chamber" (Bergsmo and Pejić, 2008, p. 585, para. 9). The phrasing has to be put into context with the followings words: "investigation" and *"proprio motu"*.

Under this paragraph, the Prosecutor may not start full investigations, despite the wording, but may only initiate preliminary examinations. Taking a glance at the whole provision of Article 15, its accompanying rules 48 and 104 of the Rule of Procedure and Evidence and regulations 25 and 29 of the OTP Regulations, paragraph 1 of Article 15 should not be misconstrued. Paragraph 6 of Article 15 refers to the "preliminary examination referred to in paragraphs 1 and 2 (emphasis added)". This preliminary state can be clearly distinguished from the investigation stage under Article 54 ICC Statute.

"Proprio motu" means on his or her own initiative without any formal referral by a third party. Article 13(c) of the ICC Statute names Article 15 ICC Statute as one of three trigger mechanisms, on equal footing with Articles 13(a), 14, and Article 13(b).

In consequence, the discretionary "may" under paragraph 1 simply means that the Prosecutor has the right to pre-investigate gathered information if he/she thinks fit. Full investigations, however, require authorisation under paragraph 3 of Article 15 ICC Statute. The decision of the PTC to authorise full investigations under Article 15(4) ICC Statute is then – procedurally – on equal footing with the Article 53(1) ICC Statute. Only after this decision one may speak of investigations in the narrow sense.

Article 15 therefore embraces two different levels: First, preliminary examination methods are regulated in paragraphs 1, 2, and 6. Second, an intermediary phase is foreseen during which the Pre-Trial Chamber "checks and balances" the proprio motu power of the Prosecutor in accordance with paragraphs 3, 4, and 5.

Author: Ignaz Stegmiller.

[189] The Prosecutor "shall" analyse "the seriousness" of the "information received". In practice, the Office of the Prosecutor uses "communication" as an abbreviation and short term rather than "information received" or "information on crimes within the jurisdiction of the Court". The latter terms are statutory language, but the former ("communication") is not. In regulation 26 of the OTP Regulations it is held that all information shall be registered. The newly drafted OTP Regulations also depart from the term "communication" and the Prosecutor seems to acknowledge the legal notion of "information received".

intergovernmental or non-governmental organizations, or other reliable sources that he or she deems appropriate, and may receive written or oral testimony at the seat of the Court.[190]

The term "shall" indicates a legal duty to analyse all information received. A qualified member of the Office of the Prosecutor must analyse all incoming information. Once information is classified as such under Article 15 ICC Statute, there is thus a statutory obligation to conduct a preliminary examination and inform the information provider of the result. This duty is acknowledged pursuant to regulation 28(1) OTP Regulation (see further below at Article 15 paragraph 6 ICC Statute).

Public reports may be made available if confidentiality concerns allow pursuant to rule 46 Rules of Procedure and Evidence, regulation 28(1) OTP Regulations. The Office of the Prosecutor issued public reports with regard to examinations that were ceased in Iraq (OTP response to communications received concerning Iraq, 09 February 2006), Venezuela (OTP response to communications received concerning Venezuela, 09 February 2006), Palestine (Decision by the OTP with regard to the situation in Palestine, 03 April 2012), Korea (Article 5 Report, 23 June 2014), and Comoros (Article 53(1) Report, 6 November 2014). A policy paper further spells out the Office of the Prosecutor's understanding of preliminary examination activities (Policy Paper on Preliminary Examinations, November 2013) and general reports with regard to ongoing examinations are given annually (Report on Preliminary Examination Activities 2013, Office of the Prosecutor, November 2013).

"Seriousness" refers to a minimum threshold for information to qualify under Article 15 for further inquiries. The ICC Statute is silent of the content of "information" under Article 15. Too broad and general information might not provide a sufficient evidentiary basis for the Prosecutor to launch an investigation. It is not a test of appropriateness (Bergsmo and Pejić, 2008, p. 587, para. 13) but rather an initial assessment of information to filter out unfounded, frivolous information. For this purpose, the Office of the Prosecutor makes preliminary distinctions between matters which "manifestly fall outside the jurisdiction of the Court" and other, more profound information pursuant to regulation 27 of the OTP Regulation that is further processed. The Office of the Prosecutor has also established a filtering process comprising four phases, each phase focusing on a distinct statutory factor for analytical purpose: phase 1 deals with an initial assessment of the "seriousness" of information, phase 2 turns to the preconditions of jurisdiction under Article 12 ICC Statute, phase 3 deals with admissibility under Article 17 ICC Statute, and phase 4 examines the "interests of justice" in accordance with Article 53(1)(c) ICC Statute (Policy Paper on Preliminary Examinations, November 2013, paras. 77–84).

The Prosecutor thus understands "seriousness" as an initial evaluation of information based on its evidentiary value, taking into account the reliability of the source and the credibility of the information, and examining information from multiple sources as a means of bias control pursuant to regulation 24 of the OTP Regulations. "Seriousness" is an evidentiary assessment linked to the legal factors of Article 53(1) and implies some degree of sincerity.

Author: Ignaz Stegmiller.

[190] According to the second sentence of Article 15(2) ICC Statute, the Prosecutor "may seek additional information" and "may receive written or oral testimony at the seat of the Court". The decision to seek further information is discretionary. The investigation steps are yet limited to the two mentioned possibilities and must be interpreted narrowly. The Prosecutor "cannot deploy all this investigative powers" (*Situation in the Republic of Côte d'Ivoire*, ICC PT. Ch. III, Judge Fernàndez de Gurmendi's separate and partially dissenting opinion to the Decision Pursuant to Article 15 of the ICC Statute on the Authorisation of an Investigation into the Situation in the Republic of Côte d'Ivoire, ICC-02/11-15, 3 October 2011, para. 29). Forms of cooperation from States are limited and Part 9 of the ICC Statute does not yet apply to preliminary examinations.

3. If the Prosecutor concludes that there is a reasonable basis to proceed with an investiga-
    tion, he or she shall submit to the Pre-Trial Chamber a request for authorization of an in-
    vestigation, together with any supporting material collected.[191] Victims may make repre-

---

Rule 104(2) of the Rule of Procedure and Evidence repeats the measures of Article 15(2), introducing the same method for State referrals and SC referrals. Information can be gathered from
States, organs of the United Nations, intergovernmental and non-governmental organisations
and other reliable sources. The Prosecutor may send requests for information to these sources.
Field missions for the purpose of analysing the information are possible, but have to be limited
to obtaining further information. Such field missions were conducted *inter alia* in Colombia,
Guinea, and Nigeria (Report of the Activities of the Court, International Criminal Court,
21.10.2013 (ICC-ASP/12/28, para. 72, para. 74, para. 77).

Testimony is to be received at the seat in The Hague. Rule 47 of the Rule of Procedure and
Evidence specifies this further. For example, a record in accordance with rules 47(1), 111 and
112 Rule of Procedure and Evidence is always necessary. The provision is not to be construed
as narrowly as meaning testimony has to be taken at the seat, but refers to receiving it. Therefore, testimony can be gathered through national authorities and be transmitted to The Hague.

The Prosecutor may gather information through the measures outlined in Article 93 ICC
Statute. While States might assist the Prosecutor, regardless of the application of cooperation
provisions under the ICC Statute, in the case on non-compliance, however, Articles 86 and 87
ff. ICC Statute do not apply, thus not imposing a legal duty to cooperate (Policy Paper on Preliminary Examinations, November 2013, para. 85; Informal Expert Paper, Fact-Finding and investigative functions of the Office of the Prosecutor, including co-operation, September 2003,
paras. 25–29). During preliminary examinations, the Prosecutor therefore must rely on voluntary cooperation and gather information through open sources to the extent available.

Author: Ignaz Stegmiller.

[191] The Prosecutor submits a "request for authorisation" to the Pre-Trial Chamber if preliminary
examinations provide for a "reasonable basis" to proceed with an investigation. At this stage,
the intermediary step from pre- to full investigations is foreseen, in other words, the Prosecutor
continues the inquiry after the authorisation by means of the associated powers under Article 54.

The Prosecutor determines "reasonable basis" at this stage, and he or she "shall" submit a
request for authorisation. "Shall" refers to the binding obligation to seek authorisation, in contrast to State referrals and Security Council referrals, where the Prosecutor enjoys freedom from
such an authorisation. This notwithstanding, the Prosecutor should, if a "reasonable basis" under
Article 15(3) and 53(1) ICC Statute has been reached, in principle, investigate unless exceptions
arise. The incorporation of Article 53's criteria, above all the "interests of justice", into the
Prosecutor's final determination, provides an opening for prosecutorial discretion and such an
exception.

The Prosecutor must be aware of the fact that the Pre-Trial Chamber will subsequently apply the same reasonability test under Article 15(4) ICC Statute. The content of reasonable basis
is the same under Article 15(3) and (4) and under Article 53(1) ICC Statute, which is restated by
rule 48 Rules of Procedure and Evidence.

Rule 50(2) Rules of Procedure and Evidence further states that the request shall be made in
writing. In accordance with regulation 49 Court Regulations, the Prosecutor attaches the information collected in the situation in hand to the authorisation request in annexes. As far as possible, the annexes should include a chronology of relevant events, maps detailing relevant information, including the location of the alleged crimes, and an explanatory glossary of relevant
names of persons, locations and institutions. Regulation 38(1)(e) of the Court Regulations establishes a limit of 100 pages for the document requesting the authorisation. It is thus clear that the
wording "any supporting material collected" of Article 15(3) ICC Statute does not mean "any

---

sentations to the Pre-Trial Chamber, in accordance with the Rules of Procedure and Evidence.[192]

---

and all". The Office of the Prosecutor is only obliged to forward as much supporting material as is required to demonstrate to the Pre-Trial Chamber that the conclusion to further investigate is well-founded. "Supporting material" cannot, however, be reduced to incriminating evidence only and the Office of the Prosecutor may not purposefully withhold information which does not support its conclusion. Article 54(1)(a) ICC Statute that requires the Office to investigate "incriminating and exonerating circumstances equally". In accordance with rule 46 Rule of Procedure and Evidence, supporting material can be submitted as a confidential attachment to the request.

Author: Ignaz Stegmiller.

[192] Victims may make representations to the Pre-Trial Chamber when a request under Article 15 ICC Statute is made. Information of victims may be brought to the attention of the Prosecutor under Article 15(1) and (2) ICC Statute, and as a corollary of the important role of victims in proprio motu proceedings their participation is regulated during early procedure. If the Prosecutor intends to seek a request under Article 15(3) ICC Statute, all victims known to the Prosecutor or to the Victims and Witnesses Unit ('VWU') must be informed under rule 50(1) Rules of Procedure and Evidence. Victims may then make representations in writing according to rule 50(2) and (3) Rules of Procedure and Evidence. A time limit of 30 days applies pursuant to rule 50(3) Rule of Procedure and Evidence and regulation 50(1) Court Regulations. In addition, regulation 38(2)(a) Court Regulations limits the documents submitted by victims under Article 15(3) and rule 50(3) to no more than 50 pages. The Chamber may request additional information from victims who have made representations and, "if it considers appropriate, may hold a hearing" pursuant to rule 50(4) Rules of Procedure and Evidence. In practice, victims sought participation in the situations in Kenya and Côte d'Ivoire. For the qualification as a "victim" the Chambers consulted rule 85 Rules of Procedure and Evidence (*Situation in the Republic of Côte d'Ivoire*, ICC PT. Ch. III, Order to the Victims Participation and Reparations Section Concerning Victims' Representations Pursuant to Article 15(3) of the Statute, ICC-02/11-6, 6 July 2011, para. 10). With regard to the participation procedure and victims' rights at such an early stage, jurisprudence has not yet found a common practice. The Pre-Trial Chamber in Kenya requested the Victims Participation and Reparations Section ('VPRS') to:

(1) identify, to the extent possible, the community leaders of the affected groups to act on behalf of those victims who may wish to make representations (collective representation);

(2) receive victims' representations (collective and/or individual);

(3) conduct an assessment, in accordance with paragraph 8 of this order, whether the conditions set out in rule 85 of the Rules have been met; and

(4) summarise victims' representations into one consolidated report with the original representations annexed thereto (*Situation in the Republic of Côte d'Ivoire*, ICC PT. Ch. III, Order to the Victims Participation and Reparations Section Concerning Victims' Representations Pursuant to Article 15(3) of the Statute, ICC-02/11-6, 6 July 2011, para. 9).

Pre-Trial Chamber III in Côte d'Ivoire departed from this approach and, for the sake of expeditiousness, called upon the VPRS to provide "a single, consolidated report on the collective and individual representations" (*Situation in the Republic of Côte d'Ivoire*, ICC PT. Ch. III, Order to the Victims Participation and Reparations Section Concerning Victims' Representations Pursuant to Article 15(3) of the Statute, ICC-02/11-6, 6 July 2011, para. 9; see also *Situation in the Republic of Côte d'Ivoire*, ICC PT. Ch. III, Decision Pursuant to Article 15 of the ICC Statute on the Authorisation of an Investigation into the Situation in the Republic of Côte d'Ivoire, ICC-02/11-14, 3 October 2011, para. 19).

4. If the Pre-Trial Chamber, upon examination of the request and the supporting material, considers that there is a reasonable basis to proceed with an investigation,[193] and that the

---

Author: Ignaz Stegmiller.

[193] The power to authorise an investigation *proprio motu* lies with the Pre-Trial Chamber alone. While the Prosecutor may initiate the preliminary phase, it is the Chamber's prerogative to allow for the start of a formal investigation. From the moment of authorisation, the Office of the Prosecutor is entitled to use its powers under Article 54 ICC Statute. Under rule 50(5) Rule of Procedure and Evidence, the Chamber may issue a decision, including its reasons, authorising "all or any part of the request of the Prosecutor", and it must give notice to victims that have made representations. Decisions under Article 15(4) ICC Statute can be appealed by the Prosecutor in accordance with Article 82(1)(a) or (d) ICC Statute but not by States or victims.

The Pre-Trial Chamber must consider whether there is a "reasonable basis to proceed with an investigation". The underlying purpose of this check is to control for frivolous or politically motivated charges. The same "reasonable basis" standard is used for all three trigger mechanisms to move from preliminary examinations to investigations. "Reasonable basis" appears in Articles 15(3), (4), and 53(1) ICC Statute. Rule 48 introduces the criteria of Article 53(1) ICC Statute into Article 15(3) ICC Statute, which strongly suggests that the "reasonable basis" standard is identical in Article 15(4) ICC Statute. The drafting history of Articles 15 and 53 of the Statute further reveals that the intention was to use exactly the same standard for these provisions. Therefore, the same "reasonable basis to proceed" standard applies to both the Prosecutor and the Pre-trial Chamber in Article 15(3) and (4) ICC Statute (*Situation in the Republic of Kenya*, ICC PT. Ch. II, Decision Pursuant to Article 15 of the Rome Statute on the Authorisation of an Investigation into the Situation in the Republic of Kenya, ICC-01/09-19, 31 March 2010, paras. 21–25; *Situation in the Republic of Côte d'Ivoire*, ICC PT. Ch. III, Decision Pursuant to Article 15 of the Rome Statute on the Authorisation of an Investigation into the Situation in the Republic of Côte d'Ivoire, ICC-02/11-14, 3 October 2011, para. 17).

In addition, the Pre-Trial Chamber, due to the overlap between Articles 15 and 53 ICC Statute, must first consider whether the requirements set out in Article 53(1)(a)-(c) ICC Statute are satisfied before deciding whether to authorise the commencement of an investigation. The Chamber shall consider whether

(a) the information available to the Prosecutor provides a reasonable basis to believe that a crime within the jurisdiction of the Court has been or is being committed;

(b) the case is or would be admissible under Article 17 of the Statute; and

(c) taking into account the gravity of the crime and the interests of victims, there are nonetheless substantial reasons to believe that an investigation would not serve the interests of justice (emphasis added)" (*Situation in the Republic of Côte d'Ivoire*, ICC PT. Ch. III, Decision Pursuant to Article 15 of the Rome Statute on the Authorisation of an Investigation into the Situation in the Republic of Côte d'Ivoire, ICC-02/11-14, 3 October 2011, para. 17).

In essence, the standard under Article 15(4) ICC Statute is a very low one, it is meant to "prevent the Court from proceeding with unwarranted, frivolous, or politically motivated investigations that could have a negative effect on its credibility" and the Chamber must be satisfied "that there exists a sensible or reasonable justification for a belief that a crime falling within the jurisdiction of the Court 'has been or is being committed" (*Situation in the Republic of Kenya*, ICC PT. Ch. II, Decision Pursuant to Article 15 of the Rome Statute on the Authorisation of an Investigation into the Situation in the Republic of Kenya, ICC-01/09-19, 31 March 2010, paras. 32, 35).

This notwithstanding, the question how low the threshold actually is remains unsettled in present ICC jurisprudence. Since all jurisdictional parameters must be covered by the Pre-Trial

case appears to fall within the jurisdiction of the Court, it shall authorize the commencement of the investigation, without prejudice to subsequent determinations by the Court with regard to the jurisdiction and admissibility of a case.[194]

Chamber's review, Judge Hans-Peter Kaul did not agree with the standard applied by the majority of the Chamber and issued a dissenting opinion, holding that the context element of crimes against humanity was not fulfilled:

> It is my opinion that in the present case, despite the low threshold, an examination of in particular all legal requirements of Article 7 of the Statute, which establish the *ratione materiae* jurisdiction of the Court, including the contextual elements, is still required. It is most striking that in the Prosecutor's Request of 26 November 2009 the analysis of the contextual element of crimes against humanity, this crucial point of the entire request, was inadequately explored (*Situation in the Republic of Kenya*, ICC PT. Ch. II, Decision Pursuant to Article 15 of the Rome Statute on the Authorisation of an Investigation into the Situation in the Republic of Kenya, ICC-01/09-19, 31 March 2010, Dissenting Opinion of Judge Kaul Situation in the Republic of Kenya, p. 9, para. 18).

In the different context of Côte d'Ivoire, Judge Fernàndez de Gurmendi suggests an even lower standard than the one applied by the majority in both situations of Côte d'Ivoire and Kenya, emphasising that the Chamber has no investigative powers and should largely rely upon the Prosecutor's findings:

> the examination to be conducted by the Chamber is of a limited nature, namely to ascertain the accuracy of the statement of facts and reasons of law advanced by the Prosecutor with regard to crimes and incidents identified in his own request and determine, on this basis, whether the requirements of Article 53 of the Statute are met (*Situation in the Republic of Côte d'Ivoire*, ICC PT. Ch. III, Judge Fernàndez de Gurmendi's separate and partially dissenting opinion to the Decision Pursuant to Article 15 of the Rome Statute on the Authorisation of an Investigation into the Situation in the Republic of Côte d'Ivoire, ICC-02/11-15, 3 October 2011, para. 28).

Author: Ignaz Stegmiller.

[194] The second half of the phrasing under Article 15(4) ICC Statute, "that the case appears to fall within the jurisdiction of the Court", causes confusion: first, the provision was drafted in an imprecise manner because, at the given stage, the Prosecutor is concerned with situations as opposed to cases. The term "case" should not be read in isolation from the rest of Article 15 and must be put into perspective regarding the preliminary phase. The Pre-Trial Chamber therefore construed a wide understanding of case as relating to "potential cases" within the situation at stake. Second, the phrase "jurisdiction of the Court" could suggest a double-standard as it is mentioned both under Articles 15(4) and 53(1) ICC Statute. However, jurisdiction is only checked once by the Pre-Trial Chamber and there is no need to duplicate its assessment of jurisdiction because the "analysis makes it evident that there is a degree of redundancy in Article 15(4) of the Statute insofar as the first requirement necessitates assessment of a "reasonable basis to proceed" under Article 53(1)(a) of the Statute, and the second requirement equally prescribes assessment of whether "the case appears to fall within the jurisdiction of the Court" (*Situation in the Republic of Kenya*, ICC PT. Ch. II, Decision Pursuant to Article 15 of the ICC Statute on the Authorisation of an Investigation into the Situation in the Republic of Kenya, ICC-01/09-19, 31 March 2010, para. 66).

Author: Ignaz Stegmiller.

---

5. The refusal of the Pre-Trial Chamber to authorize the investigation shall not preclude the presentation of a subsequent request by the Prosecutor based on new facts or evidence regarding the same situation.[195]

6. If, after the preliminary examination referred to in paragraphs 1 and 2, the Prosecutor concludes that the information provided does not constitute a reasonable basis for an investigation, he or she shall inform those who provided the information. This shall not preclude the Prosecutor from considering further information submitted to him or her regarding the same situation in the light of new facts or evidence.[196]

---

[195] If the Pre-Trial Chamber refuses to authorise an investigation, the Prosecutor may bring subsequent requests "based on new facts or evidence regarding the same situation". Rule 50(6) Rule of Procedure and Evidence clarifies that the new request is subject to the same procedure as the original request. The request must refer to new information. No refusal by a Pre-Trial Chamber has taken place to date. Therefore, the matter of subsequent requests is yet to be tested in ICC practice and the term "new facts or evidence" needs to be given a practical analysis.

Under this provision, it is possible that the Office of the Prosecutor keeps monitoring a conflict situation and files a new request if violence erupts again. The preliminary examination process is the Prosecutor's domain and he/she decides about usage of the Office's resources according to Article 42(2) ICC Statute.

Author: Ignaz Stegmiller.

[196] If the Prosecutor decides not to proceed to an investigation, "he or she shall inform those who provided the information". Pursuant to Rule 49(1) Rule of Procedure and Evidence, such notification must be given promptly and must include reasons for the decision. Rule 105(2) Rules of Procedure and Evidence links the decision to initiate an investigation under Article 53(1) ICC Statute to Rule 49(1) Rules of Procedure and Evidence, in the case the Prosecutor decides in the negative and does not submit a request under Article 15(4) ICC Statute. The information duty is also acknowledged by regulation 28 OTP Regulations and negative decisions by the Office of the Prosecutor are published under this provision if appropriate.

Victims, however, have neither right to a legal remedy against a (negative) decision under Article 15(3) or (4) ICC Statute, nor can they participate in a review procedure of a negative decision by the Prosecutor. A proposal by the French delegation in this respect aimed at granting victims the status of a procedural party stricto sensu, but this idea was rejected during the Rome Conference. Therefore, victims, who have provided for information under Article 15 ICC Statute, have the right to be informed, but they have limited participatory rights.

A follow-up question related to the term "those who provided the information". A narrow interpretation only covers the original information providers, thus the person who transmitted the information to the Prosecutor and filed the "communication". Beyond the statutory duty to inform the direct information providers, nothing prevents the Prosecutor from notifying other parties simultaneously. The Office of the Prosecutor has taken such a wider approach in practice and sends notification letters to anyone from whom the Prosecutor has sought additional information and persons who have given testimony.

Cross-references:
Articles 13(c) and 53.
Rules 46–50, 102–104, 111–112.
Regulation 49, 50 and 87.
OTP Regulations 25–31.
Doctrine:

---

1. Ignaz Stegmiller, *The Pre-Investigation Stage of the ICC, Criteria for Situation Selection*, Duncker and Humblot, Berlin, 2011.

2. Jo Stigen, *The Relationship between the International Criminal Court and National Jurisdiction: The Principle of Complementarity*, Martinus Nijhoff Publishers, Leiden, 2008.

3. Frank Hoffmeister and Sebastian Knoke, "Das Vorermittlungsverfahren vor dem Internationalen Strafgerichtshof – Prüfstein für die Effektivität der neuen Gerichtsbarkeit im Völkerstrafrecht", in *Zeitschrift für ausländisches und öffentliches Recht und Völkerrecht*, 1999, vol. 59, pp. 785–807.

4. Dan Sarooshi, "Prosecutorial Policy and the ICC: Prosecutor's *Proprio Motu* Action or Self-Denial?", in *Journal of International Criminal Justice*, 2006, vol. 4, no. 4, pp. 940–43.", in *Journal of International Criminal Justice*, 2006, vol. 4, no. 4, pp. 940–43.

5. Jan Wouters, Sten Verhoeven and Bruno Demeyere, "The International Criminal Court's Office of the Prosecutor: Navigating between Independence and Accountability?", in *International Criminal Law Review*, 2008, vol. 8, no. 1, pp. 273–318.

6. Morten Bergsmo and Jelena Pejić, "Article 15", in Otto Triffterer (ed.), *Commentary on the Rome Statute of the International Criminal Court: Observers' Notes, Article by Article*, 2nd ed., C.H. Beck/Hart/Nomos, Munich/Oxford/Baden-Baden, 2008, pp. 581–93.

7. Håkan Friman, "The Rules of Procedure and Evidence in the Investigation Stage", in Horst Fischer, Claus Kreß and Sascha Rolf Lüder (eds.), *International and National Prosecution of Crimes Under International Law*, Berlin Verlag Arno Spitz, Berlin, 2001, pp. 191–217.

8. Håkan Friman, "Investigation and Prosecution", in Roy S. Lee (ed.), *The International Criminal Court: Elements of Crimes and Rules of Procedure and Evidence*, Transnational Publishers, Ardsley, NY, 2001, pp. 493–539.

9. Philippe Kirsch and Darryl Robinson, "Initiation of Proceedings by the Prosecutor", in Antonio Cassese, Paola Gaeta and John R.W.D. Jones (eds.), *The Rome Statute of the ICC: A Commentary*, 2nd ed., Oxford University Press, Oxford, 2002, pp. 657–64.

10. William A. Schabas, *The International Criminal Court, A Commentary on the Rome Statute*, Oxford University Press, Oxford, 2010, pp. 314–24.

11. Giuliano Turone, "Powers and Duties of the Prosecutor", in Antonio Cassese, Paola Gaeta and John R.W.D. Jones (eds.), *The Rome Statute of the ICC: A Commentary*, 2nd ed., Oxford University Press, Oxford, 2002, pp. 1137–80.

Author: Ignaz Stegmiller.

Article 15 *bis*[5]

Exercise of jurisdiction over the crime of aggression
(State referral, *proprio motu*)[197]

---

[197] *General remarks*:

Article 15 *bis* regulates the Court's jurisdiction over the crime of aggression where situations are referred to the Court by a State, or where investigations are instigated by the Office of the Prosecutor. Referrals by the Security Council are regulated under Article 15 *ter*. The amendments on the crime of aggression will enter into force one year after the ratification or acceptance of 30 States Parties, provided that a decision is taken by at least two-thirds of the States Parties after 1 January 2017, in accordance with paragraph 3. A State Party that does not wish to be bound by the amendments may file a declaration to the Registry of the Court stating that it does not accept the amendments, which will then not be binding upon the State in question. There is still uncertainty regarding some aspects of the change to the Court's jurisdiction, especially with regard to States Parties that have neither ratified, nor opted out from the amendments in accordance with paragraph 4. While it is possible for the Prosecutor to proceed with an investigation regarding the crime of aggression without a determination by the UN Security Council that an act of aggression has been committed, this requires authorisation by the Pre-Trial Division in accordance with paragraph 8.

Preparatory works:

In accordance with the now deleted Article 5(2), the ICC would exercise jurisdiction over the crime of aggression "once a provision [was] adopted in accordance with Articles 121 and 123 defining the crime and setting out the conditions under which the Court shall exercise jurisdiction with respect to this crime". In order for the States Parties to find a definition and jurisdictional conditions that they could agree upon, the Assembly of States Parties ('ASP') decided to establish a Special Working Group on the Crime of Aggression ('SWGCA') which was to submit proposed provisions to a future Review Conference (Resolution on Continuity of Work in Respect of the Crime of Aggression, 2002). The SWGCA held several meetings between 2003 and 2009 and its draft amendments were the starting point for the discussions at the Kampala Review Conference in 2010, where Articles 8 *bis*, 15 *bis*, 15 *ter* and 25(3) *bis* were adopted.

The three main areas of controversy for the SWGCA, and later for the Review Conference, were the definition of "an act of aggression"; the individual conduct within the act; and the exercise of jurisdiction by the ICC. While the first two sets of issues are covered by Article 8 *bis*, the jurisdictional conditions are dealt with under this Article and in Article 15 *ter*.

The main questions regarding the Court's jurisdiction over the crime of aggression concerned the application of the provisions to States Parties that have not ratified or accepted the amendments, as well as the role of the Security Council in determining that an act of aggression has been committed. To start with the latter, the role of the UN Security Council was a sensitive issue in the negotiations leading up to the decision in Kampala. The drafted ICC Statute from 1994 suggested that the Court's jurisdiction over the crime of aggression should be dependent on a determination by the Security Council that an act of aggression had been committed (Report of the International Law Commission on the work of its forty-sixth session, 2 May to 22 July 1994, ILC Report, A/49/10, (F), 1994, Draft Statute of an International Court, p. 44, Article 23(2)). However, to give the Security Council, with its well documented problems and limited number of Member States such a power was considered problematic, even though it was defended by the permanent members of the Council (Kress and Holtzendorff, 2010, p. 1194). Most notably the UK and France defended the Security Council's exclusive right to determine an "act of aggression" with reference to such a right being provided to the Council by the UN Charter, to which the now deleted Article 5(2) made a direct reference.

While the majority held that the Security Council should not have an exclusive power to determine an act of aggression, the solution agreed upon in Kampala was to have different procedures in cases where the Security Council has determined that an act of aggression has been committed and where such a determination is absent. Further, it was made clear in Article 15 *bis*(8) that the right of the Security Council to defer a case in accordance with Article 16 is applicable also to the crime of aggression, just as to other crimes under the Statute.

The second major question regarding jurisdiction was that of how to regulate aggression by States Parties to the ICC Statute that have not ratified or accepted the amendments. Some argued that the amendments should be binding upon all States Parties in accordance with Article 12(1), whereas others held that States Parties had to agree to be bound by the amendments, in accordance with Article 121(5) (2009 SWGA Report, 9–11). The disagreements were largely based in different interpretations of Article 5(2), but also of Article 121(5) and its applicability to the crime of aggression.

There were several suggestions for how the conditions of jurisdictions should be determined. One was to apply the 'Adoption Model', where a two-thirds majority vote to adopt the amendments in accordance with Article 121(3) would suffice. The use of this model without any further requirement of ratification by State Parties for the entry into force of the amendments was unsatisfying to most (Kress and Holtzendorf, 2010, p. 1196). Others argued for the Article 121(5) model with a "negative understanding", which would give the Court jurisdiction over the crime of aggression for those states that had accepted the amendments, but not for others. Such an interpretation was considered problematic for several reasons, including the question of whether the crime of aggression was an amendment to Article 5, 6, 7 or 8, considering the previous existence of Article 5(1)(d) and Article 5(2) (Kress and Holtzendorff, 2010, p. 1197). A broader interpretation of Article 121(5) was provided by the supporters of the "positive understanding" model, which held that the second sentence of Article 121(5) should be read together with Article 12(2), giving the Court jurisdiction over the crime of aggression in situations where such jurisdiction had been accepted by the victim State, even if the aggressor had not ratified the amendments. Yet another suggestion was the 'Article 121(4) Model', which required the amendments to be ratified by 7/8th of the States Parties. This was considered problematic partly as it treated the provisions as amendments outside of Article 5–8, even though the crime of aggression already existed in Article 5(1)(d), but also since it would possibly bind 1/8th of the States Parties without their consent (Milanović, 2010, p. 178).

There were also some more creative suggestions trying to avoid the lock down in the interpretation of already existing paragraphs. The most notable of these were the opt-in and opt-out solutions proposed by the Chairman of the SWGCA in 2009 (Chairman's Non-Paper on the Exercise of Jurisdiction, 2009, paras. 10–12). The opt-in solution held that States would have to actively opt-in to be bound, whereas the opt-out solution gave States Parties the possibility to opt-out, in case they did not wish to be bound by the amendments. The latter would thus shift the default situation and require active action by States Parties to avoid being bound. The opt-out regime is now found in the text of Article 15 *bis*(4), but unfortunately, the large amount of compromises in the lead up to the decision in Kampala has led to the jurisdictional provision being far from clear. At the same time as a textual reading of Article 15 *bis*(4) applies the opt-out regime, the first operating paragraph of Resolution RC/Res.6 states that the crime shall enter into force in accordance with Article 121(5), which holds that a State Party is not bound by an amendment unless it has ratified or accepted it. The jurisdictional questions arising from this discussion will have to be determined by the Court in the future.

With regard to the principle of complementarity, there were some concerns around the possibility for States to exercise domestic jurisdiction over the crime of aggression. Following from this, Understanding 5 (Resolution RC/Res.6, 2010, Annex III, Understanding 5) states that the amendments do no create such a right with respect to an act of aggression committed by another

1. The Court may exercise jurisdiction over the crime of aggression in accordance with Article 13, paragraphs (a) and (c), subject to the provisions of this article.[198]

2. The Court may exercise jurisdiction only with respect to crimes of aggression committed one year after the ratification or acceptance of the amendments by thirty States Parties.[199]

3. The Court shall exercise jurisdiction over the crime of aggression in accordance with this article, subject to a decision to be taken after 1 January 2017 by the same majority of States Parties as is required for the adoption of an amendment to the Statute.[200]

4. The Court may, in accordance with article 12, exercise jurisdiction over a crime of aggression, arising from an act of aggression committed by a State Party, unless that State Party has previ-

---

State. It remains to be seen whether and how this understanding will affect domestic legislatures (Kress and Holtzendorff, 2010, p. 1216).

Author: Marie Aronsson-Storrier.

[198] Analysis of provision and sub-provisions

The Article regulates State referrals and *proprio motu*, investigations instigated by the Office of the Prosecutor. Referrals by the UN Security Council is regulated by Article 15 *ter*.

Author: Marie Aronsson-Storrier.

[199] Paragraph 2 regulates the earliest time from which the acts committed may be under the ICC's jurisdiction, as long as the requirement in paragraph 3 is fulfilled. The Understandings make clear that for the Court to have jurisdiction of a crime, one year need to have passed since the ratification of 30 State Parties and a decision needs to have been taken in accordance with paragraph 3 (Resolution RC/Res.6, 2010, Annex III, Understanding 3). That is, if 30 State Parties would have signed on 1 July 2015, the Court would not have jurisdiction over crimes committed in the second half of 2016, but would still have to await the decision taken in accordance with Article 15 *bis*(3) at the earliest on 1 January 2017.

According to Article 121(5), amendments should enter into force for a ratifying state one year after ratification. Therefore, as it is not certain whether all States Parties are bound by the provisions after the requirements in this paragraph and paragraph 3 have been met (see comment to paragraph 4), it might be the case that the Court may exercise jurisdiction over subsequent ratifying states at different times if they ratify after, or less than a year before, the provisions enter into force.

The application of the amendments with respect to States Parties that have not accepted the amendments at the time when the Court gains jurisdiction, is discussed under paragraph 4.

Author: Marie Aronsson-Storrier.

[200] According to this paragraph, the Court may only exercise jurisdiction over the crime of aggression if this is decided by at least a two-third majority after 1 January 2017, in accordance with Article 121(3). Thus, while only 30 States Parties need to actively ratify the amendments in accordance with paragraph 2, two-thirds of the States Parties must still approve of the amendments before the Court may exercise jurisdiction over the crime. Jurisdiction will apply to acts committed one year after the ratification of 30 States Parties, or after the decision taken in accordance with this paragraph, whichever comes last (Resolution RC/Res.6, 2010, Annex III, Understanding 3).

That is, if 30 States Parties have ratified or accepted the amendments by 1 December 2016, the Court will not have jurisdiction over crimes committed before 1 December 2017, even if a decision in accordance with this paragraph has been taken earlier that year.

There is no requirement for a State Parties to have ratified or otherwise accepted the amendments in order to cast a positive vote after 1 January 2017.

Author: Marie Aronsson-Storrier.

---

ously declared that it does not accept such jurisdiction by lodging a declaration with the Registrar. The withdrawal of such a declaration may be effected at any time and shall be considered by the State Party within three years.[201]

---

[201] As soon as the requirements in Article 15 *bis*(2) and (3) are met, the amendments are applicable to the States Parties that have ratified or accepted them, unless they have lodged a declaration with the registrar that they wish not to be bound. An opt-out declaration can be lodged regardless of whether or not the State in question has ratified the amendments. It further follows from the wording of this paragraph that an opt-out declaration does not affect the protection that a State has as a victim State, but merely the Court's jurisdiction in cases where the State is the aggressor.

There is significant uncertainty regarding the application of the amendments on State Parties that have not ratified, yet not lodged an opt-out declaration. This uncertainty follows from the contradiction in the adoption of Article 15 *bis*(4) and the reference to Article 121(5) in the first operational paragraph of Resolution RC/Res.6. Some hold that States Parties are bound by default, unless they opt-out (Kress and Holtzendorff, 2010, p. 1213; McDougall, 2013, pp. 258–59), whereas others argue that the provisions on the crime of aggression do not bind States Parties that have not ratified the amendments, regardless of whether or not they have opted out (Van Schaack, 2010–11, p. 598).

In addition to the uncertain relationship between Articles 15 *bis*(4) and 121(5), there are also different readings of the application of Article 12, which is referred to in this paragraph. One approach is that the Court has jurisdiction in any of the scenarios in Article 12(2), that is, cases where either the alleged aggressor State or the alleged victim State has ratified the amendments. Another approach is that a textual reading of Article 121(5) requires both the aggressor and the victim State to have ratified the amendments in order for the Court to have jurisdiction.

Kevin Jon Heller, Carrie McDougall, Marko Milanović and Astrid Reisinger Coracino have all presented illustrative and helpful tables over the jurisdiction (Heller, 2010; McDougall, 2013, p. 261; Reisinger Coracino, 2010, p. 782; Milanović, 2012, p. 182). It is agreed that the ICC has jurisdiction in situations where both the aggressor State and the victim State are Party to the ICC Statute and have ratified the amendments without lodging an opt-out declaration, and that it does not have jurisdiction under Article 15 *bis* in cases where the aggressor is a State Party that has lodged an opt-out declaration.

Where the aggressor is a State Party that has not ratified and not opted out, and the victim is a State Part that has ratified the amendments, it seems to be the view of the majority that the Court has jurisdiction in accordance with Article 12(2)(a), regardless of whether or not the victim State has lodged an opt-out declaration (McDougall, 2013, p. 261; Reisinger Coracini, 2010, p. 782; Milanović, 2012, p. 182). Those promoting a narrow interpretation of Article 121(5) however, hold that the Court could not have jurisdiction in this case, since the aggressor State has not accepted the amendments (Milanović, 2012, p. 182).

Where the aggressor is a State Party that has not ratified and not opted out and the victim is a State Party that has not ratified the amendments, the majority of scholars hold that the Court probably does not have jurisdiction, regardless of whether or not the victim State has opted out (McDougall, 2013, p. 261; Reisinger Coracini, 2010, p. 782; Milanović, 2012, p. 182). Jurisdiction in such cases might be possible if a State Party that has not ratified the amendments would be allowed to accept the Court's jurisdiction of the crime of aggression in accordance with Article 12(3), but the existence of such possibility is far from certain (McDougall, 2013, p. 264; Reisinger Coracini, 2010, p 781; Kress and Holtzendorff, 2010, p. 1214).

Where the aggressor is a State Party that has ratified and not opted out and the victim is a State Party that has not ratified the amendments, many hold that the Court has jurisdiction in accordance with this paragraph and Article 12(2)(a). Though as according to a narrow reading of

5. In respect of a State that is not a party to this Statute, the Court shall not exercise its jurisdiction over the crime of aggression when committed by that State's nationals or on its territory.[202]

6. Where the Prosecutor concludes that there is a reasonable basis to proceed with an investigation in respect of a crime of aggression, he or she shall first ascertain whether the Security Council has made a determination of an act of aggression committed by the State concerned. The Prosecutor shall notify the Secretary-General of the United Nations of the situation before the Court, including any relevant information and documents.[203]

7. Where the Security Council has made such a determination, the Prosecutor may proceed with the investigation in respect of a crime of aggression.[204]

Article 121(5) both the aggressor State and the victim State will have to have accepted the amendments, promoters of such a reading argue that the Court would not have jurisdiction in this situation (Milanović, 2013, p. 182; Akande, 2011, p. 27).

As can be seen above, there are severe uncertainties regarding the jurisdiction under this Article, and unless they are resolved before the amendments enter into force, it will be for the Court to resolve these difficult jurisdictional questions as they arise.

Author: Marie Aronsson-Storrier.

[202] Paragraph 5 excludes from the Court's jurisdiction acts of aggression committed by, or on the territory of, a non-State Party and constitutes a notable limitation of the application of the crime of aggression under this Statute.

While there have been some suggestions that Article 12(2) applies to the crime of aggression also where the victim State is not party to the ICC Statute, the majority holds that the Court does not have jurisdiction over such situations (Heller, 2010; McDougall, 2013, p. 261; Reisinger Coracino, 2010, p. 782; Milanović, 2012, p. 182). If there is some uncertainty regarding the jurisdiction in cases where a State Party that has ratified the amendments attacks a non-State Party, it is clear that the Court does not have jurisdiction over situations where the aggressor is a State Party that has not ratified the amendments, and the victim is a non-State Party. The same is true for situations where the aggressor is a State Party that has opted out, regardless of whether or not it has ratified the amendments. It is further agreed that the Court does not have jurisdiction in cases where the aggressor State is not party to the ICC Statute. A remaining question mark is whether or not it is possible for a State to accept the Court's jurisdiction *ad hoc* and it is uncertain whether Article 12(3) is applicable to the crime of aggression (Stahn, 2010, p. 880; McDougall, 2013, p. 264; Reisinger Coracini, 2010, p 781; Kress and Holtzendorff, 2010, p. 1214).

Author: Marie Aronsson-Storrier.

[203] Before proceeding with an investigation, the Prosecutor needs to establish whether or not the UN Security Council has made a determination of an act of aggression in the specific situation. While this will be an easy task in cases where the Security Council uses the phrase "act of aggression", it will be less obvious in cases where the Council might speak of a State being aggressive, or "aggressive behaviour". Questions have been raised of whether the determination needs to be in an operational paragraph, or if it is enough to just raise concerns over a State being aggressive, and it remains to be seen how the Court will interpret this. The notification of the UN Secretary-General is essential for proceeding with the investigation. In cases where the Security Council has not made a determination of an act of aggression, the waiting period of six months in paragraph 8 starts at the time of the notification.

Author: Marie Aronsson-Storrier.

[204] In cases where the Prosecutor, in accordance with paragraph 6, finds that the UN Security Council has determined an act of aggression, there is no need for a decision by the Pre-Trial Di-

8. Where no such determination is made within six months after the date of notification, the Prosecutor may proceed with the investigation in respect of a crime of aggression, provided that the Pre-Trial Division has authorized the commencement of the investigation in respect of a crime of aggression in accordance with the procedure contained in article 15, and the Security Council has not decided otherwise in accordance with Article 16.[205]

9. A determination of an act of aggression by an organ outside the Court shall be without prejudice to the Court's own findings under this Statute.[206]

10. This Article is without prejudice to the provisions relating to the exercise of jurisdiction with respect to other crimes referred to in Article 5.[207]

---

vision or by the Pre-Trial Chamber in order to proceed with the investigation. The procedure in cases where no such determination has been made is regulated in paragraph 8.

In accordance with paragraph 10, the Prosecutor may still need the authorisation by the Pre-Trial Chamber in order to proceed with the investigation of other crimes under the Statute, including in situations where this paragraph is applicable.

Author: Marie Aronsson-Storrier.

[205] In cases where the UN Security Council has not made determination of an act of aggression within six months after the UN Secretary-General was notified in accordance with paragraph 6, the Prosecutor may proceed without such a determination. Unlike cases where the Council has determined that an act of aggression has been committed, the proceeding with an investigation in the absence of such a determination is dependent on the authorisation by the Pre-Trial Division. In accordance with Article 39(1), the Pre-Trial Division consists of a minimum of six judges.

The reference to Article 15 in this paragraph clarifies that even though an authorisation for the commencement of an investigation for the crime of aggression shall come from the Pre-Trial Division rather than the Pre-Trial Chambers, the procedure is otherwise the same as for other crimes in the Statute, with the difference that the procedure in Article 15 should be followed both for State referrals and *proprio motu* investigations. In accordance with paragraph 10, the authorisation by the Pre-Trial Division of an investigation of the crime of aggression is separate from the authorisation by the Pre-Trial Chamber of the investigation of other crimes in the Statute.

The reference to Article 16 is a clarification that the Security Council's power to defer a case up to twelve months is applicable also with regard to the crime of aggression.

Author: Marie Aronsson-Storrier.

[206] Paragraph 9 ensures the independence of the ICC in determining whether an act of aggression has been committed. This, in combination with the possibility to proceed with an investigation without a determination by the UN Security Council, was a controversial issue during the negotiations.

The Court may determine that an act of aggression has been committed where such a determination is lacking, and it may also find that no act of aggression has been committed even where the Security Council, the International Court of Justice ('ICJ'), or any other organ outside the Court has made a positive determination that such an act has taken place. This paragraph will be of importance in politically sensitive situations where the veto right by the permanent members of the Security Council might stop the Council from determining an act of aggression, but it can also be used against a determination by the ICJ, or any other organ outside of the Court. The paragraph will further be applied in cases where the ICJ or the Security Council hold that there has been a breach of the prohibition of the use of force, but for various reasons do not refer to it as "aggression", and the ICC still find that the act amounts to aggression.

Author: Marie Aronsson-Storrier.

⁵ Inserted by resolution RC/Res.6 of 11 June 2010.

---

²⁰⁷ Paragraph 10 clarifies that that the special considerations applying to the crime of aggression are not to be interpreted as applying to other crimes.

In cases where a situation may entail several crimes under the Statute, additional authorisation of an investigation needs to be sought in accordance with Article 15. This is the case regardless of whether the Prosecutor proceeds with an investigation on the basis of paragraphs 7 or 8. While the need for separate procedures can be considered unsatisfactory, this solution has been adopted in order to avoid unnecessary stalling of investigations of situations where the process of the investigation of a crime of aggression has a different time frame than the investigation of other crimes (McDougall, 2013, p. 274).

It has been suggested that paragraph 10 can be read to support the view that Article 12(3) does not apply to the crime of aggression, though there is still some uncertainty as to whether or not this is correct (McDougall, 2013, p. 264; Reisinger Coracini, 2010, p 781; Kress and Holtzendorff, 2010, p. 1214).

Cross-references:

Articles 5(1)(d), 8 *bis*, 12, 15 *ter*, 121 and 123.

Doctrine:

1. Dapo Akande, "Prosecuting Aggression: The Consent Problem and the Role of the Security Council", *Oxford Legal Research Paper Series*, no. 10, 2011.
2. Kevin Jon Heller, "The Uncertain Legal Status of the Aggression Understandings", in *Journal of International Criminal Justice*, 2012, vol. 10, pp. 229–48.
3. Kevin Jon Heller, "Opt-ins and Opt-outs", in *Opinio Juris*, 2010.
4. Claus Kreß and Leonie von Holtzendorff, "The Kampala Compromise on the Crime of Aggression", in *Journal of International Criminal Justice*, 2010, vol. 8, no. 5, pp. 1179–1217.
5. Carrie McDougall, *The Crime of Aggression under the Rome Statute of the International Criminal Court*, Cambridge University Press, Cambridge, 2013, pp. 258–259, 261, 264, 274.
6. Marko Milanović, "Aggression and Legality Custom in Kampala", in *Journal of International Criminal Justice*, 2012, vol. 10, pp. 165–87.
7. Astrid Reisinger Coracini, "The International Criminal Court's Exercise of Jurisdiction Over the Crime of Aggression – at Last ... in Reach ... Over Some", in *Goettingen Journal of International Law*, 2010, vol. 2, pp. 745–89.
8. Beth Van Schaack, "Negotiating at the Interface of Power and Law: The Crime of Aggression", in *Columbia Journal of Transnational Law*, 2010–11, vol. 49, pp. 505–601.
9. Carsten Stahn, "The 'End', the Beginning of the End' or the 'End of the Beginning'? Introducing Debates and Voices on the Definition of Aggression", in *Leiden Journal of International Law*, 2010, vol. 23, no. 4, pp. 875–82.

Author: Marie Aronsson-Storrier.

Article 15 *ter*[6]

Exercise of jurisdiction over the crime of aggression
(Security Council referral)[208]

1. The Court may exercise jurisdiction over the crime of aggression in accordance with Article 13, paragraph (b), subject to the provisions of this article.[209]

2. The Court may exercise jurisdiction only with respect to crimes of aggression committed one year after the ratification or acceptance of the amendments by thirty States Parties.[210]

---

[208] *General remarks*:

Article 15 *ter* largely resembles Article 15 *bis*, and affirms that the time frame for jurisdiction of the Court is the same for Security Council referral as for State Party referral and *proprio motu* investigations. As with other crimes under this Statute, the Security Council refers the situation without the direction of the specific crime, in accordance with Article 13(b). The procedure under this Article is not affected by a determination of an act of aggression by the Security Council.

Preparatory works:

The exercise of jurisdiction over the crime of aggression through referrals by the Security Council is largely considered uncontroversial, and has thus received much less attention than State referrals and *proprio motu* investigations under Article 15 *bis*. For general comments on the lead up to the adoption of this provision in Kampala in June 2010, see comment on Article 15 *bis*.

Author: Marie Aronsson-Storrier.

[209] Security Council referrals give the Court jurisdiction over all States, including State Parties that have lodged an opt-out declaration in accordance with Article 15 *bis*(4), as well as States that are not party to the ICC Statute (Resolution RC/Res.6, 2010, Annex III, Understanding 2).

It should be noted that in accordance with Article 13(b) the Security Council may refer a situation to the ICC where one or more crimes listed in Article 5 "appears to have been committed". Thus, there might be situations where the Security Council have made a referral without having made a determination that an act of aggression is at hand (Kress and von Holtzendorff, 2010, p. 1211). That such a determination does not affect the procedure under this Article is an important difference from cases where the jurisdiction is based on state referrals or *proprio motu* investigations, where extra measures are required under Article 15 *bis*(8) in the absence of such a determination. It remains to be seen how this will affect the Security Council decisions regarding referrals to the ICC.

Author: Marie Aronsson-Storrier.

[210] Paragraph 2 regulates the time for which the acts committed may be under the ICC's jurisdiction, as long as the requirement in paragraph 3 is fulfilled. The Understandings make clear that for the Court to have jurisdiction of a crime, one year needs to have passed since the ratification of 30 States Parties and a decision needs to have been taken in accordance paragraph 3 (Resolution RC/Res.6, 2010, Annex III, Understanding 1). That is, if 30 States Parties would have signed on 1 July 2015, the Court would still not have jurisdiction over crimes committed in the second half of 2016, but would have to await the decision taken in accordance with Article 15 *ter*(3) at the earliest on 1 January 2017.

Author: Marie Aronsson-Storrier.

3. The Court shall exercise jurisdiction over the crime of aggression in accordance with this article, subject to a decision to be taken after 1 January 2017 by the same majority of States Parties as is required for the adoption of an amendment to the Statute.[211]

4. A determination of an act of aggression by an organ outside the Court shall be without prejudice to the Court's own findings under this Statute.[212]

5. This article is without prejudice to the provisions relating to the exercise of jurisdiction with respect to other crimes referred to in Article 5.[213]

[6] Inserted by resolution RC/Res.6 of 11 June 2010.

---

[211] According to this paragraph, the Court may only exercise jurisdiction over the crime of aggression if this is decided by at least a two-third majority after 1 January 2017, in accordance with Article 121(3). Thus, while only 30 Stated Parties need to actively ratify the amendments as stated in paragraph 2, two-thirds of the State Parties must still approve of the amendments before the Court may exercise jurisdiction over the crime. Jurisdiction will then apply to acts committed one year after the ratification of 30 Stated Parties, or after the decision taken in accordance with this paragraph, whichever comes last (Resolution RC/Res.6, 2010, Annex III, Understanding 1).

That is, if 30 Stated Parties have ratified or accepted the amendments by 1 December 2016, the Court will not have jurisdiction over crimes committed before 1 December 2017, even if a decision in accordance with this paragraph has been taken earlier that year.

There is no requirement for a State Party to have ratified or otherwise accepted the amendments in order to cast a positive vote after 1 January 2017.

Author: Marie Aronsson-Storrier.

[212] Paragraph 4 echoes Article 15 *bis*(9) and ensures the independence of the ICC in determining whether an act of aggression has been committed. Thus, the Court may find that no act of aggression has been committed in accordance with Article 8 *bis* even where the Security Council, the International Court of Justice, or any other organ outside the Court, have made a positive determination that such an act has taken place. That the ICC is not bound by a determination by an organ outside of the Court is not to say that findings will be without influence on the Court's analysis.

Author: Marie Aronsson-Storrier.

[213] Paragraph 5 clarifies that the delayed jurisdiction applying to the crime of aggression is not to be interpreted as applying to other crimes under the ICC Statute. While UN Security Council referrals made before the conditions in paragraph 2 and 3 are met would not give the Court jurisdiction over the crime of aggression, this does not affect its jurisdiction over the other crimes under Article 5.

Cross-references:

Articles 8 *bis*, 13 and 15 *bis*.

Doctrine:

1. Claus Kreß and Leonie von Holtzendorff, "The Kampala Compromise on the Crime of Aggression", in *Journal of International Criminal Justice*, 2010, vol. 8, no. 5, pp. 1179–1217.

Author: Marie Aronsson-Storrier

Article 16

Deferral of investigation or prosecution

No investigation or prosecution may be commenced or proceeded with under this Statute for a period of 12 months after the Security Council, in a resolution adopted under Chapter VII of the Charter of the United Nations, has requested the Court to that effect; that request may be renewed by the Council under the same conditions.[214]

---

[214] *General remarks*:

The present provision provides a vital mechanism for navigating the relationship between the responsibilities of the Security Council under the UN Charter and that of the judicial mandate of the ICC. The provision attempts to reconcile any potential conflict between the interests of peace and the interests of justice in the context of the often referred to "peace versus justice" debate.

Preparatory works:

Article 16 is rooted in Article 23 of the International Law Commission Draft Statute (Draft Statute for an International Criminal Court with commentaries, International Law Commission Report (1994) UN doc. A/49/10; Report of the ILC on the Work of its Forty-sixth session, 1 September 1994, UN doc. A/49/355, 21 February 1997) The ILC Draft proposed that any court would not have been able to proceed without prior authorisation from the Security Council if the situation falls under the auspices of Chapter VII of the UN Charter. At the Rome Conference States expressed a variety of concerns such as the risk of interference with the judicial independence of the court and inappropriate political influence by the Security Council. If a court appeared to be at the disposal of the Security Council, the impartiality and legitimacy the institution would be at risk and consequently hinder the effective execution of its judicial functions. A proposal put forward by Singapore at the Preparatory Committee in August 1997 (Proposal by Singapore on Article 23, Non-Paper/WG.3/No. 16, 8 August 1997) formed the basis of what became a difficult compromise as reflected in Article 16.

Analysis:

The language of the Article 16 would suggest that there are a number of requirements that a deferral request would need to feature. The initial point to note is the timing of when a deferral request can be activated. Article 16 refers to the commencement or proceedings of either investigations or prosecutions. This has drawn some discussion as to whether, this means a specific "investigation or prosecution" or it extends to include the preliminary stages of ICC action. Article 16 remains silent on the matter and to this commentator it would be imperative to look to other provisions of the ICC Statute for further guidance. The initiation of investigations is not the first stage of proceedings conducted under the auspices of the Prosecutor. Rather it may be inferred from Article 15(6) of the ICC Statute that there is a formal distinction between the investigative stage and that of "preliminary examinations". Thus, Article 16 can be viewed in such a manner as to refer to investigations conducted by the Prosecutor only after the Pre-Trial Chamber's authorisation under Article 15(4), but is not applicable to the activities of the Court prior to that stage. Moreover, the location of Article 16 after 14 and 15 has attracted remarks from scholars who maintain that it illustrates that the deferral request requires specific Court proceedings rather than a manifestation of preventive action by the Security Council (Stahn, 2003, p. 90). This position views Article 16 as a mechanism which may only bar the exercise of jurisdiction by the Court once a concrete "investigation" or "prosecution" is underway and indeed the criticisms of Resolutions 1422 (2002) and 1487(2003) would seem to endorse this view (El Zeidy, 2002; Stahn, 2003; Mokhtar, 2003; Zappala, 2003).

A further requirement of a deferral request under Article 16 relates to Chapter VII of the UN Charter. It requires a deferral resolution to be "adopted under Chapter VII of the Charter" which necessitates that the Security Council has determined that a particular situation constitutes a "threat to a peace, breach of the peace or an act of aggression" under Article 39 of the Charter (Bergsmo and Pejić, 1999, p. 373; Cassese *et al.*, 2002, pp. 644–46). In accordance with Article 27 of the Charter, a resolution making an Article 16 request requires nine affirmative votes from members of the Security Council and the absence of a veto from any of the five permanent members. There is no guidance in the UN Charter or the ICC Statute as to which circumstance or situation would invoke an Article 16 deferral. Thus, it remains the exclusive prerogative of the Security Council to determine whether a particular situation satisfies the threshold in Article 39. Although the question remains open as to the likelihood of the ICC undertaking a separate assessment of the validity of deferral request. To this commentator, there is a possibility that the ICC could assess the validity of a deferral resolution under Chapter VII, given the requirements under Article 16, though scholars (Schabas 2010) have noted that previously international courts have been reluctant to second-guess the Security Council in such matters (*Prosecutor v. Tadić* (Case No. IT-94-1-AR72) ICTY Appeals Chamber, Decision on the Defence Motion for Interlocutory Appeal on Jurisdiction, 2 October 1995).

Additionally, Article 16 states that a deferral request may be renewed "under the same conditions". Theoretically this could result in an indefinite deferral since Article 16 contains no limitation on the number of times a request for deferral may be renewed (Bergsmo and Pejić, 1999; Lattanzi, 2004). However, any renewal after 12 months would still have to continue to meet the threshold of Article 39 of the Charter. If one looks to the *travaux préparatoires* of Article 16 it would seem that a renewal of a deferral request may continue to assist in restoring and maintaining international peace and security, where the proceedings of the ICC in a given case would in some fashion be detrimental to the work of the Security Council.

At time of writing this commentary, there are no judicial interpretations of Article 16 offered by the ICC, yet there have been four resolutions adopted by the Security Council invoking Article 16 since the entry of the ICC Statute. Resolutions 1422 (2002), 1487(2003), 1597(2005) and 1970(2011) give some indication as to the interpretation of this provision. The Security Council adopted the first deferral request, Resolution 1422, unanimously on 12 July 2002, a few days after the ICC Statute entered into force (UN doc. SP/PV.4572). Its preamble declares that the Security Council was "acting under Chapter VII of the Charter of the United Nations". The essence of the resolution is encapsulated in operative paragraph 1, and in reference to Article 16 of the ICC Statute, it suspends, for a period of 12 months, the Court from commencing or proceeding with an investigation or prosecution of any case involving current or former official or personnel from a contributing State not a Party to the ICC Statute, relating to any UN established or authorised operation (UNSC (12 July 2002) UN doc. S/RES/1422). The second resolution was adopted on 12 June 2003, where the Security Council renewed Resolution 1422 in the form of Resolution 1487 (UNSC Resolution 1487 (12 June 2003) UN doc. S/RES/1487). This resolution substantively repeats the contents of Resolution 1422 and extends the suspension for an additional 12-month period. Further, the Security Council reiterated, in paragraph 2 its intention to renew the request to the ICC for the next 12 months period. In terms of voting, an interesting point to note is that Resolution 1487 was supported by only 12 out of the 15 members of the Security Council, as France, Germany and Syria abstained from voting in comparison to Resolution 1422 which was unanimously adopted. As opposition to the adoption of Resolution 1487 grew and members of Security Council at that time, namely France, Germany, Brazil, Chile, Romania, Spain and Benin indicated they would abstain from any decision to renew Resolution 1487(UN doc. S/PV.4772, 12 June 2003) after 12 months the resolution was left to expire. Without any judicial guidance on the matter, there remains an outstanding question as whether the Security Council has to expressly determine that the continuation of ICC proceedings would constitute a threat to international peace and security in order to defer the proceedings in accordance with Article 16. For instance, the absence of such a determination was one of the arguments made against the legality of Resolutions 1422 and 1487 as these actions were considered a pre-emptive manoeuvre the Security Council in the shadow of the United States opposition to the ICC (Stahn 2003; Lavelle 2003). The increased unpopularity of the overt political manipulation of Article 16 was demonstrated by criticisms made by the UN Secretary General and several states of the Security Council, on the basis that Article 16 did not give such a sweeping power, but only a more specific power to make a deferral request relating to a particular situation (UN doc. S/PV.4772, 12 June 2003).

The next two resolutions are referrals made under Article 13(b) and are not deferral requests *per se*, but rather make reference to Article 16 in its contents. For the purposes of this commentary, the third resolution adopted by the Security Council on 1 April 2005, referred the situation in the Darfur region of Sudan to the ICC in the form of Resolution 1593 although, notably China and the United States abstained from voting (UNSC Res 1593 (31 March 2005) UN doc. S/Res/1593). The preamble of resolution recalls the power of deferral under Article 16 and, operative paragraph 6 of the resolution excludes the jurisdiction of the ICC over "nationals, current or former officials or personnel from a contributing State outside Sudan which is not a party to the Rome Statute" participating in UN or African Union peacekeeping operations in Sudan unless "exclusive jurisdiction has been expressly waived by that contributing State". This provides blanket immunity from ICC jurisdiction to a selective group of individuals, namely nationals of non-state parties. The last resolution in question was adopted on the 26 February 2011, by a unanimous vote, where the Security Council referred the situation in Libya to the ICC. Resolution 1970 was adopted under Chapter VII of the UN Charter and was the second occasion in which the Security Council has used the referral power under Article 13(b) to extend the jurisdiction of the ICC to a state that is not party to the ICC Statute. Again, for the purposes of this commentary, the Libya referral invokes Article 16 in the same fashion as Resolution 1593. In identical language to the Sudan resolution the Security Council recalled Article 16 in the preamble and in operative paragraph 6 excludes ICC jurisdiction over "current or former officials or personnel from a State outside the Libyan Arab Jamahiriya which is not a party to the Rome Statute" involved in operations "established or authorized by the Council". There have been scholarly discussions as to the validity of including the immunity in the content of the resolution, particularly given the jurisdictional regime of Article 12 and the exclusion of immunity in Article 27 of the ICC Statute (Cryer, 2006; Trahan, 2013). While the specific referrals have been discussed in Article 15(b) of this commentary, it remains to be seen what the legal interpretation of the ICC will be in respect of the Article 16 reference and the operative paragraphs, which de facto permanently suspend action over a selective category of nationals. Given the purpose of Article 16, one explanation for the inclusion of the reference to Article 16 in the content of both referrals is the belief that States, and inevitably the Security Council are mindful of the interests of peace and the political consequences of judicial intervention by the ICC. All four resolutions discussed here have highlighted the inherent tension within Article 16, namely that the political trajectory of the Security Council may be misaligned with the judicial approach of the ICC in a given situation and could indeed come into direct conflict. All the resolutions demonstrate that the Security Council may act in a manner that could risk compromising the independence and legitimacy of the ICC.

A pertinent example of the politicisation of Article 16 is the request for a deferral of proceedings against President of Sudan. Following the arrest warrant being issued for the Al Bashir (*Prosecutor v. Omar Al Bashir*, ICC PT. Ch. I, Warrant of Arrest for Omar Hassan Ahmad Al Bashir, ICC-02/05-01/09-1, 4 March 2009), the African Union, Arab League, Non-Aligned Movement, Organisation of Islamic Conference called on the Security Council to make a deferral under Article 16. The African Union formally requested the Security Council to invoke Article 16 and suspend any indictment of the Sudanese President when it came to the extend the UNAMID mandate. However, the Security Council took no action on this matter, and Resolution 1828 (UN doc. S/RES/1828 (2008) was absent of any reference to Article 16. In the Security Council debates relating to the Al Bashir case none of the states that addressed the possibility of a deferral argued that the Council did not have the power to invoke Article 16 in that situation (UN doc. S/PV.5947, 31 July 2008). The disapproval of the African Union over the lack of an Article 16 deferral in relation to Al Bashir manifested in the first of many resolutions adopted in July 2009 reiterating its request for an Article 16 deferral and warning that until the request was heeded, African Union members would refrain from cooperating in the arrest and surrender of President Al Bashir (African Union, Assembly, Decision on the Meeting of African States Parties to the Rome Statute of the International Criminal Court (ICC), Doc. Assembly/AU/13 (XIII) 3 July 2009, Assembly/AU/Dec.245(xiii) Rev. 1, para. 8–10;). This has resulted not only in tension between the African Union and the ICC more broadly, but also specifically between the ICC and African State Parties who are not fulfilling their obligations under the ICC Statute to arrest and surrender Al Bashir due to the position taken by the AU over the lack of a deferral request (*Prosecutor v. Omar Hassan Ahmad Al Bashir*, ICC PT. Ch I, Decision pursuant to Article 87(7) of the Rome Statute on the refusal of the Republic of Chad to comply with the cooperation requests issues by the Court with respect to the arrest and surrender or Omar Hassan Ahmad Al Bashir, ICC-02/05-01/09-140-tENG, 13 December 2011; *Prosecutor v. Omar Hassan Ahmad Al Bashir*, PT. Ch, II, Decision on the Non-Compliance of the Republic of Chad with the Cooperation Requests Issued by the Court Regarding the Arrest and Surrender of Omar Hassan Ahmad Al Bashir, ICC-02/05-01/09-151, 26 March 2013; *Prosecutor v. Omar Hassan Ahmad Al Bashir*, PT. Ch. II, Decision Regarding Omar Al Bashir's potential Visit to the Republic of Chad, ICC-02/05-01/09-194, 25 March 2014).

It is worth bearing in mind one final point with respect to Article 16 of the ICC Statute and that is the notion of "interests of justice" in Article 53 of the ICC Statute. Article 53 is a means for the ICC to take into account considerations of peace. Article 53 empowers the Prosecutor with discretion to decide not to initiate either an investigation or prosecution on the grounds that to proceed would be contrary to the "interests of justice". The ICC might be viewed as not only a challenge to impunity, but additionally as a potential challenge or impediment to peace negotiations simultaneously. While it has to be made clear that the ICC Statute does not make peace deals impossible, indeed some have labeled the ICC as "part of the transitional justice project" (Moreno Ocampo, 2007; Stahn, 2005), it will impact the parties to a conflict in a manner that merits consideration. Article 16 does not dictate that peace usurps justice, or that all conflict situations require the same approach from the Security Council and the ICC. Instead, Article 16 allows for consideration of the "interests of peace" and the "interests of justice" in relation to the same situation.

Cross-references:

Article 12, Article 13(b), Article 15(6), Article 27 and Article 53.

Doctrine:

1. Morten Bergsmo and Jelena Pejić, "Article 16", in Otto Triffterer (ed.), Commentary on the Rome Statute of the International Criminal Court: Observers' Notes, Article by Article, 2nd ed., C.H. Beck/Hart/Nomos, Munich/Oxford/Baden-Baden, 2008, pp. 595–604.

2. Antonio Cassese, Paola Gaeta and John R.W.D. Jones (eds.), *The Rome Statute of the International Criminal Court: A Commentary*, Oxford University Press, Oxford 2002, pp. 644–46.

3. Robert Cryer, "Sudan, Resolution 1593, and International Criminal Justice", in *Leiden Journal of International Law*, 2006, vol. 19, pp. 195–222.

4. Mohamed El Zeidy, "The United States Dropped the Atomic Bomb of Article 16 of the ICC: Security Council Power of Deferrals and Resolution 1422", in *Vanderbilt Journal of Transnational Law*, 2002, vol. 35, pp. 1503–48.

5. Flavia Lattanzi, "The Rome Statute and the State Sovereignty: ICC Competence, Jurisdictional Links, Trigger Mechanism", in Flavia Lattanzi and William A. Schabas (eds.), *Essays on the Rome Statute of the International Criminal Court*, 2nd ed., Editrice Il Sirente, Italy 2004, pp. 51–67.

6. Roberto Lavelle, "A Vicious Storm in a Teacup: The Action by the United Nations Security Council to Narrow the Jurisdiction of the International Criminal Court", in *Criminal Law Forum*, 2003, vol. 14, no. 2, pp. 195–220.

7. Aly Mokhtar, "The Fine Art of Arm-Twisting: The US, Resolution 1422 and Security Council Deferral Power Under the Rome Statute", in *International Criminal Law Review*, 2003, vol. 3, no. 4, pp. 295–344.

8. Luis Moreno Ocampo, "Transitional Justice in Ongoing Conflicts", *International Journal of Transitional Justice*, 2007, vol. 1, no. 1, pp. 8–9.

9. William A. Schabas, *The International Criminal Court: A Commentary on the Rome Statute*, Oxford University Press, Oxford, 2010.

10. Carsten Stahn, "The Ambiguities of Security Council Resolution 1422 (2002)", in *European Journal of International Law*, 2003, vol. 14, pp. 85–104.

11. Carsten Stahn, "Complementarity, Amnesties and Alternative Forms of Justice: Some Interpretative Guidelines for the International Criminal Court", in *Journal of International Criminal Justice*, 2005, vol. 3, pp. 695–720.

12. Jennifer Trahan, "The Relationship between the International Criminal court and the UN Security Council: Parameters and Best Practices", in *Criminal Law Forum*, 2013, vol. 24, no. 4, pp. 417–73.

13. Salvatore Zappala, "Are Some Peacekeepers Better Than Others? UN Security Council Resolution 1497 (2003) and the ICC", in *Journal of International Criminal Justice*, 2003, vol. 1, no. 3, pp. 671–78.

Author: Yassin M. Brunger.

Article 17

Issues of admissibility

1. Having regard to paragraph 10 of the Preamble and article 1, the Court shall determine that a case is inadmissible where:[215]

    (a) The case is being investigated or prosecuted by a State which has jurisdiction over it, unless the State is unwilling or unable genuinely to carry out the investigation or prosecution;[216]

---

[215] *General remarks*:

Article 17 of the Statute lays down the substantive conditions for the admissibility of a case before the ICC. Under this provision, the admissibility test is composed of two main parts: the first requires the consideration of the complementarity criteria in order to determine whether the case at hand has been or is being genuinely investigated or prosecuted by a state's national judicial system. The second part of the admissibility test relates to the analysis of the "gravity threshold", in order to determine whether the case is of sufficient gravity to justify further action by the Court.

The Statute does not specify whether the two components of admissibility are to be dealt with in any particular order. For the purpose of this analysis, the complementarity test will be examined first, and the gravity threshold subsequently.

Preparatory works:

Contrary to the situation in the Statutes of the *ad hoc* tribunals which adopted the primacy principle, the ICC Statute rather opts for the principle of complementarity to regulate the relationship between the ICC and domestic jurisdictions. The negotiating history of the Statute demonstrates that the adoption of the complementarity principle was critical to secure the support of the negotiating states for the establishment of a permanent international criminal court (Holmes, 1999, pp. 41–43).

Complementarity principle:

A complementarity determination is a two-step assessment, addressing (1) whether there is a national investigation or prosecution in relation to the same case as the one before the ICC, and (2) where such proceedings exist, whether they are vitiated by unwillingness or inability.

Cross-references:

Paragraph 10 of the Preamble, Articles 1, 12–15, 17–20 and 25(1).

Regulation 112.

Author: Mohamed Abdou.

[216] A preliminary issue to be considered in the context of admissibility proceedings under Article 17 is whether there exists any investigation or prosecution at the domestic level. Failure by a state to take any measure against those involved in the commission of crimes falling within the jurisdiction of the ICC renders the case admissible before the Court (provided that the gravity threshold is satisfied). The Appeals Chamber has defined this situation, that is, where a State having jurisdiction is not investigating or prosecuting, or has not done so, as a case of "inaction" (*Prosecutor v. Germain Katanga and Mathieu Ngudjolo Chui* (Case No. ICC-01/04-01/07-1497 OA 8), ICC Appeal Chamber, Judgment on the Appeal of Mr. Germain Katanga against the Oral Decision of Trial Chamber II of 12 June 2009 on the Admissibility of the Case, 25 September 2009, para. 2). It follows that while not all "inactions" will lead to proceedings before the ICC, particularly because the Court retains the discretion to initiate cases in accordance with the Statute, a finding of inaction will however not prevent the Court from asserting jurisdiction

---

(b) The case has been investigated by a State which has jurisdiction over it and the State has decided not to prosecute the person concerned, unless the decision resulted from the unwillingness or inability of the State genuinely to prosecute;[217]

in the cases before it (*Prosecutor v. Germain Katanga and Mathieu Ngudjolo Chui* (Case No. ICC-01/04-01/07-1497 OA 8), ICC Appeal Chamber, Judgment on the Appeal of Mr. Germain Katanga against the Oral Decision of Trial Chamber II of 12 June 2009 on the Admissibility of the Case, 25 September 2009, para. 85 and fn.169). Moreover, the Appeals Chamber has established an important distinction between inaction on one hand, and unwillingness and inability on the other. In this respect, it clarified that the terms "unwillingness" and "inability" under Article 17 refers to a situation that only arises after the opening of a formal investigation by the state having jurisdiction over the case, while inaction denotes the absence of any investigative step (*Prosecutor v. Germain Katanga and Mathieu Ngudjolo Chui* (Case No. ICC-01/04-01/07-1497 OA 8), ICC Appeal Chamber, Judgment on the Appeal of Mr. Germain Katanga against the Oral Decision of Trial Chamber II of 12 June 2009 on the Admissibility of the Case, 25 September 2009, para. 76).

Consequently, for an admissibility challenge to succeed before the Court, the challenging party must establish the existence of past or ongoing investigations or prosecutions against the person concerned. Indeed, Article 17(1) prescribes that a case shall be found inadmissible if it "is being investigated" or "has been investigated" by a state which has jurisdiction. The Appeals Chamber defined the phrase "the case is being investigated" as "the taking of steps directed at ascertaining whether this individual is responsible for that conduct" (*Prosecutor v. Francis Kirimi Muthaura, Uhuru Muigai Kenyatta and Mohammed Hussein Ali* (Case No. ICC-01/09-02/11-274), ICC Appeals Chamber, Judgment on the appeal of the Republic of Kenya against the decision of Pre-Trial Chamber II of 30 May 2011 entitled "Decision on the Application by the Government of Kenya Challenging the Admissibility of the Case Pursuant to Article 19(2)(b) of the Statute", 30 August 2011, paras. 1 and 40). The Chamber provided examples of what may qualify as relevant investigative steps such as, "interviewing witnesses or suspects, collecting documentary evidence, or carrying out forensic analyses" (*Prosecutor v. Francis Kirimi Muthaura, Uhuru Muigai Kenyatta and Mohammed Hussein Ali* (Case No. ICC-01/09-02/11-274), ICC Appeals Chamber, Judgment on the appeal of the Republic of Kenya against the decision of Pre-Trial Chamber II of 30 May 2011 entitled "Decision on the Application by the Government of Kenya Challenging the Admissibility of the Case Pursuant to Article 19(2)(b) of the Statute", 30 August 2011, paras. 1 and 40). These investigative steps need to be "actually taken", the mere preparedness to take such steps is not sufficient (*Prosecutor v. Francis Kirimi Muthaura, Uhuru Muigai Kenyatta and Mohammed Hussein Ali* (Case No. ICC-01/09-02/11-274), ICC Appeals Chamber, Judgment on the appeal of the Republic of Kenya against the decision of Pre-Trial Chamber II of 30 May 2011 entitled "Decision on the Application by the Government of Kenya Challenging the Admissibility of the Case Pursuant to Article 19(2)(b) of the Statute", 30 August 2011, para. 40).

Author: Mohamed Abdou.

[217] A case is inadmissible if it has been investigated by a State which has jurisdiction over it and the State has decided not to prosecute the person concerned, unless the decision resulted from the unwillingness or inability of the State genuinely to prosecute.

In *Prosecutor v. Katanga and Chui*, Judgment on the Appeal of Mr. Germain Katanga against the Oral Decision of Trial Chamber II of 12 June 2009 on the Admissibility of the Case, 25 September 2009, the Appeals Chamber stated: "It follows that in case of inaction, the question of unwillingness or inability does not arise; inaction on the part of a State having jurisdiction (that is, the fact that a State is not investigating or prosecuting, or has not done so) renders a case admissible before the Court, subject to Article 17(1)(d) of the Statute. This interpretation of

(c) The person concerned has already been tried for conduct which is the subject of the complaint, and a trial by the Court is not permitted under Article 20, paragraph 3;[218]

Article 17(1)(a) and (b) of the Statute also finds broad support from academic writers who have commented on the provision and on the principle of complementarity" (para. 78).

In *Prosecutor v. Bemba*, Decision on the Admissibility and Abuse of Process Challenges, 24 June 2010, para. 239 the Trial Chamber considered whether the same case had been investigated by the Central African Republic ('CAR') which has jurisdiction over the alleged crimes and CAR has decided not to prosecute, rendering the case inadmissible. The Trial Chamber stated in paragraph 242 that neither of the "decisions by the national courts and the State (*viz.* to refer the case to the ICC) were decisions "not to prosecute". They were, instead, decisions closing the proceedings in the CAR – there was an order for severance that approximately coincided with the referral to the ICC (they were two days apart). It follows that the first element of Article 17(1)(b) is not met: in the sense described by the Appeals Chamber, there has not been a decision not to prosecute the accused. To the contrary, the CAR seeks his prosecution before the ICC. This decision was upheld by the Appeals Chamber, Judgment on the appeal of Mr Jean-Pierre Bemba Gombo against the decision of Trial Chamber III of 24 June 2010 entitled "Decision on the Admissibility and Abuse of Process Challenges", 19 October 2010, paras. 1, 74–75.

Author: Mohamed Abdou.

[218] *The same person*: The first prong of the "same person/same conduct" test does not raise any particular difficulty, as it refers to the specific individual(s) summoned before the Court or for whom a warrant of arrest has been issued. A case therefore cannot be found inadmissible before the ICC unless the same person is subject to an investigation or prosecution at the national level. On this issue, it is noteworthy that Pre-Trial Chamber II rejected Kenya's proposal to investigate "persons at the same level in the hierarchy being investigated by the ICC" (*Prosecutor v. Francis Kirimi Muthaura, Uhuru Muigai Kenyatta and Mohamed Hussein Ali* (Case No. ICC-01/09-02/11-96), ICC Pre-Trial Chamber II, Decision on the Application by the Government of Kenya Challenging the Admissibility of the Case Pursuant to Article 19(2)(b) of the Statute, 30 May 2011, para. 50). The Chamber indicated that the admissibility test under Article 17 is more specific and requires national proceedings to cover the same individuals who are subject to the Court's proceedings (*Prosecutor v. Francis Kirimi Muthaura, Uhuru Muigai Kenyatta and Mohamed Hussein Ali* (Case No. ICC-01/09-02/11-96), ICC Pre-Trial Chamber II, Decision on the Application by the Government of Kenya Challenging the Admissibility of the Case Pursuant to Article 19(2)(b) of the Statute, 30 May 2011, para. 50).

The same conduct: The main difficulty arises in relation to the second prong of the admissibility test, that is, the "same conduct". In the Kenyan cases, the Appeals Chamber explicitly embraced the "same person/same conduct", albeit with some adaptation. The Chamber ruled that for a case to be inadmissible, national investigations must cover the same individual "and substantially the same conduct" as alleged in the proceedings before the Court" (*Prosecutor v. Francis Kirimi Muthaura, Uhuru Muigai Kenyatta and Mohamed Hussein Ali* (Case No. ICC-01/09-02/11-96), ICC Pre-Trial Chamber II, Decision on the Application by the Government of Kenya Challenging the Admissibility of the Case Pursuant to Article 19(2)(b) of the Statute, 30 May 2011, para. 38). In doing so, the Appeals Chamber slightly modified the formulation from "same person/same conduct" to "same person/*substantially* the same conduct". The Appeals Chamber did not, however, provide further details as to the precise degree of similarity required.

Arguably, the inclusion of the qualifier "substantially" was meant to introduce some degree of flexibility to the test. Such wording suggests that a case can be found inadmissible even if the domestic case is not exactly the same as the one before the ICC. As a result, the addition of the word substantially has given rise to novel diverging views. In *Al Gaddafi*, the Prosecution argued that while the "substantially the same conduct" standard does not require national proceed-

---

ings to incorporate all the features of the ICC case, it should not however be interpreted in a manner that enables a State to only investigate limited or weak incidents (*Prosecutor v. Saif Al-Islam Gaddafi and Abdullah Al-Senussi* (Case No. ICC-01/11-01/11-276-Red2), ICC Pre-Trial Chamber I, Prosecution's Response to "Libyan Government's further submissions on issues related to the admissibility of the case against Saif Al-Islam Gaddafi", 12 February 2013, paras. 28–29). In the same vein, one author indicates that the word "substantially" means "essentially" and therefore, what should be established in admissibility proceedings mainly relates to whether the person concerned is brought before domestic courts for essentially the same conduct (Jalloh, 2012, p. 237).

A further difficulty concerning the application of the "same conduct" relates to the definition of the "conduct" itself. Indeed, in order to determine whether national proceedings cover substantially the same conduct, it is necessary to identify first its constitutive elements. As a starting point, any assessment must be made on the basis of the parameters of the "conduct" as defined in the relevant documents containing the factual allegations against the defendant. As the Appeals Chamber held, "the cases are defined by the warrant of arrest or summons to appear issued under Article 58, or the charges brought by the Prosecutor and confirmed by the Pre-Trial Chamber under Article 61" (*Prosecutor v. Francis Kirimi Muthaura et al.* (Case No. ICC-01/09-02/11-274), ICC Appeals Chamber, Judgment on the appeal of the Republic of Kenya against the decision of Pre-Trial Chamber II of 30 May 2011 entitled "Decision on the Application by the Government of Kenya Challenging the Admissibility of the Case Pursuant to Article 19(2)(b) of the Statute", 30 August 2013, para. 39). In line with this, Pre-Trial Chamber I stated that "the determination of what is substantially the same conduct as alleged in the proceedings before the Court will vary according to the concrete facts and circumstances of the case and, therefore, requires a case-by-case analysis" (*Prosecutor v. Said Al-Islam Gaddafi and Abdullah Al-Senussi* (Case No. ICC-01/11-01/11-466-Red), ICC Pre-Trial Chamber I, Decision on the admissibility of the case against Abdullah Al-Senussi, 11 October 2013, p. 34).

However, it is unclear whether the "conduct" must be interpreted as referring to the specific factual incidents as well as the underlying circumstances described in the charging documents of the Court, or whether it should be understood as referring only to the allegations of criminal responsibility against the defendant. On this issue, Pre-trial chambers have constantly held that a case before the ICC is composed of "specific incidents during which one or more crimes within the jurisdiction of the Court seem to have been committed by one or more identified suspects" (*Prosecutor v. Laurent Gbagbo* (Case No. ICC-02/11-01/11-9-Red), ICC Pre-Trial Chamber III, Decision on the Prosecutor's Application Pursuant to Article 58 for a warrant of arrest against Laurent Koudou Gbagbo, 30 November 2011, para. 10; *Prosecutor v. Thomas Lubanga Dyilo* (Case No. ICC-01/04-01/06-8-Corr), ICC Pre-Trial Chamber I, Decision concerning Pre-Trial Chamber I's Decision of 10 February 2006 and the Incorporation of Documents into the Record of the Case against Mr Thomas Lubanga Dyilo, 24 February 2006, Annex 1, para. 31; *Situation in the Democratic Republic of the Congo* (Case No. ICC-01/04-101-tEN-Corr), ICC Pre-Trial Chamber I, Decision on the applications for participation in the proceedings of VPRS 1, VPRS2, VPRS3, VPRS 4, VPRS 5 and VPRS 6, 17 January 2006, (translation notified 22 March 2006), para. 65; see also *Prosecutor v. Ahmad Harun and Ali Kushayb* (Case No. ICC-02/05-01/07-1-Corr), ICC Pre-Trial Chamber I, Decision on the Prosecution Application under Article 58(7) of the Statute, 27 April 2007, para. 14). Such approach suggests that the term conduct is "incident-specific", which implies that the challenging party must substantiate its claim that the case inadmissible with reference to the specific incidents alleged against the accused before the Court.

However, Pre-Trial Chamber I recently departed from this widely accepted approach in Al Gaddafi case. It found that, contrary to the other cases before the Court, the incidents enumerated in the warrant of arrest do not "represent unique manifestations of the form of criminality alleged against Mr Gaddafi", and therefore constitute a "non-exhaustive list" of allegations (*Prosecutor v. Saif Al-Islam Gaddafi and Abdullah Al-Senussi* (Case No. ICC-01/11-01/11-344-Red), ICC Pre-Trial Chamber I, Decision on the admissibility of the case against Saif Al-Islam Gaddafi, 31 May 2013, paras. 81–83). The Pre-Trial Chamber therefore adopted the view that the criminal conduct of the suspect may be defined by way of "illustrative examples" and that any incident investigated domestically may be relevant to the same conduct so long as it falls within the material scope of the crimes alleged in the proceedings before the ICC. According to this approach, a state may successfully challenge the admissibility of a case on the basis that it is investigating similar criminal acts without having to establish that it is investigating the same specific incidents. It is noteworthy in this regard that the Chamber specifically dismissed the Prosecutor's argument that the cases must be understood as "incident-specific", and that the criminal conduct alleged must be defined with reference to specific times and places (*Prosecutor v. Saif Al-Islam Gaddafi and Abdullah Al-Senussi* (Case No. ICC-01/11-01/11-321-Red), ICC Pre-Trial Chamber I, Prosecution's Response to "Application on behalf of the Government of Libya relating to Abdullah Al-Senussi pursuant to Article 19 of the ICC Statute", 2 May 2013, paras. 78 and fn. 175 and 176). According to the Prosecutor, the conduct identifies "criminal acts that occur in a particular location and at a specific time and in the framework of a course of conduct and series of events" (*Prosecutor v. Saif Al-Islam Gaddafi and Abdullah Al-Senussi* (Case No. ICC-01/11-01/11-321-Red), ICC Pre-Trial Chamber I, Prosecution's Response to "Application on behalf of the Government of Libya relating to Abdullah Al-Senussi pursuant to Article 19 of the ICC Statute", 2 May 2013, paras. 78 and fn. 175 and 176).

The legal characterisation, international v. ordinary crimes: One issue that appears to have been settled by the Court relates to the question as to whether Article 17 should be interpreted as requiring the State investigating the case to adopt the same legal qualification as that provided for in the ICC Statute. In other words, is the State under an obligation to enact the same crimes laid down in the Statute in order to meet the complementarity test, or it suffices to investigate the defendant for "ordinary" crimes as long as they cover all conduct that falls within the crimes of the Statute? In this respect, Pre-Trial Chamber ruled that, under Article 17, "the assessment of domestic proceedings should focus on the alleged conduct and not its legal characterisation" and that the fact that domestic investigations are carried out "with a view to prosecuting international crimes is not determinative" (*Prosecutor v. Saif Al-Islam Gaddafi and Abdullah Al-Senussi* (Case No. ICC-01/11-01/11-466-Red), ICC Pre-Trial Chamber I, Decision on the admissibility of the case against Abdullah Al-Senussi, 11 October 2013, para. 85). In reaching this conclusion, the Chamber relied on the fact that neither the complementarity provisions nor the related *ne bis in idem* principle imposes an explicit obligation on the State to adopt the same legal characterisation of the criminal conduct (*Prosecutor v. Saif Al-Islam Gaddafi and Abdullah Al-Senussi* (Case No. ICC-01/11-01/11-466-Red), ICC Pre-Trial Chamber I, Decision on the admissibility of the case against Abdullah Al-Senussi, 11 October 2013, para. 86). This analysis took also into account the *travaux préparatoires* and the expressed intent of the drafters to exclude the ordinary crimes exception provided in the ICTY and ICTR Statutes (*Prosecutor v. Saif Al-Islam Gaddafi and Abdullah Al-Senussi* (Case No. ICC-01/11-01/11-466-Red), ICC Pre-Trial Chamber I, Decision on the admissibility of the case against Abdullah Al-Senussi, 11 October 2013, para. 87).

Evidentiary threshold and burden of proof: There has been some controversy concerning the applicable evidentiary threshold and burden of proof in the context of admissibility proceedings. This is because the ICC Statute does not expressly specify any rules concerning the applicable standard of proof or allocation of the burden of proof in admissibility proceedings.

The burden to establish the inadmissibility of a case before the Court typically lies on the challenging party. In cases where such a party is a State, the Court seems to apply the burden of proof in a more stringent way. In respect of Kenya's admissibility challenge, the Chamber ruled that the state "must provide the Court with evidence with a sufficient degree of specificity and probative value that demonstrates that it is indeed investigating the case" (*Prosecutor v. Francis Kirimi Muthaura, Uhuru Muigai Kenyatta and Mohammed Hussein Ali* (Case No. ICC-01/09-02/11-274), ICC Appeals Chamber, Judgment on the appeal of the Republic of Kenya against the decision of Pre-Trial Chamber II of 30 May 2011 entitled "Decision on the Application by the Government of Kenya Challenging the Admissibility of the Case Pursuant to Article 19(2)(b) of the Statute", 30 August 2013, para. 2). It emphasised that it not merely sufficient for a state to assert that investigations are ongoing. The Appeals Chamber made clear that the burden of proof rest on the challenging party, but did not specify the standard of proof applicable to Article 17 proceedings. In cases where the Court acts on its own motion to decide on admissibility, the Prosecutor has the onus of establishing the admissibility of the case. He or she should provide sufficient evidence and information to satisfy the Court that there are either no investigative activities at the domestic level, or that the national proceedings against the defendant do not cover the same case (*Prosecutor v. Germain Katanga* (Case No. ICC-01/04-01/07-4), ICC Pre-Trial Chamber I, Decision on the evidence and information provided by the Prosecution for the issuance of a warrant of arrest for Germain Katanga, 6 July 2007).

This issue relating to the standard of proof has been addressed differently by the various chambers of the Court. In the first decision on this issue in the Bemba case, Trial Chamber III endorsed the "balance of probabilities" standard as the appropriate evidentiary threshold applicable to the admissibility proceedings. The Chamber explained that "although the Rome Statute framework again does not provide guidance, the overwhelming preponderance of national and international legal systems apply what is frequently called the 'civil standard' of proof (a balance of probabilities) when the burden lies upon the defence in criminal proceedings. There is no reason to depart from that approach in these circumstances" (*Prosecutor v. Jean-Pierre Bemba Gombo* (Case No. ICC-01/05-01/08-802), ICC Trial Chamber III, Decision on the Admissibility and Abuse of Process Challenges, 24 June 2010, para. 203). As to the burden of proof, the Trial Chamber concluded that the defence, as the challenging party, bears the evidential burden (*Prosecutor v. Jean-Pierre Bemba Gombo* (Case No. ICC-01/05-01/08-802), ICC Trial Chamber III, Decision on the Admissibility and Abuse of Process Challenges, 24 June 2010, para. 204). In Al-Gaddafi case, Pre-Trial Chamber I adopted a different approach with respect to the applicable evidentiary standard. It noted that none of the standards of proof explicitly referred to in the ICC Statute apply to the admissibility determination (*Prosecutor v. Jean-Pierre Bemba Gombo* (Case No. ICC-01/05-01/08-802), ICC Trial Chamber III, Decision on the Admissibility and Abuse of Process Challenges, 24 June 2010, paras. 54–55). Instead, the Pre-Trial Chamber reiterated the Appeals Chamber's ruling that the state, as the challenging party, must provide the Court "with evidence of sufficient degree of specificity and probative value that demonstrates that it is investigating the case" (*Prosecutor v. Saif Al-Islam Gaddafi and Abdullah Al-Senussi* (Case No. ICC-01/11-01/11-239), ICC Pre-Trial Chamber I, Decision requesting further submissions on issues related to the admissibility of the case against Saif Al-Islam Gaddafi, 7 December 2012, para. 11).

Although it may seem from the above pronouncements that the burden of proof is clearly identified, the question arose as to whether the challenging party is required not only to establish that the same case is investigated, but also that the State has the requisite willingness and ability to investigate the case domestically. In the *Al-Gaddafi and Al-Senussi* case, Libya claimed that it was only required to prove the first prong of the admissibility test namely, that it is investigating or prosecuting the same case (*Prosecutor v. Saif Al-Islam Gaddafi and Abdullah Al-Senussi* (Case No. ICC-01/11-01/11-293-Red), Libyan Government's consolidated reply to the responses of the Prosecution, OPCD, and OPCV to its further submissions on issues related to the admissibility of the case against Saif Al-Islam Gaddafi, 4 March 2013, paras. 17–21). The argument was partly approved by the Pre-Trial Chamber, which found that although the State is required to substantiate all aspects of its allegations, the "evidentiary debate on the State's unwillingness or inability will be meaningful only when doubts arise with regard to the genuineness of the domestic investigations or prosecutions" (*Prosecutor v. Saif Al-Islam Gaddafi and Abdullah Al-Senussi* (Case No. ICC-01/11-01/11-344-Red), ICC Pre-Trial Chamber I, Decision on the admissibility of the case against Saif Al-Islam Gaddafi, 31 May 2013, para. 53). This means that the Chamber has the discretion to seek additional evidence to satisfy itself that the state is both willing and able to carry out genuine proceedings.

It seems also important to clarify that the Court's analysis under Articles 17 and 19 does not extend to determining whether strong evidence is available to establish the defendant's criminal responsibility. The Court's assessment is limited to ascertaining whether domestic authorities are taking concrete and genuine investigative steps against the person concerned for the same criminal conduct. Therefore, the inadmissibility of a case "would not be negated by the fact that, upon scrutiny, the evidence may be insufficient to support a conviction by the domestic authorities" (*Prosecutor v. Saif Al-Islam Gaddafi and Abdullah Al-Senussi* (Case No. ICC-01/11-01/11-466-Red), ICC Pre-Trial Chamber I, Decision on the admissibility of the case against Abdullah Al-Senussi, 11 October 2013, para. 66 (vii)). In this regard, Pre-Trial Chamber I clarified the type of evidence that the challenging party is expected to provide to substantiate its admissibility challenge. It "may also include, depending on the circumstances, directions, orders and decisions issued by authorities in charge of the investigation as well as internal reports, updates, notifications or submissions contained in the [investigation] file" (*Prosecutor v. Saif Al-Islam Gaddafi and Abdullah Al-Senussi* (Case No. ICC-01/11-01/11-239), ICC Pre-Trial Chamber I, Decision requesting further submissions on issues related to the admissibility of the case against Saif Al-Islam Gaddafi, 7 December 2012, para. 11).

Timing: The Appeals Chamber has indicated that the admissibility of a case is determined on the basis of "the facts as they exist at the time of the proceedings concerning the admissibility challenge" (*Prosecutor v. Germain Katanga and Mathieu Ngudjolo Chui* (Case No. ICC-01/04-01/07-1479 OA 8), ICC Appeal Chamber, Judgment on the Appeal of Mr. Germain Katanga against the Oral Decision of Trial Chamber II of 12 June 2009 on the Admissibility of the Case, 25 September 2009, para. 56). It further clarified that the expression "time of the proceedings" concerns the proceedings on the admissibility challenge "before the Pre-Trial Chamber and not to the subsequent proceedings on appeal" (*Prosecutor v. William Samoei Ruto et al* (Case No. ICC-01/09-01/11 OA), ICC Appeals Chamber, Decision on the "Filing of Updated Investigation Report by the Government of Kenya in the Appeal against the Pre-Trial Chamber's Decision on Admissibility", 28 July 2011, paras. 10–11).

There remains some uncertainty as to whether the Court can limit its findings to the facts arising before the admissibility challenge is lodged. Recently, Pre-Trial Chamber I declined to take such an approach, indicating that "a decision on the admissibility of the case must be based on the circumstances prevailing at the time of its issuance"(*Prosecutor v. Saif Al-Islam Gaddafi and Abdullah Al-Senussi* (Case No. ICC-01/11-01/11-466-Red), ICC Pre-Trial Chamber I, Decision on the admissibility of the case against Abdullah Al-Senussi, 11 October 2013, para. 34). This decision suggests that should the circumstances surrounding the admissibility of the case evolve during the admissibility proceedings, the Chamber must take into consideration these developments and make its determination on the basis of the facts as they exist at the time when the admissibility decision is rendered. Such approach has important consequences, as it gives the party challenging admissibility (and notably the State) an opportunity to bolster and supplement its initial application throughout admissibility proceedings until a decision is reached by the competent chamber.

Author: Mohamed Abdou.

(d) The case is not of sufficient gravity to justify further action by the Court.[219]

---

[219] Article 17(1)(d) provides that the Court shall determine that a case is inadmissible where the case is not of sufficient gravity to justify further action by the Court. This is because the ICC was envisioned as a permanent judicial body that would preside only over cases considered to be of most serious concern to the international community as a whole. The concept of "gravity" is not defined in the Statute and the appropriate scope of the term is a subject of debate. A limited number of judicial rulings have addressed the notion of gravity, but the most important remains the decision by Pre-Trial Chamber I on 10 February 2006 concerning the issuance of an arrest warrant against Thomas Lubanga (*Prosecutor v. Thomas Lubanga* (Case No. ICC-01/04-01/06), ICC Pre-Trial Chamber I, Decision Concerning Pre-Trial Chamber I's Decision of 10 February 2006 and the Incorporation of Documents into the Record of the Case against Mr. Thomas Lubanga Dyilo, 24 February 2006, Annex 1). The main findings of the Pre-Trial Chamber are outlined below.

First, the Chamber observed that the use of the term "shall" in the chapeau of Article 17(1) of the Statute "leaves the Chamber no discretion as to the declaration of the inadmissibility of a case once it is satisfied that the case is not of sufficient gravity to justify further action by the Court" (*Prosecutor v. Thomas Lubanga* (Case No. ICC-01/04-01/06), ICC Pre-Trial Chamber I, Decision Concerning Pre-Trial Chamber I's Decision of 10 February 2006 and the Incorporation of Documents into the Record of the Case against Mr. Thomas Lubanga Dyilo, 24 February 2006, Annex 1, para. 43). The Chamber also clarified the scope of application of the gravity threshold, indicating that it applies to two different stages of the proceedings: "(i) at the stage of initiation of the investigation into a situation, the relevant situation must meet such a gravity threshold and (ii) once a case arises from the investigation of a situation, it must also meet the gravity threshold provided for in that provision" (*Prosecutor v. Thomas Lubanga* (Case No. ICC-01/04-01/06), ICC Pre-Trial Chamber I, Decision Concerning Pre-Trial Chamber I's Decision of 10 February 2006 and the Incorporation of Documents into the Record of the Case against Mr. Thomas Lubanga Dyilo, 24 February 2006, Annex 1, para. 44).

In order to determine whether a case is sufficiently grave to warrant the Court's intervention, two features must be considered: first, "the conduct which is the subject of a case must be either systematic (pattern of incidents) or large-scale". This permits to exclude isolated instances of criminal activity. Second, the assessment of gravity must give due consideration "to the social alarm such conduct may have caused in the international community" (*Prosecutor v. Thomas Lub*anga (Case No. ICC-01/04-01/06), ICC Pre-Trial Chamber I, Decision Concerning Pre-Trial Chamber I's Decision of 10 February 2006 and the Incorporation of Documents into the Record of the Case against Mr. Thomas Lubanga Dyilo, 24 February 2006, Annex 1, para. 46).

Moreover, the Chamber observed that the main reason behind the inclusion of the gravity threshold by the drafters was to maximise the Court's deterrent effect (*Prosecutor v. Thomas Lub*anga (Case No. ICC-01/04-01/06), ICC Pre-Trial Chamber I, Decision Concerning Pre-Trial Chamber I's Decision of 10 February 2006 and the Incorporation of Documents into the Record of the Case against Mr. Thomas Lubanga Dyilo, 24 February 2006, Annex 1, para. 48). Likewise, it was ruled that the reference to the insufficiency of gravity in Article 17 "is actually an additional safeguard, which prevents the Court from investigating, prosecuting and trying peripheral cases" (*Situation in the Republic of Kenya* (Case No. ICC-01/09), ICC Pre-Trial Chamber II, Decision Pursuant to Article 15 of the Rome Statute on the Authorisation of an Investigation into the Situation in the Republic of Kenya, 31 March 2010, para. 56). Several factors should be considered to ensure the objective of deterrence and prevention. First, the Court must take into account the position held by the persons against whom the Prosecution requests the initiation of a case and concentrate on the most senior leaders (*Prosecutor v. Lubanga* (Case No. ICC-01/04-01/06-8-US-Corr), ICC Pre-Trial Chamber I, Decision Concerning Pre-Trial Cham-

2. In order to determine unwillingness in a particular case, the Court shall consider, having regard to the principles of due process recognized by international law, whether one or more of the following exist, as applicable:[220]

(a) The proceedings were or are being undertaken or the national decision was made for the purpose of shielding the person concerned from criminal responsibility for crimes within the jurisdiction of the Court referred to in article 5;[221]

(b) There has been an unjustified delay in the proceedings which in the circumstances is inconsistent with an intent to bring the person concerned to justice;[222]

---

ber I's Decision of 10 February 2006 and the Incorporation of Documents into the Record of the Case against Mr. Thomas Lubanga Dyilo, 24 February 2006, Annex 1, para. 51). Second, due regard must be given to the respective roles played by the individuals concerned in the commission of systematic or large-scale crimes within the jurisdiction of the Court. Third, the Court must contemplate the role played by State entities, organisations or armed groups to which the suspects belong in the overall commission of crimes falling within the jurisdiction. In other words, ICC proceedings must be directed against those suspected of being most responsible within the relevant group (*Prosecutor v. Lubanga* (Case No. ICC-01/04-01/06-8-US-Corr), ICC Pre-Trial Chamber I, Decision Concerning Pre-Trial Chamber I's Decision of 10 February 2006 and the Incorporation of Documents into the Record of the Case against Mr. Thomas Lubanga Dyilo, 24 February 2006, paras. 51–52).

Author: Mohamed Abdou.

[220] Article 17(2) enumerates three scenarios guiding the Court's determination with respect to unwillingness. There are three factors which can ground a finding of unwillingness under Article 17(2), namely the initiation of criminal proceedings for the purpose of shielding the accused, the conduct of the proceedings in a manner that results in unjustified delays, and the lack of independent and impartial proceedings. The Court has thus far only considered the last two factors.

Cross-references:
Rule 51.

Author: Mohamed Abdou.

[221] This sub-paragraph concerns the situation when a state engages in sham proceedings to shield a person from the jurisdiction of the Court. Obvious departures from normal proceedings can be a factor that raises doubts about the legitimacy of the exercise. There is a potential overlap with this and sub-paragraph (2)(c).

Author: Mark Klamberg.

[222] In relation to unjustified delays, Pre-Trial Chamber I held that delays in the conduct of national investigations or prosecution may warrant a finding of unwillingness only where such delays appear to be inconsistent with "an intent to bring the person concerned to justice". Such a determination must be made on the basis of the "factual circumstances with a view to ultimately discerning the State's intent as concerns its ongoing domestic proceedings against the specific individual" (*Prosecutor v. Saif Al-Islam Gaddafi and Abdullah Al-Senussi* (Case No. ICC-01/11-01/11-239), ICC Pre-Trial Chamber I, Decision requesting further submissions on issues related to the admissibility of the case against Saif Al-Islam Gaddafi, 7 December 2012, para. 233). The relevant factors that the Court may consider include the chronology of domestic proceedings and the complexity of the case at hand. However, Pre-Trial Chamber I emphasised that the allegations of unjustified delay must be decided "not against an abstract ideal of justice, but against the specific circumstances surrounding the investigation concerned" (*Prosecutor v. Saif Al-Islam Gaddafi and Abdullah Al-Senussi* (Case No. ICC-01/11-01/11-239), ICC Pre-Trial Chamber I, Decision requesting further submissions on issues related to the admissibility of the case against Saif Al-Islam Gaddafi, 7 December 2012, para. 223).

(c) The proceedings were not or are not being conducted independently or impartially, and they were or are being conducted in a manner which, in the circumstances, is inconsistent with an intent to bring the person concerned to justice.[223]

3. In order to determine inability in a particular case, the Court shall consider whether, due to a total or substantial collapse or unavailability of its national judicial system, the State is unable to obtain the accused or the necessary evidence and testimony or otherwise unable to carry out its proceedings.[224]

Author: Mohamed Abdou.

[223] Article 17(2)(c) provides that the lack of independent and impartial national proceedings renders the case admissible before the ICC. In order to assess this requirement, one has to look at the manner in which the proceedings are being conducted and whether, in the circumstances of the case, there exists a lack of independence and impartiality that is inconsistent with the intent to bring the defendant to justice. The main difficulty concerning the interpretation of this provision relates to whether the Court can find a State unwilling on the ground that national proceedings violate due process. This is because the chapeau of Article 17(2) explicitly refers to the "principles of due process recognized by international law". This issue arose in the context of Al-Senussi admissibility challenge, where the defence argued that the defendant's procedural rights had been violated throughout the domestic investigation. On this specific issue, the Pre-Trial Chamber indicated that, in principle, "violations of the accused's procedural rights are not *per se* grounds for a finding of unwillingness", and that, depending on the specific circumstances of each case, "certain violations of the procedural rights of the accused may be relevant to the assessment of the independence and impartiality of the national proceedings" (*Prosecutor v. Saif Al-Islam Gaddafi and Abdullah Al-Senussi* (Case No. ICC-01/11-01/11-239), ICC Pre-Trial Chamber I, Decision requesting further submissions on issues related to the admissibility of the case against Saif Al-Islam Gaddafi, 7 December 2012, para. 235). The Chamber appears to have rejected the defence argument that a State could be found "unwilling" on the sole ground that the proceedings violate the principles of due process. Instead, the Chamber has embraced an interpretation which requires that the alleged due process violations be specifically linked to the two prongs of Article 17(2)(c), namely the absence of an intent to bring the defendant to "justice" as well as the lack of independence and impartiality of the proceedings.

In any event, the fact that the chapeau of Article 17(2)(c) specifically refers to the "principles of due process recognized by international law" suggests that due process considerations constitute an important factor and should therefore guide the analysis of all the criteria of unwillingness. The negotiating history of the Statute shows that the drafters included this reference in order to introduce an element of objectivity to the assessment of unwillingness and reduce the subjectivity inherent to the assessment of the intent of domestic authorities (Holmes, 1999, p. 50).

Author: Mohamed Abdou.

[224] Pursuant to Article 17(3), in order to determine state's "inability" in relation to a specific case, the Chamber "shall consider whether, due to a total or substantial collapse or unavailability of its national judicial system, the state is unable to obtain the accused or the necessary evidence and testimony or otherwise is unable to carry out its proceedings".

In order to find a state "unable", Article 17(3) refers to two sets of considerations: first, a total or substantial "collapse" or "unavailability" of the national judicial system, and second, whether, as a consequence of the collapse or unavailability, the state is unable to obtain the accused, or the evidence and testimony, or is otherwise unable to carry out proceedings. The manner in which Article 17 is framed suggests that the inability assessment involves an evaluation of the national judicial system as a whole. A state may thus be found unable to carry out genuine proceedings in case of civil war, public unrest or as a result of other factors that make the holding of judicial proceedings impossible, such as the lack of court personnel or qualified judges.

There is only one precedent within the ICC jurisprudence where a state was found to be lacking the requisite ability to genuinely carry out an investigation. In *Al Gaddafi* admissibility challenge, the Pre-Trial Chamber concluded that Libya is unable to investigate or prosecute the case. This finding was made after the Chamber had considered the substantial difficulties faced by the national authorities in exercising judicial powers "across the entire territory" (*Prosecutor v. Saif Al-Islam Gaddafi and Abdullah Al-Senussi* (Case No. ICC-01/11-01/11-344-Red), ICC Pre-Trial Chamber I, Decision on the admissibility of the case against Saif Al-Islam Gaddafi, 31 May 2013, para. 205). Before making an overall conclusion on Libya's ability, the Chamber found that the national judicial system is "unavailable", which in its view resulted in Libya being unable to obtain the custody of the defendant as well as the necessary testimony of some witnesses. In the Chamber's view, the specific facts of the case revealed that the suspect was being detained by uncontrolled armed militias and that authorities had failed to secure the transfer of the suspect to a government-controlled detention facility (*Prosecutor v. Saif Al-Islam Gaddafi and Abdullah Al-Senussi* (Case No. ICC-01/11-01/11-344-Red), ICC Pre-Trial Chamber I, Decision on the admissibility of the case against Saif Al-Islam Gaddafi, 31 May 2013, para. 205). The Chamber also determined that the national authorities lacked the capacity to obtain the necessary testimony, relying mainly on the absence of evidence showing the existence of witness protection programmes or other measures for witness protection (*Prosecutor v. Saif Al-Islam Gaddafi and Abdullah Al-Senussi* (Case No. ICC-01/11-01/11-344-Red), ICC Pre-Trial Chamber I, Decision on the admissibility of the case against Saif Al-Islam Gaddafi, 31 May 2013, para. 205).

Finally, the Chamber considered whether the words "otherwise unable to carry out proceedings" may be interpreted so as to include the inability of a state to secure legal representation for the defendant. Though the lack of legal representation is not explicitly provided for as a form of inability, it nevertheless constitutes an impediment to the conduct of genuine proceedings. In this respect, the Chamber held the view that the ability requirement must be assessed in accordance with the substantive and procedural domestic laws (*Prosecutor v. Saif Al-Islam Gaddafi and Abdullah Al-Senussi* (Case No. ICC-01/11-01/11-344-Red), ICC Pre-Trial Chamber I, Decision on the admissibility of the case against Saif Al-Islam Gaddafi, 31 May 2013, para. 200). The Libyan Government could not establish that a lawyer had been appointed to represent the accused at any stage of the domestic proceedings. The Chamber considered that such failure contravenes the Libyan Code of Criminal Procedure, which prescribes that no trial can take place without proper legal representation (*Prosecutor v. Saif Al-Islam Gaddafi and Abdullah Al-Senussi* (Case No. ICC-01/11-01/11-344-Red), ICC Pre-Trial Chamber I, Decision on the admissibility of the case against Saif Al-Islam Gaddafi, 31 May 2013, para. 214). Here, the inability therefore arises from the legal obstacles posed by national law.

Doctrine:

1. William W. Burke-White and Scott Kaplan, "Shaping the Contours of the Domestic Justice: The ICC and the Admissibility Challenge in the Uganda Situation", in Carsten Stahn and Göran Sluiter (eds.), *The Emerging Practice of the International Criminal Court*, Martinus Nijhoff Publishers, Leiden, 2009, pp. 79–114.

2. William W. Burke-White, "Implementing a Policy of Positive Complementarity in the Rome System of Justice", in *Criminal Law Forum*, 2008, vol. 19, no. 1, pp. 59–85.

3. Mohamed M. El Zeidy, "From Primacy to Complementarity and Backwards: (Re-)Visiting Rule 11 *bis* of the Ad Hoc Tribunals", in *International and Comparative Law Quarterly*, 2008, vol. 57, pp. 403–15.

4. Kevin Jon Heller, "The Shadow Side of Complementarity: The Effect of Article 17 of the Rome Statute on National Due Process", in *Criminal Law Forum*, 2006, vol. 17.

5. John T. Holmes, in Antonio Cassese, Paola Gaeta and John R.W.D. Jones (eds.), *The Rome Statute of the International Criminal Court: A Commentary*, Oxford University Press, Oxford, 2002, pp. 673, 675–76.

6. John T. Holmes, "The Principle of Complementarity", in Roy S. Lee (ed.), *The International Criminal Court, The Making of the Rome Statute*, Kluwer Law International, The Hague, 1999, pp. 41–43, 50, 60–65.

7. Charles Jalloh, "Kenya vs. the ICC Prosecutor", in *Harvard International Law Journal Online*, 2012, vol. 53, pp. 237.

8. Jann K. Kleffner, "The Impact of Complementarity on National Implementation of Substantive International Criminal Law", in *Journal of International Criminal Justice*, 2003, vol. 1, no. 1, pp. 86–113.

9. Ruth B. Philips, "The International Criminal Court Statute: Jurisdiction and Admissibility", in *Criminal Law Forum*, 1999, vol. 10, no. 1, pp. 61–85.

10. William A. Schabas, "Prosecutorial Discretion and Gravity", in Carsten Stahn and Göran Sluiter (eds.), *The Emerging Practice of the International Criminal Court*, Martinus Nijhoff Publishers, Leiden, 2009, pp. 229–46.

11. William A. Schabas, *The International Criminal Court, A Commentary on the Rome Statute*, Oxford University Press, Oxford, 2010, p. 365.

12. Sharon A. Williams and William A. Schabas, in Otto Triffterer (ed.), *Commentary on the Rome Statute of the International Criminal Court: Observers' Notes, Article by Article*, 2nd ed., C.H. Beck/Hart/Nomos, Munich/Oxford/Baden-Baden, 2008, pp. 605–25.

13. Carsten Stahn, "Libya, the International Criminal Court and Complementarity: A Test for 'Shared Responsibility'", in *Journal of International Criminal Justice*, 2012, vol. 10, no. 2, pp. 235–349.

Author: Mohamed Abdou.

Article 18
Preliminary rulings regarding admissibility[225]

---

[225] *General remarks*:

Whereas Article 19 permits a State to challenge admissibility after a case has been initiated before the ICC, the process delineated in Article 18 permits a State to stave off the Court's exercise of jurisdiction over potential cases in a pre-emptive manner, if the State in question is investigating or has investigated these potential cases.

It is apparent from the explicit use of the two different terms "State parties" and "States" throughout Article 18 that its complementarity regime also applies to investigations conducted by non-State parties. The Article therefore evinces a broad recognition that the Court should only intervene where domestic jurisdictions are either unwilling or unable to do so.

Notwithstanding such an overarching presumption, the procedural requirements delineated in the Article place a relatively strict onus on States to assert their right to prosecute in a diligent and expeditions manner. As enunciated by the Appeals Chamber, "the complementarity principle, as enshrined in the Statute, strikes a balance between safeguarding the primacy of domestic proceedings *vis-à-vis* the International Criminal Court on the one hand, and the goal of the ICC Statute to 'put an end to impunity' on the other hand. If States do not or cannot investigate and, where necessary, prosecute, the International Criminal Court must be able to step in" (*Prosecutor v. Katanga and Ngudjolo* (Case No. ICC-01/4-01/07-1497), ICC AC, Judgment on the Appeal of Mr. Germain Katanga against the Oral Decision of Trial Chamber II of 12 June 2009 on the Admissibility of the Case, 25 September 2009, para. 85).

Whereas States have a very limited window through which to assert their primacy over a situation as of right, the Appeals Chamber has nonetheless suggested that outside of the framework of admissibility proceedings, the Prosecution should use its discretion to enter into dialogue with States concerning the division of labour between the ICC Prosecution and States:

The Appeals Chamber accepts that there may be national legislation in existence or other impediments to a State being able to either disclose to the Court the progress of its investigations, or to take all the necessary steps to investigate. In this case, Libya has asserted, *inter alia*, that it is a State in transition; it also asserts that it was prevented from disclosing to the Court evidence as to the investigations it was undertaking as a result of Article 59 of its Code of Criminal Procedure, which it submits required it to maintain information as to investigations confidential; and it asserts that the appointment of a new Prosecutor-General was significant, therefore justifying more time. While accepting the reality that these situations can arise, the Appeals Chamber nevertheless considers that a State cannot expect that such issues will automatically affect admissibility proceedings; on the contrary, such issues should in principle be raised with the Prosecutor directly (prior to instigating admissibility proceedings), with a view to advising her as to the steps the State is taking, any impediments to those steps and allowing her to reach sensible decisions as to whether or not, in the circumstances, it is appropriate for her, at that time, to pursue a case, pending the progress of investigations by the State. It is, in principle, not the place for such issues to be raised with a Chamber in the context of admissibility proceedings" (*Prosecutor v. Gaddafi and Senussi* (Case No. ICC-01/11-01/11-547-red), ICC AC, Judgment on the appeal of Libya against the decision of Pre-Trial Chamber I of 31 May 2013 entitled "Decision on the admissibility of the case against Saif Al-Islam Gaddafi", 21 May 2014, para. 165).

The Article is primarily procedural in nature. Substantive issues concerning the definition of "inadmissibility", "willingness" and "ability" are addressed by Article 17.

---

1. When a situation has been referred to the Court pursuant to Article 13 (a) and the Prosecutor has determined that there would be a reasonable basis to commence an investigation, or the Prosecutor initiates an investigation pursuant to Articles 13 (c) and 15, the Prosecutor shall notify all States Parties and those States which, taking into account the information available, would normally exercise jurisdiction over the crimes concerned. The Prosecutor may notify such States on a confidential basis and, where the Prosecutor believes it necessary to protect persons, prevent destruction of evidence or prevent the absconding of persons, may limit the scope of the information provided to States.[226]

Article 18 has not yet been invoked in practice. Ambiguities thus remain as to whether the procedure enables States to invoke the Article in an effective manner, how the Court will interpret the notion of a "potential case", and where the burden of proof will lie.

In terms of this latter aspect, the current ICC jurisprudence concerning Article 19 has held that where a State challenges the admissibility of a case, the burden falls on the State to adduce "evidence with a sufficient degree of specificity and probative value" in order to demonstrate that all of the elements of the admissibility criteria are met (*Prosecutor v. Ruto et al.*, ICC-01/09-01/11-307, AC, Judgment on the appeal of the Republic of Kenya against the decision of Pre-Trial Chamber II of 30 May 2011 entitled "Decision on the Application by the Government of Kenya Challenging the Admissibility of the Case Pursuant to Article 19(2)(b) of the Statute", 30 August 2011, para. 2; *Prosecutor v. Gaddafi et al.*, ICC-01/11-01/11-344-Red, PTC, 'Public Redacted Decision on the Admissibility of the Case against Saif Al-Islam Gaddafi', 31 May 2013, para. 52).

It remains to be adjudicated, however, as to whether the process by which a State notifies the Prosecution that it is investigating or prosecuting 'criminal acts' is analogous to a challenge to the admissibility of a case.

Preparatory works:

A contentious issue that arose during the drafting history was whether non-State parties could invoke Article 18:

Those who favoured limiting the right to challenge to States Parties argued that non-States Parties "did not share the burden of obligations under the Statute, to share the privilege of challenging the jurisdiction of the Court" (Italy) [...] Those who favoured extending the right to non-States parties asserted that "if a State that was not a party was carrying out an effective prosecution in its own territory, there was no reason for the Court to intervene and also conduct a prosecution" (United Kingdom), *ibid.*, p. 215 and that it was more consistent with complementarity (Singapore), *ibid.*, p. 219 (Hall 2008, p. 649, fn. 42).

According to Holmes, the latter view prevailed although there was a general consensus that the right for non-States parties to challenge admissibility should not be open-ended (Holmes 1999, p. 66).

The final text does not impose any explicit limit on the rights of non-State parties. Nonetheless, in line with the view of States such as Italy that rights should be linked to obligations, a Prosecution Expert Paper on Complementarity advocates the position that a State's record of cooperation with the ICC can be a relevant factor to the ICC's determination as to whether to accept a challenge to admissibility (ICC Informal Expert Paper 2003, p. 18). It follows from this that the fact that a State has ratified the ICC Statute might militate in the State's favour, as it could be viewed as being reflective of a general willingness to cooperate with the ICC.

Author: Melinda Taylor.

[226] Article 18(1) of the Statute obliges the Prosecutor, once he or she has decided to investigate a State referral pursuant to Article 13(a) or has been authorised to initiate an investigation *proprio*

motu, to notify all State parties and States, who would normally exercise jurisdiction over the crimes concerned.

Notably, Article 18(1) omits any reference to situations referred by the Security Council pursuant to Article 13(b). If that is the case, then the ICC would exercise automatic primacy as concerns investigations into such situations, although Article 19 would permit the State concerned or the defendant to challenge the admissibility of a specific case.

Nsereko justifies this omission of Article 13(b) referrals by arguing that "the Council has primacy in matters involving international peace and security. Its decisions are binding on all States. Judicial proceedings are some of the measures that it may opt for as a means of maintaining or restoring international peace and security. Once it has opted for and sanctioned such measures there is no need for further authorization from the Pre-Trial Chamber or from any other authority" (Nsereko, 2008, p. 629).

Article 18(1) gives the Prosecution a degree of latitude to determine, on the basis of the information known to the Prosecution, which States or State Parties could exercise jurisdiction and should therefore be notified. It is therefore entirely possible that the Prosecution might fail to notify a State or State party in a timely manner, either because the Prosecution was unaware of the fact that the State in question was investigating or prosecution the same acts, or because the Prosecution had construed the definition of jurisdiction narrowly, and had therefore failed to include some States or State parties, which could potentially exercise jurisdiction.

The impact that this could have on the rights of States will be analysed in connection with Article 18(2).

A further issue is that the precise temporal and geographic parameters of a situation might not be completely defined at the time when the situation is referred to the Court by a State party. Since the purpose of Article 18 is to underscore the notion of complementarity and to enable States to fulfil their "duty [...] to exercise [...] criminal jurisdiction over those responsible for international crimes" (Preamble of the ICC Statute), it is arguable that this purpose would be frustrated if the Prosecution were to interpret its obligation as a once off obligation, as opposed to an obligation which is triggered whenever the Prosecution changes or expands the parameters of its investigations.

In the DRC situation, the Prosecution adopted both an expansive definition of the parameters of the investigation it opened into the DRC situation in 2004, and a narrow construction of its notification obligations. In its application for an arrest warrant against Calixte Mbarushimana, the Prosecution asserted that its notification to States in 2004 that it was opening an investigation into the DRC satisfied its Article 18(1) notification obligations as concerns investigations conducted much later into alleged crimes in the Kivus (*Prosecutor v. Mbarushimana*, Prosecution's Application under Article 58, ICC-01/04-01/10-11-red OTP, 20 August 2010, para. 163).

Although the Pre-Trial Chamber did not expressly address the notification issue, it ruled that in order to fall within the parameters of the initial referral from the DRC, the investigated allegations must fall "within the boundaries of the situation of crisis for which the jurisdiction of the Court was activated [...] Such a situation can include not only crimes that had already been or were being committed at the time of the referral, but also crimes committed after that time, in so far as they are sufficiently linked to the situation of crisis referred to the Court as ongoing at the time of the referral" (*Prosecutor v. Mbarushimana*, ICC PT. Ch. I, Decision on the Prosecutor's Application for an Arrest Warrant against Calixte Mbarushimana, ICC-01/04-01/10-1, 28 September 2010, para. 6).

In line with this reasoning, it follows that the Prosecution would need to reinitiate the "notification" process if the crimes being investigated are not sufficiently linked to the crimes which formed the basis of the initial notification process.

2. Within one month of receipt of that notification, a State may inform the Court that it is investigating or has investigated its nationals or others within its jurisdiction with respect to criminal acts which may constitute crimes referred to in Article 5 and which relate to the information provided in the notification to States. At the request of that State, the Prosecutor shall defer to the State's investigation of those persons unless the Pre-Trial Chamber, on the application of the Prosecutor, decides to authorize the investigation.[227]

Since Article 18 is concerned with potential rather than actual cases, the ICC Appeals Chamber has also underscored that the phrases "crimes concerned" (Article 18(1)) and "criminal acts which may constitute crimes" (Article 18(2)) should be interpreted relatively broadly, particularly as "[o]ften, no individual suspects will have been identified at this stage, nor will the exact conduct nor its legal classification be clear" (*Prosecutor v. Ruto*, Judgment on the appeal of the Republic of Kenya against the decision of Pre-Trial Chamber II of 30 May 2011 entitled "Decision on the Application by the Government of Kenya Challenging the Admissibility of the Case Pursuant to Article 19(2)(b) of the Statute", 30 August 2011, ICC-01/09-01/11-307, para. 39).

Finally, Article 18(1) permits the Prosecution to notify States on a confidential basis, and to limit the information provided to States if it believes that publicity would adversely affect the protection of persons, the integrity of evidence, or the ability of the ICC to apprehend suspects. It does not, however, appear possible for the Prosecution to rely on these reasons to refrain from notifying a State altogether. This lacuna could present problems in a situation where the target of the Prosecution's investigations is the Head of State, or an official who is likely to have access to all confidential information in the State in question.

Cross-references:
Rule 52.

Author: Melinda Taylor.

[227] Article 18(2) specifies that once States or State Parties have been notified, they have a deadline of 1 month within which to notify the Court that they are investigating or have investigated the acts in question.

Although this deadline does not run until the State has been notified by the Prosecution, if the Prosecution has, in the meantime, obtained arrested warrants in relation to the 'criminal acts in question', the State will be forced to challenge the admissibility of the case via Article 19. In so doing, it will be necessary for the State to satisfy the higher threshold of the 'same person/substantially the same conduct test', as approved by the ICC Appeals Chamber (*Prosecutor v. Ruto*, ICC A. Ch., Judgment on the appeal of the Republic of Kenya against the decision of Pre-Trial Chamber II of 30 May 2011 entitled "Decision on the Application by the Government of Kenya Challenging the Admissibility of the Case Pursuant to Article 19(2)(b) of the Statute, ICC-01/09-01/11-307, 30 August 2011, para. 1).

Accordingly, if the State is prosecuting the same crime base or incidents as the ICC but has attributed responsibility to a different person than the ICC (as was the basis of Kenya's submissions in the Ruto et al case), it will not be possible for them to successfully request the ICC to defer jurisdiction to them.

It could be argued from the perspective of States that the one month fixed deadline is inimical to the complementarity principle. Many States might be willing in principle to investigate or prosecute the 'criminal acts' but might lack the technical means to do so in the immediate aftermath of the conflict or unrest in question. They might therefore fail to meet the threshold of proving to the Court that they are investigating or have investigated the acts in question at the specific time when the Prosecution makes its Article 18 notification, although they could be ca-

3. The Prosecutor's deferral to a State's investigation shall be open to review by the Prosecutor six months after the date of deferral or at any time when there has been a significant change of circumstances based on the State's unwillingness or inability genuinely to carry out the investigation.[228]

---

pable of doing so if they had some additional time. Article 18 does not provide such States with an opportunity to either seek a reasonable extension of this deadline, or to request the Court to defer its investigations if the State can demonstrate a change in circumstances (that is, that is now conducting investigations into the acts in question).

This is but one example among many where the Statute prioritises the objective of encouraging effective and expeditious investigations and prosecutions over the presumptive right of States to exercise jurisdiction over cases.

Nonetheless, this emphasis on expedition is counterbalanced by the fact that Article 18(2) appears to establish the presumption that if a notified State requests the Prosecution to defer to its domestic investigations, the Prosecutor shall defer to the State in question. This presumption is only displaced if the Pre-Trial Chamber grants a Prosecution application to continue it investigations.

Although Article 18(2) refers to such a decision occurring upon the application of the Prosecution, it does not exclude the possibility that the Pre-Trial Chamber could rule *proprio motu* on the issue as to whether Prosecution should defer to national investigations as part of its inherent "*compétence de la compétence*".

It is arguable, however, that Article 18(2) should be construed in a manner that is consistent with Article 53 of the Statute. Article 53(3)(a) allows the State, which referred the situation, to challenge a decision of the Prosecution not to investigate a case, for reasons including an assessment that the case is inadmissible before the ICC. In contrast, the Pre-Trial Chamber cannot conduct a *proprio motu* review of a decision not to investigate if it has been made for this reason.

It follows that whereas a referring State could challenge a decision of the Prosecution to defer to the investigations of another State, in the absence of an application from either the Prosecution or the referring State, the Pre-Trial Chamber would have no competence to rule on the matter.

Cross-references:
Rule 52, 53, 54 and 55.

Regulation 38.

Author: Melinda Taylor.

[228] If the Prosecution has deferred to a State, or the Pre-Trial Chamber has rejected the Prosecutor's application for non-deferral, the Prosecution may nonetheless review the status of domestic proceedings with a view to filing a request for authorisation from the Pre-Trial Chamber to continue its investigations (Article 18(3) and Rule 65(1)). The Prosecution may do so either after 6 months has elapsed or upon a significant change of circumstances concerning whether the State's investigations meet the Article 17 criteria of willingness and ability (Article 18(3)). The existence of such a power implies that in order for this provision to be effective, the Prosecution would need to monitor the progress of domestic investigations continuously with a view to assessing whether they comport to the criteria set out in Article 17. It is unclear from the phase "at any time" whether there is any limit as concerns the number of times that the Prosecutor may review the deferral of the investigation or prosecution.

Cross-references:
Rule 56.

Author: Melinda Taylor.

4. The State concerned or the Prosecutor may appeal to the Appeals Chamber against a ruling of the Pre-Trial Chamber, in accordance with Article 82. The appeal may be heard on an expedited basis.[229]

5. When the Prosecutor has deferred an investigation in accordance with paragraph 2, the Prosecutor may request that the State concerned periodically inform the Prosecutor of the progress of its investigations and any subsequent prosecutions. States Parties shall respond to such requests without undue delay.[230]

---

[229] This Article confirms that for the purpose of Article 18 proceedings, a State can be considered as a 'party' for the purposes of initiating an automatic right to appeal pursuant to Article 82(1)(a) of the Statute. Article 82(1)(a) enables 'parties' to appeal a decision on admissibility or jurisdiction as of rights (that is, without first seeking leave to appeal from the Chamber, which issued the decision).

It has been extrapolated from the fact that Article 18(4) expressly iterates the right of States to appeal certain decisions that in the absence of such express language concerning a right for States to appeal a particular category of decisions, States cannot otherwise avail themselves of the appellate avenues set out in Articles 81 and 82 (*Prosecutor v. Lubanga*, ICC T. Ch., Decision on two requests for leave to appeal the "Decision on the request by DRC-DO1-WWWW-0019 for special protective measures relating to his asylum application, ICC-01/04-01/06-2779, 4 August 2011, para. 11).

Author: Melinda Taylor.

[230] This sub-Article specifies that where the Prosecution has deferred to a State's investigation, it may request the State in question to inform the Prosecution on a periodic basis concerning the status of its investigations and prosecutions.

Notably, the Article also specifies that "States Parties" shall respond to such requests without undue delay. The explicit reference to State Parties implies that no such obligation is imposed on non-State Parties. The absence of an obligation to submit such information renders it particularly difficult for the Prosecution to assess the progress of the case, as the Prosecution also has no right to conduct investigations in non-State parties.

Thus, whereas non-State parties can request the Prosecution to defer to its investigations, the Prosecution has no corollary power or effective ability to monitor whether the State in fact investigates and prosecutes the case in a manner, which is consistent with the admissibility criteria under Article 17.

In order to ensure that the underlying ICC Statute objectives of eliminating impunity and ensuring effective prosecutions, it is arguable that the fact that the requesting State is a non-State party might be a relevant criterion as concerns the Prosecution's decision as to whether to defer to the State's investigation, or apply to the Chamber to authorise an ICC investigation.

Similarly, even if a non-State party is not obliged to submit periodic reports, it might be appropriate to draw adverse inferences if it refuses to do so, for the purposes of deciding whether there has been a significant change of circumstances, which would warrant a reversal of the Prosecution's deferral to the investigations or prosecutions of the State.

This would be consistent with the above-cited recommendation in the ICC Informal Expert Paper on Complementarity that a State's record of cooperation with the ICC can be a relevant factor in the Court's assessment as to whether the State meets (or continues to meet) the admissibility criteria (ICC Informal Expert Paper, 2003, p. 18).

Hall has also argued that where information, which might be germane to the ICC's determination of admissibility, is within the custody of a State and the State fails to proffer it or grant

6. Pending a ruling by the Pre-Trial Chamber, or at any time when the Prosecutor has deferred an investigation under this article, the Prosecutor may, on an exceptional basis, seek authority from the Pre-Trial Chamber to pursue necessary investigative steps for the purpose of preserving evidence where there is a unique opportunity to obtain important evidence or there is a significant risk that such evidence may not be subsequently available.[231]

7. A State which has challenged a ruling of the Pre-Trial Chamber under this article may challenge the admissibility of a case under Article 19 on the grounds of additional significant facts or significant change of circumstances.[232]

---

the ICC access to it, it would be appropriate to draw adverse inferences against the State in question (Hall, 2008, pp. 645, 652).

Author: Melinda Taylor.

[231] In order to ensure that potential future prosecution or investigations before the ICC are not prejudiced during this 'ping pong' match between the jurisdiction of domestic authorities and the ICC, Article 18(6) permits the Prosecutor to apply to the Pre-Trial Chamber to take measures to preserve evidence if there is a unique opportunity to obtain important evidence or there is a significant risk that the evidence might not be subsequently available. Rule 57 specifies that such an application shall be considered on an expedited and ex parte basis. Presumably, in order to ensure that any evidence so collected would be potentially admissible during a future trial at the ICC, the invocation of a unique investigative opportunity by the Prosecution pursuant to Article 18(6) would also attract the provisions and procedures set down by Article 56 (the Role of the Pre-Trial Chamber in relation to a unique investigative opportunity). This includes the duty of the Pre-Trial Chamber to consider what measures may be necessary to "ensure the efficiency and integrity of the proceedings and, in particular, to protect the rights of the defence" (Article 56(1)(b)). These measures can include the appointment of a defence counsel to represent the interests of the defence (Article 56(2)(d)).

Cross-references:

Rule 57.

Regulation 38.

Author: Melinda Taylor.

[232] The fact that a State has unsuccessfully challenged the admissibility of a situation does not prevent it from subsequently challenging the admissibility of a particular case under Article 19, but it must then base its Article 19 challenge on additional significant facts or a significant change of circumstances (Article 18(7)).

It has been suggested that such new facts or significant change in circumstances could include "cessation of hostilities in a country that was previously embroiled in war; the coming to power of a new government that is better disposed to exercise national jurisdiction fairly and effectively; and genuine national peace and reconciliation arrangements under which the defendants might have been granted amnesty or pardon" (Nsereko, 2008, p. 636).

Doctrine:

1. Christopher K. Hall, "Article 19: Challenges to the Jurisdiction of the Court or the Admissibility of the Case", in Otto Triffterer (ed.), *Commentary on the Rome Statute of the International Criminal Court: Observers' Notes, Article by Article*, 2nd ed., C.H. Beck/Hart/Nomos, Munich/Oxford/Baden-Baden, 2008, pp. 627–36.

2. John T. Holmes, "The Principle of Complementarity", in Roy S. Lee (ed.), *The International Criminal Court. The Making of the Rome Statute,* Kluwer Law International, The Hague, 1999.

3. ICC Informal Expert Paper, *The Principle of Complementarity in Practice,* 2003.

---

4. Daniel Nsereko, "Article 18: Preliminary Rulings Regarding Admissibility", in Otto Triffterer (ed.), *Commentary on the Rome Statute of the International Criminal Court: Observers' Notes, Article by Article*, 2nd ed., C.H. Beck/Hart/Nomos, Munich/Oxford/Baden-Baden, 2008, pp. 627–36.

Author: Melinda Taylor.

Article 19

Challenges to the jurisdiction of the Court or the admissibility of a case[233]

1. The Court shall satisfy itself that it has jurisdiction in any case brought before it. The Court may, on its own motion, determine the admissibility of a case in accordance with Article 17.[234]

---

[233] *General remarks*:

Articles 17 and 19 of the ICC Statute constitute the main statutory provisions defining the complementarity regime of the ICC. While Article 17 addresses the substantive conditions for admissibility, Article 19 primarily deals with the procedural aspects related to both jurisdiction and admissibility of a case. Article 19 also differs from Article 18 (on preliminary challenges to admissibility) in that it only applies to concrete and clearly-defined cases, unlike Article 18 which governs challenges to the initiation of an investigation into a situation as a whole (Schabas, 2010, p. 365). The Article elucidates several procedural matters including, the entities having standing to make challenges, the timing, those who are entitled to participate in the proceedings and submit observations as well as the competent chamber for deciding admissibility and jurisdictional challenges (ICC Statute, Article 19, and Holmes, 1999, pp. 60–65).

Preparatory works:

The drafting history reveals that states had converging views regarding the adoption of Article 19. Among the significant questions contemplated was whether challenges should apply to both admissibility and jurisdictional matters, and there existed a common agreement among delegations regarding the conceptual differences between jurisdiction and admissibility (Holmes, 1999, p. 61). It is noteworthy that with regard to jurisdiction, it was widely accepted that it is Court's duty to satisfy itself that it has jurisdiction over a case "throughout all stages of the proceedings". As for admissibility challenges, the prevailing view was that admissibility "was less the duty of the Court to establish than a bar to the Court's consideration of a case" (Holmes, 1999, p. 61). As a result of this conceptual distinction, it was decided that the consideration of admissibility challenges should in principle be limited to the early stages of the proceedings.

Author: Mohamed Abdou.

[234] Article 19 provides that the admissibility of a given case may be examined either by the Court acting on its own initiative or in response to an admissibility challenge filed by one of the parties referred to in Article 19(2).

The significance of the Court's obligation to satisfy itself that it has jurisdiction over the case was highlighted by Pre-Trial II as follows: "notwithstanding the language of Article 19(1) of the Statute, any judicial body has the power to determine its own jurisdiction, even in the absence of an explicit reference to that effect. This is an essential element in the exercise by any judicial body of its functions. Such power is derived from the well-recognised principle of '*la compétence de la compétence*'" (*Prosecutor v. Bemba*, ICC P.T. Ch. II, Decision Pursuant to Article 61(7)(a) and (b) of the Rome Statute on the Charges of the Prosecutor Against Jean-Pierre Bemba Gombo, ICC-01/05-01/08-424, 15 June 2009, para. 23). See also *Kony et al.*, ICC P.T. Ch., Decision initiating proceedings under Article 19, requesting observations and appointing counsel for the Defence, ICC-02/04-01/05-320, 21 October 2008; *Kony et al.*, ICC P.T. Ch., Decision on the admissibility of the case under Article 19(1) of the Statute, ICC-02/04-01/05-377, 10 March 2009, para. 45 and *Ruto et al.*, ICC P.T. Ch., Decision on the Prosecutor's Application for Summons to Appear for William Samoei Ruto, Henry Kiprono Kosgey and Joshua Arap Sang, ICC-01/09-01/11-1, 08 March 2011, para. 8. In relation to admissibility challenges, it was ruled that "the existence of national proceedings is the sole reason for a possible finding of inadmissibility" (*Prosecutor v. Katanga*, ICC P.T. Ch. I, Decision on the evi-

---

2. Challenges to the admissibility of a case on the grounds referred to in Article 17 or challenges to the jurisdiction of the Court may be made by:[235]

   (a) An accused or a person for whom a warrant of arrest or a summons to appear has been issued under Article 58;

   (b) A State which has jurisdiction over a case, on the ground that it is investigating or prosecuting the case or has investigated or prosecuted; or

   (c) A State from which acceptance of jurisdiction is required under Article 12.

3. The Prosecutor may seek a ruling from the Court regarding a question of jurisdiction or admissibility. In proceedings with respect to jurisdiction or admissibility, those who have referred the situation under Article 13, as well as victims, may also submit observations to the Court.[236]

---

dence and information provided by the Prosecution for the issuance of a warrant of arrest for Germain Katanga, ICC-01/04-01/07-55, 5 November 2007, para. 20).

Cross-references:
Rules 59 and 133.

Author: Mohamed Abdou.

[235] The parties entitled to challenge admissibility or jurisdiction are identified in Article 19(2) as follows: (1) the accused or the person for whom a warrant of arrest or summon to appear has been issued; (2) a state party to the ICC Statute (3) or a state that has accepted the jurisdiction of the Court. In addition, the Statute gives the prosecution the right under Article 19(3) to seek a Court ruling on jurisdiction or admissibility.

The prosecution, the defence and the victims may participate in Article 19 proceedings. There remain however some doubts as to the status and scope of participation of states in admissibility proceedings, particularly in cases where these proceedings are triggered by a different entity, For instance, it was ruled that the State may not participate in the proceedings on admissibility when such proceedings are initiated by the defence. Pre-Trial Chamber II explained "that a State becomes a participant to the proceedings on admissibility only in particular instances where the interests of a State are envisaged by the Court's statutory documents. This is the case, for example, where the State has challenged the admissibility of the case under Article 19(2)(b) of the Statute. However, this is not the case in the context of the present proceedings as the admissibility challenge was lodged by a suspect – although this does not mean that a State will never have an interest when it is not the triggering entity of such a challenge" (*Prosecutor v. Muthaura et al.*, ICC Pre-Trial Chamber II, Decision on the "Request by the Government of Kenya in respect of the Confirmation of Charges Proceedings, ICC-01/09-02/11-340, 20 September 2011, para. 9).

Cross-references:
Rule 59.

Regulation 38(1)(c).

Author: Mohamed Abdou.

[236] The language of Article 19(3) of the Statute and Rule 59(1)(a) of the Rules makes clear that a State shall be informed about an admissibility challenge and provided with a summary of its grounds only if the situation was received by way of a State Party referral as opposed to a *proprio motu* request submitted by the Prosecutor as is the present case. This approach suggests that the drafters intended to exclude States Parties from proceedings in a scenario" (*Prosecutor v. Muthaura et al.*, ICC Pre-Trial Chamber II, Decision on the "Request by the Government of Kenya in respect of the Confirmation of Charges Proceedings, ICC-01/09-02/11-340, 20 September 2011, para. 9).

4. The admissibility of a case or the jurisdiction of the Court may be challenged only once by any person or State referred to in paragraph 2. The challenge shall take place prior to or at the commencement of the trial. In exceptional circumstances, the Court may grant leave for a challenge to be brought more than once or at a time later than the commencement of the trial. Challenges to the admissibility of a case, at the commencement of a trial, or subsequently with the leave of the Court, may be based only on Article 17, paragraph 1 (c).[237]

Cross-references:
Rules 59 and 60.

Regulation 38(2)(b).

Author: Mohamed Abdou.

[237] Pursuant to Article 19(4), the admissibility of a case or the jurisdiction of the Court may be challenged only once by the person concerned or the State, but the Court may in exceptional circumstances grant leave for a challenge to be brought more than once or at a time later than the commencement of the trial. Challenges made after the commencement of trial may only be based on Article 17(1)(c) addressing instances of double jeopardy. Challenges made after the commencement of trial are permissible only if "the person concerned has been already tried for conduct which is the subject of the complaint".

The question arose as to whether a challenge made by one of the defendants may prejudice other defendants in the same case or limit the right of the State to lodge another challenge. In this respect, Pre-Trial Chamber II indicated that "nowhere is it said that a challenge brought by either of these parties forecloses the bringing of a challenge by another equally legitimate party, nor that the right of either of the parties to bring a challenge is curtailed or otherwise affected by the Chamber's exercise of its proprio motu powers" (*Prosecutor v. Kony et al*, ICC Pre-Trial Chamber II Decision on the admissibility of the case under Article 19(1) of the Statute, ICC-02/04-01/05-377,10 March 2009, para. 25). Further, it appears from the ICC jurisprudence that it is possible for a Chamber to make several determinations on admissibility in respect of each of the defendants in the same case. In the case against Al-Gaddafi and Al-Senussi, Pre-Trial Chamber I decided that the Government's first challenge to admissibility would "be understood to only concern the case against Al-Gaddafi" (*Prosecutor v. Saif Al-Islam Gaddafi and Abdullah Al-Senussi*, ICC Pre-Trial Chamber I, Decision on the Conduct of the Proceedings Following the "Application on behalf of the Government of Libya pursuant to Article 19 of the Statute, ICC-01/11-01/11-134, 4 May 2012 para. 8). With respect to the admissibility challenge concerning Al-Senussi, the Chamber recognised that despite the close link between the two challenges the "unfolding of the proceedings following the Admissibility Challenge cannot be made dependent upon procedural steps in, or conclusion of, proceedings" concerning Mr. Al-Gaddafi (*Prosecutor v. Saif Al-Islam Gaddafi and Abdullah Al-Senussi*, ICC P.T. Ch. I, Decision on the conduct of the proceedings following the 'Application on behalf of the Government of Libya relating to Abdullah Al-Senussi pursuant to Article 19 of the ICC Statute, ICC-01/11-01/11-325, 26 April 2013, para. 10).

Timing:

As to the appropriate timing for lodging an admissibility challenge, Trial Chamber II indicated the following: "the Chamber considers that the Statute provides a three-phase approach in respect of challenges to admissibility. During the first phase, which runs until the decision on the confirmation of charges is filed with the Registry, all types of challenges to admissibility are permissible, subject to the requirement, for States, to make them at the "earliest opportunity". In the second phase, which is fairly short, running from the filing of the decision on the confirmation of charges to the constitution of the Trial Chamber, challenges may still be made if based on the *ne bis in idem* principle. In the third phase, in other words, as soon as the chamber is constituted, challenges to admissibility (based only on the *ne bis in idem* principle) are permissible

---

5. A State referred to in paragraph 2 (b) and (c) shall make a challenge at the earliest opportunity.[238]

6. Prior to the confirmation of the charges, challenges to the admissibility of a case or challenges to the jurisdiction of the Court shall be referred to the Pre-Trial Chamber. After confirmation of the charges, they shall be referred to the Trial Chamber. Decisions with respect to jurisdiction or admissibility may be appealed to the Appeals Chamber in accordance with Article 82.[239]

---

only in exceptional circumstances and with leave of the Trial Chamber" (*Prosecutor v. Katanga et al.*, ICC Trial Chamber II, Reasons for the Oral Decision on the Motion Challenging the Admissibility of the Case (Article 19 of the Statute), ICC-01/04-01/07-1213-tENG, 16 June 2009, para. 49)

While it appears clearly from this pronouncement that the Chamber has defined the commencement of trial as the date at which the Trial Chamber is constituted, it should be noted that Trial Chamber III had opted for a different approach. In the Bemba case, the Trial Chamber endorsed the view that the trial commences when "the evidence in the case is called and counsel – by speeches, submissions, statements and questioning – address the merits of the respective cases" (*Prosecutor v. Bemba*, ICC T. Ch. III, Decision on the Admissibility and Abuse of Process Challenges, ICC-01/05-01/08-802, 24 June 2010, paras. 210–211). On this basis, it concluded that the admissibility challenge occurring after the constitution of the Trial Chamber and before the delivery of the opening statements should not be treated as exceptional in the sense of Article 19(4) of the Statute (*Prosecutor v. Bemba*, ICC T. Ch. III, Decision on the Admissibility and Abuse of Process Challenges, ICC-01/05-01/08-802, 24 June 2010, paras. 210–211).

Author: Mohamed Abdou.

[238] Article 19(5) provides that the State challenging the admissibility of a case shall make the challenge at "the earliest opportunity". Moreover, the Appeals Chamber rejected the argument put forward by Kenya that the "earliest opportunity" requirement implies that the State cannot be "expected to have prepared every aspect of its Admissibility Application in detail in advance of [the date of filing]" of the challenge (*Prosecutor v. Francis Kirimi Muthaura, Uhuru Muigai Kenyatta and Mohammed Hussein Ali*, ICC A. Ch., Judgment on the appeal of the Republic of Kenya against the decision of Pre-Trial Chamber II of 30 May 2011 entitled "Decision on the Application by the Government of Kenya Challenging the Admissibility of the Case Pursuant to Article 19(2)(b) of the Statute", ICC-01/09-02/11-274, 30 August 2011, para. 45). Instead the Appeals Chamber clarified that "Article 19 (5) of the Statute requires a State to challenge admissibility as soon as possible once it is in a position to actually assert" that it is investigating the same case. Hence, the provision should not be understood as requiring "a State to challenge admissibility just because the Court has issued a summons to appear" (*Prosecutor v. Francis Kirimi Muthaura, Uhuru Muigai Kenyatta and Mohammed Hussein Ali*, ICC A. Ch., Judgment on the appeal of the Republic of Kenya against the decision of Pre-Trial Chamber II of 30 May 2011 entitled "Decision on the Application by the Government of Kenya Challenging the Admissibility of the Case Pursuant to Article 19(2)(b) of the Statute", ICC-01/09-02/11-274, 30 August 2011, para. 45).

Author: Mohamed Abdou.

[239] Article 19(6) stipulates that the decisions with respect to jurisdiction or admissibility may be appealed before the Appeals Chamber in accordance with Article 82. Article 82(1)(a) of the Statute provides that either party may appeal "a decision with respect to jurisdiction or admissibility". Decisions with respect to jurisdiction or admissibility may be directly appealed by the parties to the proceedings (the Prosecution, the Defence or the State) before the Appeals Chamber, as opposed to other interlocutory appeals brought under Article 82(1)(b), which require pri-

7. If a challenge is made by a State referred to in paragraph 2 (b) or (c), the Prosecutor shall suspend the investigation until such time as the Court makes a determination in accordance with Article 17.[240]

---

or leave from the first instance chamber. The Appeals Chamber has endorsed a narrow approach in interpreting the scope of Article 19(6), affirming that "the right to appeal a decision on jurisdiction or admissibility is intended to be limited only to those instances in which a Pre-Trial or Trial Chamber issues a ruling specifically on the jurisdiction of the Court or the admissibility of the case" (*Situation in the Republic of Kenya*, ICC Appeals Chamber, Decision on the admissibility of the "Appeal of the Government of Kenya against the 'Decision on the Request for Assistance Submitted on Behalf of the Government of the Republic of Kenya Pursuant to Article 93(10) of the Statute and Rule 194 of the Rules of Procedure and Evidence'", ICC-01/09-78, 10 August 2010, para. 16). The Chamber determined that the phrase "decision with respect to admissibility" requires "that the operative part of the decision itself must pertain directly to a question on the jurisdiction of the Court or the admissibility of a case. It is not sufficient that there is an indirect or tangential link between the underlying decision and questions of jurisdiction or admissibility" (*Situation in the Republic of Kenya*, ICC Appeals Chamber, Decision on the admissibility of the "Appeal of the Government of Kenya against the 'Decision on the Request for Assistance Submitted on Behalf of the Government of the Republic of Kenya Pursuant to Article 93(10) of the Statute and Rule 194 of the Rules of Procedure and Evidence'", ICC-01/09-78, 10 August 2010, para. 15).

Proceedings on appeal do not constitute a mere continuation of proceedings before the Trial or Pre-Trial Chamber, but rather "a separate and distinct stage of the proceedings". They are corrective in nature and not *de novo*, conducted with the purpose of reviewing the proceedings at first instance (*Prosecutor v. William Samoei Ruto et al.*, ICC Appeals Chamber, Decision on the "Filing of Updated Investigation Report by the Government of Kenya in the Appeal against the Pre-Trial Chamber's Decision on Admissibility", ICC-01/09-01/11-234, 28 July 2011, para. 13). The Appeals Chamber clarified that the proceedings on appeal are "determined by the scope of the relevant proceedings before the Pre-Trial Chamber", which entails that the appellant may not rely on new facts which postdate the admissibility decision in support of its appeal (*Prosecutor v. William Samoei Ruto et al.*, ICC Appeals Chamber, Decision on the "Filing of Updated Investigation Report by the Government of Kenya in the Appeal against the Pre-Trial Chamber's Decision on Admissibility", ICC-01/09-01/11-234, 28 July 2011, para. 13).

Cross-references:
Rule 60.

Author: Mohamed Abdou.

[240] When a State makes a challenge to the admissibility of a case before the Court, Article 19(7) provides that the Prosecutor "shall suspend the investigation until such time as the Court makes a determination". However, the Prosecutor may still seek a ruling from the Court: (a) to pursue necessary investigative steps for the purpose of preserving evidence where there is a unique opportunity to obtain important evidence or there is a significant risk that such evidence may not be subsequently available; (b) to take a statement or testimony from a witness or complete the collection and examination of evidence which had begun prior to the making of the challenge; and (c) in cooperation with the relevant States, to prevent the absconding of persons in respect of whom the Prosecutor has already requested a warrant of arrest under Article 58. Pursuant to Rules 58 and 61 of the Rules of Procedure and Evidence, the Prosecutor request for provisional measures shall be considered *ex parte* and *in camera*, and the Pre-Trial Chamber shall rule on it expeditiously.

Cross-references:
Rules 58 and 61.

---

8. Pending a ruling by the Court, the Prosecutor may seek authority from the Court:

    (a) To pursue necessary investigative steps of the kind referred to in Article 18, paragraph 6;

    (b) To take a statement or testimony from a witness or complete the collection and examination of evidence which had begun prior to the making of the challenge; and

    (c) In cooperation with the relevant States, to prevent the absconding of persons in respect of whom the Prosecutor has already requested a warrant of arrest under Article 58.

9. The making of a challenge shall not affect the validity of any act performed by the Prosecutor or any order or warrant issued by the Court prior to the making of the challenge.[241]

10. If the Court has decided that a case is inadmissible under Article 17, the Prosecutor may submit a request for a review of the decision when he or she is fully satisfied that new facts have arisen which negate the basis on which the case had previously been found inadmissible under Article 17.[242]

Regulation 38(2)(c).

Author: Mohamed Abdou.

[241] Article 19(9) specifies that the making of a challenge shall not affect the validity of any act performed by the Prosecutor or any order or warrant issued by the Court before it was made. However, it should be noted that in the *Al-Senussi* case, the Pre-Trial Chamber decided that the filing of an admissibility challenge allows the challenging State to postpone the execution of the surrender request pending the determination of the admissibility challenge in accordance with Article 95 of the Statute (*Prosecutor v. Saif Al-Islam and Abdullah Al-Senussi*, ICC Pre-Trial Chamber I, Decision on the postponement of the execution of the request for surrender of Saif Al-Islam Gaddafi pursuant to Article 95 of the Rome Statute, ICC-01/11-01/11-163, 1 June 2012, para. 37). This decision was subsequently appealed and is currently under consideration by the Appeals Chamber.

Author: Mohamed Abdou.

[242] Under Article 19(10), the prosecutor may submit a request for the review of the admissibility decision after being satisfied "that new facts have risen which negate the basis on which the case had previously been found inadmissible under Article 17 by the Court. Such a request shall be presented to the Chamber that made the ruling on admissibility, in accordance with the provisions of Rules 58, 59 and 61. The state or states that initially presented the challenge to admissibility shall be notified within a specified time limit to make their representations.

No application has been submitted by the Prosecution pursuant to Article 19(10) before the Court. In a recent decision on the admissibility of the case against Abdullah Al-Senussi, Pre-Trial Chamber I ruled that the case against the defendant was inadmissible before the Court. Despite this finding, the Chamber observed that the Prosecutor may still submit a request for review of the decision in accordance with Article 19(10) (*Prosecutor v. Saif Al-Islam and Abdullah Al-Senussi*, ICC Pre-Trial Chamber I, Decision on the admissibility of the case against Abdullah Al-Senussi, ICC-01/11-01/11-466-Red,11 October 2013, para. 312).

The language of Article 19(10) demonstrates that the admissibility assessment is not static, but must take into consideration the possible changes of circumstances that may have occurred over time. The Appeals Chamber explained that "the admissibility of a case under Article 17(1)(a), (b) and (c) of the Statute depends primarily on the investigative and prosecutorial activities of the States having jurisdiction. These activities may change over time. Thus, a case that was originally admissible may be rendered inadmissible by a change of circumstances in the concerned States and *vice versa*" (*Prosecutor v. Germain Katanga and Mathieu Ngudjolo Chui*, ICC Appeal Chamber, Judgment on the Appeal of Mr. Germain Katanga against the Oral

11. If the Prosecutor, having regard to the matters referred to in Article 17, defers an investigation, the Prosecutor may request that the relevant State make available to the Prosecutor information on the proceedings. That information shall, at the request of the State concerned, be confidential. If the Prosecutor thereafter decides to proceed with an investigation, he or she shall notify the State to which deferral of the proceedings has taken place.

Decision of Trial Chamber II of 12 June 2009 on the Admissibility of the Case, ICC-01/04-01/07-1479 OA 8, 25 September 2009, para. 56). In relation to Article 19(10), the Appeals Chamber stated that "the provision is clear evidence that the Statute assumes that the factual situation on the basis of which the admissibility of a case is established is not necessarily static, but ambulatory" (*Prosecutor v. Germain Katanga and Mathieu Ngudjolo Chui*, ICC Appeal Chamber, Judgment on the Appeal of Mr. Germain Katanga against the Oral Decision of Trial Chamber II of 12 June 2009 on the Admissibility of the Case, ICC-01/04-01/07-1479 OA 8, 25 September 2009, para. 56).

Cross-references:
Rules 62 and 185.

Doctrine:

1. John T. Holmes, "The Principle of Complementarity", in Roy S. Lee (ed.), *The International Criminal Court: The Making of the Rome Statute*, Kluwer Law International, The Hague, 1999, pp. 41–43, 50, 60–65.

2. Charles Jalloh, "Kenya vs. The ICC Prosecutor", in *Harvard International Law Journal Online*, 2012, vol. 53, p. 237.

3. William A. Schabas, *The International Criminal Court, A Commentary on the Rome Statute*, Oxford University Press, 2010, p. 361–72.

4. William W. Burke-White and Scott Kaplan, "Shaping the Contours of the Domestic Justice: The ICC and the Admissibility Challenge in the Uganda Situation", in Carsten Stahn and Göran Sluiter (eds.), *The Emerging Practice of the International Criminal Court*, Martinus Nijhoff Publishers, Leiden, 2009, pp. 79–114.

5. Mohamed El Zeidy, "From Primacy to Complementarity and Backwards: (Re-)Visiting Rule 11 Bis of the Ad hoc Tribunals", in *International and Comparative Law Quarterly*, 2008, vol. 57, pp. 403–15.

6. Jann K. Kleffner, "The Impact of Complementarity on National Implementation of Substantive International Criminal Law", in *Journal of International Criminal Justice*, 2003, vol. 1, no. 1, pp. 86–113.

7. William W. Burke-White, "Implementing a Policy of Positive Complementarity in the Rome System of Justice", in *Criminal Law Forum*, 2008, vol. 19, no. 1, pp. 59–85.

8. Carsten Stahn, "Libya, the International Criminal Court and Complementarity: A Test for 'Shared Responsibility'", in *Journal of International Criminal Justice*, 2012, vol. 10, no. 2, pp. 235–349.

9. William A. Schabas, "Prosecutorial Discretion and Gravity", in Carsten Stahn and Göran Sluiter (eds.), *The Emerging Practice of the International Criminal Court*, Martinus Nijhoff Publishers, Leiden, 2009, pp. 229–46.

10. Ruth B. Philips, "The International Criminal Court Statute: Jurisdiction and Admissibility", in *Criminal Law Forum*, 1999, vol. 10, no. 1, pp. 61–85.

Author: Mohamed Abdou.

Article 20
Ne bis in idem[7][243]

[243] *General remarks*:

1. Background to ne bis in idem

The principle that a person should not be prosecuted more than once for the same criminal conduct, reflected in the maxim *ne bis in idem* and also referred to as the rule against double jeopardy, is found among legal systems throughout the world (for example, Bassiouni, 1993, who surveys approximately 50 national constitutions containing the principle). The phrase is derived from the Roman law maxim *nemo bis vexari pro una et eadam causa* (a person shall not be twice vexed or tried for the same cause). The term "double jeopardy" is derived from the wording of the Fifth Amendment to the Constitution of the United States of America, which states, *inter alia*: "[N]or shall any person be subject for the same offence to be twice put in jeopardy of life or limb". It is the criminal law version of a broader principle, aimed at protecting the finality of judgments, and reflected in the doctrine *res judicata* (Theofanis, 2003). Although differing views can be found among writers and publicists, a substantial body of opinion has held to the view that the principle of *ne bis in idem* has not been recognised as a rule of custom, although there is somewhat more support for the rule as a general principle of international law. In the context of extradition law, *ne bis in idem* is more generally accepted as a rule of public international law, particularly as between the requested and requesting state where a prior prosecution and/or sentence has been imposed in the former (as opposed to where a prior prosecution took place in a third state) (Oehler, 1999, pp. 617–18). Support also exists, however, for the contrary view in relation to third states, that is, the view that *ne bis in idem* is not a rule of international law apart from treaty provisions where the prior trial has occurred in a third state (for example, the judgment of the German Federal Constitutional Court in BverfGE 75, 1 2 BvM 2/86). It can also be argued that an identifiable core of *ne bis in idem* can be found in international practice as a basis of a customary rule or general principle (Conway, 2003). Article 20 provides for *ne bis in idem* to apply both to prior proceedings by the ICC itself (Article 20(1)–(2)) and, somewhat more qualifiedly, to proceedings before national courts related to the same conduct (Article 20(3)).

In the context of the ICC, *ne bis in idem* can be seen as an aspect of the general issue of the complementarity of the jurisdiction of the ICC to the jurisdiction of national courts. The wording of Article 20 of the ICC Statute, on *ne bis in idem*, closely reflects the wording of Article 17 on admissibility. Article 17 and Article 20 together implement the principle of complementarity and, logically and as indicated by the practice of the ICC (see below), should be dealt with as a preliminary issue (generally see Kleffner, 2008, pp. 99–120; El Zeidy, 2008, p. 239 ff. 284–86). Complementarity was seen as a necessary limitation on the powers of the ICC in order to induce states to accept the limitations on their sovereignty that flow from ratification of the ICC Statute (UN doc. A/51/22 (1996), paras. 153–78). The ICC is permitted to exercise jurisdiction where national authorities have investigated or are investigating a case and decided not to prosecute where the decision not to prosecute resulted from an inability or unwillingness of the state concerned to pursue investigation or prosecution (Article 17(1)(a)–(b)) or where a prior national proceeding was for the purpose of shielding a person or was not conducted independently (Article 20(3), cross-referenced in Article 17(1)(c)), or on grounds of insufficient gravity (Article 17(1)(d)). In *Prosecutor v. Saif Al-Islam Gadaffi and Abdullah Al-Senussi*, the Appeals Chamber noted: "As the two provisions contain such similar language it is reasonable to assume that they were intended to have the same meaning" (*Prosecutor v. Saif Al-Islam Gadaffi and Abdullah Al-Senussi*, No. ICC-01/11-01/11 OA 6, Judgment on the appeal of Mr Abdullah Al-Senussi against the decision of Pre-Trial Chamber I of 11 October 2013 entitled "Decision on the admissibility of the case against Abdullah Al-Senussi", ICC-01/11-01/11-565, 24 July 2014, para. 222). The connection between the jurisdiction of the ICC and *ne bis in idem* means that Article 20 is "the last safeguard in allocating the tasks of national and international criminal justice according to the notion of complementarity" (Tallgren and Coracini, 2008, p. 672).

The reference to the "the Court" in Article 20 indicates that it is a vertical or upward *ne bis in idem* provision, that is, it bars prosecution by the ICC for conduct previously tried by the ICC, rather than applying *ne bis in idem* in a horizontal or 'downward' way regarding trials of conduct by other courts (on this terminology, see Ven den Wyngaert and Ongena, 2002, pp. 723–24; Kleffner, 2008, p. 119). However, implicitly, a horizontal application of *ne bis in idem* is applied in so far as the ICC is barred from prosecuting unless a previous national trial has been for the purpose of shielding a person or not conducted independently or impartially (Article 20(3)) (Kleffner, 2008, p. 119). Curiously, the wording does present the possibility that a prior trial before a different international court or tribunal would not exclude ICC jurisdiction under Article 20.

Bassiouni notes that a general understanding behind the adoption of the ICC Statute was that contracting States would enact similar crimes to those in Article 5 of the ICC Statute in their national legislation, as otherwise, States will find it difficult to exercise their right of complementarity. The possibility also exists, however, for the ICC to forgo its jurisdiction where a national court tries somebody for a lesser crime than those in Article 5, for example, a national court tries somebody for murder. He notes that "Article 20's *ne bis in idem* limitation supports such an approach, relying more on the similarity of the facts upon which a previous prosecution occurred than on the identity of the charges" (Bassiouni, 2005, p. 100). Further, it seems that Article 20 would actually automatically prevent an ICC trial after a national trial relating to the same facts or conduct due to the phrasing in Article 20(3) "conduct also proscribed under Article 6, 7 or 8", which applies *ne bis in idem* irrespective of the classification of the crime under national law (Kleffner, 2008, pp. 119–20), although the formulation is perhaps ambiguous as to whether it applies *ne bis in idem in concreto* or *in abstracto*.

2. In concreto and in abstracto applications of ne bis in idem

A central issue in the jurisprudence and literature on *ne bis in idem* is whether the principle operates to prevent further prosecution on the same facts as formed the basis of an existing conviction or acquittal facts (that is, an *in concreto* application, relating to the identity of the conduct) or if only further prosecution for the same offence or legal head of liability is prohibited (that is, an *in abstracto* application, relating to the legal identity of the offences). The latter limits the scope of the principle in that the same set of facts could ground a further prosecution so long as the subsequent prosecution charges the accused with a different offence. The Anglo-Saxon tradition has been to apply the *ne bis in idem* principle *in abstracto*, that is, more narrowly, whereas many continental or civil law countries reflect the principle *in concreto*, that is, more broadly. The practical difference between the two views could be lessened by the adoption of a *ne bis poena in idem* rule applied *in concreto* where *ne bis in idem* as such or is not accepted is only applied *in abstracto*. Article 20 of the ICC Statute contains a mixture of *ne bis in idem in concreto* and *in abstracto*. An *in concreto* formulation is used in Article 20(1), so that the ICC itself may not try an accused regarding the same conduct that formed the basis of a previous acquittal or conviction before the ICC. This seems to exclude the possibility that successive prosecutions could take place before the ICC relating to the same facts, but with a different crime being charged, over which the ICC has jurisdiction, in each prosecution, although the expression 'conduct which formed the basis of crimes' is perhaps ambiguous as to *in concreto* and *in abstracto* applications. Under Article 20(2), an *in abstracto* rule clearly applies to other courts (presumably this applies to both national and international courts other than the ICC): they may not try a person for the same crimes for which the person has already been tried before the ICC. In contrast, under Article 20(3), the ICC may not exercise jurisdiction relating to the same facts, an *in concreto* rule, as have been the subject of a national trial and, it seems, any national trial, irrespective of where it was (Bassiouni, 2005, p. 160), in a contracting State or otherwise.

Ne bis poena in idem is a related or corollary principle to that of *ne bis in idem* and is to the effect that sentencing and penalties already served or paid by an accused for the same offence or set of facts should be discounted when a subsequent penalty is imposed that relates to the same offence or facts. Unlike Article 9(3) of the Statute of the Special Court for Sierra Leone (established by Security Council resolution 1315/2000, UN doc. S/Res/1315 (2000)), the ICC Statute does not provide for *ne bis poena in idem*.

3. Comparing the ICC Statute with the Statutes of the International Criminal Tribunals

A further feature distinguishing the approach in the ICC Statute and from the Statutes of the *ad hoc* tribunals is the inclusion in the latter of the concept of "ordinary crimes": the international tribunals are prohibited from retrying someone if the accused has already been tried for acts constituting serious violations of international humanitarian law except where the act for which he or she was tried was characterised in the national court as an ordinary crime (or where the national trial was essentially a show trial). The ICC Statute eventually omitted the first exception relating to ordinary crimes, confining itself in Article 20 to the 'show trial exception', because of disagreement at the negotiations as to the compatibility of the "ordinary crimes" rule with the underlying *ne bis in idem* protection (Holmes, 1999, pp. 57–58). It seems that arguments made in favour of including the exception because the characterisation of a crime as an international one had a particular deterrent or retributive effect (greater than that associated with a conviction for ordinary crimes) were rejected (Holmes, 1999, p. 58). The effect is that the ICC Statute applies *ne bis in idem* largely *in concreto* to prior national trials, that is, more fully, and that the international criminal tribunals apply it *in abstracto* (except for the Special Tribunal for Lebanon).

In another way, the ICC Statute can be seen as restricting *ne bis in idem* (see the discussion in Finlay, 2009, pp. 221–48). The reason for this is that the ICC has jurisdiction under the complementarity principle where there has already been a trial, but where the proceedings (a) were for the purpose of shielding the person concerned from criminal responsibility for crimes within the jurisdiction of the ICC or (b) otherwise were not conducted independently or impartially. In other words, complementarity in effect institutes a qualified *ne bis in idem* principle. However, this is so in the case of most jurisdictions, given the end to ensure that the guilty are punished (Finlay, 2009, p. 224). Given the seriousness of the crimes over which the ICC has jurisdiction, the moral outrage felt against the accused is likely to be stronger than is the case with ordinary crimes, which increases the importance of ensuring the guilty are brought to justice (Finlay, 2009, p. 227).

The reason for the inclusion of *ne bis in idem* in the ICC Statute are similar to its operation at national level, albeit that the relationship with national courts in the context of State sovereignty is an additional consideration (Finlay, 2009, p. 226) (one dealt with by the complementarity principle in the context of the ICC): consideration of fairness to an accused being the primary consideration. A second trial disadvantages an accused in several respects: i. it subjects the accused to continued and more prolonged anxiety of punishment; ii. it may undermine the defence by allowing the prosecution more advance notice of what will likely be raised by the defence at trial; iii. it puts further strain on the resources of the accused to sustain a defence at trial, and iv. it increases the risk of an innocent person being convicted (Finlay, 2009, p. 223, citing Justice Black in *Green v. United States*, 355 U.S. 184, 187–88 (1957) on points i. and iv. in particular). Other reasons for *ne bis in idem* include judicial economy in avoiding repeated trials of the same conduct, the importance of finality and certainty as to the outcome of legal proceedings, and the incentivising of thorough investigations and prosecutions (because the police and prosecutors will only get one opportunity of a trial) (Finlay, 2009, p. 226).

As Kittichaisaree observes, a notable feature of the ICC Statute is that Article 20 appears in Part 2, on jurisdiction, admissibility, and applicable law, rather than Part 3, on general principles of criminal law (in which, *inter alia*, grounds for excluding criminal responsibility are set out in Article 31) (Kittichaisaree, 2001, p. 29) (the Statute of the Special Court for Sierra Leone is not organised into parts). However, this is not necessarily because *ne bis in idem* is not a general principle of criminal law in the broad sense of a general principle used in Article 38(c) of the Statute of the International Court of Justice. As Kittichaisaree notes, the placing of the *ne bis in idem* provisions in the Statute reflects the fact that *ne bis in idem* is so closely related in the scheme of the Statute to admissibility; it is a procedural bar to the ICC's jurisdiction (rather than a ground for excluding responsibility) (Kittichaisaree, 2001, p. 29). More critically, Bassiouni comments:

> Finally, there is no valid methodological explanation for the separation and placement of the provisions concerning the presumption of innocence (Article 66) in Part 6 and the provisions concerning *ne bis in idem* (Article 20) and the applicable law (Article 21) in Part 2. All of these provisions properly belong in Part 3 of the Statute, which deals with the general principles of criminal responsibility (Bassiouni, 2005, p. 85).

La Rosa points out that the admission of evidence of conduct that has sustained prior convictions, on the basis that it is evidence of a consistent pattern of conduct, may result in a violation of *ne bis in idem* in that the same evidence could ground further convictions (La Rosa, 1997, p. 323). However, given that the ICC chambers will be staffed by professional and experienced judges, the likelihood that the prejudicial effect of such evidence will unfairly tilt the Court's findings against the accused is arguably less than is the case in a jury system (the general rationale for the exclusion of character evidence in the common law tradition, as noted above, relates to the role of the jury as triers of fact). One possible approach to the issue would be to admit such evidence, but not to treat it as being alone a sufficient basis for a conviction, other accompanying or corroborating evidence being necessary. Adoption of such an approach in the ICC and other international criminal tribunals, coupled with the role of the judges as arbiters of fact, could ensure that an exaggerated significance is not attributed to evidence that has sustained a prior conviction or that such evidence might be used to compensate for a lack of compelling evidence in a current case (see generally Bogdan, 2002; Conway, 2003b, pp. 377–82).

Preparatory works:

Ne bis in idem as it is referred to now in Article 17(1)(c) was omitted from the 1994 Draft Statute prepared by the International Law Commission, as it was considered to be a self-evident principle, but was included in the final Statute subsequently for the sake of clarity after the 1998 Preparatory Committee raised the issue (Tallgren and Reisinger Coracini, 2008, p. 68).

Trial Chamber II in the case of *Prosecutor v. Germain Katanga and Mathieu Ngudjolo Chui* provided an explanation of the drafting process regarding *ne bis in idem*:

> Originally, the *ne bis in idem* principle was not included in Article 35 (current Article 17) of the Draft Statute for an International Criminal Court. The only reference to *ne bis in idem* was contained in Article 42 of the Draft Statute (current Article 20), which followed Article 41, which became the current Article 67, which defined the rights of the accused, in Part V "The Trial". This belated inclusion of the *ne bis in idem* principle in Article 17(1)(c) as a basis for challenging admissibility is therefore explained essentially by the need to protect the rights of the accused, in contrast to sub-paragraphs (a), (b) and (d) of the same Article, the purpose of which is to safeguard the sovereign rights of States and to ensure the cases brought before the Court are of sufficient gravity. Moreover, it should be recalled that the *ne bis in idem* principle is defined in Article 20 to which Article 17(1)(c) only makes reference (*Prosecutor v. Germain Katanga and*

1. Except as provided in this Statute,[244] no person shall be tried before the Court with respect to conduct which formed the basis of crimes for which the person has been convicted or acquitted by the Court.[245]

2. No person shall be tried by another court for a crime referred to in Article 5 for which that person has already been convicted or acquitted by the Court.[246]

Mathieu Ngudjolo Chui, Reasons for the Oral Decision on the Motion Challenging the Admissibility of the Case (Article 19 of the Statute), ICC-01/04-01/07-1213-tENG, 16th June 2009, para. 48).

Tallgren and Coracini note that during the last session of the Preparatory Committee in 1998, Article 20(2) was worded so as to include subsequent trials "for conduct constituting a crime referred to in Article 5", that is, a broader *in concreto* application. The committee changed the wording to ensure that a State could charge a person with a crime relating to the same conduct forming the basis of an ICC conviction, that is, a narrower *in abstracto* application. A number of delegations objected "that the proposed additions would undermine the protection of *ne bis in idem* completely" (Tallgren and Coracini, 2008, p. 686 and further references therein).

Author: Gerard Conway.

[244] This makes it clear that *ne bis in idem* is without prejudice to the appeals and revisions that are provided for under Part VIII of the ICC Statute (Finlay, 2009, p. 229).

Author: Gerard Conway.

[245] One of the main issues of interpretation that arises here is the meaning of acquittal, at what stage in proceedings is a person considered to be acquitted. In theory, it might be argued that anytime a prosecution is ceased, there is an acquittal, even if the prosecution is terminated prior to the trial of the merits occurring. The issue is yet to be decided, but has been addressed in submissions to the ICC (see case law in the comment on Article 20(3)(b)).

Author: Gerard Conway.

[246] Article 20(2) prevents a person convicted or acquitted by the ICC from being subsequently tried by another court only for the offences for which he has already been convicted or acquitted by the ICC. Thus, unlike the provision regarding prior national trials in Article 20(3), subsequent national trials are only subject to *ne bis in idem in abstracto*, that is, a national court may try an accused for the same conduct, but just not for the same offence that formed the ICC conviction. As Finlay notes, this also means that a national court could try an accused for an offence under Article 5 of the ICC Statute, so long as that offence had not formed the ICC conviction, for example, a national court could try for a crime against humanity, after an accused has been convicted for genocide before the ICC (Finlay, 2009, p. 230). This reflects that the crimes over which the ICC has jurisdiction have a very specific *mens rea* (Finlay, 2009, p. 231), which cannot be assimilated to the *mens rea* of ordinary crimes. If *ne bis in idem* prevented subsequent national trials on an *in concreto* basis, there could occur a gap in prosecution, because evidence of *mens rea* for an Article 5 crime was found to be insufficient at trial before the ICC, but any national prosecution for a 'lesser' crime would still be prevented (Finlay, 2009, p. 232).

A practical issue that may arise is the scenario whereby national proceedings, whether investigation or prosecution, would commence while ICC proceedings were ongoing, that is, where the ICC proceedings had not yet resulted. This is not addressed in Article 20(2). The issue has been raised in submissions of the prosecutor and the Libyan government in its submission in *Prosecutor v. Saif Al-Islam Gadaffi and Abdullah Al-Senussi*. The Libyan government, for example, noted that this involved a degree of speculation as to what is likely to be the result of both processes and that the test of this issue must be undertaken in a manner appropriate to the stage reached at the time of the admissibility assessment by both the domestic and the international processes and, further, that the question must be whether the co-existence of both the international and the domestic processes could violate the principle of *ne bis in idem*. Applying this test, it concluded that only where the domestic prosecution has reached a verdict could there be a question of the violation of *ne bis in idem* (The Libyan Government's further submissions in reply to the Prosecution and Gaddafi Responses to 'Document in Support of Libya's Appeal against the Decision on the admissibility of the case against Saif Al-Islam Gaddafi', *Prosecutor v. Saif Al-Islam Gadaffi and Abdullah Al-Senussi*, ICC-01/11-01/11-454-red, 23rd September 2013, paras. 32–34 (without citing any authority)). In its response, the Prosecutor commented that it did not wish to rely on *ne bis in idem*, but that jurisprudence related to *ne bis in idem* may be of assistance given the close interlink between *ne bis in idem* and the complementarity provisions, their common function in determining forum allocation and, most notably, the similarity in the inquiry regarding whether the two cases are indeed "the same", and what "same" means (Prosecution Response to 'The Libyan Government's further submissions in reply to the Prosecution and Gaddafi Responses to Document in Support of Libya's Appeal against the Decision on the admissibility of the case against Saif Al-Islam Gaddafi', *Prosecutor v. Saif Al-Islam Gadaffi and Abdullah Al-Senussi*, 30th September 2013, paras. 43–45 (without citing any authority)).

For which the person has been convicted or acquitted: As with Article 20(1), the main issue of interpretation here under Article 20(2) is what stage an accused could be said to be acquitted. At what stage or point must be reached for a prior ICC proceeding to trigger Article 20, for example, if the case is dealt with by the Pre-Trial Chamber only, or is withdrawn by the prosecutor during the trial stage, that is, before the trial chamber? This awaits a judgment from the Appeals Chamber itself, but in 2014, parties to the proceedings, including the prosecution, have argued that *ne bis in idem* applies only if there is a decision on the merits of the case resulting in a verdict of conviction or acquittal, and not at the confirmation stage before the Pre-Trial Chamber (*Prosecutor v. Uhuru Muigai Kenyatta*, Prosecutors' Submissions on the Ne Bis In Idem Principle, ICC-01/09-02/11, 10 February 2014; *Prosecutor v. Uhuru Muigai Kenyatta*, Victims' Observations on the Ne Bis In Idem Principle, ICC-01/09-02/11, 17 February 2014). For example, in Uhuru Muigai Kenyatta, the prosecutor noted that Article 20 should "apply only to res judicata and not to proceedings discontinued for technical reasons" (Prosecutors' Submissions on the Ne Bis In Idem Principle, *Prosecutor v. Uhuru Muigai Kenyatta*, p. 5, citing 1996 Preparatory Committee Report, vol. I, art. 42, para. 170). This argument was supported by the Trial Chamber in December 2014 and March 2015, when the prosecutor withdrew charges following a direction from the Trial Chamber (in December 2014) to withdraw the charges or provide an indication that the evidentiary base had improved to a degree which would justify proceeding to trial. In its decision of December 2014, it had noted the principle of ne bis in idem would not attach, and it would be open to the prosecution to bring 'new charges against the accused at a later date, based on the same or similar factual circumstances, should it obtain sufficient evidence to support such a course of action' (*Prosecutor v. Uhuru Muigai Kenyatta*, Decision of 3 December 2014, ICC-O 1/09-02111-981, para. 56, cited in Decision of 13 March 2015, ICC-01/09-02/11, para. 9).

A further issue is what significance attaches to Rule 150(1) of the Rules of Procedure and Evidence, according to which a conviction becomes non-appealable 30 days after notification of the decision or sentence. The same issue arises here, to use terminology from the United States, as to when "jeopardy attaches": is it immediately upon conviction or acquittal or 30 days after when the possibility of appeal ceases? Tallgren and Coracini note that the wording of Article 20(1) excludes *ne bis in idem* regarding appeals and revisions under Chapter VIII because it only prevents a person from being subsequently tried before the ICC "except as provided in this Statute". This wording would be superfluous if *ne bis in idem* only applied when a judgment become 'final', or non-appealable. Tallgren and Coracini note that this interpretation strengthens

3. No person who has been tried by another court for conduct also proscribed under Article 6, 7, 8 or 8 *bis* shall be tried by the Court with respect to the same conduct unless the proceedings in the other court:[247]

    (a) Were for the purpose of shielding the person concerned from criminal responsibility for crimes within the jurisdiction of the Court; or[248]

    (b) Otherwise were not conducted independently or impartially in accordance with the norms of due process recognized by international law and were conducted in a manner which, in the circumstances, was inconsistent with an intent to bring the person concerned to justice.[249]

---

the *ne bis in idem* protection for an accused (Tallgren and Coracini, 2008, pp. 683–84), that is, in relation to subsequent national trials relating to the same conduct.

Author: Gerard Conway.

[247] The main interpretative issue here relates to interpreting the 'same conduct'. No jurisprudence from the ICC exists on this issue to date. It has been the subject of submissions in *Prosecutor v. Saif Al-Islam Gadaffi and Abdullah Al-Senussi* (noted above). Essentially, this appears to be a question of fact. One approach may be to apply a *Blockburger*-style approach. In *United States v. Blockburger* (284 US 299 (1932)), the United States Supreme Court held that multiple convictions can be imposed under different statutory provisions if each statutory provision re- quires proof of a fact which the other does not. The *Blockburger* test was confirmed in *Rutledge v. United States* (517 US 292 (1996)). Applied to the same conduct scenario here, the issue is whether the same conduct could supply the elements of an offence both before the ICC and at national level. This latter test is potentially less demanding than a 'same conduct test' (see, for example, the discussion in Carter, 2010, p. 171), but would depend on how 'same conduct' was characterised, narrowly or broadly, and the two approaches could run into each other.

Author: Gerard Conway.

[248] This is among the more difficult provisions in the Statute to define. It essentially relates to the intention of prosecuting or judicial authorities, which essentially a subjective matter of the state of mind of national authorities. It is unlikely that national authorities would make explicit any intention that national proceedings were be essentially a sham to protect the accused. Thus, it seems that evidence to satisfy this provision would only emerge accidentally or without it being intended by the national authorities involved. As with almost any legal provision, Article 20(3)(a) can be interpreted narrowly or broadly. Here, the narrowness or breadth would seem to depend on what threshold of evidence is required to trigger Article 20(3)(a). By analogy with common law authority on bias as a breach of natural justice, for example, it could be interpreted quite broadly as applying where a reasonable apprehension (for example, *R v. Gough* [1993] AC 658, 668, 670 [1993], 2 All ER 724) could exist that national proceedings were for the purpose of shielding an accused and to allow circumstantial evidence to support this.

Author: Gerard Conway.

[249] Compared to Article 20(3)(a), this is a more objective test. As with that provision, it is open to broader or narrower interpretations. A broad interpretation would allow strict scrutiny of national procedural law to determine its compliance with due process. However, given that the ICC itself is a product of different national legal traditions and has many compromise elements in its procedure, it is more likely that the ICC would apply an approach based on minimum notions of due process reflected in international legal instruments.

Case law:

Ne bis in idem could arise at various stage of the trial process before the ICC. The Pre-trial Chamber may need to address the issue or it may be raised later by the defence so that the Trial

Chamber itself must address it. The Appellate Chamber will ultimately decide on issues of interpretation. To date, the Trial Chambers or Appellate Chamber have not fully dealt with Article 20, but submissions to the ICC in pending cases have been referred to above.

Case law from the Trial Chambers has dealt with the procedural question of when *ne bis in idem* should be raised. In *Prosecutor v. Mathieu Ngudjolo Chui*, the Trial Chamber held that once a trial chamber has been set up, *ne bis in idem* should only be raised exceptionally and with the permission of the Trial Chamber itself. This indicates that *ne bis in idem* should normally be dealt with by the Pre-Trial Chamber (*Prosecutor v. Mathieu Ngudjolo Chui*, Case No. ICC-01/04-01/07 (2007), Judgment of Trial Chamber II, 12 June 2009, p. 4; see also *Prosecutor v. Jean-Pierre Bemba Gombo*, Case No. ICC-01/05-01/08, Decision on the Admissibility and Abuse of Process Challenges, ICC-01/05-01/08-802, 24 June 2010, para. 209).

Cross-references:
Article 17(1)(c).

Doctrine:

1. Attila Bogdan, "Cumulative Charges, Convictions and Sentencing at the Ad Hoc International Tribunals for the Former Yugoslavia and Rwanda", in *Melbourne Journal of International Law*, 2002, vol. 3, pp. 1–32.

2. Linda E. Carter, "The Principle of Complementarity and the International Criminal Court", in *Santa Clara Journal of International Law*, 2010, vol. 8, no. 1, pp. 165–98.

3. M. Cherif Bassiouni, "Human Rights in the Context of Criminal Justice: Identifying International Procedural Protections and Equivalent Protections in National Constitutions", in *Duke Journal of Comparative and International Law*, 1993, vol. 3, pp. 235–97.

4. M. Cherif Bassiouni, *The Legislative History of the International Criminal Court: Introduction, Analysis, and Integrated Text*, Transnational Publishers, Ardsley, NY, 2005.

5. Gerard Conway, "*Ne Bis in Idem* in International Law", in *International Criminal Law Review*, 2003, vol. 3, no. 3, pp. 217–44 (Conway (2003a)).

6. Gerard Conway, "*Ne Bis in Idem* and the International Criminal Tribunals", in *Criminal Law Forum*, 2003, vol. 14, pp. 351–83 (Conway(2003b)).

7. Mohamed El Zeidy, *The Principle of Complementarity in International Criminal Law: Origin, Development and Practice*, Brill, The Hague, 2008.

8. Lorraine Finlay, "Does the International Criminal Court Protect Against Double Jeopardy: An Analysis of Article 20 of the Rome Statute", in *University of California Davis Law Review*, 2009, vol. 15, no. 2, pp. 221–48, p. 222.

9. John T. Holmes, "The Principle of Complementarity", in Roy S. Lee (ed.), *The International Criminal Court: The Making of the Rome Statute: Issues, Negotiations, Results*, Kluwer Law International, The Hague, 1999.

10. Kriangsak Kittichaisaree, *International Criminal Law*, Oxford University Press, Oxford, 2001.

11. Jann K. Kleffner, *Complementarity in the Rome Statute and National Criminal Jurisdictions*, Oxford University Press, Oxford, 2008.

12. Ann-Marie La Rosa, "A Tremendous Challenge for the International Criminal Tribunals: Reconciling the Requirements of International Humanitarian Law with Those of Fair Trial", in *International Review of the Red Cross*, 1997, no. 321, pp. 635, 637–42.

13. Dietrich Oehler, "The European System", in M. Cherif Bassiouni (ed.), *International Criminal Law: Procedural and Enforcement Mechanisms*, 2nd ed., Transnational Publishers, Berlin, 1999.

14. Immi Tallgren and Astrid Reisinger Coracini, "Article 20: *Ne bis in Idem*", in Otto Triffterer (ed.), *Commentary on the Rome Statute of the International Criminal Court: Observers' Notes, Article by Article*, 2nd ed., C.H. Beck/Hart/Nomos, Munich/Oxford/Baden-Baden, 2008, pp. 669–99.

15. Rosa Theofanis, "The Doctrine of *Res Judicata* in International Criminal Law", in *International Criminal Law Review*, 2003, vol. 3, no. 3, pp. 195–216.

16. Christine Van den Wyngaert and Tom Ongena, "*Ne Bis in Idem* Principle, including the Issue of Amnesty", in Antonio Cassese, Paola Gaeta and John R.W.D. Jones (eds.), *The Rome Statute of the International Criminal Court: A Commentary*, Oxford University Press, Oxford, 2002.

Author: Gerard Conway.

Article 21
Applicable law[250]

1. The Court shall apply:

   (a) In the first place, this Statute, Elements of Crimes and its Rules of Procedure and Evidence;[251]

---

[250] *General remarks*:

Article 38(1) of the Statute of the International Court of Justice ('ICJ') is often viewed as a provision that enumerates the "well-established sources of international law" (*Prosecutor v. Kupreškić et al.*, Judgment, TC, ICTY, 14 January 2000, para. 540). There treaty law, customary international law ('CIL') and general principles of law are named as the primary sources of international law, and judicial decisions and the doctrine as subsidiary means for the determination of rules of law. Early on the ICC Statute drafters, however, felt a need for a special provision on applicable law for the ICC (see further, for example, Schabas, 2010, pp. 383–85). The outcome was Article 21 of the ICC Statute, which includes both ICC-specific internal sources of law (Article 21(1)(a) and 21(2)) and general external sources of law (Article 21(1)(b)–(c)) (Bitti, 2009, pp. 288, 293). The aim of the Article was to modify the applicable law to better suit the criminal law context in which the Court operates (deGuzman, 2008, p. 702). This was mainly achieved by enhancing the legal relevance of the Court's internal written sources of law. As the *ad hoc* tribunals apply the general sources of public international law and the ICC its Article 21, the applicable law is a part of international criminal law where the law is fragmented.

Article 21 focuses on enumerating and ranking the applicable legal sources, rather than on elaborating how they should be identified (especially relevant in connection to non-written sources of law) or interpreted (especially relevant in connection to written sources of law). This entails that there are many aspects of the applicable law that still requires recourse to general international law. General international law, for example, guides how CIL or general principles of law should be identified. As State practice (including treaty ratifications) and case law can be relevant as evidence of more than one type of source of law, the relationship between the different international sources of law is complicated. The inclusion of external sources of law in Article 21 signifies that these complexities are also part of the ICC system of applicable law. In this regard, Cryer has noted that the "interrelationship of sources is more complex than Article 21's apparently rigid hierarchy implies" as "the overlap between the sources is too complex to reduced to simple formulae, including by reference to hierarchy" (Cryer, 2009, pp. 393–94).

Furthermore, Article 21 does not explicitly consider the legal relevance of all types of material that often are used in international legal argumentation. Article 21 is, for instance, quiet on the legal weight of international case law, the writings of highly qualified publicists, *travaux préparatoires*, and instruments adopted by international organisations, such as UN General Assembly resolutions. There are also ICC internal legal instruments, such as the Regulations of the Court, which legal position is not explicitly addressed in Article 21. Also, for example, the official actions taken by the ICC Assembly of States Parties are not included as a source of applicable law in Article 21 (*Prosecutor v. Lubanga*, Judgment on the Appeals against the "Decision Establishing the Principles and Procedures to Be Applied to Reparations" of 7 August 2012 with Amended Order for Reparations (Annex A) and Public Annexes 1 and 2, AC, 3 March 2015, para. 46).

Author: Mikaela Heikkilä.

[251] In Article 21(1)(a), the ICC Statute, the Elements of Crime ('Elements') and the Rules of Procedure and Evidence ('RPE') are enumerated as the legal sources that the Court shall apply in

---

the first place. Article 21(1) thus establishes a hierarchy between the various sources of law and puts the Court's own internal legal instruments at the top of the hierarchy. Article 21(1)(a) does not, however, clearly settle the internal relationship between these three sources of law. A hierarchy is instead established elsewhere. Article 51(5) provides that in the event of conflict between the Statute and the RPE, the Statute shall prevail. In an explanatory note to the RPE, it is furthermore emphasised that, in all cases, the RPE should be read in conjunction with and subject to the provisions of the Statute. Article 9, on its part, stipulates the Elements shall be consistent with the Statute, and that their function is to assist the Court in the interpretation and application of the crime definitions in the Statute.

The hierarchical relationship between the Statute and the RPE has been reaffirmed in the Court's case law. For example, in a decision in the Situation in Democratic Republic of the Congo, a Pre-Trial Chamber ('PTC') noted that the RPE is an instrument that is subordinate to the Statute and that a provision of the RPE cannot be interpreted in such a way as to narrow the scope of an Article of the Statute (*Situation in the Democratic Republic of the Congo*, Decision on the Applications for Participation in the Proceedings of VPRS 1, VPRS 2, VPRS 3, VPRS 4, VPRS 5 and VPRS 6, PTC, 17 January 2006, para. 47). The question to what extent the judges are obliged to follow the Elements has, however, been more controversial. Whereas Article 21(1) stipulates that the Court shall apply the Elements, Article 9 seems to give them merely an assisting role. The question has been considered in a PTC decision, where the majority held that the Elements must be applied unless a Chamber finds an irreconcilable contradiction between the Elements and the Statute (*Prosecutor v. Al Bashir*, Decision on the Prosecution's Application for a Warrant of Arrest against Omar Hassan Ahmad Al Bashir, PTC, 4 March 2009, para. 128). The minority Judge, on the other hand, held that the wording in Article 9 of the ICC Statute clearly gives forth that the Elements are not binding for the judges (*Prosecutor v.* Al Bashir, Decision on the Prosecution's Application for a Warrant of Arrest against Omar Hassan Ahmad Al Bashir, Separate and Partly Dissenting Opinion of Judge Anita Ušacka, PTC, 4 March 2009, para. 17). The minority view has been supported by a number of scholars (for example, Hochmayr, 2014, p. 658; Triffterer, 2009, pp. 387–88; von Hebel, 2001, pp. 7–8).

The ICC's internal legal sources furthermore include some instruments which hierarchical position is not explicitly settled in Article 21. Some of these are, however, anticipated in the ICC Statute. Article 44(3) stipulates that the Assembly of State Parties shall adopt Staff Regulations, and Article 52 that the judges shall adopt Regulations of the Court. The Regulations of the Office of the Prosecutor, the Regulations of the Registry, and the Code of Professional Conduct for Counsel, on the other hand, are foreseen by Rules 9, 14, respectively 8 of the ICC RPE. While it is clear that all these documents are subordinate to the three major internal sources of law, their internal relationship and relationship to the Court's external sources is not as evident. Schabas has, in this regard, submitted that "in the event of conflict judges will have to find solutions based on general principles of interpretation [...] and with reference to the authority of the body responsible for adopting the text" (Schabas, 2010, p. 387). All internal written sources of law furthermore appear to rank higher than the Court's external sources of law. In the Lubanga case, the Appeals Chamber did not find it necessary to consider whether Regulation 55 of the Court was consistent with general principles of international law. The central question was rather whether the Regulation was consistent with the Statute and the RPE (*Prosecutor v. Lubanga*, ICC A. Ch., Judgment on the Appeals of Mr Lubanga Dyilo and the Prosecutor against the Decision of Trial Chamber I of 14 July 2009 Entitled "Decision Giving Notice to the Parties and Participants that the Legal Characterisation of the Facts May be Subject to Change in Accordance with Regulation 55(2) of the Regulations of the Court", 8 December 2009, paras. 66–81).

When the judges apply the Court's internal legal instruments, the question of how the instruments should be interpreted is often the controversial question. Interpretation in general is not addressed in the ICC Statute. Article 21(3) only stipulates that interpretations must be con-

(b) In the second place, where appropriate, applicable treaties and the principles and rules of international law, including the established principles of the international law of armed conflict;[252]

---

sistent with internationally recognised human rights, and Article 22(2) that the definition of crimes shall be strictly construed and shall not be extended by analogy. As the ICC Statute is a treaty, the Court has held that guidance for interpretation can be found in the 1969 Vienna Convention on the Law of Treaties (for example, *Situation in the Democratic Republic of the Congo*, Judgment on the Prosecutor's Application for Extraordinary Review of Pre-Trial Chamber I's 31 March 2006 Decision Denying Leave to Appeal, AC, 13 July 2006, para. 33; see also *Prosecutor v. Lubanga*, PT. Ch. I, Decision on the Practices of Witness Familiarisation and Witness Proofing, 8 November 2006, para. 8). Article 31 of the Vienna Convention gives forth that in interpretation, the focus shall be on literal, contextual and teleological considerations. More specifically, the Appeals Chamber has held that:

> The rule governing the interpretation of a section of the law is its wording read in context and in light of its object and purpose. The context of a given legislative provision is defined by the particular sub-section of the law read as a whole in conjunction with the section of an enactment in its entirety. Its objects may be gathered from the chapter of the law in which the particular section is included and its purposes from the wider aims of the law as may be gathered from its preamble and general tenor of the treaty (*Situation in the Democratic Republic of the Congo*, ICC A. Ch., Judgment on the Prosecutor's Application for Extraordinary Review of Pre-Trial Chamber I's 31 March 2006 Decision Denying Leave to Appeal, 13 July 2006, para. 33)

In line with Article 32 of the Vienna Convention, the *travaux préparatoires* of the ICC Statute can be used to confirm interpretations made based on literal, contextual and teleological readings (for example, *Situation in the Democratic Republic of the Congo*, ICC A. Ch., Judgment on the Prosecutor's Application for Extraordinary Review of Pre-Trial Chamber I's 31 March 2006 Decision Denying Leave to Appeal, 13 July 2006, paras. 40–41, and *Prosecutor v. Katanga*, ICC A. Ch., Judgment on the Appeal of Mr. Germain Katanga against the Decision of Pre-Trial Chamber I Entitled "Decision on the Defence Request Concerning Languages", 27 May 2008, para. 50. See also *Prosecutor v. Lubanga*, ICC T. Ch., Judgment pursuant to Article 74 of the Statute, 14 March 2012, para. 621).

Cross-references:

Articles 9(1) and 9(3), 22(2), 44(3), 51(4)–(5) and Article 52.

Rules 8, 9, and 14.

Author: Mikaela Heikkilä.

[252] In contrast to the ICTY and ICTR statutes which "are retrospective and [...] not themselves [substantive criminal] law" but "rather, pointers to a law existing in some form in the rarefied sphere of international law" (Zahar and Sluiter, 2008, p. 80), the ICC Statute is a non-retroactive written instrument which aim is to function as a code of criminal law and procedure. As such, the role played by internal respectively external legal sources of law is different before the ICC and the *ad hoc* tribunals. Even though the aim of the ICC's internal legal sources is to comprehensively establish the legal framework according to which the Court shall function, situations can emerge where a legal question cannot be answered with reference to these instruments. As such, it is important that there are external legal sources to which the Court may rely on in situations where the Court's internal legal sources are quiet or unclear. In this regard, Article 21(1)(b) establishes that the Court shall apply, in the second place, where appropriate, applicable treaties and the principles and rules of international law, including the established principles of the international law of armed conflict.

The phrase "in the second place" emphasises that the applicable treaties and the principles and rules of international law in the ICC legal system are legal sources that hierarchically are below the legal sources mentioned in Article 21(1)(a). This has also been stressed in case law. The ICC has held that the external sources of law can only be resorted to when two conditions are met: (i) there is a lacuna in the written law contained in the Statute, the Elements and the RPE; and (ii) the lacuna cannot be filled by the application of the criteria of interpretation provided in the Vienna Convention and Article 21(3) of the ICC Statute (*Prosecutor v. Al Bashir*, ICC PT. Ch. I, Decision on the Prosecution's Application for a Warrant of Arrest against Omar Hassan Ahmad Al Bashir, 4 March 2009, para. 44. See also for example, *Prosecutor v. Ruto et al.*, ICC PT. Ch. I, Decision on the Confirmation of Charges Pursuant to Article 61(7)(a) and (b) of the ICC Statute, 23 January 2012, para. 289). In this regard, the ICC has in relation to modes of responsibility found that since the Statute in detail regulates the applicable modes of responsibility, it is not necessary to consider whether CIL admits or discards some modes of responsibility (*Prosecutor v. Katanga and Ngudjolo Chui*, ICC PT. Ch., Decision on the Confirmation of Charges, ICC-01/04-01/07-717, 30 September 2008, para. 508).

Importantly, the fact that a question is not regulated in ICC's internal legal instruments does not necessarily mean that there is a lacuna that must be filled by applying external legal sources (See further for example, *Situation in the Democratic Republic of the Congo*, Judgment on the Prosecutor's Application for Extraordinary Review of Pre-Trial Chamber I's 31 March 2006 Decision Denying Leave to Appeal, AC, 13 July 2006, paras. 33–39). Article 21(1)(b) contains the criterion of "where appropriate", which emphasises that the judges have a certain discretion in the use of the external legal sources. In connection to witness proofing, the Lubanga Trial Chamber, indicated that especially in connection to procedural questions a detailed analysis must be conducted before a norm that cannot be found in the internal "ICC legislation" is recognised based on Article 21(1)(b). More specifically, the Trial Chamber held that:

> Article 21 of the Statute requires the Chamber to apply first the Statute, Elements of Crimes and Rules of the ICC. Thereafter, if ICC legislation is not definitive on the issue, the Trial Chamber should apply, where appropriate, principles and rules of international law. In the instant case, the issue before the Chamber is procedural in nature. While this would not, ipso facto, prevent all procedural issues from scrutiny under Article 21(1)(b), the Chamber does not consider the procedural rules and jurisprudence of the ad hoc Tribunals to be automatically applicable to the ICC without detailed analysis (*Prosecutor v. Lubanga*, ICC T. Ch., Decision Regarding the Practices Used to Prepare and Familiarise Witnesses for Giving Testimony at Trial, 30 November 2007, para. 44).

Schabas has noted that Article 21(1)(b) "actually contains two distinct sources, with no suggested rank among them" (Schabas, 2010, p. 390), namely(1) applicable treaties; and (2) principles and rules of international law. As regards treaties, the meaning of the word "applicable" has been debated (see further, for example, Hochmayr, 2014, p. 666; deGuzman, 2008, pp. 705–6). It appears that applicable treaties at least include those to which the Court itself is a party, *viz.* the Negotiated Relationship Agreement between the International Criminal Court and the United Nations (2004) and the Headquarters Agreement between the International Criminal Court and the Host State (2007). A more difficult question is, however, the applicability of other treaties, such as human rights and international humanitarian law treaties. As noted by Pellet, it is difficult to see how inter-governmental treaties in general would be applicable *as treaty law* before the ICC (Pellet, 2002, pp. 1068–69). The main rule in connection to treaties is that they only are binding for those States that have ratified them (see further, for example, Milanović, 2011, p. 25 ff.). Furthermore, as regards the content of treaties, most treaties only establish State obligations to prohibit or criminalise certain behaviour (international illegality) and not international criminality *per se*. Before the ICC, the significance of treaty law is therefore primarily that it can affect the interpretation of ICC provisions and the evaluation of the existence of CIL norms.

Secondly, Article 21(1)(b) refers to the "principles and rules of international law". This concept is perplexing in that it differs from the concept of CIL that is generally used in public international law. While most scholars agree that principles and rules of international law include CIL, there are different opinions as to whether there are also other principles and rules of international law (see further, for example, deGuzman, 2008, pp. 706–7; Pellet, 2002, pp. 1070–73). It should namely be noted that general principles of law derived from national laws of legal systems of the world are covered by Article 21(1)(c). DeGuzman has, in this regard, suggested that principles and rules could be based on the international legal conscience, the nature of the international community and natural law (deGuzman, 2008, p. 707). She thus suggests that there is something that could be characterised as general principles of a genuine international origin (cf. Schlütter, 2010, p. 75) that are not created by States through their practice and will in the same way as positive international law. The existence of such international law is, however, disputed and as such deGuzman's submission must be regarded as controversial. There are also other understandings of general principles of law. Some scholars find that there are general principles of international law that generally have their origin in state practice (or the existing sources of international law), but which "have been so long and so generally accepted as to be no longer directly connected with state practice" (Brownlie, 2008, p. 19. See also, for example, Malanczuk, 1997, pp. 48–49). Exactly how such general principles emerge and how they should be identified is, however, unclear.

In this regard, it is interesting that the ICC sometimes has referred to the practice of other international/hybrid criminal tribunals by reference to Article 21(1)(b) (see, for example, *Prosecutor v. Mudacumura*, ICC PT. Ch. I, Decision on the Prosecutor's Application under Article 58, 13 July 2012, para. 63, fn. 128). The case law of these tribunals has then often been put forward as evidence of a "widely accepted practice in international criminal law" regarding a certain matter (cf. Lubanga, ICC PT. Ch. I, Decision on the Practices of Witness Familiarisation and Witness Proofing, 8 November 2006, para. 33). The ICC has also referred to case law from other courts, such as the ICJ (see, for example, *Prosecutor v. Katanga and Ngudjolo Chui*, ICC P. Ch., Decision on the Confirmation of Charges, ICC-01/04-01/07-717, 30 September 2008, para. 238). Such argumentation could be seen as evidence of a viewpoint that international case law can function as an autonomous source of law before the ICC. Despite some statements to this effect, it, however, appears that the prevailing approach of the ICC to international case law is that "decisions of other international courts and tribunals are not part of the directly applicable law under Article 21" (*Prosecutor v. Lubanga*, ICC T. Ch., Judgment pursuant to Article 74 of the Statute, 14 March 2012, para. 603). The case law can only be "indicative of a principle or rule of international law" (*Prosecutor v. Ruto et al.*, ICC PT. Ch. I, Decision on the Confirmation of Charges Pursuant to Article 61(7)(a) and (b) of the ICC Statute, 23 January 2012, para. 289), but exactly how remains unclear (on the legal relevance of international case law, see also Nerlich, 2009, pp. 305–325). While the case law of domestic, multinational (Nuremberg) and potentially hybrid (ECCC, SCSL, STL) criminal courts can be seen as evidence of State practice (relevant for, for example, the creation of CIL), the case law of international (ICTY, ICTR) criminal courts cannot readily be characterised as such. It should be noted that also the ICTY and ICTR have been criticised for their heavy reliance on jurisprudence as evidence of existing law (see, for example, Bantekas, 2006, pp. 128–32). In public international law, case law is generally regarded as a subsidiary means for the determination of rules of law (see for example, ICJ Article 38(1)(d)).

Even though the wording of Article 21 gives forth that external sources of law only exceptionally will be applicable in ICC proceedings, it is possible to find many references to treaty law, CIL and international case law in the initial case law of the Court. This may be explained

(c) Failing that, general principles of law derived by the Court from national laws of legal systems of the world including, as appropriate, the national laws of States that would normally exercise jurisdiction over the crime, provided that those principles are not inconsistent with this Statute and with international law and internationally recognized norms and standards.[253]

---

with the fact that these legal sources often have been found relevant when interpreting the Court's internal legal sources. Sometimes the phrasing of an ICC norm indicates that the drafters of the norm have been aware of a similar provision in another tribunal's statute or a convention (Cf. *Prosecutor v. Mbarushimana*, ICC A. Ch., Judgment on the Appeal of the Prosecutor against the Decision of Pre-Trial Chamber I of 16 December 2011 Entitled "Decision on the Confirmation of Charges", 30 May 2012, para. 43). In this regard, for example, the 1949 Geneva Conventions, the 1977 Additional Protocols to the Geneva Conventions, and the 1948 Genocide Convention are of importance. Regarding war crimes, the Elements explicitly stipulate that the crime shall be "interpreted within the established framework of the international law of armed conflict including, as appropriate, the international law of armed conflict applicable to armed conflict at sea". Article 8 in the ICC Statute furthermore makes some references to the 1949 Geneva Conventions. The external norms may also be directed at the same objective as the corresponding ICC provisions (*Prosecutor v. Lubanga*, ICC T. Ch., Judgment pursuant to Article 74 of the Statute, 14 March 2012, para. 603), which may make them relevant when the ICC norms are interpreted teleologically. External sources of law can, however, generally only be used as interpretational aid when the interpretation has not been predetermined by a more high-level internal norm. In the Lubanga case, the Appeals Chamber found that it did not matter if ICTY Rule 33(B) had the same wording as the ICC Regulation 24bis(1) of the Regulations of the Court, as the legal question was exhaustively settled by explicit provisions in the ICC Statute (*Prosecutor v. Lubanga*, ICC A. Ch., Decision on the "Registrar's Submissions under Regulation 24bis of the Regulations of the Court in Relation to Trial Chamber I's Decision ICC-01/04-01/06-2800" of 5 October 2011, 21 November 2011, para. 16. See also Article 21(3)).

Cross-references:
Article 8.

Author: Mikaela Heikkilä.

[253] If the ICC cannot find a solution to a legal question in its own internal sources of law or in the applicable treaties and the principles and rules of international law, it may seek for the solution in general principles of law derived from national laws of legal systems of the world. The application of this legal source is always dependent on the condition that the application is not inconsistent with the ICC Statute and with international law and internationally recognised norms and standards. The low hierarchical position of general principles of law derived from national laws of legal systems of the world has meant that the ICC has not often made inquiries into domestic legal practices based on Article 21(1)(c). When addressing the acceptability of witness proofing, the Court, however, made such an inquiry (*Prosecutor v. Lubanga*, ICC PT. Ch. I, Decision on the Practices of Witness Familiarisation and Witness Proofing, 8 November 2006, paras. 35–42). The fact that Article 31(3) refers to "a ground for excluding criminal responsibility other than those referred to [...in the Statute] where such a ground is derived from applicable law as set forth in Article 21" gives forth that general principles of law derived from national laws could also be relevant when identifying factors that can exclude criminal responsibility.

The use of general principles of law derived from national laws of legal systems of the world makes it necessary to decide what domestic legal systems should be examined, as all national laws cannot be considered and the selection of the systems may affect the result of the inquiry. Article 21(1)(c) itself stipulates that at least the national laws of States that would normally exercise jurisdiction over the crime shall be considered as appropriate. This has been found to include at least the laws of the State where the crime was committed and the laws of the State of which the accused is a national (McAuliffe deGuzman, 2008, p. 710). More generally, it has been submitted that the inquiry should include the principal legal systems of the world, including at least representatives from civil law countries and common law countries, and probably some Islamic law countries (Pellet, 2002, pp. 1073–74. See also *Prosecutor v. Lubanga*, ICC T. Ch., Decision Regarding the Practices Used to Prepare and Familiarise Witnesses for Giving Testimony, 30 November 2007, para. 41; and *Prosecutor v. Katanga and Ngudjolo*, ICC PT. Ch. I, Decision Revoking the Prohibition of Contact and Communication between Germain Katanga and Mathieu Ngidjolo Chui, 13 March 2008, p. 12). In connection to admissibility of evidence, the Court has emphasised that it is not bound by the national law of a particular State (*Prosecutor v. Lubanga*, Decision on the Confirmation of Charges, PTC, 29 January 2007, para. 69, see also Article 69(8)). The Court may hence, based on Article 21(1)(c), only derive general principles from several domestic legal systems.

The low hierarchical position of general principles of law derived from national laws of legal systems of the world means that the ICC will probably not often make inquiries into domestic legal practices. When it had to address the acceptability of witness proofing, it, however, did so (*Prosecutor v. Lubanga*, ICC PT. Ch. I, Decision on the Practices of Witness Familiarisation and Witness Proofing, 8 November 2006, paras. 35–42). In the ICC Statute, Article 31(3) furthermore explicitly stipulates that "the Court may consider a ground for excluding criminal responsibility other than those referred to [… explicitly in the Statute] where such a ground is derived from applicable law as set forth in Article 21".

While general principles of law derived from national laws rarely is an applicable legal source *per se*, practices followed in domestic legal systems can function as an interpretational aid when the Court's internal legal sources are applied. In the Katanga and Ngudjolo case, a PTC, for example, found that its interpretation of the Statute which incorporated the concept of perpetration through control over an organisation was supported by the fact that "[p]rior and subsequent to the drafting of the Statute, numerous national jurisdictions relied on the concept" (*Prosecutor v. Katanga and Ngudjolo Chui*, ICC P. Ch., Decision on the Confirmation of Charges, ICC-01/04-01/07-717, 30 September 2008, para. 502). As an interpretational aid, general principles of law derived from national laws can therefore, in practice, be influential. In his separate opinion in the *Lubanga* Trial Judgment, Judge Fulford, in this regard, criticised the Court for an imprudent reliance on domestic practices:

> In these two instances, the judges relied heavily on the scholarship of the German academic Claus Roxin as the primary authority for the control theory of co-perpetration, and in the result, this approach was imported directly from the German legal system. While Article 21(1)(c) of the Statute permits the Court to draw upon "general principles of law" derived from national legal systems, in my view before taking this step, a Chamber should undertake a careful assessment as to whether the policy considerations underlying the domestic legal doctrine are applicable at this Court, and it should investigate the doctrine's compatibility with the ICC Statute framework. This applies regardless of whether the domestic and the ICC provisions mirror each other in their formulation. It would be dangerous to apply a national statutory interpretation simply because of similarities of language, given the overall context is likely to be significantly different (*Prosecutor v. Lubanga*, ICC T. Ch., Judgment pursuant to Article 74 of the Statute, Separate Opinion of Judge Adrian Fulford, 14 March 2012, para. 10).

Similarly, Judge Van den Wyngaert has cautioned for the adoption of domestic practices under the guise of treaty interpretation:

> I believe that it is not appropriate to draw upon subsidiary sources of law [...] to justify incorporating forms of criminal responsibility that go beyond the text of the Statute. Re-

2. The Court may apply principles and rules of law as interpreted in its previous decisions.[254]

3. The application and interpretation of law pursuant to this article must be consistent with internationally recognized human rights, and be without any adverse distinction founded on grounds such as gender as defined in Article 7, paragraph 3, age, race, colour, language, religion or belief, political or other opinion, national, ethnic or social origin, wealth, birth or other status.[255]

---

liance on the control over the crime theory [...] would only be possible to the extent that it qualifies as a general principle of criminal law in the sense of Article 21(l)(c). However, in view of the radical fragmentation of national legal systems when it comes to defining modes of liability, it is almost impossible to identify general principles in this regard. [...] Moreover, even if general principles could be identified, reliance on such principles, even under the guise of treaty interpretation, in order to broaden the scope of certain forms of criminal responsibility would amount to an inappropriate expansion of the Court's jurisdiction (*Prosecutor v. Ngudjolo*, ICC T. Ch., Judgment Pursuant to Article 74 of the Statute, Concurring Opinion of Judge Christine Van den Wyngaert, 18 December 2012, para. 17).

Cross-references:
Article 31(3), Article 69(8).

Author: Mikaela Heikkilä.

[254] Article 21(2) provides that the Court has the right to apply principles and rules of law as interpreted in its previous decisions. The paragraph uses the noun "may", which emphasises that the use of precedent is discretionary. It has been noted that this provisions seems to state the obvious, as it seems evident that the application of the same legal provisions in different cases should result in similar outcomes (Pellet, 2002, p. 1066; Schabas, 2010, p. 394). The function of Article 21(2) is primarily to reject the doctrine of binding precedent or *stare decisis* that can be found in some domestic legal systems.

Author: Mikaela Heikkilä.

[255] Article 21(3) establishes that the application and interpretation of law pursuant to Article 21 must be consistent with internationally recognised human rights including the non-discrimination principle. The provision thus creates a substantial hierarchy of law which supersedes the formal hierarchy between sources established by Article 21(1) (Pellet, 2002, p. 1077). This kind of "super-legality" (Pellet, 2002, pp. 1079, 1082) is not unique for the ICC. In many domestic legal systems (and, for example, in EU law), fundamental rights or human rights are given a special legal position. Also international law there are peremptory jus cogens norms.

Article 21(3) raises the question of what those human rights are that are "internationally recognised". Of the various human rights, Article 21(3) only explicitly mentions the non-discrimination principle. While there are some human rights norms that are firmly established, there are also less established human rights norms originating in little ratified treaties and soft law instruments. In its initial case law, the ICC has frequently referred to the ECHR and the ICCPR, but also to other human rights conventions, such as the Convention on the Rights of the Child (for example, *Prosecutor v. Lubanga*, ICC T. Ch., Judgment pursuant to Article 74 of the Statute, 14 March 2012, para. 604; See also Judge Pikis separate opinion, in which he argues that: "Internationally recognized may be regarded those human rights acknowledged by customary international law and international treaties and conventions". *Prosecutor v. Lubanga*, ICC A. Ch., Decision on the Prosecutor's "Application for Leave to Reply to 'Conclusions de la défense en réponse au mémoire d'appel du Procureur'", 12 September 2006, para. 3). The Court has also mentioned soft law instruments, such as the Basic Principles and Guidelines on the Right to a Remedy and Reparation for Victims of Gross Violations of International Human

Rights Law and Serious Violations of International Humanitarian Law (for example, *Prosecutor v. Lubanga*, ICC T. Ch., Decision on Victims' Participation, 18 January 2008, para. 35) and the Cape Town Principles and Best Practices on the Recruitment of Children into the Armed Forces and on Demobilisation and Social Reintegration of Child Soldiers in Africa (*Prosecutor v. Lubanga*, ICC T. Ch., Decision Establishing the Principles and Procedures to Be Applied to Reparations, 7 August 2012, para. 185) as legally relevant. Also human rights case law has often been referred to (for example, *Prosecutor v. Lubanga*, ICC A. Ch., Judgment on the Appeal of the Prosecutor against the Decision of Trial Chamber I entitled "Decision on the Consequences of Non-Disclosure of Exculpatory Materials Covered by Article 54(3)(e) Agreements and the Application to Stay the Prosecution of the Accused, together with Certain other Issues Raised at the Status Conference on 10 June 2008", 21 October 2008, paras. 46–47). As such, the ICC seems to give the concept of internationally recognised human rights a broad reading. Also in connection to the non-discrimination principle, Article 21(3) enumerates many possible grounds for discrimination. It has been noted that the possible discriminatory grounds constituted the controversial part of the provision's negotiations and that the numeration is both provocative (starting with gender) and curious (placing age before the traditional grounds of discrimination, such as race and religion) (McAuliffe deGuzman, 2008, pp. 711–712, and Schabas, 2010, p. 400).

The Appeals Chamber has emphasised that every Article in the ICC Statute has to be interpreted and applied according to Article 21(3) (*Situation in the Democratic Republic of the Congo*, ICC A. Ch., Judgment on the Prosecutor's Application for Extraordinary Review of Pre-Trial Chamber I's 31 March 2006 Decision Denying Leave to Appeal, 13 July 2006, para. 38).

In practice, the judges must, however, make a decision whether a particular ICC norm has a human rights dimension or not. In relation to certain questions, it is evident that human rights law must be consulted, for example, in relation to the fair trial rights of the accused (Article 67, see also for example, *Prosecutor v. Bemba*, ICC PT. Ch. I, Decision on the Prosecutor's Application for a Warrant of Arrest against Jean-Pierre Bemba Gombo, 10 June 2008, para. 24). It is, however, not merely this type of provisions which interpretation and application must be guided by human rights. Human rights law, for example, can be relevant when crimes such as incitement to commit genocide and modes of responsibility such as instigation are addressed (Cf. in this regard the ICTR Media case, *Prosecutor v. Nahimana et al.*, ICTR T. Ch., Judgment and Sentence, 3 December 2003, paras. 983–999). The ICC has also held that victim participation can be considered a question which bring to the fore human rights (see for example, *Prosecutor v. Katanga*, ICC T. Ch. II, Decision of the Plenary of Judges on the Application of the Legal Representative for Victims for the Disqualification of Judge Christine Van den Wyngaert from the Case of the Prosecutor v. Germain Katanga, 18 February 2014, para. 42), even though the leading human rights instruments do not grant victim's explicit procedural rights (see further de Brouwer and Heikkilä, 2013, pp. 1337–41).

Finally, it should be noted that Article 21(3) refers to the interpretation and application of the law. In this regard, the Appeals Chamber has stressed that human rights friendly interpretation is not always enough. It must be ensured that human rights also are applied (*Prosecutor v. Lubanga*, ICC A. Ch., Judgment on the Appeal of Mr. Thomas Lubanga Dyilo against the Decision on the Defence Challenge to the Jurisdiction of the Court pursuant to Article 19(2)(a) of the Statute of 3 October 2006, 14 December 2006, para. 37). The application of human rights may support the identification of a lacuna in the ICC internal legal system, which filling demands the use of ICC's external legal sources. In this regard, the ICC has held that it is possible to order a stay of proceedings in the case of breach of accused's fundamental rights even though the Court's internal legal sources do not foresee such a response to a breach (*Prosecutor v. Lubanga*, ICC A. Ch., Judgment on the Appeal of Mr. Thomas Lubanga Dyilo against the Decision on the Defence Challenge to the Jurisdiction of the Court pursuant to Article 19(2)(a) of the Statute of 3 October 2006, 14 December 2006, paras. 37 and 39). More controversially, Article 21(3) could entail that an ICC norm, even a Statute provision, is set aside or its application is suspended.

Hochmayr has noted that this is not merely a question of "theoretical interest" (Hochmayr, 2014, p. 677). When three detained witnesses in 2011 applied for asylum in the Netherlands, the Court first based on Article 21(3) found that it was unable to return them to the Democratic Republic of Congo according to Article 93(7) to ensure their right to for example, apply for asylum was not violated (*Prosecutor v. Katanga and Ngudjolo*, ICC T. Ch. II, Decision on an Amicus Curiae application and on the "Requête tendant à obtenir présentations des témoins DRC-D02-P-0350, DRC-D02-P-0236, DRC-D02-P-0228 aux autorités néerlandaises aux fins d'asile" (Articles 68 and 93(7) of the Statute), 9 June 2011, para. 73; and, *Prosecutor v. Katanga*, ICC T. Ch. II, Decision on the application for the interim release of detained Witnesses DRCD02-P-0236, DRC-D02-P-0228 and DRC-D02-P-0350 – Dissenting Opinion of Judge Christiane Van Den Wyngaert, 1 October 2013, para. 3. Also see *Prosecutor v. Ngudjolo*, Order on the Implementation of the Cooperation Agreement between the Court and the Democratic Republic of the Congo Concluded Pursuant Article 93 (7) of the Statute, AC, 20 January 2014, paras. 26–30). More generally, it must be therefore asked to what extent Article 21(3) can function as a legal basis to challenge the internal legal framework of the ICC. In this regard, Arsanjani has noted that: "While the original intention behind this paragraph may have been to limit the court's powers in the application and interpretation of the relevant law, it could have the opposite effect and broaden the competence of the court on these matters. It provides a standard against which all the law applied by the court should be tested" (Arsanjani, 1999, p. 29). In some domestic legal systems, constitutional law provisions requiring courts to ensure adherence to fundamental human rights have significantly affected interpretations of criminal law provisions. Before the ICC, Judge Blattman has expressed concern over the fact that some judges according to him have overlooked the will of the drafters of the ICC Statute with reference to Article 21(3):

> I am concerned by the Majority application of the Basic Principles and Guidelines on the Right to a Remedy and Reparation for Victims of Gross Violations of International Human Rights Law and Serious Violations of International Humanitarian Law. While the Majority opinion lists the Basic Principles in the relevant provisions which are taken into account by the Chamber, I caution that this is not a strongly persuasive or decisive authority which the Chamber should be using in its legal determination of victims and in particular the definition of victims and participation. I support and follow Article 21(3), which requires that decisions of the Chamber must be consistent with internationally recognised human rights. However, the particular provisions relied on in the Majority decision were specifically considered and rejected during the preparatory stages of the drafting of the ICC Statute (*Lubanga*, Decision on Victims' Participation, Separate and Dissenting Opinion of Judge René Blattman, TC, 18 January 2008, para. 5).

Cross-references:
Article 67.

Doctrine:
1. Mahnoush H. Arsanjani, "The Rome Statute of the International Criminal Court", in *American Journal of International Law*, 1999, vol. 93, pp. 22–43.
2. Ilias Bantekas, "Reflections on Some Sources and Methods of International Criminal and Humanitarian Law", in *International Criminal Law Review*, 2006, vol. 6, pp. 121–36.
3. Gilbert Bitti, "Article 21 of the Statute of the International Criminal Court and the Treatment of Sources of Law in the Jurisprudence of the ICC", in Carsten Stahn and

Göran Sluiter (eds.), *The Emerging Practice of the International Criminal Court*, Martinus Nijhoff Publishers, Leiden, 2009, pp. 285–304.

4. Ian Brownlie, *Principles of Public International Law*, 2nd ed., Oxford University Press, Oxford, 2008.

5. Robert Cryer, "Royalism and the King: Article 21 of the Rome Statute and the Politics of Sources", in *New Criminal Law Review*, 2009, vol. 12, no. 3, pp. 390–405.

6. Anne-Marie de Brouwer and Mikaela Heikkilä, "Victim Issues: Participation, Protection, Reparation, and Assistance", in Göran Sluiter, Håkan Friman, Suzannah Linton, Sergey Vasiliev and Salvatore Zappalà (eds.), *International Criminal Procedure: Principles and Rules*, Oxford University Press, Oxford, 2013, pp. 1299–1374.

7. Gudrun Hochmayr, "Applicable Law in Practice and Theory – Interpreting Article 21 of the ICC Statute", in *Journal of International Criminal Justice*, 2014, vol. 12, pp. 655–79.

8. Peter Malanczuk, *Akehurst's Modern Introduction to International Law*, 7th ed., Routledge, London, 1997.

9. Marko Milanović, "Is the Rome Statute Binding on Individuals? (And Why We Should Care)", in *Journal of International Criminal Justice*, 2011, vol. 9, pp. 25–52.

10. Margaret McAuliffe deGuzman, "Article 21 – Applicable Law", in Otto Triffterer (ed.), *Commentary on the Rome Statute of the International Criminal Court: Observers' Notes, Article by Article*, 2nd ed., C.H. Beck/Hart/Nomos, Munich/Oxford/Baden-Baden, 2008, pp. 701–12.

11. Volker Nerlich, "The Status of ICTY and ICTR Precedent in Proceedings before the ICC", in Carsten Stahn and Göran Sluiter (eds.), *The Emerging Practice of the International Criminal Court*, Martinus Nijhoff Publishers, Leiden, 2009, pp. 305–25.

12. Alain Pellet, "Applicable Law", in Antonio Cassese, Paola Gaeta and John R.W.D. Jones (eds.), *The Rome Statute of the International Criminal Court: A Commentary*, 2nd ed., Oxford University Press, Oxford, 2002.

13. William A. Schabas, *The International Criminal Court: A Commentary on the Rome Statute*, Oxford University Press, Oxford, 2010.

14. Birgit Schlütter, *Developments in Customary International Law: Theory and the Practice of the International Court of Justice and the International Ad Hoc Criminal Tribunals for Rwanda and Yugoslavia*, Martinus Nijhoff Publishers, Leiden, 2010.

15. Otto Triffterer, "Can the "Elements of Crimes" Narrow or Broaden Responsibility for Criminal Behaviour Defined in the Rome Statute?", in Carsten Stahn and Göran Sluiter (eds.), *The Emerging Practice of the International Criminal Court*, Martinus Nijhoff Publishers, Leiden, 2009, pp. 381–400.

16. Herman von Hebel, "The Decision to Include Elements of Crimes in the Rome Statute", in Roy S. Lee *et al.* (eds.) *The International Criminal Court: Elements of Crimes and Rules of Procedure and Evidence*, Transnational Publishers, Ardsley, NY, 2001, pp. 4–8.

17. Alexander Zahar and Göran Sluiter, *International Criminal Law – A Critical Introduction*, Oxford University Press, Oxford, 2008.

Author: Mikaela Heikkilä.

PART 3. GENERAL PRINCIPLES OF CRIMINAL LAW

Article 22
Nullum crimen sine lege[256]

---

[256] *General remarks*:

Together with *nulla poena sine lege*, contained in Article 23 of the ICC Statute, the principle of *nullum crimen sine lege* forms the principle of legality which is of fundamental importance to international criminal law. The principles of *nullum crimen* and *nulla poena* are well-established in customary international law, a fact that was reflected by the effortlessly drafting of Articles 22 and 23 of the ICC Statute (Lamb in Cassese, 2002, p. 734–35). The need for a provision acknowledging the principle of *nullum crimen* was agreed upon already by the 1996 Preparatory Commission which stated that "the crimes within the jurisdiction of the Court should be defined with the clarity, precision and specificity required for criminal law in accordance with the principle of legality (*nullum crimen sine lege*)" (Broomhall in Otto Triffterer, 2008, p. 715). It may be noted that the statutes of the ICTY and ICTR does not contain provisions equivalent to Article 22 of the ICC Statute.

The principle of *nullum crimen* contributes to a foreseeable legal system as it stipulates that only actions which are prohibited by law can be deemed as criminal. This is an important part of the legitimacy of a legal system, and in the case of the ICC it works both in relation to the individuals under investigation and in relation to states (Broomhall in Otto Triffterer, 2008, p. 716). The principle of *nullum crimen* also acknowledges that the individual virtually always is the weaker part in the criminal process and that the individual therefore has a need to be protected from a misuse of powers by the judiciary.

Nullum crimen is harder to apply and fulfil in international criminal law than in national criminal law since international criminal law often is more vague than national law. This is a problem which was at the centre of the proceedings in Nuremberg. At the end of the Second World War the international crimes had not been exhaustively defined, which led the judges of the Nuremberg Tribunal to define many of the elements of the crimes themselves. The proceedings of Nuremberg have thus received criticism of creating new law. With regard to *nullum crimen*, the judges of Nuremberg concluded that it is a moral principle and that it is allowed to punish actions that were not prohibited at the time of the conduct in cases where it would be "unjust" not to punish the actions (Lamb in Cassese, 2002, p. 735–736).

After the Second World War and Nuremberg the principle of *nullum crimen sine lege* has been codified in a number of international treaties on human rights. The first sentence of Article 11(2) of the 1948 Universal Declaration of Human Rights states that "[n]o one shall be held guilty of any penal offence on account of any act or omission which did not constitute a penal offence, under national or international law, at the time when it was committed". The essentially identical first sentence of Article 15 of the International Covenant on Civil and Political Rights ('ICCPR') states that "[n]o one shall be held guilty of any criminal offence on account of any act or omission which did not constitute a criminal offence, under national or international law, at the time when it was committed".

When creating the ICTY the United Nations Secretary-General stated in a report that "the application of the principle nullum crimen sine lege requires that the International Tribunal should apply rules of international humanitarian law which are beyond any doubt part of customary law" (Report of the Secretary-General Pursuant to Paragraph 2 of Security Council Resolution 808 (1993), UN doc. S/25704, 3 May 1993, para. 34). The principle of *nullum crimen* has also been addressed by the ICTY, for example in *Prosecutor v. Tadić* where the Trial

1. A person shall not be criminally responsible under this Statute unless the conduct in question constitutes, at the time it takes place, a crime within the jurisdiction of the Court.[257]

Chamber found that common Article 3 of the Geneva Conventions "is beyond doubt part of customary international law, therefore the principle of *nullum crimen sine lege* is not violated by incorporating the prohibitory norms of common Article 3 in Article 3 of the Statute of the International Tribunal" (*Prosecutor v. Tadić*, Decision on the Defence Motion on Jurisdiction, 10 August 1995, para. 72) and that "[i]mposing criminal responsibility upon individuals for these violations does not violate the principle of *nullum crimen sine lege*" (para. 65).

The ICC Elements of Crimes has an important role in the fulfilling of the objectives of Article 22 since it defines the crimes within the jurisdiction of the Court. The need for the Element of Crimes was observed by the United States in the Preparatory Committee. The United States argued that the Elements of Crime were consistent with "the need to define crimes with the clarity, precision and specificity many jurisdictions require for criminal law" (Schabas, 2010, p. 407, citing the Proposal submitted by the United States of America, Elements of offences of the International Criminal Court, UN doc, A/AC.249/1998/DP.11). The need for the Elements of Crime was also stressed by Japan during the Rome Conference (Schabas 2010, p. 407).

Cross-references:
Article 23.

Author: Camilla Lind.

[257] Not only was the need for a provision on the *nullum crimen* principle noticed early in the preparation of the ICC Statute but the need for a provision on non-retroactivity, which as well was considered fundamental to a criminal legal system, was also specifically addressed by the 1996 Preparatory Committee (Lamb in Cassese, 2002, p. 751). According to Article 22(1), which states the principle of non-retroactivity, a certain conduct can only be deemed as illegal if that specific conduct was prohibited at the time when the conduct took place. In cases when the specific conduct was not criminalised at the time of the conduct Article 22(1) prescribes that the person shall not be convicted. The individual responsibility of the perpetrator of the crime does however arise directly under international law, meaning that the criminal conduct does not have to be criminalised in national law in order to fulfil the principle of *nullum crimen* (Broomhall in Triffterer, 2008, p. 718).

The term "conduct" refers both to acts and omissions. In cases where a continuous conduct is under examination Article 22(1) prescribes that all elements of the crime must be fulfilled during the time that the conduct was criminalised (Broomhall in Otto Triffterer, 2008, pp. 722–23).

Article 22(1) refers to the jurisdiction of the Court. To determine whether a person can be held criminally responsible under the ICC Statute it is therefore necessary to establish the jurisdiction of the Court. The jurisdiction *ratione materiae* of the ICC is found in Article 5 of the ICC Statute, which states that the crimes within the jurisdiction of the Court are the crimes of genocide, crimes against humanity, war crimes and the crime of aggression. However, to establish jurisdiction Article 11, stating the jurisdiction *ratione temporis* and Article 12, stating preconditions to the exercise of jurisdiction, must be taken into consideration. According to Article 11(1), the Court may only exercise jurisdiction with respect to crimes committed after the entry into force of the ICC Statute. The ICC Statute entered into force on 1 July 2002. For those states that has become parties to the ICC Statute after 1 July 2002 Article 11(2) states that the ICC may only exercise jurisdiction with respect to crimes committed after the entry into force of the ICC Statute for that individual state. Article 126(2) states further conditions on the entry into force of the ICC Statute for a state as it prescribes that the statute enters into force on the first day of the month after the 60th day following the deposit of the state's instrument of ratification, acceptance, approval or accession.

---

2. The definition of a crime shall be strictly construed and shall not be extended by analogy. In case of ambiguity, the definition shall be interpreted in favour of the person being investigated, prosecuted or convicted.[258]

Article 22(1) is not only a reminder of the principle of legality but also serves as a principle of interpretation according to which rules can be interpreted in such a way that the principle of legality is respected (Schabas 2010, p. 409). Article 22(1) has been used as a tool of interpretation in Prosecutor v. Katanga, when the Pre-Trial Chamber defined "other inhumane acts" in Article 7(1)(k) as "serious violations of international customary law and the basic rights pertaining to human beings, being drawn from the norms of international human rights law, which are of a similar nature and gravity to the acts referred to in Article 7(1) of the Statute" (*Prosecutor v. Katanga et al.*, ICC PT. Ch. I, Decision on the Confirmation of Charges, ICC-01/04-01/07-717, 30 September 2008).

i. Non-state parties and international customary law

When addressing Article 22(1) the Court will typically examine whether a certain conduct was prohibited by the ICC Statute at the time of that certain conduct. It is however possible that the Court may have to take international customary law in consideration in addressing Article 22(1) when a situation is referred to the Court by the United Nations Security Council or when a state makes a declaration of the acceptance of jurisdiction in accordance with Article 12(3). According to one view, advocated by Bruce Broomhall, the Court can only establish criminal responsibility in international customary law in such cases since the state of which the person investigated is a national of was not a party to the ICC Statute when the conduct took place. Consequently, the ICC Statute cannot provide a prohibition of that certain conduct in those cases (See Broomhall in Otto Triffterer, 2008, p. 720). This issue was however not discussed by the Pre-Trial Chamber neither when deciding to issue a warrant of arrest for president Omar Al Bashir of Sudan, a state that is not a party to the ICC (see *Prosecutor v. Al Bashir*, Decision on the Prosecution's Application for a Warrant of Arrest against Omar Hassan Ahmad Al Bashir, 4 March 2009) nor when deciding to issue warrants of arrest in relation to any of the other persons that allegedly are responsible of having committed international crimes in Sudan.

International crimes are also investigated in Côte d'Ivoire, a state that has accepted the jurisdiction of the ICC pursuant to Article 12(3) of the ICC Statute. The government of Côte d'Ivoire lodged an Article 12(3)-declaration on 18 April 2003, declaring that it accepted the jurisdiction of the court for crimes committed on its territory since the events of 19 September 2002. This declaration was reconfirmed by the President of the Côte d'Ivoire on 14 December 2010. Two cases are open in the situation of Côte d'Ivoire, the case of the *Prosecutor v. Simone Gbagbo* and of the *Prosecutor v. Laurent Gbagbo and Charles Blé Goudé*. Both cases concern alleged crimes against humanity committed in Côte d'Ivoire during the period of 16 December 2010 to 12 April 2011. Since that period occurred after the Article 12(3)-declaration on the acceptance of the jurisdiction of the ICC the Court should not, according to the view advocated by Broomhall, have to assess whether the conduct of the suspected persons was prohibited by international customary law at the time of the conduct. This issue was not addressed by the Pre-Trial Chamber II when it issued the arrest warrants of the persons allegedly responsible for crimes in Côte d'Ivoire.

Author: Camilla Lind.

[258] The rule of strict interpretation that is enshrined in Article 22(2) protects both the state parties of the ICC Statute as it ensures that the judges will interpret the Statute narrowly, and the individual that is under investigation by guarantying that the criminal responsibility of that individual will be judged according to the legislation and nothing else. According to this rule of interpretation and the prohibition of analogy the judges of the ICC cannot create new crimes as the creation of new crimes is exclusively within the power of the Assembly of States Parties. Article

22(2) is aimed at prohibiting the use of analogy for law-making, but it allows the judges of the Court to use analogies as a last resort to interpret and fill gaps in the ICC Statute (Broomhall in Triffterer, 2008, p. 725). In other words, the use of analogy as a tool of law-making is prohibited by Article 22(2) but analogy as a tool of interpretation is not prohibited (Lamb in Cassese, 2002, pp. 752–753). As Article 22(2) states that cases of ambiguity shall be interpreted in favour of the person being investigated, prosecuted or convicted it also contains the principle of *in dubio pro reo*.

Since Article 22(2) refers to the interpretation of crimes it is only applicable to Article 6–8 bis of the ICC Statute, which are Articles that contain the definitions of the crimes enlisted in Article 5 (Broomhall in Triffterer, 2008, pp. 723–724). It is however argued that Article 22(2) could also be applicable to Articles and principles that have a direct impact on the application of Articles 6–8 bis (Schabas, 2010, p. 410). Pre-Trial Chamber II has in *Prosecutor v. Bemba* referred to the principles of nullum crimen and strict interpretation in Article 22(2) when interpreting whether the chapeau of Article 28(a) includes an element of causality between a superior's dereliction of duty and the underlying crimes (*Prosecutor v. Bemba*, ICC PT. Ch. II, Decision Pursuant to Article 61(7)(a) and (b) of the Rome Statute on the Charges of the Prosecutor Against Jean-Pierre Bemba Gombo, ICC-01/05-01/08-424, 15 June 2009).

i. Al Bashir:

According to Pre-Trial Chamber I of the ICC, Article 22(2) "fully embraces the general principle of interpretation *in dubio pro reo*", which means that in cases of uncertainty the interpretation that is more favourable to the investigated person shall be used (*Prosecutor v. Al Bashir*, Decision on the Prosecution's Application for a Warrant of Arrest against Omar Hassan Ahmad Al Bashir, 4 March 2009, para. 156). In the same decision, the majority of the Pre-Trial Chamber argued that the Elements of Crimes must be applied in order to respect Article 22 (para. 131). Judge Ušacka did however in her separate opinion state that the Elements of Crime shall be consistent with the ICC Statute according to Article 9(3) and that the definitions of crime therefore only can be found in the ICC Statute itself (Separate and Partly Dissenting Opinion of Judge Anita Ušacka, para. 18).

ii. Lubanga:

On 14 March 2012 Trial Chamber I delivered the first judgment of the ICC in which Thomas Lubanga Dyilo was found guilty of war crimes consisting of enlisting and conscripting children under the age of 15 and using them to participate actively in hostilities. Article 22(2) was addressed during this process. The Defence argued in its closing submission that various interpretations made by the Pre-Trial Chamber in its Decision on the confirmation of charges was in breach with Article 22(2) (*Prosecutor v. Thomas Lubanga Dyilo*, Closing submissions of the Defence, 15 July 2011, see for example, paras. 23, 39 and 65).

In the judgment the judges used Article 22(2) as a test of whether the interpretation of Article 8(2)(e)(vii) was acceptable: "[t]herefore, consistently with Article 22 of the Statute, a child can be 'used' for the purposes of the Statute without evidence being provided as regards his or her earlier 'conscription' or 'enlistment' into the relevant armed force or group" (*Prosecutor v. Thomas Lubanga Dyilo*, Judgment pursuant to Article 74 of the Statute, 14 March 2012, para. 620).

iii. Katanga:

Article 22(2) and its impact on the interpretation was also discussed by Trial Chamber II in its judgment in *Prosecutor v. Katanga*. The Trial Chamber noted that Article 22(2) must be taken into consideration when interpreting the rules of the Rome Statue as it prescribes that "any meaning from a broad interpretation that is to the detriment of the accused" shall be discarded (*Prosecutor v. Katanga*, ICC T. Ch. II, Judgment pursuant to Article 74 of the Statute, ICC-01/04-01/07-3436-tENG, 7 March 2014, para. 50) and that the principle of legality poses "clear

3. This article shall not affect the characterization of any conduct as criminal under international law independently of this Statute.[259]

---

and explicit restrictions on all interpretative activity" (para. 51). Because of this, the judges of the Court may not create new law, but only apply already existing law (para. 53). The Chamber however also noted that the principle of in *dubio pro reo* that is enshrined in Article 22(2) only is applicable in cases of ambiguity and that it does not take precedence over the conventional method of interpretation according to Articles 31 and 32 of the Vienna Convention on the Law of Treaties (VCLT). Lastly, the Chamber concluded that the rules of interpretation in the VCLT is in accordance with Article 22(2). The Chamber hence used the general rule of interpretation in the VCLT when interpreting the rules of the ICC Statute.

Author: Camilla Lind.

[259] Article 22(3) acknowledges that the *nullum crimen* principle in Article 22 does not affect customary international law and that it applies only to the definitions of crimes in the ICC Statute (Broomhall in Otto Triffterer, 2008, p. 719). This third sub-paragraph does only limit the impact of Article 22 and not the whole ICC Statute (Lamb in Cassese, 2002, p. 754).

Cross-references:
Article 23 and 24.

Doctrine:

1. Susan Lamb, "*Nullum Crimen, Nulla Poena Sine Lege* in International Criminal Law", in Antonio Cassese, Paola Gaeta and John R.W.D. Jones (eds.), *The Rome Statute of the International Criminal Court*, Oxford University Press, Oxford, 2002, pp. 733–66.

2. Bruce Broomhall, "Article 22 – *Nullum crimen sine lege*", in Otto Triffterer (ed.), *Commentary on the Rome Statute of the International Criminal Court: Observers' Notes, Article by Article*, 2nd ed., C.H. Beck/Hart/Nomos, Munich/Oxford/Baden-Baden, 2008, pp. 713–29.

3. William A. Schabas, *The International Criminal Court: A Commentary on the Rome Statute*, Oxford University Press, Oxford, 2010, pp. 403–12.

Author: Camilla Lind.

Article 23
Nulla poena sine lege

A person convicted by the Court may be punished only in accordance with this Statute.[260]

---

[260] *General remarks*:

Article 23 contains the principle of *nulla poena sine lege*, which is part of the principle of legality and prohibits retroactive penalties. It is closely related to *nullum crimen sine lege*, a principle that prohibits retroactive application of law (see Article 22). As *nullum crimen, nulla poena* is part of a number of human rights treaties and declarations, for example the International Covenant on Civil and Political Rights (Article 15(1)) and the 1948 Universal Declaration on Human Rights (Article 11(2)). The principle of *nulla poena* is uncontroversial and was widely accepted and supported at the Rome conference (Lamb in Cassese, 2002, p. 756).

Analysis:

Article 23 shall, since *nulla poena* is a principle regarding penalties, be read together with Part 7 of the ICC Statute. Article 77(1) of the ICC Statute states the penalties available to the Court. These are imprisonment, either for a maximum of 30 years or for life, a fine or a forfeiture of proceeds, property and assets derived either directly or indirectly from the crime at hand. Factors that shall be taken into consideration when determining the sentence are stated in Article 78.

It may be noted that the drafters of the ICC Statute did not chose to regulate the penalties available to the court in the same manner as is the case in the ICTY statute. According to Article 24 of that statute, the ICTY shall, when determining sentences, consider the general practice regarding prison sentences in the former Yugoslavia. The ICTY has however, despite the fact that the national penal code of Yugoslavia did only allow sentences of a maximum of 20 years of imprisonment, concluded that it may sentence convicted persons to life imprisonment (see, for example, *Prosecutor v. Radislav Krstić* (Case No. IT-98-33-A), ICTY A. Ch., Judgment, 19 April 2004 and Lamb in Cassese, 2002, p. 759. The ICC Statute contains no reference to the penal codes of its state parties.

i. Lubanga

In its sentencing decision the Trial Chamber in *Prosecutor v. Thomas Lubanga Dyilo* acknowledged Article 23 as one of the Articles that according to Article 21(1), which states applicable law, shall be applied when passing sentence. The Trial Chamber did however not discuss it further (*Prosecutor v. Lubanga*, Decision on Sentence pursuant to Article 76 of the Statute, 10 July 2012, paras. 17–18). After acknowledging Article 23 and the principle of *nulla poena* the Trial Chamber went on with discussing and applying Articles related to sentencing. The conclusion may be drawn that the Trial Chamber was not of the opinion that Article 23 and its implications needed further discussion and that the Articles of the ICC Statute was in accordance with Article 23.

Cross-references:

Articles 22 and 77.

Doctrine:

1. Susan Lamb, "*Nullum Crimen, Nulla Poena Sine Lege* in International Criminal Law", in Antonio Cassese, Paola Gaeta and John R.W.D. Jones (eds.), *The Rome Statute of the International Criminal Court,* Oxford University Press, Oxford, 2002, pp. 733–66.

Author: Camilla Lind.

Article 24

Non-retroactivity *ratione personae*[261]

1. No person shall be criminally responsible under this Statute for conduct prior to the entry into force of the Statute.[262]

2. In the event of a change in the law applicable to a given case prior to a final judgement, the law more favourable to the person being investigated, prosecuted or convicted shall apply.[263]

---

[261] *General remarks*

Article 24 completes Articles 22 and 23, which states the principle of legality. It is also closely related to Article 11, which determines the jurisdiction *ratione temporis* of the ICC. Article 24 does however not have any predecessor in international human rights documents, as is the case for Articles 22 and 23. The need for an Article with the substance of Article 24 was noted early in the drafting process, and the drafting of Article 24 was undramatic (Schabas, 2010, p. 418).

Author: Camilla Lind.

[262] Article 24(1) provides that no person shall be held criminally responsible for conduct prior to the entry into force of the Statute. The statement is a reflection of Article 11(1) concerning jurisdiction *ratione temporis*, which provides that "[t]he Court has jurisdiction only with respect to crimes committed after the entry into force of this Statute". The ICC Statute entered into force on 1 July 2002. When determining the jurisdiction *ratione temporis* in relation to states that has ratified the ICC Statute after its entry into force, Article 126(2) must be taken into consideration. The Article states that the entry into force for such states occurs on the first day of the month after the 60th day following the deposit by that state. This day is important to the application of Article 24(1) as it prohibits criminal responsibility for conduct prior to that date.

Article 24(1) refers to "conduct", which covers both active actions and omissions. It may however prove difficult to determine when an omission takes place, and it may therefore be difficult to determine whether an omission falls within the scope of the ICC Statute (Pangalangan in Otto Triffterer, 2008, p. 740).

A difficulty with Article 24(1) and the temporal limitation of application of the ICC Statute is that the Statute does not provide a solution to the problem of continuing crimes (see Schabas, 2010, p. 419). It is possible that situations may arise when a criminal conduct begun before the entry into force of the Statute and where the criminal conduct is of a continuing nature and continues after the entry into force of the Statute. The Pre-Trial Chamber I stated in Lubanga that the crime of enlisting and conscripting children under the age of fifteen is of a continuing nature and that it continues to be committed during the time children under fifteen remain in armed groups or forces (*Prosecutor v. Lubanga*, Decision of the Confirmation of Charges, 9 January 2007, para. 248). The status of continuing crimes is however uncertain and the solution is yet to be determined by the Court.

Author: Camilla Lind.

[263] Article 24(2) states that the law most favourable to the person being investigated, prosecuted or convicted shall be applied if the law changes before the judgment. It completes the statements concerning retroactive application in Articles 22 and 23. The wording of Article 24(2) makes it broad, and it may be invoked at any stage of the proceedings before the ICC, meaning that it may also be invoked when a case reaches the Appeals Chamber (Schabas, 2010, p. 420).

Article 24(2) uses the word "law". Applicable law is determined by Article 21, which states that the Court first and foremost shall apply the Statute, the Elements of Crimes and the Rules of

Procedure and Evidence. The Court may however in second place also apply treaties and customary international law according to Article 21(1)(b). Treaties and customary international law may therefore be part of the applicable law and the Court may hence have to determine whether a change in customary international law has taken place to fully respect Article 24(2) (see Schabas, 2010, p. 420).

Cross-references:
Articles 11, 22, 23.

Doctrine:

1. Raul C. Pangalangan, "Article 24 – Non-Retroactivity *ratione personae*", in Otto Triffterer (ed.), *Commentary on the Rome Statute of the International Criminal Court: Observers' Notes, Article by Article*, 2nd ed., C.H. Beck/Hart/Nomos, Munich/Oxford/Baden-Baden, 2008, pp. 735–41.

2. William A. Schabas, *The International Criminal Court: A Commentary on the Rome Statute*, Oxford University Press, Oxford, 2010, pp. 417–20.

Author: Camilla Lind.

Article 25
Individual criminal responsibility[8][264]

1. The Court shall have jurisdiction over natural persons pursuant to this Statute.[265]

---

[264] *General remarks*:

Article 25 provides the various modes of individual liability within the jurisdiction of the ICC. This is the core of a case, providing the legal theory which connects the accused to the crimes charged. The ICC Statute provides a general framework for determining individual criminal responsibility. However, the approach taken to individual criminal responsibility differed greatly from that of previous international tribunals. As well the elements of each mode of liability have evolved through case law with various ICC Pre-Trial and Trial Chambers interpreting the diverse elements differently. The Appeals Chamber in the *Lubanga* case has issued the only decision thus far that deals with Article 25 at the appeals level, essentially confirming the approach taken at the Pre-Trial and Trial level of the case. Continued jurisprudence from the Appeals Chamber will assist in providing certainty moving forward and ending superfluous litigation over diverse opinions at the Pre-Trial and Trial level.

Compared with the previous laws on individual criminal responsibility, the provisions contained within the ICC Statute mark a turning point in regulating modes of participation under international criminal law. The *ad hoc* tribunals were in their early years during the drafting and adopting of the ICC Statute in 1998, and the modes of liability were a key focus of the development of the *ad hoc* jurisprudence during this time. In particular, and in contrast to the ICC, the *ad hoc* tribunals developed their modes of liability in the absence of guidance from their Statutes. Central to this was the concept of joint criminal enterprise ('JCE'), and the extent to which this concept falls within the ICC Statute is debatable.

The ICC Statute is much more precise than the ICTY/ICTR Statutes in that it adopts a scheme that clearly differentiates between a four-tiered system of participation. In contrast to both the ILC Draft Codes of Crimes against the Peace and Security of Mankind and the Statutes of the *ad hoc* tribunals, paragraph 3 distinguishes between perpetration and other forms of participation. In particular, perpetration corresponds to the most serious qualification of individual criminal responsibility and it is expressly provided for under letter (a) in three different forms: i) as an individual; ii) jointly with another person (co-perpetration) and iii) through another person (indirect perpetration). Based on the new drafting of the ICC Statute a new format of perpetration has emerged at the ICC based on the notion of 'indirect perpetration'. Pursuant to this new interpretation, commission of crimes encompasses the concept of 'control over the crime', including control over an organised apparatus of power, whereby indirect perpetration interacts with co-perpetration in such a way that the two forms of participation complement each other. This new doctrine on perpetration serves to make clearer the distinction between principal and accessorial liabilities within the context of the collective and multi-level commission of crimes. The Pre Trial Chamber of the ICC has taken this all one step further in a decision in the Katanga and Ngudjolo case, where the judges decided that the 'control over the crime' amounted to 'control over the organization' (*Prosecutor v. Katanga and Ngudjolo*, ICC PT. Ch. I, Confirmation of Charges Decision, ICC-01/04-01/07-717, 30 September 2008, para. 500). Now, the requirements of indirect perpetration include the existence of an organised apparatus of power, within which the direct and indirect perpetrators operate, and which enables the indirect perpetrator to secure the commission of the crimes (*Prosecutor v. Katanga and Ngudjolo*, ICC PT. Ch. I, ICC-01/04-01/07-717, 30 September 2008, paras. 515–518).

Author: Kirsten Bowman.

[265] *Preparatory works*:

---

2. A person who commits a crime within the jurisdiction of the Court shall be individually responsible and liable for punishment in accordance with this Statute.[266]

3. In accordance with this Statute, a person shall be criminally responsible and liable for punishment for a crime within the jurisdiction of the Court if that person:

(a) Commits such a crime, whether as an individual, jointly with another[267] or through another person, regardless of whether that other person is criminally responsible;[268]

Article 25(1) of the ICC Statute reads: "The Court shall have jurisdiction over natural persons pursuant to this statute". The decision regarding whether to include 'legal or 'juridical' persons within the jurisdiction of the court was controversial. During the conference in Rome there was a working paper circulated by the French delegation which articulated a proposal for ICC jurisdiction over 'juridical persons'. There was considerable debate on this point with many delegations concerned that the legal systems of their countries did not provide for such a concept or that the concept would be difficult to apply in the context of an international criminal court. The French delegation noted these concerns, but felt that the Statute should go at least as far as the Nuremberg Charter, which had provided for the criminal responsibility of criminal organisations. The debate was mainly based upon Romano-Germanic versus common law system countries. Romano-Germanic countries generally do not have mechanisms under their national systems to prosecute legal entities, effectively conferring automatic jurisdiction on the ICC in such circumstances. In the end, the concerns regarding the French proposal were too great to overcome and the ICC Statute would not accept jurisdiction over legal persons (Report of the Preparatory Committee on the Establishment of an International Criminal Court, United Nations Diplomatic Conference of Plenipotentiaries on the Establishment of an International Criminal Court Rome, Italy 15 June–17 July 1998, A/CONF.183/2).

Article 25(1) of the ICC Statute establishes the principle of 'personal jurisdiction', giving the ICC jurisdiction over natural persons accused of crimes within its jurisdiction. This provision and in particular paragraphs 1 and 2 of the Article confirm the universal acceptance of the principle of individual criminal responsibility. Sub-paragraphs (a) through (c) of paragraph 3 establish the basic concepts of individual criminal attribution. Sub-paragraph (a) refers to three forms of perpetration: on one's own, as a co-perpetrator or through another person. Sub-paragraph (b) contains different forms of participation; ordering, soliciting or inducing commission. Sub-paragraph (c) establishes criminal responsibility for aiding and abetting and sub-paragraphs (d), (e) and (f) provide for expansions of attribution: contributing to the commission or attempted commission of a crime by a group, incitement to genocide and attempt.

Author: Kirsten Bowman.

[266] Article 25(2) articulates the principle of individual criminal responsibility. "A crime within the jurisdiction of the Court" refers to genocide, crimes against humanity and war crimes according to Articles 5(1)(a)–(c) and 6–8. The possible punishment follows from Article 77.

Author: Kirsten Bowman.

[267] Sub-paragraph (a) distinguishes between three forms of perpetration: direct, co-perpetration and perpetration by means.

With respect to co-perpetration, it is no longer included in the complicity concept but recognised as an autonomous form of perpetration. Co-perpetration is characterised by a functional division of the criminal tasks between the different co-perpetrators, who are interrelated by a common plan or agreement. Every co-perpetrator fulfils a certain task which contributes to the commission of the crime and without which the commission would not be possible. The common plan or agreement forms the basis of a reciprocal or mutual attribution of the different contributions holding every co-perpetrator responsible for the whole crime.

Perpetration by means presupposes that the person who commits the crime can be used as an instrument by the indirect perpetrator as the mastermind or individual in the background. He or she is normally an innocent agent, not responsible for the criminal act.

The jurisprudence for this issue began with the Pre-Trial Chamber I's Confirmation of Charges decision in *Lubanga*. Rather than rely on any precedent established by the ICTY, the *Lubanga* Pre-Trial Chamber chose to forge a new path relying on its own theoretical analysis. The Pre-Trial Chamber noted that the ICC Statute contains a much more differentiated regime of forms of individual and joint responsibility than the ICTY Statute. It referred in particular to Article 25(3)(d) of the ICC Statute, which establishes responsibility for contributing to the activities of "a group of persons acting with a common purpose", as probably covering some forms of JCE. However, the Chamber voiced substantial reservations against accepting JCE as a form of primary liability under the ICC Statute, associating JCE with a 'subjective' approach toward distinguishing between principals and accessories, an approach that moves the focus from the objective level of contribution to the 'state of mind in which the contribution to the crime was made'.

Rather, the Pre-Trial Chamber in *Lubanga* identified five factors of individual criminal liability in order to find co-perpetration under Article 25(3)(a). These five elements were confirmed and used in the trial chamber decision of *Lubanga*, as well as by the appeals chamber decision of *Lubanga*, in order to find the accused guilty as a co-perpetrator under Article 25(3)(a). The five elements include two objective and three subjective elements.

The objective requirements:

In the confirmation of charges, the Pre-Trial Chamber set forth two objective elements: 1) the existence of a common plan between two or more persons; and 2) the coordinated essential contribution made by each co-perpetrator that results in the realisation of the objective elements of the crime. The Lubanga Trial Chamber then, following the reasoning set forth by the Pre-Trial Chamber, agreed that under the co-perpetration theory two or more individuals must act jointly within the common plan, which must include 'an element of criminality' (*Prosecutor v. Lubanga*, ICC PT. Ch. I, Decision on the Confirmation of Charges , ICC-01/04-01/06-803, 29 January 2007, para. 343). As well, the Pre-Trial Chamber found that the plan did not need to be specifically directed at the commission of a crime.

However, the *Lubanga* Trial Chamber did find that it is necessary to prove that if events followed the ordinary course of events, a crime will be committed (*Prosecutor v. Lubanga*, ICC T. Ch. I, Judgment pursuant to Article 74 of the Statute, ICC-01/04-01/06-2842, 14 March 2012, para. 2984). Noting that the crime in question need not be the overarching goal of the co-perpetrators, nor explicit in nature, the Chamber did stress that the existence of a common plan can be inferred from circumstantial evidence (*Prosecutor v. Lubanga*, Judgment, para. 988).

With regard to the requirement of an 'essential contribution' the Trial Chamber majority stated that the Statute's wording required that the offence "be the result of the combined and coordinated contributions of those involved, [...]. None of the participants' exercises, individually, control over the crime as a whole but, instead, the control of the crime is collective" (*Prosecutor v. Lubanga*, ICC T. Ch. I, Judgment, ICC-01/04-01/06-2842, 14 March 2012, para. 994). Here, the Chamber notes that the Prosecution does not have the burden to demonstrate that the contribution of the accused, if taken alone, would have caused the crime. Rather, the Prosecutor must prove mutual attribution, based on joint agreement or common plan. The Majority states that what is decisive is 'whether the co-perpetrator performs an essential role in accordance with the common plan, and it is in this sense that his contribution, as it relates to the exercise of the role and functions assigned to him, must be essential' (*Prosecutor v. Lubanga*, ICC T. Ch. I, Judgment, ICC-01/04-01/06-2842, 14 March 2012, para. 1000).

The subjective requirements:

The Lubanga Pre-Trial and Trial Chamber named the three subjective requirements, including that i) the accused was aware that by implementing the common plan, the criminal consequences would 'occur in the ordinary course of events'; ii) the accused was aware that he provided an essential contribution to the implementation of the common plan and iii) the accused was aware of the factual circumstances that established the existence of an armed conflict, and of the link between these facts and his conduct (*Prosecutor v. Lubanga*, ICC T. Ch. I, Judgment, ICC-01/04-01/06-2842, 14 March 2012, para. 1008).

The Elements of Crimes and the mental element:

It is important to note that the Chambers have chosen to examine the subjective requirements based on Article 30 – the mental element requirements, noting that "the general mental element contained in Article 30(1) (intent and knowledge) applies to all crimes under the jurisdiction of the Court 'unless otherwise provided" (*Prosecutor v. Lubanga*, ICC PT. Ch. I, ICC-01/04-01/06-803, 29 January 2007, para. 351; *Prosecutor v. Lubanga*, ICC T. Ch. I, ICC-01/04-01/06-2842, 14 March 2012, paras. 1007–1014).

At the *Lubanga* Pre-Trial stage, the chamber implicitly confirmed the status of the Elements of Crimes as law to be applied by the Court, suggesting that is equal to the Statute itself. Even in the drafting process of the Elements, some participants thought that the Elements could not provide for 'downward' departures from offence requirements listed in the Statute unless there was a clear mandate in the Statute itself (see Clark, 2001, pp. 320–21). This was exactly the situation that was presented to the Pre-Trial Chamber. The question presented to the PTC was: With respect to the age of the soldiers enlisted, does the general requirement of intention and knowledge (Article 30(1) ICC Statute) apply, or has the subjective threshold been lowered by the Elements, which require only that 'the perpetrator knew or should have known that such person or persons were under the age of 15 years' (Element (3) of Article 8(2)(b)(xxvi) ICC Statute)? The Pre-Trial Chamber stated that the crime definition in Article 8(3)(b)(xxvii) of the ICC Statute does not contain a special subjective element and Article 30 is therefore applicable. The Chamber then further specified that they "note that the third element listed in the Elements of Crimes for these specific crimes requires that, in relation to the age of the victims [t]he perpetrator knew or should have known that such person or persons were under the age of 15 years (*Prosecutor v. Lubanga*, ICC PT. Ch. I, ICC-01/04-01/06-803, 29 January 2007, para. 358). The Chamber then went on to explain that 'should have known' requires more negligence. Thus, the Pre-Trial Chamber concludes that the 'should have known' requirement is an exception to the 'intent and knowledge' requirement embodied in Article 30 of the Statute (*Prosecutor v. Lubanga*, ICC PT. Ch. I, ICC-01/04-01/06-803, 29 January 2007, para. 359).

The dissent of Judge Fulford:

Judge Fulford dissented in the Trial Chamber Judgment in the *Lubanga* case, favouring a plain text reading of Article 25(3)(a), which would result in a lower standard of proof for the Prosecution, requiring a finding that at least two persons acted to implement a common plan. Additionally, his standard would require only a 'contribution to the crime', direct or indirect. In Judge Fulford's reasoning,

a. A plain text reading of Article 25(3)(a) would establish the following elements for co-perpetration: The involvement of at least two individuals.

b. Coordination between those who commit the offence, which may take the form of an agreement, common plan or joint understanding, express or implied, to commit a crime or to undertake action that, in the ordinary course of events will lead to the commission of the crime.

c. A contribution to the crime which may be direct or indirect, provided either way there is a causal link between the individual's contribution and the crime.

d. Intent and knowledge, as defined in Article 30 of the Statute, or as 'otherwise provided' elsewhere in the Court's legal framework.

Essentially, Judge Fulford was concerned about hypothetical and counterfactual reasoning that would be required by the control theory as applied by the Chamber's approach. Because this control theory requires the 'essential contribution' finding, it is necessary to decide if the crime would have still occurred in the absence of the defendant's contribution (*Prosecutor v. Lubanga*, ICC T. Ch. I, Judgment, Separate Opinion of Judge Adrian Fulford, ICC-01/04-01/06-2842, 14 March 2012, para. 17). As well Judge Fulford discusses that the Majority's approach creates a distinction between principals and accomplices, which Judge Fulford deems unnecessary since there are no international statutory sentencing guidelines (*Prosecutor v. Lubanga*, ICC T. Ch. I, Judgment, Separate Opinion of Judge Adrian Fulford, ICC-01/04-01/06-2842, 14 March 2012, para. 9). In this discussion, he refers to the question of whether the new language of individual criminal liability found in Article 25 has created a hierarchy of seriousness in crimes (with 25(3)(a) representing the most serious of crimes and 25(3)(d) representing the least. He rejects this notion, stating that "there is no proper basis for concluding that ordering, soliciting, or inducing a crime (Article 25(3)(b)) is a less serious form of commission than committing it 'through another person' (Article 25(3)(a) [...] Similarly, I am unable to accept that the criminality of accessories (Article 25(3)(c)) is greater than those who participate within a group (Article 25(3)(d)), particularly since many of history's most serious crimes occurred as the result of the coordinated actions of groups of individuals, who jointly pursued a common goal" (*Prosecutor v. Lubanga*, ICC T. Ch. I, Judgment, Separate Opinion of Judge Adrian Fulford, ICC-01/04-01/06-2842, 14 March 2012, para. 8). Lastly, as an interesting note Judge Fulford states that within the Lubanga case, he agrees that the test laid out by the Pre-Trial Chamber should be applied as the "case has been conducted on the basis of the legal framework established by the Pre-Trial Chamber". His opinion stems from fear of prejudicing the accused's right to be informed of the charges against him. He states that, in his view, "this requirement [...] means that the accused should not only be aware of the basic outline of the legal framework against which those facts will be determined. This ensures that the accused knows, at all stages of the proceedings, what he is expected to meet" (*Prosecutor v. Lubanga*, ICC T. Ch. I, Judgment, Separate Opinion of Judge Adrian Fulford, ICC-01/04-01/06-2842, 14 March 2012, para. 20).

In the case of *Katanga and Ngudolo Chui*, Pre-Trial Chamber I in its confirmation of charges reiterated its position on Article 25(3)(a), continuing to use the formulation developed in Lubanga and adding to its analysis to incorporate the issue of perpetration through another person, found in the language of Article 25(3)(a). Here, the Pre-Trial Chamber interpreted the concept of indirect perpetration in order to charge the co-accused as co-perpetrators based on the theory that they exercised 'joint control' over the crimes committed (*Prosecutor v. Katanga*, ICC PT. Ch. I, Decision on the Confirmation of Charges , ICC-01/04-01/07-717, 30 September 2008, para. 473). The prosecutor charged the defendants, in the alternative, as accessories under Article 25(3)(b) for 'ordering' the crimes committed by the militia members. The Chamber decided that accessorial liability was 'rendered moot' by a finding of liability as principals under Article 25(3)(a) and hence did not further pursue the alternative of accessorial liability; *Ibid.*, §§ 470–471. The Chamber thus sidestepped the question whether it is permissible for the prosecutor to present alternative charges although Reg. 52(c) of the ICC Regulations requires "[a] legal characterisation of the facts to accord both with the crimes under Articles 6, 7 or 8 and the precise form of participation under Articles 25 and 28". Following its lead in *Lubanga*, the Pre-Trial Chamber of Katanga defined 'control' as the criteria for distinguishing principal and accessory liability. However, here, the Chamber expanded upon their statement, interpreting the 'control or mastermind' formula to include the situation where a person 'has control over the will of those who carry out the objective elements of the offence' (*Prosecutor v. Katanga*, ICC

PT. Ch. I, ICC-01/04-01/07-717, 30 September 2008, para. 488). As well, the Chamber concludes that 'control' over an immediate actor can be exerted by means of an organisation. Since the Article explicitly declares it irrelevant whether the person through whom the crime is committed acts culpably or not, the Chamber here concludes that the 'control' over the immediate actor can be exerted through an organisation. The Chamber notes that, "[...] the cases most relevant to international criminal law are those in which the perpetrator behind the perpetrator commits the crime through another by means of 'control over an organization'" (*Prosecutor v. Katanga*, ICC PT. Ch. I, ICC-01/04-01/07-717, 30 September 2008, para. 498). Importantly, the Pre-Trial Chamber then goes on to define the necessary elements of an 'organisation' for these purposes:

> The Chamber finds that the organization must be based on hierarchical relations between superiors and subordinates. The organization must also be composed of sufficient subordinates to guarantee that superiors' orders will be carried out, if not by one subordinate, then by another. These criteria ensure that orders given by the recognized leadership will generally be complied with by their subordinates (*Prosecutor v. Katanga*, ICC PT. Ch. I, ICC-01/04-01/07-717, 30 September 2008, para. 512).

The Chamber goes on to explain that perpetration by means of an organisation can also be committed jointly by several leaders acting in concert, provided that each leader supplied a contribution necessary for the completion of the common plan (*Prosecutor v. Katanga*, ICC PT. Ch. I, ICC-01/04-01/07-717, 30 September 2008, paras. 524–526).

In the Al Bashir arrest warrant, the Prosecution broke new ground, exclusively basing the charges on the concept of indirect perpetration. According to the Prosecutor's application, this mode of liability under Article 25(3)(a) included the following three elements: a) the Prosecution must establish the existence of a relationship such that the indirect perpetrator may impose his dominant will over the direct perpetrator to ensure that the crime is committed. Where, as in this Application, the indirect perpetrator is alleged to have committed the crime through an organisation or group, that institution must be "hierarchically organised". b) Second, the indirect perpetrator must have sufficient authority within the organisation such that he has 'the final say about the adoption and implementation' of the policies and practices at issue. c) Third, the indirect perpetrator must be 'aware of his unique role within the [organisation] and actively use it' in furtherance of the crimes charged (*Prosecutor v. Bashir*, PT. Ch. I, Public Redacted Version of the Prosecution's Application under Article 58, ICC-02/05-157-AnxA, 12 September 2008, para. 248).

The Prosecutor based his approach on the findings of Pre-Trial Chamber I in the Lubanga case (*Prosecutor v. Bashir*, PT. Ch. I, ICC-02/05-157-AnxA, 12 September 2008, para. 309). The Chamber then provided further reasoning on indirect co-perpetration based on the notion of control over an organisation within the Al Bashir Warrant of Arrest with respect to the Darfur situation. The judges contemplated three different forms of perpetration (indirect, co, and indirect co-perpetration) to qualify the participation of the accused in the alleged crimes that were directly carried out by members of the Sudanese Armed Forces, the allied militia, the Janjaweed and other individuals (*Prosecutor v. Bashir*, PT. Ch. I, Decision on the Prosecution's Application for a Warrant of Arrest against Omar Hassan Ahmad Al Bashir (ICC-02/05-01/09-3), 4 March 2009, paras. 209–223). The Chamber found that Al Bashir played an essential role in coordinating the design and the implementation of the common plan, which consisted in the unlawful attack on a part of the civilian population of Darfur, belonging to specific ethnic groups. Thus, the Chamber reiterated that, "the notion of indirect co-perpetration is applicable when some or all of the co-perpetrators carry out their respective essential contributions to the common plan through another person. As the Chamber has underscored, in these types of situations co-perpetration or joint commission through another person is not possible if the suspects behaved without the concrete intent to bring about the objective elements of the crime and if there is a low and unaccepted probability that such would be a result of their activities" (*Prosecutor v. Bashir*, PT. Ch. I, Decision on the Prosecution's Application for a Warrant of Arrest against Omar Hassan Ahmad Al Bashir ((ICC-02/05-01/09-3), 4 March 2009, para. 213).

It is important to note here though that the judges had differing views over the need to resort to indirect co-perpetration (*Prosecutor v. Bashir*, PT. Ch. I, (ICC-02/05-01/09-3), 4 March 2009, paras. 211–213; see also Separate and Partly Dissenting Opinion of Judge Usacka, paras. 103–104). Judge Usacka, offering a dissenting view, noted that because she was not able to find that Al Bashir had full control, or whether it was shared by others so that each person had the power to frustrate the completion of the crime, she would not subscribe to the Majorities assessment of indirect co-perpetration and would rather have found as the sole mode of liability indirect perpetration (*Prosecutor v. Bashir*, Separate and Partly Dissenting Opinion of Judge Usacka, PT. Ch. I, (ICC-02/05-01/09-3), 4 March 2009, para. 104).

Author: Kirsten Bowman.

[268] *Indirect Perpetration*:

A scenario often envisioned under the concept of indirect perpetration is the case of the so-called 'perpetrator behind the perpetrator', where the direct perpetrator is manipulated or exploited by the indirect perpetrator to commit the crime, but who nevertheless remains a fully responsible agent. This has been formulated by the *Lubanga* Appeals Chamber as being "being based on the notion that a person can commit a crime 'through another person'. The underlying assumption is that the accused makes use of another person, who actually carries out the incriminated conduct, by virtue of the accused's control over that person, and the latter's conduct is therefore imputed on the former" (*Prosecutor v. Lubanga*, A. Ch., Judgment on the appeal of Mr Thomas Lubanga Dyilo against his conviction, ICC-01/04-01/06-3121-Red, 1 December 2014, para. 465). This formulation was also used in the Pre-Trial Chamber decision in the *Blé Goudé* decision on the Confirmation of Charges (*Prosecutor v. Blé Goudé*, PT. Ch. I, ICC-02/11-02/11, 31 December 2014, para. 134).

When looking at the Chamber's reasoning in applying the law in this manner, rather than a plain text reading as suggested by Judge Fulford or a JCE approach as has been customary international law and established law at the *ad hoc* tribunals, the Chamber gave three reasons: 1) The notion of control over crime has been incorporated into the framework of the Statute, 2) it has been increasingly used in national jurisdictions and 3) it has been addressed in the jurisprudence of the international tribunals (*Prosecutor v. Katanga*, ICC PT. Ch. I, Decision on the Confirmation of Charges, 30 September 2008, paras. 500–510). As regards the second reasoning given, the Chamber noted that 'the control over the crime approach has been applied in a number of legal systems and is widely recognized in legal doctrine' (*Prosecutor v. Katanga*, ICC PT. Ch. I, Decision on the Confirmation of Charges, 30 September 2008, para. 485).

Indirect and co-perpetration:

The concept of indirect co-perpetration is complex. Within the Katanga decision, the Pre-Trial Chamber adopted a sophisticated and complicated line of reasoning, combining the concepts of joint commission and commission through another (*Prosecutor v. Katanga*, ICC PT. Ch. I, Decision on the Confirmation of Charges, 30 September 2008, para. 492).

The Chamber found this necessary to overcome difficulties regarding the categorisation of the responsibility of two accused as principals for the crimes carries out by members of their two military organisations under their control. In fact, the Chamber stated that though Katanga and Ngudjolo acted with a common plan, some of the members within the two organisations only accepted orders from the leader of their own ethnic group. Therefore, not all the direct perpetrators of the crime were considered to fall directly under the control of the two leaders. In order to solve this problem, the judges combined the two forms of group criminality found in Article 25(3)(a) – indirect co-perpetration.

(b) Orders, solicits or induces the commission of such a crime which in fact occurs or is attempted;[269]

> The Chamber affirmed that:
> [...] an individual who has no control over the person through whom the crimes would be committed cannot be said to commit the crime by means of that other person. However, if he acts jointly with another individual – one who controls the person used as an instrument – these crimes can be attributed to him on the basis of mutual attribution (*Prosecutor v. Katanga*, ICC PT. Ch. I, Decision on the Confirmation of Charges, 30 September 2008, para. 493).

Due to the very high threshold that the Chamber has set for both the objective elements and subjective elements and the narrow terms in which the law is being construed, a fact pattern such as that found in the Katanga case with multiple organisations and perpetrators and a complex network of criminal activity presents a complicated problem. The Court needed a way to loosen this mode of liability and by combining the second and third forms of perpetration under Article 25(3)(a) of the ICC Statute, the Chamber has endeavoured to bring certain forms of conduct under the same notion of perpetration that would otherwise remain outside of it.

The Appeals Chamber neither confirmed nor appeared to deny the validity of this form of perpetration in the Lubanga Appeals Chamber decision noting that Article 25(3)(a) of the Statute expressly provides for three forms of commission liability – individual, jointly with another person, or through another person (*Prosecutor v. Lubanga*, ICC A. Ch., Judgment on the appeal of Mr Thomas Lubanga Dyilo against his conviction, ICC-01/04-01/06-3121-Red, 1 December 2014, para. 464). The Appeals Chamber also noted that the Court's jurisprudence contained differing views on the existence of a fourth form of commission liability where a perpetrator may commit a crime jointly with another as well as through another person: indirect co-perpetration. The Appeals Chamber expresses no particular view on whether they find this form of commission liability valid, leaving the issue open to further litigation on the matter (*Prosecutor v. Lubanga*, ICC A. Ch., Judgment on the appeal of Mr Thomas Lubanga Dyilo against his conviction, ICC-01/04-01/06-3132-Red, 1 December 2014, fn. 863).

Author: Kirsten Bowman.

[269] The forms of participation listed under Article 25(3)(b) are specific and distinct from those provided for in the other sub-paragraphs. Here a person ordering a crime is not merely an accomplice, but a perpetrator by means. In fact, Article 2(3)(b) of the 1996 Draft Code was intended to provide for the criminal responsibility of mid-level officials who order their subordinates to commit crimes.

This form of individual criminal liability has not been litigated judicially within the framework of the ICC and thus, there is no jurisprudence from which to analyse. In the Katanga warrant of arrest, individual criminal responsibility was pled under 25(3)(a) or 25(3)(b) (*Prosecutor v. Katanga*, PT. Ch. I, ICC-01/04-01/07-649-AnxIA, 26 June 2008, para. 94). However, the Pre-Trial Chamber confirmed the charges based on liability under 25(3)(a), leaving no discussion or jurisprudence on sub-paragraph (b) (*Prosecutor v. Katanga*, PT. Ch. I, ICC-01/04-01/07-649-AnxIA, 26 June 2008, para. 94).

It is important to note the close relationship that sub-paragraph (b) has with Article 28 which governs command responsibility. The first alternative in sub-paragraph (b), "orders", complements the command responsibility provision in Article 28. In the Article 28 provision the superior is liable for an omission while in the case of an order to commit a crime (Article 25(3)(b)) the superior is liable for commission for having 'ordered'. According to Ambos in the Triffterer commentary, "the first alternative in sub-paragraph (b) actually belongs to the forms of perpetration provided for in sub-paragraph (a), being a form of commission 'through another

(c) For the purpose of facilitating the commission of such a crime, aids, abets or otherwise assists in its commission or its attempted commission, including providing the means for its commission;[270]

---

person'". Other commentators have pondered whether ordering a crime is not more appropriately dealt with within Article 28, rather than naming ordering a crime as a case of instigation, which could be seen as inappropriately degrading a form of perpetration to mere complicity.

Commenting on the latter two provisions within sub-paragraph (b), Ambos notes that "soliciting a crime means, inter alia, to command, encourage, request or incite another person to engage in specific conduct to commit it, while to "induce" means to influence another person to commit a crime. Inducing is an umbrella term which covers soliciting. Inducing is a broad enough term to cover any conduct which leads another person to commit a crime, including solicitation. It is important to note that neither solicitation nor inducement require a superior–subordinate relationship.

A last useful note on sub-paragraph (b) is to keep in mind that according to commentary, excesses of the perpetrator cannot be attributed to an instigator. This is key as the instigator's scope of intent limits his responsibility and is important is cases where a principal may commit a further crime than he was instigated to do. In other respects, the drafting of this sub-paragraph is consistent with previous international laws concerning instigation crimes and there is not expected to be much confusion in how to apply this law, once cases come before the Court.

Author: Kirsten Bowman.

[270] Sub-paragraph (c) is set to cover the field of complicity by assistance which falls short of instigation (sub-paragraph (b)) but goes beyond 'other contributions' such as contributing to group activities within sub-paragraph (d). This form of liability under Article 25(3)(c) has not yet been adjudicated at the ICC. However, the Mbarushimana Pre-Trial Chamber commented, with reference to this sub-provision, in its Confirmation of Charges decision that "the application of analogous modes of liability at the *ad hoc* tribunals suggests that a substantial contribution to the crime may be contemplated" (*Prosecutor v. Mbarushimana*, PT. Ch. I, Decision on the Confirmation of Charges, ICC-01/04-01/10-465-Red, 16 December 2011, para. 279).

One difference that has been pointed out with regard to sub-paragraph (c) of the ICC Statute as compared to the jurisprudence of the *ad hoc* tribunals is that the latter does not require the aider and abettor to share the intent of the perpetrator to commit the crime. With the drafting of sub-paragraph (c) "the aider and abettor must act with the purpose of facilitating the commission of that crime".

As well, there has been debate as to whether the *actus reus* required should likewise differ from the *ad hoc* tribunals' 'substantial contribution' requirement (*Prosecutor v. Mbarushimana*, PT. Ch. I, ICC-01/04-01/10-465-Red, 16 December 2011, para. 281). However, the Lubanga Trial Chamber did address the contribution threshold requirement of sub-paragraph (c) in relation to defining the contribution threshold for Article 25(3)(a) as a principal actor versus an accessorial actor suggesting that if accessories must have had 'a substantial effect on the commission of the crime' to be held liable, then co-perpetrators must have had [...] more than a substantial effect (*Prosecutor v. Lubanga*, ICC T. Ch. I, Judgment, ICC-01/04-01/06-2842, 14 March 2012, para. 997). Thus, they seem to implicitly assume or endorse the substantial effect standard for contribution as an aider and abettor.

Scholarly commentary on the sub-paragraph has noted that the language used in the *ad hoc* tribunals' 'aiding and abetting' formulation, is slightly different in the ICC Statute. The ICC Statute speaks of a person who 'aids, abets or otherwise assists' in the attempt or accomplishment of a crime, including 'providing the means for its commission'. This wording may suggest that 1) aiding and abetting are not one unit but rather each term has its own meaning, 2) aiding

(d) In any other way contributes to the commission or attempted commission of such a crime by a group of persons acting with a common purpose. Such contribution shall be intentional and shall either:[271]

---

and abetting are only two forms of possible assistance, with 'otherwise assists' being an umbrella term to encompass other forms of possible assistance and 3) 'providing the means' for the commission of a crime is merely an example of assistance.

Author: Kirsten Bowman.

[271] Article 25(3)(d) of the ICC Statute regulates a new form of criminal participation: contributing to the commission of a crime or an attempted crime by a group. Some have argued that the jurisprudence of the *ad hoc* Tribunal's JCE theory and Article 25(3)(d) of the ICC Statute might be considered 'little cousins'. In contrast, others have argued that Article 25(3)(d) 'certainly cracks open the door, but it is far from clear how much of the ICTY's complex JCE doctrine will be able to slip through it'.

In the Prosecutions submission in the *Mbarushimana* case requesting a Warrant for Arrest, they sought the arrest warrant based on the Accused's individual responsibility as a co-perpetrator under Article 25(3)(a) and in the alternative as an accessory under Article 25(3)(d) of the Statute (*Prosecutor v. Mbarushimana*, PT. Ch. I, Prosecution's Application under Article 58, ICC-01/04-573-US-Exp, 20 August 2010, p. 68).

In it's analysis on accessorial liability based on Article 25(3)(d), the Pre-Trial Chamber stated the objective and subjective elements required in order to find individual responsibility. The three objective elements were stated as: i) a crime within the jurisdiction of the Court is attempted or committed; ii) the commission or attempted commission of such a crime was carried out by a group of persons acting with a common purpose; and iii) the individual contributed to the crime in any way other than those set out in Article 25(3)(a) to (d) of the Statute. The subjective elements were elaborated as: i) the contribution shall be intentional; and ii) shall either a) be made with the aim of furthering the criminal activity or criminal purpose of the group; or b) in the knowledge of the intention of the group to commit the crime (*Prosecutor v. Mbarushimana*, PT. Ch. I, Decision on the Prosecutor's Application for a Warrant of Arrest against Callixte Mbarushimana, ICC-01/04-01/10-1, 11 October 2010, para. 39).

In its Decision on the Confirmation of Charges, the Pre-Trial Chamber rejected the idea that Article 25(3)(d) only applied to 'outside contributors' who are essentially assisting in a collective crime from the outside, but who are not themselves a member of the criminal group (*Prosecutor v. Mbarushimana*, PT. Ch. I, ICC-01/04-01/10-465-Red, 16 December 2011, para. 273). The Chamber reasoned that "[t]o adopt an essential contribution test for liability under Article 25(3)(a) of the Statute, as this Chamber has done, and accept the Defence argument that 25(3)(d) liability is limited only to non-group members would restrict criminal responsibility for group members making non-essential contributions in ways not intended [...]" (*Prosecutor v. Mbarushimana*, PT. Ch. I, ICC-01/04-01/10-465-Red, 16 December 2011, para. 273).

While not imposing the high 'essential contribution' language, the Chamber did require a threshold of 'significant contribution' for the accused to have made toward crimes committed or attempted (*Prosecutor v. Mbarushimana*, PT. Ch. I, ICC-01/04-01/10-465-Red, 16 December 2011, para. 283).

Doctrine:

1. Kai Ambos, in Otto Triffterer (ed.), *Commentary on the Rome Statute of the International Criminal Court: Observers' Notes, Article by Article*, 2nd ed., C.H. Beck/Hart/Nomos, Munich/Oxford/Baden-Baden, 2008, pp. 743–70.
2. Roger S. Clark, "The Mental Element in International Criminal Law", in *Criminal Law Forum*, 2001, vol. 12, pp. 291, 320–21.

(i) Be made with the aim of furthering the criminal activity or criminal purpose of the group, where such activity or purpose involves the commission of a crime within the jurisdiction of the Court; or

(ii) Be made in the knowledge of the intention of the group to commit the crime;

(e) In respect of the crime of genocide, directly and publicly incites others to commit genocide;[272]

(f) Attempts to commit such a crime by taking action that commences its execution by means of a substantial step, but the crime does not occur because of circumstances independent of the person's intentions. However, a person who abandons the effort to commit the crime or otherwise prevents the completion of the crime shall not be liable for punishment under this Statute for the attempt to commit that crime if that person completely and voluntarily gave up the criminal purpose.[273]

---

3. Albin Eser, in Antonio Cassese, Paola Gaeta and John R.W.D. Jones (eds.), *The Rome Statute of the International Criminal Court: A Commentary,* Oxford University Press, Oxford, 2002, pp. 767–801, 803 and 806–7.

4. Stefano Manacorda and Chantal Meloni, "Indirect Perpetration versus Joint Criminal Enterprise", in *Journal of International Justice,* 2011, vol. 9, pp. 167, 174–76.

5. Hector Olasolo, *The Criminal Responsibility of Senior Political and Military Leaders as Principals to International Crimes,* Oxford, Hart, 2009.

6. Thomas Weigend, "Intent, Mistake of Law, and Co-perpetration in the Lubanga Decision on Confirmation of Charges", in *Journal of International Criminal Justice,* 2008, vol. 6, no. 3, pp. 471–87.

Author: Kirsten Bowman.

[272] Article 25(3)(e) of the ICC Statute criminalises direct and public incitement of others to commit genocide. It is in substance identical to Article III(c) of the 1948 Convention on the Prevention and Punishment of the Crime of Genocide, and the ICTY and ICTR Statutes. Genocide is the only international crime to which public incitement has been criminalised. The reason for this provision is to prevent the early stages of genocide even prior to the preparation or attempt thereof.

To incite 'publicly' means that the call for criminal action is communicated to a number of individuals in a public place or to members of the general public at large particularly by technological means of mass communication, such as by radio or television. To incite 'directly' means that a person is specifically urging another individual to take immediate criminal action rather than merely making a vague or indirect suggestion. This incitement comes very close to, if not even substantially covered by, instigation according to Article 25(3)(b), thus losing much of its own significance. The difference between ordinary form instigation, for example, instigation on the one hand and incitement to genocide on the other, lies in the fact that the former is specifically directed towards a certain person or group of persons in private while the latter is directed to the public in general. There is one important difference between incitement to genocide and the forms of complicity under sub-paragraphs(b), (c) and (d): incitement with regard to genocide does not require the commission or even attempted commission of the actual crime, that is, genocide. As such, incitement to commit genocide is an inchoate crime.

Author: Mark Klamberg.

[273] Article 25(3)(f) provides for the criminal responsibility of an individual who attempts to commit a crime within the jurisdiction of the Court if a person commits an act to carry out his or her intention and fails to successfully complete the crime only because of some independent factor which prevents him or her from doing so. The phrase 'does not occur' recognises that the notion

3 *bis*. In respect of the crime of aggression, the provisions of this article shall apply only to persons in a position effectively to exercise control over or to direct the political or military action of a State.[274]

---

of attempt by definition only applies to situations in which an individual endeavours to commit a crime and fails in this endeavour. Thus, an individual incurs criminal responsibility for unsuccessfully attempting to commit a crime only when the following elements are present: (a) intent to commit a particular crime; (b) an act designed to commit it; and (c) non-completion of the crime for reasons independent of the perpetrator's will.

On the other hand, a person who abandons the effort to commit the crime or otherwise prevents the completion of the crime is not criminally responsible. The provision does not clarify at what stage of the commission abandonment is still admissible or under which circumstances the abandonment is voluntarily. This problem is left for the Court. However, some guidance may be sought in the phrase "by taking action commencing the execution of a crime" which is used to indicate that the individual has performed an act which constitutes a significant step towards the completion of the crime.

In *Prosecutor v. Katanga and Ngudjolo Chui*, ICC PT. Ch. I, Decision on the Confirmation of Charges, ICC-01/04-01/07-717, 30 September 2008, para. 460, PTC I endorsed the "doctrine that establishes that the attempt to commit a crime is a crime in which the objective elements are incomplete, while the subjective elements are complete. Therefore, the dolus that embodies the attempt is the same than the one that embodies the consummated act. As a consequence, in order for an attempt to commit a crime to be punished, it is necessary to infer the intent to further an action that would cause the result intended by the perpetrator, and the commencement of the execution of the act".

Doctrine:

1. Kai Ambos, in Otto Triffterer (ed.), *Commentary on the Rome Statute of the International Criminal Court: Observers' Notes, Article by Article*, 2nd ed., C.H. Beck/Hart/Nomos, Munich/Oxford/Baden-Baden, 2008, pp. 762–65.
2. Albin Eser, in Antonio Cassese, Paola Gaeta and John R.W.D. Jones (eds.), *The Rome Statute of the International Criminal Court: A Commentary*, Oxford University Press, Oxford, 2002, pp. 803–18.

Author: Mark Klamberg.

[274] Article 25(3) *bis* echoes the requirement in Article 8 *bis*(1) that a 'perpetrator was a person in a position effectively to exercise control over or to direct the political or military action of the State which committed the act of aggression'. The purpose of this paragraph is to clarify that the leadership requirement, discussed under Article 8 *bis*(1) (Section C(i)(b)), applies also when making assessments under Article 25(3). It has been suggested that as acts of aggression are general collective in nature, joint criminal enterprise will be the most applicable entry through which to assess individual responsibility (Cassese, 2007, p. 848).

While the various forms of participation is explained under Article 25(3)(a–f), it should be noted that it is uncertain whether it is possible to attempt to commit a crime of aggression in accordance with Article 25(3)(f), since the elements of the crimes clearly states that an act of aggression will have had to be committed in order for there to be a crime of aggression under the ICC Statute (Element 3). The Special Working Group on the Crime of Aggression held this to be a largely theoretical question, and decided not to actively exclude Article 25(3)(f) due to its unlikely application on the crime of aggression (Barriga, 2012, pp. 23–24).

Cross-references:

Article 8 *bis*.

Doctrine:

---

4. No provision in this Statute relating to individual criminal responsibility shall affect the responsibility of States under international law.[275]

[8] As amended by resolution RC/Res.6 of 11 June 2010 (adding paragraph 3 *bis*).

1. Stefan Barriga, "Negotiating the Amendments on the Crime of Aggression", in Stefan Barriga and Claus Kreß (eds.), *The Travaux Préparatoires of the Crime of Aggression*, Cambridge University Press, Cambridge, 2012, pp. 3–57.
2. Antonio Cassese, "On Some Problematical Aspects of the Crime of Aggression", in *Leiden Journal of International Law*, 2007, vol. 20, no. 4, pp. 841–49.

Author: Marie Aronsson-Storrier.

[275] The ICC has no direct power to ascertain State responsibility. Nevertheless, the paragraph affirms the parallel validity of the rules of state responsibility.

Doctrine:

1. Kai Ambos, in Otto Triffterer (ed.), *Commentary on the Rome Statute of the International Criminal Court: Observers' Notes, Article by Article*, 2nd ed., C.H. Beck/Hart/Nomos, Munich/Oxford/Baden-Baden, 2008, p. 765.
2. Micaela Frulli, in Antonio Cassese, Paola Gaeta and John R.W.D. Jones (eds.), *The Rome Statute of the International Criminal Court: A Commentary*, Oxford University Press, Oxford, 2002, p. 533.

Author: Mark Klamberg.

Article 26
Exclusion of jurisdiction over persons under eighteen

The Court shall have no jurisdiction over any person who was under the age of 18 at the time of the alleged commission of a crime.[276]

---

[276] The time limit of 18 is an absolute border completely independent of maturity of immaturity. The Statues of the International Military Tribunal, the UN *ad hoc* tribunals provide no age of criminal responsibility. Article 7 of the Statute of the Special Court for Sierra Leone had the limit of fifteen but no teenagers were ever prosecuted. Article 40(3)(a) of the Convention on the Rights of the Child provides that States shall seek to establish "a minimum age below which children shall be presumed not to have the capacity to infringe the penal law", without a specification of an age limit.

Turning to immaturity for person above the age of 18, responsibility of such persons may be excluded by a defence listed in Article 31(1)(a), when their immaturity results from a mental disease. It can also be a mitigating factor under Article 78(1). This Article only applies to the jurisdiction of the ICC which means that youngsters may be tried by national courts.

Doctrine:

1. Roger S. Clark and Otto Triffterer, in Otto Triffterer (ed.), *Commentary on the Rome Statute of the International Criminal Court: Observers' Notes, Article by Article*, 2nd ed., C.H. Beck/Hart/Nomos, Munich/Oxford/Baden-Baden, 2008, pp. 771–77.

2. Micaela Frulli, in Antonio Cassese, Paola Gaeta and John R.W.D. Jones (eds.), *The Rome Statute of the International Criminal Court: A Commentary*, Oxford University Press, Oxford, 2002, p. 533–35.

3. William A. Schabas, *The International Criminal Court: A Commentary on the Rome Statute*, Oxford University Press, Oxford, 2010, pp. 443–45.

Author: Mark Klamberg.

Article 27
Irrelevance of official capacity[277]

---

[277] *General remarks*:

The principles of state sovereignty and the equality of all states are fundamental to international relations and international law. As an extension of these principles certain state officials who represents their states are granted immunity from prosecution by international law. International law distinguishes between two types of immunity; immunity *ratione materiae*, which shields certain acts, and immunity *ratione personae,* which shields specific state officials.

Immunity *ratione materiae*, often also referred to as functional immunity, is attached to such acts that can be regarded as being acts of a state, that is, non-private, sovereign acts. Anyone carrying out such state acts are protected by immunity *ratione materiae*. Immunity *ratione personae* (personal immunity) on the other hand relates to a specific office held by certain state officials. It is only a small group of senior state officials who enjoy immunity *ratione personae*. The ICJ stated in the Arrest Warrant Case that such it is a firmly established principle in international law that immunity *ratione personae* attaches to heads of states and heads of government (para. 51). Furthermore the ICJ stated that also ministers of foreign affairs enjoys immunity *ratione personae*.

Since immunity *ratione personae* attaches to the office itself and not a certain category of acts it shields the state official from prosecution for both official, non-private and private acts. However, while immunity *ratione materiae* never ceases to protect the protected acts immunity ratione personae ceases to exist when the state official in question leaves his or her office. All official acts carried out during the time of office are though protected by immunity *ratione materiae* also for these persons.

The scope of immunity *ratione materiae* and immunity *ratione personae* is mainly determined by customary international law, in which an exception from immunity *ratione materiae* has developed since the Nuremberg trials. The exception provides that a state official cannot rely on immunity ratione materiae when committing international crimes (Kreß and Prost in Otto Triffterer, 2008, p. 1608). The ICTY has confirmed this exception in *Prosecutor v. Milošević* when the Trial Chamber argued that Article 7(2) of the ICTY Statute, which provides that the official capacity of a person shall not relieve him or her from criminal responsibility, reflects customary international law (*Prosecutor v. Milošević*, ICTY, T. Ch., 8 November 2001, para. 28). The Trial Chamber found that the fact that Slobodan Milošević was the former president of the Federal Republic of Yugoslavia did not stop the ICTY from having jurisdiction over him. The ICTY addressed Milošević's immunity *ratione materiae* since he no longer was the incumbent president and therefore did not enjoy immunity *ratione personae*. Two years later, the ICTY confirmed its earlier findings in *Prosecutor v. Krstić* (who was found guilty of *inter alia* aiding and abetting genocide):

It may be the case (it is unnecessary to decide here) that, between States, such a functional immunity exists against prosecution for those acts, but it would be incorrect to suggest that such an immunity exists in international criminal courts" (*Prosecutor v. Krstić*, ICTY A. Ch., 1 July 2003, para. 26).

Whether customary law provides for an exception from immunity *ratione personae* with regard to criminal proceedings before international courts is at this point not certain. The issue is though widely discussed. However, the status of immunity *ratione personae* in customary law is of no importance in the relationship between the ICC and its member states. When becoming a member state to the ICC, and consenting to Article 27 of the ICC Statute, every member state waives the immunity *ratione personae* that would otherwise be accorded to its state officials (see below). Article 27 is therefore one of the more important Articles in the ICC Statute when

1. This Statute shall apply equally to all persons without any distinction based on official capacity. In particular, official capacity as a Head of State or Government, a member of a Government or parliament, an elected representative or a government official shall in no case exempt a person from criminal responsibility under this Statute, nor shall it, in and of itself, constitute a ground for reduction of sentence.[278]

2. Immunities or special procedural rules which may attach to the official capacity of a person, whether under national or international law, shall not bar the Court from exercising its jurisdiction over such a person.[279]

---

it comes to reaching the aim set out in the preamble of putting an end to the impunity of perpetrators of international crimes since the Article grants the ICC jurisdiction over the highest state officials of the member states (Triffterer, 2008, p. 786).

Cross-references:
Article 98(1).

Author: Camilla Lind.

[278] According to Article 27(1) state officials, for example – but not exclusively – those mentioned in the Article, that would otherwise be protected by immunity *ratione materiae* or immunity *ratione personae* can be held responsible for committing international crimes (Triffterer, 2008, pp. 787–788). The aim of Article 27(1) is to remove any immunity that may be attached to any official capacity, not only the immunities applying to the official capacities mentioned in the Article. Article 27(1) therefore focuses of the functional immunity of state officials (Gaeta in Cassese, 2002, p. 990).

Cross-references:
Article 98(1)

Author: Camilla Lind.

[279] Article 27(2) aims at providing the ICC with jurisdiction over crimes committed by state officials enjoying immunity *ratione materiae* or immunity *ratione personae* (Triffterer, 2008, p. 791). Also immunity accorded to state officials by customary international law is irrelevant according to the Article since it explicitly refers to both national and international law (Schabas, 2010, p. 449).

i. Waiver of immunity for state parties

Article 27 is to be interpreted as a waiver of immunity accorded to the state officials by the state parties to the ICC Statute (Schabas, 2010, p. 450, Kreß and Prost in Otto Triffterer, 2008, p. 1607). By acceding to the ICC Statute the state consents to Article 27 and the provision stating that immunities shall not bar the court from exercising jurisdiction over their state officials. Thereby the state has waived the immunity that would otherwise be accorded to its state officials. The waiver of immunity is, according to most authors, to be interpreted as having effect not only in the relation between the state party and the ICC, but also in the relation between two or more state parties to the ICC Statute since all state parties has consented to waive the immunities of its state officials (Kreß and Prost in Otto Triffterer, 2008, p. 1607). Also, it has been argued that not giving the waiver effect in the relationship between different state parties would deprive the Article of all practical meaning. If it only would have effect in the relationship between the individual member state and the ICC the Article would be practically useless since the ICC then would have to obtain a specific waiver from the member state of a state official when requesting other member states to cooperate with the arrest and surrender of that state official (Kreß and Prost in Otto Triffterer, 2008, p. 1607, Akande, 2004, p. 420). The question of the scope of the waiver is important when discussing Article 98(1).

ii. The relationship between Article 27 of the ICC Statute and non-member states to the Statute.

When it comes to the relationship between the ICC and non-member states the general rule in Article 34 of the Vienna Convention on the Law of Treaties must be held in mind. According to that Article contracting states cannot create obligations for states that are not parties to a convention. This is true also when it comes to the ICC Statute and Article 27, meaning that state officials of non-state parties to the ICC Statute still may be accorded immunity in accordance with international law since the state parties to the ICC Statute cannot remove the immunity of state officials of non-member states (Schabas, 2010, p. 450). Article 27 has been up for discussion in two decisions by the Pre-Trial Chamber in the case of *Prosecutor v. Omar Al Bashir*. These two decisions shall be commented. When reading the decisions, it shall be kept in mind that Omar Al Bashir is currently the incumbent president of Sudan, which is a non-member state to the ICC Statute. The situation in Sudan was referred to the ICC by the United Nations Security Council by Resolution 1593 (2005) under Article 13(b) of the ICC Statute.

Pre-Trial Chamber Decision of 4 March 2009

In Prosecutor v. Omar Al Bashir, ICC PT. Ch. I, Decision on the Prosecution's Application for a Warrant of Arrest against Omar Hassan Ahmad Al Bashir, 4 March 2009, Pre-Trial Chamber I addressed the question of whether Al Bashir's status as head of state of a non-state party to the ICC would shield him from proceedings before the ICC. The conclusion of the Pre-Trial Chamber was that Al Bashir does not enjoy immunity from proceedings before the ICC (para. 41). When reaching that conclusion, the Chamber considered, among other things that one of the clearly stated goals of the ICC Statute is to end the impunity of perpetrators of international crimes (para. 42). The Chamber also relied on three core principles derived from Article 27, being that "(i) [the Rome Statute] shall apply equally to all persons without any distinction based on official capacity;" (ii) "official capacity as a Head of State or Government, a member of Government or parliament, an elected representative or a government official shall in no case exempt a person from criminal responsibility under this Statute, nor shall it, in and of itself, constitute a ground for reduction of sentence;" and (iii) "Immunities or special procedural rules which may attach to the official capacity of a person, whether under national or international law, shall not bar the Court from exercising its jurisdiction over such a person" (para. 43). The Pre-Trial Chamber also stated that there is a provision in the ICC Statute dealing with the immunity of state officials and that this provision must, according to its interpretation of Article 21 of the ICC Statute, be used also in relationship to non-party states (para. 44).

The Pre-Trial Chamber's decision of 4 March 2009 has been widely discussed. According to Schabas, the Pre-Trial Chamber has interpreted the applicability of Article 27(2) incorrectly. The Pre-Trial Chamber has interpreted Article 27 as being applicable also to states that are not parties to the ICC Statute even though the Vienna Convention on the Law of Treaties explicitly provides that a treaty cannot create obligations for third states (Schabas, 2010, p. 451). Gaeta is however of the same opinion as the Pre-Trial Chamber and argues that Article 27(2) is indeed applicable also to state officials of non-party states even though she admits that the arguments put forward by the Pre-Trial Chamber in its decision are unconvincing (Gaeta, 2009, pp. 322–325). Kreß is also of the view that Article 27(2) is applicable to state officials of non-state parties. He argues that when a situation is referred to the ICC from the United Nations Security Council, the Security Council can (and has, in the case of Sudan, indeed intended to) place a non-state party in a position that is analogous to the position of a state party. Consequently the ICC can apply the provisions of the ICC Statute regardless of whether the state concerned is a party or not to the ICC Statute (see Kreß, 2012, 241–242).

Pre-Trial Chamber Decision of 12 December 2011

In *Prosecutor v. Omar Al Bashir*, ICC PT. Ch. I, Decision Pursuant to Article 87(7) of the ICC Statute on the Failure by the Republic of Malawi to Comply with the Cooperation Requests Issued by the Court with Respect to the Arrest and Surrender of Omar Hassan Ahmad Al Bashir,

12 December 2011, the Pre-Trial Chamber stated that heads of states of non-parties to the ICC Statute do not enjoy immunity according to international law (para. 36). The Pre-Trial Chamber supports its finding by referring to the statutes of the ICTY and the ICTR, and that the ICTY has stated that the corresponding Article in the ICTY Statute is declaratory of customary international law (paras. 29–31). It is however worth noting that the statutes of the ICTY and ICTR does not explicitly waive the immunity accorded to state officials, which Article 27 of the ICC Statute does. A reference was also made by the Pre-Trial Chamber to an *obiter dictum* in the Arrest Warrant Case stating that incumbent high ranking state officials may be subject to proceedings before some international courts, including the ICC (para. 33) and to an argument given by Cassese that the underlying rationales for immunity *ratione personae* are different depending on whether a national or an international court is exercising jurisdiction (para. 34). According to the Pre-Trial Chamber Article 27 of the ICC Statute is declaratory of customary international law not only when it comes to immunity *ratione materiae* but also with regard to immunity *ratione personae*. Whether that is the case or not is however, as earlier mentioned, discussed in the literature. No certain answer to the question of the status of immunity *ratione personae* in customary law has been reached. It is however clear from the two Pre-Trial Chamber decisions that the ICC considers that there is an exception from the immunity *ratione personae* when it comes to international crimes.

Cross-references:
Article 98(1).

Doctrine:

1. Paola Gaeta, *Official Capacity and Immunities*, in Antonio Cassese, et al (eds.), *The Rome Statute of the International Criminal Court: A Commentary*, Oxford University Press, Oxford, 2002, pp. 975–1001.

2. Claus Kreß and Kimberley Prost, "Article 98 – Cooperation with Respect to Waiver of Immunity and Consent to Surrender", in Otto Triffterer (ed.), *Commentary on the Rome Statute of the International Criminal Court: Observers' Notes, Article by Article*, 2nd ed., C.H. Beck/Hart/Nomos, Munich/Oxford/Baden-Baden, 2008, pp. 1601–19.

3. Claus Kreß, "The International Criminal Court and Immunities under International Law for States Not Party to the Court's Statute", in Morten Bergsmo and Ling Yan (eds.), *State Sovereignty and International Criminal Law*, FICHL Publication Series No. 15, Torkel Opsahl Academic EPublisher, Beijing, 2012, pp. 223–65.

4. William A. Schabas, *The International Criminal Court: A Commentary on the Rome Statute*, Oxford University Press, Oxford, 2010, pp. 446–53.

5. Otto Triffterer, "Article 27 – Irrelevance of Official Capacity", in Otto Triffterer (ed.), *Commentary on the Rome Statute of the International Criminal Court: Observers' Notes, Article by Article*, 2nd ed., C.H. Beck/Hart/Nomos, Munich/Oxford/Baden-Baden, 2008, pp. 779–93.

6. Paola Gaeta, "Does President Al Bashir Enjoy Immunity from Arrest?", in *Journal of International Criminal Justice*, 2009, vol. 7, no. 2, pp. 315–32.

7. Dapo Akande, "International Law Immunities and the International Criminal Court", in *American Journal of International Law*, 2004, vol. 98, no. 3, pp. 407–33.

Author: Camilla Lind.

Article 28

Responsibility of commanders and other superiors[280]

---

[280] *General remarks*:

Article 28 sets out the parameters for how the ICC shall apply the doctrine of superior responsibility under which, in specific circumstances, military commanders, persons effectively acting as military commanders and certain other superiors are held accountable for the crimes undertaken by their subordinates, or perhaps more accurately, with regard to the crimes of their subordinates.

Superior responsibility has its origins in military law and finds its basis in the principle that armed forces always should be "commanded by a person responsible for his subordinates" as expressed in Article 1(1) of the Hague Regulations from 1899 and the corresponding legal duty of the superior to "ensure that members of the armed forces under their control are aware of their obligations" and "to prevent and repress breaches undertaken by subordinates" as expressed in Article 87 and 86 of Additional Protocol I from 1977 respectively. The doctrine has successively been developed and refined and is now understood to also cover relationships that are not military in nature (see commentary on Article 28(2)(b) below).

Article 28 has kept the old distinction between the responsibility of military commanders and persons effectively acting as military commanders on the one hand and other superiors (often referred to as 'non-military' or 'civilian superiors') on the other. The responsibility of the former is addressed in Article 28(a) whereas the responsibility of the latter, non-military superiors, are regulated in Article 28(b). Hereinafter the term 'command responsibility' will be used when referring to the responsibility under Article 28(a), the term 'non-military superior responsibility' will be used when referring to the responsibility under Article 28(b), and the term 'superior responsibility' will be used when referring to the overall responsibility covered under Article 28.

Early ICTY case law articulated a three-prong test under which one would determine whether a person could be convicted on the basis of superior responsibility under ICTY Statute Article 7(3) (the Article corresponding to the ICC Statute Article 28):

- Existence of a superior–subordinate relationship: Put in simple terms, this entails that in situations where a certain individual (military as well as non-military), in a *de jure* or *de facto* position of authority, possesses a material ability to prevent and punish subordinates from committing international crimes, there exists a superior–subordinate relationship.
- Subjective element (*Mens rea*): There are different standards set out as the subjective element for superior responsibility:
    - *Actual knowledge*: The superior has actual knowledge that his subordinates are about to commit or have committed crimes (The actual knowledge can be proven with direct or circumstantial evidence)
    - "*Reason to know*" standard: that is, the superior possesses information of a nature which would put him on notice of the risk of such offences by indicating a need for additional investigation in order to ascertain whether the crimes were about to be or had been committed.

  If fulfilled, either of these subjective elements would give rise to responsibility under the doctrine of superior responsibility.
- With regard to the superior's failure to prevent or punish the crimes, the superior can incur responsibility for either:
    - Failing to prevent the crimes before they occur, or,

In addition to other grounds of criminal responsibility under this Statute for crimes within the jurisdiction of the Court:[281]

- Failing to punish the subordinates for committing the crimes after they have occurred (Ambos, 2002, p. 833–835).

The same three elements are also present in Article 28 of the ICC Statute. The elements do however differ in some respects from the standards set out in the jurisprudence from the ICTY and other *ad hoc* tribunals. These elements, as well as some additional requirements (for example causality) and interpretations of the doctrine, will be presented and explained in the following commentary. The elements of the doctrine will however, as far as possible, be presented in the same order as they appear in the wording of the Article and will therefore follow the structure as laid out therein.

Author: Linnea Kortfält.

[281] According to the first line of the Article, superior responsibility adds to "other grounds of criminal responsibility" which are to be found elsewhere in the Statute. These "other grounds of criminal responsibility" (hereinafter referred to as 'modes of participation') are specifically listed in Article 25.

Superior responsibility is thus distinct from for example "ordering" under Article 25 which requires the superior to have actively contributed to the crime in question (*Prosecutor v. Bemba*, ICC PT Ch. II, Decision Pursuant to Article 61(7)(a) and (b) of the Rome Statute on the Charges of the Prosecutor Against Jean-Pierre Bemba Gombo, ICC-01/05-01/08, 15 June 2009, §405). With regards to accountability under Article 28, there need not be proof of any order or action undertaken by the superior him- or herself. Rather, under this doctrine, the superior incurs responsibility on the basis of his or her inaction, or more accurately, for the failure or omission to prevent or punish the actions of the perpetrators. However, the exact nature of the doctrine of superior responsibility has long been discussed and differing opinions on the subject have emerged in both academic debate and case law.

It has, for example, sometimes been questioned as to what extent the doctrine is merely disciplinary as opposed to penal or criminal in nature. This question partly originates from the wording of and the discussions held during the adoption of Article 86(2) of Additional Protocol I from 1977. Article 86(2) reads: "The fact that a breach of the Conventions or this Protocol was committed by a subordinate does not absolve his superiors from *penal* or *disciplinary* responsibility, *as the case may be*, [...]" (emphasis added) The ICC Statute has eliminated any such confusion, making Article 28 equally relevant to all "crimes within the jurisdiction of the Court" and by, at the outset of the Article, specifying that it is criminal responsibility of the superior that the Article gives rise to.

Another interesting question relating to the nature of the doctrine is precisely what the superior is held criminally responsible for if he/she is found guilty strictly on the basis of Article 28. Put in simple terms, the issue at hand is how superior responsibility relates to the "principal crime" (that is, the crime committed by the subordinates; war crime, crimes against humanity or genocide). In other words, should the superior, if convicted strictly based on the doctrine of superior responsibility, for example be held criminally responsible merely for his or her own "dereliction of duty" or should he/she be held accountable for the "principal crime"? This is not merely a theoretical question. Depending on what one believes that the superior is responsible for, there will be practical consequences, not only in relation to the stigma attached to a guilty verdict under the doctrine, but also in respect of for example sentencing considerations, evidentiary demands and possibly even the interpretation of the elements of the doctrine.

The wording of Article 28 suggests that the superior should be responsible for the crimes committed by his subordinates. A literal interpretation hereof would thus lead to the conclusion

---

that the superior should be held responsible for the "principal crime". The interpretation of the Article is nevertheless, not as clear cut as it might seem *prima facie*. The issue is still under debate and so far unresolved. A straight forward answer to these questions could hence not be provided until it has properly been addressed by the ICC, however, various thoughts have been purported in the academic debate and case law emanating from the *ad hoc* tribunals. The following is a brief presentation of a few examples of differing opinions concerning the interpretation of the nature of the doctrine.

(1) One possible interpretation as to the nature of the doctrine is that the superior is responsible for actually having participated in the commission of the "principal crime". As such the superior becomes responsible for the "principal crime" under the theory of "commission by omission".

The general rules pertaining to criminal omission is a complex area of law wherefore a few words about the meaning hereof seem to be called for in this respect. A simplified explanation of the concept (or rather one variant hereof) is that where there is a duty to act prescribed by law, a person omitting to fulfil such a duty could be held criminally responsible for the crime.

An Article dealing with a general responsibility for omission as suggested in the Draft Statute, was excluded from the final version of the ICC Statute. It could be argued that the only remnants of a rule on omission in the Statute, is enshrined in Article 28 (Ambos, 2002, p. 850)

The basis of the doctrine of superior responsibility is, unquestionably, the superior's legal duty to control subordinates. Since the adoption of Article 86(2) of AP I from 1977 there has been a clear, codified legal duty in international humanitarian law for a superior to prevent and punish criminal activities undertaken by his or her subordinates. Omitting to fulfil this legal duty gives rise to criminal responsibility. It could thus be argued that these rules are in line with general rules on commission by omission.

However, whether the criminal responsibility covers solely the superior's own "failure to supervise" or the "principal crime", with respect to theories of omission, is still under debate. The idea that superior responsibility should give rise to direct responsible for the "principal crime" under the theory of commission by omission, has been heavily criticised.

(2) Another possible interpretation of the nature of the doctrine is whether superior responsibility is a Mode of Participation and the superior in this manner is convicted as a participant in the "principal crime". Superior responsibility shares common feature with other Modes of Participation in that they are accessory to the principal crimes committed by other perpetrator/s. The difference is however that in respect of the other Modes of Participation there needs to be a positive act or, at least, a certain level of contribution to the commission of the principal crime. As stated earlier, superior responsibility is rather characterised by inaction/non-action of the superior. Despite this fact, there have been strong proponents for an interpretation of that superior responsibility should be interpreted as a Mode of Participation. (*Orić* Prosecution Appeal Brief, 18 October 2006, § 162)

Case law emanating from the aftermath of WWII tends to view superior responsibility as a Mode of Participation and the superiors were convicted for the principal crime committed by the subordinates (*US v. Leeb* (Hostage Case), TWC vol. XI, 512-543; *US v. List* (High Command Case), TWC, Vols X and XI, 1271)

The early case law from the ICTY also tend to treat superior responsibility as a Mode of Participation or at least that the superior is responsible for the principal crime (for example *Prosecutor v. Mucic et al.*, ICTY T. Ch., 16 November 1998, § 333, *Prosecutor v. Mucic et al.*, ICTY A Ch., 20 February 2001, § 198, *Prosecutor v. Aleksovski* (Case No. IT-95-14/1-T), ICTY T. Ch., Judgment, § 67). According to a survey undertaken by the Trial Chamber in the Halilović judgment, it was concluded that, up to that date, the superior had consistently been "responsible for the crimes of his subordinates [when convicted] under Article 7(3)" that is, the

(a) A military commander or person effectively acting as a military commander[282] shall be criminally responsible for crimes within the jurisdiction of the Court committed[283] by forc-

---

responsible for the "principal crime" (*Prosecutor v. Halilović*, ICTY T. Ch., Judgment, IT-01-48-T, 16 November 2005, § 53). Exactly what is meant by the fact that the superior is responsible for "the crimes of his subordinates" is however still not clear.

In the *Halilović* judgment, the Trial Chamber did however reach a different conclusion than what had been indicated in previous case law. The interpretation given in that case was that the superior is 'merely responsible for his neglect of duty with regard to the crimes committed by subordinates' (*Prosecutor v. Halilović*, ICTY T. Ch., Judgment, IT-01-48-T, 16 November 2005, § 293). This view was subsequently reiterated in for example the *Orić* and *Hadžihasanović* Trial Chamber judgments (see below).

A shift does accordingly seem to have occurred from the early case law, where superior responsibility was viewed as a Mode of Participation, alternatively that the superior in some other form was held responsible for the "principal crime", to later case law purporting a more restrictive view concerning the nature of the doctrine.

(3) A third possible interpretation of the nature of the doctrine is that the criminal responsibility of the superior is limited to his or her own failure to act with regard to, or in relation to, the "principal crime". In accordance with this interpretation, the superior is convicted, not for the "principal crime", but merely for his or her own failure to act or. This interpretation does, however, evaluate the level of responsibility, not only to the gravity of the superior's own failure, but also to the gravity of the "principal crime".

This view is supported by the *Haliliović* Trial Chamber judgment which deemed that the superior does not share the same responsibility as the subordinates and that superior responsibility solely is limited to his or her failure to perform the duties prescribed by international law. The Trial Chamber did however stress the connection to the gravity of the principal crime in the following: "The imposition of responsibility upon a commander for breach of his duty is to be weighed against the crimes of his subordinates; a commander is responsible not as though he had committed the crime himself, but his responsibility is considered *in proportion to the gravity of the offences committed*" (*Prosecutor v. Halilović*, ICTY T. Ch., 16 November 2005, § 54) (Emphasis added) The connection between the responsibility of the superior and the gravity of the "principal crime" is further developed in the Hadžihasanović Appeal Judgment (*Prosecutor v. Hadžihasanović* (Case No. IT-01-47-A), ICTY A. Ch, Judgment, 22 April 2008, §§ 312–318).

The conclusion of some is that command responsibility is a "*sui generis* form of culpable omission" which has (no equivalence / is incomparable / is distinct) from any other responsibility in either domestic or international criminal law (Melonie, Mettraux, Ambos, Shahabuddeen)

Author: Linnea Kortfält.

[282] As mentioned in the opening paragraph to the commentary on Article 28, the elements of the doctrine of superior responsibility consists of three major parts;(1) the existence of a superior–subordinate relationship, (2) the subjective element (*mens rea*), and (3) the failure to prevent and punish (*Prosecutor v. Mucic et al.*, ICTY T. Ch., 16 November 1998, § 346) This, the second paragraph of Article 28, deals with the first part; the conditions established for determining the existence of a superior–subordinate relationship.

Explained in broad strokes, the existence of a superior–subordinate relationship entails that the superior (military or non-military) is in a position of effective "command and control" or "authority and control" (as the case may be) to the extent that he/she possesses the material ability to prevent or punish the subordinate when the latter are about to or have committed crimes. There are however, several details that need further consideration and clarification. These clarifications will be offered following the structure provided by the wording of the Article. The first

---

step in the assessment of the existence of a superior–subordinate relationship, is determining the status of the superior. Secondly, the "principal crime" has to be identified and evaluated. Thirdly, the status of the subordinate as well as his or her relation to the "principal crime" has to be assessed. The forth aspect to consider is the requirements placed on the relationship as such (that is, the quality or effectiveness hereof). Finally, the link between the superior, subordinate and the "principal crime" needs to be tied together through a causality test.

As to the first step of the evaluation, that is, the status of the superior, Article 28(a) strictly deals with military commanders and persons effectively acting as a military commander (unless otherwise provided, these two will hereinafter be referred to as commanders). The particular status of and elements relating to non-military superiors are covered in Article 28(b) and are explained in the commentary provided with respect thereof. Non-military superiors are dealt with in a separate section of the Article.

A "military commander" is *generally* a member of the armed forces who is formally assigned authority to issue direct orders to subordinates or, given that there are generally several commanders in a chain-of-command, a commander may also have the authority to issue orders to commanders of units further down the chain-of-command. The rank of the commander is not of importance as such (for example be he/she a section leader, a platoon commander, a company commander, a battalion commander, a brigade commander, a division commander and others in ascending seniority), (Arnold, 2008, p. 830) wherefore a Head of State also may be considered a commander who may incur responsibility under the present doctrine (Fenrick, p. 517) Superiors high up in the line of command may be held responsible with regard to crimes undertaken by units in much lower echelons in the chain-of-command. *Prosecutor v. Orić* (Case No. IT-03-68-T), ICTY T Ch, 30 June 2006, § 313. This standpoint is also reflected in the Bemba decision: "In this respect, a military commander could be a person occupying the highest level in the chain of command or a mere leader with few soldiers under his or her command". *Prosecutor v. Bemba*, ICC PT Ch. II, 15 June 2009, §408.

It is hence not necessary that the commander is the direct superior of the subordinate who commits the principal crime. Of importance for the formal assessment of the status of the superior is whether the commander indeed possesses the authority to issue orders in a formal hierarchical structure (*Prosecutor v. Mucic et al.*, ICTY T. Ch., 16 November 1998, confirmed in *Prosecutor v. Mucic et al.*, ICTY, A. Ch., 20 February 2001, §§ 251–252)

A "person effectively acting as military commander" is a wider category and may include police officers who have been assigned command over armed police units or persons responsible for paramilitary units not incorporated into the armed forces (Fenrick, 1999, p. 517)

The above-mentioned examples deal with the determination of the legal status of the commanders who have been *formally* assigned authority to issue orders. Situations where someone is formally assigned command are referred to as being "*de jure* commanders" or having a "*de jure* position of command". In conflict situations it is nevertheless common that a person, who is *not* formally assigned command, despite this fact, assumes command over units or other subordinates. If the units indeed pay heed to the instructions of such a person (that is, if the person in reality possesses "effective command and control" or "effective authority and control"), he/she is said to be a "*de facto* commander" or having a "*de facto* position of command". The concept "person effectively acting as military commander" may accordingly also include persons who have assumed *de facto* control over armed forces, armed police units or paramilitary units (Fenrick, 1999, p. 518) That a person may be accountable under the doctrine of superior responsibility based on "*de facto* command" finds support in the case law of both the *ad hoc* Tribunals and the ICC. Representative of this opinion is the following quote from the *Čelebići* T Ch.: "Formal designation as a commander should not be considered to be a necessary prerequisite for command responsibility to attach, as such responsibility may be imposed by virtue of a person's *de facto*, as well as *de jure*, position as a commander" (*Prosecutor v. Mucic et al.*, IC-TY T. Ch., 16 November 1998, § 370) The same pronouncement is encapsulated in the following quote from the ICC: "With respect to a "person effectively acting as a military commander", the Chamber considers that this term is meant to cover a distinct as well as a broader category of commanders. This category refers to those who are not elected by law to carry out a military commander's role, yet they perform it *de facto* by exercising effective control over a group of persons through a chain of command". *Prosecutor v. Bemba*, ICC PT Ch. II, 15 June 2009, § 409.

It is furthermore not necessary that the commander is in the direct chain-of-command to the subordinate, as long as effective "command and control" or "authority and control" can be established (*Prosecutor v. Mucic et al*, ICTY A Ch., 20 February 2001, §§ 251–252)

A person who formally has been assigned the authority to issue orders may nevertheless have lost control of the subordinates in real life. Despite attempts to make the subordinates adhere to his or her orders, the commander might not be able to reach them. In these situations, the commander lacks *de facto* command notwithstanding his or her *de jure* position of command (According to Ambos, these cases should be interpreted in a restrictive manner, see below (Ambos, 2002, p. 857)) In these cases, it is of course the actual material ability of the commander that needs to be considered and the disobedience of the subordinates can instead be counted as evidence of the lack of effective control. *Prosecutor v. Blaškić* (Case No. IT-95-14-A), ICTY A Ch., Judgment, 29 July 2004, §§ 69, 399. As stated by the Trial Chamber in the Čelebići case "Instead, the factor that determines liability for this type of criminal responsibility is the actual possession, or non-possession, of powers of control over the actions of subordinates". *Prosecutor v. Mucic et al.*, ICTY T. Ch., 16 November 1998, § 370.

The status of the commander is thus closely connected to the interpretation of the elements "effective command and control" as well as "effective authority and control". These qualitative elements will be addressed below (note 333), however, first, a few thoughts about the "principal crime" and the status of the subordinates shall be presented.

Author: Linnea Kortfält.

[283] For a comment about "criminally responsible for the crimes" please refer to the discussion provided on above under the heading "In addition to other grounds of criminal responsibility under this Statute for crimes within the jurisdiction of the Court".

"Crimes within the jurisdiction of the Court" under the statute refers to genocide, crimes against humanity and war crimes according to Articles 5(1)(a)–(c) and 6–8.

According to the text of Article 28, one of the above listed "principal crimes" needs to have been "committed" in order for the superior to incur responsibility under the doctrine. There are however differing opinions as to the meaning of the term "committed" as well as the consequences that might follow from this term. One such opinion is that the term "committed" means that the crime has to have been "successfully been brought to an end" (Arnold, 2008, p. 827) Another opinion is that the word "committed" is a generic term with no particular legal significance. When viewed as a generic term there are not many problems arising from this element, however, some problems are encountered if committed should entail that the crime has to have been successfully brought to an end.

A crucial issue in this respect is whether "committed" means that the superior never could incur liability under the doctrine for so called "inchoate offences" (for example attempt, situations when the primary perpetrator voluntarily withdraws, solicitation, incitement, complicity).

Responsibility for attempted commission of the crimes in the Statute is provided under Article 25(3)(f) ICC Statute. Consequently, the ICC Statute is in general open to holding people responsible for the attempted commission of a crime (Ambos, 2008, p. 765–767) However, the term "committed" in Article 28 creates some confusion with regard to the applicability of the

es[284] under his or her effective command and control, or effective authority and control as the case may be,[285] as a result of[286] his or her failure to exercise control properly[287] over such forces, where:

doctrine of superior responsibility to attempted or inchoate crimes. The issue of inchoate offences was addressed in the Hadžihasanović case, where it was concluded that the doctrine was not applicable to inchoate offences (*Prosecutor v. Hadžihasanović*, ICTY A. Ch, 22 April 2008, § 204) The Trial Chamber in the Orić case seemed to disagree with this position. In the latter case the Trial Chamber, concluded that the duty of the superior to prevent crimes starts already at the preparation phase of the crime, and that the doctrine hence is applicable to inchoate offences (*Prosecutor v. Orić*, ICTY T Ch, 30 June 2006, § 328)

With regards to the voluntary withdrawal of the principal perpetrator, there seems to be a tendency to conclude that, as superior responsibility is accessorial to the principal crime, it would be unfair to hold the superior more liable than the principal perpetrator. Article 28 would thus not be applicable in these situations.

Another discernible problem is the issue as to whether the superior can be charged under the doctrine when the subordinates are merely convicted for the "principal crime" as an accomplices or linked to the crime under any other Mode of Participation under Article 25(3)(b–e). In the international discourse, arguments have been brought forth contending that the word "committed" should be isolated to crimes undertaken by the principal perpetrator (that is, solely those covered under ICC Statute, Article 25(3)(a)). However, Ambos asserts that a person can "commit" a crime by any Mode of Participation listed in Article 25(3), at least in the context of that same Article (Ambos, 2008, p. 747) An extensive interpretation of the term "committed" in this respect has also been preferred with regard to the ICTY Statute. An example hereof is provided by the expansion of Article 7(1) to include the concept of Joint Criminal Enterprise (via the word "committed"). The *Orić* Trial Chamber addressed the issue as to the interpretation of the term "committed" with regards to other Modes of Participation in direct connection to its applicability to the doctrine of superior responsibility; "For these and other reasons which, taking into account the relevant case law of this Tribunal, are elaborated in more detail in the *Boškoski* case, the Trial Chamber holds that the criminal responsibility of a superior under Article 7(3) of the Statue is not limited to crimes committed by subordinates in person but encompasses any modes of criminal responsibility (*Orić*, ICTY T Ch, 30 June 2006, § 301) Statements made in the Orić Appeal judgment supports such a conclusion (*Prosecutor v. Orić* (Case No. IT-03-68), ICTY A. Ch, 3 July 2008, §§ 47) The issue is however still open for debate.

Another interesting question is whether the crime can be considered to have been "committed" if the primary perpetrator is not identified or for any other reason is not convicted of the crime. It can thus be established that the *actus reus* of the crime have been perpetrated, nevertheless, since the primary perpetrator has not been identified or convicted for the crime, it cannot be fully proven that all the elements of the crime are fulfilled (for example the mental element). The question is whether the crime can be considered as "committed" despite the fact that some of the material elements of the crime thus cannot be established. The Appeals Chamber addressed the issue of unidentified subordinates in relation to the doctrine of superior responsibility in the *Orić* case: "The Appeals Chamber considers that, notwithstanding the degree of specificity with which the culpable subordinates must be identified, in any event, their existence as such must be established. If not, individual criminal liability under Article 7(3) of the Statute cannot arise" (*Orić*, ICTY A. Ch, 3 July 2008, §§ 35, 48) Reasonably, some level of identification must hence take place, however the level of specificity hereof is still open to debate.

Author: Linnea Kortfält.

[284] In the following section the status of the subordinate is addressed. Up to this point, the person that committed the "principal crime", with regard to which the superior bear's responsibility un-

der the doctrine, has been referred to as a "subordinate". This is an overarching term meant to also include the civilian aspect of the relationship. This is furthermore the term used in the IC-TY, statute Article 7(3). However, in Article 28(a) the subordinates are referred to as "forces" (as opposed to Article 28(b) which also utilises the term subordinate). The precise significance of the choice to use this term is not clear, however, if interpreted in accordance with its ordinary meaning the term ought to entail certain restrictions in line with similar definitions provided in international humanitarian law.

In order for members of irregular armed forces to be counted as combatants and granted prisoner of war status, they need to be under a command responsible for the conduct of his or her subordinates, as well as be subjected to an internal disciplinary system which enforces compliance with international humanitarian law (Geneva Convention III, Article 4(A)§2). According to Fenrick, "forces" ought to be interpreted in lines herewith and may thus signify the armed forces of a party to a conflict that is, all organised armed forces, groups and units which are under a command responsible to that party for the conduct of its subordinates (Fenrick, 1999, p. 518) According to Arnold, the concept of forces does not merely include the regular and irregular armed forces under a responsible command, but also guerrilla groups and private subcontractors (even when the illegal actions undertaken by such groups are not imputable to the state) so long as effective "command and control" or "authority and control" can be traced back to a person in a position of responsible command. Arnold also is of the view that the term forces include armed police and paramilitary units. The concept of "forces" may thus be broader than what it seems *prima facie* and might be closer to the concept of subordinates as it has been applied in most international tribunals (Arnold, 2008, p. 826)

One interesting question relating to the status of the subordinates is whether he/she needs to be the principal perpetrator of the principal crime, or whether superior–subordinate relationship also can be established between a superior and a subordinate who is merely an accomplice to the principal crime. Another question concerning to the status of the subordinates, is whether the requirements of superior–subordinate relationship can be satisfied in cases where the subordinates cannot be individually identified. These questions were addressed above under the discussions with regards to the meaning of the term "committed".

In the *Bemba* confirmation decision, it seems as if the Trial Chamber has chosen to avoid these complexities, consequently using the terms forces and subordinates synonymously (*Prosecutor v. Bemba*, ICC PT Ch. II, Decision Pursuant to Article 61(7)(a) and (b) of the Rome Statute on the Charges of the Prosecutor against Jean-Pierre Bemba Gombo, 15 June 2009, § 428).

Author: Linnea Kortfält.

[285] As for the distinction between the phrases "command and control" or "authority and control" a few thoughts have been presented in both the academic debate and ICC case law. According to Ambos, "control" is an umbrella term encompassing both command and authority (Ambos, 2002, p. 857) According to Fenrick, forces under the commander's "command and control" are subordinated to the commander in a direct chain-of-command. This chain-of-command may however, as mentioned above, be either a *de jure* or *de facto* . Forces under the "command and control" also encapsulate forces in lower echelons of the chain-of-command, as long as it can be ascertained that the commander is able to issue orders, either directly or through intermediate subordinate commanders (Fenrick, 1999, p. 518) This view is furthermore upheld in the *Prosecutor v. Orić* (Case No. IT-03-68), ICTY T Ch, Judgment, 30 June 2006, § 313.

"Authority and control" is a somewhat broader concept than "effective command and control" according to Fenrick. Effective authority and control also encompasses commanders who exercise control over forces which are not placed under him/her in a direct chain-of-command (for example third parties who do not belong directly to the chain of command or armed forces under said commander). One such example is the occupational zone commander who has the authority to give orders to all forces within their occupational zone, relating to matters of public order and safety (Fenrick, 1999, p. 518)

The definition and the distinction between these terms was addressed by the ICC in the *Bemba* case, where it was concluded that: "Article 28(a) of the Statute refers to the terms "effective command and control" or "effective authority and control" as applicable alternatives in situations of military commanders *strictu sensu* and military-like commanders. In this regard, the Chamber considers that the additional words "command" and "authority" under the two expressions has no substantial effect on the required level or standard of "control"". ... "In this context, the Chamber underlines that the term "effective command" certainly reveals or reflects "effective authority". Indeed, in the English language the word "command" is defined as "authority, especially over armed forces", and the expression "authority" refers to the "power or right to give orders and enforce obedience"". *Prosecutor v. Bemba*, ICC PT Ch. II, Decision Pursuant to Article 61(7)(a) and (b) of the Rome Statute on the Charges of the Prosecutor against Jean-Pierre Bemba Gombo, 15 June 2009, §§ 412–413.

The "command and control" as well as the "authority and control" has to be "effective". Read as a whole, this phrase encapsulates the "qualitative test" as to the nature of the superior-subordinate relationship as such; the commander needs to have effective "command and control" alternatively "effective authority and control" over forces (that is, subordinates, see discussion above) under his or her command. As a reiteration of previous statements provided above, the cornerstone of the qualitative aspect of the relationship, namely the effectiveness hereof, is that the superior possesses "the material ability to prevent or punish the criminal conduct of his or her subordinates". *Prosecutor v. Mucic et al.*, ICTY A. Ch., Judgment, 20 February 2001, § 256. The Appeals Chamber, in the same case, stresses the fact that it is not sufficient that a superior has "substantial influence" as to incur responsibility under the doctrine of superior responsibility. The interesting question to be addressed here, is however, what precisely is meant by the effectiveness prerequisite, that is, possessing the material ability to prevent and punish. The issue has been addressed in several international cases, however the Appeals Chamber in the *Blaškić* case succinctly expresses the requirement in the following terms: "The indicators of effective control are more a matter of evidence than of substantive law, and those indicators are limited to showing that the accused had the power to prevent, punish, or initiate measures leading to proceedings against the alleged perpetrators where appropriate". *Prosecutor v. Blaškić*, ICTY A Ch., Judgment, 29 July 2004, §§ 69 In order to evaluate the effectiveness of the commander's control, it is hence necessary to look on the evidence provided on a case-by-case basis. A *de jure* position of command (see above note 330) as well as the ability to issue orders can be seen as good evidence of effective control. *Prosecutor v. Mucic et al.*, ICTY, A. Ch., Judgment, 20 February 2001, §197. However, disrespect of a *de jure* commander or disobedience of orders issued from such a commander could instead be evidence of lack of effective control. *Prosecutor v. Blaškić*, ICTY A Ch., Judgment, 29 July 2004, §§ 69, 399 (Friman, 2008, p. 857) In accordance herewith, it is the *de facto* control, that is, the actual, real life, material ability of the commander that is of the highest significance when ascertaining whether effective control actually exists. Nonetheless, Ambos asserts that a duty to control may only be rejected if there is no control at all. This may be the case where the subordinate is totally out of control and no longer obeys the orders of the commander, committing widespread or isolated excesses (as the case may well be with regards to a commander with solely administrative control as opposed to operational control). In such a case, the commander is, in any way, at least supposed to use the available administrative means or sanctions to prevent the commission of crimes (Ambos, 2008, p. 857) Fenrick furthermore stresses that the lack of competence, should not be viewed as a factor which in and of itself negates the existence of the effective control prerequisite within the superior subordinate relationship all together: "The subjective competence of a commander is not a basis for an argument that the forces were not under his or her effective command and control" (Fenrick, 1999, p. 518)

However, again, the material ability has to be evaluated on a case-by-case basis. The material ability may differ depending on the distinct role and function of various commanders; whether it is operational, tactical, administrative or otherwise. The assessment of whether there is a superior–subordinate relationship is in existence and if such a relationship is effective, that is, the commander possesses the material ability to prevent and punish the principal crime, can hence not be made in isolation from the evaluation of which measures that in all actuality are within the commanders powers. The evaluation of the qualitative nature of the superior–subordinate relationship does therefore have to be made in relation to which "all necessary and reasonable measures within his or her power" are.

The ICC succinctly summarised several factors which "may indicate the existence of a superior's position of authority and effective control. These factors may include: (i) the official position of the suspect; (ii) his power to issue or give orders; (iii) the capacity to ensure compliance with the orders issued (that is, ensure that they would be executed); (iv) his position within the military structure and the actual tasks that he carried out; (v) the capacity to order forces or units under his command, whether under his immediate command or at a lower levels, to engage in hostilities; (vi) the capacity to resubordinate units or make changes to command structure; (vii) the power to promote, replace, remove or discipline any member of the forces; and (viii) the authority to send forces where hostilities take place and withdraw them at any given moment". *Prosecutor v. Bemba*, ICC PT Ch. II, Decision Pursuant to Article 61(7)(a) and (b) of the Rome Statute on the Charges of the Prosecutor against Jean-Pierre Bemba Gombo, 15 June 2009, § 417.

Author: Linnea Kortfält.

[286] These words indicate that a new, rather controversial element of superior responsibility has been introduced in Article 28, namely the need to prove a causal link between the superior and the commission of the principal crime by the subordinates. Generally, in criminal law, the existence of a causality element entails that the prosecution would have to prove that, the criminal conduct is somehow related to the action of the defendant. Normally causality is attached to a positive action, whereas in the case of superior responsibility we are dealing with inaction/non-action. This fact creates some difficulties in and of itself which has furthermore been addressed in the Bemba confirmation decision at the ICC (*Prosecutor v. Bemba*, ICC PT Ch. II, Decision Pursuant to Article 61(7)(a) and (b) of the Rome Statute on the Charges of the Prosecutor against Jean-Pierre Bemba Gombo, 15 June 2009, § 425).

It could be argued that there are different degrees of causality, where the strongest is a co called *condition sine qua non*, (meaning "without which it could not be" requirement). In the case of superior responsibility this would entail that, but for the inaction of the superior, the principal crimes would not have occurred. It becomes logically very complicated to place such a strict condition as a prerequisite for responsibility under the current doctrine. This has also been the views presented in the case law of the ICTY.

"Notwithstanding the central place assumed by the principle of causation in criminal law, causation has not traditionally been postulated as a *conditio sine qua non* for the imposition of criminal liability on superiors for their failure to prevent or punish offences committed by their subordinates. Accordingly, the Trial Chamber has found no support for the existence of a requirement of proof of causation as a separate element of superior responsibility, either in the existing body of case law, the formulation of the principle in existing treaty law, or, with one exception, in the abundant literature on this subject". *Prosecutor v. Mucic et al.*, ICTY T. Ch., Judgment, 16 November 1998, 398 At the same time, the Čelebići Trial Chamber finally concludes that "…the superior may be considered to be causally linked to the offence, in that, but for his failure to fulfil his duty to act, the acts of his subordinates would not have been committed". *Prosecutor v. Mucic et al.*, ICTY T. Ch., 16 November 1998, § 399. supported in *Prosecutor v. Blaškić*, ICTY A Ch., Judgment, 29 July 2004, § 75–77 and *Prosecutor v. Halilović*, ICTY T. Ch., Judgment, 16 November 2005, § 77.

The issue of causation becomes even more complicated when considering the fact that it is not only the superior's failure to prevent that is covered within the doctrine of superior responsibility, but also the superior's failure to punish. Providing the necessity to establish a causal link between the commission of the principal crime and the superiors' failure to punish said crime, is impossible. This difficulty has been pointed out by the *Orić* TC where the causal element was discredited in its totality: "As concerns objective causality, however, it is well established case law of the Tribunal that it is not an element of superior criminal responsibility to prove that without the superior's failure to prevent, the crimes of his subordinates would not have been committed". *Prosecutor v. Orić*, ICTY T Ch, Judgment, 30 June 2006. 338.

In dealing with the issue of the causal link between the superiors' failure to punish and the possible future commission of crimes, the Trial-Chamber in Čelebići concluded that there of course exists such a connection, however, this has no bearing on the causal connection to past crimes. *Prosecutor v. Mucic et al.*, ICTY T. Ch., Judgment, 16 November 1998, § 400

Ambos also adheres to the idea that there cannot be a *condition sine qua non* requirement between the inaction of the superior and the commission of the principal crime. Ambos states that, if there indeed would be such a causation requirement, as the text of Article 28 suggests, it must suffice that the superior's failure of supervision *increases the risk* that the subordinates commit certain crimes, also referred to as the *risk theory* (Ambos, 2002, p. 860. Emphasis added). This idea is furthermore the position taken in the Bemba confirmation decision at the ICC. However, in the *Bemba* decision the TC seems to present a causality requirement as something different from the risk theory. "There is no direct causal link that needs to be established between the superior's omission and the crime committed by his subordinates. Therefore, the Chamber considers that it is only necessary to prove that the commander's omission increased the risk of the commission of the crimes charged in order to hold him criminally responsible under Article 28(a) of the Statute". ... "Accordingly, to find a military commander or a person acting as a military commander responsible for the crimes committed by his forces, the Prosecutor must demonstrate that his failure to exercise his duty to prevent crimes increased the risk that the forces would commit these crimes". *Prosecutor v. Bemba*, ICC PT Ch. II, Decision Pursuant to Article 61(7)(a) and (b) of the Rome Statute on the Charges of the Prosecutor against Jean-Pierre Bemba Gombo, 15 June 2009, §§ 425–426. Ambos concurs with this decision in his commentary to the decision (Ambos, 2009, p. 715–726)

This requirement is hence not generally accepted as a requirement to liability under the doctrine of superior responsibility.

Author: Linnea Kortfält.

[287] Article 87 of AP from 1977 codifies a duty of commanders to take all practicable measures to ensure his forces comply with international humanitarian law. Examples of measures that the commander is obliged to undertake in order to exercise control properly could be:

- Provide adequate training in IHL
- Ensure that international IHL is regarded in operational decision making
- Ensure the existence of and properly monitor an effective reporting system
- Take corrective action if violations are under way or have been committed

(Fenrick, 1999, p. 518. Arnold, 2008, p. 834).

(i) That military commander or person either knew or, owing to the circumstances at the time, should have known that the forces were committing or about to commit such crimes;[288] and

---

Failing to exercise this control properly is one of the cornerstones of the doctrine of superior responsibility. However, the most interesting part in this phrase is not this, but rather the words "as a result of". A commentary to this element is offered in the following.

Author: Linnea Kortfält.

[288] This phrase encompasses the second part of the three-prong test to the doctrine of superior responsibility, namely the requirement of a certain mental state or attitude of the commander. Hereinafter the mental element will be referred to with the Latin term *mens rea*. For more general information concerning the *mens rea* requirement in the ICC Statute, please refer to the commentary on Article 30 and Article 25.

Article 30 of the ICC Statute states that: "*unless otherwise provided*, a person shall be criminally responsible [...] only if the material elements are committed with *intent and knowledge*" (emphasis added) Since Article 28 provides an alternative *mens rea* element, it shall hence be seen as *lex specialis* which, as such, trumps the default provision provided in Article 30. In the following section focus shall thus be given specifically to the requirements in Article 28(a) (whereas the *mens rea* standard in Article 28(b), which differs significantly, will be covered in the commentary dealing herewith).

Article 28(a)(i) establishes that the commander either needs to have known or, owing to the circumstances at the time, *should have known*, that the forces were about to or had committed the principal crime. There is thus two alternative *mens rea* standards provided in the Article;(1) actual knowledge or (2) a so-called "should have known" standard.

Several cases from the ICTY, ICTR and SCSL have dealt with the mental element of the doctrine of superior responsibility as formulated in the statutes of these tribunals (Article 7(3) and 6(3) respectively). The second alternative *mens rea* standard in Article 28(a)(i), that is, that the commander "should have known", is somewhat controversial and, according to many, differs from the standard provided in the statutes of these tribunals (*Prosecutor v. Bemba*, ICC PT Ch. II, Decision Pursuant to Article 61(7)(a) and (b) of the Rome Statute on the Charges of the Prosecutor against Jean-Pierre Bemba Gombo, 15 June 2009, § 432) The "actual knowledge" standard, however, is considered to be the same in all statutes, wherefore the jurisprudence concerning this point, can offer some insight into the interpretation of its content. In previously mentioned case law, it has been settled that actual knowledge can be proven by either direct or circumstantial evidence. These factors could be: the number, type, scope or time of the illegal acts, the type of troops or the logistics involved, as well as the location or the spread of occurrence. It was furthermore held, in the Hadžihasanović case, that "[a]ctual knowledge may be proven if, "a priori, a military commander is part of an organised structure with established reporting systems"". *Prosecutor v. Hadžihasanović*, T Ch, Judgment, 22 April 2008, § 94, as cited in *Prosecutor v. Bemba*, ICC PT Ch. II, Decision Pursuant to Article 61(7)(a) and (b) of the Rome Statute on the Charges of the Prosecutor against Jean-Pierre Bemba Gombo, 15 June 2009, §§ 431. In the Bemba confirmation decision, it was confirmed that the interpretation of actual knowledge provided in the *ad hoc* tribunals, also is applicable with respect of Article 28(a)(i). *Prosecutor v. Bemba*, ICC PT Ch. II, Decision Pursuant to Article 61(7)(a) and (b) of the Rome Statute on the Charges of the Prosecutor against Jean-Pierre Bemba Gombo, 15 June 2009, §§ 430–431

The "should have known" standard in Article 28(a)(i) is much more complicated. With regard hereto it is not as easy to take direct guidance from the jurisprudence provided in *ad hoc* tribunals. The reason for this being that these statutes provide for a "reason to know" standard, which *generally* (nevertheless not according to some scholars, see below) is considered to be

---

much higher than the "should have known" standard (Werle, 2005, p. 325. *Prosecutor v. Bemba*, ICC PT Ch. II, Decision Pursuant to Article 61(7)(a) and (b) of the Rome Statute on the Charges of the Prosecutor against Jean-Pierre Bemba Gombo, 15 June 2009, § 434).

A commander has "reason to know" according to the case law of the *ad hoc* tribunals, "[…] where he had in his possession information of a nature, which at the least, would put him on notice of the risk of such offences by indicating the need for additional investigation in order to ascertain whether such crimes were committed or were about to be committed by his subordinates" (*Prosecutor v. Mucic et al.*, ICTY T. Ch., Judgment, 16 November 1998, § 383, confirmed in *Prosecutor v. Mucic et al.*, ICTY, A. Ch., Judgment, 20 February 2001, §§ 223, 241). The concept was further explained by stating that "a showing that a superior had *some general information in his possession*, which would put him on notice of possible unlawful acts by his subordinates would be sufficient". The evaluation of the "reason to know" standard was further exemplified by "a military commander who has received information that some of the soldiers under his command have a violent or unstable character, or have been drinking prior to being sent on a mission, may be considered as having the required knowledge". *Prosecutor v. Mucic et al.*, ICTY, A. Ch., Judgment, 20 February 2001, § 238 (*emphasis added*).

In the *Bemba* confirmation decision, the Trial Chamber pointed out that the "had reason to know" standard in the statutes of the *ad hoc* tribunals differ from the "should have known" standard in the Rome Statute Article 28(a)(i). *Prosecutor v. Bemba*, ICC PT Ch. II, 15 June 2009, § 434. It concluded that the "should have know" standard merely requires that the superior has been negligent in failing to acquire knowledge of his subordinates illegal conduct *Prosecutor v. Bemba*, ICC PT Ch. II, Decision Pursuant to Article 61(7)(a) and (b) of the Rome Statute on the Charges of the Prosecutor against Jean-Pierre Bemba Gombo, 15 June 2009, § 432 and that the new standard in Article 28(a) "requires more of an active duty on the part of the superior to take the necessary measures to secure knowledge of the conduct of his troops and to inquire, *regardless of the availability of information*". *Prosecutor v. Bemba*, ICC PT Ch. II, Decision Pursuant to Article 61(7)(a) and (b) of the Rome Statute on the Charges of the Prosecutor against Jean-Pierre Bemba Gombo, 15 June 2009, § 433. The Chamber, nevertheless also makes an *obiter dictum* where it concludes that the "criteria developed by the *ad hoc* tribunals to meet the standard of "had reason to know" may also be useful when applying the "should have known" requirement.

Important to note in this context is that some scholars view both the "reason to know" and "should have known" standards, solely as different aspects of negligence. Two such proponents seem to be Ambos and Arnold (Ambos, 2002, p. 868 and Arnold, 2008, p. 837). With regards to this matter, Ambos further stresses that "it should be clear now […] that the 'should have known' standard must be understood as negligence and that it, therefore, requires neither awareness nor considers sufficient the imputation of knowledge on the basis of purely objective facts". Ambos, furthermore, makes a specific comment as to this point with regard to the Bemba confirmation decision. He thus points out that both of these standards ought to constitute a negligence standard and that it would be beneficial for the ICC to apply a restrictive interpretation of the "should have known" –standard in order to bring it closer in line with the "reason to know" standard (Ambos, 2009, p. 722). Ambos views are in stark contrast to views expressed by the ICTY and ICTR Appeals Chambers, which have rejected the negligence standards with emphasis: "(…) the Appeals Chamber recalls that the ICTR Appeals Chamber has on a previous occasion rejected criminal negligence as a basis of liability in the context of command responsibility, and that it stated that "it would be both unnecessary and unfair to hold an accused responsible under a head of responsibility which has not clearly been defined in international criminal law".(…) The Appeals Chamber expressly endorses this view". *Prosecutor v. Blaškić*, ICTY A Ch., 29 July 2004, § 63.

(ii) [289] That military commander or person failed to take all necessary and reasonable measures within his or her power[290] to prevent[291] or repress[292] their commission or to submit the matter to the competent authorities for investigation and prosecution.[293]

When comparing these standards, it is important to make note of the words "owing to the circumstances at the time". This phrase may help in the interpretation of bridging the possible gap between the concepts. However, as it stands today, the interpretation of the "should have known" standard is still undetermined and under scholastic debate.

One issue that has caused considerable debate and still is unresolved is how the low *mens rea* requirement for superior responsibility shall be reconciled with special intent crimes, such as for example genocide (for further information concerning special intent please refer to the commentary on ICC Statute Article 6 and Article 30).

Author: Linnea Kortfält.

[289] The last part of the three-prong test entails determining whether the superior has failed in his duty to control his subordinates; that is, if he/she has taken all necessary and reasonable measures within his or her power to prevent or punish the subordinate's criminal undertakings?

The wording with regards to this final prerequisite for incurring responsibility under the doctrine, is differently phrased in Article 28(a)(ii) of the ICC Statute as compared to the ICTY, ICTR and SCSL Statutes' Article 7(3) and 6(3) respectively. The *ad hoc* tribunals use the phrase: "the superior failed to take the necessary and reasonable measures to *prevent* such acts or to *punish* the perpetrators thereof" (emphasis added) when formulating this prerequisite. The duties placed on the superior in these statutes are thus two-fold. Responsibility for the superior is incurred for his or her(1) failure to prevent or (2) failure to punish. Whereas, the ICC Statute distinguishes between three separate duties which the commander may fail to undertake, hence giving rise to responsibility under the doctrine for;(1) failing to prevent (2) failing to repress or (3) failing to submit the matter to the competent authorities for investigation and prosecution. *Prima facie*, these differences may appear rather significant. However, in reality they do indicate very similar duties for the commander.

The three-stage attack to the duties of the commander signifies duties attached to different stages in the commission of the crime. The superior has a duty to(1) prevent *before* (2) repress *during* and (3) submit/report *after* the commission of the crime.

Initially it is important to note that, despite the fact that the wording of Article 28(a)(ii) signifies the three duties in the alternative (that is, by the usage of the word *or*), the commander could be convicted based on failing to undertake either one of the different duties *or* all. A commander can hence not avoid responsibility under the doctrine if he/she fails to prevent and repress, nevertheless reports the commission of the principal crime to the competent authorities *after* the completion of the crimes. The Trial Chamber in the Bemba confirmation decision thus held that "failure to prevent crimes [...] cannot be *cured* by fulfilling the duty to repress or submit the matter to the competent authorities". *Bemba*, ICC PT Ch. II, Decision Pursuant to Article 61(7)(a) and (b) of the Rome Statute on the Charges of the Prosecutor against Jean-Pierre Bemba Gombo, 15 June 2009, § 436 (emphasis added)

A commentary on each of these three duties to control subordinates will be presented separately below. However, there is one important common factor to consider when dealing with all three alternatives. The duties all need to be determined from the perspective of what is considered to be "necessary and reasonable measures" as well as within the superior's powers. This will be addressed in the subsequent paragraphs.

Author: Linnea Kortfält.

[290] This phrase corresponds to the nearly literal wording used in the statutes of the *ad hoc* tribunals as well as the prerequisites established in Article 86(2) of Additional Protocol I from 1977,

namely that the countermeasures that the superior is under a duty to carry out needs to be "feasible" (Ambos, 2002, p. 861) Any requirement that is not possible for the particular superior in question to carry out is, generally, considered to be above and beyond his or her duty, wherefore he/she may not be held responsible for a failure in this regard.

The powers of the superior, as well as what is necessary and reasonable measures, have to a certain extent already been discussed when dealing with the first part of the three-prong test, that is, the existence of a superior–subordinate relationship. In that section of this commentary, it was pointed out that the prerequisite of the commanders effective "command and control" or "authority and control" needs to be evaluated in conjunction with what is considered to be "necessary and reasonable measures within his or her power". These two issues can thus never be assessed in isolation from one another. Some reiteration of previous mentioned prerequisites will thus be necessary in the following.

The corrective measures available to the commander, are both dependent on his or her *de jure* (that is, "legal competence") and the *de facto* (that is, "material" or "actual" possibility) position of the superior to control his or her subordinates. The measures need to be commensurate to the superior's actual possession of command and control or authority and control. It is hence difficult to generalise about which measures are necessary and reasonable. What is considered to be necessary, reasonable and within the power of the commander may for instance depend on his or her position in the chain-of-command, for example the demands of a high ranking commander may be more in line with issuing orders and initiating judicial proceedings, whereas a commander lower down in the echelons of command may be charged with a duty to have a much more hands on approach, alternatively, if the low-ranking commander lacks those possibilities, he/she may nonetheless recommend that disciplinary action be taken (Fenrick, 1999, p. 520) The measures available to the commander may also depend on whether he/she obtain a position that is more operational, tactical, administrative or otherwise. The measures do therefore have to be considered on a case-by-case basis. The measures that can be expected of the superior were well presented in the Blaskic Appeals Chamber: "What constitutes such measures is not a matter of substantive law but of evidence". *Prosecutor v. Blaškić*, ICTY A Ch., Judgment, 29 July 2004, § 72.

In this connection it is important to reiterate that the subjective incompetence of a particular commander is cannot be used as an argument that forces were not under his or her effective command and control (Fenrick, p. 518). "A superior's plea of lack of authority to take the necessary measures under internal regulations does not generally free him or her from criminal responsibility". *Prosecutor v. Mucic et al.*, ICTY T. Ch., Judgment, 16 November 1998, § 396.

According to Arnold, "a commander's position and possibility to intervene shall rather be assessed on the basis of what *any* commander, in such a situation, would have *objectively* done at the time of the facts". She does however emphasise that it is important to take the available preventive measures into consideration. Arnold places much emphasis on the need for education, the responsibility of which in her view, falls on high levels of command and the government (Arnold, 2008, p. 839, emphasis added).

As presented above, there are however some objective requirements as to what is considered to be necessary and reasonable. This is based on principles developed in international humanitarian law. Examples hereof are; providing instruction in international humanitarian law, creating an effective reporting system, supervising the monitoring system, recourse to disciplinary measures or removal of rank. *Prosecutor v. Bemba*, ICC PT Ch. II, Decision Pursuant to Article 61(7)(a) and (b) of the Rome Statute on the Charges of the Prosecutor against Jean-Pierre Bemba Gombo, 15 June 2009.

As to the matter of what is considered as being within the powers of the commander, a controversial and heavily criticised part of a decision in the ICTY needs to be mentioned. In the

Hadžihasanović case, the Appeals Chamber namely held that the "principal crime" has to have been committed *while* the superior had effective control over the subordinates. The reasoning behind this decision was based on the fact that a commander who was appointed after the commission of the principal crime would not have had the possibility to prevent said crimes during their commission. Considering that the duty of the commander is three fold (or rather two fold in the ICTY statute, which was relevant to the present case), it could however be argued that the possibility exists for the commander, who assumes a position after the commission of the crime, to punish said crimes. By so doing, the superior would be fulfilling one of the main objectives of the doctrine, namely clearly condemning the actions and hence undermining chain effects hereof. It should be noted that it was a 3:2 decision with strong dissenting opinions on the matter. *Prosecutor v. Hadžihasanović*, ICTY A Ch., Judgment, 22 April 2008, § 37–56.

Author: Linnea Kortfält.

291 As mentioned above, the various duties are attached to different stages in the commission of the crime. Preventive measures are expected to be undertaken at any stage *before* the crime has been committed. The issue as to what is expected of the commander in this regard has at times been linked to the matter as to whether the doctrine is applicable to inchoate offences. As noted previously in this commentary, the relationship between the doctrine of superior responsibility and inchoate crimes has not been conclusively established in the case law of the *ad hoc* tribunals (see commentary on "committed" in note 317 on Article 25(3)(a) and inchoate offences in note 322 on Article 25(3)(f)). The *Orić* Trial Chamber did however purport the view that the commander could be responsible for inchoate crimes (*Prosecutor v. Orić*, ICTY T Ch, Judgment, 30 June 2006, § 328) The Trial Chamber in the *Orić* case correctly concluded that: "it is not only the execution and full completion of a subordinate's crimes which a superior must prevent, but the earlier planning or preparation" and that "the superior must intervene as soon as he becomes aware of the planning or preparation of crimes to be committed by his subordinates and as long as he has the effective ability to prevent them from starting or continuing" (Prosecutor v. Orić, ICTY T Ch, Judgment, 30 June 2006, § 328)

In the *Orić* case, the Trial Chamber furthermore formulated a normative yardstick in order to measure whether the superior has fulfilled his or her duty to *prevent*: "first, as a superior cannot be asked for more than what is in his or her power, the kind and extent of measures to be taken ultimately depend on the degree of effective control over the conduct of subordinates at the time a superior is expected to act; second, in order to be efficient, a superior must undertake all measures which are necessary and reasonable to prevent subordinates from planning, preparing or executing the prospective crime; third, the more grievous and/or imminent the potential crimes of subordinates appear to be, the more attentive and quicker the superior is expected to react; and fourth, since a superior is duty bound only to undertake what appears appropriate under the given conditions, he or she is not obliged to do the impossible". *Prosecutor v. Orić*, ICTY T Ch, Judgment, 30 June 2006, § 329

The *Bemba* Confirmation Decision gave further general guidance on how to evaluate specific preventive measures, such as the duty of the commander: "(i) to ensure that superior's forces are adequately trained in international humanitarian law; (ii) to secure reports that military actions were carried out in accordance with international law; (iii) to issue orders aiming at bringing the relevant practices into accord with the rules of war; (iv) to take disciplinary measures to prevent the commission of atrocities by the troops under the superior's command". *Prosecutor v. Bemba*, ICC PT Ch. II, Decision Pursuant to Article 61(7)(a) and (b) of the Rome Statute on the Charges of the Prosecutor against Jean-Pierre Bemba Gombo, 15 June 2009, § 438.

Despite these formulations of yardsticks and general guidance, it is however important to stress, that the assessment of what is considered to be necessary and reasonable preventive measures for a particular commander has to be made on a case-by-case basis. *Prosecutor v.*

Orić, ICTY T Ch, Judgment, 30 June 2006, § 330. It is hence, once again, both the *de jure* and *de facto* abilities of the commander that must be established.

Author: Linnea Kortfält.

292 *Failure to punish*

As previously mentioned, the "failure to punish" requirement in the statutes of the *ad hoc* tribunals, is formulated as two separate requirements in Article 28(a)(ii) of the ICC Statute, namely (1) to repress and (2) to report (or rather to 'submit the matter to the competent authorities for investigation and prosecution'). A few words shall first be mentioned as to the interpretation of the punish requirement provided by the *ad hoc* tribunals, after which attention subsequently shall be given to the alternative requirements found in Article 28 of the ICC Statute.

Several issues have been addressed with regard to the "failure to punish" requirement. One such issue is at what stage in the commission of the crime the punishment should be meted out. Considering that there is liability not only for completed offences in international criminal law, but also, for example, planning and attempting to commit the crime (see ICTY Statute Article 7(1), ICTR Statute Article 7(1) and ICC Statute Article 25), the conclusion must be that the punishment should be carried out as soon as any of these "punishable" actions have been undertaken. *Prosecutor v. Orić*, ICTY T. Ch., Judgment, 30 June 2006. In that same case, the distinction between at what time the preventive as opposed to the punitive measures should be carried out, was described in the following terms; "whereas measures to prevent must be taken as soon as the superior becomes aware of the risk of potential illegal acts about to be committed by subordinates, the duty to punish commences only if, and when, the commission of a crime by a subordinate can be reasonably suspected" Prosecutor v. Orić, ICTY T. Ch, Judgment, 30 June 2006, § 336.

Another issue is the precise conditions placed on the "effective control" requirement of the commander in correlation to the "duty to punish" requirement. In order for the commander to punish the subordinates he/she of course has to have effective control at the time when the punishment should be carried out. However, as already noted, the Appeals Chamber in the *Hadžihasanović* case decided that the commander also has to have had control over the subordinates during the time of the commission of the offence. *Prosecutor v. Hadžihasanović*, ICTY A. Ch., Judgment, 22 April 2008, § 37, 51. Heavy criticism has been levied against this decision. The *Orić* Trial Chamber, even expressly articulated its strong disagreement with the lack of logic in this decision. *Prosecutor v. Orić*, ICTY T Ch, Judgment, 30 June 2006, § 335. However, as it considered itself bound by the Appeals Chambers decision, it could not reach an alternative conclusion. The question of challenging this issue was avoided on appeal. *Prosecutor v. Orić*, ICTY A. Ch, Judgment, 3 July 2008, § 167.

The last issue that will be addressed within the confines of this commentary as to the conditions placed on the "duty to punish" requirement, is more precisely what measures that would be considered as appropriate for the commander to undertake in order to punish the perpetrators. If considered to be in effective control over the subordinates, at the right time, the superior has to either execute appropriate sanctions him or herself, alternatively conduct an investigation to establish the facts. The commander needs to undertake these actions either by him or herself, alternatively, if lacking such punitive measures within the ambit of his or her position, a report has to be transmitted to the competent authorities for further investigation and sanction. The superiors own lack of legal competence does not relieve him or her from pursuing these avenues, if he/she is considered to be in effective control of the perpetrators of the principal crime.

Failure to repress

Interpreted in accordance with the ordinary meaning to be given to the term, it would suggest that *repressive* measures solely entail a duty of the commander to stop the *ongoing* commission

(b) With respect to superior and subordinate relationships not described in paragraph (a),[294] a superior[295] shall be criminally responsible for crimes within the jurisdiction of the Court

---

of a crime (Ambos, p. 863), and that this concept therefore does not cover his or her obligation to *punish* the perpetrators.

However, according to the *Bemba* Confirmation Decision, the "duty to repress" arises at two different stages of the commission of the crime. Firstly, it includes the duty to stop ongoing crimes from continuing to be committed and, secondly, it entails the duty to punish the forces after their commission (*Prosecutor v. Bemba*, ICC PT Ch. II, Decision Pursuant to Article 61(7)(a) and (b) of the Rome Statute on the Charges of the Prosecutor against Jean-Pierre Bemba Gombo, 15 June 2009, § 440) Hence, repressive measures also include punishment by the commander him or herself.

The measures which ought to be taken in order to stop the ongoing crimes has to be evaluated on a case-by-case basis depending on his or her power to control as explained above (*Prosecutor v. Bemba*, ICC PT Ch. II, Decision Pursuant to Article 61(7)(a) and (b) of the Rome Statute on the Charges of the Prosecutor against Jean-Pierre Bemba Gombo, 15 June 2009, § 441). Besides punishment, these measures could include, but are certainly not limited to; conducting an investigation to establish the facts, issuing orders and securing the follow through of such orders. Perhaps, even more important would be subtler measures aiming at establishing and sustaining an environment of discipline and respect for the law. *Prosecutor v. Orić*, ICTY T Ch, Judgment, 30 June 2006, §336 and *Prosecutor v. Halilović*, ICTY T. Ch., Judgment, 16 November 2005, §§ 97–100.

The punishment after the commission of the crime could either be done by(1) the commander's own action or, if such punitive measures are limited for that particular commander, (2) by submitting the matter to the competent authorities (*Prosecutor v. Bemba*, ICC PT Ch. II, Decision Pursuant to Article 61(7)(a) and (b) of the Rome Statute on the Charges of the Prosecutor against Jean-Pierre Bemba Gombo, 15 June 2009, § 440).

Author: Linnea Kortfält.

[293] *Prima facie*, this may seem like a new requirement which differs from the Statutes of the ICTY, ICTR and SCSL. As such it would be filling the gap for those commanders who have themselves no disciplinary powers to 'repress' a crime (Ambos, 2002, p. 862) Nevertheless, despite the fact that it is not spelled out in the *ad hoc* tribunals' statutes, it has already been read into the concept of "duty to punish" according to the case law of these tribunals.

This requirement was interpreted in the Bemba Confirmation decision in the following way: "The duty to submit the matter to the competent authorities, like the duty to punish, arises after the commission of the crimes. Such a duty requires that the commander takes active steps in order to ensure that the perpetrators are brought to justice. It remedies a situation where commanders do not have the ability to sanction their forces. This includes circumstances where the superior has the ability to take measures, yet those measures do not seem to be adequate". *Prosecutor v. Bemba*, ICC PT Ch. II, Decision Pursuant to Article 61(7)(a) and (b) of the Rome Statute on the Charges of the Prosecutor against Jean-Pierre Bemba Gombo, 15 June 2009, § 442

Author: Linnea Kortfält.

[294] In this section of the commentary to Article 28, only those requirements which differ from the ones provided in paragraph 28(a), or for any other reason needs to be commented on separately, will be discussed. For comments relating to the other prerequisites, please refer back to the commentary on 28(a).

This phrase refers to the applicability of the doctrine of superior responsibility to superior–subordinate relationships that are not covered in Article 28(a), that is, the concept which, in this

---

commentary is called "non-military superior responsibility". This section of the Article hence encompasses those superiors who are *not* military commanders or effectively acting as military commanders (that is, *not* military or "quasi-military" commanders). The reasoning behind this clear separation of the requirements placed on superior responsibility for military and quasi-military commanders from the superior responsibility of non-military superiors is that there has been some controversy as to whether the doctrine should be applicable to civilians at all. Separating the requirements into distinct section of the Article consequently seemed to be an appropriate compromise during the Rome Conference (Vetter, 2000, p. 8) The jurisprudence of the *ad hoc* tribunals has, on several occasions, established that the doctrine of superior responsibility is applicable to non-military or civilian leaders.

One of the first cases, which basically paved the way for an argumentation as to the applicability of the doctrine of superior responsibility for civilian leader, was the *Čelebići* case. In the *Čelebići* case it was established that the term "superior" as used in for example the Statutes of the *ad hoc* Tribunals as well as in Article 86(2) of the Additional Protocols from 1977, is broad enough to encompass, not only strictly military commanders in a *de jure* command position, but also *de facto* superiors. A subsequent conclusion drawn hereof was that the effective control could exist in both *"civilian* and within military structures" (*Prosecutor v. Mucic et al.*, ICTY T. Ch., 16 November 1998, §§ 354, 378. emphasis added). This conclusion was supported upon appeal. *Prosecutor v. Mucic et al.*, ICTY, A. Ch., 20 February, Judgment, y 2001, § 195. The applicability of the doctrine to non-military commanders was upheld in, among others, the *Akayesu, Kayishema, Musema* and *Bagilishema* cases.

The Trial Chamber in the *Akayesu* case was not as bold in It's pronouncements as to the applicability of the doctrine to civilian leaders. It questioned whether the doctrine should at all be applicable in general terms to purely civilian leaders, since this issue, according to the Trial Chamber, still remained controversial and therefore held that "it is appropriate to assess on a case-by-case basis the power of authority actually devolved upon the Accused in order to determine whether or not he had the power to take all necessary and reasonable measures to prevent the commission of the alleged crimes or to punish the perpetrators thereof" (*Prosecutor v. Akayesu* (Case No. ICTR-96-4-T), ICTR T. Ch., Judgment, 2 September 1998, § 491) Musema was a Tea factory owner, hence, a position which was strictly civilian in nature. If studying the applicability of the doctrine to non-military superiors, this case would thus be an excellent point of reference. The Trial Chamber concluded that Article 6(3) was applicable to a person exercising *civilian authority as superiors"* (*Prosecutor v. Musema* (Case No. ICTR-96-13-A), ICTR T. Ch., Judgment, 27 January 2000, § 148) It is important to note that Musema was convicted both on the basis of 6(1), for personally having ordered the commission of the crimes, and for superior responsibility under 6(3) (*Prosecutor v. Musema*, ICTR T. Ch., Judgment, 27 January 2000, § 926 see also for example § 936) In stark contrast to the above mentioned cases, which voiced some concern as to the applicability of the doctrine to civilian superiors, the Trial Chamber in the Kayishema and Ruzindana case did not seem to find the applicability hereof to be at all problematic (*Prosecutor v. Kayishema and Ruzindana* (Case No. ICTR-95-1), ICTR T. Ch., Judgment, May 21 1999, §§ 213–215) The issue regarding the limitations of the doctrine of non-military superior responsibility was up for assessment in the *Bagilishema* Case. The Trial Chamber, had namely ruled that the doctrine was solely applicable to superiors who exercise *"military-style command authority"* over subordinates. The Appeals Chamber however clarified, once again, that the doctrine was applicable to civilian superiors (*Prosecutor v. Bagilishema* (Case No. ICTR-95-1A-A), ICTR A Ch., Judgment, 3 July 2002, §§ 47, 51). It confirmed the finding in the *Čelebići* case that it was sufficient that the civilian superior "exercise a degree of control over their subordinates which is *similar to that of military* commanders". *Prosecutor v. Bagilishema*, ICTR A Ch., Judgment, 3 July 2002, §§ 51–52 (emphasis added).

committed by subordinates[296] under his or her effective authority and control,[297] as a result of his or her failure to exercise control properly[298] over such subordinates, where:

The applicability of the doctrine to non-military superior responsibility has thus successively become established in the case law of the *ad hoc* Tribunals and the codification of such a provision in the ICC Statute is incontestable. However, the exact contours and content of the elements of this responsibility are not as clear, even in the case law from the *ad hoc* tribunals. The exact contours hereof with regard to the ICC Statute Article 28(b) is even more uncertain, however, needless to say, the text of the Article provides some guidance as to the interpretation hereof. These contours, or rather, the specific elements of the doctrine of non-military superior responsibility, shall be addressed in the following.

First however, a general comment concerning a crucial distinction between the *ad hoc* tribunals and the ICC statute, need to be mentioned. The case law of the *ad hoc* tribunals made little distinction as to the content of the doctrine of command responsibility as opposed to the doctrine of non-military superior responsibility, wherefore the question whether the superior was military, quasi-military or civilian did not lead to significant consequences. In the ICC, these consequences will however be much more significant, since the elements of the doctrine differ considerably between 28(a) and 28(b).

Author: Linnea Kortfält.

[295] *A superior:* As previously noted, Article 28(b) is only applicable when the superior cannot be considered a military or a quasi-military commander. This sub-Article is accordingly subsidiary to Article 28(a) (Arnold, 2008, p. 840) In determining whether to charge a person under Article 28(b) it is therefore of importance both to assess the status of the defendant "upwards" and "downwards"; upwards, in order to exclude the superior's status as a potential military or quasi military leader, and, downwards, by ascertaining his or her status as actually possessing effective control with the material ability to prevent or repress crimes of subordinates.

The *Kordic* case in the ICTY addressed the standard for what was not considered to be a military commander: "while he played an important role in military matters, even at times issuing orders, and exercising authority over HVO forces, he was, and remained throughout the indictment period, a civilian, who was *not part of the formal command structure of the HVO*". *Prosecutor v. Kordic* (Case No. IT-95-14), ICTY T. Ch, Judgment, 26 February 2001, § 838 (emphasis added)

It could be argued however that the importance of making a differentiation between military, quasi-military and non-military commanders are of less importance in the judgments from the *ad hoc* tribunals as opposed to the ICC since there is considerable difference between the elements in the latter and not in the former. Arnold accordingly correctly concludes that the ICC will carefully have to address this issue (Arnold, 2008, p. 840)

The matter as to the lower boundaries of the doctrine of non-military superior responsibility is still under debate. It has been established, in both case law and the academic debate, that, as long as the effective control test is satisfied (see below), non-military superiors can for instance include leaders within non military components of government and political parties (such as mayors, party leaders, Heads of State (that are not at the same time the commander-in-chief)), business leaders (for example industrial leaders, tea factory owners) as well as senior civil servants. To the category of non-military commanders have also been included prison camp commanders and chiefs of police (Fenrick, p. 521, Werle p. 132).

Author: Linnea Kortfält.

[296] Subordinates are anyone under the effective authority and control of a superior, that is, any subordinate who has a superior who can direct his work or work related activities. The middle management in a large organisation, can, needless to say, be both superiors and subordinates

---

(Fenrick, 1999, p. 521) Examples may include, but are not limited to, subordinate members of political parties, prison guards, workers in factories, civil servants, private contractors, civil personnel in a peace keeping mission, NGO workers.

These are formal, or in order to use a more familiar term at this point, *de jure* subordinates of a non-military superior. However, a relevant question is whether the doctrine also applies to so called "indirect subordinates, that is, other people or the civilian population at large, who, somehow *de facto* are under the effective control of the superior.

The issue concerning indirect subordinates was raised in the *Musema* case. Even if reaching the conclusion that Musema did not wield *de facto* control over the indirect subordinates in this particular case, it did however conclude that it would be *possible* to view people who were not employees of the superior as his or her subordinates in accordance with the doctrine of superior responsibility (*Prosecutor v. Musema*, ICTR T Ch., Judgment, 27 January 2000, §§ 144, 148, 881–883).

The range of the doctrine to indirect subordinates has, to some extent, been limited in the ICC Statute by the clause "as a result of his failure to exercise control properly" and "activities that were within the effective responsibility and control of the superior" in Article 28(b). By some scholars, these clauses have, been interpreted as limiting the reach of the superior's *de facto* control to work-related activities and consequently also limiting the fold of indirect subordinates accordingly (for example Fenrick, p. 521–522 and Arnold, p. 840–841).

Author: Linnea Kortfält.

297 In the commentary to Article 28(a) the concept of "effective control" as well as "authority and control" was discussed in relation to military and quasi-military commanders. In this section comments shall be limited to the specific interpretation of this requirement with regards to non-military superiors. For more extensive information, please refer to the previous commentary.

As already concluded, the doctrine of superior responsibility is applicable to non-military superiors so long as it can be established that a superior–subordinate relationship exists between the superior and the perpetrator of the principal crime. Some aspects of this relationship has already been discussed, namely the (possible) definition of the superior and the (possible) definition of the subordinate. These subsequent sections will however deal with the quality of the relationship as such. The relationship has to be characterised by the superiors "effective control", that is, his or her *de facto* material ability to prevent or punish the perpetrators.

Amongst others, the *Čelebići, Musema, Bagilishema* cases expressed similar views. "[I]t is [...] the Trial Chamber's conclusion that a superior, whether military or civilian, may be held liable under the principle of superior responsibility on the basis of his *de facto* position of authority [...]". "[I]n order for the principle of superior responsibility to be applicable, it is necessary that the superior have *effective control* over the persons committing the underlying violations of international humanitarian law, in the sense of having the *material ability to prevent and punish* the commission of these offences". *Prosecutor v. Mucic et al.*, ICTY T. Ch., Judgment, 16 November 1998, § 377–378 "It is also significant to note that a *civilian superior* may be charged with superior responsibility only where he has *effective control*, be it *de jure* or merely *de facto*, over the persons committing violations of international humanitarian law". *Prosecutor v. Musema*, ICTR T Ch., Judgment, 27 January 2000, § 141 "the *effective control* test applies to all superiors, whether *de jure* or *de facto*, military or *civilian*". *Prosecutor v. Bagilishema*, ICTR A Ch., Judgment, 3 July 2002, § 50 (emphasis added).

There are however some more caveats and restrictions to this "material ability" that are of particular importance with regards to civilian superiors as opposed to military or quasi-military commanders. A few of these concerns and difficulties will be addressed hereinafter.

Effective control-test does not require proof of both de jure and de facto authority

The first issue as to the interpretation of the extent of "effective control" requirement, is whether, besides proof of *de facto* authority, the court also has to be satisfied as to the existence of a *de jure* authority. The Appeals Chamber in the *Bagilishema* case had to correct the findings of the Trial Chamber on this point. The Trial Chamber had held that there needed to be proof of both *de jure* and *de facto* authority: "…the Trial Chamber wrongly held that both *de facto* and *de jure* authority need to be established before a superior can be found to exercise effective control over his or her subordinates. The Appeals Chamber reiterates that the test in all cases is whether the accused exercised effective control over his or her subordinates; this is not limited to asking whether he or she had *de jure* authority. The ICTY Appeals Chamber held in the *Čelebići* Appeal Judgment that "[a]s long as a superior has effective control over subordinates, to the extent that he can prevent them from committing crimes or punish them after they committed the crimes, he would be held responsible for the commission of the crimes if he failed to exercise such abilities of control" *Prosecutor v. Bagilishema*, ICTR A Ch., Judgment, 3 July 2002, § 61 It ought however be mentioned that the Čelebići Trial Chamber at another section of the judgment held that "[…] it is sufficient if there exists, on the part of the accused, a *de facto* exercise of authority. The Trial Chamber agrees with this view, provided the exercise of *de facto* authority is accompanied by the trappings of the exercise of *de jure* authority. By this, the Trial Chamber means the perpetrator of the underlying offence must be the subordinate of the person of higher rank and under his direct or indirect control". *Prosecutor v. Mucic et al.*, ICTY T. Ch., Judgment, 16 November 1998, § 646. Hence, the confusion of the Bagilishema Trial Chamber may be understandable.

Assessment of the effective control on a case-by-case basis

As already recognised above, the Trial Chambers in both the Akayesu and Musema case were not convinced as to the general applicability of the doctrine superior responsibility to non-military superiors. In line herewith, both Chambers expressed that the authority of the non-military superior needed to be assessed on a case-by-case basis (*Prosecutor v. Akayesu*, ICTR T. Ch., Judgment, 2 September 1998, § 491, *Prosecutor v. Musema*, ICTR T. Ch., Judgment, 27 January 2000, § 867) A thorough assessment on a case-by-case basis may be of particular importance in civilian structures, nevertheless, it should not be forgotten the importance hereof in military and quasi-military settings as well.

Broad interpretation, psychological pressure and power of influence as opposed to military-style command

The issue of how to interpret the content of the "effective authority and control" requirement of a non-military superior has been rather challenging. Differing opinions have surfaced on the subject, ranging from the authority needing to be proved solely by psychological pressure and powers of influence to the necessity of demonstrating a military style of command. The *Musema* Trial Chamber thus spoke in terms of psychological pressure: "The influence at issue in a superior–subordinate command relationship often appears in the form of psychological pressure. This is particularly relevant to the case at bar, insofar as Alfred Musema was a socially and politically prominent person in Gisovu Commune". *Prosecutor v. Musema* (Case No. ICTR-96-13-A) ICTR T. Ch., Judgment, 27 January 2000, § 140. In the Aleksovski case, the Trial Chamber stressed the need to interpret the civilian superior's authority broadly (*Prosecutor v. Aleksovski* (Case No. IT-95-14/1) ICTY T. Ch, Judgment, June 25 1999, § 78) This was subsequently restricted with an alternative view in the *Kordic* case, where the ideas of substantial influence was limited: "[A] government official will only be held liable under the doctrine of command responsibility if he was part of a superior–subordinate relationship, *even if that relationship is an indirect one*. Even though arguably effective control may be achieved through *substantial influence*, a demonstration of such powers of influence will not be sufficient in the absence of a showing that he had effective control over subordinates, in the sense of possessing the material ability to prevent subordinate offences or punish subordinate offenders after the commission of

(i) The superior either knew,[299] or consciously disregarded information which clearly in-dicated,[300] that the subordinates were committing or about to commit such crimes;

---

the crimes. A showing that the official merely was generally an influential person will not be sufficient". *Prosecutor v. Kordic and Cerkez* (Case No. IT-65-14/2) ICTY T. Ch., Judgment, 26 February 2001, §§ 415–416 (emphasis added) As noted previously (see note 342), an attempt was furthermore undertaken by the *Bagilishema* Trial Chamber, to restrict the boundaries of the doctrine of non-military superior responsibility to solely cover so called "military-style" com-mand situations. The argumentation was partly supported by the fact that the *Čelebići* Trial Chamber had concluded that the exercise of *de facto* authority had to be accompanied by the trappings of the exercise of *de jure* authority. The *Bagilishema* Trial Chamber interpreted these trappings of authority to include "for example, awareness of a chain of command, the practice of issuing and obeying orders, and the expectation that insubordination may lead to disciplinary action", and that "[i]t is by these trappings that the law distinguishes civilian superiors from mere rabble-rousers or other persons of influence". *Prosecutor v. Bagilishema* (Case No. ICTR-95-1A-A) ICTR T. Ch., 7 June 2001, §§ 42–43 This attempt was however assertively shot down by the Appeals Chamber through referring to the conclusions of the Čelebići Trial Chamber which held that civilian control solely had to be similar to that of military commanders. *Prose-cutor v. Bagilishema* (Case No. ICTR-95-1A-A), ICTR A Ch., 3 July 2002, § 52.

Author: Linnea Kortfält.

[298] This, like the same requirement under Article 28(a), indicates a new causality requirement under the doctrine of superior responsibility.

Accordingly, the principal crime undertaken by the subordinates has to be a result of the non-military superior's failure to exercise control properly. As to a discussion about the actual content of the "result" or "causality" requirement, see the commentary above.

According to many scholars, the sphere of the civilian superior's ability to "exercise control properly" has to be limited to work or work-related activities. Hence, what is expected of the non-military superior in order to "exercise control properly" is limited accordingly (Arnold, 2008, p. 840, Fenrick, 1999, p. 521). The reason being that as opposed to a military commander, a non-military superior cannot be charged with the responsibility to control his or her subordi-nates 24/7, and, furthermore he/she is normally not involved in efforts that generally increase the risk of subordinates committing international core crimes.

he/she is "obligated to establish and maintain an effective reporting system to ensure his subordinates comply with international humanitarian law in their work and work related activi-ties and, if he or she becomes aware of potential or actual violations, to take all practicable measures to prevent or repress such violations". Fenrick does however make a distinction as to the kind of workers or work that could result in IHL violations; for example care of POW's, in-terned civilians of forced labour or factories producing prison gas for use in camps. He further-more gives the example of workers in a paint factory who, outside working hours engage in genocidal activities. A non-military superior to these workers could not, according to Fenrick, be convicted under Article 28(b) for these genocidal activities (Fenrick, 1999, p. 521). Arnold, reiterates Fenrick's conclusions as to the description of that "failure to exercise control proper-ly" solely entails work-related activities (Arnold, 2008, p. 840) (For an alternative view please refer to *Prosecutor v. Musema*, ICTR T (Case No. ICTR-96-13-A), Ch., 27 January 2000, § 148)

Author: Linnea Kortfält.

[299] *Knew*: This part of the *mens rea* requirement for non-military superiors is the same as the actual knowledge standard expressed under 28(a)(i). Comments as to the content hereof are therefore referred to the information provided above.

(ii) The crimes concerned activities that were within the effective responsibility and control of the superior;[301] and

(iii) The superior failed to take all necessary and reasonable measures within his or her power to prevent or repress their commission or to submit the matter to the competent authorities for investigation and prosecution.[302]

Author: Linnea Kortfält.

[300] The "consciously disregarding information which clearly indicated" requirement in Article 28(b)(i), does however entail a much higher *mens rea* standard than what is provided for the doctrine of command responsibility (that is, the "reason to know" or "should have known" standards under ICTY Statute Article 7(3) and ICC Statute Article 28(a) respectively). This new standard has, for example, been equated to "wilful blindness", that is, that the superior is *aware* of a *high probability* of the existence of a fact (as long as he actually does not believe that it exists) and, yet, he/she decides to "turn a blind eye" to this fact. As such, it has furthermore been explained that this new criterion stands somewhere between "actual knowledge" and "recklessness" (defined as "consciously disregarding a risk") (Ambos, 2002, p. 870).

This new standard is one of the main reasons why Article 28(b) is the common understanding to provide a higher threshold and consequently more difficulties for the prosecution under the doctrine (for example Ambos, 870).

One of the reasons that there has been a much higher threshold placed upon non-military superiors is that, superiors in civilian structures generally do not have as many possibilities to receive information on the conduct of their subordinates as do military commanders (Arnold, 2008, p. 841) The standard has therefore been identified to entail that it is necessary to establish that:(1) *information* clearly indicating a significant risk that subordinates were committing or were about to commit offences existed, (2) this information was *available* to the superior, and (3) the superior, while aware that such a category of information existed, declined to refer to the category of information (Fenrick, 1999, p. 521, Ambos, 2002, p. 870, Arnold, 2008, 841) Obviously the exact content of each of these conditions could be further discussed. Fenrick briefly touched upon these additional issues in his commentary, stating for instance that considering that a superior has *a duty to be informed*, and subsequently fails to avail him- or herself of information sent to his or her office, he/she could be considered to consciously disregard said information.

Author: Linnea Kortfält.

[301] The application and interpretation of this requirement, which obviously is an additional requirement under the doctrine of non-military superior responsibility as opposed to Article 28(a), is closely connected to the comments given under "failure to exercise control properly".

Subordinates within the meaning of Article 28(b) are according to many scholars, only within the effective responsibility and control of the superior while they are at work or while engaged in work related activities. Outside these circumstances, the activities undertaken by the subordinates are not generally considered to be under the control of the superior (Fenrick, 1999, p. 522, Arnold, 2008, p. 841).

Author: Linnea Kortfält.

[302] The measures to prevent or repress the commission of the crimes by the subordinates, has to be necessary, reasonable and within the superiors' power. The duty of the superior should hence not be beyond what can reasonably be expected of him/her. Even if this condition has the same terminology as in Article 28(a), needless to say, it would entail different conditions when applied in a civilian context.

To a certain extent, the matter as to what can be considered necessary and reasonable measures within the superiors powers, are connected to what has been addressed above concern-

---

ing the requirements: "as a result of his or her failure to exercise control properly" and "activities that were within the effective responsibility and control of the superior".

The non-military superior is unlikely to have disciplinary powers. Action that can be expected of the superior in lines with his or her duty to prevention and repress could for example be issuing orders to the subordinates that the activities should cease, immediate dismissal or repatriation when stationed abroad.

If all of these possibilities do not work, of particular importance when dealing with the doctrine of non-military superior responsibility is the possibility of submitting the matter to the competent authorities for investigation (for example higher superiors, police, military and or civil/criminal judicial authorities).

All of these possible avenues would subsequently have to be followed up, especially when repatriation is involved. In this latter case it is also important to ascertain that criminal investigations are undertaken upon arrival at the country of origin (Fenrick, 1999, p. 522, Arnold, 2008, p. 841)

Doctrine:

1. Kai Ambos, "Individual Criminal Responsibility", in Otto Triffterer (ed.), *Commentary on the Rome Statute of the International Criminal Court: Observers' Notes, Article by Article*, 2nd ed., C.H. Beck/Hart/Nomos, Munich/Oxford/Baden-Baden, 2008, pp. 795–843.

2. Kai Ambos, "Critical Issues in the Bemba Decision", in *Leiden Journal of International Law*, vol. 22, 2009, pp. 715–26.

3. Kai Ambos, "Superior Responsibility", in Antonio Cassese, Paola Gaeta and John R.W.D. Jones (eds.), *The Rome Statute of the International Criminal Court – A Commentary*, Oxford University Press, Oxford, 2002, pp. 823–72.

4. Roberta Arnold, "Responsibility of Commanders and Other Superiors", in Otto Triffterer (ed.), *Commentary on the Rome Statute of the International Criminal Court: Observers' Notes, Article by Article*, 2nd ed., C.H. Beck/Hart/Nomos, Munich/Oxford/Baden-Baden, 2008, pp. 824–43.

5. Robert Cryer, Håkan Friman, Daryll Robinson and Elizabeth Wilmshurst, *An Introduction to International Criminal Law and Procedure*, Cambridge University Press, Cambridge, 2008.

6. William Fenrick, "Article 28", in Otto Triffterer (ed.), *Commentary on the Rome Statute of the International Criminal Court*, Nomos Verlagsgesellschaft, Baden-Baden, 1999, pp. 515–22.

7. Linnea Kortfält, *Occupational Zone Commanders*, LAS, Office of the Prosecutor, International Criminal Tribunal for the former Yugoslavia, 2003 (Unpublished).

8. Linnea Kortfält, "Internationellt straffansvar för befäl i multinationella styrkor", in Anders W. Berggren (ed.), *Människan i NBF: Att förbereda för internationella missioner,* FHS ILM, Stockholm, 2006.

9. Linnea Kortfält, "Skuldkravet och personliga förutsättningar för straffbarhet", in Jo Stigen and Morten Bergsmo (eds.), *Nordisk introduktion till Internationell Straffrätt*, 2010 (Unpublished).

10. Chantal Meloni, "Command Responsibility – Mode of Liability for the Crimes of Subordinates or Separate Offence of the Superior?", in *Journal of International Criminal Justice*, 2007, vol. 5, no. 3, pp. 619–37.

11. Volker Nerlich, "Supeiror Responsiblity under Article 28 ICC Statute – For what Exactly is the Superior Held Responsible", in *Journal of International Criminal Justice*, 2007, vol. 5, p. 665.

12. Maria L. Nybondas, *Command Responsibility and its Applicability to Civilian Leaders*, TMC Asser Press, Amsterdam, 2010.

13. Guénael Mettraux, *The Law of Command Responsibility*, Oxford University Press, Oxford, 2009, p. 38

14. William H. Parks, "Command Responsibility for War Crimes", in *Military Law Review*, 1973, vol. 62, pp. 1–104.

15. Greg R. Vetter, "Command Responsibility of Non-military Superiors in the International Criminal Court", in *Yale Journal of International Law*, 2000, vol. 25, no. 1, pp. 89–143.

16. Suzanne Wennberg, *Introduktion till straffrätten*, Norstedts juridik AB, Stockholm, 2001.

17. Gerhard Werle, *Principles of International Criminal Law*, TMC Asser Press, The Hague, 2005.

18. Commentary to Protocol Additional to the Geneva Conventions of 12 August 1949, and relating to the Protection of Victims of International Armed Conflicts (Protocol I), 8 June 1977, § 3527.

19. Additional Protocol to the Geneva Conventions of 12 August 1949, and relating to the Protection of Victims of International Armed Conflicts, 8 June 1977.

Author: Linnea Kortfält.

Article 29

Non-applicability of statute of limitations

The crimes within the jurisdiction of the Court shall not be subject to any statute of limitations.[303]

---

[303] *General remarks*:

Article 29 provides for the non-applicability of statutory limitations to the international crimes that are subject matter of the International Criminal Court.

Preparatory works:

The establishment of the International Criminal Court (ICC) is the result of initiatives taken by the General Assembly, the ILC, scholars and non-governmental organisations (See Kok, 2007; Page, 2004, pp, 1–35; Saland 1999; Schabas 1998, p. 400 and 1999, pp. 523–535; Van den Wyngaert and Dugard, 2001, pp. 873–888). In 1994, the ILC submitted a Draft Statute for a Permanent International Criminal Court. Even though the ILC had discussed the (non-) applicability of statutory limitations previously in the Draft Code of Offences against the Peace and Security of Mankind, this time the ILC did not address this concept (see Draft Statute for a Permanent International Criminal Court, in Report of the International Law Commission on the work of its forty-sixth session, 2 May–22 July 1994, GAOR, 49th Sess. Suppl. No. 10, UN doc. A/49/10, YILC 1994, Volume II (Part 2), pp. 20–73, at §§42–91). In 1995, an independent committee of scholars introduced in an alternative draft for an International Criminal Court, the so-called Siracusa Draft, a new provision providing that "there is no statute of limitation for genocide, serious war crimes, and crimes against humanity (or aggression)" (Association Internationale de Droit Pénal (AIDP)/International Institute of Higher Studies in Criminal Sciences (ISISC)/Max-Planck-Institute for Foreign and International Criminal Law (MPI), "Draft Statute for an International Criminal Court-Alternative to the ILC Draft", prepared by a Committee of Experts, Siracusa/Freiburg, July 1995, Article 33q). In 1995, the General Assembly established the Ad Hoc Committee on the Establishment of an International Criminal Court (Report of the Ad Hoc Committee on the Establishment of a Permanent International Criminal Court, GA 50th Sess (1995), UN doc. GAOR A/50/22). In its first report, the Ad Hoc Committee pointed at the divergences between provisions on statutory limitations contained in domestic legislation, and some delegations questioned whether they should apply with respect to serious crimes (Ibid., at §2(f), para. 127):

> Some delegations felt that the question of the statute of limitations for the crimes within the jurisdiction of the court should be addressed in the Statute in the light of divergences between national laws and bearing in mind the importance of the legal principle involved, which reflected the decreasing social importance of bringing criminals to justice and the increasing difficulties in ensuring a fair trial as time elapsed. However, other delegations questioned the applicability of the statute of limitations to the types of serious crimes under consideration and drew attention to the 1968 Convention on the Non-applicability of Statutory Limitations to War Crimes and Crimes against Humanity.

In the same year, the General Assembly established the Preparatory Committee on the Establishment of an ICC, with the task of preparing a "[w]idely acceptable consolidated text of a convention for an international criminal court" (UN GA Res, A/RES/50/46, 18 December 1995). In 1996, the Preparatory Committee submitted its first report, containing five proposals on the (non-)applicability of statutory limitations (1966 Report of the Preparatory Committee on the Establishment of an International Criminal Court, UN GA 51st Sess. Supp. No. 22, UN doc. A/51/22 (1996), Volume II, Article F). The five different proposals illustrate that the ICC drafters highly disagreed on this matter. The first proposal provided for prescription periods of an unidentified length, as well as detailed rules governing their application. The second proposal provided that statutes of limitation do not apply to crimes within the jurisdiction of the Court. The third proposal provided for the non-applicability of statutory limitations to such crimes, unless "[o]wing to the lapse of time, a person would be denied a fair trial". The fourth proposal limited the material scope of the rule to only some of the crimes within the jurisdiction of the Court. The fifth and final proposal provided for a number of detailed rules concerning the application of statutes of limitation to all crimes within the jurisdiction of the Court. The five different proposals illustrate that the delegations highly disagreed on the matter. The debate was even more complicated, since the material scope of a statute for an international court was not yet defined. Their comments have been summarised in the report as follows (Preparatory Committee on the Establishment of an International Criminal Court, 25 March–12 April 1996, A/AC.249/CRP.3/Add.l, 8 April 1996):

> Many delegations (Israel, Malaysia, and Ukraine) were of the view that owing to the serious nature of the crimes to be dealt with by the court, there should be no statute of limitations for such crimes. On the other hand, some delegations felt that such a provision was mandatory and should be included in the statute, having regard to their national laws, to ensure fairness for the accused. The view was expressed that statutory limitation might apply to lesser crimes (France). In the view of some delegations (Japan), this question should be considered in connection with the issue of the availability of sufficient evidence for a fair trial. Some delegations (Canada) suggested that instead of establishing a rigid rule the Prosecutor or President should be given flexible power to make a determination on a case-by-case basis, taking into account the right of the accused to due process. In this connection, it was noted that Article 27 of the statute was relevant to this issue. It was suggested that an accused should be allowed to apply to the court to terminate the proceedings on the basis of fairness, if there was lack of evidence owing to the passage of many years.

The proposals discussed by the Preparatory Committee on the Establishment of an ICC eventually were not consolidated in the Zutphen Report of 1998 (Report of the Inter-Sessional Meeting from 19 to 30 January 1998 in Zutphen, the Netherlands, 4 February 1998, UN doc. A/AC.249/1998/L.13, pp. 57–58, Article 21(f)). However, the 1998 Report of the Preparatory Committee on the Establishment of an International Criminal Court, which formed the basis for the negotiations during the Rome Conference, did reflect the five proposals as described supra (Draft Statute of an International Criminal Court, 14 April 1998, UN doc. A/Conf.183/2/Add.2, pp. 53–54, Article 27: "Statute of limitation"). During the Rome Conference, the Working Group on General Principles of Criminal Law proposed a provision providing for the non-applicability of statutory limitations to all crimes within the jurisdiction of the court (Working Group 2 on General Principles of Criminal Law, UN doc. A/Conf.183/C.1/WGGP/L.4, p. 4; Schabas, 1999, p. 525). Japan changed its previous position, but maintained that the passage of time should provide for a mitigating factor in allowing a prosecution to proceed before the ICC (Saland, 1999, p. 204). The drafters of the 1998 ICC Statute eventually adopted the proposal of the Working Group, which is contained in Article 29. The only disagreement on this provision can be found in the joint statement submitted by China and France in a footnote of the Working Group's Report. They firstly disagreed on the application of this rule with respect to war crimes, and secondly, stressed their concern with regard to the effect of the passage of time in terms of securing a fair trial (UN doc. A/Conf.183/C.1/WGGP/L.4, p. 4, fn. 7). However, the proposal was adopted by the Conference without changes.

Analysis:
i. Retroactivity
Article 29 is silent on its retroactive application. However, pursuant to Article 11, the ICC has jurisdiction only with regard to crimes committed after the entering into force of the 1998 ICC

Statute. The ICC Statute entered into force on 1 July 2002. The issue of retroactivity, therefore, does not arise.

ii. Complementarity

The so-called 'complementarity' provision contained in Article 17 of the 1998 ICC Statute provides that states have the main responsibility for the adjudication of international crimes. Schabas points out that a problem of complementarity may arise if the prosecution of a crime at a national level is barred by a domestic statute of limitations but still possible pursuant to the 1998 ICC Statute (Schabas, 1998, p. 103). The ICC could declare that this state is 'unable' to prosecute; the ICC would then be entitled to exercise its jurisdiction. For this reason, most states' parties that still had domestic provisions on statutes of limitation to crimes within the jurisdiction of the ICC have abolished or amended them, although not all states' parties have done so. However, if a state has not done so, it shows its unwillingness to prosecute these crimes, thus entailing that the case is admissible before the ICC. Indeed, it appears that a number of states, despite their ratification of the 1998 ICC Statute, did not (fully) amend their domestic legislation in this regard, and still apply statutes of limitation to (some) international crimes. Illustrative for the divergences between Article 29 and the domestic provisions are the implementation processes in France, Germany, and the Netherlands respectively.

First, whereas the French legal system since 1964 has provided for the imprescriptibility of crimes against humanity, war crimes remain subject to statutes of limitation (see the Journal Officiel du 29 Décembre 1964, No. 17.788 and Bulletin Législatif Dalloz, décembre 1964, p. 33). In 1999, the French Constitutional Council (Constitutional Court, Decision 98-408 DC of 22 January 1999 (Treaty on the Statute of the International Criminal Court), Journal officiel, 24 January 1999, 1317) considered that if a crime became statutorily barred due to the expiration of the prescription period provided for in the French legal system, the ICC would incur jurisdiction over the crime. Since such circumstances would infringe upon the exercise of national sovereignty, the Constitutional Court concluded that the 1994 new French Penal Code should be amended by providing for the non-applicability of statutory limitations to war crimes as well (ICRC Report 2003, p. 1).

Second, Article 5 of the German 2002 Code of Crimes against International Law, that entered into force on 30 June 2002, confines the non-applicability of statutory limitations to "serious criminal offences". As a consequence, this provision does not extend to war crimes subject to less than one-year imprisonment, such as the violation of the duty of supervision and the omission to report a crime as these sections form "less serious criminal offences" (Satzger, 2002, p. 272). These crimes remain subject to the ordinary provisions on statutory limitations, provided for in Article 78 of the German Penal Code. The German legislature exempted these crimes from imprescriptibility because it considered them of a significantly less serious nature than some ordinary crimes that remain subject to ordinary provisions on statutory limitations provided for in the Penal Code. Theoretically, the ICC could exercise its jurisdiction with respect to these minor war crimes pursuant to the complementarity provisions. However, it seems in most circumstances rather unlikely that the ICC, in effect, would start adjudicating such crimes, as the ICC aims at exercising its jurisdiction with respect to the most serious and gravest core international crimes exclusively. The Preamble 1998 ICC Statute states: "[A]ffirming that the most serious crimes of concern to the international community as a whole must not go unpunished and that their effective prosecution must be ensured by taking measures at the national level and by enhancing international cooperation; [...] Determined to these ends and for the sake of present and future generations, to establish an independent permanent International Criminal Court in relationship with the United Nations system, with jurisdiction over the most serious crimes of concern to the international community as a whole".

Third, the Dutch International Crimes Act (2003 International Crimes Act, 19 June 2003, Stb. 270, 3 July 2003, 28337), that entered into force on 1 October 2003, provides in Article 13 for the non-applicability of statutory limitations to the crimes covered by the Act. The International Crimes Act confines the material scope of Article 29 of the 1998 ICC Statute, by excluding war crimes subject to a maximum sentence of 10 years' imprisonment from its application. On the other hand, the International Crimes Act extends this provision, since it also applies with respect to the crime of torture sui generis, thus not constituting a crime against humanity. The legislature decided to extend the provision to this crime, owing to the very serious nature of the crime of torture, as well as the ius cogens character of the prohibition on torture (See the Dutch government in their explanatory memorandum on the International Crimes Act, Bijl. Hand. II 2001/2002, 28 337, No. 3, p. 33). The International Crimes Act applies retroactively with respect to the crime of torture, unless its prescription period has already expired as of the date of the entering into force of the ICC Statute (Boot-Matthijssen and van Elst, 2002, pp. 1745–1747).

International instruments and jurisprudence

i. The Statutes of the ad hoc tribunals

The Statutes of the International Criminal Court for the Former Yugoslavia (hereinafter referred to as ICTY) and the International Criminal Court for Rwanda (hereinafter referred to as ICTR) do not contain any provisions on the (non-)applicability of statutory limitations. The only reference to the aspect of time can be found in the provisions providing for the Ad Hoc Tribunal's temporal jurisdiction. The ICTY Statute provides in Article 8: "The temporal jurisdiction of the International Tribunal shall extend to a period beginning on 1 January 1991". The ICTR Statute provides in Article 7: "The temporal jurisdiction of the International Tribunal for Rwanda shall extend to a period beginning on 1 January 1994 and ending on 31 December 1994." Even though at this stage the (non-)applicability of statutory limitations to international crimes already had been addressed frequently in various international instruments, the drafters apparently considered that a provision was unnecessary. First, too little time had passed for a possible expiration of prescription periods. After all, the ICTY was established during the armed conflict in the Socialist Federal Republic of Yugoslavia, and the ICTR in a few months after the genocide terminated in Rwanda. Secondly, both the Socialist Federal Republic of Yugoslavia and Rwanda had already become parties to the 1968 UN Convention before the events occurred on the territories in the 1990s. The Socialist Federal Republic of Yugoslavia ratified the 1968 UN Convention on 9 June 1970; Rwanda acceded to the 1968 UN Convention on 16 April 1975. Moreover, the penal codes of the Former Yugoslavia and Rwanda provide for the non-applicability of statutes of limitation to international crimes.

There is some case law of the ICTY on statutes of limitation. In 1997, the Trial Chamber in the *Tadić* case (*Tadić* (Case No. IT-94-1-AR72-T), T. Ch. II, Judgment, 7 May 1997, at §§641–642) referred to a decision of a French domestic court in the French case of Barbie (Court of Appeal, Criminal Chamber, decision of 4 October 1985, ILR 125) concerning the applicability of statutory limitations to crimes against humanity. However, the Chamber itself did not express any opinion on the permissibility of the application of statutory limitation. This is different in the judgment of the Trial Chamber in the *Furundžija* case (*Furundžija* (Case No. IT-95-17/1-T), T. Ch. II, Judgment, 10 December 1998, at §156). In an *obiter dictum*, that Trial Chamber concluded that, considering the *jus cogens* character of the prohibition of torture, "it would seem that other consequences include the fact that torture may not be covered by a statute of limitations" (*Furundžija* (Case No. IT-95-17/1-T), T. Ch. II, Judgment, 10 December 1998, at §156). However, the Trial Chamber did not explain how it reached such a conclusion. In addition, the Chamber recognised this rule with respect to the crime of torture as a war crime, rather than the crime of torture sui generis (Cassese, 2003, p. 119). In later judgments, no Trial Chamber has pronounced itself on the same matter. In 2004 in the case of *Mrdja* (*Mrdja* (Case No. IT-02-59-S), T. Ch. I, Sentencing judgment, 31 March 2004, at §§103–104), the Trial Chamber discussed the difference between statutes of limitation versus the right to be tried without undue delay. In analysing the effect of the passage of time on the determination of the sanction, the Chamber recalled that:

> [T]he importance of international prosecution of the perpetrators of such serious crimes diminishes only slightly over the years, if at all. On this point, it is important to recall Article 1 of the 1968 UN Convention (ratified by the former Yugoslavia on 9 June 1970 and currently in force in Bosnia and Herzegovina), which stipulates that such crimes are not subject to statutory limitation ... [F]or crimes of a seriousness justifying their exclusion from statutory limitation, the Trial Chamber considers that a lapse of time of almost twelve years between the commission of the crimes and sentencing proceedings is not so long as to be considered a factor for mitigation.

At present, the Ad Hoc Tribunals are engaged in putting into effect so-called 'completion strategies', which imply that they will stop trying cases in the near future. Statutes of limitation play no role in these strategies.

ii. The Statutes of the Internationalised Tribunals

a) The Panels in East Timor

By its Resolution 1272 (1999) adopted on 25 October 1999, the Security Council of the United Nations, acting under Chapter VII of the Charter of the UN, decided to establish a United Nations Transitional Administration in East Timor (UNTAET). Among other things, UNTAET was empowered to exercise all legislative and executive authority, including the administration of justice. In 2000, the Representative of the UN, pursuant to the authority given to him under the Security Council Resolution, adopted UNTAET Regulation 2000/15, whereby Panels with the exclusive jurisdiction with respect to serious criminal offences were established (UNTAET Regulation on the Establishment of Panels with Exclusive Jurisdiction over Serious Criminal Offences, UNTAET/Reg./2000/15, 6 June 2000). The Regulations provide for the prosecution of genocide, war crimes, crimes against humanity, murder, sexual offences and torture. The drafters of the Regulations of the Panels did not need to fear for a possible expiration of the prescription periods as provided for in the Timor-Leste Penal Code (In Timor-Leste, Art. 78 of the Indonesia 1918 Penal Code, as well as the Portuguese Penal Code apply), since the tribunal's subject matter jurisdiction concerns crimes committed in 1999 (UNTAET/Reg./2000/15, 6 June 2000, Sec. 2(3)). Nevertheless, the Regulation provides for the non-applicability of statutory limitations to crimes of genocide, war crimes, crimes against humanity, and the crime of torture. Ordinary crimes, such as murder and sexual offences, remain subject to domestic provisions providing for statutory limitations as contained in the Timor-Leste domestic Penal Code.

b) The Special Court for Sierra Leone

In 2002, the United Nations and the government of Sierra Leone agreed on the establishment of a Special Court for Sierra Leone (Agreement between the United Nations and the Government of Sierra Leone on the Establishment of a Special Court for Sierra Leone (16 January 2002)). The Statute does not contain any provision providing for the (non-)applicability of statutory limitations (Ambos and Othman, 2003; Romano, Nollkaemper and Kleffner, 2004). Obviously, there was no reason to provide for a provision in this regard, as the Special Court has jurisdiction over crimes committed only since 30 November 1996 (Statute of the Special Court for Sierra Leone, Article 1). At the time of the Special Court's establishment (2002), too little time had passed for a possible expiration of the prescription periods. In addition, since the common law as applied within the Sierra Leonean domestic criminal law does not apply statutes of limitations to felonies, the drafters probably considered the inclusion of a provision unnecessary.

c) The Extraordinary Chambers in the Courts of Cambodia

In 2003, the UN General Assembly in its Resolution 57/222B approved a draft agreement between the United Nations and the government of Cambodia with regard to the establishment of the Extraordinary Chambers in the Courts of Cambodia for the Prosecution of Crimes Committed during the Period of Democratic Kampuchea (UNGA Res. 57/222B, 13 May 2003, 'Khmer Rouge Trials', adopted during the 85th Meeting of the 57th Sess. of the UN General Assembly). The agreement between the United Nations and the government of Cambodia was signed on 6 June of the same year, and entered into force on 29 April 2005. The (non-)applicability of statutory limitations was one of the aspects debated during the drafting stage of the Act on the Establishment of the Extraordinary Chambers in the Courts of Cambodia for the Prosecution of Crimes Committed during the Period of Democratic Kampuchea, adopted in 2001 (Cambodia, Reach Kram No. NS/RKM/0801/12, 10 August 2001 promulgating the Act on the Establishment of the Extraordinary Chambers in the Courts of Cambodia for the Prosecution of Crimes Committed during the Period of Democratic Kampuchea). This third internationalised court has jurisdiction over crimes committed almost 30 years earlier (in the period from 1975 to 1979). At the time of the adoption of the Act in 2001, and amended in 2004 pursuant to the Act on the amendment of the Act on the Establishment of the Extraordinary Chambers in the Courts of Cambodia for the Prosecution of Crimes Committed during the Period of Democratic Kampuchea (adopted by the National Assembly on 05 October 2004), many crimes had become statutorily barred pursuant to the expiration of prescription periods of a maximum of ten years as provided for in the Cambodian Criminal Code (provisions relating to the Judiciary and Criminal Law and Procedure, Applicable in Cambodia, During the Transitional Period, Decision of 10 September 1992, Article 30: Statute of Limitations: The statute of limitations is three years for misdemeanours and ten years for felonies). In order to overcome this obstacle, the 2004 Act on the Amendments of the 2001 Act on the Establishment of the Extraordinary Chambers in the Courts of Cambodia for the Prosecution of Crimes Committed during the Period of Democratic Kampuchea in Article 3 Act extends the prescription periods of common crimes by 30 years. Second, it provides for the non-applicability of statutory limitations to the crime of genocide and crimes against humanity in Article 4. It is unclear why war crimes remain subject to the ordinary statute of limitations in Article 6. It may be the case that the French approach towards statutory limitations for war crimes influenced the Cambodian legislature. The discrepancy between the core international crimes suggests that the drafters of the Act consider war crimes not of a similar grave nature as crimes against humanity and genocide. In addition, the Statute does not regulate its retroactivity with respect to crimes that have already become prescribed pursuant to Cambodian domestic law. The absence of a provision in this regard suggests that the Statute applies retroactively; it thus permits the reopening of cases involving already prescribed crimes (Swart, 2004, pp. 312–313).

Discussion on statutory limitations:

i. Scholarly organisations and scholars

Since the establishment of the ICC, scholarly organisations and scholars have broadened the discussions on the (non-)applicability of statutory limitations to core international crimes other than the ones committed during the Second World War. Finkielkraut (1992) emphasises the renewed interest for France's position during the Second World War as a consequence of the war crimes trials of Barbie and Touvier. Moreover, they also discussed this question with respect to crimes of forced disappearance of persons and the crime of torture. Poncela, 2000, pp. 887–895, points at the restrictive material scope of the French 1964 Act declaring imprescriptibility of crimes against humanity. Zaffaroni (2000) discusses this concept with respect to military junta crimes through analysing the Argentinean case law. Zimmermann (1997) carries out a similar inquiry on statutory limitations with respect to communist crimes through analysing case law and legislation in the Czech Republic, France, Germany, and Hungary. When in 1995 an independent group of experts associated with the International Association of Penal law addressed this concept for a second time, it introduced in the so-called Siracusa Draft a new provision providing that "there is no statute of limitation for genocide, serious war crimes, and crimes against humanity (or aggression)" (Association Internationale de Droit Pénal

(AIDP)/International Institute of Higher Studies in Criminal Sciences (ISISC)/Max-Planck-Institute for Foreign and International Criminal Law (MPI), Draft Statute for an International Criminal Court-Alternative to the ILC Draft, prepared by a Committee of Experts, Siracusa/Freiburg, July 1995, Art. 33(q)). Another example is provided for by the Princeton Principles adopted in 2001, which recommends in Principle 6 the adoption of a provision on the imprescriptibility of a number of international crimes. Other contemporary scholars remain hesitant in recognising the existence of a rule of customary international law or general principle of law and rather speak of the 'crystallisation' of such a rule (Abrams and Ratner, 2001, p. 143 referring to Van den Wyngaert, 1999, pp. 227 and 233; Delmas-Marty, 2002, pp. 617, 618; Gaeta, 2001, p. 766; Kreicker, 2003, p. 377; Schabas, 1999, p. 524; Zimmermann, 1997, p. 251). Some consider the imprescriptibility of international crimes a rule of customary international law, or even *jus cogens* (Bassiouni, 1999, p. 227 and 2002, p. 17; Cassese, 2003, p. 319; Page, 2004, p. 47; Schiffrin, 2003, p. 147; Van den Wyngaert and Dugard, 2001, p. 887). An example is provided for by the Advisory opinion in the case of *Bouterse*, in the proceedings before the Amsterdam Court of Appeal in 2000, in which the expert concluded that crimes against humanity are imprescriptible pursuant to customary law (*Opinion Re Bouterse*, ELRO- No. AA 8427, 7 July 2000, at §4.5.6). Notwithstanding this opinion, neither the Court of Appeal, nor the Supreme Court pronounced itself on this issue. Therefore, the expert opinion is of no significance in determining the customary character of the non-applicability of statutory limitations to international crimes. Despite discussions on various legal aspects, scholars hardly addressed the desirability of the imprescriptibility of international crimes from a criminological, philosophical, or moral perspective. An exception forms, for instance, the study carried out by the Max Planck Institute for Foreign and International Criminal Law, presented during the Conference "Strafverfolgung von Staatskriminalität, Vergeltung, Wahrheit und Versöhnung nach politischen Systemwechseln", Berlin 2004.

ii. Non-governmental organisations

In 2005, the International Committee of the Red Cross (ICRC), which carried out an extensive study on customary international humanitarian law (Henckaerts *et al.*, 2005, p. 614, volume II, chapter 43, section E) concluded that "[s]tatutes of limitation are not applicable to war crimes". Non-governmental organisations on various occasions actively called upon states not to apply statutory limitations to international crimes. A clear example of this activism is the establishment of the Women's International War Crimes Tribunal on Japan's Military Sexual Slavery, adopted by the Violence against Women in War Network Japan and other Asian women's and human rights organisations in 2000. Article 6 of its Charter provides that "[s]tatutory limitations do not apply with respect to international crimes committed against women before and during the Second World War. These crimes include, but are not limited to the following acts: sexual slavery, rape, and other forms of sexual violence, enslavement, torture, deportation, persecution, murder, and extermination." Furthermore, the International Commission of Jurists, together with Amnesty International, called upon the Argentinean authorities to recognise the imprescriptibility of various human rights violations committed by former military junta regimes. Moreover, Human Rights Watch emphasised that statutes of limitation should not preclude criminal proceedings against former Chad president Hissène Habré before Belgian or Senegalese courts. Another example is provided for by the Argentinean non-governmental organisation called Mothers of the Playa de la Mayo, which emphasised for over 30 years that the *desaperacidos* cases should not become prescribed, as long as the victims' whereabouts have not been discovered. Finally, in 2004 Human Rights First submitted an extensive analysis on statutes of limitation to the Peruvian Truth and Reconciliation Commission, established in 2000, in which this ngo concluded that crimes committed during the regime of former President Fujimori are not subject to statutes of limitation.

Doctrine:

1. Steven R. Ratner, Jason S. Abrams and James L. Bischoff, *Accountability for Human Rights Atrocities in International Law, Beyond The Nuremberg Legacy*, Oxford University Press, Oxford, 2001, p. 143.

2. Kai Ambos and Mohamed Othman, *New Approaches in International Criminal Justice: Kosovo, East Timor, Sierra Leone and Cambodia*, Edition iuscrim, Freiburg im Breisgau, 2003.

3. M. Cherif Bassiouni, *Crimes Against Humanity in International Criminal Law*, Nijhoff, Dordrecht, 1999.

4. M. Cherif Bassiouni, "Accountability for Violations of International Humanitarian Law and Other Serious Violations of Human Rights", in M. Cherif Bassiouni, *Post-Conflict Justice*, Transnational Publishers, Ardsley, NY, 2002.

5. Machteld Boot-Matthijssen and Richard van Elst, "Wetsvoorstel Internationale misdrijven, enkele knelpunten en mogelijke verbeteringen", in *Nederlands Juristenblad*, 2002, vol. 77, no. 4, p. 1729.

6. Antonio Cassese, *International Criminal Law*, Oxford University Press, Oxford, 2003.

7. Mireille Delmas-Marty, "La responsabilité pénale en échec (prescription, amnistie, immunités)", in Antonio Cassese and Mireille Delmas-Marty (eds.), *Juridictions nationales et crimes internationaux*, Presses universitaires de France, Paris, 2002.

8. Alain Finkielkraut, *Remembering in Vain: The Klaus Barbie Trial and Crimes Against Humanity*, Columbia University Press, New York, 1992.

9. Paola Gaeta, "War Crimes Trials Before Italian Criminal Courts, New Trends", in Horst Fischer, Class Kreß and Sascha Rolf Lüder (eds.), *International and National Prosecution of Crimes Under International Law: Current Developments*, Spitz, Berlin, 2001.

10. Jean Marie Henckaerts and Louise Doswald-Beck, *Customary International Humanitarian Law*, volume 1: *Rules*, Cambridge University Press, Cambridge, 2005.

11. Ruth A. Kok, *Statutory Limitations in International Criminal Law*, TMC Asser Press, The Hague, 2007.

12. Helmut Kreicker, "Allgemeine Strafbarkeitsvoraussetzungen", in Albin Eser, Helmut Kreicker and Helmut Gropengießer, *Nationale Strafverfolgung völkerrechtlicher Verbrechen*, Edition Iuscrim, Freiburg im Breisgau, 2003.

13. M.G. Page, "Article 29 of the Rome Statute", in S. Yee (ed.), *International Crimes and Punishment: Selected Issues*, 2nd ed., University Press of America, Dallas, 2004.

14. Pierette Poncela, "L'imprescriptibilité", in Alain Pellet, Adama Dieng and Malick Sow (eds.), *Droit international pénal, la formation du droit international pénal*, Pedone, Paris, 2000.

15. Per Saland., "International Criminal Law Principles", in Roy S. Lee (ed.), *The International Criminal Court: The Making of the Rome Statute*, Kluwer Law International, The Hague, 1999.

16. Helmut Satzger, "German Criminal Law and the Rome Statute: A Critical Analysis of the New German Code of Crimes Against International Law", in *International Criminal Law Review*, 2002, vol. 2, p. 261.

17. William A. Schabas, "General Principles of Criminal Law in the International Criminal Court Statute (Part III)", in *European Journal of Crime, Criminal Law, and Criminal Justice*, 1998, vol. 6, no. 4, p. 400.

18. William A. Schabas, "Article 29: Non-Applicability of Statutes of Limitations", in Otto Triffterer (ed.), *Commentary on the Rome Statute of the International Criminal Court: Ob-*

servers' Notes, Article by Article, 2nd ed., C.H. Beck/Hart/Nomos, Munich/Oxford/Baden-Baden, 2008, pp. 845–48.

19. Leopoldo Schiffrin, "De Eichmann a Schwammberger, de Priebke a Videla: la evolución de la idea de imprescriptibilidad de los delitos de lesa humanidad en el derecho argentino", in Oded Balaban and Amos Megged (eds.), *Impunidad y derechos humanos en América Latina*, Al Margen, La Plata, 2003.

20. Bert Swart, "Internationalized Courts and Substantive Criminal Law", in Cesare P.R. Romano, André Nollmaemper and Jann K. Kleffner (eds.), *Internationalized Criminal Courts and Tribunals: Sierra Leone, East Timor, Kosovo, and Cambodia*, Oxford University Press, Oxford, 2004.

21. Christine Van den Wyngaert, "War Crimes, Genocide and Crimes Against Humanity: Are States Taking National Prosecutions Seriously?", in M. Cherif Bassiouni, *International Criminal Law*, 3rd ed., Transnational Publishers, Ardsley, NY, 1999.

22. Eugenio R. Zaffaroni, "Notas sobre el fundamento de la imprescriptibilidad de los crímenes de lesa humanidad", in *Revista Nueva Doctrina Penal*, 2000, vol. 437.

23. Stefan Zimmermann, *Strafrechtliche Vergangenheitsaufarbeitung und Verjährung, Rechtsdogmatische und politische Analyse mit vergleichenden Ausblicken nach Tschechien, Ungarn und Frankreich*, Edition iuscrim, Freiburg im Breisgau, 1997.

Author: Ruth A. Kok.

Article 30
Mental element[304]

1. Unless otherwise provided, a person shall be criminally responsible and liable for punishment for a crime within the jurisdiction of the Court only if the material elements are committed with intent and knowledge.[305]

---

[304] *General remarks*

For the first time in the history of international criminal law, and unlike the Nuremberg and Tokyo Charters and the ICTY and ICTR Statutes, Article 30 of the ICC Statute has provided for a general definition of the mental element triggering the criminal responsibility of individuals for core international crimes.

This provision, which is applicable and binding within the jurisdiction of the ICC, has not put an end to the lively debate on *mens rea* that during the last two decades has confronted the jurisprudence of the ICTY and ICTR. Quite the contrary, the negotiations on Article 30 ICC Statute involved actors coming from different legal cultural experiences, who engaged in an effort of comparative law synthesis (on the drafting history of Article 30 ICC Statute see Clark, 2001). Despite the attempt to find a shared grammar, practitioners and scholars still disagree in relation to the exact meaning of the standards of culpability set out in the norm in question. Professor Joachim Vogel notes that the main reason of such confusion "is that intent and knowledge are defined in Articles 30(2) and (3) ICC Statute under clear influence of the common law principles, but in a manner that is a compromise and therefore not consistent and not without overlaps, and applies to *dolus eventualis* in the German understanding (awareness that a circumstance exists or a consequence will occur in the ordinary course of events)" (Vogel, 2009, margin 95).

Authors: Mohamed Elewa Badar and Sara Porro.

[305] Article 30 of the ICC Statute is based on a rule-exception dynamic. Criminal responsibility for core international crimes can normally be attached only to those who realised the material elements with "intent and knowledge", even though exceptions to the default rule on the mental element are to some extent allowed ("[u]nless otherwise provided" – this wording will be addressed below).

The use of the terms "intent and knowledge" could appear to point to two distinct types of mental element. However, according to the early practice of the ICC and commentators this formula refers to will and cognition as being both necessary components of the one mental element of intent (see, *inter alia, Prosecutor v. Katanga and Ngudjolo Chui*, ICC PT. Ch., Decision on the Confirmation of Charges, ICC-01/04-01/07-717, 30 September 2008, para. 529; Eser, 2002, p. 907). The choice of the terms "intent and knowledge" is rather unfortunate. Criminal systems of civil law countries generally consider 'knowledge' (*Wissen, conscience*) to be a requirement of intent alongside the element of will (*Wollen, volonté*) (on the German criminal system see Jescheck and Weigend, 1996, p. 293; on the French criminal system see Soyer, 2004, p. 98; Bell, Boyron and Whittaker, 2008, p. 225). In criminal systems of common law countries, 'knowledge' can even be a kind of intent, namely intent based on perception of the unlawful outcome with a level of likelihood bordering with certainty (on the US criminal system see s. 2.02(2)(b) US Model Penal Code; Badar, 2013, pp. 107 ff.). It can be said, hence, that "[i]n comparative criminal law [...] 'knowledge' figuratively finds its place within (and not outside) the circle of intent, either as a part (civil law) or as a form of it (common law)" (Badar and Porro, 2015, p. 651; on this aspect see also Porro, 2014, p. 176).

As a point of reference for the agent's "intent and knowledge", Article 30(1) of the ICC Statute mentions the "material elements" of the crime. The ICC Statute, however, lacks a gen-

2. For the purposes of this article, a person has intent where:[306]

    (a) In relation to conduct, that person means to engage in the conduct;[307]

---

eral provision on the definition of the material elements of the crime or *actus reus*. The deficiency is partially remedied in Article 30(2) and (3) of the ICC Statute. These provisions, which will be addressed in detail below, set out the notions of intent and knowledge in relation not to the crime as a whole, but to the elements of conduct, consequence and circumstance separately. Such a drafting technique assigns different levels of culpability to each of the material elements of the crime. This represents a notable move from an 'offence analysis' approach to *mens rea* to an 'element analysis' approach to *mens rea* (*Prosecutor v. Bemba Gombo*, ICC PT. Ch., Decision on the Confirmation of Charges, ICC-01/05-01/08-424, 15 June 2009, para. 356, endorsing *inter alia* Badar, 2008, pp. 475 ff; Badar, 2013, pp. 384 ff.) that finds a remarkable precedent in s. 2.02 of the US Model Penal Code. The move from 'offence analysis' to 'element analysis' has historically aimed to achieve "a rational, clear, and just system of criminal law" (Robinson and Grall, 1983, p. 685). Determining the level of culpability required for criminality in relation to each single material element improves the precision of the offence definition, what in turn provides fair notice of the extent of the criminal ban and reduces the possibilities of extensive interpretation (Robinson and Grall, 1983, pp. 703 ff; on this point see also Badar and Porro, 2015, p. 652).

According to the opening clause at the beginning of Article 30(1) of the ICC Statute, the requirement of "intent and knowledge" applies "[u]nless otherwise provided". It is widely accepted that this formula allows the ICC to infer exceptions to the default rule on the mental element from other provisions of the ICC Statute, such as Article 6 on genocide or Article 28 on superior responsibility. It is controversial, in contrast, whether departures from the standard of "intent and knowledge" can also derive from the Elements of Crime (in this sense, *inter alia*, Werle and Jeßberger, 2005, pp. 45 ff; Badar, 2008, p. 501; Schabas, 2010, pp. 474 ff; Porro, 2014, pp. 192 ff.), or even customary international law (in this sense, *inter alia*, Werle and Jeßberger, 2005, pp. 45 ff.). The early practice of the ICC has sustained the view that both the ICC Statute and the Elements of Crime can provide 'otherwise'. Paragraph (2) of the General Introduction to the Elements of Crime asserts in this direction that:

> [a]s stated in Article 30, unless otherwise provided, a person shall be criminally responsible and liable for punishment for a crime within the jurisdiction of the Court only if the material elements are committed with intent and knowledge. Where no reference is made in the Elements of Crime to a mental element for any particular conduct, consequence or circumstance listed, it is understood that the relevant mental element, that is, intent, knowledge or both, set out in Article 30 applies [...].

Authors: Mohamed Elewa Badar and Sara Porro.

[306] Adhering to the already mentioned 'element analysis' approach to *mens rea*, paragraph (2) of Article 30 ICC Statute defines intent in relation to the material elements of conduct and consequence separately.

Authors: Mohamed Elewa Badar and Sara Porro.

[307] Concerning the definition of intent in relation to conduct, which the early practice of the ICC has not yet addressed, commentators have proposed two competing interpretations.

According to a first approach, Article 30(2)(a) ICC Statute would merely require that the conduct be accomplished as a result of the agent's free determination to act. Intent in relation to conduct would in other words be established unless the action or omission was performed during unconsciousness, was due to an automatism, or in other ways was involuntary. To take an example, criminal responsibility for core international crimes might not be attached to an individual who, attacked by a swarm of bees, involuntarily or even automatically realised the con-

(b) In relation to a consequence, that person means to cause that consequence or is aware that it will occur in the ordinary course of events.[308]

---

duct (in this sense, *inter alia*, Eser, 2002, p. 913; Werle, 2014; Schabas, 2010, p. 477; Porro, 2014, pp. 177 ff.).

Other commentators, and in particular Ambos, have instead opined that the voluntariness to accomplish a certain conduct would be part already of the notion of act relevant to the criminal law. Article 30(2)(a) ICC Statute would impose an additional element of conscious will to engage in the conduct, or awareness to engage in it. In either case the agent would be required to have known the factual circumstances qualifying the action or omission as relevant to the criminal law (in this sense, *inter alia*, see Ambos, 2002, pp. 765 ff.; Finnin, Elements of Accessorial Modes of Liability, 2012, pp. 163 ff; Finnin, Mental Elements, 2012, pp. 341 ff; Badar, 2013, p. 388).

The latter interpretation of intent in relation to conduct relies on the concept of act relevant to the criminal law acknowledged in continental European countries such as Austria, Germany, Italy and Spain that includes a component of free determination to act (on the German criminal system see Jescheck and Weigend, 1996, pp. 219 ff.). However, this concept of criminal act has not attained worldwide diffusion, since for instance s. 1.13(2) of the US Model Penal Code provides that "'act' or 'action' means a bodily movement whether voluntary or involuntary". It can be questioned whether the notion of criminal act as including an element of voluntariness is representative enough to establish a general principle of law common to the major legal systems of the world pursuant to Article 21(1)(c) ICC Statute (Badar and Noelle, 2014). Only such a general principle of law might legitimately play a role in the interpretation of Article 30(2)(a) ICC Statute (on this point see also Porro, 2014, pp. 177 ff.).

Authors: Mohamed Elewa Badar and Sara Porro.

[308] While the former alternative of Article 30(2)(b) of the ICC Statute refers to cases where the agent aimed to bring about the consequence or result, the latter one applies to situations where the agent foresaw the result with a certain degree of likelihood.

Competing interpretations:

The main issue that has arisen in respect to intent as awareness that the result "will occur in the ordinary course of events" concerns the level of likelihood with which the agent must have foreseen the result.

A first school of thought has argued that the default rule of Article 30 of the ICC Statute would not accommodate any standard of *mens rea* below the threshold of knowledge of result in terms of practical certainty (in this sense, *inter alia*, *Prosecutor v. Bemba*, ICC PT. Ch., Decision Pursuant to Article 61(7)(a) and (b) of the Rome Statute on the Charges of the Prosecutor Against Jean-Pierre Bemba Gombo, ICC-01/05-01/08-424, 15 June 2009, paras. 359 ff; *Prosecutor v. Lubanga*, ICC T. Ch., Judgment pursuant to Article 74 of the Statute, ICC-01/04-01/06-2842, 14 March 2012, para. 1011; *Prosecutor v. Lubanga*, ICC A. Ch., Judgment on the Appeal of Mr. Thomas Lubanga Dyilo against his conviction, ICC-01/04-01/06-A-5, 1 December 2014, paras. 441 ff; Eser, 2002, pp. 915 ff; van der Vyver, 2004, pp. 70 ff; Cryer, Friman, Robinson and Wilmshurst, 2010, pp. 385 ff; Heller, 2011, p. 604; Finnin, Elements of Accessorial Modes of Liability, 2012, pp. 172 ff; Finnin, Mental Elements, 2012, p. 358; Badar, 2013, p. 392; Ohlin, 2013, p. 23; Porro, 2014, pp. 179 ff.).

Other voices have on the contrary maintained that also some forms of conscious risk-taking in relation to result that in domestic criminal laws satisfy the standards of *dolus eventualis* or recklessness could meet the requirements of Article 30 ICC Statute (in this sense, *inter alia*, *Prosecutor v. Lubanga*, ICC PT. Ch., Decision on the Confirmation of Charges, ICC-01/04-01/06-803-tEN, 29 January 2007, paras. 352 ff; *Prosecutor v. Katanga and Ngudjolo Chui*, ICC

PT. Ch., Decision on the Confirmation of Charges, ICC-01/04-01/07-717, 30 September 2008, para. 251 fn. 329; Jescheck, 2004, p. 45; Weigend, 2008, p. 484; Cassese, Gaeta, Baig, Fan, Gosnell and Whiting, 2013, p. 56; Gil Gil, 2014, pp. 86 and 107).

The Lubanga Dyilo decision on the confirmation of charges:

The early practice of ICC addressed this crucial problem already in 2007, in its first decision on the confirmation of charges issued in the Lubanga Dyilo case. PTC I of the ICC stated that the volitional element appearing in Article 30 ICC Statute includes also

> situations in which the suspect (a) is aware of the risk that the objective elements of the crime may result from his or her actions or omissions, and (b) accepts such an outcome by reconciling himself or herself with it or consenting to it (also known as *dolus eventualis*) (*Prosecutor v. Lubanga*, ICC PT. Ch., Decision on the Confirmation of Charges, ICC-01/04-01/06-803-tEN, 29 January 2007, para. 352(ii)).

After having set out a concept of *dolus eventualis* based on the idea of acceptance of a criminal risk, the Pre-Trial Chamber added the following specification:

> [t]he Chamber considers that in the latter type of situation, two kinds of scenarios are distinguishable. Firstly, if the risk of bringing about the objective elements of the crime is substantial (that is, there is a likelihood that it "will occur in the ordinary course of events"), the fact that the suspect accepts the idea of bringing about the objective elements of the crime can be inferred from:
>
> i. the awareness by the suspect of the substantial likelihood that his or her actions or omissions would result in the realisation of the objective elements of the crime; and
>
> ii. the decision by the suspect to carry out his or her actions or omissions despite such awareness.
>
> Secondly, if the risk of bringing about the objective elements of the crime is low, the suspect must have clearly or expressly accepted the idea that such objective elements may result from his or her actions or omissions (*Prosecutor v. Lubanga*, ICC PT. Ch., Decision on the Confirmation of Charges, ICC-01/04- 01/06-803-tEN, 29 January 2007, paras. 353 ff., fn. omitted).

PTC I of the ICC appears first of all to assert that a literal interpretation of the element of awareness that the result "will occur in the ordinary course of events" laid down in Article 30 ICC Statute would refer to a level of substantial criminal risk. Moreover, the Pre-Trial Chamber seems to further enlarge the concept of intent applicable within the jurisdiction of the ICC. It does so by stating that even the perception of a low risk of bringing about the objective elements of the crime can satisfy the requirements set out in the provision in question, if the agent explicitly accepted the occurrence of such objective elements. Lacking the component of acceptance of the crime – as "[t]his would be the case of a taxi driver taking the risk of driving at a very high speed on a local road, trusting that nothing would happen on account of his or her driving expertise" – the threshold of intent pursuant to Article 30 ICC Statute would not be attained (*Prosecutor v. Lubanga*, ICC P.T. Ch., Decision on the Confirmation of Charges, ICC-01/04-01/06-803-tEN, 29 January 2007, para. 355 fn. 437; on the discussion on the mental element in this decision see also Badar, 2013, pp. 394 ff; Badar and Porro, 2015, pp. 657 ff; Porro, 2014, pp. 182 ff.).

Subsequent ICC jurisprudence:

The broad interpretation of intent put forward in the *Lubanga* decision on the confirmation of charges was endorsed in principle in Katanga and Ngudjolo Chui (*Prosecutor v. Katanga and Ngudjolo Chui*, ICC PT. Ch., Decision on the Confirmation of Charges, ICC-01/04-01/07-717, 30 September 2008, para. 251 fn. 329), with Judge Anita Ušacka dissenting (Partly Dissenting Opinion of Judge Anita Ušacka to *Prosecutor v. Katanga and Ngudjolo Chui*, ICC PT.

Ch., Decision on the Confirmation of Charges, ICC-01/04-01/07-717, 30 September 2008, para. 22). Subsequently, however, it was turned down in the Bemba Gombo decision on the confirmation of charges of 2009, where PTC II of the ICC argued that:

> [w]ith respect to *dolus eventualis* as the third form of dolus, recklessness or any lower form of culpability, the Chamber is of the view that such concepts are not captured by Article 30 of the Statute. This conclusion is supported by the express language of the phrase "will occur in the ordinary course of events", which does not accommodate a lower standard than the one required by *dolus directus* in the second degree (oblique intention) (*Prosecutor v. Bemba*, ICC PT. Ch., Decision Pursuant to Article 61(7)(a) and (b) of the Rome Statute on the Charges of the Prosecutor Against Jean-Pierre Bemba Gombo, ICC-01/05-01/08-424, 15 June 2009, para. 360).

The Pre-Trial Chamber developed a reasoning based on the principles of treaty interpretation pursuant to Articles 31 and 32 of the Vienna Convention on the Law of Treaties, stressing again that a literal interpretation of "the words 'will occur', read together with the phrase 'in the ordinary course of events', clearly indicates that the required standard of occurrence is close to certainty. In this regard, the Chamber defines this standard as 'virtual certainty' or 'practical certainty'" (*Prosecutor v. Bemba Gombo*, ICC PT. Ch., Decision on the Confirmation of Charges, ICC-01/05-01/08-424, 15 June 2009, para. 362). "This standard is undoubtedly higher than the principal standard commonly agreed upon for *dolus eventualis* – namely, foreseeing the occurrence of the undesired consequences as a mere likelihood or possibility. Hence, had the drafters of the Statute intended to include *dolus eventualis* in the text of Article 30, they could have used the words 'may occur' or 'might occur in the ordinary course of events'" (*Prosecutor v. Bemba*, ICC PT. Ch., Decision Pursuant to Article 61(7)(a) and (b) of the Rome Statute on the Charges of the Prosecutor Against Jean-Pierre Bemba Gombo, ICC-01/05-01/08-424, 15 June 2009, para. 363, fn. omitted).

In support of its analysis, the *Bemba* decision on the confirmation of charges drew upon the drafting history of Article 30 of the ICC Statute, and in particular a proposal that the Preparatory Committee put forward in 1996. In the relevant parts, it reads as follows:

> 2. For the purposes of this Statute and unless otherwise provided, a person has intent where: [...] (b) In relation to a consequence, that person means to cause that consequence or is aware that it will occur in the ordinary course of events.
>
> [...]
>
> [4. For the purposes of this Statute and unless otherwise provided, where this Statute provides that a crime may be committed recklessly, a person is reckless with respect to a circumstance or a consequence if: [...]
>
> *Note. The concepts of recklessness and dolus eventualis should be further considered in view of the seriousness of the crimes considered.*
>
> *Therefore, paragraph 4 would provide a definition of "recklessness", to be used only where the Statute explicitly provides that a specific crime or element may be committed recklessly. In all situations, the general rule, as stated in paragraph 1, is that crimes must be committed intentionally and knowingly [...]* (Report of the Preparatory Committee on the Establishment of an International Criminal Court, UN GAOR, 51st Sess., Supp. No. 22A, UN doc. A/51/22 (1996) (Vol. II), reprinted in this part in Bassiouni, 2005, p. 226).

PTC II of the ICC reported that the references to *dolus eventualis* and recklessness disappeared from the general provision on the mental element at later stages of the negotiations (*Prosecutor v. Bemba*, ICC PT. Ch., Decision Pursuant to Article 61(7)(a) and (b) of the Rome Statute on the Charges of the Prosecutor Against Jean-Pierre Bemba Gombo, ICC-01/05-01/08-424, 15 June 2009, para. 366). It also highlighted that "the fact that paragraph 4 on recklessness and its accompanying footnote, which stated that 'recklessness and *dolus eventualis* should be further considered', came right after paragraph 2(b) in the same proposal, indicates that recklessness and *dolus eventualis* on the one hand, and the phrase "will occur in the ordinary course of events" on the other, were not meant to be the same notion or to set the same standard of culpability" (*Prosecutor v. Bemba*, ICC PT. Ch., Decision Pursuant to Article 61(7)(a) and (b) of the Rome Statute on the Charges of the Prosecutor Against Jean-Pierre Bemba Gombo, ICC-01/05-01/08-424, 15 June 2009, para. 368; on the drafting history of Article 30(2) the ICC Statute see Badar, 2009, pp. 444 ff.).

The Pre-Trial Chamber concluded therefore that "the suspect could not be said to have intended to commit any of the crimes charged, unless the evidence shows that he was at least aware that, in the ordinary course of events, the occurrence of such crimes was a virtually certain consequence of the implementation of the common plan" (*Prosecutor v. Bemba*, ICC PT. Ch., Decision Pursuant to Article 61(7)(a) and (b) of the Rome Statute on the Charges of the Prosecutor Against Jean-Pierre Bemba Gombo, ICC-01/05-01/08-424, 15 June 2009, para. 368; on the discussion on the mental element in this decision see also Badar, 2013, pp. 397 ff; Badar and Porro, 2015, pp. 660 f; Porro, 2014, pp. 185 f).

This restrictive interpretation of the concept of intent is at present the leading view in the early practice of the ICC.

In the first trial judgment issued in the *Lubanga* case, in 2012, TC I of the ICC accepted the approach of PTC II of the ICC to the notion of intent (*Prosecutor v. Lubanga*, ICC T. Ch., Judgment pursuant to Article 74 of the Statute, ICC-01/04-01/06-2842, 14 March 2012, para. 1011). Yet, the Trial Chamber also added in paragraph 1012 of the judgment that the prognosis underlying the awareness that result will occur in the ordinary course of events "involves consideration of the concepts of 'possibility' and 'probability', which are inherent to the notions of 'risk' and 'danger'" (*Prosecutor v. Lubanga*, ICC T. Ch., Judgment pursuant to Article 74 of the Statute, ICC-01/04-01/06-2842, 14 March 2012, para. 1012). In the context of a narrow interpretation of the concept of intent, such a mention of the notion of risk, that is a notion referring to a dimension of mere possibility as opposed to virtual certainty, was sharply criticised within the ICC itself as "potentially confusing", or even "out of place" (respectively Separate Opinion of Judge Adrian Fulford to *Prosecutor v. Lubanga*, ICC T. Ch., Judgment pursuant to Article 74 of the Statute, ICC-01/04-01/06-2842, 14 March 2012, para. 15; Concurring Opinion of Judge Christine van der Wyngaert to *Ngudjolo*, Judgment, ICC-01/04-02/12-4, 18 December 2012, para. 38).

In March 2014, Trial Chamber II of the ICC adjudicating upon Katanga opined that "the form of this criminal intent requires the person to have known that realising the acts will necessarily bring about the consequence in question, unless an unexpected intervention or unforeseen event impede it. To put it differently, it is nearly impossible for him to foresee that the consequence will not occur" (*Prosecutor v. Katanga*, ICC T. Ch., Judgment, ICC-01/04-01/07-3464, 7 March 2014, para. 777, unofficial translation S. Porro).

The Appeals Chamber of the ICC pronounced itself on the notion of intent under Article 30 ICC Statute in December 2014 (*Prosecutor v. Lubanga*, ICC A. Ch., Judgment on the Appeal of Mr. Thomas Lubanga Dyilo against his conviction, ICC-01/04-01/06-A-5, 1 December 2014, paras. 441 ff.). The *Lubanga* appeal judgment confirmed the interpretation put forward in the Bemba decision on the confirmation of charges, that under Art. 30 of the ICC Statute "the standard for the foreseeability of events is virtual certainty". The Appeals Chamber confirmed also that this standard of virtual certainty had already emerged from the Lubanga trial judgment. In relation to the use of the word "risk" by TC I of the ICC in *Lubanga*, the Appeals Chamber claimed that "[t]he Trial Chamber, in defining the requisite level of 'risk', specified [...] that

3. For the purposes of this article, "knowledge" means awareness that a circumstance exists or a consequence will occur in the ordinary course of events. "Know" and "knowingly" shall be construed accordingly.[309]

---

this entailed an 'awareness on the part of the co-perpetrators that the consequence will occur in the 'ordinary course of events' and distinguished this from a 'low risk'".

Authors: Mohamed Elewa Badar and Sara Porro.

[309] Adhering to the already mentioned 'element analysis' approach to *mens rea*, paragraph (3) of Article 30 ICC Statute defines knowledge in relation to the material elements of circumstance and consequence separately.

The early practice of the ICC has not yet addressed the definition of knowledge in relation to circumstance in Article 30(3) first sentence first alternative ICC Statute. A strict interpretation of the wording "awareness that a circumstance exists" appears to limit the meaning of this standard of culpability to actual awareness of the relevant fact. This would exclude from the notion of knowledge cases of constructive knowledge, that is, where a reasonable person would have recognised the circumstance, as well as cases of 'wilful blindness', that is, where the agent was aware that the fact probably existed, but deliberately refrained from obtaining the final confirmation (Williams, 1961, p. 159). On the plan of criminal policy, it has however also been claimed that "should reliable means to resolve one's suspicions be available, we are faced with something more than mere suspicion" (Sullivan, 2002, p. 214; on the interpretation of art. 30(3) first sentence first alternative ICC Statute see also Badar and Porro, 2015, pp. 664 f).

On the other hand, the definition of knowledge in relation to consequence or result in Article 30(3) first sentence second alternative ICC Statute overlaps substantially with the definition of intent based on foresight of result as a virtual certainty in Article 30(2)(b) second alternative ICC Statute. Due to the cumulative reference to "intent and knowledge" in Article 30(1) ICC Statute, the requirement of knowledge in relation to result should apply even to an agent who clearly wanted to bring about the result pursuant to the first alternative of Article 30(2)(b) ICC Statute. Finnin illustrates the practical outcome of this by inviting the reader to

consider the case of an accused who plants an improvised explosive device (or 'IED', which have a notoriously low success rate), which he or she intends to initiate remotely when civilians come within range. It is the perpetrator's conscious object to kill those civilians; however, unless it could be shown that he or she knew (at the time the device was initiated) that the device would explode successfully and thereby result in the death of those civilians, the perpetrator would not satisfy this gradation of intent. [...] This obviously represents an unexpected and undesired consequence of the conjunctive 'intent and knowledge' wording of Article 30 (Finnin, Elements of Accessorial Modes of Liability, 2012, p. 165; Finnin, Mental Elements, 2012, p. 343; on this point see also Badar and Porro, 2015, pp. 653 f).

Doctrine:

1. Kai Ambos, *Der Allgemeine Teil des Völkerstrafrechts: Ansätze einer Dogmatisierung*, Duncker and Humblot, Berlin, 2002.
2. Mohamed E. Badar, "*Dolus Eventualis* and the Rome Statute Without It?", in *New Criminal Law Review*, 2009, vol. 12, pp. 433–467.
3. Mohamed E. Badar, *The Concept of Mens Rea in International Criminal Law. The Case for a Unified Approach*, Hart Publishing, Oxford, 2013.
4. Mohamed E. Badar, "The Mental Element in the Rome Statute of the International Criminal Court: A Commentary from a Comparative Criminal Law Perspective", in *Criminal Law Forum*, 2008, vol. 19, pp. 473–518.

---

5. Mohamed E. Badar and Noelle Higgins, "General Principles of Law in the Early Jurisprudence of the ICC", in Triestino Mariniello (ed.), *The International Criminal Court in Search of its Purpose and Identity*, Routledge, London, 2014.

6. Mohamed E. Badar and Sara Porro, "Rethinking the Mental Elements in the Jurisprudence of the ICC", in Carsten Stahn (ed.), T*he Law and Practice of the International Criminal Court*, Oxford University Press, Oxford, 2015.

7. M. Cherif Bassiouni, *The Legislative History of the International Criminal Court: An Article-by-Article Evolution of the Statute*, 2nd ed., Transnational Publishers, Ardsley, NY, 2005.

8. John Bell, Sophie Boyron and Simon Whittaker, *Principles of French Law*, Oxford University Press, Oxford, 1998.

9. Antonio Cassese, Paola Gaeta, Laurel Baig, Mary Fan, Christopher Gosnell and Alex Whiting, in Antonio Cassese (ed.), *International Criminal Law*, 3rd ed., Oxford University Press, Oxford, 2013.

10. Roger S. Clark, "The Mental Element in International Criminal Law: The Rome Statute of the International Criminal Court and the Elements of Offences", in *Criminal Law Forum*, 2001, vol. 12, pp. 291–334.

11. Robert Cryer, Håkan Friman, Daryll Robinson and Elizabeth Wilmshurst, *An Introduction to International Criminal Law and Procedure*, 2nd ed., Cambridge University Press, Cambridge, 2010.

12. Abin Eser, "Mental Elements – Mistake of Fact and Mistake of Law", in Antonio Cassese, Paola Gaeta and John R.W.D. Jones (eds.), T*he Rome Statute of the International Criminal Court: A Commentary,* 2nd ed., Oxford University Press, Oxford, 2002, pp. 889–948.

13. Sarah Finnin, *Elements of Accessorial Modes of Liability: Article 25(3)(b) and (c) of the Rome Statute of the International Criminal Court*, Nijhoff, Leiden/Boston, 2012.

14. Sarah Finnin, "Mental Elements under Article 30 of the Rome Statute of the International Criminal Court: A Comparative Analysis", in *International and Comparative Law Quarterly*, 2001, vol. 61, x pp. 325–59.

15. Alicia Gil Gil, "Mens Rea in Co-Perpetration and Indirect Perpetration According to Article 30 of the Rome Statute. Arguments Against Punishment for Excesses Committed by the Agent or the Co-Perpetrator", in *International Criminal Law Review*, 2014, vol. 14, pp. 82–114.

16. Kevin J. Heller, "The Rome Statute of the International Criminal Court", in Kevin J. Heller and Markus D. Dubber (eds.), *The Handbook of Comparative Criminal Law*, Stanford Law Books, Stanford, 2011, pp. 593–634.

17. Hans-Heinrich Jescheck, "The General Principles of International Criminal Law Set Out in Nuremberg, as Mirrored in the ICC Statute", in *Journal of International Criminal Justice*, 2004, vol. 2, pp. 38–55.

18. Hans-Heinrich Jescheck and Thomas Weigend, *Lehrbuch des Strafrechts: allgemeiner Teil*, 5th ed., Duncker and Humblot, Berlin, 1996.

19. Jens D. Ohlin, "Targeting and the Concept of Intent", in *Michigan Journal of International Law*, 2014, vol. 35, p. 147 ff.

20. Sara Porro, *Risk and Mental Element: An Analysis of National and International Law on Core Crimes*, Nomos, Baden-Baden, 2014.

21. Paul H. Robinson and Jane A. Grall, "Element Analysis in Defining Criminal Liability: The Model Penal Code and Beyond", in *Stanford Law Review*, 1983, vol. 35, pp. 681–762.

22. William A. Schabas, *The International Criminal Court: A Commentary on the Rome Statute*, Oxford University Press, Oxford, 2010.

23. Jean-Claude Soyer, *Droit penal et procedure pénale*, 18th ed., LGDJ, Paris, 2004.

24. Robert Sullivan, "Knowledge, Belief, and Culpability", in Stephen Shute/A.P. Simester (eds.), *Criminal Law Theory: Doctrines of the General Part*, Oxford University Press, Oxford, 2002, pp. 207–226.

25. Joachim Vogel, "Vor § 15", in Heinrich Wilhelm Laufhütte, Ruth Rissing van Saan and Klaus Tiedemann (eds.), *Strafgesetzbuch Leipziger Kommentar*, 12th ed., De Gruyter, Berlin, 2007.

26. Johan D. van der Vyver, "The International Criminal Court and the Concept of Mens Rea in International Criminal Law", in *University of Miami International and Comparative Law Review*, 2004, vol. 57, pp. 57–149.

27. Thomas Weigend, "Intent, Mistake of Law, and Co-Perpetration in the Lubanga Decision on the Confirmation of Charges", in *Journal of International Criminal Justice*, 2008, vol. 6, pp. 471–87.

28. Gerhard Werle and Florian Jessberger, *Principles of International Criminal Law*, 3rd ed., Oxford University Press, Oxford, 2014.

29. Gerhard Werle and Florian Jeßberger, "Unless Otherwise Provided: Article 30 of the ICC Statute and the Mental Element of Crimes Under International Criminal Law", in *Journal of International Criminal Justice*, 2005, vol. 3, 2005, pp. 35–55.

30. William Clanville, *Criminal Law: The General Part*, 2nd ed., Stevens and Sons, London, 1961.

Authors: Mohamed Elewa Badar and Sara Porro.

Article 31

Grounds for excluding criminal responsibility[310]

1. In addition to other grounds for excluding criminal responsibility provided for in this Statute, a person shall not be criminally responsible if, at the time of that person's conduct:[311]

   (a) The person suffers from a mental disease or defect that destroys that person's capacity to appreciate the unlawfulness or nature of his or her conduct, or capacity to control his or her conduct to conform to the requirements of law;[312]

---

[310] *General remarks*

This provision concerns defences that may lead to the exclusion of criminal responsibility. Defences serves the purpose that the accused is ensured fairness in a substantive sense, meaning that prohibited acts under certain circumstances are justifiable.

The provision does not cover all defences, other defences that were neither recognised nor rejected during the negotiations of the ICC Statute include: alibi, consent of victims, conflict of interests/collision of duties, reprisals, general and/or military necessity, the *tu quoque* argument, and immunity of diplomats. Article 31(3) allows the consideration of other grounds than those referred to in paragraph 1 for excluding criminal responsibility derived from international or national sources through the reference to Article 21.

The Charter of International Military Tribunal in Nuremberg and the statutes of the *ad hoc* tribunal did not allow for defences. Instead defences such as superior orders and official capacity were excluded (IMT Charer, Articles 7 and 8, ICTY Statute, Article 7(2) and (4)). ICTR Statute, Article 6(2) and (4)).

Author: Mark Klamberg.

[311] The chapeau avoids using the common law term of "defence". Instead the provisions speak of "excluding criminal responsibility" where "criminal responsibility" should be understood in a broad sense, meaning that exclusion may not only be procured by exculpatory factors connected to the subjective capability of the actor (such as incapacity, paragraph 1(a)) but also genuine justifications concerning that may negate the objective wrongfulness of the act (such as self-defence, paragraph 1(c)).

The chapeau indicates that there are other grounds provided for in the Statute. These include: abandonment (Article 25(3)(f)), exclusion of jurisdiction of persons under 18 (Article 26), mistake of fact and mistake of law (Article 32), superior order and prescription of law (Article 33).

Author: Mark Klamberg.

[312] This defence concerns the mental state of the defendant at the time of the commission of the crime, not at the time of the trial.

One question is whether the defendant should conclusively prove the defence of insanity, or merely raise the defence shifting the burden of negating it to the prosecutor? In *Delalic et al.*, one of the accused pleaded lack of mental capacity, or insanity. The Trial Chamber considered that the accused was presumed to be sane. It was for the accused to rebut the presumption of sanity on the balance of probabilities. The Trial Chamber held that "[t]his is in accord and consistent with the general principle that the burden of proof of facts relating to a particular peculiar knowledge is on the person with such knowledge or one who raises the defence" ((case no. IT-96-21), ICTY T. Ch., 16 November 1998, paras. 78, 603, 1157–1160, 1172). Turning to the ICC, the combined effect of Articles 66(2) and 67(1)(i) would render it appropriate to rule in

(b) The person is in a state of intoxication that destroys that person's capacity to appreciate the unlawfulness or nature of his or her conduct, or capacity to control his or her conduct to conform to the requirements of law, unless the person has become voluntarily intoxicated under such circumstances that the person knew, or disregarded the risk, that, as a result of the intoxication, he or she was likely to engage in conduct constituting a crime within the jurisdiction of the Court;[313]

(c) The person acts reasonably to defend himself or herself or another person or, in the case of war crimes, property which is essential for the survival of the person or another person or property which is essential for accomplishing a military mission, against an imminent and unlawful use of force in a manner proportionate to the degree of danger to the person or the other person or property protected. The fact that the person was involved in a defensive operation conducted by forces shall not in itself constitute a ground for excluding criminal responsibility under this subparagraph;[314]

---

such cases that the accused is only required to raise a reasonable doubt as to the mental condition.

Rule 79(1) provides, *inter alia*, that the defence shall notify the Prosecutor of its intent to raise a ground for excluding criminal responsibility provided for in Article 31(1).

Author: Mark Klamberg.

[313] This provision allows a narrow defence for intoxication by alcohol or drug consumption. The defence is denied in cases of voluntary intoxication in an attempt to exclude cases were a person puts himself or herself in a state of non-responsibility with objective of committing a crime and later invoke this as a ground of excluding criminal responsibility. It is less clear whether this defence excludes cases where a defendant disregarded the risk that he or she would commit crimes when intoxicated.

Rule 79(1) provides, *inter alia*, that the defence shall notify the Prosecutor of its intent to raise a ground for excluding criminal responsibility provided for in Article 31(1).

Author: Mark Klamberg.

[314] This paragraph concerns self-defence, defence of other persons and in the case of war crimes defence of property essential for accomplishing a military mission. It does not concern the defensive use of force by States (or equivalent non-State actors) as provided for in Article 51 of the UN Charter.

The ICTY Trail Chamber in *Kordić and Čerkez* has stated that the principle of self-defence enshrined in Article 31(1)((c) "reflects provisions found in most national criminal codes and may be regarded as constituting a rule of customary international law" (*Prosecutor v. Kordić and Čerkez* (Case No. IT 95-14/2), ICTY T. Ch., Judgment, 26 February 2001, para. 451). According to the same Trial Chamber "[t]he notion of 'self-defence' may be broadly defined as providing a defence to a person who acts to defend or protect himself or his property (or another person or person's property) against attack, provided that the acts constitute a reasonable, necessary and proportionate reaction to the attack" (para. 459).

From the requirement the danger has to be "imminent" and "unlawful use of force" it follows that the defence cannot be used for pre-emption, prevention or retaliation. Further the defensive reaction must be reasonable in the sense that it is necessary and it must be proportionate.

Rule 79(1) provides, *inter alia*, that the defence shall notify the Prosecutor of its intent to raise a ground for excluding criminal responsibility provided for in Article 31(1).

Author: Mark Klamberg.

(d) The conduct which is alleged to constitute a crime within the jurisdiction of the Court has been caused by duress resulting from a threat of imminent death or of continuing or imminent serious bodily harm against that person or another person, and the person acts necessarily and reasonably to avoid this threat, provided that the person does not intend to cause a greater harm than the one sought to be avoided. Such a threat may either be:

(i) Made by other persons; or

(ii) Constituted by other circumstances beyond that person's control.[315]

2. The Court shall determine the applicability of the grounds for excluding criminal responsibility provided for in this Statute to the case before it.[316]

---

[315] The defence duress concerns the situation when a person is compelled to commit a crime as a result of a threat to his or her life or another person. Necessity is a related defence, the difference is that the threat is the result of natural circumstances. They have a close affinity and paragraph (d) is an attempt to blend into one norm the traditional necessity and duress defence, as known in national criminal justice systems. In *Aleksovski* the Appeals Chamber considered the defence of necessity, but rejected its application to the case. The Appeals Chamber considered it "unnecessary to dwell on whether necessity constitutes a defence under international law, whether it is the same as the defence of duress", see *Prosecutor v. Aleksovski* (Case No. IT-95-14/1), ICTY A. Ch., Judgment, 24 March 2000.

Duress is often confused with the defence of superior orders, but the two defences should be treated as distinct and different.

The question whether the defence of duress could amount to a ground for excluding criminal responsibility or merely a mitigating circumstance was addressed in the *Erdemović* case. The majority found that duress "cannot afford a complete defence" (*Prosecutor v. Erdemović*, ICTY A. Ch., Judgment, Joint Separate Opinion of Judge Mcdonald and Judge Vohrah, 7 October 1997, para. 88) while Judge Cassese in minority considered that the defence of duress could be accepted taking into account at minimum the following four criteria:(1) a severe threat to life or limb; (2) no adequate means to escape the threat; (3) proportionality in the means taken to avoid the threat ; (4) the situation of duress should not have been self-induced (*Prosecutor v. Erdemović*, ICTY Appeals Chamber Judgment, Separate and Dissenting Opinion of Judge Cassese, 7 October 1997, para. 41). The drafters of the ICC Statute effectively adopted the minority view of Judge Cassese.

Rule 79(1) provides, *inter alia*, that the defence shall notify the Prosecutor of its intent to raise a ground for excluding criminal responsibility provided for in Article 31(1).

Author: Mark Klamberg.

[316] Paragraph 2 dates from early drafting stages when some delegations held the view that defence should not be codified, the judges should determine them on a case-by-case basis. In the end defences were codified in paragraph 1 and paragraph 2 was a concession to those delegations that had favoured a minimalist approach. Eser argues that that "paragraph 2 provides that the Court may alter, in the interests of justice, each and every of the Statute's codified grounds for excluding criminal responsibility according to the facts of the individual case" (p. 890). Schabas finds this an "extravagant interpretation" meaning that the Court is not bound by Article 31(1) and (3). Instead he argues that paragraph 2 confirms the role of the Court in determining the applicability of various defences on a case-by-case basis within the general framework of the rest of Article 31 and other relevant provisions (pp. 491-492).

Author: Mark Klamberg.

3. At trial, the Court may consider a ground for excluding criminal responsibility other than those referred to in paragraph 1 where such a ground is derived from applicable law as set forth in Article 21. The procedures relating to the consideration of such a ground shall be provided for in the Rules of Procedure and Evidence.[317]

---

[317] Paragraph 3 concerns uncodified defences to the extent they can be found in the applicable law as set forth in Article 21. This may include the defences listed above. The reference in Article 21(b) to the "established principles of the international law of armed conflict" is of particular relevance.

Rule 79(1) provides that the defence shall notify the prosecution of its intent to raise the existence of an alibi and contains special instructions, including that the notification shall specify the place or places at which the accused claims to have been present at the time of the alleged crime and the names of witnesses and any other evidence upon which the accused intends to rely to establish the alibi. Rule 80 regulates the procedural way of how the defence may raise an exclusionary ground under paragraph 3.

Cross-references:
Rules 79 and 80.

Doctrine:

1. William A. Schabas, *The International Criminal Court: A Commentary on the Rome Statute*, Oxford University Press, Oxford, 2010, pp. 480–98.

2. Albin Eser, "Article 31 – Grounds for Excluding Criminal Responsibility", in Otto Triffterer (ed.), *Commentary on the Rome Statute of the International Criminal Court: Observers' Notes, Article by Article*, 2nd ed., C.H. Beck/Hart/Nomos, Munich/Oxford/Baden-Baden, 2008, pp. 863–93.

3. Mark Klamberg, *Evidence in International Criminal Trials: Confronting Legal Gaps and the Reconstruction of Disputed Events*, Martinus Nijhoff Publishers, Leiden, 2013, pp. 121, 124, 127.

Author: Mark Klamberg.

Article 32
Mistake of fact or mistake of law[318]

[318] *General remarks*

Throughout history defendants have sometimes relied on claims of mistake of fact or law to establish their innocence. A mistake of fact implies that the defendant mistakenly interpreted a situation or the facts of the case. It is, for example, forbidden to kill civilians in an armed conflict. If a defendant – who stands trial for killing civilians in an armed conflict – can demonstrate that he honestly mistook the civilians for soldiers he may successfully invoke the defence of mistake of fact. A mistake of law, on the other hand, implies that the defendant erroneously evaluated the law (Ambos, 2011, p. 318). A defendant who claims that he did not know that the law prohibited killing civilians in an armed conflict relies on a mistake of law. Yet, ignorance of the law can never be an excuse (*ignorantia iuris nocet*) unless the defendant acted upon superior orders or if the mistake negated the mental element of the crime (Darcy, 2011).

The defences of mistake of fact and law are codified in the ICC Statute. Article 32 of the ICC Statute provides:

1. A mistake of fact shall be a ground for excluding criminal responsibility only if it negates the mental element required by the crime.

2. A mistake of law as to whether a particular type of conduct is a crime within the jurisdiction of the Court shall not be a ground for excluding criminal responsibility. A mistake of law may, however, be a ground for excluding criminal responsibility if it negates the mental element required by such a crime or provided for in Article 33.

This commentary will discuss both defences under the ICC Statute. Before turning to both defences, it will start with describing how the defences found their way into the ICC Statute.

Preparatory works:

The question whether or not to include the defences of mistake of law and fact in the ICC Statute was for the first time discussed by the International Law Commission in 1986 during its work on a revised Draft Code of Offenses against the Peace and Security of Mankind (Triffterer, 2008, p. 897). This Code was drafted in 1954 in the wake of the Second World War; the UN General Assembly established the International Law Commission in 1948, which was tasked with undertaking the progressive development and codification of international law. In 1954, the Draft Code of Offences against Peace and Security of Mankind, consisting of four Articles, was developed. Defendants at Nuremberg had already invoked defences of mistake of fact or law during their trials before the International Military Tribunal (IMT) or in the subsequent proceedings conducted under Control Council Law No. 10 of 1945 (Triffterer, 2008, p. 897). While a defence based on a mistake of fact could be found admissible, defences based on a mistake of law were generally dismissed (Triffterer, 2008, p. 897; Milch, US NMT, 20 December 1946 – 17 April 1947, p. 64). The defence of mistake was raised in the infamous doctors' trials before the Nuremberg Military Tribunal (NMT). Physicians stood trial for war crimes as they had committed medical experiments on human beings. A defence of mistake of fact can be successful if the physician honestly and reasonably believed "that there existed factual circumstances making the conduct unlawful" (Cassese, 2003, p. 251). The mistake of fact defence was invoked in combination with the defence of superior orders. One of the arguments raised by the defendants was that the "research subjects" could avoid punishment by participating in the "medical" experiments or that they were "condemned to death and in any event marked for legal execution" (Mehring, 2011, p. 271; *United States of America v. Karl Brandt et al.* "The Doctors' Trial", Trials of War Criminals Vol. I and II, Judgment, 19 August 1947). It cannot be said, however, that the defendants lacked *mens rea* and that they were honestly and reasonably mistaken about the unlawfulness of their actions (Mehring, 2011, p. 273). In another case, the Almelo

Trial before the British Military Court for the Trial of War Criminals, the Judge Advocate advised the court that:

> "if […] the existing circumstances were such that a reasonable man might have believed that a victim whose killing was charged had been tried according to law and that a proper judicial legal execution had been carried out, than it would be open to the court to acquit the accused" (Law Reports of the Trials of War Criminals, Volume XV, Digest of Laws and Cases, 1949 p. 184, referring to the Almelo Trial, *Sandrock et al.*, BMC, 24-26 November 1945, p. 41).

Mistake of fact also surfaced in the *Hostages Trial* before the NMT:

> In determining the guilt or innocence of an army commander when charged with a failure or refusal to accord a belligerent status to captured members of the resistance forces, the situation as it appeared to him must be given first consideration. Such commander will not be permitted to ignore obvious fact in arriving at a conclusion. One trained in military science will ordinarily have no difficulty in arriving at a correct decision and if he wilfully refrains from so doing for any reason, he will be held criminally responsible for wrongs committed against those entitled to the rights of a belligerent. Where room exists for an honest error in judgment, such army commander is entitled to the benefit thereof by virtue of the presumption of his innocence" (Law Reports of the Trials of War Criminals, Volume XV, Digest of Laws and Cases, 1949, p. 184, referring to the *Hostages Trial, List et al.*, NMT, p. 58).

In 1991, however, mistake of fact and law (at that time: error of law and fact) were removed from the 1986 ILC Draft Code, which probably had to do with the sensitive nature of these defences *vis-à-vis* international crimes as well as the perceived limited function in law practice of including these defences (Triffterer, 2008, p. 898). Several reasons thereto can be identified.

First, mistake of fact and law were perceived as part of "general principles of law", as these concepts had legal standing in both national and international jurisdictions. The two defences were not incorporated in the statutes of the IMT, ICTY and ICTR; yet, the defendants could nevertheless rely on them since "generally accepted legal rules" did apply (Triffterer, 2008, p. 898). This does not take away that generally recognised principles may still be subject to controversy; the *Erdemović* case constitutes a clear example thereof. Although the defence of duress raised by Erdemović is an admissible defence in numerous domestic law systems, it was heavily disputed whether this defence could be invoked in cases of crimes against humanity (Weigend, 2004, 321; *Prosecutor v. Erdemović*, ICTY A. Ch., 7 October 1997, paras. 75-79, the Majority held that duress was not a defence if innocent life was taken). Secondly, the differences between certain legal systems may have contributed to the hesitancy in codifying these defences. In 1986, the ILC considered that written law, which predominates in certain legal systems, could not adapt and express "all the contours and nuances of a reality that is ever-changing" (United Nations, Yearbook of the International Law Commission 1986, Volume II Part One, Documents of the thirty-eighth session, para. 187). Common law systems, where written law is less relevant, evaded this problem:

> An offence is constituted by a material element, which is the act, and a moral element, which is the intention. The intervention of written law is not necessary" (United Nations, Yearbook of the International Law Commission 1986, Volume II Part One, Documents of the thirty-eighth session, para. 188).

Another reason why the defence of mistake could supposedly be excluded from the statute relates to the "mental element". For a defence on the basis of mistake of law or fact to succeed, the mistake as such is not decisive; rather the criterion is whether the defendant lacked *mens rea* (Article 32 includes the provision that a mistake of law or fact "shall be a ground for excluding criminal responsibility only if it negates the mental element required by the crime"; see also

1. A mistake of fact shall be a ground for excluding criminal responsibility only if it negates the mental element required by the crime.[319]

Dinstein, 2012, p. xxiii-xxv). Yet, this requirement was already encapsulated in Article 30 of the ICC Statute which deals with *mens rea*, providing that a person only incurs criminal responsibility if the material elements of a crime have been committed with "intent and knowledge". The defences of "mistake" in Article 32 of the ICC Statute are a reflection thereof, as the defendant must demonstrate that the mental element was lacking (lack of *mens rea*), rather than the prosecution having to prove intent and knowledge (existence of *mens rea*).

The issue whether or not to include the defence of mistake of law and fact was still not settled in the ILC's Consolidated Draft of 14 April 1998 (in fn. 20 it was stated that there were still "widely divergent views on this Article", United Nations Diplomatic Conference of Plenipotentiaries on the Establishment of an International Criminal Court, A/CONF.183/2/Add.1, 14 April 1998; see also Triffterer, 1999, p. 560). Two options for mistake of fact or law – at that time enshrined by draft Article 30 – were under consideration. The first option was:

Unavoidable mistake of fact or of law shall be a ground for excluding criminal responsibility provided that the mistake is not inconsistent with the nature of the alleged crime. Avoidable mistake of fact or of law may be considered in mitigation of punishment" (Article 30 option 1 Consolidated Draft Statute, United Nations Diplomatic Conference of Plenipotentiaries on the Establishment of an International Criminal Court, A/CONF.183/2/Add.1, 14 April 1998).

Even though this option did not make it into the final Statute, it still bears relevance for interpreting the law on mistake as the issue of (un)avoidability prominently featured in the drafting history of Article 32 (see, for example, Heller, 2008, p. 440; Cassese, 2003, p. 256). This option encompassed a *culpa in causa* element, which means that resorting to a mistake of law defence can be barred if the mistake was "avoidable". If a defendant has done everything within his power to inform himself of the law or a particular rule then the defence of mistake of law may be open to him as a result of his "excusable" ignorance (Van Sliedregt, 2003, p. 305). Despite the fact that this option was left out of the final Statute, some legal scholars argue that it is still an implicit element of mistake of law, as it is covered by general principles of criminal law (Van Sliedregt, 2003, p. 305; Triffterer, 2008, p. 908; see Article 21(1)(c) of the ICC Statute). Yet, others argue that this observation is incorrect as the common law tradition explicitly rejects the notion of reasonableness, thus, it cannot be considered as a "general principle" of criminal law (Heller, 2008, p. 441).

The second option in the Consolidated Draft consisted of two separate paragraphs; mistake of fact and mistake of law respectively. There was discussion as to whether or not to include mistake of fact as some delegations opined that it was already covered by *mens rea* (fn. 21 Consolidated Draft Statute, United Nations Diplomatic Conference of Plenipotentiaries on the Establishment of an International Criminal Court, A/CONF.183/2/Add.1, 14 April 1998). In fn. 22 to the provision on mistake of law it was observed that "whether a particular type of conduct is a crime under the Statute or whether a crime is within the jurisdiction of the Court, is not a ground for excluding criminal responsibility", which became the basis for the final wording in the ICC Statute (Triffterer, 2008, pp. 899-900).

Author: Geert-Jan Alexander Knoops.

[319] Mistake of fact actually pertains to a false representation of a material fact. If a soldier, for example, mistook a hospital for a military target, he may successfully invoke the defence of mistake of fact, as long as the mistake was reasonable (Van Sliedregt, 2003, p. 303). Even though Article 32(1) of the ICC Statute does not expressly state that the mistake must be reasonable, the likelihood of succeeding with this defence increases if the reasonableness of the mistake in-

creases. The defendant claiming a mistake of fact has the burden of making probable that he or she was honestly mistaken (Knoops, 2008, pp. 143-144).

The ILC, in its 1986 Draft Statute, underlined the distinction between avoidable and unavoidable mistakes. As follows from Article 30 of the ICC Statute crimes within the jurisdiction of the Court must have been committed with "intent and knowledge" in order to hold a person criminally responsible, unless there is a regulation that provides otherwise, such as Article 28 of the ICC Statute on command responsibility which encompasses a negligence standard. This negligence standard may apply to defendants who were mistaken about a certain fact while this could have been avoided (as opposed to an unavoidable mistake of fact) (Triffterer, 2008, p. 905). Article 28 of the ICC Statute excludes the defence of mistake of fact, if the defendant *should have known* of the relevant facts; a requirement that is also embedded in certain Elements of the Crimes (Article 8(2)(b)(xxvi) Elements of the Crimes, War crime of using, conscripting or enlisting children. A perpetrator may be held criminally responsible for this war crime if he "knew or *should have known*" that persons enlisted in the national armed forces or used to actively participate in hostilities were under the age of 15 years; see also Cryer *et al.*, 2010, p. 415). Thus, if the error was avoidable, for example, an error due to negligence or imprudence, a defendant will incur criminal responsibility. Yet, such errors may be used in mitigation of a sentence (United Nations, Yearbook of the International Law Commission 1986, Volume II Part One, Documents of the thirty-eighth session, para. 215).

In its 1986 Draft Statute, the ILC considered that a mistake of fact can be invoked as a defence against war crimes, if the defendant can demonstrate that the mistake was "unavoidable". The defence must include characteristics of *force majeure*, as only such characteristics may lift a person from criminal responsibility in this regard (United Nations, Yearbook of the International Law Commission 1986, Volume II Part One, Documents of the thirty-eighth session, para. 215). A mistake of fact can never be a defence to crimes against humanity or genocide:

> A person who mistakes the religion or race of a victim may not invoke this error as a defence, since the motive for his act was, in any case, of a racial or religious nature (United Nations, Yearbook of the International Law Commission 1986, Volume II Part One, Documents of the thirty-eighth session, para. 214).

Another question that arises is whether a mistake of fact may be a defence to perpetrators who were ignorant about the facts. According to Triffterer both states of mind (that is, ignorance and mistake) have to be treated equally as a perpetrator who does not perceive one or more of the material elements cannot fulfil the requisite mental element as the basis thereto is lacking (Triffterer, 2008, p. 903). Triffterer argues that mistake and error as well as lack of knowledge and awareness can be subsumed under the concept of "mistake of fact":

> They do not have to be differentiated because they both lead to the result that the basis to build the required *mens rea* upon is missing and, therefore, this element does not exist, which is a ground for "excluding criminal responsibility" (Triffterer, 2008, 903).

Ignorance of the law – as opposed to ignorance of the facts – can never constitute a ground for excluding criminal responsibility (Cassese, 2008, 294). The rationale thereof is clear: if defendants could successfully defend themselves by arguing that they were not aware of the existence of a legal ban, this would open the road to a state of lawlessness (Cassese, 2008, 295).

In practice, the defence of mistake of law and fact are frequently intertwined. Cassese, as did the US Military Court, cited the case against Lieutenant William A. Calley, who stood trial for a US Military Court for killing unarmed civilians in custody of US troops during the Vietnam war, as an example of mistake of fact (Cassese, 2008, 291). Calley had argued that he genuinely thought that the civilians had no right to live as they were the enemy and that he had been ordered by his superiors to kill the inhabitants of My Lai (that is, civilians). The Court held:

2. A mistake of law as to whether a particular type of conduct is a crime within the jurisdiction of the Court shall not be a ground for excluding criminal responsibility. A mistake of law may, however, be a ground for excluding criminal responsibility if it negates the mental element required by such a crime, or as provided for in Article 33.[320]

> To the extent that this state of mind reflects a mistake of fact, the governing principle is: to be exculpatory, the mistaken belief must be of such a nature that the conduct would have been lawful had the facts actually been as they were believed to be [...] An enemy in custody may not be executed summarily (*Calley v. Callaway*, 1975).

It seems that Calley was not mistaken about whether the inhabitants were civilians, but he was mistaken about the legality of killing civilians. A distinction must be made between descriptive and normative elements. The former concern mistakes of fact, which are mistakes related to the non-recognition of certain facts, and the latter concern mistakes of law, which are mistakes related to erroneous evaluations (Van Sliedregt, 2003, p. 302; according to Van Sliedregt Mistakes relating to normative elements can qualify as both mistakes of fact and mistakes of law, depending on the way the mistake is made: as failed recognition or as erroneous evaluation", p. 303). These two are often intertwined, as noted by Van Sliedregt:

> "Elements are seldom purely descriptive or purely normative. The material elements of a crime often have a double nature. After all, normative material elements are not abstract legal definitions but legal evaluations of facts, the false perception of which can qualify both as mistake of fact and law (Van Sliedregt, 2003, p. 302).

The relationship between "mistake" and "superior orders" also surfaced in the Calley case, as the Court held that superior orders will not exculpate a defendant if the order "is one which a man of ordinary sense and understanding would [...] know to be unlawful, or if the order in question is actually known to the accused to be unlawful" (*Calley v. Callaway*, 1975).

Author: Geert-Jan Alexander Knoops.

[320] Mistake of law encompasses a normative element of the definition of a certain offence. It arises if a defendant erroneously evaluated the law (Ambos, 2011, p. 318). An example thereof could be a soldier throwing a grenade to a cultural building and subsequently claiming he did not know that the law prohibited destroying cultural property during an armed conflict. Yet, as follows from Article 32(2) ICC Statute a mistake of law related to whether a particular type of conduct is a crime within the jurisdiction of the court can never exclude criminal responsibility. It stems from the principle that ignorance of the law can never be an excuse (*ignorantia iuris nocet*), unless the defendant acted upon superior orders or if the mistake negated the mental element of the crime (Darcy, 2011, pp. 231-245). This provision reflects ICTY case law which also rejected the defence of mistake of law, but accepted the defence of mistake of fact (Manual on International Criminal Defence, ADC-ICTY, 2011, para. 69). It is questionable whether a mistake of law based on an honest but unreasonable believe negates the mental element of a crime. Before turning to this question, the historical background of mistake of law will be discussed.

Early discussions on mistake of law

In its 1986 Draft Code the ILC considered the following acts as an "error of law":

> Error of law is clearly related to the implementation of an order which has been received, when the agent is called upon to assess the degree to which the order is in conformity with the law. It may also exist independently of an order, when the agent acts upon his own initiative, believing that his action is in conformity with the rules of law" (United Nations, Yearbook of the International Law Commission 1986, Volume II Part One, Documents of the thirty-eighth session, para. 204).

If there is a conflict between internal and international law, then the latter should prevail (United Nations, Yearbook of the International Law Commission 1986, Volume II Part One, Documents of the thirty-eighth session, para. 206). This principle was first established in the Nuremberg Charter and subsequently in the Control Council Law No. 10, which nullified the benefits of national amnesty laws and reinstated the criminality of the acts (United Nations, Yearbook of the International Law Commission 1986, Volume II Part One, Documents of the thirty-eighth session, para. 206). Thus, if an act would be in conformity with national legislation, while it would violate international law, then the defendant cannot rely on a defence of mistake of law.

The defence of mistake of law may not be as successful under national law as it is under international law. One is expected to know – or at least be aware – of the national legislation, while this cannot (always) be expected of all international legislation. The latter is sometimes based on "customary practice", which means that it is not based on an agreed rule. Moreover, the evolution of international law and the advent of warfare make certain concepts obsolete, while other concepts emerge, which contributes to the diffuse nature of international law (United Nations, Yearbook of the International Law Commission 1986, Volume II Part One, Documents of the thirty-eighth session, para. 207). As a result of this ambiguity mistakes about such rules may be judged more leniently. Antonio Cassese identified four factors that a court should take into account when judging upon alleged mistakes of international criminal law (Cassese, 2008, p. 296-297):

(i) The universality of the international rule that has allegedly been breached, whether the rule, on the one hand, has been written down in legal documents of which the defendant is apprised or, on the other hand, is controversial, obscure or subject to discussion;

(ii) The defendant's intellectual status (for example a layperson could more easily rely on the defence of mistake of law than a lawyer or someone working in the criminal justice system, as the latter are supposed to know the law as a result of their educational background);

(iii) The defendant's position within the military hierarchy (the higher the rank the more the defendant is expected and required to know the law);

(iv) The importance of the value of the rule that has allegedly been breached (human life and dignity are protected under both national and international rules, as such, one may be more demanding in protecting these values) (Cassese, 2008, p. 296-297).

Difficulties regarding "customary international law" were already expressed by the US Military Tribunal sitting at Nuremberg in the *I.G. Farben* case. In this case it was argued that private industrialists could not be held responsible for carrying out economic measures in occupied territories at the direction – or approval – of their government. Moreover, the limits of permissible action related to the crimes charged, were not clearly defined in international law and the Hague Regulations were said to be outdated by the concept of total warfare (*Krauch et al.*, NMT, 30 July 1948, p. 1137). Yet, this defence was dismissed as the Tribunal held that:

It is beyond the authority of any nation to authorize its citizens to commit acts in contravention of international penal law. A custom is a source of international law, customs and practices may change and find such general acceptance in the community of civilized nations as to alter the substantive content of certain of its principles [...]. Technical advancement in the weapons and tactics used in the actual waging of war may have made obsolete, in some respects, or may have rendered inapplicable, some of the provisions of the Hague Regulations having to do with the actual conduct of hostilities and what is considered legitimate warfare" (*Krauch et al.*, NMT, 30 July 1948, p. 1138).

As with mistake of fact, doubts related to the rules in question may arise with respect to the scope of war crimes, but this is much less likely for crimes against humanity. The ILC considered that mistake of law cannot be an excuse for crimes against humanity as: "No error of law can excuse a crime which is motivated by racial hatred or political prejudices". It follows that a mistake of law can also never excuse a defendant for the crime of genocide, which is, by definition, a crime motivated by hatred or political prejudices (that is, the intent to destroy certain groups; Article 6 ICC Statute defines genocide as "any of the following acts (listed sub (a)-(e)) committed with intent to destroy, in whole or in part, a national, ethnical, racial or religious group"). Given the nature of crimes against humanity and the judicial precedents, it is unimaginable that such crimes can be justified on the basis of any error, as:

> "the error must have been unavoidable [...] the agent must have brought into play all the resources of his knowledge, imagination and conscience and, despite that effort, he must have found himself unable to detect the wrongful nature of his act" (United Nations, Yearbook of the International Law Commission 1986, Volume II Part One, Documents of the thirty-eighth session, para. 209).

Faith in a certain political ideology or acts committed due to a regime's propaganda cannot exonerate a defendant for crimes against humanity on the basis of an error of law, as:

> He should have known, by consulting his conscience, that the act of which he is accused was wrongful" (United Nations, Yearbook of the International Law Commission 1986, Volume II Part One, Documents of the thirty-eighth session, para. 209).

Thus, a defence of mistake of law can only succeed if the error on part of the defendant is an *excusable* fault (United Nations, Yearbook of the International Law Commission 1986, Volume II Part One, Documents of the thirty-eighth session, para. 202). Unawareness of a certain rule of law is an inexcusable fault, as is the blindness to detect the wrongfulness of an act (United Nations, Yearbook of the International Law Commission 1986, Volume II Part One, Documents of the thirty-eighth session, para. 210).

Contemporary case law

Mistake of law surfaced in several contempt cases before the ICTY. In the Florence Hartmann case, the defendant, who was a former employee of the ICTY, faced contempt charges because she allegedly revealed confidential information through the publication of her book. The defence argued that the defendant was not aware of the illegality of her conduct, as she could reasonably believe that the information in her book was no longer confidential as a result of the public discussions in the media that took place prior to publication (*Hartmann*, ICTY Contempt Case, 14 September 2009, para. 63). The Trial Chamber rejected this argument holding that the defendant's "misunderstanding of the law does not, in itself, excuse a violation of it" (*Hartmann*, ICTY Contempt Case, 14 September 2009, para. 65). The Chamber recalled the standard set in the *Jović* case that "if mistake of law were a valid defence [...] orders would become suggestions and a Chamber's authority to control its proceedings, from which the power to punish contempt in part derives, would be hobbled" (*Hartmann*, ICTY Contempt Case, 14 September 2009, para. 65; see also Manual on International Criminal Defence, ADC-ICTY, para. 71). This consideration is congruent with the mentioned rationale behind Article 32(2) ICC Statute, namely that if defendants could successfully argue that they were not aware of the existence of a legal ban, a state of lawlessness could arise (Cassese, 2008, p. 295).

The defence team of *Kanu* before the SCSL also invoked a mistake of law. The defence held that Kanu was not aware of the unlawfulness of conscripting, enlisting or using child soldiers below the age of 15, because "the ending of childhood [in the traditional African setting] has little to do with achieving a particular age and more to do with physical capacity to perform acts reserved for adults" (*Prosecutor v. Brima et al.*, SCSL T. Ch., 20 June 2007, para. 730). Furthermore, the defence contended that various governments in Sierra Leone, prior to the war, had recruited persons under the age of 15 into the military (*Prosecutor v. Brima et al.*, SCSL T. Ch., 20 June 2007, para. 730). The Trial Chamber rejected this defence holding the crime of enlisting and conscripting child soldiers had attained the status of customary international law, and that this customary status required that the victim to be younger than 15 years of age (*Prosecutor v. Brima et al.*, SCSL T. Ch., 20 June 2007, para. 731). The Trial Chamber was furthermore not persuaded that the defence of mistake of law could be invoked in this particular case:

> The rules of customary international law are not contingent on domestic practice in one given country. Hence, it cannot be argued that a national practice creating an appearance of lawfulness can be raised as a defence of conduct violating international norms" (*Prosecutor v. Brima et al.*, SCSL T. Ch., 20 June 2007, para. 732).

The Trial Chamber rejected all defences related to the definition of childhood and the cultural differences thereto (*Prosecutor v. Brima et al.*, SCSL T. Ch., 20 June 2007, para. 1251). Likewise, mistake of law defences based on the *tu quoque* argument were also rejected. The Trial Chamber refused to evaluate evidence related to the conditions of the Sierra Leonean State prior to 1997 because this had "no bearing on the perpetration of international crimes by individuals within the state" (Brima *et al.*, T. Ch., 20 June 2007, para. 1251). Yet, when taking into account the ambiguous nature of "customary international law", as was already recognised by the ILC in 1986, while one is expected to know or be aware of national legislation, it is not surprisingly that the defendant relied on the policy practice of the Sierra Leonean government – or at least raised this as a defence.

Mistake of law also surfaced during the confirmation of the charges phase in the *Lubanga* case before the ICC. The defence team submitted that *Lubanga* could not have known that conscripting and enlisting child soldiers could result in individual criminal responsibility now that neither Uganda nor the DRC "brought to the knowledge of the inhabitants of Ituri the fact that the Rome Statute had been ratified" (*Prosecutor v. Lubanga*, ICC PT. Ch. I, ICC-01/04-01/06-803-tEN, 29 January 2007, para. 296). Under the heading "the principle of legality and mistake of law" the Trial Chamber elaborated on the issue and concluded that "absent a plea under Article 33 of the Statute, the defence of mistake of law can succeed under Article 32 only if (the defendant) was unaware of a normative objective element of the crime as a result of not realising its social significance (its everyday meaning)" (*Prosecutor v. Lubanga*, ICC PT. Ch. I, ICC-01/04-01/06-803-tEN, 29 January 2007, para. 316). Thus, the principle of morality is essential: blindness to the wrongfulness of an act is not deemed to be an excuse (United Nations, Yearbook of the International Law Commission 1986, Volume II Part One, Documents of the thirty-eighth session, para. 210).

To conclude, mistake of fact and law were heavily debated prior to their codification in the ICC Statute. It was questioned whether mistake of fact had to be included in the Statute, as it was already covered by the *mens rea* provision. Mistake of fact is deemed to be a valid defence; yet, "mistakes" are seldom of such a nature that this defence can be successfully raised in cases of international crimes. Even though mistake of law should be interpreted very strictly – as expressed in the wording of Article 32(2) ICC Statute – the defence has been raised in several cases. In principle, mistake of law cannot exonerate an accused. Yet, due to the complex nature of international criminal law, in particular related to war crimes, one should perhaps differentiate between international and national laws in terms of the unavoidability of the error. Future judgments of the ICC will have to learn whether alleged war criminals are expected to bear the same level of knowledge of international law as the level expected of own national laws. Despite the limited successfulness of a mistake of law defence, it did create case law as to its boundaries, which may serve future cases; these factors relate to a defendant's status and position, the universality of the rule and the value that the rule is trying to protect (Cassese, 2008, 296-297). The importance of these precedents cannot be underestimated, as the "general principles of criminal law" are often subject to discussion. The codification of the defence in the ICC Statute, and the discussions that preceded it, have been essential for the proliferation of international criminal law.

Doctrine:

1. Kai Ambos, "Defences in International Criminal Law", in Bertram S. Brown (ed.), *Research Handbook on International Criminal Law*, Cheltenham, Elhar, 2011.

2. Antonio Cassese, *International Criminal Law*, Oxford University Press, Oxford, 2003.

3. Antonio Cassese, *International Criminal Law*, 2nd ed., Oxford University Press, Oxford, 2008.

4. Robert Cryer, Håkan Friman, Daryll Robinson and Elizabeth Wilmshurst, *An Introduction to International Criminal Law and Procedure*, 2nd ed., Cambridge University Press, Cambridge, 2010.

5. Shane Darcy, "Defences to International Crimes", in William A. Schabas and Nadia Bernaz (eds.), *Handbook of International Criminal Law*, Routledge, 2011, pp. 231–45.

6. Yoram Dinstein, *The Defence of 'Obedience to Superior Orders' in International Law*, Oxford University Press, Oxford, 2012.

7. Kevin Jon Heller, "Mistake of Legal Element, the Common Law, and Article 32 of the Rome Statute: A Critical Analysis", in *Journal of International Criminal Justice*, 2008, vol. 6, pp. 419–45.

8. Geert-Jan Knoops, *Defenses in Contemporary International Law*, Martinus Nijhoff, Leiden, 2008.

9. Elies van Sliedregt, *The Criminal Responsibility of Individuals for Violations of International Humanitarian Law*, TMC Asser Press, The Hague, 2003.

10. Otto Triffterer, "Article 32", in Otto Triffterer (ed.), *Commentary on the Rome Statute of the International Criminal Court: Observers' Notes, Article by Article*, 2nd ed., C.H. Beck/Hart/Nomos, Munich/Oxford/Baden-Baden, 2008, pp. 895–914.

11. Thomas Weigend, "The Harmonization of General Principles of Criminal Law: The Statutes and Jurisprudence of the ICTY, ICTR, and the ICC: An Overview", in *International Criminal Law: Quo Vadis?* Association Internationale de Droit Penal, 2004.

Author: Geert-Jan Alexander Knoops.

Article 33

Superior orders and prescription of law[321]

1. The fact that a crime within the jurisdiction of the Court has been committed by a person pursuant to an order of a Government or of a superior, whether military or civilian, shall not relieve that person of criminal responsibility unless:[322]

   (a) The person was under a legal obligation to obey orders of the Government or the superior in question;[323]

   (b) The person did not know that the order was unlawful;[324] and

---

[321] *General remarks*:

Considering that the act of state doctrine after the First World War lost its previous validity in the sense that individuals may be held criminally responsible under international law, the regulation of the responsibility of subordinates became more relevant. Thus, there is a connection between Article 25 on individual criminal responsibility and Article 33 on superior orders. In addition, even if a person cannot be excused, a superior order may lead to mitigation in accordance with Article 78(1) and Rule 145.

The Statutes of the International Military Tribunals and the UN *ad hoc* tribunals denied superior orders as a valid defence (IMT Statute, Article 8, ICTY Statute Article 7(4), ICTR Statute, Article 6(4)). However, the German national court in *Ditmar and Bolt* (*Llandovery Castle*) allowed it as a defence, albeit a narrow one. The case concerned an attack against the hospital ship The Llandovery Castle and shipwrecked sailors. The Court stated that military subordinates "are under no obligation to question the order of their superior officer, and they can count upon its legality. But no such confidence can be held to exist, if such an order is universally known to everybody, including also the accused, to be without any doubt whatever against the law" (see *Ditmar and Bolt* (*Llandovery Castle*), 1922, 16 AJIL 708, p. 722). This test is derived from customary international law and codified in Article 33 of the ICC Statute (Schabas, p. 508).

The defences of duress and superior orders are often relied upon together but should be treated as distinct and separate defence.

Author: Mark Klamberg.

[322] From the words "crime within the jurisdiction of the court" follows that Article 33 is only applicable for the crimes listed in Article 5 and it does not regulate whether other crimes should be treated in the same way. However, considering that part 3 of the ICC Statute concerns "general principles of criminal law" it may be applicable also for other crimes.

Order in the sense of Article 33 should be interpreted broadly, it can be oral, written or otherwise expressed. By the use of the words "committed [...] pursuant to an order" there has to be a connection between the crime and the order.

The word "unless" is followed by three conditions set out in sub-paragraphs (a)-(c) that all have to be fulfilled in order to relive the accused of criminal responsibility.

Author: Mark Klamberg.

[323] The condition that the accused "was under a legal obligation to obey orders of the Government or the superior in question" relates to whether there was an obligation under domestic law within in which the superior and the subordinate acted.

Author: Mark Klamberg.

(c) The order was not manifestly unlawful.[325]

2. For the purposes of this article, orders to commit genocide or crimes against humanity are manifestly unlawful.[326]

---

[324] To be relieved of responsibility the person has to "not know that the order was unlawful". This is a low threshold for the defendant. In cases of doubt, the subordinate has to be treated as if he had known that the order was unlawful.

Author: Mark Klamberg.

[325] The third condition is an objective one and it is formulated in a negative way (not manifestly unlawful). It is applicable when it cannot be proven (based on the available evidence) that the order was manifestly unlawful. The condition appears to contain a contradiction in the sense that all crimes under the jurisdiction of the Court are manifestly unlawful. As Schabas argues (p. 512) even experts may disagree on the existence and scope of a prohibition which may justify a defence of superior orders.

Author: Mark Klamberg.

[326] The second paragraph makes a distinction between war crimes on the one hand where the defence of superior orders is available under the circumstances listed in the first paragraph and genocide, crimes against humanity on the other where this defence is denied. This distinction is not based on customary international law or any domestic law. This suggests that war crimes have a lower gravity than genocide, crimes against humanity. This discrepancy may be explained by the negotiating history where states some States were particularly concerned about exposing their soldiers to war crime allegations.

Doctrine:

1. William A. Schabas, *The International Criminal Court: A Commentary on the Rome Statute*, Oxford University Press, Oxford, 2010, pp. 507–14.

2. Otto Triffterer, "Article 33", in Otto Triffterer (ed.), *Commentary on the Rome Statute of the International Criminal Court: Observers' Notes, Article by Article*, 2nd ed., C.H. Beck/Hart/Nomos, Munich/Oxford/Baden-Baden, 2008, pp. 915–29.

3. Andreas Zimmerman, in Antonio Cassese, Paola Gaeta and John R.W.D. Jones (eds.), *The Rome Statute of the International Criminal Court: A Commentary*, Oxford University Press, Oxford, 2002, pp. 957–74.

Author: Mark Klamberg.

PART 4. COMPOSITION AND ADMINISTRATION OF THE COURT

Article 34
Organs of the Court

The Court shall be composed of the following organs:

(a) The Presidency;

(b) An Appeals Division, a Trial Division and a Pre-Trial Division;

(c) The Office of the Prosecutor;

(d) The Registry.[327]

---

[327] *General remarks*:

Unlike the ICTY, ICTR and SCSL, which were comprised of three organs: Chambers, the Office of the Prosecutor and the Registry, the ICC has a separate organ for the Presidency. Article 38 sets out the function and structure of the Presidency. The role and structure of the remaining organs of the ICC – Chambers, the Office of the Prosecutor, and the Registry – are elucidated in Articles 39, 42 and 43 of the Statute.

Cross-references:

Articles 39, 42 and 43.

Regulation 3.

Author: Yvonne McDermott.

Article 35
Service of judges[328]

1. All judges shall be elected as full-time members of the Court and shall be available to serve on that basis from the commencement of their terms of office.[329]

2. The judges composing the Presidency shall serve on a full-time basis as soon as they are elected.[330]

3. The Presidency may, on the basis of the workload of the Court and in consultation with its members, decide from time to time to what extent the remaining judges shall be required to serve on a full-time basis. Any such arrangement shall be without prejudice to the provisions of Article 40.[331]

---

[328] *General remarks*:

The drafters of the Statute envisioned that there may be times in the Court's lifetime when the full complement of judges would not be needed to sit on a full-time basis (Schabas, 2010). In a sense, the structure for service of judges as set out in Article 35 is akin to that of the Mechanism for the International Criminal Tribunals (MICT) and the Residual Special Court for Sierra Leone, which were established to continue the mandate of the ICTY, ICTR, and SCSL once all of their trials and appeals were completed. These residual mechanisms function with a skeleton staff and sitting Presidency, but have a roster of judges who can be called upon should any *ad hoc* functions (for example review of convictions or acquittals; contempt of court proceedings) arise. In practice, this provision has had little significance, since all of the judges have sat on a full-time basis for the majority of the Court's lifetime.

Preparatory works:

Article 35 reflects the drafters' perception of the ICC as a type of standby *ad hoc* tribunal, which could be called into action when the need arose (Schabas, 2010).

Author: Yvonne McDermott.

[329] Article 35(1), stating that elected judges are to be available "as full time members of the Court", may seem at odds with Article 35(3), which outlines that the Presidency may decide which remaining judges are to sit on a full-time basis. However, the key word here is 'available'. In principle, judges are free to take on other work, but their key priority is to the Court as full-time judges. As such, they must make themselves available as soon as the need arises (Wen-qi and Chana, 2008).

Author: Yvonne McDermott.

[330] The three judges who make up the Presidency, a stand-alone organ of the Court whose functions are set out in Article 38, are required to sit on a full-time basis from the moment they are elected. This is logical, given that the Presidency is responsible for the proper administration of the Court (except for the Office of the Prosecutor), according to Article 38. The President and two Vice-Presidents are elected for a three-year renewable term.

Author: Yvonne McDermott.

[331] The Presidency is given the discretion to decide which of the remaining judges are to sit on a full-time basis. This provision is made without prejudice to Article 40 on judicial independence. Presumably, the cross-reference is made to copper fasten the provisions in Article 40 that judges may not engage in other professional activity that may create the appearance of bias or partiality, and that judges who are sitting on a full-time basis may not take on any other employment.

In September 2003, the then-President of the Court, Philippe Kirsch, informed the Assembly of State Parties that it was expected that the judges of the Pre-Trial and Appeals Chambers

---

4. The financial arrangements for judges not required to serve on a full-time basis shall be made in accordance with Article 49.[332]

would be required to sit on a full-time basis from 2004 (Wen-qi and Chana, 2008; Schabas, 2010). By 2006, all three judicial divisions had become fully operational and only two trial judges were serving on a non-full-time basis (Assembly of States Parties, Proposed Programme Budget for 2007 of the International Criminal Court, 5th Session, 22 August 2006).

Author: Yvonne McDermott.

[332] Article 49 leaves matters of remuneration in the hands of the Assembly of States Parties, and the Assembly is charged with making financial arrangements for judges not sitting full-time. Pursuant to the 'Conditions of Service and Compensation of the Judges of the International Criminal Court', part-time judges are entitled to an annual allowance of 20,000 euros, and may have their income supplemented up to 60,000 euros if their annual declared income falls short of that amount (Wen-qi and Chana, 2008). If judges are sitting on a non-full-time basis and the need arises for them to sit full-time, they are paid from the contingency fund (Assembly of States Parties, 2006).

Cross-references:
Articles 38, 40 and 49.
Regulation 9 Term of office, para. 1.

Doctrine:
1. William A. Schabas, *The International Criminal Court: A Commentary on the Rome Statute*, Oxford University Press, Oxford, 2010, pp. 520–23.
2. Zhu Wen-qi and Sureta Chana, "Article 35", in Otto Triffterer (ed.), *Commentary on the Rome Statute of the International Criminal Court: Observers' Notes, Article by Article*, 2nd ed., C.H. Beck/Hart/Nomos, Munich/Oxford/Baden-Baden, 2008, pp. 937–39.

Author: Yvonne McDermott.

Article 36
Qualifications, nomination and election of judges[333]

1. Subject to the provisions of paragraph 2, there shall be 18 judges of the Court.[334]

2. (a) The Presidency, acting on behalf of the Court, may propose an increase in the number of judges specified in paragraph 1, indicating the reasons why this is considered necessary and appropriate. The Registrar shall promptly circulate any such proposal to all States Parties.

   (b) Any such proposal shall then be considered at a meeting of the Assembly of States Parties to be convened in accordance with Article 112. The proposal shall be considered adopted if approved at the meeting by a vote of two thirds of the members of the Assembly of States Parties and shall enter into force at such time as decided by the Assembly of States Parties.

   (c) (i) Once a proposal for an increase in the number of judges has been adopted under subparagraph (b), the election of the additional judges shall take place at the next session of the Assembly of States Parties in accordance with paragraphs 3 to 8, and Article 37, paragraph 2;

   (ii) Once a proposal for an increase in the number of judges has been adopted and brought into effect under subparagraphs (b) and (c) (i), it shall be open to the Presidency at any time thereafter, if the workload of the Court justifies it, to propose a reduction in the number of judges, provided that the number of judges shall not be reduced below that specified in paragraph 1. The proposal shall be dealt with in accordance with the procedure laid down in subparagraphs (a) and (b). In the event that the proposal is adopted, the number of judges shall be progressively decreased as the terms of office of serving judges expire, until the necessary number has been reached.[335]

---

[333] *General remarks*:

The Statute contains detailed provisions on the appointment and qualifications of judges, which are designed to ensure adequate global and gender representation. The provision on the increase and reduction of the number of judges is a pragmatic innovation, doubtlessly inspired by the issues that arose in the *ad hoc* tribunals when the workload became disproportionate to the number of judges over the course of the their lifetimes.

Preparatory works:

The key debates on this Article centred on the number of judges; whether States or the General Assembly would elect judges; and the term of office for elected judges (Schabas, 2010).

Author: Yvonne McDermott.

[334] During the negotiations there was apparently some debate as to whether 17 or 19 judges would be most appropriate (Schabas, 2010). The agreed figure of 18 judges represents a compromise in this regard.

Author: Yvonne McDermott.

[335] It may be necessary, in line with the future workload of the Court, to appoint additional judges. Article 36(2) envisions that the Presidency can propose an increase in the number of judges, which is to be considered by the Assembly of States Parties. If the proposal is passed by a two-thirds majority of the Assembly of States Parties, and Presidency later decides that additional

3. (a) The judges shall be chosen from among persons of high moral character, impartiality and integrity who possess the qualifications required in their respective States for appointment to the highest judicial offices.

    (b) Every candidate for election to the Court shall:

        (i) Have established competence in criminal law and procedure, and the necessary relevant experience, whether as judge, prosecutor, advocate or in other similar capacity, in criminal proceedings; or

        (ii) Have established competence in relevant areas of international law such as international humanitarian law and the law of human rights, and extensive experience in a professional legal capacity which is of relevance to the judicial work of the Court;

    (c) Every candidate for election to the Court shall have an excellent knowledge of and be fluent in at least one of the working languages of the Court.[336]

4. (a) Nominations of candidates for election to the Court may be made by any State Party to this Statute, and shall be made either:

        (i) By the procedure for the nomination of candidates for appointment to the highest judi- cial offices in the State in question; or

        (ii) By the procedure provided for the nomination of candidates for the International Court of Justice in the Statute of that Court.

    Nominations shall be accompanied by a statement in the necessary detail specifying how the candidate fulfils the requirements of paragraph 3.

    (b) Each State Party may put forward one candidate for any given election who need not necessarily be a national of that State Party but shall in any case be a national of a State Party.

    (c) The Assembly of States Parties may decide to establish, if appropriate, an Advisory Committee on nominations. In that event, the Committee's composition and mandate shall be established by the Assembly of States Parties.[337]

---

judges are no longer needed, it can propose a reduction in the number of judges to the Assembly of States Parties. The number of judges shall never be lower than 18.

Author: Yvonne McDermott.

[336] The Statutes of the ICTY, ICTR and SCSL stated that judges had to be persons of "high moral character, impartiality and integrity" who would be qualified to hold the highest judicial office in their home countries. However, the imprecision of these tribunals' Statutes on the qualifications required has been criticised (Bohlander, 2008; Safferling, 2012). The ICC Statute, by contrast, requires established competence and experience in either relevant fields of international law, such as international humanitarian law and human rights law, or criminal law and procedure. Given that the ICC is first and foremost a criminal court, that has to decide on the guilt or innocence of the accused, albeit for international crimes, it is logical that a slightly higher value is given to competence in criminal law over international law. The Statute dictates that at least half the judges (but no more than 13 of the 18) should be elected on the basis of their knowledge and experience of criminal law and procedure.

Author: Yvonne McDermott.

[337] States parties have the right to nominate one individual to sit as a judge of the ICC at each election. The candidate does not need to be a national of that state, but must be a national of a State Party. This contrasts with the arrangements in the International Court of Justice, where judges do not need to be nationals of states that have accepted the compulsory jurisdiction of the Court.

---

5. For the purposes of the election, there shall be two lists of candidates:

List A containing the names of candidates with the qualifications specified in paragraph 3 (b) (i); and

List B containing the names of candidates with the qualifications specified in paragraph 3 (b) (ii).

A candidate with sufficient qualifications for both lists may choose on which list to appear. At the first election to the Court, at least nine judges shall be elected from list A and at least five judges from list B. Subsequent elections shall be so organized as to maintain the equivalent proportion on the Court of judges qualified on the two lists.

6. (a) The judges shall be elected by secret ballot at a meeting of the Assembly of States Parties convened for that purpose under Article 112. Subject to paragraph 7, the persons elected to the Court shall be the 18 candidates who obtain the highest number of votes and a two-thirds majority of the States Parties present and voting.

   (b) In the event that a sufficient number of judges is not elected on the first ballot, successive ballots shall be held in accordance with the procedures laid down in subparagraph (a) until the remaining places have been filled.[338]

7. No two judges may be nationals of the same State. A person who, for the purposes of membership of the Court, could be regarded as a national of more than one State shall be deemed to be a national of the State in which that person ordinarily exercises civil and political rights.[339]

8. (a) The States Parties shall, in the selection of judges, take into account the need, within the membership of the Court, for:

Nominations can be made either through the process for nominating judges to the highest judicial offices nationally, or through the procedure followed for nominating judges to the International Court of Justice, which requires 'national groups' of sitting members of the Permanent Court of Arbitration to make nominations. States must accompany their nominations with a supporting statement, outlining why the individual nominee possesses the required amount of competence and experience in the fields of criminal or international law.

Author: Yvonne McDermott.

[338] Elections are held at a session of the Assembly of States Parties, and successful candidates are those who have received the highest number of votes, provided that two-thirds majority of the States Parties present and voting. The Bureau of the Assembly of States Parties has encouraged states to refrain from entering into reciprocal voting arrangements (Schabas, 2010)

Author: Yvonne McDermott.

[339] The ICTR and ICTY Statute required that no two permanent judges may hold the same nationality, and no two ad litem judges could hold the same nationality. Therefore, it was possible for two sitting judges to hold the same nationality, as was seen in 2014, when Judge Pocar (Italian) was the sitting President of the ICTY, and Judge Lattanzi (also Italian) was serving as a judge ad litem. The ICC Statute similarly states that no two judges may hold the same nationality, and in the case of judges who hold more than one nationality, they will be deemed to be a national of the state where they normally exercise their civil and political rights. This wording on dual nationality is a reflection of Article 12(4) of the ICTY Statute (and later Article 11(4) of the ICTR Statute), which was introduced by an amendment in 2002, via Security Council Resolution 1411 (2002).

Author: Yvonne McDermott.

(i) The representation of the principal legal systems of the world;

(ii) Equitable geographical representation; and

(iii) A fair representation of female and male judges.

(b) States Parties shall also take into account the need to include judges with legal expertise on specific issues, including, but not limited to, violence against women or children.[340]

9. (a) Subject to subparagraph (b), judges shall hold office for a term of nine years and, subject to subparagraph (c) and to Article 37, paragraph 2, shall not be eligible for re-election.

(b) At the first election, one third of the judges elected shall be selected by lot to serve for a term of three years; one third of the judges elected shall be selected by lot to serve for a term of six years; and the remainder shall serve for a term of nine years.

(c) A judge who is selected to serve for a term of three years under subparagraph (b) shall be eligible for re-election for a full term.[341]

10. Notwithstanding paragraph 9, a judge assigned to a Trial or Appeals Chamber in accordance with Article 39 shall continue in office to complete any trial or appeal the hearing of which has already commenced before that Chamber.[342]

---

[340] The ICC has been described as a "gender-sensitive court" (Oostervald, 2005). The provisions of Article 36(8) add greatly to this impression, by providing not only for gender balancing in the judicial composition of the Court, but also recommends that States Parties should take into account the need to include judges with specific expertise on issues such as violence against women and children. Such expertise will not be seen as invoking reasonable apprehension of bias on those issues, if the Furundzija Appeals Judgment is to be followed. In that case, Judge Mumba's prior involvement with the UN Commission on the Status of Women was seen as evidence of her experience in international human rights law and therefore forming part of the statutory requirements for election, as opposed to a factor that might lead to her disqualification (*Prosecutor v. Furundzija* (Case No. IT-95-17/1-A), ICTY A. Ch., Judgment, 21 July 2000, para. 201) Similarly, the SCSL held that Judge Winter's previous involvement with children's rights issues attested to her competence in the field of juvenile justice, and would not lead a reasonable observer to apprehend bias on her part (*Prosecutor v. Norman* (Case No. SCSL-2004-14), SCSL A. Ch., Decision on the Motion to Recuse Judge Winter from the Deliberation in the Preliminary Motion on the Recruitment of Child Soldiers, 28 May 2004, para. 30)

In the 2014 judicial elections, the nomination period was extended, owing to a shortage of candidates from Asia. Because only two judges from Asia were to remain in office past 2015, there was an ex ante requirement for one Asian judge and two judges from Eastern Europe to be elected. There was also a need to elect at least one male judge, to ensure an appropriate gender balance.

Author: Yvonne McDermott.

[341] As a general rule, judges serve for a period of nine years and are not eligible for re-election. The only exception to this rule is where a judge was elected for a three-year term under the transitional arrangements for the first set of elected judges of the Court, and where a judge has been elected to fill a judicial vacancy and the remainder of the predecessor's term is less than three years.

Author: Yvonne McDermott.

[342] Where a judge's term of office has completed but s/he is sitting on an ongoing case, they are permitted to remain in office until the case is complete. This was the situation of Judge Blatt-

---

mann, for example, who was elected in 2003 for a period of six years. Although he was not eligible for re-election in 2009, Judge Blattmann was permitted to remain sitting as a judge until 2012, when the *Lubanga* case ended. This arrangement is sensible and will alleviate many of the difficulties faced by the *ad hoc* tribunals when judges were not re-elected. Rule 15*bis* of the IC-TY and ICTR Rules of Procedure and Evidence were amended in 2003 to allow proceedings to continue with a substitute judge where a judge of the original bench had not been re-elected. This was less than satisfactory, because the substitute judge would not have had the opportunity to watch the witnesses testify in person and thus observe their credibility, and in cases involving protected witnesses, that testimony might not have been recorded (See *Prosecutor v. Nyiramasuhuko et al* (Case No. ICTR-97-21-T) ICTR A. Ch., Decision on the Matter of Proceedings under Rule 15bis, 24 September 2003, Dissenting Opinion of Judge David Hunt)

Cross-references:
Article 37.

Doctrine:

1. Michael Bohlander, "The International Criminal Judiciary: Problems of Judicial Selection, Independence and Ethics", in Michael Bohlander (ed.), *International Criminal Justice: A Critical Analysis of Institutions and Procedures*, Cameron May, London, 2007, pp. 325–90.

2. Valerie Oosterveld, "Prosecution of Gender-Based Crimes in International Law", in Dyan Mazurana *et al* (eds.), *Gender, Conflict and Peacekeeping*, Rowman and Littlefield Publishers Inc., Lanham, 2005, pp. 67–82.

3. Christoph Safferling, *International Criminal Procedure*, Oxford University Press, Oxford, 2012, p. 130.

4. William A. Schabas, *The International Criminal Court: A Commentary on the Rome Statute*, Oxford University Press, Oxford, 2010, pp. 524–35.

5. Zhu Wen-qi/Sureta Chana, "Article 37", in Otto Triffterer (ed.), *Commentary on the Rome Statute of the International Criminal Court: Observers' Notes, Article by Article*, 2nd ed., C.H. Beck/Hart/Nomos, Munich/Oxford/Baden-Baden, 2008, pp. 941–48.

Author: Yvonne McDermott.

Article 37
Judicial vacancies

1. In the event of a vacancy, an election shall be held in accordance with Article 36 to fill the vacancy.

2. A judge elected to fill a vacancy shall serve for the remainder of the predecessor's term and, if that period is three years or less, shall be eligible for re-election for a full term under Article 36.[343]

---

[343] *General remarks*:

This Article is relatively uncontroversial. It merely states that where a judge is unable to carry on with proceedings, a substitute judge will be elected in accordance with the procedure set out in Article 36 to serve the remainder of his or her term. The successor judge will not be eligible for re-election, unless the predecessor's remaining term of office is less than three years.

Preparatory works:

The main controversies in drafting this provision were whether the replacement judge's qualifications should match those of his or her predecessor, and the question of eligibility for re-election (Schabas, 2010). It was soon decided that any attempt to match the successor's expertise with that of their predecessor would be too complex, and the idea was abandoned (*ibid.*). The International Law Commission had initially proposed that where the predecessor's term was five years or less, the replacement judge should be eligible for re-election; this was ultimately reduced to three years (*ibid.*).

Analysis:

The wording of this provision seems to suggest that as soon as a judicial vacancy arises, an election to appoint a replacement judge shall take place. In reality, this has not been the case. In 2012, an election was held to replace the vacancies left by Judges Blattmann, Fulford and Odio-Benito. Judge Blattmann's term of office had ended in 2009, and the terms of office of his colleagues on Trial Chamber I had ended on 10 March 2012, but all three remained in office until the *Lubanga* judgment was issued on 14 March. When three replacement judges were elected, it was unclear which of the new judges had replaced Judge Blattmann, and which had succeeded the other two judges. Ultimately, lots were cast to decide upon this question (Schabas, 2010).

Under Rule 36 of the Rules of Procedure and Evidence, the Presidency must inform the Presidency of the Bureau of the Assembly of States Parties of the death of a judge, presumably so that an election for the judge's replacement can be organised. Pursuant to Rule 37, when a judge wishes to resign, they should inform the Presidency (who will in turn inform the Assembly of States Parties) with ideally six months' notice.

Cross-references:

Article 36.

Rules 36, 37, 38 and 39.

Doctrine:

1. William A. Schabas, *The International Criminal Court: A Commentary on the Rome Statute*, Oxford University Press, Oxford, 2010, pp. 536–538.

Author: Yvonne McDermott.

Article 38
The Presidency[344]

1. The President and the First and Second Vice-Presidents shall be elected by an absolute majority of the judges. They shall each serve for a term of three years or until the end of their respective terms of office as judges, whichever expires earlier. They shall be eligible for re-election once.[345]

2. The First Vice-President shall act in place of the President in the event that the President is unavailable or disqualified. The Second Vice-President shall act in place of the President in the event that both the President and the First Vice-President are unavailable or disqualified.[346]

3. The President, together with the First and Second Vice-Presidents, shall constitute the Presidency, which shall be responsible for:

   (a) The proper administration of the Court, with the exception of the Office of the Prosecutor; and

   (b) The other functions conferred upon it in accordance with this Statute.[347]

---

[344] *General remarks*:

The Presidency is a unique organ to the International Criminal Court. It is responsible for the proper administration of the Court, and other functions as set out in the ICC Statute, such as excusing judges from the exercise of their judicial functions under Article 41, and proposing an increase in the number of judges pursuant to Article 36. Some functions are conferred on the President as an individual, such as concluding the relationship agreement with the United Nations on the Court's behalf under Article 2.

Preparatory works:

One of the proposed functions of the Presidency, to determine whether the Prosecutor or Deputy Prosecutor should be disqualified on the basis of their prior involvement with a case or any other ground relating to their independence, was rejected by delegates at the Rome Conference. It was felt that such a power might risk the Presidency wielding excessive influence over the Office of the Prosecutor (Rwelamira, 1998). The final Article 38 is careful in maintaining the independence of the Prosecutor from the Presidency.

Author: Yvonne McDermott.

[345] The President and two Vice-Presidents sit for terms of office of three years each, and may be re-elected once. They are elected by a majority of the judges. The first two Presidents of the Court, Philippe Kirsch and Sang-Hyun Song, both sat for two terms of office.

Author: Yvonne McDermott.

[346] When the President is unable or disqualified from conducting one of his or her tasks, the first Vice-President acts in his or her place. If neither the President nor the first Vice-President is available, the second Vice-President will step in. In September 2013, the second Vice-President, Judge Cuno Tarfusser, corresponded with the African Union on the Court's behalf, in response to a request received to defer prosecutions in the Kenya situation before the Court.

Author: Yvonne McDermott.

[347] The Presidency is tasked with the proper administration of the Court, with the exception of the Office of the Prosecutor. It can be seen from other provisions of the Statute (for example Articles 35; 37) that there is a particular focus on organising the work of the judicial divisions of the Court in this regard. The Presidency also bears some important functions as regards the external

4. In discharging its responsibility under paragraph 3 (a), the Presidency shall coordinate with and seek the concurrence of the Prosecutor on all matters of mutual concern.[348]

relations of the Court. For example, the President presents a statement to the Association of States Parties annual meeting every year. Perhaps most importantly, the Presidency is responsible for the direct supervision of the Registrar as the principal administrative officer of the Court, pursuant to Article 43(2). There has been some jurisprudence on the meaning and precise scope of the term "proper administration of the Court" as it relates to the Presidency's functions. In 2006, the Prosecutor requested the Presidency to take steps to ensure that an individual, who had previously worked for the Office of the Prosecutor as a Legal Adviser and had gone on to become Senior Legal Adviser to the Pre-Trial Chamber in the same case, be removed from the case. The Presidency declared that it lacked competence in the matter, holding that issues relating to staff competence fell outside the scope of "proper administration of the Court", and communicated the matter to the Pre-Trial Chamber for its consideration (*Prosecutor v. Lubanga*, ICC PT. Ch., Decision on the Prosecutor's Application to Separate the Senior Legal Adviser to the Pre-Trial Division from Rendering Legal Advice Regarding the Case, ICC-01/04-01/06-623, 27 October 2006). The Appeals Chamber has thus far declined to comment on whether matters of the payment of legal assistance and the appointment of counsel could fall within the scope of the Presidency's duties, although it has held that the Registrar may "have recourse to the President for necessary advice and guidance", pursuant to Article 43(2) (*Prosecutor v. Lubanga*, Decision of the Appeals Chamber upon the Registrar's Requests of 5 April 2007, ICC-01/04-01/06-873, 27 April 2007).

Author: Yvonne McDermott.

[348] Where matters of mutual concern to both the Prosecutor and the Presidency are at issue, the Presidency shall consult with "and seek the concurrence of" the Prosecutor. Such matters might include such issues as security arrangements for defendants and witnesses, or matters concerning the functioning of the Registry (Schabas, 2010). Some have argued that this is an unwelcome provision in the Statute, on the basis that the relationship between the Presidency and the Prosecutor should not be too collegiate, and given that the Presidency is not obliged to consult the Defence on such matters of mutual concern (Jones, 2002).

Cross-references:
Articles 35, 37 and 43.

Rule 8.

Regulation 11.

Doctrine:

1. Medard R. Rwelamira, "Composition and Administration of the Court", in Roy S. Lee (ed.), *The Making of the Rome Statute*, Kluwer Law International, The Hague, 1999, pp. 153–73.

2. John R. W. D. Jones, "Composition of the Court", in Antonio Cassese, Paola Gaeta and John R.W.D. Jones (eds.), *The Rome Statute of the International Criminal Court: A Commentary*, Oxford University Press, Oxford, 2002, pp. 235–69.

3. William A. Schabas, *The International Criminal Court: A Commentary on the Rome Statute*, Oxford University Press, Oxford, 2010, pp. 539–49.

Article 39
Chambers[349]

1. As soon as possible after the election of the judges, the Court shall organize itself into the divisions specified in Article 34, paragraph (b). The Appeals Division shall be composed of the President and four other judges, the Trial Division of not less than six judges and the Pre-Trial Division of not less than six judges. The assignment of judges to divisions shall be based on the nature of the functions to be performed by each division and the qualifications and experience of the judges elected to the Court, in such a way that each division shall contain an appropriate combination of expertise in criminal law and procedure and in international law. The Trial and Pre-Trial Divisions shall be composed predominantly of judges with criminal trial experience.[350]

---

[349] *General remarks*:

The ICC's 18 judges are divided into three divisions: Appeals (five judges, including the President of the Court); Trial (six judges) and Pre-Trial (six judges), with one alternate judge.

Preparatory works:

The ILC's draft statute proposed that the Presidency would bear responsibility for assigning judges to the different divisions. Article 39 remains silent on the question of whose role it is to assign judges to divisions, simply stating that "the Court shall organise itself" into divisions. Rule 4 of the Rules of Procedure and Evidence, however, makes it clear that the judges are to decide this in plenary session.

Author: Yvonne McDermott.

[350] Regulation 10 sets the precedence of the judges. However, in the exercise of their judicial functions, the judges are of equal status.

One or more judges may remain as an alternate; Articles 39(4) and 74(1) as well as Rule 39 and Regulation 16 contain more detail on alternate judges. Considering the words "[a]ll the judges of the Trial Chamber shall be present at each stage of the trial and throughout their deliberations" in Article 74(1), it appears that it is not possible to appoint an alternate judge during the proceedings. A Danish proposal to allow the appointment of alternate judges during the proceedings was not retained in Rule 39.

The assignment of Judges shall be based on the nature of the functions to be performed by each division as well as the competence of the individual judge. Thus, the competence of the judges is an important element when they are assigned to a judicial division.

It will be recalled that under Article 36, judges are elected on 'lists' in line with their expertise; they are put forward as candidates either on the basis of their competence in international law or on the grounds of their experience in criminal law. Article 39(1) provides that each division shall be comprised of an appropriate balance between the two categories of judge and that the assignment of judges to divisions "shall be based on the qualifications and experience" of those judges. Regulation 14 permits the judges elected to each division to appoint a President of the Division (Deschênes and Staker, 2008).

According to Regulation 15 the Presidency shall be responsible for the replacement of a judge, see for example situation in Democratic Republic of the Congo, Decision replacing a judge in Pre-Trial Chamber I, 22 June 2007.

The Pre-Trial Division shall, in accordance with Regulation 17, have a duty judge.

Author: Yvonne McDermott.

---

2. (a) The judicial functions of the Court shall be carried out in each division by Chambers.[351]

    (b) (i) The Appeals Chamber shall be composed of all the judges of the Appeals Division;[352]

        (ii) The functions of the Trial Chamber shall be carried out by three judges of the Trial Division;[353]

        (iii) The functions of the Pre-Trial Chamber shall be carried out either by three judges of the Pre-Trial Division or by a single judge of that division in accordance with this Statute and the Rules of Procedure and Evidence;[354]

    (c) Nothing in this paragraph shall preclude the simultaneous constitution of more than one Trial Chamber or Pre-Trial Chamber when the efficient management of the Court's workload so requires.[355]

3. (a) Judges assigned to the Trial and Pre-Trial Divisions shall serve in those divisions for a period of three years, and thereafter until the completion of any case the hearing of which has already commenced in the division concerned.[356]

---

[351] The work of the three divisions is done through Chambers.

Author: Yvonne McDermott.

[352] Article 39(2) provides that each of the judges appointed to the Appeals Division shall make up the Appeals Chamber.

Author: Yvonne McDermott.

[353] The composition of Trial and Pre-Trial Chambers from the judges appointed to each division is a little more flexible. There can be more than one Trial Chamber and Pre-Trial Chamber in existence at any one time and judges can sit on more than one Chamber. In 2014, there were five Trial Chambers in operation, serviced by the six assigned judges and three judges who were continuing in office in order to complete their trials, pursuant to Article 36(10).

Author: Yvonne McDermott.

[354] The functions of a Pre-Trial Chamber may be carried out by a single judge of that Chamber, as was the case in the *Bemba et al.* contempt case (see for example *Prosecutor v. Jean-Pierre Bemba Gombo*, Aimé Kilolo Musamba, Jean-Jacques Mangenda Kabongo, Fidèle Babala Wandu and Narcisse Arido, Decision Requesting Observations on the 'Defence Request for the Exercise of Judicial Functions by the full Pre-Trial Chamber II', ICC-01/05-01/13-398, 14 May 2014). Each Chamber appoints a Presiding Judge. This role is distinct from that of President of the Division.

Author: Yvonne McDermott.

[355] There may be parallel Chambers within both the Pre-Trial and Trial Divisions. In addition, considering the practice of the Pre-Trial Division, it is clear that a judge may be a member of two parallel Chambers.

Author: Yvonne McDermott.

[356] Pursuant to Article 39(3)(a), judges of the Trial and Pre-Trial Divisions sit in those divisions for three years, and remain in office until any commenced hearings they were sitting on are completed. Given that judges are elected for nine-year terms, the provision suggests that judges might possibly be 'promoted' from one division to the other during their term of office (Jones, 2002). However, this raises an issue of so-called 'contaminated' judges who have served in either Trial or Pre-Trial Divisions (or, indeed, both) and who are later designated to the Appeals Chamber. They are obviously unable to sit in the appeals of the cases that they have already adjudicated on, but since there is only one Appeals Chamber, this becomes problematic. In 2009,

(b) Judges assigned to the Appeals Division shall serve in that division for their entire term of office.[357]

4. Judges assigned to the Appeals Division shall serve only in that division. Nothing in this article shall, however, preclude the temporary attachment of judges from the Trial Division to the Pre-Trial Division or vice versa, if the Presidency considers that the efficient management of the Court's workload so requires, provided that under no circumstances shall a judge who has participated in the pre-trial phase of a case be eligible to sit on the Trial Chamber hearing that case.[358]

---

two serving members of the Court, Judges Kuenyehia and Ušacka, were moved to the Appeals Chamber following the departure of two Appeals Chamber judges whose term had expired; this decision was not welcomed by the Assembly of States Parties (Schabas, 2010). There seems to be no ideal solution to this problem: if only newly-elected judges could serve on the Appeals Chamber to avoid 'contamination', then only the least experienced judges could sit on the Court's highest Chamber.

Author: Yvonne McDermott.

[357] The appeal judges sit during their full mandate, that is, nine years, and their term may not be extended.

Author: Yvonne McDermott.

[358] Once a judge has been appointed to the Appeals Chamber, he or she cannot serve in a Trial or Pre-Trial Chamber. However, Article 39(4) permits some rotation between Pre-Trial and Trial Chambers, and vice versa, provided that no judge sits on both pre-trial and trial stages of the same case. Rwelamira states that the reason for the provision on non-rotation of Appeals Chamber judges was that delegates wished to ensure that the same judge did not hear the same case at an earlier stage as well as on appeal, as discussed above. However, this possibility is precluded by Regulation 12 of the Regulations of the Court, which states that, "Under no circumstances shall a judge who has participated in the pre-trial or trial phase of a case be eligible to sit on the Appeals Chamber hearing that case", and permits for a Pre-Trial or Trial Chamber judge to be temporarily moved to the Appeals Chamber in such circumstances. Thus, the provisions formally precluding Appeals Chamber judges from mobility were probably unnecessary. Potential problems of partiality with Appeals Chamber judges who have served in other judicial divisions can and have been solved in a much more flexible manner.

Cross-references:

Articles 15, 18, 19, 54(2), 57(2), 61(7), 72, 74 and 122(1).

Rules 7 and 39.

Regulations 10, 12, 13, 14, 15, 16, 17, 18, 46, 47, 54.

Doctrine:

1. Jules Deschênes and Christopher Staker, "Article 39", in Otto Triffterer (ed.), *Commentary on the Rome Statute of the International Criminal Court: Observers' Notes, Article by Article*, 2nd ed., C.H. Beck/Hart/Nomos, Munich/Oxford/Baden-Baden, 2008, pp. 957–60.

2. John R. W. D. Jones, "Composition of the Court", in Antonio Cassese, Paola Gaeta and John R.W.D. Jones (eds.), *The Rome Statute of the International Criminal Court: A Commentary*, Oxford University Press, Oxford, 2002, pp. 235–69.

3. Socorro Flores Liera, in Roy S. Lee (ed.), *The International Criminal Court: Elements of Crimes and Rules of Procedure and Evidence*, Transnational Publishers, Ardsley, NY, 2001, pp. 310–14.

4. Medard R. Rwelamira, "Composition and Administration of the Court", in Roy S. Lee (ed.), *The Making of the Rome Statute*, Kluwer Law International, The Hague, 1999, pp. 153–73.

5. William A. Schabas, *The International Criminal Court: A Commentary on the Rome Statute*, Oxford University Press, Oxford, 2010, pp. 550–62.
Author: Yvonne McDermott.

Article 40
Independence of the judges[359]

1. The judges shall be independent in the performance of their functions.[360]

2. Judges shall not engage in any activity which is likely to interfere with their judicial functions or to affect confidence in their independence.[361]

---

[359] *General remarks*:

The right to be tried by an independent tribunal is a key component of the right to a fair trial. Article 40 sets out the conditions for judicial independence, meaning the freedom from external interference with the exercise of judicial functions.

Preparatory works:

An original proposal that a judge could not sit on a case where the accused bears the same nationality as him/her was dropped during the drafting of the ICC Statute (Jones, 2002). Article 10 of the ILC's draft statute proposed that judges could not hold office in a state concurrently with a judicial position in the ICC; in order to recognise that individuals can occasionally merely hold a title, this was later replaced with a more practical examination of whether they actively engaged in the judicial process of a state (Jones, 2002). Another proposal that the Presidency would be responsible for deciding questions of judicial independence was also replaced with the current arrangements under Article 40(4) (Jones, 2002).

Author: Yvonne McDermott.

[360] Article 40(1) states that judges shall be independent in carrying out their judicial functions. This provision is supplemented by the ICC's Code of Judicial Ethics, which was adopted in 2005. Article 3 of the Code states that judges shall uphold the "independence of their office and the authority of the Court" in their conduct, and shall not engage in any conduct that would give rise to questions about their independence. Article 9 of the Code stresses that judges have the right to freedom of expression, but that this right should be exercised in a manner consistent with their independence and impartiality, and that they should not comment on pending cases or express views "which may undermine the standing and integrity of the Court".

One issue that arises is that judges, particularly those who sit on the Presidency, have a role in the external relations of the Court and are frequently asked to give speeches on the work of the Court (Cryer, 2009). This can affect confidence in their independence and impartiality. For example, in the *Lubanga* case, the defence asked that Judge Song be recused from hearing the appeal, on the basis of remarks he had made in his capacity as President of the Court (*Prosecutor v. Lubanga*, ICC PT. Ch. I, Decision of the Plenary of Judges on the Defence Application of 20 February 2013 for the Disqualification of Judge Sang-Hyun Song from the case of The Prosecutor v. Thomas Lubanga Dyilo, ICC-01/04-01/06-3040-Anx, 11 June 2013). Judge Song had referred to the *Lubanga* conviction as a 'landmark judgment' and one that "sets a crucial precedent in the fight against impunity". The Plenary of Judges held that a fair-minded observer would not see these statements in their context as a comment on the merits of the appeal or on any legal or factual aspect of the appeal.

Author: Yvonne McDermott.

[361] The Statute and the Code of Judicial Ethics both state that judges shall not exercise any extra-judicial function that might reasonably call their independence or impartiality into question, with Article 10 of the Code adding that "judges shall not exercise any political function". In *Lubanga*, an alleged incompatibility arose between Judge Song's position as a judge and his concurrent role as President of UNICEF Korea, given that the accused was charged with the conscription and use of child soldiers. This argument was rejected by a majority of the judges

---

3. Judges required to serve on a full-time basis at the seat of the Court shall not engage in any other occupation of a professional nature.[362]

4. 4. Any question regarding the application of paragraphs 2 and 3 shall be decided by an absolute majority of the judges. Where any such question concerns an individual judge, that judge shall not take part in the decision.[363]

(*Prosecutor v. Lubanga*, Decision of the plenary of judges on the Defence Application of 20 February 2013 for the disqualification of Judge Sang-Hyun Song from the case of The Prosecutor v. Thomas Lubanga Dyilo, 11 June 2013). This decision follows precedent from the ICTY and SCSL, where involvement with related interest groups or intergovernmental organisations tends not to give rise to the dismissal of a judge on the grounds of independence or impartiality (*Prosecutor v. Norman*, SCSL PT. Ch., Decision on the Motion to Recuse Judge Winter from the Deliberation in the Preliminary Motion on the Recruitment of Child Soldiers, Case No. SCSL-2004-14-PT, 28 May 2004; *Prosecutor v. Furundžija*, Judgment, Case No. IT-95-17/1-A, 21 July 2000).

Author: Yvonne McDermott.

[362] Full-time judges may not engage in any other occupation of a professional nature. A greater leeway is afforded to judges who are not full-time members of the Court; they are merely to refrain from any activity likely to interfere with their judicial functions or give rise to questions over their independence, under Article 40(2).

Author: Yvonne McDermott.

[363] Decisions on questions of independence are to be decided by an absolute majority of the remaining judges, pursuant to Article 40(4). Although the link is not made explicit, presumably the provisions of Article 41 and the related rules on excusal, and the due process safeguards inherent thereto, would attach to such a decision.

Cross-references:
Articles 38 and 41.

Doctrine.

1. Robert Cryer, "The International Criminal Court and its Relationship to Non-Party States", in Carsten Stahn and Göran Sluiter (eds.), *The Emerging Practice of the International Criminal Court*, Nijhoff Publishers, Leiden, 2009, pp. 115–33.

2. Jules Deschênes and Christopher Staker, "Article 40", in Otto Triffterer (ed.), *Commentary on the Rome Statute of the International Criminal Court: Observers' Notes, Article by Article*, 2nd ed., C.H. Beck/Hart/Nomos, Munich/Oxford/Baden-Baden, 2008, pp. 961–65.

3. John R. W. D. Jones, "Composition of the Court", in Antonio Cassese, Paola Gaeta and John R.W.D. Jones (eds.), *The Rome Statute of the International Criminal Court: A Commentary*, Oxford University Press, Oxford, 2002, pp. 235–69.

4. Anja Seibert-Fohr, "International Judicial Ethics", in Cesare Romano *et al* (eds.), *The Oxford Handbook of International Adjudication*, Oxford University Press, Oxford, 2013, pp. 757–79.

Author: Yvonne McDermott.

Article 41
Excusing and disqualification of judges[364]

1. The Presidency may, at the request of a judge, excuse that judge from the exercise of a function under this Statute, in accordance with the Rules of Procedure and Evidence.[365]

2. (a) A judge shall not participate in any case in which his or her impartiality might reasonably be doubted on any ground. A judge shall be disqualified from a case in accordance with this paragraph if, inter alia, that judge has previously been involved in any capacity in that case before the Court or in a related criminal case at the national level involving the person being investigated or prosecuted. A judge shall also be

---

[364] *General remarks*:

While Article 40 is primarily concerned with the independence or freedom from external influence of judges, Article 41 sets out the procedure for excusal or disqualification on the grounds of perceived or actual bias on the part of the judge. Rule 35 of the Rules of Procedure and Evidence requires a judge to request recusal if any circumstances exist that might call his or her impartiality into question. Article 41 sets down some examples of such circumstances, and is complemented by Rule 34 of the Rules in this regard. It also outlines the procedure to be followed for the disqualification of a judge.

Preparatory works:

In the International Law Commission's 1993 draft, it suggested that the majority of the remaining judges in a Chamber would decide on the disqualification of their colleague, in conjunction with the Presidency (Schabas, 2010) By 1994, this had been amended to leave the decision solely to the remaining judges of the Chamber concerned. The Preparatory Committee later decided that the question should be decided by a majority of the judges of the Court, and it is this formulation that remains in Article 41(2)(c) today.

At the Rome Conference, there was some discussion as to whether States could make requests for recusal of judges, and also about whether nationality might be a factor giving rise to doubts of the impartiality of a judge (Schabas, 2010) Ultimately, these questions were answered in the negative, insofar as they were not included in the final text of Article 41. Nevertheless, it would certainly remain open to the Association of States Parties to amend the Rules of Procedure and Evidence accordingly, if it were to later decide that nationality of judges should be a factor in considering impartiality and/or that states should be able to lodge requests for disqualification of a judge.

Author: Yvonne McDermott.

[365] Article 41(1) deals with 'excusal', or what might be called 'recusal' in other courts. This is where a judge requests that he or she be excused from their judicial functions on the basis of a conflict of interest. Such requests are made in writing to the Presidency, and pursuant to Rule 33, the request and the decision are kept confidential (unless the judge involved gives his or her consent for the decision to be made public). In *Katanga*, two judges of the Appeals Chamber requested excusal from hearing an interlocutory appeal on the basis that they had previously sat on the Pre-Trial Chamber for the same case (*Prosecutor v. Katanga and Ngudjolo Chui*, ICC A. Ch., Decision on the Request to be Excused from Sitting on the Appeal against the Decision on Admissibility in the case of The Prosecutor v. Germain Katanga and Mathieu Ngudjolo Chui pursuant to Article 41 of the Rome Statute, ICC-01/04-01/07-1266-AnxII, 3 July 2009.

Author: Yvonne McDermott.

disqualified on such other grounds as may be provided for in the Rules of Procedure and Evidence.[366]

---

[366] Article 41(2) explicitly mentions *inter alia* two circumstances that might give rise to disqualification. The first is the involvement with any prior stage of the case that they have been allocated to in any capacity. For example, a new judge elected on the basis of their expertise in international law might previously have given legal assistance given to a state in challenging the admissibility of a case; this would disqualify them from later hearing that case, even though the admissibility issue has long since been settled. The second ground listed in Article 41(2) is the involvement at national level in a 'related criminal case'. An example might be where a judge who was elected on the basis of their judicial experience had earlier sat on a case involving atrocities committed by an armed group that the accused was a commander of.

Article 34 supplements this list by adding four potential further grounds for disqualification. First, if the judge has a close relationship (personal or professional) with any of the parties, his or her impartiality might reasonably be doubted. Before the ICTR, the impartiality of Judge Vaz was challenged on the basis that she was living with a member of the prosecution team. The remaining judges on the Trial Chamber dismissed this challenge, finding that there was no question of her impartiality notwithstanding this fact (*Prosecutor v. Karemera et al.* (Case No. ICTR-98-44-AR15bis.2), ICTR A. Ch., Reasons for Decision on Interlocutory Appeals Regarding the Continuation of Proceedings with a Substitute Judge and on Nzirorera's Motion for Leave to Consider New Material, 22 October 2004, para. 69). The Appeals Chamber later held that a reasonable apprehension of bias could be found against the Chamber as a whole on the basis of that decision (*Prosecutor v. Karemera et al.*, Decision on Severance of André Rwamakuba and Amendments of the Indictment, Case No. ICTR–98–44–PT, 7 December 2004, para. 22).

Second, Rule 34 states that involvement in a private capacity in any legal proceedings where the suspect or accused is an opposing party will be a ground for disqualification. It seems highly unlikely that a judge of the International Criminal Court will be involved in a civil suit against an accused before the Court, initiated either before or during their involvement in the case. One wild hypothetical might be where the accused person publishes some material or makes a statement that would seriously lower a judge's reputation in the eyes of right-thinking members of society, and the judge seeks to take a defamation action against him or her. It goes without saying that this hypothetical is exceptionally improbable, not least because judges have traditionally shown resilience in the face of insults and allegations made by obstreperous defendants in the past, but also because privilege attaches to court proceedings in many jurisdictions.

Third, the performance of functions prior to taking office "during which he or she could be expected to have formed an opinion on the case in question" or on the parties or their legal representatives that could affect their impartiality as a judge is a further potential ground for dismissal. Many international criminal judges tend to have had some scholarly involvement in the issues at hand, or have served on advisory boards, prior to their judicial appointments. This will not be a cause for recusal in and of itself, and the extent to which it affects the impartiality of the individual judge will be decided on a case-by-case basis. Before the SCSL, Judge Winter's involvement in children's rights causes generally was not seen to give rise to actual or perceived bias in a case involving chid soldiers (*Prosecutor v. Norman*, Decision on the Motion to Recuse Judge Winter from the Deliberation in the Preliminary Motion on the Recruitment of Child Soldiers, Case No. SCSL-2004-14-PT, 28 May 2004). Similarly, in *Furundžija*, it was held that Judge Mumba's past involvement with the United Nations Committee on the Status of Women similarly did not risk an appreciation of bias on her part; indeed, involvement with such organisations or interest groups may serve as proof of the judge's suit-

(b) The Prosecutor or the person being investigated or prosecuted may request the disqualification of a judge under this paragraph.[367]

---

ability for the job (*Prosecutor v. Furundžija*, Judgment, Case No. IT-95-17/1-A, 21 July 2000).

Fourth, the expression of opinions that could give rise to objective doubts as to the impartiality of the judge will be a ground for dismissal. This was the case in Sesay before the SCSL, where a judge's publication that specifically mentioned the armed group of which the accused was a member was held to give rise to a reasonable apprehension of bias (*Prosecutor v. Sesay* (Case No. SCSL-2004-15-AR15), SCSL A. Ch., Decision on Defence Motion Seeking the Disqualification of Justice Robertson from the Appeals Chamber, 13 March 2004). A request for disqualification of Judge Eboe-Osuji on the basis of a blog post was dismissed by a majority of the plenary of judges in *Banda and Jerbo* (*Prosecutor v. Banda and Jerbo*, ICC Presidency, Decision of the Plenary of the Judges on the 'Defence Request for the Disqualification of a Judge', ICC-02/05-03/09-344-Anx, 5 June 2012). The blog post, written before Judge Eboe-Osuji was appointed to the Court, discussed the relationship between the African Union and the Court and the *Situation in Sudan*, of which the *Banda and Jerbo* case was a part. The majority found that this general comment cast no doubt on the impartiality of the judge.

As mentioned above, nationality was one debated ground for impartiality challenges that ultimately did not make it into the final ICC Statute. In the *Banda and Jerbo* disqualification decision, however, the fact that Judge Eboe-Osuji shared a nationality with the alleged victims was raised as a ground in the challenge. This was dismissed by the plenary of the judges. This appears to be justified by national jurisprudence, where more often than not the judge shares the nationality of the victim; human rights law, which says nothing on nationality as a grounds for lacking impartiality, and international criminal procedure where, in courts including the SCSL and the ECCC, a certain number of domestic judges share the bench with their international counterparts.

In *Lubanga*, a question arose as to whether Article 41(2) could also apply to judicial assistants, as well as to judges. The Prosecutor argued that "[a]n adviser or clerk to a judge has no greater freedom to work on cases in which he or she has already been involved as a prosecuting lawyer, than the judge to whom the adviser or clerk provides legal advice" (*Prosecutor v. Lubanga*, ICC PT. Ch., Decision on the Prosecutor's Application to Separate the Senior Legal Adviser to the Pre-Trial Division from rendering Legal Advice regarding the Case, ICC-01/04-01/06, 27 October 2006). It would seem reasonable to suggest that an individual advising a judge on a case on which he or she previously worked for the prosecution should recuse himself or herself from that position, but there is nothing in the Statute or Rules on the impartiality of judicial advisors. The Pre-Trial Chamber ultimately requested the President to convene a plenary of judges to consider whether Article 41 could apply to a senior legal adviser to the Chamber. The President, in turn, declined this request on the basis that the remaining judges in a later meeting unanimously held that Article 41 did not apply, since the request had nothing to do with the disqualification of a judge (*Prosecutor v. Lubanga*, Decision of the President on the request of the President of the Pre-Trial Division of 20 October 2006, Case No. ICC-01/04-01/07, 7 November 2006). See also *Prosecutor v. Kony et al.*, ICC PT. Ch., III, Decision on the Prosecutor's request to Separate the Senior Legal Adviser to the Pre-Trial Division from rendering Legal Advice Regarding the Case, ICC-02/04-01/05-124, 31 October 2006.

Author: Yvonne McDermott.

[367] Procedure for disqualification

Pursuant to Rule 35, judges are expected to ask to be excused from judicial duty where circumstances exist that could give rise to doubt as to their impartiality, rather than waiting for

(c) Any question as to the disqualification of a judge shall be decided by an absolute majority of the judges. The challenged judge shall be entitled to present his or her comments on the matter, but shall not take part in the decision.

an Article 41(2) decision to be issued against them. Failure to do is a breach of duty giving rise to possible expulsion further to Article 46 (Schabas, 2010).

Under Article 41(2)(b), only the prosecution or the defence may make requests for disqualification. Rule 34 states that, "The request shall state the grounds and attach any relevant evidence, and shall be transmitted to the person concerned". The challenged judge is entitled to present written submissions in response to the request for disqualification, although of course they may not participate in the decision of their judicial colleagues. In *Katanga*, the victims' representative filed an application for the disqualification of Judge van den Wyngaert. The majority of the judges found that the request was inadmissible, as the victims had no locus standi pursuant to Article 41(2)(b). They said:

The Majority considered that the ordinary meaning of Article 41(2)(b) of the Statute was neither ambiguous nor unreasonable. Nor was there any lacuna in the law which called for further judicial interpretation. The law was plain and determinate as to who was entitled to bring an application for the disqualification of a judge. That right was limited to the Prosecutor and the person being investigated or prosecuted (*Katanga*, Decision of the Plenary of Judges on the Application of the Legal Representative for Victims for the disqualification of Judge Christine Van den Wyngaert from the case of The Prosecutor v. Germain Katanga, 22 July 2014, para. 44)

Cross-references:
Articles 40 and 46.

Rules 33, 34 and 35.

Doctrine:

1. Steven W. Becker, "The "Presumption of Impartiality" and other Errors in the International Criminal Court's Plenary Decision Concerning Judicial Disqualification of the President of the Court in The Prosecutor v. Thomas Lubanga Dyilo", in *Global Community Yearbook of International Law and Jurisprudence*, 2013, vol. 1, pp. 111–24.

2. William A. Schabas, *The International Criminal Court: A Commentary on the Rome Statute*, Oxford University Press, Oxford, 2010, pp. 568–73.

Author: Yvonne McDermott.

Article 42
The Office of the Prosecutor[368]

1. The Office of the Prosecutor shall act independently as a separate organ of the Court. It shall be responsible for receiving referrals and any substantiated information on crimes within the jurisdiction of the Court, for examining them and for conducting investigations and prosecutions before the Court. A member of the Office shall not seek or act on instructions from any external source.[369]

---

[368] *General remarks*:

In order for the ICC to retain credibility, it is imperative that it is staffed by a competent and independent Office of the Prosecutor. Article 42 sets out the functions and composition of this Office, as well as the required qualifications of the Prosecutor and Deputy Prosecutor, the process of election and disqualification, and the role of special advisers.

Preparatory works:

Very early drafts suggested that 'complaining states' would appoint the Prosecutor and take responsibility for the conduct of the case (Schabas, 2010) It quickly became clear, however, that the Prosecutor should be an independent and permanent member of staff. There was some discussion on the length of the Prosecutor's term of office and the extent of experience required, but these issues were resolved without too much difficulty (Schabas, 2010).

Author: Yvonne McDermott.

[369] Article 42(1) sets out the functions of the Office of the Prosecutor, namely: receiving referrals, pursuant to Article 14 of the Statute; receiving information on crimes and conducting investigations, pursuant to Article 15, and conducting prosecutions before the Court. In addition, Article 42(2) states that the Prosecutor has authority over the management and administration of the Office, including over its staff, facilities and resources. This is an exception to the general rule in Article 38 that tasks the Presidency with responsibility over the proper administration of the Court. As part of this administrative and management role, Rule 9 requires the Prosecutor to put in place "regulations to govern the operation of the Office". These Regulations ultimately entered into force in 2009. An additional Code of Conduct for the Office of the Prosecutor entered into force in September 2013.

Rule 10 notes that the Prosecutor bears responsibility for the retention, security and storage of information and evidence received in the course of investigations. This corresponds with the Prosecutor's power under Article 54(3)(f) to "[t]ake necessary measures, or request that necessary measures be taken, to ensure the confidentiality of information, the protection of any person or the preservation of evidence". However, there has been some tension between this apparent power of the Prosecutor to provide protective measures and the ultimate authority of the Registry under Article 43(6) to undertake ("in consultation with the Office of the Prosecutor") witness protection measures (*Prosecutor v. Katanga and Chui*, ICC A. Ch., Judgment on the Appeal of the Prosecutor against the 'Decision on Evidentiary Scope of the Confirmation Hearing, Preventative Relocation and Disclosure', ICC-01/04-01/07-776, 26 November 2008).

Although it is not explicitly listed as a role of the Office of the Prosecutor, the Prosecutor does, in practice, play a role in the external relations of the Court. For example, the Prosecutor presents a report to the Security Council every year. Further, when an arrest warrant is sought or issued, the Prosecutor tends to become the 'voice of the Court' in the press. This is not without its difficulties, as outlined below in relation to independence.

Author: Yvonne McDermott.

2. The Office shall be headed by the Prosecutor. The Prosecutor shall have full authority over the management and administration of the Office, including the staff, facilities and other resources thereof. The Prosecutor shall be assisted by one or more Deputy Prosecutors, who shall be entitled to carry out any of the acts required of the Prosecutor under this Statute. The Prosecutor and the Deputy Prosecutors shall be of different nationalities. They shall serve on a full-time basis.[370]

3. The Prosecutor and the Deputy Prosecutors shall be persons of high moral character, be highly competent in and have extensive practical experience in the prosecution or trial of criminal cases. They shall have an excellent knowledge of and be fluent in at least one of the working languages of the Court.[371]

4. The Prosecutor shall be elected by secret ballot by an absolute majority of the members of the Assembly of States Parties. The Deputy Prosecutors shall be elected in the same way

---

[370] Article 42(2) allows the Prosecutor to be assisted by 'one or more' Deputy Prosecutors. In the early days of the Court's operation, there were two Deputy Prosecutors in existence – one responsible for investigations and the other responsible for prosecutions. Since then, there has only been one Deputy Prosecutor; the most recent, James Stewart, was elected in 2012. Article 42(2) states that the Prosecutor and Deputy Prosecutors serve on a full time basis, and that they shall be of different nationalities. It is not clear whether this means that all Deputy Prosecutors and the Prosecutor must bear distinct nationalities, or merely that no Deputy Prosecutor can share a nationality with the Prosecutor. It might be possible for two Deputy Prosecutors to be of the same nationality, provided that the Prosecutor has a different nationality.

The Deputy Prosecutor(s) are entitled to "carry out any of the acts required of the Prosecutor under this Statute". Under Rule 11 of the Rules of Procedure and Evidence, either the Prosecutor or a Deputy Prosecutor may authorise staff members of the Office of the Prosecutor, other than the *gratis* personnel described under Article 44(4) of the Statute, to represent him or her in the exercise of his or her prosecutorial functions. There is an exception to this Rule, which explicitly excludes the "inherent powers of the Prosecutor set forth in the Statute, *inter alia*, those described in Articles 15 and 53." The non-exhaustive nature of the reference to Articles 15 and 53 is unhelpful; it would be much clearer if the rules explicitly set out a list of non-delegable prosecutorial functions. One might wonder, for example, whether the provisions on "unique investigative opportunities" under Article 56 classifies as an inherent power of the Prosecutor or Deputy Prosecutor, or whether it can be delegated to a more junior member of staff. Moreover, it is not entirely certain that the power to initiate investigations propio motu under Article 15 is an "inherent power" of the Prosecutor, as such. Had the drafters of the ICC Statute ultimately decided to omit the provisions of Article 15, it is difficult to imagine that the Prosecutor could nevertheless proceed with investigations propio motu, on the basis that she has the inherent power to do so.

Author: Yvonne McDermott.

[371] As might be expected, the Statute requires the Prosecutor and Deputy Prosecutor(s) to be of high moral character, be highly competent, and have fluency in at least one of the working languages of the Court. As well as 'fluency', Article 42(3) also demands that he or she should have 'excellent knowledge' in one such language – this seems rather superfluous, given that linguistic fluency and extensive knowledge of a language are broadly synonymous.

In addition, the Prosecutor and his or her Deputies must have "extensive practical experience in the prosecution or trial of criminal cases". The reference to "prosecution or trial" recognises that in some legal systems, the judiciary is a professional career that one can enter without having practiced as a lawyer beforehand.

Author: Yvonne McDermott.

---

from a list of candidates provided by the Prosecutor. The Prosecutor shall nominate three candidates for each position of Deputy Prosecutor to be filled. Unless a shorter term is decided upon at the time of their election, the Prosecutor and the Deputy Prosecutors shall hold office for a term of nine years and shall not be eligible for re-election.[372]

5. Neither the Prosecutor nor a Deputy Prosecutor shall engage in any activity which is likely to interfere with his or her prosecutorial functions or to affect confidence in his or her independence. They shall not engage in any other occupation of a professional nature.[373]

6. The Presidency may excuse the Prosecutor or a Deputy Prosecutor, at his or her request, from acting in a particular case.[374]

7. Neither the Prosecutor nor a Deputy Prosecutor shall participate in any matter in which their impartiality might reasonably be doubted on any ground. They shall be disqualified from a case in accordance with this paragraph if, inter alia, they have previously been involved in any capacity in that case before the Court or in a related criminal case at the national level involving the person being investigated or prosecuted.[375]

8. Any question as to the disqualification of the Prosecutor or a Deputy Prosecutor shall be decided by the Appeals Chamber.

(a) The person being investigated or prosecuted may at any time request the disqualification of the Prosecutor or a Deputy Prosecutor on the grounds set out in this article;

---

[372] Both the Prosecutor and Deputy Prosecutor(s) are elected via secret ballot by a majority of the Association of States Parties. The Prosecutor provides the ASP with three nominations for each Deputy Prosecutor vacancy to be filled. Each Prosecutor and Deputy Prosecutor is elected for a nine-year, non-renewable term of office. It is possible for a Deputy Prosecutor to later become Prosecutor, as was the case with the second Prosecutor of the Court, Fatou Bensouda.
Author: Yvonne McDermott.

[373] The Office of the Prosecutor is a separate organ of the Court, and Article 42(1) sets down the rule that no "member of the Office" (which presumably extends to all categories of staff enumerated in Article 44) shall seek or act upon instructions from any external source. To this end, the Prosecutor and Deputy Prosecutor(s) are prohibited from engaging in any activity likely to affect confidence in their independence. They are also prohibited from carrying out any other professional occupation or any activity likely to interfere with their prosecutorial functions.
Author: Yvonne McDermott.

[374] Akin to judges, the Prosecutor or Deputy Prosecutor can ask to excuse him or herself from acting in a particular case. Under Rule 33, this request is to be dealt with by the Presidency in confidence.
Author: Yvonne McDermott.

[375] Like Article 41 for judges, Article 42(7) makes explicit that Prosecutors or Deputy Prosecutors cannot work on cases that they have previously been involved with, at international or national levels. Rule 34 sets out four additional grounds that may give rise to disqualification: the existence of a personal or professional relationship that might call their impartiality into question; the involvement with legal proceedings involving the suspect or the accused; the existence of a prior employment that may have led him or her to form opinions about the case, the accused, or counsel; or the expression of opinions that suggest a lack of impartiality.
Author: Yvonne McDermott.

(b) The Prosecutor or the Deputy Prosecutor, as appropriate, shall be entitled to present his or her comments on the matter;[376]

9. The Prosecutor shall appoint advisers with legal expertise on specific issues, including, but not limited to, sexual and gender violence and violence against children.[377]

---

[376] Challenges to the impartiality of the Prosecutor or Deputy Prosecutor(s) are to be decided by a majority of the Appeals Chamber, pursuant to Article 42(8) and Rule 34(3).

In practice, only the fourth enumerated ground in Rule 34 – the expression of opinions that could adversely impact upon the perceived impartiality of the Prosecutor or Deputy Prosecutor – has been adjudicated to date. The remarks made by Prosecutor Luis Moreno Ocampo following the issuance of an arrest warrant for Sudanese President Omar Al Bashir might provide an example. In an article for *The Guardian*, Moreno Ocampo made statements like, "Bashir's forces continue to use different weapons to commit genocide" and failed to qualify his remarks by pointing out that these were allegations that the Court had yet to adjudge upon. The remarks were subject to a challenge brought by *ad hoc* defence counsel for Bashir, but were deemed inadmissible as falling outside of the *ad hoc* counsel's mandate (*Prosecutor v. Al Bashir*, ICC PT. Ch. I, Decision on the Application for an Order, ICC-02/05-01/09, 24 August 2009).

Author: Yvonne McDermott.

[377] The Prosecutor can appoint advisers with specific legal experience in particular areas. It would appear that these positions are pro bono, but there is nothing in the Regulations of the Office of the Prosecutor that precludes these advisors from getting paid for their assistance. Some of the areas that special advisers have been appointed in are: gender; prosecution strategies; crimes against humanity; children in armed conflict and international humanitarian law.

Cross-references:
Articles 14, 15, 38, 40, 41, 44, 53 and 54.
Rule 9, 10 and 11.
Doctrine:

1. Luc Reydams, Jan Wouters and Cedric Ryngaert, *International Prosecutors*, Oxford University Press, Oxford, 2012.
2. Arman Savarian, *Professional Ethics at the International Bar*, Oxford University Press, Oxford, 2013.
3. William A. Schabas, *The International Criminal Court: A Commentary on the Rome Statute*, Oxford University Press, Oxford, 2010, pp. 574–84.
4. Sergey Vasiliev, *The Role and Legal Status of the Prosecutor in International Criminal Trials*, Grotius Center for International Legal Studies, 2010.

Article 43
The Registry[378]

1. The Registry shall be responsible for the non-judicial aspects of the administration and servicing of the Court, without prejudice to the functions and powers of the Prosecutor in accordance with Article 42.[379]

---

[378] *General remarks*:

The Registry is the principal administrative organ of the Court. Article 43 sets out the role of the Registry and its head, the Registrar, as well as the conditions of service, means of election, and requisite qualifications of the Registrar.

Preparatory works:

One of the key debates in the drafting of the ICC Statute was the issue of responsibility over the Victims and Witnesses Unit. Some advocated for this Unit to be shared with the Office of the Prosecutor (Schabas, 2010).

Author: Yvonne McDermott.

[379] As mentioned in the commentary to Article 42, the Office of the Prosecutor is an independent organ of the Court, responsible for its own administration. Therefore, there is some interplay and possible tension between its operation and the role of the Registry. Article 43(1) underscores this by noting that the powers of the Registry are "without prejudice to the functions and powers of the Prosecutor". The Office of the Prosecutor, in creating Regulations for its operation pursuant to Rule 9, is to consult with the Registrar "on any matters that may affect the operation of the Registry".

The Registry has primary for the "non-judicial aspects of the administration and servicing of the Court", pursuant to Article 43(1). This role involves keeping records on behalf of the court (Rule 15); serving as the channel of communication of the Court (without prejudice to the OTP's right to establish such channels of communication in the course of its investigations) (Rule 13), and ensuring the security of Court premises (Rule 13). The Registrar is responsible for ensuring the safety of detained persons (see *Prosecutor v. Lubanga*, ICC Registrar, Decision to classify the "registrar's decision pursuant to Regulation 196(1) of the Regulations of the Registry" as a public document, ICC-01/04-01/06-52, 23 March 2006), for organising the surrender to the Court of suspects abroad (Rule 184); the transfer of persons in custody (Rule 192) and the transfer of convicted persons to the state where they will serve their sentence (Rule 206).

The Registry bears a significant role in ensuring that the defence rights of the accused under Article 67 are respected. It is responsible for providing "access to appropriate and reasonable administrative assistance" to defence counsel and ensuring their professional independence. According to Rule 20, for the purpose of promoting the rights of the defence, "the Registrar shall, *inter alia*:

(a) Facilitate the protection of confidentiality, as defined in Article 67, para. 1 (b);

(b) Provide support, assistance, and information to all defence counsel appearing before the Court and, as appropriate, support for professional investigators necessary for the efficient and effective conduct of the defence;

(c) Assist arrested persons, persons to whom Article 55, para. 2, applies and the accused in obtaining legal advice and the assistance of legal counsel;

(d) Advise the Prosecutor and the Chambers, as necessary, on relevant defence-related issues;

(e) Provide the defence with such facilities as may be necessary for the direct performance of the duty of the defence;

2. The Registry shall be headed by the Registrar, who shall be the principal administrative officer of the Court. The Registrar shall exercise his or her functions under the authority of the President of the Court.[380]

3. The Registrar and the Deputy Registrar shall be persons of high moral character, be highly competent and have an excellent knowledge of and be fluent in at least one of the working languages of the Court.[381]

(f) Facilitate the dissemination of information and case law of the Court to defence counsel and, as appropriate, cooperate with national defence and bar associations or any independent representative body of counsel and legal associations referred to in sub-rule 3 to promote the specialisation and training of lawyers in the law of the Statute and the Rules".

As laid out in Regulation 83 of the Regulations of the Court, adopted on 26 May 2004, the Registrar has responsibility over the payment of legal assistance. The Registrar also maintains a list of counsel eligible to practice before the Court. Pursuant to Regulation 77 of the Regulations of the Court, an Office of Public Counsel for the Defence (OPCD) was established. This Office falls under the remit of the Registry for administrative purposes but it otherwise functions independently. It is responsible for such matters as assisting counsel by providing legal research; representing suspects at the earliest stages of proceedings, and acting as duty counsel where permanent legal representation is not yet in place. In 2012, the Pre-Trial Chamber in the Libya situation appointed the OPCD to represent Saif Gaddafi in proceedings before the Court. The Libyan authorities initially refused to co-operate with the OPCD, and declined it confidentiality in its meetings with the accused. Ultimately, it was agreed that a confidential meeting between Gaddafi and OPCD representatives could take place in June 2012, but at that meeting, documents were seized and four members of OPCD staff were detained by Libyan authorities, allegedly on the basis of 'treason'. While the staff members were released a short time later, this incident shows how perilous the work of the OPCD can be when acting as legal counsel for accused persons in uncooperative states.

As well as the provisions on the Victims and Witnesses Unit in Article 43(6), the Registrar bears some responsibility for victims. Where there is a challenge to jurisdiction or admissibility, the Registrar will inform the victims who have already communicated with the Court in relation to that case or their legal representatives, as well as any referring state (Rule 59). The Registrar is also responsible for receiving applications for victims' participation under Article 68(1) of the Statute, and to provide a copy of same applications to the prosecution and defence. Akin to the OPCD, there is an autonomous organ within the Registry called the Office of Public Counsel for Victims (OPCV), which provides support and legal assistance to participating victims and their legal representatives.

Where the Registrar requests guidance on his or her functions or duties, these should be addressed to the Presidency (Article 43(2); *Prosecutor v. Lubanga*, ICC A. Ch., Decision of the Appeals Chamber upon the Registrar's Requests of 5 April 2007, ICC-01/04-01/06-873, 27 April 2007).

Author: Yvonne McDermott.

[380] The Registrar, as is obvious, is the director of the Registry and "principal administrative officer of the Court". He or she may be assisted by a Deputy Registrar, upon his or her own recommendation.

Author: Yvonne McDermott.

[381] The familiar criteria of high moral character, competence and fluency in one of the working languages of the Court also apply to the Registrar and Deputy Registrar. Like the Prosecutor and Deputy Prosecutor, the Registrar and Deputy Registrar must take an oath undertaking to perform their functions "honourably, faithfully, impartially and conscientiously". However, unlike

---

4. The judges shall elect the Registrar by an absolute majority by secret ballot, taking into account any recommendation by the Assembly of States Parties. If the need arises and upon the recommendation of the Registrar, the judges shall elect, in the same manner, a Deputy Registrar.[382]

5. The Registrar shall hold office for a term of five years, shall be eligible for re-election once and shall serve on a full-time basis. The Deputy Registrar shall hold office for a term of five years or such shorter term as may be decided upon by an absolute majority of the judges, and may be elected on the basis that the Deputy Registrar shall be called upon to serve as required.[383]

6. The Registrar shall set up a Victims and Witnesses Unit within the Registry. This Unit shall provide, in consultation with the Office of the Prosecutor, protective measures and security arrangements, counselling and other appropriate assistance for witnesses, victims who appear before the Court, and others who are at risk on account of testimony given by such witnesses. The Unit shall include staff with expertise in trauma, including trauma related to crimes of sexual violence.[384]

---

the Prosecutor and Deputy Prosecutor, there is no procedure for disqualification outlined in the Rules for a breach of impartiality for a Registrar or his or her Deputy. He or she might still be subject to removal from office under Article 46, if a serious breach of duty has occurred, or disciplinary measures under Article 47 for less serious breaches.

Author: Yvonne McDermott.

[382] A list of candidates for the post of Registrar is drawn up by the Presidency, which transmits that list to the Assembly of States Parties with a request for any recommendations (Rule 12). Having received any recommendations, the President then transmits the list and recommendations to a plenary of judges, who elect the candidate in a secret ballot by absolute majority. The Deputy Registrar is elected in the same manner, if the Registrar recommends that one be appointed.

Author: Yvonne McDermott.

[383] The Registrar holds office for a five-year term, renewable once. The Deputy Registrar's term of office is more fluid – he or she can hold office for up to five years; the term of office may be shorter if the plenary of judges deems it appropriate. The Deputy Registrar may also be elected on the basis that he or she "shall be called upon to serve as required". Lachowska notes that, in the disposable and non-essential manner of the role of Deputy Registrar as envisioned by the ICC Statute, the role bears far less weight than it did in the *ad hoc* tribunals' practice. There, the Deputy Registrar bore responsibility for the court-related servicing work of the Tribunal (Lachowska, 2009, 390) As of 2015, no Deputy Registrar had ever served before the ICC.

Author: Yvonne McDermott.

[384] Possibly the most controversial role of the Registry has been its responsibility over the Victims and Witnesses Unit (VWU), which is tasked under Article 43(6) with protective measures and security arrangements, counselling, and other appropriate assistance for those witnesses and victims that appear before the Court. There has been some tension in practice between this Unit and the Office of the Prosecutor, with the prosecution submitting that the level of protection offered by the VWU is insufficient, and refusing to disclose material on the basis of fears for the security of the witness(es) (*Prosecutor v. Lubanga*, Decision on disclosure issues, responsibilities for protective measures and other procedural matters, ICC-01/04-01/06-1295-US-Exp-Anx1, 28 April 2008).

The Registrar bears the responsibility of providing notice to victims or their representatives; assisting them in obtaining legal advice and representation; assisting their participation in accordance with the Statute and Rules, and taking gender-sensitive measures to facilitate the participation of victims of sexual violence at all stages of the proceedings (Rule 16). Some of these roles have been subsumed by the Office of Public Counsel for Victims (OPCV), created under Regulation 115, in practice. The Registry is also responsible for assisting witnesses when they are called to the Court; taking gender-sensitive measures to facilitate the testimony of victims of sexual violence; informing witnesses of their rights and obligations; assisting witnesses in obtaining medical or other requisite treatment, and ensuring witness protection. It has also been held that the practice of 'witness familiarisation' (known as 'witness proofing' in earlier international criminal tribunals) falls within the remit of the VWU and not the parties, as witnesses are to be considered witnesses of the Court, regardless of which party called them (*Prosecutor v. Lubanga*, ICC PT. Ch. I, Decision on the Practices of Witness Familiarisation and Witness Proofing, ICC-01/04-01/06-679, 8 November 2006). The Unit is also responsible for providing training to the parties and the Court on such issues as trauma, sexual violence, and confidentiality (Rule 17). As such, Rule 19 suggests a number of roles that might be filled within the Unit, including those with expertise on legal matters; psychological aspects; children; older people, and counselling. The Pre-Trial Chamber found in *Lubanga* that measures such as witness familiarisation is not only admissible but mandatory, *Prosecutor v. Lubanga*, Decision on the Practices of Witness Familiarisation and Witness Proofing, ICC-01/04-01/06-679, 8 November 2006, paras. 23 and 24

In *Katanga and Chui*, the Pre-Trial Chamber concluded that the practice of the Prosecutor to "preventively relocate" witnesses who were not included in the Protection Programme was exceeding the mandate of the Prosecutor and decided that the Prosecutor "shall immediately put an end to the practice of preventive relocation of witnesses". The Pre-Trial Chamber reasoned that Article 43 (6) of the Statute and Regulation 96 of the Regulations of the Registry establish a single Protection Programme, which is run by the Registry and in which the roles of the Prosecutor and the defence are limited to the making of applications to the Registrar (Impugned Decision, para. 22). The Pre-Trial Chamber noted that there was no provision in the Statute, the Rules of Procedure and Evidence, the Regulations of the Court or the Regulations of the Registry that expressly provides the Prosecutor with the authority to relocate witnesses preventively (*Prosecutor v. Katanga and Chui*, ICC PT. Ch. I, Decision on Evidentiary Scope of the Confirmation Hearing, Preventive Relocation and Disclosure under Article 67(2) of the Statute and Rule 77 of the Rules, ICC-01/04-01/07-428-Corr, 25 April 2008 (paras. 22–23, 32 and p. 54).

The Appeals Chamber found on appeal that any disagreement between the VWU and the Prosecutor about the relocation of a witness should ultimately be decided by the Chamber dealing with the case – and should not be resolved by the unilateral and unchecked action of the Prosecutor. The Appeals Chamber agreed with the Pre-Trial Chamber that the general mandate of the Prosecutor pursuant to Article 68(1) of the Statute does not extend to the preventive relocation of witnesses. The Appeals Chamber therefore resolves both parts of the question on this appeal (see para. 64 above) in the negative: The Prosecutor cannot unilaterally "preventively relocate" witnesses either before the Registrar has decided whether a particular witness should be relocated or after the Registrar has decided that an individual witness should not be relocated. The Appeals Chamber confirmed with a 3–2 majority the decision of the Pre-Trial Chamber (*Katanga and Chui*, ICC A. Ch., Judgment on the appeal of the Prosecutor against the "Decision on Evidentiary Scope of the Confirmation Hearing, Preventive Relocation and Disclosure under Article 67(2) of the Statute and Rule 77 of the Rules" of Pre-Trial Chamber I, ICC-01/04-01/07-776, 26 November 2008, paras. 93 and 99, para. 109).

Cross-references:

Articles 42, 46, 47 and 67.

Rules 12, 13, 14, 15, 16, 17, 18, 19, and 20.

Regulations 19 and 81.

Doctrine:

1. Marc Dubuisson, Anne-Aurore Bertrand and Natacha Schauder, "The Contribution of the Registry to Greater Respect for the Principles of Fairness and Expeditious Proceedings Before the International Criminal Court", in Göran Sluiter and Carsten Stahn (eds.), *The Emerging Practice of the International Criminal Court*, Martinus Nijhoff, 2009, pp. 565–84.

2. Anna Lachowska, "The Support Work of the Court's Registry", in José Doria, Hans-Peter Gasser and M. Cherif Bassiouni (eds.), *The Legal Regime of the International Criminal Court: Essays in Memory of Igor Blischenko*, Brill, Leiden, 2009, pp. 387–400.

Author: Yvonne McDermott.

Article 44
Staff[385]

1. The Prosecutor and the Registrar shall appoint such qualified staff as may be required to their respective offices. In the case of the Prosecutor, this shall include the appointment of investigators.[386]
2. In the employment of staff, the Prosecutor and the Registrar shall ensure the highest standards of efficiency, competency and integrity, and shall have regard, mutatis mutandis, to the criteria set forth in Article 36, paragraph 8.[387]
3. The Registrar, with the agreement of the Presidency and the Prosecutor, shall propose Staff Regulations which include the terms and conditions upon which the staff of the Court shall

---

[385] *General remarks*:

Article 44 sets out provisions on the qualifications of, and regulations applicable to, staff appointed by the Prosecutor and Registrar. Importantly, it sets out the status of so-called *gratis* personnel.

Preparatory works:

Article 44 was introduced into the Statute at a late stage of the drafting process. It was initiated by a request from a representative of the United States to include something on the statue of *gratis* personnel, and this later was subsumed into a more general provision on personnel before the Court (Schabas, 2010).

Author: Yvonne McDermott.

[386] As the Statute notes numerous times, while the Registrar is the chief administrative officer of the Court, the Prosecutor has independence over the running of his or her office under Article 42(2). Article 44(1) reiterates this distinction, stating that the Prosecutor and Registrar shall appoint such staff as may be required "to their respective offices". It adds, perhaps unnecessarily, that the Prosecutor will appoint investigators under Article 44. One possible reason for this inclusion is to underscore the fact that investigators are staff, not independent contractors, and as such, they bear all of the duties set out in the Staff Regulations.

Author: Yvonne McDermott.

[387] The Registrar and Prosecutor are to have regard to the provisions of Article 36(8) when hiring staff. In other words, they should be mindful of the need to have representation of the principal legal systems of the world, equitable geographical representation and gender balance. According to a Report released by the Registry in 2013, "as at 31 March 2013, out of 319 professionals, 54 come from Africa, 20 from the Asia-Pacific Group, 23 from Eastern Europe, 26 from the Group of Latin American and Caribbean States and 196 from the Group of Western European and Other States". The gender balance was quite good, with 49.4 percent of staff at Professional or Director level being female, and 50.6 percent being male.

Staff members are mandated by Article 44(2) to embody the highest standards of efficiency, competency and integrity. The Regulations of the Court add that they must 'uphold and respect the principles embodied in the ICC Statute, including faith in fundamental human rights, in the dignity and worth of the human person and in the equal rights of men and women. The standard reference request used by the Court asks whether the individual is free from prejudice or intolerance with regard to race, gender, religious and ethnic background. The core competencies to work at the Court are set out as including honesty, integrity, attitude towards others, temperament, and ability to work harmoniously in a large diverse multicultural environment.

Author: Yvonne McDermott.

---

be appointed, remunerated and dismissed. The Staff Regulations shall be approved by the Assembly of States Parties.[388]

4. The Court may, in exceptional circumstances, employ the expertise of gratis personnel offered by States Parties, intergovernmental organizations or non-governmental organizations to assist with the work of any of the organs of the Court. The Prosecutor may accept any such offer on behalf of the Office of the Prosecutor. Such gratis personnel shall be employed in accordance with guidelines to be established by the Assembly of States Parties.[389]

---

[388] Article 44(3) tasks the Registrar with proposing Staff Regulations including the terms and conditions on which recruitment, remuneration and dismissal of Court staff are to be based. These Regulations were adopted in 2003. They include such matters as a the independence of staff members, the confidentiality of investigations and prosecutions, disciplinary measures and payment of staff.

Author: Yvonne McDermott.

[389] Under Article 44(4), the Court can 'in exceptional circumstances' accept the services individuals on secondment from States, intergovernmental organisations or non-governmental organisations. These people are known as '*gratis* personnel', given that they are not paid directly by the Court. Guidelines for the selection and engagement of *gratis* personnel were adopted in 2005. Pursuant to these guidelines, *gratis* personnel must accept the independence of the Court, and must not accept instruction from their sending state or organisation, or indeed from any external authority. They cannot be hired to replace a paid member of staff. The Prosecutor or Deputy Prosecutor may not delegate their prosecutorial functions to *gratis* personnel serving in the Office of the Prosecutor (Rule 11).

Cross-references:
Articles 36 and 42.

Doctrine:

1. William A. Schabas, *The International Criminal Court: A Commentary on the Rome Statute*, Oxford University Press, Oxford, 2010, pp. 601–6.

2. David Tolbert and Brigitte Benoit, "Article 44", in Otto Triffterer (ed.), *Commentary on the Rome Statute of the International Criminal Court: Observers' Notes, Article by Article*, 2nd ed., C.H. Beck/Hart/Nomos, Munich/Oxford/Baden-Baden, 2008, pp. 993–99.

Author: Yvonne McDermott.

Article 45
Solemn undertaking

Before taking up their respective duties under this Statute, the judges, the Prosecutor, the Deputy Prosecutors, the Registrar and the Deputy Registrar shall each make a solemn undertaking in open court to exercise his or her respective functions impartially and conscientiously.[390]

---

[390] *General remarks*:

Article 45 sets out that judges, the Prosecutor, Deputy Prosecutor, Registrar, and Deputy Registrar shall make a 'solemn undertaking' to exercise their functions independently and conscientiously.

Preparatory works:

Early drafts of the Statute placed a duty on judges to make such an undertaking; this was later extended to other senior officers of the Court.

Analysis:

It is commonplace in the majority of legal systems that judges should make an oath declaring that they will exercise their functions impartially. At the ICC, the requirement to make such a 'solemn undertaking' extends not just to judges, but to the Prosecutor, Deputy Prosecutors, Registrar and Deputy Registrar as well. This clearly relates to the accused's right to be tried by an impartial court, under Article 67, and the duty of impartiality imposed on judges, the Prosecutor, and Deputy Prosecutors under Articles 41 and 42. Article 43 does not set down a requirement that the Registrar or Deputy Registrar be impartial, but this was clearly obvious to the drafters that this should be the case, given their inclusion in Article 45.

In some domestic legal systems, judges are required to swear an oath on a religious text. The ICC's solemn declaration under Article 45, like the solemn declaration for witnesses under Article 69(1), is non-denominational. Judges make the following declaration, set out in Rule 5: 'I solemnly undertake that I will perform my duties and exercise my powers as a judge of the International Criminal Court honourably, faithfully, impartially and conscientiously, and that I will respect the confidentiality of investigations and prosecutions and the secrecy of deliberations.' The undertaking made by the Prosecutor, Registrar, and their Deputies is almost identical, save for the 'secrecy of deliberations' element, which clearly does not apply.

Although it is not required under Article 45, the Rules also include a solemn undertaking to be made by every staff member of the Office of the Prosecutor and the Registry, to carry out their duties honourably, faithfully, impartially and conscientiously, and to respect the confidentiality of investigations. Interpreters and translators must also make a solemn undertaking, before commencing any duties, to perform their duties honourably, faithfully, impartially and conscientiously.

Cross-references:

Articles 41, 42, 43, 45, 67 and 69.

Rules 5 and 6.

Doctrine:

1. William A. Schabas, *The International Criminal Court: A Commentary on the Rome Statute*, Oxford University Press, Oxford, 2010, pp. 607–8.

Author: Yvonne McDermott.

Article 46
Removal from office[391]

1. A judge, the Prosecutor, a Deputy Prosecutor, the Registrar or the Deputy Registrar shall be removed from office if a decision to this effect is made in accordance with paragraph 2, in cases where that person:

    (a) Is found to have committed serious misconduct or a serious breach of his or her duties under this Statute, as provided for in the Rules of Procedure and Evidence; or

    (b) Is unable to exercise the functions required by this Statute.[392]

2. A decision as to the removal from office of a judge, the Prosecutor or a Deputy Prosecutor under paragraph 1 shall be made by the Assembly of States Parties, by secret ballot:

    (a) In the case of a judge, by a two-thirds majority of the States Parties upon a recommendation adopted by a two-thirds majority of the other judges;

    (b) In the case of the Prosecutor, by an absolute majority of the States Parties;

    (c) In the case of a Deputy Prosecutor, by an absolute majority of the States Parties upon the recommendation of the Prosecutor.[393]

---

[391] *General remarks*:

The Statutes of the *ad hoc* Tribunals contained no provision for removal from office of judges or any other senior staff member of the Court. Article 46 of the ICC Statute, by contrast, sets out the reasons for removal, and the process that is to be followed in reaching a decision on removal from office.

Preparatory works:

The drafting of this provision was relatively uncontroversial. Some delegations at the Rome Conference took the view that a distinction should be drawn between those who were to be removed from office because they were no longer in a position to fulfil their functions, for example because of ill health, and those whose misconduct necessitated removal from office (Schabas, 2010).

Author: Yvonne McDermott.

[392] Article 46(1) sets out two separate grounds for removal of a judge, Prosecutor, Deputy Prosecutor, Registrar, or Deputy Registrar: inability to carry out their functions under the Statute, and 'misconduct of a serious nature' or a 'serious breach of duty'. Pursuant to Rule 24, misconduct of a serious nature might include: disclosing confidential facts, where such disclosure is seriously prejudicial to the judicial proceedings or to any person; concealing information that would have precluded him or her from holding office, and abuse of office in order to obtain unwarranted favourable treatment. Such misconduct can also occur outside the course of official duties, if the conduct is 'of a grave nature causes or is likely to cause serious harm to the standing of the Court.' An obvious example would be the commission of a serious crime.

A 'serious breach of duty' implies gross negligence in the conduct of an individual's functions. Two examples are given in Rule 24: the failure to request to be excused, where there are grounds for doing so (for example if one of the judges had a close relationship with one of the parties), and (b) repeatedly causing unwarranted delay in the initiation, prosecution or trial of cases. An example of the latter might be where a Prosecutor or Deputy Prosecutor is disorganised and continually fails to file their submissions on time.

Author: Yvonne McDermott.

3. A decision as to the removal from office of the Registrar or Deputy Registrar shall be made by an absolute majority of the judges.[394]

4. A judge, Prosecutor, Deputy Prosecutor, Registrar or Deputy Registrar whose conduct or ability to exercise the functions of the office as required by this Statute is challenged under this article shall have full opportunity to present and receive evidence and to make submissions in accordance with the Rules of Procedure and Evidence. The person in question shall not otherwise participate in the consideration of the matter.[395]

---

[393] Articles 46(2) and (3) set out precisely which organ can decide on the removal of office of an individual high-ranking member of the Court's staff, and a great deal of detail is included in the Rules of Procedure and Evidence on the procedure to be followed. This is doubtless an improvement on the *ad hoc* tribunals where in practice, judges decided on the removal of a fellow judge in a plenary session, but, as Judge Shahabuddeen pointed out, there was nothing in the Statute granting this power to the plenary, and thus its competence to pass judgment on such a question was uncertain (*Prosecutor v. Delalić et al.* (Case No IT-96-21), ICTY Bureau, Decision of the bureau on motion to disqualify judges pursuant to Rule 15 or in the alternative that certain judges recuse themselves, 25 October 1999). Further, there is an added safeguard against arbitrariness in that the Assembly of State Parties makes the final decision on the question of removal of a judge, Prosecutor or Deputy Prosecutor (Article 46(2)).

For a judge to be removed from office, the other judges must meet in plenary session and a two-thirds majority must recommend that he or she be removed. This recommendation is communicated by the Presidency to the President of the Bureau of the Assembly of States Parties. The Assembly of States Parties then decides on the matter in a secret ballot; a two-thirds majority of the States Parties is needed to effectuate a removal from office. For a Prosecutor to be removed, a secret ballot of the Assembly of States Parties is taken, and an absolute majority of States Parties is needed before he or she can be removed from office. In the case of a Deputy Prosecutor, the Prosecutor must recommend his or her removal to the Assembly of States Parties, which decides on the matter by absolute majority.

Author: Yvonne McDermott.

[394] An absolute majority of the judges is needed to remove a Registrar or Deputy Registrar from office, and the Presidency then communicates that decision to the Assembly of States Parties.

[395] It may be decided that the conduct is more appropriately classified as 'misconduct of a less serious nature' pursuant to Article 47, and the individual concerned can be reprimanded accordingly.

In both Article 46 and Article 47 proceedings, due process rights attach: the individual concerned has the right to present and receive evidence, to put forward his or her own submissions on the matter, and to be represented by counsel.

Cross-references:

Article 47.

Rules 23, 24, 26, 27, 28, 29 and 31.

Regulations 119, 120, 121, 122, 123, 124 and 125.

Doctrine:

1. John R.W.D. Jones, "Duties of Officials", in Antonio Cassese, Paola Gaeta and John R.W.D. Jones (eds.), *The Rome Statute of the International Criminal Court: A Commentary*, Oxford University Press, Oxford, 2002, pp. 285–88.

2. William A. Schabas, *The International Criminal Court: A Commentary on the Rome Statute*, Oxford University Press, Oxford, 2010, pp. 609–14.

Author: Yvonne McDermott.

Article 47

Disciplinary measures

A judge, Prosecutor, Deputy Prosecutor, Registrar or Deputy Registrar who has committed misconduct of a less serious nature than that set out in Article 46, paragraph 1, shall be subject to disciplinary measures, in accordance with the Rules of Procedure and Evidence.[396]

---

[396] *General remarks*:

This short Article sets out the grounds and procedure for the invocation of disciplinary measures against senior members of the Court's staff.

Preparatory works:

There was no provision on disciplinary measures in the Statutes of the *ad hoc* tribunals, and according to Schabas, this provision only arose in the drafting of Article 46 on removal from office. One discussion arose as to whether the Rules of Procedure and Evidence or the Regulations was the best place to set out the procedure for enacting disciplinary proceedings; ultimately, this was included in the Rules (Schabas, 2010).

Analysis:

Article 47 is notable in its brevity on the types of act that might be considered 'misconduct of a less serious nature', the nature of disciplinary measures that can be imposed, and the procedure to be followed in the event of such alleged misconduct. However, it is heavily supplemented by the Rules of Procedure and Evidence.

Rule 25 defines 'misconduct of a less serious nature' as conduct that causes or is likely to cause harm to the proper internal functioning of, or administration of justice before, the Court, if committed in the course of official duties. An example might be the leaking of sensitive information that did not reach the level of seriousness envisioned under Article 46. The Rule outlines three examples of its own: interfering in the exercise of the functions of a judge, Prosecutor, Registrar, or Deputy Prosecutor or Registrar; failing to comply with request made by the Presiding Judge or the Presidency in the exercise of their lawful duty; or (in the case of judges) failing to enforce disciplinary measures when the judge is aware or should be aware of a serious breach of duty on their part. Misconduct of a less serious nature can also be committed outside the course of official duty, and is described as conduct that causes or is likely to cause harm to the standing of the Court.

Of course, the boundaries between serious misconduct and misconduct of a less serious nature are blurred, and in reality, violations as outlined in Rule 25 might constitute 'serious misconduct' or a 'serious breach of duty' giving rise to action under Article 46, depending on the circumstances. Thus, Rule 25 quite wisely notes that nothing in the rule precludes the examples set out in sub-rule 1(a) from being classified as serious misconduct or a serious breach of duty, for the purposes of Article 46.

The Rules outline two types of disciplinary measure for misconduct under Article 47 – a reprimand, or a pecuniary sanction that may not exceed six months of the salary paid by the Court to the individual concerned (Rule 32). The Rules mandate that any decision to impose a disciplinary measure on a judge, Registrar or Deputy Registrar will be taken by the Presidency. There does not seem to be any provision made for when a judge who is a member of the Presidency has carried out the alleged misconduct. Presumably, the other two judges would decide upon any disciplinary measure, but as they would be two, it would raise difficulties if they could not reach a consensus. Any decision to impose a disciplinary measure on the Prosecutor shall be made by the Bureau of the Association of States Parties, by majority. The Prosecutor can issue a reprimand to the Deputy Prosecutor, but the Bureau of the ASP, by majority, must approve pecuniary sanctions (Rule 30).

The Rules set out a procedure for complaints of alleged misconduct under Article 47 that aim to ensure procedural justice. Complaints shall be confidentially transmitted to the Presidency, which has the right to 'set aside anonymous or manifestly unfounded complaints', before transmitting any legitimate complaints to the competent organ. The 'competent organ' differs, depending on who the complaint has been made about: the Presidency for judges, Registrar or Deputy Registrar; the Bureau of the ASP for the Prosecutor, and the Prosecutor for the Deputy Prosecutor. Rule 27 establishes that the person who is subject to such disciplinary proceedings has the right to be informed of the complaint, to submit and receive evidence, to make written submissions, to answer any questions put to him or her, and to be represented by counsel.

Cross-references:

Article 46.

Rules 25, 26, 28, 30 and 32.

Doctrine:

1. Milan Marković, "The ICC Prosecutor's Missing Code of Conduct", in *Texas International Law Journal*, 2011, vol. 47, pp. 201–36.

2. William A. Schabas, *The International Criminal Court: A Commentary on the Rome Statute*, Oxford University Press, Oxford, 2010, pp. 615–18.

Author: Yvonne McDermott.

Article 48
Privileges and immunities[397]

1. The Court shall enjoy in the territory of each State Party such privileges and immunities as are necessary for the fulfilment of its purposes.[398]

2. The judges, the Prosecutor, the Deputy Prosecutors and the Registrar shall, when engaged on or with respect to the business of the Court, enjoy the same privileges and immunities as are accorded to heads of diplomatic missions and shall, after the expiry of their terms of office, continue to be accorded immunity from legal process of every kind in respect of words spoken or written and acts performed by them in their official capacity.[399]

3. The Deputy Registrar, the staff of the Office of the Prosecutor and the staff of the Registry shall enjoy the privileges and immunities and facilities necessary for the performance of

---

[397] *General remarks*:

The International Criminal Court and its staff require some privileges and immunities to exercise their functions independently and without interference from states. Article 48 recognises a 'sliding scale' of privileges and immunities, from full diplomatic privileges and immunities being afforded to judges, the Registrar and the Prosecutor and Deputy Prosecutor when they are on court business, to a limited reference to 'treatment as is necessary' given to counsel, experts, witnesses, and other persons required to be present at the seat of the Court.

Preparatory works:

It was obvious that judges should be afforded some level of diplomatic immunity when on Court business. Most of the debate in the drafting of Article 48 centred on the extent to which the Prosecutor, investigators and counsel needed and should be afforded such immunity to guarantee the effective carrying out of their functions.

Author: Yvonne McDermott.

[398] The Court itself is entitled to 'such privileges and immunities as are necessary for the fulfilment of its purposes, pursuant to Article 48(1). This means that, pursuant to the Headquarters Agreement, the property and funds of the Court are 'immune from search, seizure, requisition, confiscation, expropriation and any other form of interference, whether by executive, administrative, judicial or legislative action.'

Author: Yvonne McDermott.

[399] Judges, the Prosecutor, Registrar and Deputy Prosecutor(s) are entitled to privileges analogous to those afforded to a head of a diplomatic mission. This means, practically, that they cannot be arrested be subject to the legal process in any way; they cannot be obliged to pay taxes; they are exempt from national service and restrictions on immigration; they are entitled to repatriation in times of emergency; their official papers and documents are inviolable, as is any personal baggage carried with them, and so forth.

These individuals cannot be sued for remarks made during their time in office as part of their official functions, even after that time has expired. So, an acquitted person who was affronted by remarks made by the Prosecutor alleging him or her to be guilty of heinous crimes during trial cannot later sue the former Prosecutor for defamation.

Author: Yvonne McDermott.

---

their functions, in accordance with the agreement on the privileges and immunities of the Court.[400]

4. Counsel, experts, witnesses or any other person required to be present at the seat of the Court shall be accorded such treatment as is necessary for the proper functioning of the Court, in accordance with the agreement on the privileges and immunities of the Court.[401]

---

[400] Staff of the Office of the Prosecutor and the Registry, along with the Deputy Registrar, are entitled to such privileges and immunities as are necessary for the performance of their functions. So, for example, their right to liberty cannot be restricted by states attempting to thwart their investigations in that state. It is most unfortunate that the same functional immunity was not extended to defence counsel or members of defence investigating teams within this provision. A defence counsel practicing before the ICTR was arrested and detained by Rwanda in 2011 on charges of 'genocide denial', linked to statements made in the course of his client's defence, and four members of ICC staff acting on behalf of Saif Gaddafi were detained by Libyan authorities in 2012.

An 'Agreement on Privileges and Immunities of the ICC' was adopted by the Association of State Parties in 2002, and it came into force in 2004. The agreement defines 'counsel' as including 'defence counsel and representatives of victims'. Article 18 entitles such counsel to inviolability of documents and papers, immunity from legal process of any kind in respect of acts or words spoken as part of their official function; immunity from arrest and detention; and free communication as part of their role. Righteous as it may be, it is unlikely that this Article represents customary international law, and thus it is unfortunate that only 74 states have thus far acceded to the agreement. As regards the duty of non-Party States to the ICC, such as Libya, to respect the immunities afforded to staff under Article 48, it has been argued that this is an obligation pursuant to the Security Council's referral of that state to the ICC, demanding Libya to 'fully cooperate' with the Court (Heller, 2012).

Author: Yvonne McDermott.

[401] Article 48(4) applies to 'counsel, experts, witnesses or any other person required to be present at the seat of the Court' and states that they are entitled to 'such treatment as is necessary for the proper functioning of the Court, in accordance with the Agreement on Privileges and Immunities of the ICC. For some authors, the wording of this provision suggests that such treatment will just be afforded at the seat of the Court itself, given that it extends to 'any other person required to be present at the seat of the Court' (Schabas, 2010). The International Bar Association appears to be of the view that it applies in any state, and not just the seat of the Court (IBA, 2012).

The latter interpretation appears to be correct for two reasons. First, the word 'witnesses' is not followed by a comma in the list, which would make the terms 'witnesses' and 'any other person' disjunctive, therefore applying the 'seat of the Court' proviso to all those on the list. Without that comma, the terms are conjunctive, meaning that the treatment is owed to: (a) counsel, (b) experts, (c) witnesses required to be present at the seat of the Court, and (d) anyone else required to be present at the seat of the Court. Second, the reference to the Agreement on Privileges and Immunities of the Court would be curious if this provision were only to apply at the seat of the Court, given that the Headquarters agreement would surely be the more relevant instrument.

'Such treatment' clearly falls short of the privileges and immunities offered to others in Article 48. The Agreement on Privileges and Immunities of the Court suggests some types of treatment that may be owed to witnesses, including immunity from arrest and detention; immunity from legal processes of any kind; exemption from immigration restrictions, and inviolability

5. The privileges and immunities of:

(a) A judge or the Prosecutor may be waived by an absolute majority of the judges;

(b) The Registrar may be waived by the Presidency;

(c) The Deputy Prosecutors and staff of the Office of the Prosecutor may be waived by the Prosecutor;

(d) The Deputy Registrar and staff of the Registry may be waived by the Registrar.[402]

---

of documents, provided that such measures are necessary for their appearance before the Court for purposes of giving evidence.

Author: Yvonne McDermott.

[402] Immunities can be waived where they are not necessary for the proper functioning of the Court, for example where a member of staff has sought to avoid paying a parking fine on the basis of their immunity. Article 48(5) establishes that an absolute majority of the judges can waive the privileges and immunities of a judge or the Prosecutor; the Presidency can waive the Registrar's privileges and immunities; the Prosecutor can waive the privileges and immunities of OTP staff or the Deputy Prosecutor, and the Registrar can waive the privileges and immunities of Registry staff or the Deputy Registrar.

Doctrine:

1. Stuart Beresford, "The Privileges and Immunities of the International Criminal Court: Are they sufficient for the proper functioning of the Court or is there still room for improvement?", in *San Diego International Law Journal*, 2002, vol. 3, pp. 83–132.

2. Kevin Jon Heller, "Why I Think the Detained ICC Personnel Are Entitled to Diplomatic Immunity", in *Opinio Juris*, 15 June 2012.

3. International Bar Association, Counsel Matters before the International Criminal Court, November 2012, pp. 31–33.

4. William A. Schabas, *The International Criminal Court: A Commentary on the Rome Statute*, Oxford University Press, Oxford, 2010, pp. 619–26.

5. Hannah Woolaver, "The Immunity of Defence Team Members at the ICTR: Lessons from the Jurisprudence of the ICTR, ICTY and the ICC", in *African Yearbook of International Humanitarian Law*, 2013, vol. 134, p. 134.

Author: Yvonne McDermott.

Article 49

Salaries, allowances and expenses

The judges, the Prosecutor, the Deputy Prosecutors, the Registrar and the Deputy Registrar shall receive such salaries, allowances and expenses as may be decided upon by the Assembly of States Parties. These salaries and allowances shall not be reduced during their terms of office.[403]

---

[403] *General remarks*:

The ICC has to strike a delicate balance on salaries, allowances and expenses; it must pay a reasonable and fair wage suffice to attract the most talented individuals, but these benefits must not be so excessive as to draw criticism. In addition, these conditions must be decided by a body not directly impacted by them, but must not be subject to interference where that body is dissatisfied with some aspect of the Court's work. Article 49 attempts to strike that balance.

Preparatory works:

The International Law Commission's Draft Statute initially proposed that the judges of the Court might receive 'allowances and expenses' from the Court, with their home state paying a salary. This proposal was not successful. There was some discussion as to whether the salaries of the judges of the International Court of Justice might be used as a basis for calculation, but overall, the drafting of this provision seems to have been relatively uncontroversial (Schabas, 2010).

Analysis:

In analysing this provision, it must be borne in mind that full-time judges are not permitted to exercise any external professional function, pursuant to Article 40. In addition, it is imperative that they be seen to be independent in the exercise of their functions, so any payment that could be interfered with by one state would give rise to questions about that independence.

The Association of States Parties in its 'Conditions of Service' Resolution agreed that the remuneration for judges would be €180,000 per annum. The President receives an additional €18,000. There are allowances built in for the education of dependants, and travel/relocation allowances. Judges are entitled to join a pension scheme similar to that available to the judges of the International Court of Justice. Non-permanent judges receive an annual allowance of €20,000, but where a judge declares his or her total annual income to be less than €60,000, he or she will receive an allowance, payable monthly, to supplement his or her declared net income up to that amount.

Judges' salaries and allowances cannot be reduced during their terms of office under Article 49.

Cross-references:

Article 40.

Doctrine:

1. William A. Schabas, *The International Criminal Court: A Commentary on the Rome Statute*, Oxford University Press, Oxford, 2010, pp. 627–33.

Author: Yvonne McDermott.

Article 50
Official and working languages[404]

1. The official languages of the Court shall be Arabic, Chinese, English, French, Russian and Spanish. The judgements of the Court, as well as other decisions resolving fundamental issues before the Court, shall be published in the official languages. The Presidency shall, in accordance with the criteria established by the Rules of Procedure and Evidence, determine which decisions may be considered as resolving fundamental issues for the purposes of this paragraph.[405]

---

[404] *General remarks:*

The Statute distinguishes between 'official languages of the Court', of which there are six, and its two 'working languages', English and French. All documents must be in one of the two working languages, and certain decisions and judgments are to be published in all six official languages. Translation and interpretation are the responsibility of the Registry (Regulation 40).

Preparatory works:

Throughout the drafting process, it was clear that the working languages of the Court were to be the official languages of the United Nations, French and English. According to Schabas, the distinction between official and working languages and the addition of Arabic, Russian, Chinese and Spanish came at the final stage of negotiations, owing to intense lobbying from a group of Spanish-speaking countries (Schabas, 2010).

Author: Yvonne McDermott.

[405] It is clear that all final judgments on guilt or innocence of the accused should be published in each of the official languages. In addition, the Statute mandates that 'other decisions resolving fundamental issues before the Court' should also be published in Arabic, Chinese, English, French, Russian and Spanish. Article 50(1) permits the Presidency to determine which decisions may be considered 'fundamental' for these purposes. That authority must be exercised in accordance with the Rules of Procedure and Evidence, and Rule 40 declares four types of decision to be considered as resolving fundamental issues: all decisions of the Appeals Chamber; all admissibility and jurisdiction decisions; all Trial Chamber decisions on guilt or innocence, sentencing and reparations, and all decisions on Article 57(3)(d) (investigative steps in the absence of state cooperation). This seems to spread the net of translation, which is a costly and wieldy process, very wide. In practice, however, the Court appears to have been quite lackadaisical on its obligations to translate these documents into all of the official languages. Three years after its issuance, the *Lubanga* judgment remained available in English and French only.

Rule 40 further determines that decisions on the confirmation of charges and offences against the administration of justice shall be published in all official languages of the Court 'when the Presidency determines that they resolve fundamental issues'. This provision is rather superfluous, given that any decision is to be published in all six languages if the Presidency sees it as a decision resolving fundamental issues before the Court. The Rules offer further discretion to the Presidency to have any decisions involving 'major issues relating to the interpretation or the implementation of the Statute or concern[ing] a major issue of general interest' published in all of the official languages.

Author: Yvonne McDermott.

2. The working languages of the Court shall be English and French. The Rules of Procedure and Evidence shall determine the cases in which other official languages may be used as working languages.[406]

3. At the request of any party to a proceeding or a State allowed to intervene in a proceeding, the Court shall authorize a language other than English or French to be used by such a party or State, provided that the Court considers such authorization to be adequately justified.[407]

---

[406] English and French are the working languages of the Court. Some have criticised the Court for its excessive Anglophonism, but there is a delicate balance to be achieved between hiring staff from a wide geographic distribution and those who are competent in both working languages of the Court (Schabas, 2010).

Countries. Thus, the provisions on working languages strongly interplayed with their right to a fair trial. Pursuant to Article 67(1)(f), the accused has the right to free interpretation of proceedings into a language he or she fully understands and speaks, and to translation of any documents that are necessary to ensure fairness. The 'fully understands and speaks' proviso goes further than the 'in a language which he understands' formulation found in the ICCPR, and the 'fully' is not to be overlooked (*Prosecutor v. Katanga*, ICC A. Ch., Judgment on the appeal of Mr Germain Katanga against the decision of the Pre-Trial Chamber I entitled 'Decision on the defence request concerning languages', ICC 01/04-01/07 (OA 3), 27 May 2008). In *Lubanga*, it was held that, since the majority of the defence team spoke only French whereas the majority of the prosecution were English-speaking, the fact that simultaneous transcripts of the trial were only made available in English put the defence at a significant disadvantage *vis-à-vis* the prosecution. Thus it was ordered that live transcripts should be provided in both languages (*Prosecutor v. Lubanga*, Decision on defence's request to obtain simultaneous French transcripts, ICC-01/04-01/06, 14 December 2007).

Article 50(2) permits the Presidency to designate one of the official languages of the Court as a working language for a case. The circumstances of such an authorisation are set down in Rule 41, namely where the language is spoken by the majority of those involved in a case and any of the participants have requested it to become a working language, or where 'the Prosecutor and the defence so request'. This wording suggests that both parties need to make a request for one of the other official languages to be used as a working language. The Presidency may authorise such a request 'if it considers that it would facilitate the efficiency of the proceedings.' (Rule 41) There is no record of any such request having been made to date.

Author: Yvonne McDermott.

[407] Article 50(3) permits the Court to authorise the use of another language by any party or by any State intervening in a proceeding, provided that it believes such an authorisation to be adequately justified. There is no inherent limitation to any of the other official languages of the Court in the wording of Article 50(3), which simply refers to 'a language other than English or French'.

Cross-references:

Article 67.

Rules 40, 41, 42 and 43.

Regulation 40.

Doctrine:

1. William A. Schabas, *The International Criminal Court: A Commentary on the Rome Statute*, Oxford University Press, Oxford, 2010, pp. 634–41.

---

2. Flores Liera Socorro, "Publications, Languages and Translation", in Roy S. Lee (ed.), *The Making of the Rome Statute: Issues, Negotiations and Results*, Kluwer Law, The Hague, 1999, pp. 314–20.
3. David Tolbert and Magdalini Karagiannakis, "Article 50", in Otto Triffterer (ed.), *Commentary on the Rome Statute of the International Criminal Court: Observers' Notes, Article by Article*, 2nd ed., C.H. Beck/Hart/Nomos, Munich/Oxford/Baden-Baden, 2008, pp. 1025–31.
Author: Yvonne McDermott.

Article 51

Rules of Procedure and Evidence[408]

1. The Rules of Procedure and Evidence shall enter into force upon adoption by a two-thirds majority of the members of the Assembly of States Parties.[409]

2. Amendments to the Rules of Procedure and Evidence may be proposed by:

   (a) Any State Party;

   (b) The judges acting by an absolute majority; or

   (c) The Prosecutor.

   Such amendments shall enter into force upon adoption by a two-thirds majority of the members of the Assembly of States Parties.[410]

3. After the adoption of the Rules of Procedure and Evidence, in urgent cases where the Rules do not provide for a specific situation before the Court, the judges may, by a two-

---

[408] *General remarks:*

At the *ad hoc* Tribunals, Judges had the power to make and amend Rules of Procedure and Evidence, which led to significant fluidity of the Rules to adjust to individual circumstances (McDermott, 2013). At the ICC, this power is vested in the Association of States Parties. Article 51 sets down the conditions for the Rules of Procedure and Evidence's adoption and operation.

Preparatory works:

The main debate on this Article concerned the degree of freedom to be afforded to judges in the adoption and amendment of Rules of Procedure and Evidence. It was decided at the Rome Conference to leave the drafting of the Rules of Procedure and Evidence until after the Conference (Schabas, 2010).

Author: Yvonne McDermott.

[409] The Rules of Procedure and Evidence were drafted by the Preparatory Commission after the successful conclusion of the Rome Conference. Article 51(1) states that the Rules will be adopted by a two-thirds majority of the Assembly of States Parties, and will enter into force immediately thereafter. The Rules were adopted by consensus and entered into force in 2002.

Author: Yvonne McDermott.

[410] Rule amendments can be proposed by: any State Party; the judges acting in absolute majority, or the Prosecutor, and enter into force when adopted by a two-thirds majority of the Assembly of States Parties.

While the Rules of Procedure and Evidence are undeniably comprehensive in nature, and indeed, as Schabas notes, many procedural issues are extensively discussed in the Statute itself, there were certain issues of procedure that could not have been envisioned at the time of their drafting. For example, the Court had to deal with requests for non-attendance of high-ranking political figures in Kenya, who were simultaneously on trial before the Court. In 2013, a new Rule 134*quater* was adopted to cover the situation of those accused persons who are 'mandated to fulfil extraordinary public duties at the highest national level'. It states that the Trial Chamber shall grant a request for excusal from trial received from such persons, where it is convinced that it is in the interests of justice and not prejudicial to the rights of the accused to do so (Resolution ICC-ASP/12/Res.7, Adopted at the 12th plenary meeting on 27 November 2013 by consensus).

Author: Yvonne McDermott.

---

thirds majority, draw up provisional Rules to be applied until adopted, amended or rejected at the next ordinary or special session of the Assembly of States Parties.[411]

4. The Rules of Procedure and Evidence, amendments thereto and any provisional Rule shall be consistent with this Statute. Amendments to the Rules of Procedure and Evidence as well as provisional Rules shall not be applied retroactively to the detriment of the person who is being investigated or prosecuted or who has been convicted.[412]

5. In the event of conflict between the Statute and the Rules of Procedure and Evidence, the Statute shall prevail.[413]

---

[411] Article 51(3) allows a two-thirds majority of judges to draw up provisional Rules 'in urgent cases where the Rules do not provide for a specific situation before the Court. These Rules are to be applied until the next session of the Association of States Parties, where they can be adopted, rejected or amended.

In practice, as can be seen from the *Kenya* situation, judges tend not to draw up such provisional rules, but rather rely on judicial interpretation of the Statute to justify a particular solution or course of action. They can later seek a change of the Rules to retroactively include that solution within the Court's procedural framework.

Author: Yvonne McDermott.

[412] Importantly, Article 51(4) stresses that new or provisional Rules cannot be applied retroactively to the detriment of a suspect, accused, or convicted person. The retroactive application of amended Rules was controversial before the ICTR. In the case of *Nyiramasuhuko et al.*, Rule 15*bis* had stated that continuation of a trial in the long-term absence of one of the judges could 'only be ordered with the consent of the accused'. This was changed in May 2003 to allow the trial to continue without the accused's consent, and in November 2003, a decision was made to proceed with a substitute judge, even though five of the six accused had not consented to this.

Author: Yvonne McDermott.

[413] Article 51(4) states that the Rules and any amendments thereto must be consistent with the Statute. Pursuant to Article 51(5), the Statute shall prevail where there is any conflict between the Statute and the Rules. The primacy of the Statute over any subsidiary instruments was previously noted in *Prosecutor v. Milošević*, ICTY T. Ch., Decision on assigned counsel's motion for withdrawal, Case No IT-02-54-T, 7 December 2004, para. 13, where the ICTY held that:

The Rules and all other applicable instruments, including the Directive and the ICTY Code, are to be read and applied subject to the Statute. That is the natural relationship between an enabling instrument and any other instrument, including Rules, made thereunder – a point not specifically covered in the Statute of the ICTY, but expressly set out in the ICC Statute.

Cross-references:

Article 21.

Rule 3.

Regulation 5.

Doctrine:
1. Yvonne McDermott, "The Admissibility and Weight of Written Witness Testimony in International Criminal Law: A Socio-Legal Analysis", in *Leiden Journal of International Law*, 2013, vol. 27, pp. 971–89.
2. William A. Schabas, *The International Criminal Court: A Commentary on the Rome Statute*, Oxford University Press, Oxford, 2010, pp. 642–49.

Author: Yvonne McDermott.

Article 52
Regulations of the Court[414]

1. The judges shall, in accordance with this Statute and the Rules of Procedure and Evidence, adopt, by an absolute majority, the Regulations of the Court necessary for its routine functioning. [415]

2. The Prosecutor and the Registrar shall be consulted in the elaboration of the Regulations and any amendments thereto.[416]

3. The Regulations and any amendments thereto shall take effect upon adoption unless otherwise decided by the judges. Immediately upon adoption, they shall be circulated to States

---

[414] *General remarks*:

Article 52 entrusts judges with the power to draw up Regulations of the Court 'necessary for its routine functioning'.

Preparatory works:

Early drafts of the Statute distinguished between 'rules of the tribunal' and 'internal rules of the tribunal'. The United States of America proposed the formulation of 'Regulations of the Court' (Schabas, 2010).

Author: Yvonne McDermott.

[415] Pursuant to Article 52(1), the judges shall adopt, by majority, such Regulations as are 'necessary for the routine functioning of the Court'. The Regulations were adopted in 2004, and they cover such matters as broadcasts of Court proceedings (Regulations 20–21); the required content of the document outlining the charges; choice of defence counsel (Regulation 75), and legal aid (Regulation 84).

By far the most controversial Regulation adopted to date has been Regulation 55, which permits the Court to reclassify 'the legal characterisation of facts to accord with the crimes under Articles 6, 7 or 8, or to accord with the form of participation of the accused under Articles 25 and 28.' In *Lubanga*, the status of this rule as 'necessary for the routine functioning of the Court' was challenged, but a request to declare it contrary to Statute and Rules was denied (*Prosecutor v. Lubanga*, Decision on the status before the Trial Chamber of the evidence heard by the Pre-Trial Chamber and the decisions of the Pre-Trial Chamber in trial proceedings, and the manner in which evidence shall be submitted, ICC-01/04-01/06-1084, 13 December 2007).

More controversially, in *Katanga and Chui*, the defendants had initially been charged with co-perpetration as a mode of liability under Article 25(3)(a). In 2012, after the trial proceedings had ended, the Trial Chamber opted to use Regulation 55 to recharacterise Katanga's mode of liability to common purpose liability under Article 25(3)(d)(ii). He was later convicted, while his co-accused was acquitted (*Prosecutor v. Katanga and Chui*, ICC T. Ch., Decision on the Implementation of Regulation 55 of the Regulations of the Court and Severing the Charges against the Accused Persons, ICC-01/04-01/07-3319, 21 November 2012). Regulation 55 has been heavily criticised for its operation in the *Katanga* case and the resultant impact on the ability of the accused to prepare for trial and launch a defence against the charges, given that those charges could change at any time. In this way, it clearly risks jeopardising the right to be informed of the charges under Article 67(1).

Author: Yvonne McDermott.

[416] The Prosecutor and Registrar are to be consulted in the drafting and amendment of the Regulations (Article 52(2)).

Author: Yvonne McDermott.

Parties for comments. If within six months there are no objections from a majority of States Parties, they shall remain in force.[417]

---

[417] Although (unlike the Rules of Procedure and Evidence) drafting of the Regulations is left primarily in the hands of the judges, there is some supervision by the Assembly of States Parties over these Regulations. Article 51(3) notes that amendments shall take effect immediately upon adoption, unless otherwise decided by the judges. Upon adoption, they are to be circulated to States Parties for comments and if there are no objections from a majority of States Parties within six months, they remain in force.

Cross-references:

Articles 21 and 67.

Regulations 4 and 6.

Doctrine:

1. Sophie Rigney, "'The Words Don't Fit You': Recharacterisation of the Charges, Trial Fairness, and *Katanga*", in *Melbourne Journal of International Law*, 2015, vol. 15, pp. 515–33.
2. William A. Schabas, *The International Criminal Court: A Commentary on the Rome Statute*, Oxford University Press, Oxford, 2010, pp. 650–52.
3. Carsten Stahn, "Modification of the Legal Characterization of Facts in the ICC System: A Portrayal of Regulation", in *Criminal Law Forum*, 2005, vol. 55, pp. 1–31.

Author: Yvonne McDermott.

PART 5. INVESTIGATION AND PROSECUTION

Article 53
Initiation of an investigation[418]

---

[418] *General remarks*:

Article 53 ICC Statute becomes relevant once a situation has been triggered, be it on the basis of a referral by the Security Council or a State Party, or on the basis of the proprio motu powers of the Prosecutor. While the title suggests otherwise, Article 53 ICC Statute is not only relevant to the 'initiation of the investigation', but also governs the Prosecutor's decision not to proceed with a prosecution. Furthermore, it provides for the possibility of judicial review of a prosecutorial decision not to proceed and authorises the Prosecutor to review decisions whether to initiate an investigation or prosecution, on the basis of new facts or information.

It seems to follow from the wording of the first sentence of Article 53 that a principle of legality (Legalitätsprinzip) is incumbent on the ICC Prosecutor ('shall [...] initiate an investigation'). This provision seems to be drafted in mandatory terms, ruling out any arbitrary decision making by the Prosecutor regarding the appropriateness of an investigation (consider for example Bergsmo and Kruger, 2008, p. 1068). However, the ICC's procedural design does not offer a conclusive answer to the question whether the Prosecutor is to be guided by a principle of legality or by a principle of opportunity. Rather does the principle that guides the Prosecutor depend on the factors the Prosecutor should consider in deciding whether or not to initiate investigations into a certain situation or in deciding whether or not to prosecute a certain case (Olásolo, 2003, p. 132; Knoops, 2005, p. 377). The ICC Statute provides for at least some discretion and the Prosecutor is not under an obligation to investigate and prosecute all crimes within the Court's jurisdiction (Carsten, 2009, pp. 249 and 257). Such discretion can, for example, be found in Article 13 ICC Statute: 'The Court may exercise its jurisdiction with respect to a crime referred to in Article 5 in accordance with the provisions of this Statute if...'

Provided that Article 53(1) sets forth the factors the Prosecutor should consider in deciding whether or not to open an investigation, it follows that the investigation 'proper' is preceded by a 'pre-investigation phase', which serves the purpose of determining whether or not to proceed with an investigation. Likewise, the existence of a phase immediately preceding the investigation proper follows from the existence, under Article 53(1) of a minimum threshold for the commencement of the investigation proper, as will be discussed below. Furthermore, Article 15(1)(2), (3) and (6) as well as Rules 48 and 104 ICC RPE confirm the existence of such phase. Meanwhile, only Article 15 (6) explicitly refers to the existence of a 'preliminary examination'. The preliminary examination commences once the dormant jurisdiction of the Court is triggered and irrespective of the manner in which the jurisdiction of the Court is triggered: either on the basis of information received on crimes or upon a referral (consider for example ICC, Policy Paper on Preliminary Examinations, 2013, para. 35, 73). Therefore, while the ICC Statute uses the term 'preliminary examination' only if the Prosecutor proceeds on the basis of his or her proprio motu powers, a formal investigation does also not follow automatically in case of a referral. In all instances, the Prosecutor should assess the seriousness of the information received (Rule 104(1) ICC RPE, Article 15(2) ICC Statute). Moreover, irrespective of the triggering mechanism, in assessing whether to proceed with an investigation, the Prosecutor considers the same factors (Article 15(3) ICC Statute, Rule 48 ICC RPE and Article 53(1) ICC Statute; ICC, Policy Paper on Preliminary Examinations, 2013, para. 76). What differs is the procedural presumption (De Meester, Karel *et al.*, 2013, p. 182). With regard to referrals, it follows from the ICC Statute that the Prosecutor 'shall [...] initiate an investigation unless he or she determines that there is no reasonable basis to proceed'. Judicial review by the Pre-Trial Chamber is limited

1. The Prosecutor shall, having evaluated the information made available to him or her, initiate an investigation unless he or she determines that there is no reasonable basis to proceed under this Statute. In deciding whether to initiate an investigation, the Prosecutor shall consider whether:[419]

---

to a determination not to proceed, not of an affirmative decision to proceed (Article 53(1) ICC Statute chapeau and in fine). Hence, in such a case, there is a strong presumption in favour of the finding of a 'reasonable basis', thereby limiting prosecutorial discretion in case of a referral. In contrast, when the Prosecutor assesses information received, the starting point is that there will be no initiation of the investigation: The Prosecutor needs authorisation by the Pre-Trial Chamber to proceed with an investigation (Article 15(3) ICC Statute). It emerges that irrespective of the triggering mechanism, the pre-investigative phase is – at least in theory – almost identical (*Situation in the Republic of Côte d'Ivoire*, ICC PT. Ch. III, ICC-02/11-15-Corr, 5 October 2011, para. 24).

Neither the Statute nor the RPE regulate in detail the method for the conduct of the preliminary examination. However, Rule 104(2) ICC RPE, which details the evaluation of information by the Prosecutor under Article 53(1), provides the Prosecutor with some limited investigative powers (as does Article 15(2) ICC Statute). The Prosecutor may seek additional information from States, organs of the United Nations, intergovernmental or non-governmental organisations, or other reliable sources and he or she may receive written or oral testimony at the seat of the Court. It is stipulated that the procedural rules on the recording of the questioning during the investigation apply *mutatis mutandis* (Rules 47, 104(2), 111 and 112 ICC RPE). Other investigative powers are not mentioned and are only at the Prosecutor's disposal after the start of the investigation proper. Furthermore, no time frame has been included in the ICC Statute for the conduct of the preliminary examination. Nevertheless, Pre-Trial Chamber III held that a 'reasonable time' criterion applies to the preliminary examination of a situation pursuant to Article 53(1) ICC Statute and Rule 104 ICC RPE (*Situation in the Central African Republic*, ICC PT. Ch. III, ICC-01/05-6, 30 November 2006, p. 4). This criterion derives from Rule 105(1) ICC RPE, according to which the Prosecutor should 'promptly' inform in writing the State which referred the situation, when deciding not to commence an investigation. However, "the timing and length of preliminary examination activities will necessarily vary based on the situation". For example, since the preliminary examination process with regard to the situation in Columbia included the monitoring of national proceedings, the preliminary examination process will necessarily be longer. Consequently, some flexibility should be built into the timeframe (OTP, Policy Paper on Preliminary Examinations, 2013, para. 89).

Author: Karel De Meester.

[419]   'reasonable basis to proceed'

It follows from the wording of the chapeau of Article 53 that the threshold to start an investigation is the presence of a 'reasonable basis to proceed'. The same threshold is to be found in Article 15 (3), (4) and (6) ICC Statute and in Rule 48 ICC RPE, with regard to proprio motu investigations. A contextual interpretation clarifies that similar considerations underlie the 'reasonable basis to proceed' standard in Articles 15 and 53. More precisely, it follows from Rule 48 ICC RPE that in determining whether there exists a 'reasonable basis to proceed' under Article 15(3) ICC Statute, 'the Prosecutor shall consider the factors set out in Article 53, paragraph 1 (a) to (c)'.

This was acknowledged by Pre-Trial Chamber II, when it held that it would be illogical to dissociate the 'reasonable basis to proceed' standard in Article 15(3) and Article 53(1) (with respect to the Prosecutor) from the threshold provided for under Article 15(4) ICC Statute (with respect to the Pre-Trial Chamber) (*Situation in the Republic of Kenya*, ICC PT. Ch. II, Decision Pursuant to Article 15 of the Rome Statute on the Authorisation of an Investigation into the Sit-

---

(a) The information available to the Prosecutor provides a reasonable basis to believe that[420] a crime within the jurisdiction of the Court[421] has been or is being committed;[422]

---

uation in the Republic of Kenya, ICC-01/09-19, 31 March 2010, para. 21). The Pre-Trial Chamber emphasised that these standards are used in the same or related Articles and that they share the same purpose: the opening of an investigation (*ibid.*, para. 21). Furthermore, the *travaux préparatoires* reveal that the drafters intended to use the same standard in the different provisions and wanted to establish the link between Article 15 and 53 (*ibid.*, para. 22 – 23). Among other, this is evidenced by the *nota bene* which was included in draft Article 12 ICC Statute ("The terms "sufficient basis" used in this Article (if retained) and "reasonable basis" in Article 54, paragraph 1, should be harmonized" (see Report of the Preparatory Committee on the Establishment of an International Criminal Court, Addendum: Draft Statute for the International Criminal Court and Draft Final Act of the United Nations Diplomatic Conference of Plenipotentiaries on the establishment of an International Criminal Court, UN doc. A/CONF.183/2/Add.1, 14 April 1998, p. 37)).

A contextual interpretation of the 'reasonable basis to proceed' standard further clarifies that the 'reasonable basis to proceed' standard in the chapeau of Article 53(1) requires less certainty than the 'sufficient basis for a prosecution' standard, which is found in Article 53(2) ICC Statute. Likewise, the standard is lower than the 'reasonable grounds to believe' prerequisite for the issuance of a warrant of arrest or the existence of 'substantial grounds to believe' as required for the confirmation of the charges. For the fulfillment of the two latter standards, evidence or information is required that is directed to the individual, rather than to a situation or to events (See Ventura, 2013, p. 67). One commentator refers to "the first step of a stairway which becomes stricter with every step taken towards trial and requires more profound evidence with each level" (Stegmiller, 2008, p. 322; Stegmiller, 2011, p. 253).

With regard to Article 15(4) ICC Statute, ICC Pre-Trial Chamber III observed that the purpose of the 'reasonable basis to proceed' standard lies where it prevents "unwarranted, frivolous, or politically motivated investigations" (*Situation in the Republic of Côte d'Ivoire*, ICC PT. Ch. III, ICC-02/11-14-Corr, 15 November 2011, para. 21). On the basis of the *travaux préparatoires*, it has been argued that the identical standard in Article 53(1) serves the same purpose and was inserted "to prevent any abuse of the process not only by the Prosecutor but also by any of the other triggering parties" (Fernández de Gurmendi, 1999, p. 182).

Cross-references:

Regulation 38

Author: Karel De Meester.

[420] Sub-paragraph(1)(a) is concerned with jurisdiction. On the basis of the parameters included in this first sub-paragraph the ICC Prosecutor decided not to proceed with an investigation in the Venezuela situation and the Palestine situation (ICC, Annex to Update on Communications Received by the Office of the Prosecutor: Venezuela Response, 9 February 2006, p. 4; OTP: Situation in Palestine, 3 April 2012).

In sub-paragraph(1)(a), an additional threshold is included, 'reasonable basis to believe'. It is unclear how the 'reasonable basis to proceed' requirement in the chapeau of Article 53(1) ICC Statute and the 'reasonable basis to believe' threshold under Article 53(1)(a) mutually relate. A textual interpretation of Article 53(1) hints that a 'reasonable basis to proceed' exists once the different criteria of sub-paragraphs (a)–(c) are met. Such understanding has been confirmed by Pre-Trial Chamber II, which held that the 'reasonable basis to believe' test in Article 53(1)(a) is subsumed by the 'reasonable basis to proceed' standard referred to in the opening clause of Article 53(1) of the Statute, since the former is only one element of the latter (*Situation in the Republic of Kenya*, ICC PT. Ch. II, Decision Pursuant to Article 15 of the Rome

Statute on the Authorisation of an Investigation into the Situation in the Republic of Kenya, ICC-01/09-19, 31 March 2010, para. 26). Hence, the 'reasonable basis to proceed' requirement will be met when the requirements under Article 53(1)(a) – (c) ICC Statute are fulfilled. This conclusion is supported by the *travaux préparatoires* (Report of the Preparatory Committee on the Establishment of an International Criminal Court, Addendum: Draft Statute for the International Criminal Court and Draft Final Act of the United Nations Diplomatic Conference of Plenipotentiaries on the establishment of an International Criminal Court, UN doc. A/CONF.183/2/Add.1, 14 April 1998, p. 75). Pre-Trial Chamber II further held that any definition of the 'reasonable basis to believe' standard should reflect "the specific purpose underlying this procedure" (*ibid.*, para. 32, 35). Similar to the purpose of the 'reasonable basis to proceed' threshold in the chapeau of Article 53(1), its purpose is "to prevent the Court from proceeding with unwarranted, frivolous, or politically motivated investigations that could have a negative effect on [the Court's] credibility" (*ibid.*, para. 32). Bearing in mind that this threshold is the lowest to be found in the ICC Statute, "the information available to the Prosecutor does not have to be 'comprehensive' or 'conclusive'" (*ibid.*, para. 27). This is to be understood in light of the limited powers of the Prosecutor, prior to the start of the investigation proper. Furthermore, the Pre-Trial Chamber observed that the ECtHR's 'reasonable suspicion' threshold, upon which the Court's case law relies for the interpretation of the 'reasonable grounds to believe' standard for the issuance of an arrest warrant under Article 58, is not suitable for the interpretation of Article 53(1)(a) ICC Statute. The standard under Article 53(1)(a) "was not designed to determine whether a particular person was involved in the commission of a crime within the jurisdiction of the Court, which may justify his arrest" (*ibid.*, para. 32). Information "need not point towards only one conclusion" (*ibid.*, para. 34). The standard implies that "the Chamber must be satisfied that there is a sensible or reasonable justification for a belief that a crime falling within the Court's jurisdiction 'has been or is being committed'" (*ibid.*, para. 35). However, the Pre-Trial Chamber failed to clarify what the difference between a reasonable basis to proceed in the chapeau of Article 53(1) and a reasonable basis to believe in Article 53(1)(a) actually is. The OTP Draft Regulations defined this standard as necessitating that 'the information available to the Chief Prosecutor contains indications that make it seem possible that crimes within the jurisdiction of the Court have been or are being committed'. This will be the case "if there is a realistic prospect that the investigation will produce evidence that will lead to a prima facie case against the potential accused" or "if there is a clear indication that a person has participated in a crime within the jurisdiction of the Court" (Regulation 12.3 of the Draft Regulations of the OTP, fn. 80). However, this interpretation was not included in the final version of the Regulations of the OTP. See also *Situation in the Republic of Côte d'Ivoire*, Decision Pursuant to Article 15 of the Rome Statute on the Authorisation of an Investigation into the Situation in the Republic of Côte d'Ivoire, 3 October 2011, para. 23.

Author: Karel De Meester.

[421] The following part of the wording of this sub-paragraph ('a crime within the jurisdiction of the Court') does not cause a great deal of difficulty. It implies an examination of all necessary jurisdictional requirements (subject-matter, temporal, personal and territorial) and is devoid of any discretional traits.

Author: Karel De Meester.

[422] The last part of this provision ('has been or is being committed') seems to exclude any basis for proactive investigations by the Court. Proactive investigative efforts precede the commission of the crime. Hence, as an example, the situation when a crime 'is about to be committed' seems excluded from the realm of the provision. Prior to the moment in time when a crime within the jurisdiction of the Court is or is being committed, there is no possibility to proceed to the investigation proper.

(b) The case is or would be admissible under Article 17;[423] and

---

Author: Karel De Meester.

[423] The second sub-paragraph of Article 53(1) refers to admissibility. It encompasses both complementarity and gravity (*Situation in the Republic of Kenya*, ICC PT. Ch. II, Decision Pursuant to Article 15 of the Rome Statute on the Authorisation of an Investigation into the Situation in the Republic of Kenya, ICC-01/09-19, 31 March 2010, para. 52; Situation in the Republic of Côte d'Ivoire, ICC PT. Ch. III, ICC-02/11-14-Corr, 15 November 2011, para. 192 – 206). The admissibility assessment mainly refers to "the scenarios or conditions on the basis of which the court shall refrain from exercising its recognized jurisdiction over a given situation or case" (*Situation in the Republic of Kenya*, ICC PT. Ch. II, Decision Pursuant to Article 15 of the Rome Statute on the Authorisation of an Investigation into the Situation in the Republic of Kenya, ICC-01/09-19, 31 March 2010, para. 40). Under the ICC Statute, admissibility attaches to different stages, starting with a 'situation' up to a concrete 'case' (*ibid.*, para. 41). While the wording of Article 53(1)(b) suggests that the admissibility assessment under this sub-paragraph relates to 'cases', it is evident from a contextual reading that this assessment, in principle, relates to 'situations', rather than specific 'cases' (*ibid.*, paras. 44–46). This interpretation is confirmed by the plain reading of Article 13(a), 14(1), 15(5) and (6) and 18(1) ICC Statute. In particular, the wording of Article 53(1)(b) ICC Statute points to an assessment at a more general level than that of a particular 'case' ('or would be admissible').

Pre-Trial Chamber II offered several explanations for the peculiar wording of Article 53(1)(b) ICC Statute. Firstly, on the basis of the *travaux préparatoires* of the ICC Statute, it appears that 'case' was used in all drafts of Article 17 at the Preparatory Committee. At the Rome conference, there was a 'prevailing trend' to not reopen the 'substance' of the admissibility provisions drafted by the Preparatory Committee. Changing the terminology in Article 53 would have required revisiting the terminology of Article 17; hence, it was left unaltered. However, Pre-Trial Chamber II preferred a different explanation and held that the reference to 'case' was advertently left in all provisions on admissibility, leaving it up to the Court "to harmonize the meaning according to the different stages of the proceedings" (*ibid.*, paras. 46–47). Thus, it is for the Chamber to construe the meaning of a 'case' within the context where it is applied. In doing so, the Pre-Trial Chamber held that since "it is not possible to have a concrete case involving an identified suspect for the purpose of prosecution, prior to the commencement of the investigation, the admissibility assessment at this stage actually refers to the admissibility of one or more potential cases within the context of a situation" (*ibid.*, para. 48; *Situation in the Republic of Côte d'Ivoire*, ICC PT. Ch. III, ICC-02/11-14-Corr, 15 November 2011, para. 190). The "admissibility at the situation phase should be assessed against certain criteria defining a "potential case" such as (i) the groups of persons involved that are likely to be the focus of an investigation for the purpose of shaping the future case(s); and (ii) the crimes within the jurisdiction of the Court allegedly committed during the incidents that are likely to be the focus of an investigation for the purpose of shaping the future case(s)" (*ibid.*, para. 191; *Situation in the Republic of Kenya*, ICC PT. Ch. II, Decision Pursuant to Article 15 of the Rome Statute on the Authorisation of an Investigation into the Situation in the Republic of Kenya, ICC-01/09-19, 31 March 2010, para. 50 and 182). This selection is preliminary and not binding for future admissibility assessments (*ibid.*, para. 50).

Admissibility encompasses the three grounds of inadmissibility under Article 17(1) (complementarity, gravity and *ne bis in idem*), which are exhaustive in nature. At this stage, the admissibility assessment firstly entails "an examination as to whether the relevant State(s) is/are conducting or has/have conducted national proceedings in relation to the groups of persons and the crimes allegedly committed during those incidents, which together would likely form the object of the Court's investigation". Secondly, if the answer to this question is negative, it includes an assessment of whether the gravity threshold is met or not (*ibid.*, para. 52). It is clear that the admissibility determination for the purpose of proceedings relating to the initiation of an investigation (at the 'situation stage') differs from the admissibility determination of a concrete case (at the 'case stage'). At the case stage, the Court's jurisprudence has held that national proceedings must encompass both the same person and the same conduct (specificity test) (consider for example *Lubanga*, ICC PT. Ch. I, ICC-01/04-01/06-20-Anx2, 10 February 2006, para. 37). In contrast, at the moment of the commencement of the investigation into a situation, "the contours of the likely case will often be relatively vague because the investigations of the Prosecutor are at their initial stages" (*William Samoei Ruto, Henry Kiprono Kosgey and Joshua Arap Sang*, ICC A. Ch., ICC-01/09-01/11-307, 30 August 2011, para. 39; *Francis Kirimi Muthaura, Uhuru Muigai Kenyatta and Mohammed Hussein Ali*, ICC A. Ch., ICC-01/09-02/11-274, 30 August 2011, para. 38). "Often, no individual suspects will have been identified at this stage, nor will the exact conduct nor its legal classification be clear" (*ibid.*, para. 38). Overall, the admissibility check is more general in nature and relates to the overall conduct. For example, in its decision authorising a proprio motu investigation in Kenya, Pre-Trial Chamber II concluded that there were no national investigations regarding senior business and political leaders on the serious criminal incidents which are likely to be the focus of the Prosecutor's investigation (*Situation in the Republic of Kenya*, ICC PT. Ch. II, Decision Pursuant to Article 15 of the Rome Statute on the Authorisation of an Investigation into the Situation in the Republic of Kenya, ICC-01/09-19, 31 March 2010, para. 187). In a similar vein, in authorising a proprio motu investigation in the Republic of Côte d'Ivoire, Pre-Trial Chamber III found that Côte d'Ivoire nor any other State having jurisdiction was conducting or had conducted national proceedings against individuals or crimes that are likely to constitute the Court's future case(s) (*Situation in the Republic of Côte d'Ivoire*, ICC PT. Ch. III, ICC-02/11-14-Corr, 15 November 2011, para. 206).

On the basis of the second part of the admissibility assessment, gravity, the Prosecutor decided not to proceed with an investigation into the situation in Iraq and decided not to proceed with an investigation into the situation with respect to the 31 May 2010 Israeli raid on the Humanitarian Aid Flotilla bound for the Gaza Strip (ICC, Annex to Update on Communications Received by the Office of the Prosecutor: Iraq Response, 9 February 2006; ICC, Situation on Registered Vessels of Comoros, Greece and Cambodia, Article 53(1) Report, 6 November 2014). It was also on the basis of this parameter that the LRA, and not the UPDF, was selected for investigation in the situation in Uganda (OTP, Statement by Luis Moreno Ocampo, ICC-OTP-20051014-109, 14 October 2005, p. 3). Also gravity should be assessed in a general sense, on the basis of 'potential cases' (*Situation in the Republic of Kenya*, ICC PT. Ch. II, Decision Pursuant to Article 15 of the Rome Statute on the Authorisation of an Investigation into the Situation in the Republic of Kenya, ICC-01/09-19, 31 March 2010, para. 58; Situation in the Republic of Côte d'Ivoire, ICC PT. Ch. III, ICC-02/11-14-Corr, 15 November 2011, para. 202). Such assessment should be general in nature and compatible with the pre-investigative stage (*ibid.*, para. 203; *Situation in the Republic of Kenya*, ICC PT. Ch. II, Decision Pursuant to Article 15 of the Rome Statute on the Authorisation of an Investigation into the Situation in the Republic of Kenya, ICC-01/09-19, 31 March 2010, para. 60).

According to Pre-Trial Chambers II and III, at the Article 53(1) stage of proceedings, the gravity assessment entails a generic assessment of whether the individuals or groups of persons that are likely to be the object of an investigation capture those who may bear the greatest responsibility for the alleged crimes committed (*ibid.*, para. 60; *Situation in the Republic of Côte d'Ivoire*, ICC PT. Ch. III, ICC-02/11-14-Corr, 15 November 2011, para. 204). Besides, with regard to the crimes committed during the incidents that are likely to be the focus of an investigation for the purpose of future cases, the jurisprudence refers to the interplay between crimes and their context, entailing that the gravity of the crimes will be assessed in the context of the incidents that are likely to be the object of the investigation (*Situation in the Republic of Kenya*,

(c) Taking into account the gravity of the crime and the interests of victims, there are nonetheless substantial reasons to believe that an investigation would not serve the interests of justice.[424]

ICC PT. Ch. II, Decision Pursuant to Article 15 of the Rome Statute on the Authorisation of an Investigation into the Situation in the Republic of Kenya, ICC-01/09-19, 31 March 2010, para. 61). This assessment may include quantitative and qualitative parameters, including factors such as (i) the scale of the alleged crimes (including geographic and temporal intensity), (ii) the nature of the unlawful behaviour or of the crimes allegedly committed, (iii) the means employed for executing the crimes (manner of their commission) and (iv) the impact of the crimes and the harm caused to victims and their families (*ibid.*, para. 62). Also, any aggravating circumstances may be considered (*Situation in the Republic of Côte d'Ivoire*, ICC PT. Ch. III, ICC-02/11-14-Corr, 15 November 2011, para. 204).

Several commentators have suggested that situational gravity in Article 53(1)(b), encompasses a statutory threshold, below which the Court cannot initiate an investigation into a situation. Hence, this term is to be construed strictly legally (consider for example deGuzman, 2009, p. 1403; Stegmiller, 2011, p. 332). It follows that the gravity assessment under Article 53(1) (b) is limited to the question whether the gravity threshold is met, according to clear and pre-set criteria. So construed, it does not allow the Prosecutor to select between different situations (deGuzman, 2009, p. 1432). Nevertheless, the Prosecutor interpreted the gravity consideration in Article 53(1)(b) as allowing it to compare different situations and not to *proprio motu* initiate an investigation into the situation of British war crimes in Iraq (ICC, Annex to Update on Communications Received by the Office of the Prosecutor: Venezuela Response, 9 February 2006, pp. 8–9). Similarly, in deciding to pursue crimes committed by the LRA and not those allegedly committed by government forces in the situation in Uganda, the ICC Prosecutor compared the gravity of the crimes committed (OTP, Statement by Luis Moreno Ocampo, 14 October 2005, p. 3).

Author: Karel De Meester.

[424] While the first two sub-paragraphs of Article 53(1) encompass requirements which should be satisfied for the Prosecutor to proceed with an investigation, sub-paragraph (c) encompasses considerations which may lead the Prosecutor not to proceed with the investigation of a situation. Hence, this sub-paragraph does not require the Prosecutor to determine that the investigation is in the interests of justice in order to proceed with an investigation (*Situation in the Republic of Kenya*, ICC PT. Ch. II, Decision Pursuant to Article 15 of the Rome Statute on the Authorisation of an Investigation into the Situation in the Republic of Kenya, ICC-01/09-19, 31 March 2010, par. 63). Unlike Article 53(1)(a) and (b), which require the application of exacting legal requirements, Article 53(1)(c) ICC Statute leaves discretion with the Prosecutor to open an investigation (*Situation on the Registered Vessels of the Union of the Comoros, the Hellenic Republic and the Kingdom of Cambodia*, ICC PT. Ch. I, ICC-01/13, 16 July 2015, para. 14). The most problematic feature of sub-paragraph (c) is that the term 'interests of justice' has been left undefined. It is unclear as to whether the drafters envisaged a narrower conception of justice (as referring only to 'criminal justice') or a broader one (including 'restorative justice' interests). While this lack of clarity leaves considerable discretion with the Prosecutor, this discretion is not unchecked. The Prosecutor should inform the Pre-Trial Chamber if a decision to not initiate investigations or prosecutions was solely gauged on the 'interests of justice'. Furthermore, arbitrariness is avoided by the condition of 'substantial reasons', which requires the Prosecutor to produce convincing reasons not to open an investigation. The Prosecutor labelled this concept "one of the most complex aspects of the Treaty" (OTP, Policy Paper on the Interests of Justice, ICC-OTP-2007, September 2007, p. 2). It raises difficult issues, such as whether the reliance on

If the Prosecutor determines that there is no reasonable basis to proceed and his or her determination is based solely on subparagraph (c) above, he or she shall inform the Pre-Trial Chamber.[425]

2. If, upon investigation, the Prosecutor concludes that there is not a sufficient basis for a prosecution because:[426]

---

alternative justice mechanisms qualifies as 'unwillingness' in the sense of Article 17 ICC Statute.

The Prosecution's understanding of the 'interests of justice' concept is to be found in its 'Policy Paper on the Interests of Justice' (OTP, Policy Paper on the Interests of Justice, ICC-OTP-2007, September 2007). The Prosecution considers the interests of justice to be a "course of last resort" (*ibid.*, p. 9). The paper emphasises the exceptional nature of the 'interests of justice' criterion but does not engage in a detailed discussion of the factors that underlie it. Nevertheless, it sets out the four main considerations underlying the OTP's interpretation. Firstly, (i) the paper stresses the exceptional nature of the 'interests of justice' criterion and sets out a general presumption in favour of investigations and prosecutions. This implies that there is no precondition that an investigation is in the interests of justice. Besides, (ii) criteria are to be guided by the object and purpose of the ICC Statute (prevention of serious crimes of concern to the international community through ending impunity) and (iii) a distinction should be drawn between 'interests of justice' and 'interests of peace'. Lastly, (iv) the Prosecution is under a duty to notify the Pre-Trial Chamber of any decision not to investigate or prosecute in the interests of justice (*ibid.*, p. 1). The OTP policy paper does not detail all of the factors to be considered when a situation arises, provided that "each situation is different" (*ibid.*, pp. 1, 9).

The OTP's policy paper goes some way in clarifying the meaning of some of the other terms used in Article 53(1)(c) ICC Statute. With regard to the understanding of the 'gravity of the crime' factor, the paper refers (at the situations stage) to the same considerations as with regard to Article 53(1)(b) and 17(1)(d) ICC Statute (to know the scale of the crimes, the nature of the crimes, the manner of their commission and their impact) (*ibid.*, p. 5). This overlap is understandable, insofar that the reference was seemingly only inserted to satisfy the concern of delegations "that the interests underlying the complementarity principle sufficiently permeate the Statute" (Bergsmo and Kruger, 2008, p. 1071; Webb, 2005, p. 327).

Nevertheless, the inclusion of gravity considerations into Article 53(1)(b) would not make much sense if the criterion would be identical to the gravity requirement found in Article 53(1)(c) ICC Statute. The wording of paragraph (c) 'gravity of the crime' suggests that its meaning should be different from sub-paragraph (b). So far, however, the jurisprudence has not addressed the distinction between these two notions.

As far as the 'interests of victims' are concerned, the OTP's policy paper notes that victims have the interest 'to see justice done' but acknowledges that other considerations, such as the safety of witnesses, should be measured in (OTP, Policy Paper on the Interests of Justice, ICC-OTP-2007, September 2007, p. 5). Hence, while this factor will normally weigh in favour of investigation or prosecution, this will not always be the case.

Cross-references:

Rules 104 and 105.

Author: Karel De Meester.

[425] It follows from the last sub-paragraph of Article 53(1) that in case of a decision not to proceed, solely on the basis that continuing with an investigation is not in the interests of justice, the Prosecutor should inform the Chamber of the reasons thereof. He or she shall inform the Pre-Trial Chamber in writing and promptly after taking that decision (Rule 105(4) ICC RPE).

Author: Karel De Meester.

(a) There is not a sufficient legal or factual basis to seek a warrant or summons under Article 58;[427]

(b) The case is inadmissible under Article 17;[428] or

---

[426] The second paragraph of Article 53 concerns the situation where the Prosecutor, on the basis of information and evidence gathered during the investigation, decides whether or not there is a 'sufficient basis' to continue with a prosecution. The evaluation under Article 53(2) resembles the evaluation under Article 53(1). Like Article 53(1), the test for prosecution consists of three prongs. It follows from Regulation 29(5) of the Regulations of the OTP that in selecting potential cases for prosecution within a situation, the Prosecution will *mutatis mutandis* apply the same steps as for the selection of situations and will analyse issues of jurisdiction, admissibility (including gravity) and the interests of justice. This is not to say that there are no differences between the two paragraphs. Overall, the parameters which are found in paragraph (2) are stricter than those for the commencement of an investigation. At this stage, the contours of the likely cases will have been shaped further. The threshold of 'a sufficient basis for a prosecution' is stricter than the 'reasonable basis to proceed' threshold in Article 53(1). The threshold differs from the 'reasonable basis' test in Article 53(1) ICC Statute, insofar that it applies at a different stage. It follows from the *travaux préparatoires* that such different formulation was a deliberate choice (United Nations Diplomatic Conference of Plenipotentiaries on the establishment of an International Criminal Court, Rome, UN doc. A/CONF.183/13 (Vol. III), 15 June–17 July 1998, p. 292: "in Article 54, the words "reasonable basis" and "sufficient basis" are used intentionally in different paragraphs"). The threshold has not yet been further defined in the jurisprudence. The negative formulation of the standard under Article 53(2) ('If, upon investigation, the Prosecutor concludes that there is not a sufficient basis for a prosecution') betrays that it is presumed that one or more prosecutions will follow from an investigation into a situation.
Cross-references:
Regulation 38.
Author: Karel De Meester.

[427] Rather than requiring a 'reasonable basis to believe', Article 53(2)(a) ICC Statute refers to a stricter 'sufficient basis to seek a warrant or summons under Article 58' as the threshold for proceeding with a prosecution. It is recalled that the standard for the issuance of a warrant of arrest or a summons to appear, 'reasonable grounds to believe that the person has committed a crime within the jurisdiction of the court', has been equated by the Court's case law with the 'reasonable suspicion' standard, which can be traced back to Article 5(1)(c) ECHR (*Prosecutor v. Lubanga*, ICC PT. Ch. I, ICC-01/04-01/06, 10 February 2006, par. 12 (annexed to *Prosecutor v. Lubanga*, ICC PT. Ch. I, ICC-01/04-01/06-8, 24 February 2006)).
Author: Karel De Meester.

[428] Likewise, the consideration of admissibility under Article 53(2)(a) is more specific in nature than under Article 53(1)(b) ('the case is or would be admissible'). Pre-Trial Chamber II confirmed that while the admissibility check at the situation stage encompasses 'potential cases', "the test is more specific when it comes to an admissibility determination at the 'case' stage" (*Prosecutor v. William Samoei Ruto, Henry Kiprono Kosgey and Joshua Arap Sang*, ICC PT. Ch. II, ICC-01/09-01/11-101, 30 May 2011, para. 54; *Prosecutor v. Francis Kirimi Muthaura, Uhuru Muigai Kenyatta and Mohammed Hussein Ali*, ICC PT. Ch. II, ICC-01/09-02/11-96, 30 May 2011, para. 50). Nevertheless, although Article 53(2) is concerned with specific cases, it follows from the Court's case law that the 'case' stage only "starts with an application by the Prosecutor under Article 58 of the Statute for the issuance of a warrant of arrest or summons to appear, where one or more suspects has or have been identified" (*ibid.*, para. 50; *Prosecutor v. William Samoei Ruto, Henry Kiprono Kosgey and Joshua Arap Sang*, ICC PT. Ch. II, ICC-

(c) A prosecution is not in the interests of justice, taking into account all the circumstances, including the gravity of the crime, the interests of victims and the age or infirmity of the alleged perpetrator, and his or her role in the alleged crime;[429]

01/09-01/11-101, 30 May 2011, para. 54). That said, it is not clear why a case only exists with the 'Article 58 stage' of proceedings. It is recalled that Pre-Trial Chamber I defined a 'case' in Lubanga as including "specific incidents during which one or more crimes within the jurisdiction of the Court seem to have been committed by one or more identified suspects" (*Situation in the DRC*, ICC PT. Ch. I, ICC-01/04-101, 17 January 2006, para. 65; *Prosecutor v. Lubanga*, ICC PT. Ch. I, ICC-01/04-01/06-20-Anx2, PT. Ch. I, 10 February 2006, para. 21). Individuals will most likely already be the focus of investigations before the issuance of a warrant of arrest or a summons to appear (Safferling, 2012, p. 94 (arguing that the situation becomes a case somewhere between the identification of individuals and the decision to prosecute a case); Stegmiller, 2011, pp. 119 – 120, 419). Because of this apparent inconsistency, it has been suggested to introduce an additional distinction between 'cases in a narrower sense' and 'cases in a broader sense'. This entails that a case sensu stricto only exists after the issuance of a warrant or summons. However, a case considered in the broader sense (or 'case hypothesis') exists already earlier during investigations (*ibid.*, p. 419).

With regard to the admissibility determination at the 'case' stage, the Appeals Chamber determined that a case 'being investigated' must cover the same individual and substantially the same conduct as alleged in the proceedings before the Court (*Prosecutor v. Francis Kirimi Muthaura, Uhuru Muigai Kenyatta and Mohammed Hussein Ali*, ICC A. Ch., ICC-01/09-02/11-274, 30 August 2011, para. 39; *Prosecutor v. William Samoei Ruto, Henry Kiprono Kosgey and Joshua Arap Sang*, ICC A. Ch., ICC-01/09-01/11-307, 30 August 2011, para. 40). The test was first adopted by Pre-Trial Chamber I in the Lubanga case (ICC, *Prosecutor v. Lubanga*, ICC PT. Ch., ICC-01/04-01/06-20-Anx2, 10 February 2006, para. 37; see also *Prosecutor v. Harun and Kushayb*, ICC PT. Ch. I, ICC-02-05-01/07, 27 April 2007, paras. 24–25). While, for the reasons explained above, it remains uncertain whether the admissibility determination at the 'case' stage also applies at the Article 53(2) stage, the test will in any case be stricter than under Article 53(1)(b).

Author: Karel De Meester.

[429] Finally, also the formulation of the 'interests of justice' requirement differs slightly from the formulation in Article 53(1)(c). In line with Article 53(1), discretion regarding what cases to prosecute mainly enters through the consideration of this requirement (See for example Turone, 2002, p. 1173). The 'interests of justice' criterion in Article 53(2)(c) is formulated broader than Article 53(1)(c). From the formulation 'taking into consideration all circumstances' clearly follows the non-exhaustive nature of the enumeration of factors to be considered. Criteria expressly listed are:(1) the gravity of the crime, (2) the interests of victims, (3) the age or the infirmity of the alleged perpetrator and (4) his or her role in the alleged crime. These two latter criteria, which refer to the particular circumstances of the accused, are not included under Article 53(1)(c) given that, at that stage, the accused will often not be known yet. With regard to these 'particular circumstances of the accused' (Article 53(2)(c) ICC Statute), the OTP's strategy is to focus on those bearing the greatest degree of responsibility, and to consider factors including "the alleged status or hierarchical level of the accused or alleged implication in particularly serious or notorious crimes", or "the significance of the role of the accused in the overall commission of the crimes and the degree of the accused's involvement" (OTP, Policy Paper on the Interests of Justice, ICC-OTP-2007, September 2007, p. 7). In some instances however, these 'particular circumstances of the accused' will prevent the accused from being prosecuted; for example, if the accused were to be terminally ill or if a suspect is the victim of serious human rights abuses (*ibid.*, p. 7). Furthermore, depending on the facts of the case or the situation under

---

the Prosecutor shall inform the Pre-Trial Chamber and the State making a referral under article 14 or the Security Council in a case under Article 13, paragraph (b), of his or her conclusion and the reasons for the conclusion.

(a) At the request of the State making a referral under Article 14 or the Security Council under Article 13, paragraph (b), the Pre-Trial Chamber may review a decision of the Prosecutor under paragraph 1 or 2 not to proceed and may request the Prosecutor to reconsider that decision.

(b) In addition, the Pre-Trial Chamber may, on its own initiative, review a decision of the Prosecutor not to proceed if it is based solely on paragraph 1 (c) or 2 (c). In such a case, the decision of the Prosecutor shall be effective only if confirmed by the Pre-Trial Chamber.[430]

---

consideration, the Prosecutor's strategy is to also consider (i) other justice mechanisms and (ii) peace processes (*ibid.*, pp. 7–9).

Cross-references:

Rule 106.

Author: Karel De Meester.

[430] Sub-paragraph (3) includes an important check, in the form of judicial control, over prosecutorial discretion. Two scenarios are included. Firstly, (a) in case of a referral, the Pre-Trial Chamber may review the Prosecutor's decision to not proceed with an investigation or prosecution. The Pre-Trial Chamber may do so upon request by the referring State or the Security Council within 90 days following notification of the decision (Rule 107(1) ICC RPE). On this basis, Pre-Trial Chamber I reviewed the Prosecutor's decision not to initiate an investigation in the situation with respect to the 31 May 2010 Israeli raid on the Humanitarian Aid Flotilla bound for the Gaza Strip (*Situation on the Registered Vessels of the Union of the Comoros, the Hellenic Republic and the Kingdom of Cambodia*, ICC PT. Ch. I, ICC-01/13, 16 July 2015). The Pre-Trial Chamber clarified that its power under Article 53(3)(a) differs fundamentally from the competence it possesses pursuant to Article 15 ICC Statute – which serves as a check on the powers of an independent prosecutor – in that it presupposes the existence of a disagreement between the Prosecutor and the referring entity. Hence, the review is limited to the parameters of the disagreement and does not imply a review de novo of the Prosecutor's assessment pursuant to Article 53(1)(a) ICC Statute (*ibid.*, para. 9–10). Secondly, if a decision not to proceed is solely based on the interests of justice, the Pre-Trial Chamber may itself review a decision to not proceed within 180 days following notification (Rule 109 ICC RPE).

This review mechanism presupposes that the referring State or the Security Council (53(3)(a)) or the Pre-Trial Chamber (53(3)(b)) be informed of any prosecutorial decision taken to not investigate or to not prosecute. In this respect, a duty of notification has been included in Rules 105 and 106 ICC RPE respectively. It is in the discretionary nature of this review obligation ('the Pre-Trial Chamber may review') that potentially lays its most important limitation. No obligation is incumbent on the Pre-Trial Chamber to act upon a request. To meaningfully exercise its task, the Pre-Trial Chamber may request the Prosecutor to transmit the necessary information or documents in his or her possession or the summaries thereof. In case the Pre-Trial Chamber decides to exercise its review function upon a request by the referring State or the Security Council (Article 53(3)(a)), this power is provided for under Rule 107(2) and (3) ICC RPE. If the Prosecutor exercises its power to proprio motu review a decision by the Prosecutor not to proceed, Regulation 48(1) of the Regulations of the Court encompasses the Pre-Trial Chamber's power to 'request the Prosecutor to provide specific or additional information or documents in his or her possession, or summaries thereof, that the Pre-Trial Chamber considers necessary in order to exercise the functions and responsibilities set forth in Article 53(3)(b)'.

However, the existence of such a power, in the absence of any express decision not to proceed, has occasionally been contested by the Prosecutor. In the Uganda situation, Pre-Trial Chamber II convened a status conference in order to seek further information from the Prosecutor confirming that the Prosecution did not intend to further investigate past crimes and that the investigation was nearing completion (*Situation in Uganda*, ICC PT. Ch. II, ICC-02/04-01/05-68, 2 December 2005, paras. 8–9). The Prosecution subsequently denied that a decision not to prosecute further crimes had been taken (*Situation in Uganda*, ICC PT. Ch. II, ICC-02/04-01/05-76, 11 January 2006, para. 8). Whenever the Pre-Trial Chamber requests additional information from the Prosecutor, it should take measures to protect the documents and the safety of the victims, witnesses and family members (Rule 107(3) ICC RPE and Regulation 48(2) of the Regulations of the Court).

In the scenario of a request for review by a State or by the Security Council, the Pre-Trial Chamber may either confirm the decision by the Prosecutor or request the reconsideration of that determination, an obligation which the Prosecutor should fulfil as soon as possible. The Pre-Trial Chamber will request the Prosecutor to reconsider the decision "if it concludes that the validity of the decision is materially affected by an error, whether it is an error of procedure, an error of law, or an error of fact" (*Situation on the Registered Vessels of the Union of the Comoros, the Hellenic Republic and the Kingdom of Cambodia*, ICC PT. Ch. I, ICC-01/13, 16 July 2015, para. 12). Nothing prevents the Prosecutor from reaching the same conclusion upon reconsideration. While Article 53(3)(a) only speaks of referrals, nothing seems to prevent the information provider (other than a State Party or the Security Council) from filing a motion to the Chamber prospecting the reasons for which a judicial review on its own initiative could be desirable and practicable (Turone, 2002, p. 1158).

If a negative decision is solely based on Article 53(1)(c) or Article 53(2)(c) the Prosecution's decision may only become effective if the Pre-Trial Chamber confirms it. It follows that the Pre-Trial Chamber's revision may lead to a judicial order to investigate or prosecute ('shall') (Rule 110(2) ICC RPE). Such a possibility is known to some civil law jurisdictions. However, the term 'investigation on judicial command' only makes sense in case of a notitia criminis referred by another source. Besides, the possibility of an investigation on judicial command may be problematic insofar that nothing prevents the Prosecutor from conducting a "perfunctory and superficial" investigation (Schabas, 2007, p. 245).

Some commentators have suggested there exists a duty to review the Prosecutor's decision ("In order to be valid such decisions must be confirmed by the PTC") (Bergsmo and Kruger, 2008, p. 1075). Others have interpreted this provision as implying that the decision not to proceed with an investigation or prosecution only becomes effective if the Pre-Trial Chamber reviews the Prosecutor's decision (Razesberger, 2006, p. 108; Wouters *et al.*, 2008, pp. 297, 302). However, a textual interpretation suggests that judicial review is not a prerequisite for the Prosecutor's decision to be effective in case a decision not to proceed is solely based on the 'interests of justice'. Logically, the second sentence of paragraph (b) of Article 53(3) ICC Statute ('[i]n such a case') refers to the situation outlined in the previous sentence, and leaves discretion to the Pre-Trial Chamber whether or not to review such a decision. Overall, however, the structure of Article 53(3) suggests that closer scrutiny is provided for in case of a decision not to investigate or prosecute, solely based on the interests of justice.

In the *Situation in the DRC*, the Prosecutor submitted that no decision not to proceed against Mr. Bemba on the basis of 'the interests of justice' with respect to crimes allegedly committed in Ituri had been taken. Hence, Pre-Trial Chamber I concluded that there was no basis for it to exercise its review powers under Article 53(3)(b) (*Situation in the DRC*, ICC PT. Ch. I, Decision on the request of the legal representative of victims VPRS 3 and VPRS 6 to review an alleged decision of the Prosecutor not to proceed, ICC-01/04-582, 25 October 2010, p. 4).

4. The Prosecutor may, at any time, reconsider a decision whether to initiate an investigation or prosecution based on new facts or information.[431]

Cross-references:
Rules 107, 108, 109 and 110.
Regulation 38.
Author: Karel De Meester.

[431] Pursuant to final sub-paragraph Article 53(4), the Prosecutor possesses the discretionary power to review a decision not to proceed. The consequence of this provision is that, based on 'new facts or information', a referral may 'at any time' be reactivated. For that purpose, the Prosecutor will first reactivate the preliminary examination. For example, the ICC Prosecutor has reopened the preliminary examination in the situation in Iraq on the basis of new information. This entails that the Prosecutor will reconsider, in light of the new information, whether the criteria under Article 53(1) ICC Statute for initiating an investigation are met (OTP Press Release: Prosecutor of the International Criminal Court, Fatou Bensouda, reopens the preliminary examination of the situation in Iraq, 13 May 2014).

Cross-references:
Rule 92.

Doctrine:

1. Morten Bergsmo and Pieter Kruger, "Article 53", in Otto Triffterer (ed.), *Commentary on the Rome Statute of the International Criminal Court: Observers' Notes, Article by Article*, 2nd ed., C.H. Beck/Hart/Nomos, Munich/Oxford/Baden-Baden, 2008, pp. 1065–76.

2. Karel De Meester, Kelly Pitcher, Rod Rastan and Göran Sluiter, "Investigation, Coercive Measures, Arrest and Surrender", in Göran Sluiter, Håkan Friman, Suzannah Linton, Sergey Vasiliev and Salvatore Zappalà (eds.), *International Criminal Procedure: Principles and Rules*, Oxford University Press, Oxford, 2013, pp. 171–380, 182.

3. Margaret M. deGuzman, "Gravity and the Legitimacy of the International Criminal Court", in *Fordham International Law Journal*, 2009, vol. 32, pp. 1403, 1432.

4. Silvia A. Fernández de Gurmendi, "The Role of the International Prosecutor", in Roy S. Lee (ed.), T*he International Criminal Court: The Making of the Rome Statute, Issues, Negotiations, Results*, Kluwer Law International, The Hague, 1999, p. 182.

5. Geert-Jan Alexander Knoops, "Challenging the Legitimacy of Initiating Contemporary International Criminal Proceedings: Rethinking Prosecutorial Discretionary Powers from a Legal, Ethical and Political Perspective", in *Criminal Law Forum*, 2005, vol. 15, p. 377.

6. Héctor Olásolo, "The Prosecutor of the ICC before the Initiation of Investigations: a Quasi-Judicial or Political Body?", in *International Criminal Law Review*, 2003, vol. 3, p. 132.

7. Florian Razesberger, *The International Criminal Court: The Principle of Complementarity*, Peter Lang, Frankfurt am Main, 2006, p. 108.

8. Christopher Safferling, *International Criminal Procedure*, Oxford University Press, Oxford, 2012, p. 94.

9. William A. Schabas, *An Introduction to the International Criminal Court*, 3rd ed., Cambridge University Press, Cambridge, 2007, p. 245.

10. Carsten Stahn, "Judicial Review of Prosecutorial Discretion: Five Years on", in Carsten Stahn and Göran Sluiter (eds.), *The Emerging Practice of the International Criminal Court*, Koninklijke Brill, Leiden, 2009, pp. 247–79; 249, 257.

11. Ignaz Stegmiller, *The Pre-Investigation Stage of the ICC*, Duncker and Humblot GmbH, Berlin, 2011, pp. 119–20; 253, 332, 419.

12. Ignaz Stegmiller, "The Pre-Investigation Stage of the ICTY and the ICC Compared", in Thomas Kreussmann (ed.), *ICTY: Towards a Fair Trial?*, Neuer Wissenschaftlicher Verlag, Wien, 2008, p. 311–40.

13. Giuliano Turone, "Powers and Duties of the Prosecutor", in Antonio Cassese, Paola Gaeta and John R.W.D. Jones (eds.), *The Rome Statute of the International Criminal Court: A Commentary*, Oxford University Press, Oxford, 2002, pp. 1137–80; 1158, 1173.

14. Manuel J. Ventura, "The 'Reasonable Basis to Proceed' Threshold in the Kenya and Côte d'Ivoire Proprio Motu Investigation Decisions: The International Criminal Court's Lowest Evidentiary Standard?", in *The Law and Practice of International Courts and Tribunals*, 2013, vol. 12, p. 67.

15. Philippa Webb, "The ICC Prosecutor's Discretion not to Proceed in the 'Interests of Justice'", in *Criminal Law Quarterly*, 2005, vol. 50, p. 327.

16. Jan Wouters, Sten Verhoeven and Bruno Demeyere, "The International Criminal Court's Office of the Prosecutor: Navigating between Independence and Accountability?", in *International Criminal Law Review*, 2008, vol. 8, pp. 297, 302.

Author: Karel De Meester.

Article 54

Duties and powers of the Prosecutor with respect to investigations[432]

1. The Prosecutor shall:

    (a) In order to establish the truth, extend the investigation to cover all facts and evidence relevant to an assessment of whether there is criminal responsibility under this Statute, and, in doing so, investigate incriminating and exonerating circumstances equally;[433]

---

[432] *General remarks*:

Article 54 is the general provision detailing the duties and powers of the Prosecutor in the conduct of investigations. These duties and powers are relevant to the investigation 'proper', which follows the preliminary examination and the initiation of the investigation under Article 53(1) ICC Statute. The duties incumbent on the Prosecutor are outlined in the first paragraph of Article 54 ('The Prosecutor shall'), whereas the powers are outlined in paragraphs 2 and 3 ('The Prosecutor may').

Author: Karel De Meester.

[433] The first sub-paragraph of Article 54 posits the central objective of the Prosecutor's investigative efforts, namely 'to establish the truth'. Therefore, and notwithstanding the more adversarial design of proceedings before the Court, the Prosecutor should not solely collect evidence with the aim of securing a conviction. Moreover, it follows from the first sub-paragraph of Article 54(1) that all investigative activities should be directed towards the identification of evidence that can eventually be presented in open court (*Prosecutor v. Lubanga Dyilo*, ICC A. Ch., ICC-01/04-01/06-1486 (OA 13), 21 October 2008, para. 41).

In placing an obligation on the Prosecutor to 'investigate incriminating and exonerating circumstances equally', the ICC Statute departs from how the Prosecutor's role is conceived at the *ad hoc* tribunals. This principle of objectivity entails that the Prosecutor is expected to act as an 'officer of justice', rather than as a partisan actor. Although the jurisprudence of the *ad hoc* tribunals, the SCSL or the STL has also occasionally referred to the Prosecutor's role in terms of an 'organ of justice', this falls short of an active duty incumbent on the Prosecutor to go out and gather exonerating evidence, over and above the disclosure obligations that pertain to (potentially) exonerating information and evidence in the Prosecution's possession (compare *Prosecutor v. Kupreškić et al.*, ICTY T. Ch. II, 21 September 1998, p. 3; *Prosecutor v. Barayagwiza*, ICTR A. Ch., Separate Opinion of Judge Shahabuddeen, paras. 67–68; *Prosecutor v. Sesay*, SCSL President, 20 February 2006, para. 30; (Case No. CH/PTJ/2009/06), STL PT. J., Order Regarding the Detention of Persons Detained in Lebanon in Connection with the Case of the Attack against Prime Minister Rafiq Hariri and Others, 29 April 2009, para. 25). This principle of objectivity is typically associated with civil law criminal justice systems. It was included in the Statute "to build a bridge between the adversarial common law approach to the role of the Prosecutor and the role of the Investigating Judge in certain civil law systems" (Bergsmo and Kruger, 2008, p. 1078). It has also been incorporated in Article 49 (b) and (c) of the Code of Conduct for the Office of the Prosecutor.

The Prosecution has understood its duty to investigate into potentially exonerating information and evidence to be a 'continuous' and 'simultaneous' process. Therefore, the search for such information or evidence is not the task of a separate investigative team. In the event that the Prosecutor encounters potentially exonerating information by questioning witnesses, the Prosecution will actively pursue such leads and try to identify new witnesses and evidence (*Prosecutor v. Katanga and Ngudjolo Chui*, ICC T. Ch. II, 01/04-01/07-T-81, 25 November 2009, pp. 16–17, 34). The principle of objectivity may not always be easy to reconcile with the more adversarial nature of proceedings before the Court. A certain tension exists between the role of the Prosecutor in pursuing criminal conduct on the one hand, and to act as an officer of justice on the other hand. The difficulties for the Prosecutor to effectively realise a non-partisan attitude in the conduct of the investigation came to the front in a number of cases before the Court. In *Mbarushimana*, for example, the Prosecution was reprimanded by Pre-Trial Chamber II, which found the confrontational questioning methods used by some investigators to be inappropriate in light of their duty of objectivity and held that such techniques may significantly weaken the probative value of evidence so obtained (*Prosecutor v. Mbarushimana*, ICC PT. Ch. II, Decision on the Confirmation of Charges, ICC-01/04-01/10-465-Red, 16 December 2011, para. 51). More precisely, the Pre-Trial Chamber held that: "[t]he reader of the transcripts of interviews [of insider witnesses] is repeatedly left with the impression that the investigator is so attached to his or her theory or assumption that he or she does not refrain from putting questions in leading terms and from showing resentment, impatience or disappointment whenever the witness replies in terms which are not entirely in line with his or her expectations. Suggesting that the witness may not be "really remembering exactly what was said", complaining about having "to milk out" from the witness details which are of relevance to the investigation, lamenting that the witness does not "really understand what is important" to the investigators in the case, or hinting at the fact that the witness may be "trying to cover" for the suspect, seem hardly reconcilable with a professional and impartial technique of witness questioning" (*ibid.*, para. 51). Reference may also be made to the reliance, in the Prosecutor's investigation into the situation in the DRC, on an intermediary who previously worked for the Congolese intelligence services and who was assisted by at least one other person who, at the time being, was employed by the Congolese intelligence services. The intermediary ('P-0316') testified that he had always remained loyal to his government (*Prosecutor v. Lubanga*, ICC T. Ch. I, ICC-01/04-01/06-2842, 14 March 2012, para. 367). The Trial Chamber raised its concern "that the prosecution used an individual as an intermediary with such close ties to the government that had originally referred the situation in the DRC to the Court" (*ibid.*, para. 368).

Another feature often associated with a Prosecutor bound by a principle of objectivity, to know the possibility for the Defence to request the Prosecutor to conduct certain investigative actions, is not provided for under the ICC Statute. However, it seems that the Prosecution is willing to entertain such requests (*Prosecutor v. Katanga and Ngudjolo Chui*, ICC T. Ch. II, 01/04-01/07-T-81, 25 November 2009, p. 72).

In the *Lubanga* case, the Appeals Chamber clarified that the obligation 'to establish the truth' is not limited to the period of time prior to the confirmation of charges (*Prosecutor v. Lubanga*, ICC A. Ch., ICC-01/04-01/06-568 (OA 3), 13 October 2006, para. 52). In Kenyatta, Trial Chamber V interpreted (Judge Chile Eboe-Osuji dissenting on this point) the prosecutorial duties to 'establish the truth' and to 'extend the investigation to cover all facts and evidence relevant to an assessment of whether there is criminal responsibility under this Statute, and, in doing so, investigate incriminating and exonerating circumstances equally' under Article 54(1)(a) as imposing an obligation to properly investigate the case against the accused prior to confirmation. These obligations entail that "[t]he Prosecutor is not responsible for establishing the truth only at the trial stage by presenting a complete evidentiary record, but is also expected to present a reliable version of events at the confirmation hearing". Therefore, "[t]he Prosecutor should not seek to have the charges against a suspect confirmed before having conducted a full and thorough investigation in order to have a sufficient overview of the evidence available and the theory of the case" (*Prosecutor v. Uhuru Muigai Kenyatta*, ICC T. Ch. V, ICC-01/09-02/11-728, 26 April 2013, para. 119). *In casu*, the Trial Chamber was concerned about "the considerable volume of evidence collected by the Prosecution post-confirmation" (*ibid.*, para. 118). According to the Trial Chamber, the possibility to continue investigations post-confirmation "is not an unlimited prerogative" (*ibid.*, para. 119). This is in line with the holding of the Appeals

(b) Take appropriate measures to ensure the effective investigation and prosecution of crimes within the jurisdiction of the Court, and in doing so, respect the interests and personal circumstances of victims and witnesses, including age, gender as defined in Article 7, paragraph 3, and health, and take into account the nature of the crime, in particular where it involves sexual violence, gender violence or violence against children;[434] and

---

Chamber in the Mbarushimana case that the Prosecutor should largely have completed the investigations prior to the confirmation hearing (*Prosecutor v. Mbarushimana*, ICC A. Ch., ICC-01/04-01/10-514 (OA 4), 30 May 2012, para. 44; consider also *Prosecutor v. Lubanga*, ICC A. Ch., ICC-01/04-01/06-568 (OA 3), 13 October 2006, para. 54: "ideally, it would be desirable for the investigation to be complete by the time of the confirmation hearing"). While this does not prohibit the Prosecutor from conducting investigations post-confirmation in exceptional circumstances, for example when it concerns evidence the Prosecutor could not have obtained prior to confirmation "with reasonable diligence", the Prosecution should not continue with gathering evidence it could reasonably have been expected to have collected prior to confirmation (*Prosecutor v. Uhuru Muigai Kenyatta*, ICC T. Ch. V, ICC-01/09-02/11-728, 26 April 2013, para. 121). Moreover, post confirmation hearing investigations should be finished as soon as possible (*Prosecutor v. Abakaer Nourain and Jerbo Jamus*, ICC T. Ch. IV, ICC-02/05-03/09-158, 6 June 2011, para. 13).

The underlying problem is the silence of the ICC Statute on the temporal limitation of the investigation phase. There is no requirement in the Statute for the Prosecutor to have all investigations concluded before the confirmation of charges. The risks inherent in allowing the Prosecutor to continue with investigations post-confirmation were explained by Judge Kaul in his dissenting opinion to the Decision on the Confirmation of Charges in *Muthaura, Muigai Kenyatta and Hussein Ali*. He referred to "the possibility, if not the risk, that [the] limited permission of post-confirmation investigations in practice might be too broadly interpreted by the Prosecutor, possibly as some kind of license to investigate whenever, even after confirmation, thus enabling the Prosecutor also to allow a phased approach for the gathering of evidence" (*Prosecutor v. Francis Kirimi Muthaura, Uhuru Muigai Kenyatta and Mohammed Hussein Ali*, ICC, PT. Ch. II, ICC-01/09-02/11-382-Red, 23 January 2012, Dissenting Opinion by Judge Hans-Peter Kaul, para. 56; *Prosecutor v. William Samoei Ruto, Henry Kiprono Kosgey and Joshua Arap Sang*, ICC PT. Ch. II, ICC-01/09-01/11-373, 23 January 2012, Dissenting Opinion by Judge Hans-Peter Kaul, para. 51).

Author: Karel De Meester.

[434] Sub-paragraph (b) of the first paragraph provides the Prosecutor with the authority to determine the measures he or she considers 'appropriate'. Clearly, this provision is to be read together with the Prosecutor's obligation 'to establish the truth' which is found under sub-paragraph (a) (Bergsmo and Kruger, 2008, p. 1078). Unlike sub-paragraph (a), sub-paragraph (b) concerns both the 'investigation' and the 'prosecution'. The second part of the sentence expressly charges the Prosecutor with respecting the interests and personal circumstances of victims and witnesses. Several of such personal circumstances are included, such as age, gender, and the nature of the crime. Reference is also made to sexual violence, gender violence and violence against children. Article 54(1)(b) is not to be interpreted as to require the prior consent of a parent or guardian for the testimony of a child (*Prosecutor v. Katanga and Ngudjolo Chui*, ICC PT. Ch. I, ICC-01/04-01/07-717, 30 September 2008, paras. 144–48).

The Prosecution's understanding of its obligation to ensure 'effective investigation and prosecution' under Article 54(1)(b) is further detailed in Article 51 of the Prosecutor's Code of Conduct.

Author: Karel De Meester.

(c) Fully respect the rights of persons arising under this Statute.[435]

2. The Prosecutor may conduct investigations on the territory of a State:

(a) In accordance with the provisions of Part 9; or

(b) As authorized by the Pre-Trial Chamber under Article 57, paragraph 3 (d).[436]

---

[435] Finally, under paragraph(1), the Prosecutor is to respect the rights of all persons under the ICC Statute. In the Kenyatta case, Trial Chamber V found that the Prosecutor failed to fully respect the rights of persons under the Statute, insofar as it failed to conduct a full and thorough investigation of the case against the accused during its pre-confirmation investigation (*Prosecutor v. Uhuru Muigai Kenyatta*, Case No. ICC-01/09-02/11-728, T. Ch. V, 26 April 2013, para. 123; and the Concurring Opinion of Judge Christine Van den Wyngaert, para. 5). Likewise, Article 54(1)(c) will be breached in case confidentiality agreements concluded by the Prosecution under Article 54(3)(e) prevent it from honouring its disclosure obligations under Article 67(2) ICC Statute and Rule 77 of the RPE (*Prosecutor v. Lubanga*, ICC A. Ch., ICC-01/04-01/06-1486 (OA 13), 21 October 2008, paras. 42–43).

Author: Karel De Meester.

[436] The second paragraph of Article 54 sets out the requirements for the Prosecutor to conduct investigations directly on the territory of a State. The importance of this possibility for the Prosecutor to independently gather evidence on the territory of States is easily understood. Nevertheless, both limbs of this paragraph put significant limitations on the ability of the Prosecutor to gather evidence and information autonomously and independently on the territory of States. Article 54(2) of the Statute only allows the Prosecutor to conduct onsite investigations in two scenarios, to know 'in accordance with Part 9' or 'under Article 57, paragraph 3 (d)'. Firstly, Article 99(1) of the ICC Statute on the execution of requests for assistance provides for the general rule that the Prosecutor will have to ensure cooperation of the State concerned and that a request for assistance will be sent to the requested State. This provision allows the requested State to determine whether or not the Prosecutor can be present and assist in the execution of the investigative act on its territory. An exception is provided for under Article 99(4), which allows the Prosecutor to exceptionally execute such requests directly on the territory of a State. However, this course of action is limited to situations where it is 'without prejudice to other Articles in Part 9', where it 'is necessary for the successful execution of a request', and where the request 'can be executed without any compulsory measures'. Several examples of such non-compulsory measures are provided for: the interview of or taking evidence from a person on a voluntary basis and the examination without modification of a public site or other public place. It is clear that the above requirements substantially limit the prospects for the Prosecutor to conduct onsite investigations. For example, Article 99(4) does not allow the Prosecutor to conduct search and seizure operations directly on the territory of a State, because these operations qualify as coercive measures. This contrasts with the jurisprudence of the *ad hoc* tribunals, which allows for the direct enforcement of coercive acts on the territory of States, without directing a request for legal assistance to the national authorities concerned. For example, an ICTY Trial Chamber held in the Kordić and Čerkez case that the execution of coercive measures by the Prosecutor, encompassing the taking of enforcement action, directly on the territory of Bosnia Herzegovina, was "perfectly within the powers of the Prosecution provided for in the Statute" (*Prosecutor v. Kordić and Čerkez*, ICTY T. Ch. III, 25 June 1999, p. 6; consider also *Prosecutor v. Kordić and Čerkez* (Case No. IT-95-14/2), ICTY T. Ch. III, Transcript, 31 May 1999, pp. 2975 – 3045; *Prosecutor Naletilić and Martinović*, ICTY A. Ch., 3 May 2006, para. 238).

The second limb allows for the conduct of investigative acts directly on the territory of a State, when this has been authorised by the Pre-Trial Chamber under Article 57(3)(d). However, this avenue is limited to 'failed State' scenarios. Prior to authorising the conduct of investiga-

3. The Prosecutor may:[437]

   (a) Collect and examine evidence;[438]

   (b) Request the presence of and question persons being investigated, victims and witnesses;[439]

---

tions directly under Article 57(3)(d), the Pre-Trial Chamber should determine that 'the State is clearly unable to execute a request for cooperation due to the unavailability of any authority or any component of its judicial system competent to execute the request for cooperation under Part 9'. In contrast to Article 99(4), under Article 57(3)(d) the Pre-Trial Chamber may authorise the Prosecutor to execute coercive measures directly on the territory of a State. In such a case, the discharge of the Court's mandate and effective prosecution justify the power of the Prosecutor to exercise onsite investigations including forcible measures (Sluiter, 2002, p. 309; Guariglia *et al.*, 2008, pp. 1128–1129).

Author: Karel De Meester.

[437] The third paragraph of Article 54 contains six sub-paragraphs. They detail the necessary powers for the Prosecutor to fulfil its responsibility, under Article 42(1) ICC Statute, to conduct investigations as well as the measures he or she can take to guarantee their efficacy.

Author: Karel De Meester.

[438] The power to 'collect and examine evidence' is broadly formulated. It may include a wide array of possible investigative measures. Nevertheless, these powers should be understood in light of the limitations under paragraph 2 to the possibility for the Prosecutor to directly execute investigative acts on the territory of States.

Author: Karel De Meester.

[439] Under sub-paragraph (b), the Prosecutor is allowed to 'request the presence of and question persons being investigated, victims and witnesses' in the course of the investigation. It follows from the wording of Article 54(3)(b) ('request the presence') that this prosecutorial power is limited to taking statements on a voluntary basis. Hence, it does not offer a basis for a witness to be compelled to be interviewed by the Prosecutor in the course of the investigation. While the ICTY and the ICTR Prosecutor also lack the power to compel an unwilling party to submit to a pre-trial interview, the Trial Chamber may subpoena an unwilling person to attend at a nominated place and time in order to be interviewed (Consider for example *Prosecutor v. Krksić*, ICTY A. Ch., 30 July 2003, para. 15; *Prosecutor v. Krstić*, ICTY A. Ch., 1 July 2003, paras. 10, 17 (Judge Shahabuddeen dissenting); *Prosecutor v. Halilović*, ICTY A. Ch., 21 June 2004, para. 5). Trial Chamber I held that Article 54(3)(a) does not provide a basis for the substantive preparation of witnesses prior to trial (*Prosecutor v. Lubanga*, ICC T. Ch. I, ICC-01/04-01/06-1049, 30 November 2007, para. 36).

   A detailed regulation on the recording of suspect interviews and of interviews with victims and witnesses is laid down in Rules 112 and 111 of the ICC RPE respectively. Pursuant to Article 93(1)(b) and (c) of the ICC Statute, States Parties are under an obligation to comply with requests from the ICC to provide assistance to the taking of evidence, including testimony under oath and to the questioning of persons investigated or prosecuted. In such a case, Article 99(1) ICC Statute leaves broad discretion for the Prosecution to participate in the questioning of the suspect or accused person by the requested State. Moreover, in case this is necessary for the successful execution of the request and where the suspect participates in the interview on a voluntary basis, the Prosecutor may him or herself interview a suspect on the territory of a State party without further state assistance. The power of the Prosecutor to receive written or oral testimony at the seat of the Court in the course of the preliminary examination, is provided for under Article 15(2) ICC Statute and Rule 104(2) ICC RPE.

Author: Karel De Meester.

(c) Seek the cooperation of any State or intergovernmental organization or arrangement in accordance with its respective competence and/or mandate;[440]

(d) Enter into such arrangements or agreements, not inconsistent with this Statute, as may be necessary to facilitate the cooperation of a State, intergovernmental organization or person;[441]

(e) Agree not to disclose, at any stage of the proceedings, documents or information that the Prosecutor obtains on the condition of confidentiality and solely for the purpose of generating new evidence, unless the provider of the information consents;[442] and

---

[440] Article 54(3)(c) vests the Prosecutor with the necessary power to seek cooperation from States and other international actors.

Author: Karel De Meester.

[441] Additionally, the Prosecutor may '[e]nter into such arrangements or agreements, not inconsistent with this Statute, as may be necessary to facilitate the cooperation of a State, intergovernmental organization or person' (Article 54(3)(d)). This allows States Parties to supplement and go beyond their obligations under Part 9 and for States and international actors to cooperate with the Prosecutor on a voluntary basis. On this basis, the Office of the Prosecutor has concluded agreements with a number of States, including arrangements of modalities for the conduct of operations in territories where the Office of the Prosecutor is carrying out its investigative activities (see Report of the International Criminal Court for 2005–2006, UN doc. A/61/217, 3 August 2006, para. 52; OTP, Report on the Activities Performed During the first three Years (June 2003 – June 2006), 12 September 2006, p. 5). Within the Office of the Prosecutor, the Jurisdiction, Complementarity and Cooperation Division is charged with building a network for international cooperation, while the Investigation Division is responsible for the implementation (OTP, Strategic plan June 2012–2015, 11 October 2013, pp. 6, 16). It follows from Regulation 107(2) of the Regulations of the Court that the Prosecutor has to inform the Presidency of any arrangement or agreement it intends to negotiate, except when this would be 'inappropriate for reasons of confidentiality'. Moreover, according to Regulation 107(1), the Prosecutor's does not have the authority to negotiate arrangements or agreements with a State not party or any international organisation, when these set out a framework regarding matters which fall within the competency of more than one organ of the Court. In such a case, it is only for the President to conclude such agreements.

Cross-references:

Regulation 107.

Author: Karel De Meester.

[442] More controversial then is Article 54(3)(e), which allows the Prosecutor to conclude confidentiality agreements and to '[a]gree not to disclose, at any stage of the proceedings, documents or information that the Prosecutor obtains on the condition of confidentiality and solely for the purpose of generating new evidence, unless the provider of the information consents'. The provision is to be read together with Rule 82 of the RPE. Among others, it prevents the Prosecutor from subsequently introducing materials or information received under Article 54(3)(e) into evidence without the prior consent of the provider of the material or information and adequate prior disclosure to the accused. It is clear that such arrangements or agreements constitute an exception to the Prosecutor's disclosure obligations. When the Prosecutor accepts material on the condition of confidentiality pursuant to Article 54(3)(e), this may create tensions with the Prosecutor's disclosure obligations. The Prosecutor may be caught in a position where he either is unable to disclose materials he has to disclose, or breaches the agreement with the information provider (*Prosecutor v. Lubanga*, ICC A. Ch., Judgment on the appeal of the Prosecutor against the decision of Trial Chamber I entitled "Decision on the consequences of non-disclosure of ex-

---

culpatory materials covered by Article 54(3)(e) agreements and the application to stay the prosecution of the accused, together with certain other issues raised at the Status Conference on 10 June 2008", ICC-01/04-01/06-1486 (OA 13), 21 October 2008, para. 43).

In its investigations into the DRC situation, the Prosecutor made broad use of confidentiality agreements pursuant to Article 54 (3) (e) ICC Statute (around fifty percent of the documents gathered in the DRC: see *Prosecutor v. Lubanga*, ICC T. Ch. I, ICC-01/04-01/06-T52, 1 October 2007, p. 13). This posed challenges to the conduct of several cases before the Court, including the Lubanga case, the Katanga and Ndgujolo case as well as the Ntaganda case. This even led the Trial Chamber to stay the proceedings in Lubanga after the Prosecutor appeared unable to disclose more than 200 documents containing potentially exculpatory materials or information that is potentially material to the preparation of the Defence (*Prosecutor v. Lubanga*, ICC T. Ch. I, Decision on the consequences of non-disclosure of exculpatory materials covered by Article 54(3)(e) agreements and the application to stay the prosecution of the accused, together with certain other issues raised at the Status Conference on 10 June 2008, ICC-01/04-01/06-1401, 13 June 2008). The Prosecutor was unable to disclose these documents to the Defence because they were received on condition of confidentiality and the information providers did not subsequently agree to have confidentiality lifted. The Prosecutor was also unable to supply the majority of these documents to the Trial Chamber, while others were only supplied in redacted form. Most of this confidential information had been obtained from the United Nations. These materials included evidence that tended to suggest that the accused had acted in self-defence, that he was acting under duress or compulsion, that he had made efforts to demobilise child soldiers and that he had insufficient control over the persons who allegedly perpetrated the crimes he was charged for (*ibid.*, para. 22). The Appeals Chamber held that it follows from a textual and a contextual interpretation of Article 54(3)(e) that this provision may only be used for the purpose of generating new evidence (*Prosecutor v. Lubanga*, ICC A. Ch., Judgment on the appeal of the Prosecutor against the decision of Trial Chamber I entitled "Decision on the consequences of non-disclosure of exculpatory materials covered by Article 54(3)(e) agreements and the application to stay the prosecution of the accused, together with certain other issues raised at the Status Conference on 10 June 2008", ICC-01/04-01/06-1486 (OA 13), 21 October 2008, paras. 41, 55; consider also *Prosecutor v. Lubanga*, ICC T. Ch. I, Decision on the consequences of non-disclosure of exculpatory materials covered by Article 54(3)(e) agreements and the application to stay the prosecution of the accused, together with certain other issues raised at the Status Conference on 10 June 2008, ICC-01/04-01/06-1401, 13 June 2008, paras. 71–72). It can only be used as a stepping stone for gathering further evidence. Hence, "whenever the Prosecutor relies on Article 54(3)(e) of the Statute he must bear in mind his obligations under the Statute and apply that provision in a manner that will allow the Court to resolve the potential tension between the confidentiality to which the Prosecutor has agreed and the requirements of a fair trial" (*Prosecutor v. Lubanga*, ICC A. Ch., Judgment on the appeal of the Prosecutor against the decision of Trial Chamber I entitled "Decision on the consequences of non-disclosure of exculpatory materials covered by Article 54(3)(e) agreements and the application to stay the prosecution of the accused, together with certain other issues raised at the Status Conference on 10 June 2008", ICC-01/04-01/06-1486 (OA 13), 21 October 2008, paras. 44, 55). In particular, the Appeals Chamber expressed its concern that at the time the material was accepted, the Prosecutor agreed that he would also not disclose the materials to the Chambers, thereby preventing the Chamber from assessing whether a fair trial was still possible notwithstanding the non-disclosure of certain documents. The final assessment whether or not material gathered pursuant to Article 54(3)(e) has to be disclosed pursuant to Article 67(2) ICC Statute, had it not been obtained on the condition of confidentiality, will have to be carried out by the Trial Chamber. Therefore, the Trial Chamber should receive the material (*ibid.*, para. 2).

(f) Take necessary measures, or request that necessary measures be taken, to ensure the confidentiality of information, the protection of any person or the preservation of evidence.[443]

Whenever a conflict arises between the Prosecutor's disclosure obligations under Article 67(2) and Article 54(3)(e) the Trial Chamber has to respect the confidentiality agreement concluded by the Prosecutor and cannot order disclosure without first obtaining the prior consent by the information provider (Article 64(6)(c) ICC Statute; Rule 81(3) ICC RPE). Rather will the Chamber have to decide whether the Prosecutor would have had to disclose the material, had it not been obtained under a confidentiality arrangement. If this is the case, the Prosecutor should seek the consent of the information provider. If the provider still does not consent to disclosure, it is for the Trial Chamber to determine whether, and which counter-balancing measures can be taken to ensure that the rights of the accused are protected and the trial is fair (*ibid.*, par 48). The Appeals Chamber held that, "in particular if only small numbers of documents are concerned", the tension between confidentiality and the right to a fair trial may be resolved by other means, such as identifying new, similar exculpatory material, providing the material in summarised form, stipulating the relevant facts, or amending or withdrawing the charges (*ibid.*, paras. 44 and 28; consider also, for example, *Prosecutor v. Ntaganda*, ICC PT. Ch. II, ICC-01/04-02/06-247, 6 February 2014, paras. 14–15; *Prosecutor v. Abakaer Nourain and Jerbo Jamus*, ICC T. Ch. IV, ICC-02/05-03/09-442-Red2, 21 June 2013, para. 12).

From the foregoing, it follows that the Prosecutor should "conduct itself with extreme care" in relying on Article 54(3)(e) (*Prosecutor v. Katanga and Ngudjolo Chui*, PT. Ch. I, Decision on Article 54(3)(e) Documents Identified as Potentially Exculpatory or Otherwise Material for the Defence's Preparation for the Confirmation Hearing, ICC-01/04-01/07-621, 20 June 2008, paras. 36, 38–39). The Prosecutor has since October 2006 sought to reduce its extensive reliance on confidentiality agreements under Article 54(3)(e) ICC Statute to gather evidence (see *ibid.*, para. 51; OTP, Prosecutorial Strategy 2009 – 2012, 1 February 2010, para. 34 (b)).

Cross-references:

Rule 82.

Author: Karel De Meester.

[443] The final sub-paragraph of Article 54(3) sets forth the prosecutorial power to '[t]ake necessary measures, or request that necessary measures be taken, to ensure the confidentiality of information, the protection of any person or the preservation of evidence'. The latter part of this sentence reflects the need to preserve evidence, which is also found in Rule 10 ICC RPE. This Rule details the Prosecutor's responsibility for the retention, storage and security of information or evidence obtained in the course of investigations by his or her Office. The need to preserve evidence is also reflected by several other provisions of the ICC Statute, including Article 56 (on 'unique investigative opportunities' to gather evidence), Article 18(6) (on the possibility for the Prosecutor to request the Pre-Trial Chamber 'on an exceptional basis' to authorise it to take investigative steps when the Prosecutor has deferred an investigation or pending a preliminary ruling on admissibility), or Article 19(8) (on the necessity to preserve evidence pending a ruling on admissibility or on jurisdiction).

The power to take measures 'to ensure the confidentiality of information' is the corollary of the Prosecutor's power to conclude confidentiality agreements pursuant to Article 54(3)(e) and ensures its efficacy. From Rule 81(3) ICC RPE, which deals with disclosure, it follows that in case steps to ensure the confidentiality of information have been taken pursuant to Article 54, this information will not be disclosed, except in accordance with Article 54. Moreover, according to the first part of Rule 81(4) the Chamber should, proprio motu or at the request of the Prosecutor, the accused or any State, take the necessary steps to ensure the confidentiality of information, in accordance with Article 54. Finally, as far as measures for the 'the protection of any person' are concerned, it is clear from the wording ('any person') that it aims at protecting "anyone put at risk by the investigations of the Prosecutor" (*Prosecutor v. Katanga*, ICC A. Ch., ICC-01/04-01/07-475, A. Ch., 13 May 2008, para. 44). In turn, this provision is complemented by the second part of the aforementioned Rule 81(4) ICC RPE, which authorises the Pre-Trial Chamber to restrict disclosure and take the necessary steps to protect the safety of witnesses and victims and members of their families. While this provision seems more restrictive than Article 54(3)(f), the Appeals Chamber held (Judge Pikis dissenting) that Rule 81(4) ICC PRE should, when read together with Article 54(3)(f), be understood as to also allow restrictions on disclosure for the protection of "other persons at risk on account of the activities of the Court" (*ibid.*, paras. 55 – 56). Furthermore, the Appeals Chamber held (Judge Pikis and Judge Nsereko dissenting), that no prosecutorial power to preventively relocate witnesses can be deduced from Article 54(3)(f) ICC Statute in isolation. Rather should this provision be read in light of the Statute as a whole, which assigns the responsibility to provide protective measures to victims and witnesses specifically to the Victims and Witnesses United within the Registry (*Prosecutor v. Katanga and Ngudjolo Chui*, ICC A. Ch., ICC-01/04-01/07-776 (OA7), 26 November 2008, paras. 69 – 80). The Appeals Chamber added, obiter dictum, that it interprets Article 54(3)(f) (and Article 68(1)) as to ensure "that the Prosecutor takes general measures that ordinarily might be expected to arise on a day-to-day basis during the course of an investigation or prosecution with the aim of preventing harm from occurring to victims and witnesses". These measures may include "meeting witnesses in discrete locations rather than in public and keeping their identities confidential" (*ibid.*, para. 98).

Doctrine:

1. Morten Bergsmo and Pieter Kruger, "Article 54", in Otto Triffterer (ed.), *Commentary on the Rome Statute of the International Criminal Court: Observers' Notes, Article by Article*, 2nd ed., C.H. Beck/Hart/Nomos, Munich/Oxford/Baden-Baden, 2008, pp. 1077–87.

2. Fabricio Guariglia and Gudrun Hochmayr "Article 57", in Otto Triffterer (ed.), *Commentary on the Rome Statute of the International Criminal Court: Observers' Notes, Article by Article*, 2nd ed., C.H. Beck/Hart/Nomos, Munich/Oxford/Baden-Baden, 2008, pp. 1128–29.

3. Göran Sluiter, *International Criminal Adjudication and the Collection of Evidence*, Intersentia, Antwerp, 2002, p. 309.

Author: Karel De Meester.

Article 55

Rights of persons during an investigation[444]

---

[444] *General remarks*:

Article 55 complements Article 67(1) on rights of the accused during the trial by already guaranteeing certain rights during investigation. While all rights contained in Article 67(1) apply only to accused, Article 55 is not limited to those suspected of having committed crimes, but also includes, in its paragraph(1), some rights granted to all persons during an investigation, that is, particularly also to victims and witnesses (on rights of witnesses and suspects not expressly recognised in Article Article 55, see Hall, 1999, p. 734; Hall, 2008, pp. 1104–1105; and Zappalà, 2002, p. 1196).

Article 55 binds not only organs of the Court, but also state authorities conducting investigative steps under their obligation to cooperate with the court – this is explicitly stated in the chapeau of paragraph (2), but must also be true for the rights under paragraph(1) if this provision is to be effective in deterring violations (Hall, 1999, p. 729; and Hall, 2008, p. 1093). Additional procedural rules concerning questioning of suspects and others are contained in rules 111–113 of the Rules of Procedure and Evidence (RPE).

As an example of the ICC practice, regarding the initial Darfur investigation, Pre-Trial Chamber III referred to individuals being interviewed in Khartoum under Article 55 of the ICC Statute. The initial cooperation received from the Government of Sudan was interrupted after arrest warrants were issued against President Al Bashir (*Prosecutor v. Al Bashir*, ICC PT. Ch. II, Prosecution's request for a finding of non-compliance against the Republic of the Sudan in the case of The Prosecutor v. Omar Hassan Ahmad AL BASHIR pursuant to Article 87 (7) of the Rome Statute, ICC-02/05-01/09-219, 19 December 2014, para. 23).

In *Blé Goudé*, the defence did not argue that alleged violations were a violation of the rights of the suspect under Article 55 or a breach of other rights which may be attributed to the ICC. Accordingly, it was determined that "absent any involvement of the Court, chambers cannot proceed to make determinations of violations of the rights of a suspect while detained on the territory of a State and, therefore, such violations may not be invoked in order to halt proceedings before this Court" (*Prosecutor v. Blé Goudé*, ICC PT. Ch. I, Decision on Second Defence Request for State Party Cooperation, ICC-02/11-02/11-85, 17 June 2014, para. 12). Not every violation of Article 55 would *per se* cause that the ICC be required to decline to exercise its jurisdiction but only "violations that would amount, by themselves or in combination with other circumstances, to an abuse of process" (*Prosecutor v. Gbagbo*, ICC PT. Ch. I, Decision on the "Corrigendum of the challenge to the jurisdiction of the International Criminal Court on the basis of Articles 12(3), 19(2), 21(3), 55 an d 59 of the Rome Statute filed by the Defence for President Gbagbo (ICC- 02/11-01/11-129)", ICC-02/11-01/11-212, 15 August 2012, para. 93). If the alleged infringement is not a mere breach of Article 55 but is in itself extremely significant, it may warrant a permanent stay of proceedings (*ibid.*, paras. 93–94).

The ICC's practice has mainly so far indicated the reluctance of the ICC to act as a supervisor of national legislation and practice, which involves not only human rights of the defendant but also the principle of complementarity (see Sluiter, 2009, p. 474). Paying attention to some alleged flawed interpretation and application of two provisions fundamental for the protection of human rights in the pre-trial phase, namely, Articles 21(3) and 59 of the ICC Statute, it has been suggested that the ICC should "strengthen its grip on national activities which are an indispensable and inextricable part of the ICC proceedings" (*ibid.*, p. 475).

Preparatory works:

The text proposed by the Working Group at the 1993 session of the International Law Commission, which contained a single paragraph on the suspect's rights, was adopted in the Commis-

1. In respect of an investigation under this Statute, a person:[445]

---

sion's final version in 1994. In the Preparatory Committee, the most important issues were related to expansion of the guarantees proposed by the International Law Commission. In turn, during the Rome Conference, the provisions concerning the suspect's rights became a single Article as they were separated from the omnibus provision on investigation and the text was substantially reworked. A Working Paper, which was distributed during the first week of the Rome Conference, changed the title of the provision. This provision contained two paragraphs each with several sub-paragraphs and, thus, resembled the final text of Article 55, except for the inversed order of the two paragraphs. The final text adopted by the Working Group and then the Committee of the Whole was substantially reworked by the Drafting Committee that changed both the title and the order of the main paragraphs (see Schabas, 2010, pp. 684–685).

Cross-references:

Article 67(1), Rules 111–113.

Authors: Juan Pablo Pérez-León-Acevedo and Björn Elberling.

[445] Article 55(1) contains certain rights granted to all persons during an investigation. As stated above, it binds not only organs of the Court, but also state authorities cooperating with the court. This safeguards procedural uniformity and should be broadly interpreted to include interviewers of peacekeeping operations and international organizations (see De Meester *et al.*, 2013, p. 23; and Hall, 2008, p. 1097). Thus, the RPE and the case law suggest that the rights of all persons should be respected independently from who is conducting the investigation. Accordingly, rule 111(2) of the RPE requires that "[w]hen the Prosecutor or national authorities question a person, due regard shall be given to Article 55". In turn, in *Lubanga*, the Trial Chamber determined that a witness's right to privacy is an internationally recognised human right applicable to investigations undertaken by national authorities (*Prosecutor v. Lubanga*, ICC T. Ch. I, Decision on the Confirmation of Charges, ICC-01/04-01/06-803-tEN, 29 January 2007, paras. 62–90. See also Alamuddin, 2010, pp. 235–236).

With regard to the scope of application of Article 55(1), Pre-Trial Chamber I interpreted the expression applicable "[i]n respect of an investigation under this Statute" as encompassing "any investigative steps that are taken either by the Prosecutor or by national authorities at his or her behest" and, thus, an investigation conducted by an entity other than the Prosecutor and not related to the proceedings at the ICC "does not trigger the rights under Article 55 of the Statute" (*Prosecutor v. Gbagbo*, ICC PT. Ch. I, Decision on the "Corrigendum of the challenge to the jurisdiction of the International Criminal Court on the basis of Articles 12(3), 19(2), 21(3), 55 an d 59 of the Rome Statute filed by the Defence for President Gbagbo (ICC-02/11-01/11-129)", ICC-02/11-01/11-212, 15 August 2012, para. 96). In *Gbagbo*, it was stated that Article 55(1) was inapplicable as violations thereof were committed neither by the Prosecutor nor by the Ivorian authorities on behalf of the Prosecutor or any ICC organ. There was no relevant evidence indicating that the adoption of measures by the Ivorian authorities was on behalf of the ICC Prosecutor and, thus, the defence allegations were found to be purely speculative in nature (*ibid.*, paras. 97–98).

There is no express provision that persons have to be informed of their rights under Article 55(1), such information is, however, probably required in the interest of fairness (see Hall, 1999, p. 729; and Hall, 2008, p. 1093). Indeed, in practice, non-suspects are routinely informed of their rights by the ICC investigators (ICC Office of the Prosecutor (OTP) Regulations, regulation 40; *Prosecutor v. Katanga and Ngudjolo Chui*, ICC OTP, Prosecution's Observations regarding Admission for the Confirmation Hearing of the Transcripts of Interview of Deceased Witness 12 pursuant to Articles 61 and 69 of the Statute, ICC-01/04-01/07-336, 20 March 2008, para. 21. See also Alamuddin, 2010, p. 234). Additional procedural rules concerning questionings are contained in rules 111–113.

(a)   Shall not be compelled to incriminate himself or herself or to confess guilt;

Article 55(1)(a) contains the right against self-incrimination, based on Article 14(3)(g) of the ICCPR. Contrary to the equivalent right to silence of suspects (Article Article 55(1)(b)) and accused (Article 67(1)(g)), Article 55(1) does not contain a right to silence, showing that, for example, witnesses may not generally refuse to answer questions if the answer is not (potentially) self-incriminating. When evaluating whether the right against self-incrimination was violated, the European Court of Human Rights ('ECtHR') has considered the following factors: i) nature and degree of coercion employed to obtain the evidence; ii) the weight of the public interest in the specific investigation and punishment of the crime; iii) the existence of any relevant procedural safeguards; and iv) the use given to any material so obtained (*Jalloh v. Germany*, (Application No. 548100/00), Judgment, 11 July 2007, para. 105. See also Schabas, 2010, pp. 686–687).

Article 55(1)(b) contains the prohibition of torture and other forms of coercive treatment. The prohibition of "duress" particularly may not be unlimited – forcing a witness to testify before the court or before national authorities may well put that person in duress, especially if he or she fears repercussions from supporters of the accused, nonetheless it is hard to imagine that the court would find such an obligation to be in violation of Article 55 (cf. Hall, 1999, pp. 729–730; and Hall, 2008, p. 1094). The main aim of this provision is seemingly to protect individuals during an investigation conducted by state authorities who assist the ICC Prosecutor's investigation (see Hall, 1999, p. 730; and Hall, 2008, p. 1094).

Paragraph(1)(c) of Article 55 contains the right to translation and interpretation. The wording of this provision, including the manners in which it goes beyond human rights provisions, is largely identical to Article 67(1)(f) and for details see commentary thereto. At this point, it is however mentioned that the Appeals Chamber considered that the word "fully" refers to the intent to "raise the standard of understanding to higher than plain understanding", which consists in a level higher "than simply a language the accused understands or speaks" (*Prosecutor v. Katanga and Ngudjolo Chui*, ICC A. Ch., Judgment on the appeal of Mr. Germain Katanga against the decision of Pre-Trial Chamber I entitled "Decision on the Defence Request Concerning Languages", ICC–01/04–01/07–522, 27 May 2008, paras. 56 and 57). Thus, translation into a person's native language is not required as far as he/she fully understands the language being employed (see Hall, 2008, p. 1095).

Finally, paragraph(1)(d) sets limits to acceptable deprivations of liberty in connection with Court proceedings. It largely mirrors the language of Article 9(1) of the ICCPR. The fact that it not only refers to arrest or detention, but also to deprivation of liberty generally, shows that also limited restrictions on freedom of movement, such as, for example, house arrest or the duty to attend court proceedings, must be in conformity with the Statute (for a criticism of the unclear wording "on such grounds and in accordance with such procedures", see Zappalà, 2002, pp. 1197–1198). The prohibition in the first part of this paragraph is independent of the one contained in the second part and this paragraph should be jointly read with Article 85(1) which reads as follows: "[a]nyone who has been the victim of unlawful arrest or detention shall have an enforceable right to compensation" (see also Hall, 2008, p. 1096). Thus, there "should be some mechanism of redress in case of violations" (Zappalà, 2010, p. 140). In *Bemba*, the Appeals Chamber recalled that every person "has the right to effectively contest the deprivation of liberty" (*Prosecutor v. Bemba*, A. Ch., Judgment on the appeal of Mr. Jean–Pierre Bemba Gombo against the decision of Pre–Trial Chamber III entitled "Decision on application for interim release", ICC–01/05–01/08–323, 16 December 2008, para. 31).

Cross–references:

Articles 67(1) and 85(1), Rule 111, OTP Regulation 40.

Authors: Juan Pablo Pérez-León-Acevedo and Björn Elberling.

(b) Shall not be subjected to any form of coercion, duress or threat, to torture or to any other form of cruel, inhuman or degrading treatment or punishment;

(c) Shall, if questioned in a language other than a language the person fully understands and speaks, have, free of any cost, the assistance of a competent interpreter and such translations as are necessary to meet the requirements of fairness; and

(d) Shall not be subjected to arbitrary arrest or detention, and shall not be deprived of his or her liberty except on such grounds and in accordance with such procedures as are established in this Statute.

2. Where there are grounds to believe that a person has committed a crime within the jurisdiction of the Court and that person is about to be questioned either by the Prosecutor, or by national authorities pursuant to a request made under Part 9, that person shall also have the following rights of which he or she shall be informed prior to being questioned:

(a) To be informed, prior to being questioned, that there are grounds to believe that he or she has committed a crime within the jurisdiction of the Court;

(b) To remain silent, without such silence being a consideration in the determination of guilt or innocence;

(c) To have legal assistance of the person's choosing, or, if the person does not have legal assistance, to have legal assistance assigned to him or her, in any case where the interests of justice so require, and without payment by the person in any such case if the person does not have sufficient means to pay for it; and

(d) To be questioned in the presence of counsel unless the person has voluntarily waived his or her right to counsel.[446]

---

[446] Article 55(2) contains certain rights granted to suspects, that is, persons of whom "there are grounds to believe that [they have] committed a crime within the jurisdiction of the Court", being questioned by the prosecution or by national authorities cooperating with the Court (the term suspect is not used in the Statute, see Zappalà, 2002, pp. 1195–1196 and 1200). The provision in principle applies to those suspected of having committed crimes referenced in Article 5, rather than offences under Article 70, as shown by the reference to a "crime" as well as to state cooperation under part 9 of the Statute (cf. Article 70(2) on cooperation in proceedings concerning Article 70 offences). However, it is foreseeable that the court will find that most or all of these rights also apply to Article 70-suspects under general international law. Indeed, as seen below, for example, the ICC found that the right to legal aid (Article 55(1)(c)) applies to both crimes and offences (*Prosecutor v. Bemba et al.*, ICC T. Ch. VII, Decision on the Defence applications for judicial review of the decision of the Registrar on the allocation of resources during the trial phase, ICC-01/05-01/13-955, 21 May 2015, para. 35).

The application of Article 55(2) constitutes the most remarkable distinction between the suspect and a witness as it provides the former with certain specific rights such as the right to be informed of being a suspect, the right to remain silent, the right to have legal assistance and be questioned in presence of his or her counsel (see De Meester *et al.*, 2013, p. 233).

With regard to the steps adopted by the ICC organs to put Article 55(2) into practice, *Ntaganda* may be mentioned as an example. As part of the investigation, the ICC Prosecution met persons who had rights under Article 55(2) which include the right to have the interviews audio and/or video recorded. Then, the Prosecutor prepared transcripts of these interviews, which were time intensive and generally ran on average up to 10–15 hours each. Even though the disclosure obligation solely concerns the original form of the interview (the audio-video recording), the Prosecutor prepared and disclosed the interview transcript as an assistance mechanism to review the material (*Prosecutor v. Ntaganda*, ICC PT Ch. II, Prosecution's Urgent Request to Postpone the Date of the Confirmation Hearing, ICC-01/04-02/06-65, 23 May 2013, para. 18).

Those individuals who are subject to a warrant of arrest or a summons to appear, not yet surrendered to the ICC, "enjoy rights guaranteed elsewhere in the Statute, such as the rights relating to investigations (Article 55(2))" (*Prosecutor v. Mbarushimana*, ICC PT. Ch. I, Decision on the Defence Request for an Order to Preserve the Impartiality of the Proceedings, ICC-01/04-01/10-51, 31 January 2011, para. 8, fn. 15).

Paragraph (2)(a) grants the person the right to be informed prior to questioning of his or her status as a suspect. Such information is necessary in order to allow the person to adequately exercise the other rights under Article 55(2) which attach to this status. The "grounds to believe" is an objective test which facilitates its enforcement (see Schabas, 2010, p. 688). Under regulation 41(2) of the Regulations of the OTP, should information conveyed during the interview of a witness raise grounds to believe that the witness in question has committed a crime(s) within the ICC jurisdiction, he/she shall immediately be informed of his or her rights under Article 55(2). In the ICC Prosecutor's practice, "screening interviews" precede interviews and aim *inter alia* to establish whether the interviewee is a suspect (*Prosecutor v. Katanga and Ngudjolo Chui*, ICC T. Ch. II, Transcripts, ICC-01/04-01/07-T-81, 25 November 2009, p. 11. See also De Meester *et al.*, 2013, p. 233). Concerning how a confirmation hearing in absentia may potentially affect Article 55(2)(a), former ICC Judge Ekaterina Trendafilova has considered it as not conflicting with the "right to be properly informed of the charge", which "is made clear by a number of provisions" (Trendafilova, 2009, p. 456).

Paragraphs (2)(b) and (2)(c), whose wording is materially identical to those of Article 67(1)(d) and (g), grant suspects the rights to silence and to legal assistance. For details, see commentary to Article 67(1)(d) and (g). At this point, however, some precisions are given. First, although paragraph (2)(b) contains no explicit requirement that the suspect or the accused should be warned that his or her statement may be used as evidence in trial, rules 74 and 75 of the RPE regulate the witness's right not to incriminate himself or certain family members (see Hall, 2008, pp. 1098–1099). Indeed, the OTP's practice has consisted in a "policy of informing all persons questioned – including under Article 55(2) – that their evidence may be used in subsequent proceedings" (*Prosecutor v. Katanga and Ngudjolo Chui*, ICC OTP, Prosecution's Observations regarding Admission for the Confirmation Hearing of the Transcripts of Interview of Deceased Witness 12 pursuant to Articles 61 and 69 of the Statute, ICC-01/04-01/07-336, 20 March 2008, para. 21). This approach has been later regulated under the Regulations of the OTP (regulation 40(f). See also Karel de Meester *et al.*, 2013, p. 234). Second, concerning paragraph (2)(c), the Registrar is required to provide assistance to persons to whom Article 55(2)(c) applies in obtaining legal counsel assistance and legal advice (rule 20(c)). Third, Trial Chamber VII found no distinction between the offences under Article 70 (offences against the administration of justice) and the crimes under Article 5 (genocide, crimes against humanity, war crimes and crime of aggression) concerning the entitlement to legal aid as Article 55(2)(c) "contemplates legal aid '[w]here there are grounds to believe that a person has committed a crime within the jurisdiction of the Court.'" (*Prosecutor v. Bemba et al.*, ICC T. Ch. VII, Decision on the Defence applications for judicial review of the decision of the Registrar on the allocation of resources during the trial phase, ICC-01/05-01/13-955, 21 May 2015, para. 35).

Paragraph (2)(d) complements paragraph (2)(c) by laying down that suspects must be questioned in the presence of counsel unless they have waived this right (while the exception refers to suspects having "waived their right to counsel", it must probably also be read to cover suspects who have retained the assistance of counsel, but who consent to being questioned in the absence of said counsel). Contrary to the rules applicable to the *ad hoc* Tribunals, Article 55(2)(d) does not explicitly refer to cases where the suspect first waives the right to counsel and later withdraws this waiver; it would seem that the general rule contained in the provision also covers such cases and thus requires that questioning only continue in the presence of counsel following such withdrawal [Hall, 1999, p. 734; and Hall, 2008, p. 1103). Under Article 55(2), questioning of a person must be audio or video recorded and the recording shall be transcribed and then given to the person concerned. According to the chapeau, suspects must be informed of these rights prior to being questioned. Rules 112 and 113 of the RPE contain additional procedural rules concerning questioning of suspects, including the possibility of a medical examination of the suspect [see, for further details, Hall, 2008, pp. 1103–1104).

In *Bemba*, Pre-Trial Chamber III found that an interview for determining the suspect's identity does not probably fall within the scope of Article 55(2)(d) as were Article 55(2)(d) be applicable, the claimed "unlawful absence of the counsel would only entail a potential exclusion pursuant to Article 69 (7) of the Statute of evidence obtained in the interview" (*Prosecutor v. Bemba*, ICC PT. Ch. III, Decision concerning the public version of the "Decision on application for interim Release" of 20 August 2008, ICC-01/05-01/08-80, 26 August 2008, para. 45). The Appeals Chamber in *Banda and Jerbo* determined that the ICC Prosecutor cannot be requested, under Rule 112 (recording of questioning in particular cases), to produce organised and signed statements of a witness's interview. In accordance with Article 55(2), Rule 112 provides for that interviews of persons about whom the ICC Prosecutor has ground to believe committed a crime within the ICC jurisdiction shall be audio or video recorded [*Prosecutor v. Banda and Jerbo*, ICC A. Ch., Judgment on the appeal of the Prosecutor against the decision of Trial Chamber IV of 12 September 2011 entitled "Reasons for the Order on translation of witness statements (ICC-02/05-03/09-199) and additional instructions on translation", ICC-02/05-03/09-295, 17 February 2012, paras. 26–28).

Cross-references:

Article 67(1) and 70; Rules 21, 22, 112 and 113; Regulation 73; OTP Regulation 41(2).

Doctrine:

1. Amal Alamuddin, "Collection of Evidence", in Karim A.A. Khan, Caroline Buisman and Christopher Gosnell (eds.), *Principles of Evidence in International Criminal Justice*, Oxford University Press, Oxford, 2010, pp. 231–305.

2. Christopher K. Hall, "Article 55 – Rights of Persons During an Investigation", in Otto Triffterer (ed.), *Commentary on the Rome Statute of the International Criminal Court: Observers' Notes, Article by Article*, C.H. Nomos, Baden-Baden, 1999, pp. 727–34.

3. Christopher K. Hall, "Article 55 – Rights of Persons During an Investigation", in Otto Triffterer (ed.), *Commentary on the Rome Statute of the International Criminal Court: Observers' Notes, Article by Article*, 2nd ed., C.H. Beck/Hart/Nomos, Munich/Oxford/Baden-Baden, 2008, pp. 1089–1105.

4. Karel De Meester, Kelly Pitcher, Rod Rastan and Göran Sluiter, "Investigation, Coercive Measures, Arrest and Surrender", in Göran Sluiter, Håkan Friman, Suzannah Linton, Sergey Vasiliev and Salvatore Zappalà (eds.), *International Criminal Procedure: Principles and Rules*, Oxford University Press, Oxford, 2013, pp. 177–380.

5. William A. Schabas, *The International Criminal Court: A Commentary on the Rome Statute*, Oxford University Press, Oxford, 2010.

6. Göran Sluiter, "Human Rights Protection in the ICC Pre-trial Phase", in Carsten Stahn and Göran Sluiter (eds.), *The Emerging Practice of the International Criminal Court*, Brill/Martinus Nijhoff, Leiden, 2009, pp. 459–75.

7. Ekaterina Trendafilova, "Fairness and Expeditiousness in the International Criminal Court's Pre-trial Proceedings", in Carsten Stahn and Göran Sluiter (eds.), *The Emerging Practice of the International Criminal Court*, Brill/Martinus Nijhoff, Leiden, 2009, pp. 441–57.

8. Salvatore Zappalà, "The Rights of Persons During an Investigation", in Antonio Cassese, Paola Gaeta and John R.W.D. Jones (eds.), *The Rome Statute of the International Criminal Court: A Commentary*, 2nd ed., Oxford University Press, Oxford, 2002, pp. 1181–203.
9. Salvatore Zappalà, "The Rights of the Accused", in Antonio Cassese, Paola Gaeta and John R.W.D. Jones (eds.), *The Rome Statute of the International Criminal Court: A Commentary*, 2nd ed., Oxford University Press, Oxford, 2002, pp. 1319–54.
10. Salvatore Zappalà, "The Rights of Victims v. the Rights of the Accused", in *Journal of International Criminal Justice*, 2010, vol. 8, no. 1, p. 137–64.

Authors: Juan Pablo Pérez-León-Acevedo and Björn Elberling.

Article 56

Role of the Pre-Trial Chamber in relation to a unique investigative opportunity[447]

1. (a) Where the Prosecutor considers an investigation to present a unique opportunity to take testimony or a statement from a witness or to examine, collect or test evidence, which may not be available subsequently for the purposes of a trial, the Prosecutor shall so inform the Pre-Trial Chamber.[448]

---

[447] *General remarks*

Article 56 represents an exception from the general rule that evidence must be presented at trial. This provision allows collection of evidence under the oversight of the Pre-Trial Chamber which later is made available at trial. The rationale is that some evidence cannot be fully reproduced at trial, for example mass grave exhumation.

The purpose of the provision is to counter potential prejudice to the accused that may result from the particular nature of ICC proceedings. An accused may have difficulties to collect evidence in the country where the alleged crimes where committed when detained by the Court. Article 56 allows judicial intervention at the investigative stage.

Author: Mark Klamberg.

[448] This sub-paragraph grants the Pre-Trial Chamber a role where the Prosecution intends to perform a "unique investigative opportunity", that is, collect and test evidence that may not be available at trial.

The provision appears to focus on a scenario in which the case stage has already been reached, as evidenced in particular by the reference to the Prosecutor's obligation to provide relevant information to "the person who has been arrested or has appeared in response to a summons" in connection with the relevant investigation (Article 56, paragraph 1(c)). However, the possibility that in special circumstances Article 56 may also be applied prior to the case stage, as recognised by the jurisprudence of Pre-Trial Chamber I in *Situation in the Democratic Republic of the Congo*, Decision on the Prosecutor's Request for Measures under Article 56, 26 April 2005, cannot be discounted. Further, participation of victims in the context of the procedure set out in the said Article during the investigation of a situation may therefore be permitted, see *Prosecutor v. Joseph Kony, Vincent Otti, Okot Odhiambo and Dominic Ongwen*, ICC PT. Ch. II, Decision on victims' applications for participation a/0010/06, a/0064/06 to a/0070/06, a/0081/06 to a/0104/06 and a/0111/06 to a/0127/06 ICC-02/04-01/05-252, 10 August 2007, para. 100.

In *Situation in the Democratic Republic of the Congo*, Decision to Hold Consultation under Rule 114, 21 April 2005, PTC I considered that there is a unique investigative opportunity within the terms of Article 56 1(a) of the Statute and decided to convene an *ex parte* consultation with the Prosecutor in order to determine the measures to be taken and the modalities of their implementation.

Rule 114 provides that upon being informed by the Prosecutor, the Pre-Trial Chamber shall hold consultations with the Prosecutor and with the person who has been arrested or who has appeared before the Court pursuant to summons and his or her counsel, in order to determine the measures to be taken and the modalities of their implementation.

Cross-references:

Rule 114.

Author: Mark Klamberg.

(b) In that case, the Pre-Trial Chamber may, upon request of the Prosecutor, take such measures as may be necessary to ensure the efficiency and integrity of the proceedings and, in particular, to protect the rights of the defence.[449]

(c) Unless the Pre-Trial Chamber orders otherwise, the Prosecutor shall provide the relevant information to the person who has been arrested or appeared in response to a summons in connection with the investigation referred to in subparagraph (a), in order that he or she may be heard on the matter.[450]

2. The measures referred to in paragraph 1 (b) may include:[451]

(a) Making recommendations or orders regarding procedures to be followed;

(b) Directing that a record be made of the proceedings;

(c) Appointing an expert to assist;

---

[449] It is for the Prosecution to decide which investigative acts ought to be carried out which makes Article 56 different from an investigative judge.

The Pre-Trial Chamber's role pursuant to this paragraph is to "take such measures as may be necessary to ensure the efficiency and integrity of the proceedings and, in particular, to protect the rights of the defence" for example the production of records of forensic examinations and the appointment of an *ad hoc* counsel for the defence, see *Situation in the Democratic Republic of the Congo*, ICC PT. Ch. I, Decision on the Prosecutor's Request for Measures under Article 56, 26 April 2005. See also *Situation in the Democratic Republic of the Congo*, ICC PT. Ch. I, Decision on the Prosecutor's Communication to the Pre-Trial Chamber, 1 June 2005, where PTC I decided to approve the NFI's Investigation Plan.

Author: Mark Klamberg.

[450] Since the purpose of Article 56 is to protect the rights of the person who has been arrested or who appeared before the Court in response to a summons it follows that the Prosecution to provide relevant information regarding investigative acts taken.

The paragraph allows the Pre-Trial Chamber to order otherwise, but this should only happen on an exceptional basis taking the interests of the defence into account.

Author: Mark Klamberg.

[451] Paragraph 2 contains a non-exhaustive list of measures that the Pre-Trial Chamber may take in relation to a unique investigative opportunity. Other potential measures are added in Rule 114(1) which allows the Pre-Trial Chamber to determine on measures to ensure the right of the "suspect" under Article 67(1)(b) to communicate with counsel is protected.

Rule 112(5) provides that the Pre-Trial Chamber may, in pursuance of Article 56(2), order that the questioning of persons shall be audio- or video-recorded in accordance with the procedure set out in Rule 112.

The decision of the Pre-Trial Chamber in *Situation in the Democratic Republic of the Congo*, Decision on the Prosecutor's Request for Measures under Article 56, 26 April 2005 illustrates which measures can be taken, including the production of records of forensic examinations and the appointment of an *ad hoc* counsel for the defence.

The catch-all clause in sub-paragraph (f) uses the words "such other action" which would suggest that these measures are similar to the measures listed under (a)–(e). Guariglia and Hochmayr argue that the sub-paragraph can not be used to expand the powers of the Pre-Trial Chamber, for example to collect evidence itself (p. 1113).

Cross-references:

Rule 114.

Author: Mark Klamberg.

(d) Authorizing counsel for a person who has been arrested, or appeared before the Court in response to a summons, to participate, or where there has not yet been such an arrest or appearance or counsel has not been designated, appointing another counsel to attend and represent the interests of the defence;

(e) Naming one of its members or, if necessary, another available judge of the Pre-Trial or Trial Division to observe and make recommendations or orders regarding the collection and preservation of evidence and the questioning of persons;

(f) Taking such other action as may be necessary to collect or preserve evidence.

3. (a) Where the Prosecutor has not sought measures pursuant to this article but the Pre-Trial Chamber considers that such measures are required to preserve evidence that it deems would be essential for the defence at trial, it shall consult with the Prosecutor as to whether there is good reason for the Prosecutor's failure to request the measures. If upon consultation, the Pre-Trial Chamber concludes that the Prosecutor's failure to request such measures is unjustified, the Pre-Trial Chamber may take such measures on its own initiative.

(b) A decision of the Pre-Trial Chamber to act on its own initiative under this paragraph may be appealed by the Prosecutor. The appeal shall be heard on an expedited basis.[452]

4. The admissibility of evidence preserved or collected for trial pursuant to this article, or the record thereof, shall be governed at trial by Article 69, and given such weight as determined by the Trial Chamber.[453]

---

[452] In case the Prosecution has failed to request measures under Article 56, the Pre-Trial Chamber is empowered to take such measures on its own initiative or at the request of the defence (pursuant to Article 57(3)(b).

Pre-Trial Chamber II suggests that pursuant to Article 56(3)(a) and Article 57(3)(c), "the Chamber may even preserve evidence in favour of the defence" (*Kony et al.*, ICC PT. Ch. II, Decision on Prosecutor's applications for leave to appeal dated 15th day of March 2006 and to suspend or stay consideration of leave to appeal dated the 11th day of May 2006, ICC-02/04-01/05-90, 10 July 2006, para. 35. This is a measures that goes beyond "take measures to preserve evidence". Guariglia and Hochmayr argue that Article 56(3), on its face, does not empower the Chamber to take evidence itself.

Regulation 48 provides that the Pre-Trial Chamber may request the Prosecutor to provide specific or additional information or documents in his or her possession, or summaries thereof, that the Pre-Trial Chamber considers necessary in order to exercise the functions and responsibilities set forth in Article 56(3)(a).

Cross-references:
Regulation 48.
Author: Mark Klamberg.

[453] The use of Article 56 neither afford any weight to evidence or guarantee admissibility of the evidence. This is left for the determination of the Trial Chamber.
Doctrine:
1. William A. Schabas, *The International Criminal Court: A Commentary on the Rome Statute*, Oxford University Press, Oxford, 2010, pp. 690–94.
2. Fabricio Guariglia and Gudrun Hochmayr, "Article 56 – Role of the Pre-Trial Chamber in Relation to a Unique Investigative Opportunity", in Otto Triffterer (ed.), *Commentary on*

the Rome Statute of the International Criminal Court: Observers' Notes, Article by Article, 2nd ed., C.H. Beck/Hart/Nomos, Munich/Oxford/Baden-Baden, 2008, pp. 1107–15.
Author: Mark Klamberg.

Article 57
Functions and powers of the Pre-Trial Chamber[454]

1. Unless otherwise provided in this Statute, the Pre-Trial Chamber shall exercise its functions in accordance with the provisions of this article.[455]

2. (a) Orders or rulings of the Pre-Trial Chamber issued under Articles 15, 18, 19, 54, paragraph 2, 61, paragraph 7, and 72 must be concurred in by a majority of its judges.

   (b) In all other cases, a single judge of the Pre-Trial Chamber may exercise the functions provided for in this Statute, unless otherwise provided for in the Rules of Procedure and Evidence or by a majority of the Pre-Trial Chamber.[456]

---

[454] *General remarks*

The Pre-Trial Chamber is established by Article 39. The Pre-Trail Chamber is a compromise between different legal traditions. Judicial overview at the investigatory stage is a feature of the civil tradition, but the Pre-Trial Chamber is not an investigative chamber. It is not responsible for directing the investigations of the Prosecutor. In *Ruto et al.*, Decision on the "Request by the Victims' Representative for authorisation to make a further written submission on the views and concerns of the victims", ICC-01/09-01/11-371, 9 December 2011, para. 16, the Pre-Trial Chamber stated that "the power to conduct investigations concerning the commission of crimes and/or to direct the Prosecutor to investigate certain offences or persons do not fall among the prerogatives of the Pre-Trial Chamber as reflected in the said provision of the Statute. Pursuant to the law the power of the Pre-Trial Chamber is to evaluate, in light of the standards of proof envisaged in the Statute, the results of such investigations, namely the evidence collected and placed before the Chamber".

In addition to Article 57, there are several other provisions in the ICC Statute that concern the powers of the Pre-Trial Chamber: Articles 15(3), 18(2), 19(6), 53(3), 56, 58, 59, 60, 61, 64(4) and 72. Further, Regulation 46(2) provides that The Pre-Trial Chamber shall be responsible for any matter, request or information arising out of the situation assigned to it, save that, at the request of a Presiding Judge of a Pre-Trial Chamber, the President of the Pre-Trial Division may decide to assign a matter, request or information arising out of that situation to another Pre-Trial Chamber in the interests of the administration of justice.

Author: Mark Klamberg.

[455] The purpose of this paragraph is to avoid any inconsistencies in the ICC Statute by providing that if any other Articles contains a conflicting provision concerning the pre-trial proceedings, that provision shall prevail.

Author: Mark Klamberg.

[456] As provided for in Article 39(2)(b)(iii) the functions of the Pre-Trial Chamber shall be carried out either in plenary by three judges of the Pre-Trial Division or by a single judge.

Following this bifurcated standard for the decision-making of the Pre-Trial Chamber, Article 57(2)(a) contains a list the functions where it is required that at least two of the three judges of the Pre-Trial Chamber concur. It includes *proprio motu* investigations of the Prosecutor (Article 15), rulings on admissibility and jurisdiction (Articles 18 and 19), investigations by the Prosecutor on the territory of a State (Article 54(2)), confirmation of charges (Article 61(7)), evidence that could harm the national security of a State (Article 72).

Pursuant to Article 57(2)(b) that more routine functions may be carried out by a single judge, unless otherwise provided for in the Rules of Procedure and Evidence. This includes review of the decision of the Prosecutor not to proceed with an investigation under Article 53

3. In addition to its other functions under this Statute, the Pre-Trial Chamber may:

    (a) At the request of the Prosecutor, issue such orders and warrants as may be required for the purposes of an investigation;[457]

    (b) Upon the request of a person who has been arrested or has appeared pursuant to a summons under Article 58, issue such orders, including measures such as those described in Article 56, or seek such cooperation pursuant to Part 9 as may be necessary to assist the person in the preparation of his or her defence;[458]

(Rule 108(1) and Rule 110(1)) and decisions in respect of an unique investigative opportunity under Article 56(3) (Rule 114(2)). Further, Rule 7(3) provides that The Pre-Trial Chamber, on its own motion or, if appropriate, at the request of a party, may decide that the functions of the single judge be exercised by the full Chamber. Regulation 47 states that the single judge designated by the Pre-Trial Chamber shall, as far as possible, act for the duration of a case.

Cross-references:

Regulation 47.

Author: Mark Klamberg.

[457] Sub-paragraph 3(a) concerns the power of the Pre-Trial Chamber to issue orders and warrants.

It may be noted that the paragraph does not use the word "subpoena". If "subpoena" is considered to be covered by "order", this omission may appear irrelevant. However, it becomes more relevant subpoena is understood in the manner taken by the ICT Appeals Chamber in *Blaškić* where subpoena meant binding orders [...] under threat of penalty", see *Prosecutor v. Blaškić* (Case No. IT-95-14), ICTY A. Ch., Judgment on the request of the Republic of Croatia for the review of decision of Trial Chamber II of 18 July 1997, 29 October 1997, para. 21.

The process of making witnesses appear at the IVV is to be conducted through the Part 9 procedure concerning state cooperation. Under Article 93 there is no explicit requirement that the ICC cannot compel witnesses to testify, even less that the ICC can issue penalties. It has thus been unclear whether witnesses can be compelled to appear before the Court. However, the majority of the Trial Chamber in in *Ruto and Sang* issued a decision in which they stated that the ICC had the power to summon witnesses, and a State Party had a legal obligation to compel the witnesses concerned to appear before the court, *Prosecutor v. Ruto and Sang*, ICC T. Ch., Decision on Prosecutor's Application for Witness Summonses and resulting Request for State Party Cooperation, ICC-01/09-01/11-1274-Corr2, 17 April 2014, para. 193. The Trial Chamber stated that "when Article 64(6)(b) says that the Chamber may 'require the attendance of witnesses', the provision means that the Chamber may – as a compulsory measure – order or subpoena the appearance of witnesses" (para. 100). It would appear logical that the Pre-Trial Chamber has the same power.

Author: Mark Klamberg.

[458] Pursuant to this paragraph the Pre-Trial Chamber may issue the orders necessary to assist the person in the preparation of his or her defence, thereby giving effect to the rights granted to the accused under Article 67(1)(b). Rule 116 clarifies the threshold for an order under Article 57(3)(b), it specifies that the Pre-trial Chamber must be "satisfied [t]hat such an order would facilitate the collection of evidence that may be material to the proper determination of the issues being adjudicated, or to the proper preparation of the person's defence". There is no requirement that the evidence is exculpatory or incriminatory.

In *Prosecutor v. Katanga and Chui*, ICC PT. Ch. I, Decision on the Defence Application pursuant to Article 57(3)(b) of the Statute to Seek the Cooperation of the Democratic Republic of Congo (DRC), ICC-01/04-01/07, 25 April 2008, PTC I ruled that the Defence must first request documents and information which are likely to be in the possession or control of the Pros-

---

(c) Where necessary, provide for the protection and privacy of victims and witnesses, the preservation of evidence, the protection of persons who have been arrested or appeared in response to a summons, and the protection of national security information;[459]

---

ecution; and that the Defence of Germain Katanga in accordance with rule 77 of the Rules before seeking an order under Article 57(3)(b).

In *Prosecutor v. Banda and Jerbo*, Decision on the "Defence Application pursuant to Article 57(3)(b) of the Statute for an order for the preparation and transmission of a cooperation request to the Government of the Republic of Sudan", 15 November 2010, para. 1, the defence aimed at obtaining from the Pre-Trial Chamber a request addressed to the Republic of Sudan to provide various forms of assistance to the Defence team, with a view to allowing them to "properly prepare their case". The Single Judge observed that the Defence had stated that it "does not contest any of the material facts alleged in the DCC for the purposes of confirmation"; (ii) that, at the confirmation hearing, the Defence "shall not 'object to the charges' contained in the DCC, 'challenge the evidence presented by the Prosecutor' or otherwise 'present evidence'". As a consequence, the Single Judge found that defence statements "clarify that any investigative step which might be taken, as well as any evidentiary material which might be collected, following an order issued pursuant to Article 57(3)(b) would serve no purpose for the pre-trial phase of the case, namely in respect of the confirmation hearing which will conclude it" (paras. 3–4). The application was thus rejected. The Single Judge also rejected the defence application for leave of appeal, *Prosecutor v. Banda and Jerbo*, Decision on the "Defence Application for leave to Appeal the 'Decision on the Defence Application pursuant to Article 57(3)(b) of the Statute for an order for the preparation and transmission of a cooperation request to the Government of the Republic of Sudan' of 17 November 2010", 30 November 2010. See also *Prosecutor v. Katanga and Chui*, Ordonnance relative à la « Requête de la Défense de Mathieu Ngudjolo sollicitant l'assistance de la Chambre en vue d'obtenir de la Voice of America (VOA) la bande d'enregistrement de la déclaration de M. Thomas Lubanga à la suite et au sujet de l'attaque de Bogoro du 24 février 2003 », 15 July 2011, where the Defence requested the assistance of the Pre-Trial Chamber in order to obtain an audio clip. The Pre-Trial Chamber considered that it is for the defence, not the Registry, to take all necessary steps to get the audio recording of the statement made by Mr Thomas Lubanga. Indeed, the Defence did not show how assistance from the Registry would be required to achieve this recording (para. 9).

In *Prosecutor v. Banda and Jerbo*, Decision on "Defence Application pursuant to Articles 57(3)(b) and 64(6)(a) of the Statute for an order for the preparation and transmission of a cooperation request to the Government of the Republic of the Sudan", 1 July 2011, para. 17, the Trial Chamber stated that "the Chamber may seek cooperation under Part 9 when the requirements of (i) specificity (ii) relevance and (iii) necessity are met". The Trial Chamber found that the Defence required permission to undertake an "open-ended expedition" to the Sudan and that there was "insufficient specificity" of the application, (paras. 22, 30 and 33) This was repeated in *Prosecutor v. Banda and Jerbo*, Public Redacted Decision on the second defence's application pursuant to Articles 57(3)(b) and 64(6)(a) of the Statute, 21 December 2011, para. 13

Cross-references:

Rule 116.

Author: Mark Klamberg.

[459] Paragraph (c) empowers the Pre-Trial Chamber to take enforce a number of other provisions in the ICC Statute and the Rules of Procedure and Evidence, including the protection and privacy of victims and witnesses (Article 68), the preservation of evidence (Article 18(6), the protection of persons who have been arrested or appeared in response to a summons (Rules 117–120), protection of national security information (Article 72). There are a number of decisions where Article 57(3)(c) have been invoked.

(d) Authorize the Prosecutor to take specific investigative steps within the territory of a State Party without having secured the cooperation of that State under Part 9 if, whenever possible having regard to the views of the State concerned, the Pre-Trial Chamber has determined in that case that the State is clearly unable to execute a request for cooperation due to the unavailability of any authority or any component of its judicial system competent to execute the request for cooperation under Part 9.[460]

(e) Where a warrant of arrest or a summons has been issued under article 58, and having due regard to the strength of the evidence and the rights of the parties concerned, as provided for in this Statute and the Rules of Procedure and Evidence, seek the coop-

---

In *Prosecutor v. Kony et al.*, Decision on "Request to access documents and material", and to hold a hearing in camera and ex parte, ICC-02/04-01/05-152, 7 February 2007, PTC II, *inter alia*, rejected the OPCV's request to have access to the index of the record of the situation and of the case. In *Prosecutor v. Kony et al.*, Decision to convene a status conference on matters related to safety and security in Uganda, ICC-02/04-01/05-64, 25 November 2005, PTC II decided to hold a status conference by way of a hearing in closed session. In *Prosecutor v. Lubanga*, Decision Concerning the Reclassification of the Redacted Versions of Documents ICC-01/04-01/06-32-US-Exp and ICC-01/04-01/06-32-Conf-AnxC as Public, ICC-01/04-01/06-80, 19 April 2006, PTC I decided to reclassify certain documents as public.

In *Prosecutor v. Lubanga*, Decision on the Defence Request for Unrestricted Access to the Entire File of the Situation in the Democratic Republic of the Congo, ICC-01/04-01/06-103, 17 May 2006, PTC I rejected the Defence Request unrestricted access to the entire file of the situation in the Democratic Republic of the Congo.

In *Prosecutor v. Lubanga*, Decision Concerning Pre-Trial Chamber I's Decision of 10 February 2006 and the Incorporation of Documents into the Record of the Case against Mr. Thomas Lubanga Dyilo, ICC-01/04-01/06-8-Corr, 24 February 2006, PTC I decided, *inter alia*, that Mr. Thomas Lubanga Dyilo shall have access to redacted index of the record and to any public document contained therein.

In *the Democratic Republic of the Congo*, Decision on the Requests of the OPCV, ICC-01/04-418, 10 December 2007, the OPCV requested "(i) access to the index of the Situation record, which lists the confidential, ex parte, and under seal documents in the Situation record; (ii) the right to thereafter request any documents which the Principal Counsel believes are necessary for the fulfilment of her mandate, and (iii) two confidential documents filed in the record of the Situation in the DRC". The Single Judge rejected the request in its entirety.

Cross-references:

Regulation 48.

Author: Mark Klamberg.

[460] Pursuant to paragraph (d) the prosecutor may through a request trigger the power of the Pre-Trial Chamber to authorise the prosecutor to take specific investigative steps within the territory of a State Party without having secured the cooperation of that State. This enables investigations when dealing with a "failed State" and includes onsite investigations. The requirement on prior consultation and restrictions to non-coercive measures set in Article 99(4) does not apply to investigations authorised by the Pre-Trial Chamber.

Cross-references:

Rule 115.

Regulation 38.

Author: Mark Klamberg.

---

eration of States pursuant to Article 93, paragraph 1 (k), to take protective measures for the purpose of forfeiture, in particular for the ultimate benefit of victims.[461]

---

[461] The purpose of this provision is to ensure the right of reparations of the victims (Article 75) and the applicability of forfeiture (Article 77(2)(b)). States Parties have an obligation under Article 93(1)(k) to comply with requests by the Court to provide assistance in relation the identification, tracing and freezing or seizure of proceeds, property and assets and instrumentalities of crimes for the purpose of eventual forfeiture.

Cross-references:

Rule 99.

Doctrine:

1. Håkan Friman, in Roy S. Lee (ed.), *The International Criminal Court: Elements of Crimes and Rules of Procedure and Evidence*, Transnational Publishers, Ardsley, NY, 2001, pp. 509–12.

2. William A. Schabas, *The International Criminal Court: A Commentary on the Rome Statute*, Oxford University Press, Oxford, 2010, pp. 695–701.

3. Fabricio Guariglia, Kenneth Harris and Gudrun Hochmayr, "Article 57 – Functions and powers of the Pre-Trial Chamber", in Otto Triffterer (ed.), *Commentary on the Rome Statute of the International Criminal Court: Observers' Notes, Article by Article*, 2nd ed., C.H. Beck/Hart/Nomos, Munich/Oxford/Baden-Baden, 2008, pp. 1117–31.

4. Mark Klamberg, *Evidence in International Criminal Trials: Confronting Legal Gaps and the Reconstruction of Disputed Events*, Martinus Nijhoff Publishers, Leiden, 2013, pp. 208, 254.

Author: Mark Klamberg.

Article 58

Issuance by the Pre-Trial Chamber of a warrant of arrest or a summons to appear[462]

1. At any time after the initiation of an investigation, the Pre-Trial Chamber shall, on the application of the Prosecutor, issue a warrant of arrest of a person if, having examined the application and the evidence or other information submitted by the Prosecutor, it is satisfied that:[463]

    (a) There are reasonable grounds to believe that the person has committed a crime within the jurisdiction of the Court;[464] and

---

[462] *General remarks*:

Article 58 concerns warrant of arrest or a summons to appear *vis-à-vis* the suspect which corresponds to the "indictment" in common law jurisdictions. It applies to persons who are "suspected", but yet "accused" to have committed a crime under the jurisdiction of the Court. The status of "accused" is reserved to the stage where the Pre-Trial Chamber has confirmed the charges. The provision does not apply to offences against the administration of justice under Article 70 or witnesses.

[463] The application of an arrest warrant occurs at the start of the investigation of a case. In *Situation in Kenya*, ICC PT. Ch. II, Decision Pursuant to Article 15 of the Rome Statute on the Authorisation of an Investigation into the Situation in the Republic of Kenya, ICC-01/09-19, 31 March 2010, para. 44, the Pre-Trial Chamber stated that a "case" starts after the issuance of an arrest warrant or a summons to appear pursuant to Article 58 of the Statute.

If the requirements of paragraph 1 is fulfilled, the Pre-Trial Chamber is obliged to issue the warrant of arrest, there is no discretion.

Article 58 does not preclude the use of sealed arrest warrants in order to increase the chances of being able to arrest suspects. In *Situation in Uganda*, Decision to Hold a Hearing on the Request under Rule 176 made in the Prosecutor's Application for Warrants of Arrest Under Article 58, ICC-02/04-10, 9 June 2005, PTC II decided to hold a hearing regarding the Prosecutor's request for the transmission of warrants of arrest and requests for arrest and surrender, in closed session to be attended only by the Prosecutor and his representatives. In *Prosecutor v. Kony et al.*, ICC PT. Ch. II, Decision on the Prosecutor's Urgent Application dated 26 September 2005, ICC-02/04-01/05-27, 27 September 2005, PTC II decided, *inter alia*, authorised the Prosecutor, on a confidential basis and in situations where the Prosecutor deems it necessary to disclose information relating to the warrant of arrest In *Situation in Kenya*, ICC PT. Ch. II, Decision on the "Application for Leave to Participate in the Proceedings before the Pre-Trial Chamber relating to the Prosecutor's Application under Article 58(7)", ICC-01/09-42, 11 February 2011, para. 23, the Pre-Trial Chamber found that since the proceedings under Article 58 of the Statute are to be conducted with the exclusive participation of the Prosecutor, the person named in the Prosecutor's application pursuant to Article 58 of the Statute is not entitled to submit observations in these proceedings. The application submitted by Mohammed Hussein Ali requesting leave to participate in the proceedings related to the Prosecutor's application under Article 58 was thus rejected.

[464] The threshold "reasonable grounds" is the least demanding evidentiary requirement used in the ICC Statute.

In *Bemba*, the Pre-Trial Chamber observed "that, under Article 21(3) of the Statute, the expression 'reasonable grounds to believe' must be interpreted in a manner consistent with internationally recognized human rights". Thus, in interpreting and applying this concept, the Cham-

---

ber was specifically guided by the "reasonable suspicion" standard under Article 5(1)(c) of the ECHR, which, as interpreted by the ECtHR, "requires the existence of some facts or information which would satisfy an objective observer that the person concerned may have committed the offence". The Chamber was also guided by the jurisprudence of the Inter-American Court of Human Rights ('IACHR') on the fundamental right to liberty, as enshrined in Article 7 of the American Convention on Human Rights, *Prosecutor v. Jean-Pierre Bemba Gombo*, ICC PT. Ch. III, Decision on the Prosecutor's Application for a Warrant of Arrest against Jean-Pierre Bemba Gombo, ICC-01/05-01/08, 10 June 2008, para. 24.

In *Al Bashir* the majority of the Pre-Trial Chamber declined to issue an arrest warrant in relation to the counts concerning genocide. The background to the case is that the alleged crimes were committed as part of a counter-insurgency campaign launched by the Government of Sudan ('GoS'). The majority of the Pre-Trial Chamber stated that the "reasonable grounds" standard would be met (and a warrant would be issued) if the evidence provided by the prosecutor "show[s] that the only reasonable conclusion to be drawn therefrom is the existence of reasonable grounds to believe in the existence" of the perpetrator's dolus specialis/ specific intent to destroy in whole or in part the protected groups. *Prosecutor v. Al Bashir*, ICC PT. Ch. I, Decision on the Prosecution's Application for a Warrant of Arrest against Omar Hassan Ahmad Al Bashir, ICC-02/05-01/09-3, 4 March 2009, para. 158. Considering that the existence of a GoS's genocidal intent is only one of several reasonable conclusions available on the materials provided by the Prosecution, the Pre-Trial Chamber rejected the prosecutor's application in relation to genocide because the evidentiary standard provided for in Article 58 of the Statute was not met (paras. 153–159).

To require the prosecutor to show that it is the only reasonable conclusion in order to have an arrest warrant issued would arguably be the wrong standard of proof to use because it amounts to the higher "beyond reasonable doubt" standard. The partly dissenting Judge Ušacka noted that "[t]he Statute proscribes progressively higher evidentiary thresholds which must be met at each stage of the proceedings" and that at the arrest warrant/summons stage the Pre-Trial Chamber need only be "satisfied that there are reasonable grounds to believe that the person has committed a crime within the jurisdiction of the Court. She held that "the Prosecution need not demonstrate … an inference [of genocidal intent] is the only reasonable one at the arrest warrant stage" She was satisfied that there was reasonable grounds to issue an arrest warrant on the basis of the existence of reasonable grounds to believe that Omar Al Bashir has committed the crime of genocide (Separate and Partly Dissenting Opinion of Judge Anita Ušacka, ICC-02/05-01/09-3, paras. 8, 27–34, 84 and 105).

The Appeals Chamber accordingly reversed the decision of the Pre-Trial Chamber because it had applied an erroneous standard of proof. In the view of the Appeals Chamber, requiring that the existence of genocidal intent must be the only reasonable conclusion amounted to requiring the prosecutor to disprove any other reasonable conclusions and to eliminate any reasonable doubt. If the only reasonable conclusion based on the evidence was the existence of genocidal intent, then it could not be said that such a finding established merely "reasonable grounds to believe". The Pre-Trial Chamber was directed to decide anew, on the basis of the correct standard of proof, whether a warrant of arrest in respect of the crime of genocide should be issued. *Prosecutor v. Omar Hassan Ahmad Al Bashir*, ICC A. Ch., Judgment on the appeal of the Prosecutor against the "Decision on the Prosecution's Application for a Warrant of Arrest against Omar Hassan Ahmad Al Bashir", ICC-02/05-01/09, 3 February 2010, paras. 33 and 41.

Following the Appeals Chamber, the Pre-Trial Chamber stated in *Prosecutor v. Mudacumura*, Decision on the Prosecutor's Application under Article 58, ICC-01/04-01/12-1-RedtFRA, 13 July 2012, para. 19, that "The evidence need only establish a reasonable conclusion that the person committed a crime within the jurisdiction of the Court, and it is not required that this be the only reasonable conclusion that can be drawn from the evidence".

(b) The arrest of the person appears necessary:

  (i) To ensure the person's appearance at trial,[465]

  (ii) To ensure that the person does not obstruct or endanger the investigation or the court proceedings, or[466]

---

[465] Sub-paragraph 1(b) lists three grounds for issuing an arrest warrant. The first ground concerns the interest to ensure the suspects appearance at trial. In *Prosecutor v. Lubanga*, ICC A. Ch., Judgment on the appeal of Mr. Thomas Lubanga Dyilo against the decision of Pre-Trial Chamber I entitled "Décision sur la demande de mise en liberté provisoire de Thomas Lubanga Dyilo", ICC-01/04-01/06-824-tCMN, 13 February 2007, paras. 136–138, the Appeals Chamber upheld the finding of the single judge that the following factors should be taken into account for the purpose of Article 58(1)(b)(i) of the Statute: (i) the gravity of the crimes; (ii) the international contacts of the person, and (iii) his or her hypothetical voluntary surrender to the Court. See also *Katanga and Ngudjolo*, ICC PT. Ch. II, Decision on the Application for Interim Release of Mathieu Ngudjolo Chui, ICC-01/04-01/07-345, 27 March 2008, p. 7.

This is the main reason to detain suspects, there are several decisions where arrest warrants have been based on this ground. In *Prosecutor v. Lubanga*, Decision reviewing the "Decision on the Application for the Interim Release of Thomas Lubanga Dyilo", ICC-01/04-01/06-976, 8 October 2007, TC I concluded that the defendant was highly unlikely to attend his trial voluntarily. For these reasons TC I found it necessary to continue to detain the defendant. In *Prosecutor v. Katanga*, Warrant of arrest for Germain Katanga, ICC-01/04-01/07-1-tENG, 2 July 2007, PTC I issued an arrest warrant on two grounds, namely Articles 58(1)(b)(i) and (ii). The PTC also considered that it would state "the analysis of the evidence and other information submitted by the Prosecution will be set out in a decision to be filed subsequently" (p. 3) Subsequently, in *Prosecutor v. Katanga*, Decision on the evidence and information provided by the Prosecution for the issuance of a warrant of arrest for Germain Katanga, ICC-01/04-01/07-55, 5 November 2007, para. 64, PTC stated that "on the basis of the evidence and information contained in the Prosecution Application, the Prosecution Supporting Materials and the Prosecution Response, and without prejudice to any subsequent determination under Article 60 of the Statute and rule 119 of the Rules of Procedure and Evidence, the arrest of Germain Katanga appears necessary pursuant to Articles 58(1)(b)(i) and (ii) of the Statute, both to ensure his appearance at trial and to ensure that he does not obstruct or endanger the investigation or the court proceedings". In *Prosecutor v. Ngudjolo*, Warrant of Arrest for Mathieu Ngudjolo Chui, ICC-01/04-01/07-260-tENG, 6 July 2007, p. 7, PTC I issued an arrest warrant on two grounds, namely Articles 58(1)(b)(i) and (ii). See also *Prosecutor v. Ngudjolo*, Decision on the evidence and information provided by the Prosecution for the issuance of a warrant of arrest for Mathieu Ngudjolo Chui, ICC-01/04-01/07-262, 6 July 2007, paras. 62–68.

[466] The second ground for issuing an arrest warrant provides that if there is reason to believe that a suspect would interfere with the investigations of the Prosecution, he or she can be detained.

In *Prosecutor v. Katanga*, Warrant of arrest for Germain Katanga, 2 July 2007, PTC I issued an arrest warrant on two grounds, namely Articles 58(1)(b)(i) and (ii).The PTC also considered that it would state "the analysis of the evidence and other information submitted by the Prosecution will be set out in a decision to be filed subsequently" (p. 3) Subsequently, in *Prosecutor v. Katanga*, Decision on the evidence and information provided by the Prosecution for the issuance of a warrant of arrest for Germain Katanga, 5 November 2007, para. 64, PTC stated that "on the basis of the evidence and information contained in the Prosecution Application, the Prosecution Supporting Materials and the Prosecution Response, and without prejudice to any subsequent determination under Article 60 of the Statute and Rule 119 of the Rules of Procedure and Evidence, the arrest of Germain Katanga appears necessary pursuant to Articles

---

(iii) Where applicable, to prevent the person from continuing with the commission of that crime or a related crime which is within the jurisdiction of the Court and which arises out of the same circumstances.[467]

2. The application of the Prosecutor shall contain:

   (a) The name of the person and any other relevant identifying information;

   (b) A specific reference to the crimes within the jurisdiction of the Court which the person is alleged to have committed;

   (c) A concise statement of the facts which are alleged to constitute those crimes;

   (d) A summary of the evidence and any other information which establish reasonable grounds to believe that the person committed those crimes; and

   (e) The reason why the Prosecutor believes that the arrest of the person is necessary.[468]

3. The warrant of arrest shall contain:

   (a) The name of the person and any other relevant identifying information;

   (b) A specific reference to the crimes within the jurisdiction of the Court for which the person's arrest is sought; and

   (c) A concise statement of the facts which are alleged to constitute those crimes.[469]

4. The warrant of arrest shall remain in effect until otherwise ordered by the Court.[470]

5. On the basis of the warrant of arrest, the Court may request the provisional arrest or the arrest and surrender of the person under Part 9.[471]

58(1)(b)(i) and (ii) of the Statute, both to ensure his appearance at trial and to ensure that he does not obstruct or endanger the investigation or the court proceedings".

[467] The third ground for issuing an arrest warrant aims to prevent the suspect from continuing committing crimes. In Situation in Uganda, the Pre-Trial Chamber stated "that attacks by the LRA are still occurring and that there is therefore a likelihood that failure to arrest [...] will result in the continuation of crimes of the kind described in the Prosecutor's application; *Prosecutor v. Kony*, Warrant of Arrest for Joseph Kony issued on 8 July 2005 as amended on 27 September 2005, para. 45; *Prosecutor v. Otti*, Warrant of Arrest for Vincent Otti, 8 July 2005, para. 45; *Prosecutor v. Lukwiya*, Warrant of Arrest for Raska Lukwiya, 8 July 2005, para. 33. Warrant of Arrest for Okot Odhiambo, 8 July 2005, *Prosecutor v. Ongwen*, Warrant of Arrest for Dominic Ongwen, 8 July 2005, para. 33.

[468] Paragraph 2 lists what needs to be in the Prosecutor's application for an arrest warrant. In *Situation in the Democratic Republic of Congo*, ICC PT. Ch., Decision on the Prosecutor's Application under Article 58, paras. 5–6, the Pre-Trial Chamber dismissed the application of the Prosecutor for the lack of specificity. The Appeals Chamber has stated that the list in paragraph 2 is exhaustive, *Situation in the Democratic Republic of Congo*, ICC A. Ch., Judgment on the Prosecutor's appeal against the decision of the pre-trial chamber I entitled Decision on the Prosecutor's Application for warrants of arrest, ICC-01/04, Article 58. para. 45.

[469] Paragraph 3 lists what needs to be in the warrant of arrest. It shall encompass the information contained in the application of the Prosecutor except of the summary of evidence and the reasons why the Prosecutor considers an arrest necessary.

[470] This paragraph clarifies that only the Court has the power to lift the arrest warrant. The arrest warrant against *Lukwiya* was cancelled when convincing evidence submitted to the Pre-Trial Chamber showed that the suspect was dead, *Prosecutor v. Lukwiya*, ICC PT. Ch., Decision to Terminate the Proceedings against Raska Lukwiya, ICC-02/04-01/05-248, July 2007.

Author: Mark Klamberg.

6. The Prosecutor may request the Pre-Trial Chamber to amend the warrant of arrest by modifying or adding to the crimes specified therein. The Pre-Trial Chamber shall so amend the warrant if it is satisfied that there are reasonable grounds to believe that the person committed the modified or additional crimes.[472]

7. As an alternative to seeking a warrant of arrest, the Prosecutor may submit an application requesting that the Pre-Trial Chamber issue a summons for the person to appear. If the Pre-Trial Chamber is satisfied that there are reasonable grounds to believe that the person committed the crime alleged and that a summons is sufficient to ensure the person's appearance, it shall issue the summons, with or without conditions restricting liberty (other than detention) if provided for by national law, for the person to appear. The summons shall contain:

   (a) The name of the person and any other relevant identifying information;

   (b) The specified date on which the person is to appear;

   (c) A specific reference to the crimes within the jurisdiction of the Court which the person is alleged to have committed; and

   (d) A concise statement of the facts which are alleged to constitute the crime.[473]

---

[471] This paragraph provides that the Pre-Trial Chamber may request the provisional arrest or the arrest and surrender of the suspect. Article 92 governs provisional arrest.

[472] The Prosecutor may request the Pre-Trial Chamber to amend the warrant of arrest which refers to the information listed in paragraph 3.

Author: Mark Klamberg.

[473] As an alternative to a warrant of arrest, a suspect may be summoned to appear. The ICC Statute does not specify what is required in the Prosecutor's application for summons. Presumably it is the same as in an application for warrant of arrest, with the exception that there is no need to specify the reasons why an arrest is necessary.

In *Situation in Darfur, Sudan,* Prosecutor's Application under Article 58 (7), 27 February 2007, the Prosecutor requested that summons to appear be issued. In *Prosecutor v. Harun and Kushayb,* Decision on the Prosecution Application under Article 58(7) of the Statute, 27 April 2007, paragraph 125, PTC I was not satisfied that that the requirements of Article 58(7) of the Statute were met and instead it issued arrest warrants. In *Prosecutor v. Banda and Jerbo,* Second Decision on the Prosecutor's Application under Article 58, the Pre-Trial Chamber issued summons to appear. In *Abu Garda,* the Prosecutor applied for a warrant of arrest, but changed his position when the suspect agreed to surrender voluntarily. In *Abu Garda,* the Pre-Trial Chamber stated that it was "satisfied that that there are reasonable grounds to believe that a summons to appear is sufficient to ensure the appearance of Abu Garda before the Court within the meaning of Article 58(7) of the Statute" (*Prosecutor v. Abu Garda,* ICC PT. Ch. I, Decision on the Prosecutor's application under Article 58, 7 May 2009, para. 37). However, the Pre-Trial Chamber reserved "its right to review this finding either propio motu or at the request of the Prosecutor, however, particularly if the suspect fails to appear on the date specified in the summons or fails to comply with the orders contained in the summons to appear issued by the Chamber" (para. 38).

Cross-references:

Rules 119, 121, 122, 123.

Doctrine:

The summons shall be served on the person.

1. William A. Schabas, *The International Criminal Court: A Commentary on the Rome Statute*, Oxford University Press, Oxford, 2010, pp. 702–14.
2. Fabricio Guariglia, Kenneth Harris and Gudrun Hochmayr, "Article 58 – Issuance by the Pre-Trial Chamber of a Warrant of Arrest or a Summons to Appear", in Otto Triffterer (ed.), *Commentary on the Rome Statute of the International Criminal Court: Observers' Notes, Article by Article*, 2nd ed., C.H. Beck/Hart/Nomos, Munich/Oxford/Baden-Baden, 2008, pp. 1133–45.
3. Mark Klamberg, *Evidence in International Criminal Trials: Confronting Legal Gaps and the Reconstruction of Disputed Events*, Martinus Nijhoff Publishers, Leiden, 2013, pp. 136–39.

Author: Mark Klamberg.

Article 59

Arrest proceedings in the custodial State[474]

1. A State Party which has received a request for provisional arrest or for arrest and surrender shall immediately take steps to arrest the person in question in accordance with its laws and the provisions of Part 9.[475]

2. A person arrested shall be brought promptly before the competent judicial authority in the custodial State which shall determine, in accordance with the law of that State, that:

   (a) The warrant applies to that person;

   (b) The person has been arrested in accordance with the proper process; and

   (c) The person's rights have been respected.[476]

---

[474] *General remarks*:

Article 59 concerns arrest proceedings in the custodial state to be distinguished from the initial proceedings before the Court, regulated by Article 60. The assumption is that a suspect as a rule will be located and detained by national authorities in the territory of a State Party. This is not necessary in cases where the suspect is expected to present voluntarily in the Hague.

Article 59 imposes obligations on States Parties and is likely to be interpreted and applied by national judges.

Rule 165 exempts Article 59 from applying to proceedings concerning offences against the administration of justice. It is unclear from the provisions of Article 59 why it was exempted from such proceedings. An arrest warrant would fall under Article 70(2) of the Statute and in accordance with Rule 167(2) would be governed by the laws of the custodial State, see comment on rule 165(2).

[475] The reference to part 9 which concerns several obligations, including Article 88 that provides that States Parties shall ensure that there are procedures available under their national law. Moreover, Article 86 requires that States Parties shall cooperate fully with the Court. The requirement "immediately" should be read together with the paragraph 2 which instructs that the arrested person be brought "promptly" and paragraph 7 that the person shall be delivered to the Court "as soon as possible".

[476] Paragraph 2 is based on the assumption that the warrant of arrest by the Court is effected by a State Party rather than by an organ of the Court.

The competent judicial authority shall, in accordance with its own law, that the warrant applies to the suspect; that the arrest has followed the proper process; and that the suspect's rights have been respected. This means that the judicial authority must verify that the person arrested is the same as the person sought under the arrest warrant. Article 59 does not specify what the "proper process" is, this is ton be governed by the law of the custodial state. The rights to be respected would include both rights under national and international law, including the rights recognised under Article 55.

The jurisdiction of the Court in *Lubanga* was challenged by reference to the "doctrine of abuse of process" (*Prosecutor vs. Lubanga*, Decision on the Defence Challenge to the Jurisdiction of the Court pursuant to Article 19(2)(a) of the Statute, 3 October 2006). The defence argued that Lubanga's rights under Article 59(2) were infringed. PTC I considered that there is no evidence indicating that the arrest and detention of Thomas Lubanga Dyilo prior to the Court's cooperation request for the arrest and surrender was the result of any concerted action between the Court and the custodial State; and the Court did therefore not examine the lawfulness of the arrest and detention of Thomas Lubanga Dyilo by the custodial State prior to Court's coopera-

---

3. The person arrested shall have the right to apply to the competent authority in the custodial State for interim release pending surrender.[477]

4. In reaching a decision on any such application, the competent authority in the custodial State shall consider whether, given the gravity of the alleged crimes, there are urgent and exceptional circumstances to justify interim release and whether necessary safeguards exist to ensure that the custodial State can fulfil its duty to surrender the person to the Court. It shall not be open to the competent authority of the custodial State to consider whether the warrant of arrest was properly issued in accordance with Article 58, paragraph 1 (a) and (b).[478]

---

tion request. Thus, PTC I dismissed the challenge to the jurisdiction of the Court raised by Thomas Lubanga Dyilo pursuant to Article 19(2)(a) of the Statute and therefore rejected the request for release (pp. 11–12). In *Prosecutor vs. Lubanga*, ICC A. Ch., Judgment on the Appeal of Mr. Thomas Lubanga Dyilo against the Decision on the Defence Challenge to the Jurisdiction of the Court pursuant to Article 19(2)(a) of the Statute of 3 October 2006, 14 December 2006, paragraph 39, the Appeals Chamber ruled that Article 21(3) of the Statute makes the interpretation as well as the application of the law applicable under the Statute subject to internationally recognised human rights. It requires the exercise of the jurisdiction of the Court in accordance with internationally recognised human rights norms. The Appeals Chamber continued stating that where the breaches of the rights of the accused are such as to make it impossible for him/her to make his or her defence within the framework of his rights, no fair trial can take place and the proceedings can be stayed. The Appeals Chamber found no error in the Pre-Trial Chamber's findings (para. 42). The Pre-Trial Chamber in *Bemba* "found no indication of any irregularity or arbitrariness in the procedure followed by the competent Belgian authorities that would constitute a material breach of Article 59(2) of the Statute affecting the proceedings before the Court or render the detention of Mr Jean-Pierre Bemba on the authority of the Court otherwise unacceptable" (*Prosecutor v. Bemba*, ICC PT. Ch., Decision on application for interim release, ICC-01/05-01/08-73, 20 August 2008, para. 49)

Article 59 does not indicate what a national court should do if it finds that the "proper process" has not been respected. Article 85(1) provides that "[a]nyone who has been the victim of unlawful arrest or detention shall have an enforceable right to compensation". Hall argues that "neither the determination by the national judicial authority that the suspect's right was violated nor the remedies it adopted could prevent surrender to the Court" (Hall, p. 1152, see also Schabas, pp. 718–719).

[477] Paragraph 3 grants the suspect the right to apply for interim release pending surrender. This is determined by the "competent authority", there is no requirement that this should be a "judicial authority". This may be contrasted with the vertical order of the ICTY and ICTR where nothing in their statutes or rules permits national courts to order interim release. This feature of the ICC regime makes it more horizontal. However, the competent authorities of the custodial State cannot lift the arrest warrant issued by the Court. Paragraphs 4–6 develops the process of interim release.

[478] When considering an application interim release, the competent authority of the Custodial state shall consider factors such as: the gravity of the crimes; urgent and exceptional circumstances and there must be necessary safeguards to ensure the transfer of the arrested person to the Court. However, the competent authority of the Custodial state shall not rule on challenges to the grounds of the issuance of the warrant of arrest. Such challenges should instead be made to the Pre-Trial Chamber. Since rule 117(3) is not restricted to challenges made after surrender to the court, the arrested person could make such challenges to the Pre-Trial Chamber while still in the custodial state.

5. The Pre-Trial Chamber shall be notified of any request for interim release and shall make recommendations to the competent authority in the custodial State. The competent authority in the custodial State shall give full consideration to such recommendations, including any recommendations on measures to prevent the escape of the person, before rendering its decision.[479]

6. If the person is granted interim release, the Pre-Trial Chamber may request periodic reports on the status of the interim release.[480]

7. Once ordered to be surrendered by the custodial State, the person shall be delivered to the Court as soon as possible.[481]

---

[479] Paragraph 5 requires that the custodial State to inform the Pre-Trial Chamber of any request for interim release. The Pre-Trial Chamber is required to make recommendations to the competent authority of the custodial states. This reflects the assumption that the organs of the Court and the States Parties should work closely together on all issues of cooperation. Rule 117(4) provides that the Pre-Trial Chamber shall provide its recommendations within any time limit set by the custodial State.

[480] In the case interim release is granted, the Pre-Trial Chamber can through periodic reports control the progress of the investigation and ensure that the proceedings before the Court are secure.

[481] Paragraph 7 declares that the arrested person shall be delivered to the Court as soon as possible.

Doctrine:

1. William A. Schabas, *The International Criminal Court: A Commentary on the Rome Statute,* Oxford University Press, 2010, pp. 715–20.

2. Christopher K. Hall, "Article 59: Arrest Proceedings in the Custodial State", in Otto Triffterer (ed.), *Commentary on the Rome Statute of the International Criminal Court: Observers' Notes, Article by Article,* 2nd ed., C.H. Beck/Hart/Nomos, Munich/Oxford/Baden-Baden, 2008, pp. 1147–58.

3. Karel De Meester, "Article 59: Arrest Proceedings in the Custodial State, in Paul De Hert, Mathias Holvoet, Jean Flamme and Olivia Struyven (eds.), *Code of International Criminal Law and Procedure, Annotated,* Larcier, Ghent, 2013, pp. 247–52.

Author: Mark Klamberg.

Article 60
Initial proceedings before the Court[482]

1. Upon the surrender of the person to the Court, or the person's appearance before the Court voluntarily or pursuant to a summons, the Pre-Trial Chamber shall satisfy itself that the person has been informed of the crimes which he or she is alleged to have committed, and of his or her rights under this Statute, including the right to apply for interim release pending trial[483]

---

[482] *General remarks*:

Article 60 concerns the initial proceedings before the Court, including pre-trial release and detention. Human rights law creates a presumption that the suspect should be released pending trial, see Article 9(3) of the International Covenant on Civil and Political Rights. However, in international criminal proceedings the general rule is rather that accused are detained throughout the proceedings. The are no provisions in the ICTY and ICTR statutes on pre-trial release. This may be justified by the seriousness of the crimes in international criminal proceedings.

However, in *Bemba*, the Pre-Trial Chamber clarified that that deprivation of liberty should be an exception and not a rule is a fundamental principle, a corollary of the presumption of innocence provided in Article 66 of the Statute and the guiding principle upon which the review should be based, *Prosecutor. v. Bemba*, ICC PT. Ch., Decision on the Interim Release of Jean-Pierre Bemba Gombo and Convening Hearings with the Kingdom of Belgium, the Republic of Portugal, the Republic of France, the Federal Republic of Germany, the Italian Republic, and the Republic of South Africa, 14 August 2009, paras. 36–37.

Author: Mark Klamberg.

[483] Regardless of how a suspect was brought to the Court, the Pre-Trial Chamber must satisfy itself the person is informed of the charges against him or her and his or her rights. This is consistent with human rights law which provides that an arrested or detained person "shall be brought promptly before a judge or other office authorised by law to exercise judicial power" see ICCPR Article 9(3).

At this stage the Pre-Trial Chamber is required to notify the person the charges and accusations made under Article 58.

The Pre-Trial Chamber may authorise that initial appearance is made in public, see *Prosecutor v. Lubanga*, ICC PT. Ch. I, Order Scheduling the First Appearance of Mr Thomas Lubanga Dyilo, 17 March 2006, PTC I decided to hold a public hearing.

As indicated above, the scope and purpose of the initial appearance is limited to informing the suspect of the charges against him or her and his or her rights. Thus, the Single Judge ruled in *Ruto et al that* victims' intervention at this stage is not appropriate, see *Prosecutor v. Ruto et al*, ICC PT. Ch., Decision on the Motion by Legal Representative of Victim Applicants to Participate in Initial Appearance Proceedings, 30 March 2011, para. 6, the Single Judge held the view that victims' intervention at the stage of initial appearance is not appropriate. See also *Prosecutor v. Ruto et al*, ICC PT. Ch., Decision on the Conduct of the Proceedings Following the Application of the Government of Kenya Pursuant to Article 19 of the Rome Statute, 4 April 2011 para. 11, where the Pre-Trial Chamber held the view that to consider issues related to Article 19 proceedings during the initial appearance hearing would certainly go beyond the scope of an initial appearance hearing as defined by the Statute and Rules thereto.

Cross-references:

Regulation 51.

Author: Mark Klamberg.

---

2. A person subject to a warrant of arrest may apply for interim release pending trial. If the Pre-Trial Chamber is satisfied that the conditions set forth in Article 58, paragraph 1, are met, the person shall continue to be detained. If it is not so satisfied, the Pre-Trial Chamber shall release the person, with or without conditions.[484]

---

[484] Paragraph 2 specifies the considerations for determining the issue of interim release. These considerations are set out in Article 58(1), if they continue to exist the person shall be continued to be detained.

There are several decision concerning interim release. In *Prosecutor v. Lubanga*, ICC PT. Ch., Decision on the Application for the interim release of Thomas Lubanga Dyilo, 18 October 2006, PTC I rejected the Defence request for interim release. In *Prosecutor v. Lubanga*, ICC A. Ch, Judgment on the appeal of Mr. Thomas Lubanga Dyilo against the decision of Pre-Trial Chamber I entitled "Décision sur la demande de mise en liberté provisoire de Thomas Lubanga Dyilo", ICC-01/04-01/06-824-tCMN, 13 February 2007, the Appeals Chamber confirmed the decision of the Chamber on the application for the interim release of Thomas Lubanga Dyilo.

During the pre-trial proceedings some information may be withheld from the defence. This has to be balanced against the ability of the defence to challenge detention. In *Prosecutor v. Bemba*, ICC A. Ch., Judgment on the appeal of Mr. Jean-Pierre Bemba Gombo against the decision of Pre-Trial Chamber III entitled "Decision on application for interim release, 16 December 2008, para. 32, the Appeals Chamber ruled that defence has the right of access to documents that are essential for the purposes of applying for interim release. See also *Prosecutor v. Mbarushimana*, ICC PT. Ch., Decision on the Defence Request for Disclosure, 27 January 2011, para. 10.

The right for the parties under Article 82(1)(b) to appeal decisions granting or denying release is wide in the sense that no there is no requirement on leave to appeal. One question is what is the scope of the Appeals Chamber's review. In *Prosecutor v. Bemba*, ICC A. Ch., Judgment on the appeal of the Prosecutor against Pre-Trial Chamber II's "Decision on the Interim Release of Jean-Pierre Bemba Gombo and Convening Hearings with the Kingdom of Belgium, the Republic of Portugal, the Republic of France, the Federal Republic of Germany, the Italian Republic, and the Republic of South Africa", 02 December 2009, para. 62 the Appeals Chamber stated that it "will not review the findings of the Pre-Trial Chamber de novo, instead it will intervene in the findings of the Pre-Trial Chamber only where clear errors of law, fact or procedure are shown to exist and vitiate the Impugned Decision". See also *Prosecutor v. Mbarushimana*, ICC A. Ch., Judgment on the appeal of Mr Callixte Mbarushimana against the decision of Pre-Trial Chamber I of 19 May 2011 entitled "Decision on the 'Defence Request for Interim Release'", 14 July 2011, para. 15.

When considering conditional release, one relevant factor is the ability and willingness of the state – where accused will reside – to enforce the conditions for the release. In *Prosecutor v. Bemba*, ICC A. Ch., Judgment on the appeal of Mr Jean-Pierre Bemba Gombo against the decision of Trial Chamber III of 27 June 2011 entitled "Decision on Applications for Provisional Release", 12 September 2011, para. 1, the Appeals Chamber found that "[i]f a Chamber is considering conditional release and a State has indicated its general willingness and ability to accept a detained person and enforce conditions, the Chamber must seek observations from that State as to its ability to enforce specific conditions identified by the Chamber". The issues were remanded to the Trial Chamber for new consideration. As a consequence, the Trial Chamber considered the matter again in *Prosecutor v. Bemba*, ICC T. Ch., Public Redacted Version of the 26 September 2011 Decision on the accused's application for provisional release in light of the Appeals Chamber's judgment of 19 August 2011, 27 September 2011.

In *Bemba*, the Pre-Trial Chamber first granted the suspect conditional release, *Prosecutor v. Bemba*, ICC PT. Ch. I, Decision on the Interim Release of Jean-Pierre Bemba Gombo and Con-

---

3. The Pre-Trial Chamber shall periodically review its ruling on the release or detention of the person, and may do so at any time on the request of the Prosecutor or the person. Upon such review, it may modify its ruling as to detention, release or conditions of release, if it is satisfied that changed circumstances so require.[485]

---

vening Hearings with the Kingdom of Belgium, the Republic of Portugal, the Republic of France, the Federal Republic of Germany, the Italian Republic, and the Republic of South Africa, 14 August 2009. This was motivated, *inter alia*, with Mr Bemba's good behaviour in detention (para. 64)

On 3 September 2009 the Appeals Chamber issued in *Bemba* the "Decision on the Request of the Prosecutor for Suspensive Effect" in which it decided to grant suspensive effect in respect of operative paragraph (a) of the 14 August 2009 Decision. In *Prosecutor v. Bemba*, ICC A. Ch., Judgment on the appeal of the Prosecutor against Pre-Trial Chamber II's "Decision on the Interim Release of Jean-Pierre Bemba Gombo and Convening Hearings with the Kingdom of Belgium, the Republic of Portugal, the Republic of France, the Federal Republic of Germany, the Italian Republic, and the Republic of South Africa", 2 December 2009, the Appeals Chamber reversed the decision of Pre-Trial Chamber II. The Appeals Chamber found that "[i]n granting conditional release it is necessary to specify the appropriate conditions that make conditional release feasible, identify the State to which Mr. Bemba would be released and whether that State would be able to enforce the conditions imposed by the Court" (para. 2) The Appeals Chamber determined that the Pre-Trial Chamber erred in finding that there existed a change in circumstances that necessitated the conditional release of Mr Bemba (para. 64).

Author: Mark Klamberg.

[485] Paragraph 3 provides that the Pre-Trial Chamber periodically reviews its ruling on release or detention.

No time period for the timings if these periodic reviews are stipulated in the Statute. However, rule 118(2) requires that the Pre-Trial Chamber reviews its decision at least every 120 days. See for example *Prosecutor v. Lubanga*, ICC PT. Ch. I, Review of the "Decision on the Application for the Interim Release of Thomas Lubanga Dyilo", 14 February 2007, where PTC I after 120 days reviewed its ruling decided that Thomas Lubanga Dyilo shall continue to be detained. The Pre-Trial Chamber has the power to review the detention of a suspect even in the absence of an application for inter release. In *Prosecutor v. Katanga*, ICC PT. Ch., Decision on the powers of the Pre-Trial chamber to review proprio motu the pre-trial detention of Germain Katanga, 18 March 2008, p. 12, the Single Judge decided that she, acting on behalf of the Chamber, "has the power to undertake a proprio motu review to determine whether the conditions for the pre-trial detention of Germain Katanga continue to be met".

In *Prosecutor v. Bemba*, ICC A. Ch., Judgment on the appeal of Mr Jean-Pierre Bemba Gombo against the decision of Trial Chamber III of 28 July 2010 entitled "Decision on the review of the detention of Mr Jean-Pierre Bemba Gombo pursuant to Rule 118(2) of the Rules of Procedure and Evidence", para. 51, the Appeals Chamber clarified that while the Prosecutor does not have to re-establish circumstances that have already been established, he must show that there has been no change in those circumstances. In light of the above, a Chamber carrying out a periodic review of a ruling on detention under Article 60 (3) of the Statute must satisfy itself that the conditions under Article 58(1) of the Statute, as required by Article 60(2) of the Statute, continue to be met (para. 52). The Appeals Chamber observed that the Trial Chamber did not refer to the circumstances underpinning the ruling on detention and indicate whether these circumstances persist or whether there has been a change (para. 55) For the reasons stated above, the Appeals Chamber concluded that the Trial Chamber erred when, in carrying out a periodic review under Article 60 (3) of the Statute, it failed to revert to the ruling on detention in the manner outlined above at paragraph 52 and, instead, restricted itself to only assessing the al-

4. The Pre-Trial Chamber shall ensure that a person is not detained for an unreasonable peri-od prior to trial due to inexcusable delay by the Prosecutor. If such delay occurs, the Court shall consider releasing the person, with or without conditions.[486]

5. If necessary, the Pre-Trial Chamber may issue a warrant of arrest to secure the presence of a person who has been released.[487]

---

leged new circumstances presented by Mr Bemba (para. 57) As a consequence, the Appeals Chamber reversed the Impugned Decision. The matter was remanded to the Trial Chamber for a new review in light of paragraphs 40 to 56 of the judgment. Until, and subject to, that review, Mr Bemba was ordered to remain in detention (para. 95).

Cross-references:

Rules 118, 119, 120, 185.

Author: Mark Klamberg.

[486] Article 60(4) is independent of Article 60(2) in the sense that even if the ground for pre-trial detention set out in Article 58(1) are met, the Pre-Trial Chamber shall consider the release of the detained if the person is detained for an unreasonable period prior to trial due to inexcusable de-lay by the Prosecutor.

There are several decisions concerning Article 60(4). In *Prosecutor v. Lubanga*, ICC PT. CH. I, Second Review of the "Decision on the Application for Interim Release of Thomas Lubanga Dyilo", 11 June 2007, PTC I considered that the period of detention was reasonable and that there was no inexcusable delay caused by the Prosecution according to Article 60(4) of the Statute. It decided that Thomas Lubanga Dyilo should continue to be detained.

In *Prosecutor v. Lubanga*, ICC PT. Ch. I, Second Review of the "Decision on the Applica-tion for Interim Release of Thomas Lubanga Dyilo", 11 June 2007, PTC I considered that the period of detention was reasonable and that there was no inexcusable delay caused by the Prose-cution according to Article 60(4) of the Statute. It decided that Thomas Lubanga Dyilo should continue to be detained.

In *Prosecutor v. Lubanga*, ICC T. Ch., Decision reviewing the "Decision on the Application for the Interim Release of Thomas Lubanga Dyilo", TC I concluded that the detention of the ac-cused had not been for an unreasonable period due to inexcusable delay by the prosecution and decided that Thomas Lubanga Dyilo were to stay in detention.

However, in *Prosecutor v. Lubanga*, ICC A. Ch., Judgment on the appeal of the Prosecutor against the decision of Trial Chamber I entitled "Decision on the release of Thomas Lubanga Dyilo", 21 October 2008, the Appeals Chamber found that "[i]f a Chamber imposes a condi-tional stay of the proceedings, the unconditional release of the accused person is not the "inevi-table" consequence and "the only correct course" to take. Instead, the Chamber will have to consider all relevant circumstances and base its decision on release or detention on the criteria in Articles 60 and 58(1) of the Statute".

Cross-references:

Rule 185.

Author: Mark Klamberg.

[487] Paragraph 5 allows the Pre-Trial Chamber to issue a warrant of arrest to secure the presence of a person who has been released.

Doctrine:

1. William A Schabas, *The International Criminal Court: A Commentary on the Rome Statute*, Oxford University Press, Oxford, 2010, pp. 721–31.

---

2. Karim A.A. Khan, "Article 60 – Initial Proceedings before the Court", in Otto Triffterer (ed.), *Commentary on the Rome Statute of the International Criminal Court: Observers' Notes, Article by Article*, 2nd ed., C.H. Beck/Hart/Nomos, Munich/Oxford/Baden-Baden, 2008, pp. 1159–1169.

Author: Mark Klamberg.

Article 61
Confirmation of the charges before trial[488]

---

[488] *General remarks*:

Unique feature of the International Criminal Court

The holding of a confirmation hearing before the opening of the trial is a unique feature of the Court. No other international criminal tribunal contemplates this proceeding. Before other international criminal tribunals, the Prosecutor submits an indictment to a judge, who decides *ex parte* whether to confirm it and if so, issues an arrest warrant. The trial eventually follows on the confirmed indictment, after the remaining pre-trial proceedings have been completed. By contrast, at the Court a hearing pursuant to Article 61 of the Statute is held before three judges to confirm the charges against the person concerned, after a warrant of arrest or a summons to appear under Article 58 of the Statute has been issued *ex parte*. The person concerned may challenge those charges during the confirmation hearing and, if successful, prevent the opening of a trial against him or her. Article 61 marks the boundaries between the pre-trial and trial stages before the Court.

Purpose of the confirmation hearing

The purpose of the confirmation hearing is not to find the truth in relation to the guilt or innocence of the person against whom a warrant of arrest or a summons to appear has been issued, but to confirm the charges on which the Prosecutor intends to seek trial. The word "confirm" means to "make valid by formal authoritative assent; to ratify, sanction". Accordingly, the Pre-Trial Chamber validates the charges as formulated by the prosecution by determining whether the evidence presented is sufficient to commit said person for trial, and, in the event that the charges are confirmed, it demarcates the subject-matter of the case, designs the legal and factual framework for the subsequent trial proceedings and facilitates the preparation for trial (*Prosecutor v. Ruto and Sang*, ICC T. Ch. V, 28 December 2012, para. 14; *Kenyatta and Muthaura*, ICC T. Ch. V, 28 December 2012, para. 18; *Prosecutor v. Ruto and Sang*, ICC PT. Ch. II, 16 August 2013, para. 25). In short, the confirmation of charges hearing exists to separate those cases and charges which should go to trial from those which should not. It serves to ensure the efficiency of judicial proceedings and to protect the rights of persons by ensuring that cases and charges go to trial only when justified by sufficient evidence (*Prosecutor v. Mbarushimana*, ICC A. Ch., 30 May 2012, paras. 39 and 47).

The confirmation hearing is therefore not a "trial before the trial" or a "mini-trial", but a procedure designed to protect the suspect against unfounded accusations and to ensure judicial economy (*Prosecutor v. Lubanga*, ICC PT. Ch. I, 29 January 2007, para. 37; *Prosecutor v. Katanga and Ngudjolo*, ICC PT. Ch. I, 21 April 2008, paras. 5–6; *Prosecutor v. Katanga and Ngudjolo*, ICC PT. Ch. I, 30 September 2008, paras. 63–64; *Prosecutor v. Bemba*, ICC PT. Ch. II, 15 June 2009, para. 28; *Prosecutor v. Abu Garda*, ICC PT. Ch. I, 8 February 2010, para. 39; *Prosecutor v. Banda and Jerbo*, ICC PT. Ch. I, 8 March 2011, para. 31; *Prosecutor v. Muthaura et al.*, Decision on the Schedule for the Confirmation of Charges Hearing, 13 September 2011, para. 8; *Prosecutor v. Mbarushimana*, ICC PT. Ch. I, 16 December 2011, para. 41; *Prosecutor v. Ruto et al.*, ICC PT. Ch. II, 23 January 2012, para. 40; *Prosecutor v. Kenyatta et al.*, ICC PT. Ch. II, 23 January 2012, para. 52).

Moreover, the confirmation hearing is not intended to revisit the "reasonable grounds to believe" determination for the issuance of a warrant of arrest or to assess the manner in which the Prosecutor has conducted the investigation (*Prosecutor v. Lubanga*, ICC PT. Ch. I, 15 May 2006, Annex I, paras. 55–56; *Abu Garda*, ICC PT. Ch. I, 8 February 2010, para. 48). The confirmation hearing is only meant to assess the sufficiency of the results of the investigation to proceed to trial (*Prosecutor v. Abu Garda*, ICC PT. Ch. I, 8 February 2010, para. 48; *Prosecutor*

---

v. Ruto et al., ICC PT. Ch. II, 23 January 2012, paras. 51–53; *Prosecutor v. Kenyatta et al.*, ICC PT. Ch. II, 23 January 2012, paras. 63–65), regardless of whether the suspect agrees to consider as proven the facts alleged by the Prosecutor (*Prosecutor v. Banda and Jerbo*, ICC PT. Ch. I, 8 March 2011, para. 46).

The Court has ruled that confirmation hearings are justified by the need to provide for the early dismissal of cases lacking a substantive evidentiary basis (*Prosecutor v. Abu Garda*, ICC PT. Ch. I, 8 February 2010, Separate opinion of Judge Cuno Tarfusser, para. 4) and to identify clearly and in detail the facts of those cases deserving a trial (*Prosecutor v. Lubanga*, A. Ch., 8 December 2009, para. 90, fn. 163).

Sequence of the confirmation hearing

Article 61 of the Statute describes the sequence of events in relation to the confirmation of the charges. The proceedings leading to the confirmation of charges hearing pursuant to Article 61(7) of the Statute commence with the initial appearance of the suspect (*Prosecutor v. Gaddafi and Al-Senussi*, ICC PT. Ch. I, 30 July 2013, para. 34). Thereafter, pursuant to Article 61(3)(a) of the Statute, the Prosecutor must provide the suspect with a copy of the document containing the charges within a reasonable time before the confirmation hearing. Article 61(4) of the Statute clarifies that the provision of the document containing the charges alone does not limit the Prosecutor's flexibility with respect to the charges brought. Before the confirmation hearing, the Prosecutor may continue his investigation, amend or withdraw charges without the permission of the Pre-Trial Chamber. This flexibility of the Prosecutor is more limited after the confirmation of the charges with respect to the amendment, addition or withdrawal of charges. The Pre-Trial Chamber may confirm, decline to confirm or request the Prosecution to consider amending its charges (Article 61(7) of the Statute), but it may not add or modify the charges, which is the responsibility of the Prosecution (*Prosecutor v. Ruto and Sang*, ICC T. Ch. V, 20 November 2012, para. 4; *Prosecutor v. Kenyatta and Muthaura*, ICC T. Ch. V, 20 November 2012, para. 7). If further investigations lead the Prosecutor to reassess his theory about the suspect's liability for the crimes charged, he may seek, within the limits of Article 61(9) of the Statute, an amendment or withdrawal of the charges, as necessary. The amendment of the charges after their confirmation is only possible with the permission of the Pre-Trial Chamber. In order to add additional charges or substitute charges with more serious charges, a new confirmation hearing must be held. Withdrawal of charges after the commencement of the trial is only possible with the permission of the Trial Chamber (*Prosecutor v. Lubanga*, ICC A. Ch., 13 October 2006, paras. 53 and 56).

Preparatory works:

The drafters of the Statute did not import the ICTY/ICTR procedures. The drafters of Article 61 specifically rejected the idea of an indictment procedure which had appeared in earlier drafts of the Statute and replaced it with a new confirmation of charges hearing, which constituted part of a new "single, straightforward procedural approach, acceptable to delegations representing different national legal systems". The confirmation of an indictment at the ICTY/ICTR is an *ex parte* procedure, conducted in the absence of the defence by one judge. The confirmation of charges hearing, in comparison, was deliberately established as a hearing before a Pre-Trial Chamber of three judges at which the person charged has the right to be present and to contest the evidence and following which the Pre-Trial Chamber must assess the evidence. This process requires the Pre-Trial Chamber to go beyond looking at the Prosecutor's allegations "on their face" as is done in confirming an indictment at the ICTY/ICTR (*Prosecutor v. Mbarushimana*, ICC A. Ch., 30 May 2012, para. 43).

Author: Enrique Carnero Rojo.

1. Subject to the provisions of paragraph 2, within a reasonable time after the person's surrender or voluntary appearance before the Court, the Pre-Trial Chamber shall hold a hearing to confirm the charges on which the Prosecutor intends to seek trial. The hearing shall be held in the presence of the Prosecutor and the person charged, as well as his or her counsel.[489]

2. The Pre-Trial Chamber may, upon request of the Prosecutor or on its own motion, hold a hearing in the absence of the person charged to confirm the charges on which the Prosecutor intends to seek trial when the person has:

    (a) Waived his or her right to be present; or

    (b) Fled or cannot be found and all reasonable steps have been taken to secure his or her appearance before the Court and to inform the person of the charges and that a hearing to confirm those charges will be held.

    In that case, the person shall be represented by counsel where the Pre-Trial Chamber determines that it is in the interests of justice.[490]

---

[489] The presence of the suspect at the confirmation of charges hearing is envisaged in Article 61(1) of the Statute, which provides that the hearing "shall be held in the presence of the Prosecutor and the person charged" unless one of the conditions set forth in paragraph 2 of that provision is met (*Prosecutor v. L. Gbagbo*, ICC PT. Ch. I, 12 March 2013, para. 29). Some judges have emphasised the importance of the personal attendance of suspect at the confirmation of charges hearing, expecting the suspect's presence throughout the sessions, unless exceptional circumstances arise (*Prosecutor v. L. Gbagbo*, ICC PT. Ch. I, 13 February 2013, para. 9).

The Court does not provide the person named in the Prosecutor's application under Article 58 with any procedural instrument before the Pre-Trial Chamber allowing him or her to challenge the evidence presented by the Prosecutor other than, if and when the issuance of a warrant of arrest or a summons to appear has set in motion the process leading to the confirmation hearing, through the procedural remedies expressly provided for and within the context and for the purposes of the hearing on the confirmation of charges pursuant to Article 61(1) of the Statute (*Situation in Kenya*, ICC PT. Ch. II, 11 February 2011, para. 19).

Author: Enrique Carnero Rojo.

[490] Article 61(2) deals with a hearing to confirm charges against a person who has not yet become an accused person. In that scenario, the Statute contemplates that the proceedings may be held in his absence, if the person so chooses, considering that no judicial decision would as yet have confirmed as realistic the probability that he has a case to answer. In the absence of such a judicial decision, there would have been no appreciable juridical link that tied the suspect to the Court and its processes in a substantial way. That context is different as compared to the trial of a person who is an accused person, by virtue of a decision of a Pre-Trial Chamber following an appraisal of some evidence establishing substantial grounds to believe that the accused committed the crime charged (*Prosecutor v. Ruto and Sang*, ICC T. Ch. V(A), 18 June 2013, para. 60).

A person who wishes to waive the right to be present at the hearing must either decide to be present during the whole proceeding or may waive his right to be present throughout the entirety of the hearing (*Prosecutor v. Ruto et al*, ICC PT. Ch. II, Decision on the "Defence Request pursuant to Rule 124(1) for Mr. William Ruto to Waive his Right to be Present for part of the Confirmation of charges Hearing", 29 August 2011, para. 12.

---

2. Within a reasonable time before the hearing, the person shall:[491]

    (a) Be provided with a copy of the document containing the charges on which the Prosecutor intends to bring the person to trial;[492] and

---

Author: Enrique Carnero Rojo.

[491] By contrast with the procedure before the ICTY and ICTR, the charging document is filed by the Prosecution with the Pre-Trial Chamber for the purpose of the confirmation hearing after the suspect has voluntarily appeared, or has been surrendered to the Court, except for those exceptional situations in which the confirmation hearing is held in absentia (*Prosecutor v. Katanga and Ngudjolo*, ICC PT. Ch. I, 25 June 2008, paras. 8–9). The time limits of the Prosecution's disclosure obligations under Article 61(3) of the Statute are elaborated on by rule 121(3), (4) and (5) of the Rules, which sets specific time limits (no later than 30 days and no later than 15 days before the date of the confirmation hearing) for the Prosecution to provide the document containing the charges and the list of evidence (*Prosecutor v. Lubanga*, ICC PT. Ch. I, 15 May 2006, Annex I, para. 92; *Prosecutor v. Katanga and Ngudjolo*, ICC PT. Ch. I, 10 March 2008, p. 6).

Author: Enrique Carnero Rojo.

[492] *Purpose of the document containing the charges*

The document containing the charges is to be understood as the document which frames the confirmation hearing. This is the document which, in accordance with Article 67(1) of the Statute and rule 121 of the Rules, must establish in detail the nature, cause and content of the charges brought against the suspect and which forms the basis for preparation for the confirmation hearing (*Prosecutor v. Mbarushimana*, ICC PT. Ch. I, 16 December 2011, para. 90). Accordingly, the Chambers have limited themselves to the charges specified in the Prosecutor's document containing the charges, referring allegations concerning other crimes brought to the Chambers' attention by third parties to the scope of the "situation" within which a given case has arisen (*Prosecutor v. Lubanga*, ICC PT. Ch. I, 26 September 2006). Similarly, words such as "including but not limited to" have been found to be meaningless in the document containing the charges, noting that pursuant to Articles 61(3)(a) and 67(1)(a) of the Statute, rule 121(3) of the Rules and regulation 52 of the Regulations the suspect must be informed in detail of the facts underlying the charges against him or her before the commencement of the confirmation hearing, and that the Prosecution must know the scope of its case as well as the material facts underlying the charges that it seeks to prove, and must be in possession of the evidence necessary to prove those charges to the requisite level in advance of the confirmation hearing (*Prosecutor v. Mbarushimana*, ICC PT. Ch. I, 16 December 2011, paras. 81–83; *Prosecutor v. Ruto et al.*, ICC PT. Ch. II, 23 January 2012, para. 99).

Content of the document containing the charges

A "charge" is composed of the facts and circumstances underlying the alleged crime as well as of their legal characterisation (*Prosecutor v. Ruto et al.*, ICC PT. Ch. II, 23 January 2012, para. 44; *Prosecutor v. Kenyatta et al.*, ICC PT. Ch. II, 23 January 2012, para. 56). Pursuant to Article 67(1)(a) of the Statute, the accused has the right to be informed "in detail" of the content of the charges. This enables him to meaningfully prepare his defence. The required level of specificity of the content of the charge depends on the specific circumstances of the case (*Prosecutor v. Ruto and Sang*, ICC T. Ch. V, 28 December 2012, para. 35). Pursuant to regulation 52 of the Regulations of the Court, the document containing the charges must include a) the full name of the person and any other relevant identifying information; b) a statement of the facts, including the time and place of the alleged crimes, which provides a sufficient legal and factual basis to bring the person or persons to trial, including relevant facts for the exercise of jurisdiction by the Court; and c) a legal characterisation of the facts to accord both with the crimes under Arti-

---

(b) Be informed of the evidence on which the Prosecutor intends to rely at the hearing.[493]

cles 6, 7 or 8 and the precise form of participation under Articles 25 and 28. Consequently, the Prosecution is under no obligation to articulate in the document containing the charges its legal understanding of the various modes of liability and the alleged crimes, and it may mention events which occurred before or during the commission of the acts or omission with which the suspect is charged, especially if that would be helpful in better understanding the context in which the conduct charged occurred (*Prosecutor v. Lubanga*, ICC PT. Ch. I, 29 January 2007, paras. 151–152; *Prosecutor v. Katanga and Ngudjolo*, ICC PT. Ch. I, 25 June 2008, para. 21). Moreover, the document containing the charges may not be exhaustive in all the information in support of the charges. However, it has to provide the Defence with a sufficiently clear picture of the facts underpinning the charges against the suspect and in particular in relation to the crimes, the dates and locations of their alleged commission (*Prosecutor v. Ruto et al.*, ICC PT. Ch. II, 23 January 2012, para. 98). The document containing the charges transmitted by the Prosecution is to be read in conjunction with the Prosecution's list of evidence (*Prosecutor v. Lubanga*, ICC PT. Ch. I, 29 January 2007, para. 150; *Prosecutor v. Katanga and Ngudjolo*, ICC PT. Ch. I, 25 June 2008, para. 21).

Language of the document containing the charges

The Prosecution is usually ordered, for the purpose of its disclosure obligations to the Defence, to file its charging document in a language that the person fully understands and speaks, pursuant to Article 67(1)(a) of the Statute (*Prosecutor v. Katanga and Ngudjolo*, ICC PT. Ch. I, 10 March 2008, p. 6).

Role of the Pre-Trial Chamber

The Pre-Trial Chambers are in particular mandated to ensure the protection of the rights of the arrested person provided for in Articles 61(3) and 67 of the Statute and rule 121 of the Rules, including the right to have adequate time and facilities for the preparation of his or her defence and the right to be tried without undue delay (*Prosecutor v. Katanga and Ngudjolo*, ICC PT. Ch. I, 10 March 2008, p. 6). The Pre-Trial Chambers have a general competence under Article 61(3) of the Statute to issue orders regarding disclosure of evidence for the purposes of the confirmation of charges hearing (*Prosecutor v. Blé Goudé*, ICC PT. Ch. I, 6 May 2014, para. 6).

Author: Enrique Carnero Rojo.

[493] *Scope of evidence disclosed to the Defence*

The Defence is not entitled to full access to the entire Prosecution file of the investigation of the situation and the case because Article 61(3), together with Articles 67(1)(a) and (b), 67(2), and rules 76, 77 and 121(3) do not oblige the Prosecution to disclose to the Defence or to permit the Defence to inspect any material which the Prosecution does not intend to present at the confirmation hearing and which is neither potentially exculpatory nor material to Defence preparations for the confirmation hearing. These provisions regulate the extent, time, and manner in which the Defence can access some of the materials contained in the Prosecution record to adequately prepare for the confirmation hearing (*Prosecutor v. Lubanga*, ICC PT. Ch. I, 15 May 2006, Annex I, paras. 7–15). The intention of these provisions is that the Defence should be in a position to prepare adequately for the confirmation hearing as soon as practicable, including the decision on the scope of its defence and the selection of the evidence on which it intends to rely at the hearing (*Prosecutor v. Lubanga*, ICC PT. Ch. I, 15 May 2006, Annex I, para. 128). In accordance with these provisions, the Prosecution is usually ordered, for the purpose of its disclosure obligations to the Defence, to file a list of evidence in the case, to disclose all evidence on which it intends to rely at the confirmation hearing, including potentially exculpatory materials, and to allow the system of pre-inspection and inspection to be put in place (*Prosecutor v. Katanga and Ngudjolo*, ICC PT. Ch. I, 10 March 2008, pp. 11–14).

The Pre-Trial Chamber may issue orders regarding the disclosure of information for the purposes of the hearing.

4. Before the hearing, the Prosecutor may continue the investigation and may amend or withdraw any charges. The person shall be given reasonable notice before the hearing of any amendment to or withdrawal of charges. In case of a withdrawal of charges, the Prosecutor shall notify the Pre-Trial Chamber of the reasons for the withdrawal.[494]

5. At the hearing, the Prosecutor shall support each charge with sufficient evidence to establish substantial grounds to believe that the person committed the crime charged. The Prosecutor may rely on documentary or summary evidence and need not call the witnesses expected to testify at the trial.[495]

Author: Enrique Carnero Rojo.

[494] *Temporal limit for the Prosecution's investigation*

Article 61(4) of the Statute was initially found to provide that the Prosecution may continue its investigation until the start of the confirmation hearing and that, since the Prosecution was not expressly conferred the right to continue with its investigation after the confirmation hearing, said investigation must be completed by the time the confirmation hearing starts, barring exceptional circumstances that might justify later isolated acts of investigation (*Prosecutor v. Lubanga*, ICC PT. Ch. I, 15 May 2006, Annex I, paras. 105 and 130–131; *Prosecutor v. Lubanga*, ICC PT. Ch. I, 19 May 2006, para. 39). However, the Appeals Chamber later clarified that there is no temporal limit for the Prosecutor's investigations. In fact, the Prosecutor's flexibility with respect to the investigation that is acknowledged by Article 61(4) of the Statute remains unaffected by the confirmation of the charges, and the Prosecutor does not need to seek permission from the Pre-Trial Chamber to continue the investigation (*Prosecutor v. Lubanga*, ICC A. Ch., 13 October 2006, para. 53). Ideally, although it is not a requirement of the Statute, it would be desirable for the investigation to be complete by the time of the confirmation hearing (*Prosecutor v. Lubanga*, ICC A. Ch., 13 October 2006, para. 54; *Prosecutor v. Mbarushimana*, ICC A. Ch., 30 May 2012, para. 44). This finding has been relied upon to inquire about the reasons behind the Prosecution's apparent delays in conducting some investigations (*Prosecutor v. Kenyatta and Muthaura*, ICC PT. Ch. II, 29 January 2013, para. 9). In other occasions, this finding has been found not to exclude the possibility that the Prosecution may conduct further investigation thereafter only in certain circumstances, namely if it shows that it is necessary in order to establish the truth or certain circumstances exist that justify doing so (*Prosecutor v. Kenyatta*, ICC PT. Ch. II, 22 March 2013, para. 36; *Prosecutor v. Ruto and Sang*, ICC PT. Ch. II, 16 August 2013, para. 34). In any event, the Court's statutory documents do not oblige the Prosecutor to complete the entirety of her investigation at the beginning of the pre-trial proceedings (*Prosecutor v. Ntaganda*, ICC PT. Ch. II, 18 June 2013, para. 31).

No judicial authorisation required

Article 61(4) of the Statute clarifies that the provision of the document containing the charges alone does not limit the Prosecutor's flexibility with respect to the charges brought. Before the confirmation hearing, the Prosecutor may continue the investigation, and amend or withdraw charges without the permission of the Pre-Trial Chamber (*Prosecutor v. Lubanga*, ICC A. Ch., 13 October 2006, para. 53; *Prosecutor v. Mbarushimana*, ICC PT. Ch. I, 16 December 2011, para. 88).

Author: Enrique Carnero Rojo.

[495] *Difference between evidence and facts*

In the view of the Appeals Chamber, the evidence put forward by the Prosecutor at the confirmation hearing to support a charge pursuant to Article 61(5) of the Statute must be distinguished from the factual allegations which support each of the legal elements of the crime(s) charged. In the confirmation process, the facts must be identified with sufficient clarity and detail, meeting the standard in Article 67(1)(a) of the Statute (*Prosecutor v. Lubanga*, ICC A. Ch., 08 December 2009, fn. 163; *Prosecutor v. Lubanga*, ICC T. Ch. I, 8 January 2010, paras. 29–30).

Incriminating evidence

By contrast, the Prosecution need not present at the confirmation of charges hearing all incriminating evidence that might be in its possession, particularly that on which the Prosecution states that it places lesser reliance (*Prosecutor v. Lubanga*, ICC PT. Ch. I, 19 May 2006, para. 34). The limited purpose of the confirmation hearing is reflected in the fact that the Prosecutor may rely on documentary and summary evidence and need not call the witnesses who will testify at trial. The use of such summaries, even where the identities of witnesses are unknown to the defence and their underlying statements are not fully disclosed, is not necessarily prejudicial to or inconsistent with the rights of the accused and a fair and impartial trial. However, in such circumstances, the Pre-Trial Chamber will need to consider on a case-by-case basis, bearing in mind the character of the confirmation of charges hearing, whether and what steps may need to be taken to ensure that the use of such statements is consistent with the rights of the accused and a fair and impartial trial (*Prosecutor v. Mbarushimana*, ICC A. Ch., 30 May 2012, para. 47). In fact, the Court has ruled on occasion that the limited scope of the confirmation hearing, and its object and purpose within the criminal procedure embraced by the Statute and the Rules, require from the Prosecution a particular effort to limit the number of witnesses on whom it intends to rely at the confirmation hearing to the very core witnesses, and in general the debate of the Prosecution evidence is required to be limited to analysing the core evidence supporting the charges against the suspect (*Prosecutor v. Katanga and Ngudjolo*, ICC PT. Ch. I, 21 April 2008, paras. 78–79).

Potential witnesses

It is important to highlight that those individuals who have given a statement or have been interviewed by the Prosecution are regarded as potential witnesses due to the Prosecution's choice not to rely on them for the purpose of the confirmation hearing. Consequently, their statements, interview notes and/or interview transcripts, whether in an unredacted, redacted or summary format, are not, in principle, part of the evidentiary debate held at the confirmation hearing, nor can be used to meet the evidentiary standard provided for in Article 61(2) of the Statute, unless the Defence decides to introduce them into evidence upon the *inter partes* disclosure by the Prosecution (*Prosecutor v. Katanga and Ngudjolo*, ICC PT. Ch. I, 21 April 2008, paras. 100–101).

Use of summaries

Moreover, pursuant to Article 61(5) of the Statute, the Prosecution can rely on summaries of the statements, interview notes and interview transcripts of the relevant witnesses as long as the information provided by the witnesses is such that a summary of their statements, interview notes or interview transcripts will not identify them. The use of summaries is not only consistent with the limited scope, the object and the purpose of the confirmation hearing, but also satisfies the right of the suspects to have the confirmation hearing held within a reasonable time, without being prejudicial to or inconsistent with their other rights and with a fair and impartial trial, and, in the event that the charges are confirmed, it will also facilitate the preparation of the trial (*Prosecutor v. Katanga and Ngudjolo*, ICC PT. Ch. I, 21 April 2008, paras. 137–138).

Probative value of documentary and summary evidence

The Appeals Chamber has ruled that the Pre-Trial Chamber can evaluate the credibility of witnesses without their in-person testimony and has recognised that rules regarding orality in the pre-trial phase are more relaxed than at trial (*Prosecutor v. Mbarushimana*, ICC A. Ch., 30 May 2012, para. 45). However, the summaries of witnesses' statements have a lesser probative value than unredacted parts of redacted statements, interview notes or interview transcripts; and the difference in probative value between a summary and the unredacted parts of heavily redacted statements, interview notes or interview transcripts is minimal (*Prosecutor v. Lubanga*, ICC PT. Ch. I, 5 October 2006, pp. 4 and 6; *Prosecutor v. Katanga and Ngudjolo*, ICC PT. Ch. I, 21 April 2008, paras. 88–89). Accordingly, the use of a summary by the Prosecution diminishes, as a general rule, the probative value of such evidence (*Prosecutor v. Katanga and Ngudjolo*, ICC PT. Ch. I, 21 April 2008, para. 133). As a consequence, the Prosecutor's reliance on documentary or summary evidence *in lieu* of in-person testimony will limit the Pre-Trial Chamber's ability to evaluate the credibility of witnesses. While it may evaluate their credibility, the Pre-Trial Chamber's determinations will necessarily be presumptive, and it should take great care in finding that a witness is or is not credible. The Prosecutor's reliance on summary evidence may also mean that the Pre-Trial Chamber will not be presented with all details of the evidence in the possession of the Prosecutor (*Prosecutor v. Mbarushimana*, ICC A. Ch., 30 May 2012, para. 48) (*Prosecutor v. L. Gbagbo*, ICC PT. Ch. I, 12 June 2014, para. 21; *Prosecutor v. Blé Goudé*, ICC T. Ch. I, 11 December 2014, para. 14). Moreover, given the fact that the Defence shall not have access for the purpose of the confirmation hearing to redacted or unredacted versions of the relevant statements, interview notes and interview transcripts by the Prosecution, the probative value of said summaries when relied upon by the Defence shall only be subject to the principle of free assessment of evidence provided for in Article 69 of the Statute and rule 63 of the Rules (*Prosecutor v. Katanga and Ngudjolo*, ICC PT. Ch. I, 21 April 2008, para. 135).

Probative value of anonymous witnesses

Although anonymous witnesses' statements and summaries thereof are permitted at the pre-trial stage, this evidence may be taken to have a lower probative value in order to counterbalance the disadvantage that it might cause to the Defence and have to be evaluated on a case-by-case basis, depending on whether the information contained therein is corroborated or supported by other evidence presented into the case file (*Prosecutor v. Katanga and Ngudjolo*, ICC PT. Ch. I, 30 September 2008, paras. 159–160; *Prosecutor v. Bemba*, ICC PT. Ch. II, 15 June 2009, para. 50; *Prosecutor v. Abu Garda*, ICC PT. Ch. I, 8 February 2010, paras. 49–52; *Prosecutor v. Banda and Jerbo*, ICC PT. Ch. I, 8 March 2011, para. 41; *Prosecutor v. Mbarushimana*, ICC PT. Ch. I, 16 December 2011, para. 49; *Prosecutor v. Ruto et al.*, ICC PT. Ch. II, 23 January 2012, para. 78; *Prosecutor v. Kenyatta et al.*, ICC PT. Ch. II, 23 January 2012, para. 90). Furthermore, anonymous hearsay contained in witness statements will be used only for the purposes of corroborating other evidence, while second degree and more remote anonymous hearsay contained in witness statements will be used with caution, even as a means of corroborating other evidence (*Prosecutor v. Lubanga*, ICC PT. Ch. I, 29 January 2007, paras. 101–106; *Prosecutor v. Katanga and Ngudjolo*, ICC PT. Ch. I, 30 September 2008, paras. 118–120, 137–140; *Prosecutor v. Mbarushimana*, ICC PT. Ch. I, 16 December 2011, para. 49; *Prosecutor v. Ruto et al.*, ICC PT. Ch. II, 23 January 2012, para. 78; *Prosecutor v. Kenyatta et al.*, ICC PT. Ch. II, 23 January 2012, para. 90).

Probative value of hearsay evidence

Hearsay from a known source will be analysed on a case-by-case basis, taking into account factors such as the consistency of the information itself and its consistency with the evidence as a whole, the reliability of the source and the possibility for the Defence to challenge the source (*Prosecutor v. Katanga and Ngudjolo*, ICC PT. Ch. I, 30 September 2008, para. 141; *Prosecutor v. Mbarushimana*, ICC PT. Ch. I, 16 December 2011, para. 49).

Use of summaries instead of redactions

In any event, the use by the Prosecution of summaries rather than redactions of the relevant statements, interview notes and interview transcripts is the appropriate procedural mechanism for the Prosecution to discharge its disclosure obligations because i) the redactions authorised at

6. At the hearing, the person may:

    (a) Object to the charges;

    (b) Challenge the evidence presented by the Prosecutor; and

    (c) Present evidence.[496]

---

the confirmation hearing stage would, for the most part, be useless at the trial stage, and ii) the time required for the analysis and decision on requests for redactions would lead to a delay in the confirmation proceedings (*Prosecutor v. Katanga and Ngudjolo*, ICC PT. Ch. I, 21 April 2008, paras. 106–110). The Prosecution summaries must include all information of a potentially exculpatory nature or otherwise material for the Defence's preparation of the confirmation hearing (*Prosecutor v. Katanga and Ngudjolo*, ICC PT. Ch. I, 21 April 2008, para. 111), and need not be judicially approved if they only aim at complying with the Prosecution's disclosure obligations under Article 67(2) and rule 77 (*Prosecutor v. Katanga and Ngudjolo*, ICC PT. Ch. I, 21 April 2008, paras. 113–114, 118).

Author: Enrique Carnero Rojo.

[496] *Rights of the person charged*

Article 61(6) of the Statute enshrines the rights of the person charged to challenge the evidence presented by the Prosecutor and to present his or her own evidence. If these rights are availed of, the evidence inevitably will be contested. For these rights to have any meaning, the Pre-Trial Chamber must evaluate the contested evidence and resolve any ambiguities, contradictions, inconsistencies or doubts as to credibility introduced by the contestation of the evidence (*Prosecutor v. Mbarushimana*, ICC A. Ch., 30 May 2012, para. 40). In other words, the appropriate venue for discussing questions regarding the relevance of such factual allegations, and the relevance, admissibility and probative value of evidence is the confirmation of charges hearing which gives the Defence the opportunity to raise any apposite challenges and objections pursuant to Article 61(6) of the Statute (*Prosecutor v. Blé Goudé*, ICC PT. Ch. I, 11 September 2014, para. 8).

Scope of challenges available to the Defence

Pursuant to Article 61(6), the Defence enjoys a broad scope of action, since under this provision a suspect may contest at the confirmation hearing both matters of statutory interpretation and evidential aspects of the Prosecutor's case (*Prosecutor v. Ruto et al.*, ICC A. Ch., 24 May 2012, para. 27; *Prosecutor v. Kenyatta and Muthaura*, ICC A. Ch., 24 May 2012, para. 33).

Connection with disclosure and other defence rights

The effective exercise of the right to challenge the evidence depends on the disclosure "as soon as practicable" of any potentially exculpatory excerpts in the statements of witnesses on whose written or oral testimony the Prosecution intends to rely on at the confirmation hearing (Article 67(2) of the Statute). In turn, this right is also linked to the right of the person to have adequate time and facilities for the preparation of the defence and to communicate freely and in confidence with counsel of his or her own choice (*Prosecutor v. Lubanga*, ICC PT. Ch. I, 19 May 2006, para. 36).

Limitations in the challenges available to the Defence

It is an inherent consequence of protective measures under rule 81(4) of the Rules that in individually justified cases, the Defence's ability to raise, and the Chamber's ability to address in its decision, certain questions pertaining to the reliability of witnesses are limited (*Prosecutor v. Kenyatta et al.*, ICC PT. Ch. II, 23 January 2012, para. 94).

Author: Enrique Carnero Rojo.

---

7. The Pre-Trial Chamber shall, on the basis of the hearing, determine whether there is sufficient evidence to establish substantial grounds to believe that the person committed each of the crimes charged. Based on its determination, the Pre-Trial Chamber shall:[497]

---

[497] *Purpose of the determination*

According to Article 61(7) of the Statute, at the confirmation hearing the Pre-Trial Chamber must determine "whether there is sufficient evidence to establish substantial grounds to believe that the person committed each of the crimes charged". On this basis, the Pre-Trial Chamber is not a finder of truth in relation to the guilt or innocence of the person against whom a warrant of arrest or a summons to appear has been issued (*Prosecutor v. Lubanga*, ICC PT. Ch. I, 15 May 2006, Annex I, para. 55). However, the Pre-Trial Chamber is required to evaluate the evidence in order to make a determination as to the sufficiency of the evidence. Accordingly, the Pre-Trial Chamber must necessarily draw conclusions from the evidence where there are ambiguities, contradictions, inconsistencies or doubts as to credibility arising from the evidence and enjoys a general authority to assess the evidence pursuant to Articles 61(6) and 69(4), and rules 63(2) and 122(9) (*Prosecutor v. Mbarushimana*, ICC A. Ch., 30 May 2012, paras. 39–41). Moreover, the Pre-Trial Chamber may, pursuant to rule 58(2), consider jurisdictional issues at the confirmation hearing, deciding on them during its determination of whether the Prosecutor has submitted sufficient evidence to establish substantial grounds to believe that the charged crimes were committed (*Prosecutor v. Ruto et al.*, ICC A. Ch., 24 May 2012, para. 28; *Prosecutor v. Kenyatta and Muthaura*, ICC A. Ch., 24 May 2012, para. 34).

Definition of the evidentiary standard

The limited purpose of the confirmation of charges proceedings is reflected in the fact that the Prosecutor must only produce sufficient evidence to establish substantial grounds to believe the person committed the crimes charged. The Pre-Trial Chamber need not be convinced beyond a reasonable doubt, and the Prosecutor need not submit more evidence than is necessary to meet the threshold of substantial grounds to believe (*Prosecutor v. Abu Garda*, ICC PT. Ch. I, 8 February 2010, para. 40; *Prosecutor v. Ruto et al.*, ICC PT. Ch. II, 23 January 2012, para. 40; *Prosecutor v. Kenyatta et al.*, ICC PT. Ch. II, 23 January 2012, para. 52; *Prosecutor v. Mbarushimana*, ICC A. Ch., 30 May 2012, para. 47; *Prosecutor v. L. Gbagbo*, ICC PT. Ch. I, 3 June 2013, para. 17). Similarly, the prerequisites to issue of a warrant of arrest and to confirm the charges are different. Whereas the test for the issuance of a warrant of arrest under Article 58(1)(a) and (b) of the Statute is the presence of "reasonable grounds to believe that the person has committed a crime within the jurisdiction of the Court" coupled with the existence of grounds warranting detention, the higher standard for the confirmation of the charges is the existence of "sufficient evidence to establish substantial grounds to believe that the person committed each of the crimes charged" (Article 61(7) of the Statute) (*Prosecutor v. Lubanga*, ICC A. Ch., 13 June 2007, para. 14; *Prosecutor v. L. Gbagbo*, ICC PT. Ch. I, 3 June 2013, para. 17; *Prosecutor v. L. Gbagbo*, ICC PT. Ch. I, 12 July 2013, para. 35). This standard imposes a higher evidentiary threshold than the ICTY/ICTR's lower "reasonable grounds" standard (Rule 98 *bis* of the ICTY Rules of Procedure and Evidence), which is used in the context of the issuance of a warrant of arrest under Article 58 of the Statute (*Prosecutor v. Bemba*, ICC PT. Ch. II, 15 June 2009, para. 28; *Prosecutor v. Al Bashir*, ICC A. Ch., 3 February 2010, para. 30; *Prosecutor v. Ruto et al.*, ICC PT. Ch. II, 23 January 2012, para. 40; *Prosecutor v. Kenyatta et al.*, ICC PT. Ch. II, 23 January 2012, para. 52; *Prosecutor v. Mbarushimana*, ICC A. Ch., 30 May 2012, para. 43; *Prosecutor v. L. Gbagbo*, ICC PT. Ch. I, 3 June 2013, para. 17; *Prosecutor v. Bemba et al.*, ICC PT. Ch. II, 11 November 2014, para. 25). The standard in Article 61(7) of the Statute has therefore been defined as an "intermediate evidentiary threshold" (*Prosecutor v. Ntaganda*, ICC PT. Ch. II, 9 June 2014, para. 9).

Scope of application of the evidentiary standard

The evidentiary threshold under Article 61(7) applies to all facts and circumstances of the case and is the same for all factual allegations, whether they pertain to the individual crimes charged, contextual elements of the crimes or the criminal responsibility of the suspect (*Prosecutor v. L. Gbagbo*, ICC PT. Ch. I, 03 June 2013, paras. 19–20). By contrast, the scope of determination under Article 61(7) of the Statute does not relate to the manner in which the Prosecutor conducted his investigations, since under no circumstances will a failure on the part of the Prosecutor to properly investigate automatically justify a decision of the Chamber to decline to confirm the charges, without having examined the evidence presented (*Prosecutor v. Abu Garda*, ICC PT. Ch. I, 08 February 2010, para. 48; *Prosecutor v. Ruto et al.*, ICC PT. Ch. II, 23 January 2012, para. 51; *Prosecutor v. Kenyatta et al.*, ICC PT. Ch. II, 23 January 2012, para. 63).

Application of the evidentiary standard by the Prosecution

In order to meet this evidentiary threshold (substantial grounds to believe), the Prosecution must offer "concrete and tangible proof demonstrating a clear line of reasoning underpinning its specific allegations" (*Prosecutor v. Lubanga*, ICC PT. Ch. I, Decision on the Confirmation of Charges, 29 January 2007, para. 39; *Prosecutor v. Katanga and Ngudjolo*, ICC PT. Ch. I, Decision on the Confirmation of Charges, 30 September 2008, para. 65; *Prosecutor v. Bemba*, ICC PT. Ch. II, 15 June 2009, para. 29; *Prosecutor v. Abu Garda*, ICC PT. Ch. I, 08 February 2010, para. 37; *Prosecutor v. Mbarushimana*, ICC PT. Ch. I, 16 December 2011, para. 40; *Prosecutor v. Ruto et al.*, ICC PT. Ch. II, 23 January 2012, para. 40; *Prosecutor v. Kenyatta et al.*, ICC PT. Ch. II, 23 January 2012, para. 52; *Prosecutor v. L. Gbagbo*, ICC PT. Ch. I, 3 June 2013, para. 17; *Prosecutor v. Ntaganda*, ICC PT. Ch. II, 9 June 2014, para. 9; *Prosecutor v. L. Gbagbo*, ICC PT. Ch. I, 12 June 2014, para. 19; *Prosecutor v. Bemba et al.*, ICC PT. Ch. II, 11 November 2014, para. 25; *Prosecutor v. Blé Goudé*, ICC T. Ch. I, 11 December 2014, para. 12). At this stage the Prosecutor is requested to substantiate his allegations that the crimes charged were committed with as precise as possible data (*Prosecutor v. Ruto et al.*, ICC PT. Ch. II, 23 January 2012, para. 103).

In *Prosecutor v. Bemba*, Decision Adjourning the Hearing pursuant to Article 61(7)(c)(ii) of the Rome Statute, 3 March 2009, para. 17, the PTC stated that "a complete and in-depth analysis of all the evidence" is unwarranted during the limited examination under Article 61(7)(c)(ii). The Chamber was of the view "that the evidence submitted appears to establish a different crime within the jurisdiction of the Court" (para. 1). It also stated that "[t]he notion of a 'different crime' pursuant to Article 61(7)(c)(ii) of the Statute relates both to the crimes as defined in Articles 6, 7 and 8 of the Statute as well as to the mode of liability as referred to in Articles 25 and 28 of the Statute. The crimes and the mode of liability correlate to each other. Depending on the mode of participation as set out in Articles 25 and 28 of the Statute, the material (objective) elements of the crime are shaped differently" (para. 26) In its decision, the Chamber requested the Prosecutor to consider amending the relevant charge.

Application of the evidentiary standard by the Pre-Trial Chamber

When it comes to the Pre-Trial Chamber, the Chamber must "be thoroughly satisfied that the Prosecutor's allegations are sufficiently strong to commit the person for trial" (*Prosecutor v. Lubanga*, Decison on the Confirmation of Charges, ICC PT. Ch. I, 29 January 2007, para. 39; *Prosecutor v. L. Gbagbo*, ICC PT. Ch. I, 3 June 2013, para. 17; *Prosecutor v. Ntaganda*, ICC PT. Ch. II, 9 June 2014, para. 9; *Prosecutor v. Bemba et al.*, ICC PT. Ch. II, 11 November 2014, para. 25). It must also be noted that the Statute and the Rules of Procedure and Evidence do not grant the Pre-Trial Chamber the power to determine only the relevance or admissibility of evidence but not its weight. Indeed, no provision precludes the Chamber from evaluating the evidence as is required by Article 61(7) of the Statute or otherwise limits the Chamber's authority to freely assess evidence (*Prosecutor v. Mbarushimana*, ICC A. Ch., 30 May 2012, para. 42). In fact, in determining whether to confirm charges under Article 61 of the Statute, the Pre-Trial

Chamber may evaluate ambiguities, inconsistencies and contradictions in the evidence or doubts as to the credibility of witnesses (*Prosecutor v. Mbarushimana*, ICC PT. Ch. I, 16 December 2011, paras. 1 and 47; *Prosecutor v. Ntaganda*, ICC PT. Ch. II, 9 June 2014, para. 10). Any other interpretation would carry the risk of cases proceeding to trial although the evidence is so riddled with ambiguities, inconsistencies, contradictions or doubts as to credibility that it is insufficient to establish substantial grounds to believe the person committed the crimes charged. This is not to say that the Pre-Trial Chamber's ability to evaluate the evidence is unlimited or that its function in evaluating the evidence is identical to that of the Trial Chamber (*Prosecutor v. Mbarushimana*, ICC A. Ch., 30 May 2012, paras. 46–47). A wholesale assessment as to the admissibility of each item of evidence at this stage would unjustifiably delay the proceedings and give rise to an inappropriate pre-determination of evidentiary matters which should be properly decided in light of the whole of the evidence presented at trial. Such an approach would be incompatible with the fair trial rights of the suspect guaranteed under Article 67 of the Statute, and in particular, the right to be tried without undue delay under Article 67(1)(c) of the Statute (*Prosecutor v. Mbarushimana*, ICC PT. Ch. I, 16 December 2011, para. 44).

Assessment of the admissibility of the evidence by the Pre-Trial Chamber

Accordingly, unless a party provides information which can reasonably cast doubt on the authenticity of items presented by the opposing party, such items must be considered authentic in the context of the confirmation hearing. This principle is equally applicable to challenges raised to the admissibility of evidence under Article 69(7) of the Statute (*Prosecutor v. Lubanga*, Decison on the Confirmation of Charges, ICC PT. Ch. I, 29 January 2007, para. 97; *Prosecutor v. Mbarushimana*, ICC PT. Ch. I, 16 December 2011, para. 59; *Prosecutor v. Bemba et al.*, ICC PT. Ch. II, 11 November 2014, para. 14). Moreover, even if it were to be accepted that there were procedural shortcomings in the investigative procedures complained of, Article 69(7) of the Statute does not mandate automatic exclusion of evidence thus obtained. In each case, the striking of an appropriate balance between the Statute's fundamental values is at the discretion of the Chamber and items of evidence obtained in violation of the Statute or internationally recognised human rights will be found to be inadmissible only in circumstances where a) the violation casts substantial doubt on the reliability of the evidence, or b) the admissibility of the evidence would be antithetical to and would seriously damage the integrity of the proceedings (*Prosecutor v. Lubanga*, ICC PT. Ch. I, Decison on the Confirmation of Charges, 29 January 2007, para. 84; *Prosecutor v. Mbarushimana*, ICC PT. Ch. I, 16 December 2011, para. 61). Moreover, neither the Statute nor the Rules provide that a certain type of evidence is *per se* inadmissible. Depending on the circumstances, the Pre-Trial Chamber is vested with discretion or statutorily mandated to rule on the admissibility of the evidence pursuant to Articles 69(4) and (7) of the Statute, and rule 63(3) of the Rules (*Prosecutor v. Ruto et al.*, ICC PT. Ch. II, 23 January 2012, para. 62; *Prosecutor v. Kenyatta et al.*, ICC PT. Ch. II, 23 January 2012, para. 76).

Assessment of the relevance and probative value of the evidence by the Pre-Trial Chamber

In practical terms, the "substantial grounds to believe" standard must enable all the evidences admitted for the purposes of the confirmation hearing to be assessed as a whole (*Prosecutor v. Lubanga*, ICC PT. Ch. I, Decision on the Confirmation of Charges, 29 January 2007, para. 39). In this regard, items and documents included in the parties' lists of evidence cease to be separate pieces of evidence presented by the parties and become evidence on the record. Consequently, permitting the parties to withdraw evidence initially included in their lists will prevent the Pre-Trial Chamber from being able to make their determinations under Article 61(7) (*Prosecutor v. Lubanga*, ICC PT. Ch. I, Decision on the Confirmation of Charges, 29 January 2007, paras. 141–142).

The Appeals Chamber has held that it is not required, as a matter of principle, to fully test the reliability of every piece of evidence relied upon by the Prosecutor for the purpose of the confirmation of charges hearing (*Prosecutor v. Lubanga*, Judgment on the appeal of Mr. Thomas Lubanga Dyilo against the decision of Pre-Trial Chamber I entitled "First Decision on the Prosecution Requests and Amended Requests for Redactions under Rule 81", ICC A. Ch., 14 December 2006, para. 47; *Prosecutor v. Kenyatta et al.*, ICC PT. Ch. II, 23 January 2012, para. 94). The Pre-Trial Chamber enjoys discretion in this regard in line with the principle of free assessment of evidence, which is limited to determining, pursuant to Article 69(4) and (7) of the Statute, the admissibility, relevance and probative value of the evidence placed before it (*Prosecutor v. Bemba*, ICC PT. Ch. II, 15 June 2009, paras. 61–62; *Prosecutor v. Ruto et al.*, ICC PT. Ch. II, 23 January 2012, paras. 59–60; *Prosecutor v. Kenyatta et al.*, ICC PT. Ch. II, 23 January 2012, paras. 73–74). Thus, in determining whether there are substantial grounds to believe that the suspect committed each of the crimes charged, the Chamber is not bound by the parties' characterisation of the evidence. Rather, the Chamber makes its own independent assessment of each piece of evidence. Moreover, the Chamber will assess the relevance and probative value of the evidence, regardless of its kind or which party relied upon it (*Prosecutor v. Bemba*, ICC PT. Ch. II, 15 June 2009, para. 42; *Prosecutor v. Ruto et al.*, ICC PT. Ch. II, 23 January 2012, para. 61; *Prosecutor v. Kenyatta et al.*, ICC PT. Ch. II, 23 January 2012, para. 75).

In assessing the relevance of the evidence, the Pre-Trial Chamber must establish the extent to which this evidence is rationally linked to the fact that it tends to prove or to disprove (*Prosecutor v. Ruto et al.*, ICC PT. Ch. II, 23 January 2012, para. 66; *Prosecutor v. Kenyatta et al.*, ICC PT. Ch. II, 23 January 2012, para. 79). The determination of the probative value of a piece of evidence requires a qualitative assessment. Pursuant to the principle of free assessment of evidence enshrined in Article 69(4) of the Statute and rule 63(2) of the Rules, the Pre-Trial Chamber will give each piece of evidence the weight that it considers appropriate (*Prosecutor v. Ruto et al.*, ICC PT. Ch. II, 23 January 2012, para. 67; *Prosecutor v. Kenyatta et al.*, ICC PT. Ch. II, 23 January 2012, para. 80).

The Pre-Trial Chambers take a case-by-case approach in assessing the relevance and probative value of each piece of evidence. In doing so, they are guided by various factors, such as the nature of the evidence, its credibility, reliability, and source as well as the context in which it was obtained and its nexus to the charges of the case or the alleged perpetrator. Indicia of reliability such as voluntariness, truthfulness, and trustworthiness are considered (*Prosecutor v. Bemba*, ICC PT. Ch. II, 15 June 2009, para. 58; *Prosecutor v. Ruto et al.*, ICC PT. Ch. II, 23 January 2012, para. 68; *Prosecutor v. Kenyatta et al.*, ICC PT. Ch. II, 23 January 2012, para. 81). Accordingly, inconsistencies do not lead to an automatic rejection of the particular piece of evidence and do not bar the Chamber from using it (*Prosecutor v. Ruto et al.*, ICC PT. Ch. II, 23 January 2012, para. 86; *Prosecutor v. Kenyatta et al.*, ICC PT. Ch. II, 23 January 2012, para. 92). Likewise, the suspects or Defence witnesses who are allegedly implicated in one way or another in the crimes are not automatically considered unreliable and/or not credible nor is their evidence granted a lower probative value as a matter of principle. Rather, their final assessment and weight depend on a case-by-case basis (*Prosecutor v. Ruto et al.*, ICC PT. Ch. II, 23 January 2012, paras. 91–92). Eventually, it is not the amount of evidence presented but its probative value that is essential for the Pre-Trial Chamber's final determination on the charges presented by the Prosecutor (*Prosecutor v. Bemba*, ICC PT. Ch. II, 15 June 2009, para. 60; *Prosecutor v. Ruto et al.*, ICC PT. Ch. II, 23 January 2012, para. 68; *Prosecutor v. Kenyatta et al.*, ICC PT. Ch. II, 23 January 2012, para. 81).

Moreover, some Chambers have found that they are guided in their assessment by the principle of *in dubio pro reo* as a component of the presumption of innocence, which as a general principle in criminal procedure applies, *mutatis mutandis*, to all stages of the proceedings, including the pre-trial stage (*Prosecutor v. Ruto et al.*, ICC PT. Ch. II, 23 January 2012, para. 41; *Prosecutor v. Kenyatta et al.*, ICC PT. Ch. II, 23 January 2012, para. 53). By contrast, other Chambers have ruled that the principle of *in dubio pro reo* is not applicable to the assessment of

(a) Confirm those charges in relation to which it has determined that there is sufficient evidence, and commit the person to a Trial Chamber for trial on the charges as confirmed;[498]

---

the probative value of the evidence presented by the Prosecution at this stage of the proceedings (*Prosecutor v. Abu Garda*, ICC PT. Ch. I, 8 February 2010, para. 43).

Decision by the Pre-Trial Chamber

As a result of the evidentiary debate held at the confirmation hearing, the Pre-Trial Chamber must issue, pursuant to Article 61(7) of the Statute, a decision providing the reasons for the confirmation or not of the charges, and such a decision may be particularly detailed on the factual and legal basis for the confirmation of the charges, or some of them, contained in the Prosecution's charging document (*Prosecutor v. Katanga and Ngudjolo*, ICC PT. Ch. I, 25 June 2008, para. 11).

Time of the decision

Pursuant to Article 61(7), the decision on confirmation of charges should be delivered within 60 days following the confirmation hearing. The 60-day time limit shall commence from the date the Defence final written submissions have been filed (*Prosecutor v. Ruto et al.*, ICC PT. Ch. II, 26 October 2011, para. 9). This time limit may be extended or reduced as set out in regulation 35 of the Regulations of the Court if exceptional circumstances so warrant and when the participants have been given an opportunity to be heard (*Prosecutor v. Ruto et al.*, ICC PT. Ch. II, 26 October 2011, para. 10).

Author: Enrique Carnero Rojo.

[498] *Charges confirmed for trial*

Article 61(7)(a) states that, where appropriate, the Pre-Trial Chamber shall commit the person to a Trial Chamber for trial on the charges it has confirmed. Article 64(8)(a) of the Statute further states that at the commencement of the trial, the Trial Chamber shall have read to the accused the charges previously confirmed by the Pre-Trial Chamber. Consequently, some Trial Chambers have found that the decision on the confirmation of the charges is the only document which can serve as a reference during trial proceedings and is the authoritative document for all trial proceedings (*Prosecutor v. Katanga and Ngudjolo*, ICC T. Ch. II, 29 October 2009, para. 16; *Prosecutor v. Bemba*, ICC T. Ch. III, 21 June 2010, para. 37). Nonetheless, when the confirmation decision does not provide a readily accessible statement of the facts that underlie each confirmed charge, the confirmed document containing the charges must be provided for the purposes of the trial (*Prosecutor v. Bemba*, ICC T. Ch. III, 21 June 2010, para. 30) or a summary of the changes confirmed prepared by the Prosecution (*Prosecutor v. Katanga and Ngudjolo*, ICC T. Ch. II, 29 October 2009, paras. 12–13 and 17). Moreover, the same Trial Chambers have suggested that an annex to the confirmation decision framed in this way by the relevant Pre-Trial Chamber, including footnotes with appropriate references to paragraphs of the confirmation decision, would be of very considerable assistance during the trial (*Prosecutor v. Katanga and Ngudjolo*, ICC T. Ch. II, 29 October 2009, para. 31; *Prosecutor v. Bemba*, ICC T. Ch. III, 21 June 2010, para. 30). In this regard, other Trial Chambers have ordered the Prosecution to articulate the confirmed charges in a clearer way (*Prosecutor v. Ruto and Sang*, ICC T. Ch. V, 20 November 2012, para. 4; *Prosecutor v. Kenyatta and Muthaura*, ICC T. Ch. V, 20 November 2012, para. 7) and, more importantly, have found that the confirmation decision cannot be expected to serve as the only authoritative statement of the charges for the trial. In their view, the description of the charges in the document containing the charges, amended to harmonise it with the findings made in the confirmation decision, rather than the confirmation decision itself, provides a sufficiently authoritative statement of the charges relevant to the trial proceedings. As a result, the Pre-Trial Chamber's silence on relevant statements of fact made in the document containing the charges should not result in their removal from the post-confirmation document containing the charges (*Prosecutor v. Ruto and Sang*, ICC T. Ch. V, 28 December 2012, paras. 18–19; *Prosecutor v. Kenyatta and Muthaura*, ICC T. Ch. V, 28 December 2012, paras. 21–22). In this scenario, whenever the Prosecution refers to the charges confirmed against the accused, this should be by way of the exact language of the confirmation decision, and with specific reference to the relevant paragraph(s) (*Prosecutor v. Bemba*, ICC T. Ch. III, 21 June 2010, para. 37). In any event, it must be noted that the Pre-Trial Chambers have streamlined the confirmed charges in their latest decisions (*Prosecutor v. Bemba et al.*, ICC PT. Ch. II, 11 November 2014, pp. 47–55).

Binding character of the confirmed charges for the Trial Chamber

The "facts and circumstances" appearing in the confirmed charges, and in the confirmed charges alone, determine the factual ambit of the case for the purposes of the trial and circumscribe it by preventing the Trial Chamber from exceeding that factual ambit (*Prosecutor v. Banda and Jerbo*, ICC PT. Ch. I, 8 March 2011, para. 34; *Prosecutor v. Mbarushimana*, ICC PT. Ch. I, 16 December 2011, para. 81; *Prosecutor v. Ruto et al.*, ICC PT. Ch. II, 23 January 2012, para. 44; *Prosecutor v. Kenyatta et al.*, ICC PT. Ch. II, 23 January 2012, para. 56). The "facts described in the charges" have been defined by the Appeals Chamber as those "factual allegations which support each of the legal elements of the crime charged" (*Prosecutor v. Lubanga*, ICC A. Ch., 08 December 2009, fn. 163). These refer to the essential facts constituting the elements of the crimes charged and have been denominated "material facts and circumstances" by some Trial Chambers (*Prosecutor v. Ruto and Sang*, ICC T. Ch. V, 20 November 2012, para. 9; *Prosecutor v. Kenyatta and Muthaura*, ICC T. Ch. V, 20 November 2012, para. 12). Furthermore, according to the Appeals Chamber, the facts described in the charges are to be distinguished from "the evidence put forward by the Prosecutor at the confirmation hearing to support a charge (Article 61(5) of the Statute), as well as from background or other information that, although contained in the document containing the charges or the confirmation decision does not support the legal elements of the crime charged" (*Prosecutor v. Lubanga*, ICC A. Ch., 08 December 2009, fn. 163). On this basis, all the facts and circumstances that are referred to in the document containing the charges or in the decision on the confirmation of charges but do not appear in the confirmed charge ("facts underlying the charges") have no delimiting or constraining power as such on the Trial Chamber ("subsidiary facts"), such as facts that are referred to in the document containing the charges or in the decision on the confirmation of charges serving the purpose of demonstrating or supporting the material facts and providing background information (*Prosecutor v. Banda and Jerbo*, ICC PT. Ch. I, 8 March 2011, para. 36; *Prosecutor v. Ruto et al.*, ICC PT. Ch. II, 23 January 2012, para. 47; *Prosecutor v. Kenyatta et al.*, ICC PT. Ch. II, 23 January 2012, para. 59). However useful these "other" facts and circumstances might have been to the Pre-Trial Chamber in determining whether the Prosecution has presented evidence demonstrating a clear line of reasoning underpinning its specific allegations, and thus meeting the requisite standard of proof under Article 61(7) of the Statute, they are, in principle, to be considered only as background information or as indirect proof of the material facts, and as such, are deprived of any limiting power *vis-à-vis* the Trial Chamber pursuant to Article 74(2) of the Statute and regulation 55(1) of the Regulations (*Prosecutor v. Banda and Jerbo*, ICC PT. Ch. I, 8 March 2011, para. 37; *Prosecutor v. Ruto and Sang*, ICC T. Ch. V, 20 November 2012, para. 10; *Prosecutor v. Kenyatta and Muthaura*, ICC T. Ch. V, 20 November 2012, para. 13). Consequently, the Pre-Trial Chamber does not engage in an examination of each and every subsidiary fact which is mentioned in the document containing the charges and upon which the Prosecutor relies to prove the existence of one or more facts described in the charges (*Prosecutor v. Ruto et al.*, ICC PT. Ch. II, 23 January 2012, para. 48; *Prosecutor v. Kenyatta et al.*, ICC PT. Ch. II, 23 January 2012, para. 60). Consequently, any delimiting effect can only be ascribed to the facts and circumstances which underlie the confirmed charges and must be described therein, as opposed to

(b) Decline to confirm those charges in relation to which it has determined that there is insufficient evidence;[499]

(c) Adjourn the hearing and request the Prosecutor to consider:

(i) Providing further evidence or conducting further investigation with respect to a particular charge;[500] or

---

the factual allegations which are presented by the Prosecutor with a view to demonstrating or supporting the existence of the material facts (*Prosecutor v. Blé Goudé*, ICC PT. Ch. I, 11 September 2014, para. 6). Moreover, in conducting the trial and rendering its final decision, the Trial Chamber cannot exceed the facts and circumstances described in the charges confirmed by the Pre-Trial Chamber and framed in any eventual document containing the charges, but is not bound by the Pre-Trial Chamber's evidentiary assessments or its interpretation of the relevant provisions of the Statute (*Prosecutor v. Kenyatta*, ICC T. Ch. V, 26 April 2013, para. 107).

Binding character of the confirmed charges for the parties and participants

Parties and participants in a case are expected to prepare on the basis of the charges as confirmed which shape the subject-matter of the case, and thus, to take into consideration the evidence that is only relevant to the charges confirmed (*Prosecutor v. Ruto and Sang*, ICC PT. Ch. II, 16 August 2013, para. 40). The charges as confirmed by the Pre-Trial Chamber (eventually set out in a subsequently updated document containing the charges) serve as the basis for the trial, and not the information contained in the Prosecution's pre-trial brief (*Prosecutor v. Kenyatta*, ICC T. Ch. V, 26 April 2013, paras. 107 and 109). Likewise, the temporal scope set out in the confirmation decision is binding *vis-à-vis* the Prosecution because the charges are to be formulated by the Prosecution in the document containing the charges, but as confirmed by the confirmation decision (*Prosecutor v. Ruto and Sang*, ICC T. Ch. V, 28 December 2012, para. 28). Similarly, regarding the geographic scope of the charges, the use of the term "including" by the Prosecution suggests that the locations specified by the Prosecution are exemplary and not exhaustive and might therefore have an impact on expanding the parameters of the case confirmed by the Pre-Trial Chamber (*Prosecutor v. Ruto and Sang*, ICC T. Ch. V, 28 December 2012, paras. 32–33). In this regard, whereas the Prosecution is not necessarily required to rely on entirely the same evidence at trial as it did at the confirmation of charges stage, it cannot seek to rely at trial on facts and circumstances going beyond the confirmed charges (*Prosecutor v. Kenyatta*, ICC T. Ch. V, 26 April 2013, para. 107).

Author: Enrique Carnero Rojo.

[499] *Effects of a decision not to confirm the charges*

If in the exercise of its filtering function the Pre-Trial Chamber decides not to confirm the charges, this decision ends the prosecution of the suspect, thus avoiding superfluous proceedings as any warrant of arrest and other restrictive measures cease to have effect in accordance with Article 61(10) of the Statute (*Prosecutor v. Bemba*, ICC PT. Ch. III, 31 July 2008, para. 15). If the Pre-Trial Chamber has confirmed some allegations but dismissed others based on the lack of sufficient evidence establishing substantial grounds to believe, within the meaning of Article 61(7) of the Statute, the Prosecution should not include the discarded allegations in its subsequent, if any, formulation of the confirmed charges (*Prosecutor v. Kenyatta and Muthaura*, ICC T. Ch. V, 28 December 2012, para. 75).

Author: Enrique Carnero Rojo.

[500] *Request for further evidence*

The Pre-Trial Chamber may elect to adjourn the hearing on the confirmation of charges rather than making a final determination on the merits pursuant to Article 61(7) of the Statute where the Prosecutor's evidence, viewed as a whole, although apparently insufficient, does not appear

(ii) Amending a charge because the evidence submitted appears to establish a different crime within the jurisdiction of the Court.[501]

---

to be so lacking in relevance and probative value that it leaves the Chamber with no choice but to decline to confirm the charges, *that is,* where the Prosecutor's evidence in relation to the charges is inadequate, but remains a degree of suspicion in relation to the alleged commission of crimes and the Chamber does not exclude that the Prosecutor might be able to present or collect further evidence in relation to the alleged crimes (*Prosecutor v. L. Gbagbo,* ICC PT. Ch. I, 3 June 2013, paras. 15 and 37). In these scenarios, Article 61(7) of the Statute limits the intervention of the Pre-Trial Chamber to the possibility of requesting the Prosecution to consider the opportunity to provide additional evidence, whereas Article 69(3) of the Statute gives the competent Chamber "the authority to request the submission of all evidence that it considers necessary for the determination of the truth". Article 69(3) of the Statute is not applicable during the pre-trial proceedings conducted before the Pre-Trial Chamber because i) the Pre-Trial Chamber is not a truth-finder, and ii) according to the literal interpretation of Article 69(3) of the Statute, its application is subject to consideration of the competent Chamber that evidence other than that introduced by the Prosecution and the Defence is "necessary for the determination of the truth" (*Prosecutor v. Katanga and Ngudjolo,* ICC PT. Ch. I, 13 May 2008, para. 110). Similarly, pursuant to the Appeals Chamber, where the Pre-Trial Chamber finds the evidence insufficient because of its summary or documentary nature, the Chamber need not reject the charges but may adjourn the hearing and request the Prosecutor to provide further evidence (*Prosecutor v. Mbarushimana,* ICC A. Ch., 30 May 2012, para. 48).

Effects of adjournment

A decision adjourning the confirmation hearing under Article 61(7)(c) of the Statute is not a decision declining to confirm the charges under Article 61(7)(b) of the Statute. Pursuant to Article 61(10) of the Statute, the result of declining to confirm the charges is that the arrest warrant would cease to have effect, but no such provision exists with respect to adjournment of the hearing under Article 61(7)(c). Therefore, a decision to adjourn the confirmation hearing under Article 61(7)(c) does not represent a final disposal of the merits of the case by the Pre-Trial Chamber, but is an intermediate procedural step, and has no effect on the previous finding in relation to the warrant of arrest that there are reasonable grounds to believe that the suspect committed a crime within the jurisdiction of the Court. The fact that the available evidence does not meet the evidentiary threshold for Article 67(1) does not mean there was insufficient evidence for the purposes of issuing an arrest warrant under Article 58(1)(a) of the Statute (*Prosecutor v. L. Gbagbo,* ICC PT. Ch. I, 12 July 2013, paras. 34–35).

Author: Enrique Carnero Rojo.

[501] *Different crimes*

The Pre-Trial Chamber may, on the basis of the confirmation hearing, decide whether to confirm the charges or invite the Prosecutor to consider amending a charge if the Chamber is of the view that the evidence establishes a different crime (*Prosecutor v. Lubanga,* ICC PT. Ch. I, 24 May 2007, fn. 36). In this regard, the confirmation of the charges is possible without adjourning the proceedings and giving the Defence the right to be heard where the legal characterisation of the conflict as of an international nature has already been mentioned in the decision on the arrest warrant, the Defence itself has raised the issue of the international character of the conflict at the confirmation hearing, and all participants have had the opportunity to present their observations on the matter (*Prosecutor v. Lubanga,* ICC PT. Ch. I, 24 May 2007, para. 43).

Amendment of the charges

However, the Pre-Trial Chamber is not vested with the authority to modify the charges brought by the Prosecutor against a suspect. According to Article 61(7) of the Statute, the Pre-Trial

8. Where the Pre-Trial Chamber declines to confirm a charge, the Prosecutor shall not be precluded from subsequently requesting its confirmation if the request is supported by additional evidence.[502]

Chamber shall, on the basis of the confirmation of charges hearing, "determine whether there is sufficient evidence to establish substantial grounds to believe that the person committed each of the crimes charged". On the basis of such determination, the Pre-Trial Chamber shall then either confirm those charges or decline confirmation thereof. Accordingly, the Pre-Trial Chamber does not have the power either to confirm a charge that is not specified by the Prosecutor or to clarify that the charge includes acts in addition to those specified by the Prosecutor as being included in the charge (*Prosecutor v. Ruto et al.*, ICC PT. Ch. II, 19 August 2011, para. 7). On the contrary, when the evidence appears to establish a different crime, pursuant to Article 61(7)(c)(ii) the Pre-Trial Chamber may request the Prosecution to consider amending a charge. Importantly, it is the Prosecution which would then amend such a charge, not the Pre-Trial Chamber (*Prosecutor v. Ruto and Sang*, ICC T. Ch. V, 28 December 2012, para. 15; *Prosecutor v. Kenyatta and Muthaura*, ICC T. Ch. V, 28 December 2012, para. 19).

Request to amend the charges

At most, Article 61(7)(c)(ii) of the Statute permits the Pre-Trial Chamber, on the basis of the confirmation of charges hearing, to adjourn the hearing and request the Prosecutor to consider "[a]mending a charge because the evidence submitted appears to establish a different crime within the jurisdiction of the Court". Only the presence of the requirements provided for by the said provision may trigger, at the appropriate stage of the pre-trial proceedings, the Chamber's request to the Prosecutor to modify the charges. Such a request must be made on the basis of the confirmation of charges hearing and in light of the evidence submitted (*Prosecutor v. Ruto et al.*, ICC PT. Ch. II, 19 August 2011, paras. 8–9). Moreover, Article 61(7)(c)(ii) of the Statute allows the Chamber to request the Prosecutor, on the basis of the hearing, to consider amending a charge, *that is,* to modify the legal characterisation of facts underpinning the charges. Conversely, consistent with the principle of prosecutorial discretion, the Chamber is not vested with the authority to request the Prosecutor to consider adding a new charge, *that is,* to expand the factual ambit of the charges as originally presented (*Prosecutor v. Kenyatta et al.*, ICC PT. Ch. II, 23 January 2012, para. 285).

Effects of adjournment

A decision adjourning the confirmation hearing under Article 61(7)(c) of the Statute is not a decision declining to confirm the charges under Article 61(7)(b) of the Statute. Pursuant to Article 61(10) of the Statute, the result of declining to confirm the charges is that the arrest warrant would cease to have effect, but no such provision exists with respect to adjournment of the hearing under Article 61(7)(c). Therefore, a decision to adjourn the confirmation hearing under Article 61(7)(c) does not represent a final disposal of the merits of the case by the Pre-Trial Chamber, but is an intermediate procedural step, and has no effect on the previous finding in relation to the warrant of arrest that there are reasonable grounds to believe that the suspect committed a crime within the jurisdiction of the Court. The fact that the available evidence does not meet the evidentiary threshold for Article 67(1) does not mean there was insufficient evidence for the purposes of issuing an arrest warrant under Article 58(1)(a) of the Statute (*Prosecutor v. L. Gbagbo*, ICC PT. Ch. I, 12 July 2013, paras. 34–35).

Author: Enrique Carnero Rojo.

[502] *Subsequent request after completion of investigation*

The Pre-Trial Chamber can properly evaluate the evidence submitted by the parties even if it lacks the full evidence because the Prosecution has not completed the investigation. Eventually, if the evidence is found to be insufficient, Article 61(8) of the Statute provides that the Prosecu-

---

9. After the charges are confirmed and before the trial has begun, the Prosecutor may, with the permission of the Pre-Trial Chamber and after notice to the accused, amend the charges. If the Prosecutor seeks to add additional charges or to substitute more serious charges, a hearing under this article to confirm those charges must be held.[503] After commencement

---

tor is not precluded from subsequently requesting the confirmation of charges on the basis of additional evidence (*Prosecutor v. Mbarushimana*, ICC A. Ch., 30 May 2012, para. 44).

Author: Enrique Carnero Rojo.

[503] *Amended version of the confirmed charges*

In the event that the charges are confirmed, nothing in the Statute and the Rules of Procedure and Evidence prevents the filing in the pre-trial proceedings before the Trial Chamber of an amended charging document in which the underlined facts and their legal characterisation are adjusted in light of the Pre-Trial Chamber's decision confirming the charges (*Prosecutor v. Katanga and Ngudjolo*, ICC PT. Ch. I, 25 June 2008, para. 12).

Legal recharacterisation of the charges by the Trial Chamber

By contrast, new facts and circumstances not described in the charges may only be added under the procedure of Article 61(9) of the Statute, since the incorporation of new facts and circumstances into the subject matter of the trial would alter the fundamental scope of the trial. This is consistent with the fact that it is the Prosecutor who, pursuant to Article 54(1) of the Statute, is tasked with the investigation of crimes under the jurisdiction of the Court and who, pursuant to Article 61(1) and (3) of the Statute, proffers charges against suspects (*Prosecutor v. Lubanga*, ICC A. Ch., 8 December 2009, para. 94). Accordingly, to give the Trial Chamber the power to extend *proprio motu* the scope of a trial to facts and circumstances not alleged by the Prosecutor would be contrary to the distribution of powers under the Statute (*Prosecutor v. Lubanga*, ICC A. Ch., 08 December 2009, para. 94). At most, the Trial Chamber may, pursuant to regulation 55 of the Regulations of the Court, change the legal characterisation of the facts confirmed by the Pre-Trial Chamber (*Prosecutor v. Lubanga*, ICC A. Ch., 8 December 2009, paras. 96–97). In fact, the terms of the provision under Article 61(9) of the Statute do not exclude the possibility that a Trial Chamber modifies the legal characterisation of the facts on its own motion once the trial has commenced because Article 61(9) of the Statute and regulation 55 of the Regulations of the Court address different powers of different entities at different stages of the procedure, and the two provisions are therefore not inherently incompatible (*Prosecutor v. Lubanga*, ICC A. Ch., 8 December 2009, para. 77; *Prosecutor v. Lubanga*, ICC T. Ch. I, 8 January 2010, para. 9; *Prosecutor v. Ruto and Sang*, ICC A. Ch., 13 December 2013, para. 30).

Binding character of the charges for the Trial Chamber

Nonetheless, the Trial Chamber has no authority to ignore, strike down or declare null and void the charges as confirmed by the Pre-Trial Chamber. The power to frame the charges lies at the heart of the Pre-Trial Chamber's functions, as set out in Article 61 of the Statute. By Article 61(9), after the charges have been confirmed, control over them remains with the Pre-Trial Chamber until the commencement of the trial, since post-confirmation and "before the trial has begun", the Prosecutor may, with the permission of the Pre-Trial Chamber and on notice to the accused, amend the charges (*Prosecutor v. Lubanga*, Decision on the status before the Trial Chamber of the evidence heard by the Pre-Trial Chamber and the decisions of the Pre-Trial Chamber in trial proceedings, and the manner in which evidence shall be submitted, ICC T. Ch. I, 13 December 2007, para. 39). Although the Trial Chamber is not bound by decisions of the Pre-Trial Chamber on evidential or procedural issues, the Trial Chamber has not been given a power to review the only decision of the Pre-Trial Chamber that is definitely binding on the Trial Chamber, namely the decision on the confirmation of charges (*Prosecutor v. Lubanga*, ICC T. Ch. I, 13 December 2007, paras. 43–44). The only power which the Trial Chamber has during the stage before the trial has begun, which does not involve altering the wording or the sub-

---

stance of the charges in any way, is to rule on any application for joinder or severance of the charges against more than one accused (*Prosecutor v. Lubanga*, ICC T. Ch. I, 13 December 2007, para. 41). However, the binding character of the confirmed charges on the Trial Chamber is limited to the "facts and circumstances described in the charges" or "material facts and circumstances". By contrast, other information and evidence of the case contained in the document containing the charges may be subject to change as the trial evolves, subject to sufficient notice being provided. In any given case, whether a particular fact or circumstance is one of the "facts and circumstances described in the charges" will depend on the nature of the prosecution's allegations. By way of example, in the case of a factual allegation pertaining to a simple criminal act or omission, the "facts and circumstances" would include, as a minimum, i) the person or persons who engaged in the conduct, ii) the nature of the conduct, iii) the time, place and manner in which the conduct took place and iv) the results of the conduct, such as how it affected other persons including victims (*Prosecutor v. Ruto and Sang*, ICC T. Ch. V, 20 November 2012, paras. 10–11; *Prosecutor v. Kenyatta and Muthaura*, ICC T. Ch. V, 20 November 2012, paras. 13–14).

Moment when the trial starts

No definition is provided in the Statute or the Rules of Procedure and Evidence as to when the trial is considered to have begun and the drafters of the Statute, who deliberately adopted a hybrid procedure which borrows from different legal cultures and systems, intended the "commencement of the trial" to mean both the start of the proceedings before the Trial Chamber ("trial proceedings") and the commencement of hearings on the merits ("trial" or "hearing"), depending on the provision to be applied and the context in which it was to be applied (*Prosecutor v. Katanga and Ngudjolo*, ICC T. Ch. II, 16 June 2009, para. 41). For instance, addressing challenges under Article 19 of the Statute, some Trial Chambers have found that the trial commences as soon as the decision on the confirmation of charges is filed (*Prosecutor v. Katanga and Ngudjolo*, ICC T. Ch. II, 16 June 2009, paras. 49 and 57), whereas other Trial Chambers, addressing requests to amend the charges under Article 61(9), have relied on the language of Article 61(11) to conclude that the commencement of the trial means the true opening of the trial when the opening statements, if any, are made prior to the calling of witnesses (*Prosecutor v. Lubanga*, Decision on the status before the Trial Chamber of the evidence heard by the Pre-Trial Chamber and the decisions of the Pre-Trial Chamber in trial proceedings, and the manner in which evidence shall be submitted, ICC T. Ch. I, 13 December 2007, para. 39). Similarly, the Pre-Trial Chambers have considered requests for amendment of the charges submitted in the course of preparation for the actual commencement of the trial before the Trial Chamber to have been made "before the trial has [actually] begun" in accordance with Article 61(9) of the Statute, and consequently to fall within their competence (*Prosecutor v. Kenyatta*, ICC PT. Ch. II, 22 March 2013, para. 21; *Prosecutor v. Ruto and Sang*, ICC PT. Ch. II, 16 August 2013, paras. 28–29).

At the time of writing, the Appeals Chamber has still not clarified the meaning of the expression "before the trial has begun" for the purpose of amending the charges under Article 61(9). At most, it has found that the wording of Article 61(9) of the Statute prescribes that an amendment of the charges is no longer possible "after the trial has begun" and, in order to apply this provision, irrespective of the precise moment at which the trial begins within the meaning of Article 61 (9) of the Statute, it has considered the time of the opening statements (*Prosecutor v. Ruto and Sang*, ICC A. Ch., 13 December 2013, para. 27). Moreover, the Appeals Chamber has found that the wording of Article 61(9) of the Statute ("the Prosecutor may with the permission of the Pre-Trial Chamber [...] amend the charges") indicates that not only the request to amend the charges has to be filed before the commencement of the trial, but also that the entire process of amending the charges must be completed by that time, including the granting of permission for the amendment by the Pre-Trial Chamber because at the beginning of the trial, its parameters must be clear. Once the trial has commenced, it is no longer possible to amend or to add to the charges, irrespective of when the Prosecutor filed her request to amend the charges (*Prosecutor v. Ruto and Sang*, ICC A. Ch., 13 December 2013, paras. 29 and 31). If the Prosecutor identifies a need to seek an amendment of the charges shortly before the scheduled start of a trial, she may ask for a postponement of the trial until the amendment process, including any potential appeal in that regard, is concluded (*Prosecutor v. Ruto and Sang*, ICC A. Ch., 13 December 2013, para. 31). The only modification possible under the Court's legal framework once the trial has commenced is a change to the legal characterisation of the facts pursuant to regulation 55 of the Regulations of the Court (*Prosecutor v. Ruto and Sang*, ICC A. Ch., 13 December 2013, para. 27).

Required application by the Prosecution

After the charges have been confirmed and before the trial has begun, only the Prosecution may amend the charges (*Prosecutor v. Ruto and Sang*, ICC T. Ch. V, 20 November 2012, para. 4; *Prosecutor v. Kenyatta and Muthaura*, ICC T. Ch. V, 20 November 2012, para. 7; *Prosecutor v. Ruto and Sang*, ICC T. Ch. V, 28 December 2012, para. 15; *Prosecutor v. Kenyatta and Muthaura*, ICC T. Ch. V, 28 December 2012, para. 19). The wording of Article 61(9) of the Statute allows the Prosecutor to request permission to amend the charges up until the actual commencement of the trial, provided that a request to this effect is properly "supported and justified" (*Prosecutor v. Kenyatta*, ICC PT. Ch. II, 22 March 2013, para. 21; *Prosecutor v. Ruto and Sang*, ICC PT. Ch. II, 16 August 2013, para. 31).

Required permission by the Pre-Trial Chamber

Pursuant to Article 61(9) of the Statute, the Prosecutor may amend the charges after their confirmation only with the permission of the Pre-Trial Chamber. The Chamber's permission is a *conditio sine qua non* for any amendment of the charges at this stage, as dictated by the Statute. In order to add additional charges or substitute charges with more serious charges, a new confirmation hearing must be held (*Prosecutor v. Lubanga*, ICC A. Ch., 13 October 2006, para. 53; *Prosecutor v. Kenyatta*, ICC PT. Ch. II, 22 March 2013, para. 19; *Prosecutor v. Ruto and Sang*, ICC PT. Ch. II, 16 August 2013, para. 31). In relation to the power of the Trial Chamber to amend or alter the charges confirmed by the Pre-Trial Chamber, a joint reading of Article 61(9) and Article 61(11) demonstrates that during the preparation phase of the trial any application to amend the charges must be made to the Pre-Trial Chamber (*Prosecutor v. Lubanga*, Decision on the status before the Trial Chamber of the evidence heard by the Pre-Trial Chamber and the decisions of the Pre-Trial Chamber in trial proceedings, and the manner in which evidence shall be submitted, ICC T. Ch. I, 13 December 2007, para. 40). Granting permission pursuant to Article 61(9) of the Statute to amend the charges confirmed entails consideration of the Prosecutor's request and an evaluation of other relevant information which the Pre-Trial Chamber could seek if necessary for the purposes of its final decision (*Prosecutor v. Kenyatta*, ICC PT. Ch. II, 22 March 2013, para. 21; *Prosecutor v. Ruto and Sang*, ICC PT. Ch. II, 16 August 2013, para. 32). In arriving at a proper and balanced decision on a request to amend the charges, the Chamber must take into consideration the diverse factors affecting the case *sub judice*, including whether granting permission to amend will negatively affect other competing interests, such as the fairness and expeditiousness of the proceedings, which would result in causing prejudice to the rights of the accused to be informed promptly of the nature, cause and content of the charges, to have adequate time and facilities for the preparation of the defence and to be tried without undue delay (*Prosecutor v. Kenyatta*, ICC PT. Ch. II, 22 March 2013, paras. 21–22; *Prosecutor v. Ruto and Sang*, ICC PT. Ch. II, 16 August 2013, paras. 32 and 42). The consideration of relevant factors when entertaining any Article 61(9) request follows from the wording of Article 61(9) of the Statute. This provision allows the Prosecutor to proceed amending the charges postconfirmation only upon having received the "permission of the Pre-Trial Chamber" to do so. Whether to grant permission to amend the charges confirmed should be taken upon an assess-

of the trial, the Prosecutor may, with the permission of the Trial Chamber, withdraw the charges.[504]

---

ment of all relevant circumstances. To say otherwise would mean that the word "permission" in the text of Article 61(9) has no added value (*Prosecutor v. Ruto and Sang*, ICC PT. Ch. II, 06 September 2013, para. 33).

Required additional hearing

If a request for amendment of the charges is rejected, it is not necessary to explore further the two procedural venues provided in Article 61(9) of the Statute namely, whether the charges may be amended by the Prosecutor or whether a hearing to confirm those charges must be held (*Prosecutor v. Ruto and Sang*, ICC PT. Ch. II, 6 September 2013, para. 35).

Author: Enrique Carnero Rojo.

[504] *Moment when the trial starts*

No definition is provided in the Statute or the Rules of Procedure and Evidence as to when the trial is considered to have begun and the drafters of the Statute, who deliberately adopted a hybrid procedure which borrows from different legal cultures and systems, intended the "commencement of the trial" to mean both the start of the proceedings before the Trial Chamber ("trial proceedings") and the commencement of hearings on the merits ("trial" or "hearing"), depending on the provision to be applied and the context in which it was to be applied (*Prosecutor v. Katanga and Ngudjolo*, ICC T. Ch. II, 16 June 2009, para. 41). For instance, addressing challenges under Article 19 of the Statute, some Trial Chambers have found that the trial commences as soon as the decision on the confirmation of charges is filed (*Prosecutor v. Katanga and Ngudjolo*, ICC T. Ch. II, 16 June 2009, paras. 49 and 57), whereas other Trial Chambers, addressing requests to amend the charges under Article 61(9), have relied on the language of Article 61(11) to conclude that the commencement of the trial means the true opening of the trial when the opening statements, if any, are made prior to the calling of witnesses (*Prosecutor v. Lubanga*, Decision on the status before the Trial Chamber of the evidence heard by the Pre-Trial Chamber and the decisions of the Pre-Trial Chamber in trial proceedings, and the manner in which evidence shall be submitted, ICC T. Ch. I, 13 December 2007, para. 39). The latter interpretation has been endorsed to understand the reference to the commencement of trial included in Article 61(9) of the Statute for the withdrawal of charges (*Prosecutor v. Kenyatta and Muthaura*, ICC T. Ch. V, 18 March 2013, fn. 16).

Required permission by the Trial Chamber

After the commencement of the trial, it is only the Prosecution that can withdraw the charges (*Prosecutor v. Ruto and Sang*, ICC T. Ch. V, 20 November 2012, para. 4; *Prosecutor v. Kenyatta and Muthaura*, ICC T. Ch. V, 20 November 2012, para. 7). Withdrawal of charges after the commencement of the trial is only possible with the permission of the Trial Chamber (*Prosecutor v. Lubanga*, ICC A. Ch., 13 October 2006, para. 53). Consequently, after the trial has begun, the two additional powers given to the Trial Chamber under the ICC Statute framework in relation to the charges are to grant or reject an application by the prosecution to withdraw the charges and to modify the legal characterisation of the facts under Regulation 55 (*Prosecutor v. Lubanga*, Decision on the status before the Trial Chamber of the evidence heard by the Pre-Trial Chamber and the decisions of the Pre-Trial Chamber in trial proceedings, and the manner in which evidence shall be submitted, ICC T. Ch. I, 13 December 2007, para. 42). In deciding whether to grant or not a request by the Prosecution to withdraw the charges, the Trial Chamber assesses the Prosecution's submissions on whether the evidence supports the charges against the accused, and the latter's attitude towards the request for withdrawal of charges (*Prosecutor v. Kenyatta and Muthaura*, ICC T. Ch. V, 18 March 2013, para. 11).

Author: Enrique Carnero Rojo.

Any warrant previously issued shall cease to have effect with respect to any charges which have not been confirmed by the Pre-Trial Chamber or which have been withdrawn by the Prosecutor.[505]

11. Once the charges have been confirmed in accordance with this article, the Presidency shall constitute a Trial Chamber which, subject to paragraph 9 and to Article 64, paragraph 4, shall be responsible for the conduct of subsequent proceedings and may exercise any function of the Pre-Trial Chamber that is relevant and capable of application in those proceedings.[506]

---

[505] *Termination of the proceedings*

Upon ratification of the decision declining to confirm the charges by the Appeals Chamber, where request for leave to appeal has been granted, the decision not to confirm the charges becomes final, and subject to Article 61(8) of the Statute, proceedings related to the case at hand come to an end. Nonetheless, if there remain procedural matters pertaining to the case, triggered in the course of the proceedings, they cannot be left unresolved without judicial intervention from the Chamber, which has been seized of that case (*Prosecutor v. Mbarushimana*, ICC PT. Ch. II, 3 September 2012, para. 7). Similarly, the permission of the Trial Chamber to withdraw the charges brings about that i) the arrest or conditions imposed on the accused cease to have effect, although protective measures ordered in respect of victims and witnesses continue after the proceedings have been concluded and the classification of documents as "*ex parte*" or "confidential" remains in place until otherwise ordered by the Chamber, and ii) all pending requests or applications by the accused become moot (*Prosecutor v. Kenyatta and Muthaura*, ICC T. Ch. V, 18 March 2013, paras. 12–13).

Author: Enrique Carnero Rojo.

[506] *The Trial Chamber takes over*

Once the charges are confirmed against a person and having the Pre-Trial Chamber ruled on any leave to appeal the decision confirming the charges, the Pre-Trial Chamber is no longer seized of any matter in the case. Pursuant to Article 61(11) of the Statute, the Trial Chamber shall be responsible for the conduct of subsequent proceedings and may exercise any relevant functions of the Pre-Trial Chamber which is relevant and capable of application in those proceedings (*Prosecutor v. Lubanga*, Decision on the application for additional means under regulation 83(3) of the Regulations of the Court and on the applications to intervene as amici curiae under rule 103 of the Rules of Procedure and Evidence, ICC PT. Ch. I, 5 June 2007, pp. 3–4).

The Pre-Trial Chamber continues to have authority

As an exception, Article 61(11) qualifies the authority of the Trial Chamber when giving it responsibility for the conduct of the "subsequent proceedings" after the confirmation of the charges, by making it, *inter alia*, subject to "paragraph 9" which extends the authority of the Pre-Trial Chamber over the charges until the trial has begun (*Prosecutor v. Lubanga*, Decision on the status before the Trial Chamber of the evidence heard by the Pre-Trial Chamber and the decisions of the Pre-Trial Chamber in trial proceedings, and the manner in which evidence shall be submitted, ICC T. Ch. I, 13 December 2007, para. 40).

Functions of Pre-Trial Chambers exercised by Trial Chambers

Once the trial has begun, the Trial Chamber may exercise some functions of the Pre-Trial Chamber pursuant to Article 61(11) of the Statute, such as i) interim release reviews pursuant to Article 60 of the Statute (*Prosecutor v. L. Gbagbo*, ICC T. Ch. I, 11 November 2014, para. 31(d)), ii) requests for cooperation by an accused person pursuant to Article 59(3)(b) of the Statute (*Katanga and Ngudjolo*, ICC T. Ch. II, 6 December 2010, fn. 9; *Prosecutor v. Banda and Jerbo*, ICC T. Ch. IV, 01 July 2011, para. 6; *Prosecutor v. Banda and Jerbo*, ICC T. Ch. IV, 12 September 2013, para. 3),

---

and iii) requests for provisional release by an accused person pursuant to Article 60(3) of the Statute (*Prosecutor v. Bemba*, ICC T. Ch. III, 16 August 2011, paras. 45–47).

Referral of the confirmation decision to the Pre-Trial Chamber

Moreover, the Trial Chamber may refer to the Pre-Trial Chamber the validity of the confirmation decision as a "preliminary issue" for the Trial Chamber pursuant to Article 64(4) of the Statute (*Prosecutor v. Kenyatta*, ICC T. Ch. V, 26 April 2013, para. 84). However, in assessing whether the referral of the decision on confirmation of charges to the Pre-Trial Chamber is necessary, the Trial Chamber should not place itself in the position of the Pre-Trial Chamber when it comes to the consideration of the credibility of witnesses and assessment of the evidence presented at the confirmation hearing, and it should not determine that the confirmation decision is invalid merely on the basis that it would have assessed the evidence differently. It is only if it is self-evident that no reasonable Pre-Trial Chamber could have come to the same conclusion in light of subsequent developments that the Trial Chamber could consider a referral of the confirmation decision to the Pre-Trial Chamber (*Prosecutor v. Kenyatta*, ICC T. Ch. V, 26 April 2013, paras. 85–86). It is more efficient, expeditious and appropriate for the Trial Chamber to address the post-confirmation developments and challenges as to the sufficiency of the evidence against the accused and evaluate their impact on the Prosecution's case during the course of the trial rather than refer the case to the Pre-Trial Chamber for a "fresh" confirmation process, which can only be based on changes in the charges (as opposed to the evidence) between the confirmation of charges and the trial stages (*Prosecutor v. Kenyatta*, ICC T. Ch. V, 26 April 2013, para. 111). In any event, a request for referral of a confirmation decision under Article 64(4) of the Statute is impermissible if it amounts to an attempt to have the Trial Chamber effectively entertain an appeal of the confirmation decision because the Trial Chamber has no appellate jurisdiction over decisions of the Pre-Trial Chamber nor is the proper body to decide on a reconsideration of the evidence and credibility assessments as performed by the Pre-Trial Chamber (*Prosecutor v. Kenyatta*, ICC T. Ch. V, 26 April 2013, paras. 99–100, 104).

No power to appoint a single judge

It must also be noted that the Court has clarified that although by Article 61(11) of the Statute the Trial Chamber may exercise any function of the Pre-Trial Chamber that is relevant and capable of application in the proceedings, it is impossible to read into this provision a power by which the Trial Chamber may appoint one of the three judges to act as a single judge (*Prosecutor v. Lubanga*, ICC T. Ch. I, 22 May 2008, para. 14(a)).

Cross-references:

Article 64(4).

Rules 76, 77, 78, 92(3), 121, 122, 123, 124, 125, 126, 127, 128, 129, 130, 131 and 185.

Regulations 52 and 53.

Doctrine:

1. Fabricio Guariglia, "Investigation and Prosecution", in Roy S. Lee (ed.), *The International Criminal Court: The Making of the Rome Statute. Issues, Negotiations, Results*, Kluwer, The Hague, 1999, pp. 227–37.

2. Kuniji Shibahara, "Article 61: Confirmation of the Charges Before Trial", in Otto Triffterer (ed.), *Commentary on the Rome Statute of the International Criminal Court: Observers' Notes, Article by Article*, Nomos Verlagsgesellschaft, Baden-Baden, 1999, pp. 783–92.

3. Michele Marchesiello, *Proceedings Before the Pre-Trial Chambers*, in Antonio Cassese, Paola Gaeta and John R.W.D. Jones (eds.), *The Rome Statute of the International Criminal Court: A Commentary*, 2nd ed., Oxford University Press, 2002, pp. 1243–46.

4. Kuniji Shibahara and William A. Schabas, "Article 61: Confirmation of the Charges Before Trial", in Otto Triffterer (ed.), *Commentary on the Rome Statute of the International Crimi-*

nal Court: Observers' Notes, Article by Article, 2nd ed., C.H. Beck/Hart/Nomos, Munich/Oxford/Baden-Baden, 2008, pp. 1171–81.

5. Leïla Bourguiba, "Article 61: Confirmation des charges avant le procès", in Julian Fernandez/Xavier Pacreau (eds.), Statut de Rome de la Cour pénale international: Commentaire Article par Article, Pedone, Paris, 2012, pp. 1385–1412.

6. Enrique Carnero Rojo, "Rome Statute of the International Criminal Court – Article 61: Confirmation of the Charges Before Trial", in Paul De Hert, Mathias Holvoet, Jean Flamme and Olivia Struyven (eds.), Code of International Criminal Law and Procedure, Larcier, Brussels, 2013, pp. 258–73.

7. Håkan Friman, Helen Brady, Matteo Costi, Fabricio Guariglia and Carl-Friedrich Stuckenberg, "Charges", in Göran Sluiter, Håkan Friman, Suzannah Linton, Sergey Vasiliev and Salvatore Zappalà (eds.), International Criminal Procedure: Principles and Rules, Oxford University Press, Oxford, 2013, pp. 397–436.

Author: Enrique Carnero Rojo.

PART 6. THE TRIAL

Article 62
Place of trial

Unless otherwise decided, the place of the trial shall be the seat of the Court.[507]

---

[507] Article 62 should be read together with Article 3 which provides that the seat of the Court is at The Hague in the Netherlands and that "[t]he Court may sit elsewhere, whenever it considers it desirable, as provided in this Statute". While Article 3 encompasses all organs of the Court, Article 62 is in part 6 of the Statute which deals with the trial. Article 62 is thus not applicable for pre-trial proceedings.

Rule 100(2) provides that Prosecutor, the defence or a majority of the judges of the Court may file an application or recommendation changing the place where the Court sits. Paragraph 3 of the same provides that "[t]he Presidency shall consult the State where the Court intends to sit. If that State agrees that the Court can sit in that State, then the decision to sit in a State other than the host State shall be taken by the judges, in plenary session, by a two thirds majority".

Trial Chamber I considered holding parts of the proceedings in *Lubanga* in the Democratic Republic of Congo. A feasibility study was conducted. In the end, the Government withheld consent for holding a trial in the country. Therefore, the Trial Chamber decided that the trial in its entirety would be conducted in The Hague, see *Lubanga*, Decision on disclosure issues, responsibilities for protective measures and other procedural matters, ICC-01/04-01/06-1311-Anx2, ICC Trial Chamber, 24 April 2008, para. 105.

Doctrine:
1. William A. Schabas, *The International Criminal Court: A Commentary on the Rome Statute*, Oxford University Press, Oxford, 2010, pp. 747–49.
2. Otto Triffterer, "Article 62 – Place of the Trial", in Otto Triffterer (ed.), *Commentary on the Rome Statute of the International Criminal Court: Observers' Notes, Article by Article*, 2nd ed., C.H. Beck/Hart/Nomos, Munich/Oxford/Baden-Baden, 2008, pp. 1183–90.

Author: Mark Klamberg.

Article 63

Trial in the presence of the accused

1. The accused shall be present during the trial.[508]
2. If the accused, being present before the Court, continues to disrupt the trial, the Trial Chamber may remove the accused and shall make provision for him or her to observe the trial and instruct counsel from outside the courtroom, through the use of communications technology, if required. Such measures shall be taken only in exceptional circumstances after other reasonable alternatives have proved inadequate, and only for such duration as is strictly required.[509]

---

[508] The Article lays down the principle that the trial shall generally be conducted in the presence of the accused in order to safeguard his or her position as subject, not object of the proceedings. This principle is also safeguarded by the right of the accused to be present during trial, contained in Article 67(1)(d) (see also the commentary thereto). Article 61(2) contains a specific provision on the presence or absence of the accused at the confirmation hearing.

Article 63 only names one exception to this principle, namely the possibility of removal of the accused for disruptive behavior mentioned in para. 2. However, it is not clear whether this exhausts all possibilities for trial proceedings conducted (partially) in the absence of the accused. One other possibility would be where the accused chooses not to attend the trial. Such choice has been accepted by both *ad hoc* Tribunals and by the Special Court for Sierra Leone (See for example, *Prosecutor v. Zdravko Mucic et al.* (Case No. IT-96-21), ICTY T. Ch., Transcript of 16 April 1998, p. 11255–56; *The Prosecutor v. Théoneste Bagosora, Gratien Kabiligi, Anatole Nsengiyumva and Aloys Ntabakuze (Case* No. ICTR-98-41-I), ICTR T. Ch., Minutes of Proceedings of 2 April 2002, para. 1; *Prosecutor v. Issa Hassan Sesay, Morris Kallon and Augustine Gbao* (Case No. SCSL-2004-15), SCSL T. Ch., Ruling on the issue of the refusal of the third accused, Augustine Gbao, to attend hearing of the Special Court for Sierra Leone on 7 July 2004 and succeeding days, 12 July 2004, para. 12). On the other hand, there are also national systems which hold that presence at trial is not only a right, but also a duty of the defendant, from which he or she may only be excused under certain limited circumstances (see Sect. 230and 236 of the German Code of Criminal Procedure). In the Statute, the possibility of a waiver of the right to presence is also explicitly mentioned in Article 61(2) on the confirmation hearing (albeit referring to the confirmation hearing as a whole, not to parts of it), but whether the Court will interpret this provision as laying down a general principle also applicable to trial proceedings, or whether it will find *e contrario* that there may be no such waiver for trial proceedings as it is not explicitly laid down in Article 63, remains to be seen.

For other possibilities for trial proceedings in the absence of the accused, as well as for the question of fitness to stand trial, see commentary to Article 67(1)(d).

Cross-references:

Article 67(1)(d).

Author: Björn Elberling, revised by Mark Klamberg.

[509] Article 63(2) lays down the only clearly established exception to the principle that the accused must be present at her trial, namely his or her removal for disruptive behavior. It follows similar provisions at other tribunals, such as Rule 80 of the Rules of Procedure and Evidence at both the ICTY and the ICTR, which have seldom if ever been used.

The requirements for removal show that at the ICC too, removal of the accused must be seen as a measure of last resort which should only seldom arise: First of all, the accused must "continue [...] to disrupt the trial", in other words a single disruption, no matter how grave in itself, will not be sufficient. Rule 170 adds to this the requirement of a prior warning before re-

---

moval. Second, "other reasonable alternatives" to removal must have proved inadequate – what exactly such "reasonable alternatives" may be is left to the further jurisprudence of the Court, one that springs to mind is shutting off the microphone of the accused (The US Supreme Court has found that US law even allows binding and gagging the defendant if this is the only way to conduct the trial in his or her presence and without disruptions – Illinois v. Allen, 397 US 337, 343). Finally, removal is limited to "such duration as is strictly required" – especially where the accused has been removed from proceedings for the first time, this may require allowing him or her back into the courtroom after a sufficient "cooling off period" upon the promise to stop disrupting the trial. Whether the reference to "exceptional circumstances" must be interpreted as yet another additional requirement, or whether it is more a description of situations which fulfil the other requirements for removal, is not clear.

If the accused is removed, he or she must nonetheless be enabled to follow the proceedings and instruct counsel from outside the courtroom.

For other possibilities for trial proceedings in the absence of the accused, see commentary to Article 67(1)(d).

Cross-references:

Article 67(1)(d), Rule 170.

Doctrine:

1. William A. Schabas, in Otto Triffterer (ed.), *Commentary on the Rome Statute of the International Criminal Court: Observers' Notes, Article by Article*, 2nd ed., C.H. Beck/Hart/Nomos, Munich/Oxford/Baden-Baden, 2008, pp. 1191–98.

2. Gerhard Werle, *Principles of International Criminal Law*, TMC Asser Press, The Hague, 2005, at pp. 400–1, MN 1184–85.

3. Frank Terrier, in Antonio Cassese, Paola Gaeta and John R.W.D. Jones (eds.), *The Rome Statute of the International Criminal Court: A Commentary*, 2nd ed., Oxford University Press, Oxford, 2002, p. 1282–84.

Author: Björn Elberling, revised by Mark Klamberg.

Article 64

Functions and powers of the Trial Chamber

1. The functions and powers of the Trial Chamber set out in this article shall be exercised in accordance with this Statute and the Rules of Procedure and Evidence.[510]

2. The Trial Chamber shall ensure that a trial is fair and expeditious and is conducted with full respect for the rights of the accused and due regard for the protection of victims and witnesses.[511]

3. Upon assignment of a case for trial in accordance with this Statute, the Trial Chamber assigned to deal with the case shall:[512]

   (a) Confer with the parties and adopt such procedures as are necessary to facilitate the fair and expeditious conduct of the proceedings;[513]

---

[510] Article 64 defines most of the functions and powers of the Trial Chamber, but not all of them. Other important provisions include Articles 74–76 which concern decisions on the guilt of the accused, sentencing and decisions on reparations to victims. Article 64 should be read together with Article 21 of the ICC Statute. The provision makes a reference to the ICC Statute as well as the Rules of Procedure and Evidence. Chapter 6 of the Rules deals specifically with the proceedings to be conducted before a Trial Chamber. Chapter 4 of the Rules also deals with proceedings with importance for the Trial Chamber.

Author: Mark Klamberg.

[511] Article 64(2) gives the Trial Chamber the duty to ensure the quality of the trial. The provision instructs the Trial Chamber to ensure full respect for the rights of the accused and due regard for the protection of victims and witnesses. This two interests may come in conflict with each other when it comes to the disclosure of the names and addresses of witnesses in order to allow the accused to prepare his or her defence. One solution is to allow for delayed disclosure where the names of the witnesses are disclosed just before the trial.

Cross-references:

Rule 81.

Author: Mark Klamberg.

[512] At the beginning of the existence of the Court, pursuant to Article 61(11) the Presidency have to, once the charges have been confirmed, constitute the Trial Chamber and then assign the case to this Chamber. The Presidency may also refer the case to a previously constituted Trial Chamber pursuant to Rule 130.

Author: Mark Klamberg.

[513] The Trial Chamber is to "[c]onfer with the parties and adopt such procedures as are necessary to facilitate the fair and expeditious conduct of the proceedings". This is accomplished by means of status conferences. This is a development from the practice of the ICTY with status, pre-trial and pre-defence conferences provided for in ICTY RPE rules 65 bis, 73 bis and 73 ter.

Promptly after the Trial Chamber is constituted, ICC Rule 132(1) provides for a mandatory status conference in order to set the date of the trial. Sub-paragraph 2 provides for other status conferences in order to facilitate the fair and expeditious conduct of the proceedings. A Chamber may pursuant to regulation 30 hold status conferences by way of hearings, including by way of audio- or video-link technology or by way of written submissions. At a status conference, the Trial Chamber may, in accordance with the Statute and the Rules, issue any order in the interests of justice. Regulation 54 provides a non-exhaustive list of such issues.

Cross-references:

(b) Determine the language or languages to be used at trial;[514] and

(c) Subject to any other relevant provisions of this Statute, provide for disclosure of documents or information not previously disclosed, sufficiently in advance of the commencement of the trial to enable adequate preparation for trial.[515]

4. The Trial Chamber may, if necessary for its effective and fair functioning, refer preliminary issues to the Pre-Trial Chamber or, if necessary, to another available judge of the Pre-Trial Division.[516]

Rule 132, Regulations 30 and 54.

Author: Mark Klamberg

[514] The Trial Chamber shall determine the language or languages to be used at trial. The Court has pursuant to Article 50 of the ICC Statute two working languages, English and French. The Court shall authorise a language other than English or French provided that the Court considers such authorisation to be adequately justified. Furthermore, regulation 39 provides that "[a]ll documents and materials filed with the Registry shall be in English or French, unless otherwise provided in the Statute, Rules, these Regulations or authorised by the Chamber or the Presidency. The accused has the right according to Article 67(1)(f) to translation/interpretation into a language that he or she "fully understands and speaks".

Author: Mark Klamberg.

[515] The Trial Chamber shall provide for disclosure of documents or information not previously disclosed. It is thus the duty of the Trial Chamber, if not to review, at least to validate the work done by the Pre-Trial Chamber. The Defence may also be called upon under Article 64(3)(c) to the extent it is compatible with rights of the accused to disclose certain documents to the Prosecution. Rules 76-84 establishes a regime of disclosure, applicable with important distinctions to both the Prosecution and the Defence.

Cross-references:

Rule 134.

Author: Mark Klamberg.

[516] Pursuant to Article 61(11), echoed by Article 64(6)(a), the Trial Chamber shall be responsible for the conduct of proceedings subsequent to the confirmation of charges and may exercise any function of the Pre-Trial Chamber that is relevant in the proceedings. The present provision allows the Trial Chamber to refer preliminary issue to the Pre-Trial Chamber. It should be use restrictively.

The expression "preliminary issues" refers to Part 5 of the ICC Statute, especially Articles 56 and 57. In contrast, the provision is not a reference to Part 2 of the ICC Statute, because Article 19(6) expressly states that after confirmation of the charges, challenges to the admissibility of a case or "shall be referred to the Trial Chamber".

A decision of a Trial Chamber to refer a preliminary issue to a Pre-Trial Chamber is subject to the condition that it is "necessary for its effective and fair functioning" of the Trial Chamber.

In *Prosecutor v. Lubanga*, ICC T. Ch. I, Request for Review of Detention, 6 June 2007, the pre-trial record of proceedings had been transferred to Trial Chamber I. The Trial Chamber considered that Article 60(3) requires that a ruling on detention is subject to periodical review and that it did not "have sufficient time [...] to familiarize itself with the record in order to review Mr. Thomas Lubanga Dyilo's detention in a fair and effective manner". Thus, the Trial Chamber requested pursuant to Article 64(4) that "Pre-Trial Chamber I review its ruling on the detention of Mr. Thomas Lubanga Dyilo". For the subsequent decision by the Pre-Trial Chamber, see *Prosecutor v. Lubanga*, ICC PT. Ch. I, Second Review of the "Decision on the Application for Interim Release of Thomas Lubanga Dyilo", 11 June 2007.

5. Upon notice to the parties, the Trial Chamber may, as appropriate, direct that there be joinder or severance in respect of charges against more than one accused.[517]

6. In performing its functions prior to trial or during the course of a trial, the Trial Chamber may, as necessary:[518]

In *Prosecutor v. Lubanga*, ICC T. Ch., Decision on whether two judges alone may hold a hearing – and – Recommendations to the Presidency on whether an alternate judge should be assigned for the trial, ICC-01/04-01/06-1349, 22 May 2008, one of the Judges of the Trial Chamber was abroad and the question arose whether a hearing could be held in his absence. One of the options considered but rejected was to invoke Article 64(4). The Trial Chamber stated that in para. 14: "Although by Article 64(4) of the Statute, the Chamber may, for its effective and fair functioning, refer preliminary issues to the Pre-Trial Chamber or, if necessary, to another available judge of the Pre-Trial Division, it may be counter-productive to attempt to delegate the kind of complicated decisions that arise during this preparatory stage to a judge or to judges of another Division who have not been involved in the complex and often interrelated issues that will have arisen following the confirmation of charges. It is likely that it would be necessary for the judge or judges to place the issue referred to them in the overall context of the Trial Chamber's work to date, and that process would be exacting and time consuming".

Cross-references:

Articles 61(11) and 64(6)(a).

Author: Mark Klamberg.

[517] This provision gives the *ex officio* power explicitly to the Trial Chamber, but also implicitly to the Pre-Trial Chamber, to order joinder or severance. The Chamber must give notice to the parties. The rationale behind this rule is that the interest of justice may require that people involved in one and the same criminal undertaking should be tried at the same time in order to avoid inconsistencies and contradictions.

Rule 136 provides that persons accused jointly shall be tried together unless the Trial Chamber, on its own motion or at the request of the Prosecutor or the defence, orders severance. This mat be warranted for three purposes: 1) to avoid serious prejudice to the accused, 2) to protect the interests of justice or 3) because a person jointly accused has made an admission of guilt and can be proceeded against in accordance with Article 65, paragraph 2.

PTC I decided to join the cases against Germain Katanga and Mathieu Ngudjolo Chui in *Prosecutor v. Katanga and Ngudjolo*, ICC PT. Ch. I, Decision on the Joinder of the Cases against Germain KATANGA and Mathieu NGUDJOLO CHUI, 10 March 2008. The PTC considered that "although Article 64(5) of the Statute and rule 136 of the Rules are included in Chapter VI of the Statute and of the Rules which deals with the 'Trial Procedure', the Chamber considers that the contextual interpretation of such provisions, in light of the above-mentioned provisions relating to the Pre-Trial proceedings of a case before the Pre-Trial Chamber included in Chapter V of the Statute and the Rules, does not preclude joint proceedings at the Pre-Trial stage, but rather supports the general rule that there is a presumption of joint proceedings for persons prosecuted jointly" (pp. 8–9). See also *Prosecutor v. Katanga and Ngudjolo*, ICC PT. Ch. I, Decision on Application for Leave to Appeal by the Defence of Mathieu Ngudjolo Chui against the Decision on Joinder, April 2008, where the PTC granted leave to appeal. The Appeals Chamber upheld the decision of PTC I, Judgment on the Appeal Against the Decision on Joinder rendered on 10 March 2008 by the Pre-Trial Chamber in the Germain Katanga and Mathieu Ngudjolo Chui Cases, 9 June 2008.

Cross-references:

Rule 136.

Author: Mark Klamberg.

(a) Exercise any functions of the Pre-Trial Chamber referred to in Article 61, paragraph 11;[519]

(b) Require the attendance and testimony of witnesses and production of documents and other evidence by obtaining, if necessary, the assistance of States as provided in this Statute;[520]

(c) Provide for the protection of confidential information;[521]

---

[518] The powers of the Trial Chamber as set out in Article 64(6) applies both to the phase before the trial and its conduct as such.

Author: Mark Klamberg.

[519] Article 64(6)(a) coupled with Article 61(11) authorises the Trial Chamber to "exercise any function of the Pre-Trial Chamber that is relevant". This covers all the functions of the Pre-Trial Chamber described in Part 5 of the ICC Statute. Thus, the Trial Chamber can undertake such functions as issuance of an arrest warrant, if ever required. Considering that the Pre-Trial Chamber was created to resolve all preliminary issues it is reasonable that the power set forth in Article 64(6)(a) will be exercised only in exceptional circumstances by the Trial Chamber.

Author: Mark Klamberg.

[520] In order to facilitate the attendance and testimony of witnesses and production of documents the Trial Chamber may require and obtain the assistance of States as provided in this Statute. This is a reference to part 9 and more specifically Article 93. There appears to be an inconsistency between Article 64(6)(b) and Article 93.

Article 93(1)(e) provides that States Parties shall provide assistance with "[f]acilitating the voluntary appearance of persons as witnesses or experts before the Court". Similarly, the transfer of a person for purposes of obtaining testimony under Article 93(7) is based on the consent of that person. This is a serious weakness of the cooperation scheme in Article 93 considering that Article 69(2) expresses an aspiration that testimony of a witness at trial shall be given in person. In regard to others than the suspect or accused, the ICC Statute gives conflicting messages as to whether the Court may compel an individual to cooperate.

Göran Sluiter holds that "[o]n the basis of Article 93(1)(e) and Article 93(7)(a)(i) ... an individual has no obligation towards the Court to appear as a witness". This would imply a voluntary right of a person not to appear and testify before the Court. The preparatory works of the ICC Statute support Sluiter's conclusion. This would not only impede on the efficiency of the court but could also have negative effects from a fair trial perspective if the accused can not call witnesses.

Claus Kreß and Kimberly Prost has a slightly different approach when they illustrate how such a right would be inconsistent with Article 64(6)(b) which empowers the Trial Chamber to require the attendance and testimony of witnesses. They appear to argue that a subpoena power does exist. In addition, Article 69(2) provides that the testimony of a witness at trial shall be given in person. Kreß and Prost do not deny the inconsistency between the provisions but it should not be widened. They suggest that Article 64(6)(b) create an obligation of persons to appear and testify before the Court, but States are under no duty to enforce that obligation. This interpretation would promote the purpose of Article 64(6)(b) without violating Article 93(1)(e) and Article 93(7)(a)(i).

Cross-references:

Article 69(2) and Article 93(1)(e) and (7)(a)(i).

Author: Mark Klamberg.

[521] The Trial Chamber has an obligation to protect confidential information, including information affecting a State's national security. This includes the possibility for the Trial Chamber, on its

(d) Order the production of evidence in addition to that already collected prior to the trial or presented during the trial by the parties;[522]

(e) Provide for the protection of the accused, witnesses and victims;[523] and

(f) Rule on any other relevant matters.[524]

7. The trial shall be held in public. The Trial Chamber may, however, determine that special circumstances require that certain proceedings be in closed session for the purposes set forth in Article 68, or to protect confidential or sensitive information to be given in evidence.[525]

---

own motion, at the request of the Prosecutor, the Defence or the State concerned, to order in camera hearings.

Cross-references:

Articles 54(3)(e), 68(6), 93(8)(b) and (c).

Author: Mark Klamberg.

[522] This sub-paragraph is influenced by civil law systems and grants the Judges authority to order the parties to submit additional evidence.

Cross-references:

Article 69(3).

Author: Mark Klamberg.

[523] This sub-paragraph on protection of the participants of the trial recalls notions developed more in detail elsewhere. For example, Article 68(1) and (2) provides that the "Chambers of the Court may, to protect victims and witnesses or an accused, conduct any part of the proceedings *in camera* or allow the presentation of evidence by electronic or other special means". These measures shall not be prejudicial to or inconsistent with the rights of the accused and a fair and impartial trial.

Cross-references:

Article 68(1) and (2).

Author: Mark Klamberg.

[524] This sub-paragraph emphasises the authority of the Trial Chamber. It gives the Judges the possibility of adapting their practice and issue directions accordingly.

Author: Mark Klamberg.

[525] This sub-paragraph concerns the principle of publicity which is of interest both for the accused and the general public. It is repeated in Article 67(1). The principle of publicity may be divided up into at least two sub-principles: public access to the actual trial and the pronouncement of the judgment in public. Access for the public and the press to the courtroom, motions and decisions contributes to the fairness of the trial, by enabling third parties to assure themselves of the quality of the proceedings. The Trial Chamber in Lubanga acknowledged the principle when it stated that "all evidence will be public unless there is an order specifying otherwise", *Prosecutor v. Lubanga*, ICC T. Ch., Order on numbering of evidence, 12 May 2010. See also *Prosecutor v. Bemba*, ICC T. Ch., Public Redacted Version of the Chamber's 11 November 2011 Decision regarding the prosecution's witness schedule, 15 November 2011, para. 18 and *Prosecutor v. Katanga and Ngudjolo*, ICC PT. Ch. II, Ordonnance portant instructions en vue de favouriser la publicité de la procédure, 31 January 2012, para. 1.

Cross-references:

Article 67(1), Regulation 20.

Author: Mark Klamberg.

---

8. (a) At the commencement of the trial, the Trial Chamber shall have read to the accused the charges previously confirmed by the Pre-Trial Chamber. The Trial Chamber shall satisfy itself that the accused understands the nature of the charges. It shall afford him or her the opportunity to make an admission of guilt in accordance with Article 65 or to plead not guilty.[526]

(b) At the trial, the presiding judge may give directions for the conduct of proceedings, including to ensure that they are conducted in a fair and impartial manner. Subject to any directions of the presiding judge, the parties may submit evidence in accordance with the provisions of this Statute.[527]

---

[526] The instruction that the Trial Chamber shall read the charges refers to the charges previously confirmed by the Pre-Trial Chamber pursuant to Article 61(7)(a). The provision is also subject to the possibility of the charges being amended after the confirmation hearing (Article 61(9)).

The Trial Chamber has a responsibility at this stage to determine whether the accused is fit to stand trial and understands the nature of the charges. For this purpose, the Trial Chamber may order a medical, psychiatric or psychological examination of the accused pursuant to Rule 135. Where the Trial Chamber is satisfied that the accused is unfit to stand trial, it shall according to Rule 135(4) order that the trial be adjourned. The Trial Chamber may, on its own motion or at the request of the prosecution or the defence, review the case of the accused. In any event, the case shall be reviewed every 120 days unless there are reasons to do otherwise. If necessary, the Trial Chamber may order further examinations of the accused. When the Trial Chamber is satisfied that the accused has become fit to stand trial, it shall proceed with a status conference in accordance with Rule 132.

The procedure for guilty plea is developed in Article 65.

Cross-references:

Article 65, Rules 135 and 140.

Author: Mark Klamberg.

[527] Although the Statute outlines some general principles, it does not specify in any detail the procedure to be followed. Article 64(8)(b) grants the Presiding judge a broad discretion to determine the conduct of the proceedings, a typical civil-law feature. It may be used to control the manner of questioning the witnesses to avoid any harassment or intimidation. From a common law perspective such interventions may come in conflict with accused's interests, including the right to confront the evidence against him or her. Common law lawyers wanted to have some guidance in the rules which resulted in Rule 140. The rule has been characterised as a clash of cultures. It does not contain any sequencing instructing when the parties should examine a witness which would be normal in a common law system. However, it does provide that the defence shall have the right to be the last to examine a witness. The Trial Chamber has the right to question the witness, but is encouraged to do so before or after a witness is questioned by a party in order to avoid the judges intervening in the cross-examination of a witness and thereby frustrating a party's line of questioning. The chapeau in sub-rule 2 provides that the rules concerning questioning of witnesses apply "in all cases", which means that the right of a party to question a witness he or she has called, witnesses for the other side, and a right for the defendant to ask the last question is maintained all cases and can not be abrogated from at the discretion of the presiding judge. Thus, the possibility of cross-examination is implicitly recognised without using typical terms from either common law or civil law.

In *Prosecutor v. Lubanga*, ICC T. Ch., Decision on whether two judges alone may hold a hearing - and - Recommendations to the Presidency on whether an alternate judge should be assigned for the trial, ICC-01/04-01/06-1349, 22 May 2008, para. 12, the Trial Chamber stated that "by Article 64(8)(b), only at the trial may the presiding judge give directions for the con-

9. The Trial Chamber shall have, inter alia, the power on application of a party or on its own motion to:

   (a) Rule on the admissibility or relevance of evidence;[528] and

   (b) Take all necessary steps to maintain order in the course of a hearing.[529]

10. The Trial Chamber shall ensure that a complete record of the trial, which accurately reflects the proceedings, is made and that it is maintained and preserved by the Registrar.[530]

---

duct of the proceedings, thereby underlining that the presiding judge cannot adopt an analogous role to that of the single judge of the Pre-Trial Chamber during the preparatory phase before the trial commences".

Cross-references:

Rule 141.

Author: Mark Klamberg.

[528] Article 64(9)(a) confirms that the Trial Chamber has the power to rule on the admissibility or relevance of evidence. To a large extent it duplicates the terms in Article 69(4).

In *Prosecutor v. Lubanga*, ICC T. Ch. I, Decision on the status before the Trial Chamber of the evidence heard by the Pre-Trial Chamber and the decisions of the Pre-Trial Chamber in trial proceedings, and the manner in which evidence shall be submitted, 13 December 2007, TC I addressed the extent to which decisions of the Pre-Trial Chamber are binding on the Trial Chamber. The TC noted that "Article 64(9) of the Statute gives the Trial Chamber a seemingly unqualified power to rule on the admissibility or relevance of evidence" (para. 4) However, TC I also stated "that the Trial Chamber should only disturb the Pre-Trial Chamber's Decisions if it is necessary to do so. Not least for reasons of judicial comity, this Chamber should follow the Pre-Trial Chamber unless that would be an inappropriate approach" (para. 6).

Cross-references:

Rule 63 and 64.

Author: Mark Klamberg.

[529] In order to maintain order in the course of a hearing, the Trial Chamber has several tools, including: 1) the removal of persons, including the accused (Article 63(2)), who commit misconduct such as disruptions; 2)other sanctions for misconduct, including fines (Article 71).

Rule 170 provides that the Presiding Judge of the Chamber dealing with the matter may, after giving a warning: (a) Order a person disrupting the proceedings of the Court to leave or be removed from the courtroom; or, (b) In case of repeated misconduct, order the interdiction of that person from attending the proceedings. When the misconduct consists of deliberate refusal to comply with an oral or written direction by the Court, not covered by Rule 170, and that direction is accompanied by a warning of sanctions in case of breach, the Presiding Judge of the Chamber dealing with the matter may pursuant to Rule 171 order the interdiction of that person from the proceedings for a period not exceeding 30 days or, if the misconduct is of a more serious nature, impose a fine. The fine may not exceed 2,000 euros.

Cross-references:

Article 63(2) and 71, Rules 170 and 171.

Author: Mark Klamberg.

[530] The Trial Chamber shall ensure that a complete record of the trial, which accurately reflects the proceedings, is made and that it is maintained and preserved by the Registrar. Rule 137 provides that the Registrar shall take measures to make, and preserve, a full and accurate record of all proceedings, including transcripts, audio- and video-recordings and other means of capturing

---

sound or image. Real time transcripts of hearings shall pursuant to regulation 27 be provided in at least one of the working languages of the Court to the extent technically possible.

The record of public hearings may be a public document and distributed on conditions laid down by the either the Trial Chamber or the Registrar. By contrast, the record of hearings in camera is by nature confidential and may only be disclosed by an order of the Trial Chamber pursuant to Rule 137(2).

In *Prosecutor v. Lubanga*, ICC T. Ch., Order on numbering of evidence, 12 May 2010, the Trial Chamber pursuant to Article 64(10) adopted a revised procedure for the numbering of exhibit for the efficient administration of the record of the trial.

Cross-references:

Rule 137 and 138, regulation 27.

Doctrine:

1. Alphons Orie, in Antonio Cassese, Paola Gaeta and John R.W.D. Jones (eds.), *The Rome Statute of the International Criminal Court: A Commentary*, 2nd ed., Oxford University Press, Oxford, 2002, p. 1488.

2. Gilbert Bitti, in Otto Triffterer (ed.), *Commentary on the Rome Statute of the International Criminal Court: Observers' Notes, Article by Article*, 2nd ed., C.H. Beck/Hart/Nomos, Munich/Oxford/Baden-Baden, 2008, pp. 1199-1218.

3. Claus Kreß and Kimberly Prost, in Antonio Cassese, Paola Gaeta and John R.W.D. Jones (eds.), *The Rome Statute of the International Criminal Court: A Commentary*, 2nd ed., Oxford University Press, Oxford, 2002, pp. 1572, 1576-77, 1584.

4. Peter Lewis, in Roy S. Lee (ed.), *The International Criminal Court: Elements of Crimes and Rules of Procedure and Evidence*, Transnational Publishers, Ardsley, NY, 2001, pp. 549–50.

5. William A. Schabas, *The International Criminal Court: A Commentary on the Rome Statute*, Oxford University Press, Oxford, 2010, p. 772.

6. Frank Terrier, in Antonio Cassese, Paola Gaeta and John R.W.D. Jones (eds.), *The Rome Statute of the International Criminal Court: A Commentary*, 2nd ed., Oxford University Press, Oxford, 2002, p. 1284.

Author: Mark Klamberg.

Article 65

Proceedings on an admission of guilt[531]

1. Where the accused makes an admission of guilt pursuant to Article 64, paragraph 8 (a), the Trial Chamber shall determine whether:[532]

---

[531] *General remarks*:

Article 65 provides that if an accused admits guilt before the Trial Chamber, the Chamber may forego a full-blown trial and proceed with the case in an abbreviated fashion. The provision effectively allows for the development of a form of "plea bargaining", or "negotiated justice", whereby the accused agrees to admit guilt in exchange for more lenient treatment. In response to concerns expressed by delegates to the Rome Conference from civil-law countries, Article 65 demands a thorough inquiry by judges to ensure that an admission of guilt is supported by the facts and allows the court to require a more complete presentation of evidence in the interests of justice. The Article also expressly states that negotiations between the parties do not bind the court, emphasising that judges are the ultimate decision-makers on the facts, the charges, and the sentence.

Article 65 was drafted before plea bargaining developed at the ICTY and ICTR, and before the Rules at these Tribunals were amended to regulate the practice. Because the provisions on guilty pleas at those Tribunals are similar to those on admissions of guilt at the ICC, however, one may expect the ICC to consult Tribunal jurisprudence when interpreting Article 65. ICTY and ICTR jurisprudence is therefore mentioned in this commentary when relevant. Likewise, the commentary refers to the East Timor Special Panels on Serious Crimes (SPSC), because the SPSC accepted admissions of guilt under provisions almost identical to those of the ICC Statute. As of this writing in 2015, the ICC itself has not yet resolved any cases pursuant to the procedure in Article 65.

Preparatory works:

The negotiations of Article 65 reflected divisions between representatives of common-law countries, who viewed plea bargaining as an efficient mechanism of adjudicating complex crimes, and those of civil-law countries, who found repugnant the notion of "bargaining with justice" for serious international crimes. The International Law Commission's 1994 Final Draft of the ICC Statute included a provision for the entry of guilty pleas, without specifying the consequences of the procedure. Some delegates objected that the provision might allow for plea bargaining and that such bargaining would be inappropriate "in view of the gravity of the crimes within the jurisdiction of the court" (Schabas, p. 776, citing Ad Hoc Committee Report, para. 170). A compromise was found in a proposal submitted by Argentina and Canada, which suggested a procedure of "abbreviated proceedings on an admission of guilt" (Schabas 776). To assuage concerns about inaccurate, unfair, or overly lenient plea bargains, the final text included the provision in Article 65(5), which states that any discussions between the parties regarding the charges or the penalty would not bind the court (Schabas, p. 776-77).

Analysis:

The accused may formally admit guilt once the case reaches the Trial Chamber (ICC Statute Article 64(8)(a)). The Trial Chamber must then examine the validity of the admission under Article 65(1).

Cross-references:

Article 64(8).

Author: Jenia Iontcheva Turner.

(a) The accused understands the nature and consequences of the admission of guilt;[533]

---

[532] To determine the validity of an admission of guilt, the Chamber must examine whether the admission is knowing, voluntary, and factually based. Unlike the ICTY and ICTR Rules, the ICC Statute does not expressly require that the admission of guilt be unequivocal. Theoretically, therefore, an accused may be able to admit guilt and yet persist with a legal defence. While Article 65 does not prohibit equivocal admissions, Trial Chambers are unlikely to accept them in practice. Such admissions increase the risk that a potentially innocent defendant is convicted (*Prosecutor v. Serushago* (Case No. ICTR-98-39), ICTR T. Ch., 5 February 1999, para. 29). They also conflict with Article 65's emphasis on a full examination of the facts of the case. At the SPSC, which followed Rules identical to Article 65(1) with respect to the validity of admissions of guilt, judges required that admissions of guilt be unequivocal even though no such requirement was set out in the court's rules (UNTAET Regulation No.2000/30 on Transitional Rules of Criminal Procedure, R. 29A; *Prosecutor v. Fernandes*, SPSC; Dili District Court, Sentencing Judgment, 25 January, 2000, para. 6).

Cross-references:

Rule 139.

Author: Jenia Iontcheva Turner.

[533] The Trial Chamber must examine whether the accused "understands the nature and consequences of the admission of guilt". The ICC Statute and Rules do not interpret these terms further, but jurisprudence from the ICTY and ICTR offers some guidance.

First, the Chamber must examine whether the accused understands "the elements of the crime or crimes to which he has pleaded guilty to ensure that his understanding of the requirements of the crime reflects his actual conduct and participation as well as his state of mind or intent when he committed the crime" (*Prosecutor v. M. Nikolić* (Case No. IT-02-60/1), ICTY T. Ch., 2 December 2003, para. 12). Where the accused faces alternative charges, he must comprehend "the nature and distinction between the alternative charges and the consequences of pleading guilty to one rather than the other" (*Prosecutor v. Erdemović* (Case No. IT-96-22), ICTY A. Ch., 7 October 1997, sep. op. of Judge McDonald and Judge Vohrah), para. 14).

Second, the Chamber must inform the accused of the rights he or she is waiving by choosing to admit guilt. These include the right to a public trial, the right to prepare a defence against the charges, the right to be tried without undue delay, the right to confront adverse witnesses and obtain defence witnesses, and the right not to be compelled to testify against oneself (*Prosecutor v. Erdemović*, ICTY A. Ch., 7 October 1997 (sep. op. of Judge McDonald and Judge Vohrah), para. 15).

Third, the Chamber must confirm that the accused understands the sentencing consequences of his admission (Turner and Weigend 1381). The ICC Statute and Rules do not provide detailed guidance about sentencing. The Chamber will therefore likely have to inform the accused on only two points: 1) that it would not be bound by any sentencing agreement by the parties; and 2) that it might impose a penalty up to the maximum specified in Article 77 (a maximum sentence of 30 years, or in extremely grave cases, life imprisonment; a possible fine and forfeiture of proceeds from the crime).

Fourth, the Chamber must verify that the accused is mentally competent to understand the consequences of his actions. The ICTY and ICTR have examined mental competence when determining whether a guilty plea is voluntary, but this evaluation appears to fit more neatly under Article 65(1)(a) at the ICC. The Trial Chamber may order a psychiatric evaluation of the accused to determine his mental competence (ICC RPE Rule 135(1)). The standard for competence to enter a guilty plea is generally the same as the standard for competency to stand trial (Turner and Weigend 1379).

(b) The admission is voluntarily made by the accused after sufficient consultation with defence counsel; and[534]

(c) The admission of guilt is supported by the facts of the case that are contained in:[535]

(i) The charges brought by the Prosecutor and admitted by the accused;

(ii) Any materials presented by the Prosecutor which supplement the charges and which the accused accepts; and

(iii) Any other evidence, such as the testimony of witnesses, presented by the Prosecutor or the accused.

2. Where the Trial Chamber is satisfied that the matters referred to in paragraph 1 are established, it shall consider the admission of guilt, together with any additional evidence presented, as establishing all the essential facts that are required to prove the crime to which the admission of guilt relates, and may convict the accused of that crime.[536]

Author: Jenia Iontcheva Turner.

[534] After determining that the accused has made an informed admission of guilt, the Chamber must also inquire whether the admission is voluntary and whether it was made "after sufficient consultation with defence counsel". The admission of guilt must not be the product of any threats or inducements other than the expectation of receiving a reduced sentence or charging concessions (*Prosecutor v. Erdemović* (Case No. IT-96-22), ICTY A. Ch., 7 October 1997 (sep. op. of Judge McDonald and Judge Vohrah), para. 10; *Prosecutor v. Kambanda* (Case No. ICTR-97-23), ICTR A. Ch., 19 October 2000, para. 61). Unlike at the Tribunals, at the ICC, an admission of guilt requires consultation with defence counsel. The assistance of counsel is expected to reduce the risk that an accused person would be coerced into admitting guilt.

Author: Jenia Iontcheva Turner.

[535] The Chamber must examine the following sources to determine whether an admission of guilt is supported by the facts: 1) the charging document; 2) "[a]ny materials presented by the Prosecutor which supplement the charges and which the accused accepts; and 3) [a]ny other evidence, such as the testimony of witnesses, presented by the Prosecutor or the accused". The Article does not appear to contemplate that victims would be providing evidence (other than as witnesses) to support the factual basis of the admission.

Notably, Article 65(1) confirms that the facts on which the admission of guilt rests cannot be negotiated by the parties. This is a formal departure from ICTY and ICTR Rules, which provide that the "lack of any material disagreement between the parties about the facts of the case" could constitute sufficient factual basis for a guilty plea (ICTY RPE 62bis(iv); ICTY RPE 62(B)(iv)). In practice, however, ICTY and ICTR judges have typically conducted an independent inquiry into the facts and required evidence beyond the parties' agreement to support guilty pleas (Guariglia and Hochmayr 1229). The factual basis requirement helps to ensure that the accused is admitting responsibility only for conduct of which he is in fact guilty, and that the charges reflect the totality of his conduct (*Prosecutor v. Erdemović* (Case No. IT-96-22), ICTY A. Ch., 7 October, 1997 (sep. op. of Judge Cassese), at 11; Turner and Weigend 1382). Given the ICC's commitment to establishing an accurate record of the crimes, ICC judges may be expected to conduct a more probing inquiry into the evidence supporting admissions of guilt than is common in many national courts.

Author: Jenia Iontcheva Turner.

[536] If the Chamber concludes that the admission of guilt is valid, it "may" convict the accused. A conviction is therefore not automatic even if the court finds that the admission is valid and that the facts of the crime have been established. Under Article 65(4), the Chamber may still require additional presentation of evidence and may even order that the trial continue under ordinary

3. Where the Trial Chamber is not satisfied that the matters referred to in paragraph 1 are established, it shall consider the admission of guilt as not having been made, in which case it shall order that the trial be continued under the ordinary trial procedures provided by this Statute and may remit the case to another Trial Chamber.[537]

proceedings if it believes that this would serve the interests of justice. At the ICTY and ICTR, judges similarly had the discretion to reject a valid guilty plea if they were "not satisfied with the terms of the plea agreement", if they were concerned that the agreement did not adequately protect the rights of the accused, or if they believed that accepting the plea would not serve the interests of justice (*Prosecutor v. M. Nikolić* (Case No. IT-02-60/1) T. Ch., ICTY, 2 December 2003, para. 54; ICTY RPE R. 62bis; ICTR RPE R. 62(B); Khan and Dixon §7-161, 330).

Should the Chamber enter a conviction after the proceeding on admission of guilt, the sentencing consequences remain unspecified. Neither the Statute nor the Rules mention the admission of guilt as a mitigating factor at sentencing. However, Rule 145(2)(a)(ii) of the ICC Rules of Procedure and Evidence provides that the court should mitigate the sentence, as appropriate, based on '[t]he convicted person's conduct after the act, including any efforts by the person to compensate the victims and any cooperation with the Court'. Consistent with practice at the ICTY and ICTR, it is likely that the ICC will consider admissions of guilt as an example of cooperation with the court that deserves a sentence reduction (Turner and Weigend 1391).

The Statute and Rules are also silent on how an admission of guilt would affect the court's decisions on reparations to victims. In some civil-law countries, an accused cannot proceed with abbreviated proceedings upon admission of guilt until the court has resolved the question of reparations (Turner 146, 155). The ICC framework does not require this; as noted below, however, one may expect the court to take into account the question of reparations when consulting victims and deciding whether to require a more complete presentation of evidence under Article 65(4).

Author: Jenia Iontcheva Turner.

[537] If the court rejects an admission of guilt as invalid, it must consider the admission as "not having been made". The Chamber "shall" then order that the case proceed under the ordinary trial procedures. If the court rejects an admission of guilt as invalid, the defendant's waiver of fundamental rights is null and void and cannot result in any prejudice to him (Guariglia and Hochmayr 1230). Under this interpretation and consistent with ICTY and ICTR jurisprudence, statements made by the accused during the proceedings on admission of guilt should not be able to be used against him at trial (Turner and Weigend 1386-87; 1392). But some commentators have suggested that statements by the accused, as well as evidence introduced to support the admission of guilt, may be used as evidence at trial, if the court considers that the accused has waived his right to remain silent by admitting guilt or that the admission is reliable evidence that cannot be disregarded (Schabas 779; Damaška 1038). As a practical matter, if the court adopts this interpretation, it will discourage defendants from admitting their guilt.

If the Trial Chamber rejects the admission of guilt, it "may" remit the case to another Chamber. Transferring the case to another Chamber can help ensure that judges who have heard the admission of guilt are not prejudiced by it during their decision on the verdict. Given the small number of judges at the ICC and the few cases before the Court at any given time, it would be difficult in practice to find judges who are entirely unaware of the defendant's admission. Although complete lack of knowledge of the admission is unlikely, Article 65(3) does not require it. The provision merely allows—but does not mandate—the transfer of the case to a different Chamber, apparently under the presumption that judges could remain impartial even after hearing an accused's admission of guilt.

Author: Jenia Iontcheva Turner.

4. Where the Trial Chamber is of the opinion that a more complete presentation of the facts of the case is required in the interests of justice, in particular the interests of the victims, the Trial Chamber may:[538]

   (a) Request the Prosecutor to present additional evidence, including the testimony of witnesses; or

   (b) Order that the trial be continued under the ordinary trial procedures provided by this Statute, in which case it shall consider the admission of guilt as not having been made and may remit the case to another Trial Chamber.

5. Any discussions between the Prosecutor and the defence regarding modification of the charges, the admission of guilt or the penalty to be imposed shall not be binding on the Court.[539]

---

[538] Pursuant to sub-paragraph (a), the Trial Chamber may request the prosecution to present additional evidence where it believes that the interests of justice—and in particular the interests of victims—may require it. The Court may need to resort to this procedure if additional facts would be helpful to victims' reparation claims, to the determination of a just sentence, or to the establishment of a more complete record. No similar provision exists in the ICTY and ICTR Rules. Article 65 reflects a new approach to plea bargaining, in line with the court's goals of compiling an accurate record and protecting victims' interests (Turner and Weigend 1390).

Article 65(4)(b) of the ICC Statute provides that even when the conditions for a valid admission of guilt are met, the Chamber may nonetheless reject the admission and order the case to proceed through the ordinary trial procedure when the Chamber "is of the opinion that a more complete presentation of the facts is required in the interests of justice". The court's view of the interests of justice may override the parties' wishes to resolve the case through the Article 65 procedure (Turner and Weigend 1390).

In deciding whether to proceed under Article 65(4), the Chamber may, in accordance with Rule 139(1), invite the views of the prosecution and defence. Because the Chamber will make this determination based on the interests of justice and of victims, however, one may expect the Chamber to solicit the views of victims as well (Article 68(3); Schabas 780). This would be consistent with Rule 93, which provides that a Chamber may seek the views of victims or their legal representatives in relation to proceedings on admission of guilt (ICC RPE Rules 93, 139; Turner and Weigend 1391).

Cross-references:

Rule 139.

Author: Jenia Iontcheva Turner.

[539] Article 65(5) was included in response to concerns about allowing the parties to resolve the outcome of a case independently of the court and in a manner contrary to the interests of justice (Schabas 775). The Article acknowledges that discussions between the parties about the charges and penalty may occur, but it provides that these discussions are not binding on the court. By making the outcome of bargaining subject to judicial approval, Article 65(5) reduces the predictability and therefore the likelihood of agreements between the parties. At the same time, it reinforces the role of judges as the ultimate arbiters with respect to the accuracy and fairness of the verdict and rejects a party-driven model of negotiated justice.

So far, international tribunals have been largely reluctant to accept agreements between the parties concerning the charges and the facts, particularly when such agreements do not adequately reflect the totality of the accused's conduct and the gravity of the offences committed (*Prosecutor v. M. Nikolić* (Case No. IT-02-60/1) ICTY T. Ch., 2 December 2003, paras. 50, 65; *Prosecutor v. Deronjić* (Case No. IT-02-61) ICTY T. Ch., (dissenting op. of Judge Schomburg), March 30, 2004, para. 11). Such agreements are disfavoured because of a concern that they may leave the impression that the outcome is unjust or that the court has not established a full and credible record of the crime (*Prosecutor v. M. Nikolić* (Case No. IT-02-60/1) ICTY T. Ch., 2 December 2003, para. 65). For the same reasons, we can expect that at the ICC, too, charge bargaining will be relatively rare. If parties do enter into agreements, these are more likely to concern the sentence rather than the charges or the facts.

Cross-references:

Rule 139.

Doctrine:

1. Mirjan Damaška, "Negotiated Justice in International Criminal Courts", in *Journal of International Criminal Justice*, 2004, vol. 2, p. 1018.

2. Fabricio Guariglia and Gudrun Hochmayr, "Article 65", in Otto Triffterer (ed.), *Commentary on the Rome Statute of the International Criminal Court: Observers' Notes, Article by Article*, 2nd ed., C.H. Beck/Hart/Nomos, Munich/Oxford/Baden-Baden, 2008, pp. 1219–32.

3. Karim A.A. Khan and Rodney Dixon, *Archbold International Criminal Courts: Practice, Procedure, and Evidence*, 3rd ed., Sweet and Maxwell, London, 2009, § 7–161.

4. William A. Schabas, *The International Criminal Court: A Commentary on the Rome Statute*, Oxford University Press, Oxford, 2010.

5. Frank Terrier, "Proceedings Before the Trial Chamber", in Antonio Cassese, Paola Gaeta and John R.W.D. Jones (eds.), T*he Rome Statute of the International Criminal Court: A Commentary*, Oxford University Press, Oxford, 2002.

6. Jenia Iontcheva Turner, *Plea Bargaining Across Borders,* Aspen, New York, 2009.

7. Jenia Iontcheva Turner and Thomas Weigend, "Negotiated Justice", in Göran Sluiter, Håkan Friman, Suzannah Linton, Sergey Vasiliev and Salvatore Zappalà (eds.), *International Criminal Procedure: Principles and Rules*, Oxford University Press, Oxford, 2013.

Author: Jenia Iontcheva Turner.

Article 66

Presumption of innocence[540]

1. Everyone shall be presumed innocent until proved guilty before the Court in accordance with the applicable law.[541]

2. The onus is on the Prosecutor to prove the guilt of the accused.[542]

---

[540] *General remarks*

Article 66 contains the maxim of presumption of innocence, which is contained in all major human rights instruments, and some corollaries thereto.

While the presumption of innocence itself is not also stated as a defendant right under either Article 55(2) or Article 67(1), some of the rights contained in these Articles are corollaries of the presumption of innocence, such as the right to silence (Article 55(2)(b) , 67(1)(g)) or the right not to be burdened with a reversal of the burden of proof (Article 67(1)(i)). But also other provisions, such as those allowing interim release of accused (Articles 59(3)–(6), 60), can only be explained on the basis that all accused, including those who apply for provisional release, must be considered innocent.

Despite being placed in Part 6 on "The Trial", the presumption of innocence applies generally to all proceedings before the court concerning individual defendants (See Schabas, MN 3, MN 11-12, Zappala, p. 1342).

Author: Björn Elberling, revised by Mark Klamberg.

[541] Article 66(1) states the core of the presumption of innocence, namely that everybody must be presumed innocent until proven guilty according to the law. The wording "everyone" shows that the presumption of innocence applies not only to accused, that is, during the actual trial, but also to, for example, persons covered by Article 55(2) in the investigation phase. As to its application during sentencing and during appeals proceedings, see Schabas, MN 13-14.

The most interesting question is what legal consequences exactly attach to the principle. The major consequence, of course, is that an accused may not be convicted unless her guilt has been proven according to the applicable law (and in accordance with Article 66(2)-(3)). "According to the applicable law" in this case may also be read to imply that where evidence for guilt is not presented in accordance with applicable procedural or other norms, it may not be used to justify a conviction (see Schabas, MN 17).

Besides this consequence and those laid down in the following paragraphs or separate provisions, one can generally state that the presumption must be taken into account in all decisions concerning the defendant and that it prohibits any decision based on a preconception of his or her guilt (Generally concerning actions that may be in violation of the presumption, including acts of bodies besides the Court, see Schabas, MN 26–27)

Author: Björn Elberling, revised by Mark Klamberg.

[542] Article 66(2) lays down one important corollary to the presumption of innocence, namely that is up to the prosecution to prove the guilt of the defendant. Stated negatively, this means that it may never be up to the defendant to provide evidence of his or her innocence in the absence of direct evidence of his or her guilt. In the context of the ICC Statute, this provision is significantly strengthened by Article 67(1)(i), which prohibits any reversal of the burden of proof and thus shows that the rule contained in Article 66(2) applies generally and without exceptions.

For more on the question of reversal of the burden of proof, including examples of provisions which might pose problems under Article 66 and 67, see the commentary to Article 67(1)(i).

---

3. In order to convict the accused, the Court must be convinced of the guilt of the accused beyond reasonable doubt.[543]

Cross-references:

Article 67(1)(i).

Author: Björn Elberling, revised by Mark Klamberg.

[543] While Article 66(2) concerns the burden of proof before the ICC, this provision concerns the standard of proof to be met by the prosecution to overcome this burden. In keeping with its precursors (see references in Schabas, MN 23) as well as most national laws, the Rome Statute requires proof "beyond reasonable doubt". An exact definition of this standard may be almost impossible to find; for examples of what reasonable doubt means and what it does not mean (see Schabas, MN 25).

The standard of proof beyond reasonable doubt does not demand unanimity of the judges, rather a majority of judges is sufficient for conviction provided that these judges are convinced beyond a reasonable doubt of the guilt of the accused (see Article 74(3)).

Doctrine:

1. William A. Schabas, in Otto Triffterer (ed.), *Commentary on the Rome Statute of the International Criminal Court: Observers' Notes, Article by Article*, 2nd ed., C.H. Beck/Hart/Nomos, Munich/Oxford/Baden-Baden, 2008, pp. 1233–45.

2. Salvatore Zappala, in Antonio Cassese, Paola Gaeta and John R.W.D. Jones (eds.), *The Rome Statute of the International Criminal Court: A Commentary*, Oxford University Press, Oxford, 2002, pp. 1340–48.

Author: Björn Elberling, revised by Mark Klamberg.

Article 67
Rights of the accused[544]

1. In the determination of any charge, the accused shall be entitled to a public hearing, having regard to the provisions of this Statute, to a fair hearing conducted impartially, and to the following minimum guarantees, in full equality:[545]

---

[544] *General remarks*:

Article 67(1) contains a number of specific rights granted to the accused, most of which are taken, with some modifications, from provisions on defendant rights in human rights instruments, particularly Article 14 of the International Covenant on Civil and Political Rights ('ICCPR'). Moreover, Article 67(1) is similar to constitutional national texts. Article 67 is not only applicable to trial as their provisions are relevant to all procedural stages (*Situation in the Democratic Republic of Congo*, Decision on the Prosecution's Application for Leave to Appeal the Chamber's Decision of 17 January 2006 on the Applications for Participation in the Proceedings of VPRS 1, VPRS 2, VPRS 3, VPRS 4, VPRS 5 and VPRS 6, ICC-01/04, 31 March 2006, paras. 34-35). Besides Article 67, other Articles relevant to the rights of the accused person are: i) Article 21(3), which guarantees the application of international human rights when interpreting the ICC Statute; ii) Article 55, which fleshes out the rights of persons during an investigation; iii) Article 61(6), which contains the accused person's specific rights at the confirmation of charges hearing; iv) Article 66 (Presumption of innocence); and v) Article 74, which contains the right to a reasoned judgment. Thus, for example, by virtue of Article 21(3) of the ICC Statute, the interpretation and application of the applicable law shall be consistent with internationally recognised human rights and, thus, the broad concept of fair trial should embrace the judicial process in its entirety (*Prosecutor v. Gbagbo*, ICC PT. Ch. I, Decision on the fitness of Laurent Gbagbo to take part in the proceedings before this Court, ICC-02/11-01/11-286-Red, 2 November 2012, para. 45). It should finally be borne in mind that, as a rule, the rights of the accused have primacy "over any other conflicting interest" (Zappalà, 2010, pp. 144-145).

Preparatory works:

A provision almost identical to Article 14(3) of the ICCPR was included in the International Law Commission draft statute of 1994. Based on this draft, the Ad Hoc Committee focused its discussion on some specific issues. The Preparatory Committee, at its August 1996 session, considered the rights of the accused which led to detailed comments and suggestions. The Preparatory Committee addressed the topic again in August 1997 and, at this stage, there were many departures from the text of Article 14(3) of the ICCPR. In addition, there were many cross-references to other ICC Statute provisions. Thus, the Preparatory Committee's 1997 draft contained both modified versions of the rights included in Article 14 of the ICCPR and several new rights. This text was reproduced in the Zurphen Compilation and the final draft of the Preparatory Committee with just few changes. In turn, the Rome Conference swiftly agreed on most of Article 67 provisions and the delegates accepted the approach under which the minimum guarantees of Article 14 of the ICCPR were enlarged (on preparatory works of Article 67, see, Schabas, 1999, pp. 847-848; Schabas, 2008, 1249-1250; and Schabas, 2010, pp. 793-794).

Cross-references:

Articles 21(3), 55, 61(6), 64, 66, 74.

Authors: Juan Pablo Pérez-León-Acevedo and Björn Elberling.

[545] As to its application, the wording "in the determination of any charge" implies that in terms of substance Article 67 applies not only to crimes referenced in Article 5, but also offences against the administration of justice contained in Article 70 (Schabas, 1999, p. 849; Schabas, 2008, p.

1251; and Schabas, 2010, pp. 796–797). As to temporal application, the wording "in the determination of any charge" is largely identical to human rights norms, which apply once a person has been "substantially affected" by proceedings, that is, even before a formal indictment is brought (Schabas, 1999, p. 849; Schabas, 2008, p. 1251; and Schabas, 2010, pp. 796–797 with references). On the other hand, the fact that the norm refers to "accused" (on this terminology, see comment to Article 19(2)(a))) and that the rights of persons during an investigation are safeguarded in the separate Article 55, would seem to imply that Article 67(1) only applies once proceedings specifically against an individual accused have begun, that is, after the initial appearance of the accused. This also seems to be the approach so far taken by the Court – when Pre-Trial Chamber II in *Kony et al.* appointed an *ad hoc* counsel for the defence at a time when arrest warrants had been issued but none of the defendants had been arrested, it did so not under Article 67(1), but under its general power under Regulation 76(1) (*Prosecutor v. Kony et al.*, ICC PT. Ch. II, Decision on legal representation, appointment of counsel for the defence, protective measures and time-limit for submission of observations on applications for participation a/0010/06, a/0064/06 to a/0070/06, a/0081/06 to a/0104/06 and a/0111/06 to a/0127/06, ICC-02/04-01/05-134, 1 February 2007, para. 15). Indeed, in accordance with rule 121(1) of the Rules of Procedure and Evidence (RPE), Article 67(1) fair trial rights are applicable from the first appearance of the suspect before the Pre-Trial Chamber (*Prosecutor v. Gbagbo*, ICC PT. Ch. I, Decision on the fitness of Laurent Gbagbo to take part in the proceedings before this Court, ICC-02/11-01/11-286-Red, 2 November 2012, para. 44).

The fact that the temporal application of Article 67 is thus rather limited is partly made up by the fact that the Court is also mindful of the rights and interests of the defence generally – where Article 67 does not yet apply, but where there is a situation in which the interests of the defence generally need to be safeguarded, the Court appoints *ad hoc* counsel for the defence (for example, *Situation in Darfur, Sudan*, ICC PT. Ch. I, Decision Inviting Observations in Application of Rule 103 of the Rules of Procedure and Evidence, ICC-02/05-10, 24 July 2006; *Situation in the Democratic Republic of Congo*, PT. Ch. I, Decision on Protective Measures Requested by Applicants 01/04-1/dp to 01/04-6/dp) or assigns this task to the Office of Public Counsel for the Defence (OPCD) (for example, *Situation in Darfur*, Sudan, ICC PT. Ch. I, Decision authorising the filing of observations on applications for participation in the proceedings a/0011/06 to a/0015/06, ICC-02/05-74, 23 May 2007).

According to the chapeau of Article 67(1), all rights contained therein are granted "having regard to the provisions of this Statute". This provision, which was added rather late in the negotiating process, can best be interpreted as allowing specific limitations of the Article 67 rights to be contained elsewhere in the Statute, not as generally subordinating Article 67 to other norms of the Statute (Schabas, 1999, p. 851; Schabas, 2008, p. 1253; and Schabas, 2010, p. 798). One example for such limitations is the right to a public hearing, exceptions to which are contained in Articles 64(7), 68(2) and 72(7). On the other hand, some defence rights, such as Article 67(1)(d) on the right to be present at one's trial, explicitly refers to the Statute norms containing limitations (in this case Article 63(2)). In such cases, an argument could be made that no exceptions to these defence rights may be derived from norms not explicitly mentioned in the provision containing the defence right in question (although see commentary to Article 67(1)(d) concerning further limitations to this right).

As for Article 67(1) fair trial rights, Pre-Trial Chamber I in *Gbagbo* indicated certain necessary capacities to meaningfully exercise those rights, namely, "(i) to understand in detail the nature, cause and content of the charges; (ii) to understand the conduct of the proceedings; (iii) to instruct counsel; (iv) to understand the consequences of the proceedings; and (v) to make a statement" (*Prosecutor v. Gbagbo*, ICC PT. Ch. I, Decision on the fitness of Laurent Gbagbo to take part in the proceedings before this Court, ICC-02/11-01/11-286-Red, 2 November 2012, para. 50).

Besides provisions on the applicability of the rights of the accused, the chapeau of Article 67(1) also itself contains certain rights.

First among these is the right to a public hearing. The requirement of publicity is further elaborated upon in Regulations 20 and 21; it may require unsealing of non-public documents, if need be in a redacted form (see, for example, *Prosecutor v. Lubanga*, ICC PT. Ch. I, Decision to Unseal and Reclassify Certain Documents in the Record of the Case against Mr Thomas Lubanga Dyilo, ICC-01/04-01/06-42, 20 March 2006). There are a number of circumstances under which the publicity of hearings may be restricted – see the Articles mentioned above, as well as commentaries to these Articles (see also *Prosecutor v. Bemba*, ICC T. Ch. III, Public Redacted Version of the Chamber's 11 November 2011 Decision regarding the prosecution's witness schedule, ICC-01/05-01/08-1904-Red, 15 November 2011, para. 18; and *Prosecutor v. Katanga and Ngudjolo Chui*, ICC PT. Ch. II, Ordonnance portant instructions en vue de favouriser la publicité de la procédure, ICC-01/04-01/07-3226, 31 January 2012, para. 1). In turn, as Schabas points out, the accused person's right to privacy is not explicitly recognised in the ICC Statute (Schabas, 2010, p. 798). However, this right has been invoked by the judges in order to restrict the principle of publicity of proceedings (*Prosecutor v. Bemba*, ICC PT. Ch. III, Decision on the Second Defence's Application for Lifting the Seizure of Assets and Request for Cooperation to the Competent Authorities of the Republic of Portugal, ICC-01/05-01/08-249, 14 November 2008, paras. 27–29).

It is important to consider the (potential) tension and/or conflict between the right to a public hearing and protective measures ordered under Article 68 (for further and more detailed commentaries, see commentaries on Article 68). Under Article 68(2), these measures "[are] an exception to the principle of public hearings" and, thus, a Chamber "may, to protect victims and witnesses or an accused, conduct any part of the proceedings in camera or allow the presentation of evidence by electronic or other special means". Case law of the ICC has considered the public character of the proceedings as fundamental (*Prosecutor v. Bemba*, ICC A. Ch., Order on the reclassification as public of documents ICC-01/05-01/08-498-Conf and ICC-01/05-01/08-503-Conf, ICC-01/05-01/08-701, 24 February 2010; and *Prosecutor v. Katanga and Ngudjolo Chui*, ICC T. Ch. II, Order on protective measures for certain witnesses called by the Prosecutor and the Chamber (Rules 87 and 88 of the Rules of Procedure and Evidence), ICC-01/04-01/07-1667-Red-tENG, 9 December 2009, para. 4). However, the ICC Chambers have made exceptions to the principle of public hearings considering the protective needs of the witnesses (for example, *Prosecutor v. Lubanga*, ICC T. Ch. I, Transcripts, ICC-01/04-01/06-T-104, 16 January 2009, pp. 3–4). Article 68(2) allows a departure from the normal course of "public hearings" in order to protect victims and witnesses, when it is necessary, including "special measures" such as reading partially or totally a witness's statement in open court or in private provided that "these steps do not detract from the fairness of the proceedings" (*Prosecutor v. Lubanga*, ICC T. Ch. I, Decision on the prosecution's application for the admission of the prior recorded statements of two witnesses, ICC-01/04-01/06-1603, 15 January 2009, para. 17). In *Katanga and Ngudjolo Chui*, for example, the Chamber ordered closed sessions when certain witnesses would enter and exit the courtroom and when potentially identifying questions would be put to them (*Prosecutor v. Katanga and Ngudjolo Chui*, ICC T. Ch. II, Decision on the application for the institution of protective measures for Witnesses a/0381/09, a/0018/09, a/0191/08, pan/0363/09 and Victim a/0363/09, issued on 27 January 2011, ICC-01/04-01/07-2663-Red, 22 February 2011, para. 15).

Nevertheless, the interest of the accused person's right to a public hearing grows stronger during the trial phase. Thus, for instance, the Trial Chamber in *Lubanga* stated that it would review applications concerning protective measures, including the use of closed sessions, based on individual analysis (*Prosecutor v. Lubanga*, ICC T. Ch. I, Decision on various issues related to witnesses' testimony during trial, ICC-01/04-01/06-1140, 29 January 2008, paras. 25 and 35).

Be that as it may, during the trial in *Lubanga*, testimony was frequently heard in "private session" and, thus, the public was unable to follow it; however, the Chamber ordered the public reclassification of any portions that do not contain information which may create a security risk (*Prosecutor v. Lubanga*, ICC T. Ch. I, Judgment Pursuant to Article 74 of the Statute, ICC-01/04-01/06-2842, 14 March 2012, para. 116). Trial Chamber II followed the same approach in *Katanga and Ngudjolo Chui* (*Prosecutor v. Ngudjolo Chui*, Judgment pursuant to Article 74 of the Statute, ICC-01/04-02/12-3-tENG, 18 December 2012, para. 64). The excessive or too frequent use of in camera hearings is criticised herein as it is in detriment to the principle of public hearings, which is an important component of the accused's rights as set out under Article 67(1). Moreover, the excessive frequency of closed hearings, that is, courts sitting in private, may give the wrong impression. Accordingly, the general principle is the publicity of the ICC proceedings, as derived from Articles 67(1) and 64(7) of the ICC Statute, and protective measures in favour of witnesses and victims "shall be considered to be an exception to this principle" (*Prosecutor v. Ruto and Sang*, ICC T. Ch. V(A), Decision on the Conduct of Trial Proceedings (General Directions), ICC-01/09-01/11-847, 9 August 2013, para. 30). However, in practice, "restriction on the principle of public hearings seems to be the rule" (Schabas, 2010, p. 825).

Second, Article 67(1) also entitles the accused to a fair hearing – this reference to the rather broad and evolving principle of "fair trial" will allow the Court to keep pace with the development of defence rights in international law also insofar as they go beyond the "minimum guarantees" contained in Article 67(1) itself. The Court has already found that the reference to fair trial, read in conjunction with the wording "in full equality", lays down the principle of equality of arms which requires "that the minimum guarantees contained in Article 67(1) must be generously interpreted, so as to ensure the defence is placed insofar as possible on an equal footing with the prosecution" (*Prosecutor v. Lubanga*, ICC T. Ch. I, Decision on defence's request to obtain simultaneous French transcripts, ICC-01/04-01/06-1091, 14 December 2007, para. 18). Moreover, as concluded by Pre-Trial Chamber II, fairness is "[...] closely linked to the concept of "equality of arms", or of balance between the parties during the proceedings. As commonly understood, it concerns the ability of a party to proceedings to adequately make its case, with a view to influencing the outcome of the proceedings in its favour" (*Situation in Uganda*, ICC PT. Ch. II, Decision on Prosecutor's Application for leave to Appeal in Part Pre-Trial Chamber II's Decision on the Prosecutor's Applications for Warrants of Arrest under Article 58, ICC-02/04-01/05-20-US-Exp, 19 August 2005, para. 30). Even though "fairness" is worded in relation to the accused, it is applicable to all participants in the proceedings (*Prosecutor v. Kony et al.*, ICC PT. Ch. II, Decision on the Prosecutor's Applications for Leave to Appeal Dated the 15th Day of March 2006 and to Suspend or Stay Consideration of Leave to Appeal Dated the 11th Day of May 2006, ICC-02/04-01/15-64, 10 July 2006, para. 24).

Third, all hearings before the Court must be conducted impartially, that is, without prejudice or bias on the part of the Court (see Schabas, 1999, p. 852; Schabas, 2008, p. 1255; and Schabas, 2010, pp. 800–801). As opposed to human rights law and earlier drafts, the Statute does not refer to the requirement of independence of the court. Subjectivity is also part of the analysis of "conducted impartially" (Schabas, 2010, p. 801). As stated by the Appeals Chamber: "The absence of bias, real or apparent, is what legitimises a judicial body to administer justice" (*Prosecutor v. Katanga and Ngudjolo Chui*, ICC A. Ch., Judgment in the Appeal by *Ngudjolo Chui* of 27 March 2008 against the Decision of Pre-Trial Chamber I on the Application of the Appellant for Interim Release, ICC-01/04-01/07-572, 9 June 2008, para. 10).

Finally, the phrase "in full equality" lays down the principle that all persons shall be equal before the Court. As stated above, this phrase, read in conjunction with the general fair trial requirement, also lays down the principle of equality of arms. Whether the principle of "equality of arms" is applicable *vis-à-vis* victim participants is discussed if and when the latter apply to

(a) To be informed promptly and in detail of the nature, cause and content of the charge, in a language which the accused fully understands and speaks;[546]

---

submit evidentiary material during trial and, additionally, when ruling on the admissibility of such evidence, the Chamber considers the prejudice posed by it to a fair trial (Article 69(4)) (*Prosecutor v. Banda and Jerbo*, ICC T. Ch. IV, Decision on the defence request for a temporary stay of proceedings, ICC-02/05-03/09-410, 26 October 2012, para. 152).

Cross-references:

Articles 55, 63(2), 64(7), 67(1)(d), 68(1), (2), (4) , 69(4), 72(7).

Rule 121(1).

Regulations 20 and 21.

Authors: Juan Pablo Pérez-León-Acevedo and Björn Elberling.

[546] Article 67(1)(a) endeavours to provide the accused with information which is necessary for the defence preparation (Schabas, 1999, p. 853; Schabas, 2008, p. 1256; and Schabas, 2010, p. 802). Article 67(1)(a) contains the right of the accused to be informed of the case against him or her. This right is complemented by similar provisions during investigation (Article 55(2)(a)) and in the context of the confirmation hearing (Article 61(3)), as well as by the disclosure requirements in Article 67(2). Taken together, these provisions aim at granting the accused all the information he or she needs to be able to adequately prepare a defence. The accused must, at the minimum, be given a readable version of the warrant of arrest (*Prosecutor v. Lubanga*, ICC PT. Ch. I, Decision Concerning Pre-Trial Chamber I's Decision of 10 February 2006 and the Incorporation of Documents into the Record of the Case against Mr. Thomas Lubanga Dyilo, ICC-01/04-01/06-8-US-Corr, 24 February 2006, p. 2) and access to all public documents in the case (cf. *Prosecutor v. Lubanga*, ICC PT. Ch. I, Decision on the Defence Request for Unrestricted Access to the Entire File of the Situation in the Democratic Republic of the Congo, ICC-01/04-01/06-103, 17 May 2006). Article 67(1)(a) also generally requires that documents classified ex parte be reclassified, if need be after redactions, so that they can be made available to the defence (*Prosecutor v. Lubanga*, ICC PT. Ch. I, Decision Concerning Transcripts of in Camera Meeting Held on 17 March 2006, ICC-01/04-01/06-78, 19 April 2006). The Article does not, however, grant a right to be given access to the entire record of the case (*Prosecutor v. Lubanga*, ICC PT. Ch. I, Decision on the Defence Request for Unrestricted Access to the Entire File of the Situation in the Democratic Republic of the Congo, ICC-01/04-01/06-103, 17 May 2006).

In the context of the confirmation hearing, Rule 121(3) of the RPE states that the prosecution must provide to the defence a document containing the charges 30 days before the hearing; as to the necessary contents of this document (see *Prosecutor v. Lubanga*, ICC PT. Ch. I, Decision on the Confirmation of Charges, ICC-01/04-01/06-803-tEN, 29 January 2007, paras. 146–153).

All information must generally be in a language the accused understands and speaks. This does not mean, however, that all documents which must be provided to the defence (such as potentially exculpatory evidence under Article 67(2)) must be translated, it suffices that translations are provided for certain documents which enable the accused to get a general picture of the case against him or her (see *Prosecutor v. Lubanga*, ICC PT. Ch. I, Decision on the Requests of the Defence of 3 and 4 July 2006, ICC-01/04-01/06-268, 4 August 2006, pp. 5–6) and for those documents which other provisions require to be translated (see rule 76(3) of the RPE on statements of witnesses).

Similarly, in *Bemba*, the Pre-Trial Chamber stated that the defendant does not have an absolute right to have all documents translated into a language which he fully understands and speaks (*Prosecutor v. Bemba*, ICC PT. Ch. III, Decision on the Defence's Request Related to

---

Language Issues in the Proceedings, ICC-01/05-01/08-307, 4 December 2008, para. 11). The defendant is entitled to receive translation of such documents that inform him in detail of the nature, cause and content of the charges brought against him, namely: i) the Prosecutor's application for a warrant of arrest and the Chamber's decision thereon; ii) the Document Containing the Charges and the List of Evidence as well as any amendment thereto; and iii) the statements of prosecution witnesses (*ibid.*, para. 16).

Where it is difficult to establish which languages the accused fully understands and speaks, Chambers may request further information on this issue from the Registry (see *Prosecutor v. Katanga*, PT. Ch. I, Order for a Report of Additional Information on the Detention and Surrender of the Detainee Germain Katanga, ICC-01/04-01/07-45, 26 October 2007). Articles 67(1)(a) and (f) of the Statute do not grant the accused the right to choose the language in which he must be informed of the charges against him and in which translation of documents and interpretation must be provided. The standard is "that of a language that the arrested person or the accused 'fully understands and speaks' so as to guarantee the requirements of fairness" (see *Prosecutor v. Katanga*, ICC PT. Ch. I, Decision on Defence Request concerning languages, ICC-01/04-01/07-127, 21 December 2007, para. 30). The defence was granted leave to appeal against the aforementioned decision (*Prosecutor v. Katanga*, ICC PT. Ch. I, Decision on the Defence Application for Leave to Appeal the Decision on the Defence Request Concerning Languages, ICC-01/04-01/07-149, 18 January 2008, p. 7). Finally, the Appeals Chamber considered that an accused fully understands and speaks a language if he/she "is completely fluent in the language in ordinary, non-technical conversation; it is not required that he or she has an understanding as if he or she were trained as a lawyer or judicial officer" and, in case of any doubt, "the language requested by the person should be accommodated" (*Prosecutor v. Katanga and Ngudjolo Chui*, ICC A. Ch., Judgment on the appeal of Mr. Germain Katanga against the decision of Pre-Trial Chamber I entitled "Decision on the Defence Request Concerning Languages", ICC-01/04-01/07-522, 27 May 2008, para. 61). More recent case law has applied these findings. In *Banda and Jerbo*, the Trial Chamber ordered the Prosecution to translate into Zaghawa the witness statements intended to be relied upon for trial purposes based on Rule 76(3) and Article 67(1)(a) and (f) (*Prosecutor v. Banda and Jerbo*, ICC T. Ch. IV, Reasons for the Order on translation of witness statements (ICC-02/05-03/09-199) and additional instructions on translation, ICC-02/05-03/09-214, 12 September 2011, paras. 25–32; and *Prosecutor v. Banda and Jerbo*, ICC T. Ch. IV, Decision on the defence request for a temporary stay of proceedings (Concurring Separate Opinion of Judge Eboe-Osuji), ICC-02/05-03/09-410, 26 October 2012, paras. 130–135).

Pursuant to the objectives in Article 67(1)(a) and (b), that the accused "be informed promptly and in detail of the nature, cause and content of the charge, in a language which the accused fully understands and speaks" and must "have adequate time and facilities for the preparation of the defence", the Pre-Trial Chamber in *Bemba* ruled that the evidence exchanged between the parties and communicated to the Chamber must be the subject of a sufficiently detailed legal analysis relating the alleged facts with the constituent elements corresponding to each crime charged. This would also expedite the proceedings (*Prosecutor v. Bemba*, ICC PT. Ch. III, Decision on the Evidence Disclosure System and Setting a Timetable for Disclosure between the Parties, ICC-01/05-01/08-55, 31 July 2008, paras. 65–66, 69 and 72).

The impact of regulation 55 (change of legal characterisation of the facts) of the Regulations of the Court on the rights of the accused has been examined by the ICC. The Appeals Chamber determined that, under Article 67(1)(a) of the ICC Statute, the Trial Chamber may change the legal characterisation of the facts during trial, and without formally amending the charges, which is supported by regional human rights instruments and jurisprudence (*Prosecutor v. Lubanga*, ICC A. Ch., Judgment on the appeals of Mr Lubanga Dyilo and the Prosecutor against the Decision of Trial Chamber I of 14 July 2009 entitled "Decision giving notice to the parties and participants that the legal characterisation of the facts may be subject to change in

(b) To have adequate time and facilities for the preparation of the defence and to communicate freely with counsel of the accused's choosing in confidence;[547]

---

accordance with Regulation 55(2) of the Regulations of the Court", ICC-01/04-01/06-2205, 8 December 2009, para. 84). Accordingly, regulation 55 is not intrinsically incompatible with the accused person's rights as Article 67(1)(a) does not preclude a change of the legal characterisation of the facts during trial and without formally amending the charges (*Prosecutor v. Bemba*, ICC T. Ch. III, Decision lifting the temporary suspension of the trial proceedings and addressing additional issues raised in defence submissions ICC-01/05-01/08-2490-Red and ICC-01/05-01/08-2497, ICC-01/05-01/08-2500, 6 February 2013, para. 16).

Having said so, modifying the legal characterisation of the facts may only be conducted with regard to the facts and circumstances depicted in the charges. The restriction of the power to recharacterise facts, vested in the Trial Chamber, guarantees perfect compatibility between, on the one hand, regulation 55 and Article 74(2) of the ICC Statute and, on the other one, Article 67(1)(a) (*Prosecutor v. Katanga and Ngudjolo Chui*, ICC T. Ch. II, Decision on the implementation of regulation 55 of the Regulations of the Court and Severing the charges against the accused persons, ICC-01/04-01/07-3319-tENG/FRA, 21 November 2012, para. 21). In addition to the accused person's right to submit observations on the recharacterisation, it is pivotal to secure that "all facts underpinning the charges whose legal character is modified were clearly set out in the original indictment, from the outset" (*ibid.*, para. 22). The accused person's right to be informed promptly and in detail of charges against him/her includes both the facts and their legal characterisation and, therefore, the accused has to be timely put on notice that the legal characterisation could be modified under regulation 55 of the Regulations of the Court (*Prosecutor v. Katanga*, ICC T. Ch. II, Judgment pursuant to Article 74 of the Statute, ICC-01/04-01/07-3436-tENG, 7 March 2014, para. 1486).

Cross-references:

Articles 55(2)(a), 61(2)(b), 61(3), 67(1)(a), and 67(2), Regulation 55.

Authors: Juan Pablo Pérez-León-Acevedo and Björn Elberling.

[547] Article 67(1)(b) contains certain rights that aim at allowing the accused to mount an effective defence, namely the right to adequate time and facilities for the preparation of this defence and to free and confidential communication with counsel. It is pivotal to guarantee an appropriate preparation of the defence and, thus, the suspect or accused can confidentially and unrestrictedly communicate with his or her counsel and assistants (Gut *et al.*, 2013, p. 1210).

The notion of adequate time is hard to define precisely, especially in the context of the rather complex proceedings before international criminal tribunals. Adequate time will in any case depend on the particular circumstances of the case (see Schabas, 1999, p. 854; Schabas, 2008, p. 1258; and Schabas, 2010, p. 805). Notably, in the first pre-trial proceedings before the ICC, a defence request to postpone the confirmation hearing under this Article was rejected (see *Prosecutor v. Lubanga*, ICC PT. Ch. I, Decision on the Defence Request to Postpone the Confirmation Hearing, ICC-01/04-01/06-686, 8 November 2006). For provisions in the RPE which aim at ensuring adequate time before certain major procedural steps, see, for example, Rule 121(3). As for self-representing accused, international practice, including that of the ICC, evidences that he/she is provided with some level of facilities and legal assistance (Gut *et al.*, 2013, p. 1252).

Communication with counsel shall be free and "in confidence", that is, not within the hearing of third persons; this is further elaborated upon in Regulation 97. Further to the wording of Article 67(1)(b), the accused may also communicate freely with diplomatic and/or consular representatives of his or her state (Regulation 98).

Additionally, the right under Article 67(1)(b) is present in the robust disclosure obligations that start early in the proceedings (*Prosecutor v. Bemba*, ICC A. Ch., Judgment on the appeal of

---

Mr Jean-Pierre Bemba Gombo against the decision of Pre-Trial Chamber III entitled 'Decision on application for interim release', ICC-01/05-01/08-321, 16 December 2008, para. 33. See also Schabas, 2010, p. 805).

Concerning the modification of the legal characterisation of facts by the Trial Chamber in the course of the trial (regulation 55 of the Regulations of the Court), the Appeals Chamber considered that it must not render the trial unfair. Thus, the Appeals Chamber noted that Article 67(1)(b) of the Statute provides for the accused person's right to "have adequate time and facilities for the preparation of the defence". In order to avoid violations of this provision, regulation 55(2) and (3) contain "several stringent safeguards for the protection of the rights of the accused. How these safeguards will have to be applied to protect the rights of the accused fully and whether additional safeguards must be implemented [...] will depend on the circumstances of the case" (*Prosecutor v. Lubanga*, ICC A. Ch., Judgment on the appeals of Mr Lubanga Dyilo and the Prosecutor against the Decision of Trial Chamber I of 14 July 2009 entitled "Decision giving notice to the parties and participants that the legal characterisation of the facts may be subject to change in accordance with Regulation 55(2) of the Regulations of the Court", ICC-01/04-01/06-2205, 8 December 2009, para. 85). Thus, regulation 55 refers to Article 67(1)(b) and its stringent safeguards to protect the accused person's rights. By referring to the case law of the European Court of Human Rights (ECtHR) (*Pélissier and Sassi v. France* and *Mattei v. France*), Trial Chamber II in *Katanga and Ngudjolo Chui* noted that a breach of the accused person's fair trial rights may take place when the legal characterisation of the facts changed without providing the defence the opportunity to file observations (*Katanga and Ngudjolo Chui*, ICC T. Ch. II, Decision on the implementation of regulation 55 of the Regulations of the Court and severing the charges against the accused persons, ICC-01/04-01/07-3319-tENG/FRA, 21 November 2012, paras. 35–37).

In *Ngudjolo Chui*, the Appeals Chamber examined whether the conditions of detention of the accused, at an administrative detention centre at Schiphol Airport (The Netherlands), infringed upon his fair trial rights, in particular those laid down in Article 67(1)(b). First, under Article 3(7)(2) of the Internal Rules and Regulations for Aliens Detention Centre ("Internal Rules and Regulations"), the Appeals Chamber noted that a detainee may be visited by his or her legal assistant on every working day during working hours, and outside these hours when required by the interests of justice. The confidentiality of these communications was guaranteed by the fact that those privileged visits occurred in a visiting room without any detention centre staff member and that solely indirect surveillance was performed by a staff member outside the visiting room. Second, if the accused person's counsel is provided with hard copies of the documents necessary for the preparation of the defence and thus the accused has access to his case file, the lack of electronic access to it does not prejudice the accused person's ability to prepare his defence. Third, although whether the accused may receive calls is not explicitly mentioned in the Internal Rules and Regulations, a telephone was located in the accused person's cell and he was given some weekly telephone credit. Additionally, under Article 3(8)(2) of the Internal Rules and Regulations, telephone calls to privileged contacts cannot be monitored. Fourth, corresponds to the accused to make the necessary practical arrangements *vis-à-vis* his or her codetainee to talk confidentially with his or her lawyer. Concerning the accused person's complaints about being disturbed by his co-detainee, following the Internal Rules and Regulations, the accused needs to forward those complaints to the relevant bodies of the administrative detention centre. Therefore, based on the above-analysed considerations, the Appeals Chamber found that the conditions in the administrative detention centre did not violate the accused person's fair trial rights in relation to the proceedings before the ICC (*Prosecutor v. Ngudjolo Chui*, ICC A. Ch., Decision on "URGENT application by Mathieu Ngudjolo's Defence seeking the Appeals Chamber's instructions on the modalities of preparation for the appeals procedure in view of Mathieu Ngudjolo's current situation (Article 67 of the Rome Statute)", ICC-01/04-

(c) To be tried without undue delay;[548]

02/12-67, 24 April 2013, paras. 8–13). This decision constitutes a good example of how important is to examine Article 67(1) provisions of the ICC Statute in a systematic and contextual manner paying attention to both the whole ICC legal framework and specific circumstances of the accused person. By doing so, the ICC Chambers may accurately determine whether and to what extent the accused person's fair trial rights have been violated.

In *Banda and Jerbo*, the defence alleged its inability to conduct interviews to identify and locate potential witnesses with knowledge of the facts relevant to the case due to the obstructionist efforts of the Government of Sudan. In addressing this claim, Trial Chamber IV found that the defence failed to substantiate it properly as it was necessary to identify available evidence with sufficient specificity under the information available to it at the respective stage. Even though the Chamber may consider problems found by the defence when weighting the whole evidentiary materials, an unsubstantiated claim does not meet the high threshold required for staying the proceedings (*Prosecutor v. Banda and Jerbo*, ICC T. Ch. IV, Decision on the defence request for a temporary stay of proceedings, ICC-02/05-03/09-410, 26 October 2012, paras. 101 and 102).

Pre-Trial Chamber I in *Gbagbo*, considering the circumstances of the case, found that allowing the Prosecutor to provide more evidence or conduct further investigation for a limited period of time would affect no right of the accused as he would be "given appropriate time to respond to the new evidence presented by the Prosecutor" (*Prosecutor v. Gbagbo*, ICC PT. Ch. I, Decision adjourning the hearing on the confirmation of charges pursuant to Article 61(7)(c)(i) of the Rome Statute, ICC-02/11-01/11-432, 3 June 2013, paras. 42 and 43).

Duly meeting the requirements of Article 67(1)(b) and (e) of the Statute requires that the Chamber itself reviews the circumstances under which the recharacterisation phase of the proceedings took place, which means to dwell especially on all measures adopted to protect the accused person's rights (*Prosecutor v. Katanga*, ICC T. Ch. II, Judgment pursuant to Article 74 of the Statute, ICC-01/04-01/07-3436-Teng, 7 March 2014, para. 1539). Attention should be drawn to whether the matter of the opportunity, understood as broadly as possible, was afforded to the defence to: i) present its case on the recharacterisation envisioned and to put across its view on the correlation between the law and the evidence on record; and ii) the opportunity afforded to the defence to tender new evidence into the record, after notice of possible recharacterisation (*ibid.*).

Cross-references:

Article 67(1)(e), Rule 121(3), Regulations 55(2), 55(3), 97 and 98, Internal Rules and Regulations for Aliens Detention Centre Articles 3(7)(2), 3(8)(2).

Authors: Juan Pablo Pérez-León-Acevedo and Björn Elberling.

[548] Article 67(1)(c) grants the right to a trial without undue delay and is identical to its respective model provision under the ICCPR. What exactly this means, especially in the context of international criminal justice, is hard to determine – so far, proceedings at the Court have been similarly slow as at other international criminal tribunals. Thus, in *Lubanga*, the proceedings lasted roughly a year from initial appearance of the accused to confirmation of charges. The trial started more than three years after the initial appearance, took other three years to be completed, and the appeals phase lasted more than two years and a half. This trend has also been present in the other ICC completed trials although these have been shorter. Thus, considering the time elapsed between the accused person's first appearance before the Trial Chamber and the end of his trial, approximately 6 years and a half passed in *Katanga*, and approximately 4 years and 10 months elapsed in *Ngudjolo Chui*. As for *Bemba*, roughly 6 years and a half have passed but the Trial Chamber judgment has yet to be rendered. Two cases were joined by the Appeals Chamber paying attention to the impact of this decision on the expeditiousness of the trials (*Prosecutor v.*

Katanga and Ngudjolo Chui, ICC A. Ch., Judgment on the Appeal Against the Decision on Joinder rendered on 10 March 2008 by the Pre-Trial Chamber in the *Germain Katanga and Mathieu Ngudjolo Chui* Cases, ICC-01/04-01/07-573, 9 June 2008, para. 8). There are several factors behind slowness of international criminal proceedings, which include *inter alia* the complexity of the facts and, especially, the complexity of the proceedings (see Heinsch, 2009, pp. 481–496). Be that as it may, scholars and case law on the ICCPR indicate that the time limit is considered from the moment when the suspect or accused is informed of steps towards his or her prosecution (see Schabas, 2008, p. 1259; and Schabas, 2010, p. 806).

On the other hand, in many cases, the defence has not complained of proceedings taking too long, but has rather in some instances argued for further delays (see *Prosecutor v. Lubanga*, ICC PT. Ch. I, Decision on the Defence Request to Postpone the Confirmation Hearing, ICC-01/04-01/06-686, 8 November 2006). In fact, the full exercise of other defence rights contained in Article 67(1) may actually require certain delays, which is why the right to trial without undue delay may sometimes in effect be a limiting factor on the scope of other defence rights (see, for example, ICC PT Ch. I, *Prosecutor v. Lubanga*, Decision on the Requests of the Defence of 3 and 4 July 2006, ICC-01/04-01/06-268, 4 August 2006, p. 4). In *Lubanga*, the Appeals Chamber found that a:

> [...] conditional stay of the proceedings may be the appropriate remedy where a fair trial cannot be held at the time that the stay is imposed, but where the unfairness to the accused person is of such a nature that a fair trial might become possible at a later stage because of a change in the situation that led to the stay.

If the obstacles that led to the stay of the proceedings fall away, the Chamber that imposed the stay of the proceedings may decide to lift the stay of the proceedings in appropriate circumstances and if this would not occasion unfairness to the accused person for other reasons, in particular in light of his or her right to be tried without undue delay (see Article 67(1)(c) of the Statute) (*Prosecutor v. Lubanga*, ICC A. Ch., Judgment on the appeal of the Prosecutor against the decision of Trial Chamber I entitled "Decision on the consequences of non-disclosure of exculpatory materials covered by Article 54(3)(e) agreements and the application to stay the prosecution of the accused, together with certain other issues raised at the Status Conference on 10 June 2008", ICC-01/04-01/06-1486, 21 October 2008, paras. 4 and 5).

Thus, the Appeals Chamber determined two conditions under which a stay may be vacated: i) if the forensic obstacles leading to the stay "fall away"; and ii) if vacating the stay would not occasion unfairness to the accused "for other reasons, in particular in light of his or her right to be tried without undue delay" (*ibid.*, para. 80). The second condition is reiterated: "If a trial that is fair in all respects becomes possible as a result of changed circumstances, there would be no reason not to put on trial a person who is accused of genocide, crimes against humanity or war crimes—deeds which must not go unpunished and for which there should be no impunity [...]" (*ibid.*, para. 81). The previous judgment implies that a benign remedy of "temporary" stay may become a situation of "permanent" stay, which also takes place when vacating the stay would not be unfair to the accused due to other reasons, especially, in light of his or her "right to be tried without undue delay" (*Prosecutor v. Banda and Jerbo*, ICC T. Ch. IV, Decision on the defence request for a temporary stay of proceedings (Concurring Separate Opinion of Judge Eboe-Osuji), ICC-02/05-03/09-410, 26 October 2012, para. 12). The Appeals Chamber's consideration, in *Lubanga*, of the right to a speedy trial as an incident of a stay of proceedings tasks the discretion of the Trial Chamber which would have to choose between: i) preserving the right to a speedy trial "by requiring the case to proceed to trial, at the end of which any complaint of serious prejudice to fair trial is considered as part of the overall evaluation of the case"; and ii) staying the proceedings prior to trial for an indefinite period, "at the end of which the case may be resumed when the obstacles to fair trial fall away" (*ibid.*, para. 86).

The trial in *Lubanga* was stayed for a second time in 2010. The failure of the Prosecutor to disclose to the defence the identity of an intermediary who worked in the field on behalf of the Office of the Prosecutor (OTP) triggered the abuse of process leading to the stay of the proceedings (see McDermott, 2013, p. 797). Accordingly, the Trial Chamber found the Prosecutor's refusal to comply with its orders to be not just a smooth delay in the conduct of the proceedings but to render a fair trial impossible (*Prosecutor v. Lubanga*, ICC T. Ch. I., Redacted Decision on Intermediaries, ICC-01/04-01/06-2434-Red2, 31 May 2010, para. 20). The Appeals Chamber later overruled such stay. It determined that sanctions under Article 71 of the ICC Statute constitute the proper mechanism for a Trial Chamber to maintain control of the proceedings and, therefore, to ensure a fair trial when a party deliberately refuses to follow its directions (*Prosecutor v. Lubanga*, ICC A. Ch., Judgment on the appeal of the Prosecutor against the decision of Trial Chamber I of 8 July 2010 entitled "Decision on the Prosecution's Urgent Request for Variation of the Time-Limit to Disclose the Identity of Intermediary 143 or Alternatively to Stay Proceedings Pending Further Consultations with the VWU", ICC-01/04-01/06-2582, 8 October 2010, paras. 3 and 58). Thus, sanctions should be conducted before ordering a stay of proceedings and should be given reasonable time to trigger compliance (*ibid.*, paras. 3 and 59–62).

In *Lubanga*, between the imposition of stay and its lifting, the OTP asked the Trial Chamber to partially lift the stay to hear evidence that could be later included in the trial record in case of lifting the stay. The Trial Chamber rejected it by referring to the second prong of its decision, that is, the OTP was seemingly able to select the judicial orders to comply with based on its interpretation of its responsibilities under the ICC Statute (*Prosecutor v. Lubanga*, ICC T. Ch. I, Decision on the "Prosecution's application to take testimony while proceedings are stayed pending decision of the Appeals Chamber", ICC-01/04-01/06-2574, 24 September 2010, para. 21). The Trial Chamber established that while the Prosecutor keeps reserving to himself the right not to implement the Chamber's orders if (s)he considers them to conflict with his or her other obligations, justice can no longer be done in this case (*ibid.*, para. 22). Thus, "to ensure that the trial of the accused is conducted with full respect for his rights", and to guarantee the rule of law, the Prosecutor has to accept the Chamber's authority, which is "an irremovable and fundamental ingredient of a fair criminal trial" (*ibid.*).

The Prosecutor is only required to support each charge with "sufficient" evidence during the confirmation hearing (Article 61(5) of the ICC Statute). However, the ICC practice has understood that the investigation should be mostly complete at the hearing of confirmation of charges, which "ensures continuity in the presentation of the case and safeguards the rights of the Defence [...] [and] also ensures that the commencement of the trial is not unduly delayed and conforms with the right of the Defence to be tried without undue delay pursuant to Article 67(1)(c) of the Statute" (*Prosecutor v. Gbagbo*, ICC PT. Ch. I, Decision adjourning the hearing on the confirmation of charges pursuant to Article 61(7)(c)(i) of the Rome Statute, ICC-02/11-01/11-432, 3 June 2013, para. 25). Determining whether Article 61(7)(c)(i) (adjournment of the confirmation of charges hearing, request for the Prosecutor to provide further evidence or conduct further investigation) of the ICC Statute unduly infringes a person's right to be tried without undue delay and, in general, whether there is a violation of Article 67(1)(c) "must be determined on a case-by-case basis, taking into account the particularities of the case and in accordance with internationally recognized human rights" (*ibid.*, para. 39).

Indeed, the ICC practice evidences the application of a test which considers the following prongs. First, length of ongoing proceedings which may include extraordinary proceedings. Second, the seriousness of the charges. Third, the complexity of the case at the ICC, which normally involves multiple incidents committed by multiple perpetrators over several months or even years. Fourth, whether requesting further additional evidence is explicitly provided for in the ICC Statute (*ibid.*, paras. 40-41). Therefore, for example, in *Gbagbo*, the Chamber found that allowing the Prosecutor to provide further evidence or conduct further investigation for a limited period does not unduly breach the accused person's right to be tried without undue delay (*ibid.*, para. 42). This test to determine whether there has been undue delay is relatively similar to that applied by regional human rights courts. In international criminal law, it is common to refer to the complexity of the case (including factual or legal issues), and the situations must be examined on a case-by-case basis as well as an undue delay in criminal proceedings may be compensated by, for example, decrease in sentence (*Prosecutor v. Katanga and Ngudjolo Chui*, ICC T. Ch. II, Decision on the implementation of regulation 55 of the Regulations of the Court and severing the charges against the accused persons, ICC-01/04-01/07-3319-tENG/FRA, 21 November 2012, para. 43). The ICC Chambers may freely consider the potential impact on the accused person's rights to evaluate whether any compensatory measures are warranted (*ibid.*). Although triggering regulation 55 may increase the length of the proceedings, it "does not inevitably entail a violation of the right to be tried without undue delay" (*ibid.*, para. 46). The right to be tried without delay requires *inter alia* to reduce to a minimum the time between the end of the pre-trial phase and the beginning of the trial (*Prosecutor v. Ongwen*, ICC PT. Ch. II, Decision Postponing the Date of the Confirmation of Charges Hearing, ICC-02/04-01/15-206, 6 March 2015, para. 30).

The Appeals Chamber found "that a change of the legal characterisation of the facts pursuant to Regulation 55 as such will automatically lead to undue delay of the trial. Whether a re-characterisation leads to undue delay will depend on the specific circumstances of the case" (*Prosecutor v. Lubanga*, ICC A. Ch., Judgment on the appeals of Mr Lubanga Dyilo and the Prosecutor against the Decision of Trial Chamber I of 14 July 2009 entitled "Decision giving notice to the parties and participants that the legal characterisation of the facts may be subject to change in accordance with Regulation 55(2) of the Regulations of the Court", ICC-01/04-01/06-2205, 8 December 2009, para. 86). Thus, a change of the legal characterisation of facts under regulation 55 leads neither automatically nor inherently to undue delay of the trial as this depends on the case.

Diverse legal and practical factors may determine the need for adjournments of varying duration, including further investigation, consideration of an issue by another Chamber (appeal included), permission of an accused to be excluded (including the need for dealing with an urgent national security domestic matter), and difficulties in scheduling witnesses (*Prosecutor v. Kenyatta*, ICC T. Ch. V(B), Decision on Prosecution's applications for a finding of non-compliance pursuant to Article 87(7) and for an adjournment of the provisional trial date, ICC-01/09-02/11-908, 31 March 2014, para. 77). In contrast to the more "drastic" remedy of a stay of proceedings, the decision "on whether or not to grant the requested adjournment is based on a weighing of the interests of justice in this case, including the rights of the accused and the interests of victims" (*ibid.*, para. 78). The Chamber is obligated under Article 64(2) of the ICC Statute to ensure that the proceedings are conducted with full respect to the accused person's rights, in a form that is fair and expeditious, and consistent with internationally recognised human rights (*ibid.*, para. 80). Actually, a "further adjournment without justifiable and compelling reasons could constitute undue delay contrary to the rights of the accused" (*ibid.*).

Finally, concerning how victim participation may potentially result in undue delay of the proceedings, the ICC Statute does not authorise victim participation to be in detriment of the accused person's rights and, indeed, Article 68(3) states that such participation must take place in a way "not prejudicial to or inconsistent with the rights of the accused" (see also Zappalà, 2010, p. 146).

Cross-references:

Articles 61(5), 61(7)(c)(i), Rule 101, Regulation 55.

Authors: Juan Pablo Pérez-León-Acevedo and Björn Elberling.

(d) Subject to article 63, paragraph 2,[549] to be present at the trial, to conduct the defence in person or through legal assistance of the accused's choosing, to be informed, if the ac-

---

[549] Besides the rights to conduct a defence (see comment to next sub-paragraph), Article 67(1)(d) also contains the right of the accused to be present at trial. This generally precludes trials conducted in his or her absence. The right to presence is, however, not without limitations, the most important of which is the removal of the defendant for disruptive behavior – see Article 63(2)). Hearings in the absence of an accused who is unable to attend for health reasons, however, would be in violation of Article 67(1)(d) (see Terrier, 2002, pp. 1283–1284). Finally, an exception to the right to presence may also apply where hearings are conducted ex parte, that is, in the absence not only of the accused, but of the defence generally, for reasons of witness safety or protection of national security information (see Article 72(7), RPE rule 74(4) as well as *Prosecutor v. Lubanga*, ICC PT. Ch. I, Decision on the Defence Motion concerning the Ex parte hearing of 2 May 2006, ICC-01/04-01/06-119, 22 May 2006). Contrary to the misleading wording of Article 76(4), Article 67(1)(d) applies without exception to the hearing in which the sentence is pronounced (see Schabas, 1999, p. 856; Schabas, 2008, pp. 1259–1260; and Schabas, 2010, p. 807).

The right to be present at trial presupposes more than physical presence, but also requires that the accused be able to adequately follow and take part in the proceedings; in other words, the accused must be fit to stand trial. This requirement is not explicitly laid down in the Statute, but applies as a necessary corollary to the right to presence (see Schabas, Article 63, 1999, p. 807; and Schabas, 2010, pp. 754–755 and 757–758) and may also be deduced from Rule 135(4) of the RPE. The overall capacity needed for fitness to stand trial is the same regardless of the stage of the proceedings, that is, Article 67(1) applies to pre-trial and trial stages (*Prosecutor v. Gbagbo*, ICC PT. Ch. I, Decision on the fitness of Laurent Gbagbo to take part in the proceedings before this Court, ICC-02/11-01/11-286-Red, 2 November 2012, para. 54). In *Gbagbo*, Pre-Trial Chamber I examined whether the accused was healthy enough to stand trial-concluding in the affirmative. In interpreting the scope of Article 67(1), the Chamber referred to Article 6 of the European Convention on Human Rights ('ECHR') and the respective case law of the ECtHR as well as international and hybrid criminal courts legal sources to point out that the accused person's right to participate effectively in a criminal trial requires that he/she is not only present but that the accused can also hear and follow the proceedings (*ibid.*, paras. 46 and 49).

A special rule concerning presence of the accused at the confirmation hearing is contained in Article 61(2), it allows confirmation hearings in the absence of the accused under certain circumstances. Concerning the possibility of the confirmation hearing in absentia, some academics have considered that it may be held provided that if, after the first appearance, the defendant either cannot be found or fled (Marchesiello, 2002, p. 1244). As suggested by former ICC Judge Ekaterina Trendafilova, a close examination of the relevant provisions would indicate that a confirmation hearing in absentia absent a prior initial appearance at the ICC is compatible with both Article 67(1) rights and the RPE "A number of provisions of the Statute and the Rules make clear that the drafters intentionally provided for the possibility of a confirmation hearing in absentia under Article 61(2)(b), prior to surrender and an initial appearance before the Court" (Trendafilova, 2009, p. 453).

As a result of the 2013 amendments to the RPE (General Assembly of States Parties to the ICC Statute, Resolution ICC-ASP/12/Res.7, 27 November 2013), the scope of the right of the accused to be present at trial has been fleshed out, introducing flexible provisions which overall speaking favour the accused. Thus, rule 134bis allows the presence of the accused via video technology: "An accused subject to a summons to appear may submit a written request to the Trial Chamber to be allowed to be present through the use of video technology during part or parts of his or her trial". Under rule 134ter, an accused subject to summons to appear may request the Chamber to be excused and be represented by counsel during part(s) of his or her trial,

---

under certain conditions, namely, i) existence of exceptional circumstances, ii) inadequacy of alternative measures, iii) the accused has waived his or her right to be present at trial, and iv) fulfilment of the accused's rights during his or her absence. Finally, rule 134quarter allows an accused subject to a summons to appear to be excused from presence at trial because of his or her extraordinary public duties at the highest national level provided that "it is in the interests of justice and provided that the rights of the accused are fully ensured" and this decision on excusal from presence may be reviewed at any time. These new rules, in particular, rule 134quarter were introduced in the context of the increasing tension between the African Union States and the ICC as a consequence of the cases against the President and Vice-President of Kenya, that is, Mr. Uhuru Muigai Kenyatta (no longer prosecuted) and Mr. William Samoei Ruto respectively. Trial Chamber V(a) and (B) had excused Mr. Ruto and Mr. Kenyatta from continuous presence at trial with certain exceptions (*Prosecutor v. Ruto and Sang*, ICC T. Ch. V(a), Decision on Mr Ruto's Request for Excusal from Continuous Presence at Trial, ICC-01/09/01/11-777, 18 June 2013; and *Prosecutor v. Kenyatta*, ICC T. Ch. V(B), Decision on Defence Request for Conditional Excusal from Continuous Presence at Trial, ICC-01/09-02/11-830, 18 October 2013). However, the Appeals Chamber reversed the Trial Chamber's decision based on the following key findings:

1. Article 63(1) of the Statute does not operate as an absolute bar in all circumstances to the continuation of trial proceedings in the absence of the accused. 2. The discretion that the Trial Chamber enjoys under Article 63(1) of the Statute is limited and must be exercised with caution. The following limitations exist: (i) the absence of the accused can only take place in exceptional circumstances and must not become the rule; (ii) the possibility of alternative measures must have been considered, including, but not limited to, changes to the trial schedule or a short adjournment of the trial; (iii) any absence must be limited to that which is strictly necessary; (iv) the accused must have explicitly waived his or her right to be present at trial; (v) the rights of the accused must be fully ensured in his or her absence, in particular through representation by counsel; and (vi) the decision as to whether the accused may be excused from attending part of his or her trial must be taken on a case-by-case basis, with due regard to the subject matter of the specific hearings that the accused would not attend during the period for which excusal has been requested (*Prosecutor v. Ruto and Sang*, ICC A. Ch., Judgment on the appeal of the Prosecutor against the decision of Trial Chamber V(a) of 18 June 2013 entitled "Decision on Mr Ruto's Request for Excusal from Continuous Presence at Trial", ICC-01/09-01/11-1066, 25 October 2013).

Thus, the previously referred amendments to the RPE codified these findings of the Appeals Chamber. Finally, under Article 63(1) and rule 134quarter, the Trial Chamber in *Ruto and Sang* excused Ruto from continuous presence at trial under the condition of filing a waiver of his right to be present at trial and be physically present for certain hearings (*Prosecutor v. Ruto and Sang*, ICC T. Ch. V(a), Reasons for the Decision on Excusal from Presence at Trial under Rule 134quarter, ICC-01/09-01/11-1186, 18 February 2014, para. 10. See also *Prosecutor v. Ruto and Sang*, ICC T. Ch. V(A), Decision on 'Prosecution's application for leave to appeal the decision on excusal from presence at trial under Rule 134quarter, ICC-01/09-01/11-1246, 2 April 2014).

Cross-references:

Articles 61(2), 63(1), 63(2), 72(7) and 76(4), Rules 74(4), 135(4), 134bis, 134ter, 134quarter, 135(4).

Authors: Juan Pablo Pérez-León-Acevedo and Björn Elberling.

cused does not have legal assistance, of this right and to have legal assistance assigned by the Court in any case where the interests of justice so require, and without payment if the accused lacks sufficient means to pay for it;[550]

---

[550] Article 67(1)(d) also contains what may be termed the right to conduct a defence, which may again be subdivided into three specific rights.

First of all, the provision contains the right to conduct the defence in person, that is, the right to self-representation: The accused is generally free to choose to forego the assistance of defence counsel and to represent him- or herself, provided that she is mentally and intellectually able to do so. While the wording of Article 67(1)(d) does not contain any reference to restrictions of the right to self-representation, such restrictions are legion in the jurisprudence of other international tribunals, where the right to self-representation is guaranteed in words very similar to those of Article 67(1)(d). Exceptions accepted by other tribunals include medical reasons, fear of disruption or delay of the trial, and the potential of prejudice to co-accused (see Knoops, 2005, pp. 66–80). The accused person's self-representation should not be used to obstruct the proceedings, which requires the ICC Trial Chambers to take actions to prevent unnecessary disruption (see further Heinsch, 2009, pp. 492–494). Accordingly, self-representation is not an absolute right and may be restricted when there is a continuous and substantial obstruction of trial even if the obstruction is unintentional (see Gut *et al.*, 2013, p. 1217; Trendafilova, 2009, p. 449). Whether the ICC will follow other tribunals in limiting the right to self-representation in this way, and which consequences it will draw from any such limitations (particularly whether it will appoint defence counsel to take over the defence, standby counsel prepared to take over the defence if need be, or amici curiae to safeguard the rights of the defence independently of the accused (see, for example, Knoops, 2005, pp. 66–80) still remains to be seen.

Be that as it may, self-representation has been almost absent from the ICC's practice. Only Lubanga requested to represent himself but this took place solely for a short period and for a specific objective (*Prosecutor v. Lubanga*, ICC PT. Ch. I, Decision on the Prosecution and Defence applications for leave to appeal the Decision on the confirmation of charges, ICC-01/04-01/06-915, 24 May 2007, paras. 17–18). The meaningful exercise of the accused person's fair trial rights does not require that he/she is capable of exercising them as if/she were trained as a lawyer or a judicial officer (*Prosecutor v. Gbagbo*, ICC PT. Ch. I, Decision on the fitness of Laurent Gbagbo to take part in the proceedings before this Court, ICC-02/11-01/11-286-Red, 2 November 2012, para. 52). According to international practice, those assigned to assist a self-representing defendant need to follow the same requirements applicable to legal counsels and assistants under the general legal aid scheme (Gut *et al.*, 2013, pp. 1252–1253).

Second, the Article contains the right to be represented by counsel of one's choosing. In practice, the choice of counsel is not entirely unlimited; accused may only choose counsel who fulfil certain requirements in terms of experience and languages spoken etc. (see Rule 22 and Regulation 67 ff.). The Article also states that the accused must be informed of this right. At the ICC and other international and hybrid criminal courts, to guarantee effective representation, there is a trend aligning towards the qualifications for the accused person's assigned counsel to those for an equivalent position in the Prosecution side (Gut *et al.*, 2013, p. 1237). At the ICC and other international and hybrid criminal courts, the responsibility to guarantee effective representation has been placed on the counsel and the task of verifying the quality of the counsel's work on the accused (*ibid.*, p. 1225). The accused person's right to choose his or her legal counsel must "be reasonably exercised having regard to the principles of a fair trial. No right can be exercised in a manner frustrating the aims of a fair trial including, no doubt, the reasonableness of the time within which the proceedings must be held" (*Prosecutor v. Lubanga*, ICC A. Ch., Reasons for "Decision of the Appeals Chamber on the Defence application 'Demande de suspension de toute action ou procédure afin de permettre la désignation d'un nouveau Conseil de la Défense' filed on 20 February 2007" issued on 23 February 2007, ICC-01/04-01/06-844, 9 March 2007, para. 15). The right to counsel and legal assistance is not applicable to a defendant who has not been arrested or summoned before the ICC; however, the defendant can challenge the admissibility and jurisdiction and the issuance of the arrest warrant prior to his or her surrender to the ICC (*Prosecutor v. Kony et al.*, ICC A. Ch., Judgment on the appeal of the Defence against the "Decision on the admissibility of the case under Article 19(1) of the Statute" of 10 March 2009, ICC-02/04-01/05-408, 16 September 2009). Once the defendant has appeared before the ICC and if he/she has manifested his or her wish to be represented by a counsel, the Registry has to ensure both that a counsel is swiftly assigned and that there is no excessive gap between the moment when the counsel has resigned and when a new one has yet to be appointed (*Prosecutor v. Lubanga*, ICC A. Ch., Reasons for the Appeals Chamber's Decision to Extend Time Limits for Defence Documents issued on 3 April 2007, ICC-01/04-01/06-871, 20 April 2007, para. 6). Counsels are expected to act diligently. Otherwise, the Chamber might reject to consider motions although they are filed to secure defendant's fundamental rights (*Prosecutor v. Katanga and Ngudjolo Chui*, ICC A. Ch., Judgment on the Appeal of Mr Katanga Against the Decision of Trial Chamber II of 20 November 2009 Entitled "Decision on the Motion of the Defence for Germain Katanga for a Declaration on Unlawful Detention and Stay of Proceedings", ICC-01/04-01/07-2259, 12 July 2010).

In *Saif Gaddafi and Al-Senussi*, Pre-Trial Chamber I found that practical impediments to the provision of effective and timely legal representation to the accused Gaddafi by counsel from the OPCD made it appropriate and necessary to appoint an alternative legal representative (*Prosecutor v. Gaddafi and Al-Senussi*, ICC PT. Ch. I, Decision on the "Request to Withdraw", ICC-01/11-01/11-311-Red, 17 April 2013, para. 18). Noting the complexities of this case and in the interests of justice, the Chamber provisionally appointed a legal representative until the accused would exercise his right to freely choose counsel under Article 67(1)(d) or until admissibility challenge proceedings would be definitively disposed of, at which point the Chamber would revisit the legal representation question (*ibid.*, paras. 19–20).

The legal frameworks of the ICC and other international and hybrid criminal courts contain the fundamental right to legal representation; however, daily practice courtroom at those judicial institutions and beyond has not always complied with it, for example, legal assistance has not always been consistently applied to national proceedings related to international criminal trials (Gut *et al.*, 2013, p. 1264).

Third, where the accused is (wholly or partially) unable to pay for counsel, counsel will be assigned and paid for by the court. Following the example of Article 14(3)(d) of the ICCPR, this right is restricted to cases where the interests of justice require assignment of counsel, although it is hard to imagine that this will lead to a refusal to assign counsel in cases before the ICC. For instance, on 22 February 2008, Ngudjolo Chui was provisionally found indigent by the Registrar, which was subject to verification by the ICC and, indeed, the ICC bore the cost of his defence (see *Prosecutor v. Mathieu Ngudjolo Chui*, Case Information Sheet, ICC-01/04-02/12, updated as of 27 February 2015, p. 2). Where counsel is assigned and paid by the court, the accused does not have an unqualified right to choose counsel, although his or her wishes should be taken into account. In cases before the ICC so far, no controversies seem to have arisen in this regard. There have, however, been some controversies regarding the composition of the defence team, notably the number of legal and other assistants (see *Prosecutor v. Lubanga*, ICC T. Ch. I, Registration in the record of the case of the "Registrar's Decision on the additional means for the trial phase sought by Mr Thomas Lubanga in his 'Application for additional means under regulation 83(3) of the Regulations of the Court' filed on 3 May 2007", ICC-01/04-01/06-927-tENG, 14 June 2007; and generally Regulation 83 and the commentary thereto). Moreover, the ICC Prosecutor challenged the appointment of a defence counsel who previously worked at the

(e) To examine, or have examined, the witnesses against him or her and to obtain the attendance and examination of witnesses on his or her behalf under the same conditions as witnesses against him or her. The accused shall also be entitled to raise defences and to present other evidence admissible under this Statute;[551]

OTP; however, the Trial Chamber rejected it based on lack of evidence of both conflict of interest and awareness of relevant confidential information, which left no doubts about the counsel's integrity (*Prosecutor v. Bemba*, ICC T. Ch. I, Decision on the "Prosecution's Request to Invalidate the Appointment of Legal Consultant to the Defence Team", ICC-01/05-01/08-769, 7 May 2010, para. 45).

There is no distinction between the crimes under Article 70 (Offences against the administration of justice) and those under Article 5 (genocide, crimes against humanity, war crimes and crime of aggression) concerning the entitlement to legal aid as "Article 67(1) contemplates legal aid '[i]n the determination of any charge'" (*Prosecutor v. Bemba et al.*, ICC T. Ch. VII, Decision on the Defence applications for judicial review of the decision of the Registrar on the allocation of resources during the trial phase, ICC-01/05-01/13-955, 21 May 2015, para. 35).

When accused not wishing to represent themselves are not (yet or anymore) represented by permanent counsel, the court usually assigns duty counsel under Regulation 73 to represent the accused in the meantime (for example, *Prosecutor v. Lubanga*, ICC PT. Ch. I, Appointment of Duty Counsel, ICC-01/04-01/06-870, 19 April 2007) or requests the OPCD to do so (*Prosecutor v. Katanga*, ICC PT. Ch. I, Decision on the appointment of a duty counsel, ICC-01/04-01/07-52, 5 November 2007, p. 3); this option should, however, only be used sparingly to avoid possible conflicts of interest within the OPCD (see *ibid.*, p. 4).

Cross-references:

Rules 21 and 22, Regulation 73, 77, 83, 97 and 98.

Authors: Juan Pablo Pérez-León-Acevedo and Björn Elberling.

[551] Article 67(1)(e) has been described by the Appeals Chamber as introducing an adversarial hearing to the ICC scheme (*Prosecutor v. Lubanga*, ICC A. Ch., Decision of the Appeals Chamber on the Joint Application of Victims a/0001/06 to a/0003/06 and a/0105/06 concerning the "Directions and Decision of the Appeals Chamber" of 2 February 2007, ICC-01/04-01/06-925, 13 June 2007, para. 18). Article 67(1)(e) contains some procedural rights which are necessary for the ability of the accused to put up an effective defence at the actual trial.

First of all, this is the right to examination of witnesses against her, including witnesses called by the court (Schabas, 1999, p. 859; Schabas, 2008, p. 1265; and Schabas, 2010, p. 811). This right will foreseeably be subject to restrictions for reasons of witness protection, as foreseen by Article 68. However, such restrictions will probably not be considered to be in violation of Article 67(1)(e) as it was explicitly not formulated to include a right to confrontation and cross-examination strictu sensu (see Schabas, 1999, p. 859; Schabas, 2008, p. 1265; and Schabas, 2010, p. 811 (with references to the drafting history)).

Concerning the right to question witnesses, in *Bemba*, the Appeals Chamber examined what happens if the Prosecution witnesses become unavailable or unwilling to testify, or the Prosecution does not call particular witnesses due to any reason. In any of these situations, the Appeals Chamber noted that if these witnesses' statements are still admitted as "evidence", regardless of the fact that the accused been deprived of his or her right "to examine, or have examined, the witnesses against him or her", the defence would be required to challenge the admissibility of this "evidence" to have it excluded from the case. Nonetheless, the Appeals Chamber found it as an "impermissible burden shift to the Defence and will also put the Defence in breach of Rule 64(1) which requires that 'an issue relating to relevance or admissibility must be raised at the time when the evidence is submitted to a Chamber'" (*Prosecutor v. Bemba*, ICC A. Ch., Defence appeal against the 'Decision on the admission into evidence of material contained in the Prosecution's list of evidence' of 19 November 2010, ICC-01/05-01/08-1191, 7 February 2011, para. 51). Additionally, it was considered the Trial Chamber's adopted approach. Thus, when the evidence is used by the Prosecution, neither the defence will be aware of the purpose for admission of evidence nor the Chamber will have established whether it is required the implementation of counterbalancing measures to guarantee that:

> [...] the probative value of the evidence is not outweighed by its prejudicial impact on the rights of the defence and the fairness and impartiality of the proceedings. Since the Chamber will only be making these determinations at the end of the proceedings, the Defence will be precluded from obtaining appropriate relief [...] in a timely manner, which will further prejudice its right to examine witnesses concerning the Prosecution evidence in an effective manner" (*ibid.*, para. 52).

If the Trial Chamber indiscriminately admits all the witness statements without given consideration to whether the admission of a given statement would be inconsistent with or prejudicial to the accused person's rights, this constitutes an improper exercise of the Trial Chamber's decision and, thus, "resulted in the Chamber paying little or no regard to the principle of orality, to the rights of the accused, or to trial fairness generally. It had the potential effect of depriving Mr Bemba of his right 'to examine, or have examined the witnesses against him'" (*Prosecutor v. Bemba*, ICC A. Ch., Judgment on the appeals of Mr Jean-Pierre Bemba Gombo and the Prosecutor against the decision of Trial Chamber III entitled 'Decision on the admission into evidence of materials contained in the prosecution's list of evidence', ICC-01/05-01/08-1386, 3 May 2011, para. 79).

In interpreting Article 6(3)(d) of the ECHR, which is almost identical to Article 67(1)(e) of the ICC Statute, the ECtHR in *Kostovski v. The Netherlands* stated that, as a matter of principle, all evidence must in general be produced in the accused person's presence during a public hearing with a view to adversarial argument (*Kostovski v. The Netherlands*, (Application No. 11454/85), ECtHR, Judgment, 20 November 1989, para. 41). Nevertheless, the ECtHR added that such principle does not mean that, to be used as evidence, the statements of witnesses always need to be made during a public hearing in court (*ibid.*). Using those statements obtained at the pre-trial stage as evidence is not in itself inconsistent with Article 6 of the ECHR provided that the defence's rights have been respected. In general, those rights demand that "an accused should be given an adequate and proper opportunity to challenge and question a witness against him, either at the time the witness was making his statement or at some later stage of the proceedings [...]" (*ibid.*).

Second, the accused has the right to obtain the attendance of witnesses; however, the ICC Statute does not provide for compellability of witnesses (see further Schabas, 2008, p. 1265; and Schabas, 2010, p. 811). Even though the accused has the right to remain silent as the Prosecutor shoulders the onus of proof, the accused is entitled to submit evidence relevant to the case (Article 69(3) of the ICC Statute), which includes the right to "obtain the attendance and examination of witnesses on his or her behalf" (Article 67(1)(e) of the ICC Statute and rule 140(2)(a) of the RPE) (*Prosecutor v. Bemba*, ICC T. Ch. III, Decision lifting the temporary suspension of the trial proceedings and addressing additional issues raised in defence submissions ICC-01/05-01/08-2490-Red and ICC-01/05-01/08-2497, ICC-01/05-01/08-2500, 6 February 2013, para. 23). However, no ICC organ may be found responsible for ensuring the presence of the witnesses called to testify by a party as the party wishing to bring evidence via witness's oral testimony is the only "responsible for contacting the witness concerned, obtaining his or her voluntary consent to testify and proposing to the Chamber a feasible schedule for the appearance of witnesses, taking into account all necessary arrangements that may need to be implemented [...] to enable the witnesses to appear to testify before the Court" (*ibid.*).

Third, Article 67(1)(e) also contains the right to equality in manners concerning witnesses between the prosecution and the defence. Generally, limitations concerning attendance and, more importantly, examination of witnesses will not be in violation of Article 67(1)(e) if they are applied to both parties equally (see, however, the criticism of that "granting both the prosecutor and the defence equivalently watered-down powers does not equate to a fair trial" (Knoops, 2005, p. 57).

Fourth, the accused has the right to raise defences (with the exception, presumable, of those defences explicitly ruled out in the Statute) and to present admissible evidence besides witness statements – this rather straightforward provision is of course necessary to achieve equality of arms between the parties and to allow the accused to put up an adequate defence.

Fifth, Article 67(1)(e) rights should also be examined in the context of legal recharacterisation of facts. If at any time during the trial (regulation 55(2)) it seems to the Chamber that the legal characterisation of the facts may be subject to change, it has to give notice to the participants in the proceedings of this possibility and provide the participants with the opportunity to make submissions after having heard the evidence. In turn, regulation 55 sets out the safeguards to be respected in order to protect the accused person's rights. The safeguards to protect the accused person's rights depend on the specific circumstances of the case (*Prosecutor v. Katanga and Ngudjolo Chui*, ICC T. Ch. II, Decision on the implementation of regulation 55 of the Regulations of the Court and severing the charges against the accused persons, ICC-01/04-01/07-3319-tENG/FRA, 21 November 2012, paras. 11 and 13). Thus, the accused need to have adequate time and facilities for the effective preparation of his or her defence as well as "be given the opportunity to request the presentation of any evidence or witness that he or she considers necessary, in accordance with Article 67(1)(e)" (*ibid.*, para. 11).

In *Bemba*, when deciding on the remedial measures to be afforded to the accused, under regulation 55(3), Trial Chamber III considered the prosecution's statement whereby regulation 55 had no impact on the prosecution case and, thus, it would not submit further evidence. However, the Chamber granted the accused person's request to collect and submit additional evidence (Article 67(1)(e) of the ICC Statute). Nevertheless, as the accused person is not obliged to present evidence, he/she may voluntarily decide not to do it (*Prosecutor v. Bemba*, ICC T. Ch. III, Decision lifting the temporary suspension of the trial proceedings and addressing additional issues raised in defence submissions ICC-01/05-01/08-2490-Red and ICC-01/05-01/08-2497, ICC-01/05-01/08-2500, 6 February 2013, paras. 20 and 21). Leading new evidence following the implementation of regulation 55 may adopt several forms: "the recalling of witnesses who testified at trial, whether for the Prosecution or the Defence; the calling and the testimony of new witnesses, be they persons whom the Defence met in the course of its earlier investigations or newly identified persons; and the tendering of new documentary evidence" (*Prosecutor v. Katanga*, ICC T. Ch. II, Judgment pursuant to Article 74 of the Statute, ICC-01/04-01/07-3436-Teng, 7 March 2014, para. 1539).

Finally, it should be noted that submissions based on Article 67(1)(b) and (e) may be analysed under the principle whereby a stay of the proceedings is the ultimate remedy to be resorted only when a fair trial is impossible and there is no sufficient indication that any unfairness may be sorted out later or relieved against by the Chamber (*Prosecutor v. Banda and Jerbo*, ICC T. Ch. IV, Decision on the defence request for a temporary stay of proceedings, ICC-02/05-03/09-410, 26 October 2012, para. 97). The above-mentioned examination demands "a preliminary assessment on whether the right to be provided adequate time and facilities for the preparation of their defence and to obtain the attendance of witnesses require, as a necessary component, onsite investigations" (*ibid.*).

Cross-references:

Articles 67(1)(b), 68, 69, Rules 64(1) and 140(2)(a), Regulation 55.

(f) To have, free of any cost, the assistance of a competent interpreter and such translations as are necessary to meet the requirements of fairness, if any of the proceedings of or documents presented to the Court are not in a language which the accused fully understands and speaks;[552]

Authors: Juan Pablo Pérez-León-Acevedo and Björn Elberling.

[552] The right to interpretation and translation aims to ensure that the accused is able to adequately follow the court proceedings and thus to be "present" in a meaningful sense. Accordingly, "the right to an interpreter seems axiomatic" (Schabas, 1999, p. 860; Schabas, 2008, p. 1267; and Schabas, 2010, p. 812). The provision goes beyond the text of human rights instruments in several ways, most importantly by referring not only to the interpretation of court proceedings, but also to the translation of documents presented to the court. The right to translation of documents, however, is limited to those documents the translation of which is "necessary to meet the requirements of fairness". Thus, in *Lubanga*, Pre-Trial Chamber I denied a defence request that all procedural documents be translated into French and that deadlines only begin to run after the receipt of the French translations; it instead ordered the Registry to provide to the Defence the services of a French translator to assist the defence with documents available only in English (*Prosecutor v. Lubanga*, ICC PT. Ch. I, Decision on the Requests of the Defence of 3 and 4 July 2006, ICC-01/04-01/06-268, 4 August 2006 (with references to the jurisprudence of the ECtHR)).

The right to an interpreter needs to be jointly read with Article 67(1)(a) of the ICC Statute, under which the accused must be in a position to know both the charges and supporting evidence (*Prosecutor v. Bemba*, ICC PT. Ch. III, Decision on the Defence's Request Related to Language Issues in the Proceedings, ICC-01/05-01/08-307, 4 December 2008, para. 14).

Article 67(1)(f) does not necessarily require that interpretation or translation be into the mother tongue of the accused, translation/interpretation into a language that he or she "fully understands and speaks" is sufficient. Where it was not clear which languages the accused spoke at this level, the Court requested the Registry to provide information on this topic (see *Prosecutor v. Katanga*, ICC PT. Ch. I, Order for a Report of Additional Information on the Detention and Surrender of the Detainee Germain Katanga, ICC-01/04-01/07-45, 26 October 2007, p. 3). Articles 67(1)(a) and (f) of the Statute do not grant the accused the right to choose the language in which he must be informed of the charges against him and in which translation of documents and interpretation must be provided. The standard is "that of a language that the arrested person or the accused 'fully understands and speaks' so as to guarantee the requirements of fairness". Thus, the defence requested in *Katanga* that: i) documents in French transmitted to the accused as part of the proceedings should be accompanied by a translation into Lingala; and ii) that the accused should be granted the right to be assisted by a Lingala interpreter and translator during the proceedings was rejected (see *Prosecutor v. Katanga*, ICC PT. Ch. I, Decision on Defence Request concerning languages, ICC-01/04-01/07-127, 21 December 2007, para. 30). The Appeals Chamber found that the Single Judge erred in the interpretation of the standard to be applied under Article 67(1)(a) and (f) of the Statute because she "did not comprehensively consider the importance of the fact that the word 'fully' is included in the text, and the Article's full legislative history" (*Prosecutor v. Katanga and Ngudjolo Chui*, ICC. A. Ch., Judgment on the appeal of Mr. Germain Katanga against the decision of Pre-Trial Chamber I entitled "Decision on the Defence Request Concerning Languages", ICC-01/04-01/07-522, 27 May 2008, para. 37). In the opinion of the Appeals Chamber, the cumulative requirement "fully understands and speaks" in both paragraphs makes the applicable standard "high – higher, for example, than that applicable under the European Convention on Human Rights and the ICCPR" (*ibid.*, paras. 62 and 66). The single judge in Pre-Trial Chamber I still held "the view that the right of Germain Katanga and Mathieu Ngudjolo Chui to have the confirmation hearing held within a reasonable

(g) Not to be compelled to testify or to confess guilt and to remain silent, without such silence being a consideration in the determination of guilt or innocence;[553]

---

period of time must prevail" and decided "that, in application of the Appeals Chamber Judgment concerning Languages, Germain Katanga shall continue to be assisted by an interpreter during the hearings held in the remaining proceedings before Pre-Trial Chamber I" (*Prosecutor v. Katanga and Ngudjolo Chui*, PT. Ch. I, Decision Implementing the Appeals Chamber Judgment concerning Languages, ICC-01/04-01/07-539, 2 June 2008, para. 11).

Article 67(1)(f) does not provide that the defendant has an absolute right to have all documents translated into a language which he fully understands and speaks (*Prosecutor v. Bemba*, ICC T. Ch. III, Decision on the Defence's Request Related to Language Issues in the Proceedings, ICC-01/04-01/08-307, 4 December 2008, para. 11). The defendant is entitled to receive translation of such documents that inform him in detail of the nature, cause and content of the charges brought against him, namely: i) the Prosecutor's application for a warrant of arrest and the Chamber's decision thereon; ii) the Document Containing the Charges and the List of Evidence as well as any amendment thereto; and iii) the statements of prosecution witnesses (*ibid.*, para. 16).

In *Mbarushimana*, concerning a telephone log disclosed by the Prosecutor as incriminating evidence, the Chamber found that the Prosecutor had no obligation to provide the translation of such material to the defence, "unless he intends to rely on any of those intercepted communications for the purposes of the confirmation hearing in the present case [...]" (*Prosecutor v. Mbarushimana*, ICC PT. Ch. I, Decision on issues relating to disclosure, ICC-01/04-01/10-87, 30 March 2011, para. 16). Therefore, the Chamber rejected the defence's request for the translation of all intercepted communications since the material not sought to be relied on by the parties does not need to be filed in the case record and, thus, the language requirement set out in regulation 39 of the Regulations of the Court was found inapplicable to such material (*ibid.*, paras. 15–16).

In *Bemba et al.*, call logs (consisting to a large extent of digits) and chain-of-custody documents included in the Prosecutor's list of evidence were found not to be critical to the Defence's ability to either challenge or otherwise rely on them. Thus, the Chamber concluded that there was "no violation of Rule 121(3) of the Rules [...] and does not consider that the translation of the items concerned was necessary to meet the requirements of fairness" (*Prosecutor v. Bemba et al.*, ICC PT. Ch. II, Decision pursuant to Article 61(7)(a) and (b) of the Rome Statute, ICC-01/05-01/13-749, 11 November 2014, para. 21).

As shown by Regulation 97, the right to translation also applies to communication between the accused and his or her counsel.

Cross-references:

Article 67(1)(a), Rule 121(3), Regulations 39 and 97.

Authors: Juan Pablo Pérez-León-Acevedo and Björn Elberling.

---

[553] The right to silence, as contained in Article 67(1)(g), goes beyond the rights contained in other tribunals' Statutes and in relevant human rights provisions. First, contrary to, for example, Article 14 of the ICCPR, Article 67 does not refer to "testimony against himself", thus showing that the accused may refuse any testimony even if it might be argued that it could or would be "in favour" of the accused (Schabas, 1999, p. 861; Schabas, 2008, p. 1267; and Schabas, 2010, p. 813). The removal of the words "against himself" might also be read to imply that an accused may also refuse to testify if called as a witness in another case. This seems doubtful, however, as such cases would more appropriately be dealt with under the rules concerning the danger of self-incrimination by witnesses (see Rule 74). Certainly, the right to silence can be waived (see further Schabas, 2010, p. 814).

Second, the ICC Statute goes beyond other instruments by explicitly laying down that silence of the accused may not be considered in the determination of guilt or innocence. This precludes procedures, such as those applicable in some national jurisdictions, allowing negative conclusions to be drawn from the failure of the accused to explain, for example, his or her presence at a location where a crime had taken place.

The Trial Chamber said that "if the Defence identifies lines of defence or issues at a significantly and unnecessarily advanced stage this may have consequences for decisions that relate to disclosure to the accused" (cited in *Prosecutor v. Lubanga*, ICC A. Ch., Judgment on the appeal of Mr. Lubanga Dyilo against the Oral Decision of Trial Chamber I of 18 January 2008, ICC-01/04-01/06-1433, 11 July 2008, para. 13). The Appeals Chamber found that this "should not be read so as to place pressure on the accused to testify or to raise defences at an early stage as a condition of obtaining prosecution disclosure" (*ibid.*, paras. 1, 19, 55).

In examining Article 67(1)(g), Judge Pikis detailed that the right to silence:

[…] is in no way qualified, save in relation to the specific defences prescribed in rule 79 of the Rules. The Statute does not merely guarantee the right to silence as the inalienable right of the accused, but further provides that its exercise should draw no adverse consequences for him/her. […] In addition, the Statute assures to the accused the right "not to have imposed on him or her any reversal of the burden of proof or any onus of rebuttal". The right to silence is interwoven with the presumption of innocence of the accused (*Prosecutor v. Lubanga*, ICC A. Ch., Judgment on the appeal of Mr. Lubanga Dyilo against the Oral Decision of Trial Chamber I of 18 January 2008 – Partly dissenting opinion of Judge Georgios M. Pikis, ICC-01/04-01/06-1433, 11 July 2008, para. 14).

Although under Article 67(1)(g) the accused has the right to remain silent and cannot be compelled to testify, "once an accused voluntarily testifies under oath, he waives his right to remain silent and must answer all relevant questions, even if the answers are incriminating" (*Prosecutor v. Katanga and Ngudjolo Chui*, ICC T. Ch. II, Decision on the request of the Defence for Mathieu Ngudjolo to obtain assurances with respect to self-incrimination for the accused, ICC-01/04-01/07-3153, 13 September 2011, para. 7). Accordingly, the accused person's testimony may be used against him/her and, should he/she decline to answer a permissible question, the Chamber may as appropriate deduce any adverse inference (*ibid.*, para. 8). Additionally, the assurances under rule 74 (self-incrimination by a witness) of the RPE aim to compel witnesses to answer questions under the objection of potential self-incrimination (*ibid.*, para. 9). Thus, it is inappropriate to apply this rule to an accused who knowingly committed himself to answer all questions within the scope of cross-examination and, therefore, cross-examination must be limited to matters: i) raised during examination in chief; ii) affecting the credibility of the witness; and iii) relevant to the case for the cross-examining party (*ibid.*, para. 10).

The right not to be compelled to testify against oneself is "the corollary of the right to remain silent, both of which are intimately tied to the presumption of innocence" (*Prosecutor v. Katanga and Ngudjolo Chui*, ICC T. Ch. II, Decision on the implementation of regulation 55 of the Regulations of the Court and severing the charges against the accused persons, ICC-01/04-01/07-3319-tENG/FRA, 21 November 2012, para. 48). Although the right to remain silent and the right not to be compelled to testify against oneself or privilege against self-incrimination are not explicitly recognised in Article 6 of the ECHR, these rights are international standards pivotal to the fair trial. They endeavour to guarantee that confessions obtained via subterfuge, coercion or duress cannot be used at trial in disregard of the accused person's will to remain silent. In turn, the right to remain silent is related to, *inter alia*, have the right to decide to testify respected (*ibid.*, paras. 48 and 49).

Cross-references:

(h) To make an unsworn oral or written statement in his or her defence; and[554]

(i) Not to have imposed on him or her any reversal of the burden of proof or any onus of rebuttal.[555]

Article 66, Rule 74.

Authors: Juan Pablo Pérez-León-Acevedo and Björn Elberling.

[554] Article 67(1)(h) allows the accused to make an unsworn statement, that is, a statement made without solemn undertaking under Article 69 (and thus not subject to the penalty for false testimony under Article 70) and not subject to cross-examination. The ICC Statute thus seems to follow the civil law model, which generally does not foresee the accused taking the oath as a witness. The unsworn statement constitutes an exception to the general rule according to which testimony must be accompanied by an oath of truthfulness (see further Schabas, 1999, p. 862; Schabas, 2008, p. 1269; and Schabas, 2010, p. 815).

From the wording of Article 67(1)(h), it seems that the accused only has the right to make one statement, presumably at a specific moment in the trial, such as at the very beginning or after the presentation of all the evidence. The Statute thus does not mandate that the Chamber allows the accused to make statements throughout the trial, as is the case in certain civil law jurisdictions (see Sect. 258(1) of the German Code of Criminal Procedure). Chambers may, however, conceivably grant such rights based on their own power to control the proceedings, as at least one ICTY Trial Chambers has done (*Prosecutor v. Milomir Stakić*, Case No. IT-97-24, ICTY T. Ch., Order for Filing of Motions and Related Matters, 7 March 2002, para. 8).

As the statement is unsworn, its value as evidence is doubtful (see Schabas, 1999, p. 862; Schabas, 2008, p. 1269; and Schabas, 2010, p. 815). Defendants may therefore also wish to testify, that is, to make a sworn statement subject to cross-examination. It is unclear whether the ICC Statute allows this or whether Article 67(1)(h) in conjunction with Article 67(1)(g) must be interpreted as limiting the accused to only an unsworn statement (see pro Orie, 2002, p. 1482; contra Zappalà, 2003, p. 79). Be that as it may, concerning the use of unsworn oral statement by the accused, as an example, Mathieu Ngudjolo Chui made two oral statements in accordance with Article 67(1)(h) of the ICC Statute, that is, without oath, although he and his co-accused in general chose to testify pursuant to their right under Article 67(1)(g) of the ICC Statute. Whereas the Chamber to some extent took into account those unsworn statements, only sworn statements were considered part of the case record within the meaning of Article 74(2) of the ICC Statute (*Prosecutor v. Ngudjolo Chui*, ICC T. Ch. II, Judgment pursuant to Article 74 of the Statute, ICC-01/04-02/12-3-tENG, 18 December 2012, para. 25).

The ICC Statute imposes no restriction on the right to make an unsworn written or oral statement "as to when this right may be exercised or the form the statement should take" (*Prosecutor v. Lubanga*, ICC T. Ch. I, Decision on opening and closing statements, ICC-01/04-01/06-1346 22 May 2008, para. 14). The accused has the right to make an unsworn oral or written statement in his or her defence without this affecting his or her right to remain silent and, therefore, "cannot be compelled to testify under oath even if they make an unsworn statement" (*Prosecutor v. Katanga and Ngudjolo Chui*, ICC T. Ch. II, Corrigendum to the Directions for the conduct of the proceedings and testimony in accordance to rule 140, ICC-01/04-01/07-1665-Corr, 1 December 2009, para. 51). Nevertheless, if an accused consents to give evidence, he/she "becomes subject to the same rules [...] that are applicable to other witnesses" (*ibid.*).

Cross-references:

Articles 67(1)(g), 69, 70 and 74(2).

Authors: Juan Pablo Pérez-León-Acevedo and Björn Elberling.

[555] The right against a reversal of the burden of proof and against an onus of rebuttal is a corollary of Article 66 laying down the presumption of innocence and placing the burden of proof on the

2. In addition to any other disclosure provided for in this Statute, the Prosecutor shall, as soon as practicable, disclose to the defence evidence in the Prosecutor's possession or control which he or she believes shows or tends to show the innocence of the accused, or to mitigate the guilt of the accused, or which may affect the credibility of prosecution evidence. In case of doubt as to the application of this paragraph, the Court shall decide.[556]

---

prosecution. Article 67(1)(i) reverse onus provision has been considered as quite original since, considering the absence of typical reverse onus provisions in the ICC Statute, its real purpose would apparently be its application to judge-made reverse onus provisions (see Schabas, 2010, p. 816). By explicitly ruling out any reversal of the burden of proof, the ICC Statute goes beyond most human rights norms – the ECHR, for example, also contains the presumption of innocence, but does allow reversals within certain limits (see Schabas, Article 66, 1999, MN 22; and Schabas, 2010, pp. 784–785 with further references). Indeed, a joint, strict interpretation of Articles 66(2) and 67(1)(i) might in all circumstances lead to the burden of proof on the Prosecution which may turn to be inconsistent with criminal law under certain assumptions such as assuming the sanity of the accused person (see Sluiter, 2009, p. 462).

Article 67(1)(i) may at first glance seem of rather limited practical value as no provisions in the ICC Statute, especially in the Articles defining substantive crimes, order or allow such a reversal. The provision may, however, still be of use in guarding against reversals contained in the Elements of Crimes (of which it does not seem to be any at the moment) or in the context of other norms concerning criminal responsibility, especially those constituting the "General Part" of the substantive law (on examples concerning modes of liability and grounds for excluding criminal responsibility, see Schabas, Article 66, 1999, MN 20–21; and Schabas, 2010, pp. 785–786).

Judge Pikis detailed that "The accused is presumed to be innocent. He does not have to prove his innocence. What he must do in order to free himself from the accusation is to cast doubt on its validity: it is his right to be acquitted unless the accusations against him are proven beyond reasonable doubt" (*Prosecutor v. Lubanga*, ICC A. Ch., Judgment on the appeal of Mr. Lubanga Dyilo against the Oral Decision of Trial Chamber I of 18 January 2008 – Partly dissenting opinion of Judge Georgios M. Pikis, ICC-01/04-01/06-1433, 11 July 2008, para. 14). Pursuant to Article 66(2) and (3) of the ICC Statute, the onus of proving the accused person's guilt is on the Prosecutor and, to convict the accused, the Chamber must be convinced beyond reasonable doubt. Additionally, under Article 67(1)(g) and (i) of the ICC Statute, the accused person is entitled to remain silent and not to have imposed on him/her "any reversal of the burden of proof or any onus of rebuttal" (*Prosecutor v. Bemba*, T. Ch. III, Decision lifting the temporary suspension of the trial proceedings and addressing additional issues raised in defence submissions ICC-01/05- 01/08-2490-Red and ICC-01/05-01/08-2497, ICC-01/05-01/08-2500, 6 February 2013, para. 19).

Concerning how the rights of victims may potentially conflict with the rights of the accused, the fact that victims are authorised to participate in the ICC proceedings cannot alter, *inter alia*, the rules of burden of proof resting on the Prosecution (Article 66(2)) and the prohibition of reversal of the burden of proof (Article 67(1)(i)) (see Zappalà, 2010, p. 147).

Cross-references:

Articles 66, 67(1)(g) and 67(1)(i).

Authors: Juan Pablo Pérez-León-Acevedo and Björn Elberling.

[556] Article 67(2), which complements Article 54(1)(a) requiring the prosecution to investigate incriminating and exonerating circumstances equally, lays down the duty of the prosecution to disclose to the defence potentially exculpatory evidence. Indeed, the ICC Chambers have extended the disclosure to include any exculpatory evidence and not only evidence (for example,

Prosecutor v. Lubanga, ICC PT. Ch. I, Decision on the Final System of Disclosure and the Establishment of a Timetable, ICC-01/04-01/06-102, 15 May 2006, para. 8). Article 67(2) and the related RPE correspond to the general principle of international criminal procedure consisting in that the accused person "shall be granted reasonable access to the prosecution material in order to prepare his defence" (Tochilovsky, 2013, p. 1097).

Application of Article 67(2) may be wider than that of Article 67(1) – the Court has stated that it only applies to proceedings "pertaining to the guilt or innocence of the suspect or accused person or to the credibility of Prosecution witnesses" (*Situation in Darfur*, ICC PT. Ch. I, Decision on the Requests of the OPCD on the Production of Relevant Supporting Documentation Pursuant to Regulation 86(2)(e) of the Regulations of the Court and on the Disclosure of Exculpatory Materials by the Prosecutor, ICC-02/05-110, 3 December 2007, para. 20; and *Situation in the Democratic Republic of Congo*, ICC PT. Ch. I, Decision on the Requests of the OPCD on the Production of Relevant Supporting Documentation Pursuant to Regulation 86(2)(e) of the Regulations of the Court and on the Disclosure of Exculpatory Materials by the Prosecutor, ICC-01/04-417, 7 December 2007, para. 11). While this means that Article 67(2) does not apply to proceedings concerning applications for participation as victims in the proceedings, the decisions could be read to imply that the provision may well apply to other proceedings even in the investigation phase (*Situation in Darfur*, ICC PT. Ch. I, Decision on the Requests of the OPCD on the Production of Relevant Supporting Documentation Pursuant to Regulation 86(2)(e) of the Regulations of the Court and on the Disclosure of Exculpatory Materials by the Prosecutor, ICC-02/05-110, 3 December 2007, para. 6). Such evidence must be disclosed "in a timely manner", which also implies that the duty under Article 67(2) applies whenever the prosecution receives such material, independent of the exact stage of proceedings.

In *Lubanga*, Trial Chamber I held that "Exculpatory material [...] includes material, first, that shows or tends to show the innocence of the accused; second, which mitigates the guilt of the accused; and, third, which may affect the credibility of prosecution evidence" (*Prosecutor v. Lubanga*, ICC T. Ch. I, Decision on the consequences of non-disclosure of exculpatory materials covered by Article 54(3)(e) agreements and the application to stay the prosecution of the accused, together with certain other issues raised at the Status Conference on 10 June 2008, ICC-01/04-01/06-1401, 13 June 2008, para. 59). Thus, the disclosure duty under the first sentence of Article 67(2) is in principle applicable to all materials under the Prosecutor's possession or control and about which he/she considers that: demonstrate or tend to demonstrate the accused person's innocence, mitigate the accused person's guilt or may affect the credibility of the evidence of the Prosecution (see Schabas, 2010, p. 817). Thus, not later than a date set up by the Trial Chamber and prior to the commencement of the trial, the Prosecution must disclose: i) all incriminatory material as witness statements or any other material relied on at trial; ii) Article 67(2) and Rule 77 material in its possession for inspection to the defence teams on a rolling basis; and iii) expert witness report to be called during the Prosecution case (*Prosecutor v. Gbagbo and Blé Goudé*, ICC T. Ch. I, Order setting the commencement date for trial, ICC-02/11-01/15-58, 7 May 2015, para. 22).

Article 67(2) refers only to evidence "in the Prosecutor's possession or control", thus excluding, for example, material in the possession of information providers such as UN troops (see *Prosecutor v. Lubanga*, ICC PT. Ch. I, Decision on Defence Requests for Disclosure of Materials, ICC-01/04-01/06-718, 17 November 2006, p. 5 on material held by the UN Mission in the DRC (MONUC); in this instance the court sent a request to MONUC via the Registrar in order to gain access to such material in question, see *ibid.*, p. 7). In *Lubanga*, the Trial Chamber stated that "the disclosure regime established by the ICC Statute framework is imposed on the prosecution alone: in other words, no positive obligation is imposed on the other organs of the Court, the defence or the participants to disclose exculpatory material to the defence under Article 67(2) of the Statute, Rule 77 or Rule 76 of the Rules" (*Prosecutor v. Lubanga*, ICC T. Ch. I,

Decision on the defence application for disclosure of victims applications, ICC-01/04-01/06-1637, 21 January 2009, para. 10).

For cases in which disclosure under Article 67(2) may endanger further investigations or conflict with other obligations of the prosecution concerning evidence, Rules 81 and 82 contain certain restrictions on disclosure (see also *Prosecutor v. Lubanga*, ICC PT. Ch. I, Decision on the Information in respect of the Second Decision on Rule 81 Motions, ICC-01/04-01/06-490, 28 September 2006; *Prosecutor v. Lubanga*, ICC PT. Ch. I, Decision Further to the Information Provided by the Prosecutor on 25 October 2006, ICC-01/04-01/06-629-tEN, 30 October 2006, on conflicts with Article 54(3)(e); and *Prosecutor v. Lubanga*, ICC PT. Ch. I, Decision on the Defence Request for Order to Disclose Exculpatory Materials, ICC-01/04-01/06-649, 2 November 2006, p. 3, on witness protection issues).

While disclosure of evidence is generally directly between the parties, the court has the power to decide in cases of doubt. This is further elaborated upon in Rule 83 of the RPE. The court may also, under Rule 84, make orders for disclosure of material not yet disclosed prior to trial.

The disclosure obligation under Article 67(2) is ongoing (see *Prosecutor v. Lubanga*, ICC T. Ch. I, Decision Regarding the Timing and Manner of Disclosure and the Date of Trial, ICC-01/04-01/06-1019, 9 November 2007, para. 28; and *Prosecutor v. Katanga*, ICC PT. Ch. I, Decision Modifying the Calendar for the Disclosure of the Supporting Materials of the Prosecution Application for a Warrant of Arrest against Germain Katanga, ICC-01/04-01/07-60, 5 November 2007, p. 8).

The Prosecutor has an ongoing obligation to disclose exculpatory material (*Prosecutor v. Katanga and Ngudjolo Chui*, ICC PT. Ch. I, Decision Establishing a Calendar in the Case against Germain Katanga and Mathieu Ngudjolo Chui, ICC-01/04-01/07-259, 10 March 2008, p. 12).

As Schabas points out, the disclosure duty is seemingly attenuated with regard to confirmation charges (Schabas, 2010, p. 818). Thus, disclosing the "bulk of the materials identified as potentially exculpatory or otherwise material", also known as "the bulk rule" would suffice, that is, the Prosecutor should disclose to the defence the bulk of potentially exonerating evidence and evidence material to the preparation of the defence, before the confirmation of charges hearing (*Prosecutor v. Katanga and Ngudjolo Chui*, ICC PT. Ch. I., Decision on Article 54(3)(e) Documents Identified as Potentially Exculpatory or Otherwise Material to the Defence's Preparation for the Confirmation Hearing, ICC-01/04-01/07-621, 20 June 2008, para. 8; and *Prosecutor v. Lubanga*, ICC PT. Ch. I., Decision on the confirmation of charges, ICC-01/04-01/06-803, 29 January 2007, para. 154). In cases when relevant material is subject to redactions, the confirmation hearing is not necessarily unfair if access to certain potentially exculpatory material is denied to the defence (*Prosecutor v. Katanga*, ICC A. Ch., Judgment on the Appeal of the Prosecutor against the Decision of Pre-Trial Chamber I entitled "First Decision on the Prosecution Request for Authorisation to Redact Witnesses Statements", ICC-01/04-01/07-475, 13 May 2008, paras. 71–73). Nevertheless, judges departed from the practice developed in *Lubanga* and *Katanga and Ngudjolo Chui*, that is, the so-called "bulk-rule", since they in *Mbarushimana* and the Kenyan cases opted for the total disclosure of all said material before the confirmation of charges hearing. The Prosecutor has also been asked by the judges to prepare summaries in order to help the defence understand and identify the relevance of each evidentiary piece (*Prosecutor v. Ruto et al.*, ICC PT. Ch. II, Decision Setting the Regime for Evidence Disclosure and Other Related Matters, ICC-01/09-01/11-44, 6 April 2011, para. 6; *Prosecutor v. Mbarushimana*, ICC PT. Ch. I, Decision on issues relating to disclosure, ICC-01/04-01/10-87, 30 March 2011).

Substitutes for disclosure, for example, summaries of materials or disclosure of analogous materials, are insufficient (*Prosecutor v. Katanga and Ngudjolo Chui*, ICC PT. Ch. I., Decision on Article 54(3)(e) Documents Identified as Potentially Exculpatory or Otherwise Material to the Defence's Preparation for the Confirmation Hearing, ICC-01/04-01/07-621, 20 June 2008, para. 6). The Trial Chamber may authorise redactions of documents and summaries of exculpatory evidence are not permitted (*Prosecutor v. Lubanga*, ICC T. Ch. I, Reasons for Oral Decision Lifting the Stay of Proceedings, ICC-01/04-01/06-1644, 23 January 2009, paras. 41–47).

The Prosecutor's obligation of disclosure under Article 67(2) and the Prosecutor's power to confidentially collect evidence under Article 54(3)(c) are in tension as the latter enables to collect lead evidence used to produce other evidence rather than for production before the ICC (*Prosecutor v. Lubanga*, ICC A. Ch., Judgment on the appeal of the Prosecutor against the decision of Trial Chamber I entitled "Decision on the consequences of non-disclosure of exculpatory materials covered by Article 54(3)(e) agreements and the application to stay the prosecution of the accused, together with certain other issues raised at the Status Conference on 10 June 2008", ICC-01/04-01/06-1486, 21 October 2008, para. 43). If information provided under Article 54(3)(c) is given under confidentiality agreement, this happens to contain potentially exculpatory material and the informer denies permission to disclose, the Prosecutor may face severe problems. Precisely, the Trial Chamber in *Lubanga* ordered a stay of proceedings and only lifted it when the Prosecutor had been authorised by the informer to disclose potentially exculpatory evidence to the defence (see Schabas, 2010, p. 819).

In *Bemba*, the Appeals Chamber noted that the ICC legal framework contains no explicit disclosure regime concerning interim release applications, considered the arrested person's rights and guarantees and stated that he/she should ideally have all such information at the time of his or her initial appearance at the ICC (*Prosecutor v. Bemba*, ICC A. Ch., Judgment on the appeal of Mr Jean-Pierre Bemba Gombo against the decision of Pre-Trial Chamber III entitled 'Decision on application for interim release', ICC-01/05-01/08-323, 16 December 2008, paras. 26 and 32).

As to individuals identified by the defence and who may provide critical exculpatory evidence, the Trial Chamber may review Article 67(2) materials available to the defence to ascertain whether evidentiary materials disclosed up to that moment engage defence lines that had been made known to or are apparent to the Chamber (*Prosecutor v. Banda and Jerbo*, ICC T. Ch. IV, Decision on the defence request for a temporary stay of proceedings, ICC-02/05-03/09-410, 26 October 2012, para. 98). Then, the Chamber reviews the disclosure of the identities of potentially exculpatory witnesses and their statements as well as "issues of interviews between the defence and prosecution witnesses, issues of translation and cooperation and issues of disclosure of documents, including those exculpatory documents received by the prosecution under confidentiality agreements pursuant to Article 54(3)(e)" (*ibid.*). Before the status conference, the Trial Chamber in *Banda and Jerbo* had requested the Prosecutor to file an updated and comprehensive report on exculpatory evidence disclosed to the defence. This had the purpose to enable the Chamber to determine whether, in general, "the disclosed Article 67(2) material may support lines of defence that may reasonably arise from unavailable evidence" and the related analysis also assists "in determining whether a fair trial is impossible in the case" (*ibid.*, para. 109). Considering particular circumstances and as an alternative to the severe remedy of temporarily staying proceedings, the defence may voluntarily consider revealing one line of argument to the Prosecutor so as "to facilitate the search for, and disclosure of, relevant evidence and the investigation thereof" (*ibid.*, para. 113).

As to requests for filing additional documents before trial, the decision on the confirmation of charges defines the trial parameters (*Prosecutor v. Gbagbo and Blé Goudé*, ICC T. Ch. I, Order setting the commencement date for trial, ICC-02/11-01/15-58, 7 May 2015, para. 17). Thus, an updated document containing the charges is not needed for the accused person to prepare an effective defence under Article 67 (*ibid.*). Nevertheless, "this does not preclude the filing, by the Prosecution, of other auxiliary documents with a view of providing the Defence with further details in relation to the charges confirmed" (*ibid.*).

The second sentence of Article 67(2) makes it clear that the Trial Chamber conducts the final assessment on whether material in Prosecutor's control or possession has to be disclosed (*Prosecutor v. Lubanga*, ICC A. Ch., Judgment on the appeal of the Prosecutor against the decision of Trial Chamber I entitled "Decision on the consequences of non-disclosure of exculpatory materials covered by Article 54(3)(e) agreements and the application to stay the prosecution of the accused, together with certain other issues raised at the Status Conference on 10 June 2008", ICC-01/04-01/06-1486, 21 October 2008, para. 46). Moreover, in doing so, the Trial Chamber may provide protective measures and limitations on disclosure requested by the Prosecutor as far as those are proportionate and necessary to protect the witnesses and without causing unfairness to the defence (*Prosecutor v. Lubanga*, Transcript, ICC-01/04-01/06-T-104, 16 January 2009, p. 13). Under Rule 83 of the RPE, it is possible for the ICC Prosecutor to request a hearing before the competent Chamber in order to:

> [...] determine whether the Defence should have access to some specific materials. The presence of the Defence at this type of hearing would, in principle, defeat its very purpose because: (i) the Prosecution would be prevented from going into the details of the relevant materials, which have not yet been disclosed to the Defence; and (ii) the Defence would not be in a position to make meaningful submissions as it does not have access to such materials (*Katanga and Ngudjolo Chui*, ICC PT. Ch. I, Decision on Article 54(3)(e) Documents Identified as Potentially Exculpatory or Otherwise Material to the Defence's Preparation for the Confirmation Hearing, ICC-01/04-01/07-621, 20 June 2008, para. 2).

Pre-Trial Chamber II, in *Ruto et al.* , considered that it was fair to oblige the Prosecutor to timely make total disclosure at the pre-confirmation stage and concluded that Prosecution's objections to explanatory summaries were result of a misunderstanding of the decision (*Prosecutor v. Ruto et al.*, ICC PT. Ch. II, Decision on the 'Prosecution's Application for leave to Appeal the "Decision Setting the Regime for Evidence Disclosure and Other Related Matters", ICC-01/09-01/11-44, 2 May 2011, paras. 18 and 27). In *Mbarushimana*, Pre-Trial Chamber I found that the disclosure orders were not so burdensome to affect fairness in detriment to the Prosecution (*Prosecutor v. Mbarushimana*, ICC PT. Ch. I, Decision on the Prosecution's application for leave to Appeal the 'Decision on issues relating to disclosure', ICC-01/04-01/10-116, 21 April 2011, para. 18).

The Trial Chamber has to consider at face value whether the disclosed Article 67(2) evidence involves lines of defence that the defence intends to pursue during trial. After the Trial Chamber examines the whole evidentiary material at the end of the trial, it may arrive to conclusions and strike a balance between fairness and the fact that additional material based upon which the same argumentative lines could not have been obtained by the defence as a consequence of the absence of onsite investigations. Taking into account the case circumstances, the Trial Chamber has to determine whether a fair trial is not prospectively impossible. If a fair trial is seemingly possible, the Trial Chamber may relieve against any prejudice stemming from unfairness in the trial (*Prosecutor v. Banda and Jerbo*, ICC T. Ch. IV, Decision on the defence request for a temporary stay of proceedings, ICC-02/05-03/09-410, 26 October 2012, para. 114).

A stay of the proceedings constitutes an exceptional remedy and resorted only if the situation prompting the request for the stay neither can be resolved at a later stage nor can be cured during the trial. If the Chamber considers that the situation of the defence's access to this information has significantly improved and, thus, disclosure of critical information to the defence prior to the trial is enabled, the Chamber will most likely reject requests for stay of proceedings, even temporarily (*ibid.*, para. 121). As for defence access to Prosecution witnesses, although it corresponds to the witnesses' prerogatives, the Prosecution is encouraged to do its best to secure defence access to them (*ibid.*, para. 128).

For more on disclosure generally, including questions on procedure and timing, see the commentary on Rules 76 ff.

Cross-references:

Article 54(1)(a), 54(3)(e), 67(1), Rules 76 ff., 81–84.

Doctrine:

1. Till Gut, Stefan Kirsch, Daryl Mundis and Melinda Taylor, "Defence Issues", in Göran Sluiter, Håkan Friman, Suzannah Linton, Sergey Vasiliev and Salvatore Zappalà (eds.), *International Criminal Procedure: Principles and Rules*, Oxford University Press, Oxford, 2013, pp. 1203–97.

2. Robert Heinsch, "How to Achieve Fair and Expeditious Trial Proceedings before the ICC: Is it Time for a more Judge-dominated Approach?", in Carsten Stahn and Göran Sluiter (eds.), *The Emerging Practice of the International Criminal Court*, Brill/Martinus Nijhoff Publishers, Leiden, 2009, pp. 479–99.

3. Steven Kay and Bert Swart, "The Role of the Defence", in Antonio Cassese, Paola Gaeta and John R.W.D. Jones (eds.), *The Rome Statute of the International Criminal Court: A Commentary*, 2nd ed., Oxford University Press, Oxford, 2002, pp. 1421–37.

4. Geert-Jan Alexander Knoops, *Theory and Practice of International and Internationalized Criminal Proceedings*, Kluwer Law International, The Hague, 2005.

5. Michele Marchesiello, "Proceedings Before the Pre-Trial Chamber", in Antonio Cassese, Paola Gaeta and John R.W.D. Jones (eds.), *The Rome Statute of the International Criminal Court: A Commentary*, 2nd ed., Oxford University Press, Oxford, 2002, pp. 1231–46.

6. Yvonne McDermott, "General Duty to Ensure the Right to a Fair and Expeditious Trial", in Göran Sluiter, Håkan Friman, Suzannah Linton, Sergey Vasiliev and Salvatore Zappalà (eds.), *International Criminal Procedure: Principles and Rules*, Oxford University Press, Oxford, 2013, pp. 770–818.

7. William A. Schabas, "Article 63 – Trial in the Presence of the Accused", in Otto Triffterer (ed.), *Commentary on the Rome Statute of the International Criminal Court: Observers' Notes, Article by Article*, 2nd ed., C.H. Beck/Hart/Nomos, Munich/Oxford/Baden-Baden, 2008, pp. 803–8.

8. William A. Schabas, "Article 66 – Presumption of Innocence", in Otto Triffterer (ed.), *Commentary on the Rome Statute of the International Criminal Court: Observers' Notes, Article by Article*, Nomos, Baden-Baden, 1999, pp. 833–43.

9. William A. Schabas, "Article 67 – Rights of the Accused", in Otto Triffterer (ed.), *Commentary on the Rome Statute of the International Criminal Court: Observers' Notes, Article by Article*, Nomos, Baden-Baden, 1999, pp. 845–68.

10. William A. Schabas, "Article 63 – Trial in the Presence of the Accused", in Otto Triffterer (ed.), *Commentary on the Rome Statute of the International Criminal Court: Observers' Notes, Article by Article*, 2nd ed., C.H. Beck/Hart/Nomos, Munich/Oxford/Baden-Baden, 2008, pp. 1191–98.

11. William A. Schabas, "Article 66 – Presumption of Innocence", in Otto Triffterer (ed.), *Commentary on the Rome Statute of the International Criminal Court: Observers' Notes, Article by Article*, 2nd ed., C.H. Beck/Hart/Nomos, Munich/Oxford/Baden-Baden, 2008, pp. 1233–45.

12. William A. Schabas, "Article 67 – Rights of the Accused", in Otto Triffterer (ed.), *Commentary on the Rome Statute of the International Criminal Court: Observers' Notes, Article by Article*, 2nd ed., C.H. Beck/Hart/Nomos, Munich/Oxford/Baden-Baden, 2008, pp. 1247–74.

13. William A. Schabas, *The International Criminal Court: A Commentary on the Rome Statute*, Oxford University Press, Oxford, 2010.

14. Göran Sluiter, "Human Rights Protection in the ICC Pre-Trial Phase", in Carsten Stahn and Göran Sluiter (eds.), *The Emerging Practice of the International Criminal Court*, Brill/Martinus Nijhoff Publishers, Leiden, 2009, pp. 459–75.

15. Frank Terrier, "Procedure Before the Trial Chamber", in Antonio Cassese, Paola Gaeta and John R.W.D. Jones (eds.), *The Rome Statute of the International Criminal Court: A Commentary*, 2nd ed., Oxford University Press, Oxford, 2002, pp. 1277–1318.

16. Vladimir Tochilovsky, "Defence Access to the Prosecution Material", in Göran Sluiter, Håkan Friman, Suzannah Linton, Sergey Vasiliev and Salvatore Zappalà (eds.), *International Criminal Procedure: Principles and Rules*, Oxford University Press, Oxford, 2013, pp. 1083–98.

17. Ekaterina Trendafilova, "Fairness and Expeditiousness in the International Criminal Court's Pre-trial Proceedings", in Carsten Stahn and Göran Sluiter (eds.), *The Emerging Practice of the International Criminal Court*, Brill/Martinus Nijhoff Publishers, Leiden, 2009, pp. 441–57.

18. Alphons Orie, "Accusatorial v. Inquisitorial Approach in International Criminal Proceedings", in Antonio Cassese, Paola Gaeta and John R.W.D. Jones (eds.), *The Rome Statute of the International Criminal Court: A Commentary*, 2nd ed., Oxford University Press, Oxford, 2002, pp. 1439–1495.

19. Salvatore Zappala, *Human Rights in International Criminal Proceedings*, Oxford University Press, Oxford, 2003.

20. Salvatore Zappalà, "The Rights of Victims v. the Rights of the Accused", *Journal of International Criminal Justice*, vol. 8, no. 1, 2010, pp. 137–164.

Authors: Juan Pablo Pérez-León-Acevedo and Björn Elberling.

Article 68

Protection of the victims and witnesses and their participation in the proceedings[557]

[557] *General remarks*:

Protection of victims and witnesses

Article 68 establishes an obligation for the Court to protect victims and witnesses, in a similar manner to the obligation established for other international criminal tribunals. In fact, the protection of the victims is a recurring theme of the Statute (*Situation in the Democratic Republic of the Congo*, ICC A. Ch., Judgment on victim participation in the investigation stage of the proceedings in the appeal of the OPCD against the decision of Pre-Trial Chamber I of 7 December 2007 and in the appeals of the OPCD and the Prosecutor against the decision of Pre-Trial Chamber I of 24 December 2007, 19 December 2008, para. 54), to the point that a unit is established within the Registry to advise the Court on the protection of victims and witnesses. Moreover, the Statute and the Rules of Procedure and Evidence grant special protective measures to victims, taking into account their age and the harm they have suffered. As a result, children and victims of sexual violence are specially protected by the Court.

Participation of victims and witnesses

Victims with relevant information to pass it on to the Prosecutor may do so pursuant to Articles 15(2) and 42(1) without the need to be formally accorded a right to participate in the proceedings under Article 68 of the Statute (*Situation in the Democratic Republic of the Congo*, ICC A. Ch., Judgment on victim participation in the investigation stage of the proceedings in the appeal of the OPCD against the decision of Pre-Trial Chamber I of 7 December 2007 and in the appeals of the OPCD and the Prosecutor against the decision of Pre-Trial Chamber I of 24 December 2007, 19 December 2008, para. 53). Moreover, victims are specifically granted the right to make representations under Articles 15(3) and 19(3) of the Statute in specific procedural stages. However, the object and purpose of Article 68(3) is to provide victims with a meaningful role in criminal proceedings before the Court so that they can have a substantial impact in the proceedings (*Prosecutor v. Katanga and Ngudjolo*, ICC PT. Ch. I, Decision on the Set of Procedural Rights Attached to Procedural Status of Victim at the Pre-Trial Stage of the Case, 13 May 2008, para. 157). In this regard, the role of victims in criminal proceedings before the Court, provided for in Article 68(3) of the Statute and the corresponding Rules of Procedure and Evidence, constitutes one of the main features of the procedural framework of Court, as well as a novelty in international criminal law. In this regard, the Court has consistently clarified that the participation of victims pursuant to Article 68(3) of the Statute i) is confined to proceedings before the Court, ii) aims to afford victims an opportunity to voice their views and concerns on matters affecting their personal interests, and iii) does not equate victims to parties to the proceedings before a Chamber, restricting their participation to issues arising therein touching upon their personal interests, and then at stages and in a manner not inconsistent with the rights of the accused and a fair and impartial trial (*Prosecutor v. Lubanga*, ICC A. Ch., 13 February 2007; *Prosecutor v. Lubanga*, ICC A. Ch., Decision of the Appeals Chamber on the Joint Application of Victims a/0001/06 to a/0003/06 and a/0105/06 concerning the "Directions and Decision of the Appeals Chamber" of 2 February 2007, 13 June 2007; *Lubanga*, ICC A. Ch., Decision, in limine, on Victim Participation in the appeals of the Prosecutor and the Defence against Trial Chamber I's Decision entitled "Decision on Victims' Participation", 16 May 2008; *Situation in Darfur*, ICC A. Ch., 18 June 2008; *Situation in the Democratic Republic of the Congo*, ICC A. Ch., Decision on Victim Participation in the appeal of the Office of Public | Counsel for the Defence against Pre-Trial Chamber I's Decision of 7 December 2007 and in the appeals of the Prosecutor and the Office of Public Counsel for the Defence against Pre-Trial Chamber I's Decision of 24 December 2007, 30 June 2008; *Prosecutor v. Lubanga*, ICC A. Ch., Judgment on

1. The Court shall take appropriate measures[558] to protect the safety, physical and psychological well-being, dignity and privacy of victims and witnesses.[559] In so doing, the Court

---

the appeals of The Prosecutor and The Defence against Trial Chamber I's Decision on Victims' Participation of 18 January 2008, 11 July 2008; *Situation in the Democratic Republic of the Congo*, ICC A. Ch., Judgment on victim participation in the investigation stage of the proceedings in the appeal of the OPCD against the decision of Pre-Trial Chamber I of 7 December 2007 and in the appeals of the OPCD and the Prosecutor against the decision of Pre-Trial Chamber I of 24 December 2007, 19 December 2008).

Preparatory works:

The paragraphs of Article 68 dealing with the protection of victims and witnesses were proposed early in the negotiation of the ICC Statute, on the basis of similar provisions from the Statutes of the ICTY and the ICTR, and their discussion did not pose particular challenges (Report of the Preparatory Committee on the Establishment of an International Criminal Court, UN doc. A/51/22, 13 September 1996, Vol. II, p. 204; Decisions Taken by the Preparatory Committee at its Session Held from 4 to 15 August 1997, UN doc. A/AC.249/1997/L.8/Rev.1, 14 August 1997, pp. 36–37). By contrast, the introduction of participatory provisions in Article 68(3) does not have any precedent in other international criminal tribunal and was, as such, quite controversial during the negotiations. France made a proposal for victims to have a right to reparation (Draft Statute of the International Criminal Court, Working paper submitted by France, UN doc. A/AC.249/L.3, 6 August 1996, Articles 50(3), 126 and 130(2)) and Egypt went even further, suggesting in this sense that they become *"parties civiles"* with the capacity to submit additional evidence need to establish the basis of criminal responsibility (Proposal for Article 43 Submitted by Egypt, UN doc. A/AC.249/WP.11, 19 August 1996, Article 43(2)(b)). However, some States were against the broad scope of these proposals. As a compromise, New Zealand circulated language taken from paragraph 6(b) of the 1985 Declaration of Basic Principles of Justice for Victims of Crime and Abuse of Power (Proposal by New Zealand on Article 43, Non-Paper/WG.4/No.19, 13 August 1997, Article 43(3)). A compromise solution was eventually reached on the basis of an amended text circulated during the Rome Conference by Canada (Article 68, Protection of the Victims and Witnesses and Their Participation in the Proceedings: Proposal Submitted by Canada, UN doc. A/CONF.183/C.1/WGPM/L.58/Rev.1, 6 July 1998, Article 68(3)).

Author: Enrique Carnero Rojo.

[558] *Initiative on measures*

Article 68(1) of the ICC Statute mandates the Chambers and the other organs of the Court to take appropriate measures to protect the safety, physical and psychological well-being, dignity and privacy of the victims without prejudicing or being inconsistent with the rights of the accused and a fair and impartial trial (*Situation in the Democratic Republic of the Congo*, ICC PT. Ch. I, 22 July 2005, p. 3; *Darfur*, ICC PT. Ch. I, 8 June 2007, p. 3; *Situation in the Democratic Republic of the Congo*, ICC PT. Ch. I, 19 June 2007, pp. 5–6). This is a provision of a general nature, which aims at placing on all organs of the Court, including the Prosecution, the obligation to take "appropriate measures" for the protection of witnesses and not to attribute to any of the organs of the Court, including the Prosecution, the power to take whichever protective measure the relevant organ may consider necessary to protect a given witness. Every organ of the Court has the obligation to pay particular attention to the needs of the witnesses in performing their functions and to cooperate, whenever necessary, with those organs of the Court that are competent to adopt specific protective measures (*Prosecutor v. Katanga and Ngudjolo*, ICC PT. Ch. I, 21 April 2008, paras. 26–27).

The Pre-Trial Chambers are in particular mandated to ensure that measures are adopted for these purposes (*Prosecutor v. Katanga and Ngudjolo*, ICC PT. Ch. I, 10 March 2008, p. 6). Victims as well as witnesses may move the Court to take protective measures for their safety, physical and psychological well-being, dignity and privacy as foreseen *inter alia* in Article 68(1) and (2) of the Statute and rules 87 and 88 of the Rules (*Situation in the Democratic Republic of the Congo*, ICC A. Ch., Judgment on victim participation in the investigation stage of the proceedings in the appeal of the OPCD against the decision of Pre-Trial Chamber I of 7 December 2007 and in the appeals of the OPCD and the Prosecutor against the decision of Pre-Trial Chamber I of 24 December 2007, 19 December 2008, para. 50). Moreover, the Court may also order said measures *proprio motu* under Article 68(1), such as inviting representatives of organisations to submit observations on current and specific issues related to the protection of victims (*Situation in Darfur*, ICC PT. Ch. I, 24 July 2006, p. 4) or mandating the non-disclosure of the identity of victim applicants to the Defence (*Prosecutor v. Katanga and Ngudjolo*, ICC PT. Ch. I, Decision on the Defence Application for Leave to Appeal the "Decision authorising the filing of observations on the applications for participation in the proceedings a/0327/07 to a/0337/07 and a/0001/08", 27 February 2008, p. 5) or to the public (*Prosecutor v. Katanga and Ngudjolo*, ICC PT. Ch. I, Decision on the Set of Procedural Rights Attached to Procedural Status of Victim at the Pre-Trial Stage of the Case, 13 May 2008, paras. 21–22) for security reasons.

Control over protective measures

The Chambers of the Court may control the protective measures applied by other organs of the Court and correct them, resorting to the powers expressly entrusted by Article 57(3)(c) of the Statute, if they determine that the behaviour of another organ, such as the Registry, has created a serious risk for the witnesses' safety (*Prosecutor v. Katanga and Ngudjolo*, ICC PT. Ch. I, 21 April 2008, paras. 49–52). In this regard, the decisions of the Registrar on protective measures will only be struck down either if it has applied an incorrect approach (*for example* the wrong criteria) or if the Victims and Witnesses Unit has arrived at a conclusion which, on an assessment of the facts, is plainly wrong. The Victims and Witnesses Unit is entrusted with the discretion to consider applications for protective measures pursuant to Articles 43 and 68 of the Statute and regulation 96 of the Regulations of the Registry, and the Court may review its decisions either *proprio motu* or upon an application by the parties or the participants, applying judicial review principles (*Prosecutor v. Lubanga*, ICC T. Ch. I, 24 April 2008, para. 82).

Author: Enrique Carnero Rojo.

559 *Proportionate measures*

Article 68(1) of the ICC Statute encompasses the principle of proportionality, according to which protective measures should restrict the rights of the parties only as far as necessary, taking into account the nature and purpose of the proceedings at stake (*Situation in the Democratic Republic of the Congo*, ICC PT. Ch. I, 22 July 2005, p. 4; *Prosecutor v. Kony et al.*, ICC PT. Ch. II, Decision on legal representation, appointment of counsel for the defence, protective measures and time-limit for submission of observations on applications for participation a/0010/06, a/0064/06 to a/0070/06, a/0081/06 to a/0104/06 and a/0111/06 to a/0127/06, 1 February 2007, para. 24). Particular protective measures must be adopted on a case-by-case basis if and when the need arises (*Situation in Darfur*, ICC PT. Ch. I, 8 June 2007, p. 4; *Situation in the Democratic Republic of the Congo*, ICC PT. Ch. I, 19 June 2007, p. 7).

List of measures

The protective measures ordered by the Court under Article 68(1) of the ICC Statute include i) the redaction of the applications for participation received from victims under Article 68(3) and transmitted to the parties for a reply under rule 89(1), especially if the suspect or accused may have access to said applications (*Situation in the Democratic Republic of the Congo*, ICC PT. Ch. I, 22 July 2005, p. 3; *Lubanga*, ICC PT. Ch. I, 29 September 2006, p. 2; *Democratic Republic of the Congo*, ICC PT. Ch. I, 20 August 2007, paras. 20–21 and 28–29); ii) the redaction of submissions or decisions that are under seal before making them public (*Prosecutor v. Lubanga*,

shall have regard to all relevant factors, including age, gender as defined in Article 7, paragraph 3, and health, and the nature of the crime, in particular, but not limited to, where the crime involves sexual or gender violence or violence against children.[560] The Prosecu-

---

ICC PT. Ch. I, 17 March 2006, pp. 3–4) or the redaction of evidence before transmitting it to the suspect or accused (*Prosecutor v. Katanga and Ngudjolo*, ICC PT. Ch. I, 10 March 2008, p. 7); iii) the use of *ex parte* filings and *ex parte* hearings (*Prosecutor v. Lubanga*, ICC T. Ch. I, 26 September 2007, para. 27; *Lubanga*, ICC T. Ch. I, 24 April 2008, para. 104); iv) the use of reference numbers assigned by the Victims Participation and Reparations Section to the names of victims and witnesses (*Situation in the Democratic Republic of the Congo*, ICC PT. Ch. I, 20 August 2007, p. 24; *Democratic Republic of the Congo*, ICC PT. Ch. I, 19 March 2008, p. 52; *Prosecutor v. Katanga and Ngudjolo*, Decision on the Set of Procedural Rights Attached to Procedural Status of Victim at the Pre-Trial Stage of the Case, ICC PT. Ch. I, 13 May 2008, paras. 21–22; *Democratic Republic of the Congo*, ICC PT. Ch. I, 3 July 2008, p. 41; *Democratic Republic of the Congo*, ICC PT. Ch. I, 4 November 2008, p. 39); v) the prohibition for the parties to directly obtain confidential information on victims and witnesses, without a Chamber deciding whether to allow the parties to disclose confidential information regarding victims and witnesses (*Situation in the Democratic Republic of the Congo*, ICC PT. Ch. I, 11 September 2007, p. 7); vi) the prohibition for the parties to directly contact victims and witnesses and the obligation to do so only through their legal representatives, the VPRS or the VWU if strictly necessary (*Situation in the Democratic Republic of the Congo*, ICC PT. Ch. I, 22 July 2005, p. 6; *Situation in the Democratic Republic of the Congo*, ICC PT. Ch. I, 21 June 2007, p. 5; *Situation in Darfur*, ICC PT. Ch. I, 23 May 2007, pp. 2 and 4; *Situation in the Democratic Republic of the Congo*, ICC PT. Ch. I, 20 August 2007, p. 24; *Situation in the Democratic Republic of the Congo*, ICC PT. Ch. I, 19 March 2008, p. 52; *Situation in the Democratic Republic of the Congo*, ICC PT. Ch. I, 3 July 2008, p. 42; *Situation in the Democratic Republic of the Congo*, ICC PT. Ch. I, 4 November 2008, p. 39); vii) the non-publication of particular motions or requests, such as those requesting the issuance of warrant of arrests, until otherwise ordered by a Chamber (*Prosecutor v. Lubanga*, ICC PT. Ch. I, 17 March 2006, p. 2); viii) the holding of hearings in closed session (*Prosecutor v. Lubanga*, ICC PT. Ch. I, Decision on the Schedule and Conduct of the Confirmation Hearing, 7 November 2006, pp. 5 and 7); ix) the provision of assistance to witnesses in the experience of giving oral evidence before the Court so as to prevent them from finding themselves in a disadvantageous position or from being taken by surprise as a result of their ignorance of the process of giving oral testimony ("witness familiarisation") before the Court (*Prosecutor v. Lubanga*, ICC PT. Ch. I, 8 November 2006, paras. 20–21; *Prosecutor v. Lubanga*, ICC T. Ch. I, 30 November 2007, paras. 33–34); x) the disclosure in advance of the questions or the topics intended to be covered by the parties and participants during their questioning in order to protect traumatised or vulnerable witnesses (*Prosecutor v. Lubanga*, ICC T. Ch. I, 29 January 2008, para. 33; *Prosecutor v. Lubanga*, ICC T. Ch. I, 20 March 2008, para. 37); xi) the relocation of witnesses included in the Protection Programme of the Court (*Prosecutor v. Katanga and Ngudjolo*, ICC PT. Ch. I, 21 April 2008, paras. 23–25); xii) the denial of provisional release requested by a suspect or accused (*Prosecutor v. Bemba*, ICC T. Ch. III, 27 September 2011, para. 33; *Prosecutor v. L. Gbagbo*, ICC T. Ch. I, 11 November 2014, para. 64); and xiii) the modification of the time limits to issue decisions under Article 61 (*Prosecutor v. Ruto et al.*, ICC PT. Ch. II, 26 October 2011, paras. 13–14).

Author: Enrique Carnero Rojo.

[560] The drafters of the Statute and the Rules of Procedure and Evidence included a number of provisions specifically governing the protection of victims of sexual offences as a result of crimes within the jurisdiction of the Court. In particular, under Article 68(1) of the Statute the Court is required to take appropriate measures to protect victims and witnesses, and to have regard to all relevant factors, "in particular, but not limited to, where the crime involves sexual or gender

---

tor shall take such measures particularly during the investigation and prosecution of such crimes.[561] These measures shall not be prejudicial to or inconsistent with the rights of the accused and a fair and impartial trial.[562]

---

violence or violence against children" (*Prosecutor v. Katanga and Ngudjolo*, ICC PT. Ch. I, 23 January 2008, para. 17). More generally, protective measures must be adopted on a fact sensitive rather than a mechanical or formulistic basis, identifying the relevant criteria, assessing the level of any threat, the likelihood of harm and the overall risk to the particular individual. In this regard, the Victims and Witnesses Unit of the Court should interpret the expression "likelihood of harm" in a sufficiently flexible and purposive manner to ensure proper protection for any witness who, following careful investigation, faces an established danger of harm or death (*Prosecutor v. Lubanga*, ICC T. Ch. I, 24 April 2008, para. 79).

Author: Enrique Carnero Rojo.

[561] *Initiative on measures*

By the terms of Article 68(1) of the Statute, the Prosecutor is bound to take measures protective of the safety and well-being of victims. The Prosecutor is equally under obligation to take measures or request that measures be taken for the protection of any person including victims (*Situation in the Democratic Republic of the Congo*, ICC A. Ch., Judgment on victim participation in the investigation stage of the proceedings in the appeal of the OPCD against the decision of Pre-Trial Chamber I of 7 December 2007 and in the appeals of the OPCD and the Prosecutor against the decision of Pre-Trial Chamber I of 24 December 2007, 19 December 2008, para. 54). However, there is no provision in the legal instruments of the Court which confers upon the Prosecutor a power to preventively relocate witnesses until they are included in the Protection Programme of the Court (*Prosecutor v. Katanga and Ngudjolo*, ICC PT. Ch. I, 21 April 2008, paras. 23–25).

Protective measures vis-à-vis the Prosecutor

The statutory obligation on the Prosecution to take appropriate protective measures has sometimes been taken into account by the Chambers to exclude the application *vis-à-vis* the Prosecutor of some protective measures adopted by the judges, such as the redactions in the victims' applications for participation in the proceedings (*Situation in the Democratic Republic of the Congo*, ICC PT. Ch. I, 22 July 2005, p. 5).

Author: Enrique Carnero Rojo.

[562] *Protective measures and fair trials*

While the safety and security of victims is a key responsibility of the Court, when protecting victims the Court must ensure that the rights of the defence are respected and that the trial remains fair (*Prosecutor v. Ngudjolo*, ICC A. Ch., 23 September 2013, para. 16). The right of endangered witnesses to protection and of the defendant to a fair trial are immutable, and neither can be diminished because of the need to cater for other interests. Accordingly, if the real possibility exists that the evidence at hand may contribute to a resolution of material factual issues in the case in favour of the accused, the latter is to be provided with it, once protective measures, if relevant, have been implemented. Similarly, the right of a witness to protection cannot be diminished because of the importance of other considerations (*Prosecutor v. Lubanga*, ICC T. Ch. I, 24 April 2008, para. 94).

Consequences of no protection by the Victims and Witnesses Unit

Therefore, following a valid refusal by the VWU to provide protective measures for a particular witness or information provider who provides eyewitness or first-hand evidence of relevant events, the Prosecution must serve the Defence the potentially exculpatory material (the non-redacted witness statements and accompanying documents) in a suitably full and non-redacted

2. As an exception to the principle of public hearings provided for in article 67, the Chambers of the Court may, to protect victims and witnesses or an accused, conduct any part of the proceedings in camera or allow the presentation of evidence by electronic or other special means. In particular, such measures shall be implemented in the case of a victim of sexual violence or a child who is a victim or a witness, unless otherwise ordered by the Court, having regard to all the circumstances, particularly the views of the victim or witness.[563]

---

form, and including by revealing the identity of the witness (*Prosecutor v. Lubanga*, ICC T. Ch. I, 24 April 2008, para. 95).

Consequences of no cooperation by witnesses

For the subgroup of witnesses who provide potentially exculpatory evidence, which the Prosecution is unable to concede, and who may be at risk if their identity and involvement with the court is revealed but who either refuse offers of protection or decline to cooperate further with the court, or both, the Chambers must select a solution from the range of possibilities that satisfies both obligations under Article 68(1): i) for witnesses eventually deciding to cooperate with the judicial process, from full disclosure of the witness' identity and evidence to all parties, participants and the public, and giving evidence publicly in open court without special measures (rule 88), through to serving redacted evidence and permitting varying levels of anonymity (including the use of a pseudonym *vis-à-vis* the public), together with the witness testifying behind a screen or remotely, either via video-link or by way of pre-recorded testimony (rules 67 and 68) (*Prosecutor v. Lubanga*, ICC T. Ch. I, 24 April 2008, paras. 97–98); and ii) for witnesses not cooperating further with the Court or unable to be traced, from the disclosure to the accused of a redacted version of their statements and any other relevant material on an anonymous basis, through to eliminating the evidential value of said statement (*Prosecutor v. Lubanga*, ICC T. Ch. I, 24 April 2008, para. 99).

Author: Enrique Carnero Rojo.

[563] *Closed sessions as an exception*

Closed sessions are a protective measure granted only on an exceptional basis, as it deprives the public from understanding parts of, or the entirety of, a witness's testimony and therefore, may affect the overall fairness of the proceedings. Some Chambers have, in consultation with the parties and participants, established practices for the limited use of *in camera* hearings (*Prosecutor v. Bemba*, ICC T. Ch. III, 19 November 2010, para. 23). The Court usually calls upon parties and participants insofar as possible, to endeavour to have witnesses' testimonies given in public, and does not favour evidence being given entirely in closed session because there are other possible measures available to protect sensitive information such as witnesses' identities and identifying information –for instance, pursuant to regulation 21(2) of the Regulations of the Court, broadcasts of audio and video recordings of all hearings are delayed by at least 30 minutes (*Prosecutor v. Bemba*, ICC T. Ch. III, 19 November 2010, para. 25).

Preparation and conduct of closed sessions

The practice of the Court on closed sessions has established that i) each request for private session should specify the grounds for such protective measure in a neutral and objective fashion, and try to specify the points that will be touched upon; ii) parties and participants should provide the Chamber with reasons justifying the continuation of the private session if the reasons that motivated the Chamber's decision for such session have changed; iii) parties and participants are usually encouraged not to request that the Court goes into private session unless there is a serious and established risk which needs to be explained to the Chamber; iv) in preparing their lines of questioning, parties and participants should be endeavour to group together all the identifying questions and to ask these questions at the beginning of the testimony; v) each party calling a protected witness, must prepare and provide the Chamber, and the parties and partici-

3. Where the personal interests[564] of the victims are affected,[565] the Court shall permit their views and concerns to be presented and considered[566] at stages of the proceedings deter-

---

pants, with a list of sensitive information and related questions to be dealt with in private session; vi) in addition to the Chamber's *proprio motu* power to reclassify a document, parties and participants should draw the attention of the Chamber to any part of the transcript of a private session that could be reclassified as public after more detailed analysis or a change in circumstances (*Prosecutor v. Bemba*, ICC T. Ch. III, 19 November 2010, para. 23).

Author: Enrique Carnero Rojo.

[564] *Personal interests as additional requirement*

The "personal interests" criterion included in Article 68(3) constitutes an additional requirement to be met by victims, over and above the victim status accorded to them under rule 85, since the same criterion is not included in other provisions granting specific participatory rights to victims, such as Articles 15(3) and 19(3) of the ICC Statute (*Situation in the Democratic Republic of the Congo*, ICC PT. Ch. I, Decision on the Applications for Participation in the Proceedings of VPRS 1, VPRS 2, VPRS 3, VPRS 4, VPRS 5 and VPRS 6, 17 January 2006, para. 62). This requirement serves two interrelated purposes: in the negative, it excludes victims' participation in proceedings the outcome of which does not affect their interests; in the positive, it grounds the right of the victims to participate before the Court once the other criteria have been met. This criterion is only provided for the purposes of the participation of victims and, being *lex specialis* for a particular participant in the proceedings, cannot be applied by analogy to ground the granting of participatory rights to any person(s) (*Situation in Kenya*, ICC PT. Ch. II, 11 February 2011, para. 12).

Personal interests of victims vis-à-vis situations

The Court initially found that the investigation of a "situation" brought before the Court affected the victims' personal interests in general since the participation of victims at said stage could serve to clarify the facts, to punish the perpetrators of the crimes and to obtain reparations for the harm suffered (*Situation in the Democratic Republic of the Congo*, ICC PT. Ch. I, Decision on the Applications for Participation in the Proceedings of VPRS 1, VPRS 2, VPRS 3, VPRS 4, VPRS 5 and VPRS 6, 17 January 2006, paras. 63 and 72; *Situation in Darfur*, ICC PT. Ch. I, 14 December 2007, para. 11; *Situation in the Democratic Republic of the Congo*, ICC PT. Ch. I, 3 July 2008, para. 26). Consequently, the Court initially determined that the assessment of the personal interests of victims in specific proceedings carried out during the investigation of a situation was only to be conducted for the determination of the specific set of procedural rights enjoyed by victims (*Situation in the Democratic Republic of the Congo*, ICC PT. Ch. I, 7 December 2007, para. 3; *Situation in Darfur*, ICC PT. Ch. I, 14 December 2007, para. 13; *Situation in the Democratic Republic of the Congo*, ICC PT. Ch. I, 23 January 2008, p. 5; *Situation in Darfur*, ICC PT. Ch. I, Decision on Request for leave to appeal the "Decision on the Requests of the OPCD on the Production of Relevant Supporting Documentation Pursuant to Regulation 86(2)(e) of the Regulations of the Court and on the Disclosure of Exculpatory Materials by the Prosecutor", 23 January 2008, p. 5; *Situation in the Democratic Republic of the Congo*, ICC PT. Ch. I, 19 March 2008, para. 5). From this perspective, the Court initially concluded that the personal interests of victims could be affected during an investigation where proceedings i) were initiated *proprio motu* by the Pre-Trial Chamber under Article 56(3) and Article 57(3)(c) of the Statute, ii) were initiated by the Prosecution or the Defence, or iii) were requested by the victims themselves (*Situation in the Democratic Republic of the Congo*, ICC PT. Ch. I, Decision on the Applications for Participation in the Proceedings of VPRS 1, VPRS 2, VPRS 3, VPRS 4, VPRS 5 and VPRS 6, 17 January 2006, paras. 73–75).

The Appeals Chamber eventually overturned this understanding of Article 68(3) of the Statute, finding that victims cannot be granted a general right to participate in the investigation. The

---

participation of victims within the meaning of Article 68(3) of the Statute "can take place only within the context of judicial proceedings", including proceedings affecting investigations, provided their personal interests are affected by the issues arising for resolution (*Prosecutor v. Lubanga*, ICC A. Ch., Judgment on the appeals of The Prosecutor and The Defence against Trial Chamber I's Decision on Victims' Participation of 18 January 2008, 11 July 2008, paras. 2 and 61–62; *Situation in the Democratic Republic of the Congo*, ICC A. Ch., Judgment on victim participation in the investigation stage of the proceedings in the appeal of the OPCD against the decision of Pre-Trial Chamber I of 7 December 2007 and in the appeals of the OPCD and the Prosecutor against the decision of Pre-Trial Chamber I of 24 December 2007, 19 December 2008, paras. 45 and 56–57; *Prosecutor v. L. Gbagbo*, ICC PT. Ch. I, 4 June 2012, para. 46). In this regard, victims who have been authorised to participate in the proceedings are generally allowed to submit observations on the proposed activities by the Trust Fund for Victims, since said activities may have an impact on crucial issues before the Chamber as well as the protection and privacy of victims (*Situation in Uganda*, ICC PT. Ch. II, 5 March 2008, p. 4).

Personal interests of victims vis-à-vis cases

By contrast, the Court has considered incontrovertible from the start of its activities that the personal interests of a victim are affected in respect of a "case" relating to the very crime(s) in which that victim was allegedly involved. Accordingly, this requirement is met whenever a victim pursuant to rule 85 applies for participation in proceedings following the issuance of a warrant of arrest or of a summons to appear in a case where the said victim was allegedly involved (*Prosecutor v. Kony et al.*, ICC PT. Ch. II, Decision on victims' applications for participation a/0010/06, a/0064/06 to a/0070/06, a/0081/06 to a/0104/06 and a/0111/06 to a/0127/06, ICC-02/04-01/05-252, 10 August 2007, paras. 9–10). In some occasions, the Court has considered that to have a declaration of the truth by the competent body (*Prosecutor v. Katanga and Ngudjolo*, Decision on the Set of Procedural Rights Attached to Procedural Status of Victim at the Pre-Trial Stage of the Case, ICC PT. Ch. I, 13 May 2008, paras. 31–36), and to have the victimisers prosecuted, tried and convicted, and subjected to a certain punishment (*Prosecutor v. Katanga and Ngudjolo*, Decision on the Set of Procedural Rights Attached to Procedural Status of Victim at the Pre-Trial Stage of the Case, ICC PT. Ch. I, 13 May 2008, paras. 37–44 and 160) are among the victims' personal interests. As a result, the Court has determined at once the rights that victims authorised to participate may exercise in the pre-trial stage of the case (the so-called "systematic approach") (*Prosecutor v. Katanga and Ngudjolo*, Decision on the Set of Procedural Rights Attached to Procedural Status of Victim at the Pre-Trial Stage of the Case, ICC PT. Ch. I, 13 May 2008, para. 49).

Personal interests of victims vis-à-vis trials

In other occasions, the Court has distinguished the general interests of the victims in receiving reparations, establishing the truth, protecting their dignity, ensuring their safety, etc. from the victims' "personal interests" whose affection they need to show in order to be authorised to participate in the trial of a case. As a result, the Court has determined that the question of whether the "personal interests" of a victim are affected pursuant to Article 68(3) during a trial is necessarily fact-dependent and is determined, for instance, by the victim's involvement in or presence at a particular incident which a Chamber is considering, or if the victim has suffered identifiable harm from said incident (the so-called "casuistic approach"). In other words, pursuant to Article 68(3) a victim must show the reasons why his or her interests are affected by the evidence or issues arising in a case before a Trial Chamber, which are defined in turn by the alleged crimes the accused faces (*Prosecutor v. Lubanga*, Decision on victim's participation, ICC T. Ch. I, 18 January 2008, paras. 96–98). In practical terms, a victim who wishes to participate in relation to any identified stage of the proceedings must set out in a written application not only the nature and the detail of the proposed intervention, but also the way in which his or her personal interest is affected at said proceeding (*Prosecutor v. Lubanga*, ICC T. Ch. I, 18 January 2008, para.

102). For instance, the personal interests of victims may be affected by the outcome of the confirmation hearing to the extent that it aims at either i) confirming the charges against those responsible for perpetrating the crimes which caused harm to the victims or ii) declining to confirm the charges for those not responsible for such crimes, so that the search for those who are criminally liable can continue (*Prosecutor v. Mbarushimana*, ICC PT. Ch. I, 11 August 2011, para. 23). Similarly, the personal interests of victims may, in principle, be affected by a determination as to the fitness of a suspect to participate in the hearing on the confirmation of charges against him, in particular by any delay in the proceedings which may result therefrom (*Prosecutor v. L. Gbagbo*, ICC PT. Ch. I, 15 August 2012, para. 13), as well as by the amendment of the charges against an accused person (*Prosecutor v. Kenyatta and Muthaura*, ICC PT. Ch. II, 29 January 2013, para. 11).

Personal interests of victims vis-à-vis appeals

Following the casuistic approach, the Appeals Chamber has ruled that any determination of whether the personal interests of victims are affected in relation to a particular appeal requires careful consideration on a case-by-case basis, assessing in each case whether the interests asserted by victims do not, in fact, fall outside their personal interests and belong instead to the role assigned to the Prosecutor (*Prosecutor v. Lubanga*, ICC A. Ch., Decision of the Appeals Chamber on the Joint Application of Victims a/0001/06 to a/0003/06 and a/0105/06 concerning the "Directions and Decision of the Appeals Chamber" of 2 February 2007, 13 June 2007, para. 28; *Prosecutor v. Lubanga*, ICC A. Ch., Decision, in limine, on Victim Participation in the appeals of the Prosecutor and the Defence against Trial Chamber I's Decision entitled "Decision on Victims' Participation", 16 May 2008, para. 42; *Prosecutor v. Katanga*, ICC A. Ch., 17 January 2013, para. 9; *Prosecutor v. Banda and Jerbo*, ICC A. Ch., 06 May 2013, para. 12; *Prosecutor v. L. Gbagbo*, ICC A. Ch., 27 August 2013, para. 11; *Prosecutor v. L. Gbagbo*, ICC A. Ch., 29 August 2013, para. 10). Accordingly, the Court has ruled that in their applications to participate in any appeal victims must include a statement in relation to whether and how their personal interests are affected by the issues on the appeal at hand (*Prosecutor v. Lubanga*, ICC A. Ch., 13 February 2007, para. 43; *Prosecutor v. Lubanga*, Decision of the Appeals Chamber on the Joint Application of Victims a/0001/06 to a/0003/06 and a/0105/06 concerning the "Directions and Decision of the Appeals Chamber" of 2 February 2007, ICC A. Ch., 13 June 2007, para. 23; *Situation in the Democratic Republic of the Congo*, ICC A. Ch., 14 February 2008, p. 3; *Situation in Darfur*, ICC A. Ch., 18 June 2008, para. 49). More specifically, in seeking to demonstrate that their personal interests are affected, victims should generally ensure, *inter alia*, that express reference is made to the specific facts behind their individual applications, and the precise manner in which those facts are said to fall within the issue under consideration on appeal (*Prosecutor v. L. Gbagbo*, ICC A. Ch., 27 August 2013, para. 11). Concerning appeals against judgments brought under Article 81, the Appeals Chamber has found that the victims' personal interests are affected in the same way as they were affected during the trial in which the victims participated (*Prosecutor v. Lubanga*, ICC A. Ch., 13 December 2012, para. 3; *Prosecutor v. Ngudjolo*, ICC A. Ch., 6 March 2013, para. 3).

Author: Enrique Carnero Rojo.

565 *Rule 85 determination*

The persons referred to as "victims" in this provision are not identified in the ICC Statute but in rule 85 of the Rules of Procedure and Evidence. In this regard, the Court has determined that once said identification has been made during a phase of the proceedings, the Chambers need not inquire again whether the same persons qualify as victims in subsequent proceedings, but must proceed to the next stage of the enquiry under Article 68(3), namely, whether their personal interests are affected by the issue(s) in the proceedings at hand (*Prosecutor v. Lubanga*, ICC T. Ch. I, Decision on victim's participation, 18 January 2008, para. 101; *Situation in the Demo-*

cratic Republic of the Congo, ICC A. Ch., Decision on Victim Participation in the appeal of the Office of Public Counsel for the Defence against Pre-Trial Chamber I's Decision of 7 December 2007 and in the appeals of the Prosecutor and the Office of Public Counsel for the Defence against Pre-Trial Chamber I's Decision of 24 December 2007, 30 June 2008, para. 92).

Author: Enrique Carnero Rojo.

566 *Positive obligation vis-à-vis victims*

Article 68(3) imposes a positive obligation on the Court *vis-à-vis* victims to enable them to exercise concretely and effectively their right to access the Court. This obligation has two dimensions, namely to allow victims to present their views and concerns, and to examine them (*Situation in the Democratic Republic of the Congo,* Decision on the Applications for Participation in the Proceedings of VPRS 1, VPRS 2, VPRS 3, VPRS 4, VPRS 5 and VPRS 6, ICC PT. Ch. I, 17 January 2006, para. 71). Nonetheless, said obligations are not automatic or unconditional, since Article 68(3) entrusts the Chambers with the power to first assess and then grant requests for participation and presentation of the victims' views and concerns. Accordingly, the victims' rights under Article 68(3) are not automatic, but subject to judicial scrutiny aimed at ensuring proper and effective participation (*Situation in Uganda,* ICC PT. Ch. II, 19 December 2007, paras. 32 and 35). In other words, Article 68(3) of the Statute confers power upon a victim to participate in any proceedings if i) he/she qualifies as a victim under the definition of this term provided by rule 85 of the Rules, and ii) his or her personal interests are affected by the proceedings in hand in, *that is,* by the issues, legal or factual, raised therein (*Situation in the Democratic Republic of the Congo,* ICC A. Ch., Judgment on victim participation in the investigation stage of the proceedings in the appeal of the OPCD against the decision of Pre-Trial Chamber I of 7 December 2007 and in the appeals of the OPCD and the Prosecutor against the decision of Pre-Trial Chamber I of 24 December 2007, 19 December 2008, para. 45).

Independent voice and role of victims

The Statute grants victims an independent voice and role in the proceedings before the Court and the Court has found that such independence should be preserved, including *vis-à-vis* the Prosecutor so that the victims can represent their interests (*Situation in the Democratic Republic of the Congo,* ICC PT. Ch. II, Decision on the Applications for Participation in the Proceedings of VPRS 1, VPRS 2, VPRS 3, VPRS 4, VPRS 5 and VPRS 6, ICC PT. Ch. I, 17 January 2006, para. 51; *Prosecutor v. Kony et al.,* ICC PT. Ch. II, 9 February 2007, p. 4; *Prosecutor v. Katanga and Ngudjolo,* ICC PT. Ch. I, Decision on the Set of Procedural Rights Attached to Procedural Status of Victim at the Pre-Trial Stage of the Case, 13 May 2008, para. 155). Allowing victims to participate in the proceedings does not mean that the suspect/accused is facing two prosecutors because victims may participate if they fulfil the conditions set forth in Article 68(3) of the Statute, namely that their personal interests are affected, their participation is found to be appropriate, and the manner of their participation is not prejudicial to or inconsistent with the rights of the accused and a fair and impartial trial (*Prosecutor v. Lubanga,* ICC A. Ch., 13 February 2007, para. 55; *Prosecutor v. Lubanga,* ICC A. Ch., Decision, in limine, on Victim Participation in the appeals of the Prosecutor and the Defence against Trial Chamber I's Decision entitled "Decision on Victims' Participation", 16 May 2008, para. 36; *Situation in Darfur,* ICC A. Ch., 18 June 2008, paras. 51 and 60; *Prosecutor v. Lubanga,* ICC A. Ch., 6 August 2008, para. 7; *Prosecutor v. Mbarushimana,* ICC PT. Ch. I, 11 August 2011, para. 20; *Prosecutor v. Bemba,* ICC A. Ch., 6 March 2012, para. 11; *Prosecutor v. Katanga,* ICC A. Ch., 17 January 2013, para. 6;*Prosecutor v. Banda and Jerbo,* ICC A. Ch., 6 May 2013, para. 11; *Prosecutor v. L. Gbagbo,* ICC A. Ch., 27 August 2013, para. 9; *Prosecutor v. L. Gbagbo,* ICC A. Ch., 29 August 2013, para. 8). From this point of view, the Court has noted that victims may themselves decide to engage in preparatory enquiries, without the Chamber or the Prosecutor monitoring the activities

mined to be appropriate by the Court[567] and in a manner which is not prejudicial to or inconsistent with the rights of the accused and a fair and impartial trial.[568] Such views and

---

of the victims outside the framework of judicial proceedings (*Situation in Uganda*, ICC PT. Ch. II, 19 December 2007, para. 42).

It must be noted that victims participating in the proceeding under Article 68(3) of the Statute are only "participants" who may present their views and concerns where their personal interests are affected, and only become "parties" during reparations proceedings (*Prosecutor v. Lubanga*, ICC A. Ch., 14 December 2012, para. 67). Similarly, the fact that victims are authorised to appear before the Court in person does not necessarily mean that victim participants must be treated automatically as witnesses. Whether or not victims appearing before the Court have the status of witnesses will depend on whether they are called as witnesses during the proceedings (*Prosecutor v. Lubanga*, ICC T. Ch. I, Decision on victim's participation, 18 January 2008, para. 132).

Scope of victims' views and concerns

Addressing the scope of the "views and concerns" of the victims, the Court has found that those of victims having communicated with the Court (rule 92) may relate not only to the review procedures triggered by a State or the Security Council referral (Article 53(3)(a) of the Statute), but also to the exercise of the *proprio motu* review powers vested in the Pre-Trial Chamber under Article 53(3)(b) of the Statute. In fact, Article 53 of the Statute provides the most significant scenario where victims may play an influential role outside the context of a case due to the concrete possibility that their personal interests would be affected by the decisions of the Prosecutor (*Prosecutor v. Kony et al.*, ICC PT. Ch. II, Decision on victims' applications for participation a/0010/06, a/0064/06 to a/0070/06, a/0081/06 to a/0104/06 and a/0111/06 to a/0127/06, ICC-02/04-01/05-252, 10 August 2007, para. 95). Moreover, in some specific contexts victims applying for participation may submit their views and concerns on the protective measures to be taken by the Chamber even prior to the consideration of the merits of their applications (*Prosecutor v. Kony et al.*, ICC PT. Ch. II, 10 August 2007, para. 99).

Author: Enrique Carnero Rojo.

[567] *Judicial discretion on appropriate stages*

The Chambers have discretion as to the appropriateness of the stage of the proceedings at which the views and concerns of the victims may be presented (*Prosecutor v. Lubanga*, Decision on the applications for participation in the proceedings a/0004/06 to a/0009/06, a/0016/06 to a/0063/06, a/0071/06 to a/0080/06 and a/0105/06 in the case of The Prosecutor v. Thomas Lubanga Dyilo, ICC PT. Ch. I, 20 October 2006, p. 10). Nonetheless, the Court's discretion in determining the appropriateness of a victim's participation has to be exercised considering the impact on the personal interests of the victim, the nature and scope of the proceedings, and the personal circumstances of the particular victim (*Prosecutor v. Kony et al.*, Decision on victims' applications for participation a/0010/06, a/0064/06 to a/0070/06, a/0081/06 to a/0104/06 and a/0111/06 to a/0127/06, ICC-02/04-01/05-252, ICC PT. Ch. II, 10 August 2007, paras. 88–89). The discretion of the Chamber cannot be exercised where the stage in which victims seek to be authorised to participate has ended, such as where victims request authorisation to participate in an appeal which has since been discontinued (*Prosecutor v. Katanga*, ICC A. Ch., 24 July 2014, para. 14).

Examples of appropriate stages

Pursuant to this general approach, it is appropriate for the victims to participate in proceedings for the adoption of protective measures. In fact, it is appropriate for victims who may be affected by the protective measures to be authorised to present their views and concerns even prior to being granted victim status in a case because their personal interests may be affected by the adoption of, or the failure to adopt, measures bearing upon their security and privacy (*Prosecu-*

---

tor v. Kony et al., ICC PT. Ch. II, Decision on victims' applications for participation a/0010/06, a/0064/06 to a/0070/06, a/0081/06 to a/0104/06 and a/0111/06 to a/0127/06, ICC-02/04-01/05-252, 10 August 2007, para. 98). Similarly, subject to their intervention being restricted to the scope determined by the charges brought against the suspect, the victims may participate in the confirmation hearing by presenting their views and concerns in order to help contribute to the prosecution of the crimes from which they allegedly suffered and to, where relevant, subsequently be able to obtain reparations for the harm suffered (*Prosecutor v. Lubanga*, ICC PT. Ch. I, Decision on the Arrangements for Participation of Victims a/0001/06, a/0002/06 and a/0003/06 at the Confirmation Hearing, 22 September 2006, p. 5).

Examples of inappropriate stages

By contrast, the Court has on occasion found inappropriate the participation of victims in the proceedings, considering the increased risk to the victims arising from their contact with the legal representatives for the exercise of their rights before the Court (*Prosecutor v. Lubanga*, ICC PT. Ch. I, Decision on the applications for participation in the proceedings a/0004/06 to a/0009/06, a/0016/06 to a/0063/06, a/0071/06 to a/0080/06 and a/0105/06 in the case of The Prosecutor v. Thomas Lubanga Dyilo, 20 October 2006, p. 11), or the fact that the Court need not take measures to review the Prosecutor's decisions and preserve evidence where there is no indication that the Prosecution has failed to do so in conducting its investigation (*Situation in the Democratic Republic of the Congo*, ICC PT. Ch. I, 26 September 2007, pp. 5–6). More generally, proceedings that are to be conducted with the exclusive participation of one party (as is the case with proceedings under Article 58 of the Statute) are, by definition, not "appropriate" for the purposes of victims' participation: victims would, therefore, not be allowed to participate in any such proceedings even if their personal interests were affected by the outcome of the said proceedings (*Situation in Kenya*, ICC PT. Ch. II, 11 February 2011, para. 13).

Appropriateness regarding investigation of situations

Addressing the appropriateness of the participation of victims at different stages of the proceedings, the Court initially found that the investigation of a situation as such was included in the "proceedings" (*Situation in the Democratic Republic of the Congo*, ICC PT. Ch. I, Decision on the Applications for Participation in the Proceedings of VPRS 1, VPRS 2, VPRS 3, VPRS 4, VPRS 5 and VPRS 6, 17 January 2006, paras. 46 and 54) because, despite the fact that no case involving victims is as yet under judicial scrutiny at this stage (*Prosecutor v. Kony et al.*, ICC PT. Ch. II, 10 August 2007, para. 89), the investigation can have an effect on the identification of the victimizers and the eventual issuance of orders for reparations (*Situation in the Democratic Republic of the Congo*, Decision on the Applications for Participation in the Proceedings of VPRS 1, VPRS 2, VPRS 3, VPRS 4, VPRS 5 and VPRS 6, ICC PT. Ch. I, 17 January 2006, para. 72; *Situation in Darfur*, ICC PT. Ch. I, 3 December 2007, para. 3). The Court initially determined that the participation of victims during the procedural stage of investigation of a situation was appropriate because it did not *per se* jeopardise the appearance of integrity and objectivity of the investigation, nor was it inherently inconsistent with basic considerations of efficiency and security (*Situation in the Democratic Republic of the Congo*, ICC PT. Ch. I, Decision on the Applications for Participation in the Proceedings of VPRS 1, VPRS 2, VPRS 3, VPRS 4, VPRS 5 and VPRS 6, 17 January 2006, para. 57). On this basis, the Pre-Trial Chambers initially found it appropriate for victims to participate in the "situation stage of the proceedings", thereby becoming "victims of the situation" (*Situation in the Democratic Republic of the Congo*, ICC PT. Ch. I, 7 December 2007, para. 2; *Situation in the Democratic Republic of the Congo*, ICC PT. Ch. I, 23 January 2008, p. 5) (*Situation in Darfur*, ICC PT. Ch. I, Decision on Request for leave to appeal the "Decision on the Requests of the OPCD on the Production of Relevant Supporting Documentation Pursuant to Regulation 86(2)(e) of the Regulations of the Court and on the Disclosure of Exculpatory Materials by the Prosecutor", 23 January 2008, p. 5; *Situation in the Democratic Republic of the Congo*, ICC PT. Ch. I, 3 July 2008, para. 26).

Eventually, however, the Appeals Chamber clarified that victim status cannot be granted to victims outside a judicial proceeding and victims are therefore not entitled to participate generally in the investigatory process. Article 68(3) of the Statute correlates victim participation to "proceedings", a term denoting a judicial cause pending before a Chamber. In contrast, an investigation is not a judicial proceeding but an inquiry conducted by the Prosecutor into the commission of a crime with a view to bringing to justice those deemed responsible. Consequently, victim participation can take place only within the context of judicial proceedings (*Prosecutor v. Lubanga*, ICC A. Ch., Judgment on the appeals of The Prosecutor and The Defence against Trial Chamber I's Decision on Victims' Participation of 18 January 2008, 11 July 2008, paras. 2 and 61–62; *Situation in the Democratic Republic of the Congo*, ICC A. Ch., Judgment on victim participation in the investigation stage of the proceedings in the appeal of the OPCD against the decision of Pre-Trial Chamber I of 7 December 2007 and in the appeals of the OPCD and the Prosecutor against the decision of Pre-Trial Chamber I of 24 December 2007, 19 December 2008, paras. 45 and 57).

Appropriateness regarding appeals

Regarding the appropriateness of victims' participation in appeal proceedings, an appeal (even interlocutory ones) is considered to be a separate and distinct stage of the proceedings. As a consequence, the Appeals Chamber is not bound by a previous ruling on the appropriateness of the participation by victims before a court of first instance (*Prosecutor v. Lubanga*, ICC A. Ch., 13 February 2007, para. 43; *Situation in Darfur*, ICC A. Ch., 18 June 2008, para. 49) and must itself determine whether the participation of victims is appropriate in the appeal at hand upon an application from the victims addressing *inter alia* the reasons why it is appropriate for the Appeals Chamber to permit their views and concerns to be presented (*Prosecutor v. Lubanga*, ICC A. Ch., Decision of the Appeals Chamber on the Joint Application of Victims a/0001/06 to a/0003/06 and a/0105/06 concerning the "Directions and Decision of the Appeals Chamber" of 2 February 2007, 13 June 2007, paras. 23 and 28; *Situation in the Democratic Republic of the Congo*, ICC A. Ch., 14 February 2008, p. 3; *Situation in Darfur*, ICC A. Ch., 18 June 2008, paras. 23 and 49; *Situation in the Democratic Republic of the Congo*, ICC A. Ch., Decision on Victim Participation in the appeal of the Office of Public Counsel for the Defence against Pre-Trial Chamber I's Decision of 7 December 2007 and in the appeals of the Prosecutor and the Office of Public Counsel for the Defence against Pre-Trial Chamber I's Decision of 24 December 2007, 30 June 2008, para. 88).

Author: Enrique Carnero Rojo.

568 *Recognition as victims and rights of the defence*

The very recognition of individuals as victims with a right to participate in the proceedings has been found not to affect the rights of the defence because said recognition is not, *per se*, prejudicial to the defence (*Situation in Darfur*, ICC PT. Ch. I, 3 December 2007, para. 4; *Situation in the Democratic Republic of the Congo*, ICC PT. Ch. I, 7 December 2007, para. 4). For instance, the Court found that the victims' participation did not create an imbalance *vis-à-vis* the Defence because the victims' right to submit requests for protective measures is linked to their fundamental interest in the protection of their security (*Situation in Uganda*, ICC PT. Ch. II, 19 December 2007, para. 44).

Extent of the victims' participation and rights of the defence

However, the Court must be attentive to the rights of the accused and the requirements of a fair and impartial trial when deciding on the extent of the participation of persons recognised as victims in the proceedings because Article 68(3) of the Statute does not pre-establish all modalities of participation, leaving them to the discretion of the Chambers (*Situation in the Democratic Republic of the Congo*, ICC PT. Ch. I, 23 January 2008, p. 5; *Situation in Darfur*, ICC PT. Ch. I, Decision on Request for leave to appeal the "Decision on the Requests of the OPCD on the

Production of Relevant Supporting Documentation Pursuant to Regulation 86(2)(e) of the Regulations of the Court and on the Disclosure of Exculpatory Materials by the Prosecutor", 23 January 2008, p. 5). The modalities of participation of victims must not be prejudicial to or inconsistent with the rights of the accused and a fair and impartial trial not only during the investigation stage (*Situation in the Democratic Republic of the Congo*, ICC PT. Ch. I, 7 December 2007, para. 3; *Situation in the Democratic Republic of the Congo*, ICC PT. Ch. I, 23 January 2008, p. 5; *Situation in the Democratic Republic of the Congo*, ICC PT. Ch. I, 19 March 2008, para. 5; *Prosecutor v. Katanga and Ngudjolo*, ICC PT. Ch. I, Decision on the Set of Procedural Rights Attached to Procedural Status of Victim at the Pre-Trial Stage of the Case, 13 May 2008, para. 53; *Situation in the Democratic Republic of the Congo*, ICC A. Ch., Judgment on victim participation in the investigation stage of the proceedings in the appeal of the OPCD against the decision of Pre-Trial Chamber I of 7 December 2007 and in the appeals of the OPCD and the Prosecutor against the decision of Pre-Trial Chamber I of 24 December 2007, 19 December 2008, para. 45) but also during the subsequent stages. For instance, if the victims request that their identities remain confidential during the proceedings leading to and at the confirmation of charges hearing, limits to their participation may be imposed, such as being precluded from adding any point of fact or any evidence in order not to violate the fundamental principle prohibiting anonymous accusations, having access to public documents only, and being allowed to be present at the public hearings only (*Prosecutor v. Lubanga*, ICC PT. Ch. I, Decision on the Arrangements for Participation of Victims a/0001/06, a/0002/06 and a/0003/06 at the Confirmation Hearing, 22 September 2006, pp. 6 and 8; *Prosecutor v. Katanga and Ngudjolo*, ICC PT. Ch. I, 27 February 2008, p. 7).

Chambers to ensure no negative impact on rights of the defence

Accordingly, once the Chamber has determined that the interests of a victim or group of victims are affected, it must exercise its discretion when deciding on the modalities of the participation of the victims in the proceedings to ensure that said participation is not prejudicial to or inconsistent with the rights of the Defence and fair and expeditious proceedings (*Situation in the Democratic Republic of the Congo*, Decision on the Applications for Participation in the Proceedings of VPRS 1, VPRS 2, VPRS 3, VPRS 4, VPRS 5 and VPRS 6, ICC PT. Ch. I, 17 January 2006, para. 70; *Situation in the Democratic Republic of the Congo*, ICC PT. Ch. I, 7 December 2007, para. 2; *Prosecutor v. Lubanga*, Decision on victim's participation, ICC T. Ch. I, 18 January 2008, para. 104; *Situation in the Democratic Republic of the Congo*, ICC PT. Ch. I, 19 March 2008, para. 5; *Prosecutor v. L. Gbagbo*, ICC A. Ch., 27 August 2013, para. 14; *Prosecutor v. L. Gbagbo*, ICC A. Ch., 29 August 2013, para. 11).

Appeals Chamber to ensure no negative impact on rights of the defence

In order to ensure no negative impact on rights of the defence, the Court should analyse the impact of the victims' participation on the rights of the defence when granting them the possibility to submit their views and concerns. In proceedings before the Appeals Chamber, the victims concerned must argue why the presentation of their views and concerns would not be prejudicial to or inconsistent with the rights of the defence (*Situation in the Democratic Republic of the Congo*, ICC A. Ch., 14 February 2008, p. 3; *Prosecutor v. Lubanga*, ICC A. Ch., Decision, in limine, on Victim Participation in the appeals of the Prosecutor and the Defence against Trial Chamber I's Decision entitled "Decision on Victims' Participation", 16 May 2008, para. 48). For instance, upon declaring clearly inadmissible an appeal touching upon a suspect's fundamental right to liberty, the Appeals Chamber simply denied the victims' request to participate in said appeal because any delay for procedural reasons in the delivery of the decision on their request could have an effect on the suspect's release and on his fundamental right to liberty (*Prosecutor v. Mbarushimana*, ICC A. Ch., 24 January 2012, para. 34). In turn, the victims' views and concerns must be specifically limited solely to the issues arising in the appeal and to the extent that their personal interests are affected by the proceedings, in order for the manner of par-

concerns may be presented by the legal representatives of the victims where the Court considers it appropriate, in accordance with the Rules of Procedure and Evidence.[569]

---

ticipation of victims to comply with the rights of the suspect/accused and a fair and impartial trial (*Prosecutor v. Lubanga*, ICC A. Ch., Decision, in limine, on Victim Participation in the appeals of the Prosecutor and the Defence against Trial Chamber I's Decision entitled "Decision on Victims' Participation", 16 May 2008, para. 50; *Situation in the Democratic Republic of the Congo*, ICC A. Ch., Decision on Victim Participation in the appeal of the Office of Public Counsel for the Defence against Pre-Trial Chamber I's Decision of 7 December 2007 and in the appeals of the Prosecutor and the Office of Public Counsel for the Defence against Pre-Trial Chamber I's Decision of 24 December 2007, 30 June 2008, para. 101; *Prosecutor v. Lubanga*, ICC A. Ch., 6 August 2008, paras. 12–13).

Participation of victims as witnesses

Moreover, although a general ban on the victims' participation in the proceedings if they may be called as witnesses would be contrary to the aim and purpose of Article 68(3) of the Statute and the Chambers' obligation to establish the truth, the Court must establish whether the participation by a victim who is also a witness may adversely affect the rights of the defence at a particular stage in the case, taking into consideration the modalities of participation by victims with dual status, the need for their participation and the rights of the accused to a fair and expeditious trial (*Prosecutor v. Lubanga*, ICC T. Ch. I, Decision on Victim's Participation, 18 January 2008, paras. 133–134).

Author: Enrique Carnero Rojo.

[569] *Victims' direct participation*

The use of the term "may" in Article 68(3), the lack of reference to a legal representative in rule 89(3) and the victim's freedom to choose a legal representative foreseen in rule 90(1) entail that a victim's participation in the proceedings before the Court is not conditional upon the victim being assisted by a legal representative, even after the victim' application has been granted (*Prosecutor v. Kony et al.*, ICC PT. Ch. II, Decision on legal representation, appointment of counsel for the defence, protective measures and time-limit for submission of observations on applications for participation a/0010/06, a/0064/06 to a/0070/06, a/0081/06 to a/0104/06 and a/0111/06 to a/0127/06, 1 February 2007, paras. 3–6; *Prosecutor v. Ruto and Sang*, ICC T. Ch. V, 3 October 2012, para. 49; *Prosecutor v. Kenyatta and Muthaura*, ICC T. Ch. V, 03 October 2012, para. 48). In fact, victims have the right to participate directly in the proceedings, since Article 68(3) provides that when the Court considers it appropriate the views and concerns of victims may otherwise be presented by a legal representative (*Prosecutor v. Lubanga*, ICC T. Ch. I, Decision on Victim's Participation, 18 January 2008, para. 115; *Prosecutor v. Ruto and Sang*, ICC T. Ch. V, 3 October 2012, para. 26; *Prosecutor v. Kenyatta and Muthaura*, ICC T. Ch. V, 3 October 2012, para. 25).

Victims' participation through legal representatives

Nonetheless, the Court has found that there are at least two categories of victims: i) victims admitted to the proceedings and assisted by a legal representative, who enjoy enhanced procedural rights under rule 91, and ii) victims admitted to the proceedings but not assisted by a legal representative, who enjoy more limited rights of participation (*Prosecutor v. Kony et al.*, ICC PT. Ch. II, Decision on legal representation, appointment of counsel for the defence, protective measures and time-limit for submission of observations on applications for participation a/0010/06, a/0064/06 to a/0070/06, a/0081/06 to a/0104/06 and a/0111/06 to a/0127/06, 1 February 2007, para. 10). The latter may make opening and closing statements, but are precluded from participating in hearings and from questioning a party or a witness (*Prosecutor v. Kony et al.*, ICC PT. Ch. II, 1 February 2007, para. 7).

---

4. The Victims and Witnesses Unit may advise the Prosecutor and the Court[570] on appropriate protective measures, security arrangements, counselling and assistance as referred to in Article 43, paragraph 6.[571]

5. Where the disclosure of evidence or information pursuant to this Statute may lead to the grave endangerment of the security of a witness or his or her family, the Prosecutor may, for the purposes of any proceedings conducted prior to the commencement of the trial,[572] withhold such evidence or information and instead submit a summary thereof. Such measures shall be exercised in a manner which is not prejudicial to or inconsistent with the rights of the accused and a fair and impartial trial.[573]

Author: Enrique Carnero Rojo.

[570] *Others at risk on account of the activities of the Court as clients*

On the basis of *inter alia* Article 68(4) of the ICC Statute, the Appeals Chamber has found that specific provisions of the Statute and the Rules provide for the protection not only of witnesses and victims and members of their families, but also of others at risk on account of the activities of the Court, indicating an overarching concern to ensure that persons are not unjustifiably exposed to risk through the activities of the Court (*Prosecutor v. Katanga*, ICC A. Ch., 13 May 2008, para. 54).

Court as client

Similarly, reading Article 68(4) of the ICC Statute together with Article 43(6), the Appeals Chamber has concluded that it may be appropriate and of assistance to it to hear from the Registrar in particular appeals dealing with protective measures (*Prosecutor v. Katanga and Ngudjolo*, ICC A. Ch., 11 July 2008, para. 4).

Author: Enrique Carnero Rojo.

[571] *Victims and Witnesses Unit's exclusivity for victims' safety and security*

Article 68 of the Statute, dealing *inter alia* with the protection of victims, refers to the Registry as a whole and not to the Office of Public Counsel for Victims *per se*, since the Office falls within the remit of the Registry solely for administrative purposes. Therefore, the OPCV has no specific functions relating to any concerns victims may have for their security and safety. Consultation with the Victims and Witnesses Unit is the proper way to address the victims' safety and security issues (*Prosecutor v. Kony et al.*, ICC PT. Ch. II, 16 March 2007, pp. 5–6). Similarly, the decision of the drafters to create a single Victims and Witnesses Unit within the Registry constitutes a clear endorsement of a system of witness protection in which the core role is played by the Registry and a limited mandate is given to the Prosecution, ensuring the equality of arms between the parties as well as the effective use of the Court's resources (*Prosecutor v. Katanga and Ngudjolo*, ICC PT. Ch. I, 21 April 2008, paras. 28 and 31). Nonetheless, if the Victims and Witnesses Unit properly assesses and rejects referrals to its protection programme, thereafter it is for the referring party to decide whether to secure any other protective solution, as it considers appropriate (*Prosecutor v. Lubanga*, ICC T. Ch. I, 24 April 2008, para. 80).

Author: Enrique Carnero Rojo.

[572] The aim behind Article 68(5) – as well as behind Article 61(5) – is first and foremost to ensure the safety of Prosecution witnesses, and minimise the potentially traumatic effects of giving testimony in court by exempting witnesses from the requirement to do so twice, first before the Pre-Trial Chamber and again before the Trial Chamber (*Prosecutor v. Lubanga*, ICC PT. Ch. I, 15 May 2006, Annex I, para. 99).

Author: Enrique Carnero Rojo.

[573] Consequently, although the Defence must, in principle, have access to the non-redacted version of the prior statements of any witness on whose written or oral testimony the Prosecution in-

6. A State may make an application for necessary measures to be taken in respect of the protection of its servants or agents and the protection of confidential or sensitive information.[574]

---

tends to rely at the confirmation hearing (*Prosecutor v. Lubanga*, ICC PT. Ch. I, 15 May 2006, Annex I, para. 98), said information may be withheld and replaced with summaries when the disclosure to the Defence of said witness statements, transcripts of witness interviews and investigators' notes and reports of witness interviews would lead to the identification of the Prosecution witnesses, even with the redactions proposed by the Prosecution (*Prosecutor v. Lubanga*, ICC PT. Ch. I, First Decision on the Prosecution Requests and Amended Requests for Redactions under Rule 81, 15 September 2006, paras. 8–13).

Author: Enrique Carnero Rojo.

[574] See the commentary on Article 72.

Cross-references:

Articles 43(6), 54(1)(b), 54(3)(f) 61(5), 67(1) and 72.

Rules 16, 17, 18, 19, 43, 81, 85, 86, 87, 88, 89, 90, 91, 92 93, 119(3), 131(2), 134 and 194(3).

Regulations 20, 41, 42 and 86

Doctrine:

1. Silvia A. Fernández de Gurmendi, "The Process of Negotiations", in Roy S. Lee (ed.), T*he International Criminal Court: The Making of the Rome Statute – Issues, Negotiations, Results*, Kluwer Law International, The Hague, 1999, pp. 217–26.

2. David Donat-Cattin, "Article 68: Protection of Victims and Witnesses and their Participation in the Proceedings", in Otto Triffterer (ed.), *Commentary on the Rome Statute of the International Criminal Court: Observers' Notes, Article by Article*, Nomos Verlagsgesellschaft, Baden-Baden, 1999, pp. 869–88.

3. John R.W.D. Jones, "Protection of Victims and Witnesses", in Antonio Cassese, Paola Gaeta and John R.W.D. Jones (eds.), *The Rome Statute of the International Criminal Court: A Commentary,* 2nd ed., Oxford University Press, 2002, pp. 1355–70.

4. Claude Jorda and Jérôme de Hemptinne, "The Status and Role of the Victim", in Antonio Cassese, Paola Gaeta and John R.W.D. Jones (eds.), *The Rome Statute of the International Criminal Court: A Commentary,* 2nd ed., Oxford University Press, 2002, pp. 1387–1419.

5. Carsten Stahn, Héctor Olásolo and Kate Gibson, "Participation of Victims in Pre-Trial Proceedings of the ICC", in *Journal of International Criminal Justice*, 2006, vol. 4, no. 2, pp. 219–38.

6. David Donat-Cattin, "Article 68: Protection of Victims and Witnesses and their Participation in the Proceedings", in Otto Triffterer (ed.), *Commentary on the Rome Statute of the International Criminal Court: Observers' Notes, Article by Article*, 2nd ed., C.H. Beck/Hart/Nomos, Munich/Oxford/Baden-Baden, 2008, pp. 1275–1300.

7. Paolina Massidda and Caroline Walter, "Article 68: Protection et participation au procès des victimes et des témoins", in Julian Fernandez and Xavier Pacreau (eds.), *Statut de Rome de la Cour pénale international: Commentaire Article par Article*, Pedone, Paris, 2012, pp. 1545–76.

8. Rogier Bartels, "Rome Statute of the International Criminal Court – Article 68: Protection of Victims and Witnesses and their Participation in the Proceedings", in Paul De Hert, Mathias Holvoet, Jean Flamme and Olivia Struyven (eds.), *Code of International Criminal Law and Procedure*, Larcier, Brussels, 2013, pp. 322–43.

9. Anne-Marie De Brouwer and Mikaela Heikkilä, "Victim Issues: Participation, Protection, Reparation, and Assistance", in Göran Sluiter, Håkan Friman, Suzannah Linton, Sergey Va-

siliev and Salvatore Zappalà (eds.), *International Criminal Procedure: Principles and Rules*, Oxford University Press, Oxford, 2013, pp. 1299–1337.

Author: Enrique Carnero Rojo.

Article 69
Evidence[575]

1. Before testifying, each witness shall, in accordance with the Rules of Procedure and Evidence, give an undertaking as to the truthfulness of the evidence to be given by that witness.[576]

2. The testimony of a witness at trial shall be given in person, except to the extent provided by the measures set forth in Article 68 or in the Rules of Procedure and Evidence. The Court may also permit the giving of viva voce (oral) or recorded testimony of a witness by means of video or audio technology, as well as the introduction of documents or written transcripts, subject to this Statute and in accordance with the Rules of Procedure and Evidence. These measures shall not be prejudicial to or inconsistent with the rights of the accused.[577]

---

[575] *General remarks*:

Article 69 provides the main principles on the admissibility of evidence. The ICC Statute and the Rules of Procedure and Evidence provides for a flexible approach to the admission of evidence unhindered by technical rules. Strict and technical provisions are primarily used in common law systems where the law and fact-finding functions have been separated, allocating the former to the judge and the latter to the jury. Part of the rationale is to prevent erroneous conclusions which might be drawn by a lay jury receiving prejudicial or unreliable evidence. From a civil law perspective it is argued that there is no need to guard professional judges because they are not open to prejudice in the same way as a jury. Civil law systems combine the law and fact-finding functions by using professional judges. The ICC uses professional judges and thus there is no need for technical rules on admissibility.

While Article 69 contains more specific rules on evidence, Article 64(9)(a) provides for the general power of the Trial Chamber to "[r]ule on the admissibility or relevance of evidence".

Article 69 is contained in Part 6 concerning the trial proceedings but Article 69 refers more broadly to "the Court" rather than "the trial chamber". Rule 63(1) clarifies this ambiguity by providing that the rules of evidence together with Article 69, apply in all proceedings before all Chambers.

Author: Mark Klamberg.

[576] Before testifying, witnesses are required to give the following undertaking, as provided for in rule 66(1): "I solemnly declare that I will speak the truth, the whole truth and nothing but the truth".

Rule 66(2) further specifies that persons under the age of 18 or a person whose judgment has been impaired and who does not understand the nature of a solemn undertaking may be allowed to testify without this solemn undertaking if the Chamber considers that the person is able to describe matters of which he or she has knowledge and that the person understands the meaning of the duty to speak the truth.

Rule 66(3) provides that before testifying, the witness shall be informed that giving false testimony is an offence under Article 70(1)(a).

Cross-references:

Rules 65 and 66.

Author: Mark Klamberg.

[577] Article 69(2) expresses an aspiration that testimony of a witness at trial shall be given in person. In *Prosecutor v. Lubanga*, ICC T. Ch., Decision on the Prosecution's application for admission

---

of four documents from the bar table pursuant to Article 64(9), 20 January 2011, para. 13, the Trial Chamber states that "[t]he statutory framework of the Court establishes the clear presumption that the evidence of a witness at trial will be given orally".

However, the ICC Statute gives conflicting messages as to whether the Court may compel an individual to testify. Article 93(1)(e) provides that States Parties shall provide assistance with "[f]acilitating the voluntary appearance of persons as witnesses or experts before the Court" which suggest that it is voluntary. On the other hand, Article 64(6)(b) provides that the Trial Chamber may "[r]equire the attendance and testimony of witnesses [...] by obtaining, if necessary, the assistance of States". In *Ruto et al.*, the Trial Chamber found that that the Chamber may – as a compulsory measure – order or subpoena the appearance of witnesses. It also stated that pursuant to Article 93(1)(d) and(1) of the Statute, the Trial Chamber can, by way of requests for cooperation, obligate Kenya both to serve summonses and to assist in compelling the attendance (before the Chamber) of the witnesses summoned, *Prosecutor v. Ruto et al.*, ICC T. Ch., Decision on Prosecutor's Application for Witness Summonses and resulting Request for State Party Cooperation, ICC-01/09-01/11-1274-Corr2, 17 April 2014, paras. 100 and 193. The Appeals Chamber upheld the decision by the Trial Chamber. It found that the Trial Chamber has the power to compel witnesses to appear before it, thereby creating a legal obligation for the individuals concerned. The Appeals Chamber also stated that under Article 93(1) (b) of the Statute the Court may request a State Party to compel witnesses to appear before the Court sitting *in situ* in the State Party's territory or by way of video-link, *Prosecutor v. Ruto et al.*, ICC A. Ch., Judgment on the appeals of William Samoei Ruto and Mr Joshua Arap Sang against the decision of Trial Chamber V (A) of 17 April 2014 entitled "Decision on Prosecutor's Application for Witness Summonses and resulting Request for State Party Cooperation", ICC-01/09-01/11-1598, 9 October 2014.

The Court may also permit the giving of viva voce (oral) or recorded testimony of a witness by means of video or audio technology, as well as the introduction of documents or written transcripts, subject to this Statute and in accordance with the Rules of Procedure and Evidence. These measures shall not be prejudicial to or inconsistent with the rights of the accused.

The Court may also permit the giving of viva voce (oral) or recorded testimony of a witness by means of video or audio technology. in such cases, rule 67 requires that the witness may be examined by the prosecutor, the defence and the Chamber, primarily in order to secure the accused's right to confront the witness. In *Prosecutor v. Bemba*, ICC T. Ch., Public redacted decision on the "Prosecution request to hear Witness CAR-OTP-PPPP-0036's testimony via video-link", 3 February 2012, para. 7 the Trial Chamber stated that "[o]ne of the relevant criteria for determining whether or not a witness may be allowed to give viva voce (oral) testimony by means of video technology relates to the witness's personal circumstances, which have thus far been interpreted as being linked to, *inter alia*, the well-being of a witness".

Article 69(2) also provides that the Trial may permit the introduction of documents or transcripts as long as this is not prejudicial to or inconsistent with the rights of the accused. In *Prosecutor v. Katanga and Chui*, ICC T. Ch., Decision on Defence Request to Admit into Evidence Entirety of Document DRC-OTP-1017-0572, 25 May 2011, para. 1, a witness read a prior recorded statement in silence and the extract was admitted in evidence. The Trial Chamber rejected the motion of the defence to have the entire prior recorded statement admitted into evidence.

The *Tadić* Trial Chamber has stated that the evidentiary value of testimony provided by video-link, although weightier than that of testimony given by deposition, is not as weighty as evidence given in the courtroom (*Prosecutor v. Tadić*, ICTY T. Ch., 25 June 1996, para. 21).

Cross-references:

Rules 67 and 68.

Author: Mark Klamberg.

3. The parties may submit evidence relevant to the case, in accordance with Article 64. The Court shall have the authority to request the submission of all evidence that it considers necessary for the determination of the truth.[578]

4. The Court may rule on the relevance or admissibility of any evidence, taking into account, inter alia, the probative value of the evidence and any prejudice that such evidence may cause to a fair trial or to a fair evaluation of the testimony of a witness, in accordance with the Rules of Procedure and Evidence.[579]

---

[578] Articles 64(6)(d) and 69(3) of the ICC Statute grants the Judges authority to order the parties to submit additional evidence. This means that that the parties are not free to withhold evidence that the Court considers to be important, regardless whether it is incriminatory or exculpatory.

There is a risk that exercise of powers under Article 69(3) may favour one party at the expense of the other party. In *Lubanga*, the Trial Chamber emphasised its "statutory obligation to request the submission of all evidence that is necessary for determining the truth under Article 69(3) of the Statute, although this requirement must not displace the obligation of ensuring the accused receives a fair trial" (*Lubanga*, ICC T. Ch. I, 18 January 2008, para. 121).

In *Prosecutor v. Katanga and Ngudjolo*, the Single Judge considered "that Article 69(3) of the Statute is not applicable during the pre-trial proceedings conducted before the Pre-Trial Chamber because (i) the Pre-Trial Chamber is not a truth-finder; and (ii) according to the literal interpretation of Article 69(3) of the Statute, its application is subject to consideration of the competent Chamber that evidence other than that introduced by the Prosecution and the defence is 'necessary for the determination of the truth' " (*Prosecutor v. Katanga and Ngudjolo*, ICC PT. Ch. I, Decision on the Set of Procedural Rights Attached to Procedural Status of Victim at the Pre-Trial Stage of the Case, 13 May 2008, paras. 107–113). The Pre-Trial Chamber in *Bemba* took the opposite view when it held that "the rules concerning evidence in Article 69 of the Statute, including the authority of the Chamber to request the submission of further evidence, apply at the pre-trial stage of the proceedings, taking into account the specific purpose and limited scope of the confirmation of the charges". The Pre-Trial Chamber admitted however that the application of Article 69(3) of the ICC Statute at the confirmation stage is restricted since, in contrast to the trial stage, the Chamber does not have to determine the guilt of the person prosecuted beyond a reasonable doubt. It emphasised that "the search for truth is the principal goal of the Court as a whole" (*Prosecutor v. Bemba*, ICC PT. Ch. III, Decision on the Evidence Disclosure System and Setting a Timetable for Disclosure between the Parties, 31 July 2008, paras. 8–11).

Cross-references:
Rule 69.
Author: Mark Klamberg.

[579] As stated earlier, the ICC Statute has adopted a flexible approach. Article 69(4) provides that in addition to relevance other factors need to be considered for admissibility, including the probative value of evidence and any prejudice such evidence may cause to a fair trial or to a fair evaluation of the testimony of a witness. Rule 63 add general provisions relating to the admissibility of evidence.

During the negotiations preceding the ICC Statute it was decided as a compromise to give some guidance but leave details to the Rules and the Court's own jurisprudence. An initial French draft of rule 63 would have the principle of admissibility of all evidence (Preparatory Commission for the International Criminal Court, Proposal submitted by France concerning the Rules of Procedure and Evidence: Part 3, section 1, subsection 2, 22 February 1999, rule 37(1)), effectively undoing the compromise reached in Rome. The pendulum swung in the opposite direction and a subsequent proposal would have obliged the Court to asses all evidence for the purpose of admissibility. The adopted version of rule 63 is a compromise, which authorises, rather than obliges, a chamber "to assess freely all evidence submitted in order to determine its relevance or admissibility in accordance with Article 69" (Piragoff, 2008, 1305–1306).

Relevance

The *Katanga and Ngudjolo* Trial Chamber has clarified that "[i]f the evidence tendered makes the existence of a fact at issue more or less probable, it is relevant. Whether or not this is the case depends on the purpose for which the evidence is adduced (Prosecutor v. Katanga and Ngudjolo (Case No. ICC-01/04–01/07), ICC T. Ch. II, Decision on the Bar Table Motion of the Defence of Germain Katanga, 21 October 2011, para. 16)". In *Prosecutor v. Katanga and Ngudjolo*, ICC T. Ch., Decision on the Bar Table Motion of the Defence of Germain Katanga, 21 October 2011, paras. 16–19, the Trial Chamber excluded nine items for lack of relevance.

Reliability

During the drafting of Rule 63 there was an attempt to include reliability as a factor to be freely assessed by a Chamber in determining relevance or admissibility. As there was no consensus, the rule is silent on the issue (Piragoff, 2008, 1306). At the *ad hoc* tribunals there has been controversy as to whether reliability is a separate or inherent component of the admissibility of a particular item of evidence (May and Wierda, 2002, 107 and 109). For example, in *Delalić et al.* the defence argued that the determination of reliability was a separate component, a first hurdle to be passed before the Trial Chamber can proceed to consider the relevance and probative value of the evidence. The Trial Chamber rejected this argument and stated that "it is an implicit requirement of the Rules that the Trial Chamber give due considerations to indicia of reliability when assessing the relevance and probative value of evidence at the stage of determining its admissibility" (*Prosecutor v. Delalić et al.*, ICTY T. Ch., 19 January 1998 (I), paras. 19–20). The Pre-Trial Chamber in *Katanga and Ngudjolo* mentioned the controversy at the ICTY as to whether reliability is a separate or inherent component of the admissibility of a particular item of evidence. The Pre-Trial Chamber decided to "to consider reliability as a component of the evidence when determining its weight" (*Prosecutor v. Katanga and Ngudjolo*, ICC PT. Ch. I, 30 September 2008, para. 78).

The Chamber has a general power under Article 69(4) of the ICC Statute to exclude evidence if its probative value is substantially outweighed by the need to ensure a fair trial. In *Prosecutor v. Lubanga*, ICC T. Ch., Decision on the request by the legal representative of victims a/0001/06, a/0002/06, a/0003/06, a/0049/06, a/0007/08, a/0149/08, a/0155/07, a/0156/07, a/0404/08, a/0405/08, a/0406/08, a/0407/08, a/0409/08, a0149/07 and a/0162/07 for admission of the final report of the Panel of Experts on the illegal exploitation of natural resources and other forms of wealth of the Democratic Republic of the Congo as evidence, 22 September 2009, the Chamber weighed the potential prejudicial effect against the probative value of a report the legal representative of victims sought to introduce. Weighing the slight relevance and the low probative value of the Report and its real prejudicial potential, the Chamber was unpersuaded that it should be admitted (para. 34).

Status of Pre-Trial Chamber decisions

Rule 63(1) provides that the rules of evidence, together with Article 69, apply in all proceedings before all chambers. Does this mean that all evidentiary matters will be treated identically in all stages of the proceedings, should the Pre-Trial Chamber's assessment on admissibility be binding upon the Trial Chamber in relation to the same piece of evidence? In *Prosecutor v. Lubanga*, ICC PT. Ch. I, Decision on the Prosecution and Defence applications for leave to appeal the Decision on the confirmation of charges, 24 May 2007, PTC I noted that Pre-Trial Chamber rulings on the admissibility and probative value of evidence are not binding on a Trial Chamber.

In *Prosecutor v. Bemba*, Decision on the admission into evidence of materials contained in the prosecution's list of evidence, 19 November 2010, paras. 8–10, the majority of the Chamber

5. The Court shall respect and observe privileges on confidentiality as provided for in the Rules of Procedure and Evidence.[580]

6. The Court shall not require proof of facts of common knowledge but may take judicial notice of them.[581]

---

decided to admit *prima facie* before the start of the presentation of evidence, all statements of witnesses to be called to give evidence at trial and all the documents submitted by the prosecution in its list of evidence. The Chamber emphasised that it would evaluate the probative value and give the appropriate weight to the evidence as a whole, at the end of the case when making its final judgment. The Chamber considered "that a ruling on admissibility is not a precondition for the admission of any evidence". Judge Kuniko Ozaki dissented arguing that the concept of "prima facie admissibility" does not exist in the ICC Statute or in the Rules of Procedure and Evidence. Furthermore, he holds that Article 69(2) of the ICC Statute clearly imposes the principle of primacy of orality in proceedings before the Court. Instead, he submits that in appropriate cases, the parties may request the Chamber to admit the prior-recorded statements in order to impeach the witness, which would be exceptional in most court proceedings, *Prosecutor v. Bemba*, ICC T. Ch., Dissenting Opinion of Judge Kuniko Ozaki on the Decision on the admission into evidence of materials contained in the prosecution's list of evidence, 23 November 2010, paras. 4–6, 12. The Appeals Chamber reversed the Trial Chamber's decision and ruled that admission into evidence of the witnesses' written statements requires a cautious item-by-item analysis (*Prosecutor v. Jean-Pierre Bemba Gombo*, ICC A. Ch., Judgment on the appeals of Mr Jean-Pierre Bemba Gombo and the Prosecutor against the decision of Trial Chamber III entitled "Decision on the admission into evidence of materials contained in the prosecution's list of evidence", 3 May 2011, paras. 2–3, 45 and 70).

Cross-references:

Rules 63, 64, 70, 71 and 72.

Author: Mark Klamberg.

[580] Paragraph 5 provides that the Court shall respect and observe privileges on confidentiality as provided for in the Rules of Procedure and Evidence. Rule 73 sets out the following categories of privileged communications: 1) Lawyer–Client Privilege; 2) Communications made in the course of a confidential relationship producing a reasonable expectation of privacy and non-disclosure; and 3) information, documents or other evidence of the International Committee of the Red Cross (ICRC).

Cross-references:

Rule 73.

Author: Mark Klamberg.

[581] Judicial notice allows the fact-finder to accept facts of common knowledge. Such facts include those of which an informed and reasonable person has knowledge or which he or she can learn from reliable accessible sources.

Facts of common knowledge

UN documents, including resolutions of the Security Council will likely be regarded as facts of common knowledge before the ICC (Piragoff, 2008, p. 1330).

Adjudicated Facts

Judicial notice also allows the fact-finder to accept adjudicated facts. However, the ICC has no equivalent to rule 94(B) of the *ad hoc* tribunals, which would allow a Chamber to admit adjudicated facts under the power of judicial notice. ICC rule 68 permits the admission of written transcripts but is more restrictive than the comparable rules of the *ad hoc* tribunals; it does not mention judicial notice of adjudicated facts. Considering the specific provisions of ICC rule 68 Pira-

---

7. Evidence obtained by means of a violation of this Statute or internationally recognized human rights shall not be admissible if:

(a) The violation casts substantial doubt on the reliability of the evidence; or

(b) The admission of the evidence would be antithetical to and would seriously damage the integrity of the proceedings.[582]

---

goff holds it as unlikely that the Court will exercise its authority to admit adjudicated facts under the power of judicial notice (Piragoff, 2008, pp. 1317–1318 and 1331).

Documentary evidence

ICTR Rule 94(B) and SCSL Rule 94(b) the Chamber may take judicial notice of documentary evidence from other proceedings. Article 69(6) of the ICC Statute does not explicitly deal with judicial notice of documentary evidence. ICC rule 69 covers agreements as to facts, which are, *inter alia*, contained in the contents of a document. Piragoff argues that rule 69 and Article 69(6) do provide vehicles for bringing uncontroversial transcripts (Piragoff, 2008, p. 1317).

Author: Mark Klamberg.

[582] The issue of the admissibility of illegally or improperly obtained evidence raises contradictory and complex matters of principle. One purpose of having rules about collecting evidence, for example rules on search and seizure, is to ensure that the evidence is of good quality and thus reliable. There is also an interest in due process. Thus, an accused person who has suffered an illegal attack on his rights prior to the trial proceedings, for example through torture, should not be subject to further harm by the use of fruits of such an attack in a trial. On the other hand, in the interest of crime control, all evidence that proves that the accused is guilty should be used, even if it is illegally obtained.

During the negotiations on the ICC Statute "some delegations wanted to exclude evidence by means of a violation of human rights, but this formulation was regarded as too broad" (Behrens, p. 246). Instead the Court has to distinguish between minor infringements of procedural safeguards and more serious violations. Whereas violations of human rights law may be a ground for excluding evidence, a violation of national laws does not require exclusion, as long as it is not a violation of internationally recognised human rights. According to Article 69(8) the Court "shall not rule on the application of the State's national law ... [w]hen deciding on the relevance or admissibility of evidence collected by a State". In *Prosecutor v. Lubanga*, ICC PT. Ch. I, Decison on the Confirmation of Charges, 29 January 2007, paragraph 69, PTC I stated that the mere fact that a national court "has ruled on the unlawfulness of the search and seizure conducted by the national authorities cannot be considered binding on the Court".

In *Lubanga* the Defence requested that the Prosecution evidence should be declared inadmissible on the grounds that it had been procured in violation of Congolese rules of procedure and internationally recognised human rights. The Pre-Trial Chamber observed the following:

The mere fact that a national court has ruled on the unlawfulness of the search and seizure conducted by the national authorities cannot be considered binding on the Court. This is clear from Article 69(8) which states that "[w]hen deciding on the relevance or admissibility of evidence collected by a State, the Court shall not rule on the application of the State's national law" (*Prosecutor v. Lubanga*, ICC PT. Ch. I, 29 January 2007, paras. 62–63 and 69).

In order to determine whether there had been an illegality amounting to a violation of internationally recognised human rights or only an infringement of the domestic rules of procedure, the Chamber sought guidance from international human rights jurisprudence concerning the right to privacy. The Chamber found, in the light of ECHR jurisprudence, that the search and seizure were an infringement of the principle of proportionality and as such a violation of inter-

8. When deciding on the relevance or admissibility of evidence collected by a State, the Court shall not rule on the application of the State's national law.[583]

---

nationally recognised human rights. Even though a violation had occurred, the Judges observed that they had the discretion to seek an appropriate balance between the ICC Statute's fundamental values in their determination whether evidence is admissible. Such fundamental values would arguably include the interests of due process and crime control. In regard to the first limb of the alternative embodied in Article 69(7)(a), the Chamber held the view that the infringement of the principle of proportionality did not affect the reliability of the evidence seized. Had the search and seizure been conducted in full adherence to the principle of proportionality the content of items seized would be the same. The Chamber also considered the second limb of the alternative embodied in Article 69(7)(b), the adverse effect that the admission of such evidence could have on the integrity of the proceedings (*Prosecutor v. Lubanga*, ICC PT. Ch. I, 29 January 2007, paras. 81–86).

Cross-references:

Rules 74 and 75.

Author: Mark Klamberg.

[583] Article 69(8) is consistent with rule 63(5) that the Chambers shall not apply national laws governing evidence, except in accordance with Article 21. There is a relationship between the irrelevance of national law and the exclusionary rule in Article 69(7). In *Prosecutor v. Lubanga*, ICC PT. Ch. I, Decison on the confirmation of charges, 29 January 2007, paragraph 69, PTC I stated that the mere fact that a national court "has ruled on the unlawfulness of the search and seizure conducted by the national authorities cannot be considered binding on the Court".

Cross-references:

Regulations 43 and 44.

Doctrine:

1. Hans-Jörg Behrens, "The Trial Proceedings", in Roy S. Lee (ed.), *The International Criminal Court: the Making of the Rome Statute: Issues, Negotiations and Results*, Kluwer Law International, The Hague, 1999, pp. 238–46.
2. Gideon Boas, "Admissibility of Evidence under the Rules of Procedure and Evidence of the ICTY: Development of the 'Flexibility Principle'", in Richard May, D. Tolbert, J. Hocking, K. Roberts, B.B. Jia, D. Mundis and G. Oosthuizen (eds.), *Essays on ICTY Procedure and Evidence: In Honour of Gabrielle Kirk McDonald*, Kluwer Law International, The Hague, 2001, pp. 263–74.
3. Richard May and Marieke Wierda, *International Criminal Evidence*, Transnational Publishers, Ardsley, NY, 2002.
4. Mark Klamberg, *Evidence in International Criminal Trials: Confronting Legal Gaps and the Reconstruction of Disputed Events*, Martinus Nijhoff Publishers, Leiden, 2013.
5. Donald K. Piragoff, "Article 69 – Evidence", in Otto Triffterer (ed.), *Commentary on the Rome Statute of the International Criminal Court: Observers' Notes, Article by Article*, 2nd ed., C.H. Beck/Hart/Nomos, Munich/Oxford/Baden-Baden, 2008, pp. 1301–36.
6. William A. Schabas, *The International Criminal Court: A Commentary on the Rome Statute*, Oxford University Press, Oxford, 2010, pp. 836–51.

Author: Mark Klamberg.

Article 70
Offences against the administration of justice[584]

---

[584] *General remarks*:

Article 70 sets out an exhaustive list of the substantive offences that amount to offences against the administration of justice before the ICC. This contrasts clearly with the equivalent provisions before the ICTY, ICTR and other internationalised tribunals where this the list of which acts may constitute the offence, created solely in the Rules rather than in the respective Statute and often referred to by its common law name as contempt, is often open ended. Article 70 lists six offences divided into three general categories of offences, including: (i) providing false testimony or presenting false evidence; (ii) Interference with witnesses; and (iii) Offences by or against officials of the Court. It also limits the *mens rea* of any of these offences to those committed intentionally.

As well as creating new criminal offences, Article 70 also establishes a procedure for whether or not jurisdiction should be exercised over such offences, further delineated in Rules 162–164 thus underlining the sensitive and complicated nature of such offences and introducing an additional level of factors as to any decision on prosecution.

Although silent on the procedures for investigating and prosecuting such alleged crimes, Article 70 does proceed to establish a maximum term of 5 years or a fine in accordance with the RPE. It also details its relationship with national investigation and enforcement.

Preparatory works:

Offences against the administration of justice were not included within the 1994 Draft Statute of the International Law Commission but Article 44(2) of the Draft Statute simply required that States Parties "extend their laws of perjury to cover evidence given under this Statute by their nationals, and shall cooperate with the Court in investigating and where appropriate prosecuting any case of suspected perjury", justified by the International Law Commission on the basis that it considered that "on balance, prosecutions for perjury should be brought before the national courts" (Report of the International Law Commission on the work of its forty-sixth session (2 May–22 July 1994), UN doc. A/49/10, P.59). When the Statute was created at the Rome Conference, disagreements over the applicable procedure for the investigation and prosecution of such offences, in part whether it should be the same as that followed for the core crimes which eventually were included of Articles 5 to 8 of the ICC Statute, delayed this decision to the drafting of the Rules of Procedure and Evidence (Article 70(2)). After extensive further discussions, the Preparatory Committee included "Offenses or acts against the integrity of the Court" as Article 70 of the Draft Statute submitted to the Plenipotentiaries for discussion in Rome. This draft provision included the categories of offences ultimately included within Article 70 of the ICC Statute and covered false testimony, interfering with witnesses and illegally influencing or retaliating against officials of the court but also those relating to compliance with court orders or disruption of its processes (which eventually became "Misconduct before the Court, covered separately by Article 71 in the ICC Statute.) As well as including a *nota bene*, explaining that all the provisions of the Statute and Rules relating to jurisdiction would apply to this offence, the Draft Statute also clarified that such offences shall be tried by a different Chamber than the Chamber in which the alleged offences were committed (Draft Article 20(2). The final version of Article 70 also included provisions relating to State cooperation (Article 70(4) and the maximum sanction for the offence (Article 70(3) while leaving the procedure to be followed to the Rules of Procedure and Evidence (Article 70(2).

Author: Geoff Roberts.

---

1. The Court shall have jurisdiction over the following offences against its administration of justice when committed intentionally:[585]

   (a) Giving false testimony when under an obligation pursuant to Article 69, paragraph 1, to tell the truth;[586]

---

[585] Article 70 establishes that the ICC has jurisdiction solely over offences committed "intentionally". Under Article 30(2) of the Statute, "a person has intent where: (a) In relation to conduct, that person means to engage in the conduct; (b) In relation to a consequence, that person means to cause that consequence or is aware that it will occur in the ordinary course of events". As with much of the Statute, it is unclear whether this provision refers directly to Article 70 offences as it refers to "crimes within the jurisdiction of the Court" which on a narrow reading could refer exclusively to core crimes set out in Articles 5 to 8 . However, it has been argued that such a narrow interpretation is incorrect as, firstly, Rule 163(1) provides explicitly that the Statute and Rules shall apply *mutatis mutandis* and none of the exclusions set out therein are applicable. Secondly, in accordance with Article 21 of the Statute, the Court may be guided by Article 30 when interpreting the word "intentionally" in Article 70(1) (Piragoff, 1999, p. 1339). Indeed, for others "intent in this context cannot have a meaning other than the one ascribed to it by Article 30" (Pikis, 2010, p. 230). Regardless of which specific definition of intent applies to Article 70 offences, it would appear that this would exclude any form of liability that does not require intent. This would rule out "responsibility of commanders and other superiors" under Article 28 which is a form of liability based on omission, solely requiring proof of knowledge of the past or future crimes of subordinates.

Author: Geoff Roberts.

[586] Article 70(1)(a) establishes the offence of "Giving false testimony when under an obligation pursuant to Article 69, paragraph 1, to tell the truth". This offence may therefore only take place when a witness testifies viva voce before the Court and after having given an undertaking as to the truthfulness of the evidence to be given by that witness required by this provision. According to Pre-Trial Chamber II, "this offence is committed when a witness intentionally provides a Chamber with information that is false, or otherwise withholds information that is true" and it "relates to any type of information that the witness provides or withholds while testifying under oath" (*Prosecutor v. Bemba*, ICC PT. Ch. II, Decision pursuant to Article 61(7)(a) and (b) of the Rome Statute, ICC-01/05-01/13-749, 11 November 2014, para. 28).

In this regard, Rule 66(3) obliges the Court to inform any witness who is about to testify, of the offence under Article 70(1)(a). However, under Rule 66(2) a witness may be exempted from the requirement of giving the undertaking if they are "under the age of 18 or a person whose judgment has been impaired and who, in the opinion of the Chamber, does not understand the nature of a solemn undertaking". In such cases, no prosecution for false testimony under Article 70(1)(a) could arise. Furthermore, Article 70(1)(a) may not apply to false evidence provided to investigators and tendered by one of the parties under Rule 68.

What exactly constitutes "false testimony within the meaning of Article 69(1) has not been addressed by the court while the term "false" appears only in Articles 70(1)(a), 70(1)(b) and 84(1)(c) which relates to the discovery that decisive evidence relied upon at trial was false, forged or falsified". Distinguishing "false testimony" in the sense of Article 70(1)(a) from testimony which is vague, lacking credibility or honest but completely mistaken, is a complicated issue, accentuated by the nature of the core crimes within the Court's jurisdiction which require testimony often relating to stressful and traumatic events. Consequently, despite being faced with various instances of incorrect testimony, trial chambers have been reluctant to pursue requests for investigation for false testimony under Article 70 (in addition to their lack of authority under the Statute and Rules to order the Prosecution to investigate). Trial Chamber II held that "[inconsistencies pointed out by the Defence in the testimony of [the witness] are related

---

before everything on the credibility of his testimony, rather than on a belief that he intentionally lied to the Court" (*Prosecutor v. Katanga and Ngudjolo*, ICC T. Ch. II, Transcript of hearing, 22 September 2010, ICC-01/04-01/07-T-190-ENG Red, p. 5 lines 1–10). Similarly, Trial Chamber III recently held that while "the evidence before the Chamber may raise doubts as to [a part of the witness' testimony...] the Chamber is not persuaded that [he...] intentionally tried to mislead the Court during his testimony" (*Prosecutor v. Bemba*, ICC T. Ch. III, Public redacted version of "Decision on the 'Defence application concerning Witness CAR-OTP-WWWW-0042's evidence'" of 10 October 2013, ICC-01/05-01/08-2830-Red, 16 October 2013, para. 17). However, even in final judgment, when the Trial Chamber has been able to ultimately assess credibility and has recognised the possibility that participating victims who testified under oath have assumed a false identity in order so as to benefit from participating in the trial as victims, in light of the "consistent, credible and reliable witnesses" who contradicted them, no prosecutions for false testimony have resulted (*Prosecutor v. Lubanga*, ICC T. Ch., Judgment pursuant to Article 74 of the Statute, ICC-01/04-01/06-2842, 14 March 2012, para. 502).

At the *ad hoc* Tribunals, false testimony is covered by a separate provision from contempt and is proscribed by Rule 91. Although there have been convictions for false testimony, or soliciting false testimony, these have resulted in guilty pleas which have not contested the precise definition of false evidence (*Prosecutor v. GAA*, ICTR, Judgment and Sentence, ICTR-07-90-R77-I, 4 December 2007; *Prosecutor v. Tabaković*, ICTY T. Ch. II, Sentencing Judgment, IT-98-32/1-R77.1, 18 March 2010, para. 5). However, the Appeals Chamber, when assessing the evidence of GAA which led to his prosecution for contempt, did thoroughly assess whether his recantation of the evidence he gave before the Trial Chamber was false. In large part their assessment that his original evidence was true and the recantation was false was based on the consistency of his prior statements, the implausibility of inventing specific facts that were corroborated by other evidence as well as the witness' alleged actions when allegedly deciding to recant and tell the truth, namely by contacting the Defence rather than the Prosecution (*Prosecutor v. Kamuhanda*, AC, Judgment, ICTR-99-54A-A, 19 September 2005, paras. 216–221). This was perhaps an easier task though as the witness was recanting his own testimony and claiming the opposite to what he had already testified to the Trial Chamber. It is much more difficult to demonstrably prove that a witness is intentionally providing false evidence when the evidence that undermines or contradicts that evidence is provided by another source. This may explain why prosecutions for false testimony are so rare before International Courts, despite various examples of testimony being completely lacking in credibility.

The concept of false testimony has not therefore been adjudicated when contested before international criminal courts. It has been interpreted as "the making of a factual statement, untrue to the knowledge of the maker" (Pikis, 2010, p. 230). As set out above in relation to all offences under Article 70, the falsity of the statement must be made intentionally as recklessness or negligence as to its falsity would not suffice. In this regard, if a witness gave evidence which he thought was true or at least considered it to be reasonably likely to be true, he could not be prosecuted under Article 70 as he does not know the evidence to be false.

There appears to be no specific prerequisites for prosecuting a person for false testimony, or for any accomplice to this crime. Self-evidently, if in a trial judgment, the Chamber considers and also refers to evidence supporting a determination that a witness' evidence was completely wrong this would facilitate a prosecution under Rule 70(1)(a). However, a trial judgment is not a prerequisite for such a prosecution and at the ICC, accused have been prosecuted for core crimes while concurrently facing charges under Article 70 (*Prosecutor v. Bemba et al.*, ICC PT. Ch. II. Warrant of arrest for Jean-Pierre Bemba Gombo, Aime Kilolo Musamba, Jean-Jacques Mangenda Kabongo, Fidele Babala Wandu and Narcisse Arido, ICC-01/05-01/13, 20 November 2013).

Author: Geoff Roberts.

(b) Presenting evidence that the party knows is false or forged;[587]

---

[587] Article 70(1)(b) sets out the offence of intentionally presenting evidence that the party knows is false or forged. This offence is limited to tendering of evidence by a "party", which would apply only to the Prosecution and Defence. However, the Legal Representatives of Victims, considered to be participants in the regulatory framework of the Court, appear to therefore be exempted from Prosecution for offences under Article 70(1)(b). This appears to be supported by the interpretation by Pre-Trial Chamber II, which held that this provision only applies to "those who have the right to present evidence to a chamber in the course of proceedings before the Court" (*Prosecutor v. Bemba*, PT. Ch. II, Decision pursuant to Article 61(7)(a) and (b) of the Rome Statute, ICC-01/05-01/13-749, 11 November 2014, para. 29).

This would mean that any evidence they tender while examining the witnesses put forward by the Prosecution or Defence could not give rise to prosecution for being false or forged. Furthermore, having been granted the right to tender evidence and testify under oath, victims participating in proceedings and their legal representatives will not face any prosecution if such evidence is known by them to be false. This lacuna in the Statute must be resolved, especially in light of the findings in Lubanga that participating victims had falsified their identities (*Prosecutor v. Lubanga*, ICC T. Ch, Judgment pursuant to Article 74 of the Statute, ICC-01/04-01/06-2842, 14 March 2012, para. 502).

The term "false" in this context suffers from the same ambiguities as the term in Article 70(1)(a) but again, and for the sake of consistency, requires that the person presenting the evidence, knows it to be false. The term knows in this provision must be given the meaning set out in Article 30(3), in that the person must be aware that a circumstance exists or that a consequence will occur in the ordinary course of events. Little assistance is provided by the Statute or Rules as to the definition of "forged" as it only appears in Article 84(1)(b) relating to the revision of a conviction or sentence. It has been interpreted to mean subject to a "change or alteration of a document to read something other than it states or conveys (Pikis, 2010, p. 231). There does not appear to be any requirement that the party itself was responsible for the forgery, simply that it presented the document to the court and relied on its truthfulness. It appears therefore that false in this context is intended to cover the testimony of witnesses called by the relevant party whereas forgery covers the documents it tenders into evidence. However, the term false could also cover documentary evidence which was not manipulated but which was still factually incorrect to the knowledge of the party presenting it to the court and seeking to rely on it.

One complicated area revolves around the duties of Defence Counsel to defend their clients effectively and their obligations not to present evidence they know to be false or forged under Article 70(1)(b). Defence Counsel are disclosed large amounts of material by the Prosecutor and also collect significant information from other sources in the course of their investigations. They may well receive evidence which they consider may be false but which is in favour of their client wish they may be obliged to tender into evidence. In addition, they may have received other evidence which may strongly suggest that this evidence is false. If this contrary evidence was received by the Prosecutor he would have to disclose it to the Defence due to his obligation under Article 67 to disclose exculpatory evidence to the accused and so he would probably not present such evidence. However, the Defence has no reciprocal obligation to disclose to the Prosecutor evidence which contradicts or undermines his case under the ICC Statute and Rules. The ICTY adjudicated on this issue when Defence Counsel was prosecuted for contempt for tendering additional evidence on appeal which he allegedly knew to be false as he had been informed so by the person whose statement he tendered. In protesting his innocence, Counsel claimed that it was for the court to determine the veracity of the evidence. The Appeals Chamber, adjudicating at first instance, held that this was "not a situation in which the Tribunal could determine where the truth lay, [and that] [...] by submitting as the only evidence on the point a

(c) Corruptly influencing a witness,[588] obstructing or interfering with the attendance or testimony of a witness,[589] retaliating against a witness for giving testimony or destroying,[590] tampering with or interfering with the collection of evidence;[591]

---

statement which he knew had been repudiated by the very person who made it, denied to the Tribunal any opportunity to make any determination as to where the truth lay" and convicted him for contempt (*Prosecutor v. Tadić* (Case No. IT-94-1-A-R77) ICTY T. Ch., Judgment on Allegations of Contempt against Prior Counsel, Milan Vujin, 31 January 2000, para. 136).

Author: Geoff Roberts.

[588] The extensive list of offences in Article 70(1)(c) relating to interference with witnesses has seen the most prosecutions for contempt at the *ad hoc* Tribunals and also pending ICC cases. It is effectively subdivided into four subcategories of offences.

As held by Pre-Trial Chamber II, this provision "proscribes any conduct that may have (or is expected by the perpetrator to have) an impact or influence on the testimony to be given by a witness, inducing the witness to falsely testify or withhold information before the Court (*Prosecutor v. Bemba*, PT. Ch. II, Decision pursuant to Article 61(7)(a) and (b) of the Rome Statute, ICC-01/05-01/13-749, 11 November 2014, para. 30).

Furthermore, the same chamber considered that "the offence of corruptly influencing a witness is constituted independently from whether the pursued impact or influence is actually achieved and must therefore be understood as a conduct crime, not a result crime (*Prosecutor v. Bemba*, PT. Ch. II, Decision pursuant to Article 61(7)(a) and (b) of the Rome Statute, ICC-01/05-01/13-749, 11 November 2014, para. 30).

Corruptly influencing a witness may be considered to relate to paying a bribe to a witness to testify in a certain manner. However, it appears to be charged together with interfering with the testimony of a witness which is a larger category but which also encapsulates situations where the interference with witnesses is unwelcome. Indeed, it has been recognised at the ICTY that the *actus reus* of interfering with witnesses could include "keeping a witness out of the way, by bribery or otherwise, so as to avoid or prevent service of a subpoena; assaulting, threatening or intimidating a witness or a person likely to be called as a witness; endeavouring to influence a witness against a party by, for instance, disparagement of the party; or endeavouring by bribery to induce a witness to suppress evidence" (*Prosecutor v. Radoslav Brđanin* (Case No. IT-99-36-R77) ICTY T. Ch., Concerning Allegations Against Milka Maglov, Decision on Motion for Acquittal pursuant to Rule 98bis, 19 March 2004, para. 28 footnotes omitted).

It must be noted that any of the forms of interference under this provision must be with a "witness" which, on a narrow reading, could limit its application to those who testify in accordance with Article 69(1). However, it is possible that such an offence could also cover situations where a person who was corruptly influenced, did not testify because of what he had said or denied when interviewed before giving evidence. Such an offence could be equally damaging to the administration of justice which Article 70 seeks to protect. In this regard ICTY Rule 77(A)(iv), covering almost identical offences, applies also to "potential witnesses".

Exactly what constitutes a bribe has been interpreted at the ICTY as "an inducement offered to procure illegal or dishonest action in favour of the giver [and] ... a price, reward, gift or favour bestowed on promised with a view to pervert the judgment of or influence the action of a person in a position of trust" (*Prosecutor v. Begaj* (Case No. IT-03-66-T-R77), ICTY T. Ch. I, Judgment on contempt allegations, 27 May 2005, para. 18). There does not appear to be any requirement that the inducement offered must be of monetary value. Furthermore, proof is not required that the conduct intended to influence the nature of the witness's evidence produced a result (*Prosecutor v. Begaj* (Case No. IT-03-66-T-R77), ICTY T. Ch. I, Judgment on contempt allegations, 27 May 2005, para. 21). Therefore, if the witness was going to testify in a certain manner anyway and was provided with a gift, arguably this would not constitute the offence of corruptly influencing a witness under Article 70(1)(c). Indeed, the ICTY Appeals Chamber, acting in first instance, acquitted an accused of bribery of witnesses where the evidence of a later payment to a witness which was well after the witness was interviewed and unconnected with his testimony, undermined accusations of bribery based on a previous payment for "difficult financial and emotional circumstances" and demonstrated a lack of intent of bribery (*Prosecutor v. Tadić* (Case No. IT-94-1-A-R77), ICTY A. Ch., Judgment on Allegations of Contempt against Prior Counsel, Milan Vujin, 31 January 2000, para. 158).

Author: Geoff Roberts.

[589] The obstruction or interference with witness testimony is a general provision covering most forms of interference with prospective witnesses. It most closely equates to Rule 77(a)(iv), which prosecutes for contempt "any person who threatens, intimidates, [...], or otherwise interferes with, a witness". ICTY jurisprudence, which also includes bribery within this provision considers the following definitions of these provisions: "threat is defined as a communicated intent to inflict harm or damage of some kind to a witness and/or the witness' property, and/or a third person and/or his property, so as to influence or overcome the will of the witness to whom the threat is addressed" (*Prosecutor v. Begaj* (Case No. IT-03-66-T-R77), ICTY T. Ch. I, Judgment on contempt allegations, 27 May 2005, para. 13); intimidation consists of acts or culpable omissions likely to constitute direct, indirect or potential threats to a witness, which may interfere with or influence the witness' testimony" (*Prosecutor v. Brdjanin* (Case No. IT-99-36-R77) ICTY T. Ch., Concerning Allegations Against Milka Maglov, Decision on Motion for Acquittal pursuant to Rule 98bis, 19 March 2004, para. 22); "Otherwise interfering with a witness" is an open ended provision which encompasses acts or omissions, other than threatening, intimidating, causing injury or offering a bribe, capable of and likely to deter a witness from giving full and truthful testimony or in any other way influence the nation of the witness' evidence (*Prosecutor v. Brđanin* (Case No. IT-99-36-R77) ICTY T. Ch., Concerning Allegations Against Milka Maglov, Decision on Motion for Acquittal pursuant to Rule 98bis, 19 March 2004, para. 27). Furthermore, to establish responsibility, it is immaterial whether the witness actually felt threatened or intimidated, or was deterred or influenced (*Prosecutor v. Begaj* (Case No. IT-03-66-T-R77), ICTY T. Ch., Judgment on contempt allegations, 27 May 2005, para. 21; *Prosecutor v. Haraqija, and Morina* (Case No. IT-04-84-R77.4), ICTY T. Ch., Judgment on Allegations of Contempt, 17 December 2008, para. 61). Furthermore, even when it was the witness who initiated the communication by calling the accused, and the accused requested that the witness provide another statement denying knowledge of certain people and come and "fix something up" this can amount to otherwise interfering with a witness (*Prosecutor v. Begaj* (Case No. IT-03-66-T-R77), ICTY T. Ch., Judgment on contempt allegations, 27 May 2005, para. 38). The interference need not also be in favour of an accused's client and Defence Counsel have been convicted for witness interference when preventing witnesses from naming other perpetrators (*Prosecutor v. Tadić* (Case No. IT-94-1-A-R77) ICTY A. Ch., Judgment on Allegations of Contempt against Prior Counsel, Milan Vujin, 31 January 2000, para. 150).

The *mens rea* for this offence has been held to require proof of a "specific intent to interfere with the administration of justice" (*Prosecutor v. Begaj* (Case No. IT-03-66-T-R77), ICTY T. Ch., Judgment on contempt allegations, 27 May 2005, para. 22).

Author: Geoff Roberts.

[590] By its very nature, retaliation must occur after the giving of testimony, whether to a court or to an investigator for use in court. Indeed, "retaliation is an act of revenge; avenging one who you believe has damned you" (Pikis, 2010, p. 232) There are few clues as to the nature of the retaliation required, but presumably it may encapsulate the different forms of interference that can occur in elsewhere in Article 70(1)(c), such as intimidation, threats or other attempts at interfer-

(d) Impeding, intimidating or corruptly influencing an official of the Court for the purpose of forcing or persuading the official not to perform, or to perform improperly, his or her duties;[592]

(e) Retaliating against an official of the Court on account of duties performed by that or another official;[593]

---

ence. It would include physical harm to a witness but not require it and may also be directed at a witness' property or a third party's property in order to hurt the witness.

Author: Geoff Roberts.

[591] Forming the last part of Article 70(1)(c), the offence of destroying, tampering with or interfering with the collection of evidence has no direct equivalent before the ICTY. Little guidance is provided by the Statute and Rules as to the meanings of these terms.

One complicated area is the obligation on Defence Counsel to retain or provide any evidence to the Prosecutor. There is no obligation on Defence Counsel to inform the Prosecutor of the existence of evidence which may be incriminating to their client. In addition, there is no obligation to secure or protect such evidence. As such, and taken in conjunction with Article 70(1) which provides that all offences against the administration of justice must require intent, it would only be if there was an overt intentional act to destroy, tamper with, hide or remove evidence that liability could potentially result.

Author: Geoff Roberts.

[592] Sub-paragraphs (d)–(f) concerns offences involving officials of the Court.

Neither the Statute nor Rules define the phrase "official of the court". However, to give proper effect to this provision, it must encompass "every person holding office in any department of the Court, not just in the judicial branch (Pikis, 2010, p. 232), or at least, in accordance with Article 34, it "encompasses representation of all four organs of the Court mentioned here" (Triffterer, p. 1341). However, this definition would exclude from its ambit any offences against either Defence or Victims' Counsel, who are not "officials of the Court" but rather independent practising lawyers. It would also exclude offences committed by or against "intermediaries" who are, used primarily by the Office of the Prosecutor to make contact with and communicate with potential witnesses. As such, impeding, retaliating against or bribing Defence Counsel would not fall under this definition.

Article 70(1)(d) makes it an offence to impede, intimidate or corruptly influence an official of the Court. The purpose of this offence must be to force or persuade the official not to perform, or perform improperly, his or her duties. There is no indication of exactly what duties are covered by this provision and whether they must in any way relate to a particular case or situation but it would appear that no nexus is so required. There appears also to be no requirement that the official did not perform or perform improperly, his or her duties.

Author: Geoff Roberts.

[593] Article 70(1)(e) criminalises retaliation against officials of the Court for the official duties they perform. Again, retaliation is not further defined by the Statute or Rules but should be interpreted in the same way as this term is used in Article 70(1)(c). As such it would logically include but not be limited to intimidation, threats or other attempts at interference as interpreted by the ICTY in relation to contempt cases brought under ICTY Rule 77(a)(iv). No prosecutions under this provision have occurred at the ICC yet, but one prime example of a situation that would normally fall within this definition would be the illegal arrest, interrogation and detention of four ICC staff members by the Libyan authorities in 2012. No investigation of these actions appears to have been undertaken by the Office of the Prosecutor who retains exclusive jurisdiction to prosecute Article 70 offences under Rule 165.

(f) Soliciting or accepting a bribe as an official of the Court in connection with his or her official duties.[594]

2. The principles and procedures governing the Court's exercise of jurisdiction over offences under this article shall be those provided for in the Rules of Procedure and Evidence.[595] The conditions for providing international cooperation to the Court with respect to its proceedings under this article shall be governed by the domestic laws of the requested State.[596]

3. In the event of conviction, the Court may impose a term of imprisonment not exceeding five years, or a fine in accordance with the Rules of Procedure and Evidence, or both.[597]

Retaliation against the officials of the court requires proof of the specific intent that the retaliation occurred "on account of duties performed by that or another official". Therefore, if the retaliation against the ICC official was for a distinct purpose, this would not entail liability under Article 70.

Author: Geoff Roberts.

[594] Article 70(1)(f) criminalises both the solicitation or acceptance of a bribe as an official of the Court in connection with his or her official duties. Solicitation will presumably be given the same definition as that provided in Article 25(3)(b) of the court. Similarly, bribery of officials in the context of this provision will be interpreted in the same manner as "corruptly influencing" in Article 70(1)(f). Whether a bribe is solicited or simply accepted by an official of the court, it must be "in connection with his official duties" to warrant prosecution under this provision. How closely connected is not defined. However, this would exclude bribery solicited for private actions which may be offences under the ICC staff rules or domestic criminal legislation but not under Article 70.

Cross-references:

Rule 169 Immediate arrest.

Author: Geoff Roberts.

[595] The exercise of jurisdiction by the Court was left to the Rules of Procedure and Evidence which, in Rule 162, derogated from the normal jurisdictional limitations in Article 13 of the Statute for core crimes and established various discretionary factors which may be taken into account when the Court exercises jurisdiction in Article 70 proceedings.

Cross-references:

Rules 163, 164, 165, 170 and 171.

Author: Geoff Roberts.

[596] Article 70(2) provides that the conditions for providing international cooperation to the Court with respect to Article 70 proceedings shall be governed by the domestic laws of the requested State. The requests could include requests to arrest, detain and transfer an accused, requests to interview certain persons or indeed requests for the search and seizure of certain evidence. By allowing the domestic laws of the requested State to govern whether the conditions for fulfilling such requests have been met, the Court grants significant power to the individual States to accept or reject these requests and therefore maintain control over these proceedings. The specifics of how this is implemented is addressed in relation to Rule 167(2).

Cross-references:

Rule 167.

Author: Geoff Roberts.

[597] Article 70(3) provides for a sentence of imprisonment not exceeding five years for an offence against the administration of justice or a fine or a combination. Rule 166 further establishes the

4. (a) Each State Party shall extend its criminal laws penalizing offences against the integrity of its own investigative or judicial process to offences against the administration of justice referred to in this article, committed on its territory, or by one of its nationals;

   (b) Upon request by the Court, whenever it deems it proper, the State Party shall submit the case to its competent authorities for the purpose of prosecution. Those authorities shall treat such cases with diligence and devote sufficient resources to enable them to be conducted effectively.[598]

---

procedure for imposing fines and forfeiture orders. In is unclear whether an accused may receive multiple consecutive sentences for Article 70 offences or whether five years is considered to be the maximum sentence for all convictions combined. Article 77, which regulates penalties for core crimes, establishes under Article 77(1)(a) that the "penalty may not exceed a maximum of 30 years" and separately sets life imprisonment under Article 77(1)(b) "when justified by the extreme gravity of the crime and the individual circumstances of the convicted person". In light of the fact that Article 70 does not propose an exception to the limit of 5 years, it is to be presumed that this would be the absolute maximum even for consecutive offences for offences under Article 70.

Cross-references:

Rule 166.

Author: Geoff Roberts.

[598] The obligation upon all State Parties to "extend its criminal laws penalising offences against the integrity of its own investigative or judicial process to offences against the administration of justice referred to in this Article, committed on its territory, or by one of its nationals" in Article 70(4)(a) most closely replicates the original provision in the ILC Draft Statute. It seeks to place the burden on national states to investigate and prosecute these offences rather than the Court itself. Article 70(4)(b) reinforces this burden sharing by obliging State Parties to submit a case to the competent authorities for the purpose of prosecution whenever it is deemed proper. Once submitted, the competent authorities, are further obliged to treat such cases with diligence and devote sufficient resources to enable them to be conducted effectively. This provision appears to demonstrate the concern of the Court that simply referring to the general obligation upon States Parties to cooperate under Article 86, is not sufficient in terms of prosecuting Article 70 offences and that an additional more extensive obligation is necessary.

Cross-references:

Articles 5–8, 30(2), 34, 69(1), 71, 77, 86.

Rules 162–169.

Doctrine:

1. Georghios M. Pikis, "The Rome Statute for the International Criminal Court, Analysis of the Statute, the Rules of Procedure and Evidence", *The Regulations of the Court and Supplementary Instruments*, Brill, Nijhoff, pp. 230–32, 2010.

2. Donald K. Piragoff, "Article 70: Offences Against the Administration of Justice", in Otto Triffterer (ed.), *Commentary on the Rome Statute of the International Criminal Court: Observers' Notes, Article by Article*, 2nd ed., C.H. Beck/Hart/Nomos, Munich/Oxford/Baden-Baden, 2008, pp. 1337–45.

Author: Geoff Roberts.

Article 71

Sanctions for misconduct before the Court[599]

1. The Court may sanction persons present before it who commit misconduct, including disruption of its proceedings or deliberate refusal to comply with its directions, by administrative measures other than imprisonment, such as temporary or permanent removal from the courtroom, a fine or other similar measures provided for in the Rules of Procedure and Evidence.[600]

2. The procedures governing the imposition of the measures set forth in paragraph 1 shall be those provided for in the Rules of Procedure and Evidence.[601]

---

[599] *General remarks*:

Article 71 concerns contempt of court, that is, conduct that takes place in the court and that defies the authority or dignity of the court. Reactions towards such behaviour is accepted in most legal systems of the world, but differences do exist as to line between punishable behaviour and less severe conduct. Sanctions may vary, from exclusion from the courtroom to fines and imprisonment. The purpose of Article 71 is thus to avoid behaviour which prevent proper proceedings, for example intimidation of witnesses, disruptions, witnesses refusing or failing to answering a question.

Author: Mark Klamberg.

[600] From the words "persons before it" follows that the provision only applies to misconduct committed inside the courtroom and not conduct outside the courtroom.

Although Article 71 is contained in Part 6 "The Trial" of the ICC Statute, it also applies to the proceedings of the Pre-Trial Chamber. It applies to public as well as closed sessions (Triffterer, p. 1351).

When the Court is in doubt whether the conduct is acceptable, it should advise the person concern and express a warning before issuing a sanction. This is consistent with rule 71(5) which provides that "[t]he person concerned shall be given an opportunity to be heard before a sanction for misconduct, as described in this rule, is imposed".

The paragraph lists two examples of misconduct: disruption of proceedings and deliberate refusal to comply with directions. However, the word "including" suggests that these are only examples and other behaviour may also fall within the scope of Article 71.

Author: Mark Klamberg.

[601] During the negotiations of the ICC Statute some issues were left without agreement to be resolved by the Rules of Procedure and Evidence. The rules have not managed to fill these gaps in a satisfactory manner. For example, it is unclear whether Sates Parties have an obligation to cooperate and give judicial assistance to the Court in relation to fines imposed for misconduct. The Court could potentially rely upon the second sentence in Article 70(2), paras (3) and (4). Misconduct covered by Article 71 ma also amount to a violation covered by Article 70 which make the rules enacted pursuant to Article 70 applicable (Triffterer, p. 1359 and Schabas, p. 860).

Cross-references:

Rules 170, 171 and 172.

Regulation 29.

Doctrine:

1. William A. Schabas, *The International Criminal Court: A Commentary on the Rome Statute*, Oxford University Press, Oxford, 2010, pp. 859–60.

---

2. Otto Triffterer, "Article 71", in Otto Triffterer (ed.), *Commentary on the Rome Statute of the International Criminal Court: Observers' Notes, Article by Article*, 2nd ed., C.H. Beck/Hart/Nomos, Munich/Oxford/Baden-Baden, 2008, pp. 1347–60.

Author: Mark Klamberg.

Article 72

Protection of national security information[602]

1. This article applies in any case where the disclosure of the information or documents of a State would, in the opinion of that State, prejudice its national security interests. Such cases include those falling within the scope of Article 56, paragraphs 2 and 3, Article 61 paragraph 3, Article 64, paragraph 3, Article 67, paragraph 2, Article 68, paragraph 6, Article 87, paragraph 6 and Article 93, as well as cases arising at any other stage of the proceedings where such disclosure may be at issue.[603]

2. This article shall also apply when a person who has been requested to give information or evidence has refused to do so or has referred the matter to the State on the ground that disclosure would prejudice the national security interests of a State and the State concerned confirms that it is of the opinion that disclosure would prejudice its national security interests.[604]

---

[602] *General remarks*:

Article 72 sets out the rules and procedure on how the Court should handle the disclosure of information and documents that a State considers to "prejudice its national security interests". It is a compromise between several interests: national security concerns, the effective functioning of the Court, to establish the guilt or innocence of the accused and the defendant's right to a fair trial. It represents the conflict between two different views, one that nly the State can properly asses when its national security is in jeopardy, the other that the Court should be the ultimate arbiter in such issues. In the end the balance was tilted towards the States. The Court may make determinations on whether information or documents are relevant, necessary and should be disclosed but the decisions are not enforceable (Dixon, Duffy and Hall, pp, 1363–1364).

[603] National security is closely related to the concept of vital interest of States, which is protected by customary international law as recognised as the *domaine réservé* of States.

The term "national" implies that there must be a danger to the country as a whole. A narrow understanding of the word "security" would include the "threat or use of force against the territorial integrity or political independence of [another] state" as understood in Article 2(4) of the UN Charter. However, a broader definition of national security would include the State's territorial integrity, sovereignty, national defence issues, military operations, international freedom f action, foreign relations or anything else affecting the State's national interests The danger with a broad definition of national security is that the concept becomes meaningless (Dixon, Duffy and Hall, pp. 1365–1366).

The words "at any other stage of the proceedings" confirms the broad scope of the provision.

Disclosure in relation to national security interests has a broader meaning than in the sense of prosecution disclosure *vis-à-vis* the defence. Article 72(1) employs the term in sense of information being revealed generally (Schabas, p. 866).

[604] Article 72(2) protects a cooperative witness from being required to reveal sensitive information during examination. The provision is triggered when the individual asked to give evidence invokes the Article. Te matter is then referred to the State concerned. Thus, the assessment of national security concerns is done by the State and not the individual (Dixon, Duffy and Hall, p. 1369 and Schabas, p. 866).

---

3. Nothing in this article shall prejudice the requirements of confidentiality applicable under Article 54, paragraph 3 (e) and (f), or the application of Article 73.[605]

4. If a State learns that information or documents of the State are being, or are likely to be, disclosed at any stage of the proceedings, and it is of the opinion that disclosure would prejudice its national security interests, that State shall have the right to intervene in order to obtain resolution of the issue in accordance with this article.[606]

5. If, in the opinion of a State, disclosure of information would prejudice its national security interests, all reasonable steps will be taken by the State, acting in conjunction with the Prosecutor, the defence or the Pre-Trial Chamber or Trial Chamber, as the case may be, to seek to resolve the matter by cooperative means. Such steps may include:

   (a) Modification or clarification of the request;

   (b) A determination by the Court regarding the relevance of the information or evidence sought, or a determination as to whether the evidence, though relevant, could be or has been obtained from a source other than the requested State;

   (c) Obtaining the information or evidence from a different source or in a different form; or

   (d) Agreement on conditions under which the assistance could be provided including, among other things, providing summaries or redactions, limitations on disclosure, use of in camera or ex parte proceedings, or other protective measures permissible under the Statute and the Rules of Procedure and Evidence.[607]

6. Once all reasonable steps have been taken to resolve the matter through cooperative means, and if the State considers that there are no means or conditions under which the information or documents could be provided or disclosed without prejudice to its national security interests, it shall so notify the Prosecutor or the Court of the specific reasons for its decision, unless a specific description of the reasons would itself necessarily result in such prejudice to the State's national security interests.[608]

7. Thereafter, if the Court determines that the evidence is relevant and necessary for the establishment of the guilt or innocence of the accused, the Court may undertake the following actions:

---

[605] Paragraph 3 clarifies that other provisions which impose requirements of confidentiality do not depend on meeting the "national security" threshold. This includes lead evidence (Article 54(3)(e)) and evidence provided in confidence (Article 73).

[606] Paragraph 4 establishes the right of the State to intervene at any stage of the proceedings in relation to information or documents which the State believes would be prejudicial to its national security interests. It reinforces paragraph 1 of Article 72 in this regard.

[607] Paragraph 5 provides a list of measures whereby resolution between conflicting interests may be resolved. It follows from the word "may" that the list is non-exhaustive. This modelled on the *Blaškić* case (*Prosecutor v. Blaškić* (Case No. IT-95-14-A), ICTY A. Ch., Judgment on the Request of the Republic of Croatia for Review of the Decision of the Trial Chamber II of 18 July 1997, 29 October 1997, paras. 67–69).

[608] Paragraph 6 imposes on obligation for States to cooperate with the Court to resolve conflicts relating to national security interests. If the matter cannot be resolved the State must declare "that there are no means or conditions under which the information or documents could be provided or disclosed without prejudice to its national security interests". The State is also obliged to explains its reasons, except in cases when would itself prejudice national security.

(a) Where disclosure of the information or document is sought pursuant to a request for cooperation under Part 9 or the circumstances described in paragraph 2, and the State has invoked the ground for refusal referred to in Article 93, paragraph 4:

    (i) The Court may, before making any conclusion referred to in subparagraph 7 (a) (ii), request further consultations for the purpose of considering the State's representations, which may include, as appropriate, hearings in camera and ex parte;

    (ii) If the Court concludes that, by invoking the ground for refusal under Article 93, paragraph 4, in the circumstances of the case, the requested State is not acting in accordance with its obligations under this Statute, the Court may refer the matter in accordance with Article 87, paragraph 7, specifying the reasons for its conclusion; and

    (iii) The Court may make such inference in the trial of the accused as to the existence or non-existence of a fact, as may be appropriate in the circumstances; or

(b) In all other circumstances:

    (i) Order disclosure; or

    (ii) To the extent it does not order disclosure, make such inference in the trial of the accused as to the existence or non-existence of a fact, as may be appropriate in the circumstances.[609]

---

[609] After the state makes the declaration under paragraph 6, the procedure under paragraph 7 follows.

The Court must first determine whether the evidence is "relevant and necessary for the establishment of the guilt or innocence of the accused".

This is done to exclude cases where the evidence sought is not really necessary for the proceedings.

If the Court finds that the evidence is "relevant and necessary"

The Court is denied the ability to make orders as to disclosure where the State has declared itself unable to do so because of prejudice to national security interests. However, paragraph 7(a)(ii) states that the Court may make a finding that the state is not acting in accordance with its obligations and refer the matter to the Assembly of States Parties or, where the Security Council referred the matter to the Court, to the Security Council.

However, paragraph 7(b)(i) empowers the Court to order to disclosure "[i]n all other circumstances". Such circumstances would include where the information is already in the hands of teh Court, defence or a third party (Dixon, Duffy and Hall, p. 1374).

Doctrine:

1. William A. Schabas, *The International Criminal Court: A Commentary on the Rome Statute* Oxford University Press, Oxford, 2010, pp. 861–69.

2. Rodney Dixon, Helen Duffy and Christopher K. Hall, "Article 72", in Otto Triffterer (ed.), *Commentary on the Rome Statute of the International Criminal Court: Observers' Notes, Article by Article*, 2nd ed., C.H. Beck/Hart/Nomos, Munich/Oxford/Baden-Baden, 2008, pp. 1361–78.

Author: Mark Klamberg.

Article 73

Third-party information or documents

If a State Party is requested by the Court to provide a document or information in its custody, possession or control, which was disclosed to it in confidence by a State, intergovernmental organization or international organization, it shall seek the consent of the originator to disclose that document or information. If the originator is a State Party, it shall either consent to disclosure of the information or document or undertake to resolve the issue of disclosure with the Court, subject to the provisions of Article 72. If the originator is not a State Party and refuses to consent to disclosure, the requested State shall inform the Court that it is unable to provide the document or information because of a pre-existing obligation of confidentiality to the originator.[610]

---

[610] *General remarks*:

Article 73 concerns the flow of information between States, and between States and organisations. The provision might have been better placed in Part 9 governing State cooperation because it limits the duty of States to provide assistance to the Court.

Analysis:

Articles 73 and 93(9)(b) allow a State party to refuse to provide documents or information disclosed to it in confidence by a third State or an international organisation, if the consent to disclosure is refused by the originator.

The provision only relates to States Parties and not to Non-States Parties. Non-States Parties can enter into agreement to cooperate with the Court under Article 87(5) but in absence of such agreement there is no obligation to cooperate.

The second sentence provides that if the originator is a State Party, information and evidence can only be withheld if the originator State invokes national security concerns under Article 72. Requests where the originator is a State Party is in essence a request to the that State Party. A more straightforward approach for the Court would be to ask that State in the first place which makes this part of Article 73 appear redundant (Schabas, p. 871).

If the originator is not a State Party and refuses to consent to disclosure, the requested State shall inform the Court of the refusal.

The words "in confidence" should be construed narrowly to prevent illegitimate use of Article 73, such as to protect evidence of crimes committed by a State's own nationals (Duffy and Hall, p. 1383).

Doctrine:

1. Annalisa Ciampi, "The Obligation to Cooperate", in Antonio Cassese, Paola Gaeta and John R.W.D. Jones (eds.), *The Rome Statute of the International Criminal Court: A Commentary*, Oxford University Press, Oxford, 2002, pp. 1607–38.

2. Helen Duffy and Christopher K. Hall, in Otto Triffterer (ed.), *Commentary on the Rome Statute of the International Criminal Court: Observers' Notes, Article by Article*, 2nd ed., C.H. Beck/Hart/Nomos, Munich/Oxford/Baden-Baden, 2008, pp. 1379–85.

3. William A. Schabas, *The International Criminal Court: A Commentary on the Rome Statute* Oxford University Press, Oxford, 2010, pp. 870–71.

Author: Mark Klamberg.

Article 74
Requirements for the decision[611]

---

[611] *General remarks*

Article 74 regulates the key aspects of judicial deliberations in the Trial Chamber on the issue of the guilt or innocence of the accused and sets requirements towards the format and content of the judgment on the merits. This includes the judges' presence requirement as a precondition of the decision's validity (Article 74(1)), the admissible basis and scope of the decision (Article 74(2)), the judicial duty to strive for unanimity and the majority rule (Article 74(3)), the principle of secrecy of judicial deliberations (Article 74(4)), and the requirements regarding the format, reasoning, and the delivery of decisions (Article 74(5)). Notably, deliberations and delivery of judgment are the only interval of the trial stage of the ICC proceedings that is subject to a fairly detailed regulation in the Statute. Other segments of trial, in particular the order and manner in which evidence is to be submitted, are left for the determination of the Trial Chamber, which will confer with the parties and issue directions for the conduct of the proceedings (Article 64(3)(a) and (8)(b)).

Neither the title of Article 74 nor its sub-paragraphs state what category of decisions is covered by the provision. However, sub-paragraph 2 provides that the decision 'shall be based on [...] the *entire* proceeding', and sub-paragraph 5 stipulates that it 'shall contain a *full* and reasoned statement of the Trial Chamber's findings on the evidence and *conclusions*'. This language implies that the provision deals solely with the verdicts at trial. Interlocutory decisions of the Trial Chamber may neither be expected to be based on the entire proceeding nor contain findings on the evidence and conclusions. Moreover, Article 81, entitled 'Appeal against decision of acquittal or conviction or against sentence' establishes in sub-paragraph 1 the grounds on which the Prosecutor and the convicted person may appeal '[a] decision under Article 74'. Article 81(2) addresses appeals against sentencing decisions pursuant to Article 76, while Article 82 covers appeals against 'other' (interlocutory) decisions (Article 82(1) and (2)). The combined reading of Articles 74 and 81–82 makes it clear that 'decision under Article 74' can only be interpreted as referring to the final decision regarding guilt or innocence at trial (see also Triffterer 2008, p. 1391; Safferling 2010, p. 522).

However, this does not rule out the application of parts of Article 74 by analogy, and *mutatis mutandis*, to other decisions, to the extent that they are not subject to special regulation. While Article 83(4) and (5) set the requirements towards the judgments of the Appeals Chamber, a statutory gap with respect to the Pre-Trial Chambers' decisions (see for example Article 61(7)) may be covered through the application of Article 74 by analogy. In particular, the judicial duty to provide reasoned opinions is a general requirement that holds for all decisions affecting the legal status and interests of parties and participants, although the required degree of detail may legitimately vary by type of decision. In a similar vein, the Pre-Trial Chambers' decisions are subject to the duty of judges to genuinely deliberate with one another but may also be rendered by majority, in line with Article 74(3) (Triffterer 2008, p. 1391). By the same token, the requirement in Article 74(2) that the judgment must be limited to evidence on the record must apply to any other decisions that involve the making of factual findings (Jørgensen and Zahar 2013, p. 1155).

Unlike the ICTY and ICTR Statutes (Article 23 and 22 respectively), Article 74 of the ICC Statute avoids the term 'judgment'. By contrast, all rulings of the ICC Appeals Chamber are denominated as 'judgments'. The downside of this approach is that the Statute does not make a traditional distinction between interlocutory and final decisions, whether for the purpose of trial or appeals, which may appear confusing (Boas *et al.* 2011, p. 377). The reason for this legislative choice is not self-evident and cannot readily be inferred from the drafting history. The draft Statute as submitted to the Preparatory Committee referred to 'judgment' in Articles 72 and 80

---

1. All the judges of the Trial Chamber shall be present at each stage of the trial and through-out their deliberations. The Presidency may, on a case-by-case basis, designate, as available, one or more alternate judges to be present at each stage of the trial and to replace a member of the Trial Chamber if that member is unable to continue attending.[612]

(UN doc. A/CONF.183/2, cited in Schabas 2011, p. 319). However, the term was rejected in Rome in favour of a more general term 'decision' upon recommendation by the Working Group on Procedural Matters (UN doc. A/CONF.183/C.1/WGPM/L.2, cited in Schabas 2011, p. 319 fn. 20). As a result, the Committee of the Whole informed the Drafting Committee that 'the phrase "final decision of acquittal or conviction and sentence" should be used to refer to the final decision of the Trial Chamber throughout the Statute', without clarifying the rationale behind this choice ('Note regarding part 6 and Article 72 contained in the transmittal letters from the Chairman of the Committee of the Whole to the Chairman of the Drafting Committee dated 10 and 11 July 1998', UN doc. A/CONF.183/DC/R. 145 and Corr. 1, cited in Schabas 2010, p. 874).

It has been suggested that the omission of the word 'judgment' from Article 74 is a result of the drafters' attempt to avoid a nomenclature associated with particular legal traditions (Schabas 2011, p. 301), although this does not explain why that term was retained for appellate rulings. It is also possible that the drafters wished to reserve the term 'judgment' for decisions that are genuinely final, given that the Trial Chamber's decisions on criminal responsibility are potentially subject to appellate review and may be reversed or amended. Ultimately, the nuances of terminology have proved to be of little practical relevance. Initially, the ICC Trial Chambers referred to decision on the merits as 'Article 74 decision' (*Prosecutor v. Lubanga*, ICC T. Ch., Decision on the press interview with Ms Le Fraper du Hellen, ICC-01/04-01/06-2433, 12 May 2010, para. 51; *Prosecutor v. Lubanga*, ICC T. Ch., Decision on the translation of the Article 74 Decision and related procedural issues, ICC-01/04-01/06-2834, 15 December 2011, passim, cf. para. 1). But the verdicts delivered in the first cases bear the conventional label 'judgment', which means that, despite what the drafters may have had in mind, the judges still preferred the conventional taxonomy (*Prosecutor v. Lubanga*, ICC T. Ch., Judgment pursuant to Article 74 of the Statute, ICC-01/04-01/06-2842, 14 March 2012; *Prosecutor v. Ngudjolo*, ICC T. Ch., Judgment pursuant to Article 74 of the Statute, ICC-01/04-02/12-3-tENG, 18 December 2012; *Prosecutor v. Katanga*, ICC T. Ch., Jugement rendu en application de l'Article 74 du Statut, ICC-01/04-01/07-3464, 7 March 2014; *Prosecutor v. Bemba*, ICC T. Ch., Judgment pursuant to Article 74 of the Statute, ICC-01/05-01/08-3343, 21 March 2016).

Cross-references:

Articles 64(3)(a) and (8)(b), 81, 82(1) and (2), 83(4) and (5).

Author: Sergey Vasiliev.

[612] In order for the Trial Chamber to be properly constituted at each stage of the trial and be competent to issue a valid verdict, Article 74(1) requires that all three judges of the Chamber (Article 39(2)(b)(ii)) must have participated throughout the trial and deliberations. In *Lubanga*, the Trial Chamber considered this provision to make it 'clear beyond doubt that during the trial the three judges shall function *in banco*' (*Prosecutor v. Lubanga*, ICC T. Ch., Decision on whether two judges alone may hold a hearing – and – Recommendations to the Presidency on whether an alternate judge should be assigned for the trial, ICC-01/04-01/06-1349, 22 May 2008, para. 12).

The requirement of the presence at trial ensures that the judgment is rendered by the bench each member of which is in a position to evaluate 'the entire proceedings' (Article 74(2)). This implies the highest degree of knowledge of the evidence and issues discussed during the trial (Triffterer 2008, p. 1391). The same degree of knowledge may be difficult to achieve for a judge who has absented from one or more of the trial hearings. In respect of the evidentiary hearings, no subsequent familiarisation with the transcript of testimony or a summary of evidence would be sufficient to remedy the absent judge's inability to directly observe the demeanour of a witness, which is crucial for the credibility assessment.

Moreover, the familiarity with the trial record will not always compensate for the absence of a judge because the ICC judges' role during the trial is not limited to passive presence. Depending on the specific context, it might require active contributions to the court's inquiry by posing questions to witnesses and experts (Rule 140(2)(c)) and by deciding whether the submission of evidence should be ordered (Article 69(3)). While being the primary responsibility of the Presiding Judge, the conduct of trial hearings is a collective effort. All judges of the Trial Chamber are expected to participate in this process, and to be available for consultation (Regulation 43).

By establishing a formal duty of the judges to be present 'throughout deliberations', the Statute extends the presence requirement to all deliberation conferences. Due to the secrecy of the internal workings of the Chambers (Article 74(3)), the judicial attendance during deliberations is more difficult for the public to police than the judges' presence at trial. But as a matter of law, there is an unconditional duty incumbent on all members of the Trial Chamber to be directly and personally involved in every stage of the final decision-making. This involvement extends beyond taking part 'at the decisive parts of deliberations' and during voting (cf. Triffterer 2008, p. 1392). The bulk of deliberations may consist in the exchange of drafts and written memoranda among the Trial Chamber judges. But the participation by a judge in the deliberations on the judgment solely through written submissions whereas other members of the bench convene for deliberation in person would arguably fail to meet the Article 74(1) requirement. In the interests of preserving collegiality and avoiding an early split in the Chamber, this provision invites the trial judges to plan their deliberation conferences around the dates when one of them is absent from the seat of the Court.

Notably, the Statute contains no provision obliging all judges of the Trial Chamber to be present at all times during the preparatory stage following the confirmation of charges and leading up to the commencement of the trial. Unlike with the Pre-Trial Chambers, whose functions may be carried out by a single judge (Article 39(2)(b)(iii)), the Statute envisions no possibility for a single judge to exercise the functions of the Trial Chamber. Therefore, the *Lubanga* Chamber interpreted the statutory framework as providing for the duty of all three members, next to their attendance at trial as mandated by Article 74(1), to 'be present for each hearing and status conference during the period following the confirmation of charges and leading up to the beginning of the trial' (*Prosecutor v. Lubanga*, ICC T. Ch., Decision on whether two judges alone may hold a hearing – and – Recommendations to the Presidency on whether an alternate judge should be assigned for the trial, ICC-01/04-01/06-1349, 22 May 2008, para. 15). This meant that, during the preparatory stage, 'any urgent issues that arise during the absence of a judge from the seat of the Court will be dealt with solely on the basis of written representations.' (*ibid.*).

Given the evident inefficiency of requiring the presence of a full bench throughout the preparatory stage of trial proceedings due to what appears to have been an accidental lacuna in the Statute, Rule 132*bis* was adopted in 2012 (Resolution ICC-ASP/11/Res.2 adopted at the 8th plenary meeting, on 21 November 2012, by consensus, Amendment of the Rules of Procedure and Evidence). The new Rule authorises a Trial Chamber to 'designate one or more of its members for the purposes of ensuring the preparation of the trial'. A single judge of the Trial Chamber has broad powers in preparing the case for the trial, in consultation with the Chamber (Rule 132*bis*(2)–(5)). But he or she 'shall not render decisions which significantly affect the rights of the accused or which touch upon the central legal and factual issues in the case'; except for deciding on the applications of victims for participation at trial, a single judge may not 'make decisions that affect the substantive rights of victims' (Rule 132*bis*(6)).

2. The Trial Chamber's decision shall be based on its evaluation of the evidence and the entire proceedings.[613] The decision shall not exceed the facts and circumstances described in

---

The same procedural rationale of preserving the continuity of adjudication at trial and the completeness of the basis for the decision, underlies the rule contained in the second sentence of Article 74(1). It envisages the possibility for the Presidency to assign, on a case-by-case basis, one or more alternate judges that could replace a judge who is unable to continue attending. The excusals and disqualification of the judge are the specific examples of such situations contemplated by the Statute (Article 41). Rule 38 details this provision by stating that a judge may be replaced for 'objective and justified reasons', which include (but are not limited to) resignation; accepted excuse; disqualification; removal from office; and death. Regulation 15(1) provides additionally that in replacing a judge, the Presidency shall take into account, to the extent possible, 'gender and equitable geographical representation'.

On several occasions, the Presidency granted judges' requests for excusal from the exercise of functions as members of their Trial Chambers prior to the commencement of the trial in the respective cases. Thus, the Presidency excused two of the judges of the *Lubanga* Chamber from presiding over the *Bemba* trial in which they had served in the preparatory stage, with reference to their workload in the *Lubanga* case and, in particular, the 'possible lengthy overlap between the two trials' (*Prosecutor v. Bemba*, Decision replacing judges in Trial Chamber III, Presidency, 20 July 2010, pp. 3–4 and Decision on the request to be excused from the exercise of judicial functions in Trial Chamber III, pursuant to Article 41 of the Rome Statute, Presidency, 15 July 2010, p. 3).

When faced with a situation of temporary absence of one of its members during the preparatory stage of the trial, the *Lubanga* Trial Chamber pointed out the absence of a pre-determined procedure (*Prosecutor v. Lubanga*, ICC T. Ch., Decision on whether two judges alone may hold a hearing – and – Recommendations to the Presidency on whether an alternate judge should be assigned for the trial, ICC-01/04-01/06-1349, 22 May 2008, para. 16). Acting *proprio motu* and by majority, it took upon itself to consider whether to recommend the Presidency to designate an alternate judge for the trial and ultimately opined that no alternate judge should be appointed. Trial Chamber I referred to the non-extensive scope of the charges and prosecution evidence and the absence of 'known personal circumstances relating to any of the judges which raise any concerns that one of more of them will be unable to complete this trial' (*ibid.*, paras. 19–23). In no other case so far has the need to designate an alternate judge been raised and considered. The practice relating to Article 74(1) (second sentence), Rule 39, and Regulation 16 is lacking at present.

Cross-references:

Articles 39(2)(b)(ii), 41, 69(3).

Rules 39, 41, 132bis, 140(2)(c).

Regulations 15, 16, and 43.

Author: Sergey Vasiliev.

[613] Article 74(2) lays down three closely interrelated principles restricting the admissible factual scope and evidentiary basis of the Trial Chamber's decision on criminal responsibility, while at the same time safeguarding the Chamber's adjudicative autonomy. It does so by prescribing what relationship should exist between the Pre-Trial Chamber and the Trial Chamber, given the likely overlap between the decision to confirm charges and the judgment pursuant to Article 74. Such overlaps may in particular arise in part of findings on, and evaluation of, the evidence that is relied upon for the purpose of confirming charges and that forms part of the record transmitted to the Trial Chamber under Rule 130.

The first sentence of Article 74(2) stipulates that the judgment must be based on the Trial Chamber's evaluation of evidence and the entire proceedings. In *Lubanga*, the Trial Chamber held that it would assess the reliability of individual pieces of evidence and their probative value for the purpose of the decision on the merits in the context of other admissible and probative material (*Prosecutor v. Lubanga*, ICC T. Ch., Judgment pursuant to Article 74 of the Statute, ICC-01/04-01/06-2842, 14 March 2012, para. 94). The parties were responsible for specifically identifying the parts of oral and written evidence relied upon and they were expected to explain its relevance to the Article 74 decision in their final submissions (*ibid.*, paras. 95–96; *Prosecutor v. Lubanga*, Transcript, ICC-01/04-01/06-T-342-ENG, 1 April 2011, pp. 64–65). Moreover, in ruling on the admissibility of evidence, the Chamber is guided by the duty to avoid prejudice for a fair trial and ensure a 'fair evaluation' in accordance with Article 69(4). The principle of 'fair evaluation' mandates the court to rely only on the material that is admissible. The parameters of admissibility of the evidence are its relevance, probative value, and non-prejudicial nature (*Prosecutor v. Bemba*, ICC A. Ch., Judgment on the appeals of Mr Jean-Pierre Bemba Gombo and the Prosecutor against the decision of Trial Chamber III entitled "Decision on the admission into evidence of materials contained in the prosecution's list of evidence", ICC-01/05-01/08-1386, 3 May 2011, para. 37). The latter prong can only be determined if the Chamber duly considers the context and procedural history of the case, in particular any past—and anticipated—delays that are potentially problematic in light of Article 67(1)(c).

Although the Court's legal instruments do not clarify the meaning of 'the entire proceedings', this element can be interpreted as requiring the Court to adopt a holistic approach to the evaluation of evidence when deciding on the merits of the case. The evaluation should be informed by the consideration of the procedural context in which the evidence is submitted and the conduct of the relevant actors in the courtroom, which are the pertinent aspects of 'entire proceedings'. This includes, for example, the demeanour of the witness, 'the manner in which he or she gave evidence' (*Prosecutor v. Lubanga*, ICC T. Ch., Judgment pursuant to Article 74 of the Statute, ICC-01/04-01/06-2842, para. 102), and the accused's attitude and reactions to the evidence (Trifferer 2008, p. 1395). The temporal aspect of 'entire proceedings' is that the evidence may be admitted even after the formal close of the submission of evidence pursuant to Rule 141(1), subject to 'the reopening of oral proceedings to hear adversarial submissions as to the appropriate weight to be attached in the light of the whole case file' (*Katanga and Ngudjolo Chui*, Decision on the request by the Defence for Germain Katanga seeking to admit excerpts from the judgment rendered in *Prosecutor v. Lubanga*, TC, 26 April 2012, para. 14).

The qualification '*its* evaluation' in Article 74(2) underscores that the evaluation of evidence by the Trial Chamber should be its own, rather than that of any other Chamber. The evidence submitted during the confirmation hearing and relied upon in the decision to confirm charges is highly likely to be discussed at trial. Even though at the confirmation stage the Prosecutor may rely principally on documentary or summary evidence and need not call witnesses expected to testify at trial (Article 61(5)), the ICC's initial practice demonstrates that there will normally be a partial overlap in evidence between the two stages. While this increases a chance that multiple and divergent judicial evaluations will be given to the same evidence in the same case, Article 74(2) reaffirms the Trial Chamber's competence to evaluate evidence independently.

Its adjudicative autonomy *vis-à-vis* the Pre-Trial Chamber involved in the same case follows from the distinct purposes of the confirmation and the trial as well as the fundamentally different functions of Pre-Trial and Trial Chambers. Importantly, the standards of proof for the purpose of confirmation of charges and conviction are not the same, both in terms of the quantity of evidence and its persuasiveness as to the guilt (for example *Prosecutor v. Katanga and Ngudjolo*, ICC T. Ch., Decision on the Filing of a Summary of the Charges by the Prosecutor, ICC-01/04-01/07-1547-tENG, 21 October 2009, para. 25). Article 61(7) requires 'sufficient evidence to establish substantial grounds to believe that the person committed each of the crimes charged' for the Pre-Trial Chamber to confirm the charges, but Article 66(3) sets the threshold for conviction at 'beyond reasonable doubt' and thus compels the prosecution to present additional evidence that can meet that burden. Because the Pre-Trial and Trial Chambers as a matter of principle labour under the different standards of proof, the Trial Chamber must conduct a fully independent assessment of both the admissibility and weight of evidence.

As held by Trial Chamber I, Article 64(9) provides the Trial Chamber with an 'unfettered authority ... to rule on the admissibility or relevance of evidence', while Rule 64(1) authorises it 'to assess freely' all evidence when determining admissibility and relevance (*Prosecutor v. Lubanga*, ICC T. Ch., Decision on the status before the Trial Chamber of the evidence heard by the Pre-Trial Chamber and the decisions of the Pre-Trial Chamber in trial proceedings, and the manner in which evidence shall be submitted, ICC-01/04-01/06-1084, 13 December 2007, paras. 4–5). The evidence admitted by the Pre-Trial Chamber and constituting a part of the record of the proceedings transmitted to the Trial Chamber pursuant to Rule 130, cannot be introduced into the trial automatically: it requires a *de novo* consideration (*ibid.*, para. 8). This implies that the Trial Chamber shall not be guided, and much less bound, by the evaluations of the evidence by the Pre-Trial Chamber in the same case.

The Trial Chamber that is trying the case may also be confronted with another trial bench's findings or evaluation of evidence in another case (particularly in the context of the same situation), which can be relevant to the Trial Chamber's assessment of the credibility of evidence before it. The question of the status before the Trial Chamber of evaluations and findings from another trial arose in *Katanga and Ngudjolo Chui*. In that case, the defence requested Trial Chamber II to admit excerpts from the *Lubanga* trial judgment containing Trial Chamber I's discussion of the role of intermediaries P-143 and P-316 and their impact on the credibility of witnesses, given that the same intermediaries had had contact with witnesses in the *Katanga and Ngudjolo Chui* trial.

Trial Chamber II held the *Lubanga* judgment to constitute 'new material' as an appropriate basis for reopening the oral proceedings, the issue of intermediaries relevant to the case, and the *Lubanga* Chamber's findings probative and highly reliable (*Katanga and Ngudjolo Chui*, Decision on the request by the Defence for Germain Katanga seeking to admit excerpts from the judgment rendered in *Lubanga*, TC, 26 April 2012, paras. 15–16). However, Trial Chamber II turned down the admission request, among others, on the ground that Trial Chamber I's findings on the behaviour of the intermediaries towards witnesses not involved in the present case would not have 'an appreciably more significant impact on the assessment ... of the credibility of the witnesses concerned' than the evidence already on the trial record (*ibid.*, paras. 16–20). Trial Chamber II assured that it did not artificially dissociate the role of intermediaries in the *Lubanga* case from their role in the present case (*ibid.*, para. 15).

However, the minority opinion to the *Katanga* trial judgment criticised the majority's disregard of the *Lubanga* findings when assessing the credibility of key witnesses (P-28 and P-132) involved with intermediary P-143. The dissenting judge held that oral proceedings must have been reopened to introduce the relevant sections of the *Lubanga* judgment (*Prosecutor v. Katanga*, ICC T. Ch., Minority Opinion of Judge Christine Van den Wyngaert, Jugement rendu en application de l'Article 74 du Statut, ICC-01/04-01/07-3464-AnxI, 7 March 2014, paras. 161–163). The Trial Chambers' adjudicative autonomy *vis-à-vis* each other in part of admissibility rulings and the evaluation of evidence and the 'entire proceedings' does not require insulation from the findings on shared issues reached in adjacent cases. On the contrary, where such evaluations point to the material evidence missing from the record in the present case and any circumstances relevant for the fair evaluation of the record, the presumption of innocence (Article 66) and the *in dubio pro reo* principle as its component (*Prosecutor v. Bemba*, ICC PT. Ch., Decision Pursuant to Article 61(7)(a) and (b) of the Rome Statute on the Charges of the

the charges and any amendments to the charges.[614] The Court may base its decision only on evidence submitted and discussed before it at the trial.[615]

Prosecutor Against Jean-Pierre Bemba Gombo, ICC-01/05-01/08-424, 15 June 2009, para. 31) militate against an overly restrictive and isolationist approach in this regard.

Author: Sergey Vasiliev.

[614] The second principle in Article 74(2), namely that the decision 'shall not exceed the facts and circumstances described in the charges and any amendments' thereto, imposes a duty on the Trial Chamber to adjudicate strictly within the factual boundaries of the charges as confirmed or amended by the Pre-Trial Chamber. In the period after the confirmation of charges and before the commencement of trial, the Prosecutor may amend the charges with the permission of the Pre-Trial Chamber and after notice to the accused; adding or substituting more serious charges requires that a confirmation hearing be held on those additional charges; after the commencement of the trial, the charges may be withdrawn with the permission of the Trial Chamber (Article 61(9); *Prosecutor v. Katanga and Ngudjolo*, ICC T. Ch., Decision on the Filing of a Summary of the Charges by the Prosecutor, ICC-01/04-01/07-1547-tENG, 21 October 2009, para. 21). The decision to confirm the charges and any subsequent amendments are binding on the Trial Chamber in part of the factual scope of the case at trial (*Prosecutor v. Lubanga*, ICC A. Ch., Judgment on the appeals of Mr Lubanga Dyilo and the Prosecutor against the Decision of Trial Chamber I of 14 July 2009 entitled "Decision giving notice to the parties and participants that the legal characterisation of the facts may be subject to change in accordance with Regulation 55(2) of the Regulations of the Court", ICC-01/04-01/06-2205, 8 December 2009, para. 91; *Prosecutor v. Lubanga*, ICC T. Ch., Judgment pursuant to Article 74 of the Statute, ICC-01/04-01/06-2842, 14 March 2012, para. 3; *Prosecutor v. Katanga and Ngudjolo Chui*, ICC T. Ch., Decision on the implementation of regulation 55 of the Regulations of the Court and severing the charges against the accused persons, ICC-01/04-01/07-3319-tENG/FRA, 21 November 2012, para. 10). It demarcates the ambit of the Trial Chamber's authority over the case by fixing and settling its factual basis, thereby providing the accused with a clear notice of the relevant 'facts and circumstances' within the meaning of Article 74(2) and precluding related disputes at trial (*Prosecutor v. Katanga and Ngudjolo*, Decision on the Filing of a Summary of the Charges by the Prosecutor, 21 October 2009, paras. 22 and 31).

Next to the amendment and withdrawal of charges pursuant to Article 61(9), Regulation 55 constitutes an avenue—albeit a narrow one—through which charges may be modified. It is a reflection of the civil law principle of *iura novit curia*, which was extensively debated during the negotiations on the Statute and the Rules but ultimately not incorporated into the primary instruments owing to significant differences between legal cultures (see Friman *et al.* 2013, p. 431–432). The application of this provision proved contentious, confused, and highly controversial in the ICC's practice. Regulation 55(1) authorises the Trial Chamber to change the legal characterisation of facts to accord with crime definitions or with the forms of participation, but it prohibits the Chamber to exceed 'the facts and circumstances described in the charges and any amendments to the charges' when doing so (*Prosecutor v. Lubanga*, ICC A. Ch., Judgment on the appeals of Mr Lubanga Dyilo and the Prosecutor against the Decision of Trial Chamber I of 14 July 2009 entitled "Decision giving notice to the parties and participants that the legal characterisation of the facts may be subject to change in accordance with Regulation 55(2) of the Regulations of the Court", ICC-01/04-01/06-2205, 8 December 2009, paras. 88–93). The Appeals Chamber defined 'facts' as 'the factual allegations which support each of the legal elements of the crime charged', distinguishable from 'the evidence put forward by the Prosecutor at the confirmation hearing to support a charge ... as well as from background or other information that, although contained in the document containing the charges or the confirmation decision, does not support the legal elements of the crime charged'. Facts 'must be identified with sufficient clarity and detail, meeting the standard in Article 67(1)(a) of the Statute' (*ibid.*, para. 90 n163). On that basis, the Appeals Chamber rejected the *Lubanga* Trial Chamber's interpretation of Regulation 55 as allowing it to change the legal characterisation 'based on facts and circumstances that, although not contained in the charges and any amendments thereto, build a procedural unity with the latter and are established by the evidence at trial' (*ibid.*, paras. 88, 90–93). Reliance on additional facts not properly described in the charges but introduced into the trial via the change of legal characterisation is inconsistent with Article 74(2) and Regulation 55(1), just as a change in the statement of facts rather than in their legal characterisation (*ibid.*, para. 97).

In *Katanga*, the change of legal characterisation of facts by the Trial Chamber's majority from Article 25(3)(a) initially charged to the Article 25(3)(d)(ii) liability, on the basis of which the accused was ultimately convicted, was highly controversial. As a way of deflecting critique based on the violation of Article 74(2), the Trial Chamber's majority assured that it did not exceed the facts and circumstances underlying the charges confirmed, but it nevertheless might legitimately place more emphasis on certain facts than on the others and disregard certain facts in favour of the others (*Prosecutor v. Katanga and Ngudjolo Chui*, ICC T. Ch., Decision on the implementation of regulation 55 of the Regulations of the Court and severing the charges against the accused persons, ICC-01/04-01/07-3319-tENG/FRA, 21 November 2012, paras. 31–34).

But, in her dissents to both the Regulation 55 decision and Katanga's subsequent conviction, Judge Van den Wyngaert held that the majority's use of Regulation 55 not only was fundamentally unfair towards the accused but also violated the terms of Article 74(2) and Regulation 55(1) itself. First, in requalifying Katanga's mode of liability, the majority relied on 'subsidiary facts' falling outside the 'facts and circumstances' underlying the confirmation decision, as opposed to 'material facts' that properly constitute the factual allegations supporting the legal elements of the crimes charged. Since subsidiary facts are not part of the 'facts and circumstances described in the charges' they may not be subject to legal recharacterisation under Regulation 55. Second, by recasting the facts under a different mode of liability, the majority amended the narrative of the facts underlying the charges so drastically that it exceeded the facts and circumstances described in the charges (Dissenting Opinion of Judge Christine Van Den Wyngaert, *Prosecutor v. Katanga and Ngudjolo Chui*, ICC T. Ch., Decision on the implementation of regulation 55 of the Regulations of the Court and severing the charges against the accused persons, ICC-01/04-01/07-3319-tENG/FRA, 21 November 2012, paras. 13–23; *Prosecutor v. Katanga*, ICC T. Ch., Minority Opinion of Judge Christine Van den Wyngaert, Jugement rendu en application de l'Article 74 du Statut, ICC-01/04-01/07-3464-AnxI, 7 March 2014, paras. 2, 12, 16–49). While the dissenting judge agreed with the majority that it is not forbidden for there to be any change of factual narrative for the purpose of legal recharacterisation of facts (*Prosecutor v. Katanga*, ICC T. Ch., Jugement rendu en application de l'Article 74 du Statut, ICC-01/04-01/07-3464, 7 March 2014, para. 1472), whether such a change violates Article 74 is 'a question of fact and degree' (*Prosecutor v. Lubanga*, ICC T. Ch., Minority Opinion on the "Decision giving notice to the parties and participants that the legal characterisation of facts may be subject to change in accordance with Regulation 55(2) of the Regulations of the Court", ICC-01/04-01/06-2049, 14 July 2009, para. 19; *Prosecutor v. Katanga*, ICC T. Ch., Minority Opinion of Judge Christine Van den Wyngaert, Jugement rendu en application de l'Article 74 du Statut, ICC-01/04-01/07-3464-AnxI, 7 March 2014, para. 29).

Author: Sergey Vasiliev.

[615] The third principle contained in Article 74(2), restricts the evidentiary basis for the Trial Chamber's decision to 'evidence submitted and discussed before it at the trial'. 'Evidence submitted … at the trial' refers to the evidence presented by the parties or ordered by the Trial Chamber (including the evidence of victim participants) pursuant to Articles 64(6)(d) and 69(3). Next to

3. The judges shall attempt to achieve unanimity in their decision, failing which the decision shall be taken by a majority of the judges.[616]

---

oral testimony, documents, and video recordings 'discussed' during the trial hearings, the evidence discussed before the Trial Chamber encompasses also 'any items of evidence "discussed" in the written submissions of the parties and the participants at any stage during the trial (for example documents introduced by counsel pursuant to a written application)'. It is essential that all evidence constituting the basis for the judgment 'must have been introduced during the trial and have become part of the trial record, through the assignment of the evidence (EVD) number' and that 'the parties should have had an opportunity to make submissions as to each item of evidence' (*Prosecutor v. Lubanga*, ICC T. Ch., Judgment pursuant to Article 74 of the Statute, ICC-01/04-01/06-2842, para. 98; *Prosecutor v. Ngudjolo*, ICC T. Ch., Judgment pursuant to Article 74 of the Statute, ICC-01/04-02/12-3-tENG, 18 December 2012, para. 44; *Prosecutor v. Katanga*, ICC T. Ch., Jugement rendu en application de l'Article 74 du Statut, ICC-01/04-01/07-3464, 7 March 2014, para. 78).

Therefore, the Trial Chamber's judgment may only be based on the evidence that has been produced before it and that the accused person had an opportunity to confront in accordance with Article 67(1)(e). The only exception to the principles of adversarial argument and immediacy is allowed for those alleged facts contained in the charges, the contents of a document, the expected testimony of a witness or other evidence that are not contested among the parties. Such agreed facts may be considered by the Chamber as being proven without a substantive discussion and detailed examination, unless the court is of the opinion that a more complete presentation of the alleged facts is necessary in the interests of justice, in particular in the interests of the victims (Rule 69). Other than that, the Trial Chamber shall ignore any information generated outside of the trial process, as not having been 'discussed before it at trial', including the evidence produced for the purpose of the confirmation of charges. This bolsters the first principle of Article 74(2) discussed above to the effect that the trial judgment must be based on the Trial Chamber's own evaluation of evidence.

Cross-references:

Articles 25(3)(a) and (d)(ii), 61(5), (7), and (9), 64(6)(d) and (9), 66(3), 67(1)(a), (c), (d) and (e), and 69(3).

Rules 64(1), 69, and 130.

Regulation 55.

Author: Sergey Vasiliev.

[616] Paragraph 3 addresses the process of deliberation of the Trial Chamber, which commences upon the delivery of closing statements in the case (Rule 141(1)). The provision is remarkable in several respects. It lays down the judges' duty to deliberate with one another by prescribing that they must *attempt* to achieve unanimity before deciding by majority. This requires each and every member of the Trial Chamber, and not only the Presiding Judge *ex officio*, to be fully invested in the search for consensus (see also Triffterer 2008, p. 1397). The obligation to strive for unanimity is an innovation of the ICC Statute. Except for the ECCC Internal Rule 98(4), it does not feature in the legal texts of other international or hybrid courts.

The duty of the members of the Trial Chamber to actively participate in the deliberations can also be inferred from Rule 39. It stipulates that where the Presidency assigns an alternate judge to a Trial Chamber in accordance with Article 74(1), he or she shall sit through all proceedings and deliberations, but may not take any part therein unless and until he or she is required to replace a member of the Trial Chamber who is unable to continue attending. The prerogative to deliberate is what distinguishes the regular members of the Trial Chamber from alternates. Notably, Article 83(4) that governs deliberation and judgment of the Appeals Chamber only mentions the lack of unanimity as the situation in which the 'judgment of the Appeals Chamber' shall contain the views of the majority or the minority and a judge may deliver a 'separate or dissenting opinion on a question of law'. But since it does not articulate a duty to attempt to achieve unanimity in their decision, it is unclear whether appellate judges are bound by it by analogy, or whether they are exempt from it – for example because dissents on the issues of law are deemed beneficial for the progressive development of jurisprudence.

Article 74(3) reflects a recognition of 'the importance of authoritative, preferably unanimous, judgments' (Sluiter 2009, p. 511). But it clearly falls short of instituting a preference or demand for unanimity. The provision results from a compromise in the Preparatory Committee between the proponents of the majority rule and the advocates of unanimity in decision-making (Report of the Preparatory Committee on the Establishment of an International Criminal Court, Vol. I (Proceedings of the Preparatory Committee during March—April and August 1996), UN doc. A/51/22, para. 291). The prescription that the ICC trial judges engage in a joint deliberation with one another is meant to strengthen the collegiate character of decision-making, by preventing a premature split on the trial bench and the proliferation of avoidable dissenting opinions. While the commentators have described the effects of the codified duty to strive for unanimity as 'highly uncertain', and the provision itself as 'purely hortatory', they recognise that the striving for unanimity inheres in any effort of collegiate decision-making and is good practice (Sluiter 2011, p. 203; Schabas 2010, p. 876).

Apart from the general consideration that deliberations enhance the quality of legal reasoning, the duty to strive for unanimity has several specific rationales in the ICC context. First, the consensus on the verdict and on the underlying reasons at least among two trial judges is a precondition for the Trial Chamber's ability to pass a decision. Only two verdicts are available to the ICC Trial Chamber: guilty or not guilty. The latter verdict equals to a legal recognition of innocence – in this sense, the statement by Trial Chamber II that 'finding an accused person not guilty does not necessarily mean that the Chamber considers him or her to be innocent' is based on a misunderstanding of the presumption of innocence (Article 66(1)) (*Prosecutor v. Ngudjolo*, ICC T. Ch., Judgment pursuant to Article 74 of the Statute, ICC-01/04-02/12-3-tENG, 18 December 2012, para. 36; *Prosecutor v. Katanga*, ICC T. Ch., Jugement rendu en application de l'Article 74 du Statut, ICC-01/04-01/07-3464, 7 March 2014, para. 70). Given the binary nature of decision-making on the issue of guilt or innocence, it is in theory possible for two judges to arrive at the same verdict via separate reasoning routes, without deliberation oriented at consensus, and to form the majority in respect of the verdict as opposed to the third judge who has voted in favour of another verdict. However, the reasoning forms an integral part of the decision. In the scenario described above, despite that two votes are cast in favour of the majority verdict, there will be three separate opinions but no 'majority decision' within the meaning of Article 74(3). Mere coincidence of verdicts between two judges does not make a judgment. Consensus and possible compromises will also need to cover the reasons controlling the majority decision. This means that joint deliberations are not desirable but also unavoidable if the Trial Chamber is to issue a judgment at all.

Second, the expectation that the Trial Chamber judges will engage in joint deliberation is also a corollary of the system for the nomination and election of candidates, which is based on the areas of competence. Article 36(5) envisages that two lists containing the names of candidates with different qualifications will be compiled. List A will contain the names of candidates who '[h]ave established competence in criminal law and procedure, and the necessary relevant experience, whether as judge, prosecutor, advocate or in other similar capacity, in criminal proceedings', whereas list B will contain the names of candidates with 'established competence in relevant areas of international law such as international humanitarian law and the law of human rights, and extensive experience in a professional legal capacity which is of relevance to the judicial work of the Court' (Article 36(3)(b) and (5)). The Trial and Pre-Trial Divisions shall be

4. The deliberations of the Trial Chamber shall remain secret.[617]

---

composed predominantly of judges with criminal trial experience (Article 39(1)). But it is possible that a member of the Trial Chamber will have been elected from among the candidates on List B as a specialist in international (humanitarian) law. It may thus be particularly important for the judges to approach the adjudicative task collegially in order to benefit from each other's expertise. This will enrich the deliberation by insights from the relevant disciplines and, arguably, enhance the quality of the judgment.

Contrary to the view that the duty under Article 74(3) did not require codification (Sluiter 2011, p. 203), there is no reason to lament its inclusion. Given that the ICC judges come from different legal-cultural and professional backgrounds, the provision usefully clarifies what minimal duties judges have in respect of the deliberation process. Notably, the RPE, Regulations of the Court, and the Code of Judicial Ethics do not provide further standards to govern judicial deliberations. Rule 142(2) merely prescribes that the judges decide separately on each charge and on each accused where there are several charges or accused. The provision of Article 74(3) goes some way to compensating for the scarcity of the ICC law in this area and precluding deliberation irregularities, even if does not rule out split judgments entirely.

Cross-references:

Article 36(3)(b) and (5), 39(1), and 83(4).

Rules 39 and 142(1) and (2).

Author: Sergey Vasiliev.

[617] Article 74(4) enshrines the fundamental principle of secrecy of judicial deliberations, which is well established in most domestic jurisdictions. How votes have been cast will be evident from the judgment's disposition, but the principle of secrecy of deliberations forbids the members of the Trial Chamber to disclose to the public the details of debates in the Chambers, including the positions initially held, adjusted, or withdrawn by the judges in the course of deliberations. Being an outgrowth of the guarantees of judicial independence and impartiality, the principle is meant to enable the judges to exchange their views freely in the expectation that whatever is said in the deliberation room will stay there. The rationale for the prohibition on making the content of judicial discussions public is that unless the judges are assured that secrecy shall be respected, they might feel deterred from expressing their views. If that is so, the trust and collegiality in the Chamber would be undermined, which will likely congeal and impoverish the deliberation of judges on the issues relevant to the case.

Besides Article 74(4), the principle of secrete deliberations is given expression in numerous other provisions of the ICC's legal framework. Thus, the pledge to respect secrecy of deliberations is a constituent element of the solemn undertaking each judge shall make before exercising his or her functions under the Statute (see Rule 5(1)(a)). Article 6 of the Code of Judicial Ethics, ICC-BD/02-01-05, entitled 'Confidentiality', provides that 'Judges shall respect the confidentiality of consultations which relate to their judicial functions and the secrecy of deliberations.' Therefore, although it is not restated in respect of the judges of the Pre-Trial Chambers and the Appeals Chamber (see Articles 57 and 83), the principle is of general application and holds equally for all judges.

Unlike ICTY, ICTR, and SCSL Rule 29 ('The deliberations of the Chambers shall take place in private and remain secret.'), Article 74 does not make a distinction between 'privacy' (a confidential character of the process itself), on the one hand, and 'secrecy' (a confidential character of the contents of judicial debates after their close), on the other hand. However, the French language version of Article 74(4) covers both aspects of confidentiality ('Les deliberations de la Chambre de première instance *sont et demeurent secrètes*.'). In addition, Rule 142(1) states that 'after the closing statements, the Trial Chambers shall retire to deliberate, *in camera*.'

5. The decision shall be in writing and shall contain a full and reasoned statement of the Trial Chamber's findings on the evidence and conclusions.[618] The Trial Chamber shall issue one

---

In essence, this means that deliberations shall take place in private. Thus, the substance of judicial consultations that does not form part of 'a full and reasoned statement of the Trial Chamber's findings on the evidence and conclusions' (Article 74(5)) shall remain confidential indefinitely (Triffterer 2008, p. 1397).

Cross-references:

Articles 57 and 83.

Rules 5(1)(a), 142(1).

Code of Judicial Ethics, Article 6.

Author: Sergey Vasiliev.

[618] While Article 74(2) provides for the admissible scope and content of trial judgments, paragraph 5 establishes the requirements as to their form and reasoning, the number of decisions and the accommodation of dissenting views, and the delivery of judgments in open court.

Some interlocutory decisions at trial may be delivered orally, but a trial judgment self-evidently should be rendered in writing. Thus the parties are enabled to exercise effectively their right to appeal the judgment under Article 81(1). For the same reason, the judgment shall contain 'a full and reasoned statement of ... findings on the evidence and conclusions'. This requirement is a rendition of the right to a reasoned opinion that is recognised in international human rights jurisprudence as a component of the right to a fair trial and, in particular, the right of the accused to have his or her conviction reviewed by a higher tribunal (Article 14(5) ICCPR; Article 2 Protocol No. 7, ECHR). The Human Rights Committee stated that '[t]he right to have one's conviction reviewed can only be exercised effectively if the convicted person is entitled to have access to a duly reasoned, written judgment of the trial court' (General Comment No. 32, Article 14: Right to equality before courts and tribunals and to a fair trial, UN doc. CCPR/C/GC/32, 23 August 2007, para. 49). Similarly, the European Court of Human Rights has recognised the obligation of courts to adequately state reasons for their judgments (albeit without requiring a detailed answer to every argument) as an integral element of the right of the accused to a fair trial under Article 6(1) ECHR and a principle 'linked to the proper administration of justice' (*Van der Hurk v. Netherlands*, 16034/90, 19 April 1994, para. 61; *Hiro Balani v. Spain*, 18064/91, 9 December 1994, para. 27; *Ruiz Torija v. Spain*, 18390/91, 9 December 1994, para. 29; *Higgins et al. v. France*, 20124/92, 19 February 1998, para. 42; *Garcia Ruiz v. Spain*, 30544/96, 21 January 1999, para. 26; *Hadjianastassiou v. Greece*, 12945/87, 16 December 1992, para. 33). By contrast, a judgment of the Appeals Chamber 'shall state the reasons on which it is based' (Article 83(4)), which appears to be a lower threshold than which applies to trial judgments. As the court of last resort, the Appeals Chamber need not necessarily provide a full statement of reasons.

The Appeals Chamber is yet to pronounce itself on the meaning of a 'full and reasoned statement' in the context of appellate review of decisions pursuant to Article 74. Its jurisprudence thus far has discussed the requirement that rulings must be reasoned in relation to decisions of a Pre-Trial Chamber in the following terms: 'it is essential that it [the decision – SV] indicates with sufficient clarity the basis of the decision. Such reasoning will not necessarily require reciting each and every factor that was before the Pre-Trial Chamber to be individually set out, but it must identify which facts it found to be relevant in coming to its conclusion.' (*Prosecutor v. Lubanga*, ICC A. Ch., Judgment on the appeal of Mr. Thomas Lubanga Dyilo against the decision of Pre-Trial Chamber I entitled "First Decision on the Prosecution Requests and Amended Requests for Redactions under Rule 81", ICC-01/04-01/06-773, 14 December 2006, para. 20). In another judgment, the Appeals Chamber observed that '[t]he reasons for a decision should be comprehensible from the decision itself. It is not sufficient for the Chamber to identi-

decision. When there is no unanimity, the Trial Chamber's decision shall contain the views of the majority and the minority.[619] The decision or a summary thereof shall be delivered in open court.[620]

---

fy simply which filings were before it. The decision must set out which of the relevant facts and legal arguments that were before the Chamber were found to be persuasive for the determination it reached.' (*Prosecutor v. Lubanga*, ICC A. Ch., Judgment on the Appeal of Mr. Thomas Lubanga Dyilo against the Decision of Pre-Trial Chamber I Entitled "Second Decision on the Prosecution Requests and Amended Requests for Redactions under Rule 81", 14 December 2006, para. 33). Although these rulings concern the reasoning in the decisions of Pre-Trial Chambers rather than Article 74 decisions, the same rationales, at minimum, apply to the latter decisions, if they are to meet the requirement of a full and reasoned statement of the findings on evidence and conclusions.

In light of the grounds of appellate review (Articles 81(1) and 83(2)), a 'full and reasoned statement' of 'findings on evidence and conclusions' should be such as to persuade the Appeals Chamber that the Trial Chamber has not committed any errors of fact or errors of law materially affecting the decision, or other errors affecting fairness or reliability of the decision (Triffterer 2008, p. 1398). The final decision at trial that satisfies the parameters of Article 74(5) must state the applicable law and relevant facts, each established by the evidence on the trial record, and explain how the Chamber arrived at the legal conclusions based on the application of law to facts. Furthermore, the reasoning underlying the trial judgment must be presented in a way that allows a meaningful inquiry by the Appeals Chamber into the alleged errors and demonstrates the soundness of the Trial Chamber's findings and conclusions. In other words, the statement of findings and conclusions must be complete, well structured, comprehensible, transparent, and logical. At the same time, the judgment must not stray beyond the boundaries of factual and legal relevance set by the Pre-Trial Chamber's decision on the confirmation of charges, as required by Article 74(2) and Regulation 55 discussed above.

The first Article 74 judgments delivered thus far have departed from the template of the *ad hoc* tribunals' judgments and adopted a structure and legal drafting technique distinct from those typically used by the ICC's predecessors. All of them are highly detailed, heavily referenced, and fairly lengthy, especially considering that they deal with the cases involving limited charges against single accused. Thus, the *Lubanga* trial judgment is 593 pp (excluding two separate and dissenting opinions); the *Ngudjolo* trial judgment 198 pp (excluding a concurring opinion); and the *Katanga* trial judgment 881 pp (including a 170-page minority opinion, but excluding a concurring opinion). One commentator's concern that 'new records in verbosity may well be set' (Schabas 2010, p. 875) has rather not been confirmed, at least not in the sense that the length of the opinions was excessive and unjustified. In terms of discursive transparency and candour, the judicial style adopted by the ICC trial judges when setting out issues and analysing the evidence, including its deficiencies and overall complexities of fact-finding, is comparable to that of the *ad hoc* tribunals.

Author: Sergey Vasiliev.

[619] When there is no unanimity, the Trial Chamber's decision shall contain the views of the majority and the minority. Turning to the issue of the number of decisions and the accommodation of dissenting views, Article 74(5) – which should be read jointly with paragraph 3 providing for the judicial duty to attempt to achieve unanimity – states that '[t]he Trial Chamber shall issue one decision' and '[w]hen there is no unanimity, the Trial Chamber's decision shall contain the views of the majority and the minority.' In contrast with the allowance made for the judges of the Appeals Chamber to 'deliver a separate or dissenting opinion on a question of law' (Article 83(4)), the trial judges are not explicitly authorised to append separate (concurring or dissenting) individually signed opinions to their judgment (see also Sluiter 2009, p. 511; but cf. Scha-

bas 2010, p. 876). Moreover, while Article 83(4) does not feature the requirement of 'one decision' in respect of the Appeals Chamber's judgment, Article 74(5) does envisage the issuance of a single decision containing the views of both the majority and the minority. On that basis, some scholars have argued that this provision 'clearly intends to discourage the writing of separate and dissenting opinions on a purely individual basis and to prevent the publication of separate and dissenting voices some time after the publication of the judgment.' (Sluiter 2009, p. 511).

However, in practice the trial judges have not adopted the interpretation of Article 74(5) as prescribing them to issue a single consolidated decision and precluding them from appending separate opinions to the trial judgment. The trial judgments issued thus far were all accompanied by individual opinions that do not qualify as 'minority opinions' within the meaning of Article 74(5) (*Prosecutor v. Lubanga*, ICC T. Ch., Separate opinion of Judge Adrian Fulford and Separate and Dissenting Opinion of Judge Odio Benito, Judgment pursuant to Article 74 of the Statute, ICC-01/04-01/06-2842, 14 March 2014; *Prosecutor v. Ngudjolo*, ICC T. Ch., Concurring Opinion of Judge Christine Van den Wyngaert, Judgment pursuant to Article 74 of the Statute, ICC-01/04-02/12-4, 18 December 2012; *Prosecutor v. Katanga*, ICC T. Ch., Concurring opinion of Judges Fatoumata Diarra and Bruno Cotte, Judgment pursuant to Article 74 of the Statute, ICC-01/04-01/07-3464-AnxII, 7 March 2014). On these instances, the conclusions on the question of guilt or innocence of the accused were reached unanimously, but the verdicts were still accompanied by individual opinions on discrete issues, delivered on the same date as the judgment and bearing the same individual number. Apparently, the judges did not construe the 'one decision' requirement restrictively, but chose to append any dissenting views on the majority's reasoning as separate documents within the same filing, instead of including them as the 'minority opinion' within the body of the verdict itself. The implications of the requirement that where there is no unanimity the decision 'shall contain the views of the majority and the minority' are uncertain. The text allows several interpretations. First, the body of the trial judgment could include the minority position and attribute it to the judge. The example of this approach is provided by the judgment of the Trial Chamber of the Extraordinary Chambers in the Courts of Cambodia in Case 001, whereby a dissenting opinion of Judge Cartwright was incorporated into the text of the judgment itself (*Kaing Guek Eav* (Case No. 001/18-07-2007), ECCC T. Ch., Judgment, 26 July 2010, paras. 397–399). Second, the trial judgment could blend both positions of the majority and the minority in a consolidated reasoning and present the latter as a set of counterarguments ultimately rejected by the court as erroneous or unconvincing (see for example Triffterer 2008, p. 1398: 'different findings on the evidence and/or different conclusions ought to be mentioned within the decision of the majority, without, however, indicating any assignment to a specific judge.'). Third, the minority opinion may be stated separately from the majority opinion while still forming part of the same filing. For instance, Judge Van den Wyngaert's 'minority opinion' in *Katanga* (which in fact amounts to a partially dissenting opinion) was appended to the 'majority opinion' (denominated as judgment). The dissent stated that 'this constitutes the Minority Opinion and forms an integral part of Trial Chamber II's judgment on the charges pursuant to Article 74' (*Prosecutor v. Katanga*, ICC T. Ch., Minority Opinion of Judge Christine Van den Wyngaert, Jugement rendu en application de l'Article 74 du Statut, ICC-01/04-01/07-3464-AnxI, 7 March 2014, fn. 1). If the 'minority opinion' is attributed (the options 1 and 3 above), there is no principled difference between such an opinion and a traditional 'dissenting opinion'. The arguments *a contrario* and by analogy based on textual differences between Articles 74(5) and 83(4) are a tenuous basis for claiming that the Rome Statute authorises – or forbids – the Trial Chamber judges to append separate and dissenting opinions to Articles 74 decisions. The drafting history of the ICC Statute does not provide clarity in this respect either. The issue of allowing for individual opinions was sidelined at the decisive stages of negotiations in Rome. However, it did receive attention during the drafting of the ILC Statute of 1994. The draft's Article 45(5) ruled out the possibility for the judges to append separate opinions to the final decision and contained the requirement of the 'sole judgment' (Draft Statute for an International Criminal Court, Report of the International Law Commission on the work of its forty-sixth session, 2 May—22 July 1994, Yearbook of the International Law Commission, 1994, vol. II (Part Two), UN doc. A/CN.4/SER./1994/Add.1 (Part 2), at 59). The commentary on the Article justified this choice with reference to the prevailing view that allowing separate or dissenting opinions 'could undermine the authority of the court and its judgments.' (*ibid.*). Since the negotiation record of the ICC Statute contains no traces of similar debates, its *travaux préparatoires* are of a limited value in interpreting Article 74(5).

Author: Sergey Vasiliev.

620 While it is meant to serve an expressive function (see for example Schabas 2010, p. 877), the public delivery of the judgment, in the presence of the parties and participants, also constitutes an important aspect of the principle of a public hearing (Articles 64(7) and 67(1)) and is mandated by human rights law (Article 6(1) ECHR and Article 14 ICCPR). Thus, the ECtHR held that the pronouncement of judgments in public or making them public or available to those who established interest (depending on the special features of the proceedings) ensures 'scrutiny of the judiciary by the public with a view to safeguarding the right to a fair trial'. It protects litigants against the 'administration of justice in secret with no public scrutiny' and contributes to the maintenance of confidence in the courts and 'the achievement of a fair trial' (*Pretto et al. v. Italy*, 7984/77, 8 December 1983, paras. 20–27; *Biryukov v. Russia*, 14810/02, 17 January 2008, paras. 30 and 45). A similar rationale was expressed by Judge Pikis when he held that the publication of ICC decisions is mandated by 'the significance of judgments and decisions as a source of law, a fact expressly acknowledged by Article 21(2) of the Statute... Making the case law known is a condition of its applicability. Withholding publication of judgments/decisions is tantamount to secreting their existence, making the principles deriving therefrom inaccessible to the public (*Prosecutor v. Kony et al.*, ICC A. Ch., Separate Opinion of Judge Georghios M. Pikis, Decision of the Appeals Chamber on the Unsealing of Documents, ICC-02/04-01/05-266, 4 February 2008, para. 9).

The reading out of the summary is intended to replace the pronouncement of the full text of judgments, which will usually be of a considerable length. In principle, as has often been the practice at the ICTR, the summary may be pronounced before the drafting of the full text of the decision is completed and the judgment can be made public. This may be the way to give a notice of the verdict to the parties and remove the uncertainty about the outcome as early as possible (which is particularly important in case of an acquittal). However, the summary is an unofficial document that does not contain a 'full and reasoned statement' and does not enable the parties to prepare a notice of appeal. Furthermore, there is a risk that the reasons stated in the summary might diverge from the written reasons ultimately given in the judgment (Triffterer 2008, p. 1398). It is therefore advisable for the ICC to avoid – as it has done thus far – the unfortunate practice of other tribunals not to make full reasons available on the same day when the oral summary is delivered in open court.

Indeed, the ICC Trial Chambers took care to publish both the decisions pursuant to Article 74 (in the original language) as well as the summaries on the day of the pronouncement of the judgment. According to the practice in the first cases, at the hearing for the delivery of the judgment, the President reads out the summary of the judgment in open court. Where the verdict is unanimous but accompanied by individual opinions, a note of that is made in the summary of the judgment but it does not include the summary of such opinions, and separate opinions are not read out (*Prosecutor v. Lubanga*, ICC T. Ch., Summary of the "Judgment pursuant to Article 74 of the Statute", ICC-01/04-01/06-2843, 14 March 2012, para. 41; *Prosecutor v. Ngudjolo*, Résumé du jugement rendu en application de l'Article 74 du Statut dans l'affaire Le Procureur c. Mathieu Ngudjolo le 18 décembre 2012 par la Chambre de première instance II, T. Ch., 18 December 2012, para. 47). However, in case of a non-unanimous verdict, a minority opinion is incorporated into the summary that is read out by the Presiding Judge in open court (*Prosecutor v. Katanga*, Summary of Trial Chamber II's Judgment of 7 March 2014, pursuant to Article 74 of the Statute in the case of The Prosecutor v. Germain Katanga, T. Ch., 7 March 2014, paras. 54–60).

Given that delayed issuance of judgments used to be a recurring problem in other tribunals (in particular, the ICTR), the time of the delivery of the decision and the admissible duration of deliberations are important issues raised by the consideration of Article 74(5). Rule 142(1) provides for the duty of the Trial Chamber to 'inform all those who participated in the proceedings of the date on which the Trial Chamber will pronounce its decision' and adds that '[t]he pronouncement shall be made within a reasonable period of time after the Trial Chamber has retired to deliberate'. The practical implications and enforceability of this rule are uncertain. There is a tension between the need for a carefully researched and drafted judgment satisfying the requirements of Article 74(5) and the interest in obtaining a prompt judgment, which is an aspect of a fair and expeditious trial and the right of the accused to be tried without undue delay. Since the optimal balance between these interests will vary by case and depend on the case's complexity and any other contingencies encountered in the preparation of the judgment, setting a time limit *in abstracto* may be inexpedient. In the absence of a fixed time limit, what a 'reasonable period of time' amounts to is to be determined on a case-by-case basis.

This issue generated debates when drafting the ICC Rules. Some delegations to the Preparatory Commission felt that defendants should not remain incarcerated indefinitely while waiting for the judgment. The Mexican delegation proposed setting a fixed time limit for the issuance of the decision on the charges (Lewis 2001, p. 551). However, for many delegations, the Mexico proposal could not be pursued due to the difficulty of agreeing on the reasonable time limit and uncertainty as to what sanctions or consequences, if any, were to attach to non-compliance with the deadline (*ibid.*). The delegates to the Preparatory Committee benefited from the recommendation by then ICTY President Jorda on this point, who strongly advised to refrain from imposing specific deadlines because that would have been unreasonable in the circumstances of international trials (*ibid.*, pp. 551–552). The result was the current compromise solution that the Chamber is to notify the parties and participants of the date for the pronouncement of the decision in advance, and that such date is to be set 'within a reasonable period of time', rather than within a term fixed by law. This was hoped to 'discipline' the judges and put 'moral pressure' on them to deliver the final decision as soon as possible while at the same time allowing for reasonable flexibility (*ibid.*, para. 522).

Cross-references:

Articles 76(4), 81(1), 83(2) and (4).

Rules 142(1), 144.

Regulation 55.

Doctrine:

1. Gideon Boas, James L. Bischoff and Nathalie L. Reid, *International Criminal Law Practitioner Library Series*. Volume III: *International Criminal Procedure*, Cambridge University Press, Cambridge, 2011, p. 377.

2. Håkan Friman, Helen Brady, Matteo Costi, Fabricio Guariglia and Carl-Friedrich Stuckenberg, "Charges", in Göran Sluiter, Håkan Friman, Suzannah Linton, Sergey Vasiliev and Salvatore Zappalà (eds.), *International Criminal Procedure: Principles and Rules*, Oxford University Press, Oxford, 2013, pp. 431–32.

3. Nina Jørgensen and Alexander Zahar, "Deliberation, Dissent, Judgment", in Göran Sluiter, Håkan Friman, Suzannah Linton, Sergey Vasiliev and Salvatore Zappalà (eds.), *Interna-*

tional Criminal Procedure: Principles and Rules, Oxford University Press, Oxford, 2013, p. 1155.

4. P. Lewis, "Trial Procedure", in Roy S. Lee (ed.), *The International Criminal Court: Elements of Crimes and Rules of Procedure and Evidence*, Transnational Publishers, Ardsley, NY, 2001, pp. 551, 553.

5. Christoph Safferling, *International Criminal Procedure*, Oxford University Press, Oxford, 2010, p. 522.

6. William A. Schabas, *The International Criminal Court: A Commentary on the Rome Statute*, Oxford University Press, Oxford, 2010, pp. 875–77.

7. William A. Schabas, *An Introduction to the International Criminal Court*, 4th ed., Cambridge University Press, Cambridge, 2011, pp. 301, 319.

8. Göran Sluiter, "Separate and Dissenting Opinions", in Antonio Cassese, Paola Gaeta and John R.W.D. Jones (eds.), *The Oxford Companion to International Criminal Justice*, Oxford University Press, Oxford, 2009, pp. 511–12.

9. Göran Sluiter, "Unity and Division in Decision Making: The Law and Practice on Individual Opinions at the ICTY", in Bert Swart, Alexander Zahar and Göran Sluiter (eds.), *The Legacy of the International Criminal Tribunal for the Former Yugoslavia*, Oxford University Press, Oxford, 2011, p. 203.

10. Otto Triffterer, "Article 74", in Otto Triffterer (ed.), *Commentary on the Rome Statute of the International Criminal Court: Observers' Notes, Article by Article*, 2nd ed., C.H. Beck/Hart/Nomos, Munich/Oxford/Baden-Baden, 2008, pp. 1387–98.

Author: Sergey Vasiliev.

Article 75
Reparations to victims[621]

1. The Court shall establish principles relating to reparations[622] to, or in respect of, victims,[623] including restitution, compensation and rehabilitation.[624] On this basis, in its decision the

---

[621] *General remarks*:

Article 75, which deals with reparations to victims, is a novelty in international law as it allows victims to file claims against, and be awarded reparations from, an individual perpetrator of a crime in an international criminal process. The reparations scheme is considered a key feature of the Statute, on which the success of the Court is partly depending (*Prosecutor v. Lubanga*, ICC PT. Ch., Corrigendum of Decision on the Prosecutor's Application for a Warrant of Arrest, Article 58, ICC-01/04-01/06-1, 10 February 2006, para. 150). Logically, Article 75 implies that victims possess a right of reparations under international law and that this right can be satisfied in the framework of international criminal proceedings (Zappalà, pp. 159–160). A general concern, however, is that the perpetrator-centred reparation regime, which is also complex and requires expert advice, might create hierarchies or dividing lines among victims who falls inside or outside of the regime (Kendall and Nouwen).

The first, and so far only, decisions on reparations were handed down in *Lubanga* by the Trial Chamber on 7 August 2012 (*Prosecutor v. Lubanga*, ICC T. Ch., Decision establishing the principles and procedures to be applied to reparations, ICC-01/04-01/06-2904, 7 August 2012), and by the Appeals Chamber on 3 March 2015 (*Prosecutor v. Lubanga*, ICC A. Ch., Judgment on the appeals against the "Decision establishing the principles and procedures to be applied to reparations" of 7 August 2012 with AMENDED order for reparations (Annex A) and public annexes 1 and 2, ICC-01/04-01/06-3129, 3 March 2015).

Preparatory works:

The 1994 ILC Draft Statute did not contain any provision on reparations to victims (Report of the International Law Commission on the work of its 46th session 2 May–22 July 1994, UN doc. A/49/10, 1994). Some proposals were made in the negotiations of the ICC Statute (for example Article 45, subheading G, Report of the Preparatory Committee, UN doc A/51/22, Vol. II, 1996, at 224), but they were discussed in earnest first at the last session of the Preparatory Committee in March/April 1998. These discussions were based upon three alternative proposals reproduced in the so-called Zutphen Draft (Article 66, Draft Report of the Intersessional Meeting from 19 to 30 January 1998 in Zutphen, The Netherlands) and a joint proposal by France and the United Kingdom. The result was a draft Article, within brackets, transmitted to the Diplomatic Conference for further discussions as to whether there should be any Article at all and, if so, its content (Article 73, Report of the Preparatory Committee on the Establishment of an International Criminal Court, UN doc. A/CONF.183/2 (1998)). The Article, finally the current Article 75, was substantially redrafted by the Working Group on Procedures and finally adopted by the Diplomatic Conference. The legal principles and procedures for reparations in Article 75 are outlined only in very general terms and it was clear that implementing provisions were necessary in the Rules of Procedure and Evidence. In order to air the issues and create a deeper understanding, the French Government arranged an international seminar on 27–29 April 1999 (the Paris Seminar). The Report from the Paris Seminar (UN doc. PCNICC/1999/WGRPE/INF/2) then served as a point of departure for the drafting of the Rules. An account of the negotiations is provided in Friman and Lewis, 2001.

Author: Håkan Friman.

[622] The Court has settled for a case specific approach to the stipulation of the Court's reparation principles. The question of pre-established general principles has been discussed but rejected by

the plenary of judges in 2006 and 2008 (Report of the Court on principles relating to victims' reparations, ICC-ASP12/39 of 8 October 2013, paras. 3 and 17–18). The case-by-case approach was also underlined by the Trial Chamber in the *Lubanga* decision on reparations (*Prosecutor v. Lubanga*, ICC T. Ch., ICC-01/04-01/06-2904, 7 August 2012, para. 181) and approved by the Appeals Chamber (*Lubanga*, ICC A. Ch., ICC-01/04-01/06-3129, 3 March 2015, para. 55).

The ASP, on the other hand, has requested the Court to ensure court-wide and coherent principles relating to reparations to be "established in accordance with Article 75, paragraph 1" based on which individual orders may be issued (Resolution ICC-ASP/10/Res.3, op. 1, adopted on 20 December 2011 by consensus). The approach by the Court has also been criticised by others as contrary to the spirit and letter of Article 75(1) (for example Redress, 2011).

In *Lubanga*, the Appeals Chamber stressed that the principles relevant to the circumstances of a case must be distinguished from the order of reparations: "principles should be general concepts that, while formulated in light of the circumstances of a specific case, can nonetheless be applied, adapted, expanded upon, or added to by future Trial Chambers", while the order is "the Trial Chamber's holdings, determinations and findings based upon those principles" (*Lubanga*, ICC A. Ch., ICC-01/04-01/06-3129, 3 March 2015, paras. 3 and 55). Accordingly, the Appeals Chamber presented the principles separate from the order for reparations. Moreover, the Appeals Chamber held that both individual and collective awards made against the convicted person, regardless of whether they are made directly or through the Trust Fund for Victims, must be based on the relevant Article 75(1) principles (paras. 52–53).

In *Lubanga*, the Trial Chamber laid down a number of general principles (*Prosecutor v. Lubanga*, ICC T. Ch., ICC-01/04-01/06-2904, 7 August 2012). General aims of reparations are to repair the harm caused and to provide accountability (para. 179). The Appeals Chamber agreed (*Lubanga*, ICC A. Ch., ICC-01/04-01/06-3129, 3 March 2015, Annex A, para. 2). A number of international soft law instruments (principles and declarations), certain significant human rights reports (by van Boven and Bassiouni) as well as the jurisprudence of regional human rights courts and national and international mechanisms may be consulted for guidance (*Lubanga*, ICC T. Ch., ICC-01/04-01/06-2904, 7 August 2012, paras. 185–186).

As a general principle, victims "should receive appropriate, adequate and prompt reparations" (*Lubanga*, ICC A. Ch., ICC-01/04-01/06-3129, 3 March 2015, Annex A, para. 44). The awards ought to be proportionate to the harm, injury, loss and damage as established by the Court (Annex A, para. 45). Importantly, the Appeals Chamber concluded that a reparation order in all circumstances – whether individual or collective, direct or made through the Trust Fund for Victims – must be issued against the convicted person (*Lubanga*, ICC A. Ch., ICC-01/04-01/06-3129, 3 March 2015, paras. 64–76 and Annex A, para. 20). The convicted person's liability for reparations must be proportionate to the harm caused and, *inter alia*, his or her participation the in the commission of the crimes for which he or she was found guilty, in the specific circumstances of the case (paras. 6 and 118, Annex A, para. 21).

Under the heading "Dignity, non-discrimination and non-stigmatisation", the Trial Chamber held that 'all victims are to be treated fairly and equally as regards reparations, irrespective of whether they participated in the trial proceedings', as the Trial Chamber considered it inappropriate to limit reparations to the rather small group of participating victims (*Lubanga*, ICC T. Ch., ICC-01/04-01/06-2904, 7 August 2012, para. 187). The victims, as defined in rule 85, shall enjoy equal access to information and assistance from the Court, and the Court shall take into account the needs of all the victims but pay special attention to victims who are children, elderly, have disabilities or are victims of sexual or gender violence (paras. 188–189). When deciding on reparations, the Court shall treat the victims with humanity, respect their dignity and human rights and implement appropriate measures to ensure their safety, physical and psychological wellbeing and privacy, and apply the non-discrimination principle set forth in Article 21(3) (paras. 190–191). These principles were upheld by the Appeals Chamber (*Lubanga*, ICC A. Ch., ICC-01/04-01/06-3129, 3 March 2015, Annex A, paras. 12–19).

In line with theories of so-called transformative justice, the Trial Chamber found that reparations must address any underlying injustices and be implemented so as to avoid replicating discriminatory practices or structures that predated the crimes and to avoid further stigmatisation of the victims and discrimination by their families and communities (*Lubanga*, ICC T. Ch., ICC-01/04-01/06-2904, 7 August 2012, paras. 192 and 227). Whenever possible, reparations should secure reconciliation (para. 193). A particular aim is to reconcile the victims with their families and all the communities affected by the charges (para. 244). Also in these respects the Appeals Chamber concurred (*Lubanga*, ICC A. Ch., ICC-01/04-01/06-3129, 3 March 2015, Annex A, paras. 17 and 46).

The Trial Chamber also adhered to the concept of gender justice stating that a gender-inclusive approach should guide the design of the principles and that gender parity in all aspects of reparations is an important goal of the Court (*Lubanga*, ICC T. Ch., ICC-01/04-01/06-2904, 7 August 2012, para. 202). Reparations are to be awarded on a non-discriminatory and gender-inclusive basis (paras. 218 and 243). The Appeals Chamber upheld these principles (*Lubanga*, ICC A. Ch., ICC-01/04-01/06-3129, 3 March 2015, Annex A, paras. 12 and 18). The Trial Chamber took the issue further by stating that appropriate and gender-sensitive reparations must be formulated and implemented with respect to victims of sexual or gender-based violence (*Lubanga*, ICC T. Ch., ICC-01/04-01/06-2904, 7 August 2012, paras. 207–209). However, the Appeals Chamber noted that the conviction in the case at hand did not include responsibility for sexual and gender-based violence and thus that such violence could not be defined as a harm resulting from the convicted crimes (*Lubanga*, ICC A. Ch., ICC-01/04-01/06-3129, 3 March 2015, paras. 196–198). Hence, the convicted person could not be held liable for reparations in respect of such harm.

As for child victims, the age-related harm experienced as well as their needs must be considered and the Court should be guided by the principle of the "best interest of the child" as enshrined in the Convention on the Rights of the Child as well as other guidelines in the Convention and other international instruments (*Lubanga*, ICC A. Ch., ICC-01/04-01/06-3129, 3 March 2015, Annex A, paras. 23–24).

Reparations should also, whenever possible, reflect local cultural and customary practices, unless these are discriminatory, exclusive or deny victims equal access to their rights (*Lubanga*, ICC A. Ch., ICC-01/04-01/06-3129, 3 March 2015, Annex A, para. 47).

Author: Håkan Friman.

[623] Article 75(1) and (2) refer to reparations "to, or in respect of victims", and a definition is provided in rule 85, but the Court has found it necessary to give further clarifications. With reference to rule 85, reparations may be granted to direct and indirect victims, including family members to direct victims, anyone who attempted to prevent one or more of the relevant crimes, and those who suffered personal harm as a result of these offences (*Lubanga*, ICC T. Ch., Decision establishing the principles and procedures to be applied to reparations, ICC-01/04-01/06-2904, 7 August 2012, para. 194). Unless it is someone who suffered harm when helping or intervening on behalf of a direct victim (para. 196; see also *Lubanga*, ICC T. Ch., Redacted version of "Decision on 'indirect victims'", ICC-01/04-01/06-1813, 8 April 2009, para. 51), an indirect victim should have a close personal relationship with a direct victim and in considering the relationship the applicable social and familial structures ought to be regarded (para. 195; see also *Lubanga*, ICC A. Ch., Judgment on the appeals of the Prosecutor and the Defence against Trial Chamber I's Decision on Victims' Participation of 18 January 2008, ICC-01/04-01/06-1432, 11 July 2008, para. 32). In an earlier decision, the Trial Chamber clarified that indirect victims must establish that, as a result of their relationship with the direct victim, the loss, inju-

ry, or damage suffered by the latter gives rise to harm to them; hence, the harm suffered by indirect victims must arise out of the harm suffered by direct victims, brought about by the commission of the crimes charged (*Lubanga*, ICC T. Ch., Redacted version of "Decision on 'indirect victims'", ICC-01/04-01/06-1813, 8 April 2009, para. 49). Reparations can also be granted to legal entities (para. 197).

The Appeals Chamber has recognised that the concept of "family" may have many different cultural variations and that the Court should have regard to the applicable societal and familial structures, but also the widely accepted presumption that an individual is succeeded by his or her spouse and children (*Lubanga*, ICC A. Ch., ICC-01/04-01/06-3129, 3 March 2015, Annex A, para. 7). Priority may need to be given to certain particularly vulnerable victims or victims who require urgent assistance (*Lubanga*, ICC T. Ch., ICC-01/04-01/06-2904, 7 August 2012, para. 200, and ICC A. Ch., ICC-01/04-01/06-3129, 3 March 2015, Annex A, para. 19). Examples are victims of sexual or gender-based violence, individuals who require immediate medical case (for example plastic surgery or HIV treatment) or severely traumatised children. Hence, the Chamber may adopt "measures that constitute affirmative action in order to guarantee equal, effective and safe access to reparations for particularly vulnerable victims".

The *Lubanga* Trial Chamber took a very broad approach to which victims may benefit from reparations, including victims who did not request reparations although they participated in the trial proceedings (*Lubanga*, ICC T. Ch., Scheduling order concerning timetable for sentencing and reparations, ICC-01/04-01/06-2844, 14 March 2012, para. 8). The Chamber also held that a collective approach to reparations should ensure that reparations reach also those victims who are currently unidentified (*Lubanga*, ICC T. Ch., ICC-01/04-01/06-2904, 7 August 2012, para. 219). The Appeals Chamber, noting that the reparations proceedings are a distinct process and that rule 94 does not require participation in the criminal proceedings (in accordance with rule 89), has generally accepted the broad approach (*Prosecutor v. Lubanga*, ICC A. Ch., Decision on the admissibility of the appeals against Trial Chamber I's "Decision establishing the principles and procedures to be applied to reparations" and directions on the further conduct of proceedings, ICC-01/04-01/06-2953, 14 December 2012, paras. 69–72). However, the Appeals Chamber rejected, for the purpose of an appeal, the inclusion of unidentified individuals since it was impossible to discern who belongs to this group (para. 72).

Author: Håkan Friman.

624   According to the Appeals Chamber, also a community – understood as a group of victims– may be awarded collective reparations (*Lubanga*, ICC A. Ch., ICC-01/04-01/06-3129, 3 March 2015, paras. 211–212). However, this does apply only to members of the community meeting the relevant criteria for eligibility and, thus, the Trial Chamber must establish the criteria for this distinction (para. 214 and Annex A, para. 54).

As to the modalities of reparations, the *Lubanga* Trial Chamber concluded that the list in Article 75(1) is not exclusive and that also, for example, reparations with a symbolic, preventative or transformative value may be appropriate (*Lubanga*, ICC T. Ch., ICC-01/04-01/06-2904, 7 August 2012, para. 222). Other modalities of reparations may include campaigns, certificates of harm suffered, outreach and promotional programmes, and educational measures (para. 239). Measures to address shame and to prevent further victimisation may also be considered, and the Chamber noted that the accused is able to contribute by way of a voluntary apology to individual victims or groups of victims on a public or confidential basis (paras. 240–241).

The Appeals Chamber, while agreeing with these findings, stressed that the Trial Chamber must identify in the reparation order the most appropriate modalities of reparations in the case at hand, and that this question is interlinked to the identification of the harm caused to the direct and indirect victims (*Lubanga*, ICC A. Ch., ICC-01/04-01/06-3129, 3 March 2015, paras. 200 and 202–203, and Annex A, paras. 34 and 67). Individual and collective reparations are not mu-

Court may, either upon request or on its own motion[625] in exceptional circumstances, determine the scope and extent of any damage, loss and injury to, or in respect of, victims and will state the principles on which it is acting.[626]

---

tually exclusive and may be awarded concurrently (Annex A, para. 33). Once the appropriate modalities are established by the Trial Chamber, it may be left to the Trust Fund for Victims to design the concrete awards for reparations to the victims (paras. 200–201).

Restitution, which is mentioned in Article 75(1), is directed at the restoration of an individual's life and should as far as possible restore the victim to his or her circumstances before the crime was committed (*Lubanga*, ICC T. Ch., ICC-01/04- 01/06-2904, 7 August 2012, paras. 223–224, and ICC A. Ch., ICC-01/04-01/06-3129, 3 March 2015, Annex A, paras. 35 and 67). It may be an appropriate modality for legal bodies (Annex A, para. 36).

Compensation should be considered when the economic harm is sufficiently quantifiable, an award of this kind would be appropriate and proportionate, and there are available funds to make the result feasible (*Lubanga*, ICC A. Ch., ICC-01/04-01/06-3129, 3 March 2015, Annex A, para. 37). Compensation requires a broad application to encompass all forms of damage, loss and injury, including physical harm, moral and non-material damage resulting in physical, mental and emotional suffering, material damage, lost opportunities (employment, education, etcetera), and costs of legal or other relevant experts, medical services, psychological and social assistance ((Annex A, paras. 39–40).

Rehabilitation shall include the provision of medical services and health care, psychological, psychiatric and social assistance to support those suffering from grief and trauma, and any relevant legal and social services (*Lubanga*, ICC A. Ch., ICC-01/04-01/06-3129, 3 March 2015, Annex A, para. 42). Rehabilitation may include measures that are directed at facilitating the reintegration into society, such as education, vocational training and sustainable work opportunities (Annex A, para. 67). Compensation and rehabilitation shall be approached on a gender-inclusive basis (Annex A, paras. 38, 41 and 67).

With reference to decisions by the Inter-American Court of Human Rights, the *Lubanga* Trial Chamber stated that the conviction and sentence are also examples of reparations, "given they are likely to have significance for the victims, their families and communities" (*Lubanga*, ICC T. Ch., ICC-01/04- 01/06-2904, 7 August 2012, para. 237). This part of the decision has been criticised, however, for conflating retributive and reparative justice by making the former a part of the latter (Hoyle and Ullrich, p. 698). Nonetheless, the Appeals Chamber upheld the Trial Chamber's conclusion (*Lubanga*, ICC A. Ch., ICC-01/04-01/06-3129, 3 March 2015, Annex A, para. 43).

For a further discussion on modalities of reparations (that is, restitution, compensation, different forms of satisfaction), see McCarthy, pp. 158–182.

Author: Håkan Friman.

[625] Article 75(1) makes clear that reparations may be decided upon request or, in exceptional circumstances, on the Court's own motion. The *Lubanga* Trial Chamber, however, established that reparations are "entirely voluntary" and that the informed consent of the recipient is required prior to any award (*Lubanga*, ICC T. Ch., ICC-01/04-01/06-2904, 7 August 2012, para. 204). The Appeals Chamber agreed (*Lubanga*, ICC A. Ch., ICC-01/04-01/06-3129, 3 March 2015, paras. 159–160). Consequently, even in case the Court moves on the issue on its own motion, informed consent must be obtained from each victim concerned.

Author: Håkan Friman.

[626] The concepts "damage, loss and injury", as set forth in Article 75(1), are synonymous with "harm" (see rule 85(a), and *Lubanga*, ICC A. Ch., Judgment of the Appeals of the Prosecutor and the Defence against Trial Chamber I's Decision on Victims' Participation', ICC-01/04-

2. The Court may make an order directly against a convicted person specifying appropriate reparations to, or in respect of, victims, including restitution, compensation and rehabilitation.

01/06-1432, 11 July 2008, para. 31). It is not necessary that he harm is direct, but it must be personal to the victim, and it can consist of material, physical or psychological harm (para. 32). Nonetheless, in its decision on reparations the *Lubanga* Trial Chamber sometimes placed the four terms side by side (*Lubanga*, ICC T. Ch., ICC-01/04-01/06-2904, 7 August 2012, para. 243), thus confusing the terminology. Whether the harm should be of a recoverable nature was not addressed by the Chambers, although the Appeals Chamber noted with respect to compensation that some forms of damage are "essentially unquantifiable in financial terms" (Lubanga, ICC A. Ch., ICC-01/04-01/06-3129, 3 March 2015, Annex A, para. 40). For a general discussion, see McCarthy pp. 100–101).

The Appeals Chamber stressed that the Trial Chamber must clearly identify the harm to direct and indirect victims caused by the crimes in the case at hand and form part of the reparation order (*Lubanga*, ICC A. Ch., ICC-01/04-01/06-3129, 3 March 2015, paras. 181 and 184). Amending the Trial Chambers order in *Lubanga* (para. 191 and Annex A, para. 58), the Appeals Chamber held that the harm of direct victims consisted of: a) physical injury and trauma; b) psychological trauma and the development of psychological disorders (suicidal tendencies, etcetera); c) interruption and loss of schooling; d) separation from families; e) exposure to an environment of violence and fear; f) difficulties socialising within their families and communities; g) difficulties in controlling aggressive impulses; and h) the non-development of "civilian life skills" resulting in the victim being at a disadvantage, particularly as regards employment. Indirect victims suffered harm such as: a) psychological suffering experiences as a result of the sudden loss of a family member; b) material deprivation that accompanies the loss of family members' contributions; c) loss, injury or damage suffered by the intervening person from attempting to prevent the child from being further harmed as a result of a relevant crime; and d) psychological and/or material sufferings as a result of aggressiveness on the part of former child soldiers relocated to their families and communities.

Causation

In *Lubanga*, the Trial Chamber concluded that that there must be a causal link between the relevant crimes and the "damage, loss and injury" which form the basis of the reparation claim (*Lubanga*, ICC T. Ch., ICC-01/04-01/06-2904, 7 August 2012, para. 247). But there was some ambiguity as to whether the Chamber required the harm to be linked to the crimes of which the accused was actually convicted. It referred more neutrally to the type of offences concerned ("the crimes of enlisting and conscripting children under the age of 15 and using them to participate actively in the hostilities" paras. 247 and 249). Further, the Chamber stated that the relevant standard of causation needs to reflect and balance the divergent interests and rights of the victims and convicted person (para. 250). Nonetheless, the linkage between the harm and the crimes of which the accused was convicted was established by a "but/for" relationship between the crime and the harm (para. 250). Instead of requiring direct harm or immediate effects of the crimes, the Chamber concluded that a looser standard of "proximate cause" should be applied (para. 249).

The Appeals Chamber considered that the casual link between the crime and the harm for the purposes of reparations is to be determined in light of the specificities of the case (*Lubanga*, ICC A. Ch., ICC-01/04-01/06-3129, 3 March 2015, para. 80). It upheld the but/for relationship and "proximate cause" standard of causation (paras. 124–129 and Annex A, para. 59).

Author: Håkan Friman.

Where appropriate, the Court may order that the award for reparations be made through the Trust Fund provided for in Article 79.[627]

---

[627] *Reparation orders and awards*

Article 75(2) refers to an order of reparations as well as an award for reparations to be made through the Trust Fund for Victims. The terms are intended to be synonymous as they are in the French and Spanish versions of the Statute.

An order of reparations may be made against a person only once he or she is convicted. The post-conviction nature of the reparations proceedings follows also from Article 76(3).

In *Lubanga*, the Appeals Chamber established that a reparation order must contain, at a minimum, five essential elements: 1) it must be directed against the convicted person; 2) it must establish and inform the convicted person of his or her liability with respect to the reparations awarded in the order; 3) it must specify, and provide reasons for, the type of reparations ordered, either collective, individual or both, pursuant to rules 97(1) and 98; 4) it must define the harm caused to direct and indirect victims as a result of the crimes for which the person was convicted, as well as identify the modalities of reparations that are considered appropriate based on the specific circumstances of the specific case at hand; and 5) it must identify the victims eligible to benefit from the awards for reparations or set out criteria of eligibility based upon the link between the harm suffered by the victims and the crimes for which the person was convicted (*Lubanga*, ICC A. Ch., ICC-01/04-01/06-3129, 3 March 2015, para. 1).

a) Direct orders and awards through the Trust Fund

In *Lubanga*, the Trial Chamber was drawing extensively on the Trust Fund for Victim to make determinations and award reparations, but also to make use of funds available to the Fund from its own resources (*Lubanga*, ICC T. Ch., ICC-01/04-01/06-2904, 7 August 2012). Instead of examining individual applications for reparations, the Chamber endorsed an implementation plan suggested by the Trust Fund (paras. 281–283 and 289).

This caused the Appeal Chamber to settle a number of questions with respect to the responsibilities of the Trial Chamber and the relationship to the Trust Fund and its various mandates. The fundamental principle was that reparations, irrespective of whether they are ordered directly or through the Trust Fund, must be directed against the convicted person (*Lubanga*, ICC A. Ch., ICC-01/04-01/06-3129, 3 March 2015, paras. 1 and 69–76). Although the Trial Chamber's decision in *Lubanga* did not explicitly award reparations to any victim, the Appeals Chamber found that it should be deemed to be an order for reparations (*Lubanga*, ICC A. Ch., ICC-01/04-01/06-2953, 14 December 2012, para. 51). Decisive for this determination was the fact that apart from establishing principles, the decision also established procedures to be applied and tasked the Trust Fund for Victims to carry out the implementation which could only be done based upon a reparation order (paras. 51–64).

As long as the Trial Chamber concludes that the convicted person is liable for the reparations awarded, identifies the harms to direct and indirect victims, and set the criteria for the assessment, as well as identifies the most appropriate modalities of reparations (based upon the specific circumstances), the Chamber may delegate to the Trust Fund to assess the harm suffered by the victims and decide the nature and size of the awards (*Lubanga*, ICC A. Ch., ICC-01/04-01/06-2953, 14 December 2012, paras. 101, 181–184 and 200–203). It is possible that not all the modalities will ultimately be reflected in the actual awards and, if so, the Trust Fund must explain why (para. 201 and Annex A, paras. 68–70). In addition, the order must identify the victims eligible to benefit from reparations, or set out criteria of eligibility (paras. 205 and 210–215). The indigence of the convicted person is irrelevant for the liability (*Lubanga*, ICC A. Ch., ICC-01/04-01/06-2953, 14 December 2012, paras. 102–15; compare ICC T. Ch., ICC-01/04-01/06-2904, 7 August 2012, paras. 269–271). Moreover, the so-called "other resources"

3. Before making an order under this article, the Court may invite and shall take account of representations from or on behalf of the convicted person, victims, other interested persons or interested States.[628]

---

of the Trust Fund fall solely under the control of the Fund and, thus, are not subject to an order by the Court, although the Fund might voluntarily make use of these resources without exonerating the convicted person from liability (*Lubanga*, ICC A. Ch., ICC-01/04-01/06-2953, 14 December 2012, paras. 4–5 and 106–117; compare ICC T. Ch., ICC-01/04-01/06-2904, 7 August 2012, paras. 270–273). These "other resources" may also be utilised for victims that fall outside of the Court's reparations award (*Lubanga*, ICC A. Ch., ICC-01/04-01/06-2953, 14 December 2012, para. 215).

b) Individual and collective reparations

While Article 75(2) distinguishes between orders directed against the convicted person and awards made through the Trust Fund for Victims, rule 97(1) makes clear that reparations may be awarded on an individualised basis, or on a collective one, or by a combination of the two. Individual and collective reparations are not mutually exclusive and may be awarded concurrently (*Lubanga*, ICC T. Ch., ICC-01/04-01/06-2904, 7 August 2012, para. 220, and ICC A. Ch., ICC-01/04-01/06-3129, 3 March 2015, Annex A, para. 33).

According to rule 98(1), individual awards for reparations shall be made directly against the convicted person. But under certain conditions the Court may, under rule 98(2), order that such awards be deposited with the Trust Fund. In addition, rule 98(3) allows collective awards against a convicted person be made through the Trust Fund. A collective approach was preferred in *Lubanga* to ensure that reparations reach those victims who were currently unidentified (*Lubanga*, ICC T. Ch., ICC-01/04-01/06-2904, 7 August 2012, para. 219). In case of collective awards only, the Appeals Chambers agreed that the Trial Chamber is not required to rule on the merits of the individual requests, but instead – if applicable – to deny, as a category, individual awards (*Lubanga*, ICC A. Ch., ICC-01/04-01/06-3129, 3 March 2015, para. 152). Collective reparations may be awarded also without an application to that effect (para. 151). Individual claims may be disregarded (para. 7).

Collective awards may be motivated by a considerable number of victims, particularly when only a limited number of individuals have applied for reparations (*Lubanga*, ICC A. Ch., ICC-01/04-01/06-3129, 3 March 2015, para. 153). Further, both the Trial Chamber and the Appeals Chamber held that reparations need to support programmes that are self-sustaining so that they can be beneficial over an extended period of time (*Lubanga*, ICC T. Ch., ICC-01/04-01/06-2904, 7 August 2012, para. 246, and ICC A. Ch., ICC-01/04-01/06-3129, 3 March 2015, Annex A, para. 48). For example, if pensions are paid they should be periodic rather than paid by way of a lump payment.

Author: Håkan Friman.

[628] *a) Reparation proceedings*

The procedures before a Trial Chamber leading to the issuance of an order for reparations are regulated in particular by Articles 75 and 76(3) of the Statute and rules 94, 95, 97 and 143 of the RPE. The first part is the establishment of principles relating to reparations to, or in respect of, victims, which concludes with the issuance of an order for reparations under Article 75(2) or a decision not to award reparations. The second part of the proceedings consists of the implementation phase, which is regulated primarily by Article 75(2) and rule 98 (*Lubanga*, ICC A. Ch., ICC-01/04-01/06-2953, 14 December 2012, paras. 54–55).

The reparations proceedings are considered to be distinct and not forming part of the trial *strictu sensu*, which means, for example, that a Chamber different from the Trial Chamber convicting the accused may be constituted (*Prosecutor v. Katanga*, ICC Pres., Decision on conclusion of term of office of Judges Bruno Cotte and Fatoumata Dembele Diarra, ICC-01/04-01/07-3468-AnxI (2014/PRES/115), 16 April 2014). Similarly, the *Lubanga* Trial Chamber concluded that a different Chamber could monitor and supervise reparations to be awarded through the Trust Fund for Victims (*Lubanga*, ICC T. Ch., ICC-01/04-01/06-2904, 7 August 2012, paras. 260–262). This solution was upheld by the Appeals Chamber, which also devised a more detailed scheme for issues to be adjudicated by the Chamber (*Lubanga*, ICC A. Ch., ICC-01/04-01/06-3129, 3 March 2015, paras. 167, 232–236 and Annex A, paras. 75–81).

An important feature of the reparations proceedings is that the victims are parties and not merely participants to the proceedings (for example Zappalà, 2010, p. 157, and Friman, 2009, p. 496). This is also true with respect to the appeals stage (*Lubanga*, ICC A. Ch., ICC-01/04-01/06-2953, 14 December 2012, para. 67).

b) Representations

In seeking inspiration regarding the principles to be established, the Trial Chambers have reached out within and outside of the Court. In *Lubanga*, written instructions were issued by email of 16 March 2011 whereby the Chamber requested a consolidated and updated joint filing on reparations from the Trust Fund for Victims and the Registry (*Prosecutor v. Lubanga*, ICC TFV, Public Redacted Version of ICC-01/04-01/06-2803-Conf-Exp-Trust Fund for Victims' First Report on Reparations, ICC-01/04-01/06, 1 September 2011).

Moreover, five organisations were granted leave to make written representations concerning reparations (*Prosecutor v. Lubanga*, ICC T. Ch., Decision granting leave to make representations in the reparations proceedings, ICC-01/04-01/06-2870, 20 April 2012). The defence argued that such intervention was only possible under rule 103 of the RPE (amicus curiae), but the Trial Chamber concluded that the proceedings set out in Article 75(3) are distinct from those of rule 103(2)–(3) and they require the Court to take representations that it has received into account (paras. 11 and 20).

In the appeals process, however, the Appeals Chamber opted to rely upon Article 103 (*Lubanga*, ICC A. Ch., ICC-01/04-01/06-2953, 14 December 2012, para. 77). Once submitted, the Appeals Chamber rejected the various requests to submit amicus curiae observations (*Lubanga*, ICC A. Ch., ICC-01/04-01/06-3129, 3 March 2015, paras. 247–251).

c) Requests for reparations and other procedural issues

Rule 94 of the RPE contains provisions on the procedure to follow in case of a victim's request for reparations. According to the rule, the request shall contain, *inter alia*, the identity and address of the claimant, a description of the injury, loss or harm, and information on concerning the incident and, if possible, the person responsible. These requirements may be too onerous considering the actual situation, however, and the Court has accepted different means of identification, including official or unofficial identification documents or a statement signed by two credible witnesses (*Prosecutor v. Lubanga*, ICC T. Ch., Decision on victims' participation, ICC-01/04-01/06-1119, 18 January 2008, paras. 87–88, and *Lubanga*, ICC T. Ch., ICC-01/04-01/06-2904, 7 August 2012, para. 198).

Rule 95 sets out the procedure when the Court intends to proceed with awarding reparations on its own motion. The threshold for the application of this rule ("exceptional circumstances") is different from that applicable to collective reparations ("more appropriate") (*Lubanga*, ICC A. Ch., ICC-01/04-01/06-3129, 3 March 2015, para. 148 c.).

The Registry is tasked with providing a standard form for reparations claims as well as to assist the victims and make certain inquiries (regulation 88). In *Katanga*, the Registry was requested to assist in clarifying and updating the requests for reparations by contacting the victims and report back to the Trial Chamber (including information on the harm suffered and the reparations sought) (*Prosecutor v. Katanga*, ICC T. Ch., Order instructing the Registry to report on applications for reparations, ICC-01/04-01/07-3508, 27 August 2014).

4. In exercising its power under this article, the Court may, after a person is convicted of a crime within the jurisdiction of the Court, determine whether, in order to give effect to an order which it may make under this article, it is necessary to seek measures under Article 93, paragraph 1.[629]

The *Lubanga* Trial Chamber stressed that the victims, together with their families and communities, should be able to participate throughout the reparations process and receive adequate support to make their participation substantive and effective (*Lubanga*, ICC T. Ch., ICC-01/04-01/06-2904, 7 August 2012, para. 203). The Registry was tasked with deciding the most appropriate form of participation in the proceedings (para. 268). Moreover, the Chamber addressed outreach activities, communication, and consultations (paras. 205–206).

In the same case, the OPCV was designated to act as the legal representative of unrepresented applicants for reparations until their status is determined or until the Registrar arranges a legal representative to act on their behalf; and to represent the interests of victims who have not submitted applications but who may benefit from an award for collective reparations, pursuant to Rules 97 and 98 of the RPE (*Prosecutor v. Lubanga*, ICC T. Ch., Decision on the OPCV's request to participate in the reparations proceedings, ICC-01/04-01/06-2858, 5 April 2012).

d) Standard and burden of proof

No agreement on rules on evidence with respect to reparations could be reached in the negotiations of the RPE (Friman and Lewis, pp. 484–486). The *Lubanga* Trial Chamber found that the standard of "a balance of probabilities" was sufficient and proportionate concerning an order directed against the convicted person (*Lubanga*, ICC T. Ch., ICC-01/04-01/06-2904, 7 August 2012, para. 253). On the other hand, the Trial Chamber considered that no such standard was required when reparations are awarded through the Trust Fund and instead "a wholly flexible approach to determining factual matters is appropriate" (para. 254).

The Appeal Chamber disagreed and established that the "balance of probabilities" standard applies in both instances (*Lubanga*, ICC A. Ch., ICC-01/04-01/06-3129, 3 March 2015, para. 83 and Annex A, para. 22). The Appeals Chamber added that the applicant shall provide sufficient proof of the causal link between the crime and the harm suffered, based on the specific circumstances of the case (para. 81).

e) Expert assistance

According to rule 97(2), the Court may appoint experts to assist it in determining the scope, extent of any damage, loss or injury to or in respect of victims, and to suggest various options concerning the types and modalities of reparations. The *Lubanga* Trial Chamber strongly recommended that a multidisciplinary team of experts be retained to provide assistance and delegated the issue to the Trust Fund (*Lubanga*, ICC T. Ch., ICC-01/04-01/06-2904, 7 August 2012, paras. 263–265). The Appeals Chamber stressed that expert assistance could be obtained both before the reparation order, and after (that is, at the implementation stage) (*Lubanga*, ICC A. Ch., ICC-01/04-01/06-3129, 3 March 2015, para. 178).

f) Publicity

The responsibility of the Registry to give publicity to the reparations proceedings is laid down in rule 96. While the rule is primarily aimed at publicity to ensure that victims could file claims and take part in the proceedings (Friman and Lewis, p. 482), the *Lubanga* Trial Chamber found it applicable also to publicity of the principles that the Chamber had established (*Lubanga*, ICC T. Ch., ICC-01/04-01/06-2904, 7 August 2012, para. 258; see also ICC A. Ch., ICC-01/04-01/06-3129, 3 March 2015, Annex A, paras. 51–52).

Author: Håkan Friman.

[629] *a) Seeking state cooperation to give effect to an order*

---

5. A State Party shall give effect to a decision under this article as if the provisions of Article 109 were applicable to this article.[630]

Unlike Article 75(5) which deals with enforcement of an issued reparation order, Article 75(4) empowers the Court to seek measures in order to secure the enforcement of a future reparation order. The provision refers to international cooperation measures under Article 93(1), which includes the identification, tracing and freezing or seizure of proceeds, property and assets and instrumentalities of crimes for the purpose of eventual forfeiture (Article 93(1)(k)). Article 75(4) explicitly apply only subsequent to the conviction of the perpetrator concerned by the Court (and, arguably, only to convictions concerning a core crime under the Court's jurisdiction). The assistance by States Parties, and invited non-States Parties that commit themselves to cooperate (Article 87(5)(a)), shall be timely, effective and provided at the earliest possible stage of the proceedings (ASP Resolution ICC-ASP/10/Res.3 of 20 December 2011).

The *Lubanga* Trial Chamber, which did not distinguish between Article 75(4) and (5), generally noted the identification and freezing of any assets of the convicted person as a fundamental element in securing effective reparations, and handed the issue over to the Registry and the Trust Fund with the recommendation to establish standard operating procedures, confidentiality protocols and financial reporting obligations (*Lubanga*, ICC T. Ch., ICC-01/04-01/06-2904, 7 August 2012, paras. 277 and 280). The Appeals Chamber merely recalled the States Parties' obligation to cooperate (*Lubanga*, ICC A. Ch., ICC-01/04-01/06-3129, 3 March 2015, Annex A, para. 50). The Chambers did not elaborate on to what extent, if any, issues concerning international cooperation and enforcements would fall under the (newly constituted judicial) Chamber's remaining monitoring and oversight functions; the reference in the Chamber's "conclusions" is limited to functions in accordance with Article 64(2) and (3)(a) appears to exclude such issues.

b) Interim protective measures

In this context, protective measures under Article 57(3)(e) should also be noted since the provision does also encompass measures to secure future forfeiture "for the ultimate benefit of victims". Clearly, forfeiture as a penalty (Article 77(2)(b)) may benefit victims through an order by the Court. In accordance with Article 79(2), that money or other property collected through fines or forfeiture be transferred to the Trust Fund. But the question has arisen as to whether protective measures under Article 57(3)(e) may be ordered by the Pre-Trial Chamber for the direct purpose of a future reparation order. In *Kenyatta*, the majority of the Trial Chamber answered this question in the affirmative (*Prosecutor v. Kenyatta*, ICC T. Ch., Decision on the implementation of the request to freeze assets, ICC-01/09-02/11-931, 8 July 2014, para. 12). One judge dissented, however, and found that protective measures to secure a future reparation order is possible only post-conviction in accordance with Article 75(4) (Dissenting opinion of Judge Henderson, para. 3). Although less explicit, earlier Pre-Trial Chamber decisions have also made the connection between the protective measures under Article 57(3)(e) and future reparations awards (for example *Prosecutor v. Lubanga*, ICC PT. Ch., Request to the Democratic Republic of the Congo for the purpose of obtaining the identification, tracing, freezing and seizure of property and assets belonging to Mr. Thomas Lubanga Dyilo, ICC-01/04-01/06-22, 9 March 2006, and *Prosecutor v. Bemba*, ICC PT. Ch., Decision et demande en vue d'obtenir l'identification, la localisation, le gel et la saisie des biens et avoirs adressées a la République portugaise, ICC-01/05-01/08-8, 27 May 2008).

Author: Håkan Friman.

[630] Without effective enforcement, the reparation awards will be merely symbolic. Enforcement of fines and forfeiture orders are regulated in Article 109 and the term 'give effect to' (instead of 'enforce') is used in order to set forth the material obligation but leave the States with discretion concerning the procedures for doing so (Draft Report of the Working Group on Enforcement, 4

6. Nothing in this article shall be interpreted as prejudicing the rights of victims under national or international law.[631]

July 1998, A/CONF.183/C.1/WGE/L.13 p. 5). Article 75(5) provides the equivalent obligation of States Parties to "give effect to" a decision on reparations "as if the provisions of Article 109 were applicable".

Further directions are given in the Rules. Rule 217 provides for the role of the Presidency in seeking cooperation and enforcement and rule 218 the content of relevant orders to allow for their effective enforcement. The reparations ordered may not be modified by the enforcing State according to rule 219. The Presidency is responsible for the disposition or allocation of property or assets realised through the realisation of a Court order (rule 221) and it may assist with service of notifications and other matters in furtherance of the enforcement (rule 222). The Presidency shall establish an enforcement unit (regulation 113) and the Registry may be enlisted to assist with certain tasks, which may include ongoing monitoring of a sentenced person's financial situation (regulations 116–117)

The *Lubanga* Trial Chamber merely noted that in order for a reparations award to have effect, the Court "requires the cooperation of States Parties and non-states parties" and in particular close cooperation with the "DRC local government" (*Lubanga*, ICC T. Ch., ICC-01/04-01/06-2904, 7 August 2012, para. 278).

Author: Håkan Friman.

[631] In *Lubanga*, the Chambers underlined that the decision was not intended to affect the rights of victims to reparations in other cases, whether before the ICC or national, regional or other international bodies (*Lubanga*, ICC T. Ch., ICC-01/04-01/06-2904, 7 August 2012, para. 181, and ICC A. Ch., ICC-01/04-01/06-3129, 3 March 2015, Annex A, para. 4). Although decisions by other national or international bodies do not affect the rights to reparations under Article 75, the Court may take other orders and awards into account in order to guarantee that reparations are not applied unfairly or in discriminatory manner (*Lubanga*, ICC T. Ch., ICC-01/04-01/06-2904, 7 August 2012, para. 201).

Cross-references:

Rules 94, 95, 96 and 97.

Regulations 38, 56 and 88.

Doctrine:

1. Anne-Marie de Brouwer and Mikaela Heikkilä, "Victim Issues: Participation, Protection, Reparation, and Assistance", in Göran Sluiter, Håkan Friman, Suzannah Linton, Sergey Vasiliev and Salvatore Zappalà (eds.), *International Criminal Procedure: Principles and Rules*, Oxford University Press, Oxford, 2013.

2. David Donat-Cattin, "Article 75", in Otto Triffterer (ed.), *Commentary on the Rome Statute of the International Criminal Court: Observers' Notes, Article by Article*, 2nd ed., C.H. Beck/Hart/Nomos, Munich/Oxford/Baden-Baden, 2008, pp. 1399–1412.

3. Eva Dwertmann, *The Reparation System of the International Criminal Court*, Martinus Nijhoff Publishers, Leiden/Boston, 2010.

4. Christine Evans, *The Right to Reparation in International Law for Victims of Armed Conflict*, Cambridge University Press, Cambridge, 2012.

5. Carla Ferstman *et al.*, *Reparations for Victims of Genocide, War Crimes and Crimes against Humanity: Systems in Place and Systems in the Making*, Martinus Nijhoff Publishers, 2009.

6. Håkan Friman, "The International Criminal Court and Participation of Victims: A Third Party to the Proceedings?", in *Leiden Journal of International Law*, 2009, vol. 22, pp. 485–500.

7. Håkan Friman and Peter Lewis, "Reparations to Victims", in Roy S. Lee (ed.), *The International Criminal Court: Elements of Crimes and Rules of Procedure and Evidence*, Transnational Publishers, Ardsley, NY, 2001, pp. 474–491.

8. Carolyn Hoyle and Leila Ullrich, "New Court, New Justice?" in *Journal of International Criminal Justice*, 2014, vol. 12, no. 4, pp. 681–703.

9. Sara Kendall and Sarah Nouwen, "Representational Practices at the International Criminal Court: The Gap between Juridified and Abstract Victimhood", in *Law and Contemporary Problems*, 2013,vol. 76, nos. 3/4, pp. 235–62.

10. Conor McCarthy, *Reparations and Victim Support in the International Criminal Court*, Cambridge University Press, Cambridge, 2012.

11. Luke Moffett, *Justice for Victims before the International Criminal Court*, Routledge, London, 2014.

12. Christopher Muttukumaru, "Reparation to Victims", in Roy S. Lee (ed.), *The International Criminal Court: The Making of the Rome Statute*, Kluwer Law International, The Hague, 1999, pp. 262–70.

13. Juan Carlos Ochoa, *The Rights of Victims in Criminal Justice Proceedings for Serious Human Rights Violations*, Martinus Nijhoff Publishers, 2013.

14. Valentina Spiga, "No Redress without Justice: Victims and International Criminal Law", in *Journal of International Criminal Justice*, 2012, vol. 10, no. 5, pp. 1377–94.

15. Carsten Stahn, "Reparative Justice after the Lubanga Appeals Judgment on Principles and Procedures of Reparation", in *European Journal of International Law: Talk!*, 7 April 2015.

16. Salvatore Zappalà, "The Rights of Victims v. the Rights of the Accused", in *Journal of International Criminal Justice*, 2010, vol. 8, no. 1, pp. 137–64.

17. Liesbeth Zegveld, "Victims' Reparations Claims and International Criminal Courts", in *Journal of International Criminal Justice*, 2010, vol. 8, no. 1, pp. 79–111.

Author: Håkan Friman.

Article 76
Sentencing[632]

1. In the event of a conviction, the Trial Chamber shall consider the appropriate sentence to be imposed and shall take into account the evidence presented and submissions made during the trial that are relevant to the sentence.[633]

2. Except where Article 65 applies and before the completion of the trial, the Trial Chamber may on its own motion and shall, at the request of the Prosecutor or the accused, hold a further hearing to hear any additional evidence or submissions relevant to the sentence, in accordance with the Rules of Procedure and Evidence.[634]

---

[632] *General remarks*:

Article 76 was adopted without difficulty at the Rome conference. In international criminal proceedings it is possible to identify two major choices of presenting evidence and making submissions relating to sentencing. The first option is to have submissions and evidence on sentencing considered at one (or more) distinct hearings to be held after the pronouncement of a verdict of guilt ("bifurcated trial). The other option is hearing all of the evidence and submissions together without issuing a separate decision on guilt ("single trial"), see (Acquaviva, p. 534.

Distinct sentencing hearings are familiar to common laws systems in order to protect the jury. Even in the absence of juries in international criminal proceedings, Safferling argues from a human rights perspective in favour of separation of the hearing into two stages perspective so as to safeguard the judges' impartiality (Safferling, 2001, pp. 269–272, 372).

The *ad hoc* tribunals initially adopted a policy of distinct sentencing hearings (rule 100 of the original ICTY Rules of Procedure and Evidence). This approach was later abandoned because the judges of the *ad hoc* tribunals though separate sentencing hearings were unnecessary in the absence of jury trials (ICTY RPE Rule 85(A)(vi), ICTR RPE Rule 85(A)(vi)). There were complaints about this procedure, the defence argued in *Brđanin* that the accused was forced to "give up his right against self-incrimination in order to present evidence relevant to his sentencing". The Trial Chamber dismissed this objection with reference to the Appeals Chamber in *Vasiljević* where the later stated that "an accused can express sincere regret without admitting his participation in a crime" (*Prosecutor v. Brđanin* (Case No. IT-99-36-T), ICTY T. Ch., Judgment 1 September 2004, para. 1081; *Prosecutor v. Vasiljević*, ICTY A. Ch., Appeal Judgment, 25 February 2004, para. 17, Schabas, 2010, pp. 884–885).

At the ICC, Article 76 creates a strong presumption in favour of separate sentencing hearings.

Author: Mark Klamberg.

[633] Paragraph 1 provides that if the accused is convicted, the Trial Chamber shall take into account the evidence presented and submissions made during the trial. This includes mitigating and aggravating circumstances relating to both the crime and circumstances both of the convicted person.

Author: Mark Klamberg.

[634] Paragraph 2 present that holding a distinct sentencing hearing is an option. However, considering that such a hearing is mandatory at the request of the Prosecutor or accused, it appears likely that there will be a separate sentencing in all cases. Rule 143 provides that this hearing can be postponed by the Trial Chamber, in exceptional circumstances.

In *Lubanga* the Trial Chamber decided, at the request of the defence that there would be a separate sentencing hearing if the accused is convicted, see *Prosecutor v. Lubanga*, Judgment pursuant to Article 74 of the Statute, ICC-01/04-01/06-2842, 14 March 2012, para. 12. The Trial

---

3. Where paragraph 2 applies, any representations under Article 75 shall be heard during the further hearing referred to in paragraph 2 and, if necessary, during any additional hearing.[635]

4. The sentence shall be pronounced in public and, wherever possible, in the presence of the accused.[636]

Chamber issued its sentence after a separate sentencing hearing, *Prosecutor v. Lubanga*, T. Ch., Decision on Sentence pursuant to Article 76 of the Statute, ICC-01/04-01/06-2901, 10 July 2012.

This provision does not operate when Article 65 applies, that is in cases of a guilty plea.

Author: Mark Klamberg.

[635] Paragraph 3 provides that the in cases with distinct sentencing hearings, such hearings shall also include the presentation of evidence and submissions relating to reparations.

Author: Mark Klamberg.

[636] Whereas the accused is to be present during trial, paragraph 4 suggests a less strict approach by the use of the words "wherever possible".

Cross-references:

Rule 143.

Doctrine:

1. Guido Acquaviva, "Single and Bifurcated Trials", in Göran Sluiter, Håkan Friman, Suzannah Linton, Sergey Vasiliev and Salvatore Zappalà (eds.), *International Criminal Procedure: Principles and Rules*, Oxford University Press, Oxford, 2013, pp. 534–43.

2. Christoph J.M. Safferling, *Towards an International Criminal Procedure*, Oxford University Press, Oxford, 2001.

3. William A. Schabas, *The International Criminal Court: A Commentary on the Rome Statute*, Oxford University Press, Oxford, 2010, pp. 884–88.

4. William A. Schabas, "Article 76", in Otto Triffterer (ed.), *Commentary on the Rome Statute of the International Criminal Court: Observers' Notes, Article by Article*, 2nd ed., C.H. Beck/Hart/Nomos, Munich/Oxford/Baden-Baden, 2008, pp. 1413–17

Author: Mark Klamberg.

PART 7. PENALTIES

Article 77
Applicable penalties[637]

1. Subject to Article 110, the Court may impose one of the following penalties on a person convicted of a crime referred to in Article 5 of this Statute:[638]

    (a) Imprisonment for a specified number of years, which may not exceed a maximum of 30 years;[639] or

---

[637] *General remarks*:

Under Article 77 the International Criminal Court may impose a penalty against a person convicted of a crime under its jurisdiction, that is, one or more of the crimes specified in Article 5 of the ICC Statute. This list of penalties is exhaustive in accordance with the *nulla poena sine lege* principle found in Article 23. Notably, the only punishment that the Court can impose is imprisonment, which, further to Article 22(2), can be followed but not replaced by a fine or forfeiture of proceeds, property and assets derived directly or indirectly from the crime. Evidently, the drafters of the ICC Statute did not leave it open to the Court to impose the death penalty, a non-custodial or a suspended sentence. It should be noted that, once a convicted person has been sentenced, the Court relies on the cooperation and assistance of States Parties for the enforcement of the sentence, pursuant to Article 103. Article 110 is relevant for post-conviction measures, for example as regards a reduction of the sentence, stipulating that the Court shall review the sentence to determine whether it should be reduced once two-thirds of a fixed-term sentence have been served, or 25 years in the event of life imprisonment. Article 110 provides merely that a review shall not be conducted before such time and should not be read as giving the convicted person an automatic right to release upon having served the proportion of the sentence stipulated in the Article. As the Court relies on States for the enforcement of its sentences, pursuant to Article 103, Article 110(1) is fundamental in stating that the Court alone shall have the right to decide any reduction of sentence.

Preparatory works:

A Working Group on Penalties was created to discuss all matters related to the penalties to be open to the Court, both before and during the United Nations Diplomatic Conference of Plenipotentiaries on the Establishment of an International Criminal Court (A/CONF.183/13 (Vol. 1), with a Norwegian diplomat, Rolf Einar Fife, as chair. Discussions on penalties were not without contentions, with State representatives disagreeing whether to include capital punishment, life imprisonment and minimum fixed term sentences. Rolf Einar Fife has remarked that the negotiations at the Diplomatic Conference on these issues were made difficult and time consuming by "the marked differences in national values, norms, standards and judicial practices" of the participants (Triffterer, 2008, p. 1423).

Author: Dejana Radisavljevic.

[638] Use of the terminology "person" indicates that the Court's jurisdiction is limited to natural persons and, as such, does not extend to legal persons. In accordance with Article 26, Article 77(1) is to be read as giving the Court jurisdiction over natural persons over 18 years of age. Moreover, the penalties enumerated in Article 77 may only be imposed against persons "convicted of a crime referred to in Article 5". As a consequence offences against the administration of justice, covered in Article 70, and misconduct before the Court, covered by Article 71 are implicitly excluded.

Author: Dejana Radisavljevic.

[639] `Pursuant to Article 77(1)(a), the Court cannot impose a fixed-term sentence that exceeds 30 years' imprisonment. There is no provision on the minimum fixed-term sentence imposable, although the wording "imprisonment for a specified number of *years*" (emphasis added) has led some commentators such as Silvia D'Ascoli to deduce that the minimum sentence must be expressed in years (2011, p. 1901). Notably lacking in this sub-paragraph is recognition of the different crimes enumerated in Article 5 and their respective gravity; that is, there is no mention of a range of sentences for the different crimes. This leaves the Court's judiciary significant discretion in determining a sentence for a specific crime, although, as the commentary on Article 78 will illustrate, the ICC Statute and the Rules of Procedure and Evidence do provide guidance on the factors to consider when imposing a sentence.

The Court is not alone in excluding a provision on the maximum fixed-term sentence imposable and providing for a range of sentences based on the different crimes, as such provisions are lacking in the Statutes of the *ad hoc* tribunals preceding the Court – the International Criminal Tribunal for the former Yugoslavia ('ICTY'), the International Criminal Tribunal for Rwanda ('ICTR'), the Special Court for Sierra Leone ('SCSL') and the Special Tribunal for Lebanon ('STL'). Article 24(1) of the ICTY Statute and Article 23(1) of the ICTR Statute provide only that "[t]he penalty imposed by the Trial Chamber shall be limited to imprisonment", while Article 19 of the SCSL Statute and Article 24 of the STL Statute provide that imprisonment shall be "for a specified number of years". In practice, fixed-term sentences imposed by the ICTY range from 6 years' imprisonment, imposed on Dražen Erdemović (IT-96-22-A, Judgment, 7 October 1997), to 40 years' imprisonment, imposed on Milomir Stakić (IT-97-24-A, Judgment, 22 March 2006) and Goran Jelisić (IT-95-10-A, Judgment, 5 July 2001). Sentences handed down by the ICTR range from 6 years' imprisonment imposed on Michel Bagaragaza (ICTR-05-86, Judgment, 17 November 2009), to 45 years' imprisonment imposed on Juvenal Kajelijeli (ICTR-98-44A, Judgment, 23 May 2005). While lacking specificity, the fact that the ICTY and ICTR were established to try persons in two specific conflicts made it possible to include that "in determining the terms of imprisonment, the Trial Chambers shall have recourse to the general practice regarding prison sentences in the courts" of the former Yugoslavia and Rwanda respectively. In contrast, the reference to national sentencing practices is missing in Article 77 of the ICC Statute. Ralf Einar Fife has remarked that this, along with the lack of a range of sentences for the different crimes is in recognition of the flexibility required of a court that will deal with crimes relating to any number of different conflicts across the globe, and allows the Court to treat equally all convicted persons, regardless of their nationality (Triffterer, 2008, p. 1420 and 1423).

In practice, the Court has only pronounced two convictions, both in relation to the situation in the Democratic Republic of the Congo, where four cases have been brought before the Trial Chambers: *Lubanga*, *Ntaganda*, *Katanga*, *Ngudjolo* and *Mbarushimana*. The first sentence handed down by the Court was in the case of the Prosecutor v. Thomas Lubanga Dyilo. On 1 December 2014, the Appeals Chamber confirmed the conviction and sentence against Thomas Lubanga Dyilo (ICC-01/04-01/06-3121-Red), imposing a sentence of 14 years' imprisonment. In its second conviction, on 23 May 2014, Trial Chamber II sentenced Germain Katanga (ICC-01/04-01/07-3484) to 12 years' imprisonment. Although a sentence at the first instance, it is final as the Defence and Office of the Prosecutor both dropped their appeals against the judgment, on 25 June 2014.

A third trial, that of Bosco Ntaganda, who voluntarily surrendered to the Court, commenced on 2 September 2015.

Author: Dejana Radisavljevic.

(b) A term of life imprisonment when justified by the extreme gravity of the crime and the individual circumstances of the convicted person.[640]

---

[640] The possibility of imposing a sentence of life imprisonment is explicitly provided in Article 77(1)(b), as an alternative to a fixed-term sentence. Life imprisonment is only an option in exceptional circumstances, where "the extreme gravity of the crime and the individual circumstances of the convicted person" justify its imposition. These two justifications are cumulative and as such the judges imposing the sentence must be convinced that consideration of both factors justifies imposing a life sentence. This requirement of justification is connected to the debates during the Diplomatic Conference on the appropriateness of including life imprisonment. As Rolf Einar Fife has reported, some States viewed life imprisonment as a "prerequisite for the credibility of the Court and its deterrent functions" (Triffterer, 2008, p. 1420), while others opposed it, based on their national laws.

In contrast, the Statutes of the ICTY and ICTR do not explicitly pronounce themselves on the possibility of imposing a sentence of life imprisonment. It is only in the Rules of Procedure and Evidence that life imprisonment is referred to, with Rule 101(A) of the ICTY stating that "[a] convicted person may be sentenced to imprisonment for a term up to and including the remainder of the convicted person's life". Rule 101(A) of the ICTR similarly states that "[a] person convicted by the Tribunal may be sentenced to imprisonment for a fixed term or the remainder of his life". The Statute of the SCSL in Article 19, on the other hand, provides that imprisonment shall be for "a specified number of years", thus implicitly excluding the possibility of imposing a sentence of life imprisonment. This is perhaps one of the reasons behind the fact that the SCSL has handed out the lengthiest fixed-term sentences of all international tribunals, imposing 52 years' imprisonment on Issa Sesay (SCSL-04-15-T, Sentencing Judgment, 8 April 2009). The jurisprudence of the ICTY and ICTR in this context is instructive for the ICC, as the ICTY has handed down five life sentences and, the ICTR has imposed 19 life sentences, three of which are currently on appeal. The STL, on the other hand, allows for the imposition of life sentences, with Article 24 of the Statute providing that the Trial Chamber "shall impose upon a convicted person imprisonment for life or for a specified number of years". The option of life imprisonment as a penalty precedes imposition of a fixed-term sentence and, as such, may be regarded as a usual sentence rather than one requiring particular justification. This remains to be seen in practice, as the STL has yet to impose a sentence.

Unlike the STL, the Court, by providing for life imprisonment as an alternative only to be imposed when "justified by the extreme gravity of the crime and the individual circumstances of the convicted person", effectively restricted its imposition. As William Schabas has commented, these words were "added as part of a delicate compromise aimed at winning the agreement of some States for whom life imprisonment was deemed to be cruel, inhuman and degrading treatment or punishment" (Schabas, 2010, p. 895). For Schabas, life imprisonment was included on the assumption that it would rarely come to use. Indeed, the Court can only prosecute individuals for crimes of a particularly heinous nature, thus adding the additional caveat of extreme gravity of the crime in order to impose life imprisonment leans towards limiting its use.

As a result of compromise during the Diplomatic Conference, sentences of life imprisonment are subject to a mandatory review after 25 years have been served, pursuant to Rule 145(3). It is important to note that this Rule does not provide that a person serving a life sentence has a right to be released upon having served 25 years of his or her sentence, stipulating only that the Court is obliged to review the sentence. Nonetheless, it provides a measure of certainty for the convicted person and his or her counsel and is an important factor in ensuring that convicted persons are treated equally regardless of the State in which the sentence is being served. Commentators such as William Schabas have described the Court's approach as more lenient than that of the *ad hoc* tribunals, noting the ruling of the European Court of Human

2. In addition to imprisonment, the Court may order:

    (a) A fine under the criteria provided for in the Rules of Procedure and Evidence;

    (b) A forfeiture of proceeds, property and assets derived directly or indirectly from that crime, without prejudice to the rights of bona fide third parties.[641]

Rights where judges pointed to the ICC Statute as evidence of a "more universal trend towards attenuating the rigours of lengthy prison sentences" (Schabas, 2010, p. 895) This is also much more coherent an approach than that taken by the Court's predecessors who have failed to set any benchmarks in the enforcement of life sentences.

In his first decision on the early release of a person serving a sentence of life imprisonment, the President of the Mechanism for International Criminal Tribunals (mandated *inter alia* to supervise the enforcement of ICTY and ICTR sentences) denied the early release of Stanislav Galic (Public Redacted Version of the 5 December 2014 Decision with Reasons to Follow on the Early Release of Stanislav Galic (MICT-14-83-ES)) On 23 June 2015, the President issued the Public Redacted Version of Reasons for the President's Decision to Deny the Early Release of Stanislav Galic and Decision on Prosecution Motion, in which he pronounced that the existing threshold of considering those convicted by the ICTR, the ICTY or the Mechanism eligible for early release upon having served two-thirds of their sentence would similarly be applicable to persons serving life sentences. As regards how a life sentence, and the early release eligibility threshold thereof, would be calculated, the President decided that "a sentence of life imprisonment is to be treated as equivalent to more than a sentence of 45 years" – the lengthiest sentence imposed by the ICTR, the ICTY or the Mechanism, in the case of Mr. Juvenal Kajelijeli (*Prosecutor v. Kajelijeli* (Case No. ICTR-98-44A), ICTR A. Ch., Judgment, 23 May 2005, para. 325) Calculating the two-thirds threshold on this basis, the President concluded, at paragraph 36 that Galic should be considered eligible for early release upon having served more than 30 years of his sentence. Noting that a fixed-term sentence higher than 45 years may be imposed by the ICTY, the ICTR or the Mechanism in the future, the President concluded at paragraph 38, "the interests of justice and the principle of legal certainty require that no change in the present calculation of the eligibility threshold for those sentenced to life imprisonment take place". Finally, at paragraph 38, the President explained that "[t]he consequences of this decision for those on whom a fixed-term of more than 45 years is imposed in the future, and who would therefore reach two-thirds of their sentences after Galic and others sentenced to the higher sentence of life imprisonment were eligible for early release will be considered if and as necessary in light of the principle of treating similarly situated persons equally".

Author: Dejana Radisavljevic.

[641] In addition to imprisonment, the Court may order the convicted person to pay a fine and/or a forfeiture of proceeds, property and assets, for any of the crimes enumerated in Article 5. Fines and forfeitures are not alternatives to imprisonment, but can be imposed additionally. Interestingly, reference to a forfeiture of proceeds, property and assets derived directly or indirectly from the crime, as Rolf Einar Fife has remarked, implicitly excludes the Court from ordering forfeiture of "property used or intended to be used to commit the crime" (Triffterer, 2008, 1430)

Article 77(2)(a) directs the Court to the criteria provided in Rule 146 of the Rules of Procedure and Evidence, which states that the Court, in determining whether to order a fine

shall determine whether imprisonment is a sufficient penalty", giving "due consideration to the financial capacity of the convicted person, including any orders for forfeiture in accordance with Article 77, paragraph 2(b), and, as appropriate, any orders for reparation in accordance with Article 75.

Moreover, Rule 146 states that the Court shall take into account "whether and to what degree the crime was motivated by personal financial gain". A fine shall be set "at an appropriate level", taking into consideration "the damage and injuries caused as well as the proportionate gains derived from the crime by the perpetrator" and must not "exceed 75 percent of the value of the convicted person's identifiable assets, liquid or realizable, and property, after deduction of an appropriate amount that would satisfy the financial needs of the convicted person and his or her dependants". Where a fine has been imposed, Regulation 116 of the Regulations of the Court state that the enforcement of fines, forfeiture orders and reparation orders lies with the Presidency, who shall:

> Receive payment of fines as described in Article 77, paragraph 2 (a); Receive, as described in Article 109, paragraph 3, property or the proceeds of the sale of real property or, where appropriate, the sale of other property; Account for interest gained on money received under (a) and (b) above; Ensure the transfer of money to the Trust Fund or to victims, as appropriate.

Rule 146(2) states that the convicted person shall be allowed a reasonable period in which to pay the fine, which may be made either through a lump sum or in instalments. Moreover, the Court has the possibility to calculate the fine "according to a system of daily fines", the minimum duration of which is 30 days and the maximum duration of which is 5 years. The amount of such payments shall be determined "in the light of the individual circumstances of the convicted person, including the financial needs of his or her dependants". In enforcing a fine, forfeiture or reparation order, the President shall, pursuant to Rule 217 and as appropriate, seek the cooperation of a State with which the convicted person has a direct connection. Rule 217 specifies that a direct connection between a State and the convicted person can be established either by "nationality, domicile or habitual residence or by virtue of the location of the sentenced person's assets and property or with which the victim has such connection". This should be read in conjunction with Article 109, which stipulates that "States Parties shall give effect to fines or forfeitures ordered by the Court under Part 7, without prejudice to the rights of bona fide third parties and in accordance with the procedure of their national law". In the case of continued willful non-payment of a fine, the Presidency, on its own motion or at the request of the Prosecutor, pursuant to Rule 146, "may as a last resort extend the term of imprisonment for a period not to exceed a quarter of such term or five years, whichever is less", provided that it is "satisfied that all available enforcement measures have been exhausted". This is an important enforcement incentive, which, as William Schabas has remarked, is the sole example of the Presidency exercising a judicial power in the ICC Statute.

The practical implications of the Court's power to impose fines and forfeitures and the difficulties in enforcing them has yet to be seen as the Trial Chambers in the *Lubanga* and *Katanga* cases did not order the payment of a fine or forfeiture. In the *Lubanga* case, the Trial Chamber considered it inappropriate to impose a fine in addition to the prison term, given the financial situation of Mr Lubanga" (*Prosecutor v. Lubanga*, ICC T. Ch., Public Decision on Sentence pursuant to Article 76 of the Statute, ICC-01/04-01/06-2901, 10 July 2012, para. 106). Similarly, the Trial Chamber in the *Katanga case* decided against imposing a fine, noting that Mr Katanga's financial situation had not changed since his indigency during trial (*Prosecutor v. Katanga*, ICC T. Ch., Public Decision on Sentence pursuant to Article 76 of the Statute, ICC-01/04-01/07-3484, 23 May 2014, para. 169).

The provision of forfeiture of proceeds, property and assets derived from the crime is part of traditional criminal law rationale that a criminal should not profit from his or her crime (Triffterer, 2008, p. 1425). However, their explicit inclusion in the ICC Statute is unprecedented in international criminal justice. Aside from giving this power to the Court, one must look to the Rules of Procedure and Evidence for further provisions on such orders. Rule 147 is instructive in stating that "at any hearing to consider an order of forfeiture, the Chamber shall hear evidence as to the identification and location of specific proceeds, property or assets which have been derived directly or indirectly from the crime". Having heard the evidence, the Chamber may issue an order of forfeiture in relation to specific proceeds, property or assets. Once again, the Chamber will have considerable discretion in ordering forfeitures, as there is no definition of property or assets. . For guidance on the meaning of these terms as well as "derived directly or indirectly form that crime" (a rather broad and vague wording) the Court will have to turn to other courts or international or European Conventions. Notably, there is no mention of the standard of proof, except that the Court must be "satisfied" that the proceeds, property and or assets have been derived directly or indirectly from the crime, pursuant to Rule 147.

The power of the Court to impose fines under Article 77(2)(a) exceeds the powers of the ICTY and ICTR, who can only impose a fine for administrative offences such as, contempt of court, in accordance with Rule 77(g) of the Rules of Procedure and Evidence, and for false testimony, in accordance with Rule 91(g). Moreover, the *ad hoc* tribunals' Rules of Procedure and Evidence restrict the imposition of fines by setting the maximum value of such a fine at 100,000 EUR for the ICTY and 10,000 USD for the ICTR. As regards forfeiture, Article 24(3) of the ICTY Statute and 23(3) of the ICTR Statute further permit the respective *ad hoc* tribunals to "order the return of any property and proceeds acquired by criminal conduct, including by means of duress, to their rightful owners". Accordingly, the Court's authority to proscribe fines, forfeiture measures and reparation orders has been described as "a novel system within the history of international criminal law due to its comprehensiveness" (Abtahi and Koh, 2012, p. 4)

The provision that forfeiture may be ordered "without prejudice to the rights of bona fide third parties" is in respect of the general principles of law and the need to respect third parties' rights. However, such a provision is not without its difficulties, particularly in the case of armed conflicts where property rights may be difficult to establish. Moreover, this proviso restricts the Court's jurisdiction in a way that the ICTY, ICTR and SCSL have avoided. Thus, the ICTY, ICTR and SCSL may order restitution of property or the proceeds thereof, "even in the hands of third parties, not otherwise connected with the crime of which the convicted person has been found guilty".

The general difficulties inherent in ordering and enforcing forfeitures have been remarked by Rolf Einar Fife, particularly in terms of determining ownership, the standards for burden of proof and choice of law in determining ownership and where "victims, property and thirds parties are located in different jurisdictions" (Triffterer, 2008, 1430) Moreover, as noted above, the Court relies on State cooperation in the enforcement of any fines and forfeiture, pursuant to Rule 217. The obligations of States Parties to provide the Court with assistance in this regard is established in Article 93. An incentive for convicted persons to assist the Court can be found in Article 110(4)(b) which provides the Court with the possibility of reducing a sentence where *inter alia* the convicted person has "provided assistance in locating assets subject to orders of fine, forfeiture or reparation which may be for the benefit of victims".

Finally, pursuant to Article 79(2), the collection of fines or forfeitures can be to the benefit of the victims and their families as the Chamber may order the transfer of any such fines or forfeitures to the Trust Fund for victims. In this regard, Rule 148 provides that "[b]efore making an order pursuant to Article 79 paragraph 2, a Chamber may request the representatives of the Trust Fund to submit written or oral observations to it".

Cross-references:

Articles 5, 22, 23, 24, 26, 70, 71, 76, 78, 79, 93, 103, 109, 110.

Rules 145, 146, 147, 148, 212, 217.

Regulations 116 and 118.

Doctrine:

1. Hirad Abtahi and Steven Arrigg Koh, "The Emerging Enforcement Practice of the International Criminal Court", in *Cornell International Law Journal*, 2012, vol. 45, no. 1, pp. 1–23.

2. Gideon Boas, James L. Biscoff and Nathalie L. Reid, *International Criminal Law Practitioner Library*. Vol. II: *Elements of Crime under International Criminal Law*, Cambridge University Press, Cambridge, 2008.

3. Karin Calvo-Goller, *The Trial Proceedings of the International Criminal Court: ICTY and ICTR Precedents*, Martinus Nijhoff Publishers, 2005.

4. Silvia D'Ascoli, *Sentencing in International Criminal Law: The Approach of the two Ad Hoc Tribunals and Future Perspectives for the International Criminal Court*, Hart Publishing, Oxford, 2011.

5. William A. Schabas, *The International Criminal Court: A Commentary on the Rome Statute*, Oxford University Press, Oxford, 2010, pp. 891–97.

6. William A. Schabas, *War Crimes and Human Rights: Essays on the Death Penalty Justice and Accountability*, Cameron May, London, 2008.

7. Rolf Einar Fife, "Article 77 – Applicable Penalties", in Otto Triffterer (ed.), *Commentary on the Rome Statute of the International Criminal Court: Observers' Notes, Article by Article*, 2nd ed., C.H. Beck/Hart/Nomos, Munich/Oxford/Baden-Baden, 2008, pp. 1419–32.

Author: Dejana Radisavljevic.

Article 78
Determination of the sentence[642]

1. In determining the sentence, the Court shall, in accordance with the Rules of Procedure and Evidence, take into account such factors as the gravity of the crime and the individual circumstances of the convicted person.[643]

---

[642] *General remarks*:

Article 78 relates to the determination of sentences imposable by the Court, which, as Article 77(1) provides, must be a sentence of imprisonment whether for a fixed term of up to 30 years' imprisonment or life imprisonment. Article 78 does not concern any fines or forfeiture of proceeds, property and assets that are provided in Article 77(2). Article 78 deals with three specific matters regarding such sentences of imprisonment: the factors to be taken into account in determining a sentence; the deduction of time spent in detention; and, instances where a person has been convicted of multiple crimes.

Author: Dejana Radisavljevic.

[643] Article 78(1) provides the factors to be taken into consideration when determining the length of a sentence: the gravity of the crime committed – an aggravating factor – and the individual circumstances of the convicted person – a mitigating factor. Significantly, the list is merely illustrative. There is no evident hierarchy between the two factors, but the importance of gravity as a consideration in determining a sentence is apparent in the jurisprudence of the ICTY and ICTR where it has been noted that "[b]y far the most important consideration, which may be regarded as the litmus test for the appropriate sentence, is the gravity of the offence" (*Prosecutor v. Mucic* (Case No. IT-96-21-T), ICTY T. Ch., Trial Judgment, 16 November 1998, para. 1225) There is, however, no indication of the factors deemed relevant in determining the gravity of the crime.

It appears that the drafters of the Statute intended the Rules of Procedure and Evidence to provide further guidance, as evident in the scarce provisions in Article 78 and the words "in accordance with the Rules of Procedure and Evidence". Thus, Rule 145(1)(a) states that the Court is to "bear in mind that the totality of any sentence of imprisonment and fine, as the case may be, imposed under Article 77 must reflect the culpability of the convicted person". This is in recognition of the heinous nature of international crimes as well as the notion that the sentence imposed on the individual should not exceed his or her culpability. The ICTY in *Mucic et al.* articulated this as meaning that the sentence must be "both just and appropriate" (*Prosecutor v. Mucic et al.* (Case No. IT-96-21-A), ICTY A. Ch., Appeals Judgment, 20 February 2001, para. 429) While an uncontroversial principle, this is the first mention of culpability in the regulations of an international court, as Silvia D'Ascoli notes (2011, p. 29). Rule 145(1)(b) is of further assistance, stipulating that the Court is to balance all the relevant factors, "including any mitigating and aggravating factors and consider the circumstances both of the convicted person and of the crime". Use of the term "including" implies that the list of factors, as in Article 78, is not exhaustive. In the same vein, Rule 145(1)(c) provides additional, illustrative, factors to take into consideration in determining a sentence, namely the extent of the damage caused, in particular the harm caused, and the nature of the behaviour and the means employed to execute the crime, all of which go towards considering the gravity of the crime. Moreover, Rule 145(1)(c) states that the Court shall consider the degree of participation of the convicted person, the degree of his or her intent, the circumstances, time and location as well as the age, education, social and economic condition of the convicted person. In addition to the already substantial list of factors, Rule 145(2) provides a further list of mitigating and aggravating circumstances for the Court to take into account´. Use of the term "such as" in Rule 145(1)(a) reiterates that the list of mitigating factors is merely illustrative. While there is a notable lack of words like "such as" and "*inter alia*" preceding the list of aggravating circumstances, thus insinuating that the list provided is exhaustive, the words in Rule 145(2)(b)(vi) "other circumstances which, although not enumerated above, by virtue of their nature are similar to those mentioned", leave some room for additional factors to be taken into account. This discretion provided to the judges is important in giving scope for the development of aggravating and mitigating factors, allowing the judiciary to consider factors relevant to each individual case.

Finally, Rule 145(3) addresses life imprisonment, reiterating the words used in Article 77 of the Statute, that "life imprisonment only be imposed when justified by the extreme gravity of the crime and the individual circumstances of the convicted person". Rule 145(3) further adds that these are evidenced "by the existence of one or more aggravating circumstances" – presumably including those illustrated in Rule 145.

As William Schabas has noted, there is nothing to indicate the standard of proof for mitigating or aggravating factors (2008, p. 904) The Trial Chamber in *Lubanga*, thus had no guidance from the Statute or Rules of Procedure and Evidence, and declared that it was for the Chamber to establish the standard of proof (*Prosecutor v. Lubanga*, Decision on Sentence pursuant to Article 76 of the Statute, ICC-01/04-01/06-2901, 10 July 2012, para. 33). As there is nothing in the basic legal texts of the Court to guide the Chamber, the jurisprudence of the ICTY and ICTR may prove an important source of information. In this regard, the ICTY and the ICTR have established that the burden of proof for aggravating factors lies with the prosecution and that such factors must be proven beyond a reasonable doubt (*Prosecutor v. Mucic et al.* (Case No. IT-96-21-A), ICTY A. Ch., Appeals Judgment, 20 February 2001, para. 763; *Prosecutor v. Bralo* (Case No. IT-95-17), ICTY T. Ch., Trial Judgment, 7 December 2005, para. 27; *Prosecutor v. Brđanin* (Case No. IT-99-36), ICTY T. Ch., Trial Judgment, 1 September 2004, para. 1096; *Prosecutor v. Kunarac, Kovač and Vuković* (Case No. IT-96-23&23/1), ICTY T. Ch., Trial Judgment, 22 February 2001, para. 847). As regards mitigating factors on the other hand, the ICTY has established that the burden of proof is on the balance of probabilities (*Prosecutor v. Blaskic* (Case No. IT-95-14), ICTY A. Ch., Appeals Judgment, 29 July 2004, para. 697; *Prosecutor v. Blagojević and Jokić* (Case No. IT-02-60) ICTY T. Ch., Trial Judgment, 17 January 2005, para. 850; *Prosecutor v. Babić* (Case No. IT-03-72), ICTY A. Ch., Appeals Judgment, 18 July 2005, para. 43).

While this jurisprudence may be of assistance to the Court, it is not bound to follow it and is free to set its own standard of proof. The Trial Chamber in *Lubanga*, the Court's first conviction, stated in its Decision on Sentence pursuant to Article 76 of the Statute that:

> It is for the Chamber to establish the standard of proof for the purposes of sentencing, given the Statute and the Rules do not provide any guidance. Since any aggravating factors established by the Chamber may have a significant effect on the overall length of the sentence Mr. Lubanga will serve, it is necessary that they are established to the criminal standard of proof, namely beyond a reasonable doubt (*Prosecutor v. Lubanga*, ICC T. Ch., Decision on Sentence pursuant to Article 76 of the Statute, ICC-01/04-01/06-2901, 10 July 2012, para. 33).

Moreover, the Trial Chamber accepted the defence submission that "the mitigating factors are not limited to the facts and circumstances described in the Decision [on the Confirmation of Charges]" adding that "as to the standard of proof, the Chamber is of the view that the in *dubio pro reo* principle applies at the sentencing stage of the proceedings, and any mitigating circumstances are to be established on a balance of the probabilities" (para. 34) Finally, the Trial Chamber stated that "any factors that are to be taken into account when assessing the gravity of the crime will not additionally be taken into account as aggravating circumstances and vice versa" (para. 35)

The Trial Chamber in *Lubanga* noted that while the Statute fails to identify which factors are to be taken into account when considering "the individual circumstances of the convicted person", as referred to in Article 78(1), Rule 145(c) of the Rules of Procedure and Evidence refer to "the age, education, social and economic situation of the convicted person" (para. 54). In this regard, the Trial Chamber in its Decision, para. 56, noted that "Mr Lubanga is clearly an intelligent and well-educated individual, who would have understood the seriousness of the crimes of which he has been found guilty. This marked level of awareness on his part is a relevant factor in determining the appropriate sentence (*Prosecutor v. Lubanga*, ICC T. Ch., Decision on Sentence pursuant to Article 76 of the Statute, ICC-01/04-01/06-2901, 10 July 2012)". The Prosecution in *Lubanga* submitted harsh conditions and treatment in the camps, and the commission of sexual violence and rape as aggravating circumstances, which, they argued also showed that "the harms committed were gender based", and an abuse of Thomas Lubanga's power or official capacity, where the victim was particularly defenceless (in this case due to very young age), noting the broader social impact of the crimes on the families and communities affected. In its judgment, the Trial Chamber decided that it had not been demonstrated that "the individual punishments referred to by the Chamber were the responsibility of Mr Lubanga, and in any event the Chamber has not taken this into account as an aggravating factor in the determination of his sentence" (para. 59). As regards sexual violence, the Trial Chamber, in para. 67, noted that:

> The prosecution's failure to charge Thomas Lubanga Dyilo with rape and other forms of sexual violence as separate crimes within the jurisdiction of the Court is not determinative of the question of whether that activity is a relevant factor in the determination of the sentence. The Chamber is entitled to consider sexual violence under Rule 145(1)(c) of the Rules as part of: (i) the harm suffered by the victims; (ii) the nature of the unlawful behaviour; and (iii) the circumstances of manner in which the crime was committed; additionally, this can be considered under Rule 145(2)(b)(iv) as showing the crime was committed with particular cruelty.

Nonetheless, para. 75, the Chamber found that, as a result of the prosecution's failure to introduce evidence on this issue during the sentencing hearing, "the link between Mr Lubanga and sexual violence, in the context of the charges, has not been established beyond reasonable doubt. Therefore, this factor cannot properly form part of the assessment of his culpability for the purposes of sentence".

As for the prosecution's submission that the crimes were committed against particularly defenceless victims, the Trial Chamber found that "[a]s already indicated, the factors that are relevant for determining the gravity of the crime cannot additionally be taken into account as aggravating circumstances. Therefore, the age of the children does not both define the gravity of the crime and act as an aggravating factor. Accordingly, the age of the children does not constitute an aggravating factor as regard these offences" (para. 78) As regards gender based violence, the Trial Chamber judged that "the Court has not been provided with any evidence that Mr Lubanga deliberately discriminated against women in committing these offences, in the sense suggested by the prosecution or the victims. In any event, 'motive involving discrimination' pursuant to Rule 145(2)(b)(v) has not been treated as an aggravating factor".

Lubanga's defence submitted a number of mitigating factors: necessity, peaceful motives, demobilisation orders and Mr. Lubanga's cooperation with the Court. As regards peaceful motive, the Trial Chamber accepted that "Mr Lubanga hoped that peace would return to Ituri once he had secured his objectives", but found this only of limited relevance given the persistent recruitment of child soldiers during the period covered by the charges. However, the Trial Chamber in this regard noted Lubanga's notable cooperation with the Court and the fact that he was respectful and cooperative throughout the proceedings, "notwithstanding some particularly onerous circumstances" (para. 91) The precedent on standard of proof for mitigating and aggravating circumstances set in the *Lubanga* case was adopted by the Trial Chamber in the Court's second case, that is, the case against Germain Katanga. Citing *Lubanga*, the Trial Chamber in *Katanga* affirmed the notion that "any factors that are to be taken into account when assessing the gravity of the crime will not additionally be taken into account as aggravating circumstances and vice versa" (*Prosecutor v. Katanga*, ICC T. Ch., Decision on Sentence pursuant to Article 76 of the Statute, ICC-01/04-01/07-3484, 23 May, 2014, para. 35)

Interestingly, the Trial Chamber in *Katanga* spoke to the aims of imprisonment, referring to the Statute's Preamble and deducing that "*Il s'agit donc de sanctionner les crimes qui 'menacent la paix, la sécurité et le bien-être du monde' et de faire en sorte que la peine ait un effet réellement dissuasive*" (own translation: The Court is to punish crimes that "threaten the peace, security and wellbeing of the world" and to ensure that the penalty acts as a real deterrent.) The Trial Chamber went on to explain that "*[e]lle considère que la peine a donc deux fonctions importantes : le châtiment d'une part, c'est-à-dire l'expression de la réprobation sociale qui entoure l'acte criminel et son auteur et qui est aussi une manière de reconnaitre le préjudice et les souffrances causées aux victimes ; la dissuasion d'autre part, dont l'objectif est de détourner de leur projet d'éventuels candidats à la perpétration de crimes similaires*" (own translation: the Trial Chamber considers that the sentence has two important functions: on the one hand condemnation of the criminal act and its perpetrator, as a way of recognising the harm done to the victims; and on the other hand, deterrence, with the objective of deterring others from committing similar crimes. As concerns deterrence, the Trial Chamber evoked the ICTY's sentiment that it is not the length of the sentence but its inevitability which is of importance (*Prosecutor v. Furundžija* (Case No. IT-95-17/1), ICTY T. Ch., Trial Judgment, 10 December 1998, para. 290. Moreover, the Trial Chamber added that pursuant to Rule 145(1), the sentence should be proportionate and contribute to the restoration of peace and reconciliation and must encourage the rehabilitation of the convicted person. Interestingly, the Trial Chamber referred to Jennings who has asserted that all crimes are not of equal gravity and, as such, "the Court will have to consider the nature and scale of crimes in determining their gravity" (Jennings, p. 1436 and *Prosecutor v. Katanga*, ICC T. Ch., ICC-01/04-01/07-3484, 23 May, 2014, para. 43).

In *Katanga*, the Trial Chamber discussed only one aggravating factor: whether Katanga abused his authority, considering that the other factors submitted by the prosecution had already been taken into account in determining the gravity of the crimes. In this case, the Trial Chamber judged that the one aggravating factor had not been proven beyond a reasonable doubt. As for mitigating factors, the defence relied on Katanga's young age, the nature of the role he played, the exceptional circumstances in which he found himself, his willingness to change, and the cooperation given to the court as well as asking the Trial Chamber to take into consideration his personal and family life. The Trial Chamber accepted that Katanga's young age, his family situation, as a father of six children, and protective and watchful eye over the civilian population could be considered as mitigating factors. However, these factors could not have a determinative role in view of the nature of the crimes committed. Following the precedent set by the ICTY in *Prosecutor v. Blagojević and Jokić* (Case No. IT-02-60), ICTY T. Ch., Trial Judgment, 7 January 2005, paras. 858–860) and *Prosecutor v. Plavšić (Case* No. IT-00-39&40/1), ICTY T. Ch., Sentencing Judgment, 27 February 2003, paras. 85–94 and 110), the Trial Chamber noted that efforts to promote peace and reconciliation should be taken into consideration in determining the sentence. While the Trial Chamber did not conclude that it had been proven on the balance of probabilities that Katanga had made efforts to actively encourage the peace process, evidence did demonstrate that he played a positive role in the disarmament and demobilisation of child soldiers, which was given more weight than his young age and personal circumstances. The Trial Chamber further considered Katanga's statements of remorse and the expressions of sympathy and compassion towards the victims, distinguishing the two and giving the latter less weight. In so doing, the Trial Chamber referred to the ICTY jurisprudence, finding that Katanga's words

2. In imposing a sentence of imprisonment, the Court shall deduct the time, if any, previously spent in detention in accordance with an order of the Court. The Court may deduct any time otherwise spent in detention in connection with conduct underlying the crime.[644]

---

of remorse remained conventional in nature and noting that he was not easily able to acknowledge his crimes. Such words of remorse were thus not considered a mitigating circumstance.

As regards cooperation with the prosecution, the Trial Chamber distinguished the wording used in Rule 145 from the requirement in Rule 101 of the Rules of Procedure and Evidence of the ICTY and ICTR, which require substantial cooperation, while also noting that the ICTY has exercised a certain discretion in interpreting this requirement. In judging what would be considered as cooperation, the Trial Chamber noted that it must go beyond good behaviour in court and noted Katanga's testimony, the fact that he responded to questions from both parties and the information that he brought before the court. The Chamber declined to comment on the importance of Katanga's good behaviour in detention. Moreover, the Trial Chamber relied on *Semanza* (Case No. ICTR-97-20), ICTR T. Ch., Trial Judgment, 15 May 2003; *Nahimana et al* (Case No. ICTR-99-52), ICTR T. Ch., Trial Judgment, 3 December 2003) and *Kajelijeli* (Case No. ICTR-98-44-A), ICTR A. Ch., Appeals Judgment, 23 May 2005) in stating that the violation of fundamental human rights during detention could be considered as mitigating factors. The Trial Chamber however found that it could only judge on Katanga's detention further to an order of the Court and thus could not pass judgment on his detention in the Democratic Republic of the Congo ('DRC').

Author: Dejana Radisavljevic.

[644] Pursuant to Article 78(2) of the Statute, the Court "shall deduct the time, if any, previously spent in detention in accordance with an order of the Court and may deduct any time otherwise spent in detention in connection with conduct underlying the crime". This provides the convicted person with an automatic right to have the time already spent in detention pursuant to an order of the Court, that is, the arrest warrant, deducted from his or her sentence. Additionally, the Chamber has the discretion to deduct any time spent in detention other than by an order of the Court, as long as the detention is "in connection with conduct underlying the crime". This is an important and necessary discretion because, pursuant to Article 20, "national convictions are not an absolute bar to prosecutions before the Court" (Triffterer, 2008, 1434) However, Article 78(2) neither stipulates the factors that the Court will take into account when exercising this discretion nor the relevant standard of proof.

The formulation in Article 78(2) is arguably broader than that of the *ad hoc* tribunals, as it "presumably could include detention by order of a national or other international court, and time spent in pre-trial detention, during trial, or serving a sentence imposed by that court" (Boas *et al.*, 2011, p. 409) In this respect, Rule 101(c) of the Rules of Procedure and Evidence of the ICTY and Rule 101(d) of the ICTR state that "[c]redit shall be given to the convicted person for the period, if any, during which the convicted person was detained in custody pending surrender to the Tribunal or pending trial or appeal". While the terminology used differs in that the Court refers to a deduction of time where the ICTY and ICTR refer to credit for time spent in detention, their impact remains the same. Along with this obligation to deduct time spent in detention pending surrender, trial or appeal, the ICTY and ICTR have discretion similar to that found in Article 78(2) of the Court's Statute. Thus, Article 10(3) of the ICTY Statute and Article 9(3) of the ICTR Statute stipulate that "[i]n considering the penalty to be imposed on a person convicted of a crime under the present Statute, the International Tribunal shall take into account the extent to which any penalty imposed by a national court on the same person for the same act has already been served". As noted above, this is potentially a narrower discretion than that provided to the judiciary of the Court. While there is no indication of the factors to take into account when exercising its discretion, the ICTY in its first trial, that of *Tadić*, ruled that fairness required that account be taken of the period he had spent in detention in the Federal Republic of Germany prior to the issuance of the ICTY's formal request for deferral" (*Prosecutor v. Tadić*, IT-94-1-A and IT-94-1-A bis, Judgment in Sentencing Appeals, 26 January 2000, para. 38).

The *Lubanga* case was the first instance in which the Court was required to consider the application of Article 78(2). Lubanga's defence submitted that his house arrest and detention by the Democratic Republic of the Congo ("DRC") authorities between 2003 and 2006 should be deducted from his sentence, arguing that, in accordance with Article78(2), the detention was imposed as a result of the same conduct underlying the crimes for which he was convicted by the Court (Defence Observations on Sentence, 3 June 2012, ICC-01/04-01/06-2891-Red, paras. 133–140).

However, the Trial Chamber, in paragraph 102 of the Decision on Sentence pursuant to Article 76 of the Statute, ICC-01/04-01/06-2901, judged that the defence failed to established on the balance of probabilities that there was sufficient evidence that Lubanga was detained in the DRC for conduct underlying the crimes for which he was convicted by the Court, namely the conscription and enlistment of children under the age of 15 and their active participation in hostilities. As such, the Chamber refused to deduct any time Lubanga spent in detention prior to the DRC acting on the Court's arrest warrant. The Appeals Chamber, in its Judgment on the appeals of the Prosecutor and Mr Thomas Lubanga Dyilo against the Decision on Sentence pursuant to Article 76 of the Statute, ICC-01/04-01/06-3122, 1 December 2014, refused to intervene in the Trial Chamber's finding.

In the second case before the Court, the Trial Chamber in *Katanga* started counting Katanga's sentence from the date at which the Congolese authorities were informed of the arrest warrant issued by the Court. The period in detention spent before this period was judged as neither having been pursuant to an order of the Court nor connected with the crimes for which Katanga was convicted by the Court. Accordingly, this time spent in detention was not deducted under Article 78(2).

The formulation in Article 78(2) is arguably broader than that of the *ad hoc* tribunals, as it "presumably could include detention by order of a national or other international court, and time spent in pre-trial detention, during trial, or serving a sentence imposed by that court" (Boas *et al.*, 2011, p. 409) In this respect, Rule 101(c) of the Rules of Procedure and Evidence of the ICTY and Rule 101(d) of the ICTR state that "[c]redit shall be given to the convicted person for the period, if any, during which the convicted person was detained in custody pending surrender to the Tribunal or pending trial or appeal". While the terminology used differs in that the Court refers to a deduction of time and the ICTY and ICTR refer to credit for time spent in detention, their impact is the same. Along with this obligation to deduct time spent in detention pending surrender, trial or appeal, the ICTY and ICTR have discretion similar to that found in Article 78(2) of the Court's Statute. Namely, Article 10(3) of the ICTY Statute and Article 9(3) of the ICTR Statute further state that "[i]n considering the penalty to be imposed on a person convicted of a crime under the present Statute, the International Tribunal shall take into account the extent to which any penalty imposed by a national court on the same person for the same act has already been served". Although as noted above, this is potentially a narrower discretion that that provided to the judiciary of the Court. While there is no indication of the factors to take into account when exercising its discretion, the ICTY in its first trial, that of *Tadić*, ruled that fairness required that account be taken of the period he had spent in detention in the Federal Republic of Germany prior to the issuance of the ICTY's formal request for deferral" (*Prosecutor v. Tadić* (Case No. IT-94-1-A and IT-94-1-A bis), ICTY T. Ch., Judgment in Sentencing Appeals, 26 January 2000, para. 38).

Author: Dejana Radisavljevic.

3. When a person has been convicted of more than one crime, the Court shall pronounce a sentence for each crime and a joint sentence specifying the total period of imprisonment. This period shall be no less than the highest individual sentence pronounced and shall not exceed 30 years imprisonment or a sentence of life imprisonment in conformity with Article 77, paragraph 1 (b).[645]

---

[645] Article 78(3) requires the Court to pronounce a sentence for each crime followed by a joint sentence specifying the total period of imprisonment. The joint sentence cannot exceed the maximum fixed term sentence imposable, that is 30 years' imprisonment, pursuant to Article 77(1)(a), or life imprisonment further to Article 77(1)(b). As there is no determined hierarchy of crimes enumerated in Article 5, the obligation to pronounce a separate sentence for each crime is an opportunity for the Court to ascertain the different degrees of gravity of the crimes, remarked as crucial by Silvia D'Ascoli (2011, p. 267). Only the jurisprudence of the Court, as it develops, will tell whether clear degrees of gravity will be established.

In contrast, the ICTY and the ICTR have no such obligation to impose a sentence for each crime and a joint sentence specifying the total period of imprisonment. Rule 87(c) of the Rules of Procedure and Evidence of the ICTY and ICTR state:

If the Trial Chamber finds the accused guilty on one or more of the charges contained in the indictment, it shall impose a sentence in respect of each finding of guilt and indicate whether such sentences shall be served consecutively or concurrently, unless it decides to exercise its power to impose a single sentence reflecting the totality of the criminal conduct of the accused.

Similarly, Rule 87(c) of the SCSL Rules of Procedure and Evidence state that "[t]he Trial Chamber shall indicate whether multiple sentences shall be served consecutively or concurrently". In practice, international judges have tended to impose a single sentence without specifying individual sentences for each crime. As a result, a hierarchy of crimes is not clear from the jurisprudence of these tribunals, with the exception of genocide, which has been regarded as the most serious crime (*Prosecutor v. Kambanda* (Case No. ICTR-97-23-S), ICTR T. Ch., Trial Judgment and Sentence, 4 September 1998, paras. 10–16; *Prosecutor v. Krstić* (Case No. IT-98-33-T), ICTY T. Ch., Trial Judgment, 2 August 2001, para. 700).

In its first judgment, the Court sentenced Lubanga to 13 years' imprisonment for having committed, jointly with other persons, the crime of conscripting children under the age of 15 into the Union of Congolese Patriots ('UPC'); to 12 years' imprisonment for having committed, jointly with other persons, the crime of enlisting children under the age of 15 into the UPC; and, to 14 years' imprisonment for having committed, jointly with other persons, the crime of using children under the age of 15 to participate actively in hostilities. The Trial Chamber then rendered a joint sentence of 14 years' imprisonment, which was confirmed by the Appeals Chamber in its Judgment on the appeals of the Prosecutor and Mr Thomas Lubanga Dyilo against the "Decision on Sentence pursuant to Article 76 of the Statute" (*Prosecutor v. Lubanga*, ICC A. Ch, Judgment, ICC-01/04-01/06-3121-Red, 1 December 2014).

In its second verdict, on 23 May 2014, the Trial Chamber sentenced Germain Katanga to 12 years' imprisonment for murder constituting a crime against humanity; 12 years' imprisonment for murder as a war crime; 12 years' imprisonment for directing an attack against the civilian population as such or against individual civilians not taking direct part in hostilities as a war crime; 10 years' imprisonment for destroying the enemy's property as a war crime; and, 10 years' imprisonment for pillaging constituting a war crime. The Trial Chamber pronounced a joint sentence of 12 years' imprisonment, as an accessory within the meaning of Article 25(3)(d), against Katanga. In its determination, the Trial Chamber noted, at paragraph 145 of the Decision on Sentence pursuant to Article 76 of the Statute, ICC-01/04-01/07-3484, its intention to distinguish between murder and attacks against civilians and the destruction of property and pillaging. Thus, the Trial Chamber considered it appropriate to punish more severely crimes against the person than against property, which was evident by the Court's sentencing Katanga to 12 years for crimes against the person and 10 years for crimes against property.

Cross-references:

Article 20.

Rule 145.

Doctrine:

1. Gideon Boas, James L. Biscoff and Nathalie L. Reid, *International Criminal Law Practitioner Library*. Vol. II: *Elements of Crime under International Criminal Law*, Cambridge University Press, Cambridge, 2008.

2. Antonio Cassese, Paola Gaeta and John R.W.D. Jones, *The Oxford Companion to International Criminal Justice*, Oxford University Press, Oxford, 2009.

3. Karin Calvo-Goller, *The Trial Proceedings of the International Criminal Court: ICTY and ICTR Precedents*, Martinus Nijhoff Publishers, Leiden, 2005.

4. Silvia D'Ascoli, *Sentencing in International Criminal Law: The Approach of the two Ad Hoc Tribunals and Future Perspectives for the International Criminal Court,* Hart Publishing, Oxford, 2011.

5. Human Rights Watch, *Genocide, War Crimes and Crimes Against Humanity: A Topical Digest of the Case Law of the International Criminal Tribunal for the former Yugoslavia*, 2006.

6. Michael Kurth, "The Lubanga Case of the International Criminal Court: A Critical Analysis of the Trial Chamber's Findings on Issues of Active Use, Age and Gravity", in *Goettingen Journal of International Law*, 2013, vol. 5, no. 2, pp. 431–53.

7. William A. Schabas, *The International Criminal Court: A Commentary on the Rome Statute*, Oxford University Press, Oxford, 2010, pp. 898–908.

8. Mark Jennings, "Article 78 – Determination of the Sentence", in Otto Triffterer (ed.), *Commentary on the Rome Statute of the International Criminal Court: Observers' Notes, Article by Article*, 2nd ed., C.H. Beck/Hart/Nomos, Munich/Oxford/Baden-Baden, 2008, pp. 1433–37.

Author: Dejana Radisavljevic.

Article 79
Trust Fund[646]

1. A Trust Fund shall be established by decision of the Assembly of States Parties.[647] for the benefit of victims of crimes within the jurisdiction of the Court, and of the families of such victims.[648]

---

[646] *General remarks*

The ICC Statute created two independent institutions: the International Criminal Court and the Trust Fund for Victims ('TFV'). It is aimed to establish a system which combines retributive and restorative justice (*Prosecutor v. Lubanga*, ICC T. Ch., Decision establishing the principles and procedures to be applied to reparations, ICC-01/04-01/06-2904, 7 August 2012, para. 177).

The TFV's two mandates are:(1) Reparations Mandate: implementing awards for reparations ordered by the Court against a convicted person (Article 75(2), Rule 98 (1–4)); (2) Assistance Mandate: using other resources (voluntary contributions and private donations) to provide victims and their families in situations where the Court is active with physical rehabilitation, psychological rehabilitation, and/or material support (Rule 98 (5); Reg. 50, Regulations of TFV; for details, see, for example, TFV Programme Progress Report Summer 2014).

The TFV's first mandate is linked to specific cases. Resources are collected through fines or forfeiture and awards for reparations (Regs. 43–46, Regulations of TFV) and complemented with "other resources of the Trust Fund" if the Board of the Directors so determines (Reg. 56). The Board of directors may launch a public donor appeal supported by reparations order (Reg. 20).

The assistance mandate of the TFV envisions the possibility of victims and their families to receive assistance separate from and prior to a court conviction, using resources the TFV has raised through voluntary contributions. The TFV started field operations related to the assistance mandate in northern Uganda and Democratic Republic of Congo (DRC) in 2008 (TFV Programme Progress Report Summer 2014, p. 6). The Board of Directors shall notify the relevant Chamber before undertaking activities under this mandate (Reg. 50; for example, *Situation in the Democratic Republic of the Congo*, TFV, Notification of the Board of Directors of the Trust Fund for Victims in accordance with Regulation 50 of the Regulations of the Trust Fund for Victims with Confidential Annex, ICC-01/04-439, 24 January 2008; *Situation in the Democratic Republic of the Congo*, ICC PT. Ch. I, Decision on the Notification of the Board of Directors of the Trust Fund for Victims in accordance with Regulation 50 of the Regulations of the Trust Fund, ICC-01/04-492, 11 April 2008).

Author: SONG Tianying.

[647] In 2002, the TFV was established by Assembly of States Parties (Establishment of a fund for the benefit of victims of crimes within the jurisdiction of the Court, and of the families of such victims, ICC-ASP/1/Res.6, 9 September 2002). The TFV is consisted of Board of Directors and its Secretariat. The Board of Directors is the decision-making body of TFV (Annex to ICC-ASP/1/Res.6, 9 September 2002, para. 7). The Board of Directors report annually on TFV activities to the Committee on Budget and Finance and the External Auditor and the Assembly of States Parties (Reg. 76). The Secretariat is under the full authority of the Board of Directors and provides assistance to it. For administrative purposes, the Secretariat is attached to the Registry of the Court and as part of the staff of the Registry and, as such, of the Court, the staff of the Secretariat enjoy the same rights, duties, privileges, immunities and benefits. Although the Board and the Secretariat are independent from the Court, the Registrar of the Court may provide necessary assistance for their proper functioning (Establishment of the Secretariat of the Trust Fund for Victims, ICC-ASP/3/Res.7, 10 September 2004; Regs. 18–19).

For example, the Registry assists in developing and disseminating standard application forms for reparations, receiving and treating submitted applications, seeking additional information from victims and generally assisting victims in relation to reparations (Rule 94, Rules of Procedure and Evidence; Regs. 86, 88, Regulations of the Court). The Victims Participation and Reparation Section of the Registry is responsible for such matters (Reg. 86(9), Regulations of the Court).

The TFV is funded by:

(a) Voluntary contributions from Governments, international organisations, individuals, corporations and other entities, in accordance with relevant criteria adopted by the Assembly of States Parties;

(b) Money and other property collected through fines or forfeiture transferred to the Trust Fund if ordered by the Court pursuant to Article 79, paragraph 2, of the Statute;

(c) Resources collected through awards for reparations if ordered by the Court pursuant to rule 98 of the Rules of Procedure and Evidence;

(d) Such resources, other than assessed contributions, as the Assembly of States Parties may decide to allocate to the Trust Fund (Establishment of a fund for the benefit of victims of crimes within the jurisdiction of the Court, and of the families of such victims, ICC-ASP/1/Res.6, 9 September 2002, para. 2; Reg. 21, TFV Regulations).

Author: SONG Tianying.

[648] On the implementation level, the TFV uses two definitions of victims pursuant to its two mandates. For Court-ordered reparations, victims are defined in Rule 85 of the Rules of Procedure and Evidence and may apply to receive reparations in the context of a particular case according to orders made under Article 75 of the ICC Statute (see above commentary to Article 75(1), "to, or in respect of, victims").

Under the TFV's assistance mandate, the category of "victims" is broader, encompassing all victims of crimes within the jurisdiction of the Court and their families (TFV Report 2014 Summer, p. 8). For example, the Appeals Chamber held in the *Lubanga* case that "it is appropriate for the Board of Directors of the Trust Fund to consider, in the exercise of its mandate under Regulation 50(a) of the Regulations of the Trust Fund, the possibility of including members of the affected communities in the assistance programmes operating in the situation area in the DRC, where such persons do not meet" the eligibility criterion for Court-ordered reparations (*Prosecutor v. Lubanga*, ICC A. Ch., Judgment on the appeals against the "Decision establishing the principles and procedures to be applied to reparations" of 7 August 2012 with AMENDED order for reparations (Annex A) and public annexes 1 and 2, ICC-01/04-01/06-3129-AnxA, 3 March 2015, para. 55).

While maximising the scope of beneficiaries, the TFV should notify the Court of its planned activities to ensure such activities would not "pre-determine any issue to be determined by the Court, including the determination of jurisdiction pursuant to Article 19, admissibility pursuant to Articles 17 and 18, or violate the presumption of innocence pursuant to Article 66, or be prejudicial to or inconsistent with the rights of the accused and a fair and impartial trial" (Reg. 50(a)); *Situation in the Democratic Republic of the Congo*, TFV, Notification of the Board of Directors of the Trust Fund for Victims in accordance with Regulation 50 of the Regulations of the Trust Fund for Victims with Confidential Annex, ICC-01/04-439, 24 January 2008, para. 31; *Situation in the Democratic Republic of the Congo*, ICC PT. Ch. I, Decision on the Notification of the Board of Directors of the Trust Fund for Victims in accordance with Regulation 50 of the Regulations of the Trust Fund, ICC-01/04-492, 11 April 2008).

Author: SONG Tianying.

2. The Court may order money and other property collected through fines or forfeiture to be transferred, by order of the Court, to the Trust Fund.[649]

3. The Trust Fund shall be managed according to criteria to be determined by the Assembly of States Parties.[650]

---

[649] The Board of Directors shall, at the request of the Chamber, make written or oral observations on the transfer of fines or forfeitures to the Trust Fund (Reg. 31; Rule 148, Rules of Procedure and Evidence). The Board of Directors shall determine the uses of such resources in accordance with any stipulations or instructions contained in such orders, in particular on the scope of beneficiaries and the nature and amount of the award(s) (Reg. 43). The Board of Directors may seek further instructions from the relevant Chamber on the implementation of its orders (Reg. 45). The TFV shall submit to the relevant Chamber, via the Registrar, the draft implementation plan for approval and shall consult and update the relevant Chamber on the implementation of the award (Regs. 57, 58).

Resources collected through awards for reparations may only benefit victims as defined in rule 85 of the Rules of Procedure and Evidence, and, where natural persons are concerned, their families, affected directly or indirectly by the crimes committed by the convicted person (Reg. 46). The Board of Directors has discretion as to whether to complement the resources collected through awards for reparations with "other resources of the Trust Fund" and shall advise the Court accordingly (Reg. 56).

In the Lubanga case, the convicted person was declared indigent. No assets or property of the convicted person was identified for the purposes of reparations (*Prosecutor v. Lubanga*, ICC T. Ch., Decision establishing the principles and procedures to be applied to reparations, ICC-01/04-01/06-2904, 7 August 2012, para. 269). The Appeals Chamber held that should the TFV provide "other resources of the Trust Fund" for reparation, the convicted person remains liable and must reimburse the Trust Fund (*Prosecutor v. Lubanga*, A. Ch., Judgment on the appeals against the "Decision establishing the principles and procedures to be applied to reparations" of 7 August 2012 with AMENDED order for reparations (Annex A) and public annexes 1 and 2, ICC-01/04-01/06-3129-AnxA, 3 March 2015, paras. 114, 115). The TFV will be able to claim the advanced resources from Lubanga. His financial situation shall be monitored pursuant to Regulation 117 of the Regulations of the Court (para. 116).

Author: SONG Tianying.

[650] The Assembly of States Parties adopted the Regulations of the Trust Fund in 2005, with a view to ensure the proper and effective functioning of the Trust Fund (Regulations of the Trust Fund for Victims, ICC-ASP/4/Res.3, 3 December 2005). They contain provisions regulating:

- the management and oversight of the TFV;
- the receipt of funds;
- the activities and projects of the TFV; and
- the TFV's reporting requirements.

Cross-references:

Rules 94, 98 and 148.

Regulations 86, 88 and 116.

Doctrine:

1. William A. Schabas, *The International Criminal Court: A Commentary on the Rome Statute*, Oxford University Press, 2010, pp. 909–17.

2. Mark Jennings, "Article 79 – Trust Fund", in Otto Triffterer (ed.), *Commentary on the Rome Statute of the International Criminal Court: Observers' Notes, Article by Article*, 2nd ed., C.H. Beck/Hart/Nomos, Munich/Oxford/Baden-Baden, 2008, pp. 1439–42.

Author: SONG Tianying.

Article 80
Non-prejudice to national application of penalties and national laws

Nothing in this Part affects the application by States of penalties prescribed by their national law, nor the law of States which do not provide for penalties prescribed in this Part.[651]

---

[651] *General remarks*:

Article 80 was introduced in the final draft of the ICC Statute in order to calm the minority of states that had campaigned to include the capital punishment within the available penalties. Some of these states were concerned that the exclusion of the death penalty could be interpreted as part of trend and an emerging norm of customary international law on the matter (Schabas, p. 918).

Analysis:

The element "Nothing in this Part affects the application by States of penalties prescribed by their national law" means that the penalties system set out in Part 7 only applies to the ICC and does not affect national criminal justice systems. This is relevant for example in relation to the non-inclusion of the death penalty.

The element "nor the law of States which do not provide for penalties prescribed in this Part" is based on the same assumption. It means that the inclusion of certain penalties in the ICC Statute and other criteria for their applicability does not affect national criminal justice systems which do not provide for such penalties. This is relevant for the inclusion of the ICC Statute of life imprisonment, a penalty not used by all states.

Doctrine:

1. William A. Schabas, *The International Criminal Court: A Commentary on the Rome Statute*, Oxford University Press, Oxford, 2010, pp. 918–26.
2. Rolf Einar Fife, "Article 80", in Otto Triffterer (ed.), *Commentary on the Rome Statute of the International Criminal Court: Observers' Notes, Article by Article*, 2nd ed., C.H. Beck/Hart/Nomos, Munich/Oxford/Baden-Baden, 2008, pp. 1443–48.

Author: Mark Klamberg.

PART 8. APPEAL AND REVISION

Article 81

Appeal against decision of acquittal or conviction or against sentence[652]

1. A decision under Article 74 may be appealed in accordance with the Rules of Procedure and Evidence as follows:

   (a) The Prosecutor may make an appeal on any of the following grounds:

      (i) Procedural error,

      (ii) Error of fact, or

      (iii) Error of law;

   (b) The convicted person, or the Prosecutor on that person's behalf, may make an appeal on any of the following grounds:

      (i) Procedural error,

      (ii) Error of fact,

      (iii) Error of law, or

      (iv) Any other ground that affects the fairness or reliability of the proceedings or decision.[653]

---

[652] *General remarks*

Article 81 concerns the appeal of the final decision on conviction or acquittal. The possibility of the defendant to appeal a criminal conviction is a human right pursuant to Article 14(5) of the ICCPR.

One question is whether the appeal proceedings are intended to be a trial *de novo* or are more of a corrective procedure. Brady argues that the specified grounds for appeal in Article 81 of the ICC Statute would suggest that the appeal is more in nature with a corrective procedure (Brady, p. 583). Staker holds a similar view (Staker, p. 1455). Roth and Henzelin are more cautious and they are more open towards trial *de novo*. They argue that the case law from the ECtHR which allows more corrective appeal proceedings has been applied to minor cases and not to cases of the nature that the ICC is concerned with (Roth and Henzelin, pp. 1552–1555).

Article 81 contain distinct provisions for an appeal of the verdict and an appeal of the sentence. Only the prosecutor or the convicted person may file an appeal. Although this excludes victims, they may participate in the appeals if there personal interests are affected by the appeal to the extent that it is not "prejudicial to or inconsistent with the rights of the accused and a fair and impartial trial" (*Prosecutor v. Lubanga*, ICC A. Ch., Decision on the participation of victims in the appeal, ICC-01/04-01/06-1453, 6 August 2008, para. 7). Pursuant to rule 103 the Appeals Chamber may, if it considers it appropriate, invite or grant leave to a State, organisation or person to submit observations.

Cross-references:

Rule 152.

Author: Mark Klamberg.

[653] Paragraph 1 provides for three grounds on which the Prosecution may bring an appeal, and four grounds on which the convicted person can appeal.

---

2. (a) A sentence may be appealed, in accordance with the Rules of Procedure and Evidence, by the Prosecutor or the convicted person on the ground of disproportion between the crime and the sentence;

   (b) If on an appeal against sentence the Court considers that there are grounds on which the conviction might be set aside, wholly or in part, it may invite the Prosecutor and the convicted person to submit grounds under Article 81, paragraph 1 (a) or (b), and may render a decision on conviction in accordance with Article 83;

   (c) The same procedure applies when the Court, on an appeal against conviction only, considers that there are grounds to reduce the sentence under paragraph 2 (a).[654]

3. (a) Unless the Trial Chamber orders otherwise, a convicted person shall remain in custody pending an appeal;

   (b) When a convicted person's time in custody exceeds the sentence of imprisonment imposed, that person shall be released, except that if the Prosecutor is also appealing, the release may be subject to the conditions under subparagraph (c) below;

   (c) In case of an acquittal, the accused shall be released immediately, subject to the following:

       (i) Under exceptional circumstances, and having regard, inter alia, to the concrete risk of flight, the seriousness of the offence charged and the probability of success on appeal, the Trial Chamber, at the request of the Prosecutor, may maintain the detention of the person pending appeal;

       (ii) A decision by the Trial Chamber under subparagraph (c) (i) may be appealed in accordance with the Rules of Procedure and Evidence.[655]

Procedural errors include non-compliance with mandatory procedural requirements of the Statute and the RPE as well as errors relating to the exercise of the discretion by a Trial Chamber (for example: on admissibility of evidence)

Errors of fact includes two types of errors. The first type is when it is alleged that the Trial Chamber erred in reaching the conclusions of fact it did on the basis of the evidence that was before it. The second type concerns the type when the Trial Chamber was justified in reaching the final conclusion on the evidence presented at trial, but where additional evidence present on appeal casts doubt on those findings (Staker, p. 1459–1465).

Errors of law may concern any determination made by a Trial Chamber on a question of the substantive or procedural law of the Court.

The phrase "any other ground that affects the fairness or reliability of the proceedings or decision" is a "catch-all" provision that may add little to the other specified grounds of appeal.

Author: Mark Klamberg.

[654] Paragraph 2 provides for appeal against the sentence. In contrast to paragraph 1(b), there is no express provision for the Prosecutor to bring an appeal of the convicted person, although nothing in the wording of paragraph 2 would prevent it (Staker, p. 1454).

The paragraph only provides for ground for appeal is that there is "disproportion between the crime and the sentence". However, it follows from Article 83(2) that appeals may also be brought against a sentence based on allegations of "error of fact or law or procedural error". This could include: failure to hold a hearing under Article 76(2); determining the sentence based on matters that are factually wrong; and/or misconstruing a provision of the Statute or the Rules.

Author: Mark Klamberg.

4. Subject to the provisions of paragraph 3 (a) and (b), execution of the decision or sentence shall be suspended during the period allowed for appeal and for the duration of the appeal proceedings.[656]

---

[655] A convicted person shall remain in custody pending an appeal unless the Trial Chamber orders otherwise. This is based on the assumption that the convicted person is already in custody, which is not necessarily the case.

    If the person has been acquitted the person is to be released immediately. However, the Prosecutor may request the Trial Chamber to maintain the detention of the person pending appeal in "exceptional circumstances" taking into consideration, *inter alia*, "the concrete risk of flight, the seriousness of the offence charged and the probability of success on appeal".

Author: Mark Klamberg.

[656] Apart from the fact that the person convicted normally remain in custody, as provided for in paragraph 3, execution of the decision or sentence shall be suspended during the period allowed for appeal and for the duration of the appeal proceedings.

Cross-references:

Rules 149, Rule 150, 151, 152, 154.

Regulations 57, 58, 59, 60, 61, 63.

Doctrine:

1. Helen Brady, "Appeal", in Roy S. Lee (ed.), *The International Criminal Court: Elements of Crimes and Rules of Procedure and Evidence*, Transnational Publishers, Ardsley, NY, 2001, pp. 575–96.

2. Robert Roth and Marc Henzelin, "The Appeal Procedure of the ICC", in Antonio Cassese, Paola Gaeta and John R.W.D. Jones (eds.), *The Rome Statute of the International Criminal Court*, Oxford University Press, Oxford, 2002, pp. 1535–58.

3. William A. Schabas, *The International Criminal Court: A Commentary on the Rome Statute*, Oxford University Press, Oxford, 2010, pp. 929–37.

4. Christopher Staker, "Article 81 – Appeal Against Decision or Acquittal or Conviction or Against Sentence", in Otto Triffterer (ed.), *Commentary on the Rome Statute of the International Criminal Court: Observers' Notes, Article by Article*, 2nd ed., C.H. Beck/Hart/Nomos, Munich/Oxford/Baden-Baden, 2008, pp. 1449–74.

Author: Mark Klamberg.

Article 82
Appeal against other decisions[657]

---

[657] *General remarks*:

Article 82(1)–(2) addresses interlocutory appeals against certain decisions by the Pre-Trial or Trial Chamber. Paragraphs 1(a)–(c) and (2) set out decisions against which an interlocutory appeal is always permitted. Paragraph 1(d) provides a system for certification – leave to appeal – regarding other decisions. A decision that may not be appealed separately, or for which leave to appeal is not granted, can be challenged in an appeal against the final decision in the case.

Article 82(3) deals with suspensive effects of an appeal and Article 82(4) with appeals against reparation orders, provisions that are not confined to interlocutory appeals (see also *Prosecutor v. Ngudjolo Chui*, ICC A. Ch., Decision on the Public document request of the Prosecutor of 19 December 2012 for suspensive effect, ICC-01/04-02/12-12, 20 December 2012, para. 15).

i) Grounds for and standards of review

As to the grounds for appeal, the Appeals Chamber has accepted that the categories of errors in Article 81(1)(a) be transposed to interlocutory appeals: procedural error, error of fact and error of law (*Situation in the Democratic Republic of Congo*, ICC A. Ch., Judgment on the Prosecutor's Appeal against the decision of the Pre-Trial Chamber I entitled "Decision on the Prosecutor's Application for Warrants of Arrest, Article 58". ICC-01/04-169, 13 July 2006, paras. 34–35). Hence, the appellant may rely on procedural errors as the basis also for impugning a decision concerning the admissibility of the case (for example *Prosecutor v. Kony, Otti, Odhiambo and Ongwen*, ICC A. Ch., Judgment on the appeal of the Defence against the "Decision on the admissibility of the case under Article 19(1) of the Statute" of 10 March 2009, ICC-02/04-01/05-408, 16 September 2009, para. 47).

The Appeals Chamber may confirm, reverse or amend the decision appealed (rule 158(2)). Initially it was not clear whether the requirements set forth for reversal or amendment in Article 83(2) are applicable also in case of an appeal in accordance with Article 82 (*Situation in the DRC*, ICC A. Ch., ICC-01/04-169, 13 July 2006, para. 83). But later the Appeals Chamber has clarified that Article 83(2) does not apply to appeals under Article 82 (*Prosecutor v. Lubanga*, ICC A. Ch., Judgment on the Prosecutor's appeal against the decision of Pre-Trial Chamber I entitled "Decision Establishing General Principles Governing Applications to Restrict Disclosure pursuant to Rule 81 (2) and (4) of the Rules of Procedure and Evidence", ICC-01/04-01/06-568, 13 October 2006, para. 13).

Nonetheless, the Appeals Chamber has regularly applied the requirement, found in Article 83(2), that the error of fact or law or procedural error must have "materially affected" the decision (for example *Situation in Uganda*, ICC A. Ch., Judgment on the appeals of the Defence against the decisions entitled "Decision on victims' applications for participation a/0010/06, a/0064/06 to a/0070/06, a/0081/06, a/0082/06, a/0084/06 to a/0089/06, a/0091/06 to a/0097/06, a/0099/06, a/0100/06, a/0102/06 to a/0104/06, a/0111/06, a/0113/06 to a/0117/06, a/0120/06, a/0121/06 and a/0123/06 to a/0127/06" of Pre-Trial Chamber II, ICC-02/04-179, 23 February 2009, para. 40; *Prosecutor v. Lubanga*, ICC A. Ch., Judgment on the appeal of the Prosecutor against the decision of Trial Chamber I entitled "Decision on the release of Thomas Lubanga Dyilo", ICC-01/04-01/06-1487, 21 October 2008, para. 44; *Prosecutor v. Katanga and Ngudjolo Chui*, ICC A. Ch., Judgment on the Appeal of Mr. Germain Katanga against the Oral Decision of Trial Chamber II of 12 June 2009 on the Admissibility of the Case, ICC-01/04-01/07-1497, 25 September 2009, para. 38). The impugned decision is materially affected by the error if the decision would otherwise have been "substantially different" (*Situation in the Democratic Republic of Congo*, ICC A. Ch., ICC-01/04-169, 13 July 2006, para. 83).

The Appeals Chamber will not interfere with a discretionary decision by another Chamber unless that decision is vitiated by a legal error, a factual error or a procedural error, and only if the error materially affected the decision, which includes assessing whether the other Chamber erred in law, gave undue weight to extraneous factors, or failed to consider relevant factors (*Prosecutor v. Katanga and Ngudjolo Chui*, ICC A. Ch., Judgment on the Appeal of Mr Katanga Against the Decision of Trial Chamber II of 20 November 2009 Entitled "Decision on the Motion of the Defence for Germain Katanga for a Declaration on Unlawful Detention and Stay of Proceedings", ICC-01/04-01/07-2259, 12 July 2010, para. 34). Under this standard of review, the Appeals Chamber will not reverse the impugned decision simply because it would have decided differently, but only when it finds that the Trial Chamber exercised its discretion incorrectly. In applying this "margin of appreciation", the Appeals Chamber will interfere only in the case of a clear error, namely where it cannot discern how the Chamber's conclusion could have reasonably been reached from the evidence before it (*Prosecutor v. Mbarushimana*, ICC A. Ch., Judgment on the appeal of Mr Callixte Mbarushimana against the decision of Pre-Trial Chamber I of 19 May 2011 entitled "Decision on the 'Defence Request for Interim Release", ICC-01/04-01/10-283, 14 July 2011, para. 17).

One example of improper application of discretion was the Pre-Trial Chamber (Single Judge) ordering the production and submission of so-called "in-depth analysis charts" without first receiving submissions from the parties concerning the utility of the ordered scheme (*Prosecutor v. Ongwen*, ICC A. Ch., Judgment on the appeal of the Prosecutor against the decision of Pre-Trial Chamber II entitled "Decision Setting the Regime for Evidence Disclosure and Other Related Matters", ICC-02/04-01/15-251, 17 June 2015, para. 46). This exercise of discretion was considered to be "unfair and unreasonable and had a material effect on the Impugned Decision".

ii) Errors of law

On legal errors, the Appeals Chamber has stated that it "will not defer to the Trial Chamber's interpretation of the law", but instead that "it will arrive at its own conclusions as to the appropriate law and determine whether or not the Trial Chamber misinterpreted the law" (*Prosecutor v. Banda and Jerbo*, ICC A. Ch., Judgment on the appeal of the Prosecutor against the decision of Trial Chamber IV of 12 September 2011 entitled "Reasons for the Order on translation of witness statements (ICC-02/05-03/09-199) and additional instructions on translation", ICC-02/05-03/09-295, 17 February 2012, para. 20). In case of an error of law, the Appeals Chamber will only intervene if the error materially affected the impugned decision (para. 20). Insufficient reasoning may amount to an error of law (for example *Prosecutor v. Gbagbo*, ICC A. Ch., Judgment on the appeal of Mr Laurent Koudou Gbagbo against the decision of Pre-Trial Chamber I of 13 July 2012 entitled "Decision on the 'Requête de la Défense demandant la mise en liberté provisoire du président Gbagbo", ICC-02/11-01/11-278, 26 October 2012, paras. 46–47 and the dissenting opinions of judges Ušacka and Kourula). Where the appellant, while alleging an error of law, challenges the factual finding based on that law, the Appeals Chamber will consider such an alleged error as an error of fact (*Prosecutor v. Simone Gbagbo*, ICC A. Ch., Judgment on the appeal of Côte d'Ivoire against the decision of Pre-Trial Chamber I of 11 December 2014 entitled "Decision on Côte d'Ivoire's challenge to the admissibility of the case against Simone Gbagbo", ICC-02/11-01/12-75, 27 May 2015, paras. 70 and 78).

iii) Errors of fact

On factual errors, the Appeals Chamber has stated that it will not interfere with factual findings of a first-instance Chamber unless it is shown that that Chamber "committed a clear error, namely: misappreciated the facts, took into account irrelevant facts or failed to take into account relevant facts" (for example *Prosecutor v. Gaddafi and Al-Senussi*, ICC A. Ch., Judgment on the Appeal of Libya against the decision of Pre-Trial Chamber I of 31 May 2013 entitled "Decision on the admissibility of the case against Saif Al-Islam Gaddafi", ICC-01/11-01/11-547, 21 May 2014, para. 93). Hence, the appraisal of evidence lies, in the first place, with the relevant Chamber and the Appeals Chamber will "defer or accord a margin of appreciation both to the inferences [the Trial Chamber] drew from the available evidence and to the weight it accorded to the different factors militating for or against detention" (*Prosecutor v. Bemba*, ICC A. Ch., Judgment on the appeal of Mr Jean-Pierre Bemba Gombo against the decision of Trial Chamber III of 6 January 2012 entitled 'Decision on the defence's 28 December 2011 "Requête de Mise en liberté provisoire de M. Jean-Pierre Bemba Gombo", ICC-01/05-01/08-2151, 5 March 2012, para. 16). The appellant's mere disagreement with the conclusions that the Chamber drew from the available facts or the weight it accorded to particular factors is not enough to establish a clear error (*Prosecutor v. Mbarushimana*, ICC A. Ch., ICC-01/04-01/10-283, 14 July 2011, para. 17).

iv) Procedural errors

On procedural errors, the guiding question for the Appeals Chamber's review is whether the procedure the Pre-Trial or Trial Chamber adopted was so unfair and unreasonable as to constitute an abuse of discretion (for example *Prosecutor v. Gaddafi and Al-Senussi*, ICC A. Ch., Judgment on the Appeal of Libya against the decision of Pre-Trial Chamber I of 31 May 2013 entitled "Decision on the admissibility of the case against Saif Al-Islam Gaddafi", ICC-01/11-01/11-547, 21 May 2014, para. 162).

v) Additional evidence on appeal

The corrective function of the Appeals Chamber and the fact that the scope of proceedings on appeal is determined by the scope of the relevant proceedings before the Pre-Trial or Trial Chamber have been held against accepting additional evidence on appeal (for example *Prosecutor v. Ruto and Sang*, ICC A. Ch., Decision on the "Filing of Updated Investigation Report by the Government of Kenya in the Appeal against the Pre-Trial Chamber's Decision on Admissibility", ICC-01/09-01/11-234, 28 July 2011, paras. 9–14; *Prosecutor v. Gaddafi and Al-Senussi*, ICC A. Ch., Judgment on the appeal of Libya against the decision of Pre-Trial Chamber I of 31 May 2013 entitled 'Decision on the admissibility of the case against Saif Al-Islam Gaddafi', ICC-01/11-01/11-547, 21 May 2014, para. 43). It would, according to the Appeals Chamber, not be appropriate for it to consider the information (some of which post-dated the impugned decision) when the Pre-Trial Chamber had not done so (*Prosecutor v. Gaddafi and Al-Senussi*, ICC A. Ch., Judgment on the appeal of Mr Abdullah Al-Senussi against the decision of Pre-Trial Chamber I of 11 October 2013 entitled "Decision on the admissibility of the case against Abdullah Al-Senussi", ICC-01/11-01/11-565, 24 July 2014, para. 58). Likewise, the Appeals Chamber did not take into account, in the circumstances of the case at hand, any other factual matters that post-date the impugned decision or were not before the Pre-Trial Chamber (para. 59).

vi) Other procedural issues

Some procedural provisions are provided in the Rules. As a general principle, Parts 5 and 6 of the Statute and the rules governing proceedings and the submission of evidence in the Pre-Trial and Trial Chambers are also applicable, *mutatis mutandis*, to the proceedings in the Appeals Chamber (rule 149). The filing of interlocutory appeals is addressed in rule 154 (no leave to appeal required) and rule 155 (leave for appeal required). The procedure before the Appeals Chamber, directly or upon leave to appeal, is set out in rule 156. Further directions are given in regulations 64 and 65. An appeal may be discontinued at any time before the judgment (rule 157). Apart from setting out the power of the Appeals Chamber to confirm, reverse or amend the impugned decision, rule 158 provides that the judgment shall be delivered in accordance with Article 83(4).

The Appeals Chamber may decide to render a single judgment on multiple appeals when the impugned decision is identical (*Prosecutor v. Kony, Otti, Odhiambo and Ongwen*, ICC A. Ch.,

1. Either party may appeal any of the following decisions in accordance with the Rules of Procedure and Evidence:[658]

Judgment on the appeals of the Defence against the decisions entitled "Decision on victims' applications for participation a/0010/06, a/0064/06 to a/0070/06, a/0081/06, a/0082/06, a/0084/06 to a/0089/06, a/0091/06 to a/0097/06, a/0099/06, a/0100/06, a/0102/06 to a/0104/06, a/0111/06, a/0113/06 to a/0117/06, a/0120/06, a/0121/06 and a/0123/06 to a/0127/06" of Pre-Trial Chamber II, ICC-02/04-01/05-371, 23 February 2009, para. 12). The same approach has also been taken when the subject-matter of each one of the appeals under review is identical (for example *Situation in Darfur*, Sudan, ICC A. Ch., Judgment on victim participation in the investigation stage of the proceedings in the appeal of the OPCD against the decision of Pre-Trial Chamber I of 3 December 2007 and in the appeals of the OPCD and the Prosecutor against the decision of Pre-Trial Chamber I of 6 December 2007, ICC-02/05-177, 2 February 2009).

Preparatory works:

As with the rest of the ICC Statute, there is a lack of pertinent *travaux préparatoires* for the purpose of assisting in the interpretation and application of the provisions. The 1994 ILC Draft Statute contained only brief provisions on appeals and revision, inspired by the provisions of the ICTY Statute (Articles 48–50, Report of the International Law Commission on the work of its 46th session 2 May–22 July 1994, UN doc. A/49/10, 1994, pp. 125–129). The subsequent negotiations in the Preparatory Committee generated a large number of additional proposals with respect to appeals, which were listed in a compilation – "the telephone book" (Article 48, Report of the Preparatory Committee, UN doc A/51/22, Vol. II, 1996, pp. 235–242). In order to further compile and clarify the alternatives, and to create a higher degree of compatibility and consistency among the proposals, delegations met at an intersessional meeting in Siracusa in May and June 1997. Although the new compilation was an informal document, it proved very influential as a point of departure in the further negotiations.

Another compiled draft Statute – the Zutphen draft – formed the basis of the final session of the Preparatory Committee and it contained more elaborated texts on appeals, albeit with various options (Articles 73–74, Draft Report of the Intersessional Meeting from 19 to 30 January 1998 in Zutphen, The Netherlands). The Report of the Preparatory Committee, which was the basis for the Rome Diplomatic Conference, contained further refined provisions, including an Article specifically addressing interlocutory appeals (Article 81, Report of the Preparatory Committee on the Establishment of an International Criminal Court, UN doc. A/CONF.183/2 (1998), pp. 64–66). This draft provision also included a default rule on leave to appeal which was similar to the final Article 82(1)(d).

Author: Håkan Friman.

[658] Article 82(1) designates the right to appeal to "either party". The Appeals Chamber has concluded that "the Statute defines exhaustively the right to appeal" and further held that the limitation of the right to bring interlocutory appeals to those subjects listed in Article 82 of the Statute is fully consistent with internationally recognised human rights (*Situation in the Democratic Republic of Congo*, ICC A. Ch., Judgment on the Prosecutor's Application for Extraordinary Review of Pre-Trial Chamber I's 31 March 2006 Decision Denying Leave to Appeal, ICC-01/04-168, 13 July 2006, paras. 38–39). This means that no one else than a party may appeal or be granted leave to appeal (*Prosecutor v. Lubanga*, ICC A. Ch., Decision on the "Urgent Request for Directions" of the Kingdom of the Netherlands of 17 August 2011, ICC-01/04-01/06-2799, 26 August 2011, para. 8).

As part of the reasons in support of the application of a ground of appeal, an appellant is obliged not only to set out the alleged error, but also to indicate, with sufficient precision, how this error would have materially affected the impugned decision (*Prosecutor v. Kony, Otti, Odhiambo and Ongwen*, ICC A. Ch., Judgment on the appeal of the Defence against the "Deci-

(a) A decision with respect to jurisdiction or admissibility;[659]

---

sion on the admissibility of the case under Article 19(1) of the Statute" of 10 March 2009, ICC-02/04-01/05-408, 16 September 2009, para. 48). This may include explaining how the decision would have been substantially different without the error, such as by referring to arguments that the appellant would have made in response to an incorrectly handled submission and that could have led to a different decision (*Prosecutor v. Gbagbo*, ICC A. Ch., Judgment on the appeal of Mr Laurent Koudou Gbagbo against the decision of Pre-Trial Chamber I on jurisdiction and stay of the proceedings, ICC-02/11-01/11-321, 12 December 2012, para. 44). If these requirements are not met, the Appeals Chamber may dismiss arguments *in limine*, without full consideration of their merits (for example *Prosecutor v. Ntaganda*, ICC A. Ch., Judgment on the appeal of Mr Bosco Ntaganda against the decision of Pre-Trial Chamber II of 18 November 2013 entitled "Decision on the Defence's Application for Interim Release", ICC-01/04-02/06-271, 5 March 2014, para. 32).

Author: Håkan Friman.

[659] The Appeals Chamber is the competent Chamber to decide whether the defence may avail itself of the procedural remedy of an appeal under Article 82(1)(a) and thus to decide on related matters such as the extension of time limits (*Prosecutor v. Lubanga*, ICC PT. Ch., Decision on the Application by the Duty Counsel for the Defence Dated 20 March 2006, ICC-01/04-01/06-50, 22 March 2006). The function of the Appeals Chamber in respect of appeals brought under Article 82(1)(a) is to determine whether the determination on the admissibility of the case or the jurisdiction of the Court was in accord with the law (*Prosecutor v. Kony, Otti, Odhiambo and Ongwen*, ICC A. Ch., ICC-02/04-01/05-408, 16 September 2009, para. 80). Hence, its function is not to decide anew on the admissibility of the case (for example *Prosecutor v. Muthaura, Kenyatta and Ali*, ICC A. Ch., Decision on the "Filing of Updated Investigation Report by the Government of Kenya in the Appeal against the Pre-Trial Chamber's Decision on Admissibility", ICC-01/09- 02/11-202, 28 July 2011, paras. 9 and 11).

In light of the limitation in Article 19(4) concerning the number of challenges that a person or a State may raise with respect to the jurisdiction of the Court or the admissibility of the case, an appellant may wish to preserve the right to challenge by discontinuing an appeal. However, the Appeals Chamber has concluded that discontinuance of an appeal cannot be made subject to reservations and found as invalid a notice of discontinuance subject to the appellants retaining the right to challenge the admissibility of the case (*Prosecutor v. Lubanga*, ICC A. Ch., Decision on Thomas Lubanga Dyilo's Brief Relative to Discontinuance of Appeal, ICC-01/04-01/06-176, 3 July 2006). Further, the Appeals Chamber has rejected the appellants request that the matter be referred to the Pre-Trial Chamber (see Article 19(6)) and instead deemed the appeal as abandoned and dismissed (*Prosecutor v. Lubanga*, ICC A. Ch., Decision on Thomas Lubanga Dyilo's Application for Referral to the pre-Trial Chamber/in the Alternative, Discontinuance of Appeal, ICC-01/04-01/06-393, 6 September 2006).

The phrase "decision with respect to" is interpreted to mean that the operative part of the decision itself must pertain directly to a question on the jurisdiction of the Court or the admissibility of a case, and it is not sufficient that there is an indirect or tangential link between the underlying decision and questions of jurisdiction or admissibility (*Situation in Kenya*, ICC A. Ch., Decision on the admissibility of the "Appeal of the Government of Kenya against the 'Decision on the Request for Assistance Submitted on Behalf of the Government of the Republic of Kenya Pursuant to Article 93(10) of the Statute and Rule 194 of the Rules of Procedure and Evidence'", ICC-01/09-78, 10 August 2011, paras. 15–16; *Prosecutor v. Gaddafi and Al-Senussi*, ICC A. Ch., Decision on the admissibility of the "Appeal Against Decision on Application Under Rule 103" of Ms Mishana Hosseinioun of 7 February 2012, ICC-01/11-01/11-74, 9 March 2012, para. 10). Hence, an appeal was not allowed on this ground against a decision concerning assistance to and cooperation with the Court just because it was related to a challenge to the admissibility of two cases that the appellant had lodged. Likewise, an appeal was rejected when the impugned decision concerned a request for the postponement of surrender under Article 95 but contained no determination concerning the admissibility of the case (*Prosecutor v. Gaddafi and Al-Senussi*, ICC A. Ch., Decision on "Government of Libya's Appeal Against the 'Decision Regarding the Second Request by the Government of Libya for Postponement of the Surrender of Saif Al-Islam Gaddafi'" of 10 April 2012, ICC-01/11-01/11-126, 25 April 2012, para. 14).

The notion of "jurisdiction" is not entirely the same in different legal traditions and there may be different opinions as to what constitutes a jurisdictional issue. In *Lubanga*, the defence challenged the jurisdiction of the Court by reference to the "doctrine of abuse of process". In the appeal against the Pre-Trial Chamber's decision establishing jurisdiction (and the admissibility of the case), the Appeals Chamber rejected the submission that a challenge based upon this doctrine raises a challenge to the jurisdiction of the Court (*Prosecutor v. Lubanga*, ICC A. Ch., Judgment on the Appeal of Mr. Thomas Lubanga Dyilo against the Decision on the Defence Challenge to the Jurisdiction of the Court pursuant to Article 19(2)(a) of the Statute of 3 October 2006, ICC-01/04-01/06-772, 14 December 2006, para. 24). Instead, the doctrine should be considered a sui generis application to stay the proceedings and release the suspect, that is, to relinquish jurisdiction. Nonetheless, the appeals, referring to Article 82(1)(a), were addressed in substance by the Chamber.

In *Gbagbo*, on the other hand, the Appeals Chamber stated that a decision to reject a request to stay the proceedings is not a "decision with respect to jurisdiction" in terms of Article 82(1)(a) and may therefore be appealed only with the leave of the Chamber under Article 82(1)(d) (*Gbagbo*, ICC A. Ch., ICC-02/11-01/11-321, 12 December 2012, para. 101). Conversely, a decision that is subject to an appeal under Article 82(1)(a) may not be appealed pursuant to Article 82(1)(d) (*Prosecutor v. Gaddafi and Al-Senussi*, ICC PT. Ch. I, Decision on Libya application for leave to appeal and request for reconsideration of the "Decision on the 'Urgent Defence Request'", ICC-01/11-01/11-316, 24 April 2013, para. 30).

Also the concept "subject-matter jurisdiction" may be understood differently. In *Lubanga*, the Appeals Chamber concluded that "[j]urisdiction under Article 19 of the Statute denotes competence to deal with a criminal cause or matter under the Statute" (*Prosecutor v. Lubanga*, ICC A. Ch., ICC-01/04-01/06-772, 14 December 2006, para. 24). An appeal which challenged the Pre-Trial Chamber's interpretation of the requirement of an "organisational policy" for crimes against humanity (see Article 7(2)(a)) was held to relate to the substantive merits of the case as opposed to the issue whether the Court has subject-matter jurisdiction to consider the question (*Prosecutor v. Ruto, Kosgey and Sang*, ICC A. Ch., Decision on the appeals of Mr William Samoei Ruto and Mr Joshua Arap Sang against the decision of Pre-Trial Chamber II of 23 January 2012 entitled "Decision on the Confirmation of Charges Pursuant to Article 61(7)(a) and (b) of the Rome Statute", ICC-01/09-01/11-414, 24 May 2012, paras. 23–33). Hence, the appeal should be lodged pursuant to Article 82(1)(d) and not under Article 82(1)(a) (paras. 29 and 33; similarly, see *Prosecutor v. Muthaura, Kenyatta and Ali*, ICC A. Ch., Decision on the appeal of Mr Francis Kirimi Muthaura and Mr Uhuru Muigai Kenyatta against the decision of Pre-Trial Chamber II of 23 January 2012 entitled "Decision on the Confirmation of Charges Pursuant to Article 61(7)(a) and (b) of the Rome Statute", ICC-01/09-02/11-425, 24 May 2012).

The purpose of an admissibility challenge and, by extension, an appeal under Article 82(1)(a), is to determine whether or not a case is admissible, and generally speaking, the admissibility of a case must be determined on the basis of the facts as they exist at the time of the proceedings concerning the admissibility challenge (*Prosecutor v. Katanga and Ngudjolo Chui*, ICC A. Ch., ICC-01/04-01/07-1497, 25 September 2009, para. 56).

(b) A decision granting or denying release of the person being investigated or prosecuted;[660]

Questions of admissibility of the case may arise at different junctures of the process and interlocutory appeals have been accepted under this ground against a decision to deny a request to issue an arrest warrant because of inadmissibility (*Situation in the DRC*, ICC A. Ch., Judgment on the Prosecutor's Appeal against the decision of the Pre-Trial Chamber I entitled "Decision on the Prosecutor's Application for Warrants of Arrest, Article 58". ICC-01/04-169, 13 July 2006). However, the Appeals Chamber made clear that the admissibility of the case is not a criterion for the issuance of an arrest warrant (para. 45) and further that the circumstances were not such that a separate assessment of this issue was motivated (paras. 46–53).

Author: Håkan Friman.

[660] This ground for interlocutory appeal applies to decisions by the Pre-Trial or Trial Chamber "granting or denying release". However, it is not applicable to any decision having an impact on the detention or release of the person, such as a decision to confirm charges, and the effect or implications of a decision do not qualify or alter the character of the decision (*Prosecutor v. Lubanga*, ICC A. Ch., Decision on the admissibility of the appeal of Mr. Thomas Lubanga Dyilo against the decision of Pre-Trial Chamber I entitled "Décision sur la confirmation des charges" of 29 January 2007", ICC-01/04-01/06-926, 13 June 2007, paras. 10–11, 15–16). With other words: "it is the nature or character of a decision and not its implications or effects which determine whether a party is entitled to bring an appeal pursuant to Article 82(1)(b)" (*Prosecutor v. Mbarushimana*, ICC A. Ch., Decision on the admissibility of the appeal of Mr Callixte Mbarushimana against the decision of Pre-Trial Chamber I of 28 July 2011 entitled "Decision on "Second Defence request for interim release", ICC-01/04-01/10-438, 21 September 2011, para. 17). A decision rejecting a request that the Pre-Trial Chamber consider the admissibility of the case as it stood at the time of the issuance of the arrest warrant and, based on this, the validity of the arrest warrant was not considered a decision on the question of whether to grant or deny the appellants release (para. 17). Further, interlocutory appeal against a decision on the issuance of a warrant of arrest does also not fall under this provision and instead requires leave for appeal (see for example *Prosecutor v. Al Bashir*, ICC A. Ch., Judgment on the appeal of the Prosecutor against the "Decision on the Prosecution's Application for a Warrant of Arrest against Omar Hassan Ahmad Al Bashir", ICC-02/05-01/09-73, 3 February 2010).

A decision on a request for staying an already ordered release is also not a "decision granting or denying release" and cannot be appealed under Article 82(1)(b) (*Prosecutor v. Mbarushimana*, ICC A. Ch., Reasons for "Decision on the appeal of the Prosecutor of 19 December 2011 against the 'Decision on the confirmation of the charges' and, in the alternative, against the 'Decision on the Prosecution's Request for stay of order to release Callixte Mbarushimana' and on the victims' request for participation" of 20 December 2011, ICC-01/04-01/10-483, 24 January 2012, para. 31).

A decision granting conditional release is "a decision granting or denying release" regardless of the fact that implementation of the decision has been deferred (*Prosecutor v. Bemba*, ICC A. Ch., Judgment on the appeal of the Prosecutor against Pre-Trial Chamber II's "Decision on the Interim Release of Jean-Pierre Bemba Gombo and Convening Hearings with the Kingdom of Belgium, the Republic of Portugal, the Republic of France, the Federal Republic of Germany, the Italian Republic, and the Republic of South Africa", ICC-01/05-01/08-631, 2 December 2009, para. 36).

Moreover, the decision must concern the "person being investigated or prosecuted" by the Court, which excludes, for example, detained witnesses who have been transferred from a State to the Court for giving evidence but who are not subject to a warrant of arrest issued by the Court (*Prosecutor v. Katanga*, ICC A. Ch., Decision on the admissibility of the appeal against the "Decision on the application for the interim release of detained Witnesses DRC-D02-P0236,

(c) A decision of the Pre-Trial Chamber to act on its own initiative under Article 56, paragraph 3;[661]

(d) A decision that involves an issue that would significantly affect the fair and expeditious conduct of the proceedings or the outcome of the trial, and for which, in the opinion of the Pre-Trial or Trial Chamber, an immediate resolution by the Appeals Chamber may materially advance the proceedings.[662]

DRC-D02-P0228 and DRC-D02-P0350", ICC-01/04-01/07-3424, 20 January 2014, paras. 37–38).

In addition, the error must relate to the "decision appealed", which follows from rule 158(1), and a challenge that relates to something which was only assessed in previous decision, such as the risk of flight, may not be brought up in the appeal against a subsequent decision (*Prosecutor v. Bemba*, ICC A. Ch., Judgment on the appeal of Mr Jean-Pierre Bemba Gombo against the decision of Trial Chamber III of 6 January 2012 entitled "Decision on the defence's 28 December 2011 'Requête de Mise en liberté provisoire de M. Jean-Pierre Bemba Gombo'", ICC-01/05-01/08-2151, 5 March 2012, para. 29).

It may be noted that the periodic review of a ruling on release or detention, under Article 60(3), is considered to be triggered first when a request for interim release has already been submitted and ruled upon and the warrant of arrest is not sufficient to trigger the review obligation (*Prosecutor v. Lubanga*, ICC A. Ch., Judgment on the appeal of Mr. Thomas Lubanga Dyilo against the decision of Pre-Trial Chamber I entitled "Décision sur la demande de mise en liberté proviso ire de Thomas Lubanga Dyilo", ICC-01/04-01/06-824, 13 February 2007, paras. 94–100). Hence, the absence of such review prior to a decision based on a request for interim release cannot be challenged on appeal. Further, a decision in response to a request for release, other than interim release, does not trigger the periodic reviews under Article 60(3) (paras. 103–106).

The grounds for arrest in Article 58(1)(b)(i)–(iii) are stated in the alternative and the conclusion that the assessment of one ground is affected by a procedural error does not mean that the decision must be reversed as long as continued detention is justified under one of the other grounds (*Prosecutor v. Bemba*, ICC A. Ch., Judgment on the appeal of Mr Jean-Pierre Bemba Gombo against the decision of Trial Chamber III of 26 September 2011 entitled "Decision on the accused's application for provisional release in light of the Appeals Chamber's judgment of 19 August 2011", ICC-01/05-01/08-1937, 23 November 2011, para. 68). In case of a reversal of the impugned decision due to procedural errors, the Appeals Chamber may remand the matter to the lower Chamber for new consideration, while ordering the person to remain in detention subject to the other Chamber's decision on the matter (for example *Prosecutor v. Bemba*, ICC A. Ch., Judgment on the appeal of Mr Jean-Pierre Bemba Gombo against the decision of Trial Chamber III of 27 June 2011 entitled "Decision on Applications for Provisional Release", ICC-01/05-01/08-1626, 19 August 2011, para. 87).

Author: Håkan Friman.

[661] There has not yet been a decision whereby a Pre-Trial Chamber has acted on its own motion with respect to a unique investigative opportunity in accordance with Article 56(3) and, thus, no appeal regarding this matter.

Author: Håkan Friman.

[662] All other decisions may, with leave for appeal, be subject to interlocutory appeal if it is a decision that involves an issue that would significantly affect the fair and expeditious conduct of the proceedings or the outcome of the trial, and for which, in the opinion of the Pre-Trial or Trial Chamber, an immediate resolution by the Appeals Chamber may materially advance the proceedings.

Initially, the Pre-Trial and Trial Chambers were very reluctant to grant leave for appeal. An attempt by the Prosecutor to seek extraordinary review of a decision ruling out an appeal was rejected by the Appeals Chamber finding no room for such a review in the law of the Court (*Situation in the DRC*, ICC A. Ch., ICC-01/04-168, 13 July 2006). Hence, the certification process is put exclusively in the hands of the Chamber that rendered the challenged decision. Later, however, leave for appeal was granted more frequently. It is not a question of defending the impugned decision, but instead the application of a test (*Prosecutor v. Muthaura, Kenyatta and Ali*, ICC PT. Ch. II, Decision on the "Prosecution's Application for Leave to Appeal the 'Decision with Respect to the Question of Invalidating the Appointment of Counsel to the Defence (ICC-01/09-02/11-185)'", ICC-01/09-02/11-253, 18 August 2011, para. 28).

The consistent practice on leave to appeal, first established by the Appeals Chamber (*Situation in the Democratic Republic of Congo*, ICC A. Ch., ICC-01/04-168, 13 July 2006), is a two-component test.

The first component is to identify whether there exists an "issue" that may be the subject of appeal – an "issue" is an identifiable subject or topic requiring a decision for its resolution that is not merely a question over which there is disagreement or conflicting opinion (*Situation in the Democratic Republic of Congo*, ICC A. Ch., ICC-01/04-168, 13 July 2006, para. 9). Put differently an "issue" is "constituted by a subject the resolution of which is essential for the determination of matters arising in the judicial cause under examination" and it may legal or factual or a mixed one (para. 9). Moreover, the "issue" must be one apt to significantly affect, in a material way, either the fair and expeditious conduct of the proceedings or the outcome of the trial (para. 10). The term "fair" is associated with the norms of a fair trial, which also include the expeditiousness of the proceedings, and it must be interpreted and applied and accordance with internationally recognised human rights (para. 11; see also Articles 64(2), 69(1) and 21(3)). The principles of a fair trial are not confined to the trial proceedings but apply to the criminal investigation and pre-trial proceedings as well (para. 11). The term "proceedings" also includes prior and subsequent proceedings (para. 12). A forecast must be made of the possible implications of the given issue being wrongly decided on the outcome of the case (para. 13).

The second component of the test is whether the "issue" is one "for which, in the opinion of the Pre-Trial or Trial Chamber, an immediate resolution by the Appeals Chamber may materially advance the proceedings". Hence, the "issue" must be such "that its immediate resolution by the Appeals Chamber will settle the matter posing for decision through its authoritative determination, ridding thereby the judicial process of possible mistakes that might taint either the fairness of the proceedings or mar the outcome of the trial" (*Situation in the Democratic Republic of Congo*, ICC A. Ch., ICC-01/04-168, 13 July 2006, para. 14). The term "advance" should be understood as moving the case forward by ensuring that the proceedings follow the right course (para. 15). Here too, the term "proceedings" should be understood broadly (para. 17). By the term "immediate" is required the prompt reference of the issue to the Appeals Chamber and this Chamber, in turn, must render its decision as soon as possible (para. 18).

Consequently, the Chambers have generally applied the following scheme (for example *Prosecutor v. Lubanga*, ICC T. Ch. I, Decision on the Prosecution's Application for Leave to Appeal the 'Decision on the consequences of non-disclosure of exculpatory materials covered by Article 54(3)(e) agreements and the application to stay the prosecution of the accused', ICC-01/04-01/06-1417, 2 July 2008, paras. 17–18). The criteria are: a) Whether the matter is an "appealable issue"; b) Whether the issue at hand could significantly affect: i) the fair and expeditious conduct of the proceedings, or ii) the outcome of the trial; and c) Whether in the opinion of the Trial Chamber, an immediate resolution by the Appeals Chamber could materially advance the proceedings. The requirements a), b) and c) are cumulative and therefore the failure to fulfil one or more of them is fatal to an application for leave to appeal. Assessing whether the issue would indeed significantly affect one of the elements of justice in i) or ii), the Chamber "must ponder the implications of a given issue being wrongly decided" on the fairness and expeditiousness of the proceedings or the outcome of the trial, performing an "exercise [that] involves a forecast of the consequences of such an occurrence" (*Situation in the Democratic Republic of Congo*, ICC A. Ch., ICC-01/04-168, 13 July 2006, para. 9).

It has been held that the 'outcome of the trial' at the trial level can only be a judgment (pursuant to Article 74) in which an accused is found individually criminally responsible for all or parts of the counts as confirmed, or not to be; with other words a pronouncement of guilt or an acquittal. During the subsequent appeals proceedings, however, the Statute provides the Appeals Chamber with other options in which it can 'significantly affect' the outcome of the trial proceedings, including the repetition of (certain parts of) the trial proceedings as envisaged by the Prosecution (*Prosecutor v. Ruto and Sang*, ICC T. Ch. V(a), Decision on Prosecution's Application for Leave to Appeal the "Decision on Mr Ruto's Request for Excusal from Continuous Presence at Trial", ICC-01/09-01/11-817, 18 July 2013, para. 22).

It is not sufficient for the purposes of granting leave to appeal that the issue for which leave to appeal is sought is of general interest or that it may arise in future pre-trial or trial proceedings (*Situation in Uganda*, ICC PT. Ch. II, Decision on Prosecutor's Application for Leave to Appeal in part Pre-Trial Chamber II's Decision on the Prosecutor's Applications for Warrants of Arrest under Article 58, ICC-02/04-01/05-20, 19 August 2005, para. 30). It is also insufficient that an appeal may be legitimate or even necessary at some future stage, as opposed to requiring immediate resolution by the Appeals Chamber in order to materially advance the proceedings (*Prosecutor v. Bemba*, ICC T. Ch., Decision on the prosecution and defence applications for leave to appeal the "Decision on the admission into evidence of materials contained in the prosecution's list of evidence", ICC-01/05-01/08-1169, 26 January 2011, para. 25).

The applicant for leave is required to identify a specific issue which has been dealt with in the relevant decision and which constitutes the appealable subject. In *Gbagbo*, the Pre-Trial Chamber sought, to the extent possible, to give the defence submissions an "effective interpretation, rather than rejecting proposed issues for incompleteness of argument" (*Prosecutor v. Gbagbo*, ICC PT. Ch. I, Decision on the Defence request for leave to appeal the "Decision on the Confirmation of Charges against Laurent Gbagbo", ICC-02/11-01/11-680, 11 September 2014, para. 10). Nonetheless, the Chamber concluded that none of the issues identified by the defence met the criteria of Article 82(1)(d) because: (i) some issues proposed by the defence were in fact extraneous to the decision; (ii) other issues misrepresented the decision or involved various disagreements with the decision with no identifiable impact on the confirmation of charges against Gbagbo; (iii) other issues arose out of the decision but, in the conclusion of the Chamber, did not significantly affect the fair and expeditious conduct of the proceedings or the outcome of the trial. The Chamber then provided detailed reasons concerning each of the proposed issues.

In practice, the Appeals Chamber has generally accepted the Pre-Trial or Trial Chamber's determination of what is an appealable issue (for example *Situation in Uganda*, ICC A. Ch., ICC-02/04-179, 23 February 2009, cf. the dissenting opinion of Judge Pikis; *Prosecutor v. Lubanga*, ICC A. Ch., Judgment on the appeal of Mr. Lubanga Dyilo against the Oral Decision of Trial Chamber I of 18 January 2008, ICC-01/04-01/06-1433, 11 July 2008, para. 11, cf. dissenting opinion of Judge Song). However, the Appeals Chamber may address various certified "issues" together (for example *Prosecutor v. Muthaura, Kenyatta and Ali*, ICC A. Ch., Judgment on the appeal of the Prosecutor against the decision of Pre-Trial Chamber II dated 20 July 2011 entitled "Decision with Respect to the Question of Invalidating the Appointment of Counsel to the Defence", ICC-01/09-02/11-365, 10 November 2011, para. 44). Further, the Appeals Chamber may clarify or amend the "issue" (for example *Prosecutor v. Katanga*, ICC A. Ch., Judgment on the appeal of Mr Germain Katanga against the decision of Pre-Trial Chamber I entitled "First Decision on the Prosecution Request for Authorisation to Redact Witness State-

2. A decision of the Pre-Trial Chamber under Article 57, paragraph 3 (d), may be appealed against by the State concerned or by the Prosecutor, with the leave of the Pre-Trial Chamber. The appeal shall be heard on an expedited basis.[663]

3. An appeal shall not of itself have suspensive effect unless the Appeals Chamber so orders, upon request, in accordance with the Rules of Procedure and Evidence.[664]

---

ments", ICC-01/04-01/07-476, 13 May 2008, para. 46; *Prosecutor v. Katanga and Ngudjolo Chui*, ICC A. Ch., Judgment on the Appeal of Mr Katanga Against the Decision of Trial Chamber II of 22 January 2010 Entitled "Decision on the Modalities of Victim Participation at Trial", ICC-01/04-01/07-2288, 16 July 2010, paras. 56–57, 88–90). A certified issue may also be rendered moot by a subsequent decision (for example *Prosecutor v. Katanga and Ngudjolo Chui*, ICC A. Ch., Judgment on the appeal of the Prosecutor against the "Decision on Evidentiary Scope of the Confirmation Hearing, Preventive Relocation and Disclosure under Article 67(2) of the Statute and Rule 77 of the Rules" of Pre-Trial Chamber I, ICC-01/04-01/07-776, 26 November 2008, para. 11).

Author: Håkan Friman.

[663] The Pre-Trial Chamber's power, under Article 57(3)(d), to authorise the Prosecutor to take specific investigative steps within the territory of a State Party without having secured the cooperation of that State under Part 9, was very controversial during the negotiations of the Statute (see Friman, 2001, pp. 507–509). Hence, an explicit provision on interlocutory appeals, to be heard on an expedited basis, was introduced. Since no such authorisation has been granted there are not yet any appeals on this ground.

Author: Håkan Friman.

[664] Neither Article 82(3) nor rule 156(5) stipulate in which circumstances suspensive effect should be ordered, and thus, this decision is left to the discretion of the Appeals Chamber which will determine the matter on a case-by-case basis (*Prosecutor v. Lubanga*, ICC A. Ch., Decision on the request of Mr. Thomas Lubanga Dyilo for suspensive effect of his appeal against the oral decision of Trial Chamber I of 18 January 2008, ICC-01/04-01/06-1290 , 22 April 2008, para. 7). When examining a request for suspensive effect, the Appeals Chamber "will consider the specific circumstances of the case and the factors it considers relevant for the exercise of its discretion under these circumstances" (for example *Prosecutor v. Bemba, Musamba, Kabongo, Wandu and Arido*, ICC A. Ch., Decision on the Prosecutor's urgent request for suspensive effect of the "Decision ordering the release of Aimé Kilolo Musamba, Jean-Jacques Mangenda Kabongo, Fidèle Babala Wandu and Narcisse Arido" of 21 October 2014, ICC-01/05-01/13-718, 22 October 2014, para. 5).

The Appeals Chamber may require that the implementation of the impugned decision would create an irreversible situation that could not be corrected if the Appeals Chamber eventually were to find in favour of the appellant (para. 8). The suspension could, for example, relate to the release of the suspect although the detention is considered necessary to secure his or her presence at trial (*Prosecutor v. Lubanga*, ICC A. Ch., Reasons for the decision on the request of the Prosecutor for suspensive effect of his appeal against the "Decision on the release of Thomas Lubanga Dyilo", ICC-01/04-01/06-1444, 22 July 2008, and *Prosecutor v. Lubanga*, ICC A. Ch., Decision on the Prosecutor's request to give suspensive effect to the appeal against Trial Chamber I's oral decision to release Mr Thomas Lubanga Dyilo, ICC-01/04-01/06-2536, 23 July 2010). Another reason may be that the decision "could potentially defeat the purpose of the [...] appeal" (*Prosecutor v. Lubanga*, ICC A. Ch., Reasons for the decision on the request of the Prosecutor for suspensive effect of his appeal against the "Decision on the release of Thomas Lubanga Dyilo", ICC-01/04-01/06-1444, 22 July 2008, para. 10). The standard is not met in case the Appeals Chamber is able to reverse, confirm or amend the impugned decision irrespective of whether the proceedings before Trial Chamber continue (*Prosecutor v. Bemba*, ICC A.

Ch., Decision on the Request of Mr Bemba to Give Suspensive Effect to the Appeal Against the "Decision on the Admissibility and Abuse of Process Challenges", ICC-01/05-01/08-817, 9 July 2010, para. 11; *Prosecutor v. Ruto, Kosgey and Sang*, ICC A. Ch., Decision on the requests of Mr Ruto and Mr Sang for suspensive effect, ICC-01/09-01/11-391, 29 February 2012, para. 10; *Prosecutor v. Muthaura, Kenyatta and Ali*, ICC A. Ch., Decision on the request of Mr Kenyatta and Mr Muthaura for suspensive effect, ICC-01/09-02/11-401, 29 February 2012, para. 10).

Resolution of the question whether the accused's absence from the upcoming trial hearings would be permitted, met the requirements because the decision, if overturned, would mean that the trial had to restart in his presence and that witnesses who testified in his absence may be unwilling or unable to return to testify again (*Prosecutor v. Ruto and Sang*, ICC A. Ch., Decision on the request for suspensive effect, ICC-01/09-01/11-862, 20 August 2013). But it is not sufficient that the potential effect that the enforcement of the impugned decision might have on the witnesses is largely speculative (*Prosecutor v. Ruto and Sang*, ICC A. Ch., Decision on Mr William Samoei Ruto's request for suspensive effect, ICC-01/09-01/11-1370, 17 June 2014, para. 9).

However, the threshold need not be so high. It may be sufficient that, absent a resolution by the Appeals Chamber, the Trial Chamber could be considering additional material with resulting effects on the fairness and expeditiousness of the trial and the outcome and that there is a risk for unnecessary appeals (*Prosecutor v. Lubanga*, ICC A. Ch., Decision on the requests of the Prosecutor and the Defence for suspensive effect of the appeals against Trial Chamber I's Decision on Victim's Participation of 18 January 2008, ICC-01/04-01/06-1347, 22 May 2008, paras. 19–20). Other considerations are the need to preserve the integrity of the proceedings, and the delay that a suspension would cause weighed against the impact that continuing the proceedings before the Trial Chamber based on the impugned decision could have, in particular, on the rights of the accused, should the Appeals Chamber eventually reverse or amend the decision (*Prosecutor v. Katanga*, ICC A. Ch., Decision on the request for suspensive effect of the appeal against Trial Chamber II's decision on the implementation of regulation 55 of the Regulations of the Court, ICC-01/04-01/07-3344, 16 January 2013, paras. 8–9).

In any case, a party claiming suspensive effect must present persuasive reasons why the absence of a stay would have consequences that "would be very difficult to correct" or that "may be irreversible" (cf. *Prosecutor v. Gbagbo*, ICC A. Ch., Decision on Côte d'Ivoire's request for suspensive effect of its appeal against the "Decision on Côte d'Ivoire's challenge to the admissibility of the case against Simone Gbagbo" of 11 December 2014, ICC-02/11-01/12-56, 20 January 2015, paras. 14–18).

An order for suspensive effect is aimed at preserving the situation existing prior to the issuance of the impugned decision and the suspension may not go beyond that scope, for example by being directed to domestic proceedings (*Prosecutor v. Gaddafi and Al-Senussi*, ICC A. Ch., Decision on the request for suspensive effect and the request to file a consolidated reply, ICC-01/11-01/11-480, 22 November 2013, paras. 15–18).

Quite apart from this provision on suspensive effects of an appeal is the issue of a stay of the entire process. The Appeals Chamber has unanimously held that it has no power to order stay of all proceedings before another Chamber (*Prosecutor v. Lubanga*, ICC A. Ch., Reasons for "Decision of the Appeals Chamber on the Defence application 'Demande de suspension de toute action ou procédure afin de permettre la désignation d'un nouveau Conseil de la Défense' filed on 20 February 2007" issued on 23 February 2007, ICC-01/04-01/06-844, 9 March 2007, para. 3). Nonetheless, the suspension of the decision that is subject to an appeal may well affect the proceedings of the Chamber which has issued the impugned decision and this is accepted insofar it does not by implication necessitate the suspension of all the proceedings before the other Chamber (*Prosecutor v. Lubanga*, ICC A. Ch., Decision on the requests of the Prosecutor and

4. A legal representative of the victims, the convicted person or a bona fide owner of property adversely affected by an order under Article 75 may appeal against the order for reparations, as provided in the Rules of Procedure and Evidence.[665]

---

the Defence for suspensive effect of the appeals against Trial Chamber I's Decision on Victim's Participation of 18 January 2008, ICC-01/04-01/06-1347, 22 May 2008, para. 25). Furthermore, the Appeals Chamber has accepted a power to stay the entire proceedings because of breaches of the fundamental rights of the suspect or the accused by his or her accusers, which may be either a permanent stay (*Prosecutor v. Lubanga*, ICC A. Ch., Judgment on the Appeal of Mr. Thomas Lubanga Dyilo against the Decision on the Defence Challenge to the Jurisdiction of the Court pursuant to Article 19(2)(a) of the Statute of 3 October 2006, ICC-01/04-01/06-772, 14 December 2006, paras. 37–39) or a conditional one (*Prosecutor v. Lubanga*, A. Ch., Judgment on the appeal of the Prosecutor against the decision of Trial Chamber I entitled "Decision on the consequences of non-disclosure of exculpatory materials covered by Article 54(3)(e) agreements and the application to stay the prosecution of the accused, together with certain other issues raised at the Status Conference on 10 June 2008", ICC-01/04-01/06-1486, 21 October 2008, paras. 80–83). Such a stay is not, however, based upon Article 82(3).

Author: Håkan Friman.

[665] The "Decision establishing the principles and procedures to be applied to reparations" by the *Lubanga* Trial Chamber (*Lubanga*, ICC T. Ch. I, ICC-01/04-01/06-2904, 7 August 2012) established principles relating to reparations as well as some procedures. Due to the latter feature, the Appeals Chamber was persuaded to consider the decision as an order for reparations and, thus, subject to appeal in accordance with Article 82(4) (*Prosecutor v. Lubanga*, ICC A. Ch., Decision on the admissibility of the appeals against Trial Chamber I's "Decision establishing the principles and procedures to be applied to reparations" and directions on the further conduct of proceedings, ICC-01/04-01/06-2953, 14 December 2012, para. 51). An order for reparations may not be appealed in accordance with Article 82(1)(d) (para. 64).

The convicted person has an unencumbered right to appeal orders for reparations, and this right is not limited to monetary awards (*Lubanga*, ICC A. Ch., ICC-01/04-01/06-2953, 14 December 2012, para. 66). Victims are considered parties to the reparations proceedings and hence they may be entitled to bring an appeal (para. 67). Such victims may also include individuals who did not participate in the proceedings concerning the accused person's guilt or innocence or the sentence insofar they have requested reparations (para. 69). Since the reparations proceedings are a distinct stage of the process, also victims who's right to participate was withdrawn or rejected and victims who participated in the proceedings concerning guilt or innocence or on sentencing may have a right to appeal (paras. 70–71). However, an appeal cannot be made with reference to the interests of unidentified victims who have not made requests but who may benefit from a collective award (para. 72).

An appeal pursuant to Article 82(4) does not mean the automatic suspension of the order for reparations. Instead a request for suspensive effect must be made in accordance with Article 82(3) and rule 156(5), notwithstanding the fact that the wording of rule 156(5) does not cover appeals against reparation orders under Article 82(4) ((*Lubanga*, ICC A. Ch., ICC-01/04-01/06-2953, paras. 79–80). In suspending the execution of the reparation order, the Appeals Chamber attached weight to the undesirability of having to halt or revise later the ongoing engagement with victims in accordance with the order and the fact that the order could not in any case be executed until the accused's conviction had been confirmed on appeal (paras. 83 and 86).

The standard of review with respect to appeals against a reparations order is the same as for all other appeals (*Prosecutor v. Lubanga*, ICC A. Ch., Judgment on the appeals against the "Decision establishing the principles and procedures to be applied to reparations" of 7 August 2012 with AMENDED order for reparations (Annex A) and public annexes 1 and 2, ICC-01/04-01/06-3129, 3 March 2015, para. 40).

Cross-references:

Rules 154, 155 and 156.

Regulations 64 and 65.

Doctrine:

1. Gideon Boas *et al.*, "Appeals, Reviews, and Reconsideration", in Göran Sluiter, Håkan Friman, Suzannah Linton, Sergey Vasiliev and Salvatore Zappalà (eds.), *International Criminal Procedure: Principles and Rules*, Oxford University Press, Oxford, 2013, Ch. 6.

2. Helen Brady, "Appeals and Revision", in Roy S. Lee (ed.), *The International Criminal Court: Elements of Crimes and Rules of Procedure and Evidence*, Transnational Publishers, Ardsley, NY, 2001, pp. 575–603.

3. Håkan Friman, "Interlocutory Appeals in the Early Practice of the International Criminal Court", in Carsten Stahn/Göran Sluiter (eds.), *The Emerging Practice of the International Criminal Court*, Martinus Nijhoff Publishers, Leiden, 2009.

4. Håkan Friman, "Investigation and Prosecution", in Roy S. Lee (ed.), *The International Criminal Court: Elements of Crimes and Rules of Procedure and Evidence*, Transnational Publishers, Ardsley, NY, 2001.

5. Alena Hartwig, "Appeal and Revision", in Christoph Safferling (ed.), *International Criminal Procedure*, Oxford University Press, Oxford, 2012, pp. 531–39.

6. Robert Roth and Marc Henzlin, "The Appeal Procedure of the ICC", in Antonio Cassese, Paola Gaeta and John R.W.D. Jones (eds.), *The Rome Statute of the International Criminal Court: A Commentary*, 2nd ed., Oxford University Press, Oxford, 2002, pp. 1535–58.

7. Christopher Staker, "Article 82", in Otto Triffterer (ed.), *Commentary on the Rome Statute of the International Criminal Court: Observers' Notes, Article by Article*, 2nd ed., C.H. Beck/Hart/Nomos, Munich/Oxford/Baden-Baden, 2008, pp. 1475–80.

Author: Håkan Friman.

Article 83

Proceedings on appeal[666]

1. For the purposes of proceedings under Article 81 and this article, the Appeals Chamber shall have all the powers of the Trial Chamber.[667]

2. If the Appeals Chamber finds that the proceedings appealed from were unfair in a way that affected the reliability of the decision or sentence, or that the decision or sentence appealed from was materially affected by error of fact or law or procedural error, it may:

   (a) Reverse or amend the decision or sentence; or

   (b) Order a new trial before a different Trial Chamber.

   For these purposes, the Appeals Chamber may remand a factual issue to the original Trial Chamber for it to determine the issue and to report back accordingly, or may itself call evidence to determine the issue. When the decision or sentence has been appealed only by the person convicted, or the Prosecutor on that person's behalf, it cannot be amended to his or her detriment.[668]

3. If in an appeal against sentence the Appeals Chamber finds that the sentence is disproportionate to the crime, it may vary the sentence in accordance with Part 7.[669]

4. The judgement of the Appeals Chamber shall be taken by a majority of the judges and shall be delivered in open court. The judgement shall state the reasons on which it is based. When there is no unanimity, the judgement of the Appeals Chamber shall contain the views of the majority and the minority, but a judge may deliver a separate or dissenting opinion on a question of law.[670]

---

[666] *General remarks*:

Article 83 deals with powers and procedures of the Appeals Chamber in the context of appellate proceedings. The provision performs the same role as Article 57 on the "Functions and Powers of the Pre-Trial Chamber" and Article 64 on "Functions and Powers of the Trial Chamber".

[667] Article 83(1) only applies to proceedings under Article 81, which excludes interlocutory appeals. This is confirmed later in subsequent paragraphs: appeals against the decisions on conviction or acquittal (paragraph 2(a)), ordering a new trial (paragraph 2(b)) and sentence (paragraph 3) (*Prosecutor v. Lubanga*, Judgment on the Prosecutor's appeal against the decision of Pre-Trial Chamber I entitled "Decision Establishing General Principles Governing Applications to Restrict Disclosure pursuant to Rule 81 (2) and (4) of the Rules of Procedure and Evidence", ICC-01/04-01/06-568, ICC A. Ch. 13 October 2006, para. 16).

[668] This provision allows the Appeals Chamber to reverse as well as amend the decision and sentence. This means that the Appeals Chamber may itself determine issue of fact. However, as already indicated in the comment on Article 81, the Statute envisages that trial proceedings, involving fact-finding, will be held before the Trial Chambers, not the Appeals Chamber.

[669] As already indicated in the comment on Article 81(2), the Appeals Chamber may vary the sentence if there is a disproportion between the crime and the sentence.

[670] During the drafting of the ICC Statute there was debate whether the Appeals Chamber was unanimity was required for a decision or simply a majority (Staker, p. 1484 and Schabas, p. 956). The wording for paragraph 4 seems to suggest that concern of the majority and minority in relation to a procedural error or error of fact should be expressed within the judgment whereas a judge may deliver a separate or dissenting opinion on a question of law. In practice dissenting

5. The Appeals Chamber may deliver its judgement in the absence of the person acquitted or convicted.[671]

---

and separate opinions have included not only questions of law but also views on procedural facts and errors of fact (*Prosecutor v. Lubanga*, Judgment on the appeals of the Prosecutor and Mr Thomas Lubanga Dyilo against the "Decision on Sentence pursuant to Article 76 of the Statute", Dissenting Opinion of Judge Anita Ušacka, ICC A. Ch., 1 December 2014).

[671] Paragraph 5 is an exception if the rejection of *in absentia* proceedings and may be contrasted with Articles 63 76(4) the later providing that "[t]he sentence shall be pronounced in public and, wherever possible, in the presence of the accused".

Cross-references:

Rules 156, 157, 153, 158.

Doctrine:

1. William A. Schabas, *The International Criminal Court: A Commentary on the Rome Statute*, Oxford University Press, Oxford, 2010, pp. 950–57.

2. Christopher Staker, "Article 83 – Proceedings on Appeal", in Otto Triffterer (ed.), *Commentary on the Rome Statute of the International Criminal Court: Observers' Notes, Article by Article*, 2nd ed., C.H. Beck/Hart/Nomos, Munich/Oxford/Baden-Baden, 2008, pp. 1481–85.

Author: Mark Klamberg.

Article 84

Revision of conviction or sentence[672]

1. The convicted person or, after death, spouses, children, parents or one person alive at the time of the accused's death who has been given express written instructions from the accused to bring such a claim, or the Prosecutor on the person's behalf, may apply to the Appeals Chamber to revise the final judgement of conviction or sentence on the grounds that:

   (a) New evidence has been discovered that:

      (i) Was not available at the time of trial, and such unavailability was not wholly or partially attributable to the party making application; and

      (ii) Is sufficiently important that had it been proved at trial it would have been likely to have resulted in a different verdict;

   (b) It has been newly discovered that decisive evidence, taken into account at trial and upon which the conviction depends, was false, forged or falsified;

   (c) One or more of the judges who participated in conviction or confirmation of the charges has committed, in that case, an act of serious misconduct or serious breach of duty of sufficient gravity to justify the removal of that judge or those judges from office under Article 46.[673]

---

[672] *General remarks*:

This provision provides for revision which is different from appeal in the sense that revision does challenge the conclusions of the Trial Chamber. Instead it reviews a decision based upon facts that were not available at trial. The mechanism of revision is familiar both at the international level and many national jurisdictions although there may differences when the mechanism may be applied. Proceedings of this kind is normally regarded as an extraordinary remedy and are more common in civil law systems. In common law systems this type of proceedings are brought before a court of appeal (Staker, p. 1488, Schabas, p. 959).

At the *ad hoc* tribunals it is called "review", see ICTY Statute, Article 26 and ICTR Statute, Article 25.

[673] Revisions proceedings can only be brought by the person convicted or certain others on behalf of the convicted. This includes the Prosecutor. However, the Prosecutor can only bring revision against a conviction, not against an acquittal.

Sub-paragraph (a) provides for revision when "new evidence" has been discovered. For revision, it is required that this new evidence was not available at the time of the trial and is sufficiently important in the sense that it would have affected the outcome of the trial.

Revision is also possible under sub-paragraph (b) if it is newly discovered that the evidence was false, forged or falsified.

Finally, revision is possible under sub-paragraph (c) when "[o]ne or more of the judges who participated in conviction or confirmation of the charges has committed, in that case, an act of serious misconduct or serious breach of duty".

Cross-references:

Rules 159, 160, 161.

Regulations 62, 66.

Author: Mark Klamberg.

2. The Appeals Chamber shall reject the application if it considers it to be unfounded. If it determines that the application is meritorious, it may, as appropriate:

(a) Reconvene the original Trial Chamber;

(b) Constitute a new Trial Chamber; or

(c) Retain jurisdiction over the matter,

with a view to, after hearing the parties in the manner set forth in the Rules of Procedure and Evidence, arriving at a determination on whether the judgement should be revised.[674]

---

[674] Paragraph 2 provides for the procedure on revision which is divided in two stages which establishes a "filter" mechanism for revision applications. The purpose is to prevent "frivolous applications" (Staker, p. 1495).

First, the Appeals shall consider whether the application is "unfounded". If the Appeals Chamber finds the application meritorious it may reconvene the original Trial Chamber; constitute a new Trial Chamber; or retain jurisdiction over the matter, "with a view to, after hearing the parties in the manner set forth in the Rules of Procedure and Evidence, arriving at a determination on whether the judgment should be revised".

Doctrine:

1. William A. Schabas, *The International Criminal Court: A Commentary on the Rome Statute*, Oxford University Press, Oxford, 2010, pp. 958–63.

2. Christopher Staker, "Article 83 – Proceedings on Appeal", in Otto Triffterer (ed.), *Commentary on the Rome Statute of the International Criminal Court: Observers' Notes, Article by Article*, 2nd ed., C.H. Beck/Hart/Nomos, Munich/Oxford/Baden-Baden, 2008, pp. 1487–97.

Author: Mark Klamberg.

Article 85

Compensation to an arrested or convicted person[675]

1. Anyone who has been the victim of unlawful arrest or detention shall have an enforceable right to compensation.[676]

2. When a person has by a final decision been convicted of a criminal offence, and when subsequently his or her conviction has been reversed on the ground that a new or newly discovered fact shows conclusively that there has been a miscarriage of justice, the person

---

[675] *General remarks*:

Article 85 contains a number of provisions concerning compensation to defendants for unjust arrest, detention or conviction. Paras. 1 and 2 are taken almost verbatim from relevant human rights instruments (see Article 9(5), 14(6) ICCPR; Article 5(5) ECHR, Article 3 of Additional Protocol No. 7 to the ECHR; similarly Article 10 ACHR) . There are no comparable norms in the legal texts of other international tribunals, although the ad hoc Tribunals have in principle allowed claims for compensation for miscarriages of justice or violations of defence rights (see Zappala, at pp. 1579–1582). Procedural rules for claims under Article 85 are contained in Rules 173–175.

The wording of several provisions ("enforceable right", "compensated according to law") might be interpreted as a sign that compensation under Article 85 may be claimed not only from the Court, but also from states under national proceedings mandated by Article 85 (Staker, MN. 6). Those peculiarities in the wording are, however, most likely due to the fact that Article 85(1) and (2) were imported almost verbatim from human rights treaties (see Zappala at 1582); in fact, Rules 173–175 refer solely to compensation claimed directly from the Court.

As Rule 173(3) shows, Article 85 refers only to monetary compensation, not to, for example, claims that a violation of the defendant's rights must lead to a termination of proceedings. However, as Article 85(3) presupposes, such claims may in principle be made under the Statute – the Court had occasion to pronounce on this question, under Article 21(3), in the Lubanga case (see the commentary to Article 20(3), as well as ICC-01/04-01/06-512 of 3 October 2006; ICC-01/04-01/06-772 of 14 December 2006).

Cross-references:

Rules 173, 174, 175.

Author: Björn Elberling, revised by Mark Klamberg.

[676] Article 85(1) deals with compensation for unlawful arrest and/or detention. Its wording is substantially identical to Article 9(5) ICCPR and Article 5(5) ECHR. An arrest or detention is, first of all, unlawful under Article 85(1) if it is in violation of the Statute. The wording is not clear on whether a violation of other norms of international law would also render an arrest or detention unlawful under Article 85(1), but one may presume that this is the case given the applicability of general international law under Article 21 and the drafting history of Article 85(1) (see Staker, MN 2). Given that it is states which will arrest suspects, the most interesting question is whether Article 85(1) also applies to arrest and detention by State authorities in connection with Court proceedings, which may be unlawful also under national law. One argument for applying Article 85(1) to such situations is that Article 59(1) specifies that arrest shall be in accordance with national laws, thus making compliance with national laws a requirement also under the Statute (Cf. Staker, MN. 2)

Cross-references:

Rules 173, 174.

Author: Björn Elberling, revised by Mark Klamberg.

who has suffered punishment as a result of such conviction shall be compensated according to law, unless it is proved that the non-disclosure of the unknown fact in time is wholly or partly attributable to him or her.[677]

3. In exceptional circumstances, where the Court finds conclusive facts showing that there has been a grave and manifest miscarriage of justice, it may in its discretion award compensation, according to the criteria provided in the Rules of Procedure and Evidence, to a person who has been released from detention following a final decision of acquittal or a termination of the proceedings for that reason.[678]

---

[677] Article 85(2) applies to compensation for unjust conviction. Its wording is substantially identical to that of Article 14(6) ICCPR and Article 3 of the Additional Protocol No. 7 to the ECHR (Article 85(2) does not contain a reference to a person being pardoned after a finding that there had been a miscarriage of justice – this because a power of pardon is not foreseen in the ICC Statute.) The provision sets up four requirements for such compensation: First, the person must have been convicted by a final decision (that is, not only by a judgment in first instance still open to appeal) and must have suffered punishment as a result of this judgment. Second, the conviction must have been reversed, presumably after a revision pursuant to Article 84. Third, this reversal must have been based on evidence showing a miscarriage of justice – the exact definition of this term will have to be left to the future jurisprudence of the Court. Finally, the late disclosure of this evidence must not be wholly or partially attributable to the convicted person – this requirement basically repeats what is already a requirement for the availability of the revision procedure based on new evidence under Article 84(a)(i) (see the commentary thereto; see also Zappala at 1583, who argues in favour of partial compensation, to be given at the discretion of the court, where the non-disclosure was partly attributable to the person convicted).

Cross-references:

Article 84, Rules 173, 174.

Author: Björn Elberling, revised by Mark Klamberg.

[678] Article 85(3), which goes beyond the requirements of international human rights law, refers to compensation for detention where there has been a particularly grave miscarriages of justice, namely those which are "grave and manifest" and which, moreover, lead to acquittal of the person or termination of proceedings. Which violations of defence rights fulfil these conditions must be left to the further jurisprudence of the Court – at the ICTR, even the rather grave violations in the Barayagwiza case ultimately did not lead to a termination of the proceedings (see Zappala at 1581–1582). Even where these rather strict preconditions are fulfilled, the payment of compensation is left to the Court and reserved for "exceptional circumstances" (According to Zappala, p. 1583, "exceptional circumstances" should not be interpreted as a further requirement, but rather as a description of the requirement of a grave and manifest miscarriage of justice leading to acquittal or termination of proceedings). Article 85(3) is thus rather narrow when compared to similar provisions in national law, some of which in principle grant compensation for detention to all acquitted persons (see, for example, Sect. 2 of the German Gesetz über die Entschädigung für Strafverfolgungsmaßnahmen (http://www.gesetze-im-internet.de/bundesrecht/streg/gesamt.pdf), for more example see Staker, Id., para. 4).

Where the requirements of Article 85(3) are fulfilled, Rule 175 lists some factors to be taken into account in determining the amount of compensation.

Cross-references:

Rules 173, 174, 175.

Doctrine:

1. Christopher Staker, in Otto Triffterer (ed.), *Commentary on the Rome Statute of the International Criminal Court: Observers' Notes, Article by Article*, 2nd ed., C.H. Beck/Hart/Nomos, Munich/Oxford/Baden-Baden, 2008, pp. 1499–1502.
2. Salvatore Zappala, in Cassese, Paola Gaeta and John R.W.D. Jones (eds.), *The Rome Statute of the International Criminal Court: A Commentary*, 2nd ed., Oxford University Press, Oxford, 2002, pp. 1577–83.

    Author: Björn Elberling, revised by Mark Klamberg.

PART 9. INTERNATIONAL COOPERATION AND JUDICIAL ASSISTANCE

Article 86

General obligation to cooperate

States Parties shall, in accordance with the provisions of this Statute, cooperate fully with the Court in its investigation and prosecution of crimes within the jurisdiction of the Court.[679]

---

[679] *General remarks*:

International criminal courts must get the necessities of criminal justice, including evidence, from States, other entities such as peacekeeping forces and non-consensual parties, such as the person investigated, his or her country of origin, or third-parties that have relevant information for the case. In contrast to domestic criminal courts, international tribunals have no enforcement agencies at their disposal: without the help of national authorities or other entities such as peacekeeping forces, they cannot collect evidence. In a national legal system, a prosecutor may rely upon a vertical authoritative process while at the international level all investigatory measures require either the consent of the territorial State or a binding decision from an international body such as the UN Security Council – often together with the intervention of other States. In national systems the investigations and collection of evidence are normally either the duty of the police unsupervised by any superior authority, a prosecutor or investigative judge aided by the police, or a mix thereof. International tribunals and courts dealing with international crimes lack State machinery at its disposal to investigate and collect evidence, and, as a result, they must rely first and foremost on the cooperation of the State where the crimes occurred. Without the cooperation of State authorities, international courts cannot operate. This problem also applies to national courts when witnesses reside abroad, a national court cannot subject witnesses them to the same powers as witnesses within its jurisdiction. Whereas this problem only concerns a minority of cases in domestic proceedings, every single witness is outside the jurisdiction of an international criminal court. Hence, State cooperation is inevitable in relation to every single witness.

Analysis:

i) *"State Parties"*

Article 86 distinguishes between States Parties and third States. The general obligation to cooperate with the Court in its investigation and prosecution of crimes within the jurisdiction of the Court applies only to States Parties. In principle, obligations cannot be imposed on other States.

However, the Court may establish special cooperation with States non-party to the Statute as provided for in Article 87(5). Such special cooperation regimes are based on the consent of the involved State non-party. Turning to cases referred by the Security Council to the Court of non-States Parties one has to consider the treaty-based foundation of the ICC. Such states are subject to a different regime than Part 9 of the ICC Statute. In such cases, one could conceive at least three options on how the Security Council should deal with the obligations of non-State parties.

The first scenario is that the UN Security Council would refer a situation to the Court with no instructions concerning cooperation. Such a blank referral would mean that States non-parties are under no obligation to assist the Court.

A second scenario is that the Security Council decided that all UN members shall cooperate in accordance with the regime of the ICC Statute.

Finally, the Security Council may shape a new co-operation regime, exceeding the obligations of the ICC Statute (Sluiter, 2002, 71–72).

When the UN Security Council through resolution 1593(2005) referred the *situation in Darfur* to the Court it decided "that the Government of Sudan and all other parties to the conflict in Darfur, shall cooperate fully with and provide any necessary assistance to the Court and the Prosecutor pursuant" to the resolution (Resolution 1593 (2005) UN doc. S/RES/1593, 2005). However, it is unclear what the Security Council meant by "full cooperation". Although the Council recognised "that States not party to the Rome Statute have no obligation under the Statute" it urged "all States and concerned regional and other international organizations to cooperate fully". The resolution with the referral of the *situation in Libyan Arab Jamahiriya* is drafted in an almost identical manner (Resolution 1970 (2011) UN doc. S/RES/1970, 2011).

In comparison, Resolution 827(1993) setting up the ICTY is more substantial (Resolution 827 (1993) UN doc. S/RES/827, 1993, para. 4). The resolution provides an obligation for all states 1) to "cooperate fully" with the Tribunal, 2) to take any measures necessary under their domestic law to implement the provisions of the resolution, and 3) the obligation is given concrete content with the reference to Article 29 of the ICTY Statute.

In relation to the referral of the *Darfur situation*, one may discuss whether resolution 1593(2005) establishes a cooperation regime that is similar to the vertical model of the *ad hoc* tribunals, the less vertical model of the ICC or an even weaker regime. Pre-Trial Chamber I has referred to provisions in Part 9 when dealing with execution of the arrest warrants concerning *Harun and Kushayb* (*Prosecutor v. Harun and Kushayb*, ICC PT. Ch. I, Decision on the Prosecution Application under Article 58(7) of the Statute, ICC-02/05-01/07, 27 April 2007, 56–57; Sluiter, p. 2008). Trial Chamber IV in *Banda and Jerbo* did not find that resolution 1593(2005) provides for an autonomous legal regime for cooperation that would replace the ICC regime. Instead it argued that cooperation requests remained confined to the cooperation regime of part 9 of the ICC Statute (*Prosecutor v. Banda and Jerbo*, ICC T. Ch. IV, Decision on "Defence Application pursuant to Articles 57(3)(b) and 64(6)(a) of the Statute for an order for the preparation and transmission of a cooperation request to the Government of the Republic of the Sudan", 1 July 2011, para. 15). The Pre-Trial Chamber in *Gaddafi* made a similar ruling when it stated that Part 9 is the legal framework within which Libya must comply with the surrender request (*Prosecutor v. Gaddafi et al.,* ICC PT. Ch. I, Decision on Libya's Submissions Regarding the Arrest of Saif Al-Islam Gaddafi, ICC-01/11-01/11, 7 March 2012, para. 12). A reasonable conclusion is that the Government of Sudan and State Parties are obligated to cooperate with the Court, while other non-state parties are only encouraged to cooperate with the Court. The same reasoning applies to the *situation in Libyan Arab Jamahiriya*. This does not necessarily exclude the possibility that the Security Council in the future might issue a resolution which entails binding obligations on non-state parties in general. Trial Chamber IV in *Banda and Jerbo* has stated that "the Security Council, acting under Chapter VII of the UN Charter, may oblige all UN members or some of them to cooperate with the Court in a given case, whether or not they are parties to the Statute" (*Banda and Jerbo*, ICC T. Ch. IV, 1 July 2011, para. 14). The logics of realpolitik may deny such orders, but an efficient cooperation regime is clearly in the interest of crime control.

ii) Meaning of cooperation

The reference in Article 86 to "the provisions of this Statute" indicates that the specific duties on cooperation are found elsewhere in the Statute. Thus Article 86 should be seen in the context of he subsequent rules in Part 9.

Doctrine:

1. Antonio Cassese, "The Statute of the International Criminal Court: Some Preliminary Reflections", in *European Journal of International Law*, 1999, vol. 10, pp. 144–71, p. 164.

2. Annalisa Ciampi, "Other Forms of Cooperation", in Antonio Cassese, Paola Gaeta and John R.W.D. Jones (eds.), *The Rome Statute of the International Criminal Court – A Commentary*, 2nd ed., Oxford University Press, Oxford, 2002, p. 1706.

3. Jacob Katz Cogan, "International Criminal Courts and Fair Trials: Difficulties and Prospects", in *Yale Journal of International Law*, 2002, vol. 27, pp. 111–40, p. 119.

4. Robert Cryer, Håkan Friman, Daryll Robinson and Elizabeth Wilmshurst, *An Introduction to International Criminal Law and Procedure*, 2nd ed., Cambridge University Press, Cambridge, 2010, p. 446.

5. Mark Klamberg, *Evidence in International Criminal Trials: Confronting Legal Gaps and the Reconstruction of Disputed Events*, Martinus Nijhoff Publishers, Leiden, 2013, pp. 231, 235–37.

6. Claus Kreß and Kimberly Prost, "Article 86 – General Obligation to Cooperate", in Otto Triffterer (ed.), *Commentary on the Rome Statute of the International Criminal Court: Observers' Notes, Article by Article*, 2nd ed., C.H. Beck/Hart/Nomos, Munich/Oxford/ Baden-Baden, 2008, pp. 1513–16.

7. Eric Mathias, "The Balance of Power Between the Police and the Public Prosecutor", in Mireille Delmas-Marty and J.R. Spencer (eds.), *European Criminal Procedures*, Cambridge University Press, Cambridge, 2005, p. 459.

8. Christoph J.M. Safferling, *Towards an International Criminal Procedure*, Oxford University Press, Oxford, 2001, pp. 64–66.

9. Göran Sluiter, *International Criminal Adjudication and the Collection of Evidence: Obligations of States*, Intersentia, Antwerpen, 2002.

10. Göran Sluiter, "Obtaining Cooperation from Sudan – Where is the Law?", in *Journal of International Criminal Justice*, 2008, vol. 6, no. 5, pp. 876–78.

11. Göran Sluiter, "Appearance of Witnesses and Unavailability of Subpoena Powers for the Court", in Roberto Bellello (ed.), *International Criminal Justice*, Ashgate, Farnham, 2010, p. 461.

Author: Mark Klamberg.

Article 87

Requests for cooperation: general provisions[680]

1. (a) The Court shall have the authority to make requests to States Parties for cooperation. The requests shall be transmitted through the diplomatic channel or any other appropriate channel as may be designated by each State Party upon ratification, acceptance, approval or accession.

   Subsequent changes to the designation shall be made by each State Party in accordance with the Rules of Procedure and Evidence.

   (b) When appropriate, without prejudice to the provisions of subparagraph (a), requests may also be transmitted through the International Criminal Police Organization or any appropriate regional organization.[681]

2. Requests for cooperation and any documents supporting the request shall either be in or be accompanied by a translation into an official language of the requested State or one of the working languages of the Court, in accordance with the choice made by that State upon ratification, acceptance, approval or accession.

   Subsequent changes to this choice shall be made in accordance with the Rules of Procedure and Evidence.[682]

3. The requested State shall keep confidential a request for cooperation and any documents supporting the request, except to the extent that the disclosure is necessary for execution of the request.[683]

---

[680] *General remarks*

Article 87 contains general provisions for Part 9 and empowers the Court to make requests for cooperation to States Parties and that it may seek assistance of non-States-Parties and intergovernmental organisations. It also includes a mechanism for non-compliance. The provision is quite detailed in its content dealing with language, communication and confidentiality. When referring to specific State obligations the Statute uses a more traditional terminology of judicial assistance (for example requests for assistance rather than binding orders). Rules 176–180 address technical concerns relation to Article 87.

[681] The first paragraph provides for the procedure for requests for cooperation. The text of this provision is silent on which organ of the Court that has this authority, it depends on the nature of the request. The Registrar shall pursuant to Rule 176(2) transmit the requests for cooperation made by the Chambers.

The general principle is that requests shall be transmitted through the diplomatic channel. Other potential changes include the International Criminal Police Organisation (Interpol) or any appropriate regional organisation.

[682] Requests for cooperation and any documents supporting the request may be in one of the one of the working languages of the Court, that is French or English. A State may also upon ratification, acceptance, approval or accession specify that it should be in the official language of the requested State. Rule 178 clarifies that when a requested State Party has more than one official language, it may indicate upon ratification, acceptance, approval or accession that requests for cooperation and any supporting documents can be drafted in any one of its official languages.

Considering that the provision concerns "requests for cooperation" in general, the language requirement should be interpreted to apply all requests under Part 9, including those to non-States Parties and intergovernmental organisations.

---

4. In relation to any request for assistance presented under this Part, the Court may take such measures, including measures related to the protection of information, as may be necessary to ensure the safety or physical or psychological well-being of any victims, potential witnesses and their families. The Court may request that any information that is made available under this Part shall be provided and handled in a manner that protects the safety and physical or psychological well-being of any victims, potential witnesses and their families.[684]

5. (a) The Court may invite any State not party to this Statute to provide assistance under this Part on the basis of an ad hoc arrangement, an agreement with such State or any other appropriate basis.

   (b) Where a State not party to this Statute, which has entered into an ad hoc arrangement or an agreement with the Court, fails to cooperate with requests pursuant to any such arrangement or agreement, the Court may so inform the Assembly of States Parties or, where the Security Council referred the matter to the Court, the Security Council.[685]

6. The Court may ask any intergovernmental organization to provide information or documents. The Court may also ask for other forms of cooperation and assistance which may be agreed upon with such an organization and which are in accordance with its competence or mandate.[686]

---

[683] Paragraph 3 provides that a requested State shall keep confidential a request for cooperation. The provision uses the term "requested State" as opposed to "State Party" which suggests that this applies to all requests, including those submitted to a non-State Party.

[684] This paragraph supplements Article 68 which provides for general protection for victims and witnesses. Both of provisions have a reference to the safety or physical or psychological well-being of concerned individuals.

   Protection for victims and witnesses is applicable for all form of cooperation under Part 9. The provision also covers provision and handling of information.

[685] A non-State party may pursuant to Article 12(3) accept the exercise of jurisdiction by the Court. This entails a duty to co-operate with the Court. The cooperation of third States may also be obtained by *ad hoc* agreements with the Court. Such agreements may thus provide a duty to cooperate with the Court. The existence and scope of this duty depend entirely on the content of the agreement. As such the co-operation relationship between the Court and States non-parties may be more reciprocal in nature.

   Once a State has entered an *ad hoc* arrangement or an agreement with the Court, problems or failures are handled via the same channels as would be a problem with a State party. Arguably, it equally applies to the international obligations of a non-state party even when there is no *ad hoc* arrangement or an agreement but there is a UN Security Council resolution adopted under Chapter VII of the UN Charter. This finds support in the fact that the Prosecutor has reported to the UN Security Council Sudan's failure to cooperate contrary to operative paragraph 2 of resolution 1593(2005).

[686] The word "may" is used as intergovernmental organisations are not under an obligation to cooperate under Part 9. However, they may similar to non-States Parties consent to cooperate with the Court. Moreover, international organisations may be under an obligation to cooperate following a decision of the Security Council (acting under Chapter VII of the UN Charter) or where it is possible to establish an obligation to cooperate under customary international law. If an organisation is under such an obligation to cooperate, a reasonable conclusion is, in the light of *Blaškić*, that the Court "has the inherent power to make a finding as to the organization's failure to cooperate" (*Prosecutor v. Blaškić*, ICTY A. Ch., 29 October 1997, para. 33).

---

7. Where a State Party fails to comply with a request to cooperate by the Court contrary to the provisions of this Statute, thereby preventing the Court from exercising its functions and powers under this Statute, the Court may make a finding to that effect and refer the matter to the Assembly of States Parties or, where the Security Council referred the matter to the Court, to the Security Council.[687]

From the reference "competence or mandate" of the organisation follows that the Court should not ask an intergovernmental organisation to cooperate in way that would entail an *ultra vires* act.

Article 87(6) is similar to Article 54(3)(c) which provides that the prosecutor may "[s]eek the cooperation of any [...] intergovernmental organization or arrangement in accordance with its respective competence and/or mandate". The term "arrangements" was added to include peacekeeping forces. The assumption during the negotiations was that the Court could cooperate with peacekeeping forces, even in the absence of the use of the term "arrangements" (Kreß and Prost, p. 1527; Ciampi, p. 1621). For example, in *Prosecutor v. Lubanga*, ICC PT. Ch. I, Decision on Defense Requests for Disclosure of Materials, 17 November 2006, PTC I ordered the Registrar to immediately send a cooperation request to the United Nations in order to obtain notes of interviews of MONUC officials.

[687] Where a State Party fails to comply with a request to cooperate by the Court, the Court has the power, in a procedure similar to that of the *ad hoc* tribunals, to make a judicial finding and refer the matter to the Assembly of States Parties or, where the Security Council referred the matter to the Court, to the Security Council.

Moreover, when a State denies a request for assistance it shall pursuant to Article 93(6) inform the Court or the prosecutor of the reasons for such denial. In addition to making findings of non-compliance, the Court may also proceed with a) further consultations with the State, or b) deducing the existence or non-existence of a fact which may have implications for the question of guilt of an accused person.

Regulation 109 (3) contains the obligation that the State concerned must be heard prior to a finding of non-compliance.

In *Prosecutor v. Bashir*, ICC PT. Ch. I, Decision Pursuant to Article 87(7) of the ICC Statute on the Failure by the Republic of Malawi to Comply with the Cooperation Requests Issued by the Court with Respect to the Arrest and Surrender of Omar Hassan Ahmad Al Bashir including Annexes and Corrigenda, 12 December 2011, Malawi, relied on Article 98(1) of the Statute to justify its refusal to comply with the Cooperation Requests with Respect to the Arrest and Surrender of Omar Hassan Ahmad Al Bashir. The Pre-Trial Chamber found "that customary international law creates an exception to Head of State immunity when international courts seek a Head of State's arrest for the commission of international crimes. There is no conflict between Malawi's obligations towards the Court and its obligations under customary international law; therefore, Article 98(1) of the Statute does not apply" (para. 43) The Chamber therefore found, "in accordance with Article 87(7) of the Statute that the Republic of Malawi has failed to comply with the Cooperation Requests contrary to the provisions of the Statute and has thereby prevented the Court from exercising its functions and powers under this Statute. The Chamber decides to refer the matter both to the United Nations Security Council and to the Assembly of States Parties" (para. 46)

Cross-references:

Rules 176, 177, 178 , 179 and 180.

Regulation 109.

Doctrine:

1. Karin N. Calvo-Goller, *The Trial Proceedings of the International Criminal Court: ICTY and ICTR Precedents*, Koninklijke Brill NV, Leiden, 2006, p. 207.
2. Annalisa Ciampi, "The Obligation to Cooperate", in Antonio Cassese et al (eds.), *The Rome Statute of the International Criminal Court: A Commentary*, 2nd ed., Oxford University Press, Oxford, 2002, p. 1621.
3. Mark Klamberg, *Evidence in International Criminal Trials: Confronting Legal Gaps and the Reconstruction of Disputed Events*, Martinus Nijhoff Publishers, Leiden: 2013, pp. 235, 248, 249, 257 and 260.
4. Claus Kreß and Kimberly Prost, "Article 87 – Request for Cooperation: General Provisions", in Otto Triffterer (ed.), *Commentary on the Rome Statute of the International Criminal Court: Observers' Notes, Article by Article*, 2nd ed., C.H. Beck/Hart/Nomos, Munich/Oxford/Baden-Baden, 2008, pp. 1517–31.
5. Richard May and Marieke Wierda, *International Criminal Evidence*, Transnational Publishers, New York, 2002, p. 68.
6. William A. Schabas, *The International Criminal Court: A Commentary on the Rome Statute*, Oxford University Press, Oxford, 2010, pp. 978–85.

Author: Mark Klamberg.

Article 88
Availability of procedures under national law

States Parties shall ensure that there are procedures available under their national law for all of the forms of cooperation which are specified under this Part.[688]

---

[688] *General remarks*:

Cooperation models in international criminal justice are often discussed in terms of either as horizontal or vertical. International law is often described as horizontal legal system consisting of sovereign States and a lack of a supreme authority. From this follows that cooperation requires consent and a reciprocity between the involved states. The vertical relationship involves far-reaching obligations together with a lack of reciprocity and the final say in disputes is attributed to the requesting side, that is, the international tribunal or court. Article 88 and Part 9 of the Statute represents a compromise between these approaches.

Preparatory works:

The states were during the negotiations of the ICC Statute divided whether the relationship between the Court and States Parties should reflect a horizontal or vertical approach to cooperation. The present provision represents a compromise together with Articles 89 and Article 93 which provide that the obligation to comply with requests would be carried out "in accordance with the provisions of this Part and under procedures of national law".

Analysis:

Ciampi explains that Article 88 sets out an obligation of result and not one of conduct (Ciampi, p. 1625, see also Schabas, p. 987).

The phrase "ensure that there are procedures available under their national law" requires States Parties to review their national law and procedures to meet the cooperation obligations of the ICC Statute.

The word "specified" indicates that all of the measures in Part 9 are covered by the obligation under Article 88.

Doctrine:

1. Annalisa Ciampi, "The Obligation to Cooperate", in Antonio Cassese et al (eds.), *The Rome Statute of the International Criminal Court: A Commentary*, 2nd ed., Oxford University Press, Oxford, 2002, pp. 1607–38

2. Robert Cryer, Håkan Friman, Daryll Robinson and Elizabeth Wilmshurst, *An Introduction to International Criminal Law and Procedure*, 2nd ed., Cambridge University Press, Cambridge, 2010, pp. 509–10.

3. Mark Klamberg, *Evidence in International Criminal Trials: Confronting Legal Gaps and the Reconstruction of Disputed Events*, Martinus Nijhoff Publishers, Leiden, 2013, pp. 238–39.

4. Claus Kreß and Kimberly Prost, "Article 88 – Availability of Procedures under National Law", in Otto Triffterer (ed.), *Commentary on the Rome Statute of the International Criminal Court: Observers' Notes, Article by Article*, 2nd ed., C.H. Beck/Hart/Nomos, Munich/Oxford/Baden-Baden, 2008, pp. 1533–35.

5. Richard May and Marieke Wierda, *International Criminal Evidence*, Transnational Publishers, Ardsley, NY, 2002, p. 54.

6. William A. Schabas, *The International Criminal Court: A Commentary on the Rome Statute*, Oxford University Press, Oxford, 2010, pp. 986–92.

Author: Mark Klamberg.

Article 89

Surrender of persons to the Court[689]

1. The Court may transmit a request for the arrest and surrender of a person, together with the material supporting the request outlined in Article 91, to any State on the territory of which that person may be found and shall request the cooperation of that State in the arrest and surrender of such a person.[690] States Parties shall, in accordance with the provisions of this Part and the procedure under their national law, comply with requests for arrest and surrender.[691]

---

[689] *General remarks:*

The Statute separates the arrest procedure (Articles 58 and 59) from the legal assistance to be provided by states (Articles 89–92) although some overlap is plausible. Article 89 deals with surrender of person to the Court. The crucial question during the negotiations was whether the obligation to comply with requests by the Court for arrest and surrender of persons should be qualified by grounds for refusal (Kreß and Prost, p. 1538).

Author: Mark Klamberg.

[690] The first sentence of paragraph 1 should be read together with Article 58(5) which both use the word "may" which suggests that the Court has discretion to transmit a request for the arrest and surrender of a person. However, the sentence continues by saying that the Court "shall request the cooperation" of the State concerned. The Court will in general transmit a request to any State on territory of which the person sought may be found once a warrant of arrest has been issued (Kreß and Prost, pp. 1538–1539). In *Prosecutor v. Kony et al.*, ICC PT. Ch. II, Decision on the Prosecutor's Application for Warrants of Arrest under Article 58, 8 July 2005, PTC II decided, *inter alia*, that the Warrants and the Requests, be transmitted by the Registrar to the relevant States, in accordance with the terms set out in the Requests. One question was which organ would transmit the warrants and requests. The Pre-Trial Chamber stated in this regard that "the literal meaning and purpose of rule 176, sub-rule 2, of the Rules, as evident also from its drafting history, is to establish two separate and distinct procedures involving, on the one hand, the Registrar in the discharge of his responsibilities with respect to requests for cooperation made by the Chambers; and, on the other hand, the Prosecutor, in respect of the requests for cooperation made by the Prosecutor, in line with the Prosecutor's powers under Articles 42 and 54 of the Statute". Since the Pre-Trial Chamber is the only competent organ to issue and amend a warrant of arrest, it is for the Registrar to transmit a request for arrest and surrender.

Author: Mark Klamberg.

[691] The second sentence of the first paragraph contains one of the most important obligations for States Parties, namely the obligation to surrender of persons to the Court.

During the negotiations there was a divided between states favouring the horizontal or vertical approach to cooperation. In Article 87(3) option2 of the Draft Statute contained several grounds for refusal, including: a) non-acceptance of the Court's jurisdiction by the requested state; b) the person is a national of the requested State; c) parallel proceedings: the person has been investigated or has been proceeded against, convicted or acquitted in the requested State or another State for the offence for which his surrender/transfer/extradition is sought; d) the information submitted in support of the request does not meet the minimum evidentiary requirements of the requested State; e) compliance with the request would put it in breach of an existing international obligation (Report of the Preparatory Committee on the Establishment of an International Criminal Court, United Nations Diplomatic Conference of Plenipotentiaries on the Establishment of an International Criminal Court Rome, Italy 15 June–17 July 1998, A/CONF.183/2).

---

2. Where the person sought for surrender brings a challenge before a national court on the basis of the principle of ne bis in idem as provided in article 20, the requested State shall immediately consult with the Court to determine if there has been a relevant ruling on admissibility. If the case is admissible, the requested State shall proceed with the execution of the request. If an admissibility ruling is pending, the requested State may postpone the execution of the request for surrender of the person until the Court makes a determination on admissibility.[692]

3. (a) A State Party shall authorize, in accordance with its national procedural law, transportation through its territory of a person being surrendered to the Court by another State, except where transit through that State would impede or delay the surrender.

   (b) A request by the Court for transit shall be transmitted in accordance with Article 87. The request for transit shall contain:

   (i) A description of the person being transported;

   (ii) A brief statement of the facts of the case and their legal characterization; and

   (iii) The warrant for arrest and surrender;

   (c) A person being transported shall be detained in custody during the period of transit;

   (d) No authorization is required if the person is transported by air and no landing is scheduled on the territory of the transit State;

   (e) If an unscheduled landing occurs on the territory of the transit State, that State may require a request for transit from the Court as provided for in subparagraph (b). The transit State shall detain the person being transported until the request for transit is received and the transit is effected, provided that detention for purposes of this subparagraph may not be extended beyond 96 hours from the unscheduled landing unless the request is received within that time.[693]

4. If the person sought is being proceeded against or is serving a sentence in the requested State for a crime different from that for which surrender to the Court is sought, the requested State, after making its decision to grant the request, shall consult with the Court.[694]

The solution depends on the problem. Article 89(1) must be read together with Articles 89(2) and (4); Article 90, 91(2)(c) in conjunction with paragraph 4 and Article 98.

Articles 89(2) and (4) deals with parallel proceedings. Articles 90 and 98 concerns conflicting obligations for the requested state. Article 91(2)(c) in conjunction with paragraph 4 relates to national evidence requirements (Kreß and Prost, pp. 1539–1540).

Author: Mark Klamberg.

[692] The second paragraph allows a person whose surrender is sought to challenger a request on the basis of the principle of *ne bis in idem*. It is for the Court to decide the issue of admissibility.

Author: Mark Klamberg.

[693] States Parties are under an obligation to authorise, in accordance with its national procedural law, transportation through its territory of a person being surrendered to the Court by another State, except where transit through that State would impede or delay the surrender.

Author: Mark Klamberg.

[694] The fourth paragraph concerns the situation where the person whose surrender is sought is already serving a sentence in the requested state for a crime different from that for which surrender to the Court is sought. In such situation the requested State "shall consult" with the court, which suggests that the requested State has discretion to decided on the question of surrender.

This would be at odds with the general rule that States have to comply with requests for surrender.

Article 89(4) is the result of a debate during the negotiations to allow "temporary surrender", see Article 87(8) of the Draft Statute (Report of the Preparatory Committee on the Establishment of an International Criminal Court, United Nations Diplomatic Conference of Plenipotentiaries on the Establishment of an International Criminal Court Rome, Italy 15 June–17 July 1998, A/CONF.183/2). No agreement on temporary surrender was possible, the issue was left to resolve for the Court and States concerned (Kreß and Prost, p. 1547).

Cross-references:

Rules 176, 181, 182, 183 and 184.

Regulation 111.

Doctrine:

1. Karel De Meester, Kelly Pitcher, Rod Rastan and Göran Sluiter, "Investigation, Coercive Measures, Arrest and Surrender", in Göran Sluiter, Håkan Friman, Suzannah Linton, Sergey Vasiliev and Salvatore Zappalà (eds.), *International Criminal Procedure: Principles and Rules*, Oxford University Press, Oxford, 2013, pp. 171–379.

2. Claus Kreß and Kimberly Prost, "Article 89 – Surrender of Persons to the Court", in Otto Triffterer (ed.), *Commentary on the Rome Statute of the International Criminal Court: Observers' Notes, Article by Article*, 2nd ed., C.H. Beck/Hart/Nomos, Munich/Oxford/Baden-Baden, 2008, pp. 1537–1548.

3. William A. Schabas, *The International Criminal Court: A Commentary on the Rome Statute*, Oxford University Press, Oxford, 2010, pp. 993–1000.

Author: Mark Klamberg.

Article 90

Competing requests[695]

1. A State Party which receives a request from the Court for the surrender of a person under article 89 shall, if it also receives a request from any other State for the extradition of the same person for the same conduct which forms the basis of the crime for which the Court seeks the person's surrender, notify the Court and the requesting State of that fact.[696]

2. Where the requesting State is a State Party, the requested State shall give priority to the request from the Court if:

   (a) The Court has, pursuant to Article 18 or 19, made a determination that the case in respect of which surrender is sought is admissible and that determination takes into account the investigation or prosecution conducted by the requesting State in respect of its request for extradition; or

   (b) The Court makes the determination described in subparagraph (a) pursuant to the requested State's notification under paragraph 1.[697]

3. Where a determination under paragraph 2 (a) has not been made, the requested State may, at its discretion, pending the determination of the Court under paragraph 2 (b), proceed to deal with the request for extradition from the requesting State but shall not extradite the person until the Court has determined that the case is inadmissible. The Court's determination shall be made on an expedited basis.[698]

---

[695] *General remarks*:

Article 90 deals with the issue of competing requests. The substantial disagreement during the negotiations was whether the requested State's obligation *vis-à-vis* the Court should be greater, lesser or equal obligation owed to a State. Factors that were considered included: whether the competing request was from a State Party or a non-State Party, whether the competing request was based on a treaty obligation or not and whether the competing request concerned the same alleged conduct.

[696] The use of the words "any other State" mean that the first paragraph applies to ll competing requests, irrespective of whether the competing request is from a State Party or a non-State party. There is an obligation in cases of competing requests or the requested State to notify Curt and the requesting State of that fact.

[697] The second paragraph makes reference to Article 18 and 19 which deal with admissibility and together with Article 17 express and regulate the complementarity principle.

If the requesting State is a State Party, the requested State shall give priority to the request from the Court if the case is admissible. If the requesting state has jurisdiction over the crime and is not unwilling or unable to investigate or prosecute, it follows from Article 17 that the case is inadmissible. In practice, this means that Article 90(2) requires the Court to determine whether the requesting State is unwilling or unable to investigate or prosecute (Schabas, pp. 1004–1005).

[698] This paragraph concerns the situation when the Court has not yet made a ruling on the admissibility of the case. From he words "at its discretion" it follows that it is for the requested State to decide what to do with the pending request from the other State. However, the requested state shall not complete the execution of the request until the Court has determined that the case is inadmissible.

4. If the requesting State is a State not Party to this Statute the requested State, if it is not under an international obligation to extradite the person to the requesting State, shall give priority to the request for surrender from the Court, if the Court has determined that the case is admissible.[699]

5. Where a case under paragraph 4 has not been determined to be admissible by the Court, the requested State may, at its discretion, proceed to deal with the request for extradition from the requesting State.[700]

6. In cases where paragraph 4 applies except that the requested State is under an existing international obligation to extradite the person to the requesting State not Party to this Statute, the requested State shall determine whether to surrender the person to the Court or extradite the person to the requesting State. In making its decision, the requested State shall consider all the relevant factors, including but not limited to:

   (a) The respective dates of the requests;

   (b) The interests of the requesting State including, where relevant, whether the crime was committed in its territory and the nationality of the victims and of the person sought; and

   (c) The possibility of subsequent surrender between the Court and the requesting State.[701]

7. Where a State Party which receives a request from the Court for the surrender of a person also receives a request from any State for the extradition of the same person for conduct other than that which constitutes the crime for which the Court seeks the person's surrender:

---

[699] Paragraph 4 provides that the requested State must give priority to the Courts request for surrender unless it is under an international obligation to extradite the person to the requesting State.

The paragraph concerns cases when the requesting State is not party to the ICC Statute but the paragraph read in isolation does not specify whether the words "requested state" limits the scope of the paragraph to States Parties or if it also applies to non-member States.

Since the cooperation regime by default only creates obligations for States Parties, the scope of the paragraph should be limited to cases when the requested state is a State Party. This appears logical considering that paragraph 1 concerns a State Party that is requested to surrender and the entire Article is drafted to consider scenarios in sequence. Thus, the conditions in paragraph 1 also applies to paragraph 4 (Kreß and Prost, p 1553, see also Schabas, p. 1005).

[700] In situations where the Court has yet to determine admissibility (and thus are not covered by paragraph 4), the circumstances are similar to those under paragraph 3. The difference is that paragraph 5 concerns cases when the requesting state is not a party to the ICC Statute. The consequence is that the execution of the request can be completed before a decision from the Court.

[701] Paragraph 6 concerns competing requests from a non-State Party where there is an existing international obligation to extradite the person to the requesting State.

In such cases the requested State shall determine whether to surrender the person to the Court or extradite the person to the requesting State considering all relevant factors, including: a) the respective dates of the requests; 2) the interests of the requesting state; and 3) the possibility of subsequent surrender between the Court and the requesting State. The words "all relevant factors" indicates that the list in this paragraph is not exhaustive. Other factors include whether the requesting states is willing and able to investigate and prosecute.

(a) The requested State shall, if it is not under an existing international obligation to extradite the person to the requesting State, give priority to the request from the Court;

(b) The requested State shall, if it is under an existing international obligation to extradite the person to the requesting State, determine whether to surrender the person to the Court or to extradite the person to the requesting State. In making its decision, the requested State shall consider all the relevant factors, including but not limited to those set out in paragraph 6, but shall give special consideration to the relative nature and gravity of the conduct in question.[702]

8. Where pursuant to a notification under this article, the Court has determined a case to be inadmissible, and subsequently extradition to the requesting State is refused, the requested State shall notify the Court of this decision.[703]

---

[702] Paragraph 7 concerns the scenario where there are competing requests for different alleged criminal conduct. In such cases, there is no distinction to whether the requesting State is a State Party or not.

Sub-paragraph a) applies to cases where the requested State is under no international obligation to extradite the person to the requesting State. Thus, there is competing obligation. In such cases priority should be given to request from the Court.

Sub-paragraph b) applies to cases where the requested State is under an international obligation to extradite the person to the requesting State. This provision follows paragraph 6 granting some discretion to the requested state with the difference that the requested State should afford special attention to nature and gravity of the conduct in question. It is expected that the Court will deal with most serious cases which would give it priority over competing requests, but there could be exceptional situations where the requesting State are investigating and prosecuting as serious or more serious crimes than those alleged by the Court (Kreß and Prost, p. 1556).

[703] This paragraph concerns scenarios where the Court has declared a case inadmissible and extradition to the requesting State has failed. Such cases are of interest to the Court and warrants a provision on notification because failed extradition to a case may motivate the Court to reconsider its ruling on admissibility. Rule 186 provides that "the requested State shall provide the notification of its decision to the Prosecutor in order to enable him or her to act in accordance with Article 19, paragraph 10".

Cross-references:

Rule 186.

Doctrine:

1. Claus Kreß and Kimberly Prost, "Article 90 – Competing Requests", in Otto Triffterer (ed.), *Commentary on the Rome Statute of the International Criminal Court: Observers' Notes, Article by Article*, 2nd ed., C.H. Beck/Hart/Nomos, Munich/Oxford/Baden-Baden, 2008, pp. 1549–57.

2. William A. Schabas, *The International Criminal Court: A Commentary on the Rome Statute*, Oxford University Press, Oxford, 2010, pp. 1001–6.

Author: Mark Klamberg.

Article 91

Contents of request for arrest and surrender[704]

1. A request for arrest and surrender shall be made in writing. In urgent cases, a request may be made by any medium capable of delivering a written record, provided that the request shall be confirmed through the channel provided for in Article 87, paragraph 1 (a).[705]

2. In the case of a request for the arrest and surrender of a person for whom a warrant of arrest has been issued by the Pre-Trial Chamber under Article 58, the request shall contain or be supported by:

    (a) Information describing the person sought, sufficient to identify the person, and information as to that person's probable location;

    (b) A copy of the warrant of arrest; and

    (c) Such documents, statements or information as may be necessary to meet the requirements for the surrender process in the requested State, except that those requirements should not be more burdensome than those applicable to requests for extradition pursuant to treaties or arrangements between the requested State and other States and should, if possible, be less burdensome, taking into account the distinct nature of the Court.[706]

---

[704] *General remarks:*

Article 91 provides detailed requirements on the content of applications for arrest and surrender. This provision should be read together with Article 58 which, *inter alia*, concerns issuance by the Pre-Trial Chamber of a warrant of arrest.

Preparatory works:

The controversial issue of evidentiary requirements for requests for surrender as during the negotiations was less a question whether the cooperation regime should be horizontal or vertical, it was more a question of tradition where common law jurisdictions are generally more demanding (Schabas, p. 1008).

Article 88(1)(b)(v) and (c)(ii) of the Draft Statute contained provisions in brackets that reflected requirements for the production of evidence by the Court (Report of the Preparatory Committee on the Establishment of an International Criminal Court, United Nations Diplomatic Conference of Plenipotentiaries on the Establishment of an International Criminal Court Rome, Italy 15 June–17 July 1998, A/CONF.183/2).

Some civil countries opposed the inclusion of such requirements (Kreß and Prost, p. 1560). In the end a compromise was agreed upon as formulated in Article 91(2)(c).

[705] The request for arrest and surrender must be made in writing.

In urgent cases, a request may be made by any medium capable of delivering a written record, such as a fax machine or electronic communication system. Such communication should be followed by confirmation through the diplomatic channel or any other appropriate channel as stipulated in Article 87(1)(a).

[706] The content of the request depends on whether it concerns a request for the arrest and surrender of a person for whom a warrant of arrest has been issued (regulated in paragraph 2) and request for the arrest and surrender of a person already convicted (regulated in paragraph 3).

If the request concerns a request for the arrest and surrender of a person for whom a warrant of arrest has been issued, it must contain: information describing the person sought, a copy of

---

3. In the case of a request for the arrest and surrender of a person already convicted, the request shall contain or be supported by:

   (a) A copy of any warrant of arrest for that person;

   (b) A copy of the judgement of conviction;

   (c) Information to demonstrate that the person sought is the one referred to in the judgement of conviction; and

   (d) If the person sought has been sentenced, a copy of the sentence imposed and, in the case of a sentence for imprisonment, a statement of any time already served and the time remaining to be served.[707]

4. Upon the request of the Court, a State Party shall consult with the Court, either generally or with respect to a specific matter, regarding any requirements under its national law that may apply under paragraph 2 (c). During the consultations, the State Party shall advise the Court of the specific requirements of its national law.[708]

---

the warrant of arrest and documents in support of the request necessary to meet the requirement of the requested state.

Sub-paragraph 2(c) allows states to require production of documents in support of the request. It does not specify the exact standard of proof that is relevant in such procedures, that may vary depending on the requested State. However, the requirements should not be more burdensome than those applicable to requests for extradition pursuant to treaties or arrangements between the requested State and other States and should, if possible, be less burdensome, taking into account the distinct nature of the Court.

[707] If the request for the arrest and surrender concerns a person already convicted, the request shall contain or be supported by: a copy of any warrant of arrest for that person, copy of the judgment of conviction, and information to demonstrate that the person sought is the one referred to in the judgment of conviction. If the person sought has been sentenced, information on the sentence and time already served should be provided.

[708] The Court may request a State Party to consult with the Court, either generally or with respect to a specific matter, regarding any requirements under its national law that may apply under paragraph 2 (c). This paragraph was included as a part of the compromise in relation to evidentiary requirements to allow consultations on the requirements under national law for the production of evidence (Kreß and Prost, pp. 1563–1564).

Cross-references:

Rule 187.

Doctrine:

1. Claus Kreß and Kimberly Prost, "Article 91 – Contents of Request for Arrest and Surrender", in Otto Triffterer (ed.), *Commentary on the Rome Statute of the International Criminal Court: Observers' Notes, Article by Article*, 2nd ed., C.H. Beck/Hart/Nomos, Munich/Oxford/Baden-Baden, 2008, pp. 1559–64.

2. William A. Schabas, *The International Criminal Court: A Commentary on the Rome Statute*, Oxford University Press, Oxford, 2010, pp. 1007–10.

Author: Mark Klamberg.

Article 92

Provisional arrest[709]

1. In urgent cases, the Court may request the provisional arrest of the person sought, pending presentation of the request for surrender and the documents supporting the request as specified in Article 91.[710]

2. The request for provisional arrest shall be made by any medium capable of delivering a written record and shall contain:

   (a) Information describing the person sought, sufficient to identify the person, and information as to that person's probable location;

   (b) A concise statement of the crimes for which the person's arrest is sought and of the facts which are alleged to constitute those crimes, including, where possible, the date and location of the crime;

   (c) A statement of the existence of a warrant of arrest or a judgement of conviction against the person sought; and

   (d) A statement that a request for surrender of the person sought will follow.[711]

3. A person who is provisionally arrested may be released from custody if the requested State has not received the request for surrender and the documents supporting the request as specified in Article 91 within the time limits specified in the Rules of Procedure and Evi-

---

[709] *General remarks*:

Article 92 permits the Court in "urgent cases" to request the provisional arrest of the person sought. Article 89 of the draft statute was largely similar to what became Article 92 (Report of the Preparatory Committee on the Establishment of an International Criminal Court, United Nations Diplomatic Conference of Plenipotentiaries on the Establishment of an International Criminal Court Rome, Italy 15 June–17 July 1998, A/CONF.183/2).

Author: Mark Klamberg.

[710] The first paragraph provides that provisional arrest is allowed in "urgent cases". There is no exhaustive lists that explains what constitutes an urgent case. The most common is when it is necessary to ensure that they will be available for surrender or when they pose a danger to the community.

The term "provisional arrest" signifies the interim arrest of the person pending the receipt of a formal request (Kreß and Prost, p. 1566).

This provision should be read together with Article 59 which concerns arrest proceedings in the custodial State.

In *Prosecutor v. Bemba*, ICC PT. Ch. III, Warrant of Arrest for Jean-Pierre Bemba Gombo, 23 May 2008, para. 6, the Prosecutor had filed an application for request for provisional arrest under Article 92. PTC III issued a provisional warrant of arrest, see *Prosecutor v. Bemba*, Demande d'arrestation provisoire de M. Jean-Pierre Bemba Gombo adressée au Royaume de Belgique, 23 May 2008, p. 4.

Author: Mark Klamberg.

[711] In comparison with Article 91, the requirements in Article 92 on the content of requests for provisional arrests are less demanding. There is no requirement to provide "documents, statements or information".

Author: Mark Klamberg.

---

dence. However, the person may consent to surrender before the expiration of this period if permitted by the law of the requested State. In such a case, the requested State shall proceed to surrender the person to the Court as soon as possible.[712]

4. The fact that the person sought has been released from custody pursuant to paragraph 3 shall not prejudice the subsequent arrest and surrender of that person if the request for surrender and the documents supporting the request are delivered at a later date.[713]

---

[712] Provisional arrest should by its nature be limited in time. The Court shall pursuant to Article 92(3) and rule 188 provide within sixty days from the date of the provisional arrest provide documents supporting the request for surrender to the requested State. If the requested State has not received such documents within sixty days the person who is provisionally arrested may be released from custody, if interim release has not be granted already pursuant to Article 59(3)–(6).

The person may consent to surrender before the expiration of the 60-day period if permitted by the law of the requested State. Rule 189 provides that when a person has consents to surrender and the requested State proceeds to surrender the person to the Court, the Court shall not be required to provide the documents described in Article 91 unless the requested State indicates otherwise.

Author: Mark Klamberg.

[713] Even if the person sought has been released from custody pursuant to paragraph 3, paragraph 4 allows subsequent arrest and surrender of that person if the request for surrender and the documents supporting the request are delivered at a later date.

Cross-references:

Rules 188 and 189.

Doctrine:

1. Claus Kreß and Kimberly Prost, "Article 92 – Provisional Arrest", in Otto Triffterer (ed.), *Commentary on the Rome Statute of the International Criminal Court: Observers' Notes, Article by Article*, 2nd ed., C.H. Beck/Hart/Nomos, Munich/Oxford/Baden-Baden, 2008, pp. 1565–68.

2. William A. Schabas, *The International Criminal Court: A Commentary on the Rome Statute*, Oxford University Press, 2010, pp. 1010–11.

Author: Mark Klamberg.

Article 93

Other forms of cooperation

1. States Parties shall, in accordance with the provisions of this Part and under procedures of national law, comply with requests by the Court to provide the following assistance in relation to investigations or prosecutions:[714]

   (a) The identification and whereabouts of persons or the location of items:[715]

   (b) The taking of evidence, including testimony under oath, and the production of evidence, including expert opinions and reports necessary to the Court;[716]

   (c) The questioning of any person being investigated or prosecuted;[717]

   (d) The service of documents, including judicial documents;[718]

   (e) Facilitating the voluntary appearance of persons as witnesses or experts before the Court;[719]

---

[714] *General remarks*:

Article 93(1)(a–l) deals with general assistance between the Court and State Parties aside from surrender of persons. It provides a detailed and broad list of the various types of assistance in relation to investigations or prosecutions. The wording does not focus solely on legal assistance but refers broadly to any type of assistance, and could for example cover infrastructure to conduct inquiries on the territory of the requested State. To a great extent the types of assistance was drawn from the UN Model Treaty on Mutual Legal Assistance in Criminal Matters and the 1988 UN Convention Against Illicit Traffic in Narcotic Drugs and Psychotropic Substances. Most of the listed measures of assistance are self-explanatory and require no particular comment.

Author: Karin Påle-Bartes.

[715] The wording "identification and whereabouts of persons" make no distinction between a person being a suspect, a victim or a witness. The use of the word "location of items" in the same sub-paragraph restricts the cooperation to mobile objects only.

Author: Karin Påle-Bartes.

[716] "Evidence taking and the production of evidence" (b) could cover any form of evidence. However it was the understanding during the negotiations that modern intrusive and coercive measures should not be covered by the clause. Instead these measures are dealt with in littera k and l.

Author: Karin Påle-Bartes.

[717] Although the inquiry of a person being investigated or prosecuted is already covered by sub-paragraph (b), it is made clear by sub-paragraph (c) that the Court may request the questioning of an investigated or accused person. The obligation under the sub-paragraph includes an obligation to actually obtain evidence from the person through compulsion or otherwise. The sub-paragraph does not stipulate how the inquiry should be conducted.

Author: Karin Påle-Bartes.

[718] The word "documents" cover all forms of writs and judicial records as well as any other documentation. The means of transmission of the documents is not referred to in the Article but instead it is open to the Court to specify in the request the desired form of transmission.

Cross-references:

Regulation 110.

Author: Karin Påle-Bartes.

(f) The temporary transfer of persons as provided in paragraph 7;[720]

(g) The examination of places or sites, including the exhumation and examination of grave sites;[721]

(h) The execution of searches and seizures;[722]

(i) The provision of records and documents, including official records and documents;[723]

(j) The protection of victims and witnesses and the preservation of evidence;[724]

---

[719] Even though the list of forms of legal assistance is broad, it is worth noting that the Article does not oblige States Parties to compel witnesses before the Court if so requested. The non-inclusion of a State obligation to compel testimony at trial has been considered a weakness of the cooperation schema. Sub-paragraph (e) only requires the States Parties to assist in facilitating the voluntary appearance of persons and witnesses or experts before the Court, that is to encourage a witness or an expert to appear before the Court. When it comes to bearing the costs for a witness or an expert Article 100 deals with this particular issue.

According to one view there is, on top of the absence of a State duty to compel a witness to appear and to testify before the Court, an individual right of persons not to appear and testify before the Court. This rights is considered to derive from paragraph 7. Under this provision a person in custody in the requested state may be transferred to the Court only if the person consents and the same must e fortiori be true for all other witnesses the argument goes. The view has been criticised for giving far too much prominence to a provision that deals with a very specific procedural scenario.

Even if individuals may not be forced to testify, Article 93(1) however sets out an effective framework for obtaining evidence. For example States may be required to assist in "execution of searches and seizure", "provision of records and documents, including official records and documents and identification, tracing and freezing or seizure of proceeds, property and assets and instrumentalities of crimes for the purpose of eventual forfeit" (sub-paragraphs (h), (i) and (k)).

Cross-references:

Rules 74 and 190.

Author: Karin Påle-Bartes.

[720] Sub-paragraph (f) makes a reference to the temporary transfer of persons as provided in paragraph 7. Since this was not a concept that many States were familiar or comfortable with, a separate paragraph 7 was created to deal with the procedure for this type of assistance.

Author: Karin Påle-Bartes.

[721] According to sub-paragraph (g) States Parties are obliged to comply with requests to examine sites and places on its territory, including exhumation and examination of grave sites. This is probably one of the most important and common types of assistance which the Court may seek.

Author: Karin Påle-Bartes.

[722] The Court may request searches and seizure according to sub-paragraph (h). Such requests will be executed according to the procedures of the national law of the requested State. All States must have a procedure in place for search and seizure according to Article 88.

[723] Further the Court may demand the transmission of records and documents of States Parties. This is a general mandate for the production of all types of documents and records and follows from sub-paragraph (i).

Author: Karin Påle-Bartes.

[724] Sub-paragraph (j) deals with the protection of victims and witnesses and the preservation of evidence. In cases under the investigation or prosecution by the ICC the Court is primarily re-

(k) The identification, tracing and freezing or seizure of proceeds, property and assets and instrumentalities of crimes for the purpose of eventual forfeiture, without prejudice to the rights of bona fide third parties;[725] and

(l) Any other type of assistance which is not prohibited by the law of the requested State, with a view to facilitating the investigation and prosecution of crimes within the jurisdiction of the Court.[726]

2. The Court shall have the authority to provide an assurance to a witness or an expert appearing before the Court that he or she will not be prosecuted, detained or subjected to any

---

sponsible for the protection of victims and witnesses. However, such protection may require the assistance of States Parties, for example when a victim or a witness lives in that State. If the national law does not provide for protection programs the State Party may be obliged to adopt new measures to protect victims and witnesses.

Author: Karin Påle-Bartes.

[725] Sub-paragraph (k) deals with identification, tracing and freezing or seizure of proceeds, property and assets and instrumentalities of crimes. These measures are an essential part of modern international cooperation. The provision obligates States Parties to have mechanism in place which will allow for the freezing of any of the listed items. The purpose of conducting such freezing or seizure of assets is first of all to facilitate enforcement should the accused person be convicted and an order of forfeiture be imposed as part of the sentence. But freezing of assets is also important in the process of arrest and surrender, in that it helps to disrupt support networks of suspects. The question of legal assistance according to the paragraph has been raised for example in *Prosecutor v. Lubanga*, ICC PT. Ch. I, Demande adressée à la République démocratique du Congo en vue d'obtenir l'identification, la localisation, le gel et la saisie des biens et avoirs de m. Thomas Lubanga Dyilo, ICC-01/04-01/06-62, 9 March 2006, *Prosecutor v. Lubanga*, ICC PT. Ch. I, Request to States Parties to the Rome Statute for the Identification, Tracing and Freezing or Seizure of the Property and Assets of Mr Thomas Dyilo, ICC-01/04-01/06-62-tEN, 31 March 2006 and *Prosecutor v. Bemba*, ICC PT. Ch. III, Request for cooperation to Initiate an Investigation Addressed to the Competent Authorities of the Republic of Portugal, ICC-01/05-01/08-254, 17 November 2008.

Author: Karin Påle-Bartes.

[726] Sub-paragraph (l) also recognises the availability of other forms of legal assistance not specified in the list as long as there is not a prohibition under the law of the requested State. In practice this may not be a simple matter. The fact that something is "not prohibited" by national law does not automatically mean that it is permitted and although a form of cooperation "is not prohibited" the State Party might have no legislation enabling it to effect compliance. In *Prosecutor v. Banda and Jerbo*, ICC T. Ch., Decision on "Defence Application pursuant to Articles 57(3)(b) and 64(6)(a) of the Statute for an order for the preparation and transmission of a cooperation request to the Government of the Republic of the Sudan", 1 July 2011, the Trial Chamber stated that "as the type of assistance is not specified under this paragraph, it would not be appropriate to place a general obligation on a State to comply with such requests, when the nature of the obligation cannot be specified. Thus, the obligation is limited to that assistance which is not prohibited under national law".

Assistance has to be provided on the basis of a request presented by the Court. The statute does not call for a direct or spontaneous transfer of information from a national authority to the Court or vice versa. On the other hand such a transfer may be helpful and is not prohibited by Article 93(1).

Author: Karin Påle-Bartes.

---

restriction of personal freedom by the Court in respect of any act or omission that preceded the departure of that person from the requested State. [727]

3. Where execution of a particular measure of assistance detailed in a request presented under paragraph 1, is prohibited in the requested State on the basis of an existing fundamental legal principle of general application, the requested State shall promptly consult with the Court to try to resolve the matter. In the consultations, consideration should be given to whether the assistance can be rendered in another manner or subject to conditions. If after consultations the matter cannot be resolved, the Court shall modify the request as necessary. [728]

4. In accordance with Article 72, a State Party may deny a request for assistance, in whole or in part, only if the request concerns the production of any documents or disclosure of evidence which relates to its national security. [729]

---

[727] Bilateral and multilateral treaties in the field of mutual legal assistance usually provide for an assurance to a witness or an expert that they will not be prosecuted or otherwise detained with respect to an act or omission preceding their departure from the requested State. According to paragraph (2) the Court is merely empowered to provide such an assurance at its discretion. It has been described as a power likely to be used to obtain evidence from lower-level alleged perpetrators who are reluctant to testify against their superiors. In *Prosecutor v. Katanga and Ngudjolo*, ICC T. Ch., Decision on the request of the Defence for Mathieu Ngudjolo to obtain assurances with respect to self-incrimination for the accused, 13 September 2011, para. 1, the Trial Chamber stated that the position of an accused who chooses to testify in his own defence cannot be systematically equated to that of any other witness. The Trial Chamber found that Article 93(2) and rule 74 is not applicable to the accused and rejected the request.

Cross-references:

Rule 191.

Author: Karin Påle-Bartes.

[728] There are only three limited exceptions when States Parties can deny a request for cooperation presented by the Court (paragraphs 4–6). Article 93 has therefor been considered to be a rather strong regime for cooperation. Compared to a lot of other mutual assistance treaties it is worth mentioning that assistance may not be refused because the offence is characterised as a political, military or fiscal offence. There are no general provisions allowing for refusal when the execution of the request would be contrary to the public order or sovereignty of public interest of the state.

Paragraph (3) provides that where a particular measure sought in a specific request is prohibited by existing national law the requested State would have to comply with the request, unless it successfully convinces the Court that the requested measure violates a fundamental principle of general application. This means that not any prohibition can be referred to. The prohibition must rather possess a constitutional or quasi-constitutional status. Under those circumstances the requested State and the Court would consult in order to resolve the conflict. The State must consider whether cooperation can be provided subject to specified conditions or in an alternative manner. The provision emphasises the presumption that both the Court and the State will act in good faith and try to find acceptable solutions.

Author: Karin Påle-Bartes.

[729] A State Party can deny a request for assistance if it concerns the production of documents or disclosure of evidence relating to its national security according to sub-paragraph 4. The subject of national security is considered in this commentary under Article 72.

5. Before denying a request for assistance under paragraph 1 (1), the requested State shall consider whether the assistance can be provided subject to specified conditions, or whether the assistance can be provided at a later date or in an alternative manner, provided that if the Court or the Prosecutor accepts the assistance subject to conditions, the Court or the Prosecutor shall abide by them.[730]

6. If a request for assistance is denied, the requested State Party shall promptly inform the Court or the Prosecutor of the reasons for such denial.[731]

7. (a) The Court may request the temporary transfer of a person in custody for purposes of identification or for obtaining testimony or other assistance. The person may be transferred if the following conditions are fulfilled:

   (i) The person freely gives his or her informed consent to the transfer; and

   (ii) The requested State agrees to the transfer, subject to such conditions as that State and the Court may agree.

   (b) The person being transferred shall remain in custody. When the purposes of the transfer have been fulfilled, the Court shall return the person without delay to the requested State.[732]

Cross-references:

Article 72.

Author: Karin Påle-Bartes.

[730] Article 93(1)(l) requires a State to comply with a request for assistance if compliance is not prohibited by its own national law. If a state denies such a request, it must, according to paragraph 5, consider whether cooperation can be provided subject to specific conditions, or at a later date, or in an alternative manner. The Court is not obliged to accept any conditions offered by the requested State. However if the Court agrees to a particular condition it must abide that condition.

Author: Karin Påle-Bartes.

[731] If a State denies a request for assistance it is, according to paragraph 6, to inform the Court or the Prosecutor promptly of the reasons.

[732] The possibility of temporary transfer of a person in custody is featured in many mutual legal assistance schemes. Under paragraph (7) it is possible for a State to transfer an individual who is in custody for purposes of identification or to testify or provide other forms of assistance if the person is notified about the purpose of the transfer and its legal and factual consequences and the person consents to the transfer.

Further the State must also agree to the transfer. The transfer of a person in custody always raises security issues and in some cases, the security risk may be too great to permit the transfer. In most cases the Court can request the taking of evidence from the person under paragraph 1 (b), as an alternative.

The paragraph does not provide grounds for denial of transfer; but the general obligation to cooperate would require the clear and serious reason for such a refusal.

The person who is transferred remains in custody and is, according to the paragraph, returned without delay to the State once the purposes of transfer has been completed. In *Prosecutor v. Katanga and Ngudjolo*, ICC T. Ch., Decision on an Amicus Curiae application and on the "Requête tendant à obtenir présentations des témoins DRC-D02-P-0350, DRC-D02-P-0236, DRC-D02-P-0228 aux autorités néerlandaises aux fins d'asile" (Articles 68 and 93(7) of the Statute), 9 June 2011, however the Trial Chamber considered whether an immediate application of Article 93(7)) would not constitute a violation of three detained witnesses right to apply for

8. (a) The Court shall ensure the confidentiality of documents and information, except as required for the investigation and proceedings described in the request.

    (b) The requested State may, when necessary, transmit documents or information to the Prosecutor on a confidential basis. The Prosecutor may then use them solely for the purpose of generating new evidence.

    (c) The requested State may, on its own motion or at the request of the Prosecutor, subsequently consent to the disclosure of such documents or information. They may then be used as evidence pursuant to the provisions of Parts 5 and 6 and in accordance with the Rules of Procedure and Evidence.[733]

9. (a) (i) In the event that a State Party receives competing requests, other than for surrender or extradition, from the Court and from another State pursuant to an international obligation, the State Party shall endeavour, in consultation with the Court and the other State, to meet both requests, if necessary by postponing or attaching conditions to one or the other request.

       (ii) Failing that, competing requests shall be resolved in accordance with the principles established in Article 90.

    (b) Where, however, the request from the Court concerns information, property or persons which are subject to the control of a third State or an international organization by vir-

---

asylum. If the witnesses were to be returned to the Democratic Republic of Congo immediately, it would become impossible for them to exercise their right to apply for asylum in the Netherlands. As matters stood at the time, The Chamber was unable to apply Article 93(7) of the Statute in conditions which are consistent with internationally recognised human rights, as required by Article 21(3). The Chamber considered that it was incumbent upon the Registrar to authorise contact between the detained witnesses and their Dutch Counsel within the detention Center as soon as possible (paras. 72–73 and 78).

The paragraph does not cover the situation of temporary transfer of a person who is serving a sentence imposed by the Court. The Rules of Procedure and Evidence, Rule 193, specify, that the paragraph shall not apply when it comes to the temporary transfer of a person who is serving a sentence imposed by the Court for the purpose of testifying or for other matters related to legal assistance. In such a case it would not be possible for the State to authorise the transfer to the Court.

Cross-references:

Rule 192.

Rule 193.

Author: Karin Påle-Bartes.

[733] Further paragraph (8) creates a possibility of confidentiality with respect to documents and information. If a state requires confidentiality the Prosecutor may use such documents or information only for the purpose of generating new evidence. The first trial before the Court, *Prosecutor v. Lubanga* (ICC-01/04-01/06) was nearly aborted entirely because documents were provided to the Prosecutor on this basis. However it is possible for the requested State to subsequently agree to disclosure of the documents and information that it has furnished on a confidential basis. These may then be submitted as evidence in the trial.'

Author: Karin Påle-Bartes.

tue of an international agreement, the requested States shall so inform the Court and the Court shall direct its request to the third State or international organization.[734]

10. (a) The Court may, upon request, cooperate with and provide assistance to a State Party conducting an investigation into or trial in respect of conduct which constitutes a crime within the jurisdiction of the Court or which constitutes a serious crime under the national law of the requesting State.

(b) (i) The assistance provided under subparagraph (a) shall include, *inter alia*:

    a. The transmission of statements, documents or other types of evidence obtained in the course of an investigation or a trial conducted by the Court; and

    b. The questioning of any person detained by order of the Court;

    (ii) In the case of assistance under subparagraph (b) (i) a:

    a. If the documents or other types of evidence have been obtained with the assistance of a State, such transmission shall require the consent of that State;

    b. If the statements, documents or other types of evidence have been provided by a witness or expert, such transmission shall be subject to the provisions of Article 68.

(c) The Court may, under the conditions set out in this paragraph, grant a request for assistance under this paragraph from a State which is not a Party to this Statute.[735]

---

[734] Paragraph (9) deals with a procedure in the case of competing requests. If both requests cannot be met satisfactorily, the issue is to be resolved in accordance with the principles set out in Article 90 of the Statute, which deals with competing requests for arrest and surrender.

Cross-references:

Article 90.

Author: Karin Påle-Bartes.

[735] Paragraph (10) makes some provisions for the Court to assist a State Party that is conducting an investigation or a trial with respect to conduct that constitutes a crime within the jurisdiction of the Court or "a serious crime under the national law of the requesting state". The provision makes it possible even for States not Parties to the Statute to seek assistance by the Court. Under such circumstances the Court has the complete discretion to comply with such a request or not. Paragraph (10) does not cover a request for assistance to the Court by international organisations as they do not normally have the power to conduct criminal investigations and proceedings. However Article 93 does not prohibit the Court from disclosing information to an international organisation. The compliance with such a request is at the discretion of the Court.

A request for cooperation has been rejected when there is or has not been an ongoing investigation with respect to either "conduct" constituting a crime set out in Article 5 of the Statute, or in relation to "a serious crime under the national law of the requesting State. This was the case in *Situation in Kenya*, Decision on the Request for Assistance Submitted on Behalf of the Government of the Republic of Kenya Pursuant to Article 93(10) of the Statute and Rule 194 of the Rules of Procedure and Evidence, 29 June 2011.

Cross-references:

Articles 88, 100.

Rule 194.

Regulation 108.

Doctrine:

1. Annalusa Ciampi, "Other Forms of Cooperation", in Antonio Cassese, Paola Gaeta and John R.W.D. Jones (eds.), *The Rome Statute of the International Criminal Court*, Oxford University Press, Oxford, 2002, pp. 1705–47.

2. Robert Cryer, Håkan Friman, Daryll Robinson and Elizabeth Wilmshurst, *An Introduction to International Criminal Law and Procedure*, 2nd ed., Cambridge University Press, Cambridge, 2010, pp. 509–30.

3. Frederik Harhoff and Phakiso Mochocko, "International Cooperation and Judicial Assistance", in Roy S. Lee (ed.), *The International Criminal Court. Elements of Crime and Rules of Procedure and Evidence*, 2001, pp. 637–70.

4. Claus Kreβ and Kimberly Prost, "Article 93 – Other Forms of Cooperation", in Otto Triffterer (ed.), *Commentary on the Rome Statute of the International Criminal Court: Observers' Notes, Article by Article*, 2nd ed., C.H. Beck/Hart/Nomos, Munich/Oxford/Baden-Baden, 2008, pp. 1569–88.

5. Mark Klamberg, *Evidence in International Criminal Trials*, Martinus Nijhoff Publishers, Leiden, 2013, pp. 235, 242, 244–46, 253, 257, 276 and 462.

6. Karel De Meester, Kelly Pitcher, Rod Rastan and Göran Sluiter, "Investigation, Coercive Measures, Arrest and Surrender", in Göran Sluiter, Håkan Friman, Suzannah Linton, Sergey Vasiliev and Salvatore Zappalà (eds.), *International Criminal Procedure: Principles and Rules*, Oxford University Press, Oxford, 2013, pp. 292–98.

7. Phakiso Mochocko, "International Cooperation and Judicial Assistance", in Roy S. Lee (ed.), *The International Criminal Court: the Making of the Rome Statute – Issues, Negotiations and Results*, Kluwer Law International, The Hague, 1999, pp. 305–17.

8. William A. Schabas, *The International Criminal Court: A Commentary on the Rome Statute*, Oxford University Press, Oxford, 2010, pp. 1015–25.

9. Göran Sluiter, *International Criminal Adjudication and the Collection of Evidence: Obligations of States*, Intersentia, Antwerpen, 2002.

Author: Karin Påle-Bartes.

Article 94

Postponement of execution of a request in respect of ongoing investigation or prosecution[736]

1. If the immediate execution of a request would interfere with an ongoing investigation or prosecution of a case different from that to which the request relates, the requested State may postpone the execution of the request for a period of time agreed upon with the Court. However, the postponement shall be no longer than is necessary to complete the relevant investigation or prosecution in the requested State. Before making a decision to postpone, the requested State should consider whether the assistance may be immediately provided subject to certain conditions.[737]

---

[736] *General remarks*:

Article 94 together with Articles 89(2), (4) and 95 allows a State to postpone execution of a request from the Court. While Articles 89(2) and 95 concern investigation or prosecution of the same matter, Articles 89(4) and 94 concern different conduct. The difference between Article 89(4) and 94 is that the first provision concerns requests for surrender while the later provision concerns requests for forms of cooperation other than surrender (Kreβ and Prost, p. 1589 and Schabas, p. 1026). In *Prosecutor v. Gaddafi*, ICC PT. Ch. I, Decision on Libya's Submissions Regarding the Arrest of Saif Al-Islam Gaddafi, 7 March 2012, para. 15, the Pre-Trial Chamber stated that Article 94(1) allows for postponement of a cooperation request when such a situation arises, but only for requests other than requests for surrender.

Preparatory work:

The ILC draft statute required in Article 51 that States should comply with requests from the Court "without undue delay" (Report of the International Law Commission, Forty-sixth session, 2 May 1994–22 July 1994, Official Records of the General Assembly, Forty-ninth session.)

The draft statute of the preparatory committee provided in Article 90(2) grounds for refusal option 2 that "[a] State Party may deny a request for assistance, in whole or in part, only if [...] Execution of the request would interfere with an ongoing investigation or prosecution in the requested State or in another State [or with a completed investigation or prosecution that might have led to an acquittal or conviction, except that a request may not be denied if the investigation or prosecution relates to the same matter which is the subject of the request and the Court has determined that the case is admissible under Article 15]; (Report of the Preparatory Committee on the Establishment of an International Criminal Court, United Nations Diplomatic Conference of Plenipotentiaries on the Establishment of an International Criminal Court Rome, Italy 15 June–17 July 1998, A/CONF.183/2).

The final solution whereby States could delay but not refuse a request, pending an investigation into other crimes emerged in the final weeks of the Diplomatic Conference in Rome (Schabas, p. 1027).

Author: Mark Klamberg.

[737] This provision allows the requested State to postpone, but not deny execution of request by the Court if the "request would interfere with an ongoing investigation or prosecution of a case different from that to which the request relates".

The term "agreed upon with the Courts" suggests that both partes should act reasonably (Kreβ and Prost, p. 1590).

Author: Mark Klamberg.

---

2. If a decision to postpone is taken pursuant to paragraph 1, the Prosecutor may, however, seek measures to preserve evidence, pursuant to Article 93, paragraph 1 (j).[738]

---

[738] Postponement of execution of the request may cause that evidence will be unavailable when the request is finally executed. For that purpose, the second paragraph provides that the Prosecutor may seek measures to preserve evidence. Although it is not explicitly stated, the provision implies that the requested State cannot postpone the execution of requests for such measures.

Cross-references:

Articles 89(2)(4) and 95.

Doctrine:

1. Claus Kreβ and Kimberly Prost, "Article 94 – Postponement of Execution of a Request in Respect of Ongoing Investigation or Prosecution", in Otto Triffterer (ed.), *Commentary on the Rome Statute of the International Criminal Court: Observers' Notes, Article by Article*, 2nd ed., C.H. Beck/Hart/Nomos, Munich/Oxford/Baden-Baden, 2008, pp. 1589–91.

2. William A. Schabas, *The International Criminal Court: A Commentary on the Rome Statute*, Oxford University Press, Oxford, 2010, pp. 1026–28.

Author: Mark Klamberg.

Article 95

Postponement of execution of a request in respect of an admissibility challenge

Where there is an admissibility challenge under consideration by the Court pursuant to Article 18 or 19, the requested State may postpone the execution of a request under this Part pending a determination by the Court, unless the Court has specifically ordered that the Prosecutor may pursue the collection of such evidence pursuant to Article 18 or 19.[739]

---

[739] *General remarks*:

Article 95 together with Articles 89(2), (4) and 94 allows a State to postpone execution of a request from the Court. While Articles 89(4) and 94 concern different conduct, Articles 89(2) and 95 concern investigation or prosecution of the same matter and the issue of jurisdiction or admissibility is pending. The difference between Article 89(2) and 95 is that the first provision concerns requests for surrender while the later provision also cover requests for other forms of cooperation than surrender (Kreß and Prost, p. 1589 an Schabas, pp. 1026 and 1031). In *Prosecutor v. Gaddafi*, ICC PT Ch. I, Decision on the Postponement of the Execution of the Request for Surrender of Saif Al-Islam Gaddafi pursuant to Article 95 of the Rome Statute, 1 June 2012, para. 18, the OPCD asserted that "[t]he reference in Article 95 to 'the collection of such evidence' qualifies the type of request, which may be postponed, to requests concerning evidentiary issues". The Pre-Trial Chamber ruled that "Article 95 encompasses all requests for cooperation under Part IX, including requests for arrest and surrender made before or after the admissibility challenge" (para. 32)

Preparatory works:

The draft statute of the preparatory committee provided in Article 90(2) grounds for refusal option 2 that "[a] State Party may deny a request for assistance, in whole or in part, only if [...] Execution of the request would interfere with an ongoing investigation or prosecution in the requested State or in another State [or with a completed investigation or prosecution that might have led to an acquittal or conviction, except that a request may not be denied if the investigation or prosecution relates to the same matter which is the subject of the request and the Court has determined that the case is admissible under Article 15]; (Report of the Preparatory Committee on the Establishment of an International Criminal Court, United Nations Diplomatic Conference of Plenipotentiaries on the Establishment of an International Criminal Court Rome, Italy 15 June–17 July 1998, A/CONF.183/2).

There was opposition by some states during the negotiations to this ground of refusal. However, all States recognised that it would be unreasonable to require compliance where the admissibility or jurisdiction were an issue and was not yet determined by the Court (Kreß and Prost, p. 1593).

Analysis:

The provision has several similarities with Article 94. However, unlike postponement based on an ongoing investigation or prosecution, Article 95 has no requirement that the requested State should reach an agreement with Court on the measure and its duration. Thus, if here is an admissibility challenge, the requested States may postpone compliance with a request for assistance. Schabas notes that Article 95 may be difficult to reconcile with Article 18(6) which allows the Prosecutor to "seek authority from the Pre-Trial Chamber to pursue necessary investigative steps for the purpose of preserving evidence where there is a unique opportunity to obtain important evidence or there is a significant risk that such evidence may not be subsequently available". If the State Party can postpone compliance under Article 95 why would it be required to allow "necessary investigative steps" under Article 18(6)?

In *Prosecutor v. Gaddafi*, ICC PT. Ch. I, Decision Regarding the Second Request by the Government of Libya for Postponement of the Surrender of Saif Al-Islam Gaddafi, 4 April 2012, para. 18, the Pre-Trial Chamber stated that "Article 95 of the Statute only applies when there is an admissibility challenge under consideration. Though Libya has announced that an admissibility challenge is forthcoming, there is currently no such challenge before the Chamber. Therefore, the Chamber holds that Article 95 of the Statute cannot serve as a legal basis for Libya's Second Postponement Request. Consequently, the Second Postponement Request presented by the Government of Libya must be rejected. At this time, the Chamber does not consider it necessary to determine whether Article 95 of the Statute applies to surrender requests". The Chamber reiterated its request that Libya make its decision to grant the Surrender Request and proceed immediately with the surrender of Mr Gaddafi to the Court.

Cross-references:

Articles 18(6), 89(2) and (4) and 94.

Doctrine:

1. Claus Kreβ and Kimberly Prost, "Article 95 – Postponement of Execution of a Request in Respect of an Admissibility Challenge", in Otto Triffterer (ed.), *Commentary on the Rome Statute of the International Criminal Court: Observers' Notes, Article by Article*, 2nd ed., C.H. Beck/Hart/Nomos, Munich/Oxford/Baden-Baden, 2008, pp. 1593–94.

2. William A. Schabas, *The International Criminal Court: A Commentary on the Rome Statute*, Oxford University Press, Oxford, 2010, pp. 1029–31.

Author: Mark Klamberg.

Article 96

Contents of request for other forms of assistance under article 93[740]

1. A request for other forms of assistance referred to in Article 93 shall be made in writing. In urgent cases, a request may be made by any medium capable of delivering a written record, provided that the request shall be confirmed through the channel provided for in Article 87, paragraph 1 (a).[741]

2. The request shall, as applicable, contain or be supported by the following:[742]

---

[740] *General remarks*:

Article 96 provides practical information relating to Article 93 which deals with "other forms of cooperation". It provides detailed instruction to the contents of requests, therefore is procedural in nature and content (Kreß and Prost, p. 1595). In this regard Article 96 is similar to Article 91 ("contents of request for arrest and surrender"), and they share certain common paragraphs (that is, the common paragraph 1 of both Articles, and the shared text of Article 91(4) and Article 96(3)).

Article 96 is derived from Article 90 ('other forms of cooperation') paragraph 8 of the Draft Statute for the International Criminal Court, which was presented in the 1998 Report of the Preparatory Committee on the Establishment of an International Criminal Court (A/CONF.183/2). Article 90 of the draft Statute was a comprehensive clause which later became Article 93 in the final ICC Statute. The final ICC Statute makes Article 90(8) a separate provision with some modification. For instance, the former sub-paragraph 90(8)(b) concerning the protection of victims, witnesses and their families is deleted in the final Article 96, replaced by the clause on State Parties' obligation to consult (para. 3) and the applicability of this provision to requests made to the Court (para. 4).

Author: ZHANG Yueyao.

[741] Paragraph 1 corresponds to Article 91(1) dealing with contents of request for arrest and surrender. Pursuant to this paragraph, the request should be in writing in principle. Only in urgent cases may the request be transmitted by other medium capable of delivering a written record. In doing so, State Parties bear the obligation to ensure that the request should be confirmed "through the diplomatic channel or any other appropriate channel as may be designated by each State Party upon ratification, acceptance, approval or accession" as prescribed in Article 87(1)(a) (Kreß and Prost, p. 1596).

It should be noted that, the prescription on channels in Article 87(1)(a) deals with requests issued by the Court. Therefore a request submitted by a State Party or a non-State Party to the Court pursuant to Article 93(10) of the Statute does not requires such confirmation.

Author: ZHANG Yueyao.

[742] The list in paragraph 2 has fully adopted the list of Article 90(8)(a)(ii) in the ICC Preparatory Committee Draft Statute, with minor changes. For example, the final Article 96(2) reads as "contain or be supported by the following" instead of "contain the following" in the Draft Article 90. The change of terms here, together with the inclusion of para. 3 to this provision, reflects that the Court is aware of its incapacity to cover all information needed, therefore sets less strict obligation to the Court and the obligation to provide additional information is left to the requested State.

The contents of the list is also inspired by Article 5 of UN Model Treaties on Extradition and Mutual Assistance in Criminal Matters UN doc. A/RES/45/117 (annex), whose contents are all covered by the list of Article 96. The difference is that in the Model Treaty, the inclusion of the listed contents is obligatory (Eighth United Nations Congress on the Prevention of Crime

(a) A concise statement of the purpose of the request and the assistance sought, including the legal basis and the grounds for the request;[743]

(b) As much detailed information as possible about the location or identification of any person or place that must be found or identified in order for the assistance sought to be provided;

(c) A concise statement of the essential facts underlying the request;[744]

(d) The reasons for and details of any procedure or requirement to be followed;[745]

(e) Such information as may be required under the law of the requested State in order to execute the request;[746] and

(f) Any other information relevant in order for the assistance sought to be provided.[747]

3. Upon the request of the Court, a State Party shall consult with the Court, either generally or with respect to a specific matter, regarding any requirements under its national law that

---

and the Treatment of Offenders, UN Doc. A/CONF. 144/28/Rev.1, p. 80), whereas in Article 96 the obligation is less strict because of the proviso "as applicable", and "or be supported by".

Author: ZHANG Yueyao.

[743] The request should state the object of the request and describe what assistance is requested in Article 93(1). The request should also include the text of relevant laws and the reasons for requiring them (see UN Model Treaty on Extradition and Mutual Assistance in Criminal Matter, Article 5, para. 1 (c) and (e)).

Author: ZHANG Yueyao.

[744] Sub-paragraph (b) and (c) are important for efficient execution of the request. Statement of essential facts underlying the request would help the requested States decide what measures to adopt in domestic legal sphere. When deciding whether the detailed information provided in sub-paragraph (b) should be included in the request, the Court and the State Party making the request are subject to the general requirement "as applicable".

Author: ZHANG Yueyao.

[745] If the court requests certain measures to be taken or procedures to be adopted, it shall provide a reason for demanding such measures and procedures, and specify in detail. The provision does not specify what details should be provided, but reference to Article 5 of the Model Treaty reflects that such details may include a statement as to whether sworn or affirmed evidence or statements are required (Model Treaty on Mutual Assistance in Criminal Matters, UN doc. A/RES/45/117, annex, Article 5), and time-limit within which compliance with the request is desired (*ibid.*).

Author: ZHANG Yueyao.

[746] The law of the requested State may have certain procedural or evidentiary requirements on the execution of the request. Un such cases the Court the required information in the request. A similar clause is Article 91(2)(c) on the request for arrest and surrender, except that Article 91(2)(c) requires that the domestic requirements of the requested States should not be more burdensome than relevant applicable requirements in existing treaties. The "less burdensome" requirement in Article 91(2)(c) intends to reduce the obligation imposed on the Court, which could better serve the overall aim of Part 9 as to facilitate the execution of the request and cooperation. This sub-paragraph, together with sub-paragraph (f), serves as transitional clauses to paragraph 3.

[747] Sub-paragraph (f) work as compromise clauses, in case that additional information is needed to execute a request. It is also a transitional clause to paragraph 3, once such information is required, State Parties shall consult with the Court on domestic requirements.

Author: ZHANG Yueyao.

may apply under paragraph 2 (e). During the consultations, the State Party shall advise the Court of the specific requirements of its national law.[748]

4. The provisions of this article shall, where applicable, also apply in respect of a request for assistance made to the Court.[749]

---

[748] Paragraph 3 parallels Article 91(4), obliging State Parties to advise the Court of the requirements of its national law, on the condition that the Court so requests. The intention is to reduce the burden of the Court in preparation of the materials required in support of the request. When the Court requests certain information under paragraph 2(e), State Parties have the obligation to respond and advice the Court on such information. Upon receiving requests from the Court, State Parties can either advice generally to provide an overview of their domestic law requirements, or specifically over a specific matter.

Author: ZHANG Yueyao.

[749] Pursuant to paragraph 4, the provisions of this Article shall in principle apply in requests to the Court under Article 93(10). At the same time, the proviso "where applicable "sets limitation to the applicability. For instance, paragraph 3 is not applicable given the clear prescription of obligator being State Parties.

Cross-references:

Rule 194.

Doctrine:

1. Claus Kreβ and Kimberly Prost, "Article 96 – Contents of Request for Other Forms of Assistance Under Article 93", in Otto Triffterer (ed.), *Commentary on the Rome Statute of the International Criminal Court: Observers' Notes, Article by Article*, 2nd ed., C.H. Beck/Hart/Nomos, Munich/Oxford/Baden-Baden, 2008, pp. 1595–98.

2. Gabrielle Kirk McDonald, "Trial Procedures and Practices", in Gabrielle Kirk McDonald and Olivia Swaak-Goldman (eds.), *Substantive and Procedural Aspects of International Criminal Law*, Kluwer Law International, The Hague, 2000, pp. 551–620.

Author: ZHANG Yueyao.

Article 97
Consultations[750]

Where a State Party receives a request under this Part in relation to which it identifies problems which may impede or prevent the execution of the request, that State shall consult with the Court without delay in order to resolve the matter. Such problems may include, *inter alia:*[751]

(a) Insufficient information to execute the request;[752]

(b) In the case of a request for surrender, the fact that despite best efforts, the person sought cannot be located or that the investigation conducted has determined that the person in the requested State is clearly not the person named in the warrant;[753] or

(c) The fact that execution of the request in its current form would require the requested State to breach a pre-existing treaty obligation undertaken with respect to another State.[754]

---

[750] *General remarks:*

Article 97 is a clause which may be used to resolve problems that may arise in relation to requests for cooperation under Part 9. This Article intends to serve the overall purpose of Part 9 of the ICC Statute: to facilitate the execution of the request and promote cooperation. It recognises that in practice requests sent to State Parties may still be insufficient in content or not executable. State Parties have the obligation to consult with the Court 'without delay' if execution problems arise. This Article only applies to the requests issued by the Court to State Parties. Requests of assistance issued to the Court under Article 93(10) are not eligible for such consultation.

Author: ZHANG Yueyao.

[751] The intention of this Article is to promptly resolve the problems of the requests to an executable condition, and ensure good faith cooperation between State Parties and the Court. Article 93(5) reflects similar arrangement: it obliges the requested State Party to look for alternative measures to provide assistance before denying a request, provided that the Court or the Prosecutor accepts the alternative measure. State Parties and the Court would therefore negotiate over the measures to be taken and potential modifications to the request. In this way a consultation-like mechanism between the State Party and the Court is established in actuality, although without explicit terms. Article 97 is thus also applicable to the circumstances under Article 93(4) and (5).

Paragraphs (a)–(c) provides examples of problems relating to the execution of a request from the Court.

Author: ZHANG Yueyao.

[752] A State Party shall promptly consult with the Court if there is lack of information. The standard to determine such lack of information is set in the general requirement of Articles 87, the lists of Articles 91 and 96(2).

[753] When the requested State Party finds that pursuant to the request, despite best efforts, the person sought cannot be located or is not the person named in the warrant, it is necessary that both sides should promptly confirm the information of the request and determine if additional information could be provided, or corrections should be made. It is important particularly for the person mistakenly arrested or detained under the request for surrender.

[754] When the requested State identifies that execution of the request conflicts with its obligation under a pre-existing treaty, the State Party is obliged to consult with the Court for a resolution between the competing obligations.

Paragraph (c) is derived from Article 87 paragraph 3 (e) in the Draft Statute, stating that "if compliance with the request would put the requested state in breach of an existing obligation arising from [a peremptory norm of] general international law [treaty] obligation undertaken to another State", the circumstance constitutes one of the grounds for State Parties to deny a request for surrender, transfer or extradition (UN Doc. A/CONF. 183/2/Add.1, p. 68). Article 90(2)(f) in the Draft Statute also provides that if "compliance with the request would put it in breach of an existing [international law treaty] obligation undertaken to another state [non-State Party], there is a possible ground to deny a request for assistance (UN Doc. A/CONF. 183/2/Add.1, p. 73). The final ICC Statute has not kept this term and the scope of grounds of denial is limited to national security only, and in order to reinforce the obligation of State Parties to comply with the Court's request. It takes a cooperative approach to resolve the potential problems regarding competing obligations of State Parties. There is no indication as to the consequences if the requested State and the Court fail to reach a resolution, but in actuality this clause has not confronted much criticism (Kreß and Prost, p. 1599).

Doctrine:

1. Claus Kreß and Kimberly Prost, "Article 97 – Consultations", in Otto Triffterer (ed.), *Commentary on the Rome Statute of the International Criminal Court: Observers' Notes, Article by Article*, 2nd ed., C.H. Beck/Hart/Nomos, Munich/Oxford/Baden-Baden, 2008, pp. 1599–1600.

2. Roy S. Lee, "Creating an International Criminal Court: Of Procedures and Compromises", in Herman A.M. von Hebel, Johan G. Lammers and Jolien Shukking (eds.), *Reflections on the International Criminal Court*, TMC Asser Press, The Hague, 1999, pp. 141–52.

Author: ZHANG Yueyao.

Article 98

Cooperation with respect to waiver of immunity and consent to surrender[755]

1. The Court may not proceed with a request for surrender or assistance which would require the requested State to act inconsistently with its obligations under international law[756] with respect to the State or diplomatic immunity of a person or property of a third State,[757] un-

---

[755] *General remarks*:

Article 98 is placed in part 9 of the ICC Statute, which deals with international cooperation and judicial assistance. The Article represents an effort to solve conflicts that may arise between international criminal justice and the international obligations of the state parties of the ICC.

Article 98 was not among the Articles given most attention during the drafting process of the ICC Statute, but is has proven to be one of the more controversial Articles of the Statute [Schabas, 2010, p. 1038). Situations may arise where an international obligation of a state party is in conflict with the obligation to cooperate with the ICC and Article 98 provides the states parties with a possibility to rank its international obligations higher than its obligations to cooperate with the ICC. Whether a conflict between a request for cooperation from the ICC and an international obligation of the requested state is at hand or not is however ultimately determined by the Court and not the concerned state itself on a case-to-case basis [Kreß and Prost, in Triffterer, 2008, p. 1603). If a conflict of obligations is at hand the Court has a responsibility to try to achieve cooperation with the third state (sub-paragraph 1) or the sending state (sub-paragraph 2).

Article 98 also influences the effects following Article 27. Immunities enjoyed by a state official shall not, according to Article 27, bar the ICC from exercising jurisdiction over that state official. The application of Article 98 may however result in the opposite effect and may under certain circumstances in fact bar the ICC from exercising jurisdiction over a state official (Triffterer, 2008, p. 792).

Author: Camilla Lind.

[756] Article 98(1) is applicable in the situation where a state party of the ICC would have to act inconsistently with its obligations under international law concerning state or diplomatic immunity of a person or property of a third state. The application of the Article requires two definitions to be made. Firstly, "obligations under international law" means that the Article covers international immunities that exist by virtue of customary international law, treaty or general principles of law. Consequently the Article covers both immunity *ratione materiae* and immunity *ratione personae*. Immunities that exist by virtue of international agreements are however not covered by Article 98(1) but rather by Article 98(2) (Schabas, 2010, p. 1040–1041). Secondly, the term "third state" must be defined in order to determine the scope of application of Article 98(1).

Author: Camilla Lind.

[757] Article 98(1) uses another wording than Article 98(2) when it refers to "third state" rather than "sending state" as in the second sub-paragraph. To fully understand the scope of Article 98(1) the meaning of the term "third state" must be discussed. According to Article 2(1)(h) of the Vienna Convention on the Law of the Treaties "third state" is a state that is not party to the treaty at hand. However the drafters of a treaty are free to give the term "third state" another meaning. The meaning of "third state" in Article 98(1) should, according to the literature, be interpreted as meaning "state other than the requested state" since it would otherwise give rise to consequences that were not intended by the drafters (see Kreß and Prost, 2008, p. 1606 and Schabas, 2010, p. 1039).

Relationship with Article 27(2)

The third state could be both a state party to the ICC and a non-state party. This gives rise to two different situations that must be kept apart. When a third state is a state party Article 27(2) is applicable and in line with that Article the state parties of the ICC Statute has waived the immunity accorded to their state officials by international law (see the commentary to Article 27(2) ICC Statute above). Kreß and Prost argues that when the requested state and the third state are a state parties of the ICC a conflict covered by Article 98(1) cannot exist (see Kreß and Prost, 2008, p. 1607). Schabas accedes to this view (see Schabas, p. 1404). Even if the arguments put forward by Kreß and Prost and Schabas would not be accepted and a state party would be of the view that a request from the ICC would be in conflict with its international obligations the Court could obtain a waiver of immunity from the third state based on that state's consent to Article 27.

In a situation when the third state is not a state party to the ICC Statute conflicting obligations may arise. Article 98(1) is applicable in those situations. Whether there is a conflict with the international obligations of the requested state and the request from the Court will be determined on the basis of customary international law (Kreß and Prost, 2008, p. 1608). Customary international law distinguishes between immunity *ratione materiae* and immunity *ratione personae* where the first attaches to state officials performing state actions and the second attaches to the office of certain high ranking state officials (namely the head of state, head of government and the foreign minister of a state). It is now rather well established that immunity *ratione materiae* cannot shield a person from responsibility for international crimes (see the commentary to Article 27(2) above). The status of immunity *ratione personae* is however not altogether clear. What can be said is that it is quite certain that immunity *ratione personae* shields incumbent high ranking state officials from proceedings concerning responsibility for international crimes in the domestic courts of other states. However, a development can be seen with regard to proceedings before international courts. It is argued, for example by the Pre-Trial Chamber I of the ICC (see the decisions in *Prosecutor v. Omar Al Bashir*, ICC PT. Ch., Decision on the Prosecution's Application for a Warrant of Arrest against Omar Hassan Ahmad Al Bashir, ICC-02/05-01/09-3, 4 March 2009 and *Prosecutor v. Omar Al Bashir*, ICC PT. Ch., Decision Pursuant to Article 87(7) of the ICC Statute on the Failure by the Republic of Malawi to Comply with the Cooperation Requests Issued by the Court with Respect to the Arrest and Surrender of Omar Hassan Ahmad Al Bashir, ICC-02/05-01/09-139, 12 December 2011) that immunity *ratione personae* does not apply with regard to criminal proceedings before international courts. Consequently, the ICC would then have jurisdiction over incumbent high ranking state officials that are nationals of a non-state party that has not voluntarily waived the immunity of its state officials.

The distinction between national and international proceedings is not important only with regard to the jurisdiction of the ICC. It is also important with regard to the ability of state parties to fulfil a request for cooperation from the ICC without breaking its international obligations. Whether that is possible or not depends on the state party should be seen as using its own, domestic jurisdiction or if it should be considered as using the jurisdiction of the ICC when carrying out a request for cooperation. According to a decision by the Pre-Trial Chamber (see below), a state party should be considered to be an extension of the Court and thereby using the jurisdiction of the ICC instead of its own, domestic jurisdiction. This enables state parties to carry out requests for cooperation where the subject of the request is the national of a non-party state without breaking its international obligations.

Pre-Trial Chamber Decision of 12 December 2011

In a decision of 2009 the Pre-Trial Chamber I reached the conclusion that the incumbent president of Sudan, Omar Al Bashir, did not enjoy immunity from proceedings before the Court (see *Prosecutor v. Omar Al Bashir*, ICC PT. Ch., Decision on the Prosecution's Application for a Warrant of Arrest against Omar Hassan Ahmad Al Bashir, ICC-02/05-01/09-3, 4 March 2009

less the Court can first obtain the cooperation of that third State for the waiver of the immunity.

2. The Court may not proceed with a request for surrender which would require the requested State to act inconsistently with its obligations under international agreements pursuant to which the consent of a sending State is required to surrender a person of that State to the Court, unless the Court can first obtain the cooperation of the sending State for the giving of consent for the surrender.[758]

and the commentary to Article 27(2) above). In a complementing decision of 12 December 2011 (*Prosecutor v. Omar Al Bashir*, ICC PT. Ch., Decision Pursuant to Article 87(7) of the Rome Statute on the Failure by the Republic of Malawi to Comply with the Cooperation Requests Issued by the Court with Respect to the Arrest and Surrender of Omar Hassan Ahmad Al Bashir, ICC-02/05-01/09-139, 12 December 2011) a different composed Pre-Trial Chamber I concluded that a state party of the ICC must cooperate with respect to the arrest and surrender of president Al Bashir (who at the time of the decision was, and in June 2016 still is, the incumbent president of Sudan) and that Article 98(1) was not applicable to the present situation (para. 43). In that specific situation the state of Malawi had refused to cooperate with the ICC with respect to the arrest and surrender of president Al Bashir with by stating that such cooperation would be in breach with its international obligations. The Pre-Trial Chamber reached its conclusion by arguing that a state party to the ICC is an instrument of the *jus puniendi* of the Court (para. 46). In other words, the Court argued that a state party that receives a request for cooperation does not use its own domestic jurisdiction when enforcing that request but rather the international jurisdiction of the ICC. Consequently if one agrees with the view that incumbent high ranking state officials does not enjoy immunity *ratione personae* with regard to international proceedings regarding international crimes (a conclusion that also was reached by the Pre-Trial Chamber in the decision, see para. 36) there is no conflict of obligations as described in Article 98(1) at hand. This is clearly the view of the ICC and Kreß is also of this opinion as he argues that the requested state acts on behalf of the ICC (Kreß, 2012, p. 257).

The Pre-Trial Chamber also argued in its decision that a state party that denies the arrest and surrender of a incumbent high ranking state official because of immunity reasons is acting contrary to the purpose of the ICC Statute. State parties have accepted the ICC Statute by ratifying it and should, in the view of the Pre-Trial Chamber, not act contrary to it (para. 41).

Author: Camilla Lind.

[758] Article 98(2) applies to both bilateral and multilateral agreements between states, and some argue that Article 98(2) especially has so called status of forces agreements in mind. Status of forces agreements are agreements of rights and responsibilities of states when one state stations forces in the territory of another state. It was agreed during the drafting process of the ICC Statute that such agreements may create a kind of immunity (Schabas, 2010, pp. 1042–1043).

In order for Article 98(2) to be applicable, in other words in order for a conflict between the request from the ICC and the obligations of the state to arise, the state must be part of the agreement that creates the obligations that would be in conflict with the request for cooperation from the ICC (Kreß and Prost in Triffterer, 2008, p. 1614). Kreß and Prost also argues that Article 98(2) only applies to agreements that already existed when the receiving state ratified the ICC Statute (Kreß and Prost in Triffterer, 2008, pp. 1616–1618).

Cross-references:

Article 27.

Rule 195.

Doctrine:

1. Claus Kreß, "The International Criminal Court and Immunities under International Law for States Not Party to the Court's Statute", in Morten Bergsmo and LING Yan (eds.), *State Sovereignty and International Criminal Law*, FICHL Publication Series No. 15, Torkel Opsahl Academic EPublisher, Beijing, 2012, pp. 223–65.

2. Claus Kreß and Kimberly Prost, "Article 98 – Cooperation with Respect to Waiver of Immunity and Consent to Surrender", in Otto Triffterer (ed.), *Commentary on the Rome Statute of the International Criminal Court: Observers' Notes, Article by Article*, 2nd ed., C.H. Beck/Hart/Nomos, Munich/Oxford/Baden-Baden, 2008, pp. 1601–19.

3. William A. Schabas, *The International Criminal Court: A Commentary on the Rome Statute*, Oxford University Press, Oxford, 2010, pp. 1037–46.

4. Otto Triffterer, "Article 27 – Irrelevance of Official Capacity", in Otto Triffterer (ed.), *Commentary on the Rome Statute of the International Criminal Court: Observers' Notes, Article by Article*, 2nd ed., C.H. Beck/Hart/Nomos, Munich/Oxford/Baden-Baden, 2008, pp. 779–93.

Author: Camilla Lind.

Article 99

Execution of requests under articles 93 and 96[759]

1. Requests for assistance shall be executed in accordance with the relevant procedure under the law of the requested State and, unless prohibited by such law, in the manner specified in the request, including following any procedure outlined therein or permitting persons specified in the request to be present at and assist in the execution process.[760]

---

[759] *General remarks*:

Article 99 regulates the execution of requests under Articles 93 and 96, that is, requests for co-operation other than arrest and surrender. This provision reflects an attempt to strike a balance between the need of efficient and effective investigation, and States' concerns in relation to sovereignty. It reflects and follows, to a large extent, the basic principles of mutual legal assistance between States. On the other hand, it also largely deviates from the inter-State legal assistance regime by providing for the possibility of direct execution by the Prosecutor. Thus, two different situations of execution are provided for in Article 99. One is the execution by national authorities according to the national law of the requested State, which is the traditional manner for execution of a cooperation request between States. The other is the direct execution of the Prosecutor under certain circumstances.

Author: ZHANG Binxin.

[760] This provision deals with the law governing the execution of requests under Articles 93 and 96. The basic principle it sets out is that such execution should be governed by the law of the requested State. The provision stipulates, at the same time, that the Court may specify some particular manner of execution. In such case, the manner specified by the Court shall be followed, unless it is prohibited by the law of the requested State. This formula follows the general principle and common practice of mutual legal assistance between States (UN Model Treaty on Mutual Assistance in Criminal Matters, Article 6; European Convention on Mutual Assistance in Criminal Matters, Article 3).

While specifying that the execution shall be in accordance with the law of the requested State, the provision does not make clear which is the organ that shall actually carry out the execution activities. In so far as it follows the common practice in mutual legal assistance, it should normally be the national authorities of the requested State that execute the request. The situations where the Prosecutor may execute a request directly are governed by Article 99(4), or, when the Court has not secured cooperation from the State, in accordance with Article 57(3)(d).

Although the execution is to be governed by the national law of the requested State, the Court can specify the manner of execution in the request, and this shall be followed, "unless prohibited" by the national law. The provision gives one example of the manner of execution that could possibly be specified in the request, namely, "permitting persons specified in the request to be present at and assist in the execution process". This and similar manner of execution could be important to guarantee the admissibility of evidence before the Court in later stage of the proceedings. According to Article 69(7), evidence obtained by means of a violation of the Statute or internationally recognised human rights may not be admissible. Therefore, in the situation where the national law of the requested State does not accord with international human rights standards or the standards set out in the Statute, it would be very important for the request to be executed in the manner specified by the Court in the request.

The requirement of the request being executed in the manner specified therein is qualified by the wording of "unless prohibited" by the national law. The problem thus arises only when there is a prohibition in the national law. Mere absence of relevant procedure in the national law cannot be a ground for refusing cooperation requests. This interpretation is further supported by

2. In the case of an urgent request, the documents or evidence produced in response shall, at the request of the Court, be sent urgently.[761]

3. Replies from the requested State shall be transmitted in their original language and form.[762]

4. Without prejudice to other articles in this Part, where it is necessary for the successful execution of a request which can be executed without any compulsory measures, including specifically the interview of or taking evidence from a person on a voluntary basis, including doing so without the presence of the authorities of the requested State Party if it is essential for the request to be executed, and the examination without modification of a public site or other public place, the Prosecutor may execute such request directly on the territory of a State as follows:[763]

Article 88, which requires that States Parties shall ensure that they have procedures in their national law "for all of the forms of cooperation". Even if the specified manner were indeed "prohibited" by the national law, this would not necessarily grant the requested State a right to an outright refusal of execution.

According to Article 96(3), the requested State has an obligation to consult with the Court "regarding any requirements under its national law that may apply" in order to execute a request for assistance. Furthermore, Article 97 lays down a general obligation of consultations on the part of the State Party if "it identifies problems which may impede or prevent the execution of the request" (Ciampi, 2002, 1732).

Author: ZHANG Binxin.

[761] According to this provision, in the case of an urgent request, the requested State "shall" send documents or evidence urgently. No room for discretion is left to the State in this regard.

Author: ZHANG Binxin.

[762] This provision requires that the replies have to be transmitted in their original language and form. There is no need to translate them into the official working languages of the Court.

Author: ZHANG Binxin.

[763] This provision deals with the situation where the Prosecutor may execute a request under Article 93 directly on the territory of a State, and in certain circumstances, even without the presence of the national authorities. This is clearly an exceptional manner of execution, which is qualified by strict conditions. The chapeau of paragraph 4 sets out two conditions for such direct execution by the Prosecutor.

First, it must be "necessary" for the successful execution of a request. The provision does not specify how to interpret "necessary" or who can make the determination. In any case, this requirement sets out an objective condition that has to be met before the Prosecutor can execute the request directly. Such direct execution must be required by the situation of the particular case, but not subject solely to the wish of the Prosecutor.

The second condition limits the manner of direct execution. The power of the Prosecutor to execute a request directly is only limited to non-compulsory measures. Compulsory measures, such as search and seizure or the exhumation of a grave site, are not covered by this provision. Traditionally, compulsory measures can only be conducted by national authorities, but the provision does not preclude the possibility that the State authorises the Prosecutor to conduct compulsory measures directly.

The provision gives two examples of such non-compulsory measures. One is the voluntary interview or taking evidence from a person, the other is the examination of a public site. The interview and examination of a person can further be executed without the presence of the national authorities "if it is essential for the request to be executed". There are various scenarios when

(a) When the State Party requested is a State on the territory of which the crime is alleged to have been committed, and there has been a determination of admissibility pursuant to Article 18 or 19, the Prosecutor may directly execute such request following all possible consultations with the requested State Party;[764]

(b) In other cases, the Prosecutor may execute such request following consultations with the requested State Party and subject to any reasonable conditions or concerns raised by that State Party. Where the requested State Party identifies problems with the execution of a request pursuant to this subparagraph it shall, without delay, consult with the Court to resolve the matter.[765]

---

direct action by the Prosecutor and the non-presence of the national authorities become "essential". The witnesses may be intimidated by the presence of the national authorities. The national authority might seek to unduly influence the testimony of the witnesses (*Kenyatta*, ICC OTP, ICC-01/09-02/11, 10 May 2013, para. 15). This provision thus guarantees that the Prosecutor has the means to effectively collect evidence that would meet the requirement of the evidential rules of the Court. The examination of a public site or other public place is subject to the condition that such examination would not involve any modification of the site.

Author: ZHANG Binxin.

[764] The two sub-paragraphs stipulate two different situations where the Prosecutor may act directly. Sub-paragraph (a) deals with the situation of non-cooperative State Party on the territory of which the crime is alleged to have been committed, when the case has already been determined as admissible. Under such circumstance, the Prosecutor may directly execute the Court's request after "*all possible* consultations" (emphasis added) with the requested State. Sub-paragraph (b), on the other hand, stipulates that the Prosecutor may execute such request "following consultations" with the State. Thus, under sub-paragraph (a) the Prosecutor is only obliged to consult with the State Party when "possible". It might happen when consultations are not possible and do not take place at all, considering that this sub-paragraph deals with situations concerning uncooperative requested State (Ciampi, 2002, 1738). Yet under such circumstances, the need for the Prosecutor to act directly, for example to interview witnesses without the presence of national authorities, may be all the more important.

Regulation 108(2) of the Regulations of the Court stipulates that the requested State may apply for a ruling concerning the legality of the request in case of a request under Article 99(4) "within 15 days from the day on which the requested State is informed of or became aware of the direct execution". Thus, the requested State can invoke the right to challenge the legality of the request not after the consultations fail, but after the direct execution. This further confirms that the Prosecutor may proceed to direct execution under Article 99(4) when it deems that "all possible consultations" have been exhausted. On the other hand, the requested State is given a chance to challenge such decision before a competent Chamber after the direct execution takes place.

Author: ZHANG Binxin.

[765] This sub-paragraph deals with cases other than that referred to in sub-paragraph (a), that is, when the requested State is not the territorial State where the crime alleged was committed. This may happen when, for example, some witnesses have left the country where the crime was allegedly committed. It is not unusual that the Prosecutor's investigative activities take place in several countries, including countries other than the territorial State. Depending on the particular stage and situation, the Prosecutor might conduct investigations outside of the territorial State for the purpose of protecting victims and witnesses (Ocampo, Statement to the UN Security Council on Libya, para. 3; Fourth Report of the Prosecutor to the UN Security Council Pursuant to UNSCR 1593, p. 3).

5. Provisions allowing a person heard or examined by the Court under Article 72 to invoke restrictions designed to prevent disclosure of confidential information connected with national security shall also apply to the execution of requests for assistance under this article.[766]

In such cases, unlike under sub-paragraph (a), the Prosecutor has an obligation to consult with the requested State. The request can only be executed directly "following consultations". Furthermore, here the Prosecutor's power to execute the request directly is subject to a further objective standard of "any reasonable conditions or concerns" of the requested State. Thus, while in the situation of sub-paragraph (a) the Prosecutor could proceed after "possible" consultations, here there is an objective standard of "reasonable" conditions and concerns to be met. The provision does not specify who is to make the decision as to whether the conditions or concerns raised by the State Party are reasonable. It seems that the Prosecutor, being the organ that consults with the State and the one most familiar with the situation, would make the decision. Thus, the provision seems to grant the Prosecutor the power to proceed when it deems the conditions or concerns raised by the requested State unreasonable.

Once the Prosecutor executes the request directly, sub-paragraph (b) further provides that the requested State Party "*shall*, without delay, consult with the Court" (emphasis added). The word "shall" suggests that this is a requirement rather than a right on the State's part. Thus, should any problems arise with regard to the direct execution, the State has an obligation to further consult with *the Court*, with the purpose of solving the matter. The provision does not specify which organ of the Court the State shall consult with. It might well be still the Prosecutor, when, for example, the State has agreed with the execution but later identifies problems during the execution process.

Should such consultations fail and no further consultations be possible, it would meet the requirement of exhaustion of consultations under Regulation 108(2) of the Regulations of the Court. In that case, the requested State would be able to seek a ruling concerning the legality of the direct execution before the competent Chamber after it became aware of such execution.

Author: ZHANG Binxin.

[766] This provision is to reaffirm that measures and procedures designed to protect national security information under Article 72 also apply to the execution of requests under Article 99. As Article 99 says nothing about national security information, and Article 72 applies "in any case" where the State considers the disclosure of such information at issue, Article 72 would apply to the execution of requests even without this provision. It is nevertheless included in Article 99 and leaves no ambiguity on the matter, which might have been considered necessary due to the utter importance and sensitivity of this issue. Thus, when concerns or objections concerning national security information are raised, relevant provisions in Article 72 will govern the matter. This applies to the execution by national authorities as well as direct execution by the Prosecutor. In the latter case, national security concerns might well be raised during the consultations or as "reasonable conditions and concerns" under sub-paragraph 4 by the requested State.

Doctrine:

1. Annalusa Ciampi, "Other Forms of Cooperation", in Antonio Cassese, Paola Gaeta and John R.W.D. Jones (eds.), *The Rome Statute of the International Criminal Court*, Oxford University Press, Oxford, 2002, pp. 1732, 1738.

2. Claus Kreß and Kimberly Prost, "Article 99", in Otto Triffterer (ed.), *Commentary on the Rome Statute of the International Criminal Court: Observers' Notes, Article by Article*, 2nd ed., C.H. Beck/Hart/Nomos, Munich/Oxford/Baden-Baden, 2008, p. 1621–29.

3. Rod Rastan, "Testing Co-operation: The International Criminal Court and National Authorities", in *Leiden Journal of International Law*, 2008, vol. 21, no. 2, pp. 431–56.

4. Alex Whiting, "Dynamic Investigative Practice at the International Criminal Court", in *Law and Contemporary Problems*, 2013, vol. 76, p. 163.

Author: ZHANG Binxin.

Article 100

Costs[767]

1. The ordinary costs for execution of requests in the territory of the requested State shall be borne by that State, except for the following, which shall be borne by the Court:[768]

   (a) Costs associated with the travel and security of witnesses and experts or the transfer under Article 93 of persons in custody;[769]

   (b) Costs of translation, interpretation and transcription;[770]

   (c) Travel and subsistence costs of the judges, the Prosecutor, the Deputy Prosecutors, the Registrar, the Deputy Registrar and staff of any organ of the Court;[771]

   (d) Costs of any expert opinion or report requested by the Court;

---

[767] *General remarks*:

Article 100 deals with the costs of executing a request. It divides the responsibility to bear the relevant costs in line with the traditional principles of mutual legal cooperation and assistance between States (UN Model Treaty on Mutual Assistance in Criminal Matters, Article 20). Thus, generally the costs involved in the requested actions are borne by the requesting party, while ordinary functioning costs are borne by the requested State, the national authorities of which would execute the requests.

Author: ZHANG Binxin.

[768] In the situation of a request for cooperation from the Court, paragraph one stipulates that the "ordinary costs" for the execution of such a request shall be borne by the State on whose territory the execution takes place. It then lists the costs that do not belong to "ordinary costs" and should be borne by the Court. This is an exhaustive list, including five categories of clearly specified costs, and one catch-all clause which covers all other "extraordinary costs".

Author: ZHANG Binxin.

[769] The first category of costs listed is that associated with the travel and security of witnesses and experts or the transfer of persons. If the meeting and interview of witnesses and experts involve the travel of these persons, such costs shall be borne by the requesting party, here the Court. When security measures are needed to protect the witnesses, this would also be an extra burden to the requested State, outside of the "ordinary costs" of the functioning of relevant national authorities, and thus should be borne by the Court. The transfer of persons here refers to that under Article 93, not the surrender of a person, which is governed by sub-paragraph (e), according to which the costs for the transport of persons being surrendered to the Court should also be borne by the Court itself.

Author: ZHANG Binxin.

[770] Costs of translation, interpretation and transcription are to be borne by the Court. As made clear by Article 99, replies to the requests from the Court shall be transmitted in their original language. There is no requirement for translation on the part of the requested State. If the Court needs translation or interpretation, when interviewing witnesses, for example, such costs shall be borne by the Court.

Author: ZHANG Binxin.

[771] The Court shall, without doubt, bear the costs for the travel and subsistence costs of judges, the Prosecutor, the Registrar and other staff of the Court. When the Court seeks the opinion from an expert through a request, the costs thus involved shall also be borne by the Court.

Author: ZHANG Binxin.

(e) Costs associated with the transport of a person being surrendered to the Court by a custodial State; and

(f) Following consultations, any extraordinary costs that may result from the execution of a request.[772]

2. The provisions of paragraph 1 shall, as appropriate, apply to requests from States Parties to the Court. In that case, the Court shall bear the ordinary costs of execution.[773]

---

[772] Lastly, paragraph 1 contains a catch-all clause, which stipulates that "any extraordinary costs that may result from the execution" shall be borne by the Court. This is to include "extraordinary costs" that are not covered by the above-mentioned specifically listed categories. This clause guarantees that as long as the costs are not "ordinary costs" that the normal execution activities of the relevant national authorities would usually involve, such costs shall be borne by the Court. In the *Kenyatta* case, the Government of Kenya requested that the ICC Prosecution reimburse it for the costs of certain proceedings in its national court. These proceedings were concerned with the issuance of a preliminary injunction prohibiting a national judge from taking evidence for the purpose of the ICC (*Prosecutor v. Kenyatta*, ICC OTP, ICC-01/09-02/11-733-Red, 10 May 2013, paras. 21–23). Although it is unclear whether or not these costs constitute "extraordinary costs" under Article 100(1)(f), this serves as an example when such problems may arise.

For such "extraordinary costs", sub-paragraph (f) provides for a consultation process. The Court will only bear the costs after consultations with the State. As usually it is the national authorities that carry out the execution acts, the Court may not always be aware of or be very clear about the costs of various activities involved. The requirement of consultations guarantees that the Court would not be caught in surprise when the State asks the Court to bear the costs of an extraordinary nature after the spending.

The same principle also applies to the costs for the enforcement of sentences according to Rule 208 of the Rules of Procedure and Evidence. Thus, the ordinary costs for the enforcement of sentences shall be borne by the State in the territory of which the enforcement takes place, and other costs shall be borne by the Court.

Author: ZHANG Binxin.

[773] Paragraph 2 makes it clear that the provisions of paragraph 1 also apply to requests from States Parties to the Court. According to Article 93(10), the Court's assistance to States Parties includes mainly transmission of evidence obtained by the Court and the questioning of any person detained by order of the Court. If the Court agrees to cooperate with the requesting State Party, it will then bear the ordinary costs for executing such requests.

Cross-references:

Rule 208(1)(c, d, e).

Doctrine:

1. Claus Kreß and Kimberly Prost, "Article 100", in Otto Triffterer (ed.), *Commentary on the Rome Statute of the International Criminal Court: Observers' Notes, Article by Article*, 2nd ed., C.H. Beck/Hart/Nomos, Munich/Oxford/Baden-Baden, 2008, pp. 1631–33.

2. Rod Rastan, "Testing Co-operation: The International Criminal Court and National Authorities", in *Leiden Journal of International Law*, 2008, vol. 21, no. 2, pp. 431–56.

Author: ZHANG Binxin.

Article 101

Rule of speciality[774]

1. A person surrendered to the Court under this Statute shall not be proceeded against, punished or detained for any conduct committed prior to surrender, other than the conduct or

---

[774] *General remarks*:

Article 101 contains the rule of specialty which restricts the requesting jurisdiction to bringing proceedings only with respect to the crimes for which the person was surrendered.

The basis for the rule of speciality is States' sovereignty as the requesting State can only exercise jurisdiction if the requested State cooperates. If the requested by virtue of its sovereignty could refuse extradition for certain offences, it should also have the right to exclude offences being included in the proceedings in the requesting jurisdiction after extradition (Wilkitzki, p. 1636.)

There are different views on whether the rule of speciality is a rule of customary international law. Justice Miller delivered the opinion of the US Supreme Court in *United States v. Rauscher*, 119 U.S. 407 (1886) after having carefully examined the terms and history of the Webster Ashburton Treaty of 1842; the practice of nations in regards to extradition treaties; the case law from the states; and the writings of commentators, and reached the following conclusion:

> [A] person who has been brought within the jurisdiction of the court *by virtue of proceedings under an extradition treaty*, can only be tried for one of the offences described in that treaty, and for the offence with which he is charged in the proceedings for his extradition, until a reasonable time and opportunity have been given him, after his release or trial upon such charge, to return to the country from whose asylum he had been forcibly taken under those proceedings"., *United States v. Rauscher* at 430 (emphasis added). See also *United States v. Alvarez-Machain*, 504 U.S. 655 (1992)

However, statues of the *ad hoc* tribunals do contain a rule of speciality. The Appeals Chamber in *Kovačević* stated that "if there exists such a customary international law principle, it is associated with the institution of extradition as between states and does not apply in relation to the operations of the International Tribunal (*Prosecutor v. Kovačević* (Case No. IT-01-42) ICTY A. Ch., Decision Stating Reasons for Appeals Chamber's Order of 29 May 1998, 2 July 1998, para, 37).

Schabas explains the existence of Article 101 in the ICC Statute with the tension between the "horizontal" and "vertical" view of the relationship between the States and the ICC. The inclusion of Article 101 is expression of the vision of the ICC's surrender regimes to be analogous to that of extradition between sovereign States (Schabas, pp. 1054–1055).

Preparatory works:

Article 55 of the ILC Draft Statute is very similar to the provision finally adopted and stated that "[a] person transferred to the Court under Article 53 shall not be subject to prosecution or punishment for any crime other than that for which the person was transferred" (Report of the International Law Commission, Forty-sixth session, 2 May 1994–22 July 1994, Official Records of the General Assembly, Forty-ninth session (International Law Commission 1994). The rule of speciality is to be found in Article 92 of the Preparatory Committee Draft Statute (Report of the Preparatory Committee on the Establishment of an International Criminal Court, United Nations Diplomatic Conference of Plenipotentiaries on the Establishment of an International Criminal Court Rome, Italy 15 June–17 July 1998, A/CONF.183/2).

Author: Mark Klamberg.

---

course of conduct which forms the basis of the crimes for which that person has been surrendered.[775]

2. The Court may request a waiver of the requirements of paragraph 1 from the State which surrendered the person to the Court and, if necessary, the Court shall provide additional information in accordance with Article 91. States Parties shall have the authority to provide a waiver to the Court and should endeavour to do so.[776]

---

[775] The first paragraph expresses the rule of speciality in a way similar to multilateral extradition treaties.

The provision only applies to "conduct committed prior to surrender", which means that the Court is no limited to speciality considerations in relation to offence committed after the person has been surrendered to the Court. This clause may become relevant in the unlikely scenario that the person is released pending trial and commits crimes or commits crimes while in detention (Schabas, p. 1639).

In *Prosecutor v. Muthaura et al.*, ICC Pt. Ch., Decision on the "Preliminary Motion Alleging Defects in the Documents Containing the Charges (DCC) and List of Evidence (LoE) and Request that the OTP be ordered to re-file an Amended DCC and LoE" and the "Defence Request for a Status Conference Concerning the Prosecution's Disclosure of 19 August 2011 and the Document Containing the Charges and Article 101 of the Rome Statute", 12 September 2011, para. 16, the Single Judge stated that "that the rationale of Article 101 of the Statute is to protect State sovereignty. The Defence argued that " [a]rticle 101 does not make any distinction between a person, who is arrested pursuant to an arrest warrant, and a person, who voluntarily surrenders to the Court pursuant to a summons to appear". To the contrary, the Single Judge observed that the application of the rule of speciality is limited to the scenarios in which the person is arrested and is surrendered as a result of a request submitted by the Court to the State. This distinction between a person who is surrendered and a person who voluntarily appears before the Court can be educed from the statutory provisions, such as Articles 58(5) and 61(1) of the Statute.

Author: Mark Klamberg.

[776] The State that surrenders the person may waive the rule of speciality which corresponds well with established extradition standards and the rationale underlying the rule.

Cross-references:

Rules 196 and 197.

Doctrine:

1. Robert Cryer, Håkan Friman, Daryll Robinson and Elizabeth Wilmshurst, *An Introduction to International Criminal Law and Procedure*, 3rd ed., Cambridge University Press, Cambridge, 2014, p. 95.

2. William A. Schabas, *The International Criminal Court: A Commentary on the Rome Statute*, Oxford University Press, Oxford, 2010, pp. 1054–57.

3. Peter Wilkitzki, "Article 101 – Postponement of Execution of a Request in Respect of an Admissibility Challenge", in Otto Triffterer (ed.), *Commentary on the Rome Statute of the International Criminal Court: Observers' Notes, Article by Article*, 2nd ed., C.H. Beck/Hart/Nomos, Munich/Oxford/Baden-Baden, 2008, pp. 1635–44.

Author: Mark Klamberg.

Article 102

Use of terms

For the purposes of this Statute:

(a) "surrender" means the delivering up of a person by a State to the Court, pursuant to this Statute.

(b) "extradition" means the delivering up of a person by one State to another as provided by treaty, convention or national legislation.[777]

---

[777] *General remarks*:

The Article clarifies the Statute's terminological distinction between delivering up a person in the interstate context (extradition) and in the relationship "State to Court" (surrender). With the term "extradition" follows in general a lot of safe guards for the individual. For example, many States prohibit the extradition of their nationals. Article 102 is an attempt to address potential difficulties in this area by specifying that transfer of a person by a State to the Court is not extradition but surrender.

The Article does not oblige States Parties to make use of the same terminological distinction in their respective national legislation since the opening wording is "for the purpose of this Statute".

Doctrine:

1. William A. Schabas, *The International Criminal Court: a Commentary on the Rome Statute*, Oxford University Press, Oxford, 2010, pp. 1058–61.

2. Claus Kreß and Kimberly Prost, "Article 102 – Use of Terms", in Otto Triffterer (ed.), *Commentary on the Rome Statute of the International Criminal Court: Observers' Notes, Article by Article*, 2nd ed., C.H. Beck/Hart/Nomos, Munich/Oxford/Baden-Baden, 2008, pp. 1645–46.

Author: Karin Påle-Bartes.

PART 10. ENFORCEMENT

Article 103

Role of States in enforcement of sentences of imprisonment[778]

---

[778] *General remarks*:

International criminal law is intended "to put an end to impunity" so that the enforcement of sentences represents the fulfilment of its mission. Although rarely at the centre of political and academic interest, the manner how sentences passed by international criminal tribunals are enforced is a crucial determinant of the legitimacy of the whole enterprise of international criminal justice (Holá/van Wijk, 2014, pp. 110 f., 132; Kreß/Sluiter, 2002, pp. 1752 f., 1820; Nemitz, 2006, p. 144; Penrose, 2000b, p. 557).

Notably, the execution of long-term custodial sentences poses special problems since international courts up to now lack executive organs, thus depending on the cooperation of states. Accordingly, enforcement of sentences is just one form of necessary cooperation and, interestingly, it usually is the field of cooperation where the legal position of the international tribunal is at its weakest. States are extremely reluctant to make a general commitment to the burdensome and costly task of enforcing long-term prison sentences of international criminals. As a result, the enforcement regime still appears to be the least advanced part of international criminal justice, plagued by a number of structural problems which the conclusion of the ICC Statute could defuse in part but not resolve either.

The ICC Statute makes a terminological distinction reflected in its regulatory scheme between "Cooperation" in Part 9 – encompassing cooperation before and during trial – and "Enforcement" in Part 10 which covers cooperation after trial. In sharp contrast to the cooperation regime which with regard to States Parties has a fairly hierarchical or vertical structure, the enforcement regime is based on voluntariness – this has been deplored as a step back from the resolve that the prosecution of international crimes is a matter of joint concern of the international community (Kreß/Sluiter, 2002, pp. 1818 f.).

The ICC does not operate an international prison for persons sentenced by the Court, but relies on States to enforce its judgments. Unlike the scheme of the IMT (joint enforcement of the prison sentences by the four Allied powers in a prison in Berlin-Spandau) and the IMTFE (enforcement of the prison sentences initially by the USA as occupying power and later by Japan in Sugamo prison in Tokyo), the approach of the ICC Statute may be described as "decentralised", largely identical to the regime of the UN *ad hoc* tribunals, namely ICTY and ICTR. Although there were some expressions of sympathy for an international prison (UN doc. A/CN.4/449, § 121; UN doc. A/49/10, p. 66 f.; cf. *Prosecutor v. Erdemović* (Case No. IT-96-22-T), ICTY T. Ch., Sentencing Judgment, 29 November 1996, § 71: "institutional lacuna"; Abels, 2012, pp. 504–506; Mulgrew, 2009, pp. 395 f.; Penrose, 2000a, p. 390; 2000b, pp. 583–587), delegations in Rome favoured the "traditional" scheme of the *ad hoc* tribunals, presumably as it can rely on existing national infrastructures (Kreß/Sluiter, 2002, pp. 1817 f.). However, this type of "*ad hoc* approach to imprisonment" (Weinberg de Roca/Rassi, 2008, p. 44) has been subject to criticism, as it puts the Court in a "penitentiary predicament" (Strijards, 2008, Article 103 mgn. 18; Tolbert, 1998, p. 658), since there is no general legal obligation of States Parties to recognise and enforce prison sentences of the ICC, so that the Court is (almost) entirely dependent on the goodwill of States (cf. Strijards, 2008, Article 103 mgn. 18). Others argue that the "lottery" which State will be designated in a particular case affects both the equality and uniformity of the enforcement of international sentences, for example due to significantly different understandings of a "life sentence" (Hoffmann, 2011, p. 838 f., 841) or living standards (cf. Zahar/Sluiter, 2008, p. 319).

1. (a) A sentence of imprisonment shall be served in a State designated by the Court from a list of States which have indicated to the Court their willingness to accept sentenced persons.[779]

Yet, the ultimate responsibility for the enforcement of its sentences rests at all times with the Court, as is reflected in the supervisory powers (*viz.* "primacy", Strijards, 2008, Article 103 mgn. 7–15; Kreß/Sluiter, 2002, pp. 1819–1821) accorded to it throughout Part 10. These powers are generally vested in the Presidency (Rule 199) and, in contrast to the *ad hoc* tribunals, in the Appeals Chamber with respect to the reduction of the sentence (Article 110, Rule 223).

Preparatory works:

During the negotiations in Rome it was proposed that States should be bound by the Court's designation as State of enforcement (UN doc. A/CONF.183/2/Add.1, p. 151: Option 1 for Article 94; UN doc. A/50/22, § 239), but this suggestion was rejected by the majority of delegations as too "inflexible" (Chimimba, 1999/2002, p. 350; Kreß/Sluiter, 2002, p. 1787; Marchesi, 1999, pp. 427–430) and because States shied away from the burdens and risks involved (cf. Gartner, 2001, p. 441). Therefore, as opposed to the general duty to cooperate with the Court (Article 86) and the obligation to enforce fines, forfeiture and reparation orders (Article 75(5), 109), States' participation in enforcement of custodial services is entirely voluntarily (Schabas, 2010, p. 1067), even after having declared their general willingness to enforce (Article 103(1)(a)) and later being designated as potential State of enforcement by the Court (Article 103(1)(c)).

It was further discussed whether States should be allowed to attach conditions to their willingness to accept prisoners. Although this could further distort the uniformity of the enforcement of international sentences, the majority of delegations favoured the possibility of conditions in order to enhance the willingness of States to volunteer for enforcement (cf. Strijards, 2008, Article 103 mgn. 24). For this reason, the proposal was eventually adopted (Chimimba, 1999/2002, p. 350; Prost, 2001, p. 675) and has become Article 103(1)(b). However, as a compromise, the State of enforcement has to notify the Court according to Article 103(2)(a) at least 45 days before the exercise of such a condition which could materially affect the punishment.

Authors: Michael Stiel and Carl-Friedrich Stuckenberg.

[779] The wording "a State designated" was deliberately chosen to include non-State Parties as possible States of enforcement, although such a situation does not seem very likely (Prost, 2001, p. 679; Schabas, 2010, p. 1070). It must be taken into account, however, that non-States Parties are not bound by the provisions of the Statute and its Part 10 so that the conclusion of an enforcement agreement (cf. Rule 200(5)) might be indispensable before including the State on the list (or even making a designation under Article 103(1)(c)).

The State of enforcement shall be designated from a list of States that have indicated their willingness to accept sentenced persons. Such a declaration upon ratification of the Statute has been made to date by nine States Parties: Andorra, Czech Republic, Honduras, Liechtenstein, Lithuania, Luxembourg, Slovakia, Spain and Switzerland. All of them have attached conditions to this declaration, which are discussed below. In addition, all seven Enforcement Agreements that have entered into force to date note in their preamble the willingness of the respective State to receive prisoners. In this way, the States listed below have declared their interest to join the list.

Although the Statute itself does not provide for this, Rule 200(5) and the Court's practice follow the model of the *ad hoc* tribunals by concluding bilateral agreements with willing states in which the conditions and procedure of acceptance are set out. A Model Enforcement Agreement (MEA) is used which integrates all relevant provisions from the Statute, Rules and Regulations. If a State expresses its interest in joining the list, negotiations based on the MEA are initiated (Abtahi/Arrigg Koh, 2012, pp. 7 f.). As of this writing (August 2015), another eight States

(b) At the time of declaring its willingness to accept sentenced persons, a State may attach conditions to its acceptance as agreed by the Court and in accordance with this Part.[780]

Parties have concluded an Enforcement Agreement with the Court: Austria, Belgium, Colombia, Denmark, Finland, Mali, Serbia and the United Kingdom, seven of them have entered into force. For details on the practice of the Court with regard to enforcement agreements, cf. Rule 200(5).

The wording seems to imply that only States on the list may be designated, thereby excluding *ad hoc* agreements for enforcement (cf. Kreß/Sluiter, 2002, p. 1790 fn. 198) of the kind practiced by the ICTY with regard to Germany (agreements of 17 October 2000 (*Tadić*; cf. Nemitz, 2006, pp. 138 f.); 14 November 2002 (*Kunarac*); 16 December 2008 (*Galić*); 16 June 2011 (*Tarčulovski)*; 28 July 2014 (*Đorđević*); agreements are accessible at http://www.icty.org/sid/137, last retrieved on 05 August 2015"). Since States on the list have to accept the designation according to Article 103(1)(c) in each individual case anyway (by what may be called an "*ad hoc* agreement"), it is submitted that the designation of States not on the list should be possible to satisfy the needs of States that prefer not to express a general willingness to enforce the Court's sentences for whatever reasons.

The decision of the Presidency to designate a specific State is not subject to appeal, as it is not included in the exhaustive list of appealable decisions in Article 82(1). As opposed to some jurisprudence of the *ad hoc* tribunals regarding aspects of the enforcement as relevant for the sentencing judgment and thus substantive matters (cf. *Prosecutor v. Erdemović* (Case No. IT-96-22-T), ICTY T. Ch., Sentencing Judgment, 29 November 1996, § 70; *Prosecutor v. Mrđa* (Case No. IT-02-59-S), ICTY T. Ch., Sentencing Judgment, 31 March 2004, § 109), the designation is generally seen as an administrative decision after the sentence has already become final (cf. for the RSCSL: *Prosecutor v. Taylor* (Case No. RSCSL-03-01 ES), RSCSL President, Decision on Charles Ghankay Taylor's Motion for Termination of Enforcement of Sentence in the United Kingdom and for the Transfer to Rwanda AND ON Defence Application for Leave to Appeal Decision on Motion for Termination of Enforcement of Sentence in the United Kingdom and for the Transfer to Rwanda, 21 May 2015, 11 20 ff.). A sentenced person has therefore no right to appeal the designation and will have to rely on his or her right to initiate proceedings under Article 104 (for a critique see Abels, 2012, pp. 501–504).

Cross-references:

Rules 198, 199, 200, 207, 208, 225.

Regulation 114.

Authors: Michael Stiel and Carl-Friedrich Stuckenberg.

---

[780] The practice of attaching conditions to a declaration of willingness to enforce (for example nationality, residence of the convict in the declaring State) has already been known to the *ad hoc* tribunals (UN doc. A/51/292, S/1996/665, § 189; Schabas, 2010, pp. 1066 f.).

Conditions attached must be consistent with the Statute. However, this does not create a very high threshold: Given the wording of Article 105(1), even the duration of the sentence may be "subject to conditions" (cf. Kreß/Sluiter, 2002, p. 1794; Schabas, 2010, p. 1071). The Court therefore has a considerable latitude to agree on a great variety of conditions and it is likely that the Presidency will make only sparse use of its power to disagree with a certain condition, except, for example, in case a State should want to reserve the right to fall below the standards required by Article 106 (Kreß/Sluiter, 2002, pp. 1788, 1794; see also comment on Article 106). If the Presidency does not agree with the proposed conditions, it need not include that State on the list, see Rule 200(2).

Except for Article 105(2) and 106(1) and (2), there is no further guidance regarding the acceptability of conditions, neither in the Statute nor in the RPE nor in the Regulations (Schabas,

(c) A State designated in a particular case shall promptly inform the Court whether it accepts the Court's designation.[781]

2. (a) The State of enforcement shall notify the Court of any circumstances, including the exercise of any conditions agreed under paragraph 1, which could materially affect the terms or extent of the imprisonment. The Court shall be given at least 45 days' notice of any such known or foreseeable circumstances. During this period, the State of enforcement shall take no action that might prejudice its obligations under article 110.

(b) Where the Court cannot agree to the circumstances referred to in subparagraph (a), it shall notify the State of enforcement and proceed in accordance with Article 104, paragraph 1.[782]

2010, pp. 1070 f.; Strijards, 2008, Article 103 mgn. 24). This lacuna has caused concerns that States might abuse conditions (such as a reservation of "national interest" in the relevant prison facility) to withdraw via the backdoor from enforcement obligations they previously agreed upon (Strijards, 2008, Article 103 mgn. 24). However, an analysis of the conditions attached by States to date does not support this concern (cf. Abtahi/Arrigg Koh, 2012, p. 9 with respect to enforcement agreements). The majority of States having declared their willingness legitimately insist on ties to the sentenced person such as citizenship (Andorra, Czech Republic, Honduras, Liechtenstein, Lithuania, Luxembourg, Slovakia, Switzerland) or residence (Czech Republic, Liechtenstein, Luxembourg, Slovakia, Switzerland). Some require conformity with their national legislation on the maximum duration of sentences (Andorra, Honduras, Luxembourg, Spain) or a national conversion procedure (Slovakia). One has to bear in mind that States may apply conditions other than those expressed in the list when deciding whether to accept the designation in a particular case (cf. Article 103(1)(c) below). Thus, the conditions on the list are not exhaustive. Other possible conditions could include the applicability of domestic law relating to pardon, conditional release and commutation of sentence (Strijards, 2008, Article 103 mgn. 24) or other administrative issues, such as the maximum capacity of a special secured facility (UN doc. A/CONF.183/2/Add.1, p. 152; A/AC.249/1998/L.13, p. 162; Strijards, 2008, Article 103 mgn. 24).

Authors: Michael Stiel and Carl-Friedrich Stuckenberg.

[781] Even after having been designated from the list, the State in question reserves the right to reject the designation by the Court in a particular case (Abtahi/Arrigg Koh, 2012, pp. 6–10; Kreß/Sluiter, 2002, p. 1787: system of "double-consent"). The advantages of having the list are therefore quite limited. It may only give the Presidency the "most concrete idea" which State to approach in a particular case (Kreß/Sluiter, 2002, p. 1790) and have some significance for the designation decision itself, as Rule 201(b) attaches some weight to it under the criterion of "equitable distribution" in Article 103(3)(a).

In case of acceptance of the designation Rules 206–208 apply, in case of rejection Rule 205 applies.

Cross-references:

Rule 205, 206.

Authors: Michael Stiel and Carl-Friedrich Stuckenberg.

[782] According to Article 103(2)(a), the State of enforcement has to notify the Court of any circumstances that would materially affect the imprisonment, namely the exercise of a condition previously agreed upon by the Court. This is a corollary of the Court's supervisory powers regarding the enforcement of its sentences. For known or foreseeable circumstances, the notification shall be made at least 45 days in advance. This shall provide the Court with sufficient time to decide whether it can approve such action and, if necessary, to find a solution agreeable for both (Stri-

---

3. In exercising its discretion to make a designation under paragraph 1, the Court shall take into account the following:

(a) The principle that States Parties should share the responsibility for enforcing sentences of imprisonment, in accordance with principles of equitable distribution, as provided in the Rules of Procedure and Evidence;

(b) The application of widely accepted international treaty standards governing the treatment of prisoners;

(c) The views of the sentenced person;

(d) The nationality of the sentenced person;

(e) Such other factors regarding the circumstances of the crime or the person sentenced, or the effective enforcement of the sentence, as may be appropriate in designating the State of enforcement.[783]

---

jards, 2008, Article 103 mgn. 25). In the negative, Article 103(2)(b) enables the Court to prepare for a change of the State of enforcement pursuant to Article 104(1). Given the narrow time limit in this case for the complex process of selecting a new State of enforcement and preparing for the transfer of the sentenced person thereto, the Court might depend on the residual duty of the host State to detain the prisoner for the time being (in analogy to Article 103(4), proposed by Kreß/Sluiter, 2002, p. 1795 fn. 224 and provided for in Article 50(2) of the Headquarters Agreement).

The Presidency's power to decide whether the exercise of a condition is appropriate seems somewhat surprising, if one imagines a condition which affects the duration of the sentence – this is admissible under Article 105(1) –, e. g. to apply national legislation on early release or the exercise of the constitutional right of its head of state to pardon a prisoner. Article 110 and Rule 224 regard matters of reduction of the sentence as substantive questions and therefore entrust them to three judges of the Appeals Chamber (cf. Rule 224(1)). If, on the other hand, the State of enforcement wishes to make a similar decision, the Presidency is the reviewing organ, according to Article 103(2) and Rule 199 (cf. Kreß/Sluiter, 2002, p. 1795 fn. 225).

Authors: Michael Stiel and Carl-Friedrich Stuckenberg.

[783] The decision which State to designate is at the Presidency's discretion. Article 103(3) provides a non-exhaustive list of factors to be taken into account:

(a) The equitable distribution of prisoners among interested States shall be taken into account. This notion is elaborated in Rule 201.

(b) The application of widely accepted international treaty standards regarding the treatment of prisoners is another criterion. It should be noted that the reference to "treaty" standards considerably limits the scope of applicable provisions. The details are dealt with in the commentary on Article 106. Given the importance the Statute itself attaches to conformity with those standards (Article 106(1) and (2)), foreseeable non-compliance should generally preclude the designation of a particular State (Kreß/Sluiter, 2002, p. 1788).

(c) The views of the sentenced person are to be taken into account. At the *ad hoc* tribunals, it was completely left to the discretion of the President whether he wanted to conduct a hearing with the sentenced person (Hoffmann, 2011, p. 839; ICTY-Practice Direction 2009, IT/137/Rev. 1, § 5; ICTR-Practice Direction 2008, § 4; MICT-Practice Direction 2014, MICT/2 Rev. 1, § 5; SCSL-Practice Direction 2009, § 5). Under the ICC Statute, there is no doubt that the sentenced person must have an opportunity to present his or her views on the designation (Strijards, 2008, Article 103 mgn. 28), although his or her consent is not required (UN doc. A/50/22, § 240). Rule 203 outlines the relevant procedure.

4. If no State is designated under paragraph 1, the sentence of imprisonment shall be served in a prison facility made available by the host State, in accordance with the conditions set out in the headquarters agreement referred to in Article 3, paragraph 2. In such a case, the

---

(d) The criterion of the sentenced person's nationality does not necessarily point in one direction. Enforcement in the State of nationality of the sentenced person would be clearly preferable regarding his or her rehabilitation. However, such a designation bears the risk that the sentenced person will be regarded either a "hero" or, in the case of a regime change, a traitor in the eyes of his fellow citizens, both undesirable situations to be avoided when entrusting the enforcement of an international sentence to a particular State (cf. Kreß/Sluiter, 2002, pp. 1788 f.).

(e) The discretion of the Presidency is rather broad, as there is no guidance in the Rules of Procedure and Evidence what these other factors could be (Kreß/Sluiter, 2002, pp. 1788 f.).

However, the practice directions of the *ad hoc* tribunals, the MICT and the SCSL provide some additional criteria that could be applied at the ICC as well. Those include:

- whether the convict is expected to serve as a witness in further proceedings (ICTY-Practice Direction 2009, IT/137/Rev.1, § 4(b), (c); ICTR-Practice Direction 2008, § 3(ii), (iii); MICT-Practice Direction 2014, MICT/2 Rev. 1, § 4(b), (c); SCSL-Practice Direction 2009, § 4(ii), (iii);

- medical reports (ICTY-Practice Direction 2009, IT/137/Rev. 1, § 4(d); ICTR-Practice Direction 2008, § 3(iv); MICT-Practice Direction 2014, MICT/2 Rev. 1, § 4(d); SCSL-Practice Direction 2009, § 4(iv));

- the language skills of the convict (ICTY-Practice Direction 2009, IT/137/Rev. 1, § 4(e); ICTR-Practice Direction 2008, § 3(v); MICT-Practice Direction 2014, MICT/2 Rev. 1, § 4(e)); SCSL-Practice Direction 2009, § 4(v));

- the possibility of family visits, notably the financial resources of the prisoner's relatives (ICTY-Practice Direction 2009, IT/137/Rev. 1, § 4(a); ICTR-Practice Direction 2008, § 3(i); MICT-Practice Direction 2014, MICT/2 Rev. 1, § 4(a)); SCSL-Practice Direction 2009, § 4(i). This ought to be given "particular consideration" (ICTY-Practice Direction 2009, IT/137/Rev. 1, § 5; ICTR-Practice Direction 2008, § 4; MICT-Practice Direction 2014, MICT/2 Rev. 1, § 5; SCSL-Practice Direction 2009, § 5 even highlights the "desirability" of a placement in a State easily accessible for relatives);

- whether the sentenced person may be able to stay in the State of enforcement after release in case he or she cannot return to his home country for security reasons (MICT-Practice Direction 2014, MICT/2 Rev. 1, § 4(h)).

While the State in which the crime was committed was rejected as place of enforcement in case of the ICTY (cf. *Prosecutor v. Erdemović* (Case No. IT-96-22-T), ICTY T. Ch., Sentencing Judgment, 29 November 1996, § 70; cf. UN doc. S/25704, § 121), ICTR and SCSL do not preclude or, on the contrary, even favour such a designation (Article 26 ICTR Statute; cf. UN doc. S/1995/134, § 19; Article 22(1) SCSL Statute; cf. UN doc. S/2000/915, § 49). This criterion has implications similar to the nationality of the sentenced person.

The (undesired) relocation of a prisoner into another environment according to Article 104(1), possibly with major cultural and linguistic differences, may present an obstacle to his rehabilitation and thus aggravate his sentence. Therefore, the likelihood of a later transfer to another State of enforcement should bear considerable weight already in the designation phase.

Cross-references:

Rule 201, 203, 204.

Authors: Michael Stiel and Carl-Friedrich Stuckenberg.

---

costs arising out of the enforcement of a sentence of imprisonment shall be borne by the Court.[784]

---

[784] If no other State of enforcement can be found, the host State acts as a "residual custodian on behalf of the Court" (Strijards, 2008, Article 103 mgn. 29). It is the understanding of the Dutch Government that it is obliged to enforce the sentence and not only to make "a prison facility available" to the Court (Abels, 2012, pp. 459–461). Details are regulated in the agreement with the host State which merely repeats the provisions of Part 10 (Article 49(4) of the Headquarters Agreement) and therefore does not add anything substantial (Strijards, 2008, Article 103 mgn. 30).

At first glance, one could be tempted to regard this option as the nucleus of a future international prison, especially in light of the fact that many prisoners of the *ad hoc* tribunals serve their entire sentence or a large part of it at those tribunals' detention units (Culp, 2011, p. 13; Mulgrew, 2009, p. 393; Nemitz, 2006, p. 137; van Zyl Smit, 2005, p. 367; Weinberg de Roca/Rassi, 2008, p. 47) which led to the warning that this option might become the rule rather than the exception (Chimimba, 1999/2002, p. 351). However, Article 103(4) only eases the Court's predicament to find a suitable enforcement State and does not solve it because resort to the host State comes at a price, as the Court will bear the costs of such imprisonment (see below), and is not a permanent solution because the Netherlands were particularly nervous about this provision (cf. Dutch declaration on the Rome Conference emphasising the "exceptional character" of the residual duty, UN doc. A/CONF.183/12) and consequently, the Headquarters Agreement requires the Court to "endeavour" to seek another State of enforcement (Article 49(1), (3)). Therefore, on the one hand, the residual duty cannot be used to avoid the complex designation process under Article 103(1)–(3) altogether. Only when the remaining time to be served is less than six months, the Court will first consider whether the sentence may be enforced in the Court's detention centre instead of designating another enforcement State (Article 50(1) of the Headquarters Agreement; cf. Abels, 2012, p. 496). On the other hand, the Court would not be bound to give priority to another State willing to enforce when it deems the transfer thereto completely inappropriate (Kreß/Sluiter, 2002, pp. 1790 f.).

The costs of enforcement in this situation are borne by the Court, as an exception from the general rule set out in Rule 208. This provision had been insisted upon by the Netherlands (Chimimba, 1999/2002, p. 351) and seems fair insofar as the sentence is not enforced by the host State after accepting an individual designation (Article 103(1)(c)).

Cross-references:

Article 104.

Rules 198–208.

Regulation 114.

Doctrine:

1. Denis Abels, *Prisoners of the International Community: The Legal Position of Persons Detained at International Criminal Tribunals*, TMC Asser Press/Springer, The Hague, 2012.

2. Hirad Abtahi, "L'exécution de la peine", in Hervé Ascensio, Emmanuel Decaux and Alain Pellet (eds.), *Droit pénal international*, 2nd ed., Pedone, Paris, 2012, pp. 989–96.

3. Hirad Abtahi and Steven Arrigg Koh, "The Emerging Enforcement Practice of the International Criminal Court", in *Cornell International Law Journal*, 2012, vol. 45, no. 1, pp. 1–23.

4. Trevor Pascal Chimimba, "Chapter 11 – Establishing An Enforcement Regime", in Roy S. Lee (ed.), *The International Criminal Court: The Making of the Rome Statute*, Kluwer Law International, The Hague, 2002, pp. 345–56.

5. Richard Culp, *Enforcement and Monitoring of Sentences in the Modern War Crimes Process: Equal Treatment before the Law?*, 2011.
6. Irene Gartner, "The Rules of Procedure and Evidence on Co-operation and Enforcement", in Horst Fischer, Claus Kreß and Sascha Rolf Lüder (eds.), *International and National Prosecution of Crimes Under International Law*, Berlin Verlag, Berlin, 2001, pp. 423–45.
7. Klaus Hoffmann, "Some Remarks on the Enforcement on International Sentences in Light of the Galic case at the ICTY", in *Zeitschrift für Internationale Strafrechtsdogmatik* (ZIS), 2011, pp. 838–42.
8. Barbora Holá and Joris van Wijk, "Life after Conviction at International Criminal Tribunals", in *Journal of International Criminal Justice*, 2014, vol. 12, pp. 109–32.
9. André Klip, "Enforcement of Sanctions Imposed by the International Criminal Tribunals for Rwanda and the Former Yugoslavia", in *European Journal of Crime, Criminal Law and Criminal Justice*, 1997, vol. 5, pp. 144–64.
10. Claus Kreß and Göran Sluiter, "Imprisonment", in Antonio Cassese, *et al* (eds.), *The Rome Statute of the International Criminal Court: A Commentary*, 2nd ed., Oxford University Press, Oxford, 2002, pp. 1757–1821.
11. Antonio Marchesi, "The Enforcement of Sentences of the International Criminal Court", in Flavia Lattanzi and William A. Schabas (eds.), *Essays on the Rome Statute of the International Criminal Court*, il Sirente, Ripa Fagnano Alto, 1999, pp. 427–45.
12. Róisín Mulgrew, "On the Enforcement of Sentences Imposed by International Courts", in *Journal of International Criminal Justice*, 2009, vol. 7, pp. 373–96.
13. Jan Christoph Nemitz, "Execution of Sanctions Imposed by Supranational Criminal Tribunals", in Roelof Haveman and Olaoluwa Olusanya (eds.), *Sentencing and Sanctioning in Supranational Criminal Law*, Intersentia, Antwerp, 2006, pp. 125–44.
14. Faustin Z. Ntoubandi, "Article 103", in Julian Fernandez and Xavier Pacreau (eds.), *Statut de Rome de la Cour pénale internationale*, Commentaire Article par Article, Vol. II, Éditions Pedone, Paris, 2012.
15. Mary Margaret Penrose, "Lest We Fail: The Importance of Enforcement in International Criminal Law", in *American University International Law Review*, 2000, vol. 15, pp. 321–94.
16. Mary Margaret Penrose, "Spandau Revisited: The Question of Detention for International War Crimes", in *New York Law School Journal of Human Rights*, 2000, vol. 16, pp. 553–91.
17. Kimberly Prost, "Chapter 14 – Enforcement", in Roy S. Lee (ed.), *The International Criminal Court: Elements of Crimes and Rules of Procedure and Evidence*, Transnational Publishers, Ardsley, NY, 2001, pp. 673–703.
18. William A. Schabas, Article 103, *The International Criminal Court: A Commentary on the Rome Statute*, Oxford University Press, Oxford, 2010.
19. Gerard A. M. Strijards, "Article 103", in Otto Triffterer (ed.), *Commentary on the Rome Statute of the International Criminal Court: Observers' Notes, Article by Article*, 2nd ed., C.H. Beck/Hart/Nomos, Munich/Oxford/Baden-Baden, 2008, pp. 1647–57.
20. David Tolbert, "The International Tribunal for the Former Yugoslavia and the Enforcement of Sentences", in *Leiden Journal of International Law*, 1998, vol. 11, pp. 655–69.
21. Dirk van Zyl Smit, "International Imprisonment", in *International and Comparative Law Quarterly*, 2005, vol. 54, pp. 357–86.
22. Inés Mónica Weinberg de Roca and Christopher M. Rassi, "Sentencing and Incarceration in the Ad Hoc Tribunals", in *Stanford Journal of International Law*, 2008, vol. 44, pp. 1–62.

23. Alexander Zahar and Göran Sluiter, *International Criminal Law: A Critical Introduction*, Oxford University Press, Oxford, 2008.

Authors: Michael Stiel and Carl-Friedrich Stuckenberg.

Article 104

Change in designation of State of enforcement[785]

1. The Court may, at any time, decide to transfer a sentenced person to a prison of another State.[786]

---

[785] *General remarks*:

The option to transfer the sentenced person back into the Court's custody or to another State of enforcement was developed by the *ad hoc* tribunals in their bilateral enforcement agreements (cf., being the first one, Agreement between the Government of the Italian Republic and the United Nations on the Enforcement of Sentences of the ICTY, Article 9(2)) for the hypothesis that national sentence reduction measures could not be agreed upon by the Court (Cassese, 2013, p. 397). Only one person convicted by the ICTY has been relocated so far. Radislav Krstić was moved upon his request from a prison in the United Kingdom first back to the UN Detention Unit and later to Poland (cf. *Prosecutor v. Krstić* (Case No. MICT-13-46-ES.1/IT-98-33-ES), MICT President, Order designating the State in which Radislav Krstić is to serve the remainder of his sentence, 19 July 2013). However, the motion of Charles Taylor for relocation from the UK to Rwanda has been denied by the RSCSL. The Court argued that his situation was not comparable to that of Krstić (cf. *Prosecutor v. Taylor* (Case No. RSCSL-03-01 ES), RSCSL T. Ch., Decision on Public with Public and Confidential Annexes Charles Ghankay Taylor's Motion for Termination of Enforcement of Sentence in the United Kingdom and for the Transfer to Rwanda, 30 January 2015, mgn. 114–120).

The provision was not present in any of the preceding drafts but was added during the Rome Conference (Schabas, 2010, p. 1075) because some delegations made its inclusion the condition to accept Article 106 on supervision (UN doc. A/CONF.183/C.1/WGE/L.14, fn. 241 to Article 106 II), as Article 104 ensures that the Court retains ultimate control over the enforcement of the sentence (Kreß/Sluiter, 2002, p. 1791). In fact, changing the enforcement State is the only power the Court has to influence the modalities of enforcement and ensure compliance with prescribed standards, since it lacks the authority to order modifications of the conditions of detention (a provision to that effect, still contained in the Draft Statute, UN doc. A/CONF.183/2/Add.1, Article 96(2)(option 1), was dropped during the negotiations, Kreß/Sluiter, 2002, pp. 1799 f.). Simultaneously, transferring the sentenced person is the ultimate form of remedy he or she may apply for in the decentralised enforcement system of the ICTY, ICTR and ICC (Kreß/Sluiter, 2002, p. 1808). The character as an individual right is underscored by Article 104(2). There is, however, no clear priority of the transfer procedure under Article 104 over domestic remedies available to the prisoner (cf. Article 106(2)). It is expected that the Presidency will await the outcome of any procedures at the national level before making its decision (Kreß/Sluiter, 2002, pp. 1808 f.).

Bearing in mind the difficulties of an (undesired) relocation of the sentenced person (cf. commentary on Article 103(3)(e)), it is submitted that the exercise of this competence of last resort should be avoided as far as possible and restricted to exceptional and unforeseeable circumstances.

Authors: Michael Stiel and Carl-Friedrich Stuckenberg.

[786] Criteria for the exercise of this power are not provided in the ICC Statute or the Rules of Procedure and Evidence (Strijards, 2008, Article 104 mgn. 2), but could well include the following:

(i) If the Court is notified of the upcoming exercise of a condition in accordance with Article 103(2)(a) and cannot agree to this (Kreß/Sluiter, 2002, pp. 1791, 1795; Strijards, 2008, Article 104 mgn. 2)

2. A sentenced person may, at any time, apply to the Court to be transferred from the State of enforcement.[787]

(ii) or if the conditions of imprisonment fall below the necessary standard (Kreß/Sluiter, 2002, p. 1791).

The Court may decide to transfer the prisoner "at any time".

Cross-references:

Rules 202, 205, 209.

Authors: Michael Stiel and Carl-Friedrich Stuckenberg.

[787] Article 104(2) sets forth the right of the sentenced person to apply to the Court for the exercise of its power under Article 104(1). This would have been the case even without a specific provision in the Statute (Strijards, 2008, Article 104 mgn. 2). Article 104(2) is to be read together with Article 106(3) which provides for the prisoner's right to confidential communication with the Court regarding his or her conditions of imprisonment.

The convict may apply "at any time". This clarifies that applications may be made repeatedly (Strijards, 2008, Article 104 mgn. 2) and without any time limits, as opposed to Rule 224(3).

Cross-references:

Article 103(2), 106.

Rules 209, 210.

Doctrine:

1. Antonio Cassese, Paola Gaeta and John R.W.D. Jones, *International Criminal Law*, 3rd ed., Oxford University Press, Oxford, 2013.

2. Claus Kreß and Göran Sluiter, "Imprisonment", in Antonio Cassese, Paola Gaeta and John R.W.D. Jones (eds.), *The Rome Statute of the International Criminal Court: A Commentary*, 2nd ed., Oxford University Press, Oxford, 2002, pp. 1757–1821.

3. Faustin Z. Ntoubandi, "Article 104", in Julian Fernandez and Xavier Pacreau (eds.), *Statut de Rome de la Cour pénale internationale*, Commentaire Article par Article, Vol. II, Éditions Pedone, Paris, 2012.

4. William A. Schabas, Article 104, *The International Criminal Court: A Commentary on the Rome Statute*, Oxford University Press, Oxford, 2010.

5. Gerard A.M. Strijards, "Article 104", in Otto Triffterer (ed.), *Commentary on the Rome Statute of the International Criminal Court: Observers' Notes, Article by Article*, 2nd ed., C.H. Beck/Hart/Nomos, Munich/Oxford/Baden-Baden, 2008, p. 1659.

Authors: Michael Stiel and Carl-Friedrich Stuckenberg.

Article 105
Enforcement of the sentence[788]

1. Subject to conditions which a State may have specified in accordance with Article 103, paragraph 1 (b), the sentence of imprisonment shall be binding on the States Parties, which shall in no case modify it.[789]

---

[788] *General remarks*:

It is a "matter of principle" that the sentence imposed by the Court is binding on States Parties, as the State of enforcement is acting on behalf of the international community (Hoffmann, 2011, p. 839; cf. *Prosecutor v. Erdemović* (Case No. IT-96-22-T), ICTY T. Ch., Sentencing Judgment, 29 November 1996, § 71; Clark, 2008, Article 105 mgn. 1). The provision is closely connected with Article 110 which provides for an international procedure to reduce the sentence (Kreß/Sluiter, 2002, pp. 1792–1794.; Schabas, 2010, p. 1077). This principle is also in line with inter-State prisoner exchange treaties (Clark, 2008, Article 105 mgn. 1). During the negotiations in Rome, this exclusive power of the Court to determine the sentence was favoured over the general applicability of national procedures, subject to the consent of the Court in each individual case, as was the practice of the *ad hoc* tribunals (Kreß/Sluiter, 2002, p. 1791 f.; Schabas, 2010, p. 1078). The latter approach could have tempted trial judges to include in their considerations possible reviews of their sentence in the State of enforcement, as it occurred at the ICTY (cf. *Prosecutor v. Stakić* (Case No. IT-97-24-T), ICTY T. Ch., Judgment, 31 July 2003, p. 253 f. imposing a detailed review obligation on the State of enforcement to review the sentence after 20 years, which was later successfully appealed), and thus would have led to considerable inequality (Schabas, 2010, p. 1078).

However, the wording of Article 105(1) includes a qualification. It explicitly refers to conditions accepted by the Presidency according to Article 103(1)(b) that may deviate from the obligation of the State of enforcement to respect the duration of the sentence, and therefore makes an "exceptional case scenario" possible (Kreß/Sluiter, 2002, p. 1792; cf. Ntoubandi, 2012, p. 1972: "dualist regime"). This is difficult to reconcile with the general principle of non-modification of an international sentence (Prost, 2001, p. 675), but the qualification is the corollary of the decision to allow conditional acceptance of prisoners (cf. commentary on Article 103(1)(b)) and will not cause serious problems in practice, as the Court's prior consent to such conditions is required in every case (Clark, 2008, Article 105 mgn. 2; Ntoubandi, 2012, p. 1973; Schabas, 2010, p. 1078).

Authors: Michael Stiel and Carl-Friedrich Stuckenberg.

[789] Article 105(1) sets forth the general rule that sentences pronounced by the Court are "binding". This means that a possible exequatur procedure is limited to the decision between accepting or rejecting the designation, and national law on pardon, parole, commutation or early release is not to be applied (Kreß/Sluiter, 2002, pp. 1792 f.). An acceptance of the designation with modifications affecting the duration or nature of the sentence would be in breach of Article 105(1). States Parties therefore have to ensure that they have their "legislative and administrative house in order" (Clark, 2008, Article 105 mgn. 2).

It is doubtful whether Article 105(1) also applies to States Parties other than the State of enforcement by establishing a negative duty to refrain from any possible interferences with the enforcement process (Marchesi, 1999, p. 437).

Article 105(1) is repeated in all seven Enforcement Agreements which have entered into force so far: cf. the Agreement between the Court and Austria (Article 4(1); ICC-PRES/01-01-05), Belgium (Article 4(1); ICC-PRES/16-03-14), Denmark (Article 4(1); ICC-PRES/12-02-12), Finland (Article 4(1); ICC-PRES/07-01-11), Mali (Article 1(3); ICC-PRES/11-01-12), Ser-

2. The Court alone shall have the right to decide any application for appeal and revision. The State of enforcement shall not impede the making of any such application by a sentenced person.[790]

---

bia (Article 4(1); ICC-PRES/09-03-11) and the United Kingdom (Article 4(1); ICC-PRES/04-01-07). Including the present provision in an enforcement agreement is imperative in case a non-State Party would be chosen as State of enforcement, as the sentence would not be binding by way of Article 105(1), which only refers to "States Parties".

Authors: Michael Stiel and Carl-Friedrich Stuckenberg.

[790] The Court reserves the exclusive right to decide on any issues "surrounding the original conviction" (Clark, 2008, Article 105 mgn. 4). Article 105(2) sent. 1 prohibits any procedures to modify the conviction or sentence in the State of enforcement, the wording "appeal or revision" was only inserted to create consistency with Part 8 (Schabas, 2010, p. 1078).

Since Article 105(1) already covers appeal and revision procedures, Article 105(2) sent. 1 seems superfluous at first sight. However, the latter's prohibition is unqualified, as the reference to conditions under Article 103(1)(c) is omitted there. It follows that a condition which allows for national review of the original conviction is not acceptable under any circumstances. The provision is repeated in all seven Enforcement Agreements currently in force, that is, between the Court and Austria (Article 11(1); ICC-PRES/01-01-05), Belgium (Article 12(1); ICC-PRES/16-03-14), Denmark (Article 11(1); ICC-PRES/12-02-12), Finland (Article 11(1); ICC-PRES/07-01-11), Mali (Article 6(2); ICC-PRES/11-01-12), Serbia (Article 11(1); ICC-PRES/09-03-11) and the United Kingdom (Article 10; ICC-PRES/04-01-07).

The second sentence in Article 105(2) requires the State of Enforcement not to impede the making of an application for appeal or revision. While it seems highly unlikely for a prisoner already transferred to the State of enforcement to make an application for appeal in light of Rule 202, the situation could well arise with regard to revision procedures. Some authors submit that, despite the wording ("shall not impede"), there is even a positive obligation of the State to facilitate the communication of the prisoner with the Court in this respect (Clark, 2008, Article 105 mgn. 5). The provision is only repeated in the Enforcement Agreements with Belgium (Article 12(1) sent. 2; ICC-PRES/16-03-14), Denmark (Article 11; ICC-PRES/12-02-12), Finland (Article 11(1); ICC-PRES/07-01-11), Mali (Article 6(2); ICC-PRES/11-01-12), Serbia (Article 11(1); ICC-PRES/09-03-11) – as the two other Enforcement Agreements are concluded with States Parties as well, Article 105(2) sent. 2 will nevertheless apply to them without being explicitly repeated in the Agreement.

Cross-references:

Articles 103(1)(b), 110.

Doctrine:

1. Roger S. Clark, "Article 105", in Otto Triffterer (ed.), *Commentary on the Rome Statute of the International Criminal Court: Observers' Notes, Article by Article*, 2nd ed., C.H. Beck/Hart/Nomos, Munich/Oxford/Baden-Baden, 2008, pp. 1661–62.

2. Klaus Hoffmann, "Some Remarks on the Enforcement on International Sentences in Light of the Galic Case at the ICTY", in *Zeitschrift für Internationale Strafrechtsdogmatik* (ZIS), 2011, pp. 838–42.

3. Claus Kreß and Göran Sluiter, "Imprisonment", in Antonio Cassese, Paola Gaeta and John R.W.D. Jones (eds.), *The Rome Statute of the International Criminal Court: A Commentary*, 2nd ed., Oxford University Press, Oxford, 2002, pp. 1757–1821.

4. Antonio Marchesi, "The Enforcement of Sentences of the International Criminal Court", in Flavia Lattanzi and William, A. Schabas (eds.), *Essays on the Rome Statute of the International Criminal Court*, il Sirente, Ripa Fagnano Alto, 1999, pp. 427–45.

---

5. Faustin Z. Ntoubandi, "Article 105", in Julian Fernandez and Xavier Pacreau (eds.), *Statut de Rome de la Cour pénale internationale, Commentaire Article par Article*, 2nd ed., Éditions Pedone, Paris, 2012.

6. Kimberly Prost, "Chapter 14 – Enforcement", in Roy S. Lee (ed.), *The International Criminal Court: Elements of Crimes and Rules of Procedure and Evidence*, Transnational Publishers, Ardsley, NY, 2001, pp. 673–703.

7. William A. Schabas, Article 105, *The International Criminal Court: A Commentary on the Rome Statute*, Oxford University Press, Oxford, 2010.

Authors: Michael Stiel and Carl-Friedrich Stuckenberg.

Article 106
Supervision of enforcement of sentences and conditions of imprisonment[791]

1. The enforcement of a sentence of imprisonment shall be subject to the supervision of the Court and shall be consistent with widely accepted international treaty standards governing treatment of prisoners.[792]

---

[791] *General remarks*:

Article 106 endeavours to strike a balance between two equally valid interests. On the one hand, as a matter of principle the State of enforcement's prison infrastructure is used, so it seems quite natural that its national law should govern the day-to-day-life in prison – otherwise the Court would have had to set up its own prison norms (Schabas, 2010, p. 1082). On the other hand, there is the need for the Court to guarantee a certain uniformity of prison conditions and thereby ensuring equal treatment of all international prisoners (Prost, 2001, p. 675; cf. Chimimba, 1999/2002, pp. 351 f. and options for Article 96(2) in UN doc. A/CONF.183/2/Add.1, p. 153). The compromise enshrined in Article 106 is that the Court exercises general penitentiary supervision (para. 1), whereas the national law of the State of enforcement and its application by the competent authorities govern the daily life in prison without interference by the Court, but have to comply with certain minimum standards (para. 2). It remains dubious, how precisely "supervision" is to be understood, cf. below.

Authors: Michael Stiel and Carl-Friedrich Stuckenberg.

[792] In contrast to para. 2, which deals with the day-to-day execution of the sentence in a national prison, para. 1 refers to the administration of the sentence as a whole by the Court. Clark, 2008, Article 106 mgn. 4 argues that it would be inconsistent with the relevant international standards (in concreto: Article 7 ICCPR – for details on the applicable law cf. below) if the convict for example were sentenced to hard labour wearing a ball and chain. This is obviously true – nonetheless it remains dubious whether such a sentence would not a priori be excluded by Articles 77(1), 21(3).

The Court is designated as the body to supervise any decisions in the execution of the sentence, as "enforcement", it is argued, must be understood to include not only the enforcement of the sentence as such but also the modalities of this enforcement (the "conditions of enforcement", Article 106(2)), which is indicated by the reference to "standards governing the treatment of prisoners" in both paragraphs and further supported by Rule 211(1)(a) (Kreß/Sluiter, 2002, pp. 1804 f.).

Article 106(1) is silent on the question which powers the Court has for the exercise of that function. However, the Presidency is vested with the right to request all relevant information, especially from the State of enforcement, in Rule 211. If it deems it necessary after careful assessment of all available information, it may transfer the prisoner to another State of enforcement pursuant to Article 104(1), which can be understood as the ultimate form of exercising "supervision". Reflecting the drafting history, where a proposal to grant the Court the power to make decisions on every aspect of prison life, if deemed appropriate (UN doc. A/CONF.183/2/Add.1, p. 153), was clearly rejected (Kreß/Sluiter, 2002, pp. 1805 f.), the supervisory powers of the Court are limited to this "all or nothing" approach. It has been argued, however, that if the State of enforcement fails to respect the sentence as such (for example arbitrarily releases the prisoner in violation of Articles 105(1), 110(1)), the supervisory powers of the Court should also entail the possibility to make a formal finding to that extent, in case of a State Party pursuant to Article 87(7), but that such a finding is not authorised due to the clear intention of the States Parties (see above) in case the conditions of detention are inconsistent with the applicable human rights standards and the State therefore in breach of its obligation under

2. The conditions of imprisonment shall be governed by the law of the State of enforcement and shall be consistent with widely accepted international treaty standards governing treatment of prisoners;[793] in no case shall such conditions be more or less favourable than those available to prisoners convicted of similar offences in the State of enforcement.[794]

Article 106(2) (Kreß/Sluiter, 2002, p. 1805). It might appear doubtful, however, that the fact of the Court's having been denied the power to modify the conditions of detention necessitates the conclusion that it cannot make a finding regarding a breach of Article 106(2) either.

The *ad hoc* tribunals' Rules (Rule 104 RPE ICTY and RPE ICTR, respectively Rule 128 RPE MICT and Rule RPE SCS) allowed for supervision of their sentences by the tribunals themselves or a body designated by them (cf. Klip, 1997, pp. 150 f.; Culp, 2011, pp. 5–8). Although the ICC Statute and the RPE do neither envisage regular inspections nor the possibility that the Court may seek the assistance from other monitoring bodies, all Enforcement Agreements now in force provide for periodic inspections either by the International Committee of the Red Cross (see the Agreement with Belgium, ICC-PRES/16-03-14, Article 7; Denmark, ICC-PRES/12-02-12, Article 7; Finland, ICC-PRES/07-01-11, Article 7; Mali, ICC-PRES/11-01-12, Article 4(b); Serbia, ICC-PRES/09-03-11, Article 7), by the European Committee for the Prevention of Torture and Inhuman or Degrading Treatment or Punishment (Agreement with the United Kingdom, ICC-PRES/04-01-07, Article 6), or by the Court "or any entity designated by it" (Agreement with Austria, ICC-PRES/01-01-05, Article 7). Entrusting the ICRC with inspections continues the practice of the *ad hoc* tribunals (see above) and is in line with the fact that the Court has concluded an agreement with the ICRC the regarding the detainees at its own Detention Centre (ICC-PRES/02-01-06).

Authors: Michael Stiel and Carl-Friedrich Stuckenberg.

[793] Paragraph 2 requires that the national law which governs the conditions of imprisonment must be consistent with widely accepted international treaty standards governing treatment of prisoners. This serves the interest of the prisoner and guarantees a certain degree of uniformity, although inequalities of national laws above the international standards remain (Abels, 2012, p. 464).

Whereas the ICTY's sentencing judgment in *Prosecutor v. Erdemović* (Case No. IT-96-22-T), ICTY T. Ch., Sentencing Judgment, 29 November 1996, § 74) required conformity with "minimum principles of humanity and dignity which constitute the inspiration for the international standards governing the protection of the rights of convicted persons" and referred comprehensively to human rights treaties like Article 10 of the International Covenant on Civil and Political Rights (ICCPR, 999 UNTS 171) and regional instruments as well as to recommendatory standards like the Standard Minimum Rules for the Treatment of Prisoners (ECOSOC Res. 663 C (XXIV) of 31 July 1957, amended by Res. 2067 (LXII) of 13 May 1977), UN Basic Principles for the Treatment of Prisoners (GA Res. 111 (XXXXV), 14 December 1990), UN Body of Principles for the Protection of All Persons under Any Form of Detention or Imprisonment (GA Res. 173 (XXXXIII), 9 December 1988) etc (cf. United Nations Office of Drugs and Crime, Compendium of United Nations standards and norms in crime prevention and criminal justice, 2006), many delegations at the Rome Conference were not prepared to accept the application of these very detailed and ambitious (cf. Preliminary Observation No. 2 of the Standard Minimum Rules: "it is evident that not all of the rules are capable of application in all places and at all times"; Strijards, 2008, Article 103 mgn. 27) standards which may or may not yet have acquired the status of customary international law (Clark, 2008, Article 106 mgn. 2; Kreß/Sluiter, 2002, pp. 1798 f., 1802; Ntoubandi, 2012, pp. 1975 f.; Schabas, 2010, pp. 1080 f.). The compromise was reached to omit any reference to soft law standards (as contemplated for example in UN doc. A/49/10, p. 66) and require compliance only with the hard law of "widely accepted international treaty standards governing treatment of prisoners" now laid down in Arti-

---

cle 106(1) and (2). Thus, the negotiating history shows that this choice of words was intended to exclude the applicability of soft law like recommendatory minimum rules which the *ad hoc* Tribunals used to refer to (but see Safferling, 2001, p. 350 who rejects a literal reading). There is some ambiguity as to the criterion "widely accepted" which appears less demanding than "universally recognized" (cf. Article 7(1)(g)) or "internationally recognized" (cf. Article 21(3)) but may exclude standards only contained in regional treaties. It is equally unclear what the role of standards extant in customary international law is, as it is not mentioned in Article 106(2) (Kreß/Sluiter, 2002, p. 1803).

Which human rights instruments were specifically meant was left open (Kreß/Sluiter, 2002, p. 1799). Those will certainly include the UN Convention against Torture (1465 UNTS 85) and Article 10 of the ICCPR. While some authors declare the "Standard Minimum Rules for the Treatment of Prisoners" inapplicable with respect to the drafting history (see above; Chimimba, 1999/2002, pp. 352 f.; cf. Strijards, 2008, Article 103 mgn. 27; Zahar/Sluiter, 2008, p. 320), it is submitted by others, however, that the essence of some soft law instruments has already been assimilated into the interpretation of general treaty provisions such as the ICCPR by means of the jurisprudence of the Human Rights Committee (General Comment No. 21, UN doc. A/47/40, pp. 195 ff. §§ 5, 13; *Mukong v. Cameroon*, (Communication No. 458/1991), HRC, Views, 21 July 1994, § 9.3; *Gorij-Dinka v. Cameroon*, (Communication No. 1134/2002), HRC, Views, 17 March 2005, § 5.2; Abels, 2012, pp. 171 f., 497 f.; Clark, 2008, Article 106 mgn. 2; Kreß/Sluiter, 2002, p. 1802; Safferling, 2001, p. 344; Schabas, 2010, p. 1082; van Zyl Smit, 2005, p. 376). In addition, six out of seven Enforcement Agreements currently in force (with Austria, Belgium, Denmark, Finland, Mali, and Serbia) "recall" the Standard Minimum Rules for the Treatment of Prisoners, the Body of Principles for the Protection of all Persons under any Form of Detention or Imprisonment and the Basic Principles for the Treatment of Prisoners in their preambles, the Agreement with the United Kingdom (ICC-PRES/04-01-07, Article 5) incorporates the obligations of the United Kingdom under the European Convention for the Protection of Human Rights and Fundamental Freedoms of 1950 (ECHR, ETS No. 5; 213 UNTS 221).

Authors: Michael Stiel and Carl-Friedrich Stuckenberg.

[794] The clause that international prisoners should not be treated different from "ordinary" domestic prisoners convicted of similar offences was incorporated to guarantee that there would be no ill-treatment of ICC inmates (cf. Chimimba, 1999/2002, p. 353). Others see the provision as another manifestation of the principle of complementarity: If the ICC Statute accepts the primacy of genuine national prosecution, there should not be a different treatment of those first convicted by the ICC and later transferred back to domestic jurisdictions to serve their sentence (Clark, 2008, Article 106 mgn. 6; cf. Abels, 2012, p. 464).

"Similar offences" should be read to relate to the gravity of the offence, for example homicide, not to the legal characterisation, to provide for the necessary latitude to treat former political leaders different from low-level offenders (Kreß/Sluiter, 2002, p. 1803). Differences in treatment for other reasons are not prohibited (Kreß/Sluiter, 2002, pp. 1803 f.; for typical differences between national and international prisoners see Mulgrew, 2009, pp. 385 f.).

Following from Article 106(2), all relevant national complaint procedures must be available to the prisoner. It is submitted, that this should also include regional human rights mechanisms, where applicable, such as provided for example by the ECHR (Kreß/Sluiter, 2002, p. 1808). To date courts have been reluctant to receive applications of international prisoners (*Hirota v. MacArthur*, 338 U.S. 197, U.S. Supreme Court, Decision, 20 December 1948; *I. Hess v. The United Kingdom*, (Application No. 6231/73), ECHR, Decision, 28 May 1975, DR 2, 72), but there seems to be some development (cf. *Soering v. The United Kingdom*, (Application No. 14038/88), ECtHR, Judgment, 7 July 1989).

3. Communications between a sentenced person and the Court shall be unimpeded and confidential.[795]

Some authors expect that the prohibition of more favourable treatment for international prisoners will lead to an improvement of conditions in national prisons, as their treatment must also be consistent with international standards (Kreß/Sluiter, 2002, p. 1803; van Zyl Smit, 2005, p. 376; cf. Clark, 2008, Article 106 mgn. 6). Whereas the prohibition of discrimination is justified, the prohibition of preferential treatment may, although well-intended, turn out to be problematic. It has been observed (Abels, 2012, p. 464) that this presumably excludes a sizable number of States from the group of prospective custodial States, that is, all those states which have not yet managed to procure the required conditions of detention to the entirety of their own prison population (but see Marchesi, 1999, p. 438 who reads this as: not more favourable "provided that these [conditions] are consistent with the standards set by international law").

Authors: Michael Stiel and Carl-Friedrich Stuckenberg.

[795] Since the prisoner is the prime source of information on his living conditions, a secured channel of communication to the Court is enshrined in Article 106(3). The provision is to be read together with Article 104(2), which provides for a right to request transfer to another State of enforcement at any time (cf. Kreß/Sluiter, 2002, p. 1808). As proposals for a qualification "subject to overriding security considerations" (UN doc. A/CONF.183/C.1/WGE/L.9) were rejected at the Rome Conference, the provision is to be applied without exceptions (Kreß/Sluiter, 2002, pp. 1801 f.; Schabas, 2010, p. 1083). It is submitted, that there is even a positive obligation for the State of enforcement to facilitate communications between the prisoner and the Court (Clark, 2008, Article 106 mgn. 7).

Cross-references:

Article 104.

Rules 211, 216.

Regulation 113.

Doctrine:

1. Denis Abels, *Prisoners of the International Community: The Legal Position of Persons Detained at International Criminal Tribunals,* TMC Asser Press/Springer, The Hague, 2012.
2. Hirad Abtahi and Steven Arrigg Koh, "The Emerging Enforcement Practice of the International Criminal Court", in *Cornell International Law Journal,* 2012, vol. 45, pp. 1–23.
3. Trevor Pascal Chimimba, "Chapter 11 – Establishing An Enforcement Regime", in Roy S. Lee (ed.), *The International Criminal Court: The Making of the Rome Statute,* Kluwer Law International, The Hague, 1999/2002, pp. 345–56.
4. Roger S. Clark, "Article 106", in Otto Triffterer (ed.), *Commentary on the Rome Statute of the International Criminal Court: Observers' Notes, Article by Article,* 2nd ed., C.H. Beck/Hart/Nomos, Munich/Oxford/Baden-Baden, 2008, pp. 1663–65.
5. Richard Culp, *Enforcement and Monitoring of Sentences in the Modern War Crimes Process: Equal Treatment before the Law?,* 2011.
6. Irene Gartner, "The Rules of Procedure and Evidence on Co-operation and Enforcement", in Horst Fischer, Claus Kreß and Sascha Rolf Lüder (eds.), *International and National Prosecution of Crimes Under International Law,* Berlin Verlag, Berlin, 2001, pp. 423–45.
7. André Klip, "Enforcement of Sanctions Imposed by the International Criminal Tribunals for Rwanda and the Former Yugoslavia", in *European Journal of Crime, Criminal Law and Criminal Justice,* 1997, vol. 5, pp. 144–64.

---

8. Claus Kreß and Göran Sluiter, "Imprisonment", in Antonio Cassese, Paola Gaeta and John R.W.D. Jones (eds.), *The Rome Statute of the International Criminal Court: A Commentary*, 2nd ed., Oxford University Press, Oxford, 2002, pp. 1757–1821.

9. Antonio Marchesi, "The Enforcement of Sentences of the International Criminal Court", in Flavia Lattanzi and William A. Schabas (eds.), *Essays on the Rome Statute of the International Criminal Court*, il Sirente, Ripa Fagnano Alto, 1999, pp. 427–45.

10. Róisín Mulgrew, "On the Enforcement of Sentences Imposed by International Courts", in *Journal of International Criminal Justice*, 2009, vol. 7, pp. 373–96.

11. Faustin Z. Ntoubandi, "Article 106", in Julian Fernandez and Xavier Pacreau (eds.), *Statut de Rome de la Cour pénale internationale*, Commentaire Article par Article, Vol. II, Éditions Pedone, Paris, 2012.

12. Kimberly Prost, "Chapter 14 – Enforcement", in Roy S. Lee (ed.), *The International Criminal Court: Elements of Crimes and Rules of Procedure and Evidence*, Transnational Publishers, Ardsley, NY, 2001, pp. 673–703.

13. Nigel S. Rodley and Matt Pollard, *The Treatment of Prisoners Under International Law*, 3rd ed., Oxford University Press, Oxford, 2009.

14. Christoph J.M. Safferling, *Towards an International Criminal Procedure*, Oxford University Press, Oxford, 2001.

15. William A. Schabas, Article 106, *The International Criminal Court: A Commentary on the Rome Statute*, Oxford University Press, Oxford, 2010.

16. Gerard A.M. Strijards, "Article 103", in Otto Triffterer (ed.), *Commentary on the Rome Statute of the International Criminal Court: Observers' Notes, Article by Article*, 2nd ed., C.H. Beck/Hart/Nomos, Munich/Oxford/Baden-Baden, 2008, pp. 1647–57.

17. Dirk van Zyl Smit, "International Imprisonment", in *International and Comparative Law Quarterly*, 2005, vol. 54, pp. 357–386.

18. Alexander Zahar and Göran Sluiter, *International Criminal Law: A Critical Introduction*, Oxford University Press, Oxford, 2008.

Authors: Michael Stiel and Carl-Friedrich Stuckenberg.

Article 107
Transfer of the person upon completion of sentence[796]

1. Following completion of the sentence, a person who is not a national of the State of enforcement may, in accordance with the law of the State of enforcement, be transferred to a State which is obliged to receive him or her, or to another State which agrees to receive him or her, taking into account any wishes of the person to be transferred to that State, unless the State of enforcement authorizes the person to remain in its territory.[797]

2. If no State bears the costs arising out of transferring the person to another State pursuant to paragraph 1, such costs shall be borne by the Court.[798]

3. Subject to the provisions of Article 108, the State of enforcement may also, in accordance with its national law, extradite or otherwise surrender the person to a State which has re-

---

[796] *General remarks*:

Article 107 deals with the conflicting interests that may arise between the enforcing state and the rights of a sentence person upon completion of sentence.

Normally one would expect that a sentenced person upon completion of sentence would return to his or her State of nationality. Even national cases not involving international crimes problems may arise upon completion of sentence, human rights issues may arise when there is difficulties to transfer a person where there is risk of torture or other serious violations.

Experience shows that in relation to international criminal tribunals and courts one may expect two scenarios. The first scenario is that the prisoner wishes to return to his or her State of nationality where he or she will be welcomed as a hero. This has been the case with prisoners sentenced by the ICTY. The second scenario concerns the situations where there has been a shift in power and/or there has been a national upheaval where the released person does not want to return. It is also possible that no other state is willing to accept him or her, whereby the person effectively becomes stateless. This has been a difficulty for persons sentenced by the ICTR. States of enforcement may thus face the scenario where it will be unable to remove a person upon completion of sentence (Schabas, pp. 1084–1086, Clark, p. 1668).

Preparatory works:

Article 97 of the ICC Preparatory Committee Draft Statute (1998) contained a provision dealing with what to do with a sentenced person upon completion of sentence. Article 97(1) points out "the State of the person's nationality" as one of the options, which in the final version of Article 107(1) has been replaced by "a State which is obliged to receive him or her".

[797] It follows from the words "in accordance with the law of the State of enforcement" that the State of enforcement must have appropriate domestic legislation to deal with these details.

The concept "a State which is obliged to receive him or her" is not clear. It may include cases where the person concerned has aright under domestic law to return home.

The provision also entertains the possibility that the State of enforcement authorises the person to remain in its territory. It should be noted that the Statute does impose on obligation on the State of enforcement to provide what amounts to asylum for former criminals.

[798] The second paragraph contains an implicit hope that some State will pay for the transfer, either the State of nationality which is happy to receive its citizen back or the State of Enforcement who wants to get rid of the criminal. If no state is willing the bear the costs, it will be borne by the Court.

---

quested the extradition or surrender of the person for purposes of trial or enforcement of a sentence.[799]

---

[799] The third paragraph confirms the right of the State of enforcement to comply with requests for extradition and surrender, subject to the provisions of Article 108. Rule 213 provides that with respect to Article 107(3) the procedure set out in rules 214 and 215 shall apply, as appropriate.

Cross-references:

Rule 213.

Doctrine:

1. Roger S. Clark, "Article 107", in Otto Triffterer (ed.), *Commentary on the Rome Statute of the International Criminal Court: Observers' Notes, Article by Article*, 2nd ed., C.H. Beck/Hart/Nomos, Munich/Oxford/Baden-Baden, 2008, pp. 1667–69.

2. Kimberly Prost, "Chapter 14 – Enforcement", in Roy S. Lee (ed.), *The International Criminal Court: Elements of Crimes and Rules of Procedure and Evidence*, Transnational Publishers, Ardsley, NY, 2001, pp. 673–703.

3. William A. Schabas, *The International Criminal Court: A Commentary on the Rome Statute*, Oxford University Press, Oxford, 2010.

Author: Mark Klamberg.

Article 108
Limitation on the prosecution or punishment of other offences[800]

1. A sentenced person in the custody[801] of the State of enforcement[802] shall not be subject to prosecution or punishment or to extradition to a third State for any conduct engaged in

---

[800] *General remarks*:

The provision is modelled after the principle of specialty which is firmly embedded in the inter-State practice on extradition and often regarded as part of customary international law. Whether the principle also governs the inter-State transfer of prisoners is less clear (Gartner, 2001, p. 438; Kreß/Sluiter, 2002, p. 1809). The original rationale from the extradition context is to limit the infringement of the extraditing State's sovereignty by strict control of what the receiving state may do – in tandem with the principles of reciprocity and double criminality. Obviously, this rationale is not applicable here because no infringement of sovereignty is at issue – unlike the case of surrender, cf. Article 101 – since the ICC is neither a sovereign State nor a court of general jurisdiction (Schabas, 2008, Article 108 mgn. 7; Schabas, 2010, pp. 1092 f.; cf. Kreß/Sluiter, 2002, pp. 1809 f.). Only from the perspective of the surrendering State, the enforcement of the Court's sentence in another State amounts to re-extradition (Kreß/Sluiter, 2002, pp. 1810, 1813), yet Article 108 ignores the surrendering State completely (this is partly remedied by Rule 214(4), which requires its consultation, and Regulation 115, which calls for respect of the principles of international law on re-extradition).

Hence, the inclusion of this rule of specialty must be justified by other grounds in light of the interests at stake in the enforcement of a custodial sentence of the Court. It is submitted here that Article 108 serves to control and prevent such interferences that could frustrate the enforcement of the particular sentence or are otherwise incompatible with the aims of international criminal justice. The provision's raison d'être cannot be left undetermined because it is essential for the criteria upon which the Court may approve or reject a request for criminal prosecution, punishment or extradition (cf. Schabas, 2008, Article 108 mgn. 7).

Preparatory works:

The provision is an innovation, since the *ad hoc* tribunals' statutes do not contain a comparable rule and the tribunals never had to assess the issue in the context of a sentence being actually enforced (cf. Schabas, 2008, Article 108 mgn. 1 with fn. 1). It was introduced late in the drafting process and was adopted without much alteration (see Kreß/Sluiter, 2002, p. 1810; Schabas, 2008, Article 108 mgn. 2–3). There was some resistance against the rule of specialty in general and minor controversies arose whether the Presidency or the Court should decide on exceptions (Schabas, 2008, Article 108 mgn. 3; Schabas, 2010, pp. 1090 f.) – which is immaterial now since Rules 199, 214 and 215 entrust the Presidency with the Court's decision – and about the nature of the hearing (Gartner, 2001, pp. 438 f.).

Authors: Michael Stiel and Carl-Friedrich Stuckenberg.

[801] *Sentenced person in custody*

Article 108(1) set outs a general prohibition of prosecution or extradition of the sentenced person for conduct prior to that person's delivery to the State of enforcement which can be lifted by the approval of the Court on the request of the State of enforcement. The relevant procedure is elaborated in Rules 214 and 215.

The wording of the English version of Article 108(1) appears to be broader than the French version which uses the term "*détenu*". It has been argued that a person "in custody" is not necessarily a prisoner (a term used in earlier versions and later abandoned, Schabas, 2008, Article 108 mgn. 8) or detainee but could also be a person provisionally released or even a fugitive (Schabas, 2008, Article 108 mgn. 5). There seems to be agreement that only a broad reading in

---

prior to that person's delivery[803] to the State of enforcement, unless such prosecution, punishment[804] or extradition has been approved by the Court[805] at the request of the State of enforcement.

---

accordance with Article 33(d) of the Vienna Convention on the Law of Treaties (1155 UNTS 331) conforms to the provision's rationale (Kreß/Sluiter, 2002, p. 1811; Schabas, 2008, Article 108 mgn. 5). It is doubtful, however, whether a fugitive still is "in custody". Arguably, Article 111 is the applicable lex specialis in that case, but the question seems rather theoretical, as in practice states would wait until the fugitive has been arrested.

Authors: Michael Stiel and Carl-Friedrich Stuckenberg.

[802] State of enforcement means the State having accepted the Court's designation according to Article 103 (Schabas, 2008, Article 108 mgn. 4). It is also only the State of enforcement which can make the request in the case of extradition and not the "third State" which requested the State of enforcement to extradite the person, possibly on the basis of a bilateral extradition treaty (Schabas, 2008, Article 108 mgn. 6). After the request is made, there may be direct communication between the Court and the third State, cf. Rule 214(3).

Authors: Michael Stiel and Carl-Friedrich Stuckenberg.

[803] Conduct after the person's delivery to the State of enforcement is not covered and can be prosecuted and punished according to the enforcement State's national law without the Court's prior approval. Nevertheless, Rule 216 obliges the State of enforcement to inform the Presidency about any important events including a subsequent prosecution, as a supplement to the Court's supervisory power pursuant to Article 106 and relocation power under Article 104(1). One may doubt, however, whether the extradition to a third State for conduct following the delivery should in fact be admissible without the Court's consent; admittedly, such cases, though theoretically possible, are most unlikely. More likely are instances of prosecution and punishment for offences committed during incarceration; the disciplinary aspect is covered by Article 106, but the question whether an additional prison sentence shall be executed only after having served the full sentence pronounced by the Court, cf. Rule 215(2), is unresolved. Given the State's undertaking to execute the sentence as pronounced by the Court and following the model of Rule 215(2), it is submitted that the international sentence has to be served in full before any additional sentence in the State of enforcement can be executed. This approach is supported by Rule 216: Only prosecution by the State of enforcement subsequent to the prisoner's transfer is mentioned, arguably as enforcement (of a sentence for such conduct) will not take place.

The restriction to prior conduct is said to be in line with usual practice and the legitimate interests underlying the specialty principle (Kreß/Sluiter, 2002, p. 1811) – this reasoning appears questionable since the specialty principle is applied out of its usual context here. The restriction could be justified if Article 108 is regarded as an extension or complement of the rule of specialty enshrined in Article 101, see above, assuming that the defendant is regularly surrendered to the Court by a State other than the State of enforcement.

The use of the term "delivery" is not in line with other provisions of the Statute which use "transfer" but there is no indication that this verbal difference reflects any substantive distinction (Schabas, 2008, Article 108 mgn. 4), since Rule 214(1) also employs the term "transfer".

Authors: Michael Stiel and Carl-Friedrich Stuckenberg.

[804] The prohibition is limited to criminal proceedings, so that all other types of proceedings, for example for civil claims (Ntoubandi, 2012, p. 1987; Schabas, 2008, Article 108 mgn. 4), are admissible subject to notification according to Rule 216 ("important event concerning the sentenced person"), if appropriate.

Authors: Michael Stiel and Carl-Friedrich Stuckenberg.

---

2. The Court shall decide the matter after having heard the views of the sentenced person.[806]

3. Paragraph 1 shall cease to apply if the sentenced person remains voluntarily for more than 30 days in the territory of the State of enforcement after having served the full sentence imposed by the Court, or returns to the territory of that State after having left it.[807]

---

[805] Neither the Statute nor the Rules provide any guidance which criteria the Court shall resort to when making its decision. The usual considerations of States in extradition contexts are not pertinent here; instead, criteria must be derived from the Statute and the Court's functions and prerogatives (Kreß/Sluiter, 2002, p. 1812; Schabas, 2008, Article 108 mgn. 7). It has been put forward that the request must be denied if the principle *ne bis in idem* (Article 20) or human rights norms (Article 21(3)) would be violated or if granting the request would contribute to such violations; evolving human rights norms may be sufficient (Kreß/Sluiter, 2002, p. 1812; Schabas, 2008, Article 108 mgn. 7). The Presidency should therefore deny a request which could lead to the application of the death penalty or other cruel or degrading forms of punishment or intolerable detention conditions (Kreß/Sluiter, 2002, pp. 1812 f.; Schabas, 2008, Article 108 mgn. 7, Schabas, 2010, p. 1093) or would in some way abuse the Court's process. The Court might attach conditions to its approval in order to ensure the observance of fundamental human rights (Schabas, 2008, Article 108 mgn. 7). Absent such grounds for refusal, it has been argued that the Court should deny a request only "in exceptional cases" (Schabas, 2008, Article 108 mgn. 7; Schabas, 2010, p. 1093).

Authors: Michael Stiel and Carl-Friedrich Stuckenberg.

[806] The sentenced person shall be heard before the Courts decides on the request. It is controversial whether Article 108(2) can be regarded as formulating an individual right to specialty protecting the sentenced person (Ntoubandi, 2012, p. 1987; Schabas, 2008, Article 108 mgn. 1, 8; Schabas, 2010, p. 1089) or not (Kreß/Sluiter, 2002, p. 1811). The controversy seems to a great extent immaterial since the Presidency only has to hear the sentenced person and take his view into account and not to obtain his consent. The Statute does not prescribe how the hearing shall be conducted. Proposals for a mandatory oral hearing were rejected at the negotiations as not in line with inter-State practice which relies on written statements of the prisoner (Gartner, 2001, pp. 438 f.; Prost, 2001, pp. 690 f.). The consensus reflected in the corresponding Rules is that a written consultation is usually sufficient, since Rule 214(1)(d) directs the requesting State of enforcement to transmit a "protocol containing the views of the sentenced person" and Rule 214(6) states that the Presidency "may decide to conduct a hearing". A commentator has suggested that a fully fledged adversarial hearing would not be inconceivable which could even involve amici curiae if human rights issues are at stake (Schabas, 2008, Article 108 mgn. 9; Schabas, 2010, p. 1093).

Authors: Michael Stiel and Carl-Friedrich Stuckenberg.

[807] The prohibition of paragraph 1 ceases to apply in two hypotheses after the Court's sentence is fully served: First, when the released prisoner remains voluntarily for more than 30 days in the territory of the State of enforcement, and secondly, when he returns to that territory after having left it. This is said to be consistent with inter-State practice in bilateral extradition matters and justified because the former prisoner is deemed to have "voluntarily" relinquished the protection of the specialty rule (Schabas, 2008, Article 108 mgn. 10; Schabas, 2010, p. 1093). On the contrary, no such "voluntary" waiver exists if the person remains in the enforcement State's territory because no other State lets him enter. The second hypothesis does not contain a voluntariness requirement so that it seems that the specialty rule would not apply even if the person returns to the State of enforcement because he has been forcibly expelled from the State he wanted to enter (Ntoubandi, 2012, p. 1988; Schabas, 2008, Article 108 mgn. 10), although it is not clear that this inexplicable difference, which runs counter to principle, was really intended by the drafters (in this sense Kreß/Sluiter, 2002, p. 1813).

Cross-references:

Rules 214, 215, 216.

Regulation 115.

Doctrine:

1. Irene Gartner, "The Rules of Procedure and Evidence on Co-operation and Enforcement", in Horst Fischer, Claus Kreß and Sascha Rolf Lüder (eds.), *International and National Prosecution of Crimes Under International Law*, Berlin Verlag, Berlin, 2001, pp. 423–45.

2. Claus Kreß and Göran Sluiter, "Imprisonment", in Antonio Cassese, *et al (*eds.), *The Rome Statute of the International Criminal Court: A Commentary*, 2nd ed., Oxford University Press, Oxford, 2002, pp. 1809–13.

3. Faustin Z. Ntoubandi, "Article 108", in Julian Fernandez/Xavier Pacreau (eds.), *Statut de Rome de la Cour pénale internationale*, Commentaire Article par Article, Vol. II, Éditions Pedone, Paris, 2012.

4. Kimberly Prost, "Chapter 14 – Enforcement", in Roy S. Lee (ed.), *The International Criminal Court: Elements of Crimes and Rules of Procedure and Evidence*, Transnational Publishers, Ardsley, NY, 2001, pp. 673–703.

5. William A. Schabas, "Article 108", in Otto Triffterer (ed.), *Commentary on the Rome Statute of the International Criminal Court: Observers' Notes, Article by Article*, 2nd ed., C.H. Beck/Hart/Nomos, Munich/Oxford/Baden-Baden, 2008, pp. 1671–76.

6. William A. Schabas, Article 108, *The International Criminal Court: A Commentary on the Rome Statute*, Oxford University Press, Oxford, 2010.

Authors: Michael Stiel and Carl-Friedrich Stuckenberg.

Article 109

Enforcement of fines and forfeiture measures[808]

---

[808] *General remarks*:

Article 77(2) allows the Court to impose fines and order the forfeiture of proceeds, property and assets derived directly or indirectly from a crime in addition to custodial sentences. These powers represent a relative innovation on the international level (see Abtahi/Arrigg Koh, 2012, pp. 4 f.; Kreß/Sluiter, 2002, pp. 1823 f.), although the Court has not used them as of yet (the Trial Chambers declined to impose a fine or forfeiture order on Thomas Lubanga Dyilo and Germain Katanga as they are indigent; cf. Prose*cutor v. Lubanga*, ICC T. Ch. I, Decision on Sentence pursuant to Article 76 of the Statute, ICC-01/04-01/06-2901, 10 July 2012, mgn. 106; *Prosecutor v. Katanga*, ICC T. Ch. II, Décision relative à la peine (Article 76 du Statut), ICC-01/04-01/07-3484, 23 May 2014, mgn. 169). Provisional measures are regulated in Article 93(1)(k), the enforcement regime is contained in Article 109. The provision is applicable to reparation orders by way of referral from Article 75(5), but not to fines authorised under Article 70(3) for offences against the administration of justice.

In sharp contrast to the consensual nature of the enforcement of prison sentences, Article 109 erects an obligatory regime for the enforcement of fines and forfeiture orders, apparently a left-over of the rejected general recognition clause contained in earlier drafts (for the negotiating history see Kreß/Sluiter, 2002, pp. 1826–1828; Schabas, 2008, Article 109 mgn. 2–4; Schabas, 2010, pp. 1095–1097). The present provision could be agreed upon as the Court depends on the cooperation of a specific State in such cases (Kreß/Sluiter, 2002, p. 1831). This approach renders the ICC's "dual enforcement regime" (Abtahi/Arrigg Koh, 2012, p. 3) lamentably inconsistent; nonetheless, the obligatory nature of Article 109 is to be welcomed (Kreß/Sluiter, 2002, p. 1831).

It was debated whether the statute should provide for the direct recognition and enforcement of fines and forfeiture orders or whether the States Parties shall give effect to the Court's decisions in accordance with their national law (cf. UN doc. A/50/22, § 237 p. 44; Schabas, 2008, Article 109 mgn. 4). It is unclear what "direct enforcement" implicates (apart from the suppression of a separate recognition procedure like exequatur proceedings or a conversion requirement): Since enforcement as such needs a legally ordered procedure, either the Statute and Rules have to provide some form of *loi uniforme* to be employed (cf. Schabas, 2008, Article 109 mgn. 5; Schabas, 2010, p. 1098) – which would have been a very demanding and ambitious task – or, failing that, the domestic *lex loci executionis* is applied, possibly with some qualifications. Article 109 has chosen the latter approach which is in line with the sparse inter-State practice in this field (Kreß/Sluiter, 2002, pp. 1824–1826).

The Statute does not provide for the case that all enforcement measures with regard to a fine imposed by the Court fail, a controversial issue at the negotiations (see Kreß/Sluiter, 2002, pp. 1827 f.). Instead, Rule 146(5) authorises the Presidency in cases of "continued wilful non-payment" of a fine and "as a last resort", to extend the term of imprisonment by up to a quarter of the original term or five years, whichever is less, provided the extension does not lead to a total prison term of more than 30 years. A term of life imprisonment may not be extended. This is a remarkable power of the Presidency that is normally restricted to enforce sentences pronounced by the Chambers (Abtahi/Arrigg Koh, 2012, pp. 21 f.). It is subject to heavy criticism with regard to the *nulla poena sine lege* principle enshrined in Article 23 (cf. Mulgrew, 2013, pp. 16 f.)

Authors: Michael Stiel and Carl-Friedrich Stuckenberg.

---

1. States Parties shall give effect[809] to fines or forfeitures ordered by the Court under Part 7, without prejudice to the rights of bona fide third parties,[810] and in accordance with the procedure of their national law.[811]

---

[809] Article 109(1) obliges the States Parties to enforce fines and forfeiture orders imposed by the Court. The words "give effect" (stricter in French: "font executer") have been understood to exclude any modification of the amounts of fines and forfeiture orders (UN doc. A/CONF.183/C.1/WGE/L.14/Add.1/Corr.1 (14 July 1998), fn. to draft Article 93; Kreß/Sluiter, 2002, p. 1827). Accordingly, Rule 220 provides that the Presidency shall remind States Parties thereof.

States Parties are not expected to initiate enforcement measures on their own but only on the request of the Presidency which according to Rule 217 shall seek cooperation and enforcement measures "in accordance with Part 9". With regard to fines under Article 77, Rule 146(5) makes clear that the Presidency will first ask the sentenced person to pay voluntarily and resort to enforcement measures only in case of non-compliance.

Authors: Michael Stiel and Carl-Friedrich Stuckenberg.

[810] The only ground for refusal to enforce fines and forfeiture orders mentioned in the Statute is prejudice to the "rights of bona fide third parties", an expression nowhere defined in the Statute or RPE. Hence, it seems that national courts have to determine which rights are relevant and when a party qualifies as bona fide, which not only deviates from inter-State practice but may result in an uneven application (Kreß/Sluiter, 2002, p. 1830; Schabas, 2008, Article 109 mgn. 7; Schabas, 2010, pp. 1098 f.). It has been submitted that the Presidency should be competent to make a finding that a national court has abused that argument in a concrete case (Kreß/Sluiter, 2002, p. 1830 fn. 25) and that the Court itself might intervene in national proceedings in order to contest the priority given to a third party creditor (Schabas, 2008, Article 109 mgn. 8, Schabas, 2010, p. 1098 f.). Arguably, there should be some mechanism to provide guidance and enhance uniformity on this issue, assuming that in the future large sums could be at stake.

The restriction applies to both forfeiture orders as well as fines although the corresponding proviso is spelled out only in Article 77(2)(b) for forfeiture orders and not in Article 77(2)(a) relating to fines, as such a distinction was never mentioned during the negotiations (Schabas, 2008, Article 109 mgn. 9, Schabas, 2010, p. 1099).

Considering that the enforcement under Article 109(1) is stricter than the execution of provisional measures under Article 93(1)(k) where a "fundamental legal principle of general application" represents an additional ground for refusal pursuant to Article 93(3), commentators have, for the sake of consistency, suggested to interpret Article 109(1) accordingly (Kreß/Sluiter, 2002, p. 1829). This proposal is underscored by Rule 217 (Gartner, 2001, p. 443). Alternatively, one might argue that "fundamental legal principles of general application" can often already be taken into account in the determination of the "rights of bona fide third parties".

Authors: Michael Stiel and Carl-Friedrich Stuckenberg.

[811] States shall apply their *lex fori* when enforcing fines and forfeiture orders of the court. This is analogous to the application of national law to the enforcement of prison sentences under Article 106(2) and without alternative here, since there is no extant international legal regime on the enforcement of fines etc. The provision does not explicitly require States Parties to adjust their legislation if it proves inadequate but it is submitted that the provision has to be interpreted in that way in light of its object and purpose (Article 31(1) of the Vienna Convention on the Law of Treaties) which is made explicit for Part 9 in Articles 86, 88 and 89, the latter one only clarifying the applicability of the respective national procedure (Gartner, 2001, p. 443; Kreß/Sluiter, 2002, p. 1829; Ntoubandi, 2012, p. 1991; Schabas, 2008, Article 109 mgn. 6; Schabas, 2010, p. 1098; but see Galvis Martínez, 2014, p. 209). Rule 217 supports this view, as the Presidency

2. If a State Party is unable to give effect to an order for forfeiture, it shall take measures to recover the value of the proceeds, property or assets ordered by the Court to be forfeited, without prejudice to the rights of bona fide third parties.[812]

3. Property, or the proceeds of the sale of real property or, where appropriate, the sale of other property, which is obtained by a State Party as a result of its enforcement of a judgement of the Court shall be transferred to the Court.[813]

---

shall act in accordance with Part 9 "for the enforcement of fines ...". The opposite construction – that Article 109 obliges only those States Parties which already have suitable legislation – would render the provision largely ineffective, considering that at least some minimal implementing legislation would be needed in most cases (cf. for example Articles 43 to 45 of the German Law on Cooperation with the ICC.

Authors: Michael Stiel and Carl-Friedrich Stuckenberg.

[812] Article 109(2) directs the State Party to proceed to value confiscation if it is unable to give effect to a forfeiture order, not a fine, according to Article 109(1). The inability envisaged here is not the lack of adequate procedures in the national law since a State Party is obliged to adjust its national law in conformity with the Statute (see comment on 109(1)); Kreß/Sluiter, 2002, pp. 1829 f.; unclear Schabas, 2008, Article 109 mgn. 10 f.; Schabas, 2010, pp. 1099 f.). Rather, the inability refers to legal or factual obstacles like the rights of bona fide third parties, possibly also specific types of property immune from seizure under national law (Kreß/Sluiter, 2002, p. 1830; Schabas, 2008, Article 109 mgn. 11; Schabas, 2010, p. 1100), or the case of real property mentioned in paragraph 3. Assets may be also be unrealisable because they are subject to sanctions ordered by the Security Council or because the costs of preservation and maintenance exceed their value (for examples see Galvis Martínez, 2014, pp. 211 f.).

Again, the rights of bona fide third parties have to be respected, the determination of which is left to the national courts. This may lead to the problems set out above (see comment on 109(1)). In the case of rights of bona fide third parties hindering the seizure of property under Article 109(1), it is difficult to see how a value confiscation by, for instance, judicial sale would be feasible (Gartner, 2001, p. 444).

Authors: Michael Stiel and Carl-Friedrich Stuckenberg.

[813] Any property a State Party obtains as a result of the enforcement of a fine, forfeiture order, reparation order, or measure of value confiscation must be transferred to the Court, even where the Court awards reparations on an individual basis (cf. Rule 218(4) and Regulation 116). The Court may then order such property to be transferred to the Trust Fund according to Article 79(2).

Cross-references:

Articles 75(5), 77, 79, 93(1)(k), (3).

Rules 146(5), 212, 217, 218, 219, 220, 221, 222.

Regulations 113, 116, 117.

Doctrine:

1. Hirad Abtahi and Steven Arrigg Koh, "The Emerging Enforcement Practice of the International Criminal Court", in *Cornell International Law Journal*, 2012, vol. 45, pp. 1–23.

2. Trevor Pascal Chimimba, "Chapter 11 – Establishing An Enforcement Regime", in Roy S. Lee (ed.), *The International Criminal Court: The Making of the Rome Statute*, Kluwer Law International, The Hague, 2002, pp. 345–56.

3. Manuel Galvis Martínez, "Forfeiture of Assets at the International Criminal Court", in *Journal of International Criminal Justice*, 2014, vol. 12, pp. 193–217.

---

4. Irene Gartner, "The Rules of Procedure and Evidence on Co-operation and Enforcement", in Horst Fischer, Claus Kreß and Sascha Rolf Lüder (eds.), *International and National Prosecution of Crimes Under International Law*, Berlin Verlag, Berlin, 2001, pp. 423–45.

5. Claus Kreß and Göran Sluiter, "Fines and Forfeiture Orders", in Antonio Cassese, Paola Gaeta and John R.W.D. Jones (eds.), T*he Rome Statute of the International Criminal Court: A Commentary*, 2nd ed., Oxford University Press, Oxford, 2002, pp. 1823–38.

6. Róisín Mulgrew, *Towards the Development of the International Penal System*, Cambridge University Press, Cambridge, 2013.

7. Faustin Z. Ntoubandi, "Article 109", in Julian Fernandez and Xavier Pacreau (eds.), *Statut de Rome de la Cour pénale internationale*, Commentaire Article par Article, Vol. II, Éditions Pedone, Paris, 2012.

8. Kimberly Prost, "Chapter 14 – Enforcement", in Roy S. Lee (ed.), *The International Criminal Court: Elements of Crimes and Rules of Procedure and Evidence*, Transnational Publishers, Ardsley, NY, 2001, pp. 673–703.

9. William A. Schabas, Article 109, *The International Criminal Court: A Commentary on the Rome Statute*, Oxford University Press, Oxford, 2010.

10. William A. Schabas, "Article 109", in Otto Triffterer (ed.), *Commentary on the Rome Statute of the International Criminal Court: Observers' Notes, Article by Article*, 2nd ed., C.H. Beck/Hart/Nomos, Munich/Oxford/Baden-Baden, 2008, pp. 1677–81.

Authors: Michael Stiel and Carl-Friedrich Stuckenberg.

Article 110
Review by the Court concerning reduction of sentence[814]

---

[814] *General remarks*

Article 110 addresses the possibility to reduce the sentence after a substantial part of it has been enforced already. The main *rationale* behind this is to promote the reintegration of the prisoner into society (cf. for example German Federal Constitutional Court, (*Bundesverfassungsgericht*), Judgment of 14. 6. 1993, case no. 2 BvR 157/93, *Neue Juristische Wochenschrift* (NJW) 1994, 378). However, this idea is more than a practical consideration. Social reinsertion and reformation of prisoners is a universal human rights requirement of any penitentiary system, cf. IC-CPR, Article 10(3) (see also Schabas, 2010, 1102).

The idea of encouraging the detainee to act in accordance with the law by offering him the perspective of a life in freedom emerged during the 19th century, when the purpose of punishment was no longer seen only in retaliation and atonement, but also in general and special prevention. Sentence reduction or early release (for example under parole) exist in most domestic legal orders, however, the forms and conditions vary (a comparative study is provided by Jescheck (ed.), *Die Freiheitsstrafe und ihre Surrogate im deutschen und ausländischen Recht*, 1984, 2133 ff.). Precedents can also be found in international criminal law. At the International Military Tribunal for the Far East ('IMTFE'), all convicts, irrespective of their sentence, were released within one year following their conviction, as Japan considered the IMTFE a form of victor's vengeance and humiliation of the defeated (Bassiouni 2008, 603 ff, 605, with further references). In Germany, on the other hand, those tried by the International Military Tribunal served their sentences entirely (Bassiouni 2008, 603 ff, 605, with further references). With respect to those tried by the subsequent proceedings under Control Council Law No. 10, the United States was the only ally which had developed a formal Advisory Board on Clemency for War Criminals (Bassiouni, 2008, 605). Criteria applied by this board were "the subordinate authority and responsibility" of the defendant, the "courage to resist criminal orders at personal risk" as well as health conditions or other special circumstances of the detainee (Statement of the High Commissioner for Germany, 31 January 1951, Upon Announcing his Final Decision Concerning Requests for Clemency for War Criminals Convicted at Nuernberg, in 15 Trials of the War Criminals 1176–79 (1948)).

Both the ICTY and the ICTR Statute provide a section on "pardon or commutation of sentences" (Article 28 ICTY Statute and Article 27 ICTR Statute) and respective Rules of Procedures and Evidence (rule 125 ICTY RPE and rule 126 ICTR RPE) as well as Practice Directions. With the installation of the United Nations Mechanism for International Criminal Tribunals, these rules have been further specified by a common Practice Direction for both tribunals (Practice Direction on the Procedure for the Determination of Applications for Pardon, Commutation of Sentence, and Early Release of Persons convicted by the ICTR, the ICTY or the Mechanism (MICT/3)). When compared to the *ad hoc* Tribunals, under the ICC the possibilities for early release are more restricted: instead of pardon, parole or commutation of sentences only reduction of sentence is possible under the narrow terms of Article 110. The inclusion of pardon still formed part in the preparatory works, but was eventually omitted, due to many delegations' objection to the interference of the ICC in the administration of political decision-making process of the states (cf. infra B.).

The Statute of the Special Court for Sierra Leone (Article 23) and of the Special Tribunal for Lebanon (Article 30) provide for a similar rule. However, the Law on the Establishment of the Extraordinary Chambers of Cambodia has no such regulation. Rather the contrary, pardon and amnesties are explicitly excluded under Article 40 new of the Law on EECC.

---

1. The State of enforcement shall not release the person before expiry of the sentence pronounced by the Court.[815]

From a dogmatic viewpoint, sentence reduction is, like commutation of sentence, an adjustment of the judgment with regards to the sentence (that is, a decision relating to the merits), whereas early release or pardon refers to the possibility of the detained person to spend (for example conditionally) the remainder of his or her sentence in liberty (that is, procedural decision, cf. van Kempen 2010, 954). As a consequence, the decision is not taken by the Presidency, but by three judges of the Appeals Chamber, cf. Rule 224(1) RPE.

One of the main criteria to consider a prisoner eligible for early release is his social reinsertion, in particular the improbability of reoffending. However, in the context of war crimes, this criterion will in most cases be met as prisoners are in their vast majority first offenders and generally unlikely to recommit the war crimes they were convicted of again if socio-economic conditions have changed. If criminal law only pursued preventive purposes, in such conditions war offenders could be released immediately after their conviction. However, punishment not only aims at special and general prevention but also at retribution, deterrence, reprobation, rehabilitation, national reconciliation, protection of society and restoration of piece (see *Prosecutor v. Rwamakuba* (Case No. ICTR-98-44C-T), ICTR T. Ch. III, Decision on Appropriate Remedy, 31 January 2007, para. 48; cf. also Schabas 2010, p. 1102).

With regards to its relationship to Articles 103 and 104, one should bear in mind that the international review mechanism provided for under Article 110 is the general rule that only applies if no specific conditions were agreed upon in the Enforcement Agreement pursuant to Articles 103(1) and (2) (Hoffmann 2011, 840 with further references).

Preparatory works:

In the ILC Draft Statute for an International Criminal Court, pardon, parole or commutation of sentence was regulated under Article 60 (ILC 1994 Final Report). The terms pardon and commutation were taken from the ICTY and the ICTR Statutes. Parole was added as another possible variation of early release. Under Article 60 ILC draft statute, the principle that a prisoner should not be released before expiry of the sentence was only stipulated under para. 5. This suggests that it was an exception to the rule of early release. Moreover, the draft provision allowed the Court to delegate the decision power on pardon, commutation or parole to the custodial state. This could, however, create injustice as domestic provisions on these questions greatly vary. In the final draft of the Preparatory Committee, Article 100 governing "Pardon, parole and commutation of sentences (early release)" provided two options, the second of which was close to the finally adopted Article 110 ICC Statute (Preparatory Committee Final Draft, p. 155 ff.). However, the minimum period for life sentences was set at 20 years, not 25, as in the present rule. Concerns were also raised that pardon would involve political considerations. "Pardon, parole and commutation of sentences" was thus eventually replaced by the single "reduction of sentence". In addition, at the Preparatory Committee it was discussed to introduce a mandatory review in consideration of the severity of sentences, which was eventually included in paras. 3 and 5 of the present Article 110.

Author: Anna Oehmichen.

[815] Para. 1 stipulates the principle that the sentenced person should only be released after having served its sentence. Paras. 2 ff regulate the exceptions to this general rule, that is, reduction of sentence. Further, para. 1 clarifies that it is the ICC who determines the length of the sentence; national authorities cannot release a convict before the sentence has expired. The same principle was applied at the *ad hoc* tribunals (cf. Article 28 ICTY Statute and Article 27 ICTR Statute).

Author: Anna Oehmichen.

2. The Court alone shall have the right to decide any reduction of sentence, and shall rule on the matter after having heard the person.[816]

---

[816] It is the Court who decides upon any reduction of sentences. The exclusive power of decision of the Court as opposed to the enforcing state on this matter is also regulated in the respective enforcement agreements. *Agreement between the International Criminal Court and the Federal Government of Austria on the enforcement of sentences of the International Criminal Court*, ICC-PRES/01-01-05, Article 11(2). *Agreement between the Government of the United Kingdom of Great Britain and Northern Ireland and the International Criminal Court on the enforcement of sentences imposed by the International Criminal Court*, ICC-PRES/04-01-07, Article 10; *Agreement between the Kingdom of Denmark and the International Criminal Court on the Enforcement of Sentences of the International Criminal Court*, ICC-PRES/12-02-12, Article 12; *Agreement between the International Criminal Court and the Government of the Republic of Finland on the Enforcement of Sentences of the International Criminal Court*, ICC-PRES/07-01-11, Article 11(3); *Agreement between the Republic of Serbia and the International Criminal Court on the Enforcement of Sentences of the International Criminal Court*, ICC-PRES/09-03-11, Article 11(3); *Agreement between the International Criminal Court and the Government of the Kingdom of Belgium on the Enforcement of Sentences of the International Criminal Court*, ICC-PRES/06-01-10, Article 12(2); *Accord entre la Cour pénale internationale et le gouvernement de la République du Mali concernant l'exécution des peines prononcées par la Cour*, ICC-PRES/11-01-12, Article 6(2); see also Press Release regarding the signing of an enforcement agreement with Colombia.

However, in some agreements, it is regulated that if national authorities find further enforcement impossible for practical or legal reasons, the Court shall make arrangements for the transfer of the sentenced person (for example Agreement between the International Criminal Court and the Government of the Republic of Finland on the Enforcement of Sentences of the International Criminal Court, ICC-PRES/07-01-11, Article 16). It is argued that in such a case, the State ought to better not accept a prisoner in the first place, if certain minimum sentences are incompatible with the practical or legal requirements in that state (Scalia 2013, 493 with further references).

The responsibility for the enforcement of sentences is generally entrusted to the Presidency (see Rule 199 RPE), however, the reduction of sentences is decided by three judges of the Appeals Chamber, cf. Rule 224 RPE.

Also in the case of ICTY/ICTR, it is the tribunal that decides on pardon, commutation of sentence or early release (cf. Article 28(2) ICTY Statute and Article 27(2) ICTR Statute, see also Rule 124 RPE ICTY/Rule 125 RPE ICTR).

Although the ICC, like the *ad hoc* tribunals, delegates the detention of sentenced persons to the national states, it retains much more control over the enforcement of sentences than is the case at the *ad hoc* tribunals (Schabas 2010, 1066–67). Nonetheless, one should keep in mind that sentence remissions or reductions are also regarded as a tool of prisoner management in domestic systems. If detainees would be entitled to such reductions under national law, the ICC would be likely to grant such reduction in line with the domestic law, in order to avoid discrimination *vis-à-vis* fellow prisoners (cf. *Prosecutor v. Jelisić* (Case No. IT-95-10-ES), ICTY, Decision of the President on Sentence Remission for Goran Jelisic, 28 May 2013, para. 20).

A novelty as compared to ICTY/ICTR is that the review hearing is now regulated in the statute itself. In the case of ICTY, this was only regulated in the relevant practice direction (Practice Direction on the procedure for the determination of applications for pardon, commutation of sentence, and early release of persons convicted by the International Tribunal, IT/146/Rev.3, para. 5, cf. also the MICT's Practice Direction on the procedure for the determi-

---

3. When the person has served two thirds of the sentence, or 25 years in the case of life imprisonment, the Court shall review the sentence to determine whether it should be reduced. Such a review shall not be conducted before that time.[817]

---

nation of applications for pardon, commutation of sentence, and early release of persons convicted by the ICTR, the ICTY or the mechanism, MICT/3, para. 6). The hearing shall be conducted by three judges of the Appeals Chamber, appointed by that Chamber, unless they decide otherwise in a particular case, for exceptional reasons (Rule 224 RPE(1)). Not only the sentenced person and his or her counsel and, if applicable, interpreter, as well as the Prosecutor, but also the State of enforcement and the victims or their legal representatives may participate in this hearing or submit written observations (*ibid.*). Conversely, the MICT's Practice Direction on this matter only foresees a hearing of the sentenced person. For further details on the procedure, see Commentary on Rule 224 of the RPE.

Author: Anna Oehmichen.

[817] Stipulating a mandatory review of the sentence after a certain minimum period of time is a requirement under human rights law (*Kafkaris v. Cyprus*, (App.no. 21906/04), ECtHR, Judgment of 12 February 2008, paras. 68 ff; Scalia, 2013, p. 492 (with further references), van Kempen 2010 p. 957 f). The Committee of Ministers of the Council of Europe recommended already in 1976 that Member States should ensure that the cases of all prisoners be examined as early as possible to determine whether or not a conditional release could be granted (Resolution (76)2 on the treatment of long-term prisoners on 17 February 1976). Moreover, the European Court of Human Rights has consistently held that the imposition of an irreducible life sentence on an adult may raise an issue under Article 3 ECHR (see, *inter alia, Kafkaris v. Cyprus*, (App.no. 21906/04), ECtHR, Judgment of 12 February 2008, para. 89 with further references).

The possibility to reduce sentences was also provided for at other international tribunals. For instance, Rule 124 of the RPE of the Special Court for Sierra Leone provides for early release after two-thirds of the sentence (but does not make any provision for life-long sentences as the Statute does not provide for life-long sentence, cf. Article 19 SCSL Statute). Also the *ad hoc* tribunals granted sentence reductions (commutation of sentences or early release). However, the period of imprisonment before review was not regulated at the *ad hoc* tribunals. As a consequence, the decision depended initially upon the state in which the prisoner served his sentence, and thus dependent on the relevant domestic law, before the tribunals established a general practice of two-thirds (ICTY) or three quarters (ICTR) in their case law (cf. ICTY, *Prosecutor v. Stakić (Case* No. IT-97-24-A), ICTY A. Ch., Judgment 22 March 2006, paras. 388–393).

With regards to *fixed-term sentences*, the rule of the ICC to grant a first review after two-thirds of the sentence follows the practice of the ICTY[*]), although the latter preserved somewhat more flexibility, granting in some cases review both earlier according to the provisions under national law (cf. *Prosecutor v. Kupreskic et al* (Case No. IT-95-16-ES), ICTY Presidency, Decision of the President on the Application for Pardon and Commutation of Sentence of Vladimir Santic, 16 February 2009, para. 8), or in case of exceptionally substantial cooperation with the prosecution (*Prosecutor v. Obrenović* (Case No. IT-02-60/2-ES), ICTY Presidency, Decision of President on Early Release of Dragan Obrenovic, 21 September 2011, para. 28) later, for example because of exceptional gravity of the crime (*Prosecutor v. Blagojević* (Case No. IT-02-60-ES), ICTY Presidency, Decision of the President on Early Release of Vidoje Blagojevic (3 February 2012) para. 25), than the two-thirds threshold. Conversely, the ICTR's practice was, before the MICT became competent for them, to consider prisoners eligible to apply for early release only after they had served three-quarters of their sentence (see, for example *Prosecutor v. Tharcisse Muvunyi* (Case No. ICTR-00-59A-T), ICTR Presidency, Decision on Tharcisse Muvunyi's Application for Early Release, 6 March 2012, para. 12; *Prosecutor v. Bagaragaza* (Case No. ICTR-05-86-S), ICTR Presidency, Decision on the Early Release of Michel

Bagaragaza, 24 October 2011, para. 15; *Prosecutor v. Rugambarara* (Case No. ICTR-00-59), ICTR Presidency, Decision on the Early Release Request of Juvenal Rugambarara (P), 8 February 2012, paras. 7, 17). However, the MICT ruled that, "given that the early release practice of the ICTR was derived by reference to the long-established relevant jurisprudence and practice of the ICTY, and taking into account the *lex mitior* principle [...] all convicts supervised by the Mechanism should be considered eligible for early release upon the completion of two-thirds of their sentences, irrespective of the tribunal that convicted them" (*Prosecutor v. Paul Bisengimana (Case* No. MICT-12-07), MICT Presidency, Decision of the President on Early Release of Paul Bisengimana and on Motion to File a Public Redacted Application, 11 December 2012, para. 20; *Prosecutor v. Serushago*, No. MICT-12-28-ES, MICT, Decision of the President on Early Release of Omar Serushago, 13 December 2012, para. 16; *Prosecutor v. Kayishemana et al.* (Case No. MICT-12-10), MICT Presidency, Decision of the President on the Early Release of Obed Ruzindana, para. 14).

In view of clarity and certainty of the law, the decision of the ICC legislator to fix the two-thirds limit should be welcomed. It provides prisoners clearer guidance, which may contribute to their rehabilitation. Moreover, disparities that were observed at the ICTY and ICTR practice, due to diverging and conflicting domestic provisions on early release can thus be reduced (cf. Weinberg de Roca / Rassi 2008, 25 ff; Hoffmann 2011, 838 ff.).

However, it is worthy to bear in mind that the two-thirds period is not universal. While most domestic systems provide for the possibility of early release, there is great variety as to the specific modalities. For instance, Austrian, Beninese, Macedonian and UK law provides for release after serving half of one's sentence (cf. *Prosecutor v. Zigić* (Case No. MICT-14-81-ES.1), MICT Presidency, Public Redacted Version of the 10 November 2014 Decision of the President on the Early Release of Zoran Zigić, 23 December 2014, para. 4; *Prosecutor v. Ntakirutimana* (Case No. MICT-12-17-ES), MICT Presidency, Public Redacted Version of the 26 March 2014 Decision of the President on the Early Release of Gérard Ntakirutimana, para. 10; *Prosecutor v. Tarculovski* (Case No. IT-04-82-ES), ICTY T. Ch., Decision of President on Early Release of Johan Tarculovski, 23 June 2011, para. 12; *Prosecutor v. Krajisnik* (Case No. IT-00-39-ES), ICTY Presidency, Decision of President on Early Release of Momcilo Krajisnik, 11 July 2011, para. 20). In Germany this is also possible for first offenders, while the general rule is 2/3 (cf. s. 57(1) and (2) Criminal Code). Belgian law even provides for early release after one third has been served (cf. *Prosecutor v. Zelenović* (Case No. IT-96-23/2-ES) ICTY Presidency, Decision of President on Early Release of Dragan Zelenovic, 21 October 2011, para. 15). Under Spanish law, good behavior credits earned can be added to the time already served, so that the general two-thirds period may be shortened (cf. *Prosecutor v. Kupreskic et al.* (Case No. IT-95-16-ES), ICTY Presidency, Decision of the President on the Application for Pardon and Commutation of Sentence of Vladimir Santic, 16 February 2009, para. 8). At the *ad hoc* tribunals, different national regimes have led to great disparities among ICTY and ICTR prisoners. While the majority of jurisdictions in which the ICTY's convicts are serving their sentences require that two-thirds of the sentence be served prior to release in many African countries where ICTR convicts serve their sentence no such rules exist (for a comparison, cf. Weinberg de Roca / Rassi 2008, 29, 30).

Under the ICC statute, the first review of life-time convicts shall take place after 25 years have been served. This threshold has no precedent in international criminal law. As of now (July 2016), a clear time line in the case of life imprisonment has been established neither by statute nor by case law of the international tribunals. In *Prosecutor v. Galic* (Case No. MICT-14-83-ES), MICT Presidency, Reasons for the President's Decision to Deny the Early Release of Stanislav Galic and Decision on Prosecution Motion, 23 June 2015) the MICT, six months after the decision to deny early release had already been taken (cf. *Prosecutor v. Galic* (Case No. MICT-14-83-ES), 23 June 2015) laid out some considerations to this question regarding IC-

TY/ICTR/MICT convicts, however, without setting out any clear standard. On the one hand, it was stated that the "treatment of similarly situated prisoners" required that "two-thirds of a life time" were more than two-thirds of the highest fixed-term sentence imposed by the ICTR, the ICTY, or the Mechanism, which amounted to more than 30 years (ibid., para. 36, referring to *Kajelijeli*, who had been sentenced to 45 years). On the other, the MICT also clarified that there was nonetheless no "time-based restriction on when a convicted person who is serving his or her sentence under the supervision of the Mechanism may seek review of his or her sentence", and confirmed that the eligibility threshold recognised by the Mechanism in this case should "in no way preclude review or possible release prior to" the convict reaching that threshold (*ibid.* para. 39). Another indication of what early release may mean for life time prisoners convicted by the international tribunals was given much earlier, in the ruling of the ICTY in *Stakić*, in which the Trial Chamber stated in relation to the sentence of life imprisonment: "The then competent court [...] shall review this sentence and if appropriate suspend the execution of the remainder of the punishment of imprisonment for life and grant early release, if necessary on probation, if:(1) 20 years have been served [...]" (*Prosecutor v. Milomir Stakić* (Case No. IT-97-24-A), ICTY T. Ch., Trial Judgment, 31 July 2003, p. 253-254).

It is further notable that unlike at the *ad hoc* tribunals, where early release can be triggered by either a notification of eligibility of the enforcing state or a direct petition of the convict (cf. para. 2, 3 of MICT, Practice Direction on the Procedure for the Determination of Applications for Pardon, Commutation of Sentence, and Early Release of Persons convicted by the ICTR, ICTY or the Mechanism, MICT/3), at the ICC the review takes place automatic and mandatory once the threshold of having served two-thirds of a fixed-term sentence or 25 years in case of a life sentence has been met. As a consequence, this threshold is considered as a trigger mechanism for the commencement of the sentence review, as opposed to a trigger for automatic release (cf. also *Prosecutor v. Lubanga*, Decision on the review concerning reduction of sentence of Mr. Thomas Lubanga Dyilo, ICC-01/04/01/06, 22 September 2015, para. 20, 27; *Prosecutor v. Katanga*, Decision on the Review concerning Reduction of Sentence of Mr. Germain Katanga, ICC-01/04/01/07, 13 November 2015, para. 113).

The mandatory review also ensures equal treatment of prisoners serving their sentences in different countries, so that even if the prisoner may not be eligible for release under the domestic law of the custodial State, the ICC shall in any event review whether sentence reduction may apply (for the ICTY, cf. also *Prosecutor v. Krnojelac* (Case No. IT-97-25-ES), ICTY Presidency, Decision of the President on the Application for Pardon or Commutation of Sentence of Milorad Krnojelac, 9 July 2009; case in which release was ordered after serving two-thirds of sentence, even though the convict was not eligible for release under Italian law.)

It is not explicitly regulated whether release can also be granted in the event the two-thirds of a sentence have already been served before the decision has become final (for example pending appeal). At the ICTY, in the case of Gvero, release was granted after Gvero had been convicted in first instance and had already by then served more than four fifths of his sentence. The period to lodge an appeal had not yet expired at the moment of his release (*Prosecutor v. Gvero* (Case No. IT-05-88-ES), ICTY Presidency, Decision of President on Early Release of Milan Gvero, 28 June 2010). However, in the case of Ndindiliyimana, the MICT denied an application for early release for a person pending appeal, on the basis that the MICT had not assumed power yet over the enforcement as the judgment had not become final yet and it was up to the Appeals Chamber to decide upon provisional release (*Prosecutor v. Ndindiliyimana et al.* (Case No. MICT-13-43), Decision on Innocent Sagahutu's Notice of Eligibility for Early Release and the Prosecution's Objection thereto, 16 September 2013).

In view of the length of proceedings at the international tribunals, especially the ICC, the mandatory review should take place independent of potential appeals. Article 81(3)(a) clarifies that a convicted person shall remain in custody pending appeal unless the time in custody ex-

4. In its review under paragraph 3, the Court may reduce the sentence if it finds that one or more of the following factors are present:[818]

---

ceeds the sentence of imprisonment imposed. In the latter case, the person shall be released (Article 81(3)(b)). If only the convicted person appeals, and if the review leads to a sentence reduction so that the time in prison exceeds the (reduced) sentence, the prisoner will be released and has the choice whether to wait for the appeals decision which can, in any event, not amend the sentence to his or her detriment (prohibition against *reformatio in peius*, cf. Article 83(2)), see Cryer/Friman/Robinson/Wilmshurst 2010, 471), or to file a written notice of discontinuance of the appeal (Rule 152(1) RPE). However, if the appeal was lodged exclusively or additionally from the side of the OTP, the release may be subject to the conditions set out in Article 81(3)(c).

The review should not depend on the question whether the prisoner has already been transferred to a domestic prison or is still held at the ICC's Detention Centre. It is likely that the principles established by the *ad hoc* tribunals can be applied here as well. The ICTY ruled that fairness dictates early release also for persons serving their sentence at the United Nations Detention Unit (UNDU) (*Prosecutor v. Strugar* (Case No. IT-01-42-ES), ICTY Presidency, Decision of the President on the Application for Pardon or Commutation of Sentence for Pavle Strugar (16 January 2009) para. 9. Other cases where early release at the UNDU was granted include Blaskić, Kolundžija, Kos, Mucić, Simić, Miroslav Tadić, Simo Zarić and Kvocka, cf. Weinberg de Roca / Rassi 2008, 25 f, with further references). Similarly, the ICTR President relied on his inherent powers and applied the provisions governing early release also to persons still detained at the United Nations detention Facility (UNDF) in Arusha (for the first application see *Prosecutor v. Ruggiu* (Case No. ICTR-97-32-S), ICTR Presidency, Decision of the President on the Application for Early Release of Georges Ruggiu, 12 May 2005, cf. also *Prosecutor v. Rutaganira* (Case No. ICTR-95-IC-T), ICTR Presidency, Decision on Request for Early Release, 2 June 2006; *Prosecutor v. Imanishimwe* (Case No. ICTR-99-46-S), ICTR Presidency, Decision on Samuel Imanishimwe's Application for Early Release, 30 August 2007).
*) cf. for example *Prosecutor v. Johan Tarčulovski* (Case No. IT-04-82-ES), Decision on Early Release of Johan Tarculovski, 23 June 2011; *Prosecutor v. Predrag Banović* (Case No. IT-02-65/1-ES), Decision of the President on Commutation of Sentence, 3 September 2008; *Prosecutor v. Drazen Erdemovic* (Case No. IT-96-22-ES) Order issuing a public redacted version of decision of the President on early release, 15 July 2008; *Prosecutor v. Anto Furundzija* (Case No. IT-95-17/1), Order of the President on the Application for the Early Release of Anto Furundzija, 29 July 2004; *Prosecutor v. Damir Došen* (Case No. IT-95-8-S), Order of the President on the early release of Damir Došen, 28 February 2003; *Prosecutor v. Milan Simić* (Case No. IT-95-9/2) Order of the President on the Application for the Early Release of Milan Simic, 27 October 2003; *Prosecutor v. Kupreskic et al.* (Case No. IT-95-16-ES), Decision of the president on the application for pardon or commutation of sentence of Vladimir Santic, 16 February 2009.

Author: Anna Oehmichen.

[818] In para. 4, the Statute lists relevant factors to be taken into account when deciding on a reduction of sentence. While the first two factors are explicitly phrased in the Article, the "other factors" mentioned under sub-paragraph c) are further explained under Rule 223 RPE. While conducting the review is mandatory, the decision whether to grant early release is a discretionary one ("may", cf. also *Prosecutor v. Lubanga*, Decision on the review concerning reduction of sentence of Mr. Thomas Lubanga Dyilo, No. ICC-01/04/01/06, 22 September 2015, para. 21). The only requirement is that at least one of the factors mentioned in Article 110(4) is present. In consequence and in light of the Chamber's discretionary power, reduction of sentence is already permissible if only one of these factors is present. On the other hand, the presence of one factor does not mean that sentence reduction must be granted. Similarly, the presence of a factor mitigating against sentence reduction does not preclude the exercise of discretion. Rather, the fac-

tors must be considered and weighed against one another (*ibid.*, para. 22). At the *ad hoc* tribunals, the factors relevant for the decision of early release were not part of the Statute (cf. Article 28 ICTY Statute / Article 27 ICTR Statute) but only regulated in the RPE (Rule 125 RPE ICTY / Rule 126 RPE ICTR). The ICTY and ICTR Statutes only very generally refer to the "interests of justice" and the "general principles of law" (Articles 27 and 28, respectively). At the SCSL, Article 2 of the Practice Direction on the Conditional Early Release of Persons convicted by the Special Court for Sierra Leone of 1 October 2013 provided further criteria for eligibility for conditional early release, including some requirements that leave worrisome discretion to the authorities, such as "respect for the fairness of the process by which he was convicted" and "positive contribution to peace and reconciliation in Sierra Leone and the region". Most of these requirements relate to the specific situation of Sierra Leone. It is therefore doubtful in how far they may be applied analogously to cases of the ICC. Some of them may be considered for the interpretation of Rule 223(c) or (d) RPE.

The factors listed under Article 110 (early and continuing willingness to cooperate with the court, voluntary assistance in enabling the enforcement, as well as other factors "establishing a clear and significant change of circumstances") are all focused on the present and future, not on the past. They give regard to special preventative considerations rather than retaliation. This understanding is in line with the general principle that the execution of sentences should be mainly oriented towards rehabilitation and reinsertion, while criteria of retaliation and atonement have already been taken into account when determining the length of the sentence. Domestic constitutional law confirms this approach[*]). Moreover, the first two factors are both linked directly to and support the work of the Court. It is likely that their predominant role in the Statute (as opposed to the RPE) is a result of the practical difficulties the ICC faces when investigating in other countries, and thus reflects the ICC's strong need for cooperation of convicts in order to satisfactorily fulfil its tasks.

In light of the case law of the international tribunals, it remained unclear whether factors that already played a role for the sentencing decision may again be taken into account when deciding on a reduction of sentence (for example gravity of the crime[**]) or admission of guilt the context of a plea agreement (cf. *Prosecutor v. Ranko Cesić* (Case No. MICT-14-66-ES), Public redacted version of the 30 April 2014 decision of the President on the early release of Ranko Cesić, 28 May 2014). The wording of Article 110(4)(c) referring to changes of the situation suggests that these factors should be considered only to the extent that they continued to exist and thus influenced the enforcement of sentence, also in the period after the sentencing decision (cf. below Commentary on Article 110(4)(a)). This interpretation has recently been confirmed by the ICC's case law. The ICC has now clarified that a factor that was relevant for the determination of sentence (for example gravity of the crimes) is not a factor to be considered again when deciding on the reduction of sentence (*Prosecutor v. Lubanga*, Decision on the review concerning reduction of sentence of Mr. Thomas Lubanga Dyilo (Case No. ICC-01/04/01/06), 22 September 2015, para. 24).

The burden to establish the presence of the relevant factors rests upon the reviewing chamber. This is because – unlike at the *ad hoc* tribunals – the review of the sentence is triggered by a mandatory *proprio motu* review and not upon the individual request of the sentenced person (*Prosecutor v. Lubanga*, Decision on the review concerning reduction of sentence of Mr. Thomas Lubanga Dyilo (Case No. ICC-01/04/01/06), 22 September 2015, para. 32; see also *Prosecutor v. Katanga*, Decision on the Review concerning Reduction of Sentence of Mr. Germain Katanga (Case No. ICC-01/04/01/07), 13 November 2015, para. 21).

[*]) Under German constitutional law, for example, the decision on reduction of sentence should be limited to special preventive considerations, while matters relevant for the determination of guilt (for example gravity of the crime) may not be considered (with regard to section 57 of the

(a) The early and continuing willingness of the person to cooperate with the Court in its investigations and prosecutions;[819]

German Criminal Code, cf. Bundesverfassungsgericht, Neue Juristische Wochenschrift (NJW) 1994, 378).

**) The ICTR ruled on this matter in a contradictory manner: On the one hand, a request for early release was denied where mitigating factors were already taken into account when determining the length of the sentence (*Prosecutor v. Rutaganira* (Case No. ICTR -95-IC-T), Decision on Request for Early Release (2 June 2006)). On the other, in a different case, the request was also denied, after serving 10 of a 12-year sentence, where gravity of crimes were greater than mitigating factors, although gravity had also been decisive for the sentencing decision (cf. *Prosecutor v. Imanishimwe* (Case No. ICTR-99-46-S), Decision on Samuel Imanishimwe's Application for Early Release, 30 August 2007). Similarly, at the ICTY, in the Case of *Prosecutor v. Radić* (Case No. 98-30/1-ES), due to lack of integration in prison and high gravity of crimes, the convict from Omarska camp would only be released after serving three quarters, rather than two-thirds of his sentence (Decision of the President on Early Release of Mlado Radic (13 February 2012) para. 30. A low gravity of the crimes played, on the other hand, in favour of the early release decision in the case of Kubura, cf. *Prosecutor v. Hadžihasanović and Kubura* (Case No. IT-01-47-T), Decision of the President on Amir Kubura's Request for Early Release, 11 April 2006, para. 8).

Author: Anna Oehmichen.

[819] The first factor to take into account is the degree of cooperation shown by the prisoner with the court, the investigations and prosecutions. The prominent position within the provision indicates the importance the ICC attaches to this factor, and reflects the ICC's problematic need to rely on the cooperation of its own convicts.

To distinguish this sub-section from sub-section (b), which addresses cooperation in relation to other cases ("The voluntary assistance of the person in enabling the enforcement of the judgments and orders of the Court in other cases, and in particular providing assistance in locating assets subject to orders of fine, forfeiture or reparation which may be used for the benefit of victims"), sub-section (a) should be read as referring only to the cooperation regarding the sentenced person's *own* case.

"Substantial cooperation with the Prosecutor" (thus not willingness) was already a relevant factor at the *ad hoc* tribunals (cf. Rule 125 RPE ICTY / Rule 126 RPE ICTR). The ICTY case law shows, on the one hand, that cooperation with the OTP did come into play in many cases (cf. for example *Prosecutor v. Banović* (Case No. IT-02-65/1-ES), Decision of the President on Commutation of Sentence, 3 September 2008, para. 14, *Prosecutor v. Drazen Erdemovic* (Case No. IT-96-22-ES), Order issuing a public redacted version of decision of the President on early release, 15 July 2008; *Prosecutor v. Ivica Rajić* (Case No. IT-95-12-ES). Decision of the President on Early Release of Ivaca Rajic, 22 August 2011, para. 23; *Prosecutor v. Damir Došen* (Case No. IT-95-8-S), Order of the President on the early release of Damir Došen, 28 February 2003, p. 3; *Prosecutor v. Tadić* (Case No. IT-95-9), Decision of the President on the Application for Pardon or Commutation of Sentence of Miroslav Tadić, 3 November 2004). In the case of Obrenović, release was even granted eight months before two-thirds had been passed thanks to the exceptionally substantial cooperation with the prosecution (*Prosecutor v. Obrenović* (Case No. IT-02-60/2-ES), Decision of President on Early Release of Dragan Obrenovic, 21 September 2011, para. 28). On the other, there were also cases in which early release was granted although such a cooperation could not be established. E.g. in the case of Jokić, the defendant had even been found in contempt of the Tribunal for refusing to testify at an ICTY trial (*Prosecutor v. Dragan Jokić* (Case No. IT-02-60-ES), Decision of the President on the Application for Pardon or Commutation of Sentence of Drajan Jokic, 13 January 2010). Moreover, in many cases the cooperation with the authorities was considered as a neutral factor, as cooperation had not been sought by part of the OTP (for example *Prosecutor v. Kayishemana et al.* (Case No. MICT-12-10), MICT, Decision of the President on the Early Release of Obed Ruzindana, para. 21; *Prosecutor v. Momcilo Krajišnik* (Case No. IT-00-39-ES), ICTY, Decision of the President on Early Release of Momcilo Krajisnik, 2 July 2013, para. 29; *Prosecutor v. Vidoje Blagojević* (Case No. IT-02-60-ES), ICTY, Decision of the President on Early Release of Vidoje Blago-jevic, 3 February 2012, para. 24; *Prosecutor v. Milomir Stakić* (Case No. IT-97-24-ES), ICTY, Decision of President on Early Release of Milomir Stakic, 15 July 2011, para. 37; *Prosecutor v. Johan Tarčulovski* (Case No. IT-04-82-ES), ICTY, Decision of President on Early Release of Johan Tarculovski, 23 June 2011, para. 26; *Prosecutor v. Pavle Strugar* (Case No. IT-01-42-ES), ICTY, Decision of the President on the Application for Pardon or Commutation of Sentence of Pavle Strugar, 16 January 2009, para. 13; *Prosecutor v. Krnojelac* (Case No. IT-97-25-ES), ICTY, Decision on the Application for Pardon or Commutation of Sentence, 9 July 2009, para. 21; *Prosecutor v. Bala* (Case No. IT-03-66-ES), ICTY, Decision of President on Application of Haradin Bala for Sentence Remission, 15 October 2010, para. 27). Also in the *Tadić* case, the ICTY ruled that the ICTY prosecution was in no position to comment on the convicted person's behavior while in prison (*Prosecutor v. Dusko Tadić* (Case No. IT-97-24-ES), ICTY, Decision of the President on the Application for Pardon or Commutation of Sentence of Dusko Tadic of 17 July 2008, para. 10), in particular, as it had not sought any such cooperation after the conviction (*ibid.* para. 18). At the ICTR it seems that cooperation with the prosecution was generally an important factor for early release after serving three quarters of sentence (*Prosecutor v. Bargaragaza* (Case No. ICTR-05-86-S), Decision on the Early Release of Michel Bagaragaza, 24 October 2011, para. 13; *Prosecutor v. Rugambarara* (Case No. ICTR-00-59), Decision on the Early Release Request of Juvenal Rugambarara (P), 8 February 2012).

The cooperation with the authorities is a factor that will necessarily be considered already at the level of sentencing. Therefore, it is questionable in how far this factor should play such a prominent role again when it comes to the reduction of sentences, in particular in the case of plea agreements where substantial cooperation with the prosecution is a prerequisite for the agreed sentence.

In its recent decisions reviewing Thomas Lubanga's and Germain Katanga's sentences, the ICC concurred with the Prosecutor's submission that "ordinarily any cooperation that took place before conviction and was already considered at sentencing and does not continue post-conviction should not be considered again to reduce the sentence". However, it emphasised that the fact that a person's cooperation or assistance has not continued post-conviction and was tak-en into account in the original sentence may not always result in the automatic non-consideration of these acts, as the full impact of a person's cooperation or assistance, even where it does not continue after the conviction, may only become apparent post-sentence (*Pros-ecutor v. Lubanga*, Decision on the review concerning reduction of sentence of Mr. Thomas Lubanga Dyilo, ICC-01/04/01/06, 22 September 2015, para. 30; *Prosecutor v. Katanga*, Deci-sion on the Review concerning Reduction of Sentence of Mr. Germain Katanga, ICC-01/04/01/07, 13 November 2015, para. 26). The ICC's clear standpoint on this issue is to be welcomed, in particular as this question was not at all clear at the *ad hoc* tribunals. For instance, in the case of *Jelisić*, the ICTY qualified the entering into a plea agreement as a factor weighing in favour of a decision on remission of sentence, although the OTP's report denied any coopera-tion with the Prosecution both during and after trial (*Prosecutor v. Jelisić* (Case No. IT-95-10-ES), ICTY Presidency, Decision of the President on Sentence Remission for Goran Jelisić, 28 May 2013, para. 32, 33). On the other hand, under the SCSL's Practice Direction on the Condi-tional Early Release of Persons convicted by the Special Court for Sierra Leone of 1 October 2013, which gives very detailed regulations on early release requirements and conditions, the Registrar shall request from the Prosecutor a report, "outlining [...] any information relevant

(b) The voluntary assistance of the person in enabling the enforcement of the judgements and orders of the Court in other cases, and in particular providing assistance in locating

---

[...] of any co-operation the Convicted Person has provided to the Prosecutor that was not a consideration in sentencing" (Article 5(g)).

Moreover, the general idea to consider only post-conviction cooperation under this factor is in line with the clear wording of Article 110(4)(a): "early and continuing willingness to cooperate" suggests that cooperation before the conviction is not sufficient; further cooperation during the time serving one's sentence is required. Furthermore, this interpretation is also supported from a systematic/contextual viewpoint: As Article 110(4)(c) refers to "other" factors that establish a clear and significant change of circumstances, lit. c just provides another example of a factor that establishes such clear and significant change, implying that the factors mentioned under Articles 110(4)(a) and 110(4)(b) equally establish this change.

In the *Katanga* case, the ICC further clarified that the "cooperation" referred to as a mitigating circumstance pursuant to Rule 145(2)(a)(ii) of the RPE and referred to in Article 110 (4) (a) of the Statute may, as a general matter, be understood as having the same meaning. To the extent that a Trial Chamber qualified an accused's conduct during trial as "cooperation", within the meaning of Rule 145(2)(a)(ii) of the RPE, a panel conducting a sentence review would not generally revisit this initial determination (*Prosecutor v. Katanga*, Decision on the Review concerning Reduction of Sentence of Mr. Germain Katanga, ICC-01/04/01/07, 13 November 2015, para. 28).

In the latter decision, the ICC further had occasion to rule on the question whether the decision of a convict not to lodge an appeal against his sentencing decision could be interpreted as a form of continuous cooperation. The ICC held that the cooperation „must contribute to the efficient administration of justice at the Court". Under this aspect, the decision not to appeal one's sentence decision could be considered as "continuous cooperation" if it was taken "as a result of acknowledging that he or she is guilty of the crimes committed and publicly apologising therefor", thereby preventing an unnecessary prolongation of the proceedings (*Prosecutor v. Katanga*, Decision on the Review concerning Reduction of Sentence of Mr. Germain Katanga, ICC-01/04/01/07, 13 November 2015, para. 34). The ICC argued that the non-execution of one's right to appeal "furthermore brings finality to the proceedings against him or her and allows the reparations phase of a case to commence in a timely manner, a factor which is of particular importance in the context of the ICC" (*ibid.*).

In any event, the demonstrated will to cooperate during detention, for example the will to testify before the Court in another case, will be taken into account (cf. for example *Prosecutor v. Banović* (Case No. IT-02-65/1-ES), ICTY Presidency, Decision of the President on Commutation of Sentence, 3 September 2008, para. 14). Similarly, it is likely that a refusal to testify will not play in favour of the decision (however, cf. *Prosecutor v. Dragan Jokić* (Case No. IT-02-60-ES), ICTY Presidency, Decision of the President on the Application for Pardon or Commutation of Sentence of Drajan Jokic, 13 January 2010, where early release was granted notwithstanding contempt proceedings following the refusal to testify at an ICTY trial).

It is important that it is the (demonstrated) willingness to cooperate that may weigh in favour of release, not the actually effected (and successful) cooperation; whether cooperation will actually be possible would be a question out of reach for the detainee, and it would be unfair if a lack of cooperation would weigh against him while no authority wanted the latter from him. Convicts who do not have the opportunity to show such willingness, for example if their role was of such minor nature that they will not have any significant knowledge they could share, will have little or no chance to profit from this factor. It is likely that in such cases, as at the ICTY, this factor will be considered as a neutral one.

Author: Anna Oehmichen.

---

assets subject to orders of fine, forfeiture or reparation which may be used for the benefit of victims;[820] or

(c) Other factors establishing a clear and significant change of circumstances sufficient to justify the reduction of sentence, as provided in the Rules of Procedure and Evidence.[821]

---

[820] It is new to explicitly regulate this criterion in international criminal law. Voluntary assistance can consist in voluntary surrender as well as in locating assets. At the ICTY, voluntary assistance in enabling enforcement was taken into account in a case where the prisoner surrendered voluntarily to the ICTY (*Prosecutor v. Simić* (Case No. IT-95-9/2), Order of the President on the Application for the Early Release of Milan Simić, 27 October 2003; *Prosecutor v. Tadić* (Case No. IT-95-9), Decision of the President on the Application for Pardon or Commutation of Sentence of Miroslav Tadić, 3 November 2004). Neither the *ad hoc* tribunals nor the Special Courts for Sierra Leone and Lebanon foresee explicitly this criterion in their respective provisions governing early release. Moreover, cases may fall under this provision where people, prior to their own indictment, act as headhunters or informants or otherwise collaborate with the justice authorities in catching fugitive suspects. However, if applied in this sense one should bear in mind the risk that people turn in their political opponents, motivated not so much by the interests of justice as one might wish.

In the *Lubanga* case, the question was raised whether alleged attempts of the sentenced person to interfere with witnesses in another case (*Ntaganda*), thereby not enabling, but rather obstructing the efficient administration of justice, was a factor to be taken into account under Article 110(4)(b) (then weighing obviously against sentence reduction, cf. *Prosecutor v. Lubanga*, Decision on the review concerning reduction of sentence of Mr. Thomas Lubanga Dyilo, ICC-01/04/01/06, 22 September 2015, para. 38 ff.). This question raises actually two separate issues:(1) Are mere allegations or suspicions, substantiated by only some factual indications, sufficient basis to be taken into account when reviewing the sentence? (2) Is witness interference of the sentenced person regarding another case generally a factor that should be taken into account under Article 110(4)(b)? The ICC's Reviewing Chamber chose not to answer any of these questions, by claiming that, "mindful of the preliminary nature of the allegations", before addressing these allegations and whether they demonstrated interference in another case, it had to first establish whether there was any supportive evidence not for witness interference, but for "voluntary assistance", within the meaning of Article 110(4)(b), on part of Mr. Lubanga. By answering the latter to the negative, it found that there was no need to address the allegations of interference in the *Ntaganda* case (*ibid.*, para. 40). Bluntly put, this statement is both contradictory and disappointing. It is contradictory because if indeed the allegations of interference were of no relevance to the present case, one may wonder why the Chamber did not follow Mr. Lubanga's request to declare the filings inadmissible in the first place (cf. *Prosecutor v. Lubanga*, Decision on Mr Lubanga's request to have two filings from the Prosecutor declared inadmissible, ICC-01/04/01/06, 19 August 2015). Second, it is regrettable that the ICC missed the chance to discuss the important (and likely recurring) issue whether mere allegations / suspicions of certain conduct may influence the decision to review the sentence. The presumption of innocence should impede the judges from basing their decisions on sentence reductions on unsubstantiated allegations or suspicions. The decision on sentence reduction should, as any judicial decision, be based on factual indications that must be transparent and verifiable for the defence.

Author: Anna Oehmichen.

[821] This rather vague criterion gives the court a considerable degree of discretion and flexibility. While the first two factors concern exclusively the individual behavior of the detainee, these other "factors" may also include aspects outside of the sphere of the detainee, for example the impact of his release on society.

5. If the Court determines in its initial review under paragraph 3 that it is not appropriate to reduce the sentence, it shall thereafter review the question of reduction of sentence at such

---

As sub-section c) makes reference to the Rules of Procedure and Evidence, the "other factors" referred to here are those listed under Rule 223 RPE (conduct during detention, prospect of resocialisation, consequences of release for social stability, positive conduct towards victims and impact of release on them, as well as individual circumstances such age, sickness etc.). The wording "other factors establishing a clear and significant change of circumstances sufficient to justify the reduction of sentence" is formulated in such an open manner that it could also comprise additional factors not mentioned in Rule 223 (for example political circumstances, or the fact that the prisoner agrees to his deportation to his home country, cf. *Prosecutor v. Tadić* (Case No. IT-94-1-ES), ICTY Presidency, Decision of the President on the Application for Pardon and Commutation of Sentence of Dusko Tadić, 17 July 2008; *Prosecutor v. Vasiljević* (Case No. IT-98-32-ES), Decision of President on Application for Pardon and Commutation of Sentence of Mitar Vasiljevic, 12 March 2010). However, the explicit reference to the RPE as well as the clear guidance of Rule 223 RPE that "one or more of the following factors must be present" clarifies that the list of Article 110(4), read in conjunction with Rule 223, is – unlike Rule 125 ICTY Statute/Rule 126 ICTR statute – exhaustive (see also *Prosecutor v. Lubanga*, Decision on the Review concerning Reduction of Sentence of Mr. Thomas Lubanga Dyilo, ICC-01/04/01/06, 22 September 2015, para. 25; confirmed by *Prosecutor v. Katanga*, Decision on the Review concerning Reduction of Sentence of Mr. Germain Katanga, ICC-01/04/01/07, 13 November 2015, para. 19). Moreover, the ICC concluded from the fact that the factors under Rule 223 (b) and (c) of the RPE were going to be considered for the first time that it was necessary to find that there were changed circumstances in relation to the other factors listed in Rule 223 ((a), (d) and (e)) from the time that the sentence was imposed (*Prosecutor v. Lubanga*, Decision on the Review concerning Reduction of Sentence of Mr. Thomas Lubanga Dyilo, ICC-01/04/01/06, 22 September 2015, para. 28; confirmed by *Prosecutor v. Katanga*, Decision on the Review concerning Reduction of Sentence of Mr. Germain Katanga, ICC-01/04/01/07, 13 November 2015, para. 19).

The ICC further clarified that factors not referred to in Article 110(4) or Rule 223 are not considered as relevant factors. Specifically, the fact that a sentenced person has served two-thirds of his or her sentence does not present a relevant factor under the ICC regime, as, unlike at the *ad hoc* tribunals, the two-thirds threshold is no more than the trigger mechanism for the automatic sentence review (*Prosecutor v. Lubanga*, Decision on the Review concerning Reduction of Sentence of Mr. Thomas Lubanga Dyilo, ICC-01/04/01/06, 22 September 2015, para. 27).

In the *Lubanga* case, the Prosecution submitted that Lubanga failed to establish this criterion of "changed circumstances", based on his suspected involvement in witness interference in the *Ntaganda* case (*Prosecutor v. Lubanga*, ICC-01/04-01/06, Public redacted version of Prosecution's third notice regarding potentially relevant information to Thomas Lubanga Dyilo's sentence review, 14 August 2015, ICC-01/04-01/06-3160-Conf-Ex, 20. August 2015; see also *Prosecutor v. Lubanga*, Public Annex 1 and Public Redacted Annex 2 to 4, Third public redacted version of Prosecution's submissions regarding Thomas Lubanga Dyilo's sentence review, 10 July 2015, ICC-01/04-01/06-3150-Conf-Exp, para. 3). The Reviewing Chamber decided to address the allegations of witness interference within the context of Article 110(4)(b) (see supra comment on sub-section (b)), and saw no reason to discuss this issue separately under Article 110(4)(c), as it shares the commentator's view that Article 110(4)(c) makes exhaustive reference to the factors mentioned under Rule 223 of the RPE, without leaving discretion to consider any other factors not mentioned therein (see above).

Author: Anna Oehmichen.

---

intervals and applying such criteria as provided for in the Rules of Procedure and Evidence.[822]

---

[822] Another novelty of the ICC Statute consists in the statutory regular mandatory review in case sentence reduction is denied after the two-thirds/25-year period. The details are regulated in Rule 224(3)–(5) RPE. Three judges of the Appeal Chamber shall review the question on reduction of sentences every three years, unless in the initial review decision a shorter period is established or upon application of the sentenced person in case of a "significant change of circumstances", cf. Rule 224(3). While in the first review, a hearing of the sentenced person is mandatory (cf. Article 110(2)), in any subsequent review the three judges of the Appeals Chamber are only obliged to invite written representations from the concerned parties (that is, sentenced person or his or her counsel, the prosecutor, the State of enforcement and, to the extent possible, the victims or their legal representatives). In addition to these, a hearing is not mandatory but optional (Rule 224(4)). The decision and the reasons for the review decision shall be communicated to all those who participated in the review proceedings as soon as possible, Rule 224(5).

This provision differs from the practice at the *ad hoc* tribunals, where in case release is considered inappropriate, the decision shall specify the date on which the person will next become eligible for early release. Unlike as at the ICC, the period for the next review is not fixed and may depend on the domestic law of the State where the sentenced person serves his or her sentence (MICT, Practice Direction on the Procedure for the Determination of Applications for Pardon, Commutation of Sentence, and Early Release of Persons convicted by the ICTR, ICTY or the Mechanism, MICT/3, para. 10).

Remedies:

It is not clear whether the decision on sentence reduction is appealable. A legal basis for such an appeal could be Article 82(1)(b). However, under that provision, strictly speaking only decisions granting or denying release of the person being investigated or prosecuted can be appealed, so it would not apply to the convicted person. On the other hand, if Article 82(1)(b) should not apply in this case, the Statute would provide no other possibility of appeal against such decisions (Staker 2008 Article 82 margin no. 9 with further references). At the *ad hoc* tribunals, the President's decision on pardon, commutation of sentence or early release shall not be appealable (cf. para. 12 of the MICT's Practice Direction of 5 July 2012 on the Procedure for the Determination of Applications for Pardon, Commutation of Sentence, and Early Release of Persons Convicted by the ICTR, the ICTY or the Mechanism, MICT/3, see also ICTR, *Prosecutor v. Rutaganira*, ICTR-95-IC-A, Decision on Appeal of a Decision of the President on Early Release, 24 August 2006). Similarly, the decision on conditional early release by the SCSL was not subject to appeal (cf. Articles 2 (F), 8(E) of the Practice Direction on the Conditional Early Release of Persons convicted by the Special Court for Sierra Leone of 1 October 2013). However, one should keep in mind that contrary to the ICTY, the ICTR, and the SCSL, the ICC Statute does not provide for "early release" but for "sentence reduction", which is more of a substantive than a procedural decision and, for this reason, not taken by the President, but by three judges of the Appeals Chamber after a hearing (cf. Rule 224(1) RPE, see also above A.). It is therefore arguable that the decision whether the sentence should be reduced is, in the case of the ICC, indeed subject to appeal.

Cross-references:

Articles 77, 103, 104.

Rules 223, 224.

Doctrine:

1. Hirad Abtahi and Steven Arrigg Koh, "The Emerging Enforcement Practice of the International Criminal Court", in *Cornell International Law Journal*, 2012, vol. 45.

2. M. Cherif Bassiouni, *International Criminal Law*, vol. 3: *International Enforcement*, Martinus Nijhoff Publishers, Leiden, 2008, pp. 603–11.

3. Robert Cryer, Håkan Friman, Daryll Robinson and Elizabeth Wilmshurst, *An Introduction to International Criminal Law and Procedure*, 2nd ed., Cambridge University Press, Cambridge, 2010.

4. Klaus Hoffmann, "Some Remarks on the Enforcement of International Sentences in Light of the Galic case at the ICTY", in *Zeitschrift für Internationale Strafrechtsdogmatik* (ZIS), 2011, vol. 10, pp. 838–42.

5. Claus Kreß and Göran Sluiter, "Chapter 44 – Imprisonment", in Antonio Cassese, Paola Gaeta and John R.W.D. Jones (eds.), *The Rome Statute of the International Criminal Court: A Commentary*, 2nd ed., Oxford University Press, Oxford, 2002, pp. 1757–1821.

6. Valerie Oosterveld, "The International Criminal Court and the Closure of the Time-Limited International Hybrid Criminal Tribunals", in *Loyola University Chicago International Law Review*, 2010, vol. 13, p. 4.

7. Christoph Safferling, *Towards an International Criminal Procedure*, Oxford University Press, Oxford, 2001, pp. 363–65.

8. Damien Scalia, "Article 110", in Paul De Hert, Mathias Holvoet, Jean Flamme and Olivia Struyven (eds.), *Code of International Criminal Law and Procedure, Annotated*, Larcier, Ghent, 2013, p. 492–93.

9. Damien Scalia, "Long-Term Sentences in International Criminal Law, Do They Meet the Standards Set Out by the European Court of Human Rights?", in *Journal of International Criminal Justice*, 2011, vol. 9, no. 3, p. 669.

10. William A. Schabas, *The International Criminal Court: A Commentary on the Rome Statute*, Oxford University Press, Oxford, 2010, pp. 1101–7.

11. Christopher Staker, "Article 82 – Appeal Against Other Decisions", in Otto Triffterer (ed.), *Commentary on the Rome Statute of the International Criminal Court: Observers' Notes, Article by Article*, 2nd ed., C.H. Beck/Hart/Nomos, Munich/Oxford/Baden-Baden, 2008.

12. Gerard A.M. Strijards, "Article 103 – Role of States in Enforcement of Sentences of Imprisonment", in Otto Triffterer (ed.), *Commentary on the Rome Statute of the International Criminal Court: Observers' Notes, Article by Article*, 2nd ed., C.H. Beck/Hart/Nomos, Munich/Oxford/Baden-Baden, 2008, pp. 1647–57.

13. Gerard A.M. Strijards, "Article 110 – Review by the Court Concerning Reduction of Sentence", in Otto Triffterer (ed.), *Commentary on the Rome Statute of the International Criminal Court: Observers' Notes, Article by Article*, 2nd ed., C.H. Beck/Hart/Nomos, Munich/Oxford/Baden-Baden, 2008, p. 1683.

14. Piet Hein Van Kempen, "Early Release in the Context of International Human Rights Law. Commentary", in André Klip and Göran Sluiter (eds.), *Annotated Leading Cases of International Tribunals. The International Tribunal for Rwanda 2006–2007*, vol. 25, Intersentia, Antwerp, 2010, p. 954–62.

15. Ines Monica Weinberg de Roca and Christopher M. Rassi, "Sentencing and Incarceration in the Ad Hoc Tribunals", in *Stanford Journal of International Law*, 2008, vol. 44, no. 1, pp. 24–29.

Author: Anna Oehmichen.

Article 111
Escape[823]

---

[823] *General remarks*

The provision concerns the situation of a sentenced person escaping imprisonment and fleeing the State of enforcement. It combines two approaches, a "horizontal" and a "vertical" one, to reach the return of the sentenced person into custody as fast as possible. It is within the discretion of the State of enforcement to either seek the surrender of the fugitive from the State where he or she is currently located by means of existing bilateral or multilateral extradition treaties (for example the well-established framework of the European Convention on Extradition (CETS No. 024), comprising 50 States to date; the European arrest warrant (Council Framework Decision of 13 June 2002, 2002/584/JHA), which considerably restricts the grounds to refuse extradition; bilateral extradition treaties with non-States Parties). The State of enforcement may, however, decide to request the Court's intervention in accordance with the provisions on international cooperation and judicial assistance (cf. Articles 89; 91(1), (3); 92).

Up to date, no case of escape of a person imprisoned after conviction by an international tribunal has been reported. However, the situation envisaged by Article 111 seems not to be completely theoretical: One former detainee of the ICTY, who had been transferred to Bosnia and Herzegovina according to Rule 11bis(*Prosecutor v. Stanković* (Case No. IT-96-23/2), ICTY A. Ch., Decision on Rule 11bis referral, 1 September 2005) and received his sentence there, managed to escape while attending a dentist's office in 2007. He stayed at large until early 2012, before he was rearrested by the Bosnian authorities (OSCE press release, 23 January 2012, www.osce.org/bih/87144, last retrieved on 03 August 2015).

Given the Court's authority to supervise the enforcement (cf. Articles 105 and 110), Article 111 is a provision of merely declaratory character (Schabas, 2010, p. 1108). This assessment is supported by the drafting history: The ILC Draft (UN doc. A/49/10) did not contain any provision regarding escape from a penitentiary institution. During the sessions of the Preparatory Commission, an elaborate proposal headed "Art. Y" (UN doc. A/51/22, p. 297) on the issue was discussed. It was eventually simplified to a single, bracketed sentence (Article 101) in the Commission's final draft (UN doc. A/CONF.183/2/Add.1), underscoring the Court's authority to request the surrender of the fugitive according to Part 9 and to transfer the person to another State of enforcement. At the Rome Conference, the State's possibility to act by means of its own and potentially more effective arrangements with other States was made explicit (Kreß/Sluiter, 2002, p. 1796).

The provision does not cover a situation in which the sentenced person is at large in the territory of the State of enforcement itself. Then, however, the State has to comply with its duty to respect the sentence (established by accepting the designation under Article 103), and will re-establish custody as fast as possible (cf. Schabas, 2010, p. 1109).

Punishment for the escape (cf. for example Articles 434–27 French Penal Code) and conduct connected therewith remains to be determined according to the national law of the State of enforcement, as Article 70 does not establish the jurisdiction of the Court for such offences and Article 108 bars only the prosecution for acts committed prior to the transfer of the sentenced person (Kreß/Sluiter, 2002, p. 1797; Schabas, 2010, pp. 1109, 1111; cf. Ntoubandi, 2012, p. 2001). However, this does not exempt the Court from its supervisory function under Article 106.

Authors: Michael Stiel and Carl-Friedrich Stuckenberg.

If a convicted person escapes from custody and flees the State of enforcement, that State may, after consultation with the Court, request the person's surrender from the State in which the person is located pursuant to existing bilateral or multilateral arrangements, or may request that the Court seek the person's surrender, in accordance with Part 9.[824] It may direct that the person be delivered to the State in which he or she was serving the sentence or to another State designated by the Court.[825]

---

[824] The State of enforcement "may" request the surrender of the sentenced person, which implies a certain latitude whether it wants to act on its own (and follow the "horizontal" approach) or refer the matter ("vertically") to the Court (Schabas, 2010, p. 1109; Strijards, 2008, Article 111). Arguably, a bona fide exercise of this discretion requires the State to choose the path of action which appears to be the most promising to re-establish custody and the least burdensome to the convict (cf. Kreß/Sluiter, 2002, p. 1797). In practice, the State of enforcement will exercise its discretion in consultation with the Court as prescribed by Rule 225(1).

The wording "pursuant to existing ... arrangements" might lead to the conclusion that informal *post facto* agreements to surrender the fugitive are excluded. However, it is argued that the wording should not be interpreted in such a way: In order to bring the sentenced person back into custody most efficiently and as it is reflected in the wording of Rule 225(2) ("pursuant to either international agreements or its national legislation"), such agreements should not be excluded (cf. Schabas, 2010, p. 1110). This seems particularly important as not all extradition agreements may be directly applicable to sentences imposed not by the requesting State but an international Court (cf. France's concerns in its proposal for the Rules of Procedure and Evidence, PCNICC/1999/WGRPE[10]/DP.1, p. 13).

If the State of enforcement decides not to seek the surrender of the sentenced person itself, it is to refer the matter to the Court. The State's discretion therefore is limited to a decision between the "horizontal" and "vertical" approach (cf. Kreß/Sluiter, 2002, p. 1797). Action by the Court is imperative if the location of the fugitive is unknown, given the obligation of all States Parties to cooperate with the Court.

Authors: Michael Stiel and Carl-Friedrich Stuckenberg.

[825] The second sentence of the provision concerns the destination of a sentenced person handed over to the Court under the "vertical" approach. It may order the direct redelivery to the State of enforcement (Kreß/Sluiter, 2002, pp. 1796 f.). However, if the Court deems it appropriate, it may also have the sentenced person being transferred directly to another State, therewith preparing a change of the State of enforcement under Articles 103 and 104. Rule 225(3) provides further details on this issue.

Cross-references:

Article 86.

Rule 225.

Doctrine:

1. Claus Kreß and Göran Sluiter, "Imprisonment", in Antonio Cassese, Paola Gaeta and John R.W.D. Jones (eds.), *The Rome Statute of the International Criminal Court: A Commentary*, 2nd ed., Oxford University Press, Oxford, 2002, pp. 1757–1821.

2. Faustin Z. Ntoubandi, "Article 111", in Julian Fernandez/Xavier Pacreau (eds.), *Statut de Rome de la Cour pénale internationale*, Commentaire Article par Article, Vol. II, Éditions Pedone, Paris, 2012.

3. William A. Schabas, *The International Criminal Court: A Commentary on the Rome Statute*, Article 111, Oxford University Press, Oxford, 2010.

---

4. Gerard A. M. Strijards, "Article 111", in Otto Triffterer (ed.), *Commentary on the Rome Statute of the International Criminal Court: Observers' Notes, Article by Article*, 2nd ed., C.H. Beck/Hart/Nomos, Munich/Oxford/Baden-Baden, 2008, p. 1685.

Authors: Michael Stiel and Carl-Friedrich Stuckenberg.

PART 11. ASSEMBLY OF STATES PARTIES

Article 112
Assembly of States Parties[826]

1. An Assembly of States Parties to this Statute is hereby established. Each State Party shall have one representative in the Assembly who may be accompanied by alternates and advisers. Other States which have signed this Statute or the Final Act may be observers in the Assembly.[827]

---

[826] *General remarks*:

Although national courts are independent they all depend on political institutions in relation to issues such as financing and management. The same applies to international tribunal and courts. The United Nations Security Council, General Assembly and Secretariat all had a role in relation to the *ad hoc* tribunals. During the negotiations of the ICC Statute, the question of the Assembly of States Parties was part of the discussions on the overall question of the relationship between the United Nations and the Court. Considering that the ICC is independent of and a distinct organisation in relation to the UN an other option was sought. Considering that the Court is based on treaty it is logical that the political body is a gathering of states parties, which is normal for other treaty regimes.

Article 112 deals with participation of States Parties as well as non-States Parties, functions if the Assembly, establishment of a Bureau, decision-making, non-cooperation with the Court and default in payment of dues.

Preparatory works:

The first proposal for a general assembly of states parties was raised in the French Working Paper on the Draft Statute of the Court submitted to the Preparatory Committe in 1996, see UN doc. A/AC.249/L.3 (7 August 1996).

Author: Mark Klamberg.

[827] Paragraph 1 deals with participation in the Assembly and distinguishes between States Parties who have an inherent right to participate and other states. Other States that have signed the Statute or the Final Act may be observers in the Assembly.

Each State Party shall be represented by one representative, who may be accompanied by alternates and advisers. Each Observer State may be represented in the Assembly by one designated representative, who may be accompanied by alternates and advisers. The representative may designate an alternate or an adviser to act in his or her capacity (Rule 23 of the Rules of Procedure of the Assembly of States Parties).

Rule 92 of the Rules of Procedure of the Assembly of States Parties provides that representatives designated by entities, intergovernmental organisations and other entities that have received a standing invitation from the General Assembly of the United Nations pursuant to its relevant resolutions to participate, in the capacity of observers, in its sessions and work have the right to participate as observers, without the right to vote, in the deliberations of the Assembly. Similarly, representatives designated by regional intergovernmental organisations or other international bodies invited to the Rome Conference, accredited to the Preparatory Commission for the International Criminal Court or invited by the Assembly may participate as observers, without the right to vote, in the deliberations of the Assembly.

Even states that have not signed the Statute or the Final Act may be present during the work of the Assembly. Rule 94 of the Rules of Procedure of the Assembly of States Parties provides

---

2. The Assembly shall:

(a) Consider and adopt, as appropriate, recommendations of the Preparatory Commission;[828]

(b) Provide management oversight to the Presidency, the Prosecutor and the Registrar regarding the administration of the Court;[829]

(c) Consider the reports and activities of the Bureau established under paragraph 3 and take appropriate action in regard thereto;[830]

(d) Consider and decide the budget for the Court;[831]

(e) Decide whether to alter, in accordance with Article 36, the number of judges;[832]

---

that "At the beginning of each session of the Assembly, the President may, subject to the approval of the Assembly, invite a given State which is not a party and does not have observer status to designate a representative to be present during the work of the Assembly. A representative who is so designated may be authorized by the Assembly to make a statement".

Author: Mark Klamberg.

[828] The Preparatory commission was established at the Rome conference 1998 pursuant to Resolution F of the Final Act (UN doc. A/CONF.183/10). The Preparatory Commission was tasked to prepare proposals for practical arrangements for the establishment and coming into operation of the Court, which were all transmitted together with a report of the Commission to the Assembly of States. Pursuant to Resolution F the Commission was in existence until the conclusion of the first meeting of the Assembly of States Parties.

[829] This paragraph for the oversight function of the Assembly over the predominant representatives of the Court including the Presidency, the Prosecutor and the Registrar. There was some controversy during the negotiations whether the term "administration" covers judicial administrations in addition to the operations of the Court. Some delegations argued that this oversight should be narrow in the sense that that there was no intrusive oversight into the Court's judicial administration. In light of the negotiating history, the term "administration" should not include judicial activities of the Court (Rao, 2008, p. 1691).

[830] When it is not in session, the responsibilities of the Assembly are direct by the Bureau of Assembly established under paragraph 3. The Assembly is to consider the reports and activities of the Bureau and take appropriate action in regard thereto.

[831] The Assembly is to consider and decide the budget for the Court. It may be read together with paragraph 5(f) of Resolution F of the Final Act (UN doc. A/CONF.183/10) which provides that Preparatory Commission shall prepare a budget for the first financial year. Rule 90 of the Rules of Procedure of the Assembly of States Parties confirms that the Assembly shall decide on the budget, which shall comprise the expenses of the Court and the Assembly, including its Bureau and subsidiary bodies.

As in the case of other international organisations it is reasonable that in practice the budget is prepared by and originates from the Court, more specifically the Registrar. Paragraph 2 omits any provision that the Assembly should consult with the registrar. However, paragraph 5 provides that The President of the Court, the Prosecutor and the Registrar or their representatives may participate, as appropriate, in meetings of the Assembly and of the Bureau. This means that the Statute provides an opportunity for the Registrar to give input concerning the Court's financial requirements.

[832] The Assembly of States have the authority to alter the number of judges. The method and procedure in altering the number of judges should be in accordance the provisions of appointing judges contained in Article 36.

(f) Consider pursuant to Article 87, paragraphs 5 and 7, any question relating to non-cooperation;[833]

(g) Perform any other function consistent with this Statute or the Rules of Procedure and Evidence.[834]

3. (a) The Assembly shall have a Bureau consisting of a President, two Vice-Presidents and 18 members elected by the Assembly for three-year terms.[835]

(b) The Bureau shall have a representative character, taking into account, in particular, equitable geographical distribution and the adequate representation of the principal legal systems of the world.[836]

(c) The Bureau shall meet as often as necessary, but at least once a year. It shall assist the Assembly in the discharge of its responsibilities.[837]

4. The Assembly may establish such subsidiary bodies as may be necessary, including an independent oversight mechanism for inspection, evaluation and investigation of the Court, in order to enhance its efficiency and economy.[838]

5. The President of the Court, the Prosecutor and the Registrar or their representatives may participate, as appropriate, in meetings of the Assembly and of the Bureau.[839]

---

[833] Where a State Party fails to comply with a request to cooperate by the Court, the Court has the power pursuant to Article 87(5) and (7) to make a judicial finding and refer the matter to the Assembly of States Parties or, where the Security Council referred the matter to the Court, to the Security Council.

It is not clear whether the Assembly of States Parties can raise the issue of non-compliance on its own initiative (Schabas, p. 1124).

[834] Paragraph (g) is residual and allows the Assembly of States Parties to perform any other function consistent with this Statute or the Rules of Procedure and Evidence. Several other provisions in the ICC Statute set out responsibilities for the Assembly of States Parties, including Articles 2, 3, 9, 36(2)(c)(i), 36(4), 36(6), 42(4), 43(4) 44(3)(4), 46(2), 49, 51, 79(1), 79(3), 113, 117, 119(2) and 121(2)(3).

[835] The Statute provides that the Assembly shall have a Bureau consisting of 21 members with a President, two Vice-Presidents and eighteen members elected by the Assembly for three-year terms. It is normal for international institutions to have a bureau with administrative responsibilities operating when the Assembly is not in session.

[836] In the choice between having a bureau based on the doctrine of principal legal systems or the principle of geographical representation, both criteria are to be equally considered.

[837] The Bureau shall assist the Assembly in the discharge of its responsibilities set out in paragraph 2. In addition, paragraph 6 provides that the Bureau has the competence to convene special sessions of the Assembly on its own initiative.

[838] The Assembly may establish "subsidiary bodies [...] in order to enhance its efficiency and economy". Four such bodies have been established: the Committee on Budget and Finance; the Staff Pension Committee; the Trust Fund for Victims (Article 79); and the Oversight Committee on Permanent Premises (see Schabas, p. 1127).

[839] Although paragraph 5 provides the President of the Court, the Prosecutor and the Registrar or their representatives may participate in meetings of the Assembly and of the Bureau, it is silent whether they do so as members or as observers. One argument raised by some delegations during the negotiations in favour of restricting their roles to observers was the interest to avoid confusing the Court's judicial functions with the political and administrative role of the Assembly (Schabas, p. 1129).

6. The Assembly shall meet at the seat of the Court or at the Headquarters of the United Nations once a year and, when circumstances so require, hold special sessions. Except as otherwise specified in this Statute, special sessions shall be convened by the Bureau on its own initiative or at the request of one third of the States Parties.[840]

7. Each State Party shall have one vote. Every effort shall be made to reach decisions by consensus in the Assembly and in the Bureau. If consensus cannot be reached, except as otherwise provided in the Statute:[841]

    (a) Decisions on matters of substance must be approved by a two-thirds majority of those present and voting provided that an absolute majority of States Parties constitutes the quorum for voting;[842]

    (b) Decisions on matters of procedure shall be taken by a simple majority of States Parties present and voting.[843]

8. A State Party which is in arrears in the payment of its financial contributions towards the costs of the Court shall have no vote in the Assembly and in the Bureau if the amount of its arrears equals or exceeds the amount of the contributions due from it for the preceding two full years. The Assembly may, nevertheless, permit such a State Party to vote in the As-

---

[840] The Assembly shall meet at the seat of the Court or at the Headquarters of the United Nations once year. In addition, special sessions may be held "when circumstances so require". The Assembly may hold special sessions and fix the date of commencement and the duration of each such special session.

   Special sessions of the Assembly may also be convened by the Bureau on its own initiative or at the request of one third of the States Parties pursuant to rule 8 of the Rules of Procedure of the Assembly of States Parties.

[841] The general rule is that decisions are made by consensus. In the event of failure to reach consensus different alternatives of adopting decisions are set out depending on the character of the decision, as set in sub-paragraphs (a) and (b).

   There is a saving clause "except as otherwise provided in the Statute" which means that other provisions of the Statute will prevail over the general rules set laid down by paragraph 7. There are at least two areas where different rules apply: 1) election and removal of judges (Articles 36(6)(a) and 46(2)(a)); and 2) amendments to the ICC Statute and convening a review conference (Articles 121(4), 122(2), 123(2)).

[842] Decisions on matters of substance must be approved by a two-thirds majority of those present and voting. If the question arises whether a matter is one of procedure or of substance, the President shall rule on the question, rule 64(2) of the Rules of Procedure of the Assembly of States Parties.

   The term ""States Parties present and voting"" means States Parties present and casting an affirmative or negative vote. States Parties which abstain from the voting shall be considered as not voting (rule 66 of the Rules of Procedure of the Assembly of States Parties).

[843] Rule 65 of the Rules of Procedure of the Assembly of States Parties confirms that Decisions on amendments to proposals relating to matters of substance, and on parts of such proposals put to the vote separately, shall be made by a two-thirds majority of the States Parties present and voting.

   The term ""States Parties present and voting"" means States Parties present and casting an affirmative or negative vote. States Parties which abstain from the voting shall be considered as not voting (rule 66 of the Rules of Procedure of the Assembly of States Parties).

sembly and in the Bureau if it is satisfied that the failure to pay is due to conditions beyond the control of the State Party.[844]

9. The Assembly shall adopt its own rules of procedure.[845]

10. The official and working languages of the Assembly shall be those of the General Assembly of the United Nations.[846]

---

[844] This paragraph aims at promoting financial responsibility of the States Parties towards the Court by paying their contributions.

[845] The Assembly shall adopt its own rules of procedure. Paragraph 5(h) in the Resolution F of the Final Act (UN doc. A/CONF.183/10) provides that the Preparatory Commission shall prepare a proposal for the Rules of Procedure of the Assembly of States Parties The Rules of Procedure were adopted by consensus by the Assembly of States Parties (Official Records of the Assembly of States Parties to the Rome Statute of the International Criminal Court, First session, New York, 3–10 September 2002, ICC-ASP/1/3).

[846] The official and working languages of the Assembly shall be those of the General Assembly of the United Nations, currently: Arabic, Chinese, English, French, Russian and Spanish.

Doctrine:

1. S. Rama Rao, "Financing of the Court, Assembly of States Parties and the Preparatory Commission", in Roy S. Lee (ed.), *The International Criminal Court: The Making of the Rome Statute,* Kluwer Law International, The Hague, 1999, pp. 399–420.

2. S. Rama Rao, "Article 112 – Assembly of States Parties", in Otto Triffterer (ed.), *Commentary on the Rome Statute of the International Criminal Court: Observers' Notes, Article by Article*, 2nd ed., C.H. Beck/Hart/Nomos, Munich/Oxford/Baden-Baden, 2008, pp. 1687–97.

3. William A. Schabas, *The International Criminal Court: A Commentary on the Rome Statute*, Oxford University Press, Oxford, 2010, pp. 1115–34.

Author: Mark Klamberg.

PART 12. FINANCING

Article 113
Financial Regulations

Except as otherwise specifically provided, all financial matters related to the Court and the meetings of the Assembly of States Parties, including its Bureau and subsidiary bodies, shall be governed by this Statute and the Financial Regulations and Rules adopted by the Assembly of States Parties.[847]

---

[847] *General remarks*:

The financing of the Court was discussed during the negotiations of the ICC Statute. Two broads and different approaches emerged: should the Court be funded by the State Parties or by the United Nations from a special account following the example of peacekeeping operations? Could individuals and private organisations provide additional funding? Even if the main funding would be provided by the State Parties it was discussed whether the United Nations should pay in relation to situations referred to the Court by the UN security council. The scheme agreed is contained in Part 12 of the Statute which provides that funds would include contributions by the States as well as those provided by the United Nations, in particular in relation to the expenses incurred due to referrals by the Security Council.

The Preparatory Commission for the International Criminal Court prepared Draft Financial Regulations (PCNICC/2001/1/Add.2). The draft used as models both the UN financial regulations and the financial regulations of the International Tribunal for the Law of the Sea ("ITLOS"), as proposed by the tribunal, but not yet adopted by the Assembly of States Parties. Since the International Criminal Tribunals for the former Yugoslavia and Rwanda apply the UN financial regulations *per se* they could not provide additional models or precedents (Witschel, p. 667). The Financial Regulations were adopted by Assembly of States Parties at its first session in September 2002 (Official Records of the Assembly of States Parties to the Rome Statute of the International Criminal Court, First session, New York, 3–10 September 2002).

Analysis:

The Financial Regulations and Rules are not mentioned in the ICC Statute, not even in Article 21 on applicable law. It may appear unlikely that the Financial Regulations and Rules which concerns administration may come in conflict with the substantive law of the Statute, however in case of conflict the Statute should arguably prevail (Schabas, p. 1138).

The Registrar has the primary responsibility for managing the Court's finances (regulation 1.4, rule 101(1)(b)).

Doctrine:

1. S. Rama Rao, "Financing of the Court, Assembly of States Parties and the Preparatory Commission", in Roy S. Lee (ed.), *The International Criminal Court: The Making of the Rome Statute*, Kluwer Law International, The Hague, 1999, pp. 399–420.

2. S. Rama Rao, "Article 112 – Assembly of States Parties", in Otto Triffterer (ed.), *Commentary on the Rome Statute of the International Criminal Court: Observers' Notes, Article by Article*, 2nd ed., C.H. Beck/Hart/Nomos, Munich/Oxford/Baden-Baden, 2008, pp. 1699–1701.

3. William A. Schabas, *The International Criminal Court: A Commentary on the Rome Statute*, Oxford University Press, Oxford, 2010, pp. 1137–40.

4. Georg Witcschel, "Financial Regulations and Rules of the Court", in *Fordham International Law Journal*, 2001, vol. 25, no. 3, pp. 665–73.
Author: Mark Klamberg.

Article 114
Payment of expenses

Expenses of the Court and the Assembly of States Parties, including its Bureau and subsidiary bodies, shall be paid from the funds of the Court.[848]

---

[848] This provision provides that the expenses of the Court and the Assembly of States Parties, including its Bureau and subsidiary bodies, shall be paid from the funds of the Court. Article 114 is attempt to avoid a practice as set out in the United Nations Convention on the Law of the Sea where the Secretary General pays for the meetings of States Parties and other bodies out of the UN general budget (Arsanjani, p. 324, Schabas, p. 1142)

The term "funds" in Article 114 should be distinguished from the same term used in Article 79, the later provision concerns the Trust fund for the benefit of the victims.

Doctrine:

1. Mahmoush H. Arsanjani, "Financing", in Antonio Cassese, Paola Gaeta and John R.W.D. Jones (eds.), *The Rome Statute of the International Criminal Court: A Commentary*, Oxford University Press, Oxford, 2002, pp. 315–29.
2. S. Rama Rao, "Financing of the Court, Assembly of States Parties and the Preparatory Commission", in Roy S. Lee (ed.), *The International Criminal Court: The Making of the Rome Statute*, Kluwer Law International, The Hague, 1999, pp. 399–420.
3. S. Rama Rao, "Article 114 – Payment of Expenses", in Otto Triffterer (ed.), *Commentary on the Rome Statute of the International Criminal Court: Observers' Notes, Article by Article*, 2nd ed., C.H. Beck/Hart/Nomos, Munich/Oxford/Baden-Baden, 2008, p. 1703.
4. William A. Schabas, *The International Criminal Court: A Commentary on the Rome Statute*, Oxford University Press, Oxford, 2010, pp. 1141–43.

Author: Mark Klamberg.

Article 115
Funds of the Court and of the Assembly of States Parties

The expenses of the Court and the Assembly of States Parties, including its Bureau and subsidiary bodies, as provided for in the budget decided by the Assembly of States Parties, shall be provided by the following sources:

(a) Assessed contributions made by States Parties;

(b) Funds provided by the United Nations, subject to the approval of the General Assembly, in particular in relation to the expenses incurred due to referrals by the Security Council.[849] [845]

---

[849] *General remarks*:

Article 115 complements what has been set forth in Article, 115, namely that the Court has two sources of financing: assessed contributions made by States Parties and funds provided by the United Nations. As noted in the comment on Article 113 this is a comprise between the two main approaches set against each other during the negotiations of the ICC Statute: whether the Court should be funded by the State Parties or by the United Nations from a special account. Article 115 also confirms that the Assembly of States Parties is the budgetary authority. Pursuant to rule 90 of the Rules of Procedure of the Assembly of States Parties the Assembly "shall decide on the budget, which shall comprise the expenses of the Court and the Assembly, including its Bureau and subsidiary bodies".

Analysis:

This provision does not exclude other sources of income such as fines, reimbursement for services rendered, bank interest and rental of premises. However, the word "funds" used in Articles 114 and 115 relate to revenues which are used for approved expenses creating a "closed system" (Halff/Tolbert, p. 1705–1706). This should be distinguished from voluntary contributions which are regulated in Article 116.

Article 115(a) provides that the primary source of income are assessed contributions made by States Parties which are regulated in more detail in Article 117.

Article 115(b) implies that there are situations in which the UN should contribute to the Court's funds. This is particularly motivated in relation to Security Council referrals which may be considered as services rendered by the Court to the UN. However, the two referrals by the Security Council to the Court have explicitly excluded that possibility. Resolution 1593 referring the *Situation in Darfur, Sudan* to the Court "[r]ecognizes that none of the expenses incurred in connection with the referral including expenses related to investigations or prosecutions in connection with that referral, shall be borne by the United Nations and that such costs shall be borne by the parties to the ICC Statute and those States that wish to contribute voluntarily (para. 7)". The Court has accepted the referrals without objection or condition, and has not made financial demands on the United Nations (Schabas, p. 1147). Resolution 1970 on the *Situation in Libya* contains an identical provision (para. 8) ruling out provision of funds by the United Nations to the Court.

Doctrine:

1. Mahmoush H. Arsanjani, "Financing", in Antonio Cassese, Paola Gaeta and John R.W.D. Jones (eds.), *The Rome Statute of the International Criminal Court: A Commentary*, Oxford University Press, Oxford, 2002, pp. 315–29.

2. S. Rama Rao, "Financing of the Court, Assembly of States Parties and the Preparatory Commission", in Roy S. Lee (ed.), *The International Criminal Court: The Making of the Rome Statute*, Kluwer Law International, The Hague, 1999, pp. 399–420.

---

3. Maarten Halff and David Tolbert, "Article 115 – Funds of the Court and of the Assembly of States Parties", in Otto Triffterer (ed.), *Commentary on the Rome Statute of the International Criminal Court: Observers' Notes, Article by Article*, 2nd ed., C.H. Beck/Hart/Nomos, Munich/Oxford/Baden-Baden, 2008, pp. 1705–13.
4. William A. Schabas, *The International Criminal Court: A Commentary on the Rome Statute*, Oxford University Press, Oxford, 2010, pp. 1144–48.

Author: Mark Klamberg.

Article 116

Voluntary contributions

Without prejudice to Article 115, the Court may receive and utilize, as additional funds, voluntary contributions from Governments, international organizations, individuals, corporations and other entities, in accordance with relevant criteria adopted by the Assembly of States Parties.[850]

---

[850] *General remarks*:

It is common practice that international organisations accept voluntary contributions. Such contributions may distort the priorities of an organisation, provide wealthier and more powerful states an advantage which may come in conflict with the ideal of an independent court. In addition to the funds listed in Articles 115 and 116 provides that the Court may receive and utilise, as additional funds, voluntary contributions from Governments, international organisations, individuals, corporations and other entities.

Analysis:

Considering that voluntary contributions are not covered by Article 115 they are not "funds of the Court and of the Assembly of States Parties" within the meaning of Article 115. While Articles 114 and 115 set up a "closed system" with approved funds and approved expenses, voluntary contributions do not form part of the same calculus.

Regulation 7.2 of ICC Financial regulations and Rules provides that "[v]oluntary contributions, gifts and donations, whether or not in cash, may only be accepted by the Registrar, provided that they are consistent with the nature and functions of the Court and the criteria to be adopted by the Assembly of States Parties on the subject, in accordance with Article 116 of the ICC Statute. Acceptance of contributions which directly or indirectly involve additional financial liability for the Court shall require the prior consent of the Assembly of States Parties".

When donors specify purposes for which the voluntary contributions are to be used, it follows that when the Court's accepts such contributions shall be treated as trust funds or special accounts (regulation 7.3). When no purpose is specified for voluntary contributions such contributions shall be treated as miscellaneous income and reported as "gifts" in the accounts of the financial period (regulation 7.4).

Doctrine:

1. Mahmoush H. Arsanjani, "Financing", in Antonio Cassese, Paola Gaeta and John R.W.D. Jones (eds.), *The Rome Statute of the International Criminal Court: A Commentary*, Oxford University Press, Oxford, 2002, pp. 315–29

2. S. Rama Rao, "Financing of the Court, Assembly of States Parties and the Preparatory Commission", in Roy S. Lee (ed.), *The International Criminal Court: The Making of the Rome Statute,* Kluwer Law International, The Hague, 1999, pp. 399–420.

3. Maarten Halff and David Tolbert, "Article 115 – Funds of the Court and of the Assembly of States Parties", in Otto Triffterer (ed.), *Commentary on the Rome Statute of the International Criminal Court: Observers' Notes, Article by Article*, 2nd ed., C.H. Beck/Hart/Nomos, Munich/Oxford/Baden-Baden, 2008, pp. 1715–18.

4. William A. Schabas, *The International Criminal Court: A Commentary on the Rome Statute*, Oxford University Press, Oxford, 2010, pp. 1149–51.

Author: Mark Klamberg.

Article 117

Assessment of contributions

The contributions of States Parties shall be assessed in accordance with an agreed scale of assessment, based on the scale adopted by the United Nations for its regular budget and adjusted in accordance with the principles on which that scale is based.[851]

---

[851] *General remarks*:

As noted in the comment on Article 115(a), assessed contributions by States Parties is one of two sources of funds for the Court. Article 117 concerns how the burden of funding for this source is to be distributed between the States Parties. It acknowledges the principle of differential assessment, using the United Nations scale of assessments (Article 17 of the UN Charter, Woeste and Thomma, pp. 597–605).

Analysis:

The ICC Statute does not specify which body has the authority to adopt and adjust the scale of assessments. However, ICC RPE rule 91 and ICC Financial regulations and Rules, regulation 5.2 provides that the scale shall be adopted by the Assembly of States Parties.

Regulation 5.2 further specifies that the "scale shall be based on the scale adopted by the United Nations for its regular budget, and adjusted in accordance with the principles on which that scale is based, in order to take into account the differences in membership between the United Nations and the Court". The UN scale of assessments is based on a complex formula which takes into account the population of the country and its gross national income (GNI) and political adjustments (Woeste and Thomma, p. 597). Considering that not all UN member states are parties to the ICC Statute, the UN scale of assessments cannot be applied directly to the Court. Thus, Article 117 and regulation 5.2 provides for an adjustment following the same principles.

Doctrine:

1. Mahmoush H. Arsanjani, "Financing", in Antonio Cassese, Paola Gaeta and John R.W.D. Jones (eds.), *The Rome Statute of the International Criminal Court: A Commentary*, Oxford University Press, Oxford, 2002, pp. 315–29.

2. S. Rama Rao, "Financing of the Court, Assembly of States Parties and the Preparatory Commission", in Roy S. Lee (ed.), *The International Criminal Court: The Making of the Rome Statute*, Kluwer Law International, The Hague, 1999, pp. 399–420.

3. Maarten Halff and David Tolbert, "Article 115 – Funds of the Court and of the Assembly of States Parties", in Otto Triffterer (ed.), *Commentary on the Rome Statute of the International Criminal Court: Observers' Notes, Article by Article*, 2nd ed., C.H. Beck/Hart/Nomos, Munich/Oxford/Baden-Baden, 2008, pp. 1719–22.

4. William A. Schabas, *The International Criminal Court: A Commentary on the Rome Statute*, Oxford University Press, Oxford, 2010, pp. 1152–54.

5. Peter Woeste and Thomas Thomma, "Article 17", in Bruno Simma, Daniel-Erasmus Khan, Georg Nolte and Andreas Paulus (eds.), *The Charter of the United Nations: A Commentary*, 3rd ed., Oxford University Press, 2012, pp. 576–620.

Author: Mark Klamberg.

Article 118

Annual audit

The records, books and accounts of the Court, including its annual financial statements, shall be audited annually by an independent auditor.[852]

---

[852] *General remarks*:

Several international organisations, such as the United Nations and the European Court of Human rights have no provision in their constitutive documents requiring external audit, although it belongs to sound management practice. Article 118 is thus arguably superfluous as it would be required even in the absence of the present provision (Schabas, p. 1155).

Analysis:

The term "independent auditor" became a compromise during the negotiations of the provision in the context of other proposals including "Un auditors", "external auditors" and "internal auditors" (Rao, p. 1723).

Regulation 12 of the ICC Financial regulations and Rules provides that the Assembly of States Parties shall appoint an Auditor, which may be an internationally recognised firm of auditors or an Auditor General or an official of a State Party with an equivalent title. The Auditor shall be appointed for a period of four years and its appointment may be renewed. The Court also has an Office of Internal Audit (regulation 110.1).

Doctrine:

1. Mahmoush H. Arsanjani, "Financing", in Antonio Cassese, Paola Gaeta and John R.W.D. Jones (eds.), *The Rome Statute of the International Criminal Court: A Commentary*, Oxford University Press, Oxford, 2002, pp. 315–29.

2. S. Rama Rao, "Financing of the Court, Assembly of States Parties and the Preparatory Commission", in Roy S. Lee (ed.), *The International Criminal Court: The Making of the Rome Statute*, Kluwer Law International, The Hague, 1999, pp. 399–420.

3. S. Rama Rao, "Article 118 – Annual Audit", in Otto Triffterer (ed.), *Commentary on the Rome Statute of the International Criminal Court: Observers' Notes, Article by Article*, 2nd ed., C.H. Beck/Hart/Nomos, Munich/Oxford/Baden-Baden, 2008, p. 1723.

4. William A. Schabas, *The International Criminal Court: A Commentary on the Rome Statute*, Oxford University Press, Oxford, 2010, pp. 1155–56.

Author: Mark Klamberg.

PART 13. FINAL CLAUSES

Article 119
Settlement of disputes[853]

1. Any dispute concerning the judicial functions of the Court shall be settled by the decision of the Court.[854]

---

[853] *General remarks*:

Multilateral conventions often contain a dispute settlement clause with agreement that disputes are submitted to a third party, a common arbiter is the International Court of Justice (ICJ). Article 119 is different in the sense that it contains an intermediary stage where the Assembly of States may intervene in disputes (Schabas, p. 1161).

Preparatory works:

The ILC stated in its 1994 Report that "[t]he court will of course have to determine its own jurisdiction [...], and will accordingly have to deal with any issues of interpretation and application of the statute which arise in the exercise of that jurisdiction" (Report of the International Law Commission, Forty-sixth session, 2 May 1994–22 July 1994, Official Records of the General Assembly, Forty-ninth session, p. 70).

There was a clear will during the negotiations that the Court needed to have the competence to determine the limits of its jurisdiction. It is important the independence of the court. Some States expressed during th negotiations the belief that any disagreement or difference of opinion of any kind concerning the Court was for it alone to decide. Other States took the view that there might be different classes of disagreements where if for some would more appropriate with modes of settlement than other than the Court (Slade and Clark, p. 429; Clark, p. 1727).

The final draft report of the Preparatory committee contained four options in Article 108 on how to settle disputes: 1) disputes should be settled by the decision of the Court; 2) disputes on the interpretation or application of the Statute which is not resolved through negotiations should be referred to the Assembly of States Parties which shall make recommendations on further means of settlement of the dispute; disputes concerning the judicial functions of the Court shall be settled by the decision of the Court; and 4) no provision on dispute settlement (Report of the Preparatory Committee on the Establishment of an International Criminal Court, United Nations Diplomatic Conference of Plenipotentiaries on the Establishment of an International Criminal Court Rome, Italy 15 June–17 July 1998, A/CONF.183/2).

Article 119 is a compromise and contains two distinct approaches to settlement of dispute depending on the nature of the dispute. While the first paragraph concerns disputes "concerning the judicial functions", the second paragraph deals with "[a]ny other dispute".

Author: Mark Klamberg.

[854] Both paragraphs 1 and 2 use the word "dispute". Disputes can involve disagreement on points of law as well as facts.

The term "judicial function" also appears in Articles 39(2)(a) and 40(2) where it seems to have the meaning proceedings or trials. This includes more than merely procedural decisions but all rulings of the Court concerning ICC Statute (Schabas, pp. 1162–1163).

Clark suggests a non-exhaustive list the following areas of disagreement that fall within "judicial functions" (pp. 1729–1730):

1. questions of jurisdiction and interpretation of the definitions of crimes within the jurisdiction of the Court (Articles 5–8, 11 and 19);

2. Any other dispute between two or more States Parties relating to the interpretation or application of this Statute which is not settled through negotiations within three months of their commencement shall be referred to the Assembly of States Parties. The Assembly may itself seek to settle the dispute or may make recommendations on further means of settlement of the dispute, including referral to the International Court of Justice in conformity with the Statute of that Court.[855]

---

2. whether the preconditions to the exercise of jurisdiction have been met (Article 12);

3. issues of admissibility (Articles 17 and 19);

4. whether the case is one of *ne bis in idem* (Article 20);

5. questions involving what law applies (Article 21);

6. issues involving the judges, excusing of judges and disqualifying them (Articles 40 and 41);

7. disqualification of the Prosecutor or a Deputy prosecutor (Article 42);

8. some issues involving the Registry (Article 43 overlapping with the Assembly of States Parties);

9. removal of the Registrar or Deputy Registrar from office (Articles 46(1) and (3));

10. discipline of a judge, Prosecutor, Deputy Prosecutor, Registrar or Deputy Registrar (Article 47 and rule 30);

11. some questions involving privileges and immunities (Article 48);

12. questions involving the Rules of Procedure and Evidence (Article 51);

13. adoption of the Regulations of the Court (Article 52);

14. review of a Prosecutor not to proceed (Article 53(3));

15. rulings on various pre-trial situations (Articles 56–61);

16. making ruling on contentious issue during a trial (Articles 62–75), at sentencing (Articles 76–78), and in proceedings for appeal or revision (Articles 81–85);

17. questions concerning cooperation with and judicial assistance to the Court (Articles 86–101); and

18. questions of the modalities of enforcement of sentences (Articles 103–111).

[855] Paragraph 2 resembles dispute resolution clauses familiar to multilateral treaties. At first disputes should be settled through negotiations where a time limit of three months is set. After that time, the disputes shall in case of failure to reach a settlement "be referred to the Assembly of States Parties". The Assembly may itself seek to settle the dispute or may make recommendations on further means of settlement of the dispute, including referral to the International Court of Justice. However, Article 119(2) cannot be compared to Article IX of the Genocide Convention. Parties to the dispute still have to consent to the jurisdiction of the ICJ.

Doctrine:

1. Roger S. Clark, "Article 119 – Settlement of Disputes", in Otto Triffterer (ed.), *Commentary on the Rome Statute of the International Criminal Court: Observers' Notes, Article by Article*, 2nd ed., C.H. Beck/Hart/Nomos, Munich/Oxford/Baden-Baden, 2008, pp. 1727–35.

2. William A. Schabas, *The International Criminal Court: a Commentary on the Rome Statute*, Oxford University Press, Oxford, 2010, pp. 1159–65.

3. Tuiloma Neroni Slade and Roger S. Clark, "Preamble and Final Clauses", in Roy S. Lee (ed.), *The International Criminal Court: The Making of the Rome Statute*, Kluwer Law International, The Hague, 1999, pp. 421–50.

Author: Mark Klamberg.

Article 120
Reservations

No reservations may be made to this Statute.[856]

---

[856] *General remarks*:

Article 120 briefly stipulates that States acceding to the Statute may not make reservations. The provision appears to be concise, clear and easy to apply, but it contains a number of difficulties, which has, despite the provision in Article 120, resulted in cumbersome decisions whether declarations lodged by States acceding to the Statute would be permitted.

The possibility for a State to make use of reservations whereby it purports to exclude or to modify the legal effect of certain provisions of treaties when signing, ratifying, accepting, approving or acceding to a treaty, is governed by Articles 19 to 23 VCLT. During the beginning of the last century the unanimity principle prevailed. A reservation required the acceptance of all State parties to be valid. If one State objected to the reservation, the unanimity principle resulted in the reserving State being prevented from becoming a party to the treaty. A change in doctrine occurred in mid-2000s following the ICJ advisory opinion in the *Genocide Case* (*Genocide Case*, Advisory Opinion of 28 May 1951, I.C.J Reports 1951, p. 15). A greater emphasis was put on the principle of universality, under which a larger number of state parties to treaties is highly valued.

This shift from unanimity to universality meant that it is sufficient that a single State party accepts the reservation by the acceding State, for the latter State to become a party to the treaty. The universality principle is considered to enable a larger number of States to accede to treaties; even if the text of the treaty contains regulations acceding states may have difficulty in accepting. A flexible system for reservations to treaties was introduced and was later codified in the 1969 VCLT. In other words, a State can accede to treaties on the precondition of a reservation that modifies or excludes treaty provisions, provided that at least one State party to the treaty accepts the reservation. However, this would only be possible unless the reservation is prohibited by the treaty; the treaty provides that only specified reservations, which do not include the reservation in question, may be made; or in other cases, the reservation is incompatible with the object and purpose of the treaty, Article 19 VCLT.

The increasing number of Human Rights treaties since the mid-2000s, and the doctrine shift in terms of possibilities to formulate reservations has resulted in a growing number of accessions to international treaties. However, the possibility to formulate reservations has in many cases been misused in that obviously impermissible reservations have been formulated. Since objections to reservations must come from the other treaty parties, there might be several different reactions towards the same reservation. This has been especially frequent regarding treaties on human rights and has resulted in it being unclear to what rules treaty parties are bound, which off course is very unsatisfying (Spiliopoulou Åkermak and Mårsäter, pp. 384–385). The accelerating problem of impermissible reservations led to the issue being considered by the International Law Commission (Report of the International Law Commission, A/66/10/Add.1).

One way to overcome the above mentioned misuse of the possibility of formulating reservations is the possibility for States to object to the reservations under Article 20 VCLT. This has been done extensively under various treaties, but this could be a cumbersome way to address the problem, even if it achieves the effect that the reserving State withdraws its reservation. There is also a risk of remaining disputes regarding issues of admissibility of the reservation. Should there exist an established monitoring mechanism under the treaty, the question regarding the permissibility of the reservation can be settled by this system, provided it is an international court or another supervisory organ competent to decide on these questions. In the case of statutes where an international tribunal is established and given the task to monitor the implementation of a treaty, the tribunal may adjudicate on questions of jurisdictions, and thus also indirectly decide on the permissibility of a potentially unauthorised reservation. The latter has occurred in the Strasbourg Court, *inter alia*, when the court ruled regarding the admissibility of an interpretative declaration formulated by Switzerland, and declared that it had a modifying effect on the treaty (*Belilos v. Switzerland*, (Application No. 10328/83), ECtHR, Judgment, 18 April 1988).

Preparatory works:

In order to avoid the problems of assessing reservations, and safeguarding the integrity of treaties, it could, during the development of treaties, be considered to restrict the possibility to formulate reservations by clearly specifying which reservations may be made, or stipulating that no reservations may be formulated (cf. Article 19 VCLT).

At the Rome Conference, the latter solution was finally chosen and in order to preserve the integrity of the Statute, Article 120 stipulates, very concisely, that reservations under the treaty are impermissible.

Analysis:

By clearly formulating a prohibition to make reservations, it can be concluded that reservations *per se* have no legal effect under the Statute. States can nevertheless formulate interpretative and other declarations. These kinds of statements are not that easy to define, but an *e contrario* reading, of the definition of reservations in Article 2(1)(d) VCLT can be used in order to distinguish them from reservations. If the declaration does not purports to exclude or to modify the legal effect of certain provisions in the treaty in relation to the declaring State, it does not constitute a reservation; hence the declaration is not covered by the prohibition in Article 120 and is allowed. This interpretation of the declaration should be done with due observance of rules regarding interpretation of treaties, cf. Articles 31–32 VCLT. In other words, a properly worded declaration lacks the qualifying legal effects attached to reservations. The problematic aspect of declarations in this context is that it is not too unusual that states seek to indirectly modify the content of treaties by seeking a legal effect in formulating an improper declaration.

If the declaration has the legal effect to exclude or modify provisions of the treaty, it constitutes a disguised reservation. States are usually not required to comment on or object to declarations, and this has not been done against most of the approximately 80 declarations submitted under the Statute (see Status of Multilateral Treaties Deposited with the Secretary-General).

However, there may be reason to treat all declarations as potential reservations, and, where necessary, object to them. Uruguay formulated, when ratifying the Statute on 28 June 2002, a declaration with the wording "as a State Party to the Rome Statute, the Eastern Republic of Uruguay shall ensure its application to the full extent of the powers of the State insofar as it is competent in that respect and in strict accordance with the Constitutional provisions of the Republic". This declaration received, in contrast to other declarations under the Statute, objections from other States. Finland, Germany, the Netherlands, Sweden, Ireland, United Kingdom, Denmark and Norway objected in various ways against Uruguay's declaration, either through outright objections under the VCLT or by communication to the Secretary-General, to the effect that Uruguay's declaration in fact constituted a reservation. The objections formulated in response to Uruguay's declaration resulted in a decision by the country to withdraw the declaration on 26 February 2008 (see Status of Multilateral Treaties Deposited with the Secretary-General).

A relevant question is whether states must object to these types of impermissible reservations. One view is that such reservations are invalid, another is that the validity of reservations is dependent on the acceptance of the reservation by other states (Shaw, p. 667; Åkermak and Mårsäter, pp. 385–387). The view is divided, but an reasonable argument is that regarding reservations under treaties which explicitly does not allow formulation of reservations, it is not necessary to object in accordance with Articles 20 and 21 VCLT, since these reservations *per se* are to be seen as impermissible and the act of formulating the reservation would be an incorrect action by the reserving State that cannot be cured by other State Parties acceptance of the reservation. It is admitted that the question is more complicated when the treaty in question explicitly allows for the formulation of reservations. State practice regarding objections differs, which is also shown in the above mentioned case of Uruguay's declaration under the Statute. Finland, the Netherlands, Sweden and Ireland concluded in their respective objections that the impermissible reservation was severable, a legal effect of objections not envisaged in Article 21 VCLT, while the other objecting States seemingly followed the rules stipulated in Articles 20–21 VCLT without any conclusion regarding the severability of the reservation (see Status of Multilateral Treaties Deposited with the Secretary-General).

Whether Article 120 will have the effect of preventing States from seeking to modify or exclude regulations under the Statute, depends on how the rules regarding reservations will be developed and interpreted in the future. This applies in particular to their customary development.

Doctrine:

1. Gerhard Hafner, "Article 120 – Reservations", in Otto Triffterer (ed.), *Commentary on the Rome Statute of the International Criminal Court: Observers' Notes, Article by Article*, 2nd ed., C.H. Beck/Hart/Nomos, Munich/Oxford/Baden-Baden, 2008, pp. 1737–50.

2. William A. Schabas, *The International Criminal Court: A Commentary on the Rome Statute*, Oxford University Press, Oxford, 2010.

3. Malcolm N. Shaw, *International Law*, 7th ed., Cambridge University Press, Cambridge, 2014.

4. Sia Spiliopoulou Åkermark and Olle Mårsäter, "Otillåtna reservationer – Maldivernas reservation mot kvinnodiskrimineringskonventionen", in *Mennesker og rettigheter*, 1995, vol. 13, no. 4, pp. 382–99.

Author: Olle Mårsäter.

Article 121
Amendments[857]

1. After the expiry of seven years from the entry into force of this Statute, any State Party may propose amendments thereto. The text of any proposed amendment shall be submitted to the Secretary-General of the United Nations, who shall promptly circulate it to all States Parties.[858] [854]

2. No sooner than three months from the date of notification, the Assembly of States Parties, at its next meeting, shall, by a majority of those present and voting, decide whether to take up the proposal. The Assembly may deal with the proposal directly or convene a Review Conference if the issue involved so warrants.[859]

3. The adoption of an amendment at a meeting of the Assembly of States Parties or at a Review Conference on which consensus cannot be reached shall require a two-thirds majority of States Parties.[860]

4. Except as provided in paragraph 5, an amendment shall enter into force for all States Parties one year after instruments of ratification or acceptance have been deposited with the Secretary-General of the United Nations by seven-eighths of them.[861]

---

[857] *General remarks*:

During the negotiations of the ICC Statute some states wanted to amend the Statute as soon as the Statute came into force. This was important for states that wanted to include additional crimes such as terrorism, drug trafficking and the use of weapons of mass destruction. Other states wanted to go more slowly. The compromise was no amendments could be considered until seven years after the entry into force of the Statute.

There was also discussion on the required majority for making amendments. Most delegations accepted that a qualified majority would suffice. The ultimate resolution in paragraphs 3–6 of Article 121 will make amendments very difficult (Slade and Clark, pp. 433–434).

[858] This provision prevents any amendments until seven years after the entry into force of the Statute, that means 1 July 2009. The text of any proposed amendment is be submitted to the Secretary-General of the United Nations as the depositary of the treaty and who will notify all States Parties.

[859] This provision provides that a majority of members of the Assembly of States Parties present and voting shall decide whether to take up the proposal. Article 121(3) expresses a preference adoption by consensus, if this cannot be reached an amendment shall require the support of a two-thirds majority of States Parties.

[860] The States Parties should endeavour to adopt amendment by consensus. If this cannot be reached a two-thirds majority of States Parties is required. This higher than what is generally required for decisions on matters of substance, where it is enough with a two-thirds majority of those States Parties *present* and *voting* (Article 112(7)(a)) whereas the requirement for amendment of the ICC Statute requires the affirmative support of *all* States Parties. This means that amendments can be blocked by a combination of States Parties voting no, abstaining or by not being present during the vote together making up one-third plus one state.

[861] If the States Parties adopts an amendment under paragraph 3, paragraph 4 provides that an amendment shall enter into force for all States Parties one year after instruments of ratification or acceptance have been deposited with the Secretary-General of the United Nations by seven-

---

5. Any amendment to Articles 5, 6, 7 and 8 of this Statute shall enter into force for those States Parties which have accepted the amendment one year after the deposit of their instruments of ratification or acceptance. In respect of a State Party which has not accepted the amendment, the Court shall not exercise its jurisdiction regarding a crime covered by the amendment when committed by that State Party's nationals or on its territory.[862]

---

eighths of them. Other rules applies when dealing amendments of the substantive crimes of the Court (to which sub-paragraph 5 applies) and certain minor institutional changes (to which Article 122 applies).

[862] The general rule on the entry into force of amendments is set out in Article 121(4). Article 121(5) is an exception and applies to amendment to Articles 5, 6, 7 and 8 with consequence that amendments concerning crimes within the jurisdiction of the Court only applies to states that have accepted amendments to this Articles. This is also consistent with sub-paragraph 6 which allows withdrawals in relation to amendments under sub-paragraph 4 but not under sub-paragraph 5.

During the adoption of the provision there was a "technical error" which was corrected after the Rome conference. Initially, this provision only had a reference to Article 5 but later during the negotiations there was intent to clarify that this provision would apply also to Articles 6–8. If the provision would only apply to Article 5, the effect would be that rules of entry into force in sub-paragraph 5 would only apply to new crimes (for example adding terrorism or drug offences) meaning that amendments would apply only to accepting States Parties, whereas sub-paragraph 4 would apply to changes in Articles 6–8 meaning that such changes would apply to all States Parties. The provision was corrected with the effect that sub-paragraph 5 applies to Articles 5–8 with no objections from the States Parties (Clark, pp. 1755–1756; Schabas, pp. 1179–1180).

The matter of state consent in relation to amendments became a major issue when inclusion of the crime of aggression was negotiated, there were four different interpretations of how Article 5(2) should be interpreted in conjunction with Article 121:

1) Under the 'Adoption Model', the Court can exercise its jurisdiction over the crime of aggression in accordance with Article 12 of the ICC Statute once the new provisions have been adopted at an Assembly of States Parties meeting or at a Review Conference.

2) The "Article 121(5) Model with a Negative Understanding" is situated at the other end of the spectrum. This interpretation precludes the ICC from exercising its jurisdiction over the crime of aggression when either the State Party of nationality of the alleged offenders or the State Party on whose territory the crime is alleged to have been committed, has not accepted the provision(s) on the crime of aggression.

3) According to the 'Article 121(5) Model with a Positive Understanding', the second sentence of Article 121(5) of the ICC Statute only has the limited effect of placing non-accepting States Parties on precisely the same footing as non-States Parties for the purpose of the application of Article 12(2) of the ICC Statute. It avoids the problem of an unfair discrimination between non-accepting States Parties and non-States Parties.

4) The "Article 121(4) Model" treats the provision(s) on the crime of aggression as an amendment to the ICC Statute, but for at least one of the reasons set out above, not as an "amendment to Articles 5, 6, 7 and 8 of this Statute" within the meaning of Article 121(5) of the ICC Statute.

In order to resolve the matter, there was agreement before the Kampala conference to formulate a "special entry-into-force mechanism". The solution is to be found in Article 15 *bis* and can be described as "softly" consent based compared to the "strictly" consent based "Article

6. If an amendment has been accepted by seven-eighths of States Parties in accordance with paragraph 4, any State Party which has not accepted the amendment may withdraw from this Statute with immediate effect, notwithstanding Article 127, paragraph 1, but subject to Article 127, paragraph 2, by giving notice no later than one year after the entry into force of such amendment.[863]

7. The Secretary-General of the United Nations shall circulate to all States Parties any amendment adopted at a meeting of the Assembly of States Parties or at a Review Conference.[864]

121(5) Model with a Negative Understanding" Article 15(4) bis by adding an opt-out option (Kreß and Holtzendorf, pp. 1196–1199, 1214).

[863] A state which does not accept an amendment that has been adopted under Article 121(4) may withdraw from the Statute at any time within one year after entry force of such amendment. This provision is an exception from the general right to withdraw under Article 127(1) which takes effect only after one year of the notification. Withdrawals under Article 121(6) take effect immediately.

Author: Mark Klamberg.

[864] The Secretary-General of the United Nations shall as depositary of the treaty circulate to all States Parties any amendment adopted at a meeting of the Assembly of States Parties or at a Review Conference.

Cross-references:

Article 127.

Doctrine:

1. Roger S. Clark, "Article 121 – Amendments", in Otto Triffterer (ed.), *Commentary on the Rome Statute of the International Criminal Court: Observers' Notes, Article by Article*, 2nd ed., C.H. Beck/Hart/Nomos, Munich/Oxford/Baden-Baden, 2008, pp. 1751–57.

2. Claus Kreß and Leonievon Holtzendorff, "The Kampala Compromise on the Crime of Aggression", *Journal of International Criminal Justice*, vol. 8, 2010, pp. 1179–1217.

3. William A. Schabas, *The International Criminal Court: A Commentary on the Rome Statute*, Oxford University Press, Oxford, 2010, pp. 1155–56.

4. Tuiloma Neroni Slade and Roger S. Clark, "Preamble and Final Clauses", in Roy S. Lee (ed.), The *International Criminal Court: The Making of the Rome Statute*, Kluwer Law International, The Hague, 1999, pp. 421–50.

Author: Mark Klamberg.

Article 122

Amendments to provisions of an institutional nature[865]

1. Amendments to provisions of this Statute which are of an exclusively institutional nature, namely, Article 35, Article 36, paragraphs 8 and 9, Article 37, Article 38, Article 39, paragraphs 1 (first two sentences), 2 and 4, Article 42, paragraphs 4 to 9, Article 43, paragraphs 2 and 3, and Articles 44, 46, 47 and 49, may be proposed at any time, notwithstanding Article 121, paragraph 1, by any State Party. The text of any proposed amendment shall be submitted to the Secretary-General of the United Nations or such other person designated by the Assembly of States Parties who shall promptly circulate it to all States Parties and to others participating in the Assembly.[866]

---

[865] *General remarks*:

While Article 121 provides for amendments in general, Article 122 provides for a simplified procedure in relation to an amendments of an institutional nature. With Article 122 it is enough that two-thirds of the members of the Assembly of States Parties approves – there is no requirement that the States Parties need to ratify amendments. Moreover, there is nothing in Article 122 similar to that in Article 121 prohibiting changes during the first seven years of the life of the Court.

Preparatory works:

There was initial resistance during the negotiations to introduce a simplified amendment procedure in the final clauses. However, when negotiating Article 36 there was agreement that a simplified procedure was needed when increase the number of judges. Hence, Article 36(2) provides for such a procedure – it is enough that two-thirds of the members of the Assembly of States Parties approves an increase of judges and there is no need for the States Parties to ratify changes in this regard. The idea to have a simplified amendment procedure in the final clauses was reintroduced and Article 122 applies for such a procedure to a number of other instances (Slade and Clark, pp. 438–440; Schabas, pp. 1183–1184; Clark. p. 1759).

Author: Mark Klamberg.

[866] Article 122(1) contains an exhaustive list on the provisions of the ICC Statute that may be amended by the simplified procedure. It is:

- Article 35, service of judges,
- Article 36, paras. 8 and 9, criteria for selecting judges and term of office,
- Article 37, judicial vacancies,
- Article 38, the Presidency of the Court,
- Article 39, para. 1 (first two sentences), the Court shall organise itself into Appeals Division, Trial Division and Pre-Trial Division with a certain number of judges in each division,
- Article 39, para. 2, the Appeals Chamber shall be composed of all the judges of the Appeals Division; the functions of the Trial Chamber shall be carried out by three judges of the Trial Division; the functions of the Pre-Trial Chamber shall be carried out either by three judges of the Pre-Trial Division or by a single judge,
- Article 39, para. 4, Judges assigned to the Appeals Division shall serve only in that division. However, judges may be temporary attached from the Trial Division to the Pre-Trial Division or vice versa,
- Article 42, paras. 4 to 9, election, excuse and disqualification of the Prosecutor and Deputy Prosecutors,

2. Amendments under this article on which consensus cannot be reached shall be adopted by the Assembly of States Parties or by a Review Conference, by a two-thirds majority of States Parties. Such amendments shall enter into force for all States Parties six months after their adoption by the Assembly or, as the case may be, by the Conference.[867]

- Article 43, paras. 2 and 3, the Registry shall be headed by the Registrar
- Article 44, staff of Prosecutor and Registrar
- Article 46, removal of judge, the Prosecutor, a Deputy Prosecutor, the Registrar or the Deputy Registrar from office,
- Article 47, disciplinary measures for judges, Prosecutor, Deputy Prosecutor, Registrar or Deputy Registrar
- Article 49, salaries, allowances and expenses

The provision provides that changes to provisions may be proposed at any time under the simplified procedure in contrast to the seven-year time limit in Article 121(1). However, no amendments under the simplified procedure were submitted during the first seven years of the Court which makes this difference irrelevant.

Author: Mark Klamberg.

[867] Amendments under Article 122 are done with a two-thirds majority of States Parties. The amendment is either adopted by the Assembly of States Parties or by a Review Conference. Once the amendments is adopted, there is no need for ratification or accession. There is no requirement corresponding to Article 121(7) that the Secretary-General of the United Nations shall circulate to all States Parties any amendment adopted at a meeting of the Assembly of States Parties or at a Review Conference. The amendment enters into force for all States Parties six months after their adoption by the Assembly of Review Conference.

Doctrine:

1. Roger S. Clark, "Article 122 – Amendments to Provisions of an Institutional Nature" in Otto Triffterer (ed.), *Commentary on the Rome Statute of the International Criminal Court: Observers' Notes, Article by Article*, 2nd ed., C.H. Beck/Hart/Nomos, Munich/Oxford/Baden-Baden, 2008, pp. 1759–61.
2. William A. Schabas, *The International Criminal Court: A Commentary on the Rome Statute*, Oxford University Press, Oxford, 2010, pp. 1183–86.
3. Tuiloma Neroni Slade and Roger S. Clark, "Preamble and Final Clauses", in Roy S. Lee (ed.), *The International Criminal Court: The Making of the Rome Statute*, Kluwer Law International, The Hague, 1999, pp. 421–50.

Author: Mark Klamberg.

Article 123
Review of the Statute[868]

1. Seven years after the entry into force of this Statute the Secretary-General of the United Nations shall convene a Review Conference to consider any amendments to this Statute. Such review may include, but is not limited to, the list of crimes contained in Article 5. The Conference shall be open to those participating in the Assembly of States Parties and on the same conditions.[869]

---

[868] *General remarks*:

In addition to the amendment procedure under Article 121, Article 123 sets up an review procedure which has a set time when a first meeting must take place. Article 123 also seeks to ensure that adequate attention would be given to re-examine the crimes under the jurisdiction of the Court.

Preparatory works:

Article 21 of the 1993 draft Statute of the ILC Working group provided that "[a] Review Conference shall be held , at the request of at least [...] States Parties after this Statute has been in force for at least five years" (Report of the Working Group of the International Law Commission, Annex to the Yearbook of the International Law Commission, report of the Commission to the General Assembly on the work of its forty-fifth session, 1995, Volume II Part Two, A/CN.4/SER.A/1993/Add.1 (Part 2)).

There was no similar provision in the ILC draft Statute of 1994. Article 111 of the 1998 Preparatory Committee Draft Statute provided that after the expiry of certain number of years to be decided from the entry into force of the Statute, the meeting of the Assembly of States Parties may decide, by a two-thirds majority to convene a special meeting of the Assembly of States Parties to review the Statute.

At the Rome Conference the idea of a Review Conference was used to postpone debates on contentious issues.

Author: Mark Klamberg.

[869] The first paragraph provides that the first review is to include, but is not be limited to, the list of crimes in Article 5. The reference to Article 5 expresses the intent to expand the subject-matter jurisdiction of the Court, more specifically to cover the crime of aggression. Article 5(2) provides that "[t]he Court shall exercise jurisdiction over the crime of aggression once a provision is adopted in accordance with Articles 121 and 123 defining the crime and setting out the conditions under which the Court shall exercise jurisdiction with respect to this crime".

The reason for the limit of seven years before amendments are possible, was presumably to test how reliably the ICC functions.

The review conference is the same as for the Assembly of States Parties. Article 112 provides that each State Party shall have one representative in the Assembly.

The word "convenes" suggests that the Review Conference need to be held seven years after the entry into force of the Statute, only that it is convened by the UN Secretary General at that time and that the conference is held within a reasonable deadline thereafter (Schabas, p. 1188). The Secretary General sent a letter 7 August 2009 where he convened the conference in Kampala, Uganda. The first Review Conference was held in Kampala 31 May–11 June 2010.

The Review Conference adopted resolution 5 which added three war crimes to Article 8, paragraph 2 (e), namely the following:

(xiii) Employing poison or poisoned weapons;

2. At any time thereafter, at the request of a State Party and for the purposes set out in paragraph 1, the Secretary-General of the United Nations shall, upon approval by a majority of States Parties, convene a Review Conference.[870]

3. The provisions of Article 121, paragraphs 3 to 7, shall apply to the adoption and entry into force of any amendment to the Statute considered at a Review Conference.[871]

(xiv) Employing asphyxiating, poisonous or other gases, and all analogous liquids, materials or devices;

(xv) Employing bullets which expand or flatten easily in the human body, such as bullets with a hard envelope which does not entirely cover the core or is pierced with incisions (Resolution RC/Res.5, adopted at the 12th plenary meeting, on 10 June 2010).

The Conference also adopted resolution 6 which defines the crimes of aggression in the new provision Article 8 *bis* and new Articles 15 *bis* and 15 *ter* that sets out the conditions under which the Court shall exercise jurisdiction with respect to the crime of aggression. The resolution also amended the elements of crime accordingly. New sub-paragraph 25(3) *bis* clarifies that in respect of the crime of aggression, the provisions of Article 25 shall apply only to persons in a position effectively to exercise control over or to direct the political or military action of a State. There were some minor changes to Article 9(1) and 20(3), Resolution RC/Res.5, adopted at the 12th plenary meeting, on 11 June 2010.

Author: Mark Klamberg.

[870] After the first Review Conference, the UN Secretary-General shall at the request of a State Party and upon approval by a majority of States Parties, convene a subsequent Review Conference.

Author: Mark Klamberg.

[871] Paragraph provides that the same rules that apply for amendments done through the Assembly of States Parties shall apply to the adoption and entry into force of any amendment done through the Review Conference.

Doctrine:

1. Roger S. Clark, "Article 123 – Review of the Statute", in Otto Triffterer (ed.), *Commentary on the Rome Statute of the International Criminal Court: Observers' Notes, Article by Article*, 2nd ed., C.H. Beck/Hart/Nomos, Munich/Oxford/Baden-Baden, 2008, pp. 1763–65.

2. William A. Schabas, *The International Criminal Court: A Commentary on the Rome Statute*, Oxford University Press, Oxford, 2010, pp. 1186–91.

3. Tuiloma Neroni Slade and Roger S. Clark, "Preamble and Final Clauses", in Roy S. Lee (ed.), *The International Criminal Court: The Making of the Rome Statute*, Kluwer Law International, The Hague, 1999, pp. 421–50.

Author: Mark Klamberg.

Article 124
Transitional Provision

Notwithstanding Article 12, paragraphs 1 and 2, a State, on becoming a party to this Statute, may declare that, for a period of seven years after the entry into force of this Statute for the State concerned, it does not accept the jurisdiction of the Court with respect to the category of crimes referred to in Article 8 when a crime is alleged to have been committed by its nationals or on its territory. A declaration under this article may be withdrawn at any time. The provisions of this article shall be reviewed at the Review Conference convened in accordance with Article 123, paragraph 1.[872]

---

[872] *General remarks*:

Article 124 stipulates that a State may formulate a declaration declaring that it does not accept the jurisdiction of the Court with respect of war crimes alleged to have been committed by its nationals or on its territory over a period of seven years after the entry into force of the Statute for the State concerned. A declaration under Article 124 may be withdrawn at any time.

Analysis:

According to Article 120 it is not possible for states to modify or exclude any content in the Statute by using reservations. The disadvantage of taking a rigid stance towards State's desire to modify their obligations may have an effect of excluding the possibility for states to undertake obligations under the Statute. By allowing time limited declarations relating to the Jurisdiction of the Court an opt out model was introduced in the Statute, resulting in a compromise between a unanimity and a universality view. The use of opt out clauses can facilitate both the negotiating process and attract hesitant future State parties. The treaty basis for opt out clauses can be found in Article 17 VCLT. Article 17(1) VCLT stipulates that "Without prejudice to Articles 19 to 23, the consent of a State to be bound by part of the treaty is effective only if the treaty so permits or the other contacting States so agree". As can be seen, this partial acceptance has strong similarities with reservations (Åkermak and Mårsäter, 2005, pp. 523–27).

Article 124 can be seen as an exception to the rigid stance taken under Article 120. The regulation was criticised during the Rome Conference resulting in the decision that the provision should be reviewed at the first Review Conference in 2010. Two States, Colombia and France have made use of the possibility of formulating a declaration under Article 124. Upon ratification France declared that "[the French Republic] does not accept the jurisdiction of the Court with respect to the category of crimes referred to in Article 8 when a crime is alleged to have been committed by its nationals or on its territory". The French declaration was withdrawn on 13 August 2008 (see Status of Multilateral Treaties Deposited with the Secretary-General).

Cross-references:

Articles 8, 11 and 120.

Doctrine:

1. Sia Spilioupoulou Åkermark and Olle Mårsäter, "Treaties and the Limits of Flexibility", in *Nordic Journal of International Law*, 2005, vol. 74, pp. 509–40.
2. Gerhard Hafner, "Article 120 – Reservations", in Otto Triffterer (ed.), *Commentary on the Rome Statute of the International Criminal Court: Observers' Notes, Article by Article*, 2nd ed., C.H. Beck/Hart/Nomos, Munich/Oxford/Baden-Baden, 2008, pp. 1737–50.

Author: Olle Mårsäter.

Article 125

Signature, ratification, acceptance, approval or accession[873]

1. This Statute shall be open for signature by all States in Rome, at the headquarters of the Food and Agriculture Organization of the United Nations, on 17 July 1998. Thereafter, it shall remain open for signature in Rome at the Ministry of Foreign Affairs of Italy until 17 October 1998. After that date, the Statute shall remain open for signature in New York, at United Nations Headquarters, until 31 December 2000.[874]

2. This Statute is subject to ratification, acceptance or approval by signatory States. Instruments of ratification, acceptance or approval shall be deposited with the Secretary-General of the United Nations.[875]

3. This Statute shall be open to accession by all States. Instruments of accession shall be deposited with the Secretary-General of the United Nations.[876]

---

[873] *General remarks*:

This Article is a standard-form final clause that received little discussion during the negotiations of the Statute.

Preparatory works:

A text corresponding to the final version of Article 125 was circulated at the final session of Preparatory Committee (see Article 112 of the Draft Statute, Report of the Preparatory Committee on the Establishment of an International Criminal Court, United Nations Diplomatic Conference of Plenipotentiaries on the Establishment of an International Criminal Court Rome, Italy 15 June–17 July 1998, A/CONF.183/2.

Author: Mark Klamberg.

[874] Signature signifies the adoption and authentication of the text. Signature of the ICC Statute is subject to ratification, acceptance or approval, which means that signature alone does establish consent to be bound. However, signature expresses the intent to ratify and creates an obligation of good faith "to refrain from acts which would defeat the object and purpose of a treaty" (Article 18 of the Vienna Convention on the Law of Treaties). The Statute was open for signature until 31 December 2000.

Two states, USA and Israel, have signed the Statute but later (6 May 2002 and 28 August 2002) declared their intent not to ratify the Statute. These declarations have been referred to as "unsigning" the ICC Statute. However, signature is an act that cannot be revoked. The effect of signature can be altered by declarations such as those formulated by USA and Israel (Schabas, p. 1198).

Author: Mark Klamberg.

[875] Ratification involves two distinct procedural steps: the first the act of the appropriate organ of the State; the second is the international procedure which brings a treaty – in this case the ICC Statute – into force by a deposit of ratification with the Secretary-General of the United Nations. All three terms "ratification", "acceptance" and "approval" are colloquially referred to as "ratification". States use different terms for constitutional and historical reasons (Brownlie, pp. 582–583, Schabas, p. 1198).

Author: Mark Klamberg.

[876] Ratification is not the only way to become a State Party. States which did not sign the ICC Statute may accede the Statute and become a State Party.

Doctrine:

---

1. Ian Brownlie, *Principles of Public International Law*, 7th ed., Oxford University Press, Oxford, 2008, pp. 581–83.
2. Roger S. Clark, "Article 125 – Signature, Ratification, Acceptance, Approval or Accession", in Otto Triffterer (ed.), *Commentary on the Rome Statute of the International Criminal Court: Observers' Notes, Article by Article*, 2nd ed., C.H. Beck/Hart/Nomos, Munich/Oxford/Baden-Baden, 2008, p. 1773.
3. William A. Schabas, *The International Criminal Court: A Commentary on the Rome Statute*, Oxford University Press, Oxford, 2010, pp. 1195–1200.
4. Tuiloma Neroni Slade and Roger S. Clark, "Preamble and Final Clauses", in Roy S. Lee (ed.), *The International Criminal Court: The Making of the Rome Statute*, Kluwer Law International, The Hague, 1999, pp. 421–50.

Author: Mark Klamberg.

Article 126
Entry into force[877]

1. This Statute shall enter into force on the first day of the month after the 60th day following the date of the deposit of the 60th instrument of ratification, acceptance, approval or accession with the Secretary-General of the United Nations.[878]

2. For each State ratifying, accepting, approving or acceding to this Statute after the deposit of the 60th instrument of ratification, acceptance, approval or accession, the Statute shall

---

[877] *General remarks*:

Although this Article is a standard-form final clause, it did contain the difficult issue on the number of parties needed to bring the Statute into force.

Preparatory works:

The 1994 ILC Draft Statute stated that "The statute of the court is intended to reflect and represent the interests of the international community as a whole in relation to the prosecution of certain most serious crimes of international concern. In consequence, the statute and its covering treaty should require a substantial number of States parties before it enters into force" (Report of the International Law Commission, Forty-sixth session, 2 May 1994–22 July 1994, Official Records of the General Assembly, Forty-ninth session, p. 69)

The number of sixty first appeared in the Report of the Ad Hoc Committee on the Establishment of an International Criminal Court, 1995, Official Records of the General Assembly, Fiftieth Session, Supplement No. 22 (A/50/22) (1995), para. 15.

Article 114 of the Preparatory Committee Draft Statute followed with the same number, Report of the Preparatory Committee on the Establishment of an International Criminal Court, United Nations Diplomatic Conference of Plenipotentiaries on the Establishment of an International Criminal Court Rome, Italy 15 June–17 July 1998, A/CONF.183/2.

Some states favoured during the negotiations in Rome a lower number. Other states argued that for the institution have legitimacy it should have a decent number of parties. This is even more logical considering that the Court with the consent of the territorial State would have jurisdiction over crimes committed on that territory by nationals of non-State Parties (Slade and Clark, p. 444).

Author: Mark Klamberg.

[878] The Statute shall enter into force on sixty days after the deposit of the 60th instrument of ratification, acceptance, approval or accession. Sixty days is fairly standard waiting period in modern treaty practice for the entry into force of the Statute (Slade and Clark, p. 445).

The number of ratifications reached sixty on 13 April 2002 and thus the Statute entered into force of 1 July 2002. The entry into force is relevant for several other provisions. Article 11(1) provides that the Court has jurisdiction only with respect to crimes committed after the entry into force. Upholding the principle of legality and non-retroactivity, Article 24(1) states that no person shall be criminally responsible under this Statute for conduct prior to the entry into force of the Statute. Further, pursuant to Article 121(1) amendments are only possible after the expiry of seven years from the entry into force of the Statute. The date of the first Review Conference is also set in relation to the entry into force of the Statue according to Article 123 (Schabas, p. 1203).

Author: Mark Klamberg.

---

enter into force on the first day of the month after the 60th day following the deposit by such State of its instrument of ratification, acceptance, approval or accession.[879]

---

[879] For a State ratifying, accepting, approving or acceding to the Statute after the deposit of the sixtieth instrument of ratification – that is the 13 April 2002 – the entry into force for that State occurs on the first day of the month after the sixtieth day following the deposit by such State.

This date is relevant for Article 11(2) which provides that if a State becomes a Party to this Statute after its entry into force, the Court may exercise its jurisdiction only with respect to crimes committed after the entry into force of this Statute for that State. There are two exceptions where the Court may exercise jurisdiction for crimes committed before the ratification of that State – but still limited to acts committed after 1 July 2002: 1) if that State has made a declaration under Article 12(3); 2) jurisdiction has been established by the UN Security Council under Article 13(b).

A State may also upon ratification of the ICC Statute make a declaration in accordance with Article 124 and opt out for a period of seven years from the jurisdiction of the Court in relation to war crimes.

Cross-references:

Articles 11(1), 24(1), 121(1) and 123.

Doctrine:

1. Roger S. Clark, "Article 126 – Entry Into Force", in Otto Triffterer (ed.), *Commentary on the Rome Statute of the International Criminal Court: Observers' Notes, Article by Article*, 2nd ed., C.H. Beck/Hart/Nomos, Munich/Oxford/Baden-Baden, 2008, pp. 1775–76.

2. William A. Schabas, *The International Criminal Court: A Commentary on the Rome Statute*, Oxford University Press, Oxford, 2010, pp. 1201–4.

3. Tuiloma Neroni Slade and Roger S. Clark, "Preamble and Final Clauses", in Roy S. Lee (ed.), *The International Criminal Court: The Making of the Rome Statute,* Kluwer Law International, The Hague, 1999, pp. 421–50.

Author: Mark Klamberg.

Article 127
Withdrawal[880]

1. A State Party may, by written notification addressed to the Secretary-General of the United Nations, withdraw from this Statute. The withdrawal shall take effect one year after the date of receipt of the notification, unless the notification specifies a later date.[881]

2. A State shall not be discharged, by reason of its withdrawal, from the obligations arising from this Statute while it was a Party to the Statute, including any financial obligations which may have accrued. Its withdrawal shall not affect any cooperation with the Court in connection with criminal investigations and proceedings in relation to which the withdrawing State had a duty to cooperate and which were commenced prior to the date on which the withdrawal became effective, nor shall it prejudice in any way the continued consideration of any matter which was already under consideration by the Court prior to the date on which the withdrawal became effective.[882]

---

[880] *General remarks:*

Article 127 deals with withdrawal. It differs from the right to withdraw under Article 121(6). While Article 121(6) allows withdrawal under a narrow set of circumstances when the Statute has been amended, Article 127 is entirely open-ended. There is no limitation on what grounds a State may withdraw under Article 127. The benefit for withdrawing under Article 121(6) is the immediate effect while withdrawal under Article 127 takes a year from the date of notification of withdrawal.

Preparatory works:

There was no dispute during the negotiations that States would have the right to withdraw. Article 98 of the Draft Statute contained in the Zutphen Report was very concise (Report of the Intersessional Meeting from 19 to 30 January 1998 in Zutphen, The Netherlands A/AC.249/1998/L.13, 4 February 1998).

The discussion focused on paragraph 2 which concerns past obligation, that is obligations that arose from the Statute while the State was a Party to the Statute. Article 115 of the Draft Statute adopted by Preparatory Committee (1998) contained a draft provision of withdrawal almost identical to the adopted provision (Report of the Preparatory Committee on the Establishment of an International Criminal Court, United Nations Diplomatic Conference of Plenipotentiaries on the Establishment of an International Criminal Court Rome, Italy 15 June–17 July 1998, A/CONF.183/2).

Author: Mark Klamberg.

[881] Paragraph 1 provides that a withdrawal takes effect one year after the date of receipt of the notification of withdrawal. However, States are allows to specify a later date in its notification.

The Secretary-General of the United Nations exercises the depositary function in receiving notifications of withdrawal.

Author: Mark Klamberg.

[882] The first sentence of the second paragraph captures the principle of Article 70 of the Vienna Convention on the Law of Treaties that past obligations survive withdrawal from the treaty regime: "the termination of a treaty [...] does not affect any right, obligation or legal situation of the parties created through the execution of the treaty prior to its termination".

The second sentence deals with an example of this principle, namely cooperation in connection with investigations and prosecution.

The last part of the second sentence "nor shall it prejudice" makes it clear by the words "any matter which was already under consideration by the Court" that a State which nationals have been put under the jurisdiction of the Court by a State referral or by a Prosecutor acting *proprio motu* cannot terminate such proceedings by withdrawing from the Statute. Thus, when a State finds it, or its leaders targeted by investigations or prosecution, the ICC Statute seeks to prevent that withdrawal is used as a means of avoiding its jurisdiction.

Cross-references:

Article 12.

Doctrine:

1. Roger S. Clark, "Article 127 – Withdrawal", in Otto Triffterer (ed.), *Commentary on the Rome Statute of the International Criminal Court: Observers' Notes, Article by Article*, 2nd ed., C.H. Beck/Hart/Nomos, Munich/Oxford/Baden-Baden, 2008, pp. 1777–79.

2. William A. Schabas, *The International Criminal Court: A Commentary on the Rome Statute*, Oxford University Press, Oxford, 2010, pp. 1205–7.

3. Tuiloma Neroni Slade and Roger S. Clark, "Preamble and Final Clauses", in Roy S. Lee (ed.), *The International Criminal Court: The Making of the Rome Statute*, Kluwer Law International, The Hague, 1999, pp. 421–50.

Author: Mark Klamberg.

Article 128
Authentic texts

The original of this Statute, of which the Arabic, Chinese, English, French, Russian and Spanish texts are equally authentic, shall be deposited with the Secretary-General of the United Nations, who shall send certified copies thereof to all States.[883]

IN WITNESS WHEREOF, the undersigned, being duly authorized thereto by their respective Governments, have signed this Statute.

DONE at Rome, this 17th day of July 1998.

---

[883] *General remarks*:

Article 128 reiterates the equal authenticity principle concerning multilateral treaties stated in the Vienna Convention on the Law of Treaties (VCLT). Article 33(4) of the VCLT states when the principle is applied "the meaning which best reconciles the texts, having regard to the object and purpose of the treaty, shall be adopted".

Preparatory works:

This provision cause no controversy whatsoever and was adopted exactly on the basis of the Secretariat's draft (Slade, p. 448).

Analysis:

The languages listed are the official United Nations languages. The Secretary-General of the United Nations shall as a depositary send certified copies of the Statute to "all States", a formula that also includes states that that are not United Nations members.

Doctrine:

1. Roger S. Clark, "Article 126 – Entry Into Force", in Otto Triffterer (ed.), *Commentary on the Rome Statute of the International Criminal Court: Observers' Notes, Article by Article*, 2nd ed., C.H. Beck/Hart/Nomos, Munich/Oxford/Baden-Baden, 2008, p. 1781.

2. William A. Schabas, *The International Criminal Court: A Commentary on the Rome Statute*, Oxford University Press, Oxford, 2010, pp. 1208–10.

3. Tuiloma Neroni Slade and Roger S. Clark, "Preamble and Final Clauses", in Roy S. Lee (ed.), *The International Criminal Court: The Making of the Rome Statute*, The Hague: Kluwer Law International, 1999, pp. 421–50.

Author: Mark Klamberg.

CONTRIBUTORS

Mohamed Abdou is a Ph.D. candidate in Public international law at the University of Paris I – Panthéon Sorbonne, France. He graduated from the same University (2006) and holds an LL.M. degree in International and Comparative Law from Indiana University School of Law (2007). In 2011 he joined the Office of Public Counsel for Victims of the International Criminal Court. He is currently working on the Saif Gaddafi and Bosco Ntaganda cases. Before joining the Court, he served as an Associate Prosecutor at the Office of the Prosecutor General in Cairo. He has also previously worked for the International Labour Organisation in Geneva, and has interned with the United Nations Office of Legal Affairs.

Marie Aronsson-Storrier is a Ph.D. candidate at Melbourne Law School, Australia, researching the role of covert action in the development of the law regulating the resort to force in international relations. She teaches International Governance and Law and Human Rights in the Melbourne School of Government, and before commencing her Ph.D. candidature in 2012, she worked as a research assistant in International Humanitarian Law on the Every Casualty programme of the Oxford Research Group. She holds a Master of Laws from the University of Gothenburg.

Mohamed Elewa Badar is Associate Professor and Reader in Comparative and International Criminal Law and Islamic Law at Northumbria School of Law, Northumbria University, United Kingdom. He is the author of *The Concept of Mens Rea in International Criminal Law* (Hart, 2013) and has published more than 20 articles in refereed journals and chapters in books. His work has been cited by the International Criminal Tribunal for the former Yugoslavia, the International Criminal Court, the United Nations Extraordinary Chambers in the Courts of Cambodia, the United Nations International Law Commission and the Supreme Court of Argentina.

Paul Behrens is a Lecturer (Assistant Professor) at the University of Edinburgh, United Kingdom. He has taught in the past at the University of Leicester, is a member of the Surrey International Law Centre, Associate of the Stanley Burton Centre for Holocaust and Genocide Studies and member of the Society of Legal Scholars. He is a co-editor of *Elements of Genocide* (Routledge, 2012)) and *The Criminal Law of Genocide* (Ashgate, 2007) and has written articles and papers on various aspects of international criminal law. He also contributes regularly to newspapers (including *The Guardian*, *The Scotsman* and *Süddeutsche Zeitung*) on issues of international law and constitutional law, and has given radio interviews on these topics.

Kirsten Bowman has previously worked as a legal officer at the International Criminal Court ('ICC') and International Criminal Tribunal for Rwanda, as well as having interned with the International Criminal Tribunal for the former Yugoslavia. She spent time in both the Office of the Prosecutor as well as Chambers where, at the ICC, she worked for then Vice President Blattmann on the Lubanga case. As well, she has taught International Criminal Law and International Courts courses at Georgetown University, United States, and consults with several organisations, including Open Society Justice Initiative and the Women's Initiative for Gender Justice. She is the research director at the International Bar Association. She holds a J.D. and is a member of the New York Bar.

Yassin Brunger is a Lecturer of Human Rights Law at the School of Law, Queen's University Belfast, United Kingdom. She has held positions as a Lecturer in Socio-Legal Studies, University of Leicester and a Research Fellow, University College Dublin, Ireland. She has held Visiting Research positions at the Lauterpacht Centre for International Law at the University of Cambridge, Lucy Cavendish College and the Institute for Advanced Legal Studies, London. Her mains areas of research are the relationship between the International Criminal Court and United Nations Security Council, conflict-related gender-based violence and feminist perspectives on international law. She studied at Queen's University Belfast (Ph.D.), University of Nottingham (LL.M.) and Warwick University (LL.B.).

Enrique Carnero-Rojo is a part-time Ph.D. candidate in International Criminal Law at Utrecht University, the Netherlands. He holds a master's degree in law and economics from the University of Deusto, Spain, and an LL.M. degree in Public International Law from Leiden University, the Netherlands. Before starting his research in Utrecht, he served in the Appeals Section of the Office of the Prosecutor of the International Criminal Tribunal for the former Yugoslavia (2003) and in the Legal Advisory Section of the Office of the Prosecutor of the International Criminal Court (2004–2009). Since 2012 he has been a legal officer at the Office of Public Counsel for Victims of the International Criminal Court.

Gerard Conway is a Lecturer in Law at Brunel University London, United Kingdom, where he completed his Ph.D. He previously studied for a Master of International and Comparative Law at Uppsala University, Sweden, following which he worked as a legal trainee in the Irish Department of Foreign Affairs, as a judicial researcher in the Four Courts in Dublin, and as a legal researcher in the Irish Office of the Director of Public Prosecutions. He researches in the fields of European Union ('EU') constitutional law (especially the legal reasoning of the Court of Justice of the EU), comparative criminal and constitutional law and EU criminal law. He is the author of *The Limits of Legal Reasoning and the European Court of Justice* (Cambridge University Press, 2012) and *European Union Law* (Routledge, 2015).

Karel De Meester is a Ph.D. researcher in international criminal law at the Amsterdam Centre for International Law of the University of Amsterdam, the Netherlands, and a teaching assistant and researcher at the Leuven Institute for Human Rights and Critical Studies (LIHRICS), KU Leuven, Belgium. His research focuses on the investigation phase in international criminal procedure.

Caroline Ehlert is the author of *Prosecuting the Destruction of Cultural Property in International Criminal Law* (Martinus Nijhoff, 2014). She has previously worked for the Asian International Justice Initiative as a trial monitor at the Extraordinary Chambers in the Courts of Cambodia. She holds a Master of Laws from the University of Zurich, Switzerland, where she worked as a research assistant at the Chair for International Law and did her Ph.D. She is a member of the Zurich Bar and a lawyer specialising in criminal law in Zurich.

Ola Engdahl is Associate Professor in International Law at the Swedish Defence University and Stockholm University, Sweden. He was appointed as an Expert in the Governmental Committee of Inquiry on the implementation of certain criminal law commitments to prevent and combat terrorism. He is member of the National Commission for International Law and Disarmament and the Delegation for International Humanitarian Law Monitoring of Arms Projects in Sweden. His main research areas are international humanitarian law, human rights law and international law aspects on peace operations.

Viljam Engström currently works as University Teacher of Constitutional and International Law at the Department of Law, Åbo Akademi University, Finland. His fields of interest include international institutions, international institutional law, and the relationship between states and institutions. He has published *Constructing the Powers of International Institutions* (Martinus Nijhoff, 2012).

Håkan Friman was Senior Judge and Head of Division at Solna District Court in Sweden. He was long involved in the International Criminal Court ('ICC') and represented Sweden in the negotiations from 1996 onwards. He was a former Deputy Director-General in the Swedish Ministry of Justice, and was formerly a Professor at the University of Pretoria, South Africa, Visiting Professor at University College London, United Kingdom, and Visiting Scholar at George Washington University, USA. He published extensively concerning the ICC and is co-author of a leading textbook on international criminal law, *An Introduction to International Criminal Law and Procedure* (Cambridge University Press, 3rd ed., 2014).

Matthew Gillett is a Legal Officer in the Office of the Prosecutor of the International Criminal Tribunal for the former Yugoslavia ('ICTY'), working as an attorney on the last trial before the ICTY. He previously worked in the Immediate Office of the Prosecutor of the International Criminal Court ('ICC') and was a member of the New Zealand delegation to the Review Conference of the ICC in Kampala in 2010 where the amendments on the crime of aggression were adopted.

Barbara Goy is a Senior Appeals Counsel in the Office of the Prosecutor of the United Nations Mechanism for International Criminal Tribunals ('MICT'). Previously she worked in the Office of the Prosecutor of the International Criminal Tribunal for the former Yugoslavia ('ICTY'), in the Legal Advisory Section and the Appeals Section/Division (2003–2014). She holds a Ph.D. in law (Dr. iur.) from the University of Bonn, Germany, where she worked prior to joining the ICTY.

Mikaela Heikkilä is a post-doctoral researcher at the Institute for Human Rights at Åbo Akademi University, Finland. She has mainly conducted research within the fields of international criminal law, the rights of victims of crime, and European Union's Area of Freedom, Security and Justice. She is currently involved as a researcher in the EU Research Project FRAME (Fostering Human Rights among European (External and Internal) Policies).

Mark Klamberg is Associate Professor in International Law at Stockholm University, Sweden, and Deputy Director of the Stockholm Centre for International Law and Justice (SCILJ). He is also a visiting lecturer at Edinburgh Law School. He is the author of several publications on international criminal law and other fields of international law, including *Evidence in International Criminal Trials: Confronting Legal Gaps and the Reconstruction of Disputed Events* (Martinus Nijhoff Publishers, 2013) and *Power and Law in International Society: International Relations as the Sociology of International Law* (Routledge, 2015).

Geert-Jan Alexander Knoops is Visiting Professor of International Criminal Law at Shandong University, China. From 2003 to 2013 he was Professor of International Criminal Law at Utrecht University, the Netherlands. He holds two Ph.D. degrees, one awarded by the University of Leiden, the Netherlands (Criminal Law) and the other by the University of Ireland in the field of International Criminal Law. He has also been awarded a Master of Law degree in Public International Law and International Criminal Law by the University of Leiden. He practises as a lawyer at Knoops' Advocaten in Amsterdam. He has acted as legal counsel before various international tribunals like the European Court of Human Rights in Strasbourg, the

International Criminal Tribunal for the former Yugoslavia, the International Criminal Tribunal for Rwanda and the Special Tribunal for Sierra Leone.

Ruth Kok is a Member of the Legal Research Office (Section Criminal Law) of the Supreme Court of the Netherlands. In addition, she serves as a Substitute Judge at the District Court of Amsterdam, the Netherlands. She is also Vice-Editor-in-Chief of *Hague Yearbook of International Law*. In 2007 she received her Ph.D. from Amsterdam University for her thesis on *Statutory Limitations in International Criminal Law* (TMC Asser Press, 2007). She obtained her Law degree from Leiden University, the Netherlands. Her main expertise is (international) criminal law.

Linnea Kortfält has worked at the Swedish National Defence College, the United Nations Association of Sweden and been a Law Clerk with the Legal Advisory Section of the Office of the Prosecutor, International Criminal Tribunal for the former Yugoslavia. She started to work as a Lecturer of Law at Stockholm University, Sweden, in 2003, where she specialises in public international law, international criminal law, international humanitarian law as well as the human rights of women and children. She regularly lectures at Örebro University, the Swedish Ministry of Foreign Affairs, the Swedish Foundation for Human Rights and the Stockholm School of Theology. She is currently employed as a doctoral candidate at the Department of Law at Stockholm University.

Camilla Lind graduated from Stockholm University, Sweden, in January 2013 with a thesis on the international immunities of high-ranking state officials. She is an associate at the Stockholm law firm Kriström Advokatbyrå, where her areas of practice primarily consist of dispute resolution and criminal cases. Prior to that, she served as a law clerk at the District Court of Södertälje.

Letizia Lo Giacco is a doctoral candidate in public international law at Lund University Faculty of Law, Sweden. Her research project concerns the interplay between national and international jurisdictions in international crimes adjudication. She teaches international criminal law and international humanitarian law in the Masters in Human Rights offered by Lund University and the Raul Wallenberg Institute, and public international law in the undergraduate professional law course at Lund University. She formerly worked as an analyst on conflict diamonds at the European Commission and interned in the Chambers of the International Criminal Court and of the Special Tribunal for Lebanon as well as in the Office of the Co-Prosecutors of the Extraordinary Chambers in the Courts of Cambodia. She holds an LL.M. in international humanitarian law from the Geneva Academy of International Humanitarian Law and Human Rights.

Julie McBride specialises in human rights and the rights of children in conflict, and is the author of *The War Crime of Child Soldier Recruitment* (Springer, 2013). She has previously worked at the United Nations Office of Legal Affairs, Human Rights Watch and the International Criminal Court, and as Child Rights and Policy Adviser at War Child. She currently focuses on human rights programming for vulnerable populations at the Dutch Aids Fonds.

Yvonne McDermott is a Lecturer in Law in Bangor University, United Kingdom, where she is also Director of Teaching and Learning and Deputy Director of the Bangor Centre for International Law. She is a graduate of the National University of Ireland, Galway (B. Corp. Law, LL.B.), Leiden University, the Netherlands (LL.M. *cum laude*) and the Irish Centre for Human Rights (Ph.D.). Her research focuses on fair trial rights, international criminal procedure and international criminal law, and she has published widely in those fields.

Olle Mårsäter is a Senior Lecturer in Public International Law at the Faculty of Law of the University of Uppsala, Sweden. His key qualifications are related to research and lecturing in international law (with focus on *jus ad bellum* and *jus in bello*), human rights law, international humanitarian law, law of treaties and the law of international institutions. One of his specialities is the right to a fair trial and other aspects of access to justice under human rights law and international humanitarian law instruments, as well as under international judicial procedures.

Jonas Nilsson is a Legal Officer in Chambers, International Criminal Tribunal for the former Yugoslavia, where he has worked on a number of trials. He previously worked with human rights and refugee law at Amnesty International and the Swedish Helsinki Committee. Between 2001 and 2003, he lived in Kosovo and worked at the Ombudsperson Institution as a Legal Officer and Director of Investigations. He is working on a Ph.D. thesis on the crime of persecution and has published articles on international criminal law and human rights.

Anna Oehmichen completed a legal clerkship at the International Criminal Court in The Hague and a traineeship with Europol in the same city. She spent parts of her practical training period at a Belgian criminal defence law office and held a placement at the German Foreign Ministry. She subsequently worked as a Research Fellow at the Centre for Criminology in Wiesbaden, the National Agency for the Prevention of Torture in Wiesbaden and at the University of Gießen, all in Germany. Since October 2011 she has been a practising criminal lawyer, focusing on cross-border issues, European and international criminal defence, and white-collar cases.

Juan Pablo Pérez-León-Acevedo has been appointed as a Post-Doctoral Fellow at PluriCourts, Faculty of Law, University of Oslo, Norway. He has served in diverse capacities at, among others, the International Criminal Court, the International Criminal Tribunal for the former Yugoslavia, the United Nations, and the Centre for Human Rights, Faculty of Law, University of Pretoria, South Africa.

Sara Porro has been a visiting scholar at Cornell Law School, USA, and Max Planck Institute for Foreign and International Criminal Law, Germany, a Research Associate at the University of Turin, Italy, and a grant holder with the German Academic Exchange Service. She has also interned with the Italian Embassy and the European Union Delegation to the United States. She is a regular contributor to *Oxford Reports on International Law in Domestic Courts*, as well as a reviewer for *International Criminal Law Review*. In May 2016 she completed the practical training required for bar admission in her native Italy.

Noëlle Quénivet is an Associate Professor in International Law at the Faculty of Business and Law of the University of the West of England, United Kingdom. Prior to that she worked as Researcher at the Institute for International Law of Peace and Armed Conflict, Germany. She has published several articles relating to international humanitarian law, authored *Sexual Offences in Armed Conflict in International Law* (Transnational Publishers, 2006, winner of the Francis Lieber Honorable Mention Award) and co-edited two books, one on the relationship between international humanitarian law and human rights law and another on international law in armed conflict. Her research focuses on international humanitarian law, international criminal law, post-conflict reconstruction, and gender and children in armed conflict.

Karin Påle-Bartes is a judge in Södertörn District Court. She received her Ph.D. from Uppsala University, Sweden, in 2003 for her doctoral thesis on principles in extradition. She has worked as a university teacher during her Ph.D. studies in Uppsala. She has been an Associate Court of Appeal Judge and has worked at the Ministry of Justice, Sweden.

Dejana Radisavljević is a Ph.D. candidate at the University of Sheffield, United Kingdom, researching into international criminal sentencing. She has several years' experience with the United Nations Mechanism for International Criminal Tribunals, working as a Legal Assistant in its two branches in Tanzania and the Netherlands. She completed her master's studies in Public International Law in 2012 at the University of Leicester, United Kingdom, with a particular focus on the two *ad hoc* international criminal tribunals and the International Criminal Court.

Geoff Roberts has been assigned as Defence Counsel to protect the interest and rights of the accused Assad Sabra in the case of *Prosecutor v. Ayyash et al.* He was admitted to the New York Bar in 2006 and holds a Law Degree in English and French Law from King's College London, United Kingdom, and Université Paris I, Pantheon-Sorbonne, France, and a Masters in International Criminal Justice and Armed Conflict from the University of Nottingham. He practises internationally, almost exclusively before international and hybrid courts and tribunals. For the last four years he worked as a Legal Officer for the Defence Office of the Special Tribunal for Lebanon and subsequently for the defence team for Assad Sabra before the same tribunal. He previously worked as a legal assistant or legal consultant for the defence teams representing Naser Orić and Rasim Delić at the International Criminal Tribunal for the former Yugoslavia ('ICTY'), Thomas Lubanga at the International Criminal Court and Ieng Sary at the Extraordinary Chambers in the Courts of Cambodia. He has also previously worked as an Associate Legal Officer for the Office of the Prosecutor at the ICTY.

Maria Sjöholm is a post-doctoral researcher at the Faculty of Law, Stockholm University, Sweden. Her previous research includes the definition of rape in international law and human trafficking in the European human rights system. She is currently working on a monograph on the inclusion of women's rights in the European Convention on Human Rights and American Convention on Human Rights.

SONG Tianying has been working as a Legal Officer in the Regional Delegation for East Asia of the International Committee of the Red Cross since 2011. She holds a Master's Degree in International Law and a Bachelor's Degree in Law from China University of Political Science and Law. She passed the National Judicial Exam in 2009. As an intern, she has worked in the Office of the Prosecutor of the International Criminal Court, the Department of Judicial Assistance and Foreign Affairs of the Ministry of Justice of China, and the China International Economic and Trade Arbitration Commission.

Michael Stiel passed the first state examination in 2013 after finishing his law studies at the Rheinische Friedrich-Wilhelms-Universität Bonn, Germany. He is currently working there as a research assistant at the Institute for Criminal Law and writing a doctoral thesis on the enforcement of sanctions imposed by international criminal tribunals.

Ignaz Stegmiller works as a post-doctoral researcher at the Franz von Liszt Institute of the Justus Liebig University Gießen, Germany. He is the Coordinator for International Programmes of the Faculty of Law, Franz von Liszt Institute for International and Comparative Law, Germany.

Carl-Friedrich Stuckenberg is a Professor at Bonn University, Germany, where he teaches domestic and international criminal law, criminal procedure and comparative criminal law. He previously held a chair in International, European and Comparative Criminal Law at Saarland University, Germany. He attended the Universities of Bonn and Geneva, received a Master's Degree from Harvard Law School, USA, a doctorate from Bonn University for his thesis on the presumption of innocence and finally the *venia legendi* (*Habilitation*) for his book on intent and mistake in international criminal law. His main research interests include the general part of criminal law, criminal procedure, international and European criminal law, comparative law as well as the philosophical foundations of punishment and legal history. He has published widely in many of these fields.

Melinda Taylor is a Defence Counsel. She is currently working on the Saif Gaddafi and Jean Pierre Bemba Gombo cases. She has previously worked as Counsel/Deputy Head of the Office of Public Counsel for the Defence at the International Criminal Court, on defence cases before the International Criminal Tribunals for the former Yugoslavia and Rwanda, as a Legal Officer at the United Nations Mission in Kosovo, and for the Office of Legal Aid and Detention at the International Criminal Tribunal for the former Yugoslavia. She is admitted to practise at the New York Bar, and has a Masters in International Human Rights Law from the University of Oxford, United Kingdom.

Jenia Iontcheva Turner is a Professor at SMU Dedman School of Law, USA, where she teaches criminal procedure, comparative criminal procedure, international criminal law, European Union law and international organisations. Before joining SMU, she served as a Bigelow Fellow at the University of Chicago Law School, USA, where she taught legal research and writing and comparative criminal procedure. She attended law school at Yale University, USA. Her scholarship interests include comparative and international criminal law and procedure, and she has published *Plea Bargaining Across Borders* (Aspen Publishers, 2009), exploring plea bargaining in several national and international jurisdictions.

Sergey Vasiliev is an Assistant Professor at the Grotius Centre for International Legal Studies, Leiden University, the Netherlands. He was previously a (post-doctoral) Researcher and Lecturer in International Criminal Law and Procedure at the Faculty of Law, Vrije Universiteit Amsterdam and the Faculty of Law, University of Amsterdam, the Netherlands. He holds a Ph.D. from the University of Amsterdam, an LL.M. from Maastricht University.

ZHANG Binxin is Assistant Professor at Xiamen University Law School, China and CILRAP Research Fellow. She has previously worked as a Post-Doctoral Research Fellow at Xiamen University Law School, focusing on reparations for victims in international criminal proceedings; as a Legal Officer in the International Committee of the Red Cross Regional Delegation for East Asia; and as a trial monitor of the Asia International Justice Initiative Trial Monitoring group, monitoring the Duch case before the Extraordinary Chambers in the Courts of Cambodia. She holds a Ph.D. in International Law from Renmin University of China. Her main research interest is international criminal law and procedure. She has co-authored a book on war crimes and published several articles and book chapters on issues related to international criminal law and procedure. She teaches public international law, international criminal law and international humanitarian law.

ZHANG Yueyao is a Ph.D. candidate at the Max-Planck Institute for Comparative Public Law and International Law, Germany, where her dissertation title is *State Responsibility in the Realm of Human Rights Treaty Violation*. She holds a Master's Degree in International Law in Peking University, China. She is a fellow and on the board of editors of the Forum for International Criminal and Humanitarian Law. She has interned in the Beijing liaison office of the International Migration Organisation.

TOAEP TEAM

Dr. Cecilie Hellestveit, University of Oslo
Dr. Pablo Kalmanovitz, CIDE, Mexico City
Dr. Sangkul Kim, Korea University
Professor Jann K. Kleffner, Swedish National Defence College
Professor Kjetil Mujezinović Larsen, Norwegian Centre for Human Rights
Professor Salím A. Nakhjavání, Institute for Security Studies, Pretoria
Professor Hector Olasolo, Universidad del Rosario
Ms. Maria Paula Saffon, Dejusticia
Dr. Torunn Salomonsen, Norwegian Ministry of Justice
Professor Carsten Stahn, Leiden University
Professor Jo Stigen, University of Oslo
Dr. Philippa Webb, King's College London
Dr. WEI Xiaohong, Renmin University of China

Advisory Board
Mr. Hirad Abtahi, International Criminal Court
Ms. Silvana Arbia, former Registrar of the International Criminal Court
Professor Emeritus M. Chérif Bassiouni
Professor Olympia Bekou, University of Nottingham
Mr. Gilbert Bitti, International Criminal Court
Research Professor J. Peter Burgess, PRIO
Former Judge Advocate General Arne Willy Dahl, Norway
Professor Emeritus Yoram Dinstein, Tel Aviv University
Professor Jon Elster, Columbia University and Collège de France
Mr. James A. Goldston, Open Society Institute Justice Initiative
Mr. Richard J. Goldstone, former Chief Prosecutor,
    International Criminal Tribunal for the former Yugoslavia
Judge Hanne Sophie Greve, Gulating Court of Appeal, formerly
    European Court of Human Rights
Dr. Fabricio Guariglia, International Criminal Court
Professor Franz Günthner, Ludwig-Maximilians-Universität
Mr. Wolfgang Kaleck, European Center for Constitutional and Human Rights
Professor Emeritus Frits Kalshoven, Leiden University
Former Judge Erkki Kourula, formerly International Criminal Court
Professor Claus Kreß, Cologne University
Professor David Luban, Georgetown University
Mr. Juan E. Méndez, Special Adviser to the ICC Prosecutor on Crime Prevention,
    former President, ICTJ
Dr. Alexander Muller, Director, The Hague Institute for the Internationalisation of Law
Judge Erik Møse, European Court of Human Rights, former President,
    International Criminal Tribunal for Rwanda
Dr. Gro Nystuen, International Law and Policy Institute
Mr. William Pace, Convener, Coalition for the International Criminal Court
Ms. Jelena Pejić, International Committee of the Red Cross
Mr. Robert Petit, former International Co-Prosecutor,
    Extraordinary Chambers in the Courts of Cambodia
Dr. Joseph Rikhof, University of Ottawa
Maj-Gen (ret'd) Anthony P.V. Rogers, Cambridge University

OTHER VOLUMES IN THE
FICHL PUBLICATION SERIES

Morten Bergsmo, Mads Harlem and Nobuo Hayashi (editors):
Importing Core International Crimes into National Law
Torkel Opsahl Academic EPublisher
Oslo, 2010
FICHL Publication Series No. 1 (Second Edition, 2010)
ISBN 978-82-93081-00-5

Nobuo Hayashi (editor):
National Military Manuals on the Law of Armed Conflict
Torkel Opsahl Academic EPublisher
Oslo, 2010
FICHL Publication Series No. 2 (Second Edition, 2010)
ISBN 978-82-93081-02-9

Morten Bergsmo, Kjetil Helvig, Ilia Utmelidze and Gorana Žagovec:
The Backlog of Core International Crimes Case Files in Bosnia and Herzegovina
Torkel Opsahl Academic EPublisher
Oslo, 2010
FICHL Publication Series No. 3 (Second Edition, 2010)
ISBN 978-82-93081-04-3

Morten Bergsmo (editor):
Criteria for Prioritizing and Selecting Core International Crimes Cases
Torkel Opsahl Academic EPublisher
Oslo, 2010
FICHL Publication Series No. 4 (Second Edition, 2010)
ISBN 978-82-93081-06-7

Morten Bergsmo and Pablo Kalmanovitz (editors):
Law in Peace Negotiations
Torkel Opsahl Academic EPublisher
Oslo, 2010
FICHL Publication Series No. 5 (Second Edition, 2010)
ISBN 978-82-93081-08-1

Morten Bergsmo, César Rodríguez Garavito, Pablo Kalmanovitz and Maria Paula Saffon (editors):
Distributive Justice in Transitions
Torkel Opsahl Academic EPublisher
Oslo, 2010
FICHL Publication Series No. 6 (2010)
ISBN 978-82-93081-12-8

Morten Bergsmo, César Rodriguez-Garavito, Pablo Kalmanovitz y Maria Paula Saffon (editors):
Justicia Distributiva en Sociedades en Transición
Torkel Opsahl Academic EPublisher
Oslo, 2012
FICHL Publication Series No. 6 (2012)
ISBN 978-82-93081-10-4

Morten Bergsmo (editor):
Complementarity and the Exercise of Universal Jurisdiction for Core International Crimes
Torkel Opsahl Academic EPublisher
Oslo, 2010
FICHL Publication Series No. 7 (2010)
ISBN 978-82-93081-14-2

Morten Bergsmo (editor):
Active Complementarity: Legal Information Transfer
Torkel Opsahl Academic EPublisher
Oslo, 2011
FICHL Publication Series No. 8 (2011)
ISBN 978-82-93081-55-5 (PDF)
ISBN 978-82-93081-56-2 (print)

Morten Bergsmo (editor):
Abbreviated Criminal Procedures for Core International Crimes
Torkel Opsahl Academic EPublisher
Brussels, 2017
FICHL Publication Series No. 9 (2017)
ISBN 978-82-93081-20-3 (print) and ISBN 978-82-8348-104-4 (e-book)

Sam Muller, Stavros Zouridis, Morly Frishman and Laura Kistemaker (editors):
The Law of the Future and the Future of Law
Torkel Opsahl Academic EPublisher
Oslo, 2010
FICHL Publication Series No. 11 (2011)
ISBN 978-82-93081-27-2

Morten Bergsmo, Alf Butenschøn Skre and Elisabeth J. Wood (editors):
Understanding and Proving International Sex Crimes
Torkel Opsahl Academic EPublisher
Beijing, 2012
FICHL Publication Series No. 12 (2012)
ISBN 978-82-93081-29-6

Morten Bergsmo (editor):
Thematic Prosecution of International Sex Crimes
Torkel Opsahl Academic EPublisher
Beijing, 2012
FICHL Publication Series No. 13 (2012)
ISBN 978-82-93081-31-9

Terje Einarsen:
The Concept of Universal Crimes in International Law
Torkel Opsahl Academic EPublisher
Oslo, 2012
FICHL Publication Series No. 14 (2012)
ISBN 978-82-93081-33-3

莫滕·伯格斯默 凌岩（主编）：
国家主权与国际刑法
Torkel Opsahl Academic EPublisher
Beijing, 2012
FICHL Publication Series No. 15 (2012)
ISBN 978-82-93081-58-6

Morten Bergsmo and LING Yan (editors):
State Sovereignty and International Criminal Law
Torkel Opsahl Academic EPublisher
Beijing, 2012
FICHL Publication Series No. 15 (2012)
ISBN 978-82-93081-35-7

Morten Bergsmo and CHEAH Wui Ling (editors):
Old Evidence and Core International Crimes
Torkel Opsahl Academic EPublisher
Beijing, 2012
FICHL Publication Series No. 16 (2012)
ISBN 978-82-93081-60-9

YI Ping:
戦争と平和の間——発足期日本国際法学における「正しい戦争」
の観念とその帰結
Torkel Opsahl Academic EPublisher
Beijing, 2013
FICHL Publication Series No. 17 (2013)
ISBN 978-82-93081-66-1

Morten Bergsmo and SONG Tianying (editors):
On the Proposed Crimes Against Humanity Convention
Torkel Opsahl Academic EPublisher
Brussels, 2014
FICHL Publication Series No. 18 (2014)
ISBN 978-82-93081-96-8

Morten Bergsmo (editor):
Quality Control in Fact-Finding
Torkel Opsahl Academic EPublisher
Florence, 2013
FICHL Publication Series No. 19 (2013)
ISBN 978-82-93081-78-4

Morten Bergsmo, CHEAH Wui Ling and YI Ping (editors):
Historical Origins of International Criminal Law: Volume 1
Torkel Opsahl Academic EPublisher
Brussels, 2014
FICHL Publication Series No. 20 (2014)
ISBN 978-82-93081-11-1

Morten Bergsmo, CHEAH Wui Ling and YI Ping (editors):
Historical Origins of International Criminal Law: Volume 2
Torkel Opsahl Academic EPublisher
Brussels, 2014
FICHL Publication Series No. 21 (2014)
ISBN 978-82-93081-13-5

Morten Bergsmo, CHEAH Wui Ling, SONG Tianying and YI Ping (editors):
Historical Origins of International Criminal Law: Volume 3
Torkel Opsahl Academic EPublisher
Brussels, 2015
FICHL Publication Series No. 22 (2015)
ISBN 978-82-93081-15-3 (print) and ISBN 978-82-93081-14-6 (e-book)

Morten Bergsmo, CHEAH Wui Ling, SONG Tianying and YI Ping (editors):
Historical Origins of International Criminal Law: Volume 4
Torkel Opsahl Academic EPublisher
Brussels, 2015
FICHL Publication Series No. 23 (2015)
ISBN 978-82-93081-17-7 (print) and ISBN 978-82-93081-16-0 (e-book)

Morten Bergsmo, Klaus Rackwitz and SONG Tianying (editors):
Historical Origins of International Criminal Law: Volume 5
Torkel Opsahl Academic EPublisher
Brussels, 2017
FICHL Publication Series No. 24 (2017)
ISBN 978-82-8348-106-8 (print) and 978-82-8348-107-5 (e-book)

Morten Bergsmo and SONG Tianying (editors):
Military Self-Interest in Accountability for Core International Crimes
Torkel Opsahl Academic EPublisher
Brussels, 2015
FICHL Publication Series No. 25 (2015)
ISBN 978-82-93081-61-6 (print) and ISBN 978-82-93081-81-4 (e-book)

Wolfgang Kaleck:
Double Standards: International Criminal Law and the West
Torkel Opsahl Academic EPublisher
Brussels, 2015
FICHL Publication Series No. 26 (2015)
ISBN 978-82-93081-67-8 (print) and 978-82-93081-83-8 (e-book)

LIU Daqun and ZHANG Binxin:
Historical War Crimes Trials in Asia
Torkel Opsahl Academic EPublisher
Brussels, 2016
FICHL Publication Series No. 27 (2016)
ISBN 978-82-8348-055-9 (print) and 978-82-8348-056-6 (e-book)

CPSIA information can be obtained
at www.ICGtesting.com
Printed in the USA
BVOW06*0437311017
499048BV00014B/21/P